Baseball Players' Best Seasons

ALSO BY MICHAEL S. JONES

Baseball's Best Careers: Team by Team Rankings
(McFarland, 2001)

Baseball Players' Best Seasons

Team by Team Rankings

Michael S. Jones

McFarland & Company, Inc., Publishers
Jefferson, North Carolina, and London

Table of Contents

Preface 1
Introduction 3

Boston/Milwaukee/Atlanta Braves   11
Boston Red Sox   22
Brooklyn/Los Angeles Dodgers   34
Chicago Cubs   46
Chicago White Sox   57
Cincinnati Reds   68
Cleveland Indians   79
Detroit Tigers   90
New York/San Francisco Giants   101
New York Yankees   113
Philadelphia/Kansas City/Oakland Athletics   125
Philadelphia Phillies   136
Pittsburgh Pirates   147
St. Louis Browns/Baltimore Orioles   158
St. Louis Cardinals   169
Washington Senators/Minnesota Twins   180
American League Expansion Teams   191
National League Expansion Teams   216
Nineteenth Century Players   241
All Time Great Player Seasons   259

Index 289

Library of Congress Cataloguing-in-Publication Data

Jones, Michael S., 1956–
Baseball players' best seasons : team by team rankings / Michael S. Jones.
p.   cm.   /   Includes index.
ISBN 0-7864-1086-8 (softcover : 50# alkaline paper) ∞
1. Baseball — United States — Statistics.   2. Baseball players — Rating of — United States.   I. Title.
GV877.J65   2001   796.357 — dc21   2001030864

British Library cataloguing data are available

©2001 Michael S. Jones.   All rights reserved.   Manufactured in the United States of America

No part of this book may be reproduced or transmitted in any form or by any means, electronic or mechanical, including photocopying or recording, or by any information storage and retrieval system, without permission in writing from the publisher.

McFarland & Company, Inc., Publishers / Box 611, Jefferson, North Carolina 28640 / www.mcfarlandpub.com

PREFACE

Mark McGwire and Sammy Sosa erupted into instant fame in 1998, driving baseballs out of packed ballparks and onto front-page headlines. Their daily home run competition brought baseball back to the average fan who was alienated from the game by the 1994 players' strike. How did these two men cause such a stir with fans and the media? Did they somehow transform the game of baseball? Was it their magnetic personalities, or the way they swung the bat? No. The answer lies elsewhere, in the very soul of what makes baseball unique among major sports. With their assault on the greatest record of all sports, the single season home run record held by Roger Maris, these two men brought us back to the real magic of baseball: the ever growing heritage of baseball statistics.

More than any other sport, major league baseball is about statistics. As fans, we relate to these statistics in a powerful way. We use these statistics to settle disputes with our friends regarding the better hitter or the better pitcher. Was Sammy Sosa or Mark McGwire the better player in 1998? Were their home run accomplishments more impressive than those of Babe Ruth or Roger Maris? How do these two ball players rank historically against others who played their positions? We use their statistics to provide us with our answers. But we wish we had better statistical proof that clearly supports our arguments.

As fans, we also passionately identify with a particular team as our own. We are Yankees fans, Dodgers fans, or Braves fans. We absorb baseball statistics in the same biased fashion. Cardinals fans argue that Ozzie Smith is the greatest shortstop ever, based on his fielding statistics. Orioles fans take exception to Smith as the best, nominating Cal Ripken at short, while Pirates fans look far back in time to see Honus Wagner dominating the position. Yankees fans claim Babe Ruth as the greatest player of all time, while Red Sox fans hold dear the memory of Ted Williams, and Giants fans point to Willie Mays. We follow the current season in much the same way, supporting our team and tracking with a keen interest how the statistics of our players compare to other players in the league. And, again, we wish we could find one statistic or one set of statistics that could more clearly support our favorite players and teams.

Baseball Players' Best Seasons brings our team spirit as fans to the world of baseball statistics, giving us the statistical tools to compare the performance of players between teams and through time. Suppose, for a moment, that we are long-suffering Chicago Cubs fans. Even though our team has not won a World Series in more than ninety years, our baseball interest in recent years centers on Sammy Sosa and Mark Grace, and on Hack Wilson, Ernie Banks, and Ryne Sandberg in past years. We may even have spent hours sifting through statistical data in a baseball encyclopedia to get some sense of how our favorite Cubs players compare to each other and to their opponents. Now, this book does that analysis, sorting and comparing for us.

Rating the greatest player seasons by position for each team provides fans of every major league team unique rankings of their favorite players. Does slick fielding Ryne Sandberg have the best season ever by a Cubs second baseman? And which of his seasons is his best, the 1984 season when he hit .314 with 19 home runs for the division winning Cubs, or the 1990 season, when he hit .306 with 40 home runs? Will Johnny Evers of Tinker to Evers to Chance fame make the Cubs' all-time team at second base with his 1912 season, when he hit .341? How do other Cubs second basemen rank — players like Billy Herman, Glenn Beckert, and even Rogers Hornsby, who played for the Cubs for one full season in 1929?

This work rates and ranks each player on two levels. On the first level, players are rated according to their *rate of success* compared to their peers. A rate of success metric measures a player's performance for an individual event such as an at bat, or over a short period, such as an inning pitched, a game played, or a short series. On the second level, players are rated according to their *volume of success* during the season compared to their peers. Volume of success measures a player's performance based on his contribution for the entire season.

The rate and volume of success metrics each provide valuable information about a player's season. For example, Pedro Martinez had an incredible rate of success for Boston in 2000 but, since he worked less than half the innings of many players who pitched a hundred years ago, he ranks lower than many of these early pitchers in volume of success. Did Martinez have a better year than the best season pitched by one of these early stars? The answer depends on whether we want his great per-game performance, or the other player's greater volume of good performances. We would pick Martinez to represent us in a short series or on a team loaded with much better than average pitchers who can cover Pedro's lack of innings. We would pick the volume pitcher to represent us for a full season on a team loaded with average pitchers.

The best player seasons for each team are summarized to create two 25 player all-star teams, one for the best rate-of-success seasons, and one for the best volume-of-success seasons. We can now enjoy comparing our favorite team's lineup of star seasons to those of other teams. Which team is better: the Chicago Cubs, with a lineup of Sammy Sosa in 1998, Ernie Banks in 1959, Billy Williams in 1972, and Gabby Hartnett in 1930, backed by the arms of Three Finger Brown in 1906, Ferguson Jenkins in 1971, and Bruce Sutter in 1977? Or the St. Louis Cardinals, with Mark McGwire in 1998, Rogers Hornsby in 1924, Stan Musial in 1948, and Bob Gibson in 1968? Are the Yankees the greatest team ever assembled, led by Babe Ruth's 1921 season, Lou Gehrig in 1927, Mickey Mantle in 1956, and Joe DiMaggio in 1941? Are these players even on the all-star teams, and are these the best seasons for these players? The statistics will tell us. And there will be some surprising answers.

Finally, we bring every player season by position together to select the greatest lineups since 1900 for both the American and National leagues. These two all-star teams and the best players from the 1800s are then merged to create an all-time team featuring the 25 greatest individual player seasons of all time. This process is done by rate of success metrics, to give us the best team ever for a game or a short series, and by volume of success metrics, for the best team ever over the course of an entire season.

We now have the statistical tools to decide for ourselves who had the greatest season ever at every position for our team and for all teams. We have the tools to assemble all-star rosters for every major league team to compete in a short series or over a full season. And we have the tools to debate our friends on the relative merits of particular players and their seasons.

Another way to view the performances of our favorite players is to analyze their results over their entire career. This career perspective is especially useful in determining which players deserve to be in baseball's Hall of Fame. In my companion book, *Baseball's Best Careers: Team by Team Rankings*, the career performances of baseball's greatest stars are rated and ranked by position for each team. Next, rosters of the best 25 player careers are presented for each team, giving us a chance to play the all-time greatest players for our favorite team against the best from other teams. Finally, careers ratings are summarized to produce rosters for the best American and National League players, and a roster for the greatest players of all time. This companion book is also available from McFarland & Company, Inc., Publishers.

INTRODUCTION

Baseball Players' Best Seasons: Team by Team Rankings is more than a summary of raw, historical statistics about the men who played the game of major league baseball. Much like John Thorn and Pete Palmer's *Total Baseball*, and Bill James' *Stats All-Time Major League Handbook*, this book creates new "sabermetric" statistics from the raw statistics for the purpose of rating player performances within and between years. These new sabermetrics, or metrics for short, form the basis of all rankings found in this book.

When *The Baseball Encyclopedia* was first published in 1969, raw historic baseball statistics went from being a scarce commodity to a readily available source of enjoyment for baseball fans. However, the raw statistics have two limitations that make a historical comparison of players difficult at best. First, no one hitter's statistic, such as hits, home runs, or batting average, is sufficient to make a determination of a player's overall performance. Second, the raw statistics contain natural biases that mask a player's actual performance when compared to other players. Examples of biases are the cyclical periods of pitcher dominance and hitter dominance, the designated hitter rule employed in the American League since 1973, and the shrinking number of innings thrown by starting pitchers over time. Nonbiased metrics for evaluating and ranking players need to be developed to overcome these concerns.

Total Baseball arrived in 1989 with the first widely available metrics comparing the performances of all players in baseball history. *Total Baseball* introduced two metrics to evaluate hitters. Production, a rate of success metric, is a straightforward sum of slugging average and on-base percentage. Total Player Runs, a volume of success metric, uses several formulas to produce a composite of a player's ability to generate Batting Runs, Stolen Base Runs, and Fielding Runs. All positive and negative run factors are then converted into positive or negative wins for the team. Pitchers have a rate of success metric that compares their ERA (earned run average) to the league's average ERA for that season. Pitchers also have a second metric, the Total Pitcher's Index, a volume of success metric. This metric analyzes a pitcher's ability to affect runs through his pitching, his batting, and his fielding, with all run factors again converted into positive or negative wins for the team.

The Bill James Historical Baseball Abstract was published in 1985. It introduced the world to the concept of Runs Created as a metric to compare player performances. The basic Runs Created formula was adjusted by 14 technical variations to deal with inconsistencies in rules and data between years. The result is an elaborate list of formulas, each being applicable to certain years. Runs Created received its own voice in the world of baseball encyclopedias in 1999 with the first edition of *Stats All-Time Major League Handbook*.

This book uses the following objectives to select the appropriate metrics for rating player performance:

- Metrics are required for both rate of success and volume of success.
- The metrics used must produce accurate ratings for all players in history.
- These metrics should be simple for the average baseball fan to understand.
- These metrics should be simple for baseball fans to duplicate.

A breakthrough idea led to the development of a new set of metrics to fulfill these objectives. An all-purpose yardstick for measurement exists that allows us to accurately compare player performances across generations. This yardstick is the *historical average* performance of all hitters and of all pitchers.

The sum total of all baseball statistics from 1876 through 2000 is readily available. For instance, batters have made 13,262,794 plate appearances, producing 3,101,789 hits and 209,161 home runs. We can use this data to determine the historic average performance stated in terms of a player who plays a full 162 game schedule. This average hitter has the following statistics:

AB	BB	HBP	TAB	HITS	2B	3B	HR	BA	OB	SA	PRO
615	57	4	676	161	26	6	11	.262	.328	.377	.7059

The average pitcher, regardless of the innings we assign to him, has a 3.76 ERA, and a 4.557 RA/9. (ERA is the number of earned runs allowed per 9 innings pitched. RA/9 is the number of total runs allowed per 9 innings pitched.) We can use this historical average data for hitters and pitchers to develop the four metrics we are interested in — a rate of success metric and a volume of success metric for both hitters and pitchers.

Metrics and Definitions for the Single Season

Total Factor (TF) — A Rate of Success Metric for Hitters

The rate of success metric for hitters is called *Total Factor (TF)*. Total Factor is the sum of four other factors: a Weighted Production factor (Wtd. PRO), a stolen base factor (SBF), a fielding factor (FF), and a speed factor (SPF):TF = Wtd. PRO + SBF + FF + SPF.

These four factors measure each player's impact on creating or saving runs for his team. For ease of presentation for this book, all four factors are stated in whole numbers. This requires us to multiply Production by 1,000 to convert to a whole number. Mark McGwire's 1998 Production of 1.225 becomes 1,225. This approach will henceforth be used when discussing Production numbers.

Weighted Production (Wtd. PRO) is the primary element of the Total Factor metric. Production is the sum of on-base percentage and slugging average. Weighted Production corrects for the differences in Production levels between years by using the historic average Production of 705.9, as follows: Wtd. PRO = PRO × 705.9 / League Average PRO for that Season.

The use of a Production number is a simple and accurate means of measuring a player's value. The key to measuring a player's offensive performance is measuring that player's ability to get on base and to drive in runs. Production, a combination of on-base percentage and slugging average, provides that measurement far better than the more popular surrogates: batting average and home runs. As support for the use of Production, the authors of *Total Baseball*, who used the complex Batting Runs metric to measure performance, stated on page 633 of the 1999 edition, "the correlation between Batting Runs and Production over the course of an average team season is 99.7 percent."

Weighted Production has one additional advantage. Other published Production metrics correct for cycles in hitting by dividing a player's performance by the league average performance. The result is a ratio, rather than a Production number to which we can relate. Weighted Production, on the other hand, preserves its identity as a Production number, as illustrated by the following example.

In 1981, Mike Schmidt had a .439 on-base percentage and a .644 slugging average, which equals a 1,083 Production. The average Production for the National League that year was 686. Schmidt's Weighted Production = 1,083 × 705.9 / 686 = 1,114. Schmidt's 1,114 Weighted Production exceeds his 1,083 Production by 2.9 percent; this 2.9 percent difference is the adjustment for Schmidt hitting in a pitcher's year.

An adjustment to historic Production data is required to remove the bias related to the designated hitter rule. The DH, hitting in place of a pitcher, increases American League average Production numbers by 3.3 percent from 1973 to 1996, and by 3.0 percent from 1997 to 2000, while National League Production numbers are increased 0.3 percent from 1997 to 2000. This makes it harder for players in these seasons to compete against other players in other seasons when comparing their relative Weighted Production numbers. To correct this bias, we multiply the American League average Production by .967 for 1973–1996 seasons, and by .97 for 1997–2000 seasons. For the National League, Production numbers are multiplied by .997 for 1997–2000 seasons.

The *Stolen Base Factor (SBF)* is based on sabermetric studies that show the value of two stolen bases is negated by one time caught stealing. The formula that converts the value of stealing to a rate of success metric is: SBF = (SB - [2 × CS]) × 945 / TAB.

If a player steals 3 bases and is caught once in 676 total at bats, his Stolen Base Factor is (3 - [2 × 1]) × 945 / 676 = 1.4. (Modeling has determined that for the historic average 676 total at bats, one net stolen base above the impact of being caught stealing is equivalent to a Production value of 1.4.) In 1981, Mike Schmidt stole 12 bases and was caught stealing 4 times in 431 total at bats. Schmidt's Stolen Base Factor = (12 - [2 × 4]) × 945 / 431 = +9.

Records for caught stealing were not kept for many

seasons, including in the National League as recently as 1950. A Stolen Base Factor is not computed for those years.

Since a player must be successful two out of every three tries just to break even in Stolen Base Factor, this factor is a slightly negative number overall for the years where it applies. And Stolen Base Factor is a significantly negative number for the few years in the Dead Ball period of 1901–1919 where caught stealing data is available. Even though the number of bases stolen in that period was very high compared to modern times, the rate of successfully stealing a base was much lower. Combine the high attempts and a success rate far below 66.7 percent, and we have a very negative Stolen Base Factor. While a few players such as Ty Cobb managed a positive Stolen Base Factor in some years, in general, a player of that period is fortunate to play in a year where caught stealing information is not available.

Fielding Factor (FF) is the one calculation where, instead of relying on hard statistical data, a judgmental interpretation of this statistical data is used to measure a player's performance. Why a judgmental interpretation of statistical data? Because none of the many statistical approaches ever developed adequately measures fielding performance for all players.

For most of baseball history, fielding percentage was the main measure of fielding performance. Fielding percentage, however, tells us nothing about a player's fielding range. In response, a fielding range statistic has been developed, where range is defined as the sum of a player's putouts and assists per nine innings. Problems with the fielding range statistic include the following:

- The range statistic does not reflect errors made.
- The range statistic is not adjusted to reflect a team having more strikeouts by its pitching staff and, thus, less possible chances available for its fielders.
- Ignoring the strikeout issue, there are only 27 outs in a game to divide up among a team's fielders. A team with nine excellent fielders will have each fielder fare no better statistically than their counterparts on a team with nine average fielders, and no better than their counterparts on a team with nine poor fielders.
- A poor fielder like Albert Belle may have a high range statistic, not because he has great range, but because hitters hit more balls his way in order to avoid hitting them at better fielders.
- The range statistic does not begin to cover all the skills required of a catcher, while a first baseman's putouts are a function of the abilities of the other players in the infield.

Total Baseball's "Fielding Runs" is the best statistical approach to date. Fielding Runs rates players based on their putouts, assists, double plays, and errors compared to the league average player at that position. Unfortunately, this reliance purely on fielding statistics still produces inconsistent results. A great fielding second baseman, Bill Mazeroski, has the highest career Fielding Runs at +362, while Johnny Bench, perhaps the greatest fielding catcher of all time, has a career Fielding Runs of -80. Other players with negative fielding ratings include Mickey Mantle, Roger Maris, Dave Concepcion, Larry Bowa, and Hal Chase. Albert Belle, Jim Rice, Jose Canseco, and Bill Melton are some of the poor fielders who have positive Fielding Runs. Fielding Runs does not produce consistently reliable results because this approach suffers from some of the same problems as the range statistic. Still, more often than not, Fielding Runs approximates the reputation of the player evaluated.

Fielding Factor (FF) combines four sources of information to rate each player's fielding performance: Gold Glove recognition for players since 1957; the player's general fielding reputation, with input for players since 1900 from an independent rating source; the player's *Total Baseball* Fielding Runs rating; and the player's fielding percentage. Fielding Factor, being by nature an estimate, is stated in increments of 10. The historic sum of all Fielding Factors for each position nets to zero.

In 1981, Mike Schmidt produced a +90 Fielding Factor, one of the highest fielding ratings ever. Schmidt's 1981 Fielding Factor reflects his winning his sixth of nine straight Gold Glove awards, his reputation as the greatest fielding third baseman of all time, his solid .956 fielding percentage that year, and a very high +23 Fielding Runs rating for a 107 game schedule.

The *Speed Factor (SPF)* assigned to a player is either +10, 0, or -10. Most elements of speed are already reflected in one of the other three factors. Weighted Production incorporates a player's ability to run out a bunt or extend a single into a double. Stolen Base Factor captures a player's contribution from stealing bases. And Fielding Factor reflects a player's ability to cover ground defensively. What is not covered is a player's ability to run the bases once he is on base. Joe DiMaggio could fly on the base paths; Frank Howard and Harmon Killebrew held up traffic behind them. The sum of all Speed Factors for all players is a small positive number.

In summary, *Total Factor (TF)* enjoys an important advantage over other rate of success metrics in that it goes beyond hitting performance to also incorporate base running and fielding performance. Mike Schmidt was a player who could hit, run, steal, and play great defense. In 1981, his Weighted Production was 1,114, his Stolen Base Factor was +9, his Fielding Factor was +90, and his

Speed Factor was +10. Schmidt's Total Factor is 1,223, the highest rate of success performance for any third baseman in major league history. Unfortunately for Schmidt, 1981 was a strike year, and his team played only 107 games. As a result, Schmidt's volume-based statistics such as hits and home runs do not begin to reflect his incredible year. Schmidt's 1981 season is an example of why Total Factor, an all-encompassing rate of success metric, is needed to measure a player's performance.

Hits Contribution (HC) — A Volume of Success Metric for Hitters

Unlike other published metrics, we can convert the Total Factor rate of success metric directly into a volume of success metric, called *Hits Contribution (HC)*. The formula for calculating Hits Contribution is as follows: HC = (TF - Historic Average TF for Position) × TAB / (1000 × [Historic TAB /Historic TAB + Historic TAB/Historic AB]).

The historic TAB (total at bats) for the average player is approximately 676, while the historic AB (at bats) is approximately 615. When the first number is divided by the second, the number generated is 1.099. Inserting this new information, the suddenly simple formula for calculating Hits Contribution is now: HC = (TF - A) × TAB / 2,099 where A = Historic Average TF for Player's Position.

The difference between a player's Total Factor and the historic average Total Factor tells us how much better or worse that player's rate of success is compared to the historic average player at that position. When we multiply this difference by the second half of the equation, we convert the difference into the number of additional (or less) base hits produced by this player as compared to the historic average player at that position, given the same total at bats.

Recall that the historic sum of Fielding Factors equals zero, while a slightly negative sum of Stolen Base Factors is basically offset by a slightly positive sum of Speed Factors. As these three factors net to zero, the historic average Total Factor for *all positions* is roughly equivalent to the historic average Production factor, or 705.9. Based on an analysis of the Production figures for 80 percent of the over 13 million total at bats in history, the historic average Total Factor *for each position* is: C = 677.4, 1B = 770.0, 2B = 685.3, SS = 662.0, 3B = 716.2, OF = 757.4, P = 536.8 (1876–99), P=442.2 (1900–72), P=370.5 (1973–present).

Each player's performance is compared against the Total Factor for the position he fielded the most games at during the season. Designated hitters use the historic average Total Factor for the primary position they played in the field or, if they did not appear in the field in that season, the primary position they most recently played.

Total games played by teams vary by year, creating one of the biases making a comparison between years difficult. We already saw how Mike Schmidt's 1981 volume-based statistics are adversely impacted by that strike-shortened season. There were, in fact, many variations in games played over time. Schedules were very irregular in the early days of baseball, with a 154 game schedule not being adopted until 1904. World War I caused a reduction in games played in the 1918 and 1919 seasons. Baseball expanded to a 162 game schedule in the early sixties. And strikes shortened the 1972, 1981, 1994, and 1995 seasons. To correct the impact of this schedule bias on our volume of success metric, we make one addition to the formula: HC = (TF - A) × TAB / 2,099 × 162 / Games in Season where A = 677.4 for catchers, 770.0 for first basemen, 685.3 for second basemen, 662.0 for shortstops, 716.2 for third basemen, 757.4 for outfielders, 536.8 for pitchers (1876–99), 442.2 for pitchers (1900–72), 370.5 for pitchers (1973–present).

The "Games in Season" adjustment does not correct for games lost due to rainouts or extra games played in a season. One hundred fifty-four games are used for "Games in Season" for every year between 1904 and the introduction of expansion teams, except the 1918 and 1919 war years. Likewise, 162 games are used for every year from the introduction of expansion teams to the present, except for the strike-shortened years. For irregular schedule years such as 1896 and 1918, a league average "Games in Season" is used, regardless of the actual games played by each team. This league average "Games in Season" approach is designed to cover nineteenth century situations where teams sometimes failed in mid-year.

Mike Schmidt's 1981 Hits Contribution (tabulated in the formula [1,223 - 716.2] × 431 / 2,099 × 162 / 107) accounts for 157.5 additional base hits compared to the historic average third baseman over a 162 game schedule. Schmidt, through his hitting, his base running, and his fielding, gave the 1981 Philadelphia Phillies almost one additional base hit per game advantage over the competition!

Weighted Runs Allowed per 9 Innings (Wtd. RA/9) — A Rate of Success Metric for Pitchers

The choice of the basic measure for a pitcher's rate of success is between Runs Allowed per 9 Innings (RA/9) and the more traditional Earned Runs Allowed per 9 Innings (ERA). Supporters of Earned Run Average argue that a pitcher's performance should not suffer from errors committed by others. However, many unearned runs come after the play where the error is committed, and the pitcher certainly has a major responsibility for those runs scoring. Ultimately, the pitcher is held responsible for giving up runs, whether from legitimate hits, hits that occur because a fielder has limited range, hits from unlucky bounces, errors, walks, hit batsmen, or any other source. Bill James offered the opinion on page 483 of the *Baseball Abstract* that "the distinction between earned runs and unearned runs is silly and artificial…"

A historic analysis supports the use of RA/9 over ERA. Errors were far more prevalent in the early days of the game. In the National Association in 1874, the fielding average was .825, which means one error was committed for every six chances. In that year, RA/9 averaged 8.99, while the league's earned run average was 3.25. If we used ERA to evaluate pitchers, we would be ignoring 64 percent of all runs scored against these pitchers! Pitchers had minuscule ERAs of less than 2.00 that did not reflect their true performance. In 1903, the National League's fielding average was .946, or one error every 19 chances. The league's RA/9 was 4.88, while its ERA was 3.26. Fully one third of all runs scored were unearned. In 1998, the National League's fielding average was .981, or one error for every 53 chances. The league's RA/9 was 4.62, while its ERA was 4.23. Only 8 percent of all runs scored were unearned. As we are comparing players of all time periods, we should avoid the wide variation in results caused by not considering all runs scored.

A case-by-case analysis also typically supports the use of RA/9 over ERA. Jack Pfiester went 14–9 with an incredibly low 1.15 ERA for the 1907 Cubs. While Pfiester's ERA was 47 percent of the National League average ERA, his 2.82 RA/9 was a much higher 81 percent of the National League average RA/9. Pfiester's ERA was remarkably low only because nearly 60 percent of the runs he allowed were unearned! Carl Lundgren went 18–7 and had a superb 1.17 ERA that same year for the Cubs, but he also had a 1.83 RA/9. Lundgren's ERA was 48 percent of the National League average, and his RA/9 was a comparable 52 percent of the National League average. Carl Lundgren was clearly the superior pitcher that year. Yet Lundgren is rated lower than Pfiester based on ERA, even though Lundgren has a far superior RA/9 rating and a higher winning percentage.

Greg Maddux's two best years highlight the advantages of using RA/9. In 1994, Maddux was 16–6 with a 1.56 ERA, while in 1995 he went 19–2 with a 1.63 ERA. Nineteen ninety-four would be considered his better year based on an ERA metric. Now look again at Maddux's two best seasons. In 1994, he was 16–6 with a 1.96 RA/9, while in 1995 he went 19–2 with a 1.67 RA/9. The results are now clearly in favor of 1995.

We will use RA/9 as the basis for the pitcher's rate of success metric. The historic average RA/9 of 4.557 is used to eliminate the historic bias between years. The formula for the rate of success metric, *Weighted Runs Allowed per 9 Innings (Wtd. RA/9)*, is: Wtd. RA/9 = RA/9 × 4.557 / League Average RA/9 for that Season. Applying the Wtd. RA/9 formula to the previous examples, we determine: Wtd. RA/9 for Maddux in 1994 = 1.96 × 4.557 / 4.65 = 1.92; Wtd. RA/9 for Maddux in 1995 = 1.67 × 4.557 / 4.65 = 1.64; Wtd. RA/9 for Pfiester in 1907 = 2.82 × 4.557 / 3.49 = 3.68; Wtd. RA/9 for Lundgren in 1907 = 1.83 × 4.557 / 3.49 = 2.39.

The 1.64 Wtd. RA/9 performance by Greg Maddux in 1995 is the second best rate of success achieved by a qualifying starting pitcher in major league history, outshining the best seasons for Walter Johnson, Old Hoss Radbourn, Cy Young, Lefty Grove, and Christy Mathewson. We could never have been able to determine how awesome Maddux was that year based on his 1.63 ERA, which appears mundane against Bob Gibson's 1.12 ERA in 1968 or Walter Johnson's 1.14 ERA in 1913. Nor could we have determined his greatness by looking at an ERA-adjusted number, where even Maddux's own 1994 season would have finished ahead of the 1995 season. Given how few runs Maddux allowed in 1995 compared to his competition, is it any wonder he went 19–2?

And who was the starting pitcher with the very best rate of success season? The answer is Pedro Martinez, who blazed a 1.74 ERA and a far more remarkable 1.55 Wtd. RA/9 for the Boston Red Sox in 2000, while clearly demonstrating that great pitchers can overcome the challenges of pitching in hitter-friendly stadiums like Fenway Park.

Runs per 162 Games (Runs/162)— A Volume of Success Metric for Pitchers

The volume of success metric for pitchers is based on our rate of success metric, Wtd. RA/9. We merely add an innings volume factor, and adjust away the historic bias of uneven schedules. The formula for the volume of success metric, *Runs per 162 Games* is: Runs/162 = (4.557 - Wtd. RA/9) × IP / 9 × 162 / Games in Season. Runs/162 tells us how many runs that pitcher saved (gave up) compared to the historic average pitcher for the same number of innings worked, adjusted to a 162 game schedule. Runs/162 for Maddux in 1994 = (4.557 - 1.92) × 202 / 9 × 162 / 114.5 = 83.7. Runs/162 for Maddux in 1995 = (4.557 - 1.64) × 210 / 9 × 162 / 144 = 76.7. Maddux's 1995 season was the second best rate of success season ever. Now his 1994 season comes out on top on Runs/162? That's right. Not only does Maddux's 1994 season beat out the exemplary 1995 season, so do 32 other pitcher seasons in the twentieth century, and nearly a hundred pitcher seasons from the nineteenth century. We need two metrics for pitchers, and especially for pitchers, because of the enormous volume bias in favor of pitchers who pitched a hundred years ago. Pedro Martinez in 2000 and Greg Maddux in 1995 are the two best pitchers ever for the innings they pitched. But these two stars rate far behind the old workhorses like Old Hoss Radbourn and Al Spalding in terms of saving runs for their teams over a full season. It all depends on the question we are asking.

Defining Teams, Players, Rosters, and Other Matters

The Teams

Twenty "teams" have been assembled in this book. Sixteen of these "teams" are the original 16 teams of the twentieth century. These teams keep their identity even after they move to another city, as was the case with the Washington Senators moving to Minnesota in 1961.

Two "teams" consist of the expansion teams for the American and the National League. The expansion teams for each league are grouped together for two reasons. First, these teams have existed for such a short time that their best players do not deserve historic recognition alongside the All-Stars from the original 16 teams. Second, by combining these teams, we generate two teams whose roster can compete effectively against the other 16 teams. These two expansion teams have the disadvantage of missing out on the volume pitching years found earlier in the century. Their main advantage is that they have many quality relievers to choose from, as the relief artist came of age during expansion years.

The remaining two "teams" are comprised of players from 1876 to 1887 and from 1888 to 1899. The nineteenth century squads don't have home run hitters or pitchers with outstanding rate of success results. They do have star hitters and some incredible volume pitchers.

The Players

Players rated come from all major league teams since 1876, except for the Federal League teams of 1914–1915. Federal League teams do not logically fit in with any of the 20 teams, and are ignored here. Also excluded from consideration are player seasons from the National Association in 1871–1875. The schedules of many of the National Association teams were so short as to make their players' performances of dubious quality for comparison to players from other periods. Fortunately, many of the great players from this period, including Ross Barnes, Cap Anson, and Al Spalding, are represented in this book with at least one outstanding season from later in their careers while playing in the National League.

All players are designated to play each season at their primary position (the position they play the most games at in that year). Also, players traded between teams during a season are designated to play for the team they have the most plate appearances or innings pitched for; their season statistics appear with them for their primary team.

The Rosters

Each team roster consists of sixteen position players and nine pitchers. Eight reserves back up the eight starting infielders and outfielders, one for each position. No distinction is made in the outfield between right, center, and left fielders. Five starting pitchers and four relievers round out the roster, reflecting the days when teams did not require a big bullpen. In the case of the nineteenth century squads, when relief pitchers were basically nonexistent, nine starting pitchers have been selected.

All players are restricted to only one roster spot per team. Babe Ruth could fill the Yankees roster with at least half of his seasons, and even start at shortstop, if we let him. If a player qualifies for a roster spot at two positions, such as Ruth did at pitcher and at outfielder for the Red Sox, he is chosen for the position that gives the team its greatest overall strength. This may not be the position where the player has his best overall season, but it is the position where the team needs him the most. For the same reasons, the position chosen for the rate of success team may not be the position chosen for the volume of success team.

Average total statistics are presented for the eight starters, the eight reserves, starting pitchers and relief pitchers. A "weighted average" grand total for hitters gives twice the weighting to the eight starters as compared to the eight reserves.

Minimum Volume Requirement

This book ranks the very best players for each team. For rate of success metrics, where volume doesn't matter, we must set a minimum volume to protect the best players from being crowded out by pretenders to the throne. Major league baseball requires 502 plate appearances to qualify for certain rate of success hitting titles. But 502 is too high a minimum standard, especially for catchers. The minimum volume requirement for hitters for both hitting metrics is set at 376 plate appearances (75 percent of 502), after adjusting to a 162 game schedule. This 376-plate appearance minimum picks up just about every historically respected player's season, and provides enough catchers for a fair appraisal of players at that position.

For starting pitchers, the minimum standard for both metrics is 162 innings pitched, after adjusting to a

162 game schedule. One hundred sixty-two innings is also baseball's standard to qualify pitchers for best earned run average.

There are two minimum standards for relief pitchers. Achieving either minimum assures a pitcher's season can be evaluated for both pitcher metrics. The first minimum of at least 54 games as a reliever, after adjusting to a 162 game schedule, is designed for closers and other pure relievers. The second minimum of at least 81 innings pitched over a 162 game schedule, with an average of no more than three innings per appearance, is designed for long relievers who may occasionally start a game. Because relievers may start one or more games, the impact of these starts on the volume-based Runs/162 metric is subtracted before that reliever is considered for a spot on his team's all-star roster.

Saves and Other Pitching Statistics

Strikeout pitchers, control pitchers, and pitchers with many wins and a high winning percentage don't gain any advantage because of these attributes. A pitcher's rate of success results are determined by how many runs he gives up per 9 innings pitched, and his volume of success results are also determined by how many innings he works. Everything else is just an element of how many runs a pitcher gives up or, like wins and winning percentage, is heavily dependent on the team the pitcher performs for.

Including the save as a reduction in RA/9 (Runs Allowed per 9 Innings) would bias pitching ratings toward the modern closer. Because the role of the closer was different in the fifties and sixties, those closers would not receive as much credit as the modern closer, even though they may have more successfully prevented runs. Long relievers and set-up men, who rarely make the All-Star rosters anyway, would be practically shut out from consideration. The final rankings show a predominance of save artists, but only because they are very good at preventing runs, and not because they are save artists.

RBIs, Batting Average, and Other Batting Statistics

Runs batted in and runs scored are extremely unreliable indicators of a player's value, as they are enormously influenced by that hitter's place in the batting order, the other hitters in the lineup, and the cycles of hitter and pitcher dominance. Hack Wilson's 190 RBI record in 1930, aided by huge advantages from all of the above items, is one of the most overrated records in all sports. Another highly overrated statistic is the batting average, which measures how good a player is at hitting singles and extra base hits, but not how good he is at getting on base, hitting for power, and generating runs for his team. Finally, home runs and other batting statistics serve us only to the extent they influence the Production statistic.

The Definition of On-Base Percentage

This work does not include sacrifice flies in the denominator for computing on-base percentage. A sacrifice fly reflects a hitter doing his job, and it shouldn't penalize his on-base performance to do so. Also, sacrifice flies were not tracked before the 1950s. Instead, they were buried in with sacrifice hits, which do not affect the on-base percentage denominator. Finally, having a sacrifice fly penalize on-base percentage and not penalize batting average is logically inconsistent.

No Ballpark Adjustment

If we insist on adjusting raw statistics for biases, why don't we adjust for one of the greatest potential biases, the ballpark? The problems with a ballpark adjustment are:

- Existing ballpark adjustments demonstrate how complicated this is to accomplish. Two or three pages of extremely complex formulas and elaborate explanations violate the objective that metrics should be simple to understand.
- A ballpark adjustment violates the objective that metrics should be easy to duplicate.
- The ball park adjustment creates as many problems as it fixes. For example, Larry Walker's home games in 1997 were at incredibly hitter friendly Coors Field. Yet Walker hit 29 of his 49 home runs on the road that year. Adjusting Walker's performance would unfairly penalize him for the incorrect assumption that he hit most of his home runs at Coors. Others would be incorrectly penalized or aided when hitting in ballparks where one field has a "short porch," while the opposite field has deep dimensions. Finally, players like Wade Boggs adapt to a park regardless of its dimensions, while other players fail miserably in ballparks like Fenway because they overswing for the fences.
- Perhaps most important, when we make ball park adjustments, we are tampering with results that occur within a year. In effect, we are changing the outcome of a season, including who wins the batting title, home run title, ERA title, etc. This book does not in any way alter how one player compares to another player within a year.

Hitting in Fenway may help Fred Lynn, and pitching in Wrigley Field may hurt Ferguson Jenkins. These factors are just the breaks of the game, along with: injuries, lost seasons due to military service, rule changes affecting spitballs and other matters, no competition from black players until the 1940s, and various other factors that produce a player's results within a season.

The statistics in this book are not adjusted for ballpark factors for the above reasons. That adjustment is beyond the scope of this book and, frankly, is a suspect adjustment in metrics used in other books.

Hitter's Inflation

This term simply means the player's batting statistics are inflated by his hitting in a hitter's year, i.e., a year where the league's average Production exceeds the historic average Production of 705.9. The amount of inflation is stated in percentage terms. For example, the National League average Production for 1953 was 747, which represents a hitter's inflation of 5.8 percent when compared to the 705.9 historic average (747 / 705.9 = 1.058).

Hitter's Deflation

A player's batting statistics are deflated by his hitting in a pitcher's year. Nineteen sixty-eight was a well-known pitcher's year, as the average Production in the American League that year was only 639, representing a hitter's deflation of 10.5 percent for all American League hitters (705.9 / 639 = 1.105).

One Example of the Power of the New Metrics

Ty Cobb hit for a consistently high average during his entire career, finishing with a .366 actual batting average — and a .382 adjusted average after factoring in a 4 percent career hitter's deflation. On the surface, Ty lost nothing with age as his career progressed, other than some speed on the base paths. But once we adjust for the hitter's deflation of the Dead Ball Era, and the hitter's inflation of the roaring twenties, a completely different view of Cobb's career emerges. Adjusted for hitter's deflation, Cobb hit .405 in 1907, he batted .382 in 1908, and he then hit over .400 for an incredible ten straight years from 1909 to 1918! Cobb's real batting average performance drops off dramatically in 1920, at the same time the league's hitter's inflation takes off. The same pattern can be seen in his Total Factor and Hits Contribution results. Cobb goes from being a historically underrated phenomenon during the Dead Ball Era to an overrated veteran in the twenties.

Another Cobb fact: his highly acclaimed 1911 season, when he hit .420 with 248 hits and 79 extra base hits, was not his best season. His 1911 performance was, indeed, a very good Cobb season in a Dead Ball year that experienced a very mild 1 percent hitter's deflation. However, on a batting average basis, he hit for better adjusted results with a .436 average in both 1909 and 1910. On a rate of success Total Factor basis, 1910 and 1917 were better. And on a volume of success Hits Contribution basis, 1917 was a better season, while 1910 was about the same.

Ty Cobb's statistical stories are just the beginning of what lies ahead in this book. Welcome to a whole new world of baseball statistics.

Boston/Milwaukee/ Atlanta Braves (1900–2000)

There were two good reasons why the Braves abandoned Boston in favor of Milwaukee in 1953, becoming the first franchise in 50 years to move geographically. First, the Braves shared the fan base of a small city with a successful Red Sox club that boasted Ted Williams. Second, they were perhaps the worst performing National League team, with only two pennants and 13 winning seasons in 53 years.

The Braves struggled from the outset in the twentieth century. After they finished in 3rd place in 1902, the Braves began a decade-long slide as they finished in 6th, 7th, 7th, 8th, 7th, 6th, 8th, 8th, 8th, and 8th place from 1903 to 1912. The 1909 and 1911 teams both finished 63 games under .500, a dreadful performance in any era. The best Braves players in this era were Vic Willis, who went 27–20 with a 2.20 ERA in 1902, and Bill Sweeney, who batted .344 in 1912.

Boston had its first winning season in a dozen years in 1914, and they surprised the rest of the National League by winning the pennant that season. The Braves then stunned the baseball world by sweeping the powerful Athletics club in the World Series. Their star hitter was Joe Connolly, a one-season wonder who batted .306 with 9 home runs, for a 961 Wtd. Production. Their star pitcher was Bill James, another one-season wonder who went 26–7 with a 1.90 ERA and a 2.92 Wtd. RA/9 in 1914, but was only 11–14 over the rest of his career. Teammate Dick Rudolph was 26–10 with a 2.35 ERA, while Rabbit Maranville generated some of the best fielding statistics by a shortstop in the twentieth century. Second baseman Johnny Evers won the league's Chalmers (MVP) Award that year, while Maranville finished second, and James captured third place.

The Braves slid to second place in 1915, as Rudolph won 22 games, and to third place in 1916 behind 19 wins from Rudolph. After their brief three-year winning streak, the Braves sank into the second division again, with only one winning season in 16 years from 1917 to 1932, while often finishing in last place. A one-year appearance in 1928 by Rogers Hornsby (.387, 21 home runs, 1,076 Wtd. Production) had no impact on the team's fortunes, as the Braves finished that season with a 50–103 record.

The Braves put together four modest winning seasons in a six-year period from 1933 to 1938, led by hitting star Wally Berger. Berger began his career in 1930 with a .310 average and 38 home runs, to start a run of seven consecutive solid offensive seasons for Boston. In 1937, Jim Turner was a one-season wonder as a rookie with a 20–11 record, a league-leading 2.38 ERA, and a solid 2.79 Wtd. RA/9. After Berger was traded and Turner faded, the Braves managed to avoid last place from 1939 to 1942 only because the Phillies produced even worse teams.

Nineteen forty-two turned out to be a watershed year for the Braves, as Warren Spahn, Johnny Sain, and Tommy Holmes arrived in the big leagues. However, Spahn and Sain lost the next three seasons to the war effort. Holmes stayed behind, and starred for the 1945 team with a .352 average, and he generated league-leading numbers with 47 doubles, 28 home runs, and a 1,011 Wtd. Production.

Sain returned in 1946 to win 20 or more games three straight years. Warren Spahn waited until 1947 to blossom into a star with a 21–10 record and league-leading 2.33 ERA, for an impressive 2.65 Wtd. RA/9. Spahn had

11

14 seasons of 20 or more wins from 1947 to 1963, establishing himself as one of the greatest National League pitchers of all time. It is no coincidence that the Braves put together their first successful period in history during Spahn's tenure, as the Braves played 22 seasons of .500 or better ball in the next 29 years.

The 1948 Braves won the team's second pennant ever, led by "Spahn and Sain and two days of rain." Holmes batted .325, Jeff Heath hit .319 with 20 home runs, and Bob Elliott hit .283 with 23 home runs. These stars missed out on an all–Boston World Series when the Indians edged the Red Sox by one game.

The Braves had only one winning season between 1949 and 1952. The team moved to Milwaukee in 1953, and climbed into second place behind Spahn's best season (23–7 record, league-leading 2.10 ERA, 2.39 Wtd. RA/9) and the bat of second-year third baseman Eddie Mathews, who hit .302 with 47 home runs.

Hank Aaron arrived in the big leagues in 1954, and the Braves went on to win pennants in 1957 and 1958, while just missing in 1956 and in 1959. MVP Aaron hit .322 and led the league with 44 home runs for the 1957 squad. In 1959, Aaron hit a league-leading .355 average and 39 home runs, for a 1,012 Wtd. Production and a 1,063 Total Factor. That same year Spahn won his usual 21 games, while Mathews had his best season with a .306 average and a league-leading 46 home runs, for a 955 Wtd. Production and 985 Total Factor.

The Braves finished in the middle of the pack during the first half of the 1960s, which led to another franchise move to Atlanta in 1966. The Braves struggled the next three years as well, before winning their division in 1969. Aaron was the team's star the entire decade, hitting 375 home runs over that period. In his best season in 1963, Aaron batted .319 with 44 home runs and 31 steals in 36 attempts. Adjusted for a 5 percent hitter's deflation, Aaron hit .335 with 46 home runs, for a 1,031 Wtd. Production, a 1,089 Total Factor and 112 Hits Contribution. Other 1960s stars included catcher Joe Torre, who hit .315 with 36 home runs for a 955 Total Factor in 1966, and Felipe Alou, who batted .327 with 31 home runs that same season.

In 1970, Rico Carty hit .366 with 25 home runs for a 1,014 Wtd. Production, but the Braves weren't going anywhere due to weak pitching. Aaron put together his best Production numbers in 1971, when he hit .327 with 47 home runs, for a 1,115 Wtd. Production. In 1973, Aaron still managed to hit 40 home runs at age 39 — in just 392 at bats. That year Aaron, Darrell Evans and Davy Johnson became the only three hitters on the same team to hit more than 40 home runs in the same season, yet the team finished 9 games under .500 due to poor pitching. The 1974 team turned the tables, with strong pitching led by Phil Niekro, who went 20–13 with a 2.38 ERA, and with worse hitting, as the "Big Three" sluggers went from 124 home runs in 1973 to 60 home runs in 1974. The Braves then suffered through five losing seasons from 1975 to 1979.

Atlanta won the division in 1982 behind the bat of MVP Dale Murphy (.281, 36 home runs, 23 steals), and the pitching of crafty veteran Niekro, who was 17–4 with a 3.61 ERA. Atlanta finished second in 1983 behind MVP Murphy's .302 average, 36 homers, 30 steals, and 1,025 Total Factor in his best season. The Braves then slumped again, with seven straight losing seasons from 1984 to 1990.

In 1990, the Braves finished in last place and, as of that moment, had only 33 winning seasons in 91 years. They were perhaps the least likely franchise to win nine division titles in the next ten years, yet, they did just that. The Braves won with pitching, as Greg Maddux came from the Cubs in 1993 to join Tom Glavine and John Smoltz in forming the best rotation in baseball. Glavine won the Cy Young Award in 1991; Maddux won the same award for the Cubs in 1992 and for the Braves in 1993, 1994, and 1995. In 1995, Maddux achieved the second highest rate of success in major league history with a 1.64 Wtd. RA/9, while blazing to a 19–2 record. Smoltz won the Cy Young in 1996; Maddux finished second to Montreal's Pedro Martinez in 1997; and Glavine won the Cy Young in 1998 with his finest season (20–6, 2.47 ERA, 2.59 Wtd. RA/9). In 1999, Kevin Millwood competed for the Cy Young Award with a 18–7 record, a 2.68 ERA, and a 2.86 Wtd. RA/9. In 2000, the Braves featured two Cy Young contenders in Glavine (league-leading 21 wins) and Maddux (19–9, 3.00 ERA, 2.95 Wtd. RA/9).

Offensive contributors to these successful Braves teams included Fred McGriff (.318, 34 home runs in the strike-shortened 1994 season), Andres Galarraga (.305, 44 home runs in 1998), and 1991 MVP Terry Pendleton (.319, 22 home runs). In 1999, MVP Chipper Jones hit .319 with 45 home runs, and stole 25 bases in 28 attempts. Adjusted for 9 percent hitter's inflation, Jones batted .292 with 42 home runs, for a 986 Wtd. Production, a 1,022 Total Factor and 101.2 Hits Contribution.

Boston/Milwaukee/Atlanta Braves (1900–2000)

Boston/Milwaukee/Atlanta Braves **Hitters Volume of Success**

Pos	Year	Name	AB	BB	HBP	TAB	H	2B	3B	HR	BA	OB	SA	PRO	Wtd PRO	SB	CS	SBF	SPF	FF	R TF	V HC
C	1966	J.Torre	546	60	2	608	172	20	3	36	.315	.385	.560	945	955	0	4	(12)	(10)	20	952	79.6
1B	1994	F.McGriff	424	50	1	475	135	25	1	34	.318	.392	.623	1,014	955	7	3	2	0	0	957	59.7
2B	1928	R.Hornsby	486	107	1	594	188	42	7	21	.387	.498	.632	1,130	1,076	5			0	(20)	1,056	110.5
SS	1919	R.Maranville	480	36	1	517	128	18	10	5	.267	.319	.377	696	758	12			10	100	868	58.8
3B	1999	C.Jones	567	126	2	695	181	41	1	45	.319	.445	.633	1,078	986	25	3	26	10	0	1,022	101.2
OF	1963	H.Aaron	631	78	0	709	201	29	4	44	.319	.394	.586	980	1,031	31	5	28	10	20	1,089	112.0
OF	1945	T.Holmes	636	70	4	710	224	47	6	28	.352	.420	.577	997	1,011	15			0	20	1,031	97.3
OF	1983	D.Murphy	589	90	2	681	178	24	4	36	.302	.396	.540	936	944	30	4	31	10	40	1,025	86.8
Starters		Averages	545	77	2	624	176	31	5	31	.323	.408	.567	975	971	16	2	9	4	23	1,006	88.2
C	1998	J.Lopez	489	30	6	525	139	21	1	34	.284	.333	.540	873	831	5	3	(2)	(10)	40	859	45.5
1B	1998	A.Galarraga	555	63	25	643	169	27	1	44	.305	.400	.595	994	946	7	6	(7)	0	(10)	929	48.7
2B	1973	D.Johnson	559	81	9	649	151	25	0	43	.270	.371	.546	917	925	5	3	(1)	0	0	923	73.6
SS	1964	D.Menke	505	68	4	577	143	29	5	20	.283	.373	.479	852	875	4	2	0	0	(10)	865	55.9
3B	1959	E.Mathews	594	80	3	677	182	16	8	46	.306	.391	.593	984	955	2	1	0	10	20	985	91.4
OF	1989	L.Smith	482	76	11	569	152	34	4	21	.315	.420	.533	953	990	25	12	2	10	0	1,001	66.1
OF	1933	W.Berger	528	41	3	572	165	37	8	27	.313	.365	.566	932	969	2			10	0	979	63.4
OF	1970	R.Carty	478	77	2	557	175	23	3	25	.366	.456	.584	1,040	1,014	1	2	(5)	(10)	(20)	979	58.7
Reserves		Averages	524	65	8	596	160	27	4	33	.305	.389	.556	945	939	6	4	(2)	1	3	941	62.9
Totals		Weighted Ave.	538	73	4	614	170	29	4	32	.317	.402	.563	965	960	13	3	6	3	16	984	79.8

Pitchers Volume of Success

Pos	Year	Name	G	GS	IP	W	L	SV	SO	BB	ERA	RA/9	Wtd RA/9	R Runs /162
SP	1994	G.Maddux	25	25	202	16	6	0	156	31	1.56	1.96	1.92	83.7
SP	1953	W.Spahn	35	32	266	23	7	3	148	70	2.10	2.54	2.39	67.5
SP	1914	B.James	46	37	332	26	7	3	156	118	1.90	2.47	2.92	63.4
SP	1948	J.Sain	42	39	315	24	15	1	137	83	2.60	3.00	3.04	55.9
SP	1902	V.Willis	51	46	410	27	20	3	225	101	2.20	3.12	3.52	54.7
Starters		Averages	40	36	305	23	11	2	164	81	2.12	2.70	2.88	65.0
RP	1981	R.Camp	48	0	76	9	3	17	47	12	1.78	2.01	2.35	28.2
RP	1993	G.McMichael	74	0	92	2	3	19	89	29	2.06	2.16	2.18	24.3
RP	1974	T.House	56	0	103	6	2	11	64	27	1.93	2.27	2.49	23.6
RP	1982	S.Bedrosian	64	3	138	8	6	11	123	57	2.42	2.55	2.85	26.2
Relievers		Averages	61	1	102	6	4	15	81	31	2.10	2.29	2.52	25.6
Totals		Averages	100	37	407	29	15	17	245	112	2.11	2.60	2.79	90.6

Boston/Milwaukee/Atlanta Braves

Hitters Rate of Success

Pos	Year	Name	AB	BB	HBP	TAB	H	2B	3B	HR	BA	OB	SA	PRO	Wtd PRO	SB	CS	SBF	SPF	FF	R TF	V HC
C	1966	J.Torre	546	60	2	608	172	20	3	36	.315	.385	.560	945	955	0	4	(12)	(10)	20	952	79.6
1B	1971	H.Aaron	495	71	2	568	162	22	3	47	.327	.414	.669	1,082	1,115	1	1	(2)	10	0	1,124	95.7
2B	1928	R.Hornsby	486	107	1	594	188	42	7	21	.387	.498	.632	1,130	1,076	5			0	(20)	1,056	110.5
SS	1919	R.Maranville	480	36	1	517	128	18	10	5	.267	.319	.377	696	758	12			10	100	868	58.8
3B	1999	C.Jones	567	126	2	695	181	41	1	45	.319	.445	.633	1,078	986	25	3	26	10	0	1,022	101.2
OF	1945	T.Holmes	636	70	4	710	224	47	6	28	.352	.420	.577	997	1,011	15			0	20	1,031	97.3
OF	1983	D.Murphy	589	90	2	681	178	24	4	36	.302	.396	.540	936	944	30	4	31	10	40	1,025	86.8
OF	1989	L.Smith	482	76	11	569	152	34	4	21	.315	.420	.533	953	990	25	12	2	10	0	1,001	66.1
Starters		Averages	535	80	3	618	173	31	5	30	.324	.414	.567	981	982	14	3	5	5	20	1,013	87.0
C	1998	J.Lopez	489	30	6	525	139	21	1	34	.284	.333	.540	873	831	5	3	(2)	(10)	40	859	45.5
1B	1994	F.McGriff	424	50	1	475	135	25	1	34	.318	.392	.623	1,014	955	7	3	2	0	0	957	59.7
2B	1973	D.Johnson	559	81	9	649	151	25	0	43	.270	.371	.546	917	925	5	3	(1)	0	0	923	73.6
SS	1964	D.Menke	505	68	4	577	143	29	5	20	.283	.373	.479	852	875	4	2	0	0	(10)	865	55.9
3B	1954	E.Mathews	476	113	2	591	138	21	4	40	.290	.428	.603	1,031	977	10	3	6	10	0	993	82.1
OF	1970	R.Carty	478	77	2	557	175	23	3	25	.366	.456	.584	1,040	1,014	1	2	(5)	(10)	(20)	979	58.7
OF	1933	W.Berger	528	41	3	572	165	37	8	27	.313	.365	.566	932	969	2			10	0	979	63.4
OF	1948	J.Heath	364	51	1	416	116	26	5	20	.319	.404	.582	986	974	2			0	0	974	45.1
Reserves		Averages	478	64	4	545	145	26	3	30	.304	.390	.563	953	939	5	2	0	0	1	940	60.5
Totals		Weighted Ave.	516	74	3	594	164	29	4	30	.317	.406	.565	971	968	11	3	4	3	14	989	78.2

Pitchers Rate of Success

Pos	Year	Name	G	GS	IP	W	L	SV	SO	BB	ERA	RA/9	Wtd RA/9	R V Runs/162
SP	1995	G.Maddux	28	28	210	19	2	0	181	23	1.63	1.67	1.64	76.7
SP	1953	W.Spahn	35	32	266	23	7	3	148	70	2.10	2.54	2.39	67.5
SP	1998	T.Glavine	33	33	229	20	6	0	157	74	2.47	2.63	2.59	50.1
SP	1937	J.Turner	33	30	257	20	11	1	69	52	2.38	2.80	2.79	53.0
SP	1999	K.Millwood	33	33	228	18	7	0	205	59	2.68	3.16	2.86	43.1
Starters		Averages	32	31	238	20	7	1	152	56	2.26	2.58	2.47	58.1
RP	1993	G.McMichael	74	0	92	2	3	19	89	29	2.06	2.16	2.18	24.3
RP	1995	M.Wohlers	65	0	65	7	3	25	90	24	2.09	2.23	2.19	19.3
RP	1999	M.Remlinger	73	0	84	10	1	1	81	35	2.37	2.58	2.33	20.7
RP	1981	R.Camp	48	0	76	9	3	17	47	12	1.78	2.01	2.35	28.2
Relievers		Averages	65	0	79	7	3	16	77	25	2.08	2.25	2.26	23.1
Totals		Averages	97	31	317	27	9	16	229	81	2.22	2.50	2.42	81.2

Boston/Milwaukee/Atlanta Braves (1900–2000)

Boston/Milwaukee/Atlanta Braves
Catchers

V	R	Year	Name	AB	BB	HBP	TAB	H	2B	3B	HR	BA	OB	SA	PRO	Wtd PRO	SB	CS	SBF	SPF	FF	R TF	V HC
1	1	1966	J.Torre	546	60	2	608	172	20	3	36	.315	.385	.560	945	955	0	4	(12)	(10)	20	952	79.6
2	3	1964	J.Torre	601	36	7	644	193	36	5	20	.321	.366	.498	864	888	2	4	(9)	(10)	20	889	64.9
3	2	1965	J.Torre	523	61	8	592	152	21	1	27	.291	.373	.489	863	887	0	1	(3)	(10)	30	903	63.7
4	4	1998	J.Lopez	489	30	6	525	139	21	1	34	.284	.333	.540	873	831	5	3	(2)	(10)	40	859	45.5
5	8	1967	J.Torre	477	49	3	529	132	18	1	20	.277	.348	.444	792	829	2	2	(4)	(10)	10	825	37.2
6	7	1958	D.Crandall	427	48	4	479	116	23	1	18	.272	.351	.457	807	775	4	1	4		50	829	36.5
7	6	1997	J.Lopez	414	40	5	459	122	28	1	23	.295	.364	.534	898	852	1	1	(2)	(10)		840	35.5
8	9	1963	J.Torre	501	42	5	548	147	19	4	14	.293	.354	.431	785	826	1	5	(16)	(10)	10	810	34.7
9	10	1971	E.Williams	497	42	7	546	129	14	1	33	.260	.326	.491	817	842	0	1	(3)	(10)	(20)	808	34.1
10	17	1972	E.Williams	565	62	6	633	146	24	2	28	.258	.338	.457	795	823	0	0	0	(10)	(30)	783	33.4
11	5	1951	W.Cooper	342	28	1	371	107	14	1	18	.313	.367	.518	884	866	1	1	(3)	(10)	(10)	843	30.8
12	16	1960	D.Crandall	537	34	4	575	158	14	1	19	.294	.341	.430	771	767	4	6	(13)	(10)	40	783	30.6
13	12	1947	P.Masi	411	47	1	459	125	22	4	9	.304	.377	.443	820	794	7				10	804	29.1
14	21	1959	D.Crandall	518	46	3	567	133	19	2	21	.257	.321	.423	744	722	5	1	5		50	777	28.4
15	11	1950	W.Cooper	384	30	3	417	120	22	3	14	.313	.367	.495	862	825	1		(10)	(10)		805	26.7
16	14	1965	G.Oliver	392	36	3	431	106	20	0	21	.270	.336	.482	819	841	5	4	(7)	(10)	(30)	795	24.0
17	18	1968	J.Torre	424	34	5	463	115	11	2	10	.271	.333	.377	710	779	1	0	2	(10)	10	781	23.0
18	13	1977	B.Pocoroba	321	57	1	379	93	24	1	8	.290	.398	.445	844	819	3	4	(12)		(10)	797	21.6
19	23	1903	P.Moran	389	29	11	429	102	25	5	7	.262	.331	.406	737	766	8					766	21.0
20	15	1995	J.Lopez	333	14	2	349	105	11	4	14	.315	.347	.498	845	805	0	1	(5)		(10)	790	21.0
21	22	1945	P.Masi	371	42	1	414	101	25	4	7	.272	.348	.418	766	777	9				(10)	767	18.5
22	20	1962	D.Crandall	350	27	2	379	104	12	3	8	.297	.351	.417	768	751	3	4	(12)	(10)	50	778	18.2
23	19	1956	D.Crandall	311	35	1	347	74	14	2	16	.238	.317	.450	767	747	1	2	(8)		40	779	17.6
24	25	1955	D.Crandall	440	40	2	482	104	15	2	26	.236	.303	.457	760	728	2	1	0		20	748	17.0
25	27	1987	O.Virgil	429	47	7	483	106	13	1	27	.247	.331	.471	802	771	0	1	(4)	(10)	(10)	748	16.1

Boston/Milwaukee/Atlanta Braves
First basemen

V	R	Year	Name	AB	BB	HBP	TAB	H	2B	3B	HR	BA	OB	SA	PRO	Wtd PRO	SB	CS	SBF	SPF	FF	R TF	V HC
1	1	1971	H.Aaron	495	71	2	568	162	22	3	47	.327	.414	.669	1,082	1,115	1	1	(2)	10		1,124	95.7
2	2	1994	F.McGriff	424	50	1	475	135	25	1	34	.318	.392	.623	1,014	955	7	3	2			957	59.7
3	4	1998	A.Galarraga	555	63	25	643	169	27	1	44	.305	.400	.595	994	946	7	6	(7)		(10)	929	48.7
4	3	1972	H.Aaron	449	92	1	542	119	10	0	34	.265	.391	.514	906	937	4	0	7			944	47.4
5	5	1902	F.Tenney	489	73	5	567	154	18	3	2	.315	.409	.376	785	879	21			10	30	919	46.5
6	9	1966	F.Alou	666	24	12	702	218	32	6	31	.327	.362	.533	895	904	5	7	(12)	10		902	44.0
7	8	1970	O.Cepeda	567	47	9	623	173	33	0	34	.305	.368	.543	911	888	6	5	(6)		20	902	39.2
8	6	1990	D.Justice	439	64	0	503	124	23	2	28	.282	.374	.535	909	908	11	6	(2)	10		916	34.9
9	7	1956	J.Adcock	454	32	1	487	132	23	1	38	.291	.339	.597	936	911	1	0	2	(10)		903	32.5
10	12	1950	E.Torgeson	576	119	1	696	167	30	3	23	.290	.412	.472	885	847	15			10		857	30.4
11	10	1903	F.Tenney	447	70	8	525	140	22	3	3	.313	.415	.396	811	843	21			10	20	873	29.9
12	11	1946	J.Hopp	445	34	5	484	148	23	8	3	.333	.386	.440	827	853	21			10		863	22.6
13	15	1960	J.Adcock	514	46	1	561	153	21	4	25	.298	.357	.500	857	852	2	2	(3)	(10)		838	19.2
14	16	1907	F.Tenney	554	82	5	641	151	18	8	0	.273	.371	.334	705	808	15			10	10	828	18.7
15	13	1947	E.Torgeson	399	82	0	481	112	20	6	16	.281	.403	.481	885	857	11			10	(20)	847	18.4
16	19	1996	F.McGriff	617	68	2	687	182	37	1	28	.295	.367	.494	861	820	7	3	1			822	16.9
17	18	1906	F.Tenney	544	58	5	607	154	12	8	1	.283	.357	.340	698	794	17			10	20	824	16.5
18	14	1959	J.Adcock	404	32	0	436	118	19	2	25	.292	.344	.535	879	853	0	0	0	(10)		843	16.0
19	22	1961	J.Adcock	562	59	2	623	160	20	0	35	.285	.355	.507	862	828	2	1	0	(10)		818	14.9
20	21	1954	J.Adcock	500	44	3	547	154	27	5	23	.308	.367	.520	887	841	1	4	(12)	(10)		819	13.4
21	17	1983	C.Chambliss	447	63	0	510	125	24	3	20	.280	.369	.481	850	857	2	7	(22)	(10)		825	13.3
22	20	1973	M.Lum	513	41	6	560	151	26	6	16	.294	.354	.462	816	822	2	5	(14)	10		819	13.1
23	24	1985	B.Horner	483	50	1	534	129	25	3	27	.267	.337	.499	836	849	1	1	(2)	(10)	(20)	817	12.1
24	26	1904	F.Tenney	533	57	9	599	144	17	9	1	.270	.351	.341	692	778	17			10	20	808	11.4
25	30	1951	E.Torgeson	581	102	2	685	153	21	4	24	.263	.375	.437	812	795	20	11	(3)	10		803	11.2

Boston/Milwaukee/Atlanta Braves
Second basemen

V	R	Year	Name	AB	BB	HBP	TAB	H	2B	3B	HR	BA	OB	SA	PRO	Wtd PRO	SB	CS	SBF	SPF	FF	R TF	V HC
1	1	1928	R.Hornsby	486	107	1	594	188	42	7	21	.387	.498	.632	1,130	1,076	5				(20)	1,056	110.5
2	2	1973	D.Johnson	559	81	9	649	151	25	0	43	.270	.371	.546	917	925	5	3	(1)			923	73.6
3	3	1912	B.Sweeney	593	68	5	666	204	31	13	1	.344	.416	.445	861	856	27			10	30	896	70.4
4	4	1911	B.Sweeney	523	77	2	602	164	33	6	3	.314	.404	.417	820	838	33			10	20	868	55.2
5	6	1914	J.Evers	491	87	2	580	137	20	3	1	.279	.390	.338	728	789	12				40	829	41.8
6	10	1957	R.Schoendienst	648	33	3	684	200	31	8	15	.309	.345	.451	796	776	4	4	(6)		20	790	36.0
7	9	1936	T.Cuccinello	565	58	2	625	174	26	3	7	.308	.374	.402	776	759	1				40	799	35.6
8	7	1908	C.Ritchey	421	50	8	479	115	10	3	2	.273	.361	.325	687	801	7				20	821	32.6
9	8	1987	G.Hubbard	443	77	6	526	117	33	2	5	.264	.380	.381	762	733	1	1	(2)		70	801	28.9
10	13	1949	E.Stanky	506	113	2	621	144	24	5	1	.285	.417	.358	775	756	3				20	776	28.4
11	5	1944	C.Ryan	332	36	0	368	98	18	5	4	.295	.364	.416	780	799	13			10	30	839	28.3
12	11	1946	B.Herman	436	69	1	506	130	31	5	3	.298	.395	.413	808	834	3		(10)	(40)		784	25.0
13	14	1907	C.Ritchey	499	50	5	554	127	17	4	2	.255	.329	.317	645	739	8				30	769	23.3
14	18	1901	G.DeMontreville	577	17	1	595	173	14	4	5	.300	.321	.364	685	723	25			10	20	753	22.1
15	16	1988	R.Gant	563	46	3	612	146	28	8	19	.259	.319	.439	757	792	19	10	(2)	10	(40)	760	21.9
16	12	1984	G.Hubbard	397	55	4	456	93	27	2	9	.234	.333	.380	714	729	4	1	4		50	783	21.3
17	17	1983	G.Hubbard	517	55	4	576	136	24	6	12	.263	.339	.402	741	747	3	8	(21)		30	756	19.3
18	15	1985	G.Hubbard	439	56	4	499	102	21	0	5	.232	.325	.314	639	649	4	3	(4)		120	765	19.0
19	19	1968	F.Millan	570	22	6	598	165	22	2	1	.289	.323	.340	663	728	6	6	(9)	10	20	748	18.0
20	22	1970	F.Millan	590	35	5	630	183	25	5	2	.310	.354	.380	734	715	16	5	9	10	10	744	17.7
21	21	1971	F.Millan	577	37	3	617	167	20	8	2	.289	.335	.362	698	719	11	7	(5)	10	20	744	17.4
22	20	1986	G.Hubbard	408	66	4	478	94	16	1	4	.230	.343	.304	647	649	3	2	(2)		100	747	14.0
23	27	1937	T.Cuccinello	575	61	0	636	156	36	4	11	.271	.341	.405	746	738	2			(10)		728	13.6
24	26	1919	B.Herzog	468	23	14	505	130	12	9	1	.278	.331	.348	679	740	28			10	(20)	730	12.3
25	29	1969	F.Millan	652	34	8	694	174	23	5	6	.267	.311	.345	656	671	14	3	11	10	30	722	12.2

Boston/Milwaukee/Atlanta Braves
Shortstops

V	R	Year	Name	AB	BB	HBP	TAB	H	2B	3B	HR	BA	OB	SA	PRO	Wtd PRO	SB	CS	SBF	SPF	FF	R TF	V HC
1	1	1919	R.Maranville	480	36	1	517	128	18	10	5	.267	.319	.377	696	758	12			10	100	868	58.8
2	2	1964	D.Menke	505	68	4	577	143	29	5	20	.283	.373	.479	852	875	4	2	0		(10)	865	55.9
3	3	1914	R.Maranville	586	45	6	637	144	23	6	4	.246	.306	.326	632	685	28			10	140	835	55.3
4	7	1993	J.Blauser	597	85	16	698	182	29	2	15	.305	.405	.436	841	814	16	6	5	10	(20)	810	49.1
5	6	1911	B.Herzog	541	47	17	605	157	33	9	6	.290	.365	.418	783	800	48			10		810	44.8
6	10	1955	J.Logan	595	58	4	657	177	37	5	13	.297	.364	.442	806	772	3	3	(4)		30	797	44.6
7	11	1916	R.Maranville	604	50	2	656	142	16	13	4	.235	.296	.325	620	693	32	15	3	10	90	796	43.9
8	5	1997	J.Blauser	519	70	20	609	160	31	4	17	.308	.411	.482	892	847	5	1	5		(40)	811	43.4
9	9	1940	E.Miller	569	41	5	615	157	33	3	14	.276	.330	.418	748	753	8				50	803	43.3
10	8	1917	R.Maranville	561	40	2	603	146	19	13	3	.260	.312	.357	668	745	27			10	50	805	43.3
11	4	1925	D.Bancroft	479	64	0	543	153	29	8	2	.319	.400	.426	826	765	7	4	(2)	10	40	813	41.1
12	14	1956	J.Logan	545	46	5	596	153	27	5	15	.281	.342	.431	773	753	3	0	5		20	778	34.6
13	13	1926	D.Bancroft	453	64	2	519	141	18	6	1	.311	.399	.384	783	763	3				30	793	34.2
14	15	1948	A.Dark	543	24	2	569	175	39	6	3	.322	.353	.433	786	776	4			10	(10)	776	32.5
15	16	1908	B.Dahlen	524	35	8	567	125	23	2	3	.239	.296	.307	604	704	10				70	774	31.9
16	17	1910	B.Sweeney	499	61	2	562	133	22	4	5	.267	.349	.357	705	748	25			10		758	27.0
17	18	1915	R.Maranville	509	45	2	556	124	23	6	2	.244	.308	.324	632	697	18	12	(10)	10	60	757	26.4
18	24	1953	J.Logan	611	41	7	659	167	27	8	11	.273	.326	.398	724	684	2	2	(3)		60	741	26.2
19	12	1992	J.Blauser	343	46	4	393	90	19	3	14	.262	.356	.458	814	838	5	5	(12)	10	(40)	796	25.0
20	22	1900	H.Long	486	44	2	532	127	19	4	12	.261	.325	.391	716	717	26			10	20	747	24.9
21	25	1982	R.Ramirez	609	36	3	648	169	24	4	10	.278	.321	.379	700	711	27	14	(1)	10	20	740	24.0
22	20	1959	J.Logan	470	57	3	530	137	17	0	13	.291	.372	.411	782	760	1	3	(9)			751	23.6
23	19	1952	J.Logan	456	31	4	491	129	21	3	4	.283	.334	.368	702	711	1	2	(6)		50	756	23.0
24	21	1920	R.Maranville	493	28	0	521	131	19	15	1	.266	.305	.371	676	703	14	11	(15)	10	50	749	22.6
25	23	1957	J.Logan	494	31	4	529	135	19	7	10	.273	.321	.401	722	704	5	0	9		30	743	21.5

Boston/Milwaukee/Atlanta Braves (1900–2000)

Boston/Milwaukee/Atlanta Braves
Third basemen

V	R	Year	Name	AB	BB	HBP	TAB	H	2B	3B	HR	BA	OB	SA	PRO	Wtd PRO	SB	CS	SBF	SPF	FF	R TF	V HC
1	1	1999	C.Jones	567	126	2	695	181	41	1	45	.319	.445	.633	1,078	986	25	3	26	10		1,022	101.2
2	3	1959	E.Mathews	594	80	3	677	182	16	8	46	.306	.391	.593	984	955	2	1	0	10	20	985	91.4
3	4	1973	D.Evans	595	124	3	722	167	25	8	41	.281	.407	.556	964	972	6	3	0		10	982	91.3
4	7	1953	E.Mathews	579	99	2	680	175	31	8	47	.302	.406	.627	1,033	976	1	3	(7)	10	(20)	959	82.8
5	2	1954	E.Mathews	476	113	2	591	138	21	4	40	.290	.428	.603	1,031	977	10	3	6	10		993	82.1
6	8	1960	E.Mathews	548	111	2	661	152	19	7	39	.277	.401	.551	952	947	7	3	1	10		958	80.1
7	6	1955	E.Mathews	499	109	1	609	144	23	5	41	.289	.417	.601	1,018	975	3	4	(8)	10		978	79.8
8	5	1991	T.Pendleton	586	43	1	630	187	34	8	22	.319	.367	.517	884	901	10	2	9		70	980	79.3
9	9	1998	C.Jones	601	96	1	698	188	29	5	34	.313	.408	.547	956	910	16	6	5	10	20	945	76.1
10	10	1963	E.Mathews	547	124	1	672	144	27	4	23	.263	.400	.453	854	898	3	4	(7)	10	40	941	72.0
11	11	1961	E.Mathews	572	93	2	667	175	23	6	32	.306	.405	.535	940	903	12	7	(3)	10		910	64.7
12	12	1957	E.Mathews	572	90	0	662	167	28	9	32	.292	.388	.540	928	905	3	1	1			907	63.2
13	14	1992	T.Pendleton	640	37	0	677	199	39	1	21	.311	.349	.473	822	846	5	2	1		50	897	58.4
14	13	1947	B.Elliott	555	87	0	642	176	35	5	22	.317	.410	.517	927	897	3					897	58.3
15	17	1996	C.Jones	598	87	0	685	185	32	5	30	.309	.397	.530	927	883	14	1	17	10	(20)	890	56.7
16	15	2000	C.Jones	579	95	2	676	180	38	1	36	.311	.410	.566	976	891	14	7	0	10	(10)	891	56.2
17	16	1962	E.Mathews	536	101	2	639	142	25	6	29	.265	.383	.496	880	860	4	2	0	10	20	890	52.9
18	20	1948	B.Elliott	540	131	0	671	153	24	5	23	.283	.423	.474	897	886	6				(20)	866	50.3
19	21	1956	E.Mathews	552	91	1	644	150	21	2	37	.272	.376	.518	894	870	6	0	9		(20)	859	46.1
20	18	1907	D.Brain	509	29	5	543	142	24	9	10	.279	.324	.420	745	853	10				30	883	45.5
21	22	1965	E.Mathews	546	73	3	622	137	23	0	32	.251	.342	.469	811	834	1	0	2		20	855	41.2
22	26	1974	D.Evans	571	126	6	703	137	21	3	25	.240	.383	.419	801	814	4	2	0		20	834	39.4
23	24	1949	B.Elliott	482	90	2	574	135	29	5	17	.280	.395	.467	862	842	0		(10)		10	842	36.2
24	23	1979	B.Horner	487	22	3	512	153	15	1	33	.314	.348	.552	900	892	0	2	(7)		(30)	855	33.8
25	19	1983	B.Horner	386	50	1	437	117	25	1	20	.303	.384	.528	913	921	4	2	0	(10)	(40)	871	32.2

Boston/Milwaukee/Atlanta Braves
Outfielders

V	R	Year	Name	AB	BB	HBP	TAB	H	2B	3B	HR	BA	OB	SA	PRO	Wtd PRO	SB	CS	SBF	SPF	FF	R TF	V HC
1	1	1963	H.Aaron	631	78	0	709	201	29	4	44	.319	.394	.586	980	1,031	31	5	28	10	20	1,089	112.0
2	2	1959	H.Aaron	629	51	4	684	223	46	7	39	.355	.406	.636	1,042	1,012	8	0	11	10	30	1,063	104.8
3	7	1945	T.Holmes	636	70	4	710	224	47	6	28	.352	.420	.577	997	1,011	15				20	1,031	97.3
4	6	1967	H.Aaron	600	63	0	663	184	37	3	39	.307	.373	.573	946	989	17	6	7	10	30	1,036	88.1
5	9	1983	D.Murphy	589	90	2	681	178	24	4	36	.302	.396	.540	936	944	30	4	31	10	40	1,025	86.8
6	5	1969	H.Aaron	547	87	2	636	164	30	3	44	.300	.398	.607	1,005	1,028	9	10	(16)	10	20	1,042	86.1
7	8	1962	H.Aaron	592	66	3	661	191	28	6	45	.323	.393	.618	1,012	989	15	7	1	10	30	1,030	86.0
8	4	1965	H.Aaron	570	60	1	631	181	40	1	32	.318	.384	.560	943	969	24	4	24	10	40	1,043	85.9
9	10	1968	H.Aaron	606	64	1	671	174	33	4	29	.287	.356	.498	855	938	28	5	25	10	50	1,023	85.1
10	11	1987	D.Murphy	566	115	7	688	167	27	1	44	.295	.420	.580	1,000	961	16	6	5	10	40	1,017	85.0
11	15	1957	H.Aaron	615	57	0	672	198	27	6	44	.322	.379	.600	979	955	1	1	(1)	10	30	994	79.5
12	13	1961	H.Aaron	603	56	2	661	197	39	10	34	.327	.386	.594	979	941	21	9	4	10	40	995	78.7
13	16	1985	D.Murphy	616	90	1	707	185	32	2	37	.300	.390	.539	929	944	10	3	5	10	30	989	78.1
14	17	1984	D.Murphy	607	79	2	688	176	32	8	36	.290	.374	.547	920	940	19	7	7	10	30	987	75.3
15	14	1964	H.Aaron	570	62	0	632	187	30	2	24	.328	.394	.514	908	933	22	4	21	10	30	994	71.2
16	22	1960	H.Aaron	590	60	2	652	172	20	11	40	.292	.359	.566	925	920	16	7	3	10	40	973	70.3
17	23	1966	H.Aaron	603	76	1	680	168	23	1	44	.279	.360	.539	899	908	21	3	21	10	30	969	68.5
18	12	1989	L.Smith	482	76	11	569	152	34	4	21	.315	.420	.533	953	990	25	12	2	10		1,001	66.1
19	3	1973	H.Aaron	392	68	1	461	118	12	1	40	.301	.406	.643	1,048	1,057	1	1	(2)			1,055	65.4
20	18	1970	H.Aaron	516	74	2	592	154	26	1	38	.298	.389	.574	962	938	9	0	14	10	20	982	63.5
21	20	1933	W.Berger	528	41	3	572	165	37	8	27	.313	.365	.566	932	969	2			10		979	63.4
22	27	1958	H.Aaron	601	59	1	661	196	34	4	30	.326	.387	.546	933	896	4	1	3	10	30	939	60.1
23	19	1970	R.Carty	478	77	2	557	175	23	3	25	.366	.456	.584	1,040	1,014	1	2	(5)	(10)	(20)	979	58.7
24	30	1982	D.Murphy	598	93	3	694	168	23	2	36	.281	.380	.507	887	901	23	11	1	10	20	932	57.8
25	29	1956	H.Aaron	609	37	2	648	200	34	14	26	.328	.369	.558	927	903	2	4	(9)	10	30	934	57.3

Boston/Milwaukee/Atlanta Braves
Outfielders

V	R	Year	Name	AB	BB	HBP	TAB	H	2B	3B	HR	BA	OB	SA	PRO	Wtd PRO	SB	CS	SBF	SPF	FF	R TF	V HC
26	31	2000	A.Jones	656	59	9	724	199	36	6	36	.303	.369	.541	910	830	21	6	12	10	70	922	56.8
27	28	1907	G.Beaumont	580	37	3	620	187	19	14	4	.322	.366	.424	790	906	25			10	20	936	55.4
28	25	1978	J.Burroughs	488	117	0	605	147	30	6	23	.301	.436	.529	965	982	1	2	(5)	(10)	(20)	947	54.6
29	37	1968	F.Alou	662	48	4	714	210	37	5	11	.317	.367	.438	805	884	12	11	(13)	10	20	901	48.7
30	36	1955	H.Aaron	602	49	3	654	189	37	9	27	.314	.369	.540	908	870	3	1	1	10	20	901	47.2
31	21	1948	J.Heath	364	51	1	416	116	26	5	20	.319	.404	.582	986	974	2					974	45.1
32	26	1964	R.Carty	455	43	3	501	150	28	4	22	.330	.391	.554	945	971	1	2	(6)		(20)	945	44.9
33	35	1980	D.Murphy	569	59	1	629	160	27	2	33	.281	.350	.510	859	870	9	6	(5)	10	30	906	44.5
34	34	1998	A.Jones	582	40	4	626	158	33	8	31	.271	.323	.515	838	798	27	4	29	10	70	906	44.4
35	24	1914	J.Connolly	399	49	8	456	122	28	10	9	.306	.393	.494	886	961	12				(10)	951	44.2
36	40	1931	W.Berger	617	55	2	674	199	44	8	19	.323	.380	.512	892	873	13			10		883	42.5
37	38	1990	R.Gant	575	50	1	626	174	34	3	32	.303	.359	.539	899	897	33	16	2	10	(10)	899	42.1
38	41	1944	T.Holmes	631	61	2	694	195	42	6	13	.309	.372	.456	828	848	4				30	878	42.1
39	42	1900	B.Hamilton	520	107	3	630	173	20	5	1	.333	.449	.396	845	846	32			10	20	876	41.3
40	32	1972	D.Baker	446	45	4	495	143	27	2	17	.321	.388	.504	892	924	4	7	(19)	10		915	39.0
41	45	1935	W.Berger	589	50	4	643	174	39	4	34	.295	.355	.548	903	883	3				(10)	873	37.2
42	39	1950	S.Gordon	481	78	2	561	146	33	4	27	.304	.403	.557	960	920	2			(10)	(20)	890	37.1
43	49	1979	G.Matthews	631	60	0	691	192	34	5	27	.304	.365	.502	867	860	19	6	8	10	(10)	868	36.4
44	46	1973	D.Baker	604	67	5	676	174	29	4	21	.288	.364	.454	818	824	24	3	25	10	10	870	36.1
45	44	1930	W.Berger	555	54	4	613	172	27	14	38	.310	.375	.614	990	865	3			10		875	36.0
46	50	1999	A.Jones	592	76	9	677	163	35	5	26	.275	.366	.483	849	777	24	12	0	10	80	867	35.4
47	54	1934	W.Berger	615	49	3	667	183	35	8	34	.298	.352	.546	899	873	2				(10)	863	35.2
48	58	1986	D.Murphy	614	75	2	691	163	29	7	29	.265	.347	.477	825	827	7	7	(10)	10	30	857	32.8
49	47	1994	D.Justice	352	69	2	423	110	16	2	19	.313	.428	.531	959	903	2	4	(13)		(20)	869	31.9
50	55	1974	R.Garr	606	28	2	636	214	24	17	11	.353	.384	.503	887	901	26	16	(9)	10	(40)	862	31.7
51	60	1951	S.Jethroe	572	57	11	640	160	29	10	18	.280	.356	.460	816	799	35	5	37	10	10	856	31.6
52	33	1995	R.Klesko	329	47	2	378	102	25	2	23	.310	.399	.608	1,007	960	5	4	(8)		(40)	912	31.4
53	59	1946	T.Holmes	568	58	3	629	176	35	6	6	.310	.377	.424	801	827	7				30	857	31.3
54	61	1915	S.Magee	571	54	7	632	160	34	12	2	.280	.350	.392	742	818	15	12	(13)	10	40	855	30.9
55	62	1996	M.Grissom	671	41	3	715	207	32	10	23	.308	.351	.489	840	800	28	11	8	10	30	848	30.9
56	57	1991	R.Gant	561	71	5	637	141	35	3	32	.251	.341	.496	836	853	34	15	6	10	(10)	859	30.8
57	52	1965	F.Alou	555	31	5	591	165	29	2	23	.297	.340	.481	821	844	8	4	0	10	10	864	30.0
58	64	1937	G.Moore	561	61	4	626	159	30	10	16	.283	.358	.456	814	805	11			10	30	845	27.5
59	65	1971	R.Garr	639	30	2	671	219	24	6	9	.343	.374	.441	815	840	30	14	3	10	(10)	843	27.4
60	53	1965	M.Jones	504	29	9	542	132	18	7	31	.262	.314	.510	824	846	8	2	7	10		863	27.3
61	67	1993	R.Gant	606	67	2	675	166	27	4	36	.274	.348	.510	858	831	26	9	11	10	(10)	842	27.2
62	63	1952	S.Gordon	522	77	3	602	151	22	2	25	.289	.384	.483	866	878	0	4	(13)	(10)	(10)	845	26.4
63	43	1991	D.Justice	396	65	3	464	109	25	1	21	.275	.381	.503	884	902	8	8	(16)		(10)	875	26.1
64	71	1951	S.Gordon	550	80	5	635	158	28	1	29	.287	.383	.500	883	864	2	0	3	(10)	(20)	837	25.4
65	69	1911	D.Miller	577	43	0	620	192	36	3	7	.333	.379	.442	821	839	32					839	25.3
66	74	1993	D.Justice	585	78	3	666	158	15	4	40	.270	.359	.515	873	846	3	5	(10)			836	24.9
67	77	1977	J.Burroughs	579	86	0	665	157	19	1	41	.271	.365	.520	885	860	4	1	3	(10)	(20)	832	23.8
68	72	1912	J.Titus	502	82	10	594	155	32	11	5	.309	.416	.446	862	857	11				(20)	837	23.7
69	56	1984	C.Washington	416	59	1	476	119	21	2	17	.286	.376	.469	845	863	21	9	6	10	(20)	859	23.0
70	48	1921	W.Cruise	344	48	2	394	119	16	7	8	.346	.429	.503	932	894	10	8	(14)	10	(20)	869	22.1
71	66	1939	M.West	449	51	5	505	128	26	6	19	.285	.364	.497	861	843	1			10	(10)	843	21.7
72	70	1987	D.James	494	70	2	566	154	37	6	10	.312	.399	.472	871	838	10	8	(10)	10		838	21.6
73	68	1986	K.Griffey	490	35	1	526	150	22	3	21	.306	.354	.492	845	848	14	9	(7)			841	20.8
74	81	1941	M.West	484	72	2	558	134	28	4	12	.277	.373	.426	798	819	5			10		829	20.1
75	80	1966	R.Carty	521	60	0	581	170	25	2	15	.326	.396	.468	864	873	4	6	(13)	(10)	(20)	830	20.0

Boston/Milwaukee/Atlanta Braves
Starting Pitchers

V	R	Year	Name	G	GS	IP	W	L	SV	SO	BB	ERA	RA/9	R Wtd RA/9	V Runs /162
1	2	1994	G.Maddux	25	25	202	16	6	0	156	31	1.56	1.96	1.92	83.7
2	1	1995	G.Maddux	28	28	210	19	2	0	181	23	1.63	1.67	1.64	76.7
3	4	1953	W.Spahn	35	32	266	23	7	3	148	70	2.10	2.54	2.39	67.5
4	6	1947	W.Spahn	40	35	290	21	10	3	123	84	2.33	2.70	2.65	64.8
5	11	1914	B.James	46	37	332	26	7	3	156	118	1.90	2.47	2.92	63.4
6	3	1997	G.Maddux	33	33	233	19	4	0	177	20	2.20	2.24	2.20	60.9
7	15	1948	J.Sain	42	39	315	24	15	1	137	83	2.60	3.00	3.04	55.9
8	66	1902	V.Willis	51	46	410	27	20	3	225	101	2.20	3.12	3.52	54.7
9	25	1901	V.Willis	38	35	305	20	17	0	133	78	2.36	3.27	3.18	53.8
10	7	1998	G.Maddux	34	34	251	18	9	0	204	45	2.22	2.69	2.65	53.3
11	13	1974	P.Niekro	41	39	302	20	13	1	195	88	2.38	2.71	2.98	53.1
12	8	1937	J.Turner	33	30	257	20	11	1	69	52	2.38	2.80	2.79	53.0
13	19	1933	E.Brandt	41	32	288	18	14	4	104	77	2.60	2.70	3.07	50.1
14	5	1998	T.Glavine	33	33	229	20	6	0	157	74	2.47	2.63	2.59	50.1
15	10	1993	G.Maddux	36	36	267	20	10	0	197	52	2.36	2.87	2.89	49.4
16	40	1914	D.Rudolph	42	36	336	26	10	0	138	61	2.35	2.81	3.33	48.3
17	75	1902	T.Pittinger	46	40	389	27	16	0	174	128	2.52	3.19	3.60	48.0
18	31	1951	W.Spahn	39	36	311	22	14	0	164	109	2.98	3.21	3.27	47.0
19	21	1956	W.Spahn	39	35	281	20	11	3	128	52	2.78	2.95	3.13	46.8
20	20	1946	J.Sain	37	34	265	20	14	2	129	87	2.21	2.72	3.11	44.9
21	12	2000	G.Maddux	35	35	249	19	9	0	190	42	3.00	3.28	2.95	44.5
22	23	1936	D.MacFayden	37	31	267	17	13	0	86	66	2.87	3.27	3.14	44.1
23	9	1999	K.Millwood	33	33	228	18	7	0	205	59	2.68	3.16	2.86	43.1
24	14	1996	G.Maddux	35	35	245	15	11	0	172	28	2.72	3.12	3.02	41.9
25	43	1959	W.Spahn	40	36	292	21	15	0	143	70	2.96	3.27	3.35	41.2
26	33	1957	W.Spahn	39	35	271	21	11	3	111	78	2.69	3.12	3.27	40.8
27	28	1937	L.Fette	35	33	259	20	10	0	70	81	2.88	3.23	3.22	40.5
28	36	1969	P.Niekro	40	35	284	23	13	1	193	57	2.56	2.94	3.28	40.2
29	53	1958	W.Spahn	38	36	290	22	11	1	150	76	3.07	3.29	3.39	39.5
30	35	1961	W.Spahn	38	34	263	21	13	0	115	64	3.02	3.29	3.28	39.2
31	49	1954	W.Spahn	39	34	283	21	12	3	136	86	3.14	3.40	3.38	39.1
32	26	1996	J.Smoltz	35	35	254	24	8	0	276	55	2.94	3.30	3.19	38.5
33	34	1962	W.Spahn	34	34	269	18	14	0	118	55	3.04	3.25	3.28	38.3
34	24	1997	T.Glavine	33	33	240	14	7	0	152	79	2.96	3.22	3.17	37.0
35	70	1916	D.Rudolph	41	38	312	19	12	3	133	38	2.16	2.68	3.55	36.7
36	16	1974	B.Capra	39	27	217	16	8	1	137	84	2.28	2.78	3.05	36.3
37	32	1954	L.Burdette	38	32	238	15	14	0	79	62	2.76	3.29	3.27	35.9
38	57	1958	L.Burdette	40	36	275	20	10	0	113	50	2.91	3.34	3.44	35.8
39	41	1933	H.Betts	35	26	242	11	11	4	40	55	2.79	2.94	3.34	34.4
40	50	1931	E.Brandt	33	29	250	18	11	2	112	77	2.92	3.38	3.39	34.2
41	45	1997	J.Smoltz	35	35	256	15	12	0	241	63	3.02	3.41	3.36	34.2
42	56	1956	L.Burdette	39	35	256	19	10	1	110	52	2.70	3.23	3.43	33.7
43	69	1915	T.Hughes	50	25	280	16	14	9	171	58	2.12	2.83	3.53	33.5
44	29	1962	B.Shaw	38	29	225	15	9	2	124	44	2.80	3.20	3.23	33.3
45	44	1991	T.Glavine	34	34	247	20	11	0	192	69	2.55	3.03	3.35	33.1
46	95	1905	I.Young	43	42	378	20	21	0	156	71	2.90	3.48	3.81	32.9
47	78	1903	V.Willis	33	32	278	12	18	0	125	88	2.98	3.92	3.65	32.6
48	39	1997	D.Neagle	34	34	233	20	5	0	172	49	2.97	3.36	3.31	32.4
49	37	1993	S.Avery	35	35	223	18	6	0	125	43	2.94	3.26	3.29	31.5
50	52	2000	T.Glavine	35	35	241	21	9	0	152	65	3.40	3.77	3.39	31.2

Boston/Milwaukee/Atlanta Braves
Starting Pitchers

V	R	Year	Name	G	GS	IP	W	L	SV	SO	BB	ERA	RA/9	R Wtd RA/9	V Runs /162
51	47	1996	T.Glavine	36	36	235	15	10	0	181	85	2.98	3.48	3.37	31.1
52	17	1999	J.Smoltz	29	29	186	11	8	0	156	40	3.19	3.38	3.06	31.1
53	27	1987	D.Alexander	27	27	206	14	10	0	108	53	3.01	3.19	3.20	31.0
54	42	1957	B.Buhl	34	31	217	18	7	0	117	121	2.74	3.19	3.34	30.8
55	80	1950	W.Spahn	41	39	293	21	17	1	191	111	3.16	3.78	3.66	30.8
56	81	1952	W.Spahn	40	35	290	14	19	3	183	73	2.98	3.38	3.66	30.5
57	51	1932	H.Betts	31	27	222	13	11	1	32	35	2.80	3.41	3.39	30.4
58	63	1937	D.MacFayden	32	32	246	14	14	0	70	60	2.93	3.51	3.50	30.4
59	101	1900	B.Dinneen	40	37	321	20	14	0	107	105	3.12	4.52	3.82	30.4
60	22	1925	L.Benton	31	21	183	14	7	1	49	70	3.09	3.54	3.14	30.3
61	64	1963	W.Spahn	33	33	260	23	7	0	102	49	2.60	2.94	3.51	30.3
62	55	1931	T.Zachary	33	28	229	11	15	2	64	53	3.10	3.42	3.43	30.3
63	65	1915	P.Ragan	38	26	247	17	12	0	88	67	2.34	2.81	3.51	30.3
64	85	1949	W.Spahn	38	38	302	21	14	0	151	86	3.07	3.73	3.71	29.9
65	48	1995	T.Glavine	29	29	199	16	7	0	127	66	3.08	3.44	3.37	29.5
66	71	1933	B.Cantwell	40	29	255	20	10	2	57	54	2.62	3.14	3.57	29.5
67	58	1993	T.Glavine	36	36	239	22	6	0	120	90	3.20	3.42	3.45	29.5
68	83	1943	N.Andrews	36	34	284	14	20	0	80	75	2.57	3.17	3.69	28.9
69	38	1967	P.Niekro	46	20	207	11	9	9	129	55	1.87	2.78	3.30	28.9
70	87	1950	V.Bickford	40	39	312	19	14	0	126	122	3.47	3.89	3.76	28.9
71	18	1998	J.Smoltz	26	26	168	17	3	0	173	44	2.90	3.11	3.06	27.9
72	105	1901	B.Dinneen	37	34	309	15	18	0	141	77	2.94	3.96	3.86	27.9
73	61	1938	D.MacFayden	29	29	220	14	9	0	58	64	2.95	3.40	3.49	27.4
74	76	1955	W.Spahn	39	32	246	17	14	1	110	65	3.26	3.62	3.61	27.2
75	46	1954	G.Conley	28	27	194	14	9	0	113	79	2.96	3.39	3.37	27.0
76	73	1960	B.Buhl	36	33	239	16	9	0	121	103	3.09	3.35	3.59	27.0
77	74	1940	D.Errickson	34	29	236	12	13	4	34	90	3.16	3.47	3.59	26.6
78	93	1921	J.Oeschger	46	36	299	20	14	0	68	97	3.52	3.85	3.80	26.5
79	62	1932	T.Zachary	32	24	212	12	11	0	67	55	3.10	3.52	3.49	26.3
80	60	1995	J.Smoltz	29	29	193	12	7	0	193	72	3.18	3.55	3.48	26.0
81	79	1938	L.Fette	33	32	240	11	13	1	83	79	3.15	3.56	3.65	25.3
82	82	1941	J.Tobin	33	26	238	12	12	0	61	60	3.10	3.44	3.67	24.6
83	127	1901	K.Nichols	38	34	321	19	16	0	143	90	3.22	4.09	3.98	23.7
84	68	1959	B.Buhl	31	25	198	15	9	0	105	74	2.86	3.45	3.53	23.7
85	30	1953	B.Buhl	30	18	154	13	8	0	83	73	2.97	3.45	3.24	23.7
86	89	1934	E.Brandt	40	28	255	16	14	5	106	83	3.53	3.92	3.77	23.5
87	118	1978	P.Niekro	44	42	334	19	18	1	248	102	2.88	3.47	3.93	23.1
88	59	1916	P.Ragan	28	23	182	9	9	0	94	47	2.08	2.62	3.47	23.1
89	113	1919	D.Rudolph	37	32	274	13	18	2	76	54	2.17	3.12	3.91	22.9
90	92	1916	L.Tyler	34	28	249	17	9	1	117	58	2.02	2.86	3.79	22.4
91	96	1900	K.Nichols	29	27	231	13	16	0	53	72	3.07	4.51	3.81	22.1
92	106	1924	J.Barnes	37	32	268	15	20	0	49	53	3.23	3.86	3.86	21.9
93	84	1930	B.Smith	38	24	220	10	14	5	84	85	4.26	4.70	3.71	21.9
94	97	1930	S.Seibold	36	33	251	15	16	2	70	85	4.12	4.84	3.82	21.7
95	54	1916	T.Hughes	40	13	161	16	3	5	97	51	2.35	2.57	3.40	21.7
96	88	1934	F.Frankhouse	37	31	234	17	9	1	78	77	3.20	3.92	3.77	21.6
97	67	1953	L.Burdette	46	13	175	15	5	8	58	56	3.24	3.75	3.52	21.1
98	109	1947	J.Sain	38	35	266	21	12	1	132	79	3.52	3.96	3.88	21.0
99	86	1932	B.Brown	35	28	213	14	7	1	110	104	3.30	3.76	3.73	20.5
100	103	1968	P.Jarvis	34	34	256	16	12	0	157	50	2.60	2.88	3.84	20.5

Boston/Milwaukee/Atlanta Braves
Relief Pitchers

V	R	Year	Name	G	GS	IP	W	L	SV	SO	BB	ERA	RA/9	R Wtd RA/9	V Runs /162
1	4	1981	R.Camp	48	0	76	9	3	17	47	12	1.78	2.01	2.35	28.2
2	13	1982	S.Bedrosian	64	3	138	8	6	11	123	57	2.42	2.55	2.85	26.2
3	6	1980	R.Camp	77	0	108	6	4	22	33	29	1.91	2.16	2.44	25.4
4	1	1993	G.McMichael	74	0	92	2	3	19	89	29	2.06	2.16	2.18	24.3
5	8	1974	T.House	56	0	103	6	2	11	64	27	1.93	2.27	2.49	23.6
6	12	1978	G.Garber	65	0	117	6	5	25	85	24	2.15	2.46	2.79	23.0
7	22	1966	C.Carroll	73	3	144	8	7	11	67	29	2.37	2.81	3.12	22.9
8	20	1989	J.Acker	73	0	126	2	7	2	92	32	2.43	2.57	2.97	22.2
9	16	1954	D.Jolly	47	1	111	11	6	10	62	64	2.43	2.92	2.90	21.5
10	3	1999	M.Remlinger	73	0	84	10	1	1	81	35	2.37	2.58	2.33	20.7
11	2	1995	M.Wohlers	65	0	65	7	3	25	90	24	2.09	2.23	2.19	19.3
12	5	1983	T.Forster	56	0	79	3	2	13	54	31	2.16	2.16	2.39	19.0
13	21	1954	E.Johnson	40	4	99	5	2	2	68	34	2.81	3.09	3.07	17.2
14	11	1984	S.Bedrosian	40	4	84	9	6	11	81	33	2.37	2.47	2.76	16.8
15	24	1965	B.O'Dell	62	1	111	10	6	18	78	30	2.18	2.84	3.21	16.6
16	18	1995	G.McMichael	67	0	81	7	2	2	74	32	2.79	3.01	2.95	16.3
17	29	1982	G.Garber	69	0	119	8	10	30	68	32	2.34	3.02	3.37	15.7
18	19	1959	D.McMahon	60	0	81	5	3	15	55	37	2.57	2.89	2.96	15.1
19	10	1999	J.Rocker	74	0	72	4	5	38	104	37	2.49	2.99	2.70	14.9
20	15	1986	G.Garber	61	0	78	5	5	24	56	20	2.54	2.65	2.90	14.4
21	17	1998	K.Ligtenberg	75	0	73	3	2	30	79	24	2.71	2.96	2.91	13.3
22	7	1993	J.Howell	54	0	58	3	3	0	37	16	2.31	2.47	2.49	13.3
23	14	1999	K.McGlinchy	64	0	70	7	3	0	67	30	2.82	3.20	2.89	13.0
24	34	1969	C.Upshaw	62	0	105	6	4	27	57	29	2.91	3.09	3.45	12.9
25	31	1961	D.McMahon	53	0	92	6	4	8	55	51	2.84	3.42	3.41	12.3
26	28	1977	D.Campbell	65	0	89	0	6	13	42	33	3.05	3.24	3.36	11.9
27	36	1988	J.Alvarez	60	0	102	5	6	3	81	53	2.99	2.99	3.52	11.7
28	25	2000	M.Remlinger	71	0	73	5	3	12	72	37	3.47	3.59	3.23	10.7
29	9	1997	A.Embree	66	0	46	3	1	0	45	20	2.54	2.54	2.50	10.5
30	32	1965	D.Osinski	61	0	83	0	3	6	54	40	2.82	3.04	3.44	10.3
31	30	1996	M.Wohlers	77	0	77	2	4	39	100	21	3.03	3.49	3.38	10.1
32	33	1991	M.Stanton	74	0	78	5	5	7	54	21	2.88	3.12	3.45	9.6
33	38	1948	B.Hogue	40	1	86	8	2	2	43	19	3.23	3.56	3.61	9.6
34	37	1953	E.Johnson	36	1	81	4	3	0	36	22	2.67	3.78	3.55	9.5
35	27	1986	P.Assenmacher	61	0	68	7	3	7	56	26	2.50	3.03	3.31	9.4
36	43	1955	E.Johnson	40	2	92	5	7	4	43	55	3.42	3.72	3.71	9.1
37	39	1970	H.Wilhelm	53	0	82	6	5	13	68	42	3.40	3.62	3.64	8.3
38	23	1999	R.Seanez	56	0	54	6	1	3	41	21	3.35	3.52	3.18	8.2
39	44	1996	G.McMichael	73	0	87	5	3	2	78	27	3.22	3.84	3.72	8.1
40	35	1994	M.Stanton	49	0	46	3	1	3	35	26	3.55	3.55	3.48	7.8
41	26	2000	K.Ligtenberg	59	0	52	2	3	12	51	24	3.61	3.61	3.25	7.6
42	42	1995	B.Clontz	59	0	69	8	1	4	55	22	3.65	3.78	3.70	7.4
43	45	1988	P.Assenmacher	64	0	79	8	7	5	71	32	3.06	3.18	3.74	7.1
44	41	1997	M.Wohlers	71	0	69	5	7	33	92	38	3.50	3.76	3.70	6.6
45	49	1983	S.Bedrosian	70	1	120	9	10	19	114	51	3.60	3.75	4.15	5.5
46	40	1980	L.Bradford	56	0	55	3	4	4	32	22	2.44	3.27	3.70	5.3
47	47	1994	S.Bedrosian	46	0	46	0	2	0	43	18	3.33	3.91	3.83	5.2
48	51	1968	C.Upshaw	52	0	117	8	7	13	74	24	2.47	3.15	4.20	4.7
49	46	2000	J.Rocker	59	0	53	1	2	24	77	48	2.89	4.25	3.82	4.4
50	48	1981	G.Garber	35	0	59	4	6	2	34	20	2.61	3.53	4.14	4.2

BOSTON RED SOX (1901–2000)

Sometimes the ballpark defines the team. This is certainly the case with Fenway Park, home to the Boston Red Sox since 1912. Charming Fenway Park makes the Red Sox a fan favorite throughout the country, in the same way that Wrigley Field generates Cubs fans everywhere. The park's dimensions also bring a free-swinging focus to the team. Sox fans are proud that just three sluggers—Ted Williams, Carl Yastrzemski, and Jim Rice—patrolled left field in front of the Green Monster for nearly 50 years. But does anyone remember that Babe Ruth also roamed left field for the Red Sox?

No team regrets a baseball decision more than Boston for shipping Babe Ruth off to New York for $125,000 after the 1919 season, just after Ruth finished hitting .322 with 29 home runs, for an impressive 1,196 Total Factor. This event not only gave the Yankees a huge offensive advantage for more than a dozen years, but it also signaled the dismantling of a Red Sox dynasty by owner Harry Frazee. To this day, the Red Sox use the curse of Babe Ruth to explain why they have failed to win a World Series since 1918, when Babe won two games for the Sox against the Cubs. It is a good thing for their peace of mind that Sox fans don't dwell on the team's giving away another superstar outfielder, Tris Speaker, just three years before they sold Ruth. Just imagine the Red Sox in the 1920s with Ruth, Speaker, and the other players they sold or traded!

Before Babe's curse descended on the Red Sox, they were the American League's most successful team, matching the Athletics with six pennants, and exceeding the Athletics, White Sox, and Tigers' totals with 15 winning seasons over 18 years. They even won all five World Series they appeared in. (They also claimed a sixth title in 1904 by default when the National League champions refused to play the "minor league" champion.)

The early Red Sox teams were especially strong on the mound and in the outfield. Ruth dominated at both positions with his 1919 season, and with a 23–12 record, 1.75 ERA, and 2.87 Wtd. RA/9 as a pitcher in 1916. Star hitters Chick Stahl, Buck Freeman, and Kip Selbach played the outfield together at the turn of the century. Tris Speaker, defensive standout Harry Hooper, and Duffy Lewis formed an even stronger star-studded outfield in the 1910s. In 1912, Speaker, the Chalmers (MVP) Award winner, graced center field while hitting .383 with 10 home runs and 52 steals. Adjusted for 4 percent hitter's deflation, Tris hit .397 with 11 home runs, for a 1,069 Wtd. Production, a 1,149 Total Factor, and 131.1 Hits Contribution.

Outstanding pitchers included Cy Young, who was 33–10 with a 1.62 ERA and a career best 2.23 Wtd. RA/9 in 1901, and Smokey Joe Wood, who was 34–5 with a 1.91 ERA and a 2.75 Wtd. RA/9 in 1912. Then there was Dutch Leonard, an obscure pitcher who went 19–5 in 1914 with a twentieth century best 0.96 ERA, and a 1.68 Wtd. RA/9, fourth best in history. Other pitchers who contributed with strong seasons were Bill Dinneen, Jesse Tannehill, Ray Collins, Eddie Cicotte, Ernie Shore, Rube Foster, and Carl Mays.

When the Red Sox were good, they were very good. And when they were bad, they were very bad. No team has maintained a clearer demarcation line between good and bad eras. Boston's first losing era began in 1919, and continued unabated through the 1933 season, a stretch of 15 years. From 1922 to 1932, the team finished in last place nine times, hitting new lows with records like 47–105, 46–107, 51–103, and 43–111. One small highlight in this dark era was Earl Webb hitting .333 with a record 67 doubles in 1931.

In the 1930s, new owner Tom Yawkey bought star

players to return the Red Sox to good times. Yawkey's Sox played .500 or better ball for 20 seasons from 1934 to 1958. By 1938, Boston was in second place, thanks to Philadelphia acquisitions Jimmie Foxx and Lefty Grove, and Washington acquisition Joe Cronin. Foxx won the 1938 league MVP award with a .349 average, 50 home runs and a 1,065 Wtd. Production, while Cronin hit .325 with 17 home runs. The 1938 Sox team also had a 20-year-old star in second baseman Bobby Doerr. They added 20-year-old future legend Ted Williams in 1939, and 24-year-old rookie Dom DiMaggio in 1941.

At his peak in 1941, Williams produced a .406 average, 37 home runs, 145 walks, a .551 on-base percentage, and a .735 slugging average. Adjusted for 3 percent hitter's inflation, Ted batted .392 with 38 home runs, for a 1,244 Wtd. Production, a career-best 1,234 Total Factor, and 144.3 Hits Contribution. Despite Williams' production, Boston's road to the pennant remained blocked by the Yankees' dynasty that year. And the skills of Foxx and Grove, the team's two former Philadelphia stars, were beginning to fade rapidly. Then the war interrupted everyone's plans, although Doerr stayed long enough to hit .325 with 15 home runs in 1944, for a career best 987 Total Factor.

The nucleus of the team returned in 1946, and the Sox won their first pennant in 28 years with a 104–50 record, led by league MVP Williams (.342, 38 home runs, career best 144.9 Hits Contribution). The team stayed competitive through the Ted Williams years, as he continued to produce astronomical Production numbers. Williams won another MVP Award in 1949 (.343, 43 home runs), while Vern Stephens hit .290 with 39 home runs in his best season. The 1950 team hit .302, with all eight starters and super-sub Billy Goodman hitting .294 or better, yet Boston finished in third place. Stars on this 1950 squad included Williams, Doerr, DiMaggio, Stephens, Goodman, Johnny Pesky, Walt Dropo, Mel Parnell, Joe Dobson, and Ellis Kinder. Another star arriving in 1954 was Jackie Jensen, who earned the 1958 league MVP with a .286 average and 35 home runs. Williams put on an amazing performance in 1957, as the 38-year-old hit .388 with 38 home runs. Adjusted for 1 percent hitter's inflation, Williams batted .386 with 40 home runs, for a career best 1,251 Wtd. Production, a 1,228 Total Factor and 128.2 Hits Contribution.

The Red Sox descended into their second losing period with eight straight losing seasons from 1959 to 1966. This period saw the retirement of Ted Williams and the arrival of Carl Yastrzemski before the 1961 season. Jensen, Dick Stuart and Frank Malzone provided some offensive punch, but the team lacked talent in too many areas, especially pitching. They did have an exceptional relief pitcher in Dick Radatz. Radatz went 15–6 with 25 saves, 1.97 ERA, 2.36 Wtd. RA/9, and 162 strikeouts in 132 innings in 1963.

The Red Sox rose from ninth place in 1966 to win the pennant in 1967 in one of the most exciting races ever, edging the Tigers, Twins, and White Sox in the last week of the season. The reinvigorated and very young Sox were led by a Triple Crown MVP season from the 27-year-old Yastrzemski, who hit .326 with 44 home runs and 121 RBIs. Adjusted for 8 percent hitter's deflation, Yaz hit .351 with 46 home runs, for a 1,122 Wtd. Production, a 1,174 Total Factor and 133.8 Hits Contribution. Boston also featured a bunch of 22 to 24-year-olds in George Scott, Mike Andrews, Rico Petrocelli, Reggie Smith, and Tony Conigliaro. Twenty-five-year-old Jim Lonborg went 22–9 to lead the suspect pitching staff.

From 1967 to 2000, the Red Sox put together 28 seasons of .500 or better baseball in a span of 34 years. The Sox generated winning teams from 1968 to 1974, but failed to win another pennant. In 1969, shortstop Rico Petrocelli hit .297 with 40 home runs, earning a 1,014 Total Factor for his efforts. The next season, Yaz hit .329 with 40 home runs and 23 steals, for a 1,065 Total Factor. In 1972, rookie Carlton Fisk had his best season of his long career, hitting .293 with 22 home runs, while winning his only Gold Glove Award. Adjusted for an 8 percent hitter's deflation, Fisk batted .318 with 25 home runs, earning him the league's second best rate of success at catcher with a 1,027 Total Factor, as well as the league's second best volume of success with an 89.9 Hits Contribution.

After the stars of the 1967 squad failed to win another pennant, a new group of young upstarts led the 1975 team into the World Series. The 1975 team was so deep in outfielders, with rookies Fred Lynn (1975 MVP with a .331 average and 21 home runs) and Jim Rice joining 23-year-old defensive standout Dwight Evans, that 35-year-old Carl Yastrzemski was moved to first, and Cecil Cooper to DH. This special team also featured Carlton Fisk at catcher, Rick Burleson at short, and veteran Luis Tiant anchoring the pitching staff.

Rice and Lynn went on to have big years for the Sox, while Yaz played until he was 44, but only Rice was to participate in other Sox pennants as his career was winding down. The 1978 Sox team came close, with Rice winning the MVP Award for his .315 average, 46 home runs, and 994 Wtd. Production, and with Dennis Eckersley winning 20 games, but the Yankees overcame a 14-game Sox lead in July to win a one game playoff. In 1979, Lynn had a great year, batting .333 with 39 home runs for a career high 1,077 Total Factor. In 1981, Evans had his career year, hitting .296 with a league-leading 22 home runs, good for a 1,073 Total Factor and 113.5 Hits Contribution.

The Red Sox won pennants in 1986, 1988, and 1990,

with Rice, Evans, Wade Boggs, Ellis Burks, and Mike Greenwell providing the offense, and Roger Clemens emerging as one of the best pitchers of all time. Clemens was sharp in his MVP season of 1986, with a 24–4 record, 2.48 ERA, and 2.68 Wtd. RA/9, and even better in 1990, with a 21–6 record, 1.93 ERA, and 2.44 Wtd. RA/9. Boggs had his best season in 1987, when he batted .363, and he displayed a rare burst of power with 24 home runs. Adjusted for 4 percent hitter's inflation, Boggs batted .348 with 23 home runs, for a 1,012 Wtd. Production and a 1,024 Total Factor.

The Sox won their division in 1995 in a strike-shortened year, with league MVP Mo Vaughn (.300, 39 home runs) joining Greenwell and Clemens on top. Despite losing Clemens to the Blue Jays, the Red Sox made it to the playoffs as the wild-card team in 1998 and in 1999. The Sox were led by slugging shortstop Nomar Garciaparra (.357, 27 home runs, 988 Total Factor in 1999), and ace pitcher Pedro Martinez, who went 23–4 in 1999, with a 2.07 ERA, and an intimidating 2.05 Wtd. RA/9.

The Sox missed the playoffs in 2000 despite the magnificent pitching of Martinez, who produced the greatest rate of success for a starting pitcher in baseball history with a 1.55 Wtd. RA/9, while earning an 18–6 record and a 1.74 ERA. Teammate Garciaparra won the batting title with a .372 average, the highest batting average for a shortstop since Arky Vaughan's .385 average in 1935.

Boston Red Sox (1901–2000)

Boston Red Sox — **Hitters Volume of Success**

Pos	Year	Name	AB	BB	HBP	TAB	H	2B	3B	HR	BA	OB	SA	PRO	Wtd PRO	SB	CS	SBF	SPF	FF	R TF	V HC
C	1972	C.Fisk	457	52	4	513	134	28	9	22	.293	.370	.538	909	985	5	2	2	0	40	1,027	89.9
1B	1938	J.Foxx	565	119	0	684	197	33	9	50	.349	.462	.704	1,166	1,065	5	4	(4)	0	20	1,081	106.6
2B	1944	B.Doerr	468	58	0	526	152	30	10	15	.325	.399	.528	927	965	5	2	2	0	20	987	79.5
SS	1969	R.Petrocelli	535	98	1	634	159	32	2	40	.297	.407	.589	996	1,014	3	5	(10)	(10)	20	1,014	106.3
3B	1987	W.Boggs	551	105	2	658	200	40	6	24	.363	.467	.588	1,055	1,012	1	3	(7)	0	20	1,024	96.6
OF	1946	T.Williams	514	156	2	672	176	37	8	38	.342	.497	.667	1,164	1,188	0	0	0	0	0	1,188	144.9
OF	1967	C.Yastrzemski	579	91	4	674	189	31	4	44	.326	.421	.622	1,043	1,122	10	8	(8)	0	60	1,174	133.8
OF	1912	T.Speaker	580	82	6	668	222	53	12	10	.383	.464	.567	1,031	1,069	52			10	70	1,149	131.1
Starters		Averages	531	95	2	629	179	36	8	30	.336	.439	.603	1,042	1,058	10	3	(3)	0	31	1,086	111.1
C	1985	R.Gedman	498	50	3	551	147	30	5	18	.295	.363	.484	847	841	2	0	3	(10)	10	845	43.9
1B	1967	G.Scott	565	63	4	632	171	21	7	19	.303	.377	.465	842	906	10	8	(9)	10	20	927	47.3
2B	1958	P.Runnels	568	87	6	661	183	32	5	8	.322	.418	.438	856	855	1	2	(4)	0	20	870	61.3
SS	1999	N.Garciaparra	532	51	8	591	190	42	4	27	.357	.421	.603	1,025	945	14	3	13	10	20	988	91.8
3B	1901	J.Collins	564	34	5	603	187	42	16	6	.332	.375	.495	869	872	19			10	40	922	68.4
OF	1919	B.Ruth	432	101	6	539	139	34	12	29	.322	.456	.657	1,114	1,136	7			10	50	1,196	130.4
OF	1981	D.Evans	412	85	1	498	122	19	4	22	.296	.418	.522	940	985	3	2	(2)	10	80	1,073	113.5
OF	1979	F.Lynn	531	82	4	617	177	42	1	39	.333	.426	.637	1,063	1,040	2	2	(3)	0	40	1,077	93.9
Reserves		Averages	513	69	5	587	165	33	7	21	.321	.406	.534	940	944	7	2	(0)	5	35	984	81.3
Totals		Weighted Ave.	525	86	3	615	174	35	7	27	.331	.429	.580	1,009	1,020	9	3	(2)	2	33	1,052	101.2

Pitchers Volume of Success

Pos	Year	Name	G	GS	IP	W	L	SV	SO	BB	ERA	RA/9	Wtd RA/9	V Runs/162
SP	1901	C.Young	43	41	371	33	10	0	158	37	1.62	2.71	2.23	110.8
SP	1914	D.Leonard	36	25	225	19	5	3	176	60	0.96	1.36	1.68	75.7
SP	1912	J.Wood	43	38	344	34	5	1	258	82	1.91	2.72	2.75	72.7
SP	2000	P.Martinez	29	29	217	18	6	0	284	32	1.74	1.82	1.55	72.3
SP	1936	L.Grove	35	30	253	17	12	2	130	65	2.81	3.20	2.53	60.0
Starters		Averages	37	33	282	24	8	1	201	55	1.82	2.45	2.22	78.3
RP	1963	D.Radatz	66	0	132	15	6	25	162	51	1.97	2.11	2.36	32.3
RP	1999	D.Lowe	74	0	109	6	3	15	80	25	2.63	2.88	2.50	25.0
RP	1953	E.Kinder	69	0	107	10	6	27	39	38	1.85	2.52	2.56	24.9
RP	1982	B.Stanley	48	0	168	12	7	14	83	50	3.10	3.21	3.25	24.4
Relievers		Averages	64	0	129	11	6	20	91	41	2.45	2.72	2.72	26.7
Totals		Averages	101	33	411	35	13	21	292	96	2.02	2.53	2.38	105.0

Boston Red Sox   **Hitters Rate of Success**

Pos	Year	Name	AB	BB	HBP	TAB	H	2B	3B	HR	BA	OB	SA	PRO	Wtd PRO	SB	CS	SBF	SPF	FF	R TF	V HC
C	1972	C.Fisk	457	52	4	513	134	28	9	22	.293	.370	.538	909	985	5	2	2	0	40	1,027	89.9
1B	1939	J.Foxx	467	89	2	558	168	31	10	35	.360	.464	.694	1,158	1,077	4	3	(3)	0	30	1,104	93.3
2B	1944	B.Doerr	468	58	0	526	152	30	10	15	.325	.399	.528	927	965	5	2	2	0	20	987	79.5
SS	1969	R.Petrocelli	535	98	1	634	159	32	2	40	.297	.407	.589	996	1,014	3	5	(10)	(10)	20	1,014	106.3
3B	1987	W.Boggs	551	105	2	658	200	40	6	24	.363	.467	.588	1,055	1,012	1	3	(7)	0	20	1,024	96.6
OF	1941	T.Williams	456	145	3	604	185	33	3	37	.406	.551	.735	1,286	1,244	2	4	(9)	0	0	1,234	144.3
OF	1919	B.Ruth	432	101	6	539	139	34	12	29	.322	.456	.657	1,114	1,136	7			10	50	1,196	130.4
OF	1967	C.Yastrzemski	579	91	4	674	189	31	4	44	.326	.421	.622	1,043	1,122	10	8	(8)	0	60	1,174	133.8
Starters		Averages	493	92	3	588	166	32	7	31	.336	.443	.617	1,061	1,072	5	3	(4)	0	30	1,097	109.3
C	1985	R.Gedman	498	50	3	551	147	30	5	18	.295	.363	.484	847	841	2	0	3	(10)	10	845	43.9
1B	1909	J.Stahl	435	43	15	493	128	19	12	6	.294	.377	.434	812	938	16			0	0	938	41.5
2B	1969	M.Andrews	464	71	5	540	136	26	2	15	.293	.393	.455	847	863	1	1	(2)	0	10	871	47.9
SS	1999	N.Garciaparra	532	51	8	591	190	42	4	27	.357	.421	.603	1,025	945	14	3	13	10	20	988	91.8
3B	1901	J.Collins	564	34	5	603	187	42	16	6	.332	.375	.495	869	872	19			10	40	922	68.4
OF	1912	T.Speaker	580	82	6	668	222	53	12	10	.383	.464	.567	1,031	1,069	52			10	70	1,149	131.1
OF	1979	F.Lynn	531	82	4	617	177	42	1	39	.333	.426	.637	1,063	1,040	2	2	(3)	0	40	1,077	93.9
OF	1981	D.Evans	412	85	1	498	122	19	4	22	.296	.418	.522	940	985	3	2	(2)	10	80	1,073	113.5
Reserves		Averages	502	62	6	570	164	34	7	18	.326	.406	.529	935	948	14	1	1	4	34	986	79.0
Totals		Weighted Ave.	496	82	4	582	165	33	7	26	.333	.431	.587	1,019	1,030	8	3	(3)	1	31	1,060	99.2

Pitchers Rate of Success

Pos	Year	Name	G	GS	IP	W	L	SV	SO	BB	ERA	RA/9	Wtd RA/9	R V Runs /162
SP	2000	P.Martinez	29	29	217	18	6	0	284	32	1.74	1.82	1.55	72.3
SP	1914	D.Leonard	36	25	225	19	5	3	176	60	0.96	1.36	1.68	75.7
SP	1915	J.Wood	25	16	157	15	5	2	63	44	1.49	1.83	2.09	45.3
SP	1901	C.Young	43	41	371	33	10	0	158	37	1.62	2.71	2.23	110.8
SP	1990	R.Clemens	31	31	228	21	6	0	209	54	1.93	2.33	2.44	53.6
Starters		Averages	33	28	240	21	6	1	178	45	1.56	2.11	2.03	71.5
RP	2000	D.Lowe	74	0	91	4	4	42	79	22	2.56	2.66	2.27	23.2
RP	1994	K.Ryan	42	0	48	2	3	13	32	17	2.44	2.63	2.27	17.2
RP	1995	R.Aguilera	52	0	55	3	3	32	52	13	2.60	2.60	2.31	15.4
RP	1962	D.Radatz	62	0	125	9	6	24	144	40	2.24	2.30	2.36	30.6
Relievers		Averages	58	0	80	5	4	28	77	23	2.42	2.50	2.31	21.6
Totals		Averages	90	28	319	26	10	29	255	68	1.78	2.21	2.10	93.1

Boston Red Sox
Catchers

V	R	Year	Name	AB	BB	HBP	TAB	H	2B	3B	HR	BA	OB	SA	PRO	Wtd PRO	SB	CS	SBF	SPF	FF	R TF	V HC
1	1	1972	C.Fisk	457	52	4	513	134	28	9	22	.293	.370	.538	909	985	5	2	2		40	1,027	89.9
2	2	1977	C.Fisk	536	75	9	620	169	26	3	26	.315	.408	.521	929	919	7	6	(8)		30	941	77.8
3	3	1978	C.Fisk	571	71	7	649	162	39	5	20	.284	.370	.475	844	863	7	2	4		30	898	68.1
4	4	1976	C.Fisk	487	56	6	549	124	17	5	17	.255	.339	.415	754	804	12	5	3		40	848	44.5
5	5	1985	R.Gedman	498	50	3	551	147	30	5	18	.295	.363	.484	847	841	2	0	3	(10)	10	845	43.9
6	7	1980	C.Fisk	478	36	13	527	138	25	3	18	.289	.355	.467	821	818	11	5	2		10	830	38.3
7	6	1919	W.Schang	330	71	5	406	101	16	3	0	.306	.436	.373	809	825	15				10	835	35.3
8	9	1973	C.Fisk	508	37	10	555	125	21	0	26	.246	.310	.441	751	770	7	2	5		30	805	33.7
9	8	1920	W.Schang	387	64	7	458	118	30	7	4	.305	.413	.450	862	829	7	7	(14)			815	31.5
10	10	1984	R.Gedman	449	29	1	479	121	26	4	24	.269	.315	.506	821	824	0	0	(10)	(10)		804	28.9
11	12	1934	R.Ferrell	437	66	0	503	130	29	4	1	.297	.390	.389	779	733	0	0	0		40	773	24.1
12	11	1936	R.Ferrell	410	65	0	475	128	27	5	8	.312	.406	.461	867	781	0	1	(4)	(10)	10	777	23.7
13	14	1933	R.Ferrell	493	70	2	565	143	21	4	4	.290	.381	.373	754	727	4	2	0		30	757	22.5
14	13	1964	B.Tillman	425	49	0	474	118	18	1	17	.278	.352	.445	797	806	0	0	0	(10)	(30)	766	20.0
15	16	1953	S.White	476	29	2	507	130	34	2	13	.273	.318	.435	752	738	3	2	(2)	(10)	20	746	17.4
16	18	1935	R.Ferrell	458	65	0	523	138	34	4	3	.301	.388	.413	801	751	5	8	(20)		10	741	16.6
17	17	1986	R.Gedman	462	37	4	503	119	29	0	16	.258	.318	.424	742	732	1	0	2	(10)	20	744	16.0
18	15	1996	M.Stanley	397	69	5	471	107	20	1	24	.270	.384	.506	891	815	2	0	4	(10)	(60)	749	16.0
19	19	1948	B.Tebbetts	446	62	2	510	125	26	2	5	.280	.371	.381	752	726	5	2	2		10	738	15.4
20	20	1990	T.Pena	491	43	1	535	129	19	1	7	.263	.323	.348	672	683	8	6	(7)		60	736	14.9
21	22	1954	S.White	493	21	0	514	139	25	2	14	.282	.311	.426	737	736	1	3	(9)	(10)	10	727	12.8
22	23	1999	J.Varitek	483	46	2	531	130	39	2	20	.269	.335	.482	818	754	1	2	(5)	(10)	(20)	719	10.5
23	21	1998	S.Hatteberg	359	43	5	407	99	23	1	12	.276	.361	.446	807	759	0	0	0	(10)	(20)	729	9.9
24	25	1961	J.Pagliaroni	376	55	4	435	91	17	0	16	.242	.345	.415	760	739	1	1	(2)	(10)	(10)	717	8.1
25	24	1938	G.Desautels	333	57	1	391	97	16	2	2	.291	.396	.369	766	699	1	1	(2)		20	717	7.7

Boston Red Sox
First basemen

V	R	Year	Name	AB	BB	HBP	TAB	H	2B	3B	HR	BA	OB	SA	PRO	Wtd PRO	SB	CS	SBF	SPF	FF	R TF	V HC
1	2	1938	J.Foxx	565	119	0	684	197	33	9	50	.349	.462	.704	1,166	1,065	5	4	(4)		20	1,081	106.6
2	3	1970	C.Yastrzemski	566	128	1	695	186	29	0	40	.329	.453	.592	1,045	1,049	23	13	(4)	10	10	1,065	97.8
3	1	1939	J.Foxx	467	89	2	558	168	31	10	35	.360	.464	.694	1,158	1,077	4	3	(3)		30	1,104	93.3
4	4	1936	J.Foxx	585	105	1	691	198	32	8	41	.338	.440	.631	1,071	964	13	4	7		20	991	76.5
5	7	1987	D.Evans	541	106	3	650	165	37	2	34	.305	.422	.569	991	950	4	6	(12)		(10)	929	49.2
6	6	1940	J.Foxx	515	101	0	616	153	30	4	36	.297	.412	.581	993	935	4	7	(15)		10	929	49.1
7	8	1967	G.Scott	565	63	4	632	171	21	7	19	.303	.377	.465	842	906	10	8	(9)	10	20	927	47.3
8	12	1995	M.Vaughan	550	68	14	632	165	28	3	39	.300	.391	.575	965	910	11	4	4		(10)	905	45.7
9	16	1996	M.Vaughan	635	95	14	744	207	29	1	44	.326	.425	.583	1,007	922	2	0	3		(30)	894	44.0
10	11	1998	M.Vaughan	609	61	8	678	205	31	2	40	.337	.404	.591	995	936	0	0	0	(10)	(20)	906	43.9
11	9	1974	C.Yastrzemski	515	104	3	622	155	25	2	15	.301	.421	.445	866	907	12	7	(3)	10		914	42.6
12	10	1901	B.Freeman	490	44	6	540	166	23	15	12	.339	.400	.520	920	923	17				(10)	913	42.5
13	5	1909	J.Stahl	435	43	15	493	128	19	12	6	.294	.377	.434	812	938	16					938	41.5
14	14	1994	M.Vaughan	394	57	10	461	122	25	1	26	.310	.410	.576	986	921	4	4	(8)		(10)	902	41.1
15	15	1973	C.Yastrzemski	540	105	0	645	160	25	4	19	.296	.411	.463	874	896	9	7	(7)	10		899	39.5
16	13	1941	J.Foxx	487	93	0	580	146	27	8	19	.300	.412	.505	917	887	2	5	(13)		30	904	38.9
17	18	1937	J.Foxx	569	99	1	669	162	24	6	36	.285	.392	.538	929	852	10	8	(8)		40	884	38.1
18	17	1997	M.Vaughan	527	86	12	625	166	24	0	35	.315	.422	.560	982	927	2	2	(3)	(10)	(20)	894	36.9
19	22	1950	W.Dropo	559	45	5	609	180	28	8	34	.322	.378	.583	961	894	0	0	0	(10)	(20)	864	28.6
20	21	1993	M.Vaughan	539	79	8	626	160	34	1	29	.297	.395	.525	920	897	4	3	(3)	(10)	(20)	864	28.2
21	23	1910	J.Stahl	531	42	8	581	144	19	16	10	.271	.334	.424	758	861	22					861	26.6
22	24	1965	L.Thomas	521	72	3	596	141	27	4	22	.271	.362	.464	827	856	6	2	3			859	25.3
23	25	1989	N.Esasky	564	66	3	633	156	26	5	30	.277	.355	.500	855	877	1	2	(4)	(10)	(10)	853	24.9
24	19	1956	M.Vernon	403	57	7	467	125	28	4	15	.310	.405	.511	916	877	1	0	2	(10)		869	23.2
25	20	1932	D.Alexander	392	61	1	454	144	27	3	8	.367	.454	.513	966	910	4	5	(12)	(10)	(20)	867	22.1

**Boston Red Sox
Second basemen**

															Wtd						R	V
V	R	Year	Name	AB	BB	HBP	TAB	H	2B	3B	HR	BA	OB	SA	PRO	PRO	SB	CS	SBF	SPF	FF	TF	HC
1	1	1944	B.Doerr	468	58	0	526	152	30	10	15	.325	.399	.528	927	965	5	2	2		20	987	79.5
2	2	1949	B.Doerr	541	75	0	616	167	30	9	18	.309	.393	.497	890	858	2	2	(3)		80	935	77.2
3	4	1946	B.Doerr	583	66	1	650	158	34	9	18	.271	.346	.453	799	815	5	6	(10)		90	895	68.3
4	3	1948	B.Doerr	527	83	4	614	150	23	6	27	.285	.386	.505	891	860	3	2	(2)		40	899	65.6
5	7	1958	P.Runnels	568	87	6	661	183	32	5	8	.322	.418	.438	856	855	1	2	(4)		20	870	61.3
6	5	1942	B.Doerr	545	67	1	613	158	35	5	15	.290	.369	.455	824	848	4	4	(6)		40	881	60.3
7	9	1943	B.Doerr	604	62	1	667	163	32	3	16	.270	.339	.412	751	800	8	8	(11)		60	848	54.5
8	8	1940	B.Doerr	595	57	0	652	173	37	10	22	.291	.353	.497	850	800	10	5	0		50	850	53.9
9	10	1950	B.Doerr	586	67	1	654	172	29	11	27	.294	.367	.519	886	824	3	4	(7)		30	847	52.9
10	12	1959	P.Runnels	560	95	1	656	176	33	6	6	.314	.415	.427	841	838	6	5	(6)		10	842	51.5
11	11	1997	J.Valentin	575	58	5	638	176	47	5	18	.306	.375	.499	874	825	7	4	(1)		20	843	48.0
12	6	1969	M.Andrews	464	71	5	540	136	26	2	15	.293	.393	.455	847	863	1	1	(2)		10	871	47.9
13	13	1947	B.Doerr	561	59	0	620	145	23	10	17	.258	.329	.426	755	764	3	3	(5)		70	829	44.7
14	16	1960	P.Runnels	528	71	2	601	169	29	2	2	.320	.403	.394	797	783	5	2	2		30	815	39.0
15	17	1939	B.Doerr	525	38	1	564	167	28	2	12	.318	.365	.448	813	756	1	10	(32)		80	804	33.6
16	18	1952	B.Goodman	513	48	4	565	157	27	3	4	.306	.370	.394	764	776	8	2	7		20	802	33.1
17	14	1951	B.Doerr	402	57	1	460	116	21	2	13	.289	.378	.448	826	806	2	1	0		20	826	32.5
18	15	1910	L.Gardner	413	41	4	458	117	12	10	2	.283	.354	.375	729	829	8			10	(20)	819	30.6
19	22	1990	J.Reed	598	75	4	677	173	45	0	5	.289	.372	.390	762	775	4	4	(6)		10	779	30.2
20	21	1968	M.Andrews	536	81	3	620	145	22	1	7	.271	.369	.354	724	800	3	8	(20)			780	27.9
21	26	1965	F.Mantilla	534	79	8	621	147	17	2	18	.275	.377	.416	793	820	7	3	2		(50)	772	25.6
22	25	1921	D.Pratt	521	44	1	566	169	36	10	5	.324	.378	.461	839	774	8	10	(20)	10	10	774	25.1
23	19	1980	D.Stapleton	449	13	1	463	144	33	5	7	.321	.341	.463	805	801	3	2	(2)			799	25.1
24	27	1908	A.McConnell	502	38	11	551	140	10	6	2	.279	.343	.335	678	800	31			10	(40)	770	23.4
25	28	1981	J.Remy	358	36	0	394	110	9	1	0	.307	.371	.338	709	743	9	2	12	10		765	22.7

**Boston Red Sox
Shortstops**

															Wtd							R	V
V	R	Year	Name	AB	BB	HBP	TAB	H	2B	3B	HR	BA	OB	SA	PRO	PRO	SB	CS	SBF	SPF	FF	TF	HC
1	1	1969	R.Petrocelli	535	98	1	634	159	32	2	40	.297	.407	.589	996	1,014	3	5	(10)	(10)	20	1,014	106.3
2	2	1999	N.Garciaparra	532	51	8	591	190	42	4	27	.357	.421	.603	1,025	945	14	3	13	10	20	988	91.8
3	3	2000	N.Garciaparra	529	61	2	592	197	51	3	21	.372	.439	.599	1,038	951	5	2	2	10	20	982	90.3
4	6	1949	V.Stephens	610	101	0	711	177	31	2	39	.290	.391	.539	930	897	2	2	(3)		10	905	86.4
5	4	1995	J.Valentin	520	81	10	611	155	37	2	27	.298	.403	.533	935	882	20	5	15		10	908	80.4
6	5	1938	J.Cronin	530	91	5	626	172	51	5	17	.325	.428	.536	964	880	7	5	(5)	10	20	906	76.5
7	10	1946	J.Pesky	621	65	3	689	208	43	4	2	.335	.401	.427	827	844	9	8	(10)	10	20	864	69.9
8	7	1998	N.Garciaparra	604	33	8	645	195	37	8	35	.323	.366	.584	950	894	12	6	0	10	(20)	884	68.1
9	12	1997	N.Garciaparra	684	35	6	725	209	44	11	30	.306	.345	.534	878	829	22	9	5	10	10	854	66.4
10	8	1941	J.Cronin	518	82	1	601	161	38	8	16	.311	.406	.508	914	884	1	4	(11)			873	63.4
11	14	1942	J.Pesky	620	42	2	664	205	29	9	2	.331	.375	.416	791	814	12	7	(3)	10	30	851	63.0
12	11	1903	F.Parent	560	13	6	579	170	31	17	4	.304	.326	.441	767	836	24			10	10	856	61.9
13	9	1945	E.Lake	473	106	1	580	132	27	1	11	.279	.412	.410	822	865	9	7	(8)	10		867	59.5
14	17	1948	V.Stephens	635	77	2	714	171	25	8	29	.269	.350	.471	821	793	1	0	1		30	824	58.0
15	15	1939	J.Cronin	520	87	0	607	160	33	3	19	.308	.407	.492	899	836	6	6	(9)		20	847	56.3
16	20	1950	V.Stephens	628	65	0	693	185	34	6	30	.295	.361	.511	872	811	1	0	1		10	822	55.7
17	16	1940	J.Cronin	548	83	1	632	156	35	6	24	.285	.380	.502	882	830	7	5	(4)		10	835	54.9
18	21	1937	J.Cronin	570	84	6	660	175	40	4	18	.307	.402	.486	887	814	5	3	(1)	10		822	53.0
19	18	1904	F.Parent	591	28	6	625	172	22	9	6	.291	.330	.389	719	824	20			10	(10)	824	50.6
20	24	1947	J.Pesky	638	72	0	710	207	27	8	0	.324	.393	.392	785	794	12	9	(8)	10		796	47.6
21	22	1964	E.Bressoud	566	72	1	639	166	41	3	15	.293	.374	.456	830	839	1	1	(1)		(20)	818	47.4
22	19	1951	J.Pesky	480	84	2	566	150	20	6	3	.313	.417	.398	815	796	2	2	(3)	10	20	822	45.5
23	13	1994	J.Valentin	301	42	3	346	95	26	2	9	.316	.405	.505	910	849	3	1	3			852	44.3
24	25	1962	E.Bressoud	599	46	2	647	166	40	9	14	.277	.331	.444	775	758	2	3	(6)		40	792	40.0
25	29	1970	R.Petrocelli	583	67	2	652	152	31	3	29	.261	.339	.473	812	816	1	1	(1)	(10)	(20)	784	38.0

Boston Red Sox (1901–2000)

Boston Red Sox
Third basemen

V	R	Year	Name	AB	BB	HBP	TAB	H	2B	3B	HR	BA	OB	SA	PRO	Wtd PRO	SB	CS	SBF	SPF	FF	R TF	V HC
1	1	1987	W.Boggs	551	105	2	658	200	40	6	24	.363	.467	.588	1,055	1,012	1	3	(7)		20	1,024	96.6
2	2	1988	W.Boggs	584	125	3	712	214	45	6	5	.366	.480	.490	970	986	2	3	(5)		10	991	93.2
3	4	1985	W.Boggs	653	96	4	753	240	42	3	8	.368	.452	.478	929	923	2	1	0		20	943	81.4
4	3	1983	W.Boggs	582	91	2	675	210	44	7	5	.361	.449	.486	935	934	3	3	(4)		20	950	75.1
5	5	1986	W.Boggs	580	105	0	685	207	47	2	8	.357	.455	.486	942	929	0	4	(11)		10	928	69.1
6	6	1901	J.Collins	564	34	5	603	187	42	16	6	.332	.375	.495	869	872	19			10	40	922	68.4
7	9	1989	W.Boggs	621	107	7	735	205	51	7	3	.330	.434	.449	883	906	2	6	(13)		10	903	65.3
8	7	1903	J.Collins	540	24	2	566	160	33	17	5	.296	.329	.448	777	846	23			10	60	916	62.4
9	12	1934	B.Werber	623	77	1	701	200	41	10	11	.321	.397	.472	868	817	40	15	13	10	40	881	57.9
10	8	1991	W.Boggs	546	89	0	635	181	42	2	8	.332	.425	.460	885	890	1	2	(4)		20	905	57.2
11	15	1984	W.Boggs	625	89	0	714	203	31	4	6	.325	.409	.416	825	828	3	2	(1)		50	877	54.7
12	13	1981	C.Lansford	399	34	2	435	134	23	3	4	.336	.391	.439	829	870	15	10	(11)	10	10	879	51.1
13	11	1912	L.Gardner	517	56	1	574	163	24	18	3	.315	.383	.449	832	862	25			10	10	882	47.8
14	10	1902	J.Collins	429	24	2	455	138	21	10	6	.322	.360	.459	820	827	18			10	60	897	45.2
15	17	1971	R.Petrocelli	553	91	2	646	139	24	4	28	.251	.359	.461	820	847	2	0	3	(10)	10	849	41.0
16	22	1904	J.Collins	631	27	5	663	171	33	13	3	.271	.306	.379	685	785	19			10	30	825	36.1
17	16	1953	G.Kell	460	52	5	517	141	41	2	12	.307	.383	.483	866	849	5	2	2			850	34.8
18	23	1949	J.Pesky	604	100	4	708	185	27	7	2	.306	.408	.384	792	764	8	4	0	10	40	814	34.7
19	14	1951	V.Stephens	377	38	0	415	113	21	2	17	.300	.364	.501	865	845	1	2	(7)		40	878	33.6
20	21	1950	J.Pesky	490	104	5	599	153	22	6	1	.312	.437	.388	825	767	2	1	0	10	50	827	33.4
21	18	1905	J.Collins	508	37	4	549	140	26	5	4	.276	.330	.370	700	806	18			10	20	836	32.9
22	20	1911	L.Gardner	492	64	5	561	140	17	8	4	.285	.373	.376	749	759	27			10	60	829	31.8
23	19	1916	L.Gardner	493	48	2	543	152	19	7	2	.308	.372	.387	759	831	12			10	(10)	831	31.3
24	25	1957	F.Malzone	634	31	1	666	185	31	5	15	.292	.326	.427	753	749	2	1	0		60	809	30.9
25	24	1959	F.Malzone	604	42	1	647	169	34	2	19	.280	.328	.437	765	761	6	0	9		40	810	30.5

Boston Red Sox
Outfielders

V	R	Year	Name	AB	BB	HBP	TAB	H	2B	3B	HR	BA	OB	SA	PRO	Wtd PRO	SB	CS	SBF	SPF	FF	R TF	V HC
1	4	1946	T.Williams	514	156	2	672	176	37	8	38	.342	.497	.667	1,164	1,188	0	0	0			1,188	144.9
2	1	1941	T.Williams	456	145	3	604	185	33	3	37	.406	.551	.735	1,286	1,244	2	4	(9)			1,234	144.3
3	6	1942	T.Williams	522	145	4	671	186	34	5	36	.356	.499	.648	1,147	1,180	3	2	(1)			1,179	141.6
4	7	1967	C.Yastrzemski	579	91	4	674	189	31	4	44	.326	.421	.622	1,043	1,122	10	8	(8)		60	1,174	133.8
5	9	1947	T.Williams	528	162	2	692	181	40	9	32	.343	.499	.634	1,133	1,146	0	1	(3)			1,143	133.8
6	8	1912	T.Speaker	580	82	6	668	222	53	12	10	.383	.464	.567	1,031	1,069	52			10	70	1,149	131.1
7	3	1919	B.Ruth	432	101	6	539	139	34	12	29	.322	.456	.657	1,114	1,136	7			10	50	1,196	130.4
8	2	1957	T.Williams	420	119	5	544	163	28	1	38	.388	.528	.731	1,259	1,251	0	1	(3)	(10)	(10)	1,228	128.2
9	13	1949	T.Williams	566	162	2	730	194	39	3	43	.343	.490	.650	1,141	1,100	1	1	(1)			1,099	124.8
10	18	1981	D.Evans	412	85	1	498	122	19	4	22	.296	.418	.522	940	985	3	2	(2)	10	80	1,073	113.5
11	14	1914	T.Speaker	571	77	7	655	193	46	18	4	.338	.423	.503	926	1,018	42	29	(23)	10	90	1,095	110.7
12	12	1968	C.Yastrzemski	539	119	2	660	162	32	2	23	.301	.429	.495	924	1,021	13	6	1		80	1,102	108.5
13	11	1913	T.Speaker	520	65	7	592	189	35	22	3	.363	.441	.533	974	1,040	46			10	70	1,120	107.5
14	16	1948	T.Williams	509	126	3	638	188	44	3	25	.369	.497	.615	1,112	1,074	4	0	6			1,080	103.0
15	10	1954	T.Williams	386	136	1	523	133	23	1	29	.345	.516	.635	1,151	1,149	0	0	0		(10)	1,139	100.1
16	17	1979	F.Lynn	531	82	4	617	177	42	1	39	.333	.426	.637	1,063	1,040	2	2	(3)		40	1,077	93.9
17	20	1910	T.Speaker	538	52	6	596	183	20	14	7	.340	.404	.468	873	992	35			10	60	1,062	91.0
18	5	1955	T.Williams	320	91	2	413	114	21	3	28	.356	.501	.703	1,204	1,181	2	0	5			1,185	88.6
19	19	1975	F.Lynn	528	62	3	593	175	47	7	21	.331	.405	.566	971	1,000	10	5	0	10	60	1,070	88.2
20	28	1978	J.Rice	677	58	5	740	213	25	15	46	.315	.373	.600	973	994	7	5	(4)			991	82.2
21	27	1951	T.Williams	531	144	0	675	169	28	4	30	.318	.464	.556	1,019	995	1	1	(1)			994	80.0
22	22	1909	T.Speaker	544	38	7	589	168	26	13	7	.309	.362	.443	805	930	35			10	80	1,020	77.4
23	15	1918	B.Ruth	317	57	2	376	95	26	11	11	.300	.410	.555	965	1,054	6			10	20	1,084	74.7
24	35	1982	D.Evans	609	112	1	722	178	37	7	32	.292	.403	.534	937	933	3	2	(1)		30	962	70.2
25	32	1940	T.Williams	561	96	3	660	193	43	14	23	.344	.442	.594	1,036	975	4	4	(6)			969	70.1

Boston Red Sox
Outfielders

V	R	Year	Name	AB	BB	HBP	TAB	H	2B	3B	HR	BA	OB	SA	PRO	Wtd PRO	SB	CS	SBF	SPF	FF	R TF	V HC
26	37	1984	D.Evans	630	96	4	730	186	37	8	32	.295	.392	.532	924	927	3	1	1		30	959	70.0
27	31	1963	C.Yastrzemski	570	95	1	666	183	40	3	14	.321	.419	.475	894	910	8	5	(3)	10	60	977	69.6
28	30	1944	B.Johnson	525	95	4	624	170	40	8	17	.324	.431	.528	959	998	2	7	(18)			980	69.6
29	24	1965	C.Yastrzemski	494	70	1	565	154	45	3	20	.312	.398	.536	935	967	7	6	(8)	10	40	1,009	67.7
30	34	1958	J.Jensen	548	99	3	650	157	31	0	35	.286	.398	.535	933	932	9	4	1	10	20	963	67.0
31	23	1956	T.Williams	400	102	1	503	138	28	2	24	.345	.479	.605	1,084	1,038	0	0	0	(10)	(10)	1,018	65.8
32	43	1939	T.Williams	565	107	2	674	185	44	11	31	.327	.436	.609	1,045	972	2	1	0		(20)	952	65.7
33	41	1988	M.Greenwell	590	87	9	686	192	39	8	22	.325	.420	.531	950	966	16	8	0		(10)	956	65.0
34	29	1911	T.Speaker	500	59	13	572	167	34	13	8	.334	.418	.502	920	933	25			10	40	983	64.6
35	45	1969	C.Yastrzemski	603	101	1	705	154	28	2	40	.255	.363	.507	871	887	15	7	1		60	948	64.1
36	26	1958	T.Williams	411	98	4	513	135	23	2	26	.328	.462	.584	1,046	1,044	1	0	2	(10)	(30)	1,006	64.0
37	44	1979	J.Rice	619	57	4	680	201	39	6	39	.325	.385	.596	981	960	9	4	1		(10)	952	63.0
38	38	1977	C.Yastrzemski	558	73	1	632	165	27	3	28	.296	.378	.505	884	874	11	1	13		70	957	60.2
39	46	1915	T.Speaker	547	81	7	635	176	25	12	0	.322	.416	.411	827	897	29	25	(31)	10	70	946	59.9
40	33	1968	K.Harrelson	535	69	2	606	147	17	4	35	.275	.360	.518	877	969	2	6	(16)		10	964	59.6
41	48	1959	J.Jensen	535	88	0	623	148	31	0	28	.277	.379	.492	870	867	20	5	15	10	50	942	57.6
42	21	1960	T.Williams	310	75	3	388	98	15	0	29	.316	.454	.645	1,099	1,080	1	1	(2)	(10)	(20)	1,048	56.5
43	36	1976	F.Lynn	507	48	1	556	159	32	8	10	.314	.374	.467	842	898	14	9	(7)	10	60	961	54.0
44	42	1972	R.Smith	467	68	4	539	126	25	4	21	.270	.367	.475	843	914	15	4	12	10	20	956	53.7
45	55	1942	D.DiMaggio	622	70	6	698	178	36	8	14	.286	.364	.437	801	824	16	10	(5)	10	80	909	53.0
46	25	1950	T.Williams	334	82	0	416	106	24	1	28	.317	.452	.647	1,099	1,022	3	0	7		(20)	1,009	52.4
47	51	1971	R.Smith	618	63	5	686	175	33	2	30	.283	.354	.489	843	870	11	3	7	10	30	917	52.1
48	58	1983	J.Rice	626	52	6	684	191	34	1	39	.305	.364	.550	914	912	0	2	(6)			907	48.7
49	61	1956	J.Jensen	578	89	1	668	182	23	11	20	.315	.407	.497	904	866	11	3	7	10	20	903	48.6
50	49	1978	F.Lynn	541	75	1	617	161	33	3	22	.298	.384	.492	876	895	3	6	(14)		40	922	48.3
51	62	1918	H.Hooper	474	75	4	553	137	26	13	1	.289	.391	.405	796	869	24			10	20	899	47.7
52	39	1973	R.Smith	423	68	1	492	128	23	2	21	.303	.400	.515	916	939	3	2	(2)		20	957	46.8
53	47	1908	D.Gessler	435	51	11	497	134	13	14	3	.308	.394	.423	817	965	19				(20)	945	46.7
54	54	1964	C.Yastrzemski	567	75	2	644	164	29	9	15	.289	.374	.451	826	835	6	5	(6)	10	70	909	46.6
55	65	1904	C.Stahl	587	64	7	658	170	27	19	3	.290	.366	.416	782	896	11			10	(10)	896	45.7
56	56	1970	R.Smith	580	51	4	635	176	32	7	22	.303	.364	.497	860	864	10	7	(6)	10	40	908	45.5
57	40	1980	F.Lynn	415	58	0	473	125	32	3	12	.301	.387	.480	866	863	12	0	24		70	957	44.9
58	69	1966	C.Yastrzemski	594	84	1	679	165	39	2	16	.278	.368	.431	799	835	8	9	(14)		70	891	43.1
59	57	1988	E.Burks	540	62	3	605	159	37	5	18	.294	.370	.481	852	866	25	9	11	10	20	907	43.1
60	59	1969	R.Smith	543	54	1	598	168	29	7	25	.309	.373	.527	900	916	7	13	(30)	10	10	906	42.4
61	75	1903	P.Dougherty	590	33	6	629	195	19	12	4	.331	.372	.424	796	867	35			10		877	41.4
62	66	1968	R.Smith	558	64	4	626	148	37	5	15	.265	.345	.430	775	856	22	18	(21)	10	50	895	41.1
63	67	1989	D.Evans	520	99	3	622	148	27	3	20	.285	.402	.463	865	887	3	3	(5)		10	893	40.1
64	74	1903	B.Freeman	567	30	4	601	163	39	20	13	.287	.328	.496	823	897	5				(20)	877	39.6
65	76	1931	E.Webb	589	70	0	659	196	67	3	14	.333	.404	.528	932	889	2	2	(3)		(10)	876	39.1
66	70	1988	D.Evans	559	76	1	636	164	31	7	21	.293	.379	.487	866	880	5	1	4			884	38.5
67	72	1946	D.DiMaggio	534	66	1	601	169	24	7	7	.316	.393	.427	820	836	10	6	(3)	10	40	883	37.8
68	81	1955	J.Jensen	574	89	3	666	158	27	6	26	.275	.375	.479	854	838	16	7	3	10	20	871	37.8
69	92	1985	D.Evans	617	114	5	736	162	29	1	29	.263	.382	.454	836	830	7	2	4		30	864	37.3
70	68	1965	T.Conigliaro	521	51	5	577	140	21	5	32	.269	.340	.512	852	882	4	2	0		10	892	37.0
71	84	1913	H.Hooper	586	60	5	651	169	29	12	4	.288	.359	.399	759	810	26			10	50	870	36.8
72	64	2000	C.Everett	496	52	8	556	149	32	4	34	.300	.376	.587	963	881	11	4	5	10		896	36.8
73	89	1950	D.DiMaggio	588	82	4	674	193	30	11	7	.328	.414	.452	866	806	15	4	10	10	40	866	36.5
74	86	1954	J.Jensen	580	79	2	661	160	25	7	25	.276	.365	.472	837	836	22	7	11	10	10	867	36.4
75	93	1962	C.Yastrzemski	646	66	3	715	191	43	6	19	.296	.364	.469	833	814	7	4	(1)	10	40	863	35.9

Boston Red Sox
Starting Pitchers

														R Wtd	V Net
V	R	Year	Name	G	GS	IP	W	L	SV	SO	BB	ERA	RA/9	RA/9	/162
1	5	1901	C.Young	43	41	371	33	10	0	158	37	1.62	2.71	2.23	110.8
2	17	1902	C.Young	45	43	385	32	11	0	160	53	2.15	3.18	2.90	82.1
3	2	1914	D.Leonard	36	25	225	19	5	3	176	60	0.96	1.36	1.68	75.7
4	12	1912	J.Wood	43	38	344	34	5	1	258	82	1.91	2.72	2.75	72.7
5	1	2000	P.Martinez	29	29	217	18	6	0	284	32	1.74	1.82	1.55	72.3
6	11	1908	C.Young	36	33	299	21	11	2	150	37	1.26	2.05	2.69	65.2
7	26	1904	C.Young	43	41	380	26	16	1	200	29	1.97	2.46	3.11	64.1
8	16	1916	B.Ruth	44	41	324	23	12	1	170	118	1.75	2.31	2.87	64.0
9	7	1936	L.Grove	35	30	253	17	12	2	130	65	2.81	3.20	2.53	60.0
10	3	1999	P.Martinez	31	29	213	23	4	0	313	37	2.07	2.36	2.05	59.5
11	41	1903	C.Young	40	35	342	28	9	2	176	37	2.08	3.03	3.30	55.1
12	22	1949	M.Parnell	39	33	295	25	7	2	122	134	2.77	3.11	2.98	54.3
13	50	1902	B.Dinneen	42	42	371	21	21	0	136	99	2.93	3.76	3.43	53.9
14	6	1990	R.Clemens	31	31	228	21	6	0	209	54	1.93	2.33	2.44	53.6
15	32	1917	B.Ruth	41	38	326	24	13	2	128	108	2.01	2.51	3.15	53.6
16	10	1986	R.Clemens	33	33	254	24	4	0	238	67	2.48	2.73	2.68	53.1
17	39	1907	C.Young	43	37	343	21	15	2	147	51	1.99	2.65	3.26	51.8
18	37	1903	B.Dinneen	37	34	299	21	13	2	148	66	2.26	2.95	3.22	51.5
19	18	1987	R.Clemens	36	36	282	20	9	0	256	83	2.97	3.20	2.95	50.5
20	21	1937	L.Grove	32	32	262	17	9	0	153	83	3.02	3.47	2.96	48.9
21	25	1935	L.Grove	35	30	273	20	12	1	121	65	2.70	3.46	3.07	47.3
22	33	1917	C.Mays	35	33	289	22	9	0	91	74	1.74	2.52	3.16	47.1
23	30	1942	T.Hughson	38	30	281	22	6	4	113	75	2.59	2.95	3.13	46.8
24	13	1994	R.Clemens	24	24	171	9	7	0	168	71	2.85	3.27	2.83	46.5
25	38	1921	S.Jones	40	38	299	23	16	1	98	78	3.22	3.67	3.26	45.3
26	4	1915	J.Wood	25	16	157	15	5	2	63	44	1.49	1.83	2.09	45.3
27	8	1939	L.Grove	23	23	191	15	4	0	81	58	2.54	2.97	2.55	44.7
28	15	1998	P.Martinez	33	33	234	19	7	0	251	67	2.89	3.16	2.85	44.5
29	36	1946	T.Hughson	39	35	278	20	11	3	172	51	2.75	2.88	3.20	44.1
30	47	1905	C.Young	38	33	321	18	19	0	210	30	1.82	2.78	3.40	43.5
31	29	1991	R.Clemens	35	35	271	18	10	0	241	65	2.62	3.08	3.13	43.1
32	24	1957	F.Sullivan	31	30	241	14	11	0	127	48	2.73	2.84	3.07	42.0
33	28	1915	E.Shore	38	32	247	19	8	0	102	66	1.64	2.73	3.12	41.5
34	23	1992	R.Clemens	32	32	247	18	11	0	208	62	2.41	2.92	3.07	40.9
35	14	1944	T.Hughson	28	23	203	18	5	5	112	41	2.26	2.53	2.83	40.9
36	46	1974	L.Tiant	38	38	311	22	13	0	176	82	2.92	3.06	3.39	40.2
37	9	1972	L.Tiant	43	19	179	15	6	3	123	65	1.91	2.26	2.65	40.0
38	49	1919	C.Mays	34	29	266	14	14	2	107	77	2.10	3.09	3.41	39.2
39	31	1979	D.Eckersley	33	33	247	17	10	0	150	59	2.99	3.25	3.14	39.0
40	44	1973	B.Lee	38	33	285	17	11	1	120	76	2.75	3.16	3.35	38.3
41	71	1918	C.Mays	35	33	293	21	13	0	114	81	2.21	2.89	3.64	38.2
42	51	1917	D.Leonard	37	36	294	16	17	1	144	72	2.17	2.76	3.46	37.5
43	40	1988	R.Clemens	35	35	264	18	12	0	291	62	2.93	3.17	3.28	37.4
44	20	1912	R.Collins	27	24	199	13	8	0	82	42	2.53	2.93	2.96	37.1
45	43	1915	R.Foster	37	33	255	19	8	1	82	86	2.11	2.93	3.35	36.1
46	67	1924	H.Ehmke	45	36	315	19	17	4	119	81	3.46	3.97	3.60	35.4
47	27	1995	T.Wakefield	27	27	195	16	8	0	119	68	2.95	3.50	3.12	35.1
48	74	1918	J.Bush	36	31	273	15	15	2	125	91	2.11	2.90	3.65	35.1
49	45	1910	R.Collins	35	26	245	13	11	1	109	41	1.62	2.69	3.35	34.6
50	42	1996	R.Clemens	34	34	243	10	13	0	257	106	3.63	3.93	3.30	33.8

Boston Red Sox
Starting Pitchers

V	R	Year	Name	G	GS	IP	W	L	SV	SO	BB	ERA	RA/9	R Wtd RA/9	V Net /162
51	52	1943	T.Hughson	35	32	266	12	15	2	114	73	2.64	2.94	3.48	33.5
52	58	1912	B.O'Brien	37	34	276	20	13	0	115	90	2.58	3.49	3.53	33.2
53	84	1935	W.Ferrell	41	38	322	25	14	0	110	108	3.52	4.16	3.70	32.4
54	61	1916	D.Leonard	48	34	274	18	12	6	144	66	2.36	2.86	3.55	32.2
55	66	1904	J.Tannehill	33	31	282	21	11	0	116	33	2.04	2.84	3.59	31.7
56	55	1921	J.Bush	37	32	254	16	9	1	96	93	3.50	3.93	3.49	31.6
57	19	1938	L.Grove	24	21	164	14	4	1	99	52	3.08	3.57	2.95	30.9
58	69	1911	J.Wood	44	33	276	23	17	3	231	76	2.02	3.68	3.61	30.7
59	59	1949	E.Kinder	43	30	252	23	6	4	138	99	3.36	3.68	3.53	30.2
60	63	1978	D.Eckersley	35	35	268	20	8	0	162	71	2.99	3.32	3.57	29.4
61	35	1915	D.Leonard	32	21	183	15	7	0	116	67	2.36	2.80	3.20	29.1
62	60	1919	H.Pennock	32	26	219	16	8	0	70	48	2.71	3.21	3.54	28.6
63	70	1955	F.Sullivan	35	35	260	18	13	0	129	100	2.91	3.57	3.63	28.1
64	77	1905	J.Tannehill	37	32	272	22	9	0	113	59	2.48	3.01	3.68	28.0
65	92	1936	W.Ferrell	39	38	301	20	15	0	106	119	4.19	4.78	3.78	27.5
66	68	1916	C.Mays	44	24	245	18	13	3	76	74	2.39	2.90	3.60	27.4
67	56	1993	D.Darwin	34	34	229	15	11	0	130	49	3.26	3.65	3.50	26.9
68	78	1973	L.Tiant	35	35	272	20	13	0	206	78	3.34	3.47	3.68	26.6
69	34	1986	B.Hurst	25	25	174	13	8	0	167	50	2.99	3.25	3.19	26.5
70	57	1948	M.Parnell	35	27	212	15	8	0	77	90	3.14	3.69	3.51	25.9
71	65	1947	J.Dobson	33	31	229	18	8	1	110	73	2.95	3.30	3.59	25.9
72	111	1904	B.Dinneen	37	37	336	23	14	0	153	63	2.20	3.08	3.90	25.9
73	80	1913	R.Collins	30	30	247	19	8	0	88	37	2.63	3.21	3.68	25.2
74	54	1918	B.Ruth	20	19	166	13	7	0	40	49	2.22	2.77	3.49	25.2
75	93	1930	M.Gaston	38	34	273	13	20	2	99	98	3.92	4.55	3.78	24.9
76	79	1956	T.Brewer	32	32	244	19	9	0	127	112	3.50	3.80	3.68	24.9
77	62	1914	R.Foster	32	27	212	14	8	0	89	52	1.70	2.88	3.56	24.8
78	85	1950	M.Parnell	40	31	249	18	10	3	93	106	3.61	4.19	3.72	24.3
79	75	1912	H.Bedient	41	28	231	20	9	2	122	55	2.92	3.62	3.66	24.3
80	48	1911	L.Pape	27	19	176	10	8	0	49	63	2.45	3.47	3.40	23.8
81	100	1903	T.Hughes	33	31	245	20	7	0	112	60	2.57	3.49	3.80	23.7
82	53	1941	C.Wagner	29	25	187	12	8	0	51	85	3.07	3.66	3.48	23.5
83	86	1953	M.Parnell	38	34	241	21	8	0	136	116	3.06	3.66	3.72	23.5
84	90	1989	R.Clemens	35	35	253	17	11	0	230	93	3.13	3.59	3.77	22.1
85	72	1953	M.McDermott	32	30	206	18	10	0	92	109	3.01	3.58	3.64	22.0
86	106	1985	O.Boyd	35	35	272	15	13	0	154	67	3.70	3.87	3.83	21.9
87	73	1978	L.Tiant	32	31	212	13	8	0	114	57	3.31	3.39	3.64	21.5
88	137	1901	T.Lewis	39	34	316	16	17	1	103	91	3.53	4.89	4.03	21.4
89	105	1920	H.Pennock	37	31	242	16	13	2	68	61	3.68	4.02	3.82	20.7
90	91	1971	S.Siebert	32	32	235	16	10	0	131	60	2.91	3.22	3.77	20.5
91	116	1914	R.Collins	39	30	272	20	13	0	72	56	2.51	3.17	3.91	20.4
92	76	1911	R.Collins	31	24	195	11	12	1	86	44	2.40	3.74	3.67	20.3
93	64	1993	F.Viola	29	29	184	11	8	0	91	72	3.14	3.72	3.57	20.2
94	81	1934	F.Ostermueller	33	23	199	10	13	3	75	99	3.49	4.21	3.69	20.2
95	115	1901	G.Winter	28	28	241	16	12	0	63	66	2.80	4.74	3.91	20.2
96	117	1930	D.MacFayden	36	33	269	11	14	2	76	93	4.21	4.72	3.92	20.1
97	102	1924	J.Quinn	44	25	229	12	13	7	64	52	3.27	4.21	3.81	19.9
98	94	1915	B.Ruth	32	28	218	18	8	0	112	85	2.44	3.31	3.78	19.8
99	113	1928	E.Morris	47	29	258	19	15	5	104	80	3.53	4.12	3.90	19.7
100	82	1994	A.Sele	22	22	143	8	7	0	105	60	3.83	4.27	3.69	19.4

**Boston Red Sox
Relief Pitchers**

V	R	Year	Name	G	GS	IP	W	L	SV	SO	BB	ERA	RA/9	R Wtd RA/9	V Net /162
1	5	1963	D.Radatz	66	0	132	15	6	25	162	51	1.97	2.11	2.36	32.3
2	4	1962	D.Radatz	62	0	125	9	6	24	144	40	2.24	2.30	2.36	30.6
3	12	1964	D.Radatz	79	0	157	16	9	29	181	58	2.29	2.52	2.82	30.3
4	7	1999	D.Lowe	74	0	109	6	3	15	80	25	2.63	2.88	2.50	25.0
5	8	1953	E.Kinder	69	0	107	10	6	27	39	38	1.85	2.52	2.56	24.9
6	28	1982	B.Stanley	48	0	168	12	7	14	83	50	3.10	3.21	3.25	24.4
7	17	1951	E.Kinder	63	2	127	11	2	14	84	46	2.55	2.98	2.92	24.3
8	1	2000	D.Lowe	74	0	91	4	4	42	79	22	2.56	2.66	2.27	23.2
9	21	1977	B.Campbell	69	0	140	13	9	31	114	60	2.96	3.09	3.09	22.9
10	9	1982	T.Burgmeier	40	0	102	7	0	2	44	22	2.29	2.64	2.67	21.3
11	10	1980	T.Burgmeier	62	0	99	5	4	24	54	20	2.00	2.73	2.75	19.9
12	6	1998	T.Gordon	73	0	79	7	4	46	78	25	2.72	2.72	2.45	18.5
13	22	1989	D.Lamp	42	0	112	4	2	2	61	27	2.32	2.96	3.11	18.0
14	34	1978	B.Stanley	52	3	142	15	2	10	38	34	2.60	3.18	3.42	18.0
15	2	1994	K.Ryan	42	0	48	2	3	13	32	17	2.44	2.63	2.27	17.2
16	18	1943	M.Brown	49	0	93	6	6	9	40	51	2.12	2.52	2.98	17.1
17	37	1983	B.Stanley	64	0	145	8	10	33	65	38	2.85	3.47	3.50	17.1
18	29	1960	M.Fornieles	70	0	109	10	5	14	64	49	2.64	3.14	3.25	16.6
19	11	1996	H.Slocumb	75	0	83	5	5	31	88	55	3.02	3.35	2.82	16.1
20	3	1995	R.Aguilera	52	0	55	3	3	32	52	13	2.60	2.60	2.31	15.4
21	25	1969	S.Lyle	71	0	103	8	3	17	93	48	2.54	2.89	3.22	15.3
22	24	1955	L.Kiely	33	4	90	3	3	6	36	37	2.80	3.10	3.15	14.8
23	19	1985	B.Stanley	48	0	88	6	6	10	46	30	2.87	3.08	3.05	14.7
24	15	1995	S.Belinda	63	0	70	8	1	10	57	28	3.10	3.23	2.87	14.7
25	32	1992	G.Harris	70	2	108	4	9	4	73	60	2.51	3.18	3.34	14.6
26	23	1979	T.Burgmeier	44	0	89	3	2	4	60	16	2.74	3.25	3.14	14.0
27	16	2000	R.Garces	64	0	75	8	1	1	69	23	3.25	3.38	2.88	13.9
28	33	1982	M.Clear	55	0	105	14	9	14	109	61	3.00	3.34	3.38	13.7
29	35	1989	R.Murphy	74	0	105	5	7	9	107	41	2.74	3.26	3.42	13.2
30	26	1979	D.Drago	53	1	89	10	6	13	67	21	3.03	3.34	3.22	13.2
31	20	1996	M.Stanton	81	0	79	4	4	1	60	27	3.66	3.66	3.08	13.0
32	13	1998	J.Corsi	59	0	66	3	2	0	49	23	2.59	3.14	2.83	12.7
33	36	1926	J.Russell	36	5	98	0	5	0	17	24	3.58	3.67	3.48	12.4
34	30	1959	M.Fornieles	46	0	82	5	3	11	54	29	3.07	3.18	3.30	12.0
35	31	1982	L.Aponte	40	0	85	2	2	3	44	25	3.18	3.28	3.32	11.7
36	41	1971	B.Lee	47	3	102	9	2	2	74	46	2.74	3.09	3.62	10.6
37	40	1967	J.Wyatt	60	0	93	10	7	20	68	39	2.60	2.90	3.58	10.1
38	38	1997	B.Henry	36	5	84	7	3	6	51	19	3.52	3.84	3.51	9.7
39	43	1945	F.Barrett	37	0	86	4	3	3	35	29	2.62	3.14	3.64	9.2
40	45	1988	B.Stanley	57	0	102	6	4	5	57	29	3.19	3.63	3.76	9.0
41	42	1955	T.Hurd	43	0	81	8	6	5	48	38	3.01	3.56	3.62	8.9
42	27	1991	J.Reardon	57	0	59	1	4	40	44	16	3.03	3.19	3.24	8.6
43	50	1969	V.Romo	55	11	135	8	10	11	96	53	3.13	3.59	4.00	8.4
44	44	1958	L.Kiely	47	0	81	5	2	12	26	18	3.00	3.44	3.72	7.9
45	49	1995	M.Maddux	44	4	99	5	1	1	69	18	4.10	4.47	3.98	7.2
46	46	1988	L.Smith	64	0	84	4	5	29	96	37	2.80	3.66	3.79	7.2
47	47	1966	D.McMahon	61	0	90	9	8	10	62	44	2.69	3.29	3.84	7.1
48	48	1976	J.Willoughby	54	0	99	3	12	10	37	31	2.82	3.45	3.94	6.8
49	39	1992	J.Reardon	60	0	58	5	2	30	39	9	3.41	3.41	3.58	6.3
50	57	1963	J.Lamabe	65	2	151	7	4	6	93	46	3.15	3.75	4.19	6.2

BROOKLYN/LOS ANGELES DODGERS (1900–2000)

The Dodgers' roots are buried in Brooklyn. Using hitter-friendly Ebbets Field as a launching pad, the Brooklyn Dodgers built their greatest dynasty in the 1940s and 1950s around great hitters Duke Snider, Jackie Robinson, Gil Hodges, and Roy Campanella. The dynasty ended in 1958 with the team's move to Los Angeles. In order to survive in spacious Dodgers Stadium, this East Coast hitting machine transformed into a West Coast team specializing in pitching. Duke Snider, the team's home run king, never made the transition, as his home run production dropped from 40 or more for five straight seasons in Brooklyn, to 15 in his first year in Los Angeles while playing in the Los Angeles Coliseum. The team, however, quickly made a successful transition by 1959, winning the World Series that year. By the mid–1960s, dominant pitching by legends Sandy Koufax and Don Drysdale led the Dodgers to three pennants.

Back in 1900, the Dodgers won the first pennant in the twentieth century with a collection of stars from the previous century — Willie Keeler (.362 average), Joe Kelley, Hughie Jennings, Tom Daly, Bill Dahlen, Lave Cross, Jimmy Sheckard, Fielder Jones, and Joe McGinnity (28–8, 2.94 ERA). In 1901, Sheckard hit .354 with 19 triples, 11 home runs, and 35 steals for a second place Brooklyn team. Adjusted for 5.5 percent hitter's deflation, Sheckard hit .373 with 13 home runs, for a 996 Wtd. Production and a 1,046 Total Factor.

After four winning seasons to open the century, the Dodgers played losing baseball every season from 1904 to 1914, including a 48–104 last place finish in 1905. The 1908 team hit miserably, with a .213 team average, but Nap Rucker managed to go 17–19 with a 2.08 ERA to keep the Dodgers out of last place. Zach Wheat and Jake Daubert gave the team some hitting punch after 1910, with Daubert batting .350 in 1913 to win the Chalmers (MVP) Award.

The Dodgers had their ups and downs from 1915 to 1932, with nine winning and nine losing seasons. Brooklyn won the pennant in 1916 behind the pitching of Jeff Pfeffer (25–11, 1.92 ERA), Larry Cheney (18–12, 1.92 ERA), and Rube Marquard (13–6, 1.58 ERA), while Wheat had his best season with a .312 average and 9 home runs. Adjusted for an 11 percent hitter's deflation, Wheat hit .348 with 10 home runs, for a 964 Total Factor. The Dodgers won again in 1920, as Burleigh Grimes went 23–11 with a 2.22 ERA, Pfeffer was 16–9, and Wheat batted .328. This proved to be the team's last pennant for two decades.

The 1924 team finished 1½ games out, as Dazzy Vance blazed to a 28–6 record, with a league-leading 2.16 ERA and a 2.60 Wtd. RA/9, to win the league's first ever MVP Award in his best season, while Grimes chipped in with a 22–13 record. Wheat hit .375 with 14 home runs, and Jack Fournier batted .334 with 27 home runs to lead the offense. Vance had another outstanding season in 1928 at age 37, going 22–10 with a 2.09 ERA and a career best 2.46 Wtd. RA/9. The 1930 team finished in fourth place, despite strong seasons from Babe Herman (.393 average, 35 home runs, 989 Wtd. Production) and 39-year-old Vance (17–15, league leading 2.61 ERA, 2.66 Wtd. RA/9). The Dodgers went from average to worse in the 1930s, with six straight losing seasons from 1933 to 1938.

The additions of Dolph Camilli in 1938 and Joe Medwick in 1940 turned the team around, and the Dodgers quickly put together seven winning seasons in eight years from 1939 to 1946. The Dodgers won 100 games and the pennant in 1941. MVP Camilli hit .285 with 34 home runs for a 987 Wtd. Production; Medwick hit .318 with 18 home runs; and Pete Reiser led the league in batting average (.343), doubles (39), and triples (17), for a 1,039 Total Factor in his first full season. Whit Wyatt was 22–10 with a 2.34 ERA and a 2.97 Wtd. RA/9, while Kirby Higbe also won 22 games. The 1942 team went 104–50, but finished second to the Cardinals.

The Dodgers' golden era spanned their last 11 seasons in Brooklyn from 1947 to 1957, as the team finished at least 14 games over .500 every year, while winning six pennants. The Dodgers won the pennant in 1947, as rookie Jackie Robinson broke the color barrier and hit .297 with 12 home runs and a league-leading 29 steals. Robinson also starred on the 1949 pennant winner, leading the league in hitting (.342) and steals (37) to earn the MVP Award.

The 1951 team lost a three-game playoff to the Giants. This team featured MVP Roy Campanella (.325, 33 home runs, 1,008 Total Factor), Jackie Robinson at his peak (.338, 19 home runs, 25 steals, 1,010 Total Factor, and 103.5 Hits Contribution), and two 20-game winners in Preacher Roe and Don Newcombe. The 1952 team came back to edge the Giants for the pennant behind a balanced offense and reliever Joe Black, who was 15–4 with 15 saves, a 2.15 ERA, and a 2.75 Wtd. RA/9.

The Dodgers repeated in 1953 with 105 wins and one of the greatest offenses in baseball history. MVP Campanella hit .312 with 41 home runs in his best season. Adjusted for 6 percent hitter's inflation, Campy batted .295 with 41 home runs, for a 1,000 Total Factor and 95.5 Hits Contribution. Duke Snider hit .336 with 42 home runs for a 1,012 Total Factor, Gil Hodges batted .302 with 31 home runs, Carl Furillo hit a league leading .344 with 21 home runs, and Robinson hit .329 with 12 home runs. Pitcher Carl Erskine went 20–6 with a 3.54 ERA.

The Dodgers won 98 games and another pennant in 1955. Campanella won his third MVP with a .318 average, 32 home runs, and 976 Total Factor; Snider batted .309 with 42 home runs for a career best 1,028 Total Factor; Furillo hit .314 with 26 home runs; and Don Newcombe went 20–5 with a 3.20 ERA. The Dodgers repeated in 1956, with MVP Newcombe going 27–7 with a 3.06 ERA, while Snider hit .292 with 43 home runs.

Jackie Robinson retired after the 1956 season; Roy Campanella was seriously injured in a car accident before the 1958 season; and other key players were aging. The Brooklyn dynasty was over. The team that limped into Los Angeles in 1958 was ripe for change.

The Dodgers put together seven winning seasons in nine years from 1958 to 1966. Los Angeles finished seventh in 1958, but came back to win in 1959 behind the last good year from Snider (.308, 23 home runs), while Wally Moon hit .302 with 19 home runs. Don Drysdale went 17–13 with a 3.46 ERA to head up an average pitching staff.

The Dodgers lost another three-game playoff with the Giants in 1962 to finish one back. This team featured MVP shortstop Maury Wills (.299, 104 steals), Tommy Davis (.346 average, 230 hits, 27 home runs), Don Drysdale (25–9, 2.83 ERA), and Sandy Koufax (14–7, league-leading 2.54 ERA).

The Dodgers won three pennants in the next four years behind brilliant pitching from Sandy Koufax, who won 25, 19, 26, and 27 games from 1963 to 1966, while leading the league in ERA each year, and winning the MVP Award in 1963. Koufax's best season was his last, as he went 27–9 with a 1.73 ERA, a 2.29 Wtd. RA/9, and 81.4 Runs/162. Drysdale was no slouch, either, winning 19, 18, 23, and 13 games from 1963 to 1966, with a career lows in ERA (2.18) and Wtd. RA/9 (2.88) in 1964. Ron Perranoski was the relief ace in 1963 with a 16–3 record, 21 saves, a 1.67 ERA and 2.49 Wtd. RA/9. Phil Regan was even more effective in 1966 with a 14–1 record, 21 saves, a 1.62 ERA, and 2.06 Wtd. RA/9. Wills set up the rather weak offense, stealing 40, 53, 94, and 38 bases in this period.

After Koufax retired at age 30 following the 1966 season, the Dodgers went through an eight-year dry spell before they again appeared in the playoffs. The team's best player in this period was swift outfielder Willie Davis, who won three Gold Gloves and hit around .300. In 1972, Don Sutton went 19–9 with a 2.08 ERA and a 3.01 Wtd. RA/9 in his best season, while Jim Brewer went 8–7 with 17 saves, a 1.26 ERA, and a 2.17 Wtd. RA/9.

The Dodgers won 102 games and the pennant in 1974, as MVP Steve Garvey hit .312 with 21 home runs. Andy Messersmith was 20–6 with a 2.59 ERA, Sutton went 19–9, and Tommy John went 13–3 with a 2.59 ERA before blowing out his elbow. Mike Marshall appeared in a record 106 games in relief, going 15–12 with 21 saves and a 2.42 ERA, and he saved 33.0 Runs from scoring compared to the league average performance over his 208 innings.

The Dodgers won another pennant in 1977. Garvey, Ron Cey, Reggie Smith, and Dusty Baker all hit at least 30 home runs, while Tommy John went 20–7 with a 2.78 ERA. The Dodgers won again in 1978, as Garvey hit .316 with 21 home runs, Davy Lopes batted .278 with 17 home runs and 45 steals in 49 attempts, and Burt Hooton went 19–10 with a 2.71 ERA.

After finishing one game out in 1980, the Dodgers won the World Series in the strike year of 1981 behind a balanced offensive attack and the pitching of rookie Fernando Valenzuela (13–7, 2.48 ERA, 3.01 Wtd. RA/9). The Dodgers finished one game out in 1982, and then won the division in 1983, as third baseman Pedro Guerrero hit

.298 with 32 home runs, for a 928 Total Factor. The Dodgers returned to the playoffs in 1985. Outfielder Guerrero hit .320 with 33 home runs for a 1,018 Wtd. Production, while Orel Hershisher went 19–3 with a 2.03 ERA and a 3.02 Wtd. RA/9. Los Angeles won its last World Series in 1988, as MVP Kirk Gibson hit .290 with 25 home runs and 31 steals, and Hershisher went 23–8 with a 2.26 ERA and a career low 2.90 Wtd. RA/9.

The Dodgers remained competitive in the 1990s, behind the pitching of Ramon Martinez, Hideo Nomo, and Ismael Valdes. The team's biggest star was catcher Mike Piazza. Among Piazza's several great offensive seasons was a 1997 performance that included a .362 average and 40 home runs, for a 1,019 Wtd. Production. Raul Mondesi backed Piazza up that year with a .310 average and 30 home runs. Both players departed for other teams by the turn of the century.

Brooklyn/Los Angeles Dodgers (1900–2000)

Brooklyn/Los Angeles Dodgers — **Hitters Volume of Success**

Pos	Year	Name	AB	BB	HBP	TAB	H	2B	3B	HR	BA	OB	SA	PRO	Wtd PRO	SB	CS	SBF	SPF	FF	R TF	V HC
C	1953	R.Campanella	519	67	4	590	162	26	3	41	.312	.395	.611	1,006	950	4	2	0	0	50	1,000	95.5
1B	1941	D.Camilli	529	104	4	637	151	29	6	34	.285	.407	.556	962	987	3			0	10	997	72.6
2B	1951	J.Robinson	548	79	9	636	185	33	7	19	.338	.429	.527	957	937	25	8	13	10	50	1,010	103.5
SS	1962	M.Wills	695	51	2	748	208	13	10	6	.299	.349	.373	722	706	104	13	99	10	30	844	64.9
3B	1983	P.Guerrero	584	72	2	658	174	28	6	32	.298	.377	.531	908	915	23	7	13	10	(10)	928	66.5
OF	1901	J.Sheckard	554	47	5	606	196	29	19	11	.354	.409	.534	944	996	35			10	40	1,046	96.3
OF	1954	D.Snider	584	84	4	672	199	39	10	40	.341	.427	.647	1,074	1,018	6	6	(8)	0	10	1,020	88.3
OF	1941	P.Reiser	536	46	11	593	184	39	17	14	.343	.406	.558	964	989	4			10	40	1,039	83.8
Starters		Averages	569	69	5	643	182	30	10	25	.321	.399	.537	936	932	26	5	15	6	28	980	83.9
C	1997	M.Piazza	556	69	3	628	201	32	1	40	.362	.435	.638	1,073	1,019	5	1	5	(10)	(20)	993	94.4
1B	1954	G.Hodges	579	74	1	654	176	23	5	42	.304	.384	.579	962	912	3	3	(4)	0	40	948	58.2
2B	1978	D.Lopes	587	71	0	658	163	25	4	17	.278	.356	.421	776	790	45	4	53	10	30	883	61.9
SS	1949	P.Reese	617	116	4	737	172	27	3	16	.279	.396	.410	806	787	26			10	30	827	61.0
3B	1975	R.Cey	566	78	7	651	160	29	2	25	.283	.376	.473	850	859	5	2	1	0	30	891	54.2
OF	1944	D.Walker	535	72	1	608	191	37	8	13	.357	.434	.529	963	987	6			0	10	997	72.9
OF	1930	B.Herman	614	66	4	684	241	48	11	35	.393	.455	.678	1,132	989	18			10	(30)	969	72.6
OF	1916	Z.Wheat	568	43	6	617	177	32	13	9	.312	.366	.461	828	924	19			10	30	964	64.0
Reserves		Averages	578	74	3	655	185	32	6	25	.320	.400	.523	924	906	16	1	7	4	15	931	67.4
Total		Weighted Ave.	572	70	5	647	183	30	8	25	.321	.399	.532	932	923	22	3	12	5	23	964	78.4

Pitchers Volume of Success

Pos	Year	Name	G	GS	IP	W	L	SV	SO	BB	ERA	RA/9	Wtd RA/9	V Runs /162
SP	1966	S.Koufax	41	41	323	27	9	0	317	77	1.73	2.06	2.29	81.4
SP	1924	D.Vance	35	34	308	28	6	0	262	77	2.16	2.60	2.60	70.5
SP	1975	A.Messersmith	42	40	322	19	14	1	213	96	2.29	2.57	2.84	61.6
SP	1964	D.Drysdale	40	40	321	18	16	0	237	68	2.18	2.55	2.88	59.9
SP	1911	N.Rucker	48	33	316	22	18	4	190	110	2.71	2.91	2.97	58.5
Starters		Averages	41	38	318	23	13	1	244	86	2.21	2.54	2.72	66.4
RP	1974	M.Marshall	106	0	208	15	12	21	143	56	2.42	2.85	3.13	33.0
RP	1966	P.Regan	65	0	117	14	1	21	88	24	1.62	1.85	2.06	32.5
RP	1963	R.Perranoski	69	0	129	16	3	21	75	43	1.67	2.09	2.49	29.6
RP	1952	J.Black	56	2	142	15	4	15	85	41	2.15	2.54	2.75	30.0
Relievers		Averages	74	1	149	15	5	20	98	41	2.04	2.42	2.69	31.3
Totals		Averages	115	38	467	38	18	21	342	127	2.16	2.50	2.71	97.7

Baseball Players' Best Seasons

Brooklyn/Los Angeles Dodgers — **Hitters Rate of Success**

Pos	Year	Name	AB	BB	HBP	TAB	H	2B	3B	HR	BA	OB	SA	PRO	Wtd PRO	SB	CS	SBF	SPF	FF	R TF	V HC
C	1951	R.Campanella	505	53	4	562	164	33	1	33	.325	.393	.590	983	963	1	2	(5)	0	50	1,008	93.0
1B	1941	D.Camilli	529	104	4	637	151	29	6	34	.285	.407	.556	962	987	3			0	10	997	72.6
2B	1951	J.Robinson	548	79	9	636	185	33	7	19	.338	.429	.527	957	937	25	8	13	10	50	1,010	103.5
SS	1954	P.Reese	554	90	3	647	171	35	8	10	.309	.408	.455	863	818	8	5	(3)	10	20	845	59.2
3B	1983	P.Guerrero	584	72	2	658	174	28	6	32	.298	.377	.531	908	915	23	7	13	10	(10)	928	66.5
OF	1901	J.Sheckard	554	47	5	606	196	29	19	11	.354	.409	.534	944	996	35			10	40	1,046	96.3
OF	1941	P.Reiser	536	46	11	593	184	39	17	14	.343	.406	.558	964	989	4			10	40	1,039	83.8
OF	1955	D.Snider	538	104	1	643	166	34	6	42	.309	.421	.628	1,050	1,005	9	7	(7)	0	30	1,028	87.2
Starters		Averages	544	74	5	623	174	33	9	24	.320	.406	.546	953	950	14	4	1	6	29	986	82.8
C	1997	M.Piazza	556	69	3	628	201	32	1	40	.362	.435	.638	1,073	1,019	5	1	5	(10)	(20)	993	94.4
1B	1923	J.Fournier	515	43	9	567	181	30	13	22	.351	.411	.588	999	957	11	4	5	0	(10)	952	51.8
2B	1978	D.Lopes	587	71	0	658	163	25	4	17	.278	.356	.421	776	790	45	4	53	10	30	883	61.9
SS	1962	M.Wills	695	51	2	748	208	13	10	6	.299	.349	.373	722	706	104	13	99	10	30	844	64.9
3B	1976	R.Cey	502	89	3	594	139	18	3	23	.277	.389	.462	851	878	0	4	(13)	0	40	906	53.6
OF	1944	D.Walker	535	72	1	608	191	37	8	13	.357	.434	.529	963	987	6			0	10	997	72.9
OF	1906	H.Lumley	484	48	1	533	157	23	12	9	.324	.386	.477	864	983	35			0	0	983	60.4
OF	1977	R.Smith	488	104	3	595	150	27	4	32	.307	.432	.576	1,008	979	7	5	(5)	0	0	974	61.3
Reserves		Averages	545	68	3	616	174	26	7	20	.319	.397	.502	900	904	27	4	18	1	10	933	65.2
Total		Weighted Ave.	544	72	4	621	174	30	8	23	.319	.403	.532	935	935	18	4	7	5	23	969	76.9

Pitchers Rate of Success

Pos	Year	Name	G	GS	IP	W	L	SV	SO	BB	ERA	RA/9	Wtd RA/9	V Runs /162
SP	1964	S.Koufax	29	28	223	19	5	1	223	53	1.74	1.98	2.23	57.6
SP	1928	D.Vance	38	32	280	22	10	2	200	72	2.09	2.54	2.46	68.5
SP	2000	K.Brown	33	33	230	13	6	0	216	47	2.58	2.97	2.67	48.1
SP	1980	D.Sutton	32	31	212	13	5	1	128	47	2.20	2.37	2.68	44.2
SP	1975	A.Messersmith	42	40	322	19	14	1	213	96	2.29	2.57	2.84	61.6
Starters		Averages	35	33	253	17	8	1	196	63	2.19	2.50	2.59	56.0
RP	1989	J.Howell	56	0	80	5	3	28	55	22	1.58	1.69	1.95	23.1
RP	1966	P.Regan	65	0	117	14	1	21	88	24	1.62	1.85	2.06	32.5
RP	1995	T.Worrell	59	0	62	4	1	32	61	19	2.02	2.17	2.13	18.8
RP	1972	J.Brewer	51	0	78	8	7	17	69	25	1.26	1.85	2.17	21.8
Relievers		Averages	58	0	84	8	3	25	68	23	1.60	1.87	2.07	24.1
Totals		Averages	93	33	338	25	11	26	264	86	2.04	2.34	2.46	80.1

Brooklyn/Los Angeles Dodgers (1900–2000)

Brooklyn/Los Angeles Dodgers
Catchers

V	R	Year	Name	AB	BB	HBP	TAB	H	2B	3B	HR	BA	OB	SA	PRO	Wtd PRO	SB	CS	SBF	SPF	FF	R TF	V HC
1	2	1953	R.Campanella	519	67	4	590	162	26	3	41	.312	.395	.611	1,006	950	4	2	0		50	1,000	95.5
2	3	1997	M.Piazza	556	69	3	628	201	32	1	40	.362	.435	.638	1,073	1,019	5	1	5	(10)	(20)	993	94.4
3	1	1951	R.Campanella	505	53	4	562	164	33	1	33	.325	.393	.590	983	963	1	2	(5)		50	1,008	93.0
4	4	1955	R.Campanella	446	56	6	508	142	20	1	32	.318	.402	.583	985	943	2	3	(7)	(10)	50	976	75.9
5	7	1996	M.Piazza	547	81	1	629	184	16	0	36	.336	.423	.563	986	939	0	3	(9)	(10)	(20)	900	66.8
6	5	1995	M.Piazza	434	39	1	474	150	17	0	32	.346	.401	.606	1,007	959	1	0	2	(10)	(20)	931	64.5
7	6	1950	R.Campanella	437	55	2	494	123	19	3	31	.281	.364	.551	916	877	1				40	917	59.4
8	9	1993	M.Piazza	547	46	3	596	174	24	2	35	.318	.374	.561	935	906	3	4	(8)	(10)	(10)	878	56.9
9	8	1949	R.Campanella	436	67	3	506	125	22	2	22	.287	.385	.498	883	862	3				30	892	54.5
10	10	1952	R.Campanella	468	57	3	528	126	18	1	22	.269	.352	.453	805	816	8	4	0		60	876	52.4
11	11	1973	J.Ferguson	487	87	1	575	128	26	0	25	.263	.376	.470	846	853	1	1	(2)			851	47.7
12	12	1985	M.Sciosia	429	77	5	511	127	26	3	7	.296	.409	.420	829	842	3	3	(6)	(10)	10	836	38.6
13	18	1994	M.Piazza	405	33	1	439	129	18	0	24	.319	.371	.541	912	858	1	3	(11)	(10)	(30)	808	38.5
14	17	1968	T.Haller	474	46	2	522	135	27	5	4	.285	.351	.388	739	811	1	4	(13)	(10)	20	808	32.6
15	15	1961	J.Roseboro	394	56	4	454	99	16	6	18	.251	.350	.459	810	778	6	4	(4)	10	30	813	30.9
16	13	1979	J.Ferguson	363	70	2	435	95	14	0	20	.262	.384	.466	849	842	1	0	2	(10)	(10)	824	30.5
17	14	1940	B.Phelps	370	30	1	401	109	24	5	13	.295	.349	.492	841	846	2			(10)	(20)	816	27.8
18	16	1974	J.Ferguson	349	75	0	424	88	14	1	16	.252	.384	.436	820	833	2	2	(4)	(10)	(10)	808	26.5
19	19	1937	B.Phelps	409	25	3	437	128	37	3	7	.313	.357	.469	826	817	2		(10)	(20)		787	24.0
20	20	1966	J.Roseboro	445	44	3	492	123	23	2	9	.276	.346	.398	743	751	3	2	(2)		30	779	23.7
21	23	1990	M.Sciosia	435	55	3	493	115	25	0	12	.264	.351	.405	756	754	4	1	4	(10)	20	768	21.3
22	24	1964	J.Roseboro	414	44	4	462	119	24	1	3	.287	.361	.372	733	754	3	3	(6)		20	767	19.8
23	21	1933	A.Lopez	372	21	0	393	112	11	4	3	.301	.338	.376	715	743	10				30	773	18.8
24	22	1991	M.Sciosia	345	47	3	395	91	16	2	8	.264	.357	.391	748	763	4	3	(5)	(10)	20	769	17.1
25	25	1984	M.Sciosia	341	52	1	394	93	18	0	5	.273	.371	.370	740	756	2	1	0	(10)	20	766	16.6

Brooklyn/Los Angeles Dodgers
First basemen

V	R	Year	Name	AB	BB	HBP	TAB	H	2B	3B	HR	BA	OB	SA	PRO	Wtd PRO	SB	CS	SBF	SPF	FF	R TF	V HC
1	1	1941	D.Camilli	529	104	4	637	151	29	6	34	.285	.407	.556	962	987	3				10	997	72.6
2	3	1954	G.Hodges	579	74	1	654	176	23	5	42	.304	.384	.579	962	912	3	3	(4)		40	948	58.2
3	6	1939	D.Camilli	565	110	4	679	164	30	12	26	.290	.409	.524	933	914	9				10	924	52.3
4	4	1940	D.Camilli	512	89	4	605	147	29	13	23	.287	.397	.529	926	931	9				10	941	51.9
5	2	1923	J.Fournier	515	43	9	567	181	30	13	22	.351	.411	.588	999	957	11	4	5		(10)	952	51.8
6	5	1990	E.Murray	558	82	1	641	184	22	3	26	.330	.417	.520	936	935	8	5	(3)	(10)	10	932	49.4
7	8	1924	J.Fournier	563	83	10	656	188	25	4	27	.334	.428	.536	965	934	7	5	(4)		(10)	920	49.3
8	9	1925	J.Fournier	545	86	8	639	191	21	16	22	.350	.446	.569	1,015	940	4	6	(12)		(10)	918	47.5
9	14	1951	G.Hodges	582	93	5	680	156	25	3	40	.268	.374	.527	901	882	9	7	(7)		30	905	46.1
10	10	1952	G.Hodges	508	107	2	617	129	27	1	32	.254	.386	.500	886	897	2	4	(9)		30	918	45.7
11	7	1953	G.Hodges	520	75	3	598	157	22	7	31	.302	.393	.550	943	891	1	4	(11)		40	920	45.0
12	12	1942	D.Camilli	524	97	3	624	132	23	7	26	.252	.372	.471	843	900	10				10	910	43.9
13	16	1928	D.Bissonette	587	70	4	661	188	30	13	25	.320	.396	.543	940	895	5			10	(10)	895	41.5
14	18	1978	S.Garvey	639	40	1	680	202	36	9	21	.316	.357	.499	857	871	10	5	0		20	891	39.3
15	20	1970	W.Parker	614	79	0	693	196	47	4	10	.319	.397	.458	854	833	8	2	5	10	40	889	39.1
16	19	1938	D.Camilli	509	119	0	628	128	25	11	24	.251	.393	.485	879	880	6				10	890	37.7
17	23	1945	A.Galan	576	114	2	692	177	36	7	9	.307	.423	.441	864	877	13					877	37.0
18	11	1916	J.Daubert	478	38	4	520	151	16	7	3	.316	.371	.397	769	859	21	7	13	10	30	911	36.8
19	13	1914	J.Daubert	474	30	5	509	156	17	7	6	.329	.375	.432	808	876	25			10	20	906	34.7
20	22	1957	G.Hodges	579	63	2	644	173	28	7	27	.299	.370	.511	881	859	5	3	(1)		20	877	34.6
21	15	1918	J.Daubert	396	27	5	428	122	12	15	2	.308	.360	.429	789	873	10			10	20	903	34.6
22	17	1913	J.Daubert	508	44	3	555	178	17	7	2	.350	.405	.423	829	861	25			10	20	891	33.8
23	24	1975	S.Garvey	659	33	3	695	210	38	6	18	.319	.354	.476	830	840	11	2	10		20	869	32.9
24	25	1976	S.Garvey	631	50	1	682	200	37	4	13	.317	.368	.450	818	844	19	8	4		20	868	32.0
25	26	1950	G.Hodges	561	73	1	635	159	26	2	32	.283	.367	.508	875	838	6				30	868	31.2

Brooklyn/Los Angeles Dodgers
Second basemen

V	R	Year	Name	AB	BB	HBP	TAB	H	2B	3B	HR	BA	OB	SA	PRO	Wtd PRO	SB	CS	SBF	SPF	FF	R TF	V HC
1	1	1951	J.Robinson	548	79	9	636	185	33	7	19	.338	.429	.527	957	937	25	8	13	10	50	1,010	103.5
2	2	1949	J.Robinson	593	86	8	687	203	38	12	16	.342	.432	.528	960	937	37			10	20	967	97.1
3	3	1952	J.Robinson	510	107	13	630	157	17	3	19	.308	.440	.465	904	916	24	7	15	10	20	961	87.0
4	4	1950	J.Robinson	518	80	5	603	170	39	4	14	.328	.423	.500	923	884	12			10	40	934	75.1
5	5	1978	D.Lopes	587	71	0	658	163	25	4	17	.278	.356	.421	776	790	45	4	53	10	30	883	61.9
6	6	1901	T.Daly	520	42	4	566	164	38	10	3	.315	.371	.444	815	860	31			10	(10)	860	54.6
7	8	1959	C.Neal	616	43	4	663	177	30	11	19	.287	.338	.464	802	779	17	6	7	10	50	846	53.4
8	7	1948	J.Robinson	574	57	7	638	170	38	8	12	.296	.367	.453	820	809	22			10	30	849	52.4
9	9	1986	S.Sax	633	59	3	695	210	43	4	6	.332	.391	.441	832	834	40	17	8	10	(10)	843	52.1
10	10	1979	D.Lopes	582	97	4	683	154	20	6	28	.265	.373	.464	837	830	44	4	50	10	(50)	840	50.3
11	11	1943	B.Herman	585	66	0	651	193	41	2	2	.330	.398	.417	815	856	4		(10)	(10)		836	49.2
12	15	1956	J.Gilliam	594	95	4	693	178	23	8	6	.300	.400	.396	795	774	21	9	4	10	20	808	42.8
13	14	1946	E.Stanky	483	137	2	622	132	24	7	0	.273	.436	.352	788	813	8					813	39.8
14	13	1977	D.Lopes	502	73	2	577	142	19	5	11	.283	.376	.406	782	760	47	12	38	10	20	827	39.1
15	16	1924	A.High	582	57	2	641	191	26	13	6	.328	.390	.448	838	812	3	6	(13)			799	36.4
16	20	1945	E.Stanky	555	148	4	707	143	29	5	1	.258	.417	.333	751	761	6				20	781	34.0
17	12	1900	T.Daly	343	46	6	395	107	17	3	4	.312	.403	.414	817	818	27			10		828	31.0
18	21	1923	J.Johnston	625	53	0	678	203	29	11	4	.325	.378	.426	803	769	16	13	(14)	10	10	775	30.6
19	17	1963	J.Gilliam	525	60	2	587	148	27	4	6	.282	.358	.383	741	779	19	5	14	10	(10)	794	30.3
20	18	1966	J.Lefebvre	544	48	3	595	149	23	3	24	.274	.336	.460	796	804	1	1	(2)	(10)		792	30.2
21	25	1975	D.Lopes	618	91	2	711	162	24	6	8	.262	.359	.359	718	726	77	12	70	10	(40)	766	27.5
22	24	1913	G.Cutshaw	592	39	3	634	158	23	13	7	.267	.315	.385	701	728	39			10	30	768	26.4
23	28	1953	J.Gilliam	605	100	3	708	168	31	17	6	.278	.383	.415	798	754	21	14	(9)	10		754	24.5
24	22	1958	C.Neal	473	61	5	539	120	9	6	22	.254	.345	.438	783	752	7	6	(9)	10	20	773	23.7
25	23	1911	J.Hummell	477	67	0	544	129	21	11	5	.270	.360	.392	752	769	16			10	(10)	769	22.7

Brooklyn/Los Angeles Dodgers
Shortstops

V	R	Year	Name	AB	BB	HBP	TAB	H	2B	3B	HR	BA	OB	SA	PRO	Wtd PRO	SB	CS	SBF	SPF	FF	R TF	V HC
1	2	1962	M.Wills	695	51	2	748	208	13	10	6	.299	.349	.373	722	706	104	13	99	10	30	844	64.9
2	4	1949	P.Reese	617	116	4	737	172	27	3	16	.279	.396	.410	806	787	26			10	30	827	61.0
3	1	1954	P.Reese	554	90	3	647	171	35	8	10	.309	.408	.455	863	818	8	5	(3)	10	20	845	59.2
4	3	1947	P.Reese	476	104	2	582	135	24	4	12	.284	.414	.426	841	814	7			10	20	844	53.1
5	5	1946	P.Reese	542	87	1	630	154	16	10	5	.284	.384	.378	762	787	10			10	20	817	48.9
6	6	1903	B.Dahlen	474	82	2	558	124	17	9	1	.262	.373	.342	715	743	34			10	60	813	46.4
7	7	1952	P.Reese	559	86	0	645	152	18	8	6	.272	.369	.365	734	743	30	5	29	10	20	803	45.5
8	10	1943	A.Vaughn	610	60	3	673	186	39	6	5	.305	.370	.413	783	823	20			10	(40)	793	44.1
9	9	1953	P.Reese	524	82	4	610	142	25	7	13	.271	.374	.420	794	750	22	6	15	10	20	795	40.8
10	12	1942	P.Reese	564	82	0	646	144	24	5	3	.255	.350	.332	681	728	15			10	50	788	40.7
11	15	1965	M.Wills	650	40	4	694	186	14	7	0	.286	.331	.329	661	679	94	31	44	10	50	782	39.8
12	13	1948	P.Reese	566	79	0	645	155	31	4	9	.274	.363	.390	753	744	25			10	30	784	39.3
13	8	1930	G.Wright	532	32	0	564	171	28	12	22	.321	.360	.543	903	789	2			10		799	38.7
14	14	1902	B.Dahlen	527	43	8	578	139	25	8	2	.264	.329	.353	682	763	20			10	10	783	38.4
15	22	1951	P.Reese	616	81	2	699	176	20	8	10	.286	.371	.393	763	747	20	14	(11)	10	10	757	33.1
16	17	1900	B.Dahlen	483	73	7	563	125	16	11	1	.259	.364	.344	708	709	31			10	50	769	33.1
17	11	1958	D.Zimmer	455	28	1	484	119	15	2	17	.262	.306	.415	721	693	14	2	20	10	70	792	31.6
18	16	1963	M.Wills	527	44	1	572	159	19	3	0	.302	.357	.349	706	742	40	19	3	10	20	776	31.0
19	21	1950	P.Reese	531	91	1	623	138	21	5	11	.260	.369	.380	750	718	17			10	30	758	30.0
20	20	1935	L.Frey	515	66	5	586	135	35	11	11	.262	.352	.437	788	771	6			10	(20)	761	29.0
21	18	1960	M.Wills	516	35	3	554	152	15	2	0	.295	.343	.331	674	670	50	12	44	10	40	765	28.5
22	27	1955	P.Reese	553	78	3	634	156	29	4	10	.282	.374	.403	777	744	8	7	(9)	10		745	26.5
23	19	1957	C.Neal	448	53	8	509	121	13	7	12	.270	.358	.411	768	749	11	4	6	10		765	26.2
24	25	1901	B.Dahlen	511	30	5	546	136	17	9	4	.266	.313	.358	671	708	23			10	30	748	26.0
25	26	1934	L.Frey	490	52	5	547	139	24	5	8	.284	.358	.402	760	738	11			10		748	23.7

Brooklyn/Los Angeles Dodgers (1900–2000)

Brooklyn/Los Angeles Dodgers
Third basemen

V	R	Year	Name	AB	BB	HBP	TAB	H	2B	3B	HR	BA	OB	SA	PRO	Wtd PRO	SB	CS	SBF	SPF	FF	R TF	V HC
1	1	1983	P.Guerrero	584	72	2	658	174	28	6	32	.298	.377	.531	908	915	23	7	13	10	(10)	928	66.5
2	3	1975	R.Cey	566	78	7	651	160	29	2	25	.283	.376	.473	850	859	5	2	1		30	891	54.2
3	2	1976	R.Cey	502	89	3	594	139	18	3	23	.277	.389	.462	851	878	0	4	(13)		40	906	53.6
4	5	1971	D.Allen	549	93	1	643	162	24	1	23	.295	.398	.468	866	893	8	1	9	10	(30)	882	50.6
5	4	1979	R.Cey	487	86	2	575	137	20	1	28	.281	.391	.499	890	883	3	3	(5)	(10)	20	888	47.0
6	7	1978	R.Cey	555	96	7	658	150	32	0	23	.270	.384	.452	837	851	2	5	(11)		20	860	45.0
7	8	1970	B.Grabarkewitz	529	95	6	630	153	20	8	17	.289	.403	.454	857	835	19	9	2	10		847	39.2
8	6	1981	R.Cey	312	40	3	355	90	15	2	13	.288	.375	.474	849	874	0	2	(11)	(10)	10	863	37.6
9	9	1913	R.Smith	540	45	7	592	160	40	10	6	.296	.358	.441	799	830	22				10	840	36.9
10	10	1914	R.Smith	537	58	3	598	146	27	9	7	.272	.346	.395	741	803	15				30	833	35.1
11	14	1977	R.Cey	564	93	2	659	136	22	3	30	.241	.351	.450	801	778	3	4	(7)		50	820	32.7
12	15	1921	J.Johnston	624	45	1	670	203	41	14	5	.325	.372	.460	832	798	28	16	(6)	10	10	812	32.1
13	13	1980	R.Cey	551	69	5	625	140	25	0	28	.254	.342	.452	794	804	2	2	(3)	(10)	30	821	31.3
14	18	1974	R.Cey	577	76	7	660	151	20	2	18	.262	.355	.397	751	763	1	1	(1)		40	802	26.9
15	17	1932	J.Stripp	534	36	2	572	162	36	9	6	.303	.350	.438	788	768	14			10	30	808	26.4
16	16	1984	P.Guerrero	535	49	1	585	162	29	4	16	.303	.362	.462	824	842	9	8	(11)	10	(30)	811	26.3
17	12	1928	H.Hendrick	425	54	2	481	135	15	10	11	.318	.397	.478	875	833	16			10	(20)	823	25.8
18	11	1956	J.Robinson	357	60	3	420	98	15	2	10	.275	.383	.412	795	774	12	5	5	10	40	829	23.7
19	20	1994	T.Wallach	414	46	4	464	116	21	1	23	.280	.358	.502	860	810	0	2	(8)	(10)		791	23.5
20	23	1939	C.Lavagetto	587	78	5	670	176	28	5	10	.300	.387	.416	802	785	14			10	(10)	785	23.2
21	22	1982	R.Cey	556	57	4	617	141	23	1	24	.254	.327	.428	755	767	3	2	(2)	(10)	30	786	20.4
22	21	1909	E.Lennox	435	47	2	484	114	18	9	2	.262	.337	.359	695	787	11			10	(10)	787	17.1
23	24	2000	A.Beltre	510	56	2	568	148	30	2	20	.290	.363	.475	837	764	12	5	3	10		777	16.5
24	26	1912	R.Smith	486	54	4	544	139	28	6	4	.286	.362	.393	755	751	22				20	771	14.9
25	19	1953	B.Cox	327	37	0	364	95	18	1	10	.291	.363	.443	806	762	2	2	(5)	10	30	797	14.7

Brooklyn/Los Angeles Dodgers
Outfielders

V	R	Year	Name	AB	BB	HBP	TAB	H	2B	3B	HR	BA	OB	SA	PRO	Wtd PRO	SB	CS	SBF	SPF	FF	R TF	V HC
1	1	1901	J.Sheckard	554	47	5	606	196	29	19	11	.354	.409	.534	944	996	35			10	40	1,046	96.3
2	4	1954	D.Snider	584	84	4	672	199	39	10	40	.341	.427	.647	1,074	1,018	6	6	(8)		10	1,020	88.3
3	3	1955	D.Snider	538	104	1	643	166	34	6	42	.309	.421	.628	1,050	1,005	9	7	(7)		30	1,028	87.2
4	3	1953	D.Snider	590	82	3	675	198	38	4	42	.336	.419	.627	1,046	989	16	7	3		20	1,012	86.0
5	2	1941	P.Reiser	536	46	11	593	184	39	17	14	.343	.406	.558	964	989	4			10	40	1,039	83.8
6	7	1903	J.Sheckard	515	75	6	596	171	29	9	9	.332	.423	.476	899	934	67			10	60	1,004	81.1
7	9	1956	D.Snider	542	99	1	642	158	33	2	43	.292	.402	.598	1,000	973	3	3	(4)		20	989	74.5
8	8	1944	D.Walker	535	72	1	608	191	37	8	13	.357	.434	.529	963	987	6				10	997	72.9
9	13	1930	B.Herman	614	66	4	684	241	48	11	35	.393	.455	.678	1,132	989	18			10	(30)	969	72.6
10	5	1985	P.Guerrero	487	83	6	576	156	22	2	33	.320	.425	.577	1,002	1,018	12	4	7		(10)	1,015	70.6
11	14	1916	Z.Wheat	568	43	6	617	177	32	13	9	.312	.366	.461	828	924	19			10	30	964	64.0
12	11	1977	R.Smith	488	104	3	595	150	27	4	32	.307	.432	.576	1,008	979	7	5	(5)			974	61.3
13	20	1944	A.Galan	547	101	2	650	174	43	9	12	.318	.426	.495	922	944	4					944	60.8
14	10	1906	H.Lumley	484	48	1	533	157	23	12	9	.324	.386	.477	864	983	35					983	60.4
15	24	1950	D.Snider	620	58	0	678	199	31	10	31	.321	.379	.553	932	893	16			10	30	933	59.6
16	17	1924	Z.Wheat	566	49	4	619	212	41	8	14	.375	.428	.549	978	947	3	4	(8)		10	949	59.4
17	15	1914	Z.Wheat	533	47	3	583	170	26	9	9	.319	.377	.452	830	899	20			10	50	959	59.0
18	19	1982	P.Guerrero	575	65	5	645	175	27	5	32	.304	.380	.536	915	930	22	5	18	10	(10)	947	58.4
19	16	2000	G.Sheffield	501	101	4	606	163	24	3	43	.325	.442	.643	1,085	990	4	6	(12)	10	(30)	957	57.8
20	23	1932	L.O'Doul	595	50	7	652	219	32	8	21	.368	.423	.555	978	953	11				(20)	933	57.5
21	18	1988	K.Gibson	542	73	7	622	157	28	1	25	.290	.381	.483	864	904	31	4	35	10		949	56.8
22	12	1978	R.Smith	447	70	1	518	132	27	2	29	.295	.392	.559	951	967	12	5	4			971	52.7
23	22	1957	D.Snider	508	77	1	586	139	25	7	40	.274	.370	.587	957	933	3	4	(8)		10	935	52.1
24	25	1974	J.Wynn	535	108	0	643	145	17	4	32	.271	.393	.497	891	905	18	15	(18)	10	30	927	52.0
25	29	1997	R.Mondesi	616	44	6	666	191	42	5	30	.310	.362	.541	902	857	32	15	3	10	50	919	51.4

Brooklyn/Los Angeles Dodgers
Outfielders

V	R	Year	Name	AB	BB	HBP	TAB	H	2B	3B	HR	BA	OB	SA	PRO	Wtd PRO	SB	CS	SBF	SPF	FF	R TF	V HC
26	31	1929	B.Herman	569	55	0	624	217	42	13	21	.381	.436	.612	1,047	944	21			10	(40)	914	49.1
27	37	1962	T.Davis	665	33	2	700	230	27	9	27	.346	.379	.535	914	894	18	6	8	10	(10)	902	48.1
28	27	1941	J.Medwick	538	38	1	577	171	33	10	18	.318	.364	.517	881	904	2			10	10	924	48.1
29	21	1953	C.Furillo	479	34	4	517	165	38	6	21	.344	.393	.580	973	919	1	1	(2)	(10)	30	938	46.7
30	28	1961	W.Moon	463	89	1	553	152	25	3	17	.328	.438	.505	943	906	7	5	(5)	10	10	921	45.2
31	39	1959	W.Moon	543	81	3	627	164	26	11	19	.302	.396	.495	891	865	15	6	5	10	20	900	44.7
32	26	1998	G.Sheffield	437	95	8	540	132	27	2	22	.302	.435	.524	959	913	22	7	14	10	(10)	927	43.6
33	32	1953	J.Robinson	484	74	7	565	159	34	7	12	.329	.425	.502	927	876	17	4	15	10	10	911	43.5
34	36	1952	D.Snider	534	55	0	589	162	25	7	21	.303	.368	.494	863	874	7	4	(2)		30	902	42.7
35	30	1942	P.Reiser	480	48	2	530	149	33	5	10	.310	.375	.463	838	895	20			10	10	915	41.8
36	33	1905	J.Sheckard	480	61	7	548	140	20	11	3	.292	.380	.398	777	848	23			10	50	908	41.4
37	41	1941	D.Walker	531	70	0	601	165	32	8	9	.311	.391	.452	843	865	4				30	895	41.4
38	47	1900	W.Keeler	563	30	7	600	204	13	12	4	.362	.402	.449	851	852	41			10	20	882	41.3
39	40	1987	P.Guerrero	545	74	4	623	184	25	2	27	.338	.421	.539	960	923	9	7	(8)	(10)	(10)	896	41.0
40	44	1943	A.Galan	495	103	2	600	142	26	3	9	.287	.412	.406	818	859	6				30	889	39.6
41	52	1925	Z.Wheat	616	45	1	662	221	42	14	14	.359	.403	.541	944	874	3	1	1			876	39.3
42	56	1945	D.Walker	607	75	5	687	182	42	9	8	.300	.381	.438	820	831	6				40	871	39.2
43	35	1934	L.Koenecke	460	70	1	531	147	31	7	14	.320	.411	.509	919	893	8			10		903	38.6
44	43	1900	J.Kelley	454	53	6	513	145	23	17	6	.319	.398	.485	882	883	26			10		893	38.5
45	34	1990	K.Daniels	450	68	3	521	133	23	1	27	.296	.392	.531	923	921	4	3	(4)		(10)	908	37.3
46	54	1920	Z.Wheat	583	48	6	637	191	26	13	9	.328	.385	.463	848	881	8	10	(18)		10	874	37.1
47	57	1902	W.Keeler	559	21	7	587	186	20	5	0	.333	.365	.386	751	840	19			10	20	870	36.5
48	65	1901	W.Keeler	595	21	7	623	202	18	12	2	.339	.369	.420	789	833	23			10	20	863	36.2
49	58	1995	R.Mondesi	536	33	4	573	153	23	6	26	.285	.332	.496	828	789	27	4	31	10	40	870	34.6
50	53	1919	H.Myers	512	23	2	537	157	23	14	5	.307	.339	.436	774	844	13			10	20	874	34.4
51	68	1931	B.Herman	610	50	0	660	191	43	16	18	.313	.365	.525	890	871	17			10	(20)	861	34.3
52	67	1922	Z.Wheat	600	45	7	652	201	29	12	16	.335	.388	.503	891	836	9	6	(4)		30	861	33.9
53	74	1929	J.Frederick	628	39	5	672	206	52	6	24	.328	.372	.545	917	826	6			10	20	856	33.3
54	61	1980	D.Baker	579	43	3	625	170	26	4	29	.294	.346	.503	848	859	12	10	(12)		20	867	32.6
55	64	1949	D.Snider	552	56	4	612	161	28	7	23	.292	.361	.493	854	834	12			10	20	864	32.6
56	73	1972	W.Davis	615	27	1	643	178	22	7	19	.289	.320	.441	761	788	20	3	21	10	40	858	32.5
57	75	1946	D.Walker	576	67	1	644	184	29	9	9	.319	.391	.448	839	866	14			(10)		856	31.9
58	63	1949	C.Furillo	549	37	3	589	177	27	10	18	.322	.368	.506	875	854	4				10	864	31.5
59	49	1969	W.Davis	498	33	4	535	155	23	8	11	.311	.359	.456	815	833	24	10	7	10	30	881	31.4
60	84	1945	G.Rosen	606	50	3	659	197	24	11	12	.325	.379	.460	840	852	4					852	31.1
61	45	1914	C.Stengel	412	56	5	473	130	13	10	4	.316	.404	.425	829	898	19				(10)	888	31.1
62	79	1902	J.Sheckard	501	58	5	564	133	21	10	4	.265	.348	.371	719	804	25			10	40	854	30.1
63	80	1904	H.Lumley	577	41	4	622	161	23	18	9	.279	.331	.428	759	853	30					853	29.9
64	77	1964	W.Davis	613	22	1	636	180	23	7	12	.294	.319	.413	732	752	42	13	24	10	70	856	29.8
65	55	1973	W.Crawford	457	78	1	536	135	26	2	14	.295	.399	.453	852	859	12	5	4	10		873	29.5
66	86	1971	W.Davis	641	23	0	664	198	33	10	10	.309	.333	.438	771	795	20	8	6	10	40	850	29.4
67	46	1954	J.Robinson	386	63	7	456	120	22	4	15	.311	.417	.505	922	873	7	3	2	10		886	29.3
68	48	1948	G.Hermanski	400	64	2	466	116	22	7	15	.290	.391	.493	883	872	15			10		882	29.1
69	97	1930	J.Frederick	616	46	3	665	206	44	11	17	.334	.383	.524	908	793	1			10	40	843	28.6
70	81	1970	W.Davis	593	29	1	623	181	23	16	8	.305	.339	.438	777	758	38	14	15	10	70	853	28.3
71	99	1951	D.Snider	606	62	0	668	168	26	6	29	.277	.344	.483	828	810	14	10	(8)	10	30	842	28.3
72	76	1955	C.Furillo	523	43	7	573	164	24	3	26	.314	.373	.520	894	856	4	5	(10)	(10)	20	856	28.3
73	90	1999	G.Sheffield	549	101	4	654	165	20	0	34	.301	.413	.523	936	856	11	5	1	10	(20)	847	28.0
74	66	1932	H.Wilson	481	51	1	533	143	37	5	23	.297	.366	.538	904	882	2				(20)	862	27.9
75	91	1981	D.Baker	400	29	1	430	128	17	3	9	.320	.367	.445	812	836	10	7	(9)		20	847	27.9

Brooklyn/Los Angeles Dodgers
Starting Pitchers

V	R	Year	Name	G	GS	IP	W	L	SV	SO	BB	ERA	RA/9	R Wtd RA/9	V Runs /162
1	2	1966	S.Koufax	41	41	323	27	9	0	317	77	1.73	2.06	2.29	81.4
2	3	1963	S.Koufax	40	40	311	25	5	0	306	58	1.88	1.97	2.35	76.3
3	5	1924	D.Vance	35	34	308	28	6	0	262	77	2.16	2.60	2.60	70.5
4	4	1928	D.Vance	38	32	280	22	10	2	200	72	2.09	2.54	2.46	68.5
5	9	1965	S.Koufax	43	41	336	26	8	2	382	71	2.04	2.41	2.73	68.4
6	10	1975	A.Messersmith	42	40	322	19	14	1	213	96	2.29	2.57	2.84	61.6
7	11	1964	D.Drysdale	40	40	321	18	16	0	237	68	2.18	2.55	2.88	59.9
8	17	1911	N.Rucker	48	33	316	22	18	4	190	110	2.71	2.91	2.97	58.5
9	1	1964	S.Koufax	29	28	223	19	5	1	223	53	1.74	1.98	2.23	57.6
10	6	1930	D.Vance	35	31	259	17	15	0	173	55	2.61	3.38	2.66	57.3
11	18	1912	N.Rucker	45	34	298	18	21	4	151	72	2.21	3.05	2.99	54.6
12	16	1941	W.Wyatt	38	35	288	22	10	1	176	82	2.34	2.78	2.97	53.5
13	26	1969	B.Singer	41	40	316	20	12	1	247	74	2.34	2.73	3.05	52.9
14	21	1981	F.Valenzuela	25	25	192	13	7	0	180	61	2.48	2.57	3.01	49.9
15	22	1972	D.Sutton	33	33	273	19	9	0	207	63	2.08	2.57	3.01	49.3
16	12	1988	O.Hershiser	35	34	267	23	8	1	178	73	2.26	2.46	2.90	49.3
17	49	1916	J.Pfeffer	41	36	329	25	11	1	128	63	1.92	2.49	3.30	48.4
18	7	2000	K.Brown	33	33	230	13	6	0	216	47	2.58	2.97	2.67	48.1
19	43	1969	C.Osteen	41	41	321	20	15	0	183	74	2.66	2.89	3.23	47.4
20	33	1947	R.Branca	43	36	280	21	12	1	148	98	2.67	3.21	3.15	46.2
21	34	1974	A.Messersmith	39	39	292	20	6	0	221	94	2.59	2.87	3.15	45.6
22	53	1914	J.Pfeffer	43	34	315	23	12	4	135	91	1.97	2.83	3.35	44.5
23	8	1980	D.Sutton	32	31	212	13	5	1	128	47	2.20	2.37	2.68	44.2
24	20	1973	D.Sutton	33	33	256	18	10	0	200	56	2.42	2.74	3.01	44.0
25	38	1927	D.Vance	34	32	273	16	15	1	184	69	2.70	3.23	3.19	43.7
26	25	1989	O.Hershiser	35	33	257	15	15	0	178	77	2.31	2.63	3.04	43.3
27	14	1949	P.Roe	30	27	213	15	6	1	109	44	2.79	2.92	2.91	41.1
28	23	1985	O.Hershiser	36	34	240	19	3	0	157	68	2.03	2.70	3.02	40.9
29	66	1909	N.Rucker	38	33	309	13	19	1	201	101	2.24	2.76	3.44	40.5
30	41	1951	P.Roe	34	33	258	22	3	1	113	64	3.04	3.17	3.22	40.2
31	13	1995	H.Nomo	28	28	191	13	6	0	236	78	2.54	2.96	2.90	39.5
32	24	1981	J.Reuss	22	22	153	10	4	0	51	27	2.30	2.59	3.03	39.2
33	52	1960	D.Drysdale	41	36	269	15	14	2	246	72	2.84	3.11	3.33	38.4
34	71	1920	B.Grimes	40	33	304	23	11	2	131	67	2.22	2.99	3.48	38.4
35	39	1999	K.Brown	35	35	252	18	9	0	221	59	3.00	3.53	3.19	38.3
36	76	1910	N.Rucker	41	39	320	17	18	0	147	84	2.58	3.15	3.54	38.2
37	56	1965	C.Osteen	40	40	287	15	15	0	162	78	2.79	2.98	3.37	37.9
38	45	1949	D.Newcombe	38	31	244	17	8	1	149	73	3.17	3.28	3.26	36.9
39	30	1977	B.Hooton	32	31	223	12	7	1	153	60	2.62	2.98	3.09	36.4
40	74	1921	B.Grimes	37	35	302	22	13	0	136	76	2.83	3.58	3.53	36.2
41	51	1950	P.Roe	36	32	251	19	11	1	125	66	3.30	3.44	3.33	36.0
42	73	1962	D.Drysdale	43	41	314	25	9	1	232	78	2.83	3.50	3.53	35.9
43	36	1976	D.Rau	34	32	231	16	12	0	98	69	2.57	2.77	3.16	35.8
44	40	1978	B.Hooton	32	32	236	19	10	0	104	61	2.71	2.82	3.20	35.7
45	126	1901	B.Donovan	45	38	351	25	15	3	226	152	2.77	3.87	3.77	35.6
46	55	1971	D.Sutton	38	37	265	17	12	1	194	55	2.54	2.88	3.36	35.3
47	62	1985	F.Valenzuela	35	35	272	17	10	0	208	101	2.45	3.04	3.40	34.9
48	31	1981	B.Hooton	23	23	142	11	6	0	74	33	2.28	2.66	3.12	34.4
49	68	1925	D.Vance	31	31	265	22	9	0	221	66	3.53	3.90	3.46	34.1
50	32	1916	R.Marquard	36	21	205	13	6	5	107	38	1.58	2.37	3.14	34.0

Brooklyn/Los Angeles Dodgers
Starting Pitchers

V	R	Year	Name	G	GS	IP	W	L	SV	SO	BB	ERA	RA/9	R Wtd RA/9	V Runs /162
51	29	1957	J.Podres	31	27	196	12	9	3	109	44	2.66	2.94	3.08	33.8
52	44	1957	D.Drysdale	34	29	221	17	9	0	148	61	2.69	3.10	3.25	33.8
53	35	1942	C.Davis	32	26	206	15	6	2	60	51	2.36	2.71	3.16	33.7
54	50	1931	W.Clark	34	28	233	14	10	1	96	52	3.20	3.32	3.33	33.5
55	83	1915	J.Pfeffer	40	34	292	19	14	3	84	76	2.10	2.87	3.58	33.2
56	57	1987	B.Welch	35	35	252	15	9	0	196	86	3.22	3.36	3.37	33.2
57	65	1972	C.Osteen	33	33	252	20	11	0	100	69	2.64	2.93	3.43	33.1
58	72	1927	J.Petty	42	33	272	13	18	1	101	53	2.98	3.57	3.52	32.9
59	27	1997	I.Valdes	30	30	197	10	11	0	140	47	2.65	3.11	3.06	32.7
60	61	1975	D.Sutton	35	35	254	16	13	0	175	62	2.87	3.08	3.40	32.7
61	47	1980	J.Reuss	37	29	229	18	6	3	111	40	2.51	2.90	3.28	32.5
62	19	1962	S.Koufax	28	26	184	14	7	1	216	57	2.54	2.98	3.00	31.7
63	48	2000	C.Park	34	34	226	18	10	0	217	124	3.27	3.66	3.29	31.7
64	89	1919	L.Cadore	35	27	251	14	12	0	94	39	2.37	2.87	3.59	31.1
65	101	1902	D.Newton	31	28	264	15	14	2	107	87	2.42	3.23	3.64	31.0
66	28	1948	P.Roe	34	22	178	12	8	2	86	33	2.63	3.03	3.07	31.0
67	131	1908	N.Rucker	42	37	333	17	19	1	199	125	2.08	2.75	3.77	30.5
68	63	1968	D.Drysdale	31	31	239	14	12	0	155	56	2.15	2.56	3.41	30.4
69	90	1956	D.Newcombe	38	36	268	27	7	0	139	46	3.06	3.39	3.60	29.9
70	15	1985	B.Welch	23	23	167	14	4	0	96	35	2.31	2.64	2.96	29.7
71	46	1956	S.Maglie	30	26	196	13	5	0	110	54	2.89	3.08	3.27	29.4
72	125	1934	V.Mungo	45	38	315	18	16	3	184	104	3.37	3.91	3.76	29.4
73	37	1943	W.Wyatt	26	26	181	14	5	0	80	43	2.49	2.73	3.17	29.3
74	42	1952	B.Loes	39	21	187	13	8	1	115	71	2.69	2.98	3.23	29.1
75	60	1995	I.Valdes	33	27	198	13	11	1	150	51	3.05	3.46	3.39	28.9
76	108	1929	W.Clark	41	36	279	16	19	1	140	71	3.74	4.39	3.68	28.7
77	84	1987	O.Hershiser	37	35	265	16	16	1	190	74	3.06	3.57	3.58	28.7
78	59	1952	C.Erskine	33	26	207	14	6	2	131	71	2.70	3.13	3.39	28.3
79	120	1965	D.Drysdale	44	42	308	23	12	1	210	66	2.77	3.30	3.73	28.2
80	80	1973	A.Messersmith	33	33	250	14	10	0	177	77	2.70	3.24	3.56	27.8
81	134	1936	V.Mungo	45	37	312	18	19	3	238	118	3.35	3.95	3.80	27.7
82	104	1917	J.Pfeffer	30	30	266	11	15	0	115	66	2.23	2.84	3.67	27.7
83	54	1928	W.Clark	40	19	195	12	9	3	85	50	2.68	3.46	3.35	27.4
84	78	1939	H.Casey	40	25	227	15	10	1	79	54	2.93	3.49	3.54	26.9
85	114	1982	F.Valenzuela	37	37	285	19	13	0	199	83	2.87	3.32	3.71	26.9
86	96	1953	C.Erskine	39	33	247	20	6	3	187	95	3.54	3.86	3.63	26.9
87	70	1977	T.John	31	31	220	20	7	0	123	50	2.78	3.35	3.47	26.6
88	86	1929	D.Vance	31	26	231	14	13	0	126	47	3.89	4.28	3.59	26.2
89	58	1984	A.Pena	28	28	199	12	6	0	135	46	2.48	3.03	3.38	25.9
90	75	1910	D.Scanlan	34	25	217	9	11	2	103	116	2.61	3.15	3.54	25.9
91	177	1900	J.McGinnity	44	37	343	28	8	0	93	113	2.94	4.70	3.97	25.7
92	106	1933	V.Mungo	41	28	248	16	15	0	110	84	2.72	3.23	3.67	25.7
93	85	1991	M.Morgan	34	33	236	14	10	1	140	61	2.78	3.24	3.58	25.5
94	79	1996	H.Nomo	33	33	228	16	11	0	234	85	3.19	3.67	3.55	25.5
95	91	1977	D.Sutton	33	33	240	14	8	0	150	69	3.18	3.48	3.60	25.4
96	122	1922	D.Ruether	35	35	267	21	12	0	89	92	3.53	4.15	3.74	25.3
97	113	1975	D.Rau	38	38	258	15	9	0	151	61	3.11	3.35	3.70	24.7
98	124	1913	N.Rucker	41	33	260	14	15	3	111	67	2.87	3.43	3.75	24.6
99	115	1971	A.Downing	37	36	262	20	9	0	136	84	2.68	3.19	3.72	24.4
100	139	1923	D.Vance	37	35	280	18	15	0	197	100	3.50	4.08	3.82	24.2

Brooklyn/Los Angeles Dodgers
Relief Pitchers

V	R	Year	Name	G	GS	IP	W	L	SV	SO	BB	ERA	RA/9	R Wtd RA/9	V Runs /162
1	24	1974	M.Marshall	106	0	208	15	12	21	143	56	2.42	2.85	3.13	33.0
2	2	1966	P.Regan	65	0	117	14	1	21	88	24	1.62	1.85	2.06	32.5
3	14	1952	J.Black	56	2	142	15	4	15	85	41	2.15	2.54	2.75	30.0
4	9	1963	R.Perranoksi	69	0	129	16	3	21	75	43	1.67	2.09	2.49	29.6
5	6	1983	T.Niedenfuer	66	0	95	8	3	11	66	29	1.90	2.09	2.31	23.7
6	23	1976	C.Hough	77	0	143	12	8	18	81	77	2.21	2.71	3.10	23.2
7	1	1989	J.Howell	56	0	80	5	3	28	55	22	1.58	1.69	1.95	23.1
8	4	1972	J.Brewer	51	0	78	8	7	17	69	25	1.26	1.85	2.17	21.8
9	12	1965	R.Perranoksi	59	0	105	6	6	17	53	40	2.24	2.40	2.71	21.5
10	5	1971	J.Brewer	55	0	81	6	5	22	66	24	1.88	1.88	2.19	21.3
11	29	1983	D.Stewart	54	9	135	10	4	8	78	50	2.60	2.87	3.17	20.7
12	7	1988	B.Holton	45	0	85	7	3	1	49	26	1.70	2.02	2.38	20.6
13	18	1942	H.Casey	50	2	112	6	3	13	54	44	2.25	2.57	3.00	20.4
14	19	1953	C.Labine	37	7	110	11	6	7	44	30	2.77	3.19	3.00	20.1
15	13	1982	S.Howe	66	0	99	7	5	13	49	17	2.08	2.45	2.74	20.0
16	16	1993	P.Martinez	65	2	107	10	5	2	119	57	2.61	2.86	2.88	19.9
17	3	1995	T.Worrell	59	0	62	4	1	32	61	19	2.02	2.17	2.13	18.8
18	22	1985	T.Niedenfuer	64	0	106	7	9	19	102	24	2.71	2.71	3.03	17.9
19	26	2000	M.Herges	59	4	111	11	3	1	75	40	3.17	3.50	3.14	17.4
20	10	1996	M.Guthrie	66	0	73	2	3	1	56	22	2.22	2.59	2.51	16.6
21	21	1961	R.Perranoksi	53	1	92	7	5	6	56	41	2.65	3.03	3.02	16.5
22	15	1956	D.Bessent	38	0	79	4	3	9	52	31	2.50	2.62	2.78	16.4
23	11	1993	J.Gott	62	0	78	4	8	25	67	17	2.32	2.67	2.69	16.2
24	30	1946	H.Casey	46	1	100	11	5	5	31	33	1.99	2.79	3.19	16.0
25	39	1960	E.Roebuck	58	0	117	8	3	8	77	38	2.78	3.23	3.46	15.0
26	31	1980	B.Castillo	61	0	98	8	6	5	60	45	2.75	2.84	3.21	14.7
27	47	1964	B.Miller	74	2	138	7	7	9	94	63	2.62	3.20	3.61	14.5
28	36	1962	R.Perranoksi	70	0	107	6	6	20	68	36	2.85	3.36	3.39	13.9
29	34	1988	A.Pena	60	0	94	6	7	12	83	27	1.91	2.77	3.26	13.5
30	33	1953	J.Hughes	48	0	86	4	3	9	49	41	3.47	3.47	3.26	13.0
31	8	1997	D.Hall	63	0	55	3	2	2	39	26	2.30	2.47	2.43	13.0
32	41	1967	R.Perranoksi	70	0	110	6	7	16	75	45	2.45	2.95	3.50	12.9
33	32	1992	J.Gott	68	0	88	3	3	6	75	41	2.45	2.76	3.24	12.9
34	60	1955	C.Labine	60	8	144	13	5	11	67	55	3.24	3.81	3.80	12.8
35	17	1999	J.Shaw	64	0	68	2	4	34	43	15	2.78	3.31	2.99	11.8
36	35	1981	S.Howe	41	0	54	5	3	8	32	18	2.50	2.83	3.32	11.3
37	46	1990	T.Crews	66	2	107	4	5	5	76	24	2.77	3.35	3.61	11.3
38	38	1969	J.Brewer	59	0	88	7	6	20	92	41	2.55	3.07	3.43	11.0
39	28	1982	T.Niedenfuer	55	0	70	3	4	9	60	25	2.71	2.84	3.17	10.8
40	20	1998	S.Radinsky	62	0	62	6	6	13	45	20	2.63	3.06	3.01	10.6
41	37	1996	A.Osuna	73	0	84	9	6	4	85	32	3.00	3.54	3.43	10.6
42	49	1965	B.Miller	61	1	103	6	7	9	77	26	2.97	3.23	3.65	10.4
43	48	1957	E.Roebuck	44	1	96	8	2	8	73	46	2.71	3.47	3.64	10.3
44	44	1964	J.Brewer	34	5	93	4	3	1	63	25	3.00	3.19	3.60	9.9
45	25	1997	S.Radinsky	75	0	62	5	1	3	44	21	2.89	3.18	3.13	9.8
46	62	1977	C.Hough	70	1	127	6	12	22	105	70	3.32	3.75	3.88	9.5
47	52	1968	M.Grant	37	4	95	6	4	3	35	19	2.09	2.75	3.66	9.4
48	40	1968	J.Brewer	54	0	76	8	3	14	75	33	2.48	2.61	3.48	9.1
49	50	1970	J.Brewer	58	0	89	7	6	24	91	33	3.13	3.64	3.66	8.9
50	55	1932	J.Quinn	42	0	87	3	7	8	28	24	3.30	3.72	3.69	8.8

Chicago Cubs (1900–2000)

The Chicago Cubs are the lovable losers of baseball. The Cubs broadcast a message of fun to millions of viewers, playing baseball in the friendly confines of charming Wrigley Field, where ivy vines grow in profusion on outfield walls, and where boisterous bleacher bums heave opponents' home runs back onto the playing field. Loyal fans support the team, win or lose, and for most of the past six decades they supported poor teams buried in the bottom half of the standings. No pennants have flown over Waveland Avenue since 1945. The Cubs last won a World Series more than ninety years ago in 1908, when Tinker to Evers to Chance beat a Detroit squad led by a young Ty Cobb. The team's loser image is enshrined in fond memory of the 1969 team, which had the misfortune of blowing a 9½ game August lead and then fading badly to finish 8 games behind the Miracle Mets of New York. The 1999 team is another prime example, as fans packed the ballpark to watch the Sammy Sosa home run show, while Sammy hit almost as many home runs as the last place Cubs won.

A different Chicago Cubs thrived in the first half of the twentieth century. The early Cubs teams played dominating baseball, outclassing their opponents in every aspect of the game. The Cubs started the century by briefly fielding losing teams from 1900 to 1902, although Jack Taylor provided one bright light in 1902, going 23–11 with a 1.33 ERA and a 2.68 Wtd. RA/9. The Cubs then won at least 90 games every year from 1904 through 1912. During the five-year period 1906–1910, at the high point of the Dead Ball Era, the Cubs won four pennants and finished in second in 1909 — despite a 104–49 record.

The 1906 team set the modern day record for wins and winning percentage with its 116–36 record. Never mind that the Cubs managed to lose the Series that year in six games to their weak-hitting crosstown rivals. They were an outstanding team, loaded with great talent at each position. In addition to Joe Tinker at short, Johnny Evers at second, and Frank Chance (.319, league-leading 57 steals, and 1,007 Total Factor in his best season) at first, this team featured Harry Steinfeldt (.327, 960 Total Factor), Johnny Kling (.312, 934 Total Factor), Wildfire Schulte, and Jimmy Sheckard. The hitting statistics of this lineup, representing some of the greatest players in Cubs history, suffered from playing during the Dead Ball Era, the dustbin of offensive results. Adjusted for 14 percent hitter's deflation that year, Chance hit .363, Steinfeldt batted .372, and Kling hit .355.

Cubs pitching was simply awesome in 1906, led by the starting rotation of Three Finger Brown (26–6, 1.04 ERA, career-best 2.28 Wtd. RA/9), Ed Reulbach (19–4, 1.65 ERA, 2.64 Wtd. RA/9) Jack Pfiester (20–8, 1.51 ERA, 2.83 Wtd. RA/9), Carl Lundgren, and Orvie Overall. The 1906 pitchers head up the list of post–1900 teams with the lowest Wtd. RA/9. This list includes three Cubs teams at the top:

Team	Year	ERA	Wtd. RA/9
Cubs	1906	1.75	3.09
Cubs	1905	2.04	3.10
Cubs	1909	1.75	3.12
Yankees	1939	3.31	3.19
Cardinals	1944	2.67	3.29
Cubs	1907	1.73	3.34

Excluding their World Series failure, the 1906 Cubs had the best season of any team since 1900. They won 116 games at a .763 winning percentage. They owned the best pitching staff ever with their 3.09 Wtd. RA/9. They made an impressive 25 percent fewer errors than the league average. They generated a 667 Production, which was 7.5 percent better than the league average. And, most telling, they scored a record 85 percent more runs than they gave up. The teams with the highest ratio of runs scored to runs given up (Runs Ratio) since 1900 are:

Team	Year	Runs Ratio	Record	Winning %
Cubs	1906	1.85	116–36	.763
Pirates	1902	1.76	103–36	.741
Yankees	1939	1.74	106–45	.702
Yankees	1927	1.63	110–44	.714
Cubs	1909	1.63	104–49	.680

From 1913 to 1926, the Cubs experienced one moment of success and a few standout performances. They won the pennant in 1918, as 22-year-old shortstop Charlie Hollocher hit .316 with 26 steals, Hippo Vaughn led the league in wins (22) and ERA (1.74), and Lefty Tyler was 19–8 with a 2.00 ERA. In 1920, Pete Alexander was 27–14 with a 1.91 ERA and 2.77 Wtd. RA/9 for a fifth place Cubs team. First baseman Ray Grimes produced his one good season in 1922, hitting .354 with 14 home runs. Gabby Hartnett matured into a solid hitter in 1924, hitting .299 with 16 home runs.

The Cubs also achieved a long stretch of success from 1927 through 1939. They had a record of 84–70 or better every year, and found themselves in an every-third-year cycle of winning pennants in 1929, 1932, 1935, and 1938. Their only shortcoming during this period was a failure to win any of the four World Series in which they played. Star performers included Rogers Hornsby, who was traded to his fourth team in four years in time for the 1929 season. Hornsby took home the MVP Award that year for hitting .380 with 39 home runs, for a 1,139 Production and, after adjusting for 11 percent hitter's inflation, a 1,027 Wtd. Production. A foot injury derailed Hornsby and his career the next year.

The 1930 team finished in second place, led by Hack Wilson and his statistically incredible .356 batting average, 56 home runs and a record 190 RBI, for a 1,177 Production. Adjusted for 15 percent hitter's inflation, Hack hit only .311 with 53 home runs, for a 1,029 Wtd. Production. Gabby Hartnett, who starred defensively behind the plate, generated his own impressive statistics that year, hitting .339 with 37 home runs for a 1,034 Production and, after adjusting for inflation, for a more modest 903 Wtd. Production.

Hartnett excelled in many other seasons for the Cubs, including a MVP season in 1935 (.344, 13 home runs) for a pennant winning team that went 100–54. The Cubs of this period also featured Billy Herman (.341, .334, and .335 averages from 1935 to 1937), Stan Hack, and fleet-footed Kiki Cuyler (.355, 80 extra base hits, 37 steals in 1930). Lon Warneke (22–6, 2.37 ERA, 2.71 Wtd. RA/9 in 1932) was the team's best pitcher in the 1930s.

The Cubs' winning tradition died after the 1939 season. From 1903 to 1939, the Cubs fielded 31 winning teams in 37 years, while capturing nine pennants and two World Series crowns. From 1940 through the present, only 14 of 61 Cubs teams finished over .500, with just two division crowns, one wild card team, and one pennant back in 1945 to show for six decades of effort, the worst results of any of the original 16 teams.

The Cubs and their players managed a few high points since 1939. The wartime 1945 team won the pennant, led by MVP Phil Cavaretta, who hit for a .355 average. Hank Sauer won the MVP Award in 1952, hitting .270 with a league high 37 home runs for a rare .500 Cubs team. Ernie Banks was the Cubs' highlight film on many bad Cubs teams, winning MVP awards in 1958 and 1959, while hitting 277 of his career total 512 home runs during the seven-year period 1955–1961 when he played shortstop. Banks' best season was in 1959, when he hit .304 with 45 home runs, for a 978 Total Factor and 104.5 Hits Contribution.

Billy Williams, Ron Santo, and Fergie Jenkins were the heart and soul of the competitive Cubs teams of the late sixties and early seventies. Williams won the 1972 MVP Award with a .333 batting average and 37 home runs. Adjusted for 3.5 percent hitter's deflation, Williams batted .344 with 40 home runs, while generating a Wtd. Production of 1,045, the best ever for any Cubs player. Jenkins won 20 or more games six straight years from 1967 to 1972. Santo hit over 30 home runs four straight seasons; he led the league in walks four times; and he was an outstanding defensive third baseman. Santo's best season was in 1964, when he hit .313 with 30 home runs, for a 1,035 Total Factor and 103.4 Hits Contribution.

Reliever Bruce Sutter fired a new pitch, the split finger fastball, past everyone in 1977 while posting a 7–3 record, 31 saves, a 1.34 ERA, and a Cubs record 1.82 Wtd. RA/9. Sutter went on to win the Cy Young Award in 1979 with a 6–6 record, 37 saves, and a 2.22 ERA. MVP Ryne Sandberg (.314 average, 19 triples, 19 home runs, 1,013 Total Factor, 108.0 Hits Contribution) led the surprising 1984 Cubs to the division title in 1984, as they finished over .500 for the first time since 1972. Four more losing seasons immediately followed, including the 1987 season, when Andre Dawson won the league's MVP Award for hitting 49 home runs for a last place team. Then, in 1989, Sandberg hit 30 home runs to team with slick fielding first baseman Mark Grace (.314, 13 home runs) and emerging star pitcher Greg Maddux (19–12 record) to win another division title. Maddux was the 1992 Cy Young winner with a 20–11 record, a 2.18 ERA, and a 2.68 Wtd. RA/9. In 1998, MVP Sammy Sosa hit .308 with 66 home runs, for a 977 Wtd. Production, and the Cubs earned their first playoff appearance since 1989. Sosa hit 63 home runs in 1999 for the last place Cubs, and he won his first home run title in 2000 with 50 home runs for another last place Cubs team.

Chicago Cubs

Hitters Volume of Success

Pos	Year	Name	AB	BB	HBP	TAB	H	2B	3B	HR	BA	OB	SA	PRO	Wtd PRO	SB	CS	SBF	SPF	FF	R TF	V HC
C	1930	G.Hartnett	508	55	1	564	172	31	3	37	.339	.404	.630	1,034	903	0		(10)		40	933	72.4
1B	1906	F.Chance	474	70	12	556	151	24	10	3	.319	.419	.430	849	967	57		10		30	1,007	66.1
2B	1929	R.Hornsby	602	87	1	690	229	47	8	39	.380	.459	.679	1,139	1,027	2			0	0	1,027	118.1
SS	1959	E.Banks	589	64	7	660	179	25	6	45	.304	.379	.596	975	946	2	4	(9)	10	30	978	104.5
3B	1964	R.Santo	592	86	2	680	185	33	13	30	.313	.401	.564	966	992	3	4	(7)	(10)	60	1,035	103.4
OF	1972	B.Williams	574	62	6	642	191	34	6	37	.333	.403	.606	1,010	1,045	3	1		10	0	1,057	96.3
OF	1930	H.Wilson	585	105	1	691	208	35	6	56	.356	.454	.723	1,177	1,029	3			0	(10)	1,019	90.5
OF	1998	S.Sosa	643	73	1	717	198	20	0	66	.308	.379	.647	1,026	977	18	9	0	10	(20)	967	71.5
Starters		Averages	571	75	4	650	189	31	7	39	.331	.413	.614	1,027	988	11	2	(2)	3	16	1,005	90.3
C	1993	R.Wilkins	446	50	3	499	135	23	1	30	.303	.377	.561	937	908	2	1	0	0	20	928	59.5
1B	1945	P.Cavaretta	498	81	4	583	177	34	10	6	.355	.449	.500	949	963	5			10	0	973	59.3
2B	1984	R.Sandberg	636	52	3	691	200	36	19	19	.314	.369	.520	889	909	32	7	25	10	70	1,013	108.0
SS	1908	J.Tinker	548	32	0	580	146	22	14	6	.266	.307	.391	697	814	30			0	80	894	67.4
3B	1912	H.Zimmerman	557	38	6	601	207	41	14	14	.372	.418	.571	989	983	23		(10)	(10)		963	74.3
OF	1911	W.Schulte	577	76	3	656	173	30	21	21	.300	.384	.534	918	938	23			10	20	968	69.2
OF	1901	T.Hartsel	558	74	1	633	187	25	16	7	.335	.414	.475	889	938	41			10	0	948	66.5
OF	1943	B.Nicholson	608	71	5	684	188	30	9	29	.309	.386	.531	917	963	4		(10)	(10)		943	63.8
Reserves		Averages	554	59	3	616	177	30	13	17	.319	.388	.510	898	928	20	1	3	3	21	955	71.0
Totals		Wtd. Ave.	565	70	4	639	185	31	9	32	.327	.405	.580	985	968	14	2	(0)	3	18	988	83.9

Pitchers Volume of Success

Pos	Year	Name	G	GS	IP	W	L	SV	SO	BB	ERA	RA/9	Wtd RA/9	V Runs /162
SP	1909	T.Brown	50	34	343	27	9	7	172	53	1.31	2.05	2.55	80.4
SP	1902	J.Taylor	36	33	325	23	11	1	83	43	1.33	2.38	2.68	78.2
SP	1920	P.Alexander	46	40	363	27	14	5	173	69	1.91	2.38	2.77	76.0
SP	1905	E.Reulbach	34	29	292	18	14	1	152	73	1.42	2.19	2.40	73.7
SP	1918	H.Vaughn	35	33	290	22	10	0	148	76	1.74	2.33	2.94	66.4
Starters		Averages	40	34	323	23	12	3	146	63	1.55	2.27	2.67	74.9
RP	1977	B.Sutter	62	0	107	7	3	31	129	23	1.34	1.76	1.82	32.5
RP	1983	L.Smith	66	0	103	4	10	29	91	41	1.65	2.00	2.21	26.8
RP	1959	B.Henry	65	0	134	9	8	12	115	26	2.68	2.82	2.89	26.1
RP	1980	B.Caudill	72	2	128	4	6	1	112	59	2.19	2.61	2.95	22.8
Relievers		Averages	66	1	118	6	7	18	112	37	2.02	2.34	2.52	27.1
Totals		Averages	106	34	441	29	18	21	257	100	1.67	2.29	2.63	102.0

Chicago Cubs (1900–2000)

Chicago Cubs — **Hitters Rate of Success**

Pos	Year	Name	AB	BB	HBP	TAB	H	2B	3B	HR	BA	OB	SA	PRO	Wtd PRO	SB	CS	SBF	SPF	FF	R TF	V HC
C	1937	G.Hartnett	356	43	0	399	126	21	6	12	.354	.424	.548	971	960	0			(10)	40	990	62.6
1B	1906	F.Chance	474	70	12	556	151	24	10	3	.319	.419	.430	849	967	57			10	30	1,007	66.1
2B	1929	R.Hornsby	602	87	1	690	229	47	8	39	.380	.459	.679	1,139	1,027	2			0	0	1,027	118.1
SS	1959	E.Banks	589	64	7	660	179	25	6	45	.304	.379	.596	975	946	2	4	(9)	10	30	978	104.5
3B	1964	R.Santo	592	86	2	680	185	33	13	30	.313	.401	.564	966	992	3	4	(7)	(10)	60	1,035	103.4
OF	1972	B.Williams	574	62	6	642	191	34	6	37	.333	.403	.606	1,010	1,045	3	1	1	10	0	1,057	96.3
OF	1930	H.Wilson	585	105	1	691	208	35	6	56	.356	.454	.723	1,177	1,029	3			0	(10)	1,019	90.5
OF	1911	W.Schulte	577	76	3	656	173	30	21	21	.300	.384	.534	918	938	23			10	20	968	69.2
Starters		Averages	544	74	4	622	180	31	10	30	.332	.416	.591	1,007	990	12	1	(2)	3	21	1,012	88.8
C	1906	J.Kling	343	23	1	367	107	15	8	2	.312	.357	.420	777	884	14			0	50	934	47.3
1B	1945	P.Cavaretta	498	81	4	583	177	34	10	6	.355	.449	.500	949	963	5			10	0	973	59.3
2B	1984	R.Sandberg	636	52	3	691	200	36	19	19	.314	.369	.520	889	909	32	7	25	10	70	1,013	108.0
SS	1908	J.Tinker	548	32	0	580	146	22	14	6	.266	.307	.391	697	814	30			0	80	894	67.4
3B	1912	H.Zimmerman	557	38	6	601	207	41	14	14	.372	.418	.571	989	983	23			(10)	(10)	963	74.3
OF	1998	S.Sosa	643	73	1	717	198	20	0	66	.308	.379	.647	1,026	977	18	9	0	10	(20)	967	71.5
OF	1950	A.Pafko	514	69	11	594	156	24	8	36	.304	.397	.591	989	947	4			0	10	957	59.4
OF	1970	J.Hickman	514	93	1	608	162	33	4	32	.315	.421	.582	1,003	978	0	1	(3)	(10)	(10)	955	57.1
Reserves		Averages	532	58	3	593	169	28	10	23	.318	.388	.535	923	935	16	2	3	1	21	960	68.0
Totals		Wtd. Ave.	540	69	4	612	177	30	10	28	.327	.407	.573	980	972	13	1	(0)	2	21	995	81.9

Pitchers Rate of Success

Pos	Year	Name	G	GS	IP	W	L	SV	SO	BB	ERA	RA/9	Wtd RA/9	R Runs /162
SP	1906	T.Brown	36	32	277	26	6	3	144	61	1.04	1.82	2.28	73.8
SP	1907	C.Lundgren	28	25	207	18	7	0	84	92	1.17	1.83	2.39	52.4
SP	1905	E.Reulbach	34	29	292	18	14	1	152	73	1.42	2.19	2.40	73.7
SP	1919	P.Alexander	30	27	235	16	11	1	121	38	1.72	1.95	2.44	63.9
SP	1905	B.Wicker	22	22	178	13	6	0	86	47	2.02	2.33	2.55	41.7
Starters		Averages	30	27	238	18	9	1	117	62	1.44	2.01	2.41	61.1
RP	1977	B.Sutter	62	0	107	7	3	31	129	23	1.34	1.76	1.82	32.5
RP	1983	L.Smith	66	0	103	4	10	29	91	41	1.65	2.00	2.21	26.8
RP	1983	W.Brusstar	59	0	80	3	1	1	46	37	2.35	2.35	2.60	17.4
RP	1982	M.Proly	44	1	82	5	3	1	24	22	2.30	2.41	2.69	17.0
Relievers		Averages	58	0	93	5	4	16	73	31	1.85	2.10	2.29	23.4
Totals		Averages	88	27	331	23	13	17	190	93	1.55	2.04	2.37	84.5

Chicago Cubs
Catchers

V	R	Year	Name	AB	BB	HBP	TAB	H	2B	3B	HR	BA	OB	SA	PRO	Wtd PRO	SB	CS	SBF	SPF	FF	R TF	V HC
1	5	1930	G.Hartnett	508	55	1	564	172	31	3	37	.339	.404	.630	1,034	903	0			(10)	40	933	72.4
2	1	1937	G.Hartnett	356	43	0	399	126	21	6	12	.354	.424	.548	971	960	0			(10)	40	990	62.6
3	2	1935	G.Hartnett	413	41	1	455	142	32	6	13	.344	.404	.545	949	928	1			(10)	30	948	61.7
4	6	1993	R.Wilkins	446	50	3	499	135	23	1	30	.303	.377	.561	937	908	2	1	0		20	928	59.5
5	4	1928	G.Hartnett	388	65	2	455	117	26	9	14	.302	.404	.523	928	884	3			(10)	60	934	58.4
6	7	1934	G.Hartnett	438	37	3	478	131	21	1	22	.299	.358	.502	860	835	0			(10)	70	895	52.1
7	10	1923	B.O'Farrell	452	67	1	520	144	25	4	12	.319	.408	.471	879	842	10	3	7		20	869	50.0
8	3	1906	J.Kling	343	23	1	367	107	15	8	2	.312	.357	.420	777	884	14				50	934	47.3
9	8	1924	G.Hartnett	354	39	5	398	106	17	7	16	.299	.377	.523	899	871	10	2	14	(10)		875	39.5
10	12	1922	B.O'Farrell	392	79	1	472	127	18	8	4	.324	.439	.441	880	825	5	3	(2)		20	843	39.1
11	15	1933	G.Hartnett	490	37	0	527	135	21	4	16	.276	.326	.433	759	789	1			(10)	40	819	37.4
12	11	1908	J.Kling	424	21	3	448	117	23	5	4	.276	.315	.382	697	813	16				30	843	37.2
13	9	1907	J.Kling	334	27	2	363	95	15	8	1	.284	.342	.386	728	834	9				40	874	35.8
14	13	1936	G.Hartnett	424	30	6	460	130	25	6	7	.307	.361	.443	804	786	0			(10)	50	826	34.3
15	18	1903	J.Kling	491	22	2	515	146	29	13	3	.297	.330	.428	758	788	23				10	798	34.2
16	16	1927	G.Hartnett	449	44	3	496	132	32	5	10	.294	.361	.454	815	794	2			(10)	30	814	33.9
17	20	1967	R.Hundley	539	44	2	585	144	25	3	14	.267	.325	.403	727	761	2	4	(10)	10	30	791	31.7
18	19	1983	J.Davis	510	33	2	545	138	31	2	24	.271	.317	.480	798	805	0	2	(7)	(10)	10	798	31.2
19	14	1925	G.Hartnett	398	36	2	436	115	28	3	24	.289	.351	.555	906	839	1	5	(20)	(10)	10	820	31.2
20	17	1931	G.Hartnett	380	52	1	433	107	32	1	8	.282	.370	.434	804	787	3			(10)	30	807	28.1
21	21	1932	G.Hartnett	406	51	1	458	110	25	3	12	.271	.354	.430	790	770				(10)	30	790	25.8
22	22	1969	R.Hundley	522	61	3	586	133	15	1	18	.255	.336	.391	727	744	2	3	(6)		30	767	25.1
23	25	1984	J.Davis	523	47	1	571	134	25	2	19	.256	.319	.421	739	755	5	6	(12)	(10)	20	754	20.8
24	26	1986	J.Davis	528	41	0	569	132	27	2	21	.250	.304	.428	732	734	0	1	(3)	(10)	30	751	19.9
25	27	1902	J.Kling	431	29	0	460	123	19	3	0	.285	.330	.343	674	754	24			(10)		744	16.8

Chicago Cubs
First basemen

V	R	Year	Name	AB	BB	HBP	TAB	H	2B	3B	HR	BA	OB	SA	PRO	Wtd PRO	SB	CS	SBF	SPF	FF	R TF	V HC
1	1	1906	F.Chance	474	70	12	556	151	24	10	3	.319	.419	.430	849	967	57			10	30	1,007	66.1
2	3	1945	P.Cavaretta	498	81	4	583	177	34	10	6	.355	.449	.500	949	963	5			10		973	59.3
3	2	1905	F.Chance	392	78	17	487	124	16	12	2	.316	.450	.434	883	964	38			10	30	1,004	57.1
4	6	1903	F.Chance	441	78	10	529	144	24	10	2	.327	.439	.440	878	913	67			10	30	953	53.4
5	7	1922	R.Grimes	509	75	6	590	180	45	12	14	.354	.442	.572	1,014	951	7	7	(11)	10		949	53.1
6	5	1904	F.Chance	451	36	16	503	140	16	10	6	.310	.382	.430	812	913	42			10	40	963	48.5
7	8	1989	M.Grace	510	80	0	590	160	28	3	13	.314	.407	.457	864	897	14	7	0		40	937	46.8
8	11	1995	M.Grace	552	65	2	619	180	51	3	16	.326	.399	.516	915	872	6	2	3		30	905	44.8
9	4	1975	A.Thornton	372	88	4	464	109	21	4	18	.293	.433	.516	949	960	3	2	(2)	10		968	43.8
10	15	1992	M.Grace	603	72	4	679	185	37	5	9	.307	.384	.430	814	838	6	1	6		40	883	36.6
11	13	1993	M.Grace	594	71	1	666	193	39	4	14	.325	.398	.475	873	845	8	4	0		40	885	36.5
12	9	1984	L.Durham	473	69	1	543	132	30	4	23	.279	.372	.505	877	896	16	8	0	10		906	35.2
13	12	1915	V.Saier	497	64	2	563	131	35	11	11	.264	.350	.445	795	876	29	9	18	10	(10)	895	35.2
14	16	1944	P.Cavaretta	614	67	3	684	197	35	15	5	.321	.390	.451	841	862	4			10		872	35.0
15	14	1913	V.Saier	519	62	5	586	150	15	21	14	.289	.370	.480	850	884	26			10	(10)	884	33.4
16	10	1907	F.Chance	382	51	13	446	112	19	2	1	.293	.395	.361	756	866	35			10	30	906	30.4
17	18	1981	B.Buckner	421	26	1	448	131	35	3	10	.311	.353	.480	832	857	5	2	2			859	28.7
18	22	1998	M.Grace	595	93	3	691	184	39	3	17	.309	.405	.471	876	833	4	7	(14)		30	850	26.3
19	19	1997	M.Grace	555	88	2	645	177	32	5	13	.319	.414	.465	879	834	2	4	(9)		30	855	26.2
20	21	1943	P.Cavaretta	530	75	3	608	154	27	9	8	.291	.382	.421	802	843	3			10		853	25.2
21	20	1931	C.Grimm	531	53	1	585	176	33	11	4	.331	.393	.458	851	833	1				20	853	24.3
22	23	1996	M.Grace	547	62	1	610	181	39	1	9	.331	.400	.455	855	815	2	3	(6)		40	849	22.8
23	26	1990	M.Grace	589	59	5	653	182	32	1	9	.309	.377	.413	789	788	15	6	4		50	842	22.5
24	17	1971	J.Pepitone	427	24	4	455	131	19	4	16	.307	.349	.482	832	857	1	2	(6)		20	871	21.9
25	29	1914	V.Saier	537	94	4	635	129	24	8	18	.240	.357	.415	773	838	19			10	(10)	838	21.6

Chicago Cubs
Second basemen

V	R	Year	Name	AB	BB	HBP	TAB	H	2B	3B	HR	BA	OB	SA	PRO	Wtd PRO	SB	CS	SBF	SPF	FF	R TF	V HC
1	1	1929	R.Hornsby	602	87	1	690	229	47	8	39	.380	.459	.679	1,139	1,027	2					1,027	118.1
2	2	1984	R.Sandberg	636	52	3	691	200	36	19	19	.314	.369	.520	889	909	32	7	25	10	70	1,013	108.0
3	3	1985	R.Sandberg	609	57	1	667	186	31	6	26	.305	.366	.504	870	884	54	11	45	10	60	999	99.7
4	4	1990	R.Sandberg	615	50	1	666	188	30	3	40	.306	.359	.559	918	917	25	7	16	10	50	992	97.4
5	5	1991	R.Sandberg	585	87	2	674	170	32	2	26	.291	.384	.485	870	887	22	8	8	10	70	976	93.2
6	6	1992	R.Sandberg	612	68	1	681	186	32	8	26	.304	.374	.510	884	910	17	6	7	10	30	957	88.1
7	9	1989	R.Sandberg	606	59	4	669	176	25	5	30	.290	.357	.497	854	886	15	5	7	10	40	944	82.3
8	13	1935	B.Herman	666	42	3	711	227	57	6	7	.341	.383	.476	859	839	6				60	899	76.3
9	12	1936	B.Herman	632	59	1	692	211	57	7	5	.334	.392	.470	862	842	5				60	902	75.3
10	11	1937	B.Herman	564	56	1	621	189	35	11	8	.335	.396	.479	875	865	2				40	905	68.4
11	7	1908	J.Evers	416	66	5	487	125	19	6	0	.300	.402	.375	777	907	36			10	30	947	63.9
12	10	1912	J.Evers	478	74	2	554	163	23	11	1	.341	.431	.441	873	868	16				40	908	61.8
13	8	1931	R.Hornsby	357	56	0	413	118	37	1	16	.331	.421	.574	996	975	1				(30)	945	53.7
14	17	1939	B.Herman	623	66	5	694	191	34	18	7	.307	.378	.453	830	813	9				20	833	51.3
15	14	1987	R.Sandberg	523	59	2	584	154	25	2	16	.294	.368	.442	810	779	21	2	28	10	50	866	50.4
16	15	1988	R.Sandberg	618	54	1	673	163	23	8	19	.264	.324	.419	743	777	25	10	7	10	40	834	47.7
17	16	1986	R.Sandberg	627	46	0	673	178	28	5	14	.284	.333	.411	744	746	34	11	17	10	60	833	47.4
18	18	1909	J.Evers	463	73	4	540	122	19	6	1	.263	.369	.337	705	798	28			10	20	828	38.6
19	22	1983	R.Sandberg	633	51	3	687	165	25	4	8	.261	.319	.351	669	675	37	11	21	10	90	796	36.2
20	23	1968	G.Beckert	643	31	2	676	189	28	4	4	.294	.328	.369	697	765	8	4	0		30	795	35.4
21	19	1971	G.Beckert	530	24	0	554	181	18	5	2	.342	.370	.406	776	799	3	2	(2)		20	818	34.9
22	25	1932	B.Herman	656	40	5	701	206	42	7	1	.314	.358	.404	762	743	14				40	783	34.3
23	20	1913	J.Evers	446	50	3	499	127	20	5	3	.285	.361	.372	733	762	11				50	812	31.7
24	21	1910	J.Evers	433	108	2	543	114	11	7	0	.263	.413	.321	734	777	28				20	797	30.5
25	24	1911	H.Zimmerman	535	25	5	565	164	22	17	9	.307	.343	.462	805	822	23		(10)	(20)		792	30.3

Chicago Cubs
Shortstops

V	R	Year	Name	AB	BB	HBP	TAB	H	2B	3B	HR	BA	OB	SA	PRO	Wtd PRO	SB	CS	SBF	SPF	FF	R TF	V HC
1	1	1959	E.Banks	589	64	7	660	179	25	6	45	.304	.379	.596	975	946	2	4	(9)	10	30	978	104.5
2	2	1958	E.Banks	617	52	4	673	193	23	11	47	.313	.370	.614	984	945	4	4	(6)	10	10	960	100.4
3	3	1960	E.Banks	597	71	4	672	162	32	7	41	.271	.353	.554	907	902	1	3	(7)		40	935	91.9
4	4	1957	E.Banks	594	70	3	667	169	34	6	43	.285	.363	.579	942	918	8	4	0	10		928	89.0
5	5	1955	E.Banks	596	45	2	643	176	29	9	44	.295	.347	.596	942	903	9	3	4	10	10	927	85.4
6	6	1908	J.Tinker	548	32	0	580	146	22	14	6	.266	.307	.391	697	814	30				80	894	67.4
7	8	1918	C.Hollocher	509	47	4	560	161	23	6	2	.316	.379	.397	775	858	26			10	(20)	848	63.3
8	7	1956	E.Banks	538	52	0	590	160	25	8	28	.297	.359	.530	889	866	6	9	(19)	10		856	57.5
9	12	1931	W.English	634	68	7	709	202	38	8	2	.319	.391	.413	804	787	12			10	20	817	55.1
10	9	1961	E.Banks	511	54	2	567	142	22	4	29	.278	.349	.507	856	822	1	2	(5)		10	827	46.9
11	15	1969	D.Kessinger	664	61	1	726	181	38	6	4	.273	.335	.366	701	717	11	8	(7)	10	70	790	44.4
12	11	1910	J.Tinker	473	24	0	497	136	25	9	3	.288	.322	.397	719	762	20				60	822	40.0
13	13	1909	J.Tinker	516	17	0	533	132	26	11	4	.256	.280	.372	652	737	23				70	807	38.8
14	17	1978	I.DeJesus	619	74	2	695	172	24	7	3	.278	.357	.354	711	723	41	12	23	10	20	776	37.7
15	14	1911	J.Tinker	536	39	0	575	149	24	12	4	.278	.327	.390	717	732	30				60	792	37.6
16	19	1922	C.Hollocher	592	58	5	655	201	37	8	3	.340	.388	.444	847	794	19	29	(56)	10	20	768	34.8
17	18	1937	B.Jurges	450	42	6	498	134	18	10	1	.298	.365	.389	754	746	2				30	776	28.4
18	22	1903	J.Tinker	460	37	1	498	134	21	7	2	.291	.345	.380	726	755	27			10		765	28.2
19	10	1920	C.Hollocher	301	41	3	345	96	17	2	0	.319	.406	.389	795	826	20	14	(22)	10	10	824	28.0
20	20	1990	S.Dunston	545	15	3	563	143	22	8	17	.262	.286	.426	712	711	25	5	25	10	20	766	27.8
21	16	1989	S.Dunston	471	30	1	502	131	20	6	9	.278	.323	.403	726	754	19	11	(6)	10	20	778	27.8
22	21	1919	C.Hollocher	430	44	7	481	116	14	5	3	.270	.347	.347	694	756	16			10		766	27.5
23	26	1972	D.Kessinger	577	67	2	646	158	20	6	1	.274	.351	.334	686	710	8	7	(9)	10	30	741	25.6
24	23	1933	B.Jurges	487	26	5	518	131	17	6	5	.269	.313	.359	672	699	3				60	759	25.1
25	25	1995	S.Dunston	477	10	6	493	141	30	6	14	.296	.318	.472	790	753	10	5	0			753	24.0

Chicago Cubs
Third basemen

V	R	Year	Name	AB	BB	HBP	TAB	H	2B	3B	HR	BA	OB	SA	PRO	Wtd PRO	SB	CS	SBF	SPF	FF	R TF	V HC
1	1	1964	R.Santo	592	86	2	680	185	33	13	30	.313	.401	.564	966	992	3	4	(7)	(10)	60	1,035	103.4
2	3	1967	R.Santo	586	96	3	685	176	23	4	31	.300	.401	.512	913	955	1	5	(12)	(10)	80	1,013	96.8
3	2	1966	R.Santo	561	95	6	662	175	21	8	30	.312	.417	.538	955	965	4	5	(9)	(10)	70	1,016	94.6
4	4	1965	R.Santo	608	88	5	701	173	30	4	33	.285	.379	.510	889	914	3	1	1	(10)	60	965	83.1
5	5	1912	H.Zimmerman	557	38	6	601	207	41	14	14	.372	.418	.571	989	983	23			(10)	(10)		963	74.3
6	6	1906	H.Steinfeldt	539	47	14	600	176	27	10	3	.327	.395	.430	825	940	29				20	960	73.2
7	7	1969	R.Santo	575	96	2	673	166	18	4	29	.289	.392	.485	877	898	1	3	(7)	(10)	40	921	65.6
8	11	1968	R.Santo	577	96	3	676	142	17	3	26	.246	.357	.421	778	854	3	4	(7)	(10)	60	897	58.1
9	12	1963	R.Santo	630	42	4	676	187	29	6	25	.297	.345	.481	826	869	6	4	(3)	(10)	40	896	57.8
10	15	1945	S.Hack	597	99	1	697	193	29	7	2	.323	.420	.405	826	837	12				40	877	56.3
11	17	1938	S.Hack	609	94	0	703	195	34	11	4	.320	.411	.432	843	844	16			10	20	874	55.6
12	14	1940	S.Hack	603	75	3	681	191	38	6	8	.317	.395	.439	834	839	21			10	30	879	55.6
13	10	1948	A.Pafko	548	50	5	603	171	30	2	26	.312	.375	.516	891	880	3				20	900	55.5
14	8	1976	B.Madlock	514	56	11	581	174	36	1	15	.339	.415	.500	915	944	15	11	(11)	10	(30)	913	54.4
15	9	1972	R.Santo	464	69	4	537	140	25	5	17	.302	.397	.487	884	915	1	4	(12)	(10)	20	912	52.8
16	16	1942	S.Hack	553	94	0	647	166	36	3	6	.300	.402	.409	811	866	9			10		876	51.7
17	19	1941	S.Hack	586	99	1	686	186	33	5	7	.317	.417	.427	844	865	10			10	(10)	865	51.3
18	13	1913	H.Zimmerman	447	41	6	494	140	28	12	9	.313	.379	.490	868	903	18			(10)	(10)	883	41.3
19	21	1970	R.Santo	555	92	1	648	148	30	4	26	.267	.372	.476	848	826	2	0	3	(10)	30	849	41.1
20	18	1975	B.Madlock	514	42	3	559	182	29	7	7	.354	.406	.479	885	895	9	7	(8)	(10)	(30)	866	40.0
21	23	1930	W.English	638	100	6	744	214	36	17	14	.335	.430	.511	941	822	3			10	(10)	822	39.5
22	20	1935	S.Hack	427	65	3	495	133	23	9	4	.311	.406	.436	842	823	14			10	20	853	33.9
23	25	1961	R.Santo	578	73	0	651	164	32	6	23	.284	.364	.479	843	810	2	3	(6)		10	814	31.9
24	24	1971	R.Santo	555	79	0	634	148	22	1	21	.267	.358	.423	781	805	4	0	6	(10)	20	821	31.7
25	28	1943	S.Hack	533	82	0	615	154	24	4	3	.289	.384	.366	750	787	5			10		797	25.0

Chicago Cubs
Outfielders

V	R	Year	Name	AB	BB	HBP	TAB	H	2B	3B	HR	BA	OB	SA	PRO	Wtd PRO	SB	CS	SBF	SPF	FF	R TF	V HC
1	1	1972	B.Williams	574	62	6	642	191	34	6	37	.333	.403	.606	1,010	1,045	3	1	1	10		1,057	96.3
2	2	1930	H.Wilson	585	105	1	691	208	35	6	56	.356	.454	.723	1,177	1,029	3			(10)		1,019	90.5
3	3	1970	B.Williams	636	72	2	710	205	34	4	42	.322	.393	.586	979	955	7	1	7	10	30	1,002	82.6
4	4	1965	B.Williams	645	65	3	713	203	39	6	34	.315	.380	.552	932	958	10	1	11	10	10	988	78.4
5	6	1998	S.Sosa	643	73	1	717	198	20	0	66	.308	.379	.647	1,026	977	18	9	0	10	(20)	967	71.5
6	5	1911	W.Schulte	577	76	3	656	173	30	21	21	.300	.384	.534	918	938	23			10	20	968	69.2
7	10	1901	T.Hartsel	558	74	1	633	187	25	16	7	.335	.414	.475	889	938	41			10		948	66.5
8	15	1943	B.Nicholson	608	71	5	684	188	30	9	29	.309	.386	.531	917	963	4			(10)	(10)	943	63.8
9	16	1964	B.Williams	645	59	2	706	201	39	2	33	.312	.371	.532	903	928	10	7	(5)	10	10	942	62.2
10	20	1944	B.Nicholson	582	93	6	681	167	35	8	33	.287	.391	.545	935	958	3			(10)	(10)	938	61.7
11	12	1968	B.Williams	642	48	2	692	185	30	8	30	.288	.340	.500	840	922	4	1	3	10	10	944	61.7
12	14	1963	B.Williams	612	68	2	682	175	36	9	25	.286	.359	.497	856	900	7	6	(7)	10	40	944	60.5
13	18	1929	H.Wilson	574	78	2	654	198	30	5	39	.345	.425	.618	1,044	941	3					941	60.1
14	7	1950	A.Pafko	514	69	11	594	156	24	8	36	.304	.397	.591	989	947	4				10	957	59.4
15	17	1971	B.Williams	594	77	3	674	179	27	5	28	.301	.384	.505	889	916	7	5	(4)	10	20	942	59.4
16	13	1927	H.Wilson	551	71	6	628	175	30	12	30	.318	.401	.579	980	954	13				(10)	944	58.9
17	22	2000	S.Sosa	604	91	2	697	193	38	1	50	.320	.410	.634	1,044	953	7	4	(1)	10	(30)	932	57.8
18	8	1970	J.Hickman	514	93	1	608	162	33	4	32	.315	.421	.582	1,003	978	0	1	(3)	(10)	(10)	955	57.1
19	32	1930	K.Cuyler	642	72	10	724	228	50	17	13	.355	.428	.547	975	852	37			10	40	902	52.4
20	9	1910	S.Hofman	477	65	0	542	155	24	16	3	.325	.406	.461	867	919	29			10	20	949	52.1
21	24	1928	H.Wilson	520	77	2	599	163	32	9	31	.313	.404	.588	992	945	4				(20)	925	50.5
22	28	1999	S.Sosa	625	78	3	706	180	24	2	63	.288	.370	.635	1,005	919	7	8	(12)	10	(10)	907	50.4
23	25	1926	H.Wilson	529	69	6	604	170	36	8	21	.321	.406	.539	944	921	10					921	49.5
24	21	1979	D.Kingman	532	45	4	581	153	19	5	48	.288	.348	.613	960	952	4	2	0		(20)	932	48.4
25	26	1988	A.Dawson	591	37	4	632	179	31	8	24	.303	.348	.504	852	891	12	4	6		20	917	48.2

Chicago Cubs (1900–2000)

Chicago Cubs
Outfielders

V	R	Year	Name	AB	BB	HBP	TAB	H	2B	3B	HR	BA	OB	SA	PRO	Wtd PRO	SB	CS	SBF	SPF	FF	R TF	V HC
26	36	1942	B.Nicholson	588	76	8	672	173	22	11	21	.294	.382	.476	859	917	8			(10)	(10)	897	47.0
27	37	1931	K.Cuyler	613	72	5	690	202	37	12	9	.330	.404	.473	877	859	13			10	20	889	45.5
28	35	1987	A.Dawson	621	32	7	660	178	24	2	49	.287	.329	.568	897	863	11	3	7		30	900	44.8
29	39	1967	B.Williams	634	68	2	704	176	21	12	28	.278	.349	.481	831	869	6	3	0	10	10	889	44.0
30	23	1967	A.Phillips	448	80	6	534	120	20	7	17	.268	.386	.458	843	882	24	10	7	10	30	929	43.7
31	27	1990	A.Dawson	529	42	2	573	164	28	5	27	.310	.363	.535	898	897	16	2	20	(10)	10	916	43.4
32	29	1929	K.Cuyler	509	66	5	580	183	29	7	15	.360	.438	.532	970	875	43			10	20	905	42.8
33	38	1952	H.Sauer	567	77	4	648	153	31	3	37	.270	.361	.531	892	903	1	2	(4)	(10)		889	42.7
34	30	1982	L.Durham	539	66	2	607	168	33	7	22	.312	.389	.521	910	924	28	14	0	10	(30)	904	42.5
35	19	1916	C.Williams	405	51	9	465	113	19	9	12	.279	.372	.459	831	929	6			10		939	42.2
36	41	1936	F.Demaree	605	49	1	655	212	34	3	16	.350	.400	.496	896	876	4			10		886	42.2
37	44	1911	J.Sheckard	539	147	3	689	149	26	11	4	.276	.434	.388	822	839	32			10	30	879	42.1
38	31	1962	G.Altman	534	62	5	601	170	27	5	22	.318	.394	.511	906	885	19	7	8	10		903	41.8
39	33	1976	R.Monday	534	60	2	596	145	20	5	32	.272	.347	.507	855	882	5	9	(21)	10	30	902	40.9
40	11	1939	H.Leiber	365	59	4	428	113	16	1	24	.310	.411	.556	967	947	1					947	40.7
41	53	1935	A.Galan	646	87	4	737	203	41	11	12	.314	.399	.467	866	847	22			10	10	867	40.5
42	46	1975	J.Cardenal	574	77	4	655	182	30	2	9	.317	.402	.423	825	834	34	12	14	10	20	879	37.8
43	40	1929	R.Stephenson	495	67	7	569	179	36	6	17	.362	.445	.562	1,006	907	10			(10)	(10)	887	37.0
44	52	1969	B.Williams	642	59	4	705	188	33	10	21	.293	.356	.474	830	849	3	2	(1)	10	10	867	36.9
45	55	1937	F.Demaree	615	57	1	673	199	36	6	17	.324	.382	.485	866	857	6			10		867	36.8
46	47	1910	W.Schulte	559	39	3	601	168	29	15	10	.301	.349	.460	809	858	22			10	10	878	36.2
47	42	1961	G.Altman	518	40	4	562	157	28	12	27	.303	.358	.560	917	881	6	2	3			885	35.8
48	43	1902	J.Slagle	454	53	0	507	143	11	4	0	.315	.387	.357	743	832	40			10	40	882	34.7
49	45	1933	B.Herman	508	50	0	558	147	36	12	16	.289	.353	.502	855	889	6			10	(20)	879	34.0
50	51	1974	R.Monday	538	70	2	610	158	19	7	20	.294	.377	.467	844	857	7	9	(17)	10	20	870	32.7
51	49	1940	B.Nicholson	491	50	3	544	146	27	7	25	.297	.366	.534	899	904	2			(10)	(20)	874	31.9
52	57	1946	P.Cavaretta	510	88	3	601	150	28	10	8	.294	.401	.435	836	863	2					863	31.8
53	56	1954	H.Sauer	520	70	6	596	150	18	1	41	.288	.379	.563	943	893	2	1	0	(10)	(20)	863	31.6
54	71	1966	B.Williams	648	69	4	721	179	23	5	29	.276	.350	.461	811	819	6	3	0	10	20	849	31.4
55	48	1913	T.Leach	456	77	1	534	131	23	10	6	.287	.391	.421	812	845	21				30	875	31.4
56	67	1927	R.Stephenson	579	65	6	650	199	46	9	7	.344	.415	.491	906	882	8			(10)	(20)	852	30.8
57	59	1906	W.Schulte	563	31	5	599	158	18	13	7	.281	.324	.396	720	820	25			10	30	860	30.7
58	60	1945	A.Pafko	534	45	8	587	159	24	12	12	.298	.361	.455	816	828	5				30	858	29.5
59	62	1934	K.Cuyler	559	31	4	594	189	42	8	6	.338	.377	.474	851	826	15			10	20	856	29.5
60	72	1901	D.Green	537	40	3	580	168	16	12	6	.313	.364	.421	785	828	31			10	10	848	28.9
61	68	1973	R.Monday	554	92	1	647	148	24	5	26	.267	.372	.469	842	849	5	12	(28)	10	20	851	28.9
62	63	1984	G.Matthews	491	103	3	597	143	21	2	14	.291	.417	.428	845	863	17	8	2	10	(20)	855	27.6
63	81	1962	B.Williams	618	70	4	692	184	22	8	22	.298	.373	.466	839	820	9	9	(12)	10	20	838	26.5
64	64	1940	J.Gleeson	485	54	6	545	152	39	11	5	.313	.389	.470	859	864	4			10	(20)	854	26.3
65	79	1918	D.Paskert	461	53	2	516	132	24	3	3	.286	.362	.371	733	811	20			10	20	841	26.3
66	76	1972	J.Cardenal	533	55	1	589	155	24	6	17	.291	.358	.454	812	841	25	14	(5)	10		846	26.1
67	65	1975	R.Monday	491	83	1	575	131	29	4	17	.267	.374	.446	820	829	8	3	3	10	10	853	26.1
68	34	1989	D.Smith	343	31	2	376	111	19	6	9	.324	.383	.493	876	909	9	4	3	10	(20)	902	25.8
69	69	1973	J.Cardenal	522	58	5	585	158	33	2	11	.303	.378	.437	815	821	19	7	8	10	10	850	25.7
70	80	1906	J.Sheckard	549	67	6	622	144	27	10	1	.262	.349	.353	702	800	30			10	30	840	25.6
71	90	1995	S.Sosa	564	58	5	627	151	17	3	36	.268	.341	.500	841	801	34	7	30	10	(10)	832	24.9
72	61	1940	H.Leiber	440	45	3	488	133	24	2	17	.302	.371	.482	853	857	1					857	24.5
73	66	1996	S.Sosa	498	34	5	537	136	21	2	40	.273	.326	.564	890	848	18	5	14	10	(20)	852	24.2
74	78	1974	J.Cardenal	542	56	1	599	159	35	3	13	.293	.361	.441	802	814	23	9	8	10	10	842	24.1
75	88	1973	B.Williams	576	76	1	653	166	22	2	20	.288	.372	.438	810	816	4	3	(3)		20	834	23.7

Chicago Cubs
Starting Pitchers

V	R	Year	Name	G	GS	IP	W	L	SV	SO	BB	ERA	RA/9	R Wtd RA/9	V Runs /162
1	7	1909	T.Brown	50	34	343	27	9	7	172	53	1.31	2.05	2.55	80.4
2	12	1902	J.Taylor	36	33	325	23	11	1	83	43	1.33	2.38	2.68	78.2
3	16	1920	P.Alexander	46	40	363	27	14	5	173	69	1.91	2.38	2.77	76.0
4	5	1908	T.Brown	44	31	312	29	9	5	123	49	1.47	1.84	2.53	74.1
5	1	1906	T.Brown	36	32	277	26	6	3	144	61	1.04	1.82	2.28	73.8
6	3	1905	E.Reulbach	34	29	292	18	14	1	152	73	1.42	2.19	2.40	73.7
7	23	1918	H.Vaughn	35	33	290	22	10	0	148	76	1.74	2.33	2.94	66.4
8	9	1909	O.Overall	38	32	285	20	11	3	205	80	1.42	2.08	2.59	65.5
9	4	1919	P.Alexander	30	27	235	16	11	1	121	38	1.72	1.95	2.44	63.9
10	27	1919	H.Vaughn	38	37	307	21	14	1	141	62	1.79	2.43	3.04	59.8
11	14	1932	L.Warneke	35	32	277	22	6	0	106	64	2.37	2.73	2.71	59.8
12	17	1963	D.Ellsworth	37	37	291	22	10	0	185	75	2.11	2.32	2.77	57.9
13	28	1918	L.Tyler	33	30	269	19	8	1	102	67	2.00	2.41	3.04	57.8
14	15	1907	O.Overall	36	30	268	23	7	3	141	69	1.68	2.08	2.72	57.7
15	11	1992	G.Maddux	35	35	268	20	11	0	199	70	2.18	2.28	2.68	56.0
16	8	1907	T.Brown	34	27	233	20	6	3	107	40	1.39	1.97	2.57	54.1
17	25	1933	L.Warneke	36	34	287	18	13	1	133	75	2.00	2.60	2.95	53.8
18	2	1907	C.Lundgren	28	25	207	18	7	0	84	92	1.17	1.83	2.39	52.4
19	26	1938	B.Lee	44	37	291	22	9	2	121	74	2.66	2.94	3.02	52.4
20	13	1910	K.Cole	33	29	240	20	4	1	114	130	1.80	2.40	2.69	52.3
21	19	1906	J.Pfiester	31	29	251	20	8	0	153	63	1.51	2.26	2.83	50.7
22	22	1909	E.Reulbach	35	32	263	19	10	0	105	82	1.78	2.36	2.94	49.8
23	32	1904	J.Weimer	37	37	307	20	14	0	177	97	1.91	2.81	3.19	49.2
24	10	1906	E.Reulbach	33	24	218	19	4	3	94	92	1.65	2.11	2.64	48.8
25	20	1928	S.Blake	34	29	241	17	11	1	78	101	2.47	2.99	2.90	46.7
26	31	1945	H.Wyse	38	34	278	22	10	0	77	55	2.68	3.08	3.13	46.5
27	18	1945	C.Passeau	34	27	227	17	9	1	98	59	2.46	2.78	2.82	46.0
28	39	1903	J.Weimer	35	33	282	20	8	0	128	104	2.30	3.54	3.29	45.9
29	36	1910	T.Brown	46	31	295	25	14	7	143	64	1.86	2.90	3.26	44.9
30	35	1940	C.Passeau	46	31	281	20	13	5	124	59	2.50	3.11	3.22	43.9
31	6	1905	B.Wicker	22	22	178	13	6	0	86	47	2.02	2.33	2.55	41.7
32	44	1908	E.Reulbach	46	35	298	24	7	1	133	106	2.03	2.45	3.36	41.6
33	30	1977	R.Reuschel	39	37	252	20	10	1	166	74	2.79	3.00	3.11	40.6
34	33	1911	L.Richie	36	29	253	15	11	1	78	103	2.31	3.13	3.20	40.2
35	42	1929	C.Root	43	31	272	19	6	5	124	83	3.47	3.97	3.33	39.1
36	50	1969	B.Hands	41	41	300	20	14	0	181	73	2.49	3.06	3.42	38.0
37	57	1934	L.Warneke	43	35	291	22	10	3	143	66	3.21	3.59	3.45	37.6
38	43	1935	L.Warneke	42	30	262	20	13	4	120	50	3.06	3.50	3.34	37.2
39	40	1943	H.Bithorn	39	30	250	18	12	2	86	65	2.60	2.84	3.30	36.7
40	47	1929	P.Malone	40	30	267	22	10	2	166	102	3.57	4.04	3.38	36.6
41	37	1935	L.French	42	30	246	17	10	2	90	44	2.96	3.44	3.29	36.5
42	41	1905	J.Weimer	33	30	250	18	12	1	107	80	2.26	3.02	3.31	36.5
43	67	1923	P.Alexander	39	36	305	22	12	2	72	30	3.19	3.78	3.54	36.4
44	21	1907	E.Reulbach	27	22	192	17	4	0	96	64	1.69	2.25	2.94	36.3
45	52	1926	C.Root	42	32	271	18	17	2	127	62	2.82	3.45	3.42	36.1
46	70	1912	L.Cheney	42	37	303	26	10	0	140	111	2.85	3.62	3.55	35.7
47	88	1903	J.Taylor	37	33	312	21	14	1	83	57	2.45	3.96	3.68	35.1
48	24	1952	W.Hacker	33	20	185	15	9	1	84	31	2.58	2.72	2.94	34.9
49	54	1928	P.Malone	42	25	251	18	13	2	155	99	2.84	3.55	3.44	32.7
50	89	1971	F.Jenkins	39	39	325	24	13	0	263	37	2.77	3.16	3.68	31.6

Chicago Cubs Starting Pitchers

V	R	Year	Name	G	GS	IP	W	L	SV	SO	BB	ERA	RA/9	R Wtd RA/9	V Runs /162
51	46	1944	C.Passeau	34	27	227	15	9	3	89	50	2.89	3.17	3.38	31.4
52	29	1928	A.Nehf	31	21	177	13	7	0	40	52	2.65	3.15	3.05	31.1
53	58	1948	J.Schmitz	34	30	242	18	13	1	100	97	2.64	3.42	3.46	30.9
54	68	1936	B.Lee	43	33	259	18	11	1	102	93	3.31	3.68	3.54	30.9
55	77	1938	C.Bryant	44	30	270	19	11	2	135	125	3.10	3.50	3.59	30.4
56	69	1936	L.French	43	28	252	18	9	3	104	54	3.39	3.68	3.54	30.0
57	65	1905	T.Brown	30	24	249	18	12	0	89	44	2.17	3.22	3.53	30.0
58	63	1940	L.French	40	33	246	14	14	2	107	64	3.29	3.40	3.52	29.8
59	90	1970	F.Jenkins	40	39	313	22	16	0	274	60	3.39	3.68	3.70	29.7
60	102	1913	L.Cheney	54	36	305	21	14	11	136	98	2.57	3.45	3.77	28.0
61	97	1968	F.Jenkins	40	40	308	20	15	0	260	65	2.63	2.81	3.74	27.8
62	51	1906	C.Lundgren	27	24	208	17	6	2	103	89	2.21	2.73	3.42	27.7
63	80	1935	B.Lee	39	32	252	20	6	1	100	84	2.96	3.79	3.62	27.6
64	64	1992	M.Morgan	34	34	240	16	8	0	123	79	2.55	3.00	3.52	27.6
65	76	1933	C.Root	35	30	242	15	10	0	86	61	2.60	3.16	3.59	27.3
66	91	1904	B.Briggs	34	30	277	19	11	3	112	77	2.05	3.28	3.72	27.2
67	59	1995	J.Navarro	29	29	200	14	6	0	128	56	3.28	3.55	3.48	27.0
68	66	1946	J.Schmitz	41	31	224	11	11	2	135	94	2.61	3.09	3.53	26.9
69	56	1937	T.Carleton	32	27	208	16	8	0	105	94	3.15	3.46	3.45	26.9
70	75	1925	P.Alexander	32	30	236	15	11	0	63	29	3.39	4.04	3.58	26.9
71	93	1967	F.Jenkins	38	38	289	20	13	0	236	83	2.80	3.14	3.73	26.7
72	96	1939	C.Passeau	42	35	274	15	13	3	137	73	3.28	3.68	3.73	26.3
73	34	1945	R.Prim	34	19	165	13	8	2	88	23	2.40	3.16	3.21	26.0
74	108	1917	H.Vaughn	41	38	296	23	13	0	195	91	2.01	2.95	3.81	25.9
75	84	1922	P.Alexander	33	31	246	16	13	1	48	34	3.63	4.06	3.66	25.7
76	53	1994	S.Trachsel	22	22	146	9	7	0	108	54	3.21	3.51	3.44	25.6
77	111	1916	H.Vaughn	44	35	294	17	15	1	144	67	2.20	2.88	3.82	25.5
78	99	1911	T.Brown	53	27	270	21	11	13	129	55	2.80	3.67	3.75	25.5
79	100	1929	G.Bush	50	29	271	18	7	8	82	107	3.66	4.48	3.75	25.5
80	82	1955	B.Rush	33	33	234	13	11	0	130	73	3.50	3.65	3.64	25.1
81	71	1904	T.Brown	26	23	212	15	10	1	81	50	1.86	3.14	3.56	24.7
82	105	1930	P.Malone	45	35	272	20	9	4	142	96	3.94	4.80	3.78	24.6
83	45	1923	V.Keen	35	17	177	12	8	1	46	57	3.00	3.56	3.37	24.5
84	60	1996	S.Trachsel	31	31	205	13	9	0	132	62	3.03	3.60	3.48	24.5
85	62	1995	F.Castillo	29	29	188	11	10	0	135	52	3.21	3.59	3.52	24.4
86	79	1911	K.Cole	32	27	221	18	7	0	101	99	3.13	3.54	3.62	24.3
87	61	1927	G.Bush	36	22	193	10	10	2	62	79	3.03	3.54	3.49	24.0
88	112	1903	B.Wicker	33	27	252	20	9	1	113	77	2.96	4.11	3.82	23.8
89	38	1926	G.Bush	35	16	157	13	9	2	32	42	2.86	3.32	3.29	23.3
90	48	1905	C.Lundgren	23	19	169	13	5	0	69	53	2.23	3.09	3.38	23.2
91	106	1933	G.Bush	41	32	259	20	12	2	84	68	2.75	3.34	3.80	23.0
92	49	1905	B.Briggs	20	20	168	8	8	0	68	52	2.14	3.11	3.41	22.6
93	120	1964	L.Jackson	40	38	298	24	11	0	148	58	3.14	3.44	3.88	22.4
94	55	1940	V.Olsen	34	20	173	13	9	0	71	62	2.97	3.33	3.45	22.4
95	117	1900	C.Griffith	30	30	248	14	13	0	61	51	3.05	4.57	3.86	22.1
96	132	1920	H.Vaughn	40	38	301	19	16	0	131	81	2.54	3.38	3.93	22.1
97	86	1934	B.Lee	35	29	214	13	14	1	104	74	3.40	3.83	3.68	21.9
98	83	1935	C.Root	38	18	201	15	8	2	94	47	3.08	3.81	3.64	21.5
99	104	1912	L.Richie	39	27	238	16	8	0	69	74	2.95	3.86	3.78	21.5
100	107	1931	B.Smith	36	29	240	15	12	2	63	62	3.22	3.79	3.80	21.4

Chicago Cubs
Relief Pitchers

V	R	Year	Name	G	GS	IP	W	L	SV	SO	BB	ERA	RA/9	R Wtd RA/9	V Runs /162
1	1	1977	B.Sutter	62	0	107	7	3	31	129	23	1.34	1.76	1.82	32.5
2	2	1983	L.Smith	66	0	103	4	10	29	91	41	1.65	2.00	2.21	26.8
3	7	1959	B.Henry	65	0	134	9	8	12	115	26	2.68	2.82	2.89	26.1
4	8	1980	B.Caudill	72	2	128	4	6	1	112	59	2.19	2.61	2.95	22.8
5	5	1979	B.Sutter	62	0	101	6	6	37	110	32	2.22	2.58	2.78	19.9
6	12	1993	J.Bautista	58	7	112	10	3	2	63	27	2.82	3.06	3.09	18.3
7	3	1983	W.Brusstar	59	0	80	3	1	1	46	37	2.35	2.35	2.60	17.4
8	4	1982	M.Proly	44	1	82	5	3	1	24	22	2.30	2.41	2.69	17.0
9	19	1982	L.Smith	72	5	117	2	5	17	99	37	2.69	2.92	3.26	16.8
10	14	1990	P.Assenmacher	74	1	103	7	2	10	95	36	2.80	2.88	3.10	16.6
11	15	1996	T.Adams	69	0	101	3	6	4	78	49	2.94	3.21	3.11	16.3
12	27	1968	P.Regan	73	0	135	12	5	25	67	25	2.27	2.61	3.48	16.2
13	6	1996	T.Wendell	70	0	79	4	5	18	75	44	2.84	2.95	2.85	14.9
14	17	1991	C.McElroy	71	0	101	6	2	3	92	57	1.95	2.93	3.24	14.8
15	33	1965	L.McDaniel	71	0	129	5	6	2	92	47	2.59	3.14	3.55	14.4
16	13	1958	B.Henry	44	0	81	5	4	6	58	17	2.88	3.00	3.09	13.9
17	22	1958	D.Elston	69	0	97	9	8	10	84	39	2.88	3.25	3.35	13.7
18	39	1965	T.Abernathy	84	0	136	4	6	31	104	56	2.57	3.24	3.66	13.5
19	18	1987	L.Smith	62	0	84	4	10	36	96	32	3.12	3.23	3.24	12.3
20	28	1980	B.Sutter	60	0	102	5	8	28	76	34	2.64	3.08	3.48	12.2
21	35	1977	W.Hernandez	67	1	110	8	7	4	78	28	3.03	3.44	3.56	12.2
22	16	1993	R.Myers	73	0	75	2	4	53	86	26	3.11	3.11	3.14	11.8
23	11	2000	T.Worrell	59	0	69	5	6	3	57	29	2.99	3.38	3.03	11.7
24	9	1999	R.Aguilera	61	0	68	9	4	14	45	12	2.93	3.33	3.01	11.7
25	21	1951	D.Leonard	41	1	82	10	6	3	30	28	2.64	3.29	3.35	11.6
26	20	1976	B.Sutter	52	0	83	6	3	10	73	26	2.70	2.92	3.33	11.3
27	36	1957	J.Brosnan	41	5	99	5	5	0	73	46	3.38	3.45	3.61	10.9
28	30	1986	L.Smith	66	0	90	9	9	31	93	42	3.09	3.19	3.49	10.7
29	31	1948	J.Dobernic	54	0	86	7	2	1	48	40	3.15	3.45	3.49	10.7
30	37	1985	L.Smith	65	0	98	7	4	33	112	32	3.04	3.23	3.62	10.2
31	26	1989	M.Williams	76	0	82	4	4	36	67	52	2.76	2.98	3.45	10.1
32	42	1973	B.Locker	63	0	106	10	6	18	76	42	2.54	3.40	3.73	9.7
33	34	2000	T.Van Poppel	51	2	86	4	5	2	77	48	3.75	3.96	3.56	9.6
34	32	1987	F.DiPino	69	0	80	3	3	4	61	34	3.15	3.49	3.50	9.4
35	10	1996	B.Patterson	79	0	55	3	3	8	53	22	3.13	3.13	3.03	9.3
36	40	1947	E.Kush	47	1	91	8	3	5	44	53	3.36	3.76	3.68	9.3
37	43	1959	D.Elston	65	0	98	10	8	13	82	46	3.32	3.67	3.76	9.1
38	45	1980	D.Tidrow	84	0	116	6	5	6	97	53	2.79	3.41	3.86	9.0
39	29	1982	W.Hernandez	75	0	75	4	6	10	54	24	3.00	3.12	3.48	8.9
40	55	1954	J.Davis	46	12	128	11	7	4	58	51	3.52	4.01	3.98	8.6
41	47	1998	T.Mulholland	70	6	112	6	5	3	72	39	2.89	3.94	3.88	8.5
42	25	1962	D.Elston	57	0	66	4	8	8	37	32	2.44	3.41	3.44	8.2
43	38	1998	R.Beck	81	0	80	3	4	51	81	20	3.02	3.70	3.64	8.1
44	44	1994	J.Bautista	58	0	69	4	5	1	45	17	3.89	3.89	3.81	8.1
45	49	1938	J.Russell	42	0	102	6	1	3	29	30	3.34	3.79	3.89	8.0
46	41	1995	M.Perez	68	0	71	2	6	2	49	27	3.66	3.79	3.71	7.5
47	24	1997	B.Patterson	76	0	59	1	6	0	58	10	3.34	3.49	3.43	7.4
48	23	1993	P.Assenmacher	72	0	56	4	3	0	45	22	3.38	3.38	3.41	7.2
49	54	1991	P.Assenmacher	75	0	103	7	8	15	117	31	3.24	3.59	3.97	6.7
50	46	1992	B.Scanlan	69	0	87	3	6	14	42	30	2.89	3.30	3.88	6.6

Chicago White Sox (1901–2000)

The Chicago White Sox charted an unusual and often choppy course through major league history. They began as one of the most successful American League franchises, with four league championships and 16 winning seasons in their first two decades. The Sox won the very first American League crown in 1901 behind pitcher-manager Clark Griffith and his 24 wins. The 1906 "hitless wonders," led by outfielder-manager Fielder Jones and pitchers Doc White (18–6, 1.52 ERA, 2.36 Wtd. RA/9), Big Ed Walsh, Nick Altrock, and Frank Owen, shocked the mighty Chicago Cubs in the World Series, winning in six games. In 1908, Walsh went 40–15 with a 1.42 ERA and 2.85 Wtd. RA/9, while saving 92.6 runs from scoring over 464 innings. Despite Walsh's efforts, the 1908 White Sox finished 1½ games behind Ty Cobb's Detroit squad. The 1917 team won 100 games en route to another World Series triumph, led by Eddie Cicotte's 28–12 record, 1.53 ERA, and career low 2.49 Wtd. RA/9.

In 1919, the Sox won their fourth pennant, and were heavily favored to win the World Series. Led by Shoeless Joe Jackson (.351 average), Eddie Collins, Happy Felsch, Ray Schalk, Buck Weaver, Eddie Cicotte (29–7, 1.82 ERA, 2.49 Wtd. RA/9), and Lefty Williams, the Sox were poised to challenge for the league title for many years to come.

At the pinnacle of the team's success, an event with the force of a hurricane smashed the White Sox against the rocks of fate. Because eight players threw the 1919 World Series, the Sox lost not only that moment of glory but, also, their winning ways for decades to come. Waves of controversy swamped the 1920 team, which lost many of its best players—including Jackson (.382, 12 home runs, 994 Wtd. Production)—to indictment with two weeks left in the season, although the Sox still almost managed to win the pennant with 96 wins. Marred by the Black Sox scandal, and stripped of several all-star caliber players, the White Sox sank into the second division for the next 15 years, and failed to climb above third place for 36 long seasons. The few Sox players with star power during these lost years were Collins (.349, 42 steals in 1924), Luke Appling (.388, 901 Total Factor in 1936), Red Faber (25–15, 2.48 ERA, 2.58 Wtd. RA/9 in 1921), and Ted Lyons (22–14, 2.84 ERA in 1927).

White Sox teams, good and bad, were built around pitching, defense, speed, and moving the runner over, a style of play which took advantage of cavernous Comiskey Park. The Sox were the only major league team to consistently play Dead Ball baseball for many decades, as if they were still suspended in 1919. One result of their Dead Ball style is the team's historic lack of offensive power, reflected by their all-time All-Stars having the weakest offensive statistics of any major league team.

GM Paul Richards brought in quality players to play their Dead Ball game, and the White Sox began playing consistent winning baseball in the 1950s. Luis Aparicio, Nellie Fox, Sherm Lollar, Minnie Minoso (.320, 18 triples, 19 home runs, 994 Total Factor in 1954), and Billy Pierce (15–10, 1.97 ERA, 2.22 Wtd. RA/9 in 1955) led the resurgence. Unfortunately, the Go-Go Sox were still stuck behind many strong Yankees and Indians teams for most of the decade. The Sox broke through in 1959 and won their first pennant in exactly 40 years as they went 94–60, while the Yankees sank to third with a 79–75 record in a rare off year. Fox hit .306 in 1959 to win the league MVP Award, Aparicio batted .257 with 56 steals, Lollar hit .265

with 22 home runs, and Bob Shaw was 18–6 with a 2.69 ERA and a 2.92 Wtd. RA/9.

The Sox traded talented future prospects Norm Cash and Johnny Callison for additional offensive power in order to stay on top. Their gamble failed, as the Sox could not get past the always tough Yankees with this nontraditional, heavy-hitting approach, finishing in third in 1960, and sliding to fifth place by 1962.

Young pitchers Gary Peters and Joe Horlen then propelled the Sox to three straight second place finishes, with the Sox finishing just one game behind the Yankees in 1964. Horlen had his best season in 1964, with a 13–9 record, 1.88 ERA, and career low 2.58 Wtd. RA/9. The White Sox also seriously challenged for the league title in 1967, reverting back to a "Hitless Wonders" approach, as they struggled to a .225 team batting average with 89 home runs. Horlen (19–7, 2.06 ERA, 2.84 Wtd. RA/9), Peters (16–11, 2.28 ERA), and a deep bullpen led by 43-year-old Hoyt Wilhelm (8–3, 12 saves, 1.31 ERA, 2.62 Wtd. RA/9) kept the Sox in the race until the final week. The 1967 season completed a run of 17 straight years where the White Sox finished over .500.

The White Sox reached bottom in 1970 with a 56–106 record, and the team then drifted under weak ownership for more than a decade. One very bright moment during this drab period was the sensational 1972 MVP season of Dick Allen, as he hit .308 with 37 home runs. Adjusted for 8 percent hitter's deflation, Allen hit .334 with 41 home runs, for a 1,112 Wtd. Production and a team record 1,116 Total Factor. Another unique player was Wilbur Wood, a knuckleballer, who switched from bullpen closer to become the staff ace, going 22–13 with a 1.91 ERA and a 3.00 Wtd. RA/9 in 1971. Wood was a workhorse who once started and won both games of a doubleheader, and who managed to both win and lose 20 games in the same season in 1973. The best relief performance came from young Goose Gossage, who went 9–8 with 26 saves, a 1.84 ERA, and 2.14 Wtd. RA/9 in 1975. Gossage's 38.1 runs saved from scoring over 142 innings ranks as the sixth best volume of success for relievers in league history.

Catcher Carlton Fisk joined the White Sox in 1981. Fisk led the 1983 team to a division title with a .289 average and 26 home runs, as the Sox went 99–63 and finished 20 games ahead of the second place Royals. Also starring on that "winning ugly" team were pitchers La Marr Hoyt (24–10, 3.66 ERA & Cy Young Award), Richard Dotson (22–7, 3.23 ERA), and Floyd Bannister (16–10, 3.35 ERA). The White Sox faded to 74–88 in 1984 despite a .304 average and 29 home runs from outfielder Harold Baines. The team remained reasonably competitive the rest of the decade.

The Sox won a division crown in 1993 behind their best hitter ever in MVP first baseman Frank Thomas (.317, 41 home runs), their best third baseman in Robin Ventura, and another group of young pitchers led by Cy Young winner Jack McDowell (22–10, 3.37 ERA). Thomas won a second MVP in 1994, as he powered the White Sox to another division leading record. Thomas was hitting .353 with 38 home runs, a .494 on-base percentage and a .729 slugging average — for a 1,223 Production — when a players' strike washed out the season. Adjusted for 7 percent hitter's inflation, Frank batted .330 with 52 home runs, for a 1,142 Wtd. Production, a 1,105 Total Factor, and 115.0 Hits Contribution.

For the second time in their history, events off the field caused a very good White Sox team to self-destruct at its peak. More than any other major league ball club, White Sox management reeled from the fallout from the baseball strike, while fans shunned the team in droves. Sox fans were further soured on the team after the "White Flag" trade of three key pitchers while trailing Cleveland by just 3 games in the 1997 pennant race. By the end of the decade, only a slumping Thomas remained from the 1993 division winners.

Thomas' revived bat (.328, 43 home runs, 1,066 Production) and a talented group of young players led the Sox to a 95–67 record in 2000. Like their first team in the twentieth century, the first Sox team of the new century achieved the best record in the American League. Time will tell whether the new century will be kinder to a franchise that began with great promise.

Chicago White Sox (1901–2000)

Chicago White Sox — **Hitters Volume of Success**

Pos	Year	Name	AB	BB	HBP	TAB	H	2B	3B	HR	BA	OB	SA	PRO	Wtd PRO	SB	CS	SBF	SPF	FF	R TF	V HC
C	1959	S.Lollar	505	55	9	569	134	22	3	22	.265	.348	.451	799	796	4	3	(3)	(10)	80	863	52.8
1B	1994	F.Thomas	399	109	2	510	141	34	1	38	.353	.494	.729	1,223	1,142	2	3	(7)	0	(30)	1,105	115.0
2B	1915	E.Collins	521	119	5	645	173	22	10	4	.332	.460	.436	896	972	46	30	(21)	10	70	1,031	111.8
SS	1943	L.Appling	585	90	1	676	192	33	2	3	.328	.419	.407	825	879	27	8	15	0	10	904	82.1
3B	1992	R.Ventura	592	93	0	685	167	38	1	16	.282	.380	.431	810	826	2	4	(8)	0	90	908	62.5
OF	1954	M.Minoso	568	77	16	661	182	29	18	19	.320	.416	.535	951	950	18	11	(6)	10	40	994	78.4
OF	1998	A.Belle	609	81	1	691	200	48	2	49	.328	.408	.655	1,063	1,000	6	4	(3)	0	(20)	977	72.3
OF	1920	J.Jackson	570	56	7	633	218	42	20	12	.382	.444	.589	1,033	994	9	12	(22)	10	0	981	71.1
Starters		Averages	544	85	5	634	176	34	7	20	.324	.420	.524	944	941	14	9	(7)	3	30	966	80.8
C	1983	C.Fisk	488	46	6	540	141	26	4	26	.289	.357	.518	876	875	9	6	(5)	0	10	879	52.0
1B	1972	D.Allen	506	99	1	606	156	28	5	37	.308	.422	.603	1,025	1,112	19	8	5	10	(10)	1,116	105.2
2B	1957	N.Fox	619	75	16	710	196	27	8	6	.317	.404	.415	819	815	5	6	(9)	0	70	875	67.6
SS	1905	G.Davis	550	60	4	614	153	29	1	1	.278	.353	.340	693	799	31			10	50	859	60.5
3B	1971	B.Melton	543	61	11	615	146	18	2	33	.269	.354	.492	846	873	3	3	(5)	0	20	889	50.5
OF	1920	H.Felsch	556	37	4	597	188	40	15	14	.338	.384	.540	923	888	8	13	(28)	10	70	939	54.4
OF	1984	H.Baines	569	54	0	623	173	28	10	29	.304	.364	.541	906	909	1	2	(5)	10	10	925	49.7
OF	1926	J.Mostil	600	79	10	689	197	41	15	4	.328	.415	.467	882	838	35	14	10	10	40	897	48.3
Reserves		Averages	554	64	7	624	169	30	8	19	.305	.383	.487	870	886	14	7	(5)	6	33	920	61.0
Totals		Weighted Ave.	547	78	6	631	174	32	7	20	.317	.408	.511	919	923	14	8	(6)	4	31	951	74.2

Pitchers Volume of Success

Pos	Year	Name	G	GS	IP	W	L	SV	SO	BB	ERA	RA/9	Wtd RA/9	R V Runs /162
SP	1908	E.Walsh	66	49	464	40	15	6	269	56	1.42	2.17	2.85	92.6
SP	1917	E.Cicotte	49	35	347	28	12	4	150	70	1.53	1.98	2.49	84.0
SP	1921	R.Faber	43	39	331	25	15	1	124	87	2.48	2.91	2.58	76.3
SP	1941	T.Lee	35	34	300	22	11	1	130	92	2.37	2.94	2.80	61.7
SP	1913	R.Russell	52	36	317	22	16	4	122	79	1.90	2.53	2.90	61.2
Starters		Averages	49	39	352	27	14	3	159	77	1.89	2.47	2.73	75.2
RP	1975	R.Gossage	62	0	142	9	8	26	130	70	1.84	2.03	2.14	38.1
RP	1965	H.Wilhelm	66	0	144	7	7	20	106	32	1.81	2.13	2.45	33.7
RP	1999	K.Foulke	67	0	105	3	3	9	123	21	2.22	2.39	2.07	29.1
RP	1968	W.Wood	88	2	159	13	12	16	74	33	1.87	2.22	2.94	28.5
Relievers		Averages	71	1	138	8	8	18	108	39	1.91	2.18	2.44	32.4
Totals		Averages	120	39	489	35	21	21	267	116	1.90	2.39	2.65	107.5

Chicago White Sox — **Hitters Rate of Success**

Pos	Year	Name	AB	BB	HBP	TAB	H	2B	3B	HR	BA	OB	SA	PRO	Wtd PRO	SB	CS	SBF	SPF	FF	R TF	V HC
C	1983	C.Fisk	488	46	6	540	141	26	4	26	.289	.357	.518	876	875	9	6	(5)	0	10	879	52.0
1B	1972	D.Allen	506	99	1	606	156	28	5	37	.308	.422	.603	1,025	1,112	19	8	5	10	(10)	1,116	105.2
2B	1915	E.Collins	521	119	5	645	173	22	10	4	.332	.460	.436	896	972	46	30	(21)	10	70	1,031	111.8
SS	1943	L.Appling	585	90	1	676	192	33	2	3	.328	.419	.407	825	879	27	8	15	0	10	904	82.1
3B	1992	R.Ventura	592	93	0	685	167	38	1	16	.282	.380	.431	810	826	2	4	(8)	0	90	908	62.5
OF	1954	M.Minoso	568	77	16	661	182	29	18	19	.320	.416	.535	951	950	18	11	(6)	10	40	994	78.4
OF	1920	J.Jackson	570	56	7	633	218	42	20	12	.382	.444	.589	1,033	994	9	12	(22)	10	0	981	71.1
OF	1998	A.Belle	609	81	1	691	200	48	2	49	.328	.408	.655	1,063	1,000	6	4	(3)	0	(20)	977	72.3
Starters		Averages	555	83	5	642	179	33	8	21	.322	.414	.522	936	950	17	10	(6)	5	24	973	79.4
C	1959	S.Lollar	505	55	9	569	134	22	3	22	.265	.348	.451	799	796	4	3	(3)	(10)	80	863	52.8
1B	1994	F.Thomas	399	109	2	510	141	34	1	38	.353	.494	.729	1,223	1,142	2	5	(7)	0	(30)	1,105	115.0
2B	1905	F.Isbell	341	15	5	361	101	21	11	2	.296	.335	.440	775	893	15			10	(10)	893	37.5
SS	1970	L.Aparicio	552	53	1	606	173	29	3	5	.313	.375	.404	779	782	8	3	3	10	70	865	58.6
3B	1971	B.Melton	543	61	11	615	146	18	2	33	.269	.354	.492	846	873	3	3	(5)	0	20	889	50.5
OF	1920	H.Felsch	556	37	4	597	188	40	15	14	.338	.384	.540	923	888	8	13	(28)	10	70	939	54.4
OF/DH	1977	O.Gamble	408	54	6	468	121	22	2	31	.297	.387	.588	975	964	1	2	(6)	10	(30)	938	40.3
OF	1978	C.Lemon	357	39	8	404	107	24	6	13	.300	.381	.510	891	911	5	9	(30)	10	40	931	33.3
Reserves		Averages	458	53	6	516	139	26	5	20	.303	.383	.514	896	900	6	5	(10)	5	26	922	55.3
Totals		Weighted Ave.	522	73	5	600	165	31	7	20	.316	.404	.519	923	933	13	8	(7)	5	25	956	71.4

Pitchers Rate of Success

Pos	Year	Name	G	GS	IP	W	L	SV	SO	BB	ERA	RA/9	Wtd RA/9	V Runs/162
SP	1955	B.Pierce	33	26	206	15	10	1	157	64	1.97	2.18	2.22	56.3
SP	1906	D.White	28	24	219	18	6	0	95	38	1.52	1.93	2.36	56.3
SP	1917	E.Cicotte	49	35	347	28	12	4	150	70	1.53	1.98	2.49	84.0
SP	1937	M.Stratton	22	21	165	15	5	0	69	37	2.40	3.00	2.56	38.5
SP	1964	J.Horlen	32	28	211	13	9	0	138	55	1.88	2.30	2.58	46.5
Starters		Averages	33	27	230	18	8	1	122	53	1.80	2.21	2.44	56.3
RP	1996	R.Hernandez	72	0	85	6	5	38	85	38	1.91	2.23	1.87	26.6
RP	1999	K.Foulke	67	0	105	3	3	9	123	21	2.22	2.39	2.07	29.1
RP	1990	B.Thigpen	77	0	89	4	6	57	70	32	1.83	2.03	2.13	25.3
RP	1975	R.Gossage	62	0	142	9	8	26	130	70	1.84	2.03	2.14	38.1
Relievers		Averages	70	0	105	6	6	33	102	40	1.95	2.16	2.07	29.8
Totals		Averages	102	27	335	23	14	34	224	93	1.84	2.20	2.32	86.1

Chicago White Sox (1901–2000)

Chicago White Sox
Catchers

V	R	Year	Name	AB	BB	HBP	TAB	H	2B	3B	HR	BA	OB	SA	PRO	Wtd PRO	SB	CS	SBF	SPF	FF	R TF	V HC
1	2	1959	S.Lollar	505	55	9	569	134	22	3	22	.265	.348	.451	799	796	4	3	(3)	(10)	80	863	52.8
2	1	1983	C.Fisk	488	46	6	540	141	26	4	26	.289	.357	.518	876	875	9	6	(5)		10	879	52.0
3	4	1956	S.Lollar	450	53	16	519	132	28	2	11	.293	.387	.438	825	790	2	0	4	(10)	70	854	45.9
4	5	1958	S.Lollar	421	57	8	486	115	16	0	20	.273	.370	.454	824	823	2	1	0	(10)	40	853	42.7
5	6	1990	C.Fisk	452	61	7	520	129	21	0	18	.285	.379	.451	830	844	7	2	5	(10)	10	849	42.6
6	7	1955	S.Lollar	426	68	10	504	111	13	1	16	.261	.375	.408	783	768	2	2	(4)	(10)	70	824	37.1
7	10	1985	C.Fisk	543	52	17	612	129	23	1	37	.238	.324	.488	812	806	17	9	(2)	(10)	10	804	37.1
8	9	1922	R.Schalk	442	67	3	512	124	22	3	4	.281	.379	.371	750	710	12	4	7		100	817	35.8
9	3	1989	C.Fisk	375	36	3	414	110	25	2	13	.293	.360	.475	835	856	1	0	2	(10)	10	858	35.6
10	8	1953	S.Lollar	334	47	8	389	96	19	0	8	.287	.388	.416	804	789	1	0	2	(10)	40	821	28.0
11	15	1982	C.Fisk	476	46	6	528	127	17	3	14	.267	.339	.403	742	739	17	2	23		10	773	23.9
12	18	1981	C.Fisk	338	38	12	388	89	12	0	7	.263	.358	.361	719	754	3	2	(2)		10	762	23.6
13	11	1965	J.Romano	356	59	5	420	86	11	0	18	.242	.357	.424	781	809	0	2	(9)	(10)		790	22.5
14	22	1920	R.Schalk	485	68	2	555	131	25	5	1	.270	.362	.348	711	683	10	4	3		70	757	22.1
15	20	1919	R.Schalk	394	51	2	447	111	9	3	0	.282	.367	.320	687	700	11				60	760	20.5
16	13	1957	S.Lollar	351	35	13	399	90	11	2	11	.256	.346	.393	739	735	2	0	5	(10)	50	779	20.4
17	21	1915	R.Schalk	413	62	3	478	110	14	4	1	.266	.366	.327	693	751	15	18	(42)		50	760	19.8
18	17	1916	R.Schalk	410	41	6	457	95	12	9	0	.232	.311	.305	616	674	30	13	8		80	762	19.4
19	12	1977	J.Essian	322	52	1	375	88	18	2	10	.273	.376	.435	811	802	1	4	(18)			784	19.1
20	19	1952	S.Lollar	375	54	12	441	90	15	0	13	.240	.354	.384	738	749	1	0	2	(10)	20	761	18.6
21	14	1966	J.Romano	329	58	1	388	76	12	0	15	.231	.348	.404	752	785	0	0	0	(10)		775	18.1
22	16	1984	C.Fisk	359	26	5	390	83	20	1	21	.231	.292	.468	760	763	6	0	15		(10)	768	16.8
23	23	1914	R.Schalk	392	38	8	438	106	13	2	0	.270	.347	.314	661	727	24	11	4		20	751	16.1
24	29	1917	R.Schalk	424	59	7	490	96	12	5	2	.226	.331	.292	623	689	19				50	739	15.2
25	28	1987	C.Fisk	454	39	8	501	116	22	1	23	.256	.325	.460	786	754	1	4	(13)	(10)	10	740	15.1

Chicago White Sox
First basemen

V	R	Year	Name	AB	BB	HBP	TAB	H	2B	3B	HR	BA	OB	SA	PRO	Wtd PRO	SB	CS	SBF	SPF	FF	R TF	V HC
1	2	1994	F.Thomas	399	109	2	510	141	34	1	38	.353	.494	.729	1,223	1,142	2	3	(7)		(30)	1,105	115.0
2	1	1972	D.Allen	506	99	1	606	156	28	5	37	.308	.422	.603	1,025	1,112	19	8	5	10	(10)	1,116	105.2
3	5	1995	F.Thomas	493	136	6	635	152	27	0	40	.308	.463	.606	1,069	1,009	3	2	(1)		(30)	977	70.5
4	4	1993	F.Thomas	549	112	2	663	174	36	0	41	.317	.434	.607	1,041	1,016	4	2	0		(30)	986	68.2
5	8	1992	F.Thomas	573	122	5	700	185	46	2	24	.323	.446	.536	981	1,001	6	3	0		(30)	971	66.9
6	7	1997	F.Thomas	530	109	3	642	184	35	0	35	.347	.461	.611	1,072	1,012	1	1	(1)		(40)	971	61.4
7	9	1996	F.Thomas	527	109	5	641	184	26	0	40	.349	.465	.626	1,091	998	1	1	(1)		(30)	967	60.0
8	3	1915	J.Fournier	422	64	15	501	136	20	18	5	.322	.429	.491	920	997	21	16	(21)	10		986	54.4
9	6	1974	D.Allen	462	57	1	520	139	23	1	32	.301	.379	.563	942	986	7	1	9	10	(30)	975	50.9
10	10	1960	R.Sievers	444	74	3	521	131	22	0	28	.295	.399	.534	933	917	1	1	(2)	(10)	(10)	895	32.8
11	12	1961	R.Sievers	492	61	6	559	145	26	6	27	.295	.379	.537	916	890	1	0	2	(10)	(10)	872	27.2
12	11	1937	Z.Bonura	447	49	2	498	154	41	2	19	.345	.412	.573	984	902	5	1	6	(10)	(20)	878	27.0
13	15	1952	E.Robinson	594	70	12	676	176	33	1	22	.296	.382	.466	848	861	2	0	3	(10)	(10)	844	25.1
14	13	1984	G.Walker	442	35	2	479	130	29	2	24	.294	.349	.532	880	884	8	5	(4)	(10)		870	22.8
15	19	1940	J.Kuhel	603	87	3	693	169	28	8	27	.280	.374	.488	861	811	12	5	3	10	10	833	22.0
16	14	1914	J.Fournier	379	31	3	413	118	14	9	6	.311	.368	.443	811	892	10	13	(37)	10		865	19.8
17	18	1934	Z.Bonura	510	64	0	574	154	35	4	27	.302	.380	.545	925	871	0	2	(7)	(10)	(20)	834	18.4
18	20	1905	J.Donahue	533	44	4	581	153	22	4	1	.287	.346	.349	695	800	32		10	20		830	17.5
19	21	1939	J.Kuhel	546	64	2	612	164	24	9	15	.300	.376	.460	836	777	18	5	12	10	20	819	15.2
20	23	1931	L.Blue	589	127	3	719	179	23	15	1	.304	.430	.399	829	791	13	3	9	10		810	14.3
21	22	1951	E.Robinson	564	77	3	644	159	23	5	29	.282	.371	.495	866	845	2	5	(12)	(10)	(10)	814	14.1
22	16	1957	E.Torgeson	301	61	0	362	86	13	3	8	.286	.406	.429	835	830	7	3	3	10		842	13.1
23	17	1982	T.Paciorek	382	24	9	415	119	27	4	11	.312	.366	.490	856	852	3	3	(7)	(10)		835	12.9
24	25	1962	J.Cunningham	526	101	7	634	155	32	7	8	.295	.415	.428	843	824	3	3	(4)		(10)	809	11.9
25	26	1971	C.May	500	62	6	568	147	21	7	7	.294	.379	.406	785	810	16	7	3	10	(20)	803	8.9

Chicago White Sox
Second basemen

V	R	Year	Name	AB	BB	HBP	TAB	H	2B	3B	HR	BA	OB	SA	PRO	Wtd PRO	SB	CS	SBF	SPF	FF	R TF	V HC
1	1	1915	E.Collins	521	119	5	645	173	22	10	4	.332	.460	.436	896	972	46	30	(21)	10	70	1,031	111.8
2	2	1920	E.Collins	602	69	2	673	224	38	13	3	.372	.438	.493	932	896	20	8	6	10	60	972	96.6
3	3	1916	E.Collins	545	86	3	634	168	14	17	0	.308	.405	.396	802	877	40	21	(3)	10	40	924	76.0
4	5	1924	E.Collins	556	89	3	648	194	27	7	6	.349	.441	.455	896	838	42	17	12	10	40	900	69.6
5	8	1957	N.Fox	619	75	16	710	196	27	8	6	.317	.404	.415	819	815	5	6	(9)		70	875	67.6
6	4	1923	E.Collins	505	84	4	593	182	22	5	5	.360	.455	.453	909	868	48	29	(16)	10	40	902	64.4
7	10	1919	E.Collins	518	68	2	588	165	19	7	4	.319	.400	.405	805	821	33			10	40	871	60.3
8	11	1917	E.Collins	564	89	3	656	163	18	12	0	.289	.389	.363	752	832	53			10	10	852	54.9
9	14	1955	N.Fox	636	38	17	691	198	28	7	6	.311	.366	.406	772	757	7	9	(15)	10	80	832	50.7
10	12	1921	E.Collins	526	66	2	594	177	20	10	2	.337	.412	.424	836	772	12	10	(13)	10	80	849	48.8
11	9	1925	E.Collins	425	87	4	516	147	26	3	3	.346	.461	.442	904	831	19	6	13	10	20	873	48.6
12	19	1954	N.Fox	631	51	5	687	201	24	8	2	.319	.374	.391	766	764	16	9	(3)	10	40	812	43.5
13	17	1949	C.Michaels	561	101	3	665	173	27	9	6	.308	.417	.421	837	807	5	7	(13)		20	815	43.1
14	7	1926	E.Collins	375	62	3	440	129	32	4	1	.344	.441	.459	900	855	13	8	(6)	10	20	878	42.5
15	20	1922	E.Collins	598	73	3	674	194	20	12	1	.324	.401	.403	804	760	20	12	(6)	10	40	805	40.4
16	22	1959	N.Fox	624	71	7	702	191	34	6	2	.306	.383	.389	773	769	5	6	(9)		40	800	40.3
17	13	1918	E.Collins	330	73	0	403	91	8	2	2	.276	.407	.330	737	806	22			10	30	846	39.3
18	6	1905	F.Isbell	341	15	5	361	101	21	11	2	.296	.335	.440	775	893	15			10	(10)	893	37.5
19	16	1975	J.Orta	542	48	4	594	165	26	10	11	.304	.365	.450	816	840	16	9	(3)	10	(30)	816	37.1
20	18	1974	J.Orta	525	40	3	568	166	31	2	10	.316	.368	.440	808	846	9	5	(2)	10	(40)	815	35.0
21	21	1982	T.Bernazard	540	67	2	609	138	25	9	11	.256	.340	.396	736	733	11	0	17	10	40	800	33.3
22	23	1981	T.Bernazard	384	54	2	440	106	14	4	6	.276	.368	.380	748	785	4	4	(9)	10		786	32.1
23	26	1952	N.Fox	648	34	3	685	192	25	10	0	.296	.334	.366	700	711	5	5	(7)		60	774	30.5
24	25	1951	N.Fox	604	43	14	661	189	32	12	4	.313	.372	.425	798	779	9	12	(21)	10	10	777	30.5
25	27	1998	R.Durham	635	73	6	714	181	35	8	19	.285	.364	.455	819	770	36	9	24	10	(30)	774	30.2

Chicago White Sox
Shortstops

V	R	Year	Name	AB	BB	HBP	TAB	H	2B	3B	HR	BA	OB	SA	PRO	Wtd PRO	SB	CS	SBF	SPF	FF	R TF	V HC
1	1	1943	L.Appling	585	90	1	676	192	33	2	3	.328	.419	.407	825	879	27	8	15		10	904	82.1
2	2	1936	L.Appling	526	85	1	612	204	31	7	6	.388	.474	.508	981	884	10	6	(3)		20	901	73.2
3	4	1905	G.Davis	550	60	4	614	153	29	1	1	.278	.353	.340	693	799	31			10	50	859	60.5
4	3	1970	L.Aparicio	552	53	1	606	173	29	3	5	.313	.375	.404	779	782	8	3	3	10	70	865	58.6
5	5	1969	L.Aparicio	599	66	2	667	168	24	5	5	.280	.354	.362	716	729	24	4	23	10	80	842	57.2
6	8	1960	L.Aparicio	600	43	1	644	166	20	7	2	.277	.326	.343	669	658	51	8	51	10	100	819	50.8
7	7	1902	G.Davis	485	65	4	554	145	27	7	3	.299	.386	.402	788	795	31			10	20	825	49.8
8	9	1935	L.Appling	525	122	0	647	161	28	6	1	.307	.437	.389	826	774	12	6	0		40	814	49.4
9	11	1904	G.Davis	563	43	5	611	142	27	15	1	.252	.311	.359	670	768	32			10	30	808	44.6
10	6	1906	G.Davis	484	41	4	529	134	26	6	0	.277	.338	.355	694	789	27			10	30	829	44.2
11	12	1940	L.Appling	566	69	1	636	197	27	13	0	.348	.420	.442	862	811	3	5	(10)			800	44.1
12	10	2000	J.Valentin	568	59	4	631	155	37	6	25	.273	.345	.491	837	766	19	2	22	10	10	808	44.0
13	16	1937	L.Appling	574	86	1	661	182	42	8	4	.317	.407	.439	846	776	18	10	(3)		20	793	43.3
14	13	1964	R.Hansen	575	73	6	654	150	25	3	20	.261	.350	.419	769	778	1	0	1	(10)	30	799	42.8
15	17	1933	L.Appling	612	56	0	668	197	36	10	6	.322	.379	.443	822	792	6	11	(23)		20	790	42.7
16	20	1946	L.Appling	582	71	0	653	180	27	5	1	.309	.384	.378	762	778	6	4	(3)		10	785	40.2
17	19	1968	L.Aparicio	622	33	2	657	164	24	4	4	.264	.303	.334	637	704	17	11	(7)	10	80	787	39.1
18	15	1913	B.Weaver	533	15	8	556	145	17	8	4	.272	.302	.356	659	703	20			10	80	793	36.6
19	18	1947	L.Appling	503	64	1	568	154	29	0	8	.306	.386	.412	797	806	8	6	(7)		(10)	789	36.3
20	14	1981	B.Almon	349	21	2	372	105	10	2	4	.301	.344	.375	719	755	16	6	10	10		795	35.6
21	21	1949	L.Appling	492	121	0	613	148	21	5	5	.301	.439	.394	833	803	7	12	(26)		(10)	767	32.3
22	23	1941	L.Appling	592	82	1	675	186	26	8	1	.314	.399	.390	789	763	12	8	(6)			757	32.2
23	27	1954	C.Carrasquel	620	85	5	710	158	28	3	12	.255	.349	.368	717	716	7	6	(7)	10	30	749	31.1
24	24	1961	L.Aparicio	625	38	1	664	170	24	4	6	.272	.315	.352	667	648	53	13	38	10	60	757	30.0
25	26	1959	L.Aparicio	612	53	3	668	157	18	5	6	.257	.319	.332	651	648	56	13	42	10	50	750	29.5

Chicago White Sox (1901–2000)

Chicago White Sox
Third basemen

V	R	Year	Name	AB	BB	HBP	TAB	H	2B	3B	HR	BA	OB	SA	PRO	Wtd PRO	SB	CS	SBF	SPF	FF	R TF	V HC
1	1	1992	R.Ventura	592	93	0	685	167	38	1	16	.282	.380	.431	810	826	2	4	(8)		90	908	62.5
2	2	1971	B.Melton	543	61	11	615	146	18	2	33	.269	.354	.492	846	873	3	3	(5)		20	889	50.5
3	4	1996	R.Ventura	586	78	2	666	168	31	2	34	.287	.372	.520	893	817	1	3	(7)		50	860	45.5
4	3	1995	R.Ventura	492	75	1	568	145	22	0	26	.295	.389	.498	887	837	4	3	(3)		30	863	44.8
5	5	1991	R.Ventura	606	80	4	690	172	25	1	23	.284	.371	.442	813	818	2	4	(8)		40	850	43.8
6	6	1964	P.Ward	539	56	2	597	152	28	3	23	.282	.352	.473	825	834	1	1	(2)		10	843	36.0
7	8	1963	P.Ward	600	52	5	657	177	34	6	22	.295	.356	.482	838	852	7	6	(7)		(20)	825	34.1
8	9	1993	R.Ventura	554	105	3	662	145	27	1	22	.262	.382	.433	815	796	1	6	(16)		40	820	32.8
9	7	1977	E.Soderholm	460	47	4	511	129	20	3	25	.280	.352	.500	852	843	2	4	(11)		10	842	30.6
10	13	1928	W.Kamm	552	73	2	627	170	30	12	1	.308	.391	.411	802	764	17	9	(2)	10	40	812	30.3
11	10	1926	W.Kamm	480	77	4	561	141	24	10	0	.294	.396	.385	781	742	12	4	7	10	60	819	28.9
12	11	1961	A.Smith	532	56	5	593	148	29	4	28	.278	.352	.506	858	834	4	4	(6)	10	(20)	818	28.7
13	12	1970	B.Melton	514	56	9	579	135	15	1	33	.263	.345	.488	834	837	2	4	(10)	(10)		817	27.9
14	15	1973	B.Melton	560	75	2	637	155	29	1	20	.277	.364	.439	803	824	4	4	(6)	(10)		808	27.8
15	17	1994	R.Ventura	401	61	2	464	113	15	1	18	.282	.379	.459	838	782	3	1	2		10	794	24.5
16	21	1998	R.Ventura	590	79	1	670	155	31	4	21	.263	.351	.436	786	739	1	1	(1)	(10)	60	788	22.9
17	14	1917	B.Weaver	447	27	5	479	127	16	5	3	.284	.332	.362	694	768	19			10	30	808	22.1
18	20	1911	H.Lord	561	32	6	599	180	18	18	3	.321	.364	.433	797	808	43			10	(30)	788	21.7
19	19	1901	F.Hartman	473	25	9	507	146	23	13	3	.309	.355	.431	786	788	31			10	(10)	788	20.2
20	16	1945	T.Cuccinello	402	45	1	448	124	25	3	2	.308	.379	.400	780	821	6	2	4		(20)	805	19.9
21	23	1923	W.Kamm	544	62	1	607	159	39	9	6	.292	.366	.430	796	760	18	13	(12)	10	20	778	18.7
22	18	1955	G.Kell	429	51	6	486	134	24	1	8	.312	.393	.429	822	806	2	2	(4)		(10)	792	18.4
23	25	1969	B.Melton	556	56	5	617	142	26	2	23	.255	.329	.433	762	777	1	2	(5)			772	16.4
24	22	1943	R.Hodgin	407	20	6	433	128	22	8	1	.314	.356	.415	771	821	3	5	(15)		(20)	785	15.0
25	24	1903	N.Callahan	439	20	1	460	128	26	5	2	.292	.324	.387	711	775	24			10	(10)	775	14.8

Chicago White Sox
Outfielders

V	R	Year	Name	AB	BB	HBP	TAB	H	2B	3B	HR	BA	OB	SA	PRO	Wtd PRO	SB	CS	SBF	SPF	FF	R TF	V HC
1	1	1954	M.Minoso	568	77	16	661	182	29	18	19	.320	.416	.535	951	950	18	11	(6)	10	40	994	78.4
2	3	1998	A.Belle	609	81	1	691	200	48	2	49	.328	.408	.655	1,063	1,000	6	4	(3)		(20)	977	72.3
3	2	1920	J.Jackson	570	56	7	633	218	42	20	12	.382	.444	.589	1,033	994	9	12	(22)	10		981	71.1
4	4	1916	J.Jackson	592	46	5	643	202	40	21	3	.341	.393	.495	888	972	24	14	(6)	10		976	70.6
5	6	1956	M.Minoso	545	86	23	654	172	29	11	21	.316	.430	.525	954	914	12	6	0	10	30	954	64.5
6	5	1919	J.Jackson	516	60	4	580	181	31	14	7	.351	.422	.506	928	947	9			10		957	63.8
7	7	1920	H.Felsch	556	37	4	597	188	40	15	14	.338	.384	.540	923	888	8	13	(28)	10	70	939	54.4
8	9	1984	H.Baines	569	54	0	623	173	28	10	29	.304	.364	.541	906	909	1	2	(5)	10	10	925	49.7
9	12	1951	M.Minoso	530	72	16	618	173	34	14	10	.326	.422	.500	922	901	31	10	17	10	(10)	917	49.5
10	11	1917	J.Jackson	538	57	7	602	162	20	17	5	.301	.375	.429	805	890	13			10	20	920	49.2
11	13	1917	H.Felsch	575	33	6	614	177	17	10	6	.308	.352	.403	755	836	26			10	70	916	48.7
12	19	1926	J.Mostil	600	79	10	689	197	41	15	4	.328	.415	.467	882	838	35	14	10	10	40	897	48.3
13	15	1972	C.May	523	79	9	611	161	26	3	12	.308	.408	.438	845	917	23	14	(8)	10	(10)	909	46.4
14	20	1957	M.Minoso	568	79	21	668	176	36	5	12	.310	.413	.454	867	862	18	15	(17)	10	40	895	46.2
15	16	1934	A.Simmons	558	53	2	613	192	36	7	18	.344	.403	.530	933	879	3	2	(2)		30	907	46.0
16	14	1930	C.Reynolds	563	20	7	590	202	25	18	22	.359	.388	.584	973	889	16	4	13	10		912	45.7
17	10	1981	C.Lemon	328	33	13	374	99	23	6	9	.302	.388	.491	879	921	5	8	(28)	10	20	924	44.9
18	18	1974	K.Henderson	602	66	2	670	176	35	5	20	.292	.364	.467	831	870	12	7	(3)	10	20	897	44.7
19	17	1961	J.Landis	534	65	4	603	151	18	8	22	.283	.365	.470	835	812	19	5	14	10	70	906	42.7
20	23	1933	A.Simmons	605	39	2	646	200	29	10	14	.331	.373	.481	854	824	5	1	4		60	888	42.3
21	22	1992	T.Raines	551	81	0	632	162	22	9	7	.294	.384	.405	789	805	45	6	49	10	30	894	41.1
22	28	1953	M.Minoso	556	74	17	647	174	24	8	15	.313	.410	.466	875	858	25	16	(10)	10	20	878	39.1
23	24	2000	M.Ordonez	588	60	2	650	185	34	3	32	.315	.380	.546	926	848	18	4	15	10	10	882	38.6
24	29	1960	M.Minoso	591	52	13	656	184	32	4	20	.311	.380	.481	860	846	17	13	(13)	10	30	873	37.9
25	31	1966	T. Agee	629	41	10	680	172	27	8	22	.273	.328	.447	775	809	44	18	11	10	40	870	36.5

Chicago White Sox
Outfielders

V	R	Year	Name	AB	BB	HBP	TAB	H	2B	3B	HR	BA	OB	SA	PRO	Wtd PRO	SB	CS	SBF	SPF	FF	R TF	V HC
26	27	1979	C.Lemon	556	56	13	625	177	44	2	17	.318	.394	.496	890	871	7	11	(23)	10	20	878	36.0
27	25	1916	H.Felsch	546	31	3	580	164	24	12	7	.300	.341	.427	768	841	13			10	30	881	35.8
28	26	1977	C.Lemon	553	52	11	616	151	38	4	19	.273	.347	.459	807	798	8	7	(9)	10	80	879	35.6
29	33	1945	W.Moses	569	69	2	640	168	35	15	2	.295	.373	.420	793	835	11	5	1	10	20	866	34.9
30	30	1903	D.Green	499	47	6	552	154	26	7	6	.309	.375	.425	800	871	29			10	(10)	871	34.7
31	8	1978	C.Lemon	357	39	8	404	107	24	6	13	.300	.381	.510	891	911	5	9	(30)	10	40	931	33.3
32	21	1993	T.Raines	415	64	3	482	127	16	4	16	.306	.402	.480	882	861	21	7	14	10	10	894	31.5
33	35	1987	I.Calderon	542	60	1	603	159	38	2	28	.293	.365	.526	891	854	10	5	0		10	864	30.7
34	32	1924	H.Hooper	476	65	4	545	156	27	8	10	.328	.413	.481	894	836	16	13	(17)		50	868	30.3
35	39	1923	J.Mostil	546	62	12	620	159	37	15	3	.291	.376	.430	806	770	41	16	14	10	60	854	30.0
36	41	1926	B.Falk	566	66	2	634	195	43	4	8	.345	.415	.477	892	847	9	10	(16)		20	851	29.7
37	40	1955	M.Minoso	517	76	10	603	149	26	7	10	.288	.390	.424	813	797	19	8	5	10	40	852	28.6
38	48	1985	H.Baines	640	42	1	683	198	29	3	22	.309	.353	.467	820	814	1	1	(1)		30	843	27.9
39	42	1919	H.Felsch	502	40	6	548	138	34	11	7	.275	.336	.428	764	779	19			10	60	849	27.8
40	49	1962	F.Robinson	600	72	2	674	187	45	10	11	.312	.387	.475	862	843	4	2	0	10	(10)	843	27.5
41	38	1909	P.Dougherty	491	51	6	548	140	23	13	1	.285	.359	.391	751	867	36			10	(20)	857	27.4
42	44	1980	C.Lemon	514	71	12	597	150	32	6	11	.292	.390	.442	832	829	6	6	(9)	10	20	849	26.1
43	50	1956	L.Doby	504	102	4	610	135	22	3	24	.268	.395	.466	861	825	0	1	(3)		20	842	25.8
44	46	1924	B.Falk	526	47	1	574	185	37	8	6	.352	.406	.487	893	835	6	6	(10)	10	10	845	25.1
45	55	1999	M.Ordonez	624	47	1	672	188	34	3	30	.301	.351	.510	861	794	13	6	1	10	30	835	25.0
46	47	1941	T.Wright	513	60	6	579	165	35	5	10	.322	.399	.468	867	838	5	4	(5)	10		843	24.9
47	52	1960	A.Smith	536	50	3	589	169	31	3	12	.315	.377	.451	828	814	8	3	3	10	10	838	23.7
48	56	1959	J.Landis	515	78	8	601	140	26	7	5	.272	.376	.379	755	751	20	9	3	10	70	835	23.2
49	57	1939	M.Kreevich	541	59	0	600	175	30	8	5	.323	.390	.436	826	768	23	10	5	10	50	833	22.8
50	62	1952	M.Minoso	569	71	14	654	160	24	9	13	.281	.375	.424	798	811	22	16	(14)	10	20	826	22.6
51	36	1915	B.Roth	384	51	5	440	103	10	17	7	.268	.361	.438	799	866	26	10	13	10	(30)	859	22.4
52	34	1969	C.May	367	58	6	431	103	18	2	18	.281	.387	.488	875	892	1	4	(15)		(10)	866	22.3
53	58	1958	J.Landis	523	52	8	583	145	23	7	15	.277	.352	.434	786	784	19	7	8	10	30	833	22.0
54	45	1999	C.Singleton	496	22	1	519	149	31	6	17	.300	.331	.490	821	758	20	5	18	10	60	846	21.8
55	67	1901	D.Hoy	527	86	14	627	155	28	11	2	.294	.407	.400	807	809	27			10		819	21.4
56	43	1961	F.Robinson	432	52	4	488	134	20	7	11	.310	.389	.465	855	831	7	4	(2)	10	10	849	21.3
57	37	1981	H.Baines	280	12	2	294	80	11	7	10	.286	.320	.482	802	841	6	2	6	10		857	21.2
58	59	1977	R.Zisk	531	55	3	589	154	17	6	30	.290	.360	.514	874	865	0	4	(13)	(10)	(10)	832	20.9
59	61	1986	H.Baines	570	38	2	610	169	29	2	21	.296	.343	.465	808	797	2	1	0		30	827	20.1
60	71	1995	L.Johnson	607	32	1	640	186	18	12	10	.306	.342	.425	767	724	40	6	41	10	40	815	19.7
61	70	1902	F.Jones	532	57	3	592	171	16	5	0	.321	.390	.370	761	767	33			10	40	817	19.4
62	60	1993	L.Johnson	540	36	0	576	168	18	14	0	.311	.354	.396	750	732	35	7	34	10	50	827	19.1
63	53	1921	H.Hooper	419	55	1	475	137	26	5	8	.327	.406	.470	876	809	13	7	(2)	10	20	837	18.9
64	54	1957	L.Doby	416	56	2	474	120	27	2	14	.288	.376	.464	839	835	2	3	(8)		10	837	18.8
65	65	1927	B.Falk	535	52	4	591	175	35	6	9	.327	.391	.465	856	805	5	7	(14)		30	820	18.7
66	69	1982	H.Baines	608	49	0	657	165	29	8	25	.271	.326	.469	794	791	10	3	6	10	10	817	18.6
67	64	1960	J.Landis	494	80	9	583	125	25	6	10	.253	.367	.389	756	743	23	6	18	10	50	821	18.5
68	75	1925	J.Mostil	605	90	12	707	181	36	16	2	.299	.384	.421	822	755	43	20	4	10	40	809	18.4
69	63	1945	J.Dickshot	486	48	1	535	147	19	10	4	.302	.366	.407	774	814	18	3	21	10	(20)	825	18.2
70	73	1905	F.Jones	568	73	4	645	139	17	12	2	.245	.335	.327	662	763	20			10	40	813	17.9
71	51	1997	M.Cameron	379	55	5	439	98	18	3	14	.259	.360	.433	793	748	23	2	41	10	40	839	17.1
72	68	1908	P.Dougherty	482	58	10	550	134	11	6	0	.278	.367	.326	693	818	47			10	(10)	818	16.7
73	77	1911	M.McIntyre	569	64	5	638	184	19	11	1	.323	.397	.401	797	809	17					809	16.4
74	66	1922	J.Mostil	458	38	14	510	139	28	14	7	.303	.375	.472	846	801	14	10	(11)	10	20	820	15.9
75	79	1904	D.Green	536	63	9	608	142	16	10	2	.265	.352	.343	695	797	28			10		807	15.0

Chicago White Sox (1901–2000)

Chicago White Sox
Starting Pitchers

V	R	Year	Name	G	GS	IP	W	L	SVS	SO	BB	ERA	RA/9	R Wtd RA/9	V Runs /162
1	15	1908	E.Walsh	66	49	464	40	15	6	269	56	1.42	2.17	2.85	92.6
2	3	1917	E.Cicotte	49	35	347	28	12	4	150	70	1.53	1.98	2.49	84.0
3	4	1919	E.Cicotte	40	35	307	29	7	1	110	49	1.82	2.26	2.49	81.4
4	9	1910	E.Walsh	45	36	370	18	20	5	258	61	1.27	2.19	2.73	79.2
5	17	1912	E.Walsh	62	41	393	27	17	10	254	94	2.15	2.86	2.89	76.6
6	7	1921	R.Faber	43	39	331	25	15	1	124	87	2.48	2.91	2.58	76.3
7	29	1907	E.Walsh	56	46	422	24	18	4	206	87	1.60	2.56	3.15	69.3
8	23	1911	E.Walsh	56	37	369	27	18	4	255	72	2.22	3.05	2.99	67.6
9	12	1941	T.Lee	35	34	300	22	11	1	130	92	2.37	2.94	2.80	61.7
10	18	1913	R.Russell	52	36	317	22	16	4	122	79	1.90	2.53	2.90	61.2
11	28	1922	R.Faber	43	38	352	21	17	2	148	83	2.81	3.26	3.12	59.1
12	21	1927	T.Thomas	40	36	308	19	16	1	107	94	2.98	3.21	2.94	58.1
13	24	1971	W.Wood	44	42	334	22	13	1	210	62	1.91	2.56	3.00	57.8
14	1	1955	B.Pierce	33	26	206	15	10	1	157	64	1.97	2.18	2.22	56.3
15	2	1906	D.White	28	24	219	18	6	0	95	38	1.52	1.93	2.36	56.3
16	27	1905	N.Altrock	38	34	316	23	12	0	97	63	1.88	2.53	3.09	54.1
17	13	1905	D.White	36	33	260	17	13	0	120	58	1.76	2.32	2.83	52.3
18	61	1909	F.Smith	51	40	365	25	17	1	177	70	1.80	2.56	3.35	51.4
19	8	1909	E.Walsh	31	28	230	15	11	2	127	50	1.41	2.03	2.66	51.0
20	35	1913	J.Scott	48	38	312	20	21	1	158	86	1.90	2.77	3.18	50.2
21	22	1913	E.Cicotte	41	30	268	18	12	1	121	73	1.58	2.59	2.97	49.6
22	14	1967	J.Horlen	35	35	258	19	7	0	103	58	2.06	2.30	2.84	49.2
23	20	1952	B.Pierce	33	32	255	15	12	1	144	79	2.57	2.68	2.92	48.7
24	32	1901	C.Griffith	35	30	267	24	7	1	67	50	2.67	3.85	3.17	47.5
25	6	1964	J.Horlen	32	28	211	13	9	0	138	55	1.88	2.30	2.58	46.5
26	16	1963	G.Peters	41	30	243	19	8	1	189	68	2.33	2.56	2.86	45.8
27	19	1959	B.Shaw	47	26	231	18	6	3	89	54	2.69	2.81	2.92	44.3
28	34	1953	B.Pierce	40	33	271	18	12	3	186	102	2.72	3.12	3.17	43.8
29	44	1926	T.Lyons	39	31	284	18	16	2	51	106	3.01	3.42	3.24	43.7
30	58	1927	T.Lyons	39	34	308	22	14	2	71	67	2.84	3.65	3.35	43.6
31	36	1954	V.Trucks	40	33	265	19	12	3	152	95	2.79	2.95	3.19	42.5
32	49	1906	E.Walsh	41	31	278	17	13	2	171	58	1.88	2.68	3.27	41.7
33	74	1904	F.Owen	37	36	315	21	15	1	103	61	1.94	2.71	3.43	41.5
34	81	1919	L.Williams	41	40	297	23	11	1	125	58	2.64	3.15	3.48	41.3
35	11	1966	G.Peters	30	27	205	12	10	0	129	45	1.98	2.37	2.77	40.7
36	69	1915	J.Scott	48	35	296	24	11	2	120	78	2.03	2.98	3.40	39.9
37	68	1902	R.Patterson	34	30	268	19	14	0	61	67	3.06	3.73	3.40	39.9
38	48	1964	G.Peters	37	36	274	20	8	0	205	104	2.50	2.92	3.27	39.2
39	53	1925	T.Lyons	43	32	263	21	11	3	45	83	3.26	3.80	3.30	38.7
40	67	1940	J.Rigney	39	33	281	14	18	3	141	90	3.11	3.75	3.38	38.5
41	5	1937	M.Stratton	22	21	165	15	5	0	69	37	2.40	3.00	2.56	38.5
42	25	1902	N.Garvin	25	21	193	11	11	0	62	47	2.09	3.31	3.02	38.2
43	42	1996	A.Fernandez	35	35	258	16	10	0	200	72	3.45	3.84	3.23	38.1
44	10	1942	T.Lyons	20	20	180	14	6	0	50	26	2.10	2.60	2.76	37.8
45	31	1925	T.Blankenship	40	23	232	17	8	1	81	69	3.03	3.65	3.17	37.7
46	64	1953	V.Trucks	40	33	264	20	10	3	149	99	2.93	3.30	3.36	37.0
47	75	1928	T.Thomas	36	32	283	17	16	2	129	76	3.08	3.63	3.44	37.0
48	71	1956	B.Pierce	35	33	276	20	9	1	192	100	3.32	3.52	3.41	36.9
49	30	1980	B.Burns	34	32	238	15	13	0	133	63	2.84	3.14	3.17	36.8
50	102	1905	F.Owen	42	38	334	21	13	0	125	56	2.10	2.96	3.62	36.7

Chicago White Sox
Starting Pitchers

V	R	Year	Name	G	GS	IP	W	L	SVS	SO	BB	ERA	RA/9	R Wtd RA/9	V Runs /162
51	43	1901	N.Callahan	27	22	215	15	8	0	70	50	2.42	3.93	3.24	36.4
52	129	1972	W.Wood	49	49	377	24	17	0	193	74	2.51	2.85	3.73	36.4
53	54	1958	B.Pierce	35	32	245	17	11	2	144	66	2.68	3.05	3.30	36.0
54	92	1907	D.White	46	35	291	27	13	1	141	38	2.26	2.88	3.55	34.4
55	47	1956	J.Harshman	34	30	227	15	11	0	143	102	3.10	3.37	3.27	34.2
56	70	1947	E.Lopat	31	31	253	16	13	0	109	73	2.81	3.13	3.40	34.1
57	38	1951	S.Rogovin	27	26	217	12	8	0	82	74	2.78	3.28	3.21	34.1
58	56	1993	A.Fernandez	34	34	247	18	9	0	169	67	3.13	3.46	3.32	34.0
59	114	1920	R.Faber	40	39	319	23	13	1	108	88	2.99	3.84	3.65	33.7
60	51	1964	J.Pizarro	33	33	239	19	9	0	162	55	2.56	2.94	3.29	33.6
61	100	1920	E.Cicotte	37	35	303	21	10	2	87	74	3.26	3.80	3.62	33.4
62	83	1941	E.Smith	34	33	263	13	17	1	111	114	3.18	3.66	3.48	33.0
63	65	1915	J.Benz	39	28	238	15	11	0	81	43	2.11	2.95	3.37	33.0
64	57	1981	B.Burns	24	23	157	10	6	0	108	49	2.64	2.99	3.33	32.4
65	77	1992	J.McDowell	34	34	261	20	10	0	178	75	3.18	3.28	3.44	32.3
66	37	1966	J.Horlen	37	29	211	10	13	1	124	53	2.43	2.73	3.19	32.1
67	73	1951	B.Pierce	37	28	240	15	14	2	113	73	3.03	3.49	3.42	31.9
68	79	1967	G.Peters	38	36	260	16	11	0	215	91	2.28	2.80	3.46	31.8
69	41	1963	J.Pizarro	32	28	215	16	8	1	163	63	2.39	2.89	3.23	31.8
70	105	1906	N.Altrock	38	30	288	20	13	0	99	42	2.06	2.97	3.63	31.3
71	40	1952	J.Dobson	29	25	201	14	10	1	101	60	2.51	2.96	3.23	31.2
72	59	1957	D.Donovan	28	28	221	16	6	0	88	45	2.77	3.10	3.35	31.2
73	112	1905	F.Smith	39	31	292	19	13	0	171	107	2.13	2.99	3.65	30.9
74	39	1923	S.Thurston	46	13	196	7	8	4	55	38	3.13	3.40	3.22	30.6
75	46	1993	W.Alvarez	31	31	208	15	8	0	155	122	2.95	3.38	3.24	30.4
76	87	1993	J.McDowell	34	34	257	22	10	0	158	69	3.37	3.65	3.50	30.1
77	85	1991	J.McDowell	35	35	254	17	10	0	191	82	3.41	3.44	3.49	30.1
78	26	1968	T.John	25	25	177	10	5	0	117	49	1.98	2.28	3.04	29.9
79	90	1994	J.McDowell	25	25	181	10	9	0	127	42	3.73	4.08	3.53	29.3
80	132	1907	F.Smith	41	37	310	23	10	0	139	111	2.47	3.05	3.76	29.0
81	82	1983	R.Dotson	35	35	240	22	7	0	137	106	3.23	3.45	3.48	28.8
82	89	1932	T.Lyons	33	26	231	10	15	2	58	71	3.28	4.05	3.51	28.3
83	45	1981	D.Lamp	27	10	127	7	6	0	71	43	2.41	2.91	3.24	28.1
84	33	1939	T.Lyons	21	21	173	14	6	0	65	26	2.76	3.69	3.17	28.0
85	55	1935	T.Lyons	23	22	191	15	8	0	54	56	3.02	3.72	3.30	28.0
86	88	1962	R.Herbert	35	35	237	20	9	0	115	74	3.27	3.42	3.50	27.8
87	80	1994	W.Alvarez	24	24	162	12	8	0	108	62	3.45	4.01	3.47	27.7
88	72	1937	T.Lee	30	25	205	12	10	0	80	60	3.52	4.00	3.41	27.4
89	101	1958	D.Donovan	34	34	248	15	14	0	127	53	3.01	3.34	3.62	27.3
90	78	1950	B.Wight	30	28	206	10	16	0	62	79	3.58	3.89	3.46	26.5
91	93	1940	T.Lee	28	27	228	12	13	0	87	56	3.47	3.95	3.56	26.5
92	160	1901	R.Patterson	41	35	312	20	15	0	127	62	3.37	4.73	3.90	26.4
93	140	1908	D.White	41	37	296	18	13	0	126	69	2.55	2.89	3.80	26.4
94	62	1916	E.Cicotte	44	19	187	15	7	5	91	70	1.78	2.70	3.35	26.3
95	63	1961	J.Pizarro	39	25	195	14	7	2	188	89	3.05	3.37	3.35	26.1
96	144	1908	F.Smith	41	35	298	16	17	1	129	73	2.03	2.90	3.81	26.1
97	139	1975	J.Kaat	43	41	304	20	14	0	142	77	3.11	3.59	3.79	26.0
98	125	1916	R.Russell	56	25	264	18	11	3	112	42	2.42	3.00	3.73	25.7
99	159	1903	D.White	37	36	300	17	16	0	114	69	2.13	3.57	3.89	25.7
100	119	1957	B.Pierce	37	34	257	20	12	2	171	71	3.26	3.43	3.70	25.6

Chicago White Sox (1901–2000)

Chicago White Sox
Relief Pitchers

V	R	Year	Name	G	GS	IP	W	L	SVS	SO	BB	ERA	RA/9	R Wtd RA/9	V Runs /162
1	4	1975	R.Gossage	62	0	142	9	8	26	130	70	1.84	2.03	2.14	38.1
2	7	1965	H.Wilhelm	66	0	144	7	7	20	106	32	1.81	2.13	2.45	33.7
3	2	1999	K.Foulke	67	0	105	3	3	9	123	21	2.22	2.39	2.07	29.1
4	24	1968	W.Wood	88	2	159	13	12	16	74	33	1.87	2.21	2.94	28.5
5	16	1964	H.Wilhelm	73	0	131	12	9	27	95	30	1.99	2.40	2.69	27.2
6	1	1996	R.Hernandez	72	0	85	6	5	38	85	38	1.91	2.23	1.87	26.6
7	10	1957	G.Staley	47	0	105	5	1	7	44	27	2.06	2.31	2.49	25.3
8	3	1990	B.Thigpen	77	0	89	4	6	57	70	32	1.83	2.03	2.13	25.3
9	11	1985	B.James	69	0	110	8	7	32	88	23	2.13	2.54	2.52	24.9
10	38	1965	E.Fisher	82	0	165	15	7	24	90	43	2.40	2.78	3.20	24.9
11	40	1960	G.Staley	64	0	115	13	8	10	52	25	2.42	3.13	3.24	23.8
12	28	1967	B.Locker	77	0	125	7	5	20	80	23	2.09	2.45	3.03	22.4
13	5	1993	R.Hernandez	70	0	79	3	4	38	71	20	2.29	2.40	2.30	22.3
14	30	1955	S.Consuegra	44	7	126	6	5	7	35	18	2.64	3.00	3.05	22.2
15	9	1983	S.Barojas	52	0	87	3	3	12	38	32	2.47	2.47	2.49	21.0
16	12	1968	H.Wilhelm	72	0	94	4	4	12	72	24	1.73	1.91	2.54	21.0
17	26	1967	D.McMahon	63	0	109	6	2	5	84	40	1.98	2.39	2.95	20.5
18	14	1967	H.Wilhelm	49	0	89	8	3	12	76	34	1.31	2.12	2.62	20.2
19	23	1977	L.LaGrow	66	0	99	7	3	25	63	35	2.46	2.92	2.92	19.0
20	8	1997	R.Hernandez	74	0	81	10	3	31	82	38	2.45	2.68	2.45	18.9
21	36	1959	G.Staley	67	0	116	8	5	14	54	25	2.24	3.03	3.15	18.2
22	17	2000	K.Foulke	72	0	88	3	1	34	91	22	2.97	3.17	2.71	18.1
23	6	1991	S.Radinsky	67	0	71	5	5	8	49	23	2.02	2.27	2.30	17.8
24	15	1968	D.McMahon	45	0	82	5	2	1	65	30	1.98	1.98	2.64	17.5
25	21	1987	B.Thigpen	51	0	89	7	5	16	52	24	2.73	3.03	2.79	17.5
26	34	1954	H.Dorish	37	6	109	6	4	6	48	29	2.72	2.89	3.12	17.4
27	25	1973	C.Acosta	48	0	97	10	6	18	60	39	2.23	2.78	2.95	17.4
28	13	1990	B.Jones	65	0	74	11	4	1	45	33	2.31	2.43	2.55	16.5
29	19	1966	H.Wilhelm	46	0	81	5	2	6	61	17	1.66	2.33	2.72	16.5
30	53	1963	H.Wilhelm	55	3	136	5	8	21	111	30	2.64	3.11	3.47	16.4
31	52	1964	E.Fisher	59	2	125	6	3	9	74	32	3.02	3.10	3.47	15.9
32	35	1943	G.Maltzberger	37	0	99	7	4	14	48	24	2.46	2.64	3.12	15.8
33	33	1946	E.Caldwell	39	0	91	13	4	8	42	29	2.08	2.77	3.08	15.7
34	29	1966	D.Higgins	42	1	93	1	0	5	86	33	2.52	2.61	3.05	15.6
35	27	1952	H.Dorish	39	1	91	8	4	11	47	42	2.47	2.77	3.02	15.5
36	37	1999	S.Lowe	64	0	96	4	1	0	62	46	3.67	3.67	3.18	14.6
37	39	1959	T.Lown	60	0	93	9	2	15	63	42	2.89	3.10	3.22	14.6
38	51	1933	J.Heving	40	6	118	7	5	6	47	27	2.67	3.81	3.46	14.4
39	44	1961	T.Lown	59	0	101	7	5	11	50	35	2.76	3.30	3.28	14.3
40	61	1953	H.Dorish	55	6	146	10	6	18	69	52	3.40	3.64	3.70	13.9
41	22	2000	B.Howry	65	0	71	2	4	7	60	29	3.17	3.30	2.81	13.8
42	54	1962	F.Baumann	40	10	120	7	6	4	55	36	3.38	3.45	3.53	13.7
43	49	1942	J.Haynes	40	1	103	8	5	6	35	47	2.62	3.23	3.43	13.6
44	47	1980	E.Farmer	64	0	100	7	9	30	54	56	3.34	3.34	3.37	13.2
45	20	2000	K.Wunsch	83	0	61	6	3	1	51	29	2.93	3.23	2.75	12.3
46	48	1986	B.Dawley	46	0	98	0	7	2	66	28	3.32	3.50	3.43	12.3
47	50	1944	G.Maltzberger	46	0	91	10	5	12	49	19	2.96	3.07	3.44	11.3
48	31	2000	B.Simas	60	0	68	2	3	0	49	22	3.46	3.59	3.06	11.2
49	56	1966	B.Locker	56	0	95	9	8	12	70	23	2.46	3.03	3.54	10.7
50	59	1972	T.Forster	62	0	100	6	5	29	104	44	2.25	2.79	3.65	10.6

Cincinnati Reds (1900–2000)

The Reds produced only 20 winning seasons and three pennants in the first half of the twentieth century, trailing five other National League clubs in both categories. In the second half of the century, the Reds emerged as one of the league's powers, peaking with the Big Red Machine teams of the 1970s.

Cincinnati began the twentieth century with four seasons at .500 or better in its first six years. Sam Crawford was the team's first star, hitting .330 with a career-best 16 home runs in 1901, and he then batted .333 with 23 triples in 1902. Crawford then left for the Tigers of the upstart American League in 1903. Fortunately, the Reds had already effectively replaced Crawford with Cy Seymour, who hit .340 in 1902 after joining the team in midyear. Seymour then batted .342 and .313 the next two years, before enjoying one of the greatest seasons ever by a Reds player in 1905. Seymour batted .377 with 40 doubles, 21 triples, and 8 home runs, for a 988 Production. Adjusted for a 9 percent hitter's deflation, he batted .411 with 9 home runs, for a team record 1,078 Wtd. Production, a 1,128 Total Factor, and 117.9 Hits Contribution.

Seymour was traded to the Giants during the 1906 season, and the Reds then stumbled to just one winning season from 1906 to 1916. Fred Toney joined the team for the 1915 season, and proceeded to post the team's best performance during this period with a 17–6 record and a 1.58 ERA. His 2.32 Wtd. RA/9 gave Toney the best rate of success for any Reds starting pitcher in team history.

In 1917, Edd Roush hit .341 to win the batting title, Heinie Groh hit .304 in his best season, and Toney was 24–16 with a 2.20 ERA, beginning a Reds streak of ten winning seasons over a 12-year period. The 1919 squad won the team's first pennant with a 96–44 record, while winning eight more regular season games than their highly favored World Series opponent, the White Sox. Roush won his last batting title that year with a .321 average, while Heinie Groh hit .310. Superb pitching was provided by Slim Sallee (21–7, 2.06 ERA), Dutch Ruether (19–6, 1.82 ERA), and Hod Eller (19–9, 2.39 ERA).

Pitching continued to be the team's strong suite in the 1920s. In 1922, Eppa Rixey came from the Phillies to win 25 games. In 1923, Dolf Luque was outstanding with a 27–8 record, a 1.93 ERA, a 2.36 Wtd. RA/9, and a team record 82.8 Runs saved from scoring. Catcher Bubbles Hargrave gave the 1923 team a lift with a .333 average and 10 home runs, while Roush hit .351 that year. Roush was traded to the Giants before the 1928 season, which turned out to be the last winning season the Reds would see in ten years.

The Reds sunk to seventh place in both 1929 and 1930, and then finished dead last from 1931 to 1934, and again in 1937. The Reds were unable to reverse their fortunes by bringing in aging veterans Harry Heilmann, Bob Meusel, Edd Roush, Babe Herman, Chick Hafey, George Grantham, and Jim Bottomley. Ponderous catcher Ernie Lombardi emerged as the team's best offensive weapon, hitting .343, .333, and .334 from 1935 to 1937, followed in 1938 by a league leading .342 average and 19 home runs, earning him MVP honors.

Cincinnati won pennants in 1939 and 1940, in the midst of seven straight winning seasons from 1938 to 1944. In 1939, Bucky Walters led the league with 27 wins, a 2.29 ERA, and a 2.80 Wtd. RA/9 to win the MVP Award, while Paul Derringer went 25–7 with a 2.93 ERA, and slick-fielding first baseman Frank McCormick hit .332 with 18 home runs. In 1940, McCormick hit .309 with 19 home runs to win the MVP award, while Walters and Derringer again posted 20 win seasons.

The team struggled after World War II, with only two winning seasons from 1945 to 1960. Ted Kluszewski was the team's best player during this period, batting over .300 seven times and slugging 40, 49, and 47 home runs from 1953 to 1955. The best team in this period was the 1956 club, which hit 221 home runs, led by Kluszewski (35 home runs), Ed Bailey (28), Wally Post (36), Gus Bell (29), and rookie Frank Robinson (38).

The Reds posted 19 winning records in 21 years during their golden period from 1961 to 1981, while appearing in the postseason seven times. In 1961, the Reds won their fourth pennant. Robinson was the league's MVP that year, as he batted .323 with 37 home runs and 22 stolen bases, for a 1,045 Total Factor. Gold Glove winner Vada Pinson was the team's other star, hitting .343 with 16 home runs and 23 steals. Robinson had another super year in 1962, hitting .342 with 39 home runs and 92 extra base hits, for a 1,064 Total Factor, as the third place Reds won 98 games. The 1965 team led the league in offense, while Jim Maloney went 20–9 with a 2.54 ERA and a 3.08 Wtd. RA/9, but the Reds still finished in fourth place. The team's poor showing led to Robinson being traded to Baltimore after the 1965 season.

The Big Red Machine began to emerge in the late 1960s. Johnny Bench, Tony Perez, and Lee May developed into stars, while Pete Rose moved from second base to the outfield and won batting titles in 1968 (.335) and 1969 (.348). Adjusted for 2 percent hitter's deflation, Rose hit .356 with 16 home runs in 1969, earning him a career best 989 Total Factor.

The Big Red Machine blossomed in 1970, winning 102 games and the team's fifth pennant that year. Twenty-two-year-old Gold Glove winner Bench hit .293 with 45 home runs, for a 1,015 Total Factor and the league's MVP Award. Fellow slugger Tony Perez batted .317 with 40 home runs, Rose and Bobby Tolan each hit .316, and rookie Bernie Carbo chipped in with a .310 average and 21 home runs. Gary Nolan was 18–7 with a 3.27 ERA in a rare injury-free year, while Wayne Granger and Clay Carroll were the league's best 1–2 bullpen punch.

The Big Red Machine won another pennant in 1972, led by MVP Johnny Bench, who hit .270, drew 100 walks, and led the league with 40 home runs. Adjusted for 3.5 percent hitter's deflation, Bench batted .279 with 43 home runs, for a career high 959 Wtd. Production. Bench's 1,040 Total Factor and 116.4 Hits Contribution rank as the best volume and rate of success results for any National League catcher. Joe Morgan came from Houston in one of history's most lopsided trades, and added a .292 average, 115 walks, 16 home runs, and 58 steals. Nolan was the staff ace, with a 15–5 record and 1.99 ERA, while Carroll saved 37 games and posted a 2.25 ERA.

Reaching its peak in 1975 with 108 wins and the team's seventh pennant, the Big Red Machine featured a starting lineup of Bench (C), Perez (1B), Morgan (2B), Concepcion (SS), Rose (3B), Foster (OF), Griffey (OF), and Geronimo (OF). League MVP Morgan hit .327 with 17 homers and 67 steals, added 132 walks for a career-best .471 on-base percentage, and achieved a 1,110 Total Factor. Don Gullett was 15–4 with a 2.42 ERA to lead the pitching staff, and Nolan went 15–9 with a 3.16 ERA. This powerful team fought off a young Red Sox ball club to win a memorable World Series in seven games.

The 1976 Reds won 102 games and another World Series. Morgan repeated as league MVP and won another Gold Glove, while hitting .320 with 27 home runs, 60 steals, and 114 walks, for a 1,062 Wtd. Production, and the league's all-time best 1,160 Total Factor at his position. Morgan also generated a 132.8 Hits Contribution that year, which represents the league's fourth best volume of success at second base.

The Reds finished second in 1977 despite 52 home runs, a .320 average and a 1,015 Total Factor from MVP George Foster, and a 14–3 record and 2.35 ERA from Tom Seaver, who was obtained from the Mets in midseason to shore up a shaky pitching rotation. The 1979 team won another division crown behind a balanced attack and Seaver's 16 wins. In the strike-shortened season of 1981, Seaver was 14–2 with a 2.54 ERA in his last great season to lead the Reds to the league's best record at 66–42, but the team failed to win either "half" of the season and were denied a playoff appearance. Cincinnati then slumped to last place in 1982 and 1983.

The Reds produced four straight second place finishes in 1985–1988. In 1985, Dave Parker hit .312 with 34 home runs and 80 extra-base hits. In 1987, Eric Davis hit .293 with 37 home runs and 50 steals for a 1,090 Total Factor, while Kal Daniels chipped in with a .334 average, 26 home runs, 26 steals and a 1,028 Total Factor. In 1988, John Franco earned a 6–6 record, 39 saves, a 1.57 ERA, and a 2.21 Wtd. RA/9.

The Reds won their last World Series in 1990. This team featured Davis, Barry Larkin, Chris Sabo, and Hal Morris. The team's bullpen excelled, as Rob Dibble was 8–3 with 11 saves, a 1.74 ERA and 2.18 Wtd. RA/9, while Randy Myers was 4–6 with 31 saves, a 2.08 ERA, and 2.68 Wtd. RA/9.

The 1995 team won its division, as league MVP Larkin won a Gold Glove while hitting .319 with 15 home runs and 51 steals, and Reggie Sanders hit .306 with 28 home runs and 36 steals. Larkin had his best season in 1996 for a .500 ballclub, as he hit .298 with 33 home runs, while stealing 36 bases, for a 1,009 Total Factor and 102.5 Hits Contribution. The 1999 team won 96 games behind a deep bullpen led by 23-year-old rookie Scott Williamson (12–7, 19 saves, 2.41 ERA, 2.53 Wtd. RA/9), and just missed earning a wild card spot in the playoffs.

Cincinnati Reds **Hitters Volume of Success**

Pos	Year	Name	AB	BB	HBP	TAB	H	2B	3B	HR	BA	OB	SA	PRO	Wtd PRO	SB	CS	SBF	SPF	FF	R TF	V HC
C	1972	J.Bench	538	100	2	640	145	22	2	40	.270	.386	.541	927	959	6	6	(9)	0	90	1,040	116.4
1B	1954	T.Kluszewski	573	78	3	654	187	28	3	49	.326	.410	.642	1,052	997	0	2	(6)	(10)	(10)	971	65.9
2B	1976	J.Morgan	472	114	1	587	151	30	5	27	.320	.453	.576	1,029	1,062	60	9	68	10	20	1,160	132.8
SS	1996	B.Larkin	517	96	7	620	154	32	4	33	.298	.415	.567	981	935	36	10	24	10	40	1,009	102.5
3B	1917	H.Groh	599	71	8	678	182	39	11	1	.304	.385	.411	796	887	15			10	60	957	81.9
OF	1905	C.Seymour	581	51	2	634	219	40	21	8	.377	.429	.559	988	1,078	21			10	40	1,128	117.9
OF	1962	F.Robinson	609	76	11	696	208	51	2	39	.342	.424	.624	1,048	1,024	18	9	0	10	30	1,064	101.8
OF	1987	E.Davis	474	84	1	559	139	23	4	37	.293	.401	.593	994	956	50	6	64	10	60	1,090	88.5
Starters		Averages	545	84	4	634	173	33	7	29	.317	.412	.563	975	987	26	5	18	6	41	1,052	101.0
C	1938	E.Lombardi	489	40	0	529	167	30	1	19	.342	.391	.524	915	916	0		(10)	0		906	60.6
1B	1916	H.Chase	542	19	1	562	184	29	12	4	.339	.363	.459	822	919	22	11	0	10	40	969	55.9
2B	1905	M.Huggins	564	103	7	674	154	11	8	1	.273	.392	.326	718	783	27			10	60	853	56.7
SS	1976	D.Concepcion	576	49	1	626	162	28	7	9	.281	.339	.401	740	763	21	10	2	10	70	845	54.5
3B	1970	T.Perez	587	83	4	674	186	28	6	40	.317	.405	.589	994	970	8	3	3	(10)	(20)	942	72.6
OF	1977	G.Foster	615	61	5	681	197	31	2	52	.320	.386	.631	1,017	988	6	4	(3)	10	20	1,015	83.5
OF	1969	P.Rose	627	88	5	720	218	33	11	16	.348	.432	.512	944	966	7	10	(17)	10	30	989	79.3
OF	1902	S.Crawford	555	47	1	603	185	16	23	3	.333	.386	.461	848	948	16			10	20	978	73.4
Reserves		Averages	569	61	3	634	182	26	9	18	.319	.388	.490	878	907	13	5	(2)	5	28	938	67.1
Totals		Weighted Ave.	553	76	4	634	176	31	7	26	.318	.404	.539	943	960	22	5	11	6	37	1,014	89.7

Pitchers Volume of Success

Pos	Year	Name	G	GS	IP	W	L	SV	SO	BB	ERA	Wtd RA/9	R RA/9	V Runs/162
SP	1923	D.Luque	41	37	322	27	8	2	151	88	1.93	2.52	2.36	82.8
SP	1939	B.Walters	39	36	319	27	11	0	137	109	2.29	2.76	2.80	65.5
SP	1902	N.Hahn	36	36	321	23	12	0	142	58	1.77	2.72	3.07	61.4
SP	1915	F.Toney	36	23	223	17	6	2	108	73	1.58	1.86	2.32	58.2
SP	1993	J.Rijo	36	36	257	14	9	0	227	62	2.48	2.66	2.68	53.5
Starters		Averages	38	34	288	22	9	1	153	78	2.02	2.54	2.67	64.3
RP	1967	T.Abernathy	70	0	106	6	3	28	88	41	1.27	1.61	1.91	31.2
RP	1990	R.Dibble	68	0	98	8	3	11	136	34	1.74	2.02	2.18	25.9
RP	1973	P.Borbon	80	0	121	11	4	14	60	35	2.16	2.45	2.69	25.1
RP	1978	D.Bair	70	0	100	7	6	28	91	38	1.97	2.06	2.34	24.7
Relievers		Averages	72	0	106	8	4	20	94	37	1.80	2.05	2.30	26.7
Totals		Averages	110	34	395	30	13	21	247	115	1.96	2.41	2.57	91.0

Cincinnati Reds (1900–2000)

Cincinnati Reds — **Hitters Rate of Success**

Pos	Year	Name	AB	BB	HBP	TAB	H	2B	3B	HR	BA	OB	SA	PRO	Wtd PRO	SB	CS	SBF	SPF	FF	R TF	V HC
C	1972	J.Bench	538	100	2	640	145	22	2	40	.270	.386	.541	927	959	6	6	(9)	0	90	1,040	116.4
1B	1954	T.Kluszewski	573	78	3	654	187	28	3	49	.326	.410	.642	1,052	997	0	2	(6)	(10)	(10)	971	65.9
2B	1976	J.Morgan	472	114	1	587	151	30	5	27	.320	.453	.576	1,029	1,062	60	9	68	10	20	1,160	132.8
SS	1996	B.Larkin	517	96	7	620	154	32	4	33	.298	.415	.567	981	935	36	10	24	10	40	1,009	102.5
3B	1917	H.Groh	599	71	8	678	182	39	11	1	.304	.385	.411	796	887	15			10	60	957	81.9
OF	1905	C.Seymour	581	51	2	634	219	40	21	8	.377	.429	.559	988	1,078	21			10	40	1,128	117.9
OF	1987	E.Davis	474	84	1	559	139	23	4	37	.293	.401	.593	994	956	50	6	64	10	60	1,090	88.5
OF	1962	F.Robinson	609	76	11	696	208	51	2	39	.342	.424	.624	1,048	1,024	18	9	0	10	30	1,064	101.8
Starters		Averages	545	84	4	634	173	33	7	29	.317	.412	.563	975	987	26	5	18	6	41	1,052	101.0
C	1956	E.Bailey	383	52	3	438	115	8	2	28	.300	.388	.551	939	914	2	0	4	(10)	10	919	52.9
1B	1916	H.Chase	542	19	1	562	184	29	12	4	.339	.363	.459	822	919	22	11	0	10	40	969	55.9
2B	1906	M.Huggins	545	71	3	619	159	11	7	0	.292	.376	.338	714	813	10			10	40	863	55.1
SS	1913	J.Tinker	382	20	1	403	121	20	13	1	.317	.352	.445	797	829	10			(10)	40	859	39.8
3B	1970	T.Perez	587	83	4	674	186	28	6	40	.317	.405	.589	994	970	8	3	3	(10)	(20)	942	72.6
OF	1994	K.Mitchell	310	59	3	372	101	18	1	30	.326	.438	.681	1,119	1,053	2	0	5	(10)	(20)	1,028	67.9
OF	1987	K.Daniels	368	60	1	429	123	24	1	26	.334	.429	.617	1,046	1,006	26	8	22	10	(10)	1,028	55.3
OF	1977	G.Foster	615	61	5	681	197	31	2	52	.320	.386	.631	1,017	988	6	4	(3)	10	20	1,015	83.5
Reserves		Averages	467	53	3	522	148	21	6	23	.318	.391	.532	923	934	15	3	4	0	13	951	60.4
Totals		Weighted Ave.	519	74	4	596	165	29	6	27	.318	.405	.553	958	969	22	5	13	4	32	1,018	87.4

Pitchers Rate of Success

Pos	Year	Name	G	GS	IP	W	L	SV	SO	BB	ERA	RA/9	Wtd RA/9	V Runs /162
SP	1915	F.Toney	36	23	223	17	6	2	108	73	1.58	1.86	2.32	58.2
SP	1923	D.Luque	41	37	322	27	8	2	151	88	1.93	2.52	2.36	82.8
SP	1993	J.Rijo	36	36	257	14	9	0	227	62	2.48	2.66	2.68	53.5
SP	1977	T.Seaver	33	33	261	21	6	0	196	66	2.58	2.69	2.79	51.4
SP	1939	B.Walters	39	36	319	27	11	0	137	109	2.29	2.76	2.80	65.5
Starters		Averages	37	33	276	21	8	1	164	80	2.18	2.53	2.60	62.3
RP	1967	T.Abernathy	70	0	106	6	3	28	88	41	1.27	1.61	1.91	31.2
RP	1990	R.Dibble	68	0	98	8	3	11	136	34	1.74	2.02	2.18	25.9
RP	1988	J.Franco	70	0	86	6	6	39	46	27	1.57	1.88	2.21	22.4
RP	1994	M.McElroy	52	0	58	1	2	5	38	15	2.34	2.34	2.29	20.6
Relievers		Averages	65	0	87	5	4	21	77	29	1.65	1.91	2.12	25.0
Totals		Averages	102	33	363	26	12	22	241	109	2.06	2.38	2.48	87.3

Cincinnati Reds
Catchers

V	R	Year	Name	AB	BB	HBP	TAB	H	2B	3B	HR	BA	OB	SA	PRO	Wtd PRO	SB	CS	SBF	SPF	FF	R TF	V HC
1	1	1972	J.Bench	538	100	2	640	145	22	2	40	.270	.386	.541	927	959	6	6	(9)		90	1,040	116.4
2	2	1970	J.Bench	605	54	0	659	177	35	4	45	.293	.351	.587	937	914	5	2	1		100	1,015	106.1
3	4	1974	J.Bench	621	80	3	704	174	38	2	33	.280	.365	.507	872	886	5	4	(4)		90	972	98.8
4	3	1975	J.Bench	530	65	2	597	150	39	1	28	.283	.363	.519	882	892	11	0	17		100	1,010	94.5
5	5	1969	J.Bench	532	49	4	585	156	23	1	26	.293	.357	.487	844	864	6	6	(10)		90	944	74.3
6	6	1977	J.Bench	494	58	1	553	136	34	2	31	.275	.353	.540	893	867	2	4	(10)		70	927	65.7
7	9	1973	J.Bench	557	83	0	640	141	17	3	25	.253	.350	.429	779	786	4	1	3		100	889	64.4
8	8	1938	E.Lombardi	489	40	0	529	167	30	1	19	.342	.391	.524	915	916	0		(10)			906	60.6
9	10	1968	J.Bench	564	31	2	597	155	40	2	15	.275	.315	.433	748	821	1	5	(14)		80	886	59.4
10	7	1956	E.Bailey	383	52	3	438	115	8	2	28	.300	.388	.551	939	914	2	0	4	(10)	10	919	52.9
11	14	1976	J.Bench	465	81	2	548	109	24	1	16	.234	.350	.394	744	768	13	2	16		90	873	51.1
12	17	1979	J.Bench	464	67	0	531	128	19	0	22	.276	.367	.459	826	819	4	2	0	(10)	40	849	43.5
13	11	1978	J.Bench	393	50	1	444	102	17	1	23	.260	.345	.483	828	842	4	2	0	(10)	50	882	43.3
14	20	1971	J.Bench	562	49	0	611	134	19	2	27	.238	.300	.423	723	745	2	1	0		80	825	43.0
15	16	1923	B.Hargrave	378	44	12	434	126	23	9	10	.333	.419	.521	941	901	4	5	(13)	(10)	(10)	868	41.4
16	13	1940	E.Lombardi	376	31	7	414	120	22	0	14	.319	.382	.489	871	876	0		(10)		10	876	41.2
17	15	1965	J.Edwards	371	50	1	422	99	22	2	17	.267	.355	.474	830	853	0	0	0		20	873	39.3
18	12	1926	B.Hargrave	326	25	4	355	115	22	8	6	.353	.406	.525	930	907	2			(10)	(20)	877	35.5
19	18	1936	E.Lombardi	387	19	7	413	129	23	2	12	.333	.375	.496	871	852	1		(10)			842	34.1
20	22	1939	E.Lombardi	450	35	3	488	129	26	2	20	.287	.342	.487	829	812	0		(10)		10	812	32.8
21	23	1955	S.Burgess	442	50	1	493	133	17	3	21	.301	.373	.495	869	832	1	1	(2)	(10)	(10)	810	32.8
22	19	1980	J.Bench	360	41	2	403	90	12	0	24	.250	.330	.483	813	824	4	2	0	(10)	20	834	30.0
23	24	1957	E.Bailey	391	73	2	466	102	15	2	20	.261	.380	.463	843	822	5	3	(2)	(10)	(10)	800	28.6
24	31	1944	R.Mueller	555	53	4	612	159	24	4	10	.286	.353	.398	751	770	4		(10)		10	770	28.3
25	28	1963	J.Edwards	495	45	4	544	128	19	4	11	.259	.325	.380	705	742	1	5	(16)		60	786	28.2

Cincinnati Reds
First basemen

V	R	Year	Name	AB	BB	HBP	TAB	H	2B	3B	HR	BA	OB	SA	PRO	Wtd PRO	SB	CS	SBF	SPF	FF	R TF	V HC
1	1	1960	F.Robinson	464	82	9	555	138	33	6	31	.297	.413	.595	1,007	1,002	13	6	2	10		1,013	67.7
2	2	1954	T.Kluszewski	573	78	3	654	187	28	3	49	.326	.410	.642	1,052	997	0	2	(6)	(10)	(10)	971	65.9
3	4	1959	F.Robinson	540	69	8	617	168	31	4	36	.311	.397	.583	980	952	18	8	3	10		965	60.3
4	3	1916	H.Chase	542	19	1	562	184	29	12	4	.339	.363	.459	822	919	22	11	0	10	40	969	55.9
5	7	1955	T.Kluszewski	612	66	4	682	192	25	0	47	.314	.384	.585	969	928	1	1	(1)	(10)	(10)	907	46.8
6	5	1973	T.Perez	564	74	3	641	177	33	3	27	.314	.396	.527	923	931	3	1	1	(10)		922	46.5
7	6	1944	F.McCormick	581	57	4	642	177	37	3	20	.305	.371	.482	853	874	7				40	914	46.2
8	8	1939	F.McCormick	630	40	2	672	209	41	4	18	.332	.374	.495	869	851	1				40	891	40.6
9	9	1902	J.Beckley	531	34	6	571	175	23	7	5	.330	.377	.427	804	899	15			(10)		889	37.6
10	14	1940	F.McCormick	618	52	5	675	191	44	3	19	.309	.367	.482	850	854	2				20	874	35.3
11	11	1971	L.May	553	42	4	599	154	17	3	39	.278	.334	.532	866	892	3	0	5	(10)		887	33.3
12	15	1953	T.Kluszewski	570	55	4	629	180	25	0	40	.316	.380	.570	950	898	2	0	3	(10)	(20)	871	31.8
13	17	1969	L.May	607	45	6	658	169	32	3	38	.278	.334	.529	863	883	5	4	(4)	(10)		869	31.0
14	12	1952	T.Kluszewski	497	47	4	548	159	24	11	16	.320	.383	.509	892	904	3	3	(5)	(10)	(10)	878	29.8
15	10	1991	H.Morris	478	46	1	525	152	33	1	14	.318	.379	.479	858	875	10	4	4		10	889	29.8
16	13	1909	D.Hoblitzell	517	44	2	563	159	23	11	4	.308	.364	.418	782	885	17			(10)		875	29.5
17	16	1972	T.Perez	515	55	0	570	146	33	7	21	.283	.353	.497	850	879	4	2	0	(10)		869	28.4
18	18	1918	S.Magee	400	37	9	446	119	15	13	2	.298	.370	.415	785	868	14			10	(10)	868	26.7
19	19	1956	T.Kluszewski	517	49	3	569	156	14	1	35	.302	.366	.536	901	878	1	0	2	(10)	(10)	859	25.5
20	20	1968	L.May	559	34	6	599	162	32	1	22	.290	.337	.469	806	885	4	7	(16)	(10)		859	25.4
21	23	1994	H.Morris	436	34	5	475	146	30	4	10	.335	.389	.491	880	829	6	2	4		10	843	23.2
22	21	1977	D.Driessen	536	64	3	603	161	31	4	17	.300	.378	.468	846	822	31	13	8	10	10	850	22.9
23	29	1922	J.Daubert	610	56	3	669	205	15	22	12	.336	.395	.492	886	831	14	17	(28)	10	20	833	21.0
24	24	1980	D.Driessen	524	93	6	623	139	36	1	14	.265	.382	.418	800	810	19	6	11	10	10	841	21.0
25	27	1999	S.Casey	594	61	9	664	197	42	3	25	.332	.402	.539	941	861	0	2	(6)	(10)	(10)	835	20.5

Cincinnati Reds
Second basemen

V	R	Year	Name	AB	BB	HBP	TAB	H	2B	3B	HR	BA	OB	SA	PRO	Wtd PRO	SB	CS	SBF	SPF	FF	R TF	V HC
1	1	1976	J.Morgan	472	114	1	587	151	30	5	27	.320	.453	.576	1,029	1,062	60	9	68	10	20	1,160	132.8
2	2	1975	J.Morgan	498	132	3	633	163	27	6	17	.327	.471	.508	979	990	67	10	70	10	40	1,110	128.1
3	4	1973	J.Morgan	576	111	4	691	167	35	2	26	.290	.408	.493	901	909	67	15	51	10	40	1,009	106.7
4	3	1974	J.Morgan	512	120	3	635	150	31	3	22	.293	.430	.494	924	939	58	12	51	10	20	1,019	101.0
5	5	1972	J.Morgan	552	115	6	673	161	23	4	16	.292	.419	.435	854	884	58	17	34	10	30	957	91.8
6	6	1977	J.Morgan	521	117	2	640	150	21	6	22	.288	.420	.478	898	872	49	10	43	10	30	955	82.2
7	8	1905	M.Huggins	564	103	7	674	154	11	8	1	.273	.392	.326	718	783	27			10	60	853	56.7
8	7	1906	M.Huggins	545	71	3	619	159	11	7	0	.292	.376	.338	714	813	41			10	40	863	55.1
9	10	1965	P.Rose	670	69	8	747	209	35	11	11	.312	.383	.446	829	852	8	3	3	10	(30)	834	53.1
10	9	1939	L.Frey	484	72	4	560	141	27	9	11	.291	.388	.452	840	822	5			10	20	852	46.9
11	16	1966	P.Rose	654	37	1	692	205	38	5	16	.313	.351	.460	811	819	4	9	(19)	10		810	41.2
12	15	1918	L.Magee	459	28	0	487	133	22	13	0	.290	.331	.394	725	802	19			10		812	37.5
13	14	1904	M.Huggins	491	88	2	581	129	12	7	2	.263	.377	.328	705	792	13			10	10	812	37.0
14	13	1914	H.Groh	455	64	13	532	131	18	4	2	.288	.391	.358	749	812	24			10	(10)	812	33.9
15	11	1902	H.Peitz	387	24	9	420	122	22	5	1	.315	.369	.406	775	867	7			(10)	(30)	827	32.7
16	18	1999	P.Reese	585	35	6	626	167	37	5	10	.285	.332	.417	749	685	38	7	36	10	60	792	31.7
17	20	1942	L.Frey	523	87	2	612	139	23	6	2	.266	.373	.344	717	765	9			10	10	785	30.7
18	12	1990	M.Duncan	435	24	4	463	133	22	11	10	.306	.348	.476	824	822	13	7	(2)	10	(10)	820	29.8
19	21	1998	B.Boone	583	48	4	635	155	38	1	24	.266	.326	.458	784	746	6	4	(3)	10	30	783	29.6
20	19	1994	B.Boone	381	24	8	413	122	25	2	12	.320	.373	.491	864	813	3	4	(11)	10	(20)	791	29.6
21	17	1979	J.Morgan	436	93	1	530	109	26	1	9	.250	.383	.376	759	753	28	6	29	10	10	801	29.3
22	22	1931	T.Cuccinello	575	54	0	629	181	39	11	2	.315	.374	.431	805	788	1				(10)	778	29.2
23	29	1959	J.Temple	598	72	2	672	186	35	6	8	.311	.387	.430	817	793	14	3	11	10	(50)	764	26.6
24	28	1940	L.Frey	563	80	3	646	150	23	6	8	.266	.361	.371	732	736	22			10	20	766	26.1
25	26	1981	R.Oester	354	42	0	396	96	16	7	5	.271	.348	.398	747	768	2	5	(19)	10	10	769	24.0

Cincinnati Reds
Shortstops

V	R	Year	Name	AB	BB	HBP	TAB	H	2B	3B	HR	BA	OB	SA	PRO	Wtd PRO	SB	CS	SBF	SPF	FF	R TF	V HC
1	1	1996	B.Larkin	517	96	7	620	154	32	4	33	.298	.415	.567	981	935	36	10	24	10	40	1,009	102.5
2	3	1995	B.Larkin	496	61	3	560	158	29	6	15	.319	.396	.492	888	846	51	5	69	10	30	955	88.1
3	2	1991	B.Larkin	464	55	3	522	140	27	4	20	.302	.379	.506	886	904	24	6	22	10	70	1,005	85.4
4	4	1992	B.Larkin	533	63	4	600	162	32	6	12	.304	.382	.454	836	860	15	4	11	10	40	921	74.0
5	5	1988	B.Larkin	588	41	8	637	174	32	5	12	.296	.350	.429	779	814	40	7	39	10	30	893	70.1
6	6	1998	B.Larkin	538	79	2	619	166	34	10	17	.309	.399	.504	903	859	26	3	31	10	(10)	890	67.1
7	9	1990	B.Larkin	614	49	7	670	185	25	6	7	.301	.360	.396	755	754	30	5	28	10	60	853	60.8
8	13	1994	B.Larkin	427	64	0	491	119	23	5	9	.279	.373	.419	792	745	26	2	42	10	40	838	58.1
9	10	1976	D.Concepcion	576	49	1	626	162	28	7	9	.281	.339	.401	740	763	21	10	2	10	70	845	54.5
10	12	1974	D.Concepcion	594	44	6	644	167	25	1	14	.281	.337	.397	734	746	41	6	43	10	40	838	54.1
11	11	1965	L.Cardenas	557	60	1	618	160	25	11	11	.287	.358	.431	788	810	1	4	(11)	10	30	839	52.3
12	16	1981	D.Concepcion	421	37	1	459	129	28	0	5	.306	.364	.409	772	795	4	5	(12)	10	20	812	49.8
13	14	1979	D.Concepcion	590	64	0	654	166	25	3	16	.281	.352	.415	767	760	19	7	7	10	40	818	48.5
14	15	1978	D.Concepcion	565	51	1	617	170	33	4	6	.301	.360	.405	765	778	23	10	5	10	20	813	44.3
15	7	1993	B.Larkin	384	51	1	436	121	20	3	8	.315	.397	.445	842	815	14	1	26	10	20	871	43.5
16	18	1982	D.Concepcion	572	45	0	617	164	25	4	5	.287	.339	.371	709	720	13	6	2	10	70	802	41.2
17	8	1913	J.Tinker	382	20	1	403	121	20	13	1	.317	.352	.445	797	829	10		(10)		40	859	39.8
18	19	1914	B.Herzog	498	42	9	549	140	14	8	1	.281	.348	.347	695	754	46			10	30	794	36.3
19	20	1956	R.McMillan	479	76	5	560	126	16	7	3	.263	.370	.344	714	695	4	3	(3)		90	782	33.7
20	24	1999	B.Larkin	583	93	2	678	171	30	4	12	.293	.392	.420	813	743	30	8	20	10	(10)	763	32.6
21	22	1977	D.Concepcion	572	46	0	618	155	26	3	8	.271	.325	.369	694	674	29	7	23	10	60	767	30.9
22	23	1947	E.Miller	545	49	4	598	146	38	4	19	.268	.333	.457	790	765	5					765	30.8
23	17	2000	B.Larkin	396	48	1	445	124	26	5	11	.313	.389	.487	876	799	14	6	4	10	(10)	804	30.0
24	21	1975	D.Concepcion	507	39	2	548	139	23	1	5	.274	.328	.353	682	689	33	6	36	10	40	775	29.6
25	25	1966	L.Cardenas	568	45	1	614	145	25	4	20	.255	.311	.419	730	737	9	4	2	10	10	759	28.3

Cincinnati Reds
Third basemen

V	R	Year	Name	AB	BB	HBP	TAB	H	2B	3B	HR	BA	OB	SA	PRO	Wtd PRO	SB	CS	SBF	SPF	FF	R TF	V HC
1	1	1917	H.Groh	599	71	8	678	182	39	11	1	.304	.385	.411	796	887	15			10	60	957	81.9
2	2	1970	T.Perez	587	83	4	674	186	28	6	40	.317	.405	.589	994	970	8	3	3	(10)	(20)	942	72.6
3	4	1918	H.Groh	493	54	7	554	158	28	3	1	.320	.395	.396	791	875	11			10	40	925	70.3
4	3	1919	H.Groh	448	56	4	508	139	17	11	5	.310	.392	.431	823	896	21			10	30	936	61.6
5	9	1976	P.Rose	665	86	6	757	215	42	6	10	.323	.406	.450	855	883	9	5	(1)	10	(10)	881	59.5
6	6	1916	H.Groh	553	84	4	641	149	24	14	2	.269	.370	.374	744	831	13			10	60	901	59.4
7	8	1969	T.Perez	629	63	2	694	185	31	2	37	.294	.360	.526	886	907	4	2	0	(10)	(10)	887	56.4
8	5	1903	H.Steinfeldt	439	47	6	492	137	32	12	6	.312	.386	.481	867	901	6				20	921	55.6
9	7	1991	C.Sabo	582	44	6	632	175	35	3	26	.301	.356	.505	861	878	19	6	10	10	(10)	889	52.0
10	11	1990	C.Sabo	567	61	4	632	153	38	2	25	.270	.345	.476	821	820	25	10	7	10	20	857	42.5
11	12	1908	H.Lobert	570	46	2	618	167	17	18	4	.293	.348	.407	755	881	47			10	(40)	851	41.7
12	10	1988	C.Sabo	538	29	6	573	146	40	2	11	.271	.316	.414	730	764	46	14	30	10	60	864	40.2
13	13	1915	H.Groh	587	50	9	646	170	32	9	3	.290	.354	.390	745	821	12	17	(32)	10	40	839	39.8
14	14	1968	T.Perez	625	51	6	682	176	25	7	18	.282	.342	.430	772	848	3	2	(1)	(10)		836	39.0
15	15	1965	D.Johnson	616	52	2	670	177	30	7	32	.287	.345	.515	859	883	0	4	(11)	(10)	(30)	832	36.9
16	17	1940	B.Werber	584	68	8	660	162	35	5	12	.277	.361	.416	777	781	16			10	30	821	34.7
17	16	1957	D.Hoak	529	74	4	607	155	39	2	19	.293	.384	.482	866	844	8	15	(34)	10	10	830	34.6
18	25	1975	P.Rose	662	89	11	762	210	47	4	7	.317	.407	.432	839	848	0	1	(2)	10	(60)	796	28.9
19	20	1986	B.Bell	568	73	5	646	158	29	3	20	.278	.365	.445	811	813	2	8	(20)		10	802	26.5
20	21	1967	T.Perez	600	33	4	637	174	28	7	26	.290	.331	.490	821	859	0	3	(9)	(10)	(40)	800	25.4
21	26	1920	H.Groh	550	60	8	618	164	28	12	0	.298	.375	.393	768	799	16	19	(34)	10	20	795	24.4
22	29	1927	C.Dressen	548	71	3	622	160	36	10	2	.292	.376	.405	781	761	7			10	20	791	23.2
23	32	1939	B.Werber	599	91	6	696	173	35	5	5	.289	.388	.389	777	761	15			10	10	781	22.5
24	34	1977	P.Rose	655	66	5	726	204	38	7	9	.311	.379	.432	811	787	16	4	10	10	(30)	778	21.3
25	28	1902	H.Steinfeldt	479	24	3	506	133	20	7	1	.278	.316	.355	671	751	12				40	791	20.8

Cincinnati Reds
Outfielders

V	R	Year	Name	AB	BB	HBP	TAB	H	2B	3B	HR	BA	OB	SA	PRO	Wtd PRO	SB	CS	SBF	SPF	FF	R TF	V HC
1	1	1905	C.Seymour	581	51	2	634	219	40	21	8	.377	.429	.559	988	1,078	21			10	40	1,128	117.9
2	3	1962	F.Robinson	609	76	11	696	208	51	2	39	.342	.424	.624	1,048	1,024	18	9	0	10	30	1,064	101.8
3	4	1961	F.Robinson	545	71	10	626	176	32	7	37	.323	.411	.611	1,022	981	22	3	24	10	30	1,045	90.3
4	2	1987	E.Davis	474	84	1	559	139	23	4	37	.293	.401	.593	994	956	50	6	64	10	60	1,090	88.5
5	9	1977	G.Foster	615	61	5	681	197	31	2	52	.320	.386	.631	1,017	988	6	4	(3)	10	20	1,015	83.5
6	8	1964	F.Robinson	568	79	9	656	174	38	6	29	.306	.399	.548	947	973	23	5	19	10	20	1,022	82.6
7	10	1969	P.Rose	627	88	5	720	218	33	11	16	.348	.432	.512	944	966	7	10	(17)	10	30	989	79.3
8	14	1902	S.Crawford	555	47	1	603	185	16	23	3	.333	.386	.461	848	948	16			10	20	978	73.4
9	15	1965	F.Robinson	582	70	18	670	172	33	5	33	.296	.388	.540	928	953	13	9	(7)	10	20	976	69.8
10	12	1903	M.Donlin	496	56	3	555	174	25	18	7	.351	.420	.516	936	973	26			10		983	69.0
11	13	1901	S.Crawford	515	37	3	555	170	20	16	16	.330	.378	.524	903	952	13			10	20	982	68.9
12	6	1994	K.Mitchell	310	59	3	372	101	18	1	30	.326	.438	.681	1,119	1,053	2	0	5	(10)	(20)	1,028	67.9
13	19	1963	V.Pinson	652	36	1	689	204	37	14	22	.313	.350	.514	864	909	27	8	15	10	30	964	67.7
14	20	1968	P.Rose	626	56	4	686	210	42	6	10	.335	.394	.470	863	948	3	7	(15)	10	20	963	67.0
15	24	1965	V.Pinson	669	43	7	719	204	34	10	22	.305	.353	.484	838	861	21	8	7	10	70	947	65.0
16	16	1995	R.Sanders	484	69	8	561	148	36	6	28	.306	.401	.579	980	933	36	12	20	10	10	973	64.9
17	31	1959	V.Pinson	648	55	1	704	205	47	9	20	.316	.371	.509	880	854	21	6	12	10	60	937	63.2
18	5	1986	E.Davis	415	68	1	484	115	15	3	27	.277	.380	.523	903	905	80	11	113	10		1,029	62.6
19	27	1957	F.Robinson	611	44	12	667	197	29	5	29	.322	.379	.529	908	885	10	2	9	10	40	944	62.3
20	25	1956	F.Robinson	572	64	20	656	166	27	6	38	.290	.381	.558	939	914	8	4	0	10	20	944	61.4
21	21	1976	G.Foster	562	52	4	618	172	21	9	29	.306	.369	.530	899	928	17	3	17	10		955	58.1
22	33	1981	G.Foster	414	51	3	468	122	23	2	22	.295	.376	.519	895	921	4	0	8			929	58.1
23	11	1989	E.Davis	462	68	1	531	130	14	2	34	.281	.375	.541	916	951	21	7	12	10	10	983	57.1
24	34	1978	G.Foster	604	70	7	681	170	26	7	40	.281	.363	.546	909	925	4	4	(6)	10		929	55.7
25	7	1987	K.Daniels	368	60	1	429	123	24	1	26	.334	.429	.617	1,046	1,006	26	8	22	10	(10)	1,028	55.3

Cincinnati Reds Outfielders

V	R	Year	Name	AB	BB	HBP	TAB	H	2B	3B	HR	BA	OB	SA	PRO	Wtd PRO	SB	CS	SBF	SPF	FF	R TF	V HC
26	29	2000	K.Griffey Jr.	520	94	9	623	141	22	3	40	.271	.392	.556	947	864	6	4	(3)	10	70	941	54.6
27	26	1909	M.Mitchell	523	57	0	580	162	17	17	4	.310	.378	.430	808	914	37			10	20	944	54.2
28	23	1904	C.Seymour	531	29	3	563	166	26	13	5	.313	.352	.439	790	889	11			10	50	949	53.9
29	22	1917	E.Roush	522	27	5	554	178	19	14	4	.341	.379	.454	833	929	21			10	10	949	53.2
30	18	1988	E.Davis	472	65	3	540	129	18	3	26	.273	.365	.489	854	893	35	3	51	10	10	964	53.2
31	37	1938	I.Goodman	568	53	15	636	166	27	10	30	.292	.368	.533	901	903	3			10	10	923	52.6
32	40	1903	C.Seymour	558	33	3	594	191	25	15	7	.342	.382	.478	861	895	25			10	10	915	51.5
33	41	1985	D.Parker	635	52	3	690	198	42	4	34	.312	.367	.551	918	932	5	13	(29)		10	913	51.3
34	30	1918	E.Roush	435	22	2	459	145	18	10	5	.333	.368	.455	823	911	24			10	20	941	51.2
35	47	1973	P.Rose	680	65	6	751	230	36	8	5	.338	.401	.437	838	845	10	7	(5)	10	50	900	50.9
36	36	1919	E.Roush	504	42	6	552	162	19	12	4	.321	.380	.431	811	883	20			10	30	923	50.5
37	32	1988	K.Daniels	495	87	3	585	144	29	1	18	.291	.400	.463	863	902	27	6	24	10		936	49.9
38	44	1955	W.Post	601	60	2	663	186	33	3	40	.309	.374	.574	948	908	7	4	(1)			907	49.6
39	51	1972	P.Rose	645	73	7	725	198	31	11	6	.307	.383	.417	801	829	10	3	5	10	50	894	49.5
40	43	1961	V.Pinson	607	39	1	647	208	34	8	16	.343	.383	.504	887	852	23	10	4	10	40	907	48.4
41	17	1970	B.Carbo	365	94	4	463	113	19	3	21	.310	.456	.551	1,006	981	10	4	4		(20)	965	45.9
42	46	1920	E.Roush	579	42	3	624	196	22	16	4	.339	.386	.453	839	872	36	24	(18)	10	40	904	45.8
43	50	1932	B.Herman	577	60	0	637	188	38	19	16	.326	.389	.541	930	907	7			10	(20)	897	44.5
44	39	1963	F.Robinson	482	81	14	577	125	19	3	21	.259	.381	.442	823	866	26	10	10	10	30	916	43.6
45	56	1970	P.Rose	649	73	2	724	205	37	9	15	.316	.387	.470	857	835	12	7	(3)	10	40	883	43.2
46	38	1939	I.Goodman	470	54	7	531	152	37	16	7	.323	.401	.515	916	897	2			10	10	917	42.4
47	48	1976	K.Griffey	562	62	1	625	189	28	9	6	.336	.403	.450	853	881	34	11	18	10	(10)	899	42.1
48	53	1970	B.Tolan	589	62	8	659	186	34	6	16	.316	.388	.475	864	842	57	20	24	10	10	887	40.6
49	42	1995	R.Gant	410	74	3	487	113	19	4	29	.276	.390	.554	944	899	23	8	14	10	(10)	913	40.5
50	35	1979	G.Foster	440	59	3	502	133	18	3	30	.302	.388	.561	950	942	0	2	(8)	(10)		924	39.9
51	57	1958	F.Robinson	554	62	7	623	149	25	6	31	.269	.350	.504	854	820	10	1	12	10	40	882	38.9
52	28	1904	M.Donlin	368	28	4	400	121	18	10	3	.329	.383	.457	839	943	2			10	(10)	943	37.2
53	54	1923	E.Roush	527	46	3	576	185	41	18	6	.351	.406	.531	938	898	10	15	(33)	10	10	885	36.9
54	58	1907	M.Mitchell	558	37	3	598	163	17	12	3	.292	.339	.382	721	826	17			10	40	876	35.7
55	63	1962	V.Pinson	619	45	4	668	181	31	7	23	.292	.344	.477	821	803	26	8	14	10	40	867	34.8
56	45	1996	E.Davis	415	70	6	491	119	20	0	26	.287	.397	.523	920	876	23	9	10	10	10	906	34.8
57	64	1969	B.Tolan	637	27	15	679	194	25	10	21	.305	.348	.474	822	841	26	12	3	10	10	863	34.3
58	78	1974	P.Rose	652	106	5	763	185	45	7	3	.284	.388	.388	776	788	2	4	(7)	10	60	851	33.9
59	59	1980	K.Griffey	544	62	1	607	160	28	10	13	.294	.367	.454	821	832	23	1	33	10		875	33.9
60	49	1975	G.Foster	463	40	3	506	139	24	4	23	.300	.360	.518	878	888	2	1	0	10		898	33.9
61	55	1976	C.Geronimo	486	56	6	548	149	24	11	2	.307	.385	.414	799	824	22	5	21	10	30	885	33.3
62	52	1990	E.Davis	453	60	2	515	118	26	2	24	.260	.350	.486	835	834	21	3	28	10	20	891	32.9
63	61	1980	G.Foster	528	75	1	604	144	21	5	25	.273	.364	.473	838	848	1	0	2		20	870	32.4
64	79	1960	V.Pinson	652	47	5	704	187	37	12	20	.287	.339	.472	812	807	32	12	11	10	20	848	31.9
65	75	1971	P.Rose	632	68	3	703	192	27	4	13	.304	.374	.421	795	819	13	9	(7)	10	30	853	31.9
66	69	1906	C.Seymour	576	42	4	622	165	19	5	8	.286	.339	.378	718	817	29			10	30	857	31.1
67	77	1967	V.Pinson	650	26	3	679	187	28	13	18	.288	.318	.454	772	807	26	8	14	10	20	851	30.3
68	66	1991	P.O'Neill	532	73	1	606	136	36	0	28	.256	.347	.481	828	844	12	7	(3)		20	861	30.0
69	71	1967	P.Rose	585	56	3	644	176	32	8	12	.301	.365	.444	809	846	11	6	(1)	10		855	29.9
70	67	1943	E.Tipton	493	85	2	580	142	26	7	9	.288	.395	.424	819	860	1					860	29.8
71	73	1977	K.Griffey	585	69	0	654	186	35	8	12	.318	.390	.467	857	832	17	8	1	10	10	853	29.8
72	65	1992	B.Roberts	532	62	2	596	172	34	6	4	.323	.396	.432	828	852	44	16	19	10	(20)	861	29.5
73	80	1936	K.Cuyler	567	47	2	616	185	29	11	7	.326	.380	.453	833	815	16			10	20	845	26.9
74	85	1953	G.Bell	610	48	3	661	183	37	5	30	.300	.354	.525	879	830	0	2	(6)		10	835	25.6
75	62	1921	E.Roush	418	31	5	454	147	27	12	4	.352	.403	.502	905	868	19	17	(31)	10	20	867	25.0

Cincinnati Reds
Starting Pitchers

V	R	Year	Name	G	GS	IP	W	L	SV	SO	BB	ERA	RA/9	R Wtd RA/9	V Runs /162
1	2	1923	D.Luque	41	37	322	27	8	2	151	88	1.93	2.52	2.36	82.8
2	5	1939	B.Walters	39	36	319	27	11	0	137	109	2.29	2.76	2.80	65.5
3	13	1902	N.Hahn	36	36	321	23	12	0	142	58	1.77	2.72	3.07	61.4
4	7	1940	B.Walters	36	36	305	22	10	0	115	92	2.48	2.80	2.90	59.1
5	1	1915	F.Toney	36	23	223	17	6	2	108	73	1.58	1.86	2.32	58.2
6	3	1993	J.Rijo	36	36	257	14	9	0	227	62	2.48	2.66	2.68	53.5
7	10	1925	D.Luque	36	36	291	16	18	0	140	78	2.63	3.37	2.99	53.4
8	9	1947	E.Blackwell	33	33	273	22	8	0	193	95	2.47	3.00	2.94	51.6
9	4	1977	T.Seaver	33	33	261	21	6	0	196	66	2.58	2.69	2.79	51.4
10	12	1925	E.Rixey	39	36	287	21	11	1	69	47	2.88	3.42	3.03	51.2
11	16	1944	B.Walters	34	32	285	23	8	1	77	87	2.40	2.91	3.10	48.6
12	21	1925	P.Donohue	42	38	301	21	14	2	78	49	3.08	3.65	3.24	46.5
13	27	1938	P.Derringer	41	37	307	21	14	3	132	49	2.93	3.22	3.30	44.9
14	39	1923	E.Rixey	42	37	309	20	15	1	97	65	2.80	3.61	3.38	42.6
15	19	1919	D.Ruether	33	29	243	19	6	0	78	83	1.82	2.56	3.20	42.2
16	17	1919	S.Sallee	29	28	228	21	7	0	24	20	2.06	2.49	3.12	42.2
17	15	1965	J.Maloney	33	33	255	20	9	0	244	110	2.54	2.72	3.08	42.0
18	91	1901	N.Hahn	42	42	375	22	19	0	239	69	2.71	3.81	3.71	40.8
19	65	1900	N.Hahn	39	37	311	16	20	0	132	89	3.27	4.19	3.54	40.6
20	30	1942	R.Starr	37	33	277	15	13	0	83	106	2.67	2.86	3.33	39.6
21	45	1941	B.Walters	37	35	302	19	15	2	129	88	2.83	3.22	3.44	39.6
22	11	1941	E.Riddle	33	22	217	19	4	1	80	59	2.24	2.82	3.01	39.2
23	63	1903	N.Hahn	34	34	296	22	12	0	127	47	2.52	3.80	3.53	38.9
24	28	1929	R.Lucas	32	32	270	19	12	0	72	58	3.60	3.97	3.33	38.9
25	38	1909	A.Fromme	37	34	279	19	13	2	126	101	1.90	2.71	3.37	38.6
26	47	1940	P.Derringer	37	37	297	20	12	0	115	48	3.06	3.33	3.45	38.5
27	51	1939	P.Derringer	38	35	301	25	7	0	128	35	2.93	3.44	3.49	37.5
28	52	1904	N.Hahn	35	34	298	16	18	0	98	35	2.06	3.08	3.49	37.1
29	20	1981	T.Seaver	23	23	166	14	2	0	87	66	2.54	2.76	3.23	37.0
30	8	1944	E.Heusser	30	23	193	13	11	2	42	42	2.38	2.75	2.93	36.7
31	22	1924	E.Rixey	35	29	238	15	14	1	57	47	2.76	3.25	3.25	36.4
32	46	1962	B.Purkey	37	37	288	23	5	0	141	64	2.81	3.41	3.44	35.8
33	42	1920	D.Ruether	37	33	266	16	12	3	99	96	2.47	2.94	3.42	35.4
34	6	1972	G.Nolan	25	25	176	15	5	0	90	30	1.99	2.45	2.87	34.7
35	33	1952	K.Raffensberger	38	33	247	17	13	1	93	45	2.81	3.10	3.36	34.7
36	85	1907	B.Ewing	41	37	333	17	19	0	147	85	1.73	2.81	3.67	34.6
37	34	1942	J.Vander Meer	33	33	244	18	12	0	186	102	2.43	2.88	3.36	34.2
38	49	1932	R.Lucas	31	31	269	13	17	0	63	35	2.94	3.51	3.48	33.7
39	68	1926	C.Mays	39	33	281	19	12	1	58	53	3.14	3.59	3.56	32.9
40	43	1982	M.Soto	35	34	258	14	13	0	274	71	2.79	3.07	3.43	32.3
41	53	1983	M.Soto	34	34	274	17	13	0	242	95	2.70	3.16	3.50	32.3
42	56	1950	E.Blackwell	40	32	261	17	15	4	188	112	2.97	3.62	3.50	32.2
43	55	1943	E.Riddle	36	33	260	21	11	3	69	107	2.63	3.01	3.50	32.1
44	25	1964	J.O'Toole	30	30	220	17	7	0	145	51	2.66	2.90	3.27	31.4
45	23	1920	D.Luque	37	23	208	13	9	1	72	60	2.51	2.81	3.27	31.4
46	54	1988	D.Jackson	35	35	261	23	8	0	161	71	2.73	2.97	3.50	30.7
47	31	1966	J.Maloney	32	32	225	16	8	0	216	90	2.80	3.00	3.33	30.6
48	24	1919	J.Ring	32	18	183	10	9	3	61	51	2.26	2.61	3.27	30.3
49	48	1911	B.Keefe	39	26	234	12	13	3	105	76	2.69	3.38	3.45	30.2
50	18	1990	J.Rijo	29	29	197	14	8	0	152	78	2.70	2.97	3.20	29.7

**Cincinnati Reds
Starting Pitchers**

V	R	Year	Name	G	GS	IP	W	L	SV	SO	BB	ERA	RA/9	R Wtd RA/9	V Runs /162
51	78	1919	H.Eller	38	30	248	19	9	2	137	50	2.39	2.90	3.63	29.5
52	29	1995	P.Schourek	29	29	190	18	7	0	160	45	3.22	3.40	3.33	29.1
53	88	1943	J.Vander Meer	36	36	289	15	16	0	174	162	2.87	3.18	3.70	29.1
54	72	1961	J.O'Toole	39	35	253	19	9	2	178	93	3.10	3.59	3.58	28.9
55	26	1946	E.Blackwell	33	25	194	9	13	0	100	79	2.45	2.88	3.29	28.7
56	44	1967	G.Nolan	33	32	227	14	8	0	206	62	2.58	2.89	3.43	28.4
57	81	1910	G.Suggs	35	30	266	20	12	3	91	48	2.40	3.25	3.65	28.3
58	66	1927	R.Lucas	37	23	240	18	11	2	51	39	3.38	3.60	3.55	28.2
59	40	1964	J.Maloney	31	31	216	15	10	0	214	83	2.71	3.00	3.38	28.2
60	32	1998	P.Harnisch	32	32	209	14	7	0	157	64	3.14	3.40	3.35	28.1
61	35	1992	J.Rijo	33	33	211	15	10	0	171	44	2.56	2.86	3.36	28.1
62	103	1922	E.Rixey	40	38	313	25	13	0	80	45	3.53	4.20	3.79	28.1
63	96	1912	A.Fromme	43	37	296	16	18	0	120	88	2.74	3.83	3.75	27.8
64	101	1921	E.Rixey	40	37	301	19	18	1	76	66	2.78	3.83	3.78	27.4
65	36	1991	J.Rijo	30	30	204	15	6	0	172	55	2.51	3.04	3.36	27.1
66	62	1941	J.Vander Meer	33	32	226	16	13	0	202	126	2.82	3.31	3.53	27.1
67	14	1988	J.Rijo	49	19	162	13	8	0	160	63	2.39	2.61	3.07	26.7
68	89	1918	H.Eller	37	22	218	16	12	1	84	59	2.36	2.93	3.70	26.5
69	75	1963	J.Maloney	33	33	250	23	7	0	265	88	2.77	3.02	3.60	26.5
70	70	1937	L.Grissom	50	30	224	12	17	6	149	93	3.26	3.58	3.57	25.8
71	41	1946	J.Beggs	28	22	190	12	10	1	38	39	2.32	2.98	3.40	25.6
72	58	1971	D.Gullett	35	31	218	16	6	0	107	64	2.65	3.01	3.51	25.4
73	107	1928	E.Rixey	43	37	291	19	18	2	58	67	3.43	3.93	3.81	25.4
74	99	1973	J.Billingham	40	40	293	19	10	0	155	95	3.04	3.44	3.78	25.4
75	113	1912	G.Suggs	42	36	303	19	16	3	104	56	2.94	3.92	3.84	25.3
76	71	1904	T.Walker	24	24	217	15	8	0	64	53	2.24	3.15	3.57	25.0
77	102	1910	H.Gaspar	48	31	275	15	17	7	74	75	2.59	3.37	3.78	24.9
78	115	1921	D.Luque	41	36	304	17	19	3	102	64	3.38	3.91	3.86	24.9
79	87	1922	P.Donohue	33	30	242	18	9	1	66	43	3.12	4.09	3.69	24.5
80	90	1961	J.Jay	34	34	247	21	10	0	157	92	3.53	3.72	3.71	24.5
81	77	1959	D.Newcombe	30	29	222	13	8	1	100	27	3.16	3.53	3.61	24.4
82	110	1906	B.Ewing	33	32	288	13	14	0	145	60	2.38	3.06	3.83	24.4
83	86	1970	G.Nolan	37	37	251	18	7	0	181	96	3.27	3.66	3.68	24.4
84	121	1906	J.Weimer	41	39	305	20	14	1	141	99	2.22	3.10	3.88	24.1
85	61	1975	G.Nolan	32	32	211	15	9	0	74	29	3.16	3.20	3.53	24.1
86	82	1938	J.Vander Meer	32	29	225	15	10	0	125	103	3.12	3.56	3.65	23.8
87	69	1992	G.Swindell	31	30	214	12	8	0	138	41	2.70	3.03	3.56	23.7
88	98	1955	J.Nuxhall	50	33	257	17	12	3	98	78	3.47	3.78	3.77	23.7
89	37	1945	B.Walters	22	22	168	10	10	0	45	51	2.68	3.32	3.37	23.3
90	50	1940	J.Turner	24	23	187	14	7	0	53	32	2.89	3.37	3.49	23.3
91	60	1976	P.Zachry	38	28	204	14	7	0	143	83	2.74	3.09	3.53	23.3
92	124	1916	F.Toney	41	38	300	14	17	1	146	78	2.28	2.94	3.89	23.2
93	76	1963	J.Nuxhall	35	29	217	15	8	2	169	39	2.61	3.03	3.61	22.7
94	59	1999	P.Harnisch	33	33	198	16	10	0	120	57	3.68	3.90	3.53	22.7
95	80	1928	R.Kolp	44	24	209	13	10	3	61	55	3.19	3.75	3.64	22.5
96	67	1919	R.Fisher	26	20	174	14	5	1	41	38	2.17	2.84	3.56	22.4
97	108	1922	D.Luque	39	33	261	13	23	1	79	72	3.31	4.24	3.83	22.3
98	94	1994	J.Rijo	26	26	172	9	6	0	171	52	3.08	3.81	3.73	22.3
99	135	1905	B.Ewing	40	34	312	20	11	0	164	79	2.51	3.61	3.95	22.0
100	131	1904	J.Harper	35	35	294	23	9	0	125	85	2.30	3.46	3.92	21.8

Cincinnati Reds
Relief Pitchers

V	R	Year	Name	G	GS	IP	W	L	SV	SO	BB	ERA	RA/9	R Wtd RA/9	V Runs /162
1	1	1967	T.Abernathy	70	0	106	6	3	28	88	41	1.27	1.61	1.91	31.2
2	2	1990	R.Dibble	68	0	98	8	3	11	136	34	1.74	2.02	2.18	25.9
3	16	1973	P.Borbon	80	0	121	11	4	14	60	35	2.16	2.45	2.69	25.1
4	7	1978	D.Bair	70	0	100	7	6	28	91	38	1.97	2.06	2.34	24.7
5	38	1979	T.Hume	57	12	163	10	9	17	80	33	2.76	2.98	3.21	24.4
6	8	1989	R.Dibble	74	0	99	10	5	2	141	39	2.09	2.09	2.42	23.5
7	9	1997	J.Shaw	78	0	95	4	2	42	74	12	2.38	2.47	2.43	22.4
8	3	1988	J.Franco	70	0	86	6	6	39	46	27	1.57	1.88	2.21	22.4
9	13	1974	C.Carroll	57	3	101	12	5	6	46	30	2.15	2.41	2.65	21.4
10	5	1998	J.Shaw	73	0	85	3	8	48	55	19	2.12	2.33	2.29	21.4
11	10	1999	S.Williamson	62	0	93	12	7	19	107	43	2.41	2.80	2.53	21.0
12	47	1990	N.Charlton	56	16	154	12	9	2	117	70	2.74	3.09	3.33	21.0
13	4	1994	C.McElroy	52	0	58	1	2	5	38	15	2.34	2.34	2.29	20.6
14	26	1999	S.Sullivan	79	0	114	5	4	3	78	47	3.01	3.25	2.94	20.5
15	6	1940	J.Beggs	37	1	77	12	3	7	25	21	2.00	2.22	2.30	20.3
16	23	1976	R.Eastwick	71	0	108	11	5	26	70	27	2.09	2.51	2.87	20.3
17	21	1996	J.Shaw	78	0	105	8	6	4	69	29	2.49	2.92	2.83	20.2
18	18	1985	J.Franco	67	0	99	12	3	12	61	40	2.18	2.45	2.74	20.0
19	41	1980	T.Hume	78	0	137	9	10	25	68	38	2.56	2.89	3.27	19.6
20	12	1956	T.Acker	29	7	84	4	3	1	54	29	2.37	2.46	2.61	19.1
21	34	1964	S.Ellis	52	5	122	10	3	14	125	28	2.57	2.80	3.16	19.0
22	17	1994	J.Brantley	50	0	65	6	6	15	63	28	2.48	2.76	2.70	18.9
23	19	2000	D.Graves	66	0	91	10	5	30	53	42	2.56	3.05	2.75	18.4
24	31	1999	D.Graves	75	0	111	8	7	27	69	49	3.08	3.41	3.08	18.2
25	15	1990	R.Myers	66	0	87	4	6	31	98	38	2.08	2.49	2.68	18.1
26	28	1960	J.Brosnan	57	2	99	7	2	12	62	22	2.36	2.82	3.02	17.7
27	30	1966	B.McCool	57	0	105	8	8	18	104	41	2.48	2.74	3.05	17.6
28	39	1935	D.Brennan	38	5	114	5	5	5	48	44	3.15	3.39	3.24	17.6
29	27	1955	H.Freeman	54	0	93	7	4	11	38	31	2.11	2.97	2.96	17.3
30	25	1971	C.Carroll	61	0	94	10	4	15	64	42	2.50	2.49	2.90	17.3
31	29	1972	C.Carroll	65	0	96	6	4	37	51	32	2.25	2.59	3.03	17.1
32	24	1975	R.Eastwick	58	0	90	5	3	22	61	25	2.60	2.60	2.87	16.9
33	14	1994	H.Carrasco	45	0	56	5	6	6	41	30	2.24	2.72	2.67	16.7
34	35	1987	F.Williams	85	0	106	4	0	2	60	39	2.30	3.15	3.16	16.4
35	40	2000	S.Williamson	48	10	112	5	8	6	136	75	3.29	3.62	3.25	16.3
36	20	1995	J.Brantley	56	0	70	3	2	28	62	20	2.82	2.82	2.76	15.7
37	11	1996	J.Brantley	66	0	71	1	2	44	76	28	2.41	2.66	2.57	15.6
38	33	1975	C.Carroll	56	2	96	7	5	7	44	32	2.62	2.81	3.10	15.5
39	22	1987	J.Franco	68	0	82	8	5	32	61	27	2.52	2.85	2.86	15.5
40	54	1943	J.Beggs	39	4	115	7	6	6	28	25	2.34	2.97	3.45	14.8
41	57	1977	P.Borbon	73	0	127	10	5	18	48	24	3.19	3.40	3.52	14.6
42	32	1964	B.McCool	40	3	89	6	5	7	87	29	2.42	2.73	3.08	14.6
43	45	1970	C.Carroll	65	0	104	9	4	16	63	27	2.59	3.29	3.31	14.4
44	48	2000	S.Sullivan	79	0	106	3	6	3	96	38	3.47	3.72	3.35	14.3
45	42	1994	J.Ruffin	51	0	70	7	2	1	44	27	3.09	3.34	3.27	14.1
46	36	1975	W.McEnaney	70	0	91	5	2	15	48	23	2.47	2.87	3.17	14.1
47	51	1991	N.Charlton	39	11	108	3	5	1	77	34	2.91	3.07	3.40	13.9
48	46	1987	R.Murphy	87	0	101	8	5	3	99	32	3.04	3.31	3.32	13.9
49	53	1984	T.Power	78	0	109	9	7	11	81	46	2.82	3.06	3.42	13.8
50	43	1997	S.Sullivan	59	0	97	5	3	1	96	30	3.24	3.33	3.28	13.8

CLEVELAND INDIANS (1901–2000)

Throughout most of their history, the Indians were a relatively weak franchise, winning only three pennants and two World Series titles in their first eight decades. Cleveland fielded especially bad teams from 1960 to 1993. The Tribe finally put together a winning tradition beginning in 1994, and their future looks bright as they enter the new century.

The franchise was also very competitive at the start of the twentieth century, with six winning seasons in Cleveland's first eight years, including a ½ game out, second place finish in 1908. Cleveland was led by one of baseball's greatest talents ever in second baseman Nap Lajoie. Napoleon produced his best season with Cleveland in 1910, when he batted .384. Adjusted for a 14 percent hitter's deflation, Lajoie hit .437 with 264 hits that year, for a 1,091 Wtd. Production, a 1,171 Total Factor and an incredibly high 159.6 Hits Contribution. The Indians also featured Bill Bradley (.340 average in 1902), Elmer Flick (league-leading .308 average in 1905), and ace pitcher Addie Joss, who produced the second lowest career ERA in major league history at 1.89, while earning a 160–97 record in just nine years before his untimely death in 1911. Joss' best season was in 1908, when he went 24–11 with a sparkling 1.16 ERA, and a 2.80 Wtd. RA/9.

In 1911, 21-year-old Shoeless Joe Jackson hit .408 with 41 steals in his first full season. Adjusted for 1 percent hitter's deflation, Jackson batted .414 with a 1,103 Total Factor. Teammate Vean Gregg went 23–7 with a 1.80 ERA and team all-time best 2.42 Wtd. RA/9. In 1912, Shoeless Joe hit .395 with 26 triples and 35 steals. Adjusted for 4 percent hitter's deflation, Jackson batted .410, for a 1,074 Wtd. Production, a 1,104 Total Factor, and 110.9 Hits Contribution in his best season ever. The Indians finished in third place in 1911 and in 1913, but otherwise played under .500 from 1909 through 1915, and they even shipped Jackson off to the White Sox during the 1915 season.

Cleveland's fortunes improved in 1916 when they purchased the contract of superstar Tris Speaker to replace Jackson. The team reached .500 in 1916, with Speaker hitting for an inflation-adjusted .423 average, and the Indians then played winning ball for the next seven seasons. In addition to Speaker and Ray Chapman (.302, 52 steals in his best year in 1917), pitchers Stan Coveleski and Jim Bagby played key roles in the Tribe's success. In 1920, Bagby won 31 games and Coveleski added 24 wins, while Speaker hit .388 with a 1,042 Total Factor, leading the Tribe to their first pennant. Although Chapman died in a tragic beaning on August 16, 1920, the Indians were able to overcome his loss with the emergence of Joe Sewell at the same position.

The Indians remained competitive through the 1926 season due to the performances of player-manager Speaker (.380, 17 home runs, 1,077 Total Factor in 1923), Sewell (.353 average in 1923), George Burns (.358, 64 doubles, MVP Award in 1926), and pitcher George Uhle (27–11, 2.83 ERA in 1926). Thirty-nine-year-old Speaker was traded to Washington before the 1927 season, and the Indians dipped below .500 for two years.

The Tribe came back with 11 winning seasons over the 12 year period 1929–1940, led by hitters Earl Averill (.378, 28 home runs, 959 Wtd. Production in 1936), Hal Trosky (.330, 35 home runs in 1934), Joe Vosmik, and Odell Hale. The best pitchers were Wes Ferrell, Mel Harder, and Johnny Allen (15–1, 2.55 ERA, 2.44 Wtd. RA/9 in 1937). The best Indians team in this period was the 1940 squad, which finished one game behind Detroit in second place. This team featured slugger Trosky, 22-year-old Lou Boudreau, and 23-year-old Ken Keltner, but they received no help from slumping young star Jeff Heath and his .219 batting average. Twenty-one-year-old ace Bob Feller was 27–11 with a 2.61 ERA and a 2.59 Wtd. RA/9 to lead the pitching staff.

In 1948, the superb hitting and fielding of player-manager Lou Boudreau led the Indians to their first pennant in nearly three decades. Boudreau had a career year in home runs (18) and batting average (.355), for the league's fifth best shortstop performance ever with a 982 Total Factor and 105.7 Hits Contribution. Keltner and Joe Gordon each hit over 30 home runs, and 24-year-old rookie Larry Doby hit .301. Feller, Bob Lemon, and Gene Bearden led the pitching staff with a combined 59 wins.

The Indians played winning baseball in 12 of 13 seasons from 1947 to 1959, while often finishing 1-2-3 behind the Yankees and ahead of the White Sox. Al Rosen had a career year in 1953, hitting .336 with 43 home runs, for a 1,014 Wtd. Production. Cleveland's best season ever was in 1954, as the Tribe won 111 games against only 43 losses. Bobby Avila hit .341 to win the batting title, Doby led the league in home runs with 32, and Rosen displayed a .300 average and 24 home runs. Bob Lemon and Early Wynn each won 23 games to lead the league, Mike Garcia won 19, and 35-year-old Bob Feller produced his last effective season with a 13–3 record.

The Indians began a long slide into the second division in 1960, fielding losing teams in all but seven of their next 34 years, while playing in front of empty seats in huge, dreary Cleveland Stadium. The best players in this challenging period were Johnny Romano, Julio Franco, Graig Nettles, Buddy Bell, Luis Tiant, Doug Jones, and Gaylord Perry (24–16, 1.92 ERA, 2.71 Wtd. RA/9 in 1972). The most intriguing team was the 1968 squad that finished third, while boasting the league's best ERA, as Tiant went 21–9 with a league-leading 1.60 ERA and a 2.47 Wtd. RA/9, while Sam McDowell added a 15–14 record and a 1.81 ERA.

With the opening of Jacobs Field in 1994, a new era dawned for the Cleveland organization and its fans. The team began to win, and the fans came to see both the team and the wonderful new stadium. There was a sudden infusion of cash, and the team's owner was now able to compete in the new baseball economics for the best available players.

The Indians put together a strong second place showing in the new Central Division in 1994 before the players' strike ended the season after 113 games. Albert Belle had his best season, hitting .357 with 36 home runs for a 1,156 Production. Adjusted for 7 percent hitter's inflation and a 162 game schedule, Albert hit .333 with 48 home runs, for a 1,079 Wtd. Production, 1,053 Total Factor, and 94.6 Hits Contribution. Teammate Kenny Lofton led off for this powerful ball club, batting .349 with 60 stolen bases, for a 1,006 Total Factor.

The Tribe won five straight division titles from 1995 to 1999. The best of these teams was the 1995 squad that went 100–44, with a powerful lineup led by Belle, who hit .317 with 50 home runs and 103 extra base hits. After Belle left for the White Sox in 1997, Manny Ramirez took his place as the team's key slugger. Ramirez hit 45 home runs in 1998 and 44 home runs in 1999. In 2000, Manny batted .351 with 38 home runs in just 528 total at bats, for a 1,059 Wtd. Production and a 1,048 Total Factor.

Also contributing to these winning Indians teams were defensive whiz Omar Vizquel (.333, 42 steals in 1999), Jim Thome (.311, 123 walks, 38 home runs in 1996), and Roberto Alomar (.323, 24 home runs, 37 steals, 994 Total Factor and 98.3 Hits Contribution in 1999). Relievers Jose Mesa and Mike Jackson each achieved a special season that ranks as one of the best rates of success in history. Mesa was 3–0, with 46 saves, a 1.13 ERA, and a 1.13 Wtd. RA/9 in 1995. Jackson was 1–1, with 40 saves, a 1.55 ERA, and a 1.40 Wtd. RA/9 in 1998.

Cleveland Indians (1901–2000)

Cleveland Indians — Hitters Volume of Success

Pos	Year	Name	AB	BB	HBP	TAB	H	2B	3B	HR	BA	OB	SA	PRO	Wtd PRO	SB	CS	SBF	SPF	FF	R TF	V HC
C	1970	R.Fosse	450	39	1	490	138	17	1	18	.307	.363	.469	832	836	1	5	(17)	0	40	858	42.2
1B	1934	H.Trosky	625	58	2	685	206	45	9	35	.330	.388	.598	987	929	2	2	(3)	0	0	926	53.5
2B	1910	N.Lajoie	591	60	5	656	227	51	7	4	.384	.445	.514	960	1,091	26			0	80	1,171	159.6
SS	1948	L.Boudreau	560	98	2	660	199	34	6	18	.355	.453	.534	987	953	3	2	(1)	(10)	40	982	105.7
3B	1953	A.Rosen	599	85	4	688	201	27	5	43	.336	.422	.613	1,034	1,014	8	7	(8)	0	0	1,006	85.6
OF	1912	J.Jackson	572	54	12	638	226	44	26	3	.395	.458	.579	1,036	1,074	35			10	20	1,104	110.9
OF	1923	T.Speaker	574	93	4	671	218	59	11	17	.380	.469	.610	1,079	1,031	8	9	(14)	10	50	1,077	107.4
OF	1994	A.Belle	412	58	5	475	147	35	2	36	.357	.442	.714	1,156	1,079	9	6	(6)	0	(20)	1,053	94.6
Starters		Averages	548	68	4	620	195	39	8	22	.356	.432	.577	1,009	1,003	12	4	(6)	1	26	1,024	94.9
C	1961	J.Romano	509	61	5	575	152	29	1	21	.299	.379	.483	862	839	0	0	0	0	(10)	829	41.4
1B	1930	E.Morgan	584	62	1	647	204	47	11	26	.349	.413	.601	1,014	927	8	4	0	10	(10)	927	50.9
2B	1999	R.Alomar	563	99	7	669	182	40	3	24	.323	.430	.533	963	889	37	6	35	10	60	994	98.3
SS	1917	R.Chapman	563	61	0	624	170	28	13	2	.302	.370	.409	779	862	52			10	50	922	81.2
3B	1903	B.Bradley	536	25	3	564	168	36	22	6	.313	.348	.496	844	919	21			10	30	959	62.7
OF	1994	K.Lofton	459	52	2	513	160	32	9	12	.349	.417	.536	953	890	60	12	66	10	40	1,006	86.0
OF	1999	M.Ramirez	522	96	13	631	174	34	3	44	.333	.448	.663	1,111	1,025	2	4	(9)	0	0	1,016	77.8
OF	1958	R.Colavito	489	84	2	575	148	26	3	41	.303	.407	.620	1,027	1,025	0	2	(7)	(10)	10	1,018	75.2
Reserves		Averages	528	68	4	600	170	34	8	22	.321	.402	.542	944	922	23	4	11	5	21	959	71.7
Totals		Weighted Ave.	541	68	4	614	187	37	8	22	.345	.422	.566	988	976	15	4	(1)	3	25	1,003	87.2

Pitchers Volume of Success

Pos	Year	Name	G	GS	IP	W	L	SV	SO	BB	ERA	RA/9	Wtd RA/9	R Runs /162
SP	1946	B.Feller	48	42	371	26	15	4	348	153	2.18	2.45	2.72	79.5
SP	1972	G.Perry	41	40	343	24	16	1	234	82	1.92	2.07	2.71	74.0
SP	1908	A.Joss	42	35	325	24	11	2	130	30	1.16	2.13	2.80	66.8
SP	1911	V.Gregg	34	26	245	23	7	0	125	86	1.80	2.47	2.42	61.2
SP	1968	L.Tiant	34	32	258	21	9	0	264	73	1.60	1.85	2.47	60.0
Starters		Averages	40	35	308	24	12	1	220	85	1.75	2.20	2.65	68.3
RP	1979	S.Monge	76	0	131	12	10	19	108	64	2.40	2.54	2.45	30.6
RP	1995	J.Mesa	62	0	64	3	0	46	58	17	1.13	1.27	1.13	27.4
RP	1982	D.Spillner	65	0	134	12	10	21	90	45	2.49	2.96	3.00	23.2
RP	1998	M.Jackson	69	0	64	1	1	40	55	13	1.55	1.55	1.40	22.5
Relievers		Averages	68	0	98	7	5	32	78	35	2.09	2.32	2.25	25.9
Totals		Averages	108	35	407	31	17	33	298	120	1.83	2.23	2.55	94.2

Cleveland Indians **Hitters Rate of Success**

Pos	Year	Name	AB	BB	HBP	TAB	H	2B	3B	HR	BA	OB	SA	PRO	Wtd PRO	SB	CS	SBF	SPF	FF	R TF	V HC
C	1970	R.Fosse	450	39	1	490	138	17	1	18	.307	.363	.469	832	836	1	5	(17)	0	40	858	42.2
1B	1997	J.Thome	496	120	3	619	142	25	0	40	.286	.428	.579	1,007	950	1	1	(2)	0	(10)	939	49.8
2B	1910	N.Lajoie	591	60	5	656	227	51	7	4	.384	.445	.514	960	1,091	26			0	80	1,171	159.6
SS	1948	L.Boudreau	560	98	2	660	199	34	6	18	.355	.453	.534	987	953	3	2	(1)	(10)	40	982	105.7
3B	1953	A.Rosen	599	85	4	688	201	27	5	43	.336	.422	.613	1,034	1,014	8	7	(8)	0	0	1,006	85.6
OF	1912	J.Jackson	572	54	12	638	226	44	26	3	.395	.458	.579	1,036	1,074	35			10	20	1,104	110.9
OF	1922	T.Speaker	426	77	1	504	161	48	8	11	.378	.474	.606	1,080	1,022	8	3	4	10	60	1,096	85.4
OF	1994	A.Belle	412	58	5	475	147	35	2	36	.357	.442	.714	1,156	1,079	9	6	(6)	0	(20)	1,053	94.6
Starters		Averages	513	74	4	591	180	35	7	22	.351	.437	.573	1,009	1,005	11	3	(4)	1	26	1,028	91.7
C	1997	S.Alomar	451	19	3	473	146	37	0	21	.324	.355	.545	901	850	0	2	(8)	0	10	852	39.4
1B	1939	H.Trosky	448	52	1	501	150	31	4	25	.335	.405	.589	994	925	2	3	(8)	0	10	927	39.5
2B	1999	R.Alomar	563	99	7	669	182	40	3	24	.323	.430	.533	963	889	37	6	35	10	60	994	98.3
SS	1917	R.Chapman	563	61	0	624	170	28	13	2	.302	.370	.409	779	862	52		10	10	50	922	81.2
3B	1903	B.Bradley	536	25	3	564	168	36	22	6	.313	.348	.496	844	919	21		10	10	30	959	62.7
OF	2000	M.Ramirez	439	86	3	528	154	34	2	38	.351	.460	.697	1,157	1,059	1	1	(2)	0	(10)	1,048	73.0
OF	1958	R.Colavito	489	84	2	575	148	26	3	41	.303	.407	.620	1,027	1,025	0	2	(7)	(10)	10	1,018	75.2
OF	1994	K.Lofton	459	52	2	513	160	32	9	12	.349	.417	.536	953	890	60	12	66	10	40	1,006	86.0
Reserves		Averages	494	60	3	556	160	33	7	21	.324	.400	.547	947	927	22	3	10	4	25	965	69.4
Totals		Weighted Ave.	507	69	4	579	173	34	7	21	.342	.425	.564	989	979	15	3	1	2	26	1,007	84.3

Pitchers Rate of Success

Pos	Year	Name	G	GS	IP	W	L	SV	SO	BB	ERA	RA/9	Wtd RA/9	R V Runs /162
SP	1911	V.Gregg	34	26	245	23	7	0	125	86	1.80	2.47	2.42	61.2
SP	1937	J.Allen	24	20	173	15	1	0	87	60	2.55	2.86	2.44	42.8
SP	1968	L.Tiant	34	32	258	21	9	0	264	73	1.60	1.85	2.47	60.0
SP	1949	M.Garcia	41	20	176	14	5	2	94	60	2.36	2.61	2.50	42.2
SP	1940	B.Feller	43	37	320	27	11	4	261	118	2.61	2.87	2.59	73.6
Starters		Averages	35	27	234	20	7	1	166	79	2.17	2.52	2.49	56.0
RP	1995	J.Mesa	62	0	64	3	0	46	58	17	1.13	1.27	1.13	27.4
RP	1998	M.Jackson	69	0	64	1	1	40	55	13	1.55	1.55	1.40	22.5
RP	1971	S.Mingori	54	0	57	1	2	4	45	24	1.43	1.58	1.85	17.1
RP	1992	D.Lilliquist	71	0	62	5	3	6	47	18	1.75	1.90	2.00	17.6
Relievers		Averages	64	0	62	3	2	24	51	18	1.46	1.57	1.58	21.2
Totals		Averages	99	27	296	23	8	25	217	97	2.02	2.32	2.30	77.1

Cleveland Indians Catchers

V	R	Year	Name	AB	BB	HBP	TAB	H	2B	3B	HR	BA	OB	SA	PRO	Wtd PRO	SB	CS	SBF	SPF	FF	R TF	V HC
1	1	1970	R.Fosse	450	39	1	490	138	17	1	18	.307	.363	.469	832	836	1	5	(17)		40	858	42.2
2	5	1961	J.Romano	509	61	5	575	152	29	1	21	.299	.379	.483	862	839	0	0	0		(10)	829	41.4
3	2	1997	S.Alomar	451	19	3	473	146	37	0	21	.324	.355	.545	901	850	0	2	(8)		10	852	39.4
4	8	1920	S.O'Neill	489	69	3	561	157	39	5	3	.321	.408	.440	848	815	3	5	(12)	(10)	20	814	38.3
5	6	1919	S.O'Neill	398	48	5	451	115	35	7	2	.289	.373	.427	800	816	4			(10)	20	826	36.9
6	11	1962	J.Romano	459	73	5	537	120	19	3	25	.261	.369	.479	848	829	0	1	(4)	(10)	(10)	806	32.8
7	3	1924	G.Myatt	342	33	1	376	117	22	7	8	.342	.402	.518	919	859	6	1	10		(20)	849	32.4
8	4	1970	D.Sims	345	46	6	397	91	12	0	23	.264	.360	.499	859	862	0	4	(19)	(10)		833	29.5
9	9	1994	S.Alomar	292	25	2	319	84	15	1	14	.288	.348	.490	838	782	8	4	0		30	812	28.9
10	7	1968	D.Sims	361	62	5	428	90	21	0	11	.249	.367	.399	766	846	1	3	(11)	(10)	(10)	815	28.0
11	12	1907	N.Clarke	390	35	2	427	105	19	6	3	.269	.333	.372	704	814	3				(10)	804	27.0
12	17	1971	R.Fosse	486	36	4	526	134	21	1	12	.276	.331	.397	728	751	4	1	4		30	785	26.9
13	20	1948	J.Hegan	472	48	0	520	117	21	6	14	.248	.317	.407	724	699	6	3	0		80	779	26.5
14	15	1990	S.Alomar	445	25	2	472	129	26	2	9	.290	.331	.418	748	761	4	1	4		30	795	26.4
15	13	1980	R.Hassey	390	49	1	440	124	18	4	8	.318	.395	.446	842	838	0	2	(9)	(10)	(20)	800	25.6
16	10	1910	T.Easterly	363	21	0	384	111	16	6	0	.306	.344	.383	727	826	10				(20)	806	24.8
17	19	1922	S.O'Neill	392	73	3	468	122	27	4	2	.311	.423	.416	839	794	2	2	(4)	(10)		780	24.0
18	14	1969	D.Sims	326	66	6	398	77	8	0	18	.236	.374	.426	801	816	1	2	(7)	(10)		799	23.0
19	16	1964	J.Romano	352	51	7	410	85	18	1	19	.241	.349	.460	809	818	2	2	(5)	(10)	(10)	794	22.7
20	22	1937	F.Pytlak	397	52	7	456	125	15	6	1	.315	.404	.390	794	728	16	5	12	10	20	770	21.2
21	18	1960	J.Romano	316	37	3	356	86	12	2	16	.272	.354	.475	829	815	0	0	0		(30)	785	19.1
22	25	1972	R.Fosse	457	45	3	505	110	20	1	10	.241	.313	.354	667	724	5	1	6		20	749	18.2
23	23	1921	S.O'Neill	335	57	2	394	108	22	1	1	.322	.424	.403	827	763	0	1	(5)	(10)	20	768	17.9
24	21	1968	J.Azcue	357	28	0	385	100	10	0	4	.280	.332	.342	674	745	1	1	(2)	(10)	40	772	17.4
25	24	1902	H.Bemis	317	19	8	344	99	12	7	1	.312	.366	.404	770	777	3			10	(20)	767	16.9

Cleveland Indians First basemen

V	R	Year	Name	AB	BB	HBP	TAB	H	2B	3B	HR	BA	OB	SA	PRO	Wtd PRO	SB	CS	SBF	SPF	FF	R TF	V HC
1	5	1934	H.Trosky	625	58	2	685	206	45	9	35	.330	.388	.598	987	929	2	2	(3)			926	53.5
2	4	1930	E.Morgan	584	62	1	647	204	47	11	26	.349	.413	.601	1,014	927	8	4	0	10	(10)	927	50.9
3	1	1997	J.Thome	496	120	3	619	142	25	0	40	.286	.428	.579	1,007	950	1	1	(2)		(10)	939	49.8
4	6	1936	H.Trosky	629	36	3	668	216	45	9	42	.343	.382	.644	1,026	923	6	5	(6)			918	49.5
5	2	1998	J.Thome	440	90	3	533	129	34	2	30	.293	.417	.584	1,001	941	1	0	2		(10)	933	41.3
6	8	1902	C.Hickman	534	15	7	556	193	36	13	11	.361	.387	.539	926	934	9				(30)	904	41.0
7	11	1929	L.Fonseca	566	50	6	622	209	44	15	6	.369	.426	.532	958	894	19	11	(5)	10		900	40.5
8	3	1939	H.Trosky	448	52	1	501	150	31	4	25	.335	.405	.589	994	925	2	3	(8)		10	927	39.5
9	10	1978	A.Thornton	508	93	6	607	133	22	4	33	.262	.382	.516	898	918	4	7	(16)			902	38.3
10	7	1931	E.Morgan	462	83	1	546	162	33	4	11	.351	.451	.511	961	917	4	5	(10)	10	(10)	907	37.4
11	14	1938	H.Trosky	554	67	1	622	185	40	9	19	.334	.407	.542	948	866	5	1	5		10	881	34.4
12	13	1999	J.Thome	494	127	4	625	137	27	2	33	.277	.429	.540	969	894	0	0	0	(10)		884	34.0
13	9	1975	B.Powell	435	59	1	495	129	18	0	27	.297	.382	.524	906	933	1	3	(10)	(10)	(10)	903	31.4
14	15	1958	V.Power	590	20	1	611	184	37	10	16	.312	.336	.490	825	824	3	2	(2)	10	40	873	31.4
15	12	1977	A.Thornton	433	70	11	514	114	20	5	28	.263	.379	.527	906	896	3	4	(9)			887	28.6
16	18	1942	L.Fleming	548	106	6	660	160	27	4	14	.292	.412	.432	845	869	6	8	(14)	10	(10)	855	28.0
17	16	1940	H.Trosky	522	79	4	605	154	39	4	25	.295	.392	.529	920	866	1	2	(5)			862	27.8
18	17	1981	M.Hargrove	322	60	5	387	102	21	0	2	.317	.432	.401	832	873	5	4	(7)	(10)		855	23.9
19	23	1937	H.Trosky	601	65	1	667	179	36	9	32	.298	.367	.547	915	839	3	1	1			840	23.4
20	22	1926	G.Burns	603	28	8	639	216	64	3	4	.358	.394	.494	889	844	13	7	(1)			843	23.3
21	19	1908	G.Stovall	534	17	2	553	156	29	6	2	.292	.316	.380	697	822	14				30	852	22.8
22	26	2000	J.Thome	557	118	4	679	150	33	1	37	.269	.401	.531	932	853	1	0	1	(10)	(10)	835	20.9
23	20	1923	F.Brower	397	62	8	467	113	25	8	16	.285	.392	.509	901	860	6	5	(8)			852	19.2
24	27	1957	V.Wertz	515	78	2	595	145	21	0	28	.282	.378	.485	864	859	2	3	(6)	(10)	(10)	832	18.6
25	29	1903	C.Hickman	522	17	6	545	154	31	11	12	.295	.325	.466	790	861	14				(30)	831	18.3

Cleveland Indians
Second basemen

V	R	Year	Name	AB	BB	HBP	TAB	H	2B	3B	HR	BA	OB	SA	PRO	Wtd Rating	SB	CS	SBF	SPF	FF	R TF	V HC
1	1	1910	N.Lajoie	591	60	5	656	227	51	7	4	.384	.445	.514	960	1,091	26				80	1,171	159.6
2	2	1904	N.Lajoie	553	27	8	588	208	49	15	5	.376	.413	.546	959	1,099	29			10	50	1,159	139.7
3	5	1906	N.Lajoie	602	30	6	638	214	48	9	0	.355	.392	.465	857	974	20			10	90	1,074	124.3
4	4	1903	N.Lajoie	485	24	3	512	167	41	11	7	.344	.379	.518	896	977	21			10	100	1,087	113.2
5	7	1999	R.Alomar	563	99	7	669	182	40	3	24	.323	.430	.533	963	889	37	6	35	10	60	994	98.3
6	8	1908	N.Lajoie	581	47	9	637	168	32	6	2	.289	.352	.375	727	858	15			10	120	988	96.6
7	3	1902	N.Lajoie	352	19	6	377	133	35	5	7	.378	.419	.565	984	993	20			10	110	1,113	88.8
8	6	1909	N.Lajoie	469	35	6	510	152	33	7	1	.324	.378	.431	809	935	13				80	1,015	84.2
9	9	1907	N.Lajoie	509	30	6	545	152	30	6	2	.299	.345	.393	738	852	24			10	120	982	81.2
10	12	1954	B.Avila	555	59	1	615	189	27	2	15	.341	.405	.477	882	881	9	7	(8)	10	20	903	67.2
11	13	2000	R.Alomar	610	64	6	680	189	40	2	19	.310	.381	.475	856	784	39	4	43	10	40	877	62.1
12	10	1912	N.Lajoie	448	28	7	483	165	34	4	0	.368	.414	.462	876	908	18				30	938	61.2
13	11	1913	N.Lajoie	465	33	15	513	156	25	2	1	.335	.398	.404	802	856	17				50	906	56.9
14	14	1947	J.Gordon	562	62	1	625	153	27	6	29	.272	.346	.496	842	852	7	3	2		10	863	55.7
15	15	1948	J.Gordon	550	77	3	630	154	21	4	32	.280	.371	.507	879	849	5	2	2		10	860	55.2
16	16	1992	C.Baerga	657	35	13	705	205	32	1	20	.312	.359	.455	814	830	10	2	8		10	848	54.6
17	17	1993	C.Baerga	624	34	6	664	200	28	6	21	.321	.361	.486	847	827	15	4	10		10	847	51.0
18	18	1930	J.Hodapp	635	32	1	668	225	51	8	9	.354	.386	.502	889	813	6	5	(6)		30	837	50.7
19	19	1994	C.Baerga	442	10	6	458	139	32	2	19	.314	.338	.525	863	806	8	3	8		10	824	42.9
20	20	1986	T.Bernazard	562	53	6	621	169	28	4	17	.301	.367	.456	823	812	17	8	2			813	37.8
21	21	1934	O.Hale	563	48	0	611	170	44	6	13	.302	.357	.471	827	779	8	12	(25)	10	40	804	36.4
22	23	1995	C.Baerga	557	35	3	595	175	28	2	15	.314	.358	.452	810	764	11	2	11		10	785	31.9
23	24	1988	J.Franco	613	56	2	671	186	23	6	10	.303	.364	.409	773	786	25	11	4	10	(20)	780	30.3
24	25	1955	B.Avila	537	82	2	621	146	22	4	13	.272	.370	.400	771	756	1	4	(11)	10	20	775	27.9
25	27	1952	B.Avila	597	67	1	665	179	26	11	7	.300	.371	.415	787	799	12	10	(11)	10	(30)	768	27.5

Cleveland Indians
Shortstops

V	R	Year	Name	AB	BB	HBP	TAB	H	2B	3B	HR	BA	OB	SA	PRO	Wtd PRO	SB	CS	SBF	SPF	FF	R TF	V HC
1	1	1948	L.Boudreau	560	98	2	660	199	34	6	18	.355	.453	.534	987	953	3	2	(1)	(10)	40	982	105.7
2	2	1944	L.Boudreau	584	73	5	662	191	45	5	3	.327	.406	.437	843	878	11	3	7		90	975	103.8
3	3	1917	R.Chapman	563	61	0	624	170	28	13	2	.302	.370	.409	779	862	52			10	50	922	81.2
4	5	1923	J.Sewell	553	98	7	658	195	41	10	3	.353	.456	.479	935	893	9	6	(4)		10	899	78.1
5	4	1943	L.Boudreau	539	90	0	629	154	32	7	3	.286	.388	.388	776	826	4	7	(15)		90	901	75.3
6	6	1947	L.Boudreau	538	67	4	609	165	45	3	4	.307	.388	.424	811	820	1	0	2	(10)	80	892	70.2
7	8	1906	T.Turner	584	35	6	625	170	27	7	2	.291	.338	.372	709	806	27			10	40	856	60.8
8	9	1928	J.Sewell	588	58	7	653	190	40	2	4	.323	.391	.418	809	771	7	1	7		70	848	60.8
9	7	1999	O.Vizquel	574	65	1	640	191	36	4	5	.333	.402	.436	837	772	42	9	35	10	40	858	59.6
10	10	1918	R.Chapman	446	84	6	536	119	19	8	1	.267	.390	.352	742	811	30			10	10	831	55.0
11	12	1940	L.Boudreau	627	73	2	702	185	46	10	9	.295	.370	.443	814	766	6	3	0		50	816	54.1
12	13	1915	R.Chapman	570	70	3	643	154	14	17	3	.270	.353	.370	723	784	36	15	9	10	10	813	48.7
13	16	1926	J.Sewell	578	65	8	651	187	41	5	4	.324	.399	.433	832	790	17	7	4		10	805	46.6
14	18	1924	J.Sewell	594	67	2	663	188	45	5	4	.316	.388	.429	817	764	3	3	(4)		40	800	45.7
15	20	1941	L.Boudreau	579	85	3	667	149	45	8	10	.257	.355	.415	770	744	9	4	1		50	796	44.7
16	22	1925	J.Sewell	608	64	4	676	204	37	7	1	.336	.402	.424	827	760	7	6	(7)		40	793	44.3
17	14	1946	L.Boudreau	515	40	1	556	151	30	6	6	.293	.345	.410	755	770	6	7	(14)	(10)	60	807	40.3
18	23	1998	O.Vizquel	576	62	4	642	166	30	6	2	.288	.361	.372	733	689	37	12	19	10	70	788	38.6
19	26	1921	J.Sewell	572	80	11	663	182	36	12	4	.318	.412	.444	856	790	7	6	(7)		(10)	773	36.7
20	24	1996	O.Vizquel	542	56	4	602	161	36	1	9	.297	.367	.417	784	717	35	9	27	10	30	784	35.0
21	19	1919	R.Chapman	433	31	3	467	130	23	10	3	.300	.351	.420	772	787	18			10		797	34.8
22	25	1961	W.Held	509	69	3	581	136	23	5	23	.267	.358	.468	826	803	0	0	0		(20)	783	33.4
23	21	1920	R.Chapman	435	52	2	489	132	27	8	3	.303	.380	.423	803	773	13	9	(10)		30	793	32.1
24	11	1945	L.Boudreau	345	35	2	382	106	24	1	3	.307	.374	.409	783	824	0	4	(20)	(10)	30	824	31.0
25	15	1960	W.Held	376	44	5	425	97	15	1	21	.258	.344	.471	814	801	0	1	(4)		10	806	30.7

Cleveland Indians (1901–2000)

Cleveland Indians
Third basemen

V	R	Year	Name	AB	BB	HBP	TAB	H	2B	3B	HR	BA	OB	SA	PRO	Wtd PRO	SB	CS	SBF	SPF	FF	R TF	V HC
1	1	1953	A.Rosen	599	85	4	688	201	27	5	43	.336	.422	.613	1,034	1,014	8	7	(8)			1,006	85.6
2	2	1903	B.Bradley	536	25	3	564	168	36	22	6	.313	.348	.496	844	919	21			10	30	959	62.7
3	3	1996	J.Thome	505	123	6	634	157	28	5	38	.311	.451	.612	1,063	972	2	2	(3)		(20)	949	58.0
4	4	1902	B.Bradley	550	27	4	581	187	39	12	11	.340	.375	.515	890	897	11			10	30	937	57.6
5	5	1971	G.Nettles	598	82	3	683	156	18	1	28	.261	.353	.435	788	813	7	4	(1)		100	911	50.1
6	6	1944	K.Keltner	573	53	0	626	169	41	9	13	.295	.355	.466	821	854	4	3	(3)		60	911	48.3
7	8	1948	K.Keltner	558	89	1	648	166	24	4	31	.297	.395	.522	917	885	2	1	0		20	905	48.0
8	9	1904	B.Bradley	609	26	5	640	183	32	8	6	.300	.334	.409	743	852	23			10	40	902	46.3
9	7	1995	J.Thome	452	97	5	554	142	29	3	25	.314	.440	.558	998	941	4	3	(3)		(30)	908	44.7
10	12	1952	A.Rosen	567	75	4	646	171	32	5	28	.302	.387	.524	911	925	8	6	(6)		(40)	879	39.4
11	14	1982	T.Harrah	602	84	12	698	183	29	4	25	.304	.400	.490	890	886	17	3	15		(30)	871	37.8
12	11	1987	B.Jacoby	540	75	3	618	162	26	4	32	.300	.388	.541	929	891	2	3	(6)			885	37.6
13	15	1950	A.Rosen	554	100	10	664	159	23	4	37	.287	.405	.543	948	882	5	7	(13)			869	37.2
14	10	1954	A.Rosen	466	85	3	554	140	20	2	24	.300	.412	.506	918	917	6	2	3		(30)	890	36.8
15	13	2000	T.Fryman	574	73	1	648	184	38	4	22	.321	.398	.516	914	837	1	1	(1)		40	875	36.3
16	16	1941	K.Keltner	581	51	2	634	156	31	13	23	.269	.330	.485	815	788	2	2	(3)		80	865	34.2
17	17	1939	K.Keltner	587	51	0	638	191	35	11	13	.325	.379	.489	868	807	6	6	(9)		50	849	29.2
18	19	1936	O.Hale	620	64	0	684	196	50	13	14	.316	.380	.506	887	798	8	5	(3)		30	825	23.3
19	18	1905	B.Bradley	541	27	15	583	145	34	6	0	.268	.321	.353	674	776	22			10	40	826	20.0
20	20	1972	G.Nettles	557	57	4	618	141	28	0	17	.253	.327	.395	722	783	2	3	(6)		40	817	18.3
21	21	1970	G.Nettles	549	81	3	633	129	13	1	26	.235	.336	.404	741	744	3	1	1		70	815	17.5
22	22	1997	M.Williams	596	34	4	634	157	32	3	32	.263	.308	.488	796	751	12	4	6		50	807	15.0
23	23	1963	M.Alvis	602	36	10	648	165	32	7	22	.274	.326	.460	786	799	9	7	(7)	10		802	13.7
24	25	1935	O.Hale	589	52	1	642	179	37	11	16	.304	.361	.486	847	794	15	13	(16)	10	10	798	13.0
25	26	1981	T.Harrah	361	57	1	419	105	12	4	5	.291	.389	.388	777	815	12	1	23		(40)	797	12.1

Cleveland Indians
Outfielders

V	R	Year	Name	AB	BB	HBP	TAB	H	2B	3B	HR	BA	OB	SA	PRO	Wtd PRO	SB	CS	SBF	SPF	FF	R TF	V HC
1	1	1912	J.Jackson	572	54	12	638	226	44	26	3	.395	.458	.579	1,036	1,074	35			10	20	1,104	110.9
2	2	1911	J.Jackson	571	56	8	635	233	45	19	7	.408	.468	.590	1,058	1,073	41			10	20	1,103	110.0
3	7	1923	T.Speaker	574	93	4	671	218	59	11	17	.380	.469	.610	1,079	1,031	8	9	(14)	10	50	1,077	107.4
4	4	1916	T.Speaker	546	82	4	632	211	41	8	2	.386	.470	.502	972	1,064	35	27	(28)	10	50	1,095	107.0
5	5	1913	J.Jackson	528	80	5	613	197	39	17	7	.373	.460	.551	1,011	1,080	26			10		1,090	102.1
6	6	1917	T.Speaker	523	67	7	597	184	42	11	2	.352	.432	.486	918	1,016	30			10	60	1,086	98.2
7	8	1994	A.Belle	412	58	5	475	147	35	2	36	.357	.442	.714	1,156	1,079	9	6	(6)		(20)	1,053	94.6
8	10	1920	T.Speaker	552	97	5	654	214	50	11	8	.388	.483	.562	1,045	1,005	10	13	(23)	10	50	1,042	93.2
9	12	1995	A.Belle	546	73	6	625	173	52	1	50	.317	.403	.690	1,094	1,031	5	2	2		(10)	1,023	89.0
10	15	1994	K.Lofton	459	52	2	513	160	32	9	12	.349	.417	.536	953	890	60	12	66	10	40	1,006	86.0
11	3	1922	T.Speaker	426	77	1	504	161	48	8	11	.378	.474	.606	1,080	1,022	8	3	4	10	60	1,096	85.4
12	14	1999	M.Ramirez	522	96	13	631	174	34	3	44	.333	.448	.663	1,111	1,025	2	4	(9)			1,016	77.8
13	13	1958	R.Colavito	489	84	2	575	148	26	3	41	.303	.407	.620	1,027	1,025	0	2	(7)	(10)	10	1,018	75.2
14	9	2000	M.Ramirez	439	86	3	528	154	34	2	38	.351	.460	.697	1,157	1,059	1	1	(2)		(10)	1,048	73.0
15	19	1918	T.Speaker	471	64	3	538	150	33	11	0	.318	.403	.435	839	916	27			10	50	976	71.6
16	18	1904	E.Flick	579	51	9	639	177	31	17	6	.306	.371	.449	820	940	38			10	30	980	71.2
17	11	1925	T.Speaker	429	70	4	503	167	35	5	12	.389	.479	.578	1,057	972	5	2	2	10	50	1,034	69.6
18	17	1952	L.Doby	519	90	0	609	143	26	8	32	.276	.383	.541	924	939	5	2	2	10	30	980	68.0
19	16	1905	E.Flick	500	53	8	561	154	29	18	4	.308	.383	.462	845	973	35			10	10	993	66.3
20	24	1936	E.Averill	614	65	1	680	232	39	15	28	.378	.438	.627	1,065	959	3	3	(4)		(10)	945	63.9
21	25	1996	A.Belle	602	99	7	708	187	38	3	48	.311	.414	.623	1,037	948	11	0	15		(20)	943	62.6
22	21	1921	T.Speaker	506	68	2	576	183	52	14	3	.362	.439	.538	977	901	2	4	(10)	10	70	971	61.8
23	27	1941	J.Heath	585	50	4	639	199	32	20	24	.340	.396	.586	982	950	18	12	(9)	10	(10)	941	58.8
24	33	1934	E.Averill	598	99	4	701	187	48	6	31	.313	.414	.569	982	924	5	3	(1)			923	58.2
25	34	1931	E.Averill	627	68	6	701	209	36	10	32	.333	.404	.576	979	934	9	9	(12)			922	57.9

85

Baseball Players' Best Seasons

Cleveland Indians
Outfielders

V	R	Year	Name	AB	BB	HBP	TAB	H	2B	3B	HR	BA	OB	SA	PRO	Wtd PRO	SB	CS	SBF	SPF	FF	R TF	V HC
26	32	1906	E.Flick	624	54	7	685	194	34	22	1	.311	.372	.441	813	924	39			10	(10)	924	57.2
27	28	1919	T.Speaker	494	73	8	575	146	38	12	2	.296	.395	.433	828	845	15			10	80	935	56.2
28	29	1907	E.Flick	549	64	11	624	166	15	18	3	.302	.386	.412	798	922	41			10		932	54.5
29	30	1950	L.Doby	503	98	6	607	164	25	5	25	.326	.442	.545	986	917	8	6	(6)	10	10	931	52.8
30	37	1993	A.Belle	594	76	8	678	172	36	3	38	.290	.378	.552	930	907	23	12	(1)		10	916	51.2
31	35	1998	M.Ramirez	571	76	6	653	168	35	2	45	.294	.383	.599	982	923	5	3	(1)			922	51.1
32	26	1951	L.Doby	447	101	3	551	132	27	5	20	.295	.428	.512	941	918	4	1	3	10	10	942	50.9
33	23	1914	J.Jackson	453	41	5	499	153	22	13	3	.338	.399	.464	862	948	22	15	(15)	10	10	953	48.9
34	40	1926	T.Speaker	539	94	0	633	164	52	8	7	.304	.408	.469	877	833	6	1	6	10	60	909	48.1
35	20	1959	T.Francona	399	35	3	437	145	17	2	20	.363	.419	.566	985	981	2	0	4		(10)	975	47.7
36	31	1997	D.Justice	495	80	0	575	163	31	1	33	.329	.423	.596	1,019	961	3	5	(12)		(20)	930	47.3
37	48	1932	E.Averill	631	75	6	712	198	37	14	32	.314	.392	.569	961	904	5	8	(15)			890	47.2
38	41	1993	K.Lofton	569	81	1	651	185	28	8	1	.325	.410	.408	818	798	70	14	61	10	40	909	47.1
39	39	1996	M.Ramirez	550	85	3	638	170	45	3	33	.309	.404	.582	986	902	8	5	(3)		10	909	46.1
40	47	1954	L.Doby	577	85	3	665	157	18	4	32	.272	.368	.484	852	851	3	1	1	10	30	892	44.9
41	46	1965	R.Colavito	592	93	3	688	170	25	2	26	.287	.387	.468	855	884	1	1	(1)	(10)	20	893	44.5
42	52	1935	J.Vosmik	620	59	4	683	216	47	20	10	.348	.408	.537	946	886	2	1	0			886	44.2
43	43	1958	M.Minoso	556	59	15	630	168	25	2	24	.302	.384	.484	868	867	14	14	(21)	10	40	896	43.6
44	44	1985	B.Butler	591	63	1	655	184	28	14	5	.311	.379	.431	810	805	47	20	10	10	70	895	42.8
45	22	1945	J.Heath	370	56	1	427	113	16	7	15	.305	.398	.508	906	953	3	1	2	10	(10)	956	42.4
46	42	1924	T.Speaker	486	72	4	562	167	36	9	9	.344	.432	.510	943	881	5	7	(15)	10	30	906	41.9
47	54	1959	M.Minoso	570	54	17	641	172	32	0	21	.302	.379	.468	848	844	8	10	(18)	10	50	886	41.4
48	38	1938	J.Heath	502	33	0	535	172	31	18	21	.343	.383	.602	985	899	3	1	2	10		911	41.2
49	36	1957	G.Woodling	430	64	3	497	138	25	2	19	.321	.412	.521	933	928	0	5	(19)		10	919	40.3
50	50	1995	M.Ramirez	484	75	5	564	149	26	1	31	.308	.406	.558	964	909	6	6	(10)		(10)	889	39.8
51	53	1997	M.Ramirez	561	79	7	647	184	40	0	26	.328	.417	.538	956	902	2	3	(6)		(10)	886	39.7
52	45	1955	L.Doby	491	61	2	554	143	17	5	26	.291	.372	.505	877	860	2	0	3	10	20	893	37.7
53	49	1965	L.Wagner	517	60	3	580	152	18	1	28	.294	.371	.495	866	896	12	2	13		(20)	889	36.4
54	59	1903	E.Flick	523	51	8	582	155	23	16	2	.296	.368	.413	781	850	24			10	10	870	36.3
55	57	1953	L.Doby	513	96	6	615	135	18	5	29	.263	.385	.487	873	856	3	2	(2)	10	10	874	36.0
56	56	1938	E.Averill	482	81	3	566	159	27	15	14	.330	.429	.535	965	881	5	2	2			883	35.5
57	58	1992	K.Lofton	576	68	2	646	164	15	8	5	.285	.362	.365	727	741	66	12	61	10	60	872	35.4
58	70	1955	A.Smith	607	93	15	715	186	27	4	22	.306	.411	.473	884	867	11	6	(1)	10	(20)	855	35.1
59	63	1959	R.Colavito	588	71	2	661	151	24	0	42	.257	.339	.512	851	847	3	3	(4)	(10)	30	863	34.9
60	64	1986	J.Carter	663	32	5	700	200	36	9	29	.302	.339	.514	853	841	29	7	20	10	(10)	862	34.8
61	73	1996	K.Lofton	662	61	0	723	210	35	4	14	.317	.375	.446	820	751	75	17	54	10	40	854	33.3
62	51	1961	J.Piersall	484	43	2	529	156	26	7	6	.322	.380	.442	822	799	8	2	7	10	70	886	32.5
63	74	1944	R.Cullenbine	571	87	2	660	162	34	5	16	.284	.380	.445	825	859	4	4	(6)			853	31.7
64	62	1987	B.Butler	522	91	1	614	154	25	8	9	.295	.401	.425	826	792	33	16	2	10	60	864	31.1
65	55	1943	J.Heath	424	63	1	488	116	22	6	18	.274	.369	.481	850	905	5	8	(21)	10	(10)	884	30.9
66	77	1988	J.Carter	621	35	7	663	168	36	6	27	.271	.317	.478	795	808	27	5	24	10	10	853	30.0
67	79	1929	E.Averill	597	63	3	663	198	43	13	18	.332	.398	.538	936	874	13	13	(19)		(10)	845	29.2
68	71	1943	R.Cullenbine	488	96	1	585	141	24	4	8	.289	.407	.404	811	863	3	4	(8)			855	28.6
69	60	1946	H.Edwards	458	43	0	501	138	33	16	10	.301	.361	.509	870	887	1	3	(9)	(10)		868	27.8
70	65	1988	C.Snyder	511	42	1	554	139	24	3	26	.272	.329	.483	812	825	5	1	5		30	861	27.2
71	72	1995	K.Lofton	481	40	1	522	149	22	13	7	.310	.364	.453	817	771	54	15	43	10	30	854	27.1
72	68	1980	M.Dilone	528	28	2	558	180	30	9	0	.341	.376	.432	808	805	61	18	42	10		857	26.5
73	67	1918	B.Roth	375	53	8	436	106	21	12	1	.283	.383	.411	794	867	35			10	(20)	857	26.5
74	66	1920	E.Smith	456	53	3	512	144	37	10	12	.316	.391	.520	910	876	5	4	(6)		(10)	860	26.3
75	80	1930	E.Averill	534	56	2	592	181	33	8	19	.339	.404	.537	941	861	10	7	(6)		(10)	844	25.8

Cleveland Indians (1901–2000)

Cleveland Indians Starting Pitchers

V	R	Year	Name	G	GS	IP	W	L	SV	SO	BB	ERA	RA/9	R Wtd RA/9	V Runs /162
1	9	1946	B.Feller	48	42	371	26	15	4	348	153	2.18	2.45	2.72	79.5
2	8	1972	G.Perry	41	40	343	24	16	1	234	82	1.92	2.07	2.71	74.0
3	5	1940	B.Feller	43	37	320	27	11	4	261	118	2.61	2.87	2.59	73.6
4	11	1908	A.Joss	42	35	325	24	11	2	130	30	1.16	2.13	2.80	66.8
5	10	1939	B.Feller	39	35	297	24	9	1	246	142	2.85	3.18	2.73	63.3
6	1	1911	V.Gregg	34	26	245	23	7	0	125	86	1.80	2.47	2.42	61.2
7	3	1968	L.Tiant	34	32	258	21	9	0	264	73	1.60	1.85	2.47	60.0
8	25	1920	J.Bagby	48	38	340	31	12	0	73	79	2.89	3.23	3.07	59.0
9	16	1920	S.Coveleski	41	38	315	24	14	2	133	65	2.49	3.14	2.99	57.8
10	39	1918	S.Coveleski	38	33	311	22	13	1	87	76	1.82	2.60	3.27	56.6
11	15	1917	S.Coveleski	45	36	298	19	14	4	133	94	1.81	2.35	2.95	56.0
12	24	1926	G.Uhle	39	36	318	27	11	1	159	118	2.83	3.23	3.06	55.6
13	21	1974	G.Perry	37	37	322	21	13	0	216	99	2.51	2.74	3.04	54.3
14	37	1941	B.Feller	44	40	343	25	13	2	260	194	3.15	3.38	3.22	53.8
15	14	1956	E.Wynn	38	35	278	20	9	2	158	91	2.72	3.01	2.92	53.2
16	18	1948	B.Lemon	43	37	294	20	14	2	147	129	2.82	3.18	3.03	52.6
17	31	1917	J.Bagby	49	37	321	23	13	7	83	73	1.96	2.52	3.16	52.3
18	41	1907	A.Joss	42	38	339	27	11	2	127	54	1.83	2.66	3.28	50.8
19	7	1948	G.Bearden	37	29	230	20	7	1	80	106	2.43	2.82	2.68	50.4
20	12	1956	H.Score	35	33	249	20	9	0	263	129	2.53	2.96	2.87	49.1
21	13	1902	B.Bernhard	28	25	226	18	5	1	58	37	2.15	3.15	2.87	49.0
22	29	1952	M.Garcia	46	36	292	22	11	4	143	87	2.37	2.87	3.13	48.7
23	33	1947	B.Feller	42	37	299	20	11	3	196	127	2.68	2.92	3.18	48.3
24	6	1913	W.Mitchell	35	22	217	14	8	0	141	88	1.91	2.32	2.66	48.0
25	26	1913	C.Falkenberg	39	36	276	23	10	0	166	88	2.22	2.68	3.08	47.8
26	28	1949	B.Lemon	37	33	280	22	10	1	138	137	2.99	3.25	3.12	47.1
27	17	1934	M.Harder	44	29	255	20	12	4	91	81	2.61	3.42	3.00	46.5
28	22	1965	S.McDowell	42	35	273	17	11	4	325	132	2.18	2.64	3.04	46.1
29	32	1906	A.Joss	34	31	282	21	9	1	106	43	1.72	2.59	3.16	45.9
30	48	1906	B.Rhoads	38	34	315	22	10	0	89	92	1.80	2.71	3.31	45.9
31	45	1952	B.Lemon	42	36	310	22	11	4	131	105	2.50	3.02	3.29	45.8
32	50	1919	S.Coveleski	43	34	286	24	12	4	118	60	2.61	3.01	3.32	45.4
33	56	1906	O.Hess	43	36	334	20	17	3	167	85	1.83	2.80	3.42	44.4
34	2	1937	J.Allen	24	20	173	15	1	0	87	60	2.55	2.86	2.44	42.8
35	4	1949	M.Garcia	41	20	176	14	5	2	94	60	2.36	2.61	2.50	42.2
36	35	1954	M.Garcia	45	34	259	19	8	5	129	71	2.64	2.95	3.19	41.5
37	53	1935	M.Harder	42	35	287	22	11	2	95	53	3.29	3.76	3.34	40.8
38	42	1951	E.Wynn	37	34	274	20	13	1	133	107	3.02	3.35	3.28	40.8
39	62	1921	S.Coveleski	43	40	315	23	13	2	99	84	3.37	3.90	3.46	40.2
40	30	1936	J.Allen	36	31	243	20	10	1	165	97	3.44	4.00	3.16	39.7
41	49	1912	V.Gregg	37	34	271	20	13	2	184	90	2.59	3.28	3.31	39.4
42	52	1954	E.Wynn	40	36	271	23	11	2	155	83	2.73	3.09	3.34	38.7
43	36	1915	G.Morton	34	27	240	16	15	1	134	60	2.14	2.81	3.21	37.8
44	20	1996	C.Nagy	32	32	222	17	5	0	167	61	3.41	3.61	3.04	37.5
45	61	1905	A.Joss	33	32	286	20	12	0	132	46	2.01	2.83	3.46	36.8
46	64	1970	S.McDowell	39	39	305	20	12	0	304	131	2.92	3.19	3.48	36.6
47	51	1945	S.Gromek	33	30	251	19	9	1	101	66	2.55	2.87	3.33	36.1
48	38	1984	B.Blyleven	33	32	245	19	7	0	170	74	2.87	3.16	3.24	36.0
49	23	1995	D.Martinez	28	28	187	12	5	0	99	46	3.08	3.42	3.04	35.4
50	76	1930	W.Ferrell	43	35	297	25	13	3	143	106	3.31	4.27	3.54	35.2

Cleveland Indians
Starting Pitchers

V	R	Year	Name	G	GS	IP	W	L	SV	SO	BB	ERA	RA/9	R Wtd RA/9	V Runs /162
51	86	1903	A.Joss	32	31	284	18	13	0	120	37	2.19	3.30	3.60	35.0
52	46	1994	D.Martinez	24	24	177	11	6	0	92	44	3.52	3.82	3.30	34.9
53	19	1904	A.Joss	25	24	192	14	10	0	83	30	1.59	2.39	3.03	34.4
54	40	1981	B.Blyleven	20	20	159	11	7	0	107	40	2.88	2.94	3.28	34.3
55	74	1952	E.Wynn	42	33	286	23	12	3	153	132	2.90	3.24	3.53	34.3
56	65	1903	E.Moore	29	27	248	19	9	1	148	62	1.74	3.20	3.49	34.1
57	73	1929	W.Hudlin	40	33	280	17	15	1	60	73	3.34	3.92	3.53	33.6
58	54	1950	B.Feller	35	34	247	16	11	0	119	103	3.43	3.83	3.40	33.3
59	63	1968	S.McDowell	38	37	269	15	14	0	283	110	1.81	2.61	3.48	32.3
60	55	1992	C.Nagy	33	33	252	17	10	0	169	57	2.96	3.25	3.41	32.0
61	44	1950	E.Wynn	32	28	214	18	8	0	143	101	3.20	3.70	3.29	31.8
62	60	1909	A.Joss	33	28	243	14	13	0	67	31	1.71	2.63	3.44	31.6
63	81	1953	M.Garcia	38	35	272	18	9	0	134	81	3.25	3.51	3.57	31.4
64	98	1902	A.Joss	32	29	269	17	13	0	106	75	2.77	4.01	3.65	31.2
65	69	1951	M.Garcia	47	30	254	20	13	6	118	82	3.15	3.58	3.51	31.1
66	84	1908	B.Rhoads	37	30	270	18	12	0	62	73	1.77	2.73	3.59	30.7
67	72	1956	B.Lemon	39	35	255	20	14	3	94	89	3.03	3.64	3.53	30.6
68	58	1955	E.Wynn	32	31	230	17	11	0	122	80	2.82	3.37	3.43	30.4
69	47	1939	M.Harder	29	26	208	15	9	1	67	64	3.50	3.85	3.31	30.3
70	27	1975	D.Eckersley	34	24	187	13	7	2	152	90	2.60	2.94	3.10	30.2
71	90	1938	B.Feller	39	36	278	17	11	1	240	208	4.08	4.40	3.63	30.0
72	59	1955	H.Score	33	32	227	16	10	0	245	154	2.85	3.37	3.43	30.0
73	82	1954	B.Lemon	36	33	258	23	7	0	110	92	2.72	3.31	3.57	29.6
74	34	1965	S.Siebert	39	27	189	16	8	1	191	46	2.43	2.76	3.18	29.0
75	103	1985	B.Blyleven	37	37	294	17	16	0	206	75	3.16	3.71	3.68	28.8
76	119	1904	B.Bernhard	38	37	321	23	13	0	137	55	2.13	3.00	3.80	28.5
77	67	1994	C.Nagy	23	23	169	10	8	0	108	48	3.45	4.04	3.49	28.3
78	78	1938	M.Harder	38	29	240	17	10	4	102	62	3.83	4.31	3.56	28.0
79	88	1924	S.Smith	39	27	248	12	14	1	34	42	3.02	3.99	3.61	27.3
80	57	1982	R.Sutcliffe	34	27	216	14	8	1	142	98	2.96	3.38	3.42	27.2
81	43	1966	S.Hargan	38	21	192	13	10	0	132	45	2.48	2.81	3.28	27.2
82	108	1942	J.Bagby	38	35	271	17	9	1	54	64	2.96	3.49	3.71	26.9
83	96	1933	M.Harder	43	31	253	15	17	4	81	67	2.95	4.02	3.65	26.8
84	111	1922	S.Coveleski	35	33	277	17	14	2	98	64	3.32	3.90	3.73	26.7
85	115	1948	B.Feller	44	38	280	19	15	3	164	116	3.56	3.95	3.76	26.2
86	118	1953	B.Lemon	41	36	287	21	15	1	98	110	3.36	3.73	3.79	25.6
87	91	1977	D.Eckersley	33	33	247	14	13	0	191	54	3.53	3.64	3.64	25.2
88	107	1951	B.Feller	33	32	250	22	8	0	111	95	3.50	3.78	3.70	24.9
89	124	1932	W.Ferrell	38	34	288	23	13	1	105	104	3.66	4.41	3.82	24.8
90	77	1939	A.Milnar	37	26	209	14	12	3	76	99	3.79	4.13	3.55	24.6
91	121	1901	E.Moore	31	30	251	16	14	0	99	107	2.90	4.62	3.81	24.2
92	151	1923	G.Uhle	54	44	358	26	16	5	109	102	3.77	4.20	3.98	24.2
93	127	1913	V.Gregg	44	34	286	20	13	3	166	124	2.24	3.35	3.85	23.8
94	99	1923	S.Coveleski	33	31	228	13	14	2	54	42	2.76	3.87	3.67	23.7
95	104	1935	W.Hudlin	36	29	232	15	11	5	45	61	3.69	4.15	3.69	23.6
96	68	1925	J.Miller	32	22	190	10	13	2	51	62	3.31	4.03	3.50	23.5
97	109	1974	J.Perry	36	36	252	17	12	0	71	64	2.96	3.36	3.73	23.3
98	112	1929	W.Ferrell	43	25	243	21	10	5	100	109	3.60	4.15	3.74	23.3
99	79	1908	H.Berger	29	24	199	13	8	0	101	66	2.12	2.71	3.56	23.2
100	126	1931	W.Ferrell	40	35	276	22	12	3	123	130	3.75	4.37	3.84	23.0

Cleveland Indians (1901–2000)

Cleveland Indians Relief Pitchers

V	R	Year	Name	G	GS	IP	W	L	SV	SO	BB	ERA	RA/9	R Wtd RA/9	V Runs /162
1	11	1979	S.Monge	76	0	131	12	10	19	108	64	2.40	2.54	2.45	30.6
2	1	1995	J.Mesa	62	0	64	3	0	46	58	17	1.13	1.27	1.13	27.4
3	7	1954	D.Mossi	40	5	93	6	1	7	55	39	1.94	2.13	2.30	24.5
4	26	1982	D.Spillner	65	0	134	12	10	21	90	45	2.49	2.96	3.00	23.2
5	2	1998	M.Jackson	69	0	64	1	1	40	55	13	1.55	1.55	1.40	22.5
6	5	1996	E.Plunk	56	0	78	3	2	2	85	34	2.43	2.43	2.04	21.8
7	6	1968	V.Romo	41	1	84	5	3	12	54	32	1.60	1.71	2.28	21.3
8	8	1942	T.Ferrick	31	2	81	3	2	3	28	32	1.99	2.22	2.36	20.8
9	16	1994	E.Plunk	41	0	71	7	2	3	73	37	2.54	3.17	2.74	20.3
10	12	1976	D.LaRoche	61	0	96	1	4	21	104	49	2.24	2.34	2.67	20.1
11	15	1954	R.Narleski	42	2	89	3	3	13	52	44	2.22	2.53	2.73	19.0
12	20	1984	E.Camacho	69	0	100	5	9	23	48	37	2.43	2.79	2.86	18.9
13	10	1989	J.Orosco	69	0	78	3	4	3	79	26	2.08	2.31	2.43	18.5
14	13	1992	S.Olin	72	0	88	8	5	29	47	27	2.34	2.55	2.68	18.4
15	4	1992	D.Lilliquist	71	0	62	5	3	6	47	18	1.75	1.90	2.00	17.6
16	9	1995	E.Plunk	56	0	64	6	2	2	71	27	2.67	2.67	2.38	17.4
17	3	1971	S.Mingori	54	0	57	1	2	4	45	24	1.43	1.58	1.85	17.1
18	17	1948	E.Klieman	44	0	80	3	2	4	18	46	2.60	2.92	2.78	16.6
19	29	1964	D.McMahon	70	0	101	6	4	16	92	52	2.41	2.76	3.09	16.5
20	41	1935	L.Brown	42	8	122	8	7	4	45	37	3.61	3.84	3.41	16.3
21	35	1976	J.Kern	50	2	118	10	7	15	111	50	2.37	2.91	3.32	16.2
22	18	1997	J.Mesa	66	0	82	4	4	16	69	28	2.40	3.06	2.80	16.0
23	32	1976	S.Thomas	37	7	106	4	4	6	54	41	2.30	2.80	3.20	16.0
24	31	1992	T.Power	64	0	99	3	3	6	51	35	2.54	2.99	3.14	15.6
25	21	1990	D.Jones	66	0	84	5	5	43	55	22	2.56	2.77	2.90	15.4
26	22	1988	D.Jones	51	0	83	3	4	37	72	16	2.27	2.81	2.91	15.2
27	27	1949	S.Paige	31	5	83	4	7	5	54	33	3.04	3.14	3.01	15.0
28	24	1989	D.Jones	59	0	81	7	10	32	65	13	2.34	2.79	2.93	14.6
29	45	1944	J.Heving	63	1	120	8	3	10	46	41	1.96	3.15	3.53	14.4
30	25	1975	D.LaRoche	61	0	82	5	3	17	94	57	2.19	2.84	3.00	14.2
31	30	1955	D.Mossi	57	1	82	4	3	9	69	18	2.42	3.07	3.12	13.7
32	36	1984	T.Waddell	58	0	97	7	4	6	59	37	3.06	3.25	3.33	13.2
33	14	1993	D.Lilliquist	56	2	64	4	4	10	40	19	2.25	2.81	2.70	13.2
34	40	1947	E.Klieman	58	0	92	5	4	17	21	39	3.03	3.13	3.40	12.4
35	38	1995	J.Tavarez	57	0	85	10	2	0	68	21	2.44	3.81	3.39	12.4
36	44	1994	J.Mesa	51	0	73	7	5	2	63	26	3.82	4.07	3.52	11.9
37	39	1961	F.Funk	56	0	92	11	11	11	64	31	3.31	3.42	3.40	11.8
38	43	1978	J.Kern	58	0	99	10	10	13	95	58	3.08	3.26	3.50	11.6
39	48	1977	D.Hood	41	5	105	2	1	0	62	49	3.00	3.60	3.60	11.2
40	50	1982	E.Whitson	40	9	108	4	2	2	61	58	3.26	3.59	3.64	11.1
41	55	1951	L.Brissie	56	6	126	4	5	9	53	69	3.58	3.89	3.81	11.0
42	28	2000	P.Shuey	57	0	64	4	2	0	69	30	3.39	3.53	3.02	10.9
43	34	2000	S.Karsay	72	0	77	5	9	20	66	25	3.76	3.87	3.31	10.7
44	37	1996	J.Mesa	69	0	72	2	7	39	64	28	3.73	3.98	3.35	9.7
45	42	1984	M.Jeffcoat	63	1	75	5	2	1	41	24	2.99	3.35	3.43	9.4
46	59	1955	R.Narleski	60	1	112	9	1	19	94	52	3.71	3.78	3.84	9.3
47	47	1999	P.Shuey	72	0	82	8	5	6	103	40	3.53	4.08	3.53	9.3
48	19	1997	P.Assenmacher	75	0	49	5	0	4	53	15	2.94	3.12	2.85	9.3
49	23	1996	P.Assenmacher	63	0	47	4	2	1	44	14	3.09	3.47	2.92	8.6
50	51	1980	S.Monge	67	0	94	3	5	14	61	40	3.53	3.72	3.75	8.4

DETROIT TIGERS (1901–2000)

The Tigers started the twentieth century slowly, with two winning seasons in their first six years. Ty Cobb matured into a superstar in 1907, and the franchise was off and running. From 1907 to 1988, the Tigers put together 57 winning seasons, 24 losing seasons, and one .500 year, the second best performance in the American League, trailing only the Yankees. Detroit won nine pennants and two additional division titles in that period. After this extended period of success, the Tigers fizzled, with just two winning seasons in the last eleven years of the twentieth century, and another losing record in 2000. Detroit's on-field problems stemmed from their being unable to economically compete with an aging stadium in a small market city.

Detroit's success began a long time ago, in the early days of the American League, when a 20-year-old demon from Georgia became the most unstoppable force in Dead Ball baseball. This young star, Tyrus Cobb, hit for adjusted batting averages of .405, .382, and .436 in 1907–1909 to push the Tigers to a three-year reign at the top of the league. Cobb received support from fellow outfielder Sam Crawford (.323 average, 17 triples, 1,004 Total Factor in his best year in 1907), and from pitchers Wild Bill Donovan (25-4 in 1907), Ed Killian (25 wins in 1907), Ed Summers (24 wins in 1908) and George Mullin (league-high 29 wins in 1909).

Violent, driven, and extremely talented, Ty Cobb stayed at the top of his game for more than a decade, while hitting an adjusted average of .400 or better for ten straight years from 1909 to 1918. Cobb's outstanding 1911 season, in which he hit .420 with 248 hits, 47 doubles, 24 triples, 8 home runs, and 83 steals, for a 1,143 Total Factor, earned him the Chalmers (MVP) Award. While the Tigers had many winning seasons during the Cobb years, they were unable to win another pennant after 1909. The 1915 team came close, with a 100–54 record, to finish 2½ games behind Boston. Outfielders Cobb, Crawford, and Bobby Veach provided most of the team's offense that year. Cobb hit an adjusted .401, with an adjusted 101 stolen bases, in one of his better years. Cobb's best season in his career was in 1917, as he batted .383 with 6 home runs and 55 steals. Adjusted for 11 percent hitter's deflation, Cobb batted .423 with a .491 on-base percentage, a 1,122 Wtd. Production, a 1,172 Total Factor, and 135.6 Hits Contribution.

Cobb became the team's player-manager in the 1920s, just as his real performance was declining substantially, and as home-run king Babe Ruth was changing the rules of how to play the game. As manager, Cobb discouraged his players from swinging for the fences, insisting that the team continue to play the Dead Ball game of going for singles and aggressively running the basepaths. The result was a Tigers team sporting one of the league's best batting averages every year, but lacking the power to compete with the Yankees and other free-swinging clubs. Harry Heilmann hit around .400 and won four batting titles in 1921, 1923, 1925, and 1927. Heilmann's best season was in 1923, when he batted .403 with 18 home runs, for a 1,063 Wtd. Production. Heinie Manush won a batting title in 1926 with a .378 average. Even catcher Johnny Bassler got into the swing of things, hitting .346 in 1924. Cobb, meanwhile, hit as high as .401 in 1922, but failed to win any batting titles in the 1920s. In 1927, the 40-year-old Cobb was traded to Philadelphia, and the next season the Tigers began a mini-slump, with only one winning season from 1928 to 1933.

The Tigers rebuilt in 1934 around 23-year-old Hank Greenberg, Charlie Gehringer, and pitchers Schoolboy Rowe and Tommy Bridges. Mickey Cochrane was purchased from the Athletics before the 1934 season, and the new player-manager led his hungry squad to pennants in 1934 and 1935. Cochrane was even selected the 1934 AL MVP, hitting for a .320 average. Greenberg (1935 MVP) provided the power, hitting 194 extra base hits over those two seasons, while Gehringer hit .356 in 1934 and .330 in 1935. Pitchers Bridges and Rowe each won 43 games for these two pennant teams.

The Tigers were very competitive from 1934 to 1950, with 15 winning seasons in 17 years. Greenberg hit .315 with 58 home runs in 1938, for a 1,024 Wtd. Production. The Tigers won another pennant in 1940, with MVP Greenberg moving to the outfield in order to get Rudy York's bat (and weak glove) into the lineup at first base. Greenberg batted .340 with 41 home runs and 99 extra base hits for a career-best 1,039 Wtd. Production, while York hit .316 with 33 home runs and 85 extra base hits. Bobo Newsom, traded 16 times over his career, led the team's pitchers with a 21–5 record and 2.83 ERA. Rowe and Bridges supported him with 28 wins between them.

The Tigers remained successful during the war years despite losing Greenberg and others to military service. In 1944, the Tigers finished one game out due to a 56–23 record from their two best pitchers. Twenty-three-year-old MVP Hal Newhouser was 29–9 with a 2.22 ERA and 3.03 Wtd. RA/9. Dizzy Trout was even more impressive, with a 27–14 record, league-leading 2.12 ERA, and a 2.98 Wtd. RA/9. In 1945, Detroit won the pennant and the World Series behind Newhouser, who won his second straight MVP Award for going 25–9 with a league best 1.81 ERA and a 2.44 Wtd. RA/9. Newhouser showed he could still pitch when the veterans came home in 1946, leading the league in wins with 26, and in ERA at 1.94, while producing a 2.63 Wtd. RA/9, as the Tigers finished in second place. Greenberg led the league with 44 home runs, while Roy Cullenbine hit .335 and drew 88 walks in just 417 total at bats for a .477 on-base percentage, while producing a 1,034 Wtd. Production.

The Tigers started the 1950s with a second place finish, three games behind the Yankees. The final standings would have been different if ace pitcher Virgil Trucks hadn't been limited to seven starts with a sore arm. The offense was paced by George Kell, who hit .340, and Vic Wertz, who hit .308 with 27 home runs. Then came four losing seasons.

The winning tradition returned in 1955, when another 20-year-old, Al Kaline, hit 27 home runs and led the league with a .340 average for a 952 Wtd. Production, establishing himself as the star to whom the Tigers could anchor their team for nearly two decades. From 1955 to 1973, Kaline led the Tigers to 15 seasons of .500 or better ball in a 19-year period. Kaline never hit more than 29 home runs in a season, but he played solid defense and was consistently one of the league's top three outfielders in both Total Factor and Hits Contribution. His best season was in 1967, when he hit .308 with 25 home runs, while winning his last Gold Glove. Adjusted for 8 percent hitter's deflation, Kaline batted .331 with 26 home runs that year, for a career-best 1,029 Wtd. Production, and a 1,076 Total Factor.

The 1961 Tigers were 101–61, but finished 8 games behind the Yankees. Detroit featured Norm Cash, who had a blockbuster year with a .361 average, 124 walks, and 41 home runs, for a 1,118 Wtd. Production. Rocky Colavito hit .290 with 45 home runs, while Kaline hit 19 round trippers to go with his .324 average. Pitcher Frank Lary was 23–9, and Jim Bunning went 17–11.

The 1968 Tigers team may have been Detroit's best team ever, despite starting a shortstop who batted .135 with 1 home run. Detroit won 103 games, and came back to beat the Cardinals in the World Series after trailing 3 games to 1. Bill Freehan earned the best league volume of success season ever for a catcher with a 94.8 Hits Contribution, achieved by a .263 average, 25 home runs, and superb defense. The 1968 Tigers also featured Cash, Kaline (.287 average), Jim Northrup (21 home runs) and Willie Horton (36 home runs). MVP Denny McLain was the last person to win 30 games when he went 31–6 with a 1.96 ERA and a 3.06 Wtd. RA/9, while Mickey Lolich added 17 wins.

McLain self-destructed after the 1969 season, but the other veterans were still around in 1972 as Detroit edged Boston for a division title, with Lolich winning 22 games. The aging Tigers produced another winning season in 1973, as reliever John Hiller had a brilliant season, with a 10–5 record, a league-leading 38 saves, a 1.44 ERA, and 1.60 Wtd. RA/9. Hiller saved 41.1 runs from scoring over 125 innings—the third best volume of success for relievers in league history. In 1974, Detroit slid into last place, and the team stayed below .500 for four seasons.

The Tigers returned to their winning ways in 1978 when 20-year-old shortstop Alan Trammell and 21-year-old second baseman Lou Whitaker broke into the starting lineup. This double play tandem anchored Detroit infields for more than a decade. The 1984 squad won 104 games and the World Series, led by Trammell (.314), Whitaker (.289), Lance Parrish (33 home runs), Kirk Gibson (27 home runs), and Chet Lemon (20 home runs, great defense). Pitcher Jack Morris was 19–11, while league MVP Willie Hernandez was 9–3 with 32 saves, a 1.92 ERA, and 1.97 Wtd. RA/9. The 1987 team earned Detroit's last postseason appearance, as Trammell hit .343 with 28 home runs for a career-best 962 Total Factor and 94.5 Hits Contribution, and Morris went 18–11. Detroit's last winning season was in 1993, when 35-year-old Trammell hit .329 and 36-year-old Whitaker hit .290.

Detroit Tigers   **Hitters Volume of Success**

														Wtd						R	V
Pos	Year	Name	AB	BB	HBP	TAB	H	2B	3B	HR	BA	OB	SA	PRO	PRO	SB	CS	SBF	SPF	FF	TF	HC
C	1968	B.Freehan	540	65	24	629	142	24	2	25	.263	.367	.454	821	907	0	1	(3)	10	80	994	94.8
1B	1961	N.Cash	535	124	9	668	193	22	8	41	.361	.488	.662	1,150	1,118	11	5	1	0	20	1,139	117.5
2B	1936	C.Gehringer	641	83	4	728	227	60	12	15	.354	.431	.555	987	888	4	1	3	0	70	961	100.6
SS	1987	A.Trammell	597	60	3	660	205	34	3	28	.343	.406	.551	957	918	21	2	24	10	10	962	94.5
3B	1953	R.Boone	497	72	5	574	147	17	8	26	.296	.390	.519	909	892	3	3	(5)	0	10	897	51.9
OF	1917	T.Cobb	588	61	4	653	225	44	24	6	.383	.444	.570	1,014	1,122	55		10		40	1,172	135.6
OF	1940	H.Greenberg	573	93	1	667	195	50	8	41	.340	.433	.670	1,103	1,039	6	3	0	0	(10)	1,029	90.6
OF	1923	H.Heilmann	524	74	5	603	211	44	11	18	.403	.481	.632	1,113	1,063	9	7	(8)	(10)	(10)	1,035	83.9
Starters		Averages	562	79	7	648	193	37	10	25	.344	.431	.577	1,007	993	14	3	2	3	26	1,024	96.2
C	1938	R.York	463	92	2	557	138	27	2	33	.298	.417	.579	995	909	1	2	(5)	0	(30)	874	54.8
1B	1990	C.Fielder	573	90	5	668	159	25	1	51	.277	.380	.592	972	988	0	1	(3)	(10)	(10)	965	62.1
2B	1983	L.Whitaker	643	67	0	710	206	40	6	12	.320	.385	.457	842	841	17	10	(4)	10	30	877	64.7
SS	1901	K.Elberfeld	432	57	7	496	133	21	11	3	.308	.397	.428	825	828	23			10	40	878	59.0
3B	1959	E.Yost	521	135	12	668	145	19	0	21	.278	.437	.436	873	869	9	2	7	0	(10)	866	50.2
OF	1967	A.Kaline	458	83	1	542	141	28	2	25	.308	.415	.541	957	1,029	8	2	7	0	40	1,076	82.4
OF	1907	S.Crawford	582	37	2	621	188	34	17	4	.323	.366	.460	826	954	18			10	40	1,004	76.8
OF	1961	R.Colavito	583	113	2	698	169	30	2	45	.290	.407	.580	987	959	1	2	(4)	(10)	20	965	69.1
Reserves		Averages	532	84	4	620	160	28	5	24	.301	.400	.509	909	922	10	2	(0)	1	15	938	64.9
Totals		Weighted Ave.	552	81	6	639	182	34	8	25	.330	.421	.555	976	970	12	3	1	2	23	995	85.8

Pitchers Volume of Success

Pos	Year	Name	G	GS	IP	W	L	SV	SO	BB	ERA	RA/9	Wtd RA/9	V Runs /162
SP	1945	H.Newhouser	40	36	313	25	9	2	212	110	1.81	2.10	2.44	77.6
SP	1944	D.Trout	49	40	352	27	14	0	144	83	2.12	2.66	2.98	65.0
SP	1968	D.McLain	41	41	336	31	6	0	280	63	1.96	2.30	3.06	55.7
SP	1949	V.Trucks	41	32	275	19	11	4	153	124	2.81	3.11	2.98	50.6
SP	1903	B.Donovan	35	34	307	17	16	0	187	95	2.29	3.05	3.33	48.6
Starters		Averages	41	37	317	24	11	1	195	95	2.18	2.63	2.96	59.5
RP	1973	J.Hiller	65	0	125	10	5	38	124	39	1.44	1.51	1.60	41.1
RP	1984	W.Hernandez	80	0	140	9	3	32	112	36	1.92	1.92	1.97	40.3
RP	1979	A.Lopez	61	0	127	10	5	21	106	51	2.41	2.62	2.53	28.6
RP	1988	M.Henneman	65	0	91	9	6	22	58	24	1.87	2.27	2.35	22.3
Relievers		Averages	68	0	121	10	5	28	100	38	1.92	2.06	2.09	33.1
Totals		Averages	109	37	437	33	16	29	295	133	2.11	2.47	2.72	92.6

Detroit Tigers

Hitters Rate of Success

Pos	Year	Name	AB	BB	HBP	TAB	H	2B	3B	HR	BA	OB	SA	PRO	Wtd PRO	SB	CS	SBF	SPF	FF	R TF	V HC
C	1968	B.Freehan	540	65	24	629	142	24	2	25	.263	.367	.454	821	907	0	1	(3)	10	80	994	94.8
1B	1961	N.Cash	535	124	9	668	193	22	8	41	.361	.488	.662	1150	1118	11	5	1	0	20	1,139	117.5
2B	1936	C.Gehringer	641	83	4	728	227	60	12	15	.354	.431	.555	987	888	4	1	3	0	70	961	100.6
SS	1987	A.Trammell	597	60	3	660	205	34	3	28	.343	.406	.551	957	918	21	2	24	10	10	962	94.5
3B	1953	R.Boone	497	72	5	574	147	17	8	26	.296	.390	.519	909	892	3	3	(5)	0	10	897	51.9
OF	1910	T.Cobb	506	64	4	574	194	35	13	8	.383	.456	.551	1008	1146	65			10	30	1,186	123.2
OF	1967	A.Kaline	458	83	1	542	141	28	2	25	.308	.415	.541	957	1029	8	2	7	0	40	1,076	82.4
OF	1946	R.Cullenbine	328	88	1	417	110	21	0	15	.335	.477	.537	1014	1034	3	0	7	0	0	1,041	59.3
Starters		Averages	513	80	6	599	170	30	6	23	.331	.428	.547	975	987	14	2	4	4	33	1,032	90.5
C	1935	M.Cochrane	411	96	4	511	131	33	3	5	.319	.452	.450	902	846	5	5	(9)	0	50	886	53.5
1B	1938	H.Greenberg	556	119	3	678	175	23	4	58	.315	.438	.683	1122	1024	7	5	(4)	0	10	1,030	88.3
2B	1991	L.Whitaker	470	90	2	562	131	26	2	23	.279	.397	.489	886	891	4	2	0	0	20	911	60.4
SS	1966	D.McAuliffe	430	66	3	499	118	16	8	23	.274	.375	.509	884	923	5	7	(17)	10	(20)	896	55.7
3B	1959	E.Yost	521	135	12	668	145	19	0	21	.278	.437	.436	873	869	9	2	7	0	(10)	866	50.2
OF	1923	H.Heilmann	524	74	5	603	211	44	11	18	.403	.481	.632	1113	1063	9	7	(8)	(10)	(10)	1,035	83.9
OF	1907	S.Crawford	582	37	2	621	188	34	17	4	.323	.366	.460	826	954	18			10	40	1,004	76.8
OF	1961	R.Colavito	583	113	2	698	169	30	2	45	.290	.407	.580	987	959	1	2	(4)	(10)	20	965	69.1
Reserves		Averages	510	91	4	605	159	28	6	25	.311	.420	.534	954	945	7	4	(4)	0	13	949	67.2
Totals		Weighted Ave.	512	84	6	601	166	29	6	23	.325	.425	.543	968	973	12	2	1	3	26	1,004	82.8

Pitchers Rate of Success

Pos	Year	Name	G	GS	IP	W	L	SV	SO	BB	ERA	RA/9	R Wtd RA/9	V Runs /162
SP	1945	H.Newhouser	40	36	313	25	9	2	212	110	1.81	2.10	2.44	77.6
SP	1962	H.Aguirre	42	22	216	16	8	3	156	65	2.21	2.79	2.86	40.8
SP	1944	D.Trout	49	40	352	27	14	0	144	83	2.12	2.66	2.98	65.0
SP	1949	V.Trucks	41	32	275	19	11	4	153	124	2.81	3.11	2.98	50.6
SP	1997	J.Thompson	32	32	223	15	11	0	151	66	3.02	3.30	3.02	38.1
Starters		Averages	41	32	276	20	11	2	163	90	2.35	2.75	2.85	54.4
RP	1973	J.Hiller	65	0	125	10	5	38	124	39	1.44	1.51	1.60	41.1
RP	1995	M.Henneman	50	0	50	0	2	26	43	13	2.15	2.15	1.91	16.5
RP	1984	W.Hernandez	80	0	140	9	3	32	112	36	1.92	1.92	1.97	40.3
RP	1999	D.Brocail	70	0	82	4	4	2	78	25	2.52	2.52	2.19	21.6
Relievers		Averages	66	0	99	6	4	25	89	28	1.92	1.94	1.89	29.9
Totals		Averages	107	32	375	26	14	26	252	118	2.23	2.53	2.59	84.3

Detroit Tigers
Catchers

V	R	Year	Name	AB	BB	HBP	TAB	H	2B	3B	HR	BA	OB	SA	PRO	Wtd PRO	SB	CS	SBF	SPF	FF	R TF	V HC
1	1	1968	B.Freehan	540	65	24	629	142	24	2	25	.263	.367	.454	821	907	0	1	(3)	10	80	994	94.8
2	2	1967	B.Freehan	517	73	20	610	146	23	1	20	.282	.392	.447	839	902	1	2	(5)	10	50	958	81.5
3	5	1938	R.York	463	92	2	557	138	27	2	33	.298	.417	.579	995	909	1	2	(5)		(30)	874	54.8
4	3	1935	M.Cochrane	411	96	4	511	131	33	3	5	.319	.452	.450	902	846	5	5	(9)		50	886	53.5
5	4	1982	L.Parrish	486	40	1	527	138	19	2	32	.284	.340	.529	868	865	3	4	(9)	(10)	30	876	49.8
6	7	1964	B.Freehan	520	36	8	564	156	14	8	18	.300	.355	.462	816	825	5	1	5	10	20	860	49.2
7	14	1983	L.Parrish	605	44	1	650	163	42	3	27	.269	.320	.483	803	802	1	3	(7)	(10)	50	834	48.6
8	8	1971	B.Freehan	516	54	9	579	143	26	4	21	.277	.356	.465	821	847	2	7	(20)		20	848	46.9
9	12	1991	M.Tettleton	501	101	2	604	132	17	2	31	.263	.389	.491	880	885	3	3	(5)	(10)	(30)	840	46.9
10	11	1934	M.Cochrane	437	78	4	519	140	32	1	2	.320	.428	.412	840	790	8	4	0		50	840	42.4
11	17	1992	M.Tettleton	525	122	1	648	125	25	0	32	.238	.383	.469	851	868	0	6	(18)	(10)	(30)	810	41.1
12	6	1937	R.York	375	41	0	416	115	18	3	35	.307	.375	.651	1,026	940	3	2	(2)		(70)	868	39.7
13	15	1969	B.Freehan	489	53	8	550	128	16	3	16	.262	.344	.405	749	762	1	2	(5)		70	827	39.3
14	18	1980	L.Parrish	553	31	3	587	158	34	6	24	.286	.327	.499	826	823	6	4	(3)	(10)		810	37.0
15	10	1972	B.Freehan	374	48	6	428	98	18	2	10	.262	.355	.401	756	820	0	1	(4)		30	846	36.1
16	19	1985	L.Parrish	549	41	2	592	150	27	1	28	.273	.326	.479	805	800	2	6	(16)	(10)	30	804	35.6
17	9	1993	C.Kreuter	374	49	3	426	107	23	3	15	.286	.373	.484	857	837	2	1	0		10	847	34.3
18	16	1924	J.Bassler	379	62	3	444	131	20	3	1	.346	.441	.422	864	807	2	1	0	(10)	20	817	31.2
19	13	1939	R.York	329	41	2	372	101	16	1	20	.307	.387	.544	931	866	5	0	13		(40)	839	30.1
20	21	1994	M.Tettleton	339	97	5	441	84	18	2	17	.248	.422	.463	885	826	0	1	(4)	(10)	(40)	772	28.0
21	22	1984	L.Parrish	578	41	2	621	137	16	2	33	.237	.290	.443	733	736	2	3	(6)	(10)	50	770	27.3
22	20	1987	M.Nokes	461	35	6	502	133	14	2	32	.289	.347	.536	882	846	2	1	0		(60)	786	26.1
23	23	1966	B.Freehan	492	40	3	535	115	22	0	12	.234	.295	.352	647	676	5	2	2	10	80	767	22.9
24	26	1979	L.Parrish	493	49	2	544	136	26	3	19	.276	.344	.456	800	783	6	7	(14)	(10)		759	21.2
25	27	1999	B.Ausmus	458	51	14	523	126	25	6	9	.275	.365	.415	780	719	12	9	(11)	10	40	759	20.2

Detroit Tigers
First basemen

V	R	Year	Name	AB	BB	HBP	TAB	H	2B	3B	HR	BA	OB	SA	PRO	Wtd PRO	SB	CS	SBF	SPF	FF	R TF	V HC
1	1	1961	N.Cash	535	124	9	668	193	22	8	41	.361	.488	.662	1,150	1,118	11	5	1		20	1,139	117.5
2	3	1937	H.Greenberg	594	102	3	699	200	49	14	40	.337	.436	.668	1,105	1,013	8	3	3		10	1,025	89.5
3	2	1938	H.Greenberg	556	119	3	678	175	23	4	58	.315	.438	.683	1,122	1,024	7	5	(4)		10	1,030	88.3
4	6	1935	H.Greenberg	619	87	0	706	203	46	16	36	.328	.411	.628	1,039	974	4	3	(3)		10	982	74.8
5	4	1946	H.Greenberg	523	80	0	603	145	29	5	44	.277	.373	.604	977	997	5	1	5			1,002	70.0
6	5	1939	H.Greenberg	500	91	2	593	156	42	7	33	.312	.420	.622	1,042	969	8	3	3		10	982	63.1
7	7	1990	C.Fielder	573	90	5	668	159	25	1	51	.277	.380	.592	972	988	0	1	(3)	(10)	(10)	965	62.1
8	8	1934	H.Greenberg	593	63	2	658	201	63	7	26	.339	.404	.600	1,005	946	9	5	(1)		10	954	60.7
9	10	1943	R.York	571	84	1	656	155	22	11	34	.271	.366	.527	893	951	5	5	(7)		(10)	934	53.8
10	12	1940	R.York	588	89	4	681	186	46	6	33	.316	.410	.583	993	935	3	2	(1)		(10)	923	52.3
11	9	1971	N.Cash	452	59	7	518	128	10	3	32	.283	.375	.531	905	934	1	0	2	(10)	10	936	41.0
12	11	1965	N.Cash	467	77	4	548	124	23	1	30	.266	.374	.512	886	917	6	6	(10)		20	927	40.9
13	14	1962	N.Cash	507	104	13	624	123	16	2	39	.243	.385	.513	897	877	6	3	0		20	897	37.9
14	16	1963	N.Cash	493	89	6	588	133	19	1	26	.270	.388	.471	858	873	2	3	(6)		20	887	32.7
15	20	1929	D.Alexander	626	56	0	682	215	43	15	25	.343	.397	.580	977	912	5	9	(18)	(10)	(20)	864	32.3
16	19	1966	N.Cash	603	66	4	673	168	18	3	32	.279	.354	.478	831	868	2	1	0	(10)	10	868	31.4
17	17	1908	C.Rossman	524	27	1	552	154	33	13	2	.294	.330	.418	748	883	8					883	31.1
18	13	1968	N.Cash	411	39	3	453	108	15	1	25	.263	.331	.487	818	903	1	1	(2)	(10)	20	911	30.5
19	23	1911	J.Delahanty	542	56	10	608	184	30	14	3	.339	.411	.463	874	887	15				(30)	857	26.4
20	15	1960	N.Cash	353	65	6	424	101	16	3	18	.286	.406	.501	907	892	4	2	0			892	25.9
21	21	1967	N.Cash	488	81	4	573	118	16	5	22	.242	.354	.430	785	844	3	2	(2)	(10)	30	863	25.3
22	18	1974	B.Freehan	445	42	5	492	132	17	5	18	.297	.364	.479	842	882	2	0	4	(10)		876	24.9
23	24	1978	J.Thompson	589	74	0	663	169	25	3	26	.287	.367	.472	839	857	0	0	0		(10)	847	24.4
24	22	1969	N.Cash	483	63	6	552	135	15	4	22	.280	.370	.464	833	849	2	1	0	(10)	20	859	23.4
25	31	1991	C.Fielder	624	78	6	708	163	25	0	44	.261	.349	.513	862	866	0	0	0	(10)	(20)	836	22.4

Detroit Tigers
Second basemen

V	R	Year	Name	AB	BB	HBP	TAB	H	2B	3B	HR	BA	OB	SA	PRO	Wtd PRO	SB	CS	SBF	SPF	FF	R TF	V HC
1	1	1936	C.Gehringer	641	83	4	728	227	60	12	15	.354	.431	.555	987	888	4	1	3		70	961	100.6
2	3	1934	C.Gehringer	601	99	3	703	214	50	7	11	.356	.450	.517	967	910	11	8	(7)		40	943	90.9
3	2	1937	C.Gehringer	564	90	1	655	209	40	1	14	.371	.458	.520	978	896	11	4	4		50	950	87.0
4	4	1929	C.Gehringer	634	64	6	704	215	45	19	13	.339	.405	.532	936	874	27	9	12	10	30	926	85.1
5	7	1935	C.Gehringer	610	79	3	692	201	32	8	19	.330	.409	.502	911	854	11	4	4		40	898	73.7
6	8	1930	C.Gehringer	610	69	7	686	201	47	15	16	.330	.404	.534	938	858	19	15	(15)	10	30	883	67.9
7	9	1933	C.Gehringer	628	68	3	699	204	42	6	12	.325	.393	.468	862	831	5	4	(4)	10	40	877	67.1
8	10	1983	L.Whitaker	643	67	0	710	206	40	6	12	.320	.385	.457	842	841	17	10	(4)	10	30	877	64.7
9	13	1938	C.Gehringer	568	113	4	685	174	32	5	20	.306	.425	.486	911	832	14	1	17		20	868	62.8
10	6	1991	L.Whitaker	470	90	2	562	131	26	2	23	.279	.397	.489	886	891	4	2	0		20	911	60.4
11	5	1939	C.Gehringer	406	68	1	475	132	29	6	16	.325	.423	.544	967	900	4	3	(4)		30	926	57.3
12	15	1985	L.Whitaker	609	80	2	691	170	29	8	21	.279	.365	.456	821	816	6	4	(3)	10	30	853	55.2
13	12	1989	L.Whitaker	509	89	3	601	128	21	1	28	.251	.366	.462	828	849	6	3	0		20	869	52.5
14	17	1928	C.Gehringer	603	69	6	678	193	29	16	6	.320	.395	.451	846	806	15	9	(4)	10	20	832	49.9
15	22	1932	C.Gehringer	618	68	3	689	184	44	11	19	.298	.370	.497	867	816	9	8	(10)	10	10	826	48.7
16	11	1992	L.Whitaker	453	81	1	535	126	26	0	19	.278	.389	.461	850	867	6	4	(4)		10	873	47.9
17	16	1927	C.Gehringer	508	52	2	562	161	29	11	4	.317	.383	.441	824	774	17	8	2	10	60	846	45.2
18	19	1998	D.Easley	594	39	16	649	161	38	2	27	.271	.333	.478	811	762	15	5	7	10	50	830	44.7
19	21	1940	C.Gehringer	515	101	3	619	161	33	3	10	.313	.428	.447	875	823	10	0	15		(10)	829	44.4
20	18	1982	L.Whitaker	560	48	1	609	160	22	8	15	.286	.343	.434	777	774	11	3	8	10	40	832	42.5
21	26	1968	D.McAuliffe	570	82	2	654	142	24	10	16	.249	.346	.411	756	835	8	7	(9)	10	(20)	817	40.9
22	27	1967	D.McAuliffe	557	105	7	669	133	16	7	22	.239	.366	.411	777	836	6	5	(6)		(20)	811	40.0
23	14	1993	L.Whitaker	383	78	4	465	111	32	1	9	.290	.415	.449	864	843	3	3	(6)		20	857	38.1
24	25	1945	E.Mayo	501	47	0	548	143	24	3	10	.285	.347	.405	752	791	7	7	(12)		40	819	36.7
25	30	1984	L.Whitaker	558	62	0	620	161	25	1	13	.289	.360	.407	766	770	6	5	(6)	10	30	804	34.9

Detroit Tigers
Shortstops

V	R	Year	Name	AB	BB	HBP	TAB	H	2B	3B	HR	BA	OB	SA	PRO	Wtd PRO	SB	CS	SBF	SPF	FF	R TF	V HC
1	1	1987	A.Trammell	597	60	3	660	205	34	3	28	.343	.406	.551	957	918	21	2	24	10	10	962	94.5
2	2	1983	A.Trammell	505	57	0	562	161	31	2	14	.319	.388	.471	859	858	30	10	17	10	30	915	67.7
3	4	1984	A.Trammell	555	60	3	618	174	34	5	14	.314	.383	.468	852	855	19	13	(11)	10	30	885	65.6
4	7	1990	A.Trammell	559	68	1	628	170	37	1	14	.304	.381	.449	830	843	12	10	(12)	10	20	861	59.7
5	5	1901	K.Elberfeld	432	57	7	496	133	21	11	3	.308	.397	.428	825	828	23			10	40	878	59.0
6	3	1966	D.McAuliffe	430	66	3	499	118	16	8	23	.274	.375	.509	884	923	5	7	(17)	10	(20)	896	55.7
7	11	1993	T.Fryman	607	77	4	688	182	37	5	22	.300	.382	.486	868	847	9	4	1		(20)	829	54.7
8	8	1986	A.Trammell	574	59	5	638	159	33	7	21	.277	.350	.469	818	807	25	12	1	10	20	839	53.7
9	6	1988	A.Trammell	466	46	4	516	145	24	1	15	.311	.378	.464	841	855	7	4	(2)	10	10	874	52.0
10	12	1909	D.Bush	532	88	4	624	145	18	2	0	.273	.380	.314	694	801	53			10	10	821	49.9
11	10	1910	D.Bush	496	78	2	576	130	13	4	3	.262	.365	.323	687	781	49			10	40	831	48.8
12	15	1914	D.Bush	596	112	3	711	150	18	4	0	.252	.373	.295	668	735	35	26	(23)	10	70	792	46.3
13	14	1956	H.Kuenn	591	55	3	649	196	32	7	12	.332	.391	.470	862	825	9	5	(1)		(30)	794	42.9
14	16	1933	B.Rogell	587	79	3	669	173	42	11	0	.295	.381	.404	785	757	6	9	(17)	10	40	790	42.9
15	13	1980	A.Trammell	560	69	3	632	168	21	5	9	.300	.380	.404	783	780	12	12	(18)	10	30	802	42.2
16	9	1993	A.Trammell	401	38	2	441	132	25	3	12	.329	.390	.496	886	865	12	8	(9)		(20)	836	36.6
17	19	1934	B.Rogell	592	74	0	666	175	32	8	3	.296	.374	.392	766	721	13	3	10	10	30	771	36.3
18	17	1924	T.Rigney	499	102	1	602	144	29	9	4	.289	.410	.407	817	764	11	11	(17)	10	20	777	34.6
19	18	1908	G.Schaefer	584	37	1	622	151	20	10	3	.259	.304	.342	646	763	40			10		773	34.6
20	21	1981	A.Trammell	392	49	3	444	101	15	3	2	.258	.345	.327	671	704	10	3	9	10	40	762	32.2
21	20	1912	D.Bush	511	117	3	631	118	14	8	2	.231	.377	.301	679	703	35			10	50	763	32.1
22	25	1917	D.Bush	581	80	2	663	163	18	3	0	.281	.370	.322	691	765	34			10	(20)	755	30.9
23	22	1964	D.McAuliffe	557	77	3	637	134	18	7	24	.241	.336	.427	763	772	8	5	(3)	10	(20)	759	29.4
24	28	1913	D.Bush	597	80	4	681	150	19	10	1	.251	.344	.322	665	710	44			10	20	740	26.8
25	29	1992	T.Fryman	659	45	6	710	175	31	4	20	.266	.318	.416	734	748	8	4	0		(10)	738	25.9

Detroit Tigers
Third basemen

V	R	Year	Name	AB	BB	HBP	TAB	H	2B	3B	HR	BA	OB	SA	PRO	Wtd PRO	SB	CS	SBF	SPF	FF	R TF	V HC
1	1	1953	R.Boone	497	72	5	574	147	17	8	26	.296	.390	.519	909	892	3	3	(5)		10	897	51.9
2	3	1959	E.Yost	521	135	12	668	145	19	0	21	.278	.437	.436	873	869	9	2	7		(10)	866	50.2
3	2	1956	R.Boone	481	77	3	561	148	14	6	25	.308	.406	.518	924	885	0	0	0	(10)		875	44.7
4	4	1949	G.Kell	522	71	3	596	179	38	9	3	.343	.424	.467	892	860	7	5	(5)		10	865	44.6
5	7	1950	G.Kell	641	66	1	708	218	56	6	8	.340	.403	.484	886	824	3	3	(4)		20	840	44.0
6	6	1954	R.Boone	543	71	2	616	160	19	7	20	.295	.378	.466	844	843	4	2	0		10	853	42.2
7	5	1946	G.Kell	521	40	1	562	168	25	10	4	.322	.372	.432	804	820	3	2	(2)		40	858	40.0
8	9	1947	G.Kell	588	61	3	652	188	29	5	5	.320	.387	.412	798	807	9	11	(19)		40	828	36.6
9	8	1930	M.McManus	484	59	2	545	155	40	4	9	.320	.396	.475	872	797	23	8	12	10	20	839	33.6
10	10	1951	G.Kell	598	61	4	663	191	36	3	2	.319	.386	.400	786	767	10	3	6		40	813	32.1
11	12	1944	P.Higgins	543	81	4	628	161	32	4	7	.297	.392	.409	801	834	4	4	(6)	(10)	(20)	797	25.6
12	11	1955	R.Boone	500	50	1	551	142	22	7	20	.284	.350	.476	826	810	1	1	(2)			808	25.5
13	14	1997	T.Fryman	595	46	5	646	163	27	3	22	.274	.331	.440	772	728	16	3	15		40	783	20.5
14	15	1915	O.Vitt	560	80	4	644	140	18	13	1	.250	.348	.334	682	739	26	18	(15)	10	40	775	18.8
15	13	1986	D.Coles	521	45	6	572	142	30	2	20	.273	.337	.453	790	780	6	2	3	10	(10)	783	18.2
16	16	1934	M.Owen	565	59	4	628	179	34	9	8	.317	.385	.451	837	787	3	3	(5)		(10)	773	17.9
17	18	1995	T.Fryman	567	63	3	633	156	21	5	15	.275	.351	.409	760	717	4	2	0		50	767	17.1
18	19	1929	M.McManus	599	60	1	660	168	32	8	18	.280	.347	.451	798	745	16	11	(9)	10	20	766	16.6
19	20	1965	D.Wert	609	73	3	685	159	22	2	12	.261	.343	.363	706	731	5	6	(10)		40	761	14.6
20	21	1941	P.Higgins	540	67	2	609	161	28	3	11	.298	.378	.422	800	773	5	4	(5)		(10)	759	13.0
21	17	1909	G.Moriarity	473	24	1	498	129	20	4	1	.273	.309	.338	648	748	34			10	10	768	12.9
22	23	1996	T.Fryman	616	57	4	677	165	32	3	22	.268	.334	.437	771	705	4	3	(3)		50	752	11.6
23	28	1916	O.Vitt	597	75	1	673	135	17	12	0	.226	.314	.295	608	666	18			10	70	746	10.0
24	25	1999	D.Palmer	560	57	10	627	147	25	2	38	.263	.341	.518	859	792	3	3	(5)	(10)	(30)	748	9.5
25	26	1966	D.Wert	559	64	2	625	150	20	2	11	.268	.346	.370	716	748	6	3	0			748	9.3

Detroit Tigers
Outfielders

V	R	Year	Name	AB	BB	HBP	TAB	H	2B	3B	HR	BA	OB	SA	PRO	Wtd PRO	SB	CS	SBF	SPF	FF	R TF	V HC
1	2	1917	T.Cobb	588	61	4	653	225	44	24	6	.383	.444	.570	1,014	1,122	55			10	40	1,172	135.6
2	3	1911	T.Cobb	591	44	8	643	248	47	24	8	.420	.467	.621	1,088	1,103	83			10	30	1,143	124.3
3	1	1910	T.Cobb	506	64	4	574	194	35	13	8	.383	.456	.551	1,008	1,146	65			10	30	1,186	123.2
4	5	1915	T.Cobb	563	118	10	691	208	31	13	3	.369	.486	.487	973	1,055	96	38	27	10	10	1,102	119.5
5	4	1909	T.Cobb	573	48	6	627	216	33	10	9	.377	.431	.517	947	1,094	76			10	20	1,124	115.3
6	6	1912	T.Cobb	553	43	5	601	226	30	23	7	.409	.456	.584	1,040	1,078	61			10	10	1,098	102.6
7	8	1916	T.Cobb	542	78	2	622	201	31	10	5	.371	.452	.493	944	1,034	68	24	30	10	10	1,084	101.8
8	14	1940	H.Greenberg	573	93	1	667	195	50	8	41	.340	.433	.670	1,103	1,039	6	3	0		(10)	1,029	90.6
9	11	1918	T.Cobb	421	41	2	464	161	19	14	3	.382	.440	.515	955	1,044	34			10	20	1,074	89.2
10	13	1923	H.Heilmann	524	74	5	603	211	44	11	18	.403	.481	.632	1,113	1,063	9	7	(8)	(10)	(10)	1,035	83.9
11	16	1907	T.Cobb	605	24	5	634	212	28	14	5	.350	.380	.468	848	980	49			10	30	1,020	83.3
12	15	1908	T.Cobb	581	34	6	621	188	36	20	4	.324	.367	.475	842	994	39			10	20	1,024	83.0
13	10	1967	A.Kaline	458	83	1	542	141	28	2	25	.308	.415	.541	957	1,029	8	2	7		40	1,076	82.4
14	7	1913	T.Cobb	428	58	4	490	167	18	16	4	.390	.467	.535	1,002	1,070	51			10	10	1,090	81.8
15	18	1907	S.Crawford	582	37	2	621	188	34	17	4	.323	.366	.460	826	954	18			10	40	1,004	76.8
16	26	1955	A.Kaline	588	82	5	675	200	24	8	27	.340	.425	.546	971	952	6	8	(14)	10	30	978	74.7
17	21	1959	A.Kaline	511	72	4	587	167	19	2	27	.327	.414	.530	944	940	10	4	3	10	50	1,003	72.4
18	32	1956	A.Kaline	617	70	1	688	194	32	10	27	.314	.385	.530	915	877	7	1	7	10	70	963	71.0
19	23	1961	A.Kaline	586	66	4	656	190	41	7	19	.324	.396	.515	912	886	14	1	17	10	70	984	70.7
20	27	1911	S.Crawford	574	61	0	635	217	36	14	7	.378	.438	.526	964	978	37					978	70.1
21	20	1921	T.Cobb	507	56	3	566	197	37	16	12	.389	.452	.596	1,048	967	22	15	(13)	10	40	1,004	69.8
22	22	1927	H.Heilmann	505	72	2	579	201	50	9	14	.398	.475	.616	1,091	1,025	11	5	2	(10)	(20)	997	69.5
23	30	1961	R.Colavito	583	113	2	698	169	30	2	45	.290	.407	.580	987	959	1	2	(4)	(10)	20	965	69.1
24	31	1908	M.McIntyre	569	83	7	659	168	24	13	0	.295	.392	.383	775	914	20				50	964	68.4
25	24	1919	T.Cobb	497	38	1	536	191	36	13	1	.384	.429	.515	944	963	28			10	10	983	66.7

Detroit Tigers
Outfielders

V	R	Year	Name	AB	BB	HBP	TAB	H	2B	3B	HR	BA	OB	SA	PRO	Wtd PRO	SB	CS	SBF	SPF	FF	R TF	V HC
26	29	1908	S.Crawford	591	37	3	631	184	33	16	7	.311	.355	.457	812	958	15				10	968	66.7
27	19	1966	A.Kaline	479	81	5	565	138	29	1	29	.288	.396	.534	931	972	5	5	(8)		40	1,004	66.3
28	9	1914	T.Cobb	345	57	6	408	127	22	11	2	.368	.466	.513	979	1,076	35	17	2	10	(10)	1,078	65.6
29	33	1903	S.Crawford	550	25	2	577	184	23	25	4	.335	.366	.489	855	931	18			10	20	961	64.8
30	28	1922	T.Cobb	526	55	4	585	211	42	16	4	.401	.462	.565	1,026	971	9	13	(27)	10	20	974	63.4
31	36	1909	S.Crawford	589	47	1	637	185	35	14	6	.314	.366	.452	817	944	30				10	954	62.9
32	35	1919	B.Veach	538	33	5	576	191	45	17	3	.355	.398	.519	916	935	19			10	10	955	62.6
33	34	1905	S.Crawford	575	50	3	628	171	38	10	6	.297	.357	.430	786	905	22			10	40	955	62.3
34	39	1917	B.Veach	571	61	9	641	182	31	12	8	.319	.393	.457	850	941	21			10		951	62.1
35	12	1946	R.Cullenbine	328	88	1	417	110	21	0	15	.335	.477	.537	1,014	1,034	3	0	7			1,041	59.3
36	37	1958	A.Kaline	543	54	2	599	170	34	7	16	.313	.377	.490	867	866	7	4	(2)	10	80	954	59.1
37	44	1914	S.Crawford	582	69	1	652	183	22	26	8	.314	.388	.483	871	958	25	16	(10)		(10)	937	58.8
38	17	1962	A.Kaline	398	47	1	446	121	16	6	29	.304	.379	.593	972	950	4	0	8	10	50	1,019	55.5
39	48	1921	H.Heilmann	602	53	2	657	237	43	14	19	.394	.444	.606	1,051	970	2	6	(14)	(10)	(20)	925	55.2
40	41	1964	A.Kaline	525	75	3	603	154	31	5	17	.293	.385	.469	853	863	4	1	3	10	70	946	54.2
41	25	1925	T.Cobb	415	65	5	485	157	31	12	12	.378	.468	.598	1,066	979	13	9	(10)	10		980	54.0
42	43	1963	A.Kaline	551	54	4	609	172	24	3	27	.312	.378	.514	891	907	6	4	(3)	10	30	943	54.0
43	38	1968	W.Horton	512	49	8	569	146	20	2	36	.285	.357	.543	900	994	0	3	(10)	(10)	(20)	954	53.3
44	40	1926	H.Manush	498	31	6	535	188	35	8	14	.378	.421	.564	985	936	11	5	2	10		947	50.9
45	53	1945	R.Cullenbine	536	113	3	652	146	28	5	18	.272	.402	.444	846	890	2	0	3		20	913	50.8
46	52	1925	H.Heilmann	573	67	1	641	225	40	11	13	.393	.457	.569	1,026	943	6	6	(9)	(10)	(10)	914	50.4
47	54	1913	S.Crawford	609	52	0	661	193	32	23	9	.317	.371	.489	860	918	13			(10)		908	50.0
48	60	1962	R.Colavito	601	96	2	699	164	30	2	37	.273	.375	.514	889	869	2	0	3	(10)	40	902	48.1
49	50	1956	C.Maxwell	500	79	2	581	163	14	3	28	.326	.420	.534	954	914	1	1	(2)		10	922	48.0
50	46	1984	C.Lemon	509	51	7	567	146	34	6	20	.287	.360	.495	855	858	5	5	(8)	10	70	930	46.6
51	62	1903	J.Barrett	517	74	6	597	163	13	10	2	.315	.407	.391	798	869	27			10	20	899	46.6
52	45	1922	H.Heilmann	455	58	3	516	162	27	10	21	.356	.432	.598	1,030	975	8	4	0	(10)	(30)	935	45.8
53	57	1985	K.Gibson	581	71	5	657	167	37	5	29	.287	.370	.518	888	882	30	4	32	10	(20)	904	45.7
54	55	1959	H.Kuenn	561	48	1	610	198	42	7	9	.353	.405	.501	906	902	7	2	5			906	45.6
55	69	1924	H.Heilmann	570	78	4	652	197	45	16	10	.346	.428	.533	961	899	13	5	4	(10)		893	44.3
56	61	1950	H.Evers	526	71	4	601	170	35	11	21	.323	.408	.551	959	892	5	9	(20)		30	901	43.4
57	42	1965	A.Kaline	399	72	0	471	112	18	2	18	.281	.391	.471	862	892	6	0	12	10	30	944	41.9
58	63	1976	R.LeFlore	544	51	2	597	172	23	8	4	.316	.377	.410	787	840	58	20	28	10	20	898	40.0
59	64	1926	H.Heilmann	502	67	4	573	184	41	8	9	.367	.445	.534	979	930	6	7	(13)	(10)	(10)	897	40.0
60	71	1906	S.Crawford	563	38	1	602	166	25	16	2	.295	.341	.407	747	849	24			10	30	889	39.8
61	74	1921	B.Veach	612	48	1	661	207	43	13	16	.338	.387	.529	917	846	14	10	(9)	10	30	877	39.7
62	56	1979	S.Kemp	490	68	2	560	156	26	3	26	.318	.404	.543	946	926	5	6	(12)		(10)	904	39.2
63	66	1984	K.Gibson	531	63	8	602	150	23	10	27	.282	.367	.516	883	887	29	9	17	10	(20)	894	39.2
64	67	1969	J.Northrup	543	52	3	598	160	31	5	25	.295	.360	.508	868	884	4	2	0	10		894	38.9
65	51	1971	A.Kaline	405	82	7	494	119	19	2	15	.294	.421	.462	883	911	4	6	(15)		20	916	37.3
66	75	1916	B.Veach	566	52	3	621	173	33	15	3	.306	.367	.433	800	876	24	15	(9)	10		876	37.0
67	77	1915	B.Veach	569	68	4	641	178	40	10	3	.313	.390	.434	824	894	16	19	(32)	10		871	36.6
68	65	1986	K.Gibson	441	68	7	516	118	11	2	28	.268	.374	.492	866	854	34	6	40	10	(10)	895	33.7
69	80	2000	B.Higginson	597	74	2	673	179	44	4	30	.300	.379	.538	917	839	15	3	13		10	862	33.4
70	76	1957	C.Maxwell	492	76	5	573	136	23	3	24	.276	.379	.482	860	855	3	2	(2)		20	874	33.4
71	79	1912	S.Crawford	581	42	2	625	189	30	21	4	.325	.373	.470	843	873	41				(10)	863	33.2
72	68	1952	V.Wertz	415	69	1	485	115	20	3	23	.277	.381	.506	887	901	1	0	2	(10)		893	33.0
73	81	1957	A.Kaline	577	43	3	623	170	29	4	23	.295	.347	.478	825	820	11	9	(11)	10	40	860	31.9
74	82	1910	S.Crawford	588	37	1	626	170	26	19	5	.289	.332	.423	756	859	20					859	31.9
75	73	1925	A.Wingo	440	69	0	509	163	34	10	5	.370	.456	.527	983	904	14	13	(22)			881	31.6

Detroit Tigers
Starting Pitchers

V	R	Year	Name	G	GS	IP	W	L	SV	SO	BB	ERA	RA/9	R Wtd RA/9	V Runs /162
1	1	1945	H.Newhouser	40	36	313	25	9	2	212	110	1.81	2.10	2.44	77.6
2	2	1946	H.Newhouser	37	34	293	26	9	1	275	98	1.94	2.37	2.63	65.9
3	4	1944	D.Trout	49	40	352	27	14	0	144	83	2.12	2.66	2.98	65.0
4	9	1968	D.McLain	41	41	336	31	6	0	280	63	1.96	2.30	3.06	55.7
5	7	1944	H.Newhouser	47	34	312	29	9	2	187	102	2.22	2.71	3.03	55.5
6	5	1949	V.Trucks	41	32	275	19	11	4	153	124	2.81	3.11	2.98	50.6
7	22	1903	B.Donovan	35	34	307	17	16	0	187	95	2.29	3.05	3.33	48.6
8	10	1946	D.Trout	38	32	276	17	13	3	151	97	2.34	2.77	3.08	47.7
9	16	1969	D.McLain	42	41	325	24	9	0	181	67	2.80	2.91	3.24	47.5
10	18	1950	A.Houtteman	41	34	275	19	12	4	88	99	3.54	3.67	3.26	41.7
11	23	1939	B.Newsom	41	37	292	20	11	2	192	126	3.58	3.88	3.34	41.7
12	3	1962	H.Aguirre	42	22	216	16	8	3	156	65	2.21	2.79	2.86	40.8
13	17	1934	S.Rowe	45	30	266	24	8	1	149	81	3.45	3.72	3.26	40.3
14	28	1936	T.Bridges	39	38	295	23	11	0	175	115	3.60	4.30	3.40	40.0
15	11	1976	M.Fidrych	31	29	250	19	9	0	97	53	2.34	2.73	3.12	40.0
16	21	1957	J.Bunning	45	30	267	20	8	1	182	72	2.69	3.07	3.32	38.8
17	25	1934	T.Bridges	36	35	275	22	11	1	151	104	3.67	3.83	3.36	38.6
18	19	1954	S.Gromek	36	32	253	18	16	1	102	57	2.74	3.02	3.26	38.3
19	36	1956	F.Lary	41	38	294	21	13	1	165	116	3.15	3.55	3.44	38.3
20	6	1997	J.Thompson	32	32	223	15	11	0	151	66	3.02	3.30	3.02	38.1
21	12	1955	B.Hoeft	32	29	220	16	7	0	133	75	2.99	3.07	3.12	36.9
22	51	1972	M.Lolich	41	41	327	22	14	0	250	74	2.50	2.75	3.60	36.5
23	41	1949	H.Newhouser	38	35	292	18	11	1	144	111	3.36	3.64	3.49	36.3
24	27	1940	B.Newsom	36	34	264	21	5	0	164	100	2.83	3.75	3.38	36.2
25	54	1916	H.Coveleski	44	39	324	21	11	2	108	63	1.97	2.91	3.61	35.7
26	37	1922	H.Pillette	40	37	275	19	12	1	71	95	2.85	3.60	3.45	35.7
27	33	1948	H.Newhouser	39	35	272	21	12	1	143	99	3.01	3.61	3.43	35.7
28	42	1981	J.Morris	25	25	198	14	7	0	97	78	3.05	3.14	3.50	35.3
29	31	1958	F.Lary	39	34	260	16	15	1	131	68	2.90	3.15	3.41	34.9
30	76	1971	M.Lolich	45	45	376	25	14	0	308	92	2.92	3.18	3.73	34.7
31	81	1901	R.Miller	38	36	332	23	13	1	79	98	2.95	4.55	3.75	34.5
32	60	1907	E.Killian	42	34	314	25	13	1	96	91	1.78	2.95	3.63	33.9
33	30	1960	J.Bunning	36	34	252	11	14	0	201	64	2.79	3.29	3.41	33.9
34	43	1935	S.Rowe	42	34	276	19	13	3	140	68	3.69	3.95	3.51	33.8
35	14	1902	E.Siever	25	23	188	8	11	1	36	32	1.91	3.49	3.18	33.3
36	26	1933	F.Marberry	37	32	238	16	11	2	84	61	3.29	3.71	3.37	33.1
37	38	1987	J.Morris	34	34	266	18	11	0	208	93	3.38	3.76	3.46	32.4
38	39	1986	J.Morris	35	35	267	21	8	0	223	82	3.27	3.54	3.47	32.3
39	53	1947	H.Newhouser	40	36	285	17	17	2	176	110	2.87	3.32	3.61	31.5
40	13	1943	T.Bridges	25	22	192	12	7	0	124	61	2.39	2.67	3.16	31.3
41	34	1930	G.Uhle	33	29	239	12	12	3	117	75	3.65	4.14	3.44	31.3
42	50	1907	E.Siever	39	33	275	18	11	1	88	52	2.16	2.92	3.60	30.9
43	56	1983	J.Morris	37	37	294	20	13	0	232	83	3.34	3.59	3.62	30.6
44	8	1909	E.Killian	25	19	173	11	9	1	54	49	1.71	2.34	3.06	30.2
45	15	1949	F.Hutchinson	33	21	189	15	7	1	54	52	2.96	3.33	3.19	30.1
46	77	1909	G.Mullin	40	35	304	29	8	1	124	78	2.22	2.85	3.73	29.3
47	46	1985	J.Morris	35	35	257	16	11	0	191	110	3.33	3.57	3.54	29.1
48	82	1902	W.Mercer	35	33	282	15	18	1	40	80	3.04	4.12	3.75	29.1
49	91	1923	H.Dauss	50	39	316	21	13	3	105	78	3.62	3.99	3.78	28.7
50	47	1943	D.Trout	44	30	247	20	12	6	111	101	2.48	3.02	3.57	28.4

Detroit Tigers (1901–2000)

Detroit Tigers
Starting Pitchers

V	R	Year	Name	G	GS	IP	W	L	SV	SO	BB	ERA	RA/9	R Wtd RA/9	V Runs /162
51	96	1905	E.Killian	39	37	313	23	14	0	110	102	2.27	3.11	3.80	27.7
52	40	1995	D.Wells	29	29	203	16	8	0	133	53	3.24	3.90	3.47	27.6
53	35	1965	D.McLain	33	29	220	16	6	1	192	62	2.61	2.99	3.44	27.3
54	98	1915	H.Dauss	46	35	310	24	13	2	132	115	2.50	3.34	3.81	26.9
55	29	1939	T.Bridges	29	26	198	17	7	2	129	61	3.50	3.95	3.40	26.9
56	24	1979	J.Morris	27	27	198	17	7	0	113	59	3.28	3.46	3.34	26.8
57	48	1933	T.Bridges	33	28	233	14	12	2	120	110	3.09	3.94	3.58	26.7
58	112	1903	G.Mullin	41	36	321	19	15	2	170	106	2.25	3.59	3.91	26.5
59	45	1942	H.White	34	25	217	12	12	1	93	82	2.91	3.32	3.53	26.1
60	20	1940	S.Rowe	27	23	169	16	3	0	61	43	3.46	3.62	3.27	25.5
61	66	1954	N.Garver	35	32	246	14	11	1	93	62	2.81	3.40	3.67	25.5
62	84	1935	T.Bridges	36	34	274	21	10	1	163	113	3.51	4.24	3.77	25.3
63	61	1982	D.Petry	35	35	246	15	9	0	132	100	3.22	3.59	3.64	25.2
64	95	1909	E.Summers	35	32	282	19	9	1	107	52	2.24	2.90	3.80	25.0
65	57	1961	D.Mossi	35	34	240	15	7	1	137	47	2.96	3.64	3.62	24.9
66	68	1981	M.Wilcox	24	24	166	12	9	0	79	52	3.03	3.30	3.68	24.6
67	78	1966	E.Wilson	38	37	264	18	11	0	200	74	3.07	3.20	3.74	24.0
68	94	1919	B.Boland	35	30	243	14	16	1	71	80	3.04	3.44	3.80	23.8
69	65	1985	D.Petry	34	34	239	15	13	0	109	81	3.36	3.70	3.67	23.7
70	64	1942	A.Benton	35	30	227	7	13	2	110	84	2.90	3.45	3.66	23.7
71	44	1935	E.Auker	36	25	195	18	7	0	63	61	3.83	3.97	3.53	23.5
72	49	1977	D.Rozema	28	28	218	15	7	0	92	34	3.09	3.59	3.59	23.5
73	88	1961	J.Bunning	38	37	268	17	11	1	194	71	3.19	3.79	3.77	23.4
74	55	1957	P.Foytack	38	27	212	14	11	1	118	104	3.14	3.35	3.62	23.3
75	70	1928	O.Carroll	34	28	231	16	12	2	51	87	3.27	3.90	3.69	23.3
76	74	1930	V.Sorrell	35	30	233	16	11	1	97	106	3.86	4.48	3.72	22.8
77	97	1961	F.Lary	36	36	275	23	9	0	146	66	3.24	3.83	3.81	22.8
78	75	1911	G.Mullin	30	29	234	18	10	0	87	61	3.07	3.80	3.72	22.8
79	73	1984	D.Petry	35	35	233	18	8	0	144	66	3.24	3.63	3.72	21.7
80	93	1908	B.Donovan	29	28	243	18	7	0	141	53	2.08	2.89	3.80	21.6
81	52	1931	G.Uhle	29	18	193	11	12	2	63	49	3.50	4.10	3.61	21.4
82	100	1918	B.Boland	29	25	204	14	10	0	63	67	2.65	3.04	3.83	21.1
83	32	1941	A.Benton	38	14	158	15	6	7	63	65	2.97	3.59	3.42	21.1
84	85	1925	H.Dauss	35	30	228	16	11	1	58	85	3.16	4.34	3.77	21.0
85	87	1959	D.Mossi	34	30	228	17	9	0	125	49	3.36	3.63	3.77	21.0
86	79	1947	F.Hutchinson	33	25	220	18	10	2	113	61	3.03	3.44	3.74	21.0
87	63	1940	T.Bridges	29	28	198	12	9	0	133	88	3.37	4.05	3.65	20.9
88	103	1937	E.Auker	39	32	253	17	9	1	73	97	3.88	4.52	3.86	20.7
89	80	1924	R.Collins	34	30	216	14	7	0	75	63	3.21	4.13	3.74	20.6
90	69	1932	T.Bridges	34	26	201	14	12	1	108	119	3.36	4.25	3.68	20.6
91	111	1971	J.Coleman	39	38	286	20	9	0	236	96	3.15	3.34	3.91	20.5
92	104	1912	J.Dubuc	37	26	250	17	10	3	97	109	2.77	3.82	3.86	20.4
93	124	1914	H.Coveleski	44	36	303	22	12	2	124	100	2.49	3.23	3.99	20.1
94	67	1949	T.Gray	34	27	195	10	10	1	96	103	3.51	3.83	3.67	20.1
95	107	1956	P.Foytack	43	33	256	15	13	1	184	142	3.59	4.01	3.89	20.0
96	59	1950	D.Trout	34	20	185	13	5	4	88	64	3.75	4.09	3.63	20.0
97	116	1907	B.Donovan	32	28	271	25	4	1	123	82	2.19	3.19	3.93	19.9
98	102	1927	E.Whitehill	41	31	236	16	14	3	95	105	3.36	4.19	3.84	19.7
99	135	1904	E.Killian	40	34	332	14	20	1	124	93	2.44	3.20	4.05	19.6
100	71	1945	A.Benton	31	27	192	13	8	3	76	63	2.02	3.19	3.70	19.3

Detroit Tigers
Relief Pitchers

V	R	Year	Name	G	GS	IP	W	L	SV	SO	BB	ERA	RA/9	R Wtd RA/9	V Runs /162
1	1	1973	J.Hiller	65	0	125	10	5	38	124	39	1.44	1.51	1.60	41.1
2	3	1984	W.Hernandez	80	0	140	9	3	32	112	36	1.92	1.92	1.97	40.3
3	7	1979	A.Lopez	61	0	127	10	5	21	106	51	2.41	2.62	2.53	28.6
4	6	1988	M.Henneman	65	0	91	9	6	22	58	24	1.87	2.27	2.35	22.3
5	10	1983	A.Lopez	57	0	115	9	8	18	90	49	2.81	2.81	2.83	22.0
6	4	1999	D.Brocail	70	0	82	4	4	2	78	25	2.52	2.52	2.19	21.6
7	25	1974	J.Hiller	59	0	150	17	14	13	134	62	2.64	3.06	3.39	19.4
8	16	1976	J.Hiller	56	1	121	12	8	13	117	67	2.38	2.75	3.14	19.0
9	5	1981	K.Saucier	38	0	49	4	2	13	23	21	1.65	2.02	2.25	19.0
10	9	1978	J.Hiller	51	0	92	9	4	15	74	35	2.34	2.63	2.83	17.7
11	27	1984	A.Lopez	71	0	138	10	1	14	94	52	2.94	3.33	3.41	17.6
12	8	1960	D.Sisler	41	0	80	7	5	6	47	45	2.47	2.59	2.68	17.5
13	12	1960	H.Aguirre	37	6	95	5	3	10	80	30	2.85	2.94	3.04	16.8
14	2	1995	M.Henneman	50	0	50	0	2	26	43	13	2.15	2.15	1.91	16.5
15	19	1985	W.Hernandez	74	0	107	8	10	31	76	14	2.70	3.21	3.18	16.4
16	14	1987	M.Henneman	55	0	97	11	3	7	75	30	2.98	3.35	3.08	15.9
17	18	1981	D.Tobik	27	0	60	2	2	1	32	33	2.69	2.83	3.15	14.2
18	13	1990	J.Gleaton	57	0	83	1	3	13	56	25	2.94	2.94	3.08	13.6
19	15	1991	M.Henneman	60	0	84	10	2	21	61	34	2.88	3.09	3.14	13.3
20	33	1971	F.Scherman	69	1	113	11	6	20	46	49	2.71	3.03	3.55	12.6
21	22	1988	P.Gibson	40	1	92	4	2	0	50	34	2.93	3.23	3.35	12.4
22	30	1990	P.Gibson	61	0	97	5	4	3	56	44	3.05	3.33	3.49	11.5
23	40	1968	P.Dobson	47	10	125	5	8	7	93	48	2.66	2.81	3.74	11.3
24	20	1997	D.Brocail	61	4	78	3	4	2	60	36	3.23	3.58	3.28	11.1
25	11	1998	D.Brocail	60	0	63	5	2	0	55	18	2.73	3.30	2.97	11.1
26	29	1986	W.Hernandez	64	0	89	8	7	24	77	21	3.55	3.55	3.48	10.7
27	36	1970	J.Hiller	47	5	104	6	6	3	89	46	3.03	3.38	3.68	10.1
28	34	1990	M.Henneman	69	0	94	8	6	22	50	33	3.05	3.43	3.59	10.1
29	39	1935	C.Hogsett	40	0	97	6	6	5	39	49	3.54	4.18	3.71	9.6
30	21	1988	W.Hernandez	63	0	68	6	5	10	59	31	3.06	3.19	3.30	9.5
31	24	1993	M.Henneman	63	0	72	5	3	24	58	32	2.64	3.52	3.38	9.4
32	42	1994	J.Boever	46	0	81	9	2	3	49	37	3.98	4.43	3.83	9.2
33	28	1997	T.Jones	68	0	70	5	4	31	70	35	3.09	3.73	3.41	8.9
34	23	2000	T.Jones	67	0	64	2	4	42	67	25	3.52	3.94	3.36	8.5
35	35	1955	A.Aber	39	1	80	6	3	3	37	28	3.37	3.60	3.66	8.4
36	41	1996	R.Lewis	72	0	90	4	6	2	78	65	4.18	4.48	3.77	7.9
37	38	1914	R.Reynolds	26	7	78	5	3	0	31	39	2.08	3.00	3.70	7.8
38	32	1999	T.Jones	65	0	66	4	4	30	64	35	3.80	4.07	3.53	7.6
39	17	1992	M.Munoz	65	0	48	1	2	2	23	25	3.00	3.00	3.15	7.5
40	31	2000	D.Patterson	58	0	57	5	1	0	29	14	3.97	4.13	3.52	6.5
41	44	1980	A.Lopez	67	1	124	13	6	21	97	45	3.77	4.06	4.09	6.4
42	45	1972	C.Seelbach	61	3	112	9	8	14	76	39	2.89	3.13	4.10	6.0
43	43	1967	D.Wickersham	36	4	85	4	5	4	44	33	2.74	3.18	3.93	5.9
44	26	1994	B.Groom	40	0	32	0	1	1	27	13	3.94	3.94	3.41	5.8
45	46	1980	P.Underwood	49	7	113	3	6	5	60	35	3.59	4.07	4.10	5.7
46	49	1981	A.Lopez	29	3	82	5	2	3	53	31	3.64	3.75	4.18	5.2
47	37	1998	S.Runyan	88	0	50	1	4	1	39	28	3.58	4.11	3.70	4.8
48	48	1982	D.Tobik	51	1	99	4	9	9	63	38	3.56	4.10	4.15	4.5
49	47	1984	D.Bair	47	1	94	5	3	4	57	36	3.75	4.04	4.14	4.4
50	52	1950	H.White	42	8	111	9	6	1	53	65	4.54	4.78	4.25	4.0

New York/San Francisco Giants (1900–2000)

From start to finish, the Giants proved to be one of the most successful teams in the twentieth century. Led by short, feisty manager John McGraw, the Giants emerged in 1903, finishing in second place thanks to two 30-game winners in Joe McGinnity and Christy Mathewson, and a .350 batting average from catcher-turned-outfielder Roger Bresnahan. Adjusted for 4 percent hitter's deflation, Bresnahan batted .364, for a 973 Wtd. Production and a 1,003 Total Factor in his best season.

In 1904, the Giants went 106–47 to capture their first pennant. McGinnity was 35–8 with a 1.61 ERA, a 2.57 Wtd. RA/9, and he saved 94.6 runs from scoring over 408 innings, for the league's best ever volume of success. Mathewson, the team's second best pitcher, went 33–12 with a 2.03 ERA and 3.33 Wtd. RA/9, Dummy Taylor was 21–15 with a 2.34 ERA, Hooks Wiltse went 13–3, and the rest of the pitching staff was 4–9. New York won again in 1905 with a 105–48 record, as Mathewson went 31–9 with a 1.28 ERA and a 2.48 Wtd. RA/9, McGinnity added 21 wins, and Mike Donlin led the offense with a .356 average, 7 home runs, and 990 Wtd. Production.

New York won 98 games in 1908, but finished one game out due to the famous "bonehead" baserunning by young Fred Merkle. Mathewson was 37–11 with a 1.43 ERA, a 2.69 Wtd. RA/9, and a career-best 85.3 runs saved from scoring, while 37-year-old McGinnity faded to an 11–7 record in his last season. In 1909, Mathewson was 25–6 with a 1.14 ERA and a career-best 2.34 Wtd. RA/9, but the team slipped to third place.

The Giants won another pennant in 1911, as Mathewson went 26–13 with a 1.99 ERA, and Rube Marquard added a 24–7 record with a 2.50 ERA. Larry Doyle batted .310 with 25 triples and 13 home runs to win the Chalmers (MVP) Award. The Giants repeated as champs in 1912 with 103 wins, as Mathewson went 23–12, Marquard was 26–11, Chief Meyers hit .358, Doyle batted .330 with 10 home runs, and Merkle hit .309 with 11 home runs. The team won its third straight pennant in 1913 behind Mathewson, still going strong with a 25–11 record and 2.06 ERA. Marquard went 23–10 and Jeff Tesreau was 22–13 to round out a strong starting rotation.

After a three-year pause, the Giants won again in 1917 without Mathewson and Marquard. Fast outfielders Benny Kauff (.308, 30 steals) and George Burns (.302, 40 steals) led the offense, while new ace pitcher Ferdie Schupp went 21–7 with a 1.95 ERA.

McGraw's Giants, led by a powerful lineup, won four straight pennants from 1921 to 1924. George Kelly hit 77 home runs over that stretch, Frankie Frisch stole 131 bases, and nearly everyone hit for high batting averages:

	1921	1922	1923	1924
Kelly (1B)	.308	.328	.307	.324
Frisch (2B/3B)	.341	.327	.348	.328
Bancroft/Jackson (SS)	.318	.321	.304	.302
Youngs (OF)	.327	.331	.336	.355
I. Meusel (OF)	.329	.331	.297	.310

Beginning in 1925, the Giants went through a nine year dry spell without a pennant. In the meantime, they changed their cast of stars. Rogers Hornsby played one season for the Giants, hitting .361 with 26 home runs, for a 1,027 Total Factor in 1927. Twenty-year-old Mel Ott starred in 1929, hitting .328 with 42 home runs, for a 977 Wtd. Production. The 1930 Giants led the league with a

.319 batting average, yet finished in third place. Bill Terry led the hit parade with a .401 average and 23 home runs. However, Terry hit only .351 after adjusting for the league's 15 percent hitter's inflation that year, for a 935 Wtd. Production. Other hitters with inflated averages included Travis Jackson (.339), Fred Lindstrom (.379), Ott (.349), Freddy Leach (.327), and Shanty Hogan (.339).

The Giants won the pennant in 1933 by returning to an old strength: pitching. MVP Carl Hubbell, the team's best pitcher since Mathewson, was 23–12 with a 1.66 ERA and a team record 2.28 Wtd. RA/9. Hal Schumacher was 19–12 with a 2.16 ERA, and Freddie Fitzsimmons was 16–11 with a 2.90 ERA. The Giants won another pennant in 1936, carried again by Hubbell's arm, as he went 26–6 with a 2.31 ERA and a 2.31 Wtd. RA/9 to earn his second MVP Award, while Ott hit .328 and led the league with 33 home runs. New York repeated in 1937, as Hubbell went 22–8, Cliff Melton was 20–9 with a 2.61 ERA, Ott led the league with 31 home runs, and shortstop Dick Bartell hit .306 with 14 home runs. The team slid to third place in 1938 as Hubbell faded with a sore arm. Ott had his best season that year, hitting .311 with 36 home runs for a career-best 1,025 Wtd. Production, while playing 113 games at third base.

After putting together 34 winning seasons in 37 years from 1903 to 1939, the Giants had a mild midlife crisis in the 1940s, with only four winning seasons and no pennants. These Giants teams were led by Ott until he retired in 1946. The 1947 team hit 221 home runs, led by Johnny Mize (.302, 51 home runs, 967 Wtd. Production) and Walker Cooper (.305, 35 home runs), while Larry Jansen went 21–5 with a 3.16 ERA. That 1947 team finished in fourth place due to the poor pitching results behind Jansen.

The Giants rebounded in 1950, and went on to achieve 19 winning seasons over a 22-year period from 1950 to 1971. The 1951 team was famous for Bobby Thomson's climatic game-winning home run against the Dodgers in the playoffs, while 20-year-old Willie Mays arrived in the majors to hit .274 with 20 home runs, and Jansen and Sal Maglie each won 23 games.

Mays went into military service the next two years, and the Giants waited for his return to win again. In 1954, MVP Mays hit .345 with 41 home runs for a 1,113 Total Factor, super-sub Dusty Rhodes hit .341 with 15 home runs in just 164 at bats, and Johnny Antonelli went 21–7 with a league-leading 2.30 ERA and an impressive 2.69 Wtd. RA/9. The bullpen featured Hoyt Wilhelm (12–4, 2.10 ERA, 2.57 Wtd. RA/9) and Marv Grissom (10–7, 2.35 ERA, 2.71 Wtd. RA/9).

The Giants of the late 1950s were Mays' team. He hit 51, 36, 35, 29, and 34 home runs from 1955 to 1959, while batting as high as .347 in 1958, and leading the league in steals four consecutive seasons. He also won Gold Glove honors from 1957 to 1968, the first 12 seasons the award was presented.

The 1962 team hit 204 home runs on their way to a pennant, with Mays leading the league with 49 home runs for a 1,087 Total Factor, while Orlando Cepeda hit 35 round trippers. Jack Sanford went 24–7, Juan Marichal was 18–11, and veteran Billy Pierce was 16–6. In 1965, Mays earned his second MVP Award in his best season, hitting .317 with 52 home runs for a career-best 1,073 Wtd. Production, a 1,164 Total Factor and 122.9 Hits Contribution. McCovey hit 39 home runs that year; Marichal was 22–13 with a 2.13 ERA and a 2.69 Wtd RA/9; and reliever Frank Linzy was 9–3 with 21 saves and a 1.43 ERA for a team that finished 2 games behind Los Angeles. In 1966, the team was still stuck in second, 1½ games behind the Dodgers, as Marichal went 25–6 with a 2.23 ERA and 2.87 Wtd. RA/9, while Gaylord Perry was 21–8 with a 2.99 ERA.

Willie McCovey took over as the team's leading slugger in 1967, and he proceeded to hit 31, 36, 45, and 39 home runs the next four years. McCovey won the MVP Award for his 1969 performance, when he hit .320 with 45 home runs and 121 walks for a second place club. Adjusted for 2 percent hitter's deflation, McCovey batted .327 with 46 home runs, for a 1,139 Wtd. Production. Marichal also starred in 1969, going 21–11 with a league-leading 2.10 ERA and a 3.02 Wtd. RA/9.

The Giants ended their Mays-dominated winning era on a high note in 1971, as the 41-year-old led them to a division title, hitting .271 with 18 home runs, 23 steals, and 112 walks. Bobby Bonds hit .288 with 33 home runs and 26 steals, while Marichal won 18 games and Perry added 16 wins.

The Giants produced only four winning seasons from 1972 to 1985. In 1973, Bonds hit .283 with 39 home runs and 43 steals—just missing becoming the first 40-40 player in his best season. In 1978, 22-year-old Jack Clark emerged as the team leader as he hit .306 with 25 home runs. In 1982, Greg Minton was the bullpen stopper, with a 10–4 record, 30 saves, 1.83 ERA, and 2.37 Wtd. RA/9.

The Giants won their division in 1987, as Will Clark hit .308 with 35 home runs, although he was also caught stealing 17 times in 22 attempts. The Giants then made it to the World Series in 1989. Clark hit .333 with 23 home runs for a 1,028 Total Factor, while MVP Kevin Mitchell hit .291 with 47 home runs for a 1,066 Wtd. Production and a 1,059 Total Factor. Veteran Rick Reuschel led the pitching staff with a 17–8 record and a 2.94 ERA.

The Giants added Barry Bonds in 1993, they won 100 games, and ... just missed winning their own division, as the Braves won 101 games. MVP Bonds hit .336 with 46 home runs, 126 walks and 29 steals, for a 1,104 Wtd. Production, a 1,171 Total Factor, and 131.6 Hits Contribution.

Rob Thompson hit .312 with 19 home runs, and Matt Williams batted .294 with 38 home runs. John Burkett went 22–7, Bob Swift was 21–8, and Rod Beck led the bullpen with a 3–1 record, 48 saves, 2.16 ERA, and 2.29 Wtd. RA/9.

Bonds was the backbone of the team for the rest of the 1990s, including a 40-40 season in 1996, when he hit 42 home runs and stole 40 bases, for a 1,126 Total Factor. In 1994, Williams led the league with 43 home runs in just 115 games before the season ended due to the player's strike — he was on pace to hit 61 homers that year. The 1997 team won their division, and the 1998 team just missed the postseason when they lost a one game playoff to the Cubs.

The Giants won the division title in 2000, as Bonds hit .306 with a career best 49 home runs for a 1,101 Total Factor, while MPV Jeff Kent batted .334 with 33 home runs. Bullpen stopper Robb Nen was 4–3 with 41 saves, a 1.50 ERA, and a 1.84 Wtd. RA/9.

New York/San Francisco Giants — Hitters Volume of Success

Pos	Year	Name	AB	BB	HBP	TAB	H	2B	3B	HR	BA	OB	SA	PRO	Wtd PRO	SB	CS	SBF	SPF	FF	R TF	V HC
C	1906	R.Bresnahan	405	81	15	501	114	22	4	0	.281	.419	.356	775	882	25			10	30	922	61.4
1B	1969	W.McCovey	491	121	4	616	157	26	2	45	.320	.458	.656	1,114	1,139	0	0	0	(10)	0	1,129	105.4
2B	1927	R.Hornsby	568	86	4	658	205	32	9	26	.361	.448	.586	1,035	1,007	9		0		20	1,027	112.8
SS	1937	D.Bartell	516	40	10	566	158	38	2	14	.306	.367	.469	836	827	5			10	90	927	75.2
3B	1938	M.Ott	527	118	5	650	164	23	6	36	.311	.442	.583	1,024	1,025	2			0	0	1,025	100.7
OF	1993	B.Bonds	539	126	2	667	181	38	4	46	.336	.463	.677	1,140	1,104	29	12	7	10	50	1,171	131.6
OF	1955	W.Mays	580	79	4	663	185	18	13	51	.319	.404	.659	1,063	1,018	24	4	23	10	80	1,131	124.1
OF	1989	K.Mitchell	543	87	3	633	158	34	6	47	.291	.392	.635	1,027	1,066	3	4	(7)	10	(10)	1,059	90.9
Starters		Averages	521	92	6	619	165	29	6	33	.317	.425	.585	1,011	1,015	12	3	3	5	33	1,055	100.3
C	1970	D.Dietz	493	109	3	605	148	36	2	22	.300	.430	.515	945	921	0	1	(3)	(10)	(20)	888	60.8
1B	1989	W.Clark	588	74	5	667	196	38	9	23	.333	.412	.546	958	995	8	3	3	10	20	1,028	81.8
2B	2000	J.Kent	587	90	9	686	196	41	7	33	.334	.430	.596	1,026	936	12	9	(8)	10	(10)	928	79.4
SS	1921	D.Bancroft	606	66	4	676	193	26	15	6	.318	.389	.441	830	796	17	10	(4)	10	70	872	71.0
3B	1906	A.Devlin	498	74	6	578	149	23	8	2	.299	.396	.390	786	895	54			10	60	965	72.0
OF	1905	M.Donlin	606	56	2	664	216	31	16	7	.356	.413	.495	908	990	33			10	(20)	980	74.2
OF	1973	B.Bonds	643	87	4	734	182	34	4	39	.283	.372	.530	902	910	43	17	12	10	30	961	71.4
OF	1951	M.Irvin	558	89	9	656	174	19	11	24	.312	.415	.514	929	910	12	2	12	10	40	971	70.2
Reserves		Averages	572	81	5	658	182	31	9	20	.318	.407	.505	912	919	22	5	1	8	21	949	72.6
Totals		Weighted Ave.	538	88	6	632	171	30	7	29	.317	.419	.557	976	983	16	3	2	6	29	1,020	91.0

Pitchers Volume of Success

Pos	Year	Name	G	GS	IP	W	L	SV	SO	BB	ERA	RA/9	Wtd RA/9	R Runs /162	V
SP	1904	J.McGinnity	51	44	408	35	8	5	144	86	1.61	2.27	2.57	94.6	
SP	1908	C.Mathewson	56	44	391	37	11	5	259	42	1.43	1.96	2.69	85.3	
SP	1933	C.Hubbell	45	33	309	23	12	5	156	47	1.66	2.01	2.28	82.1	
SP	1965	J.Marichal	39	37	295	22	13	1	240	46	2.13	2.38	2.69	61.2	
SP	1928	L.Benton	42	35	310	25	9	4	90	71	2.73	3.08	2.99	56.9	
Starters		Averages	47	39	343	28	11	4	178	58	1.87	2.32	2.64	76.0	
RP	1982	G.Minton	78	0	123	10	4	30	58	42	1.83	2.12	2.37	29.9	
RP	1954	H.Wilhelm	57	0	111	12	4	7	64	52	2.10	2.59	2.57	25.8	
RP	1990	J.Brantley	55	0	87	5	3	19	61	33	1.56	1.87	2.01	24.6	
RP	1998	R.Nen	78	0	89	7	7	40	110	25	1.52	2.13	2.10	24.3	
Relievers		Averages	67	0	103	9	5	24	73	38	1.78	2.20	2.29	26.2	
Totals		Averages	114	39	445	37	15	28	251	96	1.85	2.29	2.56	102.2	

New York/San Francisco Giants (1900–2000) 105

New York/San Francisco Giants — **Hitters Rate of Success**

Pos	Year	Name	AB	BB	HBP	TAB	H	2B	3B	HR	BA	OB	SA	PRO	Wtd PRO	SB	CS	SBF	SPF	FF	R TF	V HC
C	1912	C.Meyers	371	47	8	426	133	16	5	6	.358	.441	.477	918	913	8			(10)	10	913	50.3
1B	1969	W.McCovey	491	121	4	616	157	26	2	45	.320	.458	.656	1,114	1,139	0	0	0	(10)	0	1,129	105.4
2B	1927	R.Hornsby	568	86	4	658	205	32	9	26	.361	.448	.586	1,035	1,007	9			0	20	1,027	112.8
SS	1937	D.Bartell	516	40	10	566	158	38	2	14	.306	.367	.469	836	827	5			10	90	927	75.2
3B	1938	M.Ott	527	118	5	650	164	23	6	36	.311	.442	.583	1,024	1,025	2			0	0	1,025	100.7
OF	1993	B.Bonds	539	126	2	667	181	38	4	46	.336	.463	.677	1,140	1,104	29	12	7	10	50	1,171	131.6
OF	1965	W.Mays	558	76	0	634	177	21	3	52	.317	.399	.645	1,044	1,073	9	4	1	10	80	1,164	122.9
OF	1989	K.Mitchell	543	87	3	633	158	34	6	47	.291	.392	.635	1,027	1,066	3	4	(7)	10	(10)	1,059	90.9
Starters		Averages	514	88	5	606	167	29	5	34	.324	.427	.596	1,023	1,027	8	3	0	3	30	1,059	98.7
C	1970	D.Dietz	493	109	3	605	148	36	2	22	.300	.430	.515	945	921	0	1	(3)	(10)	(20)	888	60.8
1B	1946	J.Mize	377	62	5	444	127	18	3	22	.337	.437	.576	1,013	1,045	3			(10)	0	1,035	59.0
2B	1906	S.Strang	313	54	2	369	100	16	4	4	.319	.423	.435	857	976	21			10	(10)	976	53.8
SS	1927	T.Jackson	469	32	1	502	149	29	4	14	.318	.363	.486	849	826	8			10	40	876	53.9
3B	1906	A.Devlin	498	74	6	578	149	23	8	2	.299	.396	.390	786	895	54			10	60	965	72.0
OF	1903	R.Bresnahan	406	61	7	474	142	30	8	4	.350	.443	.493	936	973	34			10	20	1,003	64.1
OF	1905	M.Donlin	606	56	2	664	216	31	16	7	.356	.413	.495	908	990	33			10	(20)	980	74.2
OF	1951	M.Irvin	558	89	9	656	174	19	11	24	.312	.415	.514	929	910	12	2	12	10	40	971	70.2
Reserves		Averages	465	67	4	537	151	25	7	12	.324	.414	.488	902	939	21	0	1	5	14	958	63.5
Totals		Weighted Ave.	498	81	4	583	161	27	5	27	.324	.423	.562	985	997	12	2	0	3	25	1,026	87.0

Pitchers Rate of Success

Pos	Year	Name	G	GS	IP	W	L	SV	SO	BB	ERA	RA/9	Wtd RA/9	V Runs /162
SP	1933	C.Hubbell	45	33	309	23	12	5	156	47	1.66	2.01	2.28	82.1
SP	1909	C.Mathewson	37	33	275	25	6	2	149	36	1.14	1.88	2.34	71.2
SP	1904	J.McGinnity	51	44	408	35	8	5	144	86	1.61	2.27	2.57	94.6
SP	1992	B.Swift	30	22	165	10	4	1	77	43	2.08	2.24	2.63	35.3
SP	1954	J.Antonelli	39	37	259	21	7	2	152	94	2.30	2.71	2.69	56.5
Starters		Averages	40	34	283	23	7	3	136	61	1.71	2.21	2.49	67.9
RP	1956	M.Grissom	43	2	81	1	1	7	49	16	1.56	1.67	1.77	26.3
RP	2000	R.Nen	68	0	66	4	3	41	92	19	1.50	2.05	1.84	19.9
RP	1990	J.Brantley	55	0	87	5	3	19	61	33	1.56	1.87	2.01	24.6
RP	1993	R.Beck	76	0	79	3	1	48	86	13	2.16	2.27	2.29	19.9
Relievers		Averages	61	1	78	3	2	29	72	20	1.70	1.96	1.98	22.7
Totals		Averages	101	34	361	26	9	32	208	81	1.71	2.16	2.38	90.6

New York/San Francisco Giants
Catchers

V	R	Year	Name	AB	BB	HBP	TAB	H	2B	3B	HR	BA	OB	SA	Wtd PRO	PRO	SB	CS	SBF	SPF	FF	R TF	V HC
1	1	1906	R.Bresnahan	405	81	15	501	114	22	4	0	.281	.419	.356	775	882	25			10	30	922	61.4
2	5	1970	D.Dietz	493	109	3	605	148	36	2	22	.300	.430	.515	945	921	0	1	(3)	(10)	(20)	888	60.8
3	4	1908	R.Bresnahan	449	83	6	538	127	25	3	1	.283	.401	.359	760	887	14			10		897	59.2
4	7	1947	W.Cooper	515	24	3	542	157	24	8	35	.305	.339	.586	926	897	2			(10)		887	56.8
5	2	1912	C.Meyers	371	47	8	426	133	16	5	6	.358	.441	.477	918	913	8			(10)	10	913	50.3
6	10	1950	W.Westrum	437	92	2	531	103	13	3	23	.236	.371	.437	808	774	2			(10)	80	844	44.3
7	3	1905	R.Bresnahan	331	50	11	392	100	18	3	0	.302	.411	.375	785	857	11			10	30	897	43.1
8	11	1939	H.Danning	520	35	2	557	163	28	5	16	.313	.359	.479	838	820	4			(10)	20	830	42.7
9	6	1907	R.Bresnahan	328	61	6	395	83	9	7	4	.253	.380	.360	740	847	15			10	30	887	41.6
10	8	1945	E.Lombardi	368	43	5	416	113	7	1	19	.307	.387	.486	873	886	0			(10)		876	41.4
11	14	1940	H.Danning	524	35	5	564	157	34	4	13	.300	.349	.454	803	808	3			(10)	20	818	39.7
12	9	1911	C.Meyers	391	25	13	429	130	18	9	1	.332	.392	.432	824	842	7			(10)	20	852	37.5
13	13	1928	S.Hogan	411	42	8	461	137	25	2	10	.333	.406	.477	883	841	0			(10)	(10)	821	33.1
14	12	1913	C.Meyers	378	37	9	424	118	18	5	3	.312	.387	.410	797	828	7			(10)	10	828	32.1
15	15	1951	W.Westrum	361	104	5	470	79	12	0	20	.219	.400	.418	818	801	1	0	2	(10)	20	813	32.0
16	17	1971	D.Dietz	453	97	4	554	114	19	0	19	.252	.388	.419	808	832	1	3	(9)	(10)	(20)	794	30.7
17	18	1984	B.Brenly	506	48	3	557	147	28	0	20	.291	.355	.464	820	838	6	9	(20)		(30)	787	29.1
18	16	1964	T.Haller	388	55	2	445	98	14	3	16	.253	.348	.428	776	798	4	2	0		10	808	27.6
19	20	1966	T.Haller	471	53	6	530	113	19	2	27	.240	.325	.461	785	793	1	3	(9)	(10)	10	784	26.9
20	23	1967	T.Haller	455	62	4	521	114	23	5	14	.251	.345	.415	761	796	0	4	(15)	(10)	10	781	25.8
21	21	1938	H.Danning	448	23	4	475	137	26	3	9	.306	.345	.438	783	784	1			(10)	10	784	25.3
22	19	1931	S.Hogan	396	29	4	429	119	17	1	12	.301	.354	.439	794	777	1			(10)	20	787	23.6
23	22	1930	S.Hogan	389	21	3	413	132	26	2	13	.339	.378	.517	894	781	2			(10)	10	781	21.5
24	24	1987	B.Brenly	375	47	3	425	100	19	1	18	.267	.353	.467	820	788	10	7	(9)			779	20.6
25	29	1986	B.Brenly	472	74	3	549	116	26	0	16	.246	.352	.403	754	756	10	6	(3)			753	19.7

New York/San Francisco Giants
First basemen

V	R	Year	Name	AB	BB	HBP	TAB	H	2B	3B	HR	BA	OB	SA	Wtd PRO	PRO	SB	CS	SBF	SPF	FF	R TF	V HC
1	1	1969	W.McCovey	491	121	4	616	157	26	2	45	.320	.458	.656	1,114	1,139	0	0	0	(10)		1,129	105.4
2	3	1989	W.Clark	588	74	5	667	196	38	9	23	.333	.412	.546	958	995	8	3	3	10	20	1,028	81.8
3	4	1970	W.McCovey	495	137	3	635	143	39	2	39	.289	.446	.612	1,058	1,031	0	0	0	(10)		1,021	76.0
4	5	1968	W.McCovey	523	72	5	600	153	16	4	36	.293	.383	.545	928	1,019	4	2	0	(10)		1,009	68.3
5	8	1932	B.Terry	643	32	1	676	225	42	11	28	.350	.382	.580	962	938	4				30	968	67.0
6	12	1930	B.Terry	633	57	1	691	254	39	15	23	.401	.452	.619	1,071	935	8				20	955	64.2
7	6	1963	O.Cepeda	579	37	10	626	183	33	4	34	.316	.367	.563	930	979	8	3	3			982	63.2
8	11	1947	J.Mize	586	74	4	664	177	26	2	51	.302	.384	.614	998	967	2		(10)			957	62.1
9	10	1988	W.Clark	575	100	4	679	162	31	6	29	.282	.392	.508	900	941	9	1	10		10	961	61.6
10	2	1946	J.Mize	377	62	5	444	127	18	3	22	.337	.437	.576	1,013	1,045	3		(10)			1,035	59.0
11	9	1942	J.Mize	541	60	5	606	165	25	7	26	.305	.380	.521	901	962	3					962	58.3
12	7	1966	W.McCovey	502	76	6	584	148	26	6	36	.295	.394	.586	979	989	2	1	0	(10)	(10)	969	55.4
13	19	1948	J.Mize	560	94	4	658	162	26	4	40	.289	.395	.564	959	947	4		(10)	(10)		927	51.8
14	20	1931	B.Terry	611	47	2	660	213	43	20	9	.349	.397	.529	926	906	8				20	926	51.7
15	15	1991	W.Clark	565	51	2	618	170	32	7	29	.301	.361	.536	897	915	4	2	0		30	945	51.6
16	16	1961	O.Cepeda	585	39	9	633	182	28	4	46	.311	.363	.609	972	933	12	8	(6)	10		937	50.5
17	18	1964	O.Cepeda	529	43	8	580	161	27	2	31	.304	.366	.539	904	929	9	4	2			931	44.4
18	22	1965	W.McCovey	540	88	6	634	149	17	4	39	.276	.383	.539	922	948	0	4	(12)	(10)	(10)	916	44.0
19	21	1905	D.McGann	491	55	19	565	147	23	14	5	.299	.391	.434	825	900	22				20	920	42.5
20	13	1973	W.McCovey	383	105	1	489	102	14	3	29	.266	.425	.546	971	979	1	0	2	(10)	(20)	951	42.2
21	17	1967	W.McCovey	456	71	6	533	126	17	4	31	.276	.381	.535	916	958	3	3	(5)	(10)	(10)	933	41.3
22	23	1992	W.Clark	513	73	4	590	154	40	1	16	.300	.392	.476	867	892	12	7	(3)		20	909	39.1
23	25	1927	B.Terry	580	46	2	628	189	32	13	20	.326	.377	.529	907	883	1				10	893	38.7
24	14	1944	P.Weintraub	361	59	0	420	114	18	9	13	.316	.412	.524	935	958	0			(10)		948	37.6
25	26	1924	G.Kelly	571	38	5	614	185	37	9	21	.324	.371	.531	902	873	7	2	5		10	888	36.3

New York/San Francisco Giants
Second basemen

V	R	Year	Name	AB	BB	HBP	TAB	H	2B	3B	HR	BA	OB	SA	PRO	Wtd PRO	SB	CS	SBF	SPF	FF	R TF	V HC
1	1	1927	R.Hornsby	568	86	4	658	205	32	9	26	.361	.448	.586	1,035	1,007	9				20	1,027	112.8
2	3	2000	J.Kent	587	90	9	686	196	41	7	33	.334	.430	.596	1,026	936	12	9	(8)	10	(10)	928	79.4
3	9	1923	F.Frisch	641	46	4	691	223	32	10	12	.348	.395	.485	880	843	29	12	7	10	10	870	63.9
4	6	1911	L.Doyle	526	71	5	602	163	25	25	13	.310	.397	.527	924	944	38			10	(60)	894	62.8
5	8	1924	F.Frisch	603	56	2	661	198	33	15	7	.328	.387	.468	855	828	22	9	6	10	30	874	62.4
6	4	1993	R.Thompson	494	45	7	546	154	30	2	19	.312	.377	.496	873	846	10	4	3	10	50	909	58.2
7	5	1982	J.Morgan	463	85	2	550	134	19	4	14	.289	.402	.438	840	853	24	4	27	10	10	901	56.5
8	7	1998	J.Kent	526	48	9	583	156	37	3	31	.297	.365	.555	920	876	9	4	2	10		888	56.2
9	15	1950	E.Stanky	527	144	12	683	158	25	5	8	.300	.460	.412	872	835	9				10	845	54.6
10	2	1906	S.Strang	313	54	2	369	100	16	4	4	.319	.423	.435	857	976	21			10	(10)	976	53.8
11	12	1909	L.Doyle	570	45	7	622	172	27	11	6	.302	.360	.419	779	882	31			10	(40)	852	51.9
12	13	1915	L.Doyle	591	32	3	626	189	40	10	4	.320	.358	.442	799	882	22	18	(21)	10	(20)	851	51.9
13	10	1991	R.Thompson	492	63	6	561	129	24	5	19	.262	.353	.447	800	816	14	7	0	10	40	866	48.3
14	16	1912	L.Doyle	558	56	2	616	184	33	8	10	.330	.393	.471	864	859	36			10	(30)	839	47.5
15	11	1919	L.Doyle	381	31	5	417	110	14	10	7	.289	.350	.433	783	853	12			10	(10)	853	38.6
16	17	1978	B.Madlock	447	48	3	498	138	26	3	15	.309	.380	.481	861	875	16	5	11	10	(60)	837	35.9
17	18	1916	L.Doyle	479	28	4	511	133	29	11	3	.278	.323	.403	726	811	19			10		821	34.7
18	19	1999	J.Kent	511	61	5	577	148	40	2	23	.290	.371	.511	882	806	13	6	2	10	(10)	808	33.8
19	25	1910	L.Doyle	575	71	5	651	164	21	14	8	.285	.369	.412	781	828	39			10	(50)	788	33.4
20	14	1908	L.Doyle	377	22	5	404	116	16	9	0	.308	.354	.398	752	877	17			10	(40)	847	32.8
21	24	1997	J.Kent	580	48	13	641	145	38	2	29	.250	.321	.472	794	753	11	3	7	10	20	791	32.2
22	22	1922	F.Frisch	514	47	3	564	168	16	13	5	.327	.387	.438	824	773	31	17	(5)	10	20	798	31.8
23	20	1981	J.Morgan	308	66	0	374	74	16	1	8	.240	.374	.377	751	773	14	5	10	10	10	803	31.7
24	23	1989	R.Thompson	547	51	13	611	132	26	11	13	.241	.321	.400	721	749	12	2	12	10	20	791	30.8
25	29	1943	M.Witek	622	41	0	663	195	17	0	6	.314	.356	.370	726	762	1			10		772	28.9

New York/San Francisco Giants
Shortstops

V	R	Year	Name	AB	BB	HBP	TAB	H	2B	3B	HR	BA	OB	SA	PRO	Wtd PRO	SB	CS	SBF	SPF	FF	R TF	V HC
1	1	1937	D.Bartell	516	40	10	566	158	38	2	14	.306	.367	.469	836	827	5			10	90	927	75.2
2	4	1921	D.Bancroft	606	66	4	676	193	26	15	6	.318	.389	.441	830	796	17	10	(4)	10	70	872	71.0
3	3	1901	G.Davis	491	40	2	533	148	26	7	7	.301	.356	.426	782	825	27			10	40	875	62.7
4	8	1920	D.Bancroft	613	42	2	657	183	36	9	0	.299	.346	.387	732	761	8	12	(23)	10	100	848	61.3
5	15	1922	D.Bancroft	651	79	3	733	209	41	5	4	.321	.397	.418	815	764	16	11	(8)	10	60	826	60.3
6	6	1936	D.Bartell	510	40	5	555	152	31	3	8	.298	.355	.418	773	755	6			10	100	865	56.6
7	10	1929	T.Jackson	551	64	0	615	162	21	12	21	.294	.367	.490	857	773	10			10	60	843	55.8
8	2	1927	T.Jackson	469	32	1	502	149	29	4	14	.318	.363	.486	849	826	8			10	40	876	53.9
9	9	1900	G.Davis	426	35	4	465	136	20	4	3	.319	.376	.406	782	783	29			10	50	843	46.5
10	21	1951	A.Dark	646	42	6	694	196	41	7	14	.303	.352	.454	805	788	12	7	(3)	10		796	46.5
11	12	1916	A.Fletcher	500	13	14	527	143	23	8	3	.286	.323	.382	705	787	15			10	40	837	46.2
12	13	1909	A.Bridwell	476	67	4	547	140	11	5	0	.294	.386	.338	724	819	32			10		829	45.8
13	16	1917	A.Fletcher	557	23	19	599	145	24	5	4	.260	.312	.343	655	731	12			10	70	811	44.6
14	24	1953	A.Dark	647	28	6	681	194	41	6	23	.300	.335	.488	823	778	7	2	4	10		792	44.4
15	18	1952	A.Dark	589	47	5	641	177	29	3	14	.301	.357	.431	788	799	6	6	(9)	10		800	44.2
16	14	1908	A.Bridwell	467	52	6	525	133	14	1	0	.285	.364	.319	683	797	20			10	20	827	43.3
17	23	1972	C.Speier	562	82	3	647	151	25	2	15	.269	.365	.400	765	792	9	4	1	10	(10)	793	42.6
18	11	1930	T.Jackson	431	32	1	464	146	27	8	13	.339	.386	.529	915	799	6			10	30	839	41.2
19	7	1926	T.Jackson	385	20	1	406	126	24	8	8	.327	.362	.494	856	834	2			10	20	864	41.1
20	20	1931	T.Jackson	555	36	1	592	172	26	10	5	.310	.353	.420	773	757	13				40	797	40.0
21	5	1911	A.Fletcher	326	30	14	370	104	17	8	1	.319	.400	.429	829	847	20			10	10	867	38.1
22	22	1904	B.Dahlen	523	44	1	568	140	26	2	2	.268	.326	.337	662	744	47			10	40	794	37.7
23	25	1928	T.Jackson	537	56	0	593	145	35	6	14	.270	.339	.436	775	738	8			10	40	788	37.4
24	17	1923	D.Bancroft	444	62	1	507	135	33	3	1	.304	.391	.399	789	756	8	7	(11)	10	50	805	36.3
25	19	1975	C.Speier	487	70	1	558	132	30	5	10	.271	.364	.415	779	787	4	5	(10)	10	10	797	36.0

New York/San Francisco Giants
Third basemen

V	R	Year	Name	AB	BB	HBP	TAB	H	2B	3B	HR	BA	OB	SA	PRO	Wtd PRO	SB	CS	SBF	SPF	FF	R TF	V HC
1	1	1938	M.Ott	527	118	5	650	164	23	6	36	.311	.442	.583	1,024	1,025	2					1,025	100.7
2	2	1906	A.Devlin	498	74	6	578	149	23	8	2	.299	.396	.390	786	895	54			10	60	965	72.0
3	3	1994	M.Williams	445	33	2	480	119	16	3	43	.267	.321	.607	928	873	1	0	2		60	935	70.8
4	5	1928	F.Lindstrom	646	25	2	673	231	39	9	14	.358	.383	.511	894	852	15			10	50	912	66.0
5	4	1930	F.Lindstrom	609	48	0	657	231	39	7	22	.379	.425	.575	999	873	15			10	30	913	64.8
6	7	1967	J.Hart	578	77	4	659	167	26	7	29	.289	.376	.509	885	925	1	1	(1)	10	(30)	904	59.0
7	9	1921	F.Frisch	618	42	1	661	211	31	17	8	.341	.384	.485	870	834	49	13	33	10	10	887	56.6
8	8	1993	M.Williams	579	27	4	610	170	33	4	38	.294	.330	.561	891	863	1	3	(8)		40	895	51.9
9	10	1991	M.Williams	589	33	6	628	158	24	5	34	.268	.314	.499	813	829	5	5	(8)		60	882	49.5
10	11	1948	S.Gordon	521	74	3	598	156	26	4	30	.299	.390	.537	927	915	8			(10)	(30)	875	47.7
11	12	1964	J.Hart	566	47	4	617	162	15	6	31	.286	.345	.498	843	867	5	2	2	10	(10)	868	44.7
12	6	1953	H.Thompson	388	60	4	452	117	15	8	24	.302	.400	.567	967	914	6	5	(8)			906	43.0
13	14	1990	M.Williams	617	33	7	657	171	27	2	33	.277	.321	.488	809	808	7	4	(1)		40	846	40.7
14	17	1965	J.Hart	591	47	2	640	177	30	6	23	.299	.353	.487	840	864	6	4	(3)	10	(30)	841	37.9
15	16	1966	J.Hart	578	48	4	630	165	23	4	33	.285	.344	.510	855	863	2	5	(12)	10	(20)	841	37.5
16	18	1909	A.Devlin	491	65	10	566	130	19	8	0	.265	.362	.336	698	790	26			10	40	840	35.1
17	15	1904	A.Devlin	474	62	6	542	133	16	8	1	.281	.371	.354	725	815	33			10	20	845	35.1
18	20	1907	A.Devlin	491	63	15	569	136	16	2	1	.277	.376	.324	700	802	38			10	20	832	33.0
19	27	1952	B.Thomson	608	52	4	664	164	29	14	24	.270	.331	.482	813	824	5	2	1	10	(20)	815	32.9
20	21	1949	S.Gordon	489	95	3	587	139	26	2	26	.284	.404	.505	909	887	1			(10)	(50)	827	32.7
21	19	1954	H.Thompson	448	90	5	543	118	18	1	26	.263	.392	.482	874	829	3	0	5			834	32.0
22	13	1996	M.Williams	404	39	6	449	122	16	1	22	.302	.372	.510	882	840	1	2	(6)		30	864	31.6
23	24	1908	A.Devlin	534	62	14	610	135	18	4	2	.253	.346	.313	659	768	19			10	40	818	31.3
24	25	1950	H.Thompson	512	83	3	598	148	17	6	20	.289	.391	.463	854	818	8					818	30.6
25	30	1927	F.Lindstrom	562	40	2	604	172	36	8	7	.306	.354	.436	790	769	10			10	30	809	28.2

New York/San Francisco Giants
Outfielders

V	R	Year	Name	AB	BB	HBP	TAB	H	2B	3B	HR	BA	OB	SA	PRO	Wtd PRO	SB	CS	SBF	SPF	FF	R TF	V HC
1	1	1993	B.Bonds	539	126	2	667	181	38	4	46	.336	.463	.677	1,140	1,104	29	12		10	50	1,171	131.6
2	3	1955	W.Mays	580	79	4	663	185	18	13	51	.319	.404	.659	1,063	1,018	24	4	23	10	80	1,131	124.1
3	2	1965	W.Mays	558	76	0	634	177	21	3	52	.317	.399	.645	1,044	1,073	9	4	1	10	80	1,164	122.9
4	4	1996	B.Bonds	517	151	1	669	159	27	3	42	.308	.465	.615	1,080	1,029	40	7	37	10	50	1,126	117.3
5	5	1954	W.Mays	565	66	2	633	195	33	13	41	.345	.415	.667	1,083	1,026	8	5	(3)	10	80	1,113	112.8
6	6	1964	W.Mays	578	82	1	661	171	21	9	47	.296	.384	.607	992	1,019	19	5	13	10	70	1,112	111.6
7	10	1962	W.Mays	621	78	4	703	189	36	5	49	.304	.385	.615	1,001	978	18	2	19	10	80	1,087	110.4
8	8	1963	W.Mays	596	66	2	664	187	32	7	38	.314	.384	.582	966	1,017	8	3	3	10	70	1,099	108.2
9	12	1958	W.Mays	600	78	1	679	208	33	11	29	.347	.423	.583	1,006	966	31	6	26	10	70	1,073	107.3
10	11	1957	W.Mays	585	76	1	662	195	26	20	35	.333	.411	.626	1,037	1,011	38	19	0	10	60	1,081	107.2
11	9	1994	B.Bonds	391	74	6	471	122	18	1	37	.312	.429	.647	1,076	1,013	29	9	22	10	50	1,095	107.1
12	14	1995	B.Bonds	506	120	5	631	149	30	7	33	.294	.434	.577	1,011	963	31	10	16	10	70	1,060	102.3
13	13	1997	B.Bonds	532	145	8	685	155	26	5	40	.291	.450	.585	1,034	982	37	8	29	10	40	1,061	98.9
14	7	2000	B.Bonds	480	117	3	600	147	28	4	49	.306	.445	.688	1,133	1,033	11	3	8	10	50	1,101	98.3
15	16	1998	B.Bonds	552	130	8	690	167	44	7	37	.303	.442	.609	1,051	1,000	28	12	5	10	40	1,055	98.0
16	15	1989	K.Mitchell	543	87	3	633	158	34	6	47	.291	.392	.635	1,027	1,066	3	4	(7)	10	(10)	1,059	90.9
17	17	1959	W.Mays	575	65	2	642	180	43	5	34	.313	.385	.583	967	939	27	4	28	10	60	1,037	90.0
18	21	1932	M.Ott	566	100	4	670	180	30	8	38	.318	.424	.601	1,025	999	6				20	1,019	87.8
19	18	1960	W.Mays	595	61	4	660	190	29	12	29	.319	.386	.555	941	936	25	10	7	10	70	1,023	87.8
20	19	1936	M.Ott	534	111	5	650	175	28	6	33	.328	.448	.588	1,036	1,013	6				10	1,023	86.4
21	23	1961	W.Mays	572	81	2	655	176	32	3	40	.308	.395	.584	979	941	18	9	0	10	60	1,011	83.1
22	29	1929	M.Ott	545	113	6	664	179	37	2	42	.328	.449	.635	1,084	977	6			0	20	997	79.7
23	24	1956	W.Mays	578	68	1	647	171	27	8	36	.296	.371	.557	928	904	40	10	29	10	60	1,003	79.6
24	30	1942	M.Ott	549	109	3	661	162	21	0	30	.295	.415	.497	912	974	6				20	994	78.3
25	20	1966	W.Mays	552	70	2	624	159	29	4	37	.288	.370	.556	926	935	5	1	5	10	70	1,020	78.1

New York/San Francisco Giants
Outfielders

V	R	Year	Name	AB	BB	HBP	TAB	H	2B	3B	HR	BA	OB	SA	PRO	Wtd PRO	SB	CS	SBF	SPF	FF	R TF	V HC
26	32	1905	M.Donlin	606	56	2	664	216	31	16	7	.356	.413	.495	908	990	33			10	(20)	980	74.2
27	33	1934	M.Ott	582	85	3	670	190	29	10	35	.326	.415	.591	1,006	977	0					977	73.7
28	35	1935	M.Ott	593	82	3	678	191	33	6	31	.322	.407	.555	962	940	7				30	970	72.4
29	38	1973	B.Bonds	643	87	4	734	182	34	4	39	.283	.372	.530	902	910	43	17	12	10	30	961	71.4
30	34	1951	M.Irvin	558	89	9	656	174	19	11	24	.312	.415	.514	929	910	12	2	12	10	40	971	70.2
31	39	1971	B.Bonds	619	62	5	686	178	32	4	33	.288	.357	.512	869	896	26	8	14	10	40	960	66.1
32	27	1968	W.Mays	498	67	2	567	144	20	5	23	.289	.376	.488	864	948	12	6	0	10	40	998	65.0
33	22	1939	M.Ott	396	100	1	497	122	23	2	27	.308	.449	.581	1,030	1,008	2			10		1,018	64.9
34	25	1903	R.Bresnahan	406	61	7	474	142	30	8	4	.350	.443	.493	936	973	34			10	20	1,003	64.1
35	37	1908	M.Donlin	593	23	5	621	198	26	13	6	.334	.364	.452	816	952	30			10		962	63.7
36	26	1971	W.Mays	417	112	3	532	113	24	5	18	.271	.429	.482	911	938	23	3	30	10	20	999	61.1
37	51	1970	B.Bonds	663	77	2	742	200	36	10	26	.302	.376	.504	880	858	48	10	36	10	20	923	58.7
38	45	1920	R.Youngs	581	75	2	658	204	27	14	6	.351	.427	.477	904	940	18	18	(26)	10	10	934	58.2
39	40	1941	M.Ott	525	100	3	628	150	29	0	27	.286	.403	.495	898	921	5				20	941	57.9
40	31	1944	M.Ott	399	90	3	492	115	16	4	26	.288	.423	.544	967	990	2					990	57.4
41	52	1949	B.Thomson	641	44	2	687	198	35	9	27	.309	.355	.518	873	852	10			10	60	922	56.8
42	41	1924	R.Youngs	526	77	3	606	187	33	12	10	.356	.441	.521	962	931	11	9	(11)	10	10	940	55.5
43	44	1978	J.Clark	592	50	3	645	181	46	8	25	.306	.363	.537	900	915	15	11	(10)	10	20	935	54.6
44	42	1951	B.Thomson	518	73	4	595	152	27	8	32	.293	.385	.562	947	927	5	5	(8)	10	10	939	54.1
45	54	1914	G.Burns	561	89	5	655	170	35	10	3	.303	.403	.417	820	889	62			10	20	919	53.2
46	53	1937	M.Ott	545	102	3	650	160	28	2	31	.294	.408	.523	931	920	7					920	53.0
47	57	1917	G.Burns	597	75	1	673	180	25	13	5	.302	.380	.412	792	884	40			10	20	914	52.7
48	50	1930	M.Ott	521	103	2	626	182	34	5	25	.349	.458	.578	1,036	905	9				20	925	52.7
49	43	1931	M.Ott	497	80	2	579	145	23	8	29	.292	.392	.545	937	918	10				20	938	52.3
50	47	1963	W.McCovey	564	50	11	625	158	19	5	44	.280	.350	.566	916	964	1	1	(2)		(30)	932	52.0
51	63	1969	B.Bonds	622	81	10	713	161	25	6	32	.259	.353	.473	826	845	45	4	49	10		904	49.9
52	61	1900	K.Selbach	523	72	8	603	176	29	12	4	.337	.425	.461	885	886	36			10	10	906	49.6
53	28	1999	B.Bonds	355	73	3	431	93	20	2	34	.262	.392	.617	1,009	923	15	2	24	10	40	997	49.2
54	64	1919	G.Burns	534	82	0	616	162	30	9	2	.303	.396	.404	801	872	40			10	20	902	49.1
55	55	1927	G.Harper	483	84	5	572	160	19	6	16	.331	.435	.495	930	906	7			10		916	45.4
56	49	1970	W.Mays	478	79	3	560	139	15	2	28	.291	.395	.506	901	878	5	0	8	10	30	927	45.2
57	36	2000	E.Burks	393	56	1	450	135	21	5	24	.344	.427	.606	1,032	942	5	1	6		20	968	45.2
58	70	1972	B.Bonds	626	60	5	691	162	29	5	26	.259	.329	.446	774	801	44	6	44	10	30	885	44.2
59	48	1953	M.Irvin	444	55	3	502	146	21	5	21	.329	.406	.541	947	895	2	0	4	10	20	929	43.1
60	46	1910	F.Snodgrass	396	71	13	480	127	22	8	2	.321	.440	.432	871	924	33			10		934	42.4
61	68	1940	M.Ott	536	100	6	642	155	27	3	19	.289	.407	.457	864	868	6				20	888	42.2
62	58	1945	M.Ott	451	71	8	530	139	23	0	21	.308	.411	.499	910	923	1		(10)			913	41.4
63	66	1919	R.Youngs	489	51	7	547	152	31	7	2	.311	.384	.415	799	870	24			10	10	890	40.1
64	60	1984	C.Davis	499	42	1	542	157	21	6	21	.315	.369	.507	876	895	12	8	(7)	10	10	908	38.9
65	72	1974	B.Bonds	567	95	4	666	145	22	8	21	.256	.366	.434	800	813	41	11	27	10	30	880	38.8
66	56	1980	J.Clark	437	74	2	513	124	20	8	22	.284	.390	.517	907	919	2	5	(15)	10		914	38.2
67	79	1933	M.Ott	580	75	2	657	164	36	1	23	.283	.367	.467	834	867	1					867	36.1
68	77	1982	J.Clark	563	90	1	654	154	30	3	27	.274	.375	.481	856	869	6	9	(17)	10	10	872	35.7
69	80	1901	G.Van Haltren	543	51	4	598	182	23	6	1	.335	.396	.405	801	846	24			10	10	866	35.7
70	59	1904	R.Bresnahan	402	58	5	465	114	22	7	5	.284	.381	.410	791	889	13			10	10	909	35.4
71	86	1935	H.Leiber	613	48	10	671	203	37	4	22	.331	.389	.512	901	881	0				(20)	861	34.9
72	67	1907	C.Seymour	473	36	5	514	139	25	8	3	.294	.350	.400	750	859	21			10	20	889	34.0
73	73	1990	K.Mitchell	524	58	2	584	152	24	2	35	.290	.363	.544	907	905	4	7	(16)		(10)	879	33.9
74	81	1917	B.Kauff	559	59	5	623	172	22	4	5	.308	.379	.388	767	855	30			10		865	33.7
75	85	1988	B.Butler	568	97	4	669	163	27	9	6	.287	.395	.398	793	829	43	20	4	10	20	863	33.7

New York/San Francisco Giants
Starting Pitchers

V	R	Year	Name	G	GS	IP	W	L	SV	SO	BB	ERA	RA/9	R Wtd RA/9	V Runs /162
1	5	1904	J.McGinnity	51	44	408	35	8	5	144	86	1.61	2.27	2.57	94.6
2	7	1908	C.Mathewson	56	44	391	37	11	5	259	42	1.43	1.96	2.69	85.3
3	4	1905	C.Mathewson	43	37	339	31	9	3	206	64	1.28	2.26	2.48	82.5
4	1	1933	C.Hubbell	45	33	309	23	12	5	156	47	1.66	2.01	2.28	82.1
5	2	1936	C.Hubbell	42	34	304	26	6	3	123	57	2.31	2.40	2.31	79.9
6	31	1903	J.McGinnity	55	48	434	31	20	2	171	109	2.43	3.36	3.12	79.9
7	3	1909	C.Mathewson	37	33	275	25	6	2	149	36	1.14	1.88	2.34	71.2
8	29	1903	C.Mathewson	45	42	366	30	13	2	267	100	2.26	3.34	3.11	68.3
9	10	1934	C.Hubbell	49	34	313	21	12	8	118	37	2.30	2.88	2.77	65.4
10	9	1965	J.Marichal	39	37	295	22	13	1	240	46	2.13	2.38	2.69	61.2
11	13	1966	J.Marichal	37	36	307	25	6	0	222	36	2.23	2.58	2.87	57.6
12	19	1928	L.Benton	42	35	310	25	9	4	90	71	2.73	3.08	2.99	56.9
13	8	1954	J.Antonelli	39	37	259	21	7	2	152	94	2.30	2.71	2.69	56.5
14	23	1913	C.Mathewson	40	35	306	25	11	2	93	21	2.06	2.76	3.02	55.1
15	26	1912	C.Mathewson	43	34	310	23	12	4	134	34	2.12	3.11	3.05	54.7
16	27	1911	C.Mathewson	45	37	307	26	13	3	141	38	1.99	2.99	3.06	53.9
17	11	1933	H.Schumacher	35	33	259	19	12	1	96	84	2.16	2.47	2.81	53.0
18	50	1904	C.Mathewson	48	46	368	33	12	1	212	78	2.03	2.94	3.33	52.7
19	22	1969	J.Marichal	37	36	300	21	11	0	205	54	2.10	2.70	3.02	51.4
20	32	1910	C.Mathewson	38	35	318	27	9	0	184	60	1.89	2.83	3.18	51.3
21	16	1917	F.Schupp	36	32	272	21	7	0	147	70	1.95	2.28	2.94	51.3
22	24	1932	C.Hubbell	40	32	284	18	11	2	137	40	2.50	3.04	3.02	51.1
23	63	1901	C.Mathewson	40	38	336	20	17	0	221	97	2.41	3.51	3.42	49.2
24	42	1907	C.Mathewson	41	36	315	24	12	2	178	53	2.00	2.51	3.28	47.1
25	17	1931	B.Walker	37	28	239	16	9	3	121	64	2.26	2.94	2.94	45.0
26	38	1911	R.Marquard	45	33	278	24	7	3	237	106	2.50	3.18	3.25	42.5
27	71	1914	J.Tesreau	42	41	322	26	10	1	189	128	2.37	2.91	3.44	41.9
28	53	1912	R.Marquard	43	38	295	26	11	1	175	80	2.57	3.42	3.35	41.6
29	58	1951	S.Maglie	42	37	298	23	6	4	146	86	2.93	3.32	3.38	41.1
30	62	1963	J.Marichal	41	40	321	25	8	0	248	61	2.41	2.86	3.41	40.8
31	35	1931	C.Hubbell	36	30	248	14	12	3	155	67	2.65	3.19	3.19	39.5
32	52	1951	L.Jansen	39	34	279	23	11	0	145	56	3.04	3.29	3.35	39.5
33	43	1935	H.Schumacher	33	33	262	19	9	0	79	70	2.89	3.44	3.29	38.9
34	84	1908	H.Wiltse	44	38	330	23	14	2	118	73	2.24	2.59	3.56	38.6
35	54	1950	L.Jansen	40	35	275	19	13	3	161	55	3.01	3.47	3.36	38.6
36	72	1904	D.Taylor	37	36	296	21	15	0	138	75	2.34	3.04	3.45	38.4
37	66	1913	R.Marquard	42	33	288	23	10	3	151	49	2.50	3.13	3.42	38.3
38	15	1919	F.Toney	24	20	181	13	6	1	40	35	1.84	2.34	2.93	37.9
39	57	1959	S.Jones	50	35	271	21	15	4	209	109	2.83	3.29	3.37	37.6
40	40	1937	C.Melton	46	27	248	20	9	7	142	55	2.61	3.27	3.26	37.6
41	20	1950	S.Maglie	47	16	206	18	4	1	96	86	2.71	3.10	3.00	37.5
42	25	1949	D.Koslo	38	23	212	11	14	4	64	43	2.50	3.06	3.04	37.5
43	65	1913	J.Tesreau	41	38	282	22	13	0	167	119	2.17	3.13	3.42	37.5
44	47	1960	M.McCormick	40	34	253	15	12	3	154	65	2.70	3.09	3.31	36.8
45	41	1912	J.Tesreau	36	28	243	17	7	1	119	106	1.96	3.33	3.26	36.7
46	39	1925	J.Scott	36	28	240	14	15	3	87	55	3.15	3.67	3.25	36.6
47	83	1969	G.Perry	40	39	325	19	14	0	233	91	2.49	3.18	3.55	36.3
48	81	1935	C.Hubbell	42	35	303	23	12	0	150	49	3.27	3.71	3.54	35.9
49	55	1964	J.Marichal	33	33	269	21	8	0	206	52	2.48	2.98	3.36	35.7
50	49	1978	B.Knepper	36	35	260	17	11	0	147	85	2.63	2.94	3.33	35.4

New York/San Francisco Giants (1900–2000)

New York/San Francisco Giants
Starting Pitchers

V	R	Year	Name	G	GS	IP	W	L	SV	SO	BB	ERA	RA/9	R Wtd RA/9	V Runs /162
51	6	1992	B.Swift	30	22	165	10	4	1	77	43	2.08	2.24	2.63	35.3
52	36	1993	B.Swift	34	34	233	21	8	0	157	55	2.82	3.17	3.20	35.2
53	74	1959	J.Antonelli	40	38	282	19	10	1	165	76	3.10	3.41	3.49	35.1
54	90	1915	J.Tesreau	43	39	306	19	16	3	176	75	2.29	2.88	3.60	34.4
55	70	1956	J.Antonelli	41	36	258	20	13	1	145	75	2.86	3.24	3.44	33.6
56	51	1974	J.Barr	44	27	240	13	9	2	84	47	2.74	3.04	3.34	32.5
57	21	1929	B.Walker	29	23	178	14	7	0	65	57	3.09	3.59	3.01	32.2
58	69	1978	V.Blue	35	35	258	18	10	0	171	70	2.79	3.03	3.43	32.2
59	86	1967	G.Perry	39	37	293	15	17	1	230	84	2.61	3.01	3.57	32.1
60	12	1917	F.Anderson	38	18	162	8	8	3	69	34	1.44	2.22	2.87	32.0
61	34	1913	A.Demaree	31	24	200	13	4	2	76	38	2.21	2.92	3.19	31.9
62	28	1958	S.Miller	41	20	182	6	9	0	119	49	2.47	2.97	3.06	31.8
63	44	1917	P.Perritt	35	26	215	17	7	1	72	45	1.88	2.55	3.29	31.8
64	109	1919	J.Barnes	38	34	296	25	9	1	92	35	2.40	2.98	3.73	31.4
65	14	1922	P.Douglas	24	21	158	11	4	0	33	35	2.63	3.19	2.88	31.0
66	37	1964	G.Perry	44	19	206	12	11	5	155	43	2.75	2.84	3.20	31.0
67	18	1968	B.Bolin	34	19	177	10	5	0	126	46	1.99	2.24	2.98	30.9
68	30	1989	S.Garrelts	30	29	193	14	5	0	119	46	2.28	2.70	3.12	30.8
69	64	1924	V.Barnes	35	29	229	16	10	3	59	57	3.06	3.42	3.42	30.5
70	92	1929	C.Hubbell	39	35	268	18	11	1	106	67	3.69	4.30	3.60	29.9
71	73	1975	J.Montefusco	35	34	244	15	9	0	215	86	2.88	3.14	3.46	29.6
72	76	1930	C.Hubbell	37	32	242	17	12	2	117	58	3.87	4.46	3.52	29.4
73	82	1961	M.McCormick	40	35	250	13	16	0	163	75	3.20	3.56	3.55	29.4
74	67	1954	R.Gomez	37	32	222	17	9	0	106	109	2.88	3.45	3.43	29.4
75	61	1954	S.Maglie	34	32	218	14	6	2	117	70	3.26	3.43	3.41	29.3
76	87	1967	M.McCormick	40	35	262	22	10	0	150	81	2.85	3.02	3.58	28.3
77	68	1910	L.Drucke	34	27	215	12	10	0	151	82	2.47	3.06	3.43	28.2
78	78	1923	H.McQuillan	38	32	230	15	14	0	75	66	3.41	3.76	3.52	27.9
79	127	1970	G.Perry	41	41	329	23	13	0	214	84	3.20	3.78	3.80	27.6
80	91	1966	G.Perry	36	35	256	21	8	0	201	40	2.99	3.24	3.60	27.2
81	97	1947	L.Jansen	42	30	248	21	5	1	104	57	3.16	3.70	3.63	27.0
82	108	1922	A.Nehf	37	35	268	19	13	1	60	64	3.29	4.10	3.70	26.9
83	48	1924	H.McQuillan	27	23	184	14	8	3	49	43	2.69	3.33	3.33	26.4
84	80	1981	D.Alexander	24	24	152	11	7	0	77	44	2.89	3.01	3.53	26.4
85	107	1937	C.Hubbell	39	32	262	22	8	4	159	55	3.20	3.71	3.70	26.3
86	105	1921	J.Barnes	42	31	259	15	9	6	56	44	3.10	3.75	3.70	26.0
87	130	1934	H.Schumacher	41	36	297	23	10	0	112	89	3.18	3.97	3.82	25.7
88	95	1986	M.Krukow	34	34	245	20	9	0	178	55	3.05	3.31	3.62	25.6
89	98	1976	J.Montefusco	37	36	253	16	14	0	172	74	2.84	3.20	3.65	25.4
90	113	1934	F.Fitzsimmons	38	37	263	18	14	1	73	51	3.04	3.90	3.75	24.8
91	33	1965	B.Bolin	45	13	163	14	6	2	135	56	2.76	2.82	3.19	24.8
92	59	1981	V.Blue	18	18	125	8	6	0	63	54	2.45	2.89	3.39	24.6
93	126	1920	F.Toney	42	37	278	21	11	1	81	57	2.65	3.27	3.80	24.6
94	60	1916	S.Sallee	31	18	182	14	9	1	63	33	2.18	2.57	3.40	24.5
95	120	1909	H.Wiltse	37	30	269	20	11	3	119	51	2.00	3.04	3.79	24.3
96	75	1905	H.Wiltse	32	19	197	15	6	3	120	61	2.47	3.20	3.51	24.2
97	88	1980	V.Blue	31	31	224	14	10	0	129	61	2.97	3.17	3.58	24.2
98	45	1983	A.Hammaker	23	23	172	10	9	0	127	32	2.25	2.98	3.30	24.1
99	93	1952	S.Maglie	35	31	216	18	8	1	112	75	2.92	3.33	3.60	24.0
100	142	1920	J.Barnes	43	34	293	20	15	0	63	56	2.64	3.32	3.86	23.9

New York/San Francisco Giants
Relief Pitchers

V	R	Year	Name	G	GS	IP	W	L	SV	SO	BB	ERA	RA/9	R Wtd RA/9	V Runs /162
1	9	1982	G.Minton	78	0	123	10	4	30	58	42	1.83	2.12	2.37	29.9
2	1	1956	M.Grissom	43	2	81	1	1	7	49	16	1.56	1.67	1.77	26.3
3	12	1954	M.Grissom	56	3	122	10	7	19	64	50	2.35	2.73	2.71	26.3
4	10	1954	H.Wilhelm	57	0	111	12	4	7	64	52	2.10	2.59	2.57	25.8
5	3	1990	J.Brantley	55	0	87	5	3	19	61	33	1.56	1.87	2.01	24.6
6	4	1998	R.Nen	78	0	89	7	7	40	110	25	1.52	2.13	2.10	24.3
7	7	1967	F.Linzy	57	0	96	7	7	17	38	34	1.51	1.97	2.34	23.7
8	14	1977	G.Lavelle	73	0	118	7	7	20	93	37	2.05	2.66	2.75	23.6
9	6	1992	R.Beck	65	0	92	3	3	17	87	15	1.76	1.96	2.30	23.1
10	31	1981	A.Holland	47	3	101	7	5	7	78	44	2.41	2.77	3.24	22.3
11	19	1961	S.Miller	63	0	122	14	5	17	89	37	2.66	3.02	3.01	22.0
12	8	1965	F.Linzy	57	0	82	9	3	21	35	23	1.43	2.09	2.36	20.0
13	2	2000	R.Nen	68	0	66	4	3	41	92	19	1.50	2.05	1.84	19.9
14	5	1993	R.Beck	76	0	79	3	1	48	86	13	2.16	2.27	2.29	19.9
15	11	1938	J.Brown	43	0	90	5	3	5	42	28	1.80	2.60	2.67	19.9
16	27	1987	J.Robinson	81	0	123	8	9	14	101	54	2.85	3.14	3.15	19.2
17	20	1933	H.Bell	38	7	105	6	5	5	24	20	2.05	2.66	3.02	18.8
18	13	1942	A.Adams	61	0	88	7	4	11	33	31	1.84	2.35	2.74	18.7
19	15	1991	J.Brantley	67	0	95	5	2	15	81	52	2.45	2.55	2.82	18.3
20	17	1973	R.Moffitt	60	0	100	4	4	14	65	31	2.42	2.69	2.95	17.8
21	45	1953	H.Wilhelm	68	0	145	7	8	15	71	77	3.04	3.79	3.56	16.9
22	50	1952	H.Wilhelm	71	0	159	15	3	11	108	57	2.43	3.40	3.68	16.3
23	24	1979	G.Lavelle	70	0	97	7	9	20	80	42	2.51	2.89	3.11	15.6
24	23	1970	D.McMahon	61	0	94	9	5	19	74	45	2.96	3.06	3.08	15.4
25	16	2000	F.Rodriguez	76	0	82	4	2	3	95	42	2.64	3.20	2.87	15.3
26	35	1980	T.Griffin	42	4	108	5	1	0	79	49	2.76	2.93	3.31	14.9
27	42	1981	G.Minton	55	0	84	4	5	21	29	36	2.88	2.99	3.50	14.9
28	25	1980	G.Minton	68	0	91	4	6	19	42	34	2.46	2.76	3.12	14.5
29	36	1982	G.Lavelle	68	0	105	10	7	8	76	29	2.67	3.01	3.36	13.9
30	39	1976	G.Lavelle	65	0	110	10	6	12	71	52	2.69	3.02	3.45	13.5
31	53	1943	A.Adams	70	3	140	11	7	9	46	55	2.82	3.21	3.73	13.5
32	34	1924	C.Jonnard	34	3	90	4	5	5	40	24	2.41	3.30	3.30	13.2
33	37	1984	G.Lavelle	77	0	101	5	4	12	71	42	2.76	3.03	3.38	13.2
34	29	1998	J.Johnstone	70	0	88	6	5	0	86	38	3.07	3.27	3.22	13.1
35	38	1977	D.Heaverlo	56	0	99	5	1	1	58	21	2.55	3.28	3.40	12.8
36	26	1993	K.Rogers	64	0	81	2	2	0	62	28	2.68	3.12	3.15	12.7
37	41	1987	S.Garrelts	64	0	106	11	7	12	127	55	3.22	3.47	3.48	12.6
38	43	1985	S.Garrelts	74	0	106	9	6	13	106	58	2.30	3.15	3.53	12.1
39	28	1998	S.Reed	70	0	80	4	3	1	73	27	3.14	3.25	3.20	12.1
40	18	1999	J.Johnstone	62	0	66	4	6	3	56	20	2.60	3.29	2.97	11.5
41	22	1994	R.Beck	48	0	49	2	4	28	39	13	2.77	3.14	3.08	11.4
42	47	1976	R.Moffitt	58	0	103	6	6	14	50	35	2.27	3.15	3.60	11.0
43	33	1993	M.Jackson	81	0	77	6	6	1	70	24	3.03	3.26	3.29	10.9
44	44	1955	M.Grissom	55	0	89	5	4	8	49	41	2.92	3.54	3.53	10.7
45	49	1948	A.Hansen	36	9	100	5	3	1	27	36	2.97	3.60	3.65	10.7
46	40	1933	D.Luque	35	0	80	8	2	4	23	19	2.69	3.04	3.45	10.3
47	52	1989	C.Lefferts	70	0	107	2	4	20	71	22	2.69	3.20	3.70	10.2
48	60	1981	F.Breining	45	1	78	5	2	1	37	38	2.55	3.24	3.80	10.0
49	21	1999	A.Embree	68	0	59	3	2	0	53	26	3.38	3.38	3.05	9.8
50	32	1997	R.Rodriguez	71	0	65	4	3	1	32	21	3.17	3.31	3.26	9.4

New York Yankees (1901–2000)

The Bronx Bombers built more successful dynasties than any other major sports team. At their peak, the Yankees controlled a durable empire, rampaging through the major leagues for many decades. The Yankees won their very first pennant in their twenty-first season, during Babe Ruth's second season in Yankees pinstripes. By the time they finished rolling over the opposition 43 years later, they had collected 29 pennants and 20 World Series crowns, or 66 percent of all pennants and 45 percent of all World Series triumphs during the period 1921–1964. Perhaps as impressive, they had only one losing season in this period, in 1925, and only one other season where they were not at least ten games over .500! The long list of famous names behind this Yankees empire include Ruth, Gehrig, Lazzeri, Dickey, Gomez, DiMaggio, Berra, Rizzuto, Mantle, Ford, and Maris.

The Yankees' dominion over baseball since 1921 can be broken down into five player-driven dynasties. Each dynasty can be associated with a single outfielder, although no baseball dynasty would be successful without enormous talent to support the star performer. And each dynasty features a great season that stands out above the rest. What follows is a brief synopsis of these five Yankees dynasties, and of the few difficult periods in Yankees history.

New York failed to win anything during the entire Dead Ball Era. While the Red Sox, Tigers, Athletics, and White Sox captured all 19 pennants through 1919, New York was one of four American League teams that sat on the sidelines. New York did come close in 1904, when Jack Chesbro went 41–12 with a 1.82 ERA and a 3.20 Wtd. RA/9, leading the team to within 1½ games of Boston. Other solid performers in this period were Jimmy Williams (.317, 21 triples in 1901), Roger Peckinpaugh (.305 in 1919), Birdie Cree (.348, 22 triples, 48 steals in 1911), and Russ Ford (26–6, 1.65 ERA, 2.58 Wtd. RA/9 in 1910).

New York's fortunes began to change when Colonel Ruppert acquired the team in 1914. Ruppert spent freely, acquiring a dozen players from the financially troubled Athletics and Red Sox, including Frank "Home Run" Baker. The biggest of these deals, for star outfielder/pitcher Babe Ruth, ushered in the first Yankees dynasty, the Babe Ruth dynasty, which spanned 13 years (1920–1932), seven pennants and four World Series crowns.

Babe Ruth, in his prime, put together the three greatest hitting seasons of the twentieth century in 1920, 1921, and 1923, winning the MVP Award in its second year in 1923. Ruth's 1920 season produced the best slugging average, Production and Total Factor rate of success in major league history, as he hit .376 with 54 home runs in just 458 at bats, for a .530 on-base average, .847 slugging average, and 1,378 Production. Adjusted for 4 percent hitter's inflation, Ruth hit .361 with 56 home runs, for a 1,325 Wtd. Production, 1,323 Total Factor, and 172.7 Hits Contribution. Except for an off year in 1925, when he had intestinal surgery, Ruth continued to produce some of the greatest seasons ever through 1932.

The 1927 Murderer's Row team went 110–44, as Ruth hit .356 with 60 home runs for a 1,183 Wtd. Production, while MVP Lou Gehrig hit .373 with 47 round trippers for a 1,165 Wtd. Production. The two hitters made a formidable tandem, but it was still Ruth's team. Ruth produced better rate and volume of success statistics than Gehrig in every season they played together through 1932. Other key players in the Ruth dynasty were Bob Meusel, Earle Combs (.356, 23 triples in 1927), Tony Lazzeri (.354, 18 home runs in 1929), a young Bill Dickey, and a number of pitchers, including Bob Shawkey, Herb Pennock, and Red Ruffing. The Ruth dynasty came to an end in the early thirties, as an aging Ruth and "Iron Man" Gehrig could not push the Yankees beyond second place finishes in 1933 and 1934.

113

Nineteen thirty-six signaled the beginning of the second dynasty, with the arrival of Joe DiMaggio and another World Series victory. The Joe DiMaggio dynasty (1936–1942 and 1946–1951) spans Joltin' Joe's entire 13-year career, and includes ten pennants and nine World Series triumphs. Lou Gehrig starred on the first two DiMaggio teams, including a MVP season in 1936 (.354, 49 home runs, 1,057 Wtd. Production), before his performance trailed off in 1938. Other contributors in this period include:

Bill Dickey (C)	(.332, 29 home runs, 963 Total Factor in 1937)
Yogi Berra (C)	(.322, 28 home runs in 1950)
Snuffy Stirnweiss (2B)	(.319, 55 steals, 105.1 Hits Contribution in 1944)
Joe Gordon (2B)	(.322, 18 home runs & MVP in 1942)
Phil Rizzuto (SS)	(.324, 7 home runs & MVP in 1950)
Red Rolfe (3B)	(.329, 14 home runs in 1939)
Charlie Keller (OF)	(.271, 31 home runs in 1943)
Tommy Henrich (OF)	(.308, 25 home runs in 1948)
Lefty Gomez (SP)	(26–5, 2.33 ERA, 2.40 Wtd. RA/9 in 1934)
Red Ruffing (SP)	(20–7, 2.98 ERA in 1937)
Spud Chandler (SP)	(20–4, 1.64 ERA, 2.62 Wtd. RA/9 & MVP in 1943)
Joe Page (RP)	(14–8, 17 saves, 2.48 ERA in 1947)
Johnny Murphy (RP)	(8–3, 15 saves, 1.98 ERA, 2.23 Wtd. RA/9 in 1941)

Leading this group of talented players was three time MVP Joe DiMaggio, who had his famous 56 game hitting streak in 1941, a season that ranks as one of his two best. DiMaggio hit .357 with 30 home runs that year, for a 1,083 Production. Adjusted for 4 percent hitter's inflation, he batted .345 with 31 home runs, for a 1,047 Wtd. Production, 1,127 Total Factor, and career-best 115.1 Hits Contribution.

The DiMaggio dynasty peaked in 1939, when the Yankees won their fourth straight World Series. Led by awesome pitching, and by MVP DiMaggio's .381 batting average, 30 home runs, 1,041 Wtd. Production, and 1,136 Total Factor in his best rate of success season, the 1939 team posted the most impressive season statistics of any Yankees team ever. The performances of the Yankees teams with the highest winning percentages are:

Season	Record	Winning %	Runs Ratio	Wtd. PRO	Wtd. RA/9
1927	110–44	.714	1.63	820	3.56
1932	107–47	.695	1.38	781	4.01
1939	106–45	.702	1.74	767	3.19
1942	103–51	.669	1.58	761	3.53
1961	109–53	.673	1.35	753	3.78
1998	114–48	.704	1.47	755	3.65

The 1939 team had the third highest ratio of runs scored to runs given up (Runs Ratio), and the fourth best Wtd. RA/9, of any major league team since 1900. Imagine how good that team would have been if 36-year-old Lou Gehrig had not been forced to retire on May 2nd due to his tragic illness. The 1927 team produced the fourth highest Runs Ratio of any team since 1900, while the 1942 team generated the seventh highest. The 1942 team may have been the second best team in the DiMaggio dynasty, but it was also the only DiMaggio pennant winner in ten trips to the World Series that went away empty. And what a World Series matchup it was, as the Yankees played the 106–48 Cardinals, whose 1.57 Runs Ratio was eighth best since 1900.

In 1951, Mickey Mantle had an unimpressive rookie season on DiMaggio's last team. Mantle came into his own the next season, and the team was officially his. The Mickey Mantle dynasty (1952–1964) also spanned 13 years, and included eleven pennants, six World Series crowns, and three MVP awards for Mantle. Mantle's best seasons were his MVP performances of 1956 (.353, 52 home runs, 1,214 Total Factor, career-best 148.2 Hits Contribution) and 1957 (.365, 34 home runs, 146 walks, career-best 1,228 Total Factor, and 146.1 Hits Contribution).

Mantle's greatest media exposure was saved for the 1961 season, when he and league MVP Roger Maris both challenged Babe Ruth's home run record on a team that went 109–53. Mantle came up short that year due to injuries, hitting 54 home runs compared to Maris' 61 home runs, .269 average, and 969 Wtd. Production. More injuries, this time on a team-wide level, finally ended the Mantle dynasty three years later. Hitters who contributed during the Mantle dynasty include two-time league MVP Maris, three-time league MVP Yogi Berra, 1963 MVP Elston Howard (.287, 28 home runs), and multiposition talent Gil McDougald. Star pitchers included Whitey Ford (19–6, 2.47 ERA, 2.71 Wtd. RA/9 in 1956), Allie Reynolds (20–8, 2.06 ERA, 2.81 Wtd. RA/9 in 1952), and relievers Ryne Duren and Luis Arroyo.

When Mantle retired following the 1968 season, the role of team leader was passed on to Bobby Murcer. Murcer had two very good years in 1971 (.331, 25 home runs, 1,030 Total Factor) and 1972 (.292, 33 home runs, 1,016 Total Factor), but he didn't have the supporting cast to win the division. Murcer was traded away by the mid-seventies, and the Yankees rebuilt around Thurman Munson, Graig Nettles, Roy White, Catfish Hunter (23–14, 2.58 ERA in 1975), and Sparky Lyle (9–3, 15 saves, 1.66 ERA in 1974). The 1976 team won the Yankees' first pennant in a dozen years behind league MVP Munson (.302, 17 home runs) and Nettles (.254, 32 home runs), but lost to the powerful Reds in the World Series. George Steinbrenner dug into his pockets, and acquired free agent Reggie Jackson and two other starters to begin the fourth Yankees dynasty.

The Reggie Jackson dynasty spanned five years

(1977–1981), and brought the Yankees five division crowns, four pennants, and two World Series triumphs. Arguably, this dynasty was as much star pitcher Ron Guidry's doing as it was Reggie's. The real difference is that Jackson was on stage with the Yankees for just those five successful years, while Guidry continued to pitch effectively after Jackson left, but with no postseasons to show for it. Reggie Jackson did not perform at the levels of a Babe Ruth, Joe DiMaggio, or Mickey Mantle — his best season with the Yankees was in 1980, when he hit .300 with 41 homers, for a 967 Total Factor rate of success that ranks only 43rd among Yankees outfielders. But Jackson was always in the limelight and in the headlines. And he was able to rise to the occasion, earning his Mr. October nickname with his postseason exploits. Reggie awed the country when he tagged five home runs for the Yankees in the 1977 World Series, including three in game six.

Teammate Guidry achieved the best Yankees' pitching performance ever in 1978, when he went 25–3 with a 1.74 ERA and a 2.16 Wtd. RA/9. The 1978 team needed every one of Guidry's wins and new teammate Goose Gossage's 27 saves, and they showed enormous determination in clawing back from 14 games behind to beat the talented Red Sox in a one game playoff for the pennant. That special 100–63 team went on to give the Yankees their 22nd World Series crown.

The Yankees missed the postseason in each of star Don Mattingly's first 13 years from 1982 to 1994; Mattingly finally reached the playoffs in his last season in 1995, and he hit .417 against Seattle. The best Yankees team of this period was the 1985 team that finished two games behind Toronto. Mattingly hit .324 with 35 home runs to win the league MVP, while Rickey Henderson hit .314 with 24 home runs and 80 steals for a 1,079 Total Factor, Dave Winfield hit .275 with 26 home runs, and Guidry was 22–6 with a 3.27 ERA.

The current dynasty and one of its two star players, Bernie Williams, both emerged during the strike season of 1994. The Yankees were leading the league with a 70–43 record when the season was called off. The Yankees went on to appear in six straight postseasons from 1995 to 2000, winning the World Series four times— for a grand total of 26 World Series titles in 80 years. The 1998 team set an American League record, winning 114 games during the regular season. In 1998, Williams hit a league best .339, homered 26 times, and achieved a 976 Total Factor rate of success for 38th place among Yankees outfielders. Other contributors to this dynasty include co-star Derek Jeter (.349, 24 home runs, 930 Total Factor, 93.1 Hits Contribution in 1999) and Paul O'Neill (.359, 21 home runs, 996 Wtd. Production in 1994). The Yankees also featured strong pitching, led by Andy Pettitte, David Cone and relief ace Mariano Rivera (4–3, 45 saves, 1.83 ERA, 1.70 Wtd. RA/9 in 1999).

New York Yankees

Hitters Volume of Success

Pos	Year	Name	AB	BB	HBP	TAB	H	2B	3B	HR	BA	OB	SA	PRO	Wtd PRO	SB	CS	SBF	SPF	FF	R TF	V HC
C	1937	B.Dickey	530	73	4	607	176	35	2	29	.332	.417	.570	987	904	3	2	(2)	(10)	70	963	86.9
1B	1927	L.Gehrig	584	109	3	696	218	52	18	47	.373	.474	.765	1,240	1,165	10	8	(8)	0	0	1,157	135.0
2B	1944	S.Stirnweiss	643	73	1	717	205	35	16	8	.319	.389	.460	849	884	55	11	43	10	40	978	105.1
SS	1999	D.Jeter	627	91	12	730	219	37	9	24	.349	.441	.552	993	916	19	8	4	10	0	930	93.1
3B	1976	G.Nettles	583	62	4	649	148	29	2	32	.254	.330	.475	805	859	11	6	(1)	0	60	918	62.2
OF	1923	B.Ruth	522	170	4	696	205	45	13	41	.393	.545	.764	1,309	1,250	17	21	(34)	10	40	1,266	177.5
OF	1956	M.Mantle	533	112	2	647	188	22	5	52	.353	.467	.705	1,172	1,123	10	1	12	10	70	1,214	148.2
OF	1941	J.DiMaggio	541	76	4	621	193	43	11	30	.357	.440	.643	1,083	1,047	4	2	0	10	70	1,127	115.1
Starters		Averages	570	96	4	670	194	37	10	33	.340	.439	.612	1,050	1,019	16	7	2	5	44	1,070	115.4
C	1954	Y.Berra	584	56	4	644	179	28	6	22	.307	.371	.488	859	858	0	1	(3)	0	50	905	73.4
1B	1986	D.Mattingly	677	53	1	731	238	53	2	31	.352	.399	.573	973	959	0	0	0	0	40	999	79.9
2B	1942	J.Gordon	538	79	1	618	173	29	4	18	.322	.409	.491	900	926	12	6	0	0	30	956	83.9
SS	1950	P.Rizzuto	617	92	7	716	200	36	7	7	.324	.418	.439	857	797	12	8	(5)	10	40	842	64.4
3B	1994	W.Boggs	366	61	1	428	125	19	1	11	.342	.437	.489	926	864	2	1	0	(10)	50	904	54.3
OF	1985	R.Henderson	547	99	3	649	172	28	5	24	.314	.422	.516	938	931	80	10	87	10	50	1,079	99.3
OF	1972	B.Murcer	585	63	2	650	171	30	7	33	.292	.363	.537	900	976	11	9	(10)	10	40	1,016	84.1
OF	1961	R.Maris	590	94	7	691	159	16	4	61	.269	.376	.620	997	969	0	0	0	10	10	989	76.2
Reserves		Averages	563	75	3	641	177	30	5	26	.315	.398	.522	919	912	15	4	9	4	39	963	77.0
Totals		Wtd. Ave.	568	89	4	661	188	35	8	31	.332	.425	.582	1,007	984	16	6	4	5	42	1,034	102.6

Pitchers Volume of Success

Pos	Year	Name	G	GS	IP	W	L	SV	SO	BB	ERA	RA/9	Wtd RA/9	R Runs/162
SP	1978	R.Guidry	35	35	274	25	3	0	248	72	1.74	2.01	2.16	73.0
SP	1904	J.Chesbro	55	51	455	41	12	0	239	88	1.82	2.53	3.20	72.0
SP	1934	L.Gomez	38	33	282	26	5	1	158	96	2.33	2.74	2.40	71.1
SP	1910	R.Ford	36	33	300	26	6	1	209	70	1.65	2.07	2.58	69.4
SP	1943	S.Chandler	30	30	253	20	4	0	134	54	1.64	2.21	2.62	57.4
Starters		Averages	39	36	313	28	6	0	198	76	1.84	2.34	2.66	68.6
RP	1996	M.Rivera	61	0	108	8	3	5	130	34	2.09	2.09	1.76	33.6
RP	1977	S.Lyle	72	0	137	13	5	26	68	33	2.17	2.69	2.69	28.4
RP	1949	J.Page	60	0	135	13	8	27	99	75	2.59	2.93	2.81	27.6
RP	1961	L.Arroyo	65	0	119	15	5	29	87	49	2.19	2.57	2.56	26.4
Relievers		Averages	65	0	125	12	5	22	96	48	2.27	2.60	2.49	29.0
Totals		Averages	103	36	438	40	11	22	294	124	1.96	2.41	2.61	97.6

New York Yankees (1901–2000)

New York Yankees — **Hitters Rate of Success**

Pos	Year	Name	AB	BB	HBP	TAB	H	2B	3B	HR	BA	OB	SA	PRO	Wtd PRO	SB	CS	SBF	SPF	FF	R TF	V HC
C	1937	B.Dickey	530	73	4	607	176	35	2	29	.332	.417	.570	987	904	3	2	(2)	(10)	70	963	86.9
1B	1927	L.Gehrig	584	109	3	696	218	52	18	47	.373	.474	.765	1,240	1,165	10	8	(8)	0	0	1,157	135.0
2B	1944	S.Stirnweiss	643	73	1	717	205	35	16	8	.319	.389	.460	849	884	55	11	43	10	40	978	105.1
SS	1999	D.Jeter	627	91	12	730	219	37	9	24	.349	.441	.552	993	916	19	8	4	10	0	930	93.1
3B	1976	G.Nettles	583	62	4	649	148	29	2	32	.254	.330	.475	805	859	11	6	(1)	0	60	918	62.2
OF	1920	B.Ruth	458	148	3	609	172	36	9	54	.376	.530	.847	1,378	1,325	14	14	(22)	10	10	1,323	172.7
OF	1957	M.Mantle	474	146	0	620	173	28	6	34	.365	.515	.665	1,179	1,172	16	3	15	10	30	1,228	146.1
OF	1939	J.DiMaggio	462	52	4	518	176	32	6	30	.381	.448	.671	1,119	1,041	3	0	5	10	80	1,136	98.3
Starters		Averages	545	94	4	643	186	36	9	32	.341	.442	.615	1,056	1,029	16	7	4	5	36	1,074	112.4
C	1961	E.Howard	446	28	3	477	155	17	5	21	.348	.390	.549	939	913	0	3	(12)	(10)	40	931	57.7
1B	1986	D.Mattingly	677	53	1	731	238	53	2	31	.352	.399	.573	973	959	0	0	0	0	40	999	79.9
2B	1942	J.Gordon	538	79	1	618	173	29	4	18	.322	.409	.491	900	926	12	6	0	0	30	956	83.9
SS	1910	J.Knight	414	34	6	454	129	25	4	3	.312	.372	.413	785	893	23			10	(10)	893	52.5
3B	1994	W.Boggs	366	61	1	428	125	19	1	11	.342	.437	.489	926	864	2	1	0	(10)	50	904	54.3
OF	1985	R.Henderson	547	99	3	649	172	28	5	24	.314	.422	.516	938	931	80	10	87	10	50	1,079	99.3
OF	1971	B.Murcer	529	91	0	620	175	25	6	25	.331	.429	.543	972	1,003	14	8	(3)	10	20	1,030	80.4
OF	1994	P.O'Neill	368	72	0	440	132	25	1	21	.359	.464	.603	1,067	996	5	4	(6)	0	20	1,009	74.8
Reserves		Averages	486	65	2	552	162	28	4	19	.334	.415	.525	939	939	17	4	8	1	30	979	72.9
Totals		Wtd. Ave.	525	84	3	613	178	33	7	28	.339	.433	.587	1,020	999	17	6	6	4	34	1,042	99.2

Pitchers Rate of Success

Pos	Year	Name	G	GS	IP	W	L	SV	SO	BB	ERA	RA/9	Wtd RA/9	R V Runs /162
SP	1978	R.Guidry	35	35	274	25	3	0	248	72	1.74	2.01	2.16	73.0
SP	1934	L.Gomez	38	33	282	26	5	1	158	96	2.33	2.74	2.40	71.1
SP	1910	R.Ford	36	33	300	26	6	1	209	70	1.65	2.07	2.58	69.4
SP	1943	S.Chandler	30	30	253	20	4	0	134	54	1.64	2.21	2.62	57.4
SP	1927	W.Moore	50	12	213	19	7	13	75	59	2.28	2.87	2.63	47.9
Starters		Averages	38	29	264	23	5	3	165	70	1.91	2.36	2.47	63.8
RP	1994	S.Howe	40	0	40	3	0	15	18	7	1.80	1.80	1.56	18.9
RP	1999	M.Rivera	66	0	69	4	3	45	52	18	1.83	1.96	1.70	21.9
RP	1959	R.Duren	41	0	77	3	6	14	96	43	1.88	2.10	2.18	21.4
RP	1941	J.Murphy	35	0	77	8	3	15	29	40	1.98	2.34	2.23	21.0
Relievers		Averages	46	0	66	5	3	22	49	27	1.88	2.09	1.97	20.8
Totals		Averages	83	29	330	28	8	25	214	97	1.91	2.30	2.37	84.6

New York Yankees
Catchers by Year

V	R	Year	Name	AB	BB	HBP	TAB	Hits	2B	3B	HR	BA	OB	SA	PRO	Wtd PRO	SB	CS	SBF	SPF	FF	R TF	V HC
1	1	1937	B.Dickey	530	73	4	607	176	35	2	29	.332	.417	.570	987	904	3	2	(2)	(10)	70	963	86.9
2	9	1954	Y.Berra	584	56	4	644	179	28	6	22	.307	.371	.488	859	858	0	1	(3)		50	905	73.4
3	5	1956	Y.Berra	521	65	5	591	155	29	2	30	.298	.381	.534	914	876	3	2	(2)		50	924	73.1
4	13	1950	Y.Berra	597	55	4	656	192	30	6	28	.322	.383	.533	915	851	4	2	0		40	891	70.3
5	6	1939	B.Dickey	480	77	4	561	145	23	3	24	.302	.403	.513	915	851	5	0	8	(10)	70	920	68.1
6	2	1936	B.Dickey	423	46	3	472	153	26	8	22	.362	.428	.617	1,045	941	0	2	(8)	(10)	40	963	67.5
7	4	1938	B.Dickey	454	75	2	531	142	27	4	27	.313	.412	.568	981	896	3	0	5	(10)	40	931	67.5
8	12	1952	Y.Berra	534	66	4	604	146	17	1	30	.273	.358	.478	835	848	2	3	(6)		50	892	65.0
9	8	1953	Y.Berra	503	50	3	556	149	23	5	27	.296	.363	.523	886	869	0	3	(10)		50	909	64.4
10	11	1973	T.Munson	519	48	4	571	156	29	4	20	.301	.364	.487	852	873	4	6	(13)	10	30	900	60.6
11	7	1963	E.Howard	487	35	6	528	140	21	6	28	.287	.343	.528	871	885	0	0	0	(10)	40	915	59.9
12	14	1964	E.Howard	550	48	5	603	172	27	3	15	.313	.373	.455	828	837	1	1	(2)	(10)	60	885	59.8
13	3	1961	E.Howard	446	28	3	477	155	17	5	21	.348	.390	.549	939	913	0	3	(12)	(10)	40	931	57.7
14	17	1951	Y.Berra	547	44	3	594	161	19	4	27	.294	.350	.492	842	822	5	4	(5)		50	867	56.5
15	19	2000	J.Posada	505	107	8	620	145	35	1	28	.287	.419	.527	946	866	2	2	(3)	(10)	10	863	54.8
16	21	1975	T.Munson	597	45	6	648	190	24	3	12	.318	.372	.429	801	824	3	2	(1)		30	853	54.2
17	10	1993	M.Stanley	423	57	5	485	129	17	1	26	.305	.394	.534	928	906	1	1	(2)	(10)	10	904	52.3
18	24	1955	Y.Berra	541	60	7	608	147	20	3	27	.272	.352	.470	821	805	1	0	2		40	847	51.7
19	15	1933	B.Dickey	478	47	2	527	152	24	8	14	.318	.381	.490	871	840	3	4	(9)	(10)	50	871	51.1
20	23	1957	Y.Berra	482	57	1	540	121	14	2	24	.251	.331	.438	769	765	1	2	(5)		90	850	46.6
21	30	1976	T.Munson	616	29	9	654	186	27	1	17	.302	.343	.432	774	826	14	11	(12)		10	825	45.9
22	22	1959	Y.Berra	472	43	4	519	134	25	1	19	.284	.349	.462	811	807	1	2	(5)		50	852	45.3
23	16	1994	M.Stanley	290	39	2	331	87	20	0	17	.300	.387	.545	932	870	0	0	0	(10)	10	870	42.9
24	20	1958	Y.Berra	433	35	2	470	115	17	3	22	.266	.323	.471	795	793	3	0	6		60	859	42.9
25	27	1931	B.Dickey	477	39	0	516	156	17	10	6	.327	.378	.442	820	782	2	1	0	(10)	70	842	42.7

New York Yankees
First basemen

V	R	Year	Name	AB	BB	HBP	TAB	H	2B	3B	HR	BA	OB	SA	PRO	Wtd PRO	SB	CS	SBF	SPF	FF	R TF	V HC
1	1	1927	L.Gehrig	584	109	3	696	218	52	18	47	.373	.474	.765	1,240	1,165	10	8	(8)			1,157	135.0
2	2	1934	L.Gehrig	579	109	2	690	210	40	6	49	.363	.465	.706	1,172	1,103	9	5	(1)			1,101	114.6
3	3	1930	L.Gehrig	581	101	3	685	220	42	17	41	.379	.473	.721	1,194	1,092	12	14	(22)			1,070	102.9
4	5	1931	L.Gehrig	619	117	0	736	211	31	15	46	.341	.446	.662	1,108	1,057	17	12	(9)			1,048	102.5
5	4	1936	L.Gehrig	579	130	7	716	205	37	7	49	.354	.478	.696	1,174	1,057	3	4	(7)			1,050	100.5
6	6	1928	L.Gehrig	562	95	4	661	210	47	13	27	.374	.467	.648	1,115	1,062	4	11	(26)			1,037	88.3
7	7	1937	L.Gehrig	569	127	4	700	200	37	9	37	.351	.473	.643	1,116	1,023	4	3	(3)		(10)	1,010	84.4
8	8	1986	D.Mattingly	677	53	1	731	238	53	2	31	.352	.399	.573	973	959	0	0	0		40	999	79.9
9	10	1932	L.Gehrig	596	108	3	707	208	42	9	34	.349	.451	.621	1,072	1,009	4	11	(24)		(10)	975	72.6
10	11	1935	L.Gehrig	535	132	5	672	176	26	10	30	.329	.466	.583	1,049	983	8	7	(8)			975	69.0
11	12	1933	L.Gehrig	593	92	1	686	198	41	12	32	.334	.424	.605	1,030	993	9	13	(23)			969	68.6
12	13	1985	D.Mattingly	652	56	2	710	211	48	3	35	.324	.379	.567	946	940	2	2	(3)		30	967	66.7
13	9	1984	D.Mattingly	603	41	1	645	207	44	2	23	.343	.386	.537	923	927	1	1	(1)		50	976	63.2
14	14	1929	L.Gehrig	553	122	5	680	166	32	10	35	.300	.431	.584	1,015	948	4	4	(6)			942	58.7
15	15	1987	D.Mattingly	569	51	1	621	186	38	2	30	.327	.383	.559	942	904	1	4	(11)		40	933	48.2
16	16	1926	L.Gehrig	572	105	1	678	179	47	20	16	.313	.420	.549	969	921	6	5	(6)		(10)	905	46.0
17	17	1997	T.Martinez	594	75	3	672	176	31	2	44	.296	.378	.577	955	902	3	1	1	(10)	10	903	42.6
18	18	1944	N.Etten	573	97	4	674	168	25	4	22	.293	.399	.466	865	901	4	2	0	10	(20)	891	40.8
19	20	1989	D.Mattingly	631	51	1	683	191	37	2	23	.303	.356	.477	833	854	3	0	4		30	888	38.4
20	21	1906	H.Chase	597	13	3	613	193	23	10	0	.323	.341	.395	736	837	28			10	30	877	32.8
21	19	1967	M.Mantle	440	107	1	548	108	17	0	22	.245	.394	.434	828	891	1	1	(2)	10	(10)	890	31.2
22	26	1938	L.Gehrig	576	107	5	688	170	32	6	29	.295	.410	.523	932	852	6	1	5			857	30.0
23	22	1988	D.Mattingly	599	41	3	643	186	37	0	18	.311	.358	.462	820	834	1	0	1		30	865	29.2
24	27	1947	G.McQuinn	517	78	0	595	157	24	3	13	.304	.395	.437	832	842	0	2	(6)		20	855	25.4
25	23	1956	B.Skowron	464	50	6	520	143	21	6	23	.308	.383	.528	911	872	4	4	(7)			865	24.8

New York Yankees (1901–2000)

New York Yankees
Second basemen

V	R	Year	Name	AB	BB	HBP	TAB	H	2B	3B	HR	BA	OB	SA	PRO	Wtd PRO	SB	CS	SBF	SPF	FF	R TF	V HC
1	1	1944	S.Stirnweiss	643	73	1	717	205	35	16	8	.319	.389	.460	849	884	55	11	43	10	40	978	105.1
2	3	1945	S.Stirnweiss	632	78	1	711	195	32	22	10	.309	.385	.476	862	906	33	17	(1)	10	40	955	96.1
3	2	1942	J.Gordon	538	79	1	618	173	29	4	18	.322	.409	.491	900	926	12	6	0		30	956	83.9
4	4	1929	T.Lazzeri	545	68	4	617	193	37	11	18	.354	.429	.561	991	925	9	10	(17)	10	20	938	78.3
5	6	1901	J.Williams	501	56	2	559	159	26	21	7	.317	.388	.495	883	886	21				10	896	64.8
6	8	1943	J.Gordon	543	98	2	643	135	28	5	17	.249	.365	.413	778	828	4	7	(15)		60	874	60.7
7	7	1902	J.Williams	498	36	1	535	156	27	21	8	.313	.361	.500	861	868	14				10	878	56.8
8	11	1940	J.Gordon	616	52	3	671	173	32	10	30	.281	.340	.511	851	801	18	8	3		50	854	56.7
9	9	1980	W.Randolph	513	119	2	634	151	23	7	7	.294	.429	.407	836	833	30	5	30	10		873	56.6
10	10	1932	T.Lazzeri	510	82	2	594	153	28	16	15	.300	.399	.506	905	852	11	11	(18)	10	20	864	53.2
11	5	1928	T.Lazzeri	404	43	1	448	134	30	11	10	.332	.397	.535	932	888	15	5	11	10		908	50.1
12	12	1933	T.Lazzeri	523	73	2	598	154	22	12	18	.294	.383	.486	869	838	15	7	2	10		849	49.1
13	15	1927	T.Lazzeri	570	69	0	639	176	29	8	18	.309	.383	.482	866	814	22	14	(9)	10	20	835	47.9
14	16	1939	J.Gordon	567	75	2	644	161	32	5	28	.284	.370	.506	876	814	11	10	(13)		30	831	47.1
15	14	1906	J.Williams	501	44	5	550	139	25	7	3	.277	.342	.373	715	813	8				30	843	43.4
16	13	1938	J.Gordon	458	56	3	517	117	24	7	25	.255	.340	.502	843	769	11	3	9		70	849	42.3
17	19	1919	D.Pratt	527	36	4	567	154	27	7	4	.292	.342	.393	735	750	22			10	60	820	42.0
18	18	1903	J.Williams	502	39	5	546	134	30	12	3	.267	.326	.392	718	783	9				40	823	41.3
19	17	1987	W.Randolph	449	82	2	533	137	24	2	7	.305	.415	.414	829	795	11	1	16	10	10	831	37.0
20	24	1941	J.Gordon	588	72	4	664	162	26	7	24	.276	.358	.466	824	797	10	9	(11)		10	796	36.8
21	21	1904	J.Williams	559	38	4	601	147	31	7	2	.263	.314	.354	669	766	14				40	806	36.4
22	22	1955	G.McDougald	533	65	2	600	152	10	8	13	.285	.365	.407	772	757	6	4	(3)		50	804	35.7
23	23	1978	W.Randolph	499	82	4	585	139	18	6	3	.279	.385	.357	741	758	36	7	36	10		803	32.9
24	26	1930	T.Lazzeri	571	60	3	634	173	34	15	9	.303	.372	.462	835	763	4	4	(6)	10	20	787	32.4
25	27	1918	D.Pratt	477	35	2	514	131	19	7	2	.275	.327	.356	683	747	12			10	30	787	31.6

New York Yankees
Shortstops

V	R	Year	Name	AB	BB	HBP	TAB	H	2B	3B	HR	BA	OB	SA	PRO	Wtd PRO	SB	CS	SBF	SPF	FF	R TF	V HC
1	1	1999	D.Jeter	627	91	12	730	219	37	9	24	.349	.441	.552	993	916	19	8	4	10		930	93.1
2	5	1998	D.Jeter	626	57	5	688	203	25	8	19	.324	.385	.481	866	814	30	6	25	10	10	859	64.6
3	8	1950	P.Rizzuto	617	92	7	716	200	36	7	7	.324	.418	.439	857	797	12	8	(5)	10	40	842	64.4
4	3	1919	R.Peckinpaugh	453	59	4	516	138	20	2	7	.305	.390	.404	794	809	10			10	60	879	61.9
5	6	2000	D.Jeter	593	68	12	673	201	31	4	15	.339	.418	.481	898	822	22	4	20	10		852	60.9
6	7	1903	K.Elberfeld	481	33	15	529	145	23	8	0	.301	.365	.383	747	814	22			10	20	844	53.1
7	2	1910	J.Knight	414	34	6	454	129	25	4	3	.312	.372	.413	785	893	23			10	(10)	893	52.5
8	9	1942	P.Rizzuto	553	44	6	603	157	24	7	4	.284	.343	.374	718	738	22	6	16	10	70	834	52.0
9	10	1957	G.McDougald	539	59	4	602	156	25	9	13	.289	.364	.442	805	801	2	5	(13)		30	818	47.1
10	4	1906	K.Elberfeld	346	30	10	386	106	11	5	2	.306	.378	.384	763	867	19			10	(10)	867	39.6
11	18	1997	D.Jeter	654	74	10	738	190	31	7	10	.291	.371	.405	776	733	23	12	(1)	10	30	772	38.5
12	12	1907	K.Elberfeld	447	36	13	496	121	17	6	0	.271	.343	.336	678	784	22			10	10	804	35.2
13	13	1904	K.Elberfeld	445	37	13	495	117	13	5	2	.263	.337	.328	665	763	18			10	30	803	34.9
14	16	1996	D.Jeter	582	48	9	639	183	25	6	10	.314	.376	.430	805	737	14	7	0	10	30	777	34.9
15	21	1952	P.Rizzuto	578	67	5	650	147	24	10	2	.254	.337	.341	678	688	17	6	7	10	60	766	33.8
16	19	1947	P.Rizzuto	549	57	8	614	150	26	9	2	.273	.350	.364	714	723	11	6	(2)	10	40	771	33.5
17	23	1931	L.Lary	610	88	6	704	171	35	9	10	.280	.376	.416	793	756	13	10	(9)			757	33.5
18	20	1917	R.Peckinpaugh	543	64	2	609	141	24	7	0	.260	.340	.330	670	741	17			10	20	771	33.2
19	15	1901	B.Keister	442	18	8	468	145	20	21	2	.328	.365	.482	847	850	24			10	(70)	790	32.9
20	14	1956	G.McDougald	438	68	3	509	136	13	3	13	.311	.407	.443	850	814	3	8	(24)			790	32.6
21	11	1993	M.Gallego	403	50	4	457	114	20	1	10	.283	.368	.412	780	761	3	2	(2)		50	809	31.9
22	22	1916	R.Peckinpaugh	552	62	1	615	141	22	8	4	.255	.332	.346	678	742	18			10	10	762	30.7
23	17	1941	P.Rizzuto	515	27	1	543	158	20	9	3	.307	.343	.398	741	716	14	5	7	10	40	773	30.2
24	24	1962	T.Tresh	622	67	8	697	178	26	5	20	.286	.363	.441	803	786	4	8	(16)	10	(30)	749	29.0
25	28	1936	F.Crosetti	632	90	12	734	182	35	7	15	.288	.387	.437	824	742	18	7	5		(10)	737	27.5

New York Yankees
Third basemen

V	R	Year	Name	AB	BB	HBP	TAB	H	2B	3B	HR	BA	OB	SA	PRO	Wtd PRO	SB	CS	SBF	SPF	FF	R TF	V HC
1	1	1976	G.Nettles	583	62	4	649	148	29	2	32	.254	.330	.475	805	859	11	6	(1)		60	918	62.2
2	2	1994	W.Boggs	366	61	1	428	125	19	1	11	.342	.437	.489	926	864	2	1	0	(10)	50	904	54.3
3	3	1918	F.Baker	504	38	2	544	154	24	5	6	.306	.357	.409	765	836	8				40	876	52.9
4	6	1978	G.Nettles	587	59	6	652	162	23	2	27	.276	.348	.460	808	826	1	1	(1)	(10)	40	855	43.0
5	12	1939	R.Rolfe	648	81	1	730	213	46	10	14	.329	.404	.495	899	837	7	6	(6)			830	41.7
6	9	1936	R.Rolfe	568	68	0	636	181	39	15	10	.319	.392	.493	884	796	3	0	4	10	30	841	39.7
7	10	1977	G.Nettles	589	68	3	660	150	23	4	37	.255	.335	.496	831	822	2	5	(11)	(10)	40	840	39.0
8	14	1962	C.Boyer	566	51	3	620	154	24	1	18	.272	.335	.413	749	732	3	2	(2)		90	821	30.9
9	16	1917	F.Baker	553	48	5	606	156	24	2	6	.282	.345	.365	710	786	18				30	816	30.2
10	13	1965	C.Boyer	514	39	2	555	129	23	6	18	.251	.306	.424	730	756	4	1	3		70	829	29.9
11	8	1951	G.McDougald	402	56	4	462	123	23	4	14	.306	.396	.488	884	863	14	5	8		(30)	841	28.9
12	17	1973	G.Nettles	552	78	7	637	129	18	0	22	.234	.336	.386	722	740	0	0	0		70	810	28.5
13	11	1954	A.Carey	411	43	7	461	124	14	6	8	.302	.377	.423	801	800	5	5	(10)		50	839	28.4
14	15	1998	S.Brosius	530	52	10	592	159	34	0	19	.300	.373	.472	845	794	11	8	(8)		30	817	28.3
15	5	1916	F.Baker	360	36	5	401	97	23	2	10	.269	.344	.428	772	845	15				10	855	27.9
16	4	1958	A.Carey	315	34	6	355	90	19	4	12	.286	.366	.486	852	851	1	2	(8)		30	873	27.8
17	19	1974	G.Nettles	566	59	3	628	139	21	1	22	.246	.320	.403	723	757	1	0	2		50	809	27.6
18	18	1995	W.Boggs	460	74	0	534	149	22	4	5	.324	.418	.422	839	792	1	1	(2)	(10)	30	810	26.8
19	7	1905	W.Conroy	385	32	0	417	105	19	11	2	.273	.329	.395	723	833	25			10		843	26.5
20	21	1975	G.Nettles	581	51	2	634	155	24	4	21	.267	.328	.430	758	781	1	3	(7)		30	803	26.3
21	25	1938	R.Rolfe	631	74	3	708	196	36	8	10	.311	.386	.441	826	754	13	1	15	10	10	789	25.9
22	23	1915	F.Maisel	530	48	1	579	149	16	6	4	.281	.342	.357	699	757	51	12	44	10	(20)	792	21.9
23	22	1986	M.Pagliarulo	504	54	4	562	120	24	3	28	.238	.317	.464	781	770	4	1	3		20	794	20.8
24	20	1944	O.Grimes	387	59	2	448	108	17	8	5	.279	.377	.403	780	812	6	0	13		(20)	805	20.0
25	24	1966	C.Boyer	500	46	2	548	120	22	4	14	.240	.307	.384	691	721	6	0	10		60	791	19.6

New York Yankees
Outfielders

V	R	Year	Name	AB	BB	HBP	TAB	H	2B	3B	HR	BA	OB	SA	PRO	Wtd PRO	SB	CS	SBF	SPF	FF	R TF	V HC
1	3	1923	B.Ruth	522	170	4	696	205	45	13	41	.393	.545	.764	1,309	1,250	17	21	(34)	10	40	1,266	177.5
2	2	1921	B.Ruth	540	144	4	688	204	44	16	59	.378	.512	.846	1,358	1,253	17	13	(12)	10	20	1,271	177.0
3	1	1920	B.Ruth	458	148	3	609	172	36	9	54	.376	.530	.847	1,378	1,325	14	14	(22)	10	10	1,323	172.7
4	7	1927	B.Ruth	540	138	0	678	192	29	8	60	.356	.487	.772	1,259	1,183	7	6	(7)		20	1,196	149.2
5	5	1956	M.Mantle	533	112	2	647	188	22	5	52	.353	.467	.705	1,172	1,123	10	1	12	10	70	1,214	148.2
6	4	1957	M.Mantle	474	146	0	620	173	28	6	34	.365	.515	.665	1,179	1,172	16	3	15	10	30	1,228	146.1
7	6	1926	B.Ruth	495	144	3	642	184	30	5	47	.372	.516	.737	1,253	1,190	11	9	(10)		20	1,200	142.4
8	8	1924	B.Ruth	529	142	4	675	200	39	7	46	.378	.513	.739	1,252	1,170	9	13	(24)		20	1,167	138.4
9	9	1961	M.Mantle	514	126	0	640	163	16	6	54	.317	.452	.687	1,138	1,107	12	1	15	10	30	1,162	123.2
10	13	1931	B.Ruth	534	128	1	663	199	31	3	46	.373	.495	.700	1,195	1,140	5	4	(4)		(20)	1,116	119.1
11	15	1928	B.Ruth	536	135	3	674	173	29	8	54	.323	.461	.709	1,170	1,115	4	5	(8)			1,107	117.9
12	11	1941	J.DiMaggio	541	76	4	621	193	43	11	30	.357	.440	.643	1,083	1,047	4	2	0	10	70	1,127	115.1
13	14	1955	M.Mantle	517	113	3	633	158	25	11	37	.306	.433	.611	1,044	1,024	8	1	9	10	70	1,113	112.7
14	16	1930	B.Ruth	518	136	1	655	186	28	9	49	.359	.493	.732	1,225	1,120	10	10	(14)		(10)	1,095	111.0
15	17	1958	M.Mantle	519	129	2	650	158	21	1	42	.304	.445	.592	1,036	1,035	18	3	17	10	30	1,092	109.0
16	19	1937	J.DiMaggio	621	64	5	690	215	35	15	46	.346	.412	.673	1,085	994	3	0	4	10	60	1,069	107.6
17	18	1985	R.Henderson	547	99	3	649	172	28	5	24	.314	.422	.516	938	931	80	10	87	10	50	1,079	99.3
18	10	1939	J.DiMaggio	462	52	4	518	176	32	6	30	.381	.448	.671	1,119	1,041	3	0	5	10	80	1,136	98.3
19	20	1932	B.Ruth	457	130	2	589	156	13	5	41	.341	.489	.661	1,150	1,082	2	2	(3)		(20)	1,059	89.0
20	12	1962	M.Mantle	377	122	1	500	121	15	1	30	.321	.488	.605	1,093	1,068	9	0	17	10	30	1,125	87.7
21	26	1972	B.Murcer	585	63	2	650	171	30	7	33	.292	.363	.537	900	976	11	9	(10)	10	40	1,016	84.1
22	23	1929	B.Ruth	499	72	3	574	172	26	6	46	.345	.430	.697	1,128	1,053	5	3	(2)		(10)	1,041	81.7
23	25	1971	B.Murcer	529	91	0	620	175	25	6	25	.331	.429	.543	972	1,003	14	8	(3)	10	20	1,030	80.4
24	24	1940	J.DiMaggio	508	61	3	572	179	28	9	31	.352	.425	.626	1,051	989	1	2	(5)	10	40	1,034	79.3
25	22	1964	M.Mantle	465	99	0	564	141	25	2	35	.303	.426	.591	1,017	1,028	6	3	0	10	10	1,048	78.2

New York Yankees
Outfielders

V	R	Year	Name	AB	BB	HBP	TAB	H	2B	3B	HR	BA	OB	SA	PRO	Wtd PRO	SB	CS	SBF	SPF	FF	R TF	V HC
26	32	1948	J.DiMaggio	594	67	8	669	190	26	11	39	.320	.396	.598	994	960	1	1	(1)		30	988	77.4
27	29	1960	M.Mantle	527	111	1	639	145	17	6	40	.275	.402	.558	960	944	14	3	12	10	30	996	76.3
28	30	1961	R.Maris	590	94	7	691	159	16	4	61	.269	.376	.620	997	969	0	0	0	10	10	989	76.2
29	27	1994	P.O'Neill	368	72	0	440	132	25	1	21	.359	.464	.603	1,067	996	5	4	(6)		20	1,009	74.8
30	28	1943	C.Keller	512	106	0	618	139	15	11	31	.271	.396	.525	922	981	7	5	(5)	10	10	997	74.2
31	36	1942	C.Keller	544	114	2	660	159	24	9	26	.292	.417	.513	930	956	14	2	14	10		981	73.9
32	21	1922	B.Ruth	406	84	1	491	128	24	8	35	.315	.434	.672	1,106	1,047	2	5	(15)	10	10	1,051	72.3
33	35	1959	M.Mantle	541	93	2	636	154	23	4	31	.285	.392	.514	905	901	21	3	22	10	50	984	72.1
34	37	1954	M.Mantle	543	102	0	645	163	17	12	27	.300	.411	.525	936	934	5	2	1	10	30	976	70.6
35	45	1942	J.DiMaggio	610	68	2	680	186	29	13	21	.305	.376	.498	875	900	4	2	0	10	50	960	69.1
36	34	1988	D.Winfield	559	69	2	630	180	37	2	25	.322	.398	.530	928	943	9	4	2	10	30	985	68.3
37	40	1952	M.Mantle	549	75	0	624	171	37	7	23	.311	.394	.530	924	939	4	1	3	10	20	972	67.1
38	33	1960	R.Maris	499	70	3	572	141	18	7	39	.283	.374	.581	955	939	2	2	(3)	10	40	986	65.5
39	41	1941	C.Keller	507	102	1	610	151	24	10	33	.298	.416	.580	996	963	6	4	(3)	10		970	65.1
40	42	1947	J.DiMaggio	534	64	3	601	168	31	10	20	.315	.391	.522	913	924	3	0	5		40	969	63.6
41	39	1984	D.Winfield	567	53	0	620	193	34	4	19	.340	.397	.515	912	916	6	4	(3)	10	50	972	63.5
42	50	1946	C.Keller	538	113	4	655	148	29	10	30	.275	.405	.533	938	957	1	4	(10)			947	62.2
43	56	1938	J.DiMaggio	599	59	2	660	194	32	13	32	.324	.386	.581	967	883	6	1	6	10	40	939	60.1
44	43	1980	R.Jackson	514	83	2	599	154	22	4	41	.300	.399	.597	996	992	1	2	(5)		(20)	967	59.9
45	38	1998	B.Williams	499	74	1	574	169	30	5	26	.339	.425	.575	1,000	940	15	9	(5)	10	30	976	59.6
46	58	1986	R.Henderson	608	89	2	699	160	31	5	28	.263	.359	.469	828	817	87	18	69	10	40	936	59.3
47	59	1936	J.DiMaggio	637	24	4	665	206	44	15	29	.323	.352	.576	928	836	4	0	6	10	80	931	57.9
48	47	1933	B.Ruth	459	114	2	575	138	21	3	34	.301	.442	.582	1,023	987	4	5	(10)		(20)	957	57.5
49	49	1975	B.Bonds	529	89	3	621	143	26	3	32	.270	.378	.512	891	917	30	17	(6)	10	30	951	57.3
50	46	1946	J.DiMaggio	503	59	2	564	146	20	8	25	.290	.367	.511	878	896	1	0	2		60	957	56.5
51	48	1911	B.Cree	520	56	3	579	181	30	22	4	.348	.415	.513	928	941	48			10		951	56.2
52	54	1950	J.DiMaggio	525	80	1	606	158	33	10	32	.301	.394	.585	979	911	0	0	0		30	941	55.7
53	51	1971	R.White	524	86	7	617	153	22	7	19	.292	.399	.469	868	896	14	7	0	10	40	946	55.4
54	57	1988	R.Henderson	554	82	3	639	169	30	2	6	.305	.397	.399	796	810	93	13	99	10	20	939	55.2
55	63	1999	B.Williams	591	100	1	692	202	28	6	25	.342	.438	.536	974	899	9	10	(15)	10	30	924	54.8
56	52	2000	B.Williams	537	71	5	613	165	37	6	30	.307	.393	.566	959	878	13	5	5	10	50	943	54.1
57	60	1981	D.Winfield	388	43	1	432	114	25	1	13	.294	.366	.464	830	870	11	1	20	10	30	930	53.7
58	53	1997	B.Williams	509	73	1	583	167	35	6	21	.328	.413	.544	958	904	15	8	(2)	10	30	942	51.3
59	55	1982	D.Winfield	539	45	0	584	151	24	8	37	.280	.336	.560	896	892	5	3	(2)	10	40	941	51.0
60	66	1948	T.Henrich	588	76	4	668	181	42	14	25	.308	.391	.554	945	913	2	3	(6)			907	50.1
61	62	1904	W.Keeler	543	35	7	585	186	14	8	2	.343	.390	.409	799	915	21			10		925	49.2
62	69	1970	R.White	609	95	0	704	180	30	6	22	.296	.391	.473	864	867	24	10	5	10	20	902	48.7
63	75	1927	E.Combs	648	62	2	712	231	36	23	6	.356	.414	.511	925	870	15	6	4	10	10	894	48.6
64	70	1944	J.Lindell	594	44	3	641	178	33	16	18	.300	.351	.500	851	886	5	4	(4)		20	902	46.3
65	68	1983	D.Winfield	598	58	2	658	169	26	8	32	.283	.348	.513	861	860	15	6	4	10	30	905	46.1
66	61	1953	M.Mantle	461	79	0	540	136	24	3	21	.295	.398	.497	895	877	8	4	0	10	40	927	46.0
67	64	1977	R.Jackson	525	74	3	602	150	39	2	32	.286	.377	.550	928	917	17	3	17	10	(30)	915	45.1
68	73	1965	T.Tresh	602	59	5	666	168	29	6	26	.279	.348	.477	825	854	5	2	1	10	30	895	43.8
69	44	1987	R.Henderson	358	80	2	440	104	17	3	17	.291	.423	.497	920	882	41	8	54	10	20	966	43.8
70	80	1995	B.Williams	563	75	5	643	173	29	9	18	.307	.393	.487	880	830	8	6	(6)	10	50	884	43.7
71	67	1901	M.Donlin	476	53	2	531	162	23	13	5	.340	.409	.475	883	886	33			10	10	906	43.5
72	31	1966	M.Mantle	333	57	0	390	96	12	1	23	.288	.392	.538	930	971	1	1	(2)	10	10	989	42.9
73	65	1939	G.Selkirk	418	103	8	529	128	17	4	21	.306	.452	.517	969	901	12	5	4	10		914	41.6
74	87	1931	B.Chapman	600	75	5	680	189	28	11	17	.315	.396	.483	879	838	61	23	21	10	10	879	41.5
75	71	1963	T.Tresh	520	83	4	607	140	28	5	25	.269	.374	.487	861	875	3	3	(5)	10	20	901	41.4

New York Yankees
Starting Pitchers

V	R	Year	Name	G	GS	IP	W	L	SV	SO	BB	ERA	RA/9	R Wtd RA/9	V Runs /162
1	1	1978	R.Guidry	35	35	274	25	3	0	248	72	1.74	2.01	2.16	73.0
2	47	1904	J.Chesbro	55	51	455	41	12	0	239	88	1.82	2.53	3.20	72.0
3	2	1934	L.Gomez	38	33	282	26	5	1	158	96	2.33	2.74	2.40	71.1
4	4	1910	R.Ford	36	33	300	26	6	1	209	70	1.65	2.07	2.58	69.4
5	3	1937	L.Gomez	34	34	278	21	11	0	194	93	2.33	2.85	2.43	69.0
6	5	1943	S.Chandler	30	30	253	20	4	0	134	54	1.64	2.21	2.62	57.4
7	14	1920	B.Shawkey	38	31	268	20	13	2	126	85	2.45	2.97	2.83	54.2
8	12	1946	S.Chandler	34	32	257	20	8	2	138	90	2.10	2.49	2.77	53.8
9	23	1924	H.Pennock	40	34	286	21	9	3	101	64	2.83	3.27	2.96	53.3
10	37	1975	C.Hunter	39	39	328	23	14	0	177	83	2.58	2.94	3.10	53.1
11	13	1952	A.Reynolds	35	29	244	20	8	6	160	97	2.06	2.58	2.81	49.7
12	19	1927	W.Hoyt	36	32	256	22	7	1	86	54	2.63	3.16	2.90	49.7
13	9	1964	W.Ford	39	36	245	17	6	1	172	57	2.13	2.46	2.75	49.1
14	7	1956	W.Ford	31	30	226	19	6	1	141	84	2.47	2.79	2.71	48.9
15	16	1931	L.Gomez	40	26	243	21	9	3	150	85	2.67	3.26	2.87	48.0
16	6	1927	W.Moore	50	12	213	19	7	13	75	59	2.28	2.87	2.63	47.9
17	20	1946	B.Bevens	31	31	250	16	13	0	120	78	2.23	2.63	2.92	47.7
18	8	1942	T.Bonham	28	27	226	21	5	0	71	24	2.27	2.59	2.75	47.7
19	49	1922	B.Shawkey	39	34	300	20	12	1	130	98	2.91	3.36	3.22	47.0
20	28	1955	W.Ford	39	33	254	18	7	2	137	113	2.63	2.94	2.99	46.5
21	10	1958	W.Ford	30	29	219	14	7	1	145	62	2.01	2.55	2.76	46.0
22	31	1937	R.Ruffing	31	31	256	20	7	0	131	68	2.98	3.55	3.03	45.7
23	43	1916	B.Shawkey	53	27	277	24	14	8	122	81	2.21	2.54	3.15	45.4
24	35	1932	R.Ruffing	35	29	259	18	7	2	190	115	3.09	3.54	3.07	45.1
25	11	1914	R.Caldwell	31	23	213	17	9	1	92	51	1.94	2.24	2.77	44.6
26	21	1939	R.Ruffing	28	28	233	21	7	0	95	75	2.93	3.40	2.92	44.5
27	74	1921	C.Mays	49	38	337	27	9	7	70	76	3.05	3.87	3.44	44.1
28	107	1902	J.McGinnity	44	39	352	21	18	0	106	78	2.84	3.94	3.59	43.7
29	22	1997	A.Pettitte	35	35	240	18	7	0	166	65	2.88	3.22	2.95	42.9
30	24	1943	T.Bonham	28	26	226	15	8	1	71	52	2.27	2.51	2.97	41.9
31	17	1928	H.Pennock	28	24	211	17	6	3	53	40	2.56	3.03	2.87	41.6
32	39	1938	R.Ruffing	31	31	247	21	7	0	127	82	3.31	3.79	3.13	41.2
33	59	1925	H.Pennock	47	31	277	16	17	2	88	71	2.96	3.80	3.30	40.7
34	51	1968	S.Bahnsen	37	34	267	17	12	0	162	68	2.05	2.42	3.22	39.5
35	33	1979	R.Guidry	33	30	236	18	8	2	201	71	2.78	3.16	3.05	39.5
36	34	1993	J.Key	34	34	237	18	6	0	173	43	3.00	3.19	3.06	39.4
37	84	1920	C.Mays	45	37	312	26	11	2	92	84	3.06	3.66	3.48	39.2
38	48	1962	W.Ford	38	37	258	17	8	0	160	69	2.90	3.14	3.22	38.5
39	29	1934	J.Murphy	40	20	208	14	10	4	70	76	3.12	3.42	3.00	37.9
40	46	1963	J.Bouton	40	30	249	21	7	1	148	87	2.53	2.86	3.19	37.7
41	15	1997	D.Cone	29	29	195	12	6	0	222	86	2.82	3.09	2.83	37.5
42	42	1994	J.Key	25	25	168	17	4	0	97	52	3.27	3.15	3.15	37.2
43	54	1958	B.Turley	33	31	245	21	7	1	168	128	2.97	3.01	3.26	37.2
44	72	1921	W.Hoyt	43	32	282	19	13	3	102	81	3.09	3.86	3.43	37.2
45	50	1951	E.Lopat	31	31	235	21	9	0	93	71	2.91	3.29	3.22	36.6
46	44	1936	M.Pearson	33	31	223	19	7	1	118	135	3.71	4.00	3.16	36.4
47	81	1969	M.Stottlemyre	39	39	303	20	14	0	113	97	2.82	3.12	3.48	36.4
48	69	1961	W.Ford	39	39	283	25	4	0	209	92	3.21	3.43	3.41	36.0
49	45	1935	R.Ruffing	30	29	222	16	11	0	81	76	3.12	3.57	3.17	36.0
50	57	1923	H.Pennock	35	27	238	19	6	3	93	68	3.13	3.46	3.28	35.6

New York Yankees Starting Pitchers

V	R	Year	Name	G	GS	IP	W	L	SV	SO	BB	ERA	RA/9	R Wtd RA/9	V Runs /162
51	32	1942	S.Chandler	24	24	201	16	5	0	74	74	2.38	2.87	3.05	35.4
52	36	1977	R.Guidry	31	25	211	16	7	1	176	65	2.82	3.08	3.08	34.7
53	71	1979	T.John	37	36	276	21	9	0	111	65	2.96	3.55	3.43	34.6
54	27	1961	B.Stafford	36	25	195	14	9	2	101	59	2.68	3.00	2.98	34.1
55	62	1935	L.Gomez	34	30	246	12	15	1	138	86	3.18	3.80	3.38	34.0
56	86	1936	R.Ruffing	33	33	271	20	12	0	102	90	3.85	4.42	3.49	33.8
57	41	1957	T.Sturdivant	28	28	202	16	6	0	118	80	2.54	2.90	3.13	33.7
58	94	1965	M.Stottlemyre	37	37	291	20	9	0	155	88	2.63	3.06	3.52	33.5
59	65	1915	R.Fisher	30	28	248	18	11	0	97	62	2.11	2.98	3.40	33.4
60	66	1955	B.Turley	36	34	247	17	13	1	210	177	3.06	3.35	3.41	33.2
61	40	1939	L.Gomez	26	26	198	12	8	0	102	84	3.41	3.64	3.13	33.0
62	100	1919	B.Shawkey	41	27	261	20	11	5	122	92	2.72	3.24	3.57	33.0
63	26	1953	E.Lopat	25	24	178	16	4	0	50	32	2.42	2.93	2.98	32.8
64	111	1919	J.Quinn	38	31	266	15	14	0	97	65	2.61	3.27	3.61	32.5
65	137	1906	A.Orth	45	39	339	27	17	0	133	66	2.34	3.06	3.74	32.4
66	99	1923	J.Bush	37	30	276	19	15	0	125	117	3.43	3.75	3.55	32.4
67	18	1980	R.May	41	17	175	15	5	3	133	39	2.46	2.87	2.89	32.3
68	30	1942	H.Borowy	25	21	178	15	4	1	85	66	2.52	2.83	3.01	32.3
69	89	1969	F.Peterson	37	37	272	17	16	0	150	43	2.55	3.14	3.50	32.0
70	70	1938	L.Gomez	32	32	239	18	12	0	129	99	3.35	4.14	3.42	31.8
71	76	1925	U.Shocker	41	30	244	12	12	2	74	58	3.65	3.98	3.45	31.4
72	90	1963	W.Ford	38	37	269	24	7	1	189	56	2.74	3.14	3.51	31.4
73	61	1951	A.Reynolds	40	26	221	17	8	7	126	100	3.05	3.42	3.35	31.1
74	53	1998	D.Wells	30	30	214	18	4	0	163	29	3.49	3.61	3.25	31.1
75	25	1963	A.Downing	24	22	176	13	5	0	171	80	2.56	2.66	2.97	31.0
76	78	1923	W.Hoyt	37	28	239	17	9	1	60	66	3.02	3.65	3.46	30.7
77	60	1954	W.Ford	34	28	211	16	8	1	125	101	2.82	3.07	3.32	30.6
78	68	1973	D.Medich	34	32	235	14	9	0	145	74	2.95	3.22	3.41	29.9
79	73	1952	V.Raschi	31	31	223	16	6	0	127	91	2.78	3.15	3.43	29.3
80	138	1928	G.Pipgras	46	38	301	24	13	3	139	103	3.38	3.95	3.74	28.7
81	101	1985	R.Guidry	34	33	259	22	6	0	143	42	3.27	3.61	3.58	28.2
82	52	1981	R.Guidry	23	21	127	11	5	0	104	26	2.76	2.91	3.24	28.1
83	58	1953	J.Sain	40	19	189	14	7	9	84	45	3.00	3.24	3.30	27.9
84	121	1928	W.Hoyt	42	31	273	23	7	8	67	60	3.36	3.89	3.69	27.8
85	67	1953	W.Ford	32	30	207	18	6	0	110	110	3.00	3.35	3.41	27.8
86	103	1950	A.Reynolds	35	29	241	16	12	2	160	138	3.74	4.03	3.58	27.5
87	92	1940	R.Ruffing	30	30	226	15	12	0	97	76	3.38	3.90	3.52	27.4
88	136	1911	R.Ford	37	33	281	22	11	0	158	76	2.27	3.81	3.73	27.0
89	106	1983	R.Guidry	31	31	250	21	9	0	156	60	3.42	3.56	3.59	26.9
90	79	1941	M.Russo	28	27	210	14	10	1	105	87	3.09	3.64	3.46	26.9
91	77	1914	R.Fisher	29	26	209	10	12	1	86	61	2.28	2.80	3.46	26.8
92	123	1968	M.Stottlemyre	36	36	279	21	12	0	140	65	2.45	2.77	3.69	26.8
93	56	1957	B.Turley	32	23	176	13	6	3	152	85	2.71	3.02	3.26	26.7
94	108	1992	M.Perez	33	33	248	13	16	0	218	93	2.87	3.42	3.59	26.6
95	126	1922	W.Hoyt	37	31	265	19	12	0	95	76	3.43	3.87	3.70	26.4
96	55	1957	B.Shantz	30	21	173	11	5	5	72	40	2.45	3.02	3.26	26.2
97	88	1927	H.Pennock	34	26	210	19	8	2	51	48	3.00	3.81	3.49	26.1
98	38	1939	B.Hadley	26	18	154	12	6	2	65	85	2.98	3.62	3.11	26.0
99	122	1922	J.Bush	39	30	255	26	7	3	92	85	3.31	3.85	3.69	26.0
100	80	1959	A.Ditmar	38	25	202	13	9	1	96	52	2.90	3.34	3.47	25.7

New York Yankees
Relief Pitchers

V	R	Year	Name	G	GS	IP	W	L	SV	SO	BB	ERA	RA/9	R Wtd RA/9	V Runs /162
1	4	1996	M.Rivera	61	0	108	8	3	5	130	34	2.09	2.09	1.76	33.6
2	18	1977	S.Lyle	72	0	137	13	5	26	68	33	2.17	2.69	2.69	28.4
3	27	1947	J.Page	56	2	141	14	8	17	116	72	2.48	2.62	2.85	28.1
4	24	1949	J.Page	60	0	135	13	8	27	99	75	2.59	2.93	2.81	27.6
5	12	1961	L.Arroyo	65	0	119	15	5	29	87	49	2.19	2.57	2.56	26.4
6	11	1970	L.McDaniel	62	0	112	9	5	29	81	23	2.01	2.33	2.54	25.1
7	14	1974	S.Lyle	66	0	114	9	3	15	89	43	1.66	2.37	2.63	24.4
8	8	1982	R.Gossage	56	0	93	4	5	30	102	28	2.23	2.23	2.25	23.9
9	33	1978	R.Gossage	63	0	134	10	11	27	122	59	2.01	2.75	2.96	23.8
10	13	1986	D.Righetti	74	0	107	8	8	46	83	35	2.45	2.62	2.57	23.7
11	20	1972	S.Lyle	59	0	108	9	5	35	75	29	1.92	2.09	2.74	23.0
12	2	1999	M.Rivera	66	0	69	4	3	45	52	18	1.83	1.96	1.70	21.9
13	22	1985	B.Shirley	48	8	109	5	5	2	55	26	2.64	2.81	2.78	21.5
14	6	1959	R.Duren	41	0	77	3	6	14	96	43	1.88	2.10	2.18	21.4
15	7	1941	J.Murphy	35	0	77	8	3	15	29	40	1.98	2.34	2.23	21.0
16	5	1997	M.Rivera	66	0	72	6	4	43	68	20	1.88	2.13	1.95	20.9
17	17	1980	R.Gossage	64	0	99	6	2	33	103	37	2.27	2.64	2.66	20.8
18	26	1989	L.Guetterman	70	0	103	5	5	13	51	26	2.45	2.71	2.85	19.6
19	3	1998	M.Rivera	54	0	61	3	0	36	36	17	1.91	1.91	1.72	19.2
20	21	1984	D.Righetti	64	0	96	5	6	31	90	37	2.34	2.71	2.78	19.0
21	1	1994	S.Howe	40	0	40	3	0	15	18	7	1.80	1.80	1.56	18.9
22	31	1984	J.Howell	61	1	104	9	4	7	109	34	2.69	2.86	2.93	18.8
23	34	1985	D.Righetti	74	0	107	12	7	29	92	45	2.78	3.03	3.00	18.5
24	29	1994	B.Wickman	53	0	70	5	4	6	56	27	3.09	3.34	2.89	18.4
25	30	1985	B.Fisher	55	0	98	4	4	14	85	29	2.38	2.93	2.90	18.0
26	25	1991	J.Habyan	66	0	90	4	2	2	70	20	2.30	2.80	2.84	17.2
27	23	1983	R.Gossage	57	0	87	13	5	22	90	25	2.27	2.78	2.80	17.0
28	9	1997	M.Stanton	64	0	67	6	1	3	70	34	2.57	2.57	2.35	16.4
29	10	1991	S.Farr	60	0	70	5	5	23	60	20	2.19	2.44	2.48	16.2
30	15	2000	M.Rivera	66	0	76	7	4	36	58	25	2.85	3.09	2.64	16.1
31	44	1980	R.Davis	53	0	131	9	3	7	65	32	2.95	3.44	3.47	15.8
32	32	1979	R.Davis	44	0	85	14	2	9	43	28	2.85	3.06	2.95	15.1
33	39	1976	S.Lyle	64	0	104	7	8	23	61	42	2.26	2.86	3.27	14.9
34	16	2000	J.Nelson	73	0	70	8	4	0	71	45	2.45	3.10	2.65	14.8
35	38	1959	B.Shantz	33	4	95	7	3	3	66	33	2.38	3.13	3.25	14.5
36	43	1983	G.Frazier	61	0	115	4	4	8	78	45	3.43	3.43	3.46	14.0
37	37	1976	D.Tidrow	47	2	92	4	5	10	65	24	2.63	2.83	3.23	13.5
38	35	1988	C.Guante	63	0	80	5	6	12	65	26	2.82	2.94	3.04	13.4
39	36	1979	D.Hood	40	6	89	4	1	2	29	44	3.22	3.32	3.21	13.4
40	19	1996	J.Wetteland	62	0	64	2	3	43	69	21	2.83	3.25	2.73	13.0
41	28	1995	J.Wetteland	60	0	61	1	5	31	66	14	2.93	3.23	2.87	12.8
42	41	1987	T.Stoddard	57	0	93	4	3	8	78	30	3.50	3.69	3.40	12.0
43	46	1953	B.Kuzava	33	6	92	6	5	4	48	34	3.31	3.42	3.48	11.6
44	52	1959	J.Coates	37	4	100	6	1	0	64	36	2.87	3.51	3.64	10.7
45	40	1997	J.Nelson	77	0	79	3	7	2	81	37	2.86	3.66	3.35	10.6
46	47	1963	H.Reniff	48	0	89	4	3	18	56	42	2.62	3.13	3.50	10.5
47	49	1970	R.Klimkowski	45	3	98	6	7	1	40	33	2.65	3.31	3.61	10.3
48	42	1954	J.Sain	45	0	77	6	6	22	33	15	3.16	3.16	3.41	10.3
49	48	1992	R.Monteleone	47	0	93	7	3	0	62	27	3.30	3.40	3.57	10.2
50	53	1982	R.May	41	6	106	6	6	3	85	14	2.89	3.65	3.70	10.1

Philadelphia/Kansas City/ Oakland Athletics (1901–2000)

The Athletics possess a Dr. Jekyll and Mr. Hyde personality. In four periods where ownership allowed the team to realize its potential, the Athletics were .500 or better in 39 of 43 seasons, or about 90 percent of the time. In four periods where financial considerations were more important than team success, the Athletics were .500 or better in only 6 of 57 seasons, or about 10 percent of the time. Overall, the Athletics produced only 44 winning seasons in 100 years, yet they earned 20 postseason appearances, second only to the Yankees in American League history. In summary, the Athletics generally fielded bad teams, but when they were good, they dominated as effectively as the Yankees did in their winning seasons. One can only wonder how many pennants Connie Mack, Charlie Finley, and more recent owners lost when they intentionally dismantled powerful teams.

The Philadelphia Athletics put together 13 winning seasons in their first 14 years of existence, while winning six pennants and three World Series crowns. In 1901, the remarkable Nap Lajoie generated the best season of his career for Philadelphia, batting .426 with 14 home runs, for a 1,109 Wtd. Production, 1,199 Total Factor, and 164.7 Hits Contribution—which represents the highest volume of success since 1884 by any player other than Ruth. Despite losing Lajoie to Cleveland in 1902, the Athletics won their first pennant that year, as Harry Davis, Danny Murphy, Topsy Hartsel, and Socks Seybold provided the offense, while Rube Waddell (24–7, 2.05 ERA, 2.67 Wtd. RA/9) and Eddie Plank led the pitching staff. These six players, along with Chief Bender, were also the nucleus of the 1905 pennant winner. The Athletics failed to win a pennant the following four years. However, a future Hall of Famer emerged in 1909 and became an instant superstar, setting the stage for the team's return to the top. In his first full season, Eddie Collins enjoyed his best year, as he hit .347 with 67 steals. Adjusted for 15.5 percent hitter's deflation, Collins hit .401 for a 1,081 Total Factor and 126.7 Hits Contribution, the league's fourth best volume of success at second.

The Athletics won four pennants in five years from 1910 to 1914. The famous "$100,000 infield" featured Collins (.344, 58 steals, 1,051 Total Factor, Chalmers [MVP] Award in 1914) and Frank "Home Run" Baker (.347, 21 triples, 10 home runs, 40 steals, 1,030 Total Factor in 1912). Pitcher Jack Coombs was 31–9 with a 1.30 ERA and 2.35 Wtd. RA/9 in 1910, Bender went 23–5 with a 1.58 ERA and 2.83 Wtd. RA/9 that same year, and Plank was 23–8 with a 2.10 ERA and a 2.92 Wtd. RA/9 in 1911.

After the Athletics terrorized the American League for five years, owner-manager Connie Mack was forced for financial reasons to sell star players, including league MVP Eddie Collins, and the team crumbled from a 99–53 record in 1914 to a last place, 43–109 record in 1915. The Athletics piled up seven consecutive last place finishes from 1915 to 1921, with the worst of these forgettable teams being the 1919 squad, sporting a 36–104 record. In all, the Athletics produced ten consecutive losing seasons from 1915 to 1924.

Connie Mack rebuilt his Athletics into another talent-laden ballclub, with nine consecutive winning seasons from 1925 to 1933, including three pennants in a row and two World Series crowns from 1929 to 1931. Future Hall of Famers Lefty Grove (31–4, 2.06 ERA, 2.30 Wtd. RA/9, MVP in 1931), Mickey Cochrane (.349, 17 home runs, 1,014 Total Factor in 1931), and Al Simmons (.381, 36 home runs, 1,091 Total Factor in 1930) were instrumental to the team's success. Jimmie Foxx, the best hitter on this powerful team, hit .364 with 58 home runs in 1932, for a 1,146 Wtd. Production and the MVP Award. In 1933, Foxx hit .356 with 48 home runs and 163 RBI for a 1,111 Wtd. Production; these numbers earned him the Triple Crown and another MVP Award.

Connie Mack was forced to dismantle his new dynasty during the Depression. Only, this time, the aging patriarch was unable to bring his team back from the second division. The Athletics drifted through more than three decades, with two franchise moves and only four winning records in 34 seasons. A 13-year stopover in Kansas City saw the A's limp to an 829–1222 record, and a follow-up move to Oakland, where hoped-for crowds might invigorate the franchise, seemed at first to bring no change in the club's recent dark fortunes.

During much of this period, the Athletics behaved as if they were a Yankees farm club, shipping their best talent off to the Yankees to keep that dynasty going. Bob Johnson (.338, 23 home runs, 951 Total Factor in 1939) was the team's only consistent star during this period, although Eddie Joost (.263, 23 home runs, 149 walks in 1949), Ferris Fain, Elmer Valo, and 1952 MVP Bobby Shantz (24–7, 2.48 ERA) all had generated outstanding seasons.

The Athletics finally returned to the top in the late 1960s, achieving 11 winning seasons in 14 years from 1968 to 1981, including six playoff appearances and three consecutive World Series crowns in 1972–1974. The colorful Oakland A's squads of this era featured 1973 MVP Reggie Jackson (.293, 32 home runs, 22 steals), Bert Campaneris, Sal Bando, Gene Tenace, Joe Rudi, Jim "Catfish" Hunter, 1971 MVP Vida Blue (24–8, 1.82 ERA, 2.47 Wtd. RA/9), and Rollie Fingers.

Once again, the A's were dismantled at their peak, this time by owner Charlie Finley, with Jackson and Hunter leaving after the 1974 world championship season. The team managed to stay above .500, mainly because commissioner Bowie Kuhn stepped in and stopped Finley's plan to sell Fingers, Blue, and Rudi. The A's minor league system sent future superstar Rickey Henderson and a group of promising young pitchers up to the parent club. By 1981, the team returned to the playoffs with a division title.

Oakland endured a dry spell during the 1980s with five consecutive losing seasons, partly because manager Billy Martin wore out the starting pitching staff in their 1981 campaign. The sore-armed staff collapsed in 1982, and Henderson departed to the Yankees in 1985.

Jose Canseco arrived with a fine rookie season in 1986, and the A's climbed back to .500 in 1987 behind the bats of Canseco and slugger Mark McGwire, who hit 49 round trippers to set the rookie home run record. Dave Stewart led the league with 20 wins, and Dennis Eckersley came from the Cubs to anchor the bullpen. In 1988, Oakland won a pennant for the first time since 1974, with Canseco earning the MVP Award for the major leagues' first 40–40 season, as he batted .307 with 42 home runs and 40 steals, for a 1,000 Total Factor. Rickey Henderson returned in 1989, and this time Oakland had enough talent and good fortune to win the World Series.

The A's won 103 games and another pennant in 1990, as MVP Henderson produced a career year with a .325 average, 28 home runs and 65 steals, for a 1,156 Total Factor and 112.2 Hits Contribution. Eckersley was unhittable, with a 0.61 ERA, a 4–2 record and 48 saves, and with pinpoint control that yielded 73 strikeouts and only 4 walks in 73 innings. Eckersley's 1.15 Wtd. RA/9 ranks second in league rate of success for relievers. Oakland finished a run of six seasons at .500 or better with another division title in 1992, with most of the team's wins being nailed down by MVP Eckersley and his 51 saves, 1.91 ERA, and 2.01 Wtd. RA/9.

Oakland went from first place in 1992 to last place in 1993, as Canseco left for Texas, Henderson was traded in midyear to Toronto, and McGwire was limited to 84 at bats due to a foot injury. Oakland continued to lose throughout the 1990s, as their economic situation once again did not justify investing in a winner. The star during this period was McGwire, who hit .312 with 52 home runs in 1996, for a 1,199 Production. Adjusted for 9 percent hitter's inflation, McGwire hit .285 with 49 home runs, for a 1,096 Wtd. Production. Oakland traded McGwire away in the midst of a 1997 season where he hit 58 home runs.

After six straight losing seasons, Oakland assembled a new lineup of sluggers on a limited budget, and climbed to second place in 1999. They captured a spot in the postseason in 2000, led by MVP slugger Jason Giambi (.333, 43 home runs, 1,033 Wtd. Production), shortstop Miguel Tejeda (.275, 30 home runs), and 20-game winner Tim Hudson.

Philadelphia/Kansas City/Oakland Athletics

Hitters Volume of Success

Pos	Year	Name	AB	BB	HBP	TAB	H	2B	3B	HR	BA	OB	SA	PRO	Wtd PRO	SB	CS	SBF	SPF	FF	R TF	V HC
C	1932	M.Cochrane	518	100	4	622	152	35	4	23	.293	.412	.510	921	867	0	1	(3)	10	90	964	89.3
1B	1932	J.Foxx	585	116	0	701	213	33	9	58	.364	.469	.749	1,218	1,146	3	7	(15)	0	20	1,152	134.1
2B	1901	N.Lajoie	544	24	13	581	232	48	14	14	.426	.463	.643	1,106	1,109	27			10	80	1,199	164.7
SS	1949	E.Joost	525	149	4	678	138	25	3	23	.263	.429	.453	883	851	2	1	0	0	30	881	74.4
3B	1912	F.Baker	577	50	6	633	200	40	21	10	.347	.404	.541	945	980	40			10	40	1,030	99.5
OF	1990	R.Henderson	489	97	4	590	159	33	3	28	.325	.441	.577	1,017	1,034	65	10	72	10	40	1,156	112.2
OF	1930	A.Simmons	554	39	1	594	211	41	16	36	.381	.423	.708	1,130	1,033	9	2	8	0	50	1,091	99.4
OF	1969	R.Jackson	549	114	12	675	151	36	3	47	.275	.410	.608	1,019	1,038	13	5	4	10	(20)	1,032	88.3
Starters		Averages	543	86	6	634	182	36	9	30	.335	.431	.601	1,033	1,007	20	3	8	6	41	1,063	107.7
C	1975	G.Tenace	498	106	12	616	127	17	0	29	.255	.398	.464	862	887	7	4	(2)	(10)	(40)	836	46.4
1B	1996	M.McGwire	423	116	8	547	132	21	0	52	.312	.468	.730	1,199	1,096	0	0	0	(10)	0	1,086	82.4
2B	1909	E.Collins	571	62	6	639	198	30	10	3	.347	.416	.450	866	1,001	67			10	70	1,081	126.7
SS	1968	B.Campaneris	642	50	4	696	177	25	9	4	.276	.332	.361	693	766	62	22	24	10	20	820	52.5
3B	1969	S.Bando	609	111	11	731	171	25	3	31	.281	.401	.484	885	902	1	4	(9)	0	(20)	873	54.5
OF	1988	J.Canseco	610	78	10	698	187	34	0	42	.307	.394	.569	963	979	40	16	11	10	0	1,000	80.6
OF	1939	B.Johnson	544	99	0	643	184	30	9	23	.338	.440	.553	993	924	15	5	7	10	10	951	62.5
OF	1958	B.Cerv	515	50	5	570	157	20	7	38	.305	.372	.592	964	963	3	3	(5)	(10)	10	958	57.2
Subs		Averages	552	84	7	643	167	25	5	28	.302	.401	.516	917	935	24	7	3	1	6	946	70.4
Totals		Weighted Ave.	546	85	6	637	177	33	8	29	.324	.421	.573	994	983	21	4	7	5	30	1,024	95.3

Pitchers Volume of Success

Pos	Year	Name	G	GS	IP	W	L	SV	SO	BB	ERA	RA/9	Wtd RA/9	R Runs /162
SP	1910	J.Coombs	45	38	353	31	9	1	224	115	1.30	1.89	2.35	90.9
SP	1931	L.Grove	41	30	289	31	4	5	175	62	2.06	2.62	2.30	76.1
SP	1971	V.Blue	39	39	312	24	8	0	301	88	1.82	2.11	2.47	72.3
SP	1902	R.Waddell	33	27	276	24	7	0	210	64	2.05	2.93	2.67	66.9
SP	1918	S.Perry	44	36	332	20	19	2	81	111	1.98	2.63	3.31	58.6
Starters		Averages	40	34	312	26	9	2	198	88	1.82	2.41	2.63	73.0
RP	1970	M.Grant	80	0	135	8	3	24	58	32	1.87	1.93	2.10	36.8
RP	1990	D.Eckersley	63	0	73	4	2	48	73	4	0.61	1.10	1.15	27.6
RP	1966	J.Acker	66	0	113	8	4	32	68	28	1.99	2.15	2.51	25.7
RP	1964	W.Stock	64	0	114	8	3	5	115	42	2.30	2.37	2.65	24.1
Relievers		Averages	68	0	109	7	3	27	79	27	1.80	1.96	2.19	28.6
Totals		Averages	109	34	421	33	12	29	277	115	1.82	2.29	2.51	101.5

Philadelphia/Kansas City/Oakland Athletics   **Hitters Rate of Success**

Pos	Year	Name	AB	BB	HBP	TAB	H	2B	3B	HR	BA	OB	SA	PRO	Wtd PRO	SB	CS	SBF	SPF	FF	R TF	V HC
C	1931	M.Cochrane	459	56	3	518	160	31	6	17	.349	.423	.553	976	931	2	3	(7)	10	80	1,014	87.4
1B	1932	J.Foxx	585	116	0	701	213	33	9	58	.364	.469	.749	1,218	1,146	3	7	(15)	0	20	1,152	134.1
2B	1901	N.Lajoie	544	24	13	581	232	48	14	14	.426	.463	.643	1,106	1,109	27			10	80	1,199	164.7
SS	1949	E.Joost	525	149	4	678	138	25	3	23	.263	.429	.453	883	851	2	1	0	0	30	881	74.4
3B	1912	F.Baker	577	50	6	633	200	40	21	10	.347	.404	.541	945	980	40			10	40	1,030	99.5
OF	1990	R.Henderson	489	97	4	590	159	33	3	28	.325	.441	.577	1,017	1,034	65	10	72	10	40	1,156	112.2
OF	1930	A.Simmons	554	39	1	594	211	41	16	36	.381	.423	.708	1,130	1,033	9	2	8	0	50	1,091	99.4
OF	1969	R.Jackson	549	114	12	675	151	36	3	47	.275	.410	.608	1,019	1,038	13	5	4	10	(20)	1,032	88.3
Starters		Averages	535	81	5	621	183	36	9	29	.342	.433	.607	1,040	1,017	20	4	8	6	40	1,071	107.5
C	1917	W.Schang	316	29	9	354	90	14	9	3	.285	.362	.415	776	859	6			0	(20)	839	28.6
1B	1996	M.McGwire	423	116	8	547	132	21	0	52	.312	.468	.730	1,199	1,096	0	0	0	(10)	0	1,086	82.4
2B	1909	E.Collins	571	62	6	639	198	30	10	3	.347	.416	.450	866	1,001	67			10	70	1,081	126.7
SS	1929	J.Dykes	401	51	7	459	131	34	6	13	.327	.412	.539	950	887	8	3	4	0	(30)	862	45.9
3B	1996	S.Brosius	428	59	7	494	130	25	0	22	.304	.397	.516	913	835	7	2	6	0	40	881	38.8
OF	1988	J.Canseco	610	78	10	698	187	34	0	42	.307	.394	.569	963	979	40	16	11	10	0	1,000	80.6
OF	1977	M.Page	501	78	6	585	154	28	8	21	.307	.407	.521	928	918	42	5	52	10	(20)	959	56.3
OF	1958	B.Cerv	515	50	5	570	157	20	7	38	.305	.372	.592	964	963	3	3	(5)	(10)	10	958	57.2
Subs		Averages	471	65	7	543	147	26	5	24	.313	.405	.544	949	951	22	4	8	1	6	967	64.6
Totals		Weighted Ave.	514	76	6	595	171	33	8	28	.332	.424	.586	1,010	995	21	4	8	5	29	1,036	93.2

Pitchers Rate of Succes

Pos	Year	Name	G	GS	IP	W	L	SV	SO	BB	ERA	RA/9	Wtd RA/9	R Runs/162
SP	1931	L.Grove	41	30	289	31	4	5	175	62	2.06	2.62	2.30	76.1
SP	1910	J.Coombs	45	38	353	31	9	1	224	115	1.30	1.89	2.35	90.9
SP	1971	V.Blue	39	39	312	24	8	0	301	88	1.82	2.11	2.47	72.3
SP	1994	S.Ontiveros	27	13	115	6	4	0	56	26	2.65	3.04	2.63	34.9
SP	1902	R.Waddell	33	27	276	24	7	0	210	64	2.05	2.93	2.67	66.9
Starters		Averages	37	29	269	23	6	1	193	71	1.85	2.41	2.46	68.2
RP	1990	D.Eckersley	63	0	73	4	2	48	73	4	0.61	1.10	1.15	27.6
RP	1970	M.Grant	80	0	135	8	3	24	58	32	1.87	1.93	2.10	36.8
RP	1972	D.Knowles	54	0	66	5	1	11	36	37	1.37	1.64	2.15	18.6
RP	1966	J.Acker	66	0	113	8	4	32	68	28	1.99	2.15	2.51	25.7
Relievers		Averages	66	0	97	6	3	29	59	25	1.58	1.79	2.05	27.2
Totals		Averages	103	29	366	29	9	30	252	96	1.78	2.25	2.35	95.4

Philadelphia/Kansas City/Oakland Athletics
Catchers

V	R	Year	Name	AB	BB	HBP	TAB	H	2B	3B	HR	BA	OB	SA	PRO	Wtd PRO	SB	CS	SBF	SPF	FF	R TF	V HC
1	4	1932	M.Cochrane	518	100	4	622	152	35	4	23	.293	.412	.510	921	867	0	1	(3)	10	90	964	89.3
2	2	1933	M.Cochrane	429	106	3	538	138	30	4	15	.322	.459	.515	974	940	8	6	(7)	10	60	1,002	87.7
3	1	1931	M.Cochrane	459	56	3	518	160	31	6	17	.349	.423	.553	976	931	2	3	(7)	10	80	1,014	87.4
4	3	1930	M.Cochrane	487	55	1	543	174	42	5	10	.357	.424	.526	949	868	5	0	9	10	90	977	81.4
5	6	1929	M.Cochrane	514	69	2	585	170	37	8	7	.331	.412	.475	887	828	7	6	(8)	10	70	900	65.2
6	5	1927	M.Cochrane	432	50	2	484	146	20	6	12	.338	.409	.495	904	850	9	6	(6)	10	60	914	57.5
7	7	1928	M.Cochrane	468	76	3	547	137	26	12	10	.293	.395	.464	859	818	7	7	(12)	10	40	856	48.9
8	9	1975	G.Tenace	498	106	12	616	127	17	0	29	.255	.398	.464	862	887	7	4	(2)	(10)	(40)	836	46.4
9	11	1940	F.Hayes	465	61	1	527	143	23	4	16	.308	.389	.477	866	815	9	3	5		(10)	811	35.2
10	10	1925	M.Cochrane	420	44	2	466	139	21	5	6	.331	.397	.448	845	776	7	4	(2)	10	30	814	32.0
11	17	1996	T.Steinbach	514	49	6	569	140	25	1	35	.272	.343	.529	872	798	0	1	(3)	(10)		784	29.0
12	8	1917	W.Schang	316	29	9	354	90	14	9	3	.285	.362	.415	776	859	6			(20)		839	28.6
13	16	1939	F.Hayes	431	40	3	474	122	28	5	20	.283	.348	.510	859	798	4	1	4		(10)	792	27.3
14	13	1926	M.Cochrane	370	56	0	426	101	8	9	8	.273	.369	.408	777	738	5	2	2	10	50	800	26.2
15	12	1902	Schreckengost	358	9	1	368	117	17	2	2	.327	.345	.402	747	754	5		(10)		60	804	25.6
16	18	1941	F.Hayes	439	62	0	501	123	27	4	12	.280	.369	.442	811	784	2	0	4		(10)	778	25.3
17	14	1907	Schreckengost	356	17	0	373	97	16	3	0	.272	.306	.334	640	739	4			(10)	70	799	22.8
18	15	1957	H.Smith	360	14	1	375	109	26	0	13	.303	.331	.483	814	809	2	2	(5)		(10)	794	22.0
19	19	1905	Schreckengost	420	3	1	424	114	19	6	0	.271	.278	.345	624	718	9			(10)	60	768	19.3
20	21	1992	T.Steinbach	438	45	1	484	122	20	1	12	.279	.347	.411	758	773	2	3	(8)	(10)		755	17.9
21	20	1938	F.Hayes	316	54	1	371	92	19	3	11	.291	.396	.475	871	795	2	3	(10)		(20)	765	16.3
22	22	1987	T.Steinbach	391	32	9	432	111	16	3	16	.284	.352	.463	815	782	1	2	(7)		(20)	755	16.0
23	26	1994	T.Steinbach	369	26	0	395	105	21	2	11	.285	.332	.442	773	722	2	1	0	(10)	20	732	14.5
24	29	1944	F.Hayes	581	57	0	638	144	18	6	13	.248	.315	.367	682	710	2	1	0		10	720	13.5
25	25	1972	D.Duncan	403	34	5	442	88	13	0	19	.218	.287	.392	679	737	0	2	(9)	(10)	20	738	13.5

Philadelphia/Kansas City/Oakland Athletics
First basemen

V	R	Year	Name	AB	BB	HBP	TAB	H	2B	3B	HR	BA	OB	SA	PRO	Wtd PRO	SB	CS	SBF	SPF	FF	R TF	V HC
1	1	1932	J.Foxx	585	116	0	701	213	33	9	58	.364	.469	.749	1,218	1,146	3	7	(15)		20	1,152	134.1
2	2	1933	J.Foxx	573	96	1	670	204	37	9	48	.356	.449	.703	1,153	1,111	2	2	(3)		20	1,129	120.4
3	4	1934	J.Foxx	539	111	1	651	180	28	6	44	.334	.449	.653	1,102	1,037	11	2	10		20	1,067	96.9
4	6	1935	J.Foxx	535	114	0	649	185	33	7	36	.346	.461	.636	1,096	1,028	6	4	(3)		30	1,055	92.6
5	3	1996	M.McGwire	423	116	8	547	132	21	0	52	.312	.468	.730	1,199	1,096	0	0	0	(10)		1,086	82.4
6	7	1929	J.Foxx	517	103	2	622	183	23	9	33	.354	.463	.625	1,088	1,016	9	7	(8)	10	10	1,028	80.5
7	8	2000	J.Giambi	510	137	9	656	170	29	1	43	.333	.482	.647	1,129	1,033	2	0	3	(10)	(20)	1,006	73.8
8	9	1997	M.McGwire	540	101	9	650	148	27	0	58	.274	.397	.646	1,043	985	3	0	4	(10)	20	999	70.9
9	11	1930	J.Foxx	562	93	0	655	188	33	13	37	.335	.429	.637	1,066	975	7	7	(10)	10	10	985	70.5
10	5	1995	M.McGwire	317	88	11	416	87	13	0	39	.274	.447	.685	1,132	1,067	1	1	(2)	(10)		1,055	63.6
11	10	1992	M.McGwire	467	90	5	562	125	22	0	42	.268	.391	.585	976	995	0	1	(3)	(10)	10	992	59.4
12	13	1987	M.McGwire	557	71	5	633	161	28	4	49	.289	.374	.618	992	952	1	1	(1)			950	54.3
13	14	1918	G.Burns	505	23	8	536	178	22	9	6	.352	.390	.467	857	937	8			(10)		927	51.1
14	15	1906	H.Davis	551	49	5	605	161	40	8	12	.292	.355	.459	815	926	23					926	47.3
15	16	1931	J.Foxx	515	73	1	589	150	32	10	30	.291	.380	.567	947	904	4	3	(3)		20	920	44.4
16	20	1952	F.Fain	538	105	1	644	176	43	3	2	.327	.438	.429	867	881	3	5	(10)		30	901	42.1
17	22	1962	N.Siebern	600	110	1	711	185	25	6	25	.308	.416	.495	911	891	3	1	1			892	41.4
18	12	1904	H.Davis	404	23	2	429	125	21	11	10	.309	.350	.490	840	962	12					962	41.3
19	18	1972	M.Epstein	455	68	11	534	123	18	2	26	.270	.378	.490	868	942	0	1	(4)	(10)	(10)	918	39.6
20	19	1913	S.McInnis	543	45	6	594	176	30	4	4	.324	.382	.416	798	853	16			10	40	903	39.5
21	21	1990	M.McGwire	523	110	7	640	123	16	0	39	.235	.375	.489	864	879	2	1	0	(10)	30	899	39.3
22	17	1951	F.Fain	425	80	3	508	146	30	3	6	.344	.451	.471	921	900	0	3	(11)		30	918	37.8
23	23	1955	V.Power	596	35	0	631	190	34	10	19	.319	.357	.505	862	845	0	2	(6)	10	30	879	34.4
24	26	1999	J.Giambi	575	105	7	687	181	36	1	33	.315	.426	.553	980	903	1	1	(1)	(10)	(20)	872	33.4
25	24	1912	S.McInnis	568	49	3	620	186	25	13	3	.327	.384	.433	817	847	27			10	20	877	33.2

Philadelphia/Kansas City/Oakland Athletics
Second basemen

V	R	Year	Name	AB	BB	HBP	TAB	H	2B	3B	HR	BA	OB	SA	PRO	Wtd PRO	SB	CS	SBF	SPF	FF	R TF	V HC
1	1	1901	N.Lajoie	544	24	13	581	232	48	14	14	.426	.463	.643	1,106	1,109	27			10	80	1,199	164.7
2	2	1909	E.Collins	571	62	6	639	198	30	10	3	.347	.416	.450	866	1,001	67			10	70	1,081	126.7
3	3	1914	E.Collins	526	97	6	629	181	23	14	2	.344	.452	.452	904	994	58	30	(3)	10	50	1,051	115.3
4	4	1913	E.Collins	534	85	7	626	184	23	13	3	.345	.441	.453	894	955	55			10	80	1,045	112.8
5	5	1910	E.Collins	581	49	6	636	188	16	15	3	.324	.382	.418	800	910	81			10	110	1,030	109.8
6	7	1912	E.Collins	543	101	0	644	189	25	11	0	.348	.450	.435	885	917	63			10	70	997	100.7
7	6	1911	E.Collins	493	62	15	570	180	22	13	3	.365	.451	.481	932	945	38			10	50	1,005	91.3
8	8	1904	D.Murphy	557	22	5	584	160	30	17	7	.287	.320	.440	760	871	22			10	10	891	60.2
9	10	1905	D.Murphy	537	42	8	587	149	34	4	6	.277	.339	.389	728	839	23			10	(10)	839	45.1
10	14	1921	J.Dykes	613	60	15	688	168	32	13	16	.274	.353	.447	800	738	6	5	(5)		70	803	40.5
11	12	1928	M.Bishop	472	97	3	572	149	27	5	6	.316	.435	.432	868	826	9	9	(15)	10		822	39.1
12	9	1906	D.Murphy	448	21	6	475	135	28	6	2	.301	.341	.404	745	847	17			10	(10)	847	38.5
13	13	1969	D.Green	483	53	8	544	133	25	6	12	.275	.357	.427	783	798	2	3	(7)		30	821	35.1
14	15	1931	M.Bishop	497	112	2	611	146	30	4	5	.294	.426	.400	826	788	3	1	2		10	799	34.9
15	22	1962	J.Lumpe	641	44	0	685	193	34	10	10	.301	.346	.432	778	761	0	2	(6)		10	765	26.1
16	17	1907	D.Murphy	469	30	2	501	127	23	3	2	.271	.317	.345	663	766	11				20	786	25.2
17	21	1930	M.Bishop	441	128	6	575	111	27	6	10	.252	.426	.408	834	763	3	2	(2)		10	771	24.7
18	11	1908	E.Collins	330	16	3	349	90	18	7	1	.273	.312	.379	691	816	8			10		826	24.6
19	20	1992	M.Bordick	504	40	9	553	151	19	4	3	.300	.362	.371	733	747	12	6	0	10	20	777	24.2
20	19	1933	M.Bishop	391	106	1	498	115	27	1	4	.294	.446	.399	845	815	1	5	(17)		(20)	778	23.0
21	16	1924	J.Dykes	410	38	1	449	128	26	6	3	.312	.372	.427	799	747	1	3	(11)		50	786	22.7
22	18	1992	L.Blankenship	349	82	6	437	84	24	1	3	.241	.394	.341	735	749	21	7	15	10	10	784	20.6
23	23	1961	J.Lumpe	569	48	2	619	167	29	9	3	.293	.351	.392	742	722	1	0	2		30	753	20.1
24	24	1976	P.Garner	555	36	2	593	145	29	12	8	.261	.309	.400	709	756	35	13	14	10	(30)	751	18.4
25	26	1958	H.Lopez	564	49	2	615	147	28	4	17	.261	.322	.415	737	736	2	2	(3)		10	743	17.7

Philadelphia/Kansas City/Oakland Athletics
Shortstops

V	R	Year	Name	AB	BB	HBP	TAB	H	2B	3B	HR	BA	OB	SA	PRO	Wtd PRO	SB	CS	SBF	SPF	FF	R TF	V HC
1	1	1949	E.Joost	525	149	4	678	138	25	3	23	.263	.429	.453	883	851	2	1	0		30	881	74.4
2	3	1951	E.Joost	553	106	6	665	160	28	5	19	.289	.409	.461	870	850	10	8	(9)		20	861	66.3
3	5	1968	B.Campaneris	642	50	4	696	177	25	9	4	.276	.332	.361	693	766	62	22	24	10	20	820	52.5
4	4	1970	B.Campaneris	603	36	4	643	168	28	4	22	.279	.323	.448	771	774	42	10	32	10	10	827	50.5
5	6	1952	E.Joost	540	122	5	667	132	26	3	20	.244	.388	.415	803	816	5	8	(16)			800	46.2
6	2	1929	J.Dykes	401	51	7	459	131	34	6	13	.327	.412	.539	950	887	8	3	4		(30)	862	45.9
7	7	2000	M.Tejada	607	66	4	677	167	32	1	30	.275	.350	.479	829	759	6	0	8	10	20	798	43.8
8	11	1964	W.Causey	604	88	7	699	170	31	4	8	.281	.379	.386	765	774	0	1	(3)			771	36.2
9	10	1948	E.Joost	509	119	1	629	127	22	2	16	.250	.393	.395	788	761	2	4	(9)		20	772	34.5
10	8	1974	B.Campaneris	527	47	0	574	153	18	8	2	.290	.348	.366	715	748	34	15	7	10	10	775	30.9
11	12	1963	W.Causey	554	56	0	610	155	32	4	8	.280	.346	.395	741	754	4	2	0		10	764	29.6
12	9	1913	J.Barry	455	44	8	507	125	20	6	3	.275	.349	.365	714	762	15				10	772	28.1
13	14	1999	M.Tejada	593	57	10	660	149	33	4	21	.251	.327	.427	754	695	8	7	(9)	10	50	747	26.7
14	13	1966	B.Campaneris	573	25	5	603	153	29	10	5	.267	.303	.379	682	712	52	10	50	10	(20)	753	26.0
15	15	1932	E.McNair	554	28	3	585	158	47	3	18	.285	.323	.478	801	754	8	4	0		(10)	744	24.1
16	17	1965	B.Campaneris	578	41	9	628	156	23	12	6	.270	.328	.382	710	735	51	19	20	10	(30)	735	21.8
17	20	1961	D.Howser	611	92	5	708	171	29	6	3	.280	.379	.362	740	720	37	9	25	10	(30)	725	21.3
18	16	1910	J.Barry	487	52	5	544	126	19	5	3	.259	.336	.337	673	765	14			10	(40)	735	20.0
19	21	1922	C.Galloway	571	39	1	611	185	26	9	6	.324	.368	.433	801	758	10	19	(43)	10		724	19.1
20	26	1972	B.Campaneris	625	32	2	659	150	25	2	8	.240	.279	.325	604	655	52	14	34	10	20	719	18.9
21	24	1986	A.Griffin	594	35	2	631	169	23	6	4	.285	.326	.364	690	681	33	16	1	10	30	722	18.1
22	22	1969	B.Campaneris	547	30	4	581	142	15	2	2	.260	.303	.305	608	620	62	8	75	10	20	724	17.3
23	27	1950	E.Joost	476	103	3	582	111	12	3	18	.233	.373	.384	757	704	5	1	5		10	719	16.7
24	23	1917	W.Witt	452	65	0	517	114	13	4	0	.252	.346	.299	645	714	12			10		724	15.9
25	28	1976	B.Campaneris	536	63	3	602	137	14	1	1	.256	.337	.291	628	670	54	12	47	10	(10)	718	15.9

Philadelphia/Kansas City/Oakland Athletics
Third basemen

V	R	Year	Name	AB	BB	HBP	TAB	H	2B	3B	HR	BA	OB	SA	PRO	Wtd PRO	SB	CS	SBF	SPF	FF	R TF	V HC
1	1	1912	F.Baker	577	50	6	633	200	40	21	10	.347	.404	.541	945	980	40			10	40	1,030	99.5
2	2	1913	F.Baker	564	63	10	637	190	34	9	12	.337	.413	.493	906	967	34			10	20	997	89.7
3	3	1911	F.Baker	592	40	2	634	198	42	14	11	.334	.379	.508	887	900	38			10	20	930	67.8
4	4	1914	F.Baker	570	53	3	626	182	23	10	9	.319	.380	.442	822	904	19	20	(32)	10	40	922	64.7
5	5	1909	F.Baker	541	26	5	572	165	27	19	4	.305	.343	.447	790	913	20			10	(10)	913	56.3
6	8	1969	S.Bando	609	111	11	731	171	25	3	31	.281	.401	.484	885	902	1	4	(9)		(20)	873	54.5
7	10	1973	S.Bando	592	82	4	678	170	32	3	29	.287	.378	.498	876	898	4	2	0	(10)	(40)	848	42.6
8	6	1928	J.Foxx	400	60	1	461	131	29	10	13	.328	.416	.548	964	918	3	8	(27)	10	(10)	892	40.5
9	12	1902	L.Cross	559	27	2	588	191	39	8	0	.342	.374	.440	814	821	25			10	10	841	40.5
10	9	1910	F.Baker	561	34	4	599	159	25	15	2	.283	.329	.392	721	820	21			10	20	850	40.1
11	7	1996	S.Brosius	428	59	7	494	130	25	0	22	.304	.397	.516	913	835	7	2	6		40	881	38.8
12	13	1962	E.Charles	535	54	4	593	154	24	7	17	.288	.358	.454	812	794	20	4	19	10	10	833	32.9
13	15	1987	C.Lansford	554	60	9	623	160	27	4	19	.289	.368	.455	822	789	27	8	17	10	10	826	32.5
14	18	1948	H.Majeski	590	48	6	644	183	41	4	12	.310	.368	.454	822	794	2	1	0		20	814	31.6
15	11	1901	L.Cross	424	19	1	444	139	28	12	2	.328	.358	.465	823	825	23			10	10	845	31.5
16	20	1933	P.Higgins	567	61	2	630	178	34	12	13	.314	.383	.485	868	837	2	7	(18)		(10)	809	29.2
17	19	1971	S.Bando	538	86	8	632	146	23	1	24	.271	.380	.452	831	858	3	7	(16)		(30)	812	28.7
18	16	1925	J.Dykes	465	46	8	519	150	32	11	5	.323	.393	.471	864	794	3	2	(2)		30	822	27.6
19	21	1976	S.Bando	550	76	4	630	132	18	2	27	.240	.337	.427	764	815	20	6	12	(10)	(10)	807	27.3
20	23	1934	P.Higgins	543	56	0	599	179	37	6	16	.330	.392	.508	901	848	9	2	8		(50)	806	26.8
21	22	1989	C.Lansford	551	51	9	611	185	28	2	2	.336	.401	.405	806	826	37	15	11	10	(40)	807	26.4
22	27	1984	C.Lansford	597	40	3	640	179	31	5	14	.300	.347	.439	786	789	9	3	4	10	(10)	793	23.5
23	25	1947	H.Majeski	479	53	5	537	134	26	5	8	.280	.358	.405	763	771	1	0	2		30	803	23.3
24	14	1966	E.Charles	385	30	0	415	110	18	8	9	.286	.337	.444	782	816	12	5	5	10		831	22.6
25	28	1918	L.Gardner	463	43	0	506	132	22	6	1	.285	.346	.365	711	777	9			10		787	21.7

Philadelphia/Kansas City/Oakland Athletics
Outfielders

V	R	Year	Name	AB	BB	HBP	TAB	H	2B	3B	HR	BA	OB	SA	PRO	Wtd PRO	SB	CS	SBF	SPF	FF	R TF	V HC
1	1	1990	R.Henderson	489	97	4	590	159	33	3	28	.325	.441	.577	1,017	1,034	65	10	72	10	40	1,156	112.2
2	2	1930	A.Simmons	554	39	1	594	211	41	16	36	.381	.423	.708	1,130	1,033	9	2	8		50	1,091	99.4
3	3	1931	A.Simmons	513	47	3	563	200	37	13	22	.390	.444	.641	1,085	1,035	3	3	(5)		50	1,080	91.1
4	6	1969	R.Jackson	549	114	12	675	151	36	3	47	.275	.410	.608	1,019	1,038	13	5	4	10	(20)	1,032	88.3
5	5	1929	A.Simmons	581	31	1	613	212	41	9	34	.365	.398	.642	1,040	971	4	2	0		70	1,041	87.2
6	7	1988	J.Canseco	610	78	10	698	187	34	0	42	.307	.394	.569	963	979	40	16	11	10		1,000	80.6
7	9	1981	R.Henderson	423	64	2	489	135	18	7	6	.319	.411	.437	848	890	56	22	23	10	60	983	79.6
8	8	1983	R.Henderson	513	103	4	620	150	25	7	9	.292	.415	.421	836	834	108	19	107	10	40	991	69.0
9	4	1927	A.Simmons	406	31	1	438	159	36	11	15	.392	.436	.645	1,081	1,016	10	2	13		40	1,069	68.5
10	19	1980	R.Henderson	591	117	5	713	179	22	4	9	.303	.422	.399	821	818	100	26	64	10	50	942	62.6
11	15	1939	B.Johnson	544	99	0	643	184	30	9	23	.338	.440	.553	993	924	15	5	7	10	10	951	62.5
12	11	1974	R.Jackson	506	86	4	596	146	25	1	29	.289	.396	.514	910	953	25	5	24	10	(10)	977	62.3
13	21	1925	A.Simmons	654	35	1	690	253	43	12	24	.387	.419	.599	1,018	936	7	14	(29)		30	937	62.2
14	12	1993	R.Henderson	481	120	4	605	139	22	2	21	.289	.435	.474	909	887	53	8	58	10	10	965	59.7
15	18	1989	R.Henderson	541	126	3	670	148	26	3	12	.274	.413	.399	813	833	77	14	69	10	30	942	59.0
16	14	1958	B.Cerv	515	50	5	570	157	20	7	38	.305	.372	.592	964	963	3	3	(5)	(10)	10	958	57.2
17	16	1973	R.Jackson	539	76	7	622	158	28	2	32	.293	.387	.531	918	941	22	8	9	10	(10)	950	57.2
18	22	1926	A.Simmons	583	48	1	632	199	53	10	19	.341	.392	.564	957	909	11	3	7		20	936	56.7
19	13	1977	M.Page	501	78	6	585	154	28	8	21	.307	.407	.521	928	918	42	5	52	10	(20)	959	56.3
20	25	1972	J.Rudi	593	37	2	632	181	32	9	19	.305	.348	.486	834	904	3	4	(7)	10	20	927	53.6
21	10	1992	R.Henderson	396	95	6	497	112	18	3	15	.283	.429	.457	886	903	48	11	49	10	20	982	53.3
22	26	1991	J.Canseco	572	78	9	659	152	32	1	44	.266	.363	.556	919	924	26	6	20	10	(30)	924	52.2
23	24	1984	R.Henderson	502	86	5	593	147	27	4	16	.293	.401	.458	860	863	66	18	48	10	10	931	49.0
24	20	1990	J.Canseco	481	72	5	558	132	14	2	37	.274	.375	.543	917	932	19	10	(2)	10		941	48.8
25	27	1937	B.Johnson	477	98	1	576	146	32	6	25	.306	.425	.556	981	899	9	7	(8)	10	20	921	47.2

Philadelphia/Kansas City/Oakland Athletics
Outfielders

V	R	Year	Name	AB	BB	HBP	TAB	H	2B	3B	HR	BA	OB	SA	PRO	Wtd PRO	SB	CS	SBF	SPF	FF	R TF	V HC
26	28	1910	R.Oldring	546	23	4	573	168	27	14	4	.308	.340	.430	771	876	17			10	30	916	45.6
27	30	1934	B.Johnson	547	58	1	606	168	26	6	34	.307	.375	.563	938	883	12	8	(6)	10	20	906	45.2
28	34	1938	B.Johnson	563	87	2	652	176	27	9	30	.313	.406	.552	959	876	9	8	(10)	10	20	895	45.1
29	46	1932	A.Simmons	670	47	1	718	216	28	9	35	.322	.368	.548	915	862	4	2	0		20	882	44.7
30	23	1928	A.Simmons	464	31	3	498	163	33	9	15	.351	.396	.558	954	909	1	4	(13)		40	935	44.4
31	32	1902	S.Seybold	522	43	6	571	165	27	12	16	.316	.375	.506	881	888	6				10	898	44.2
32	17	1903	T.Hartsel	373	49	0	422	116	19	14	5	.311	.391	.477	868	946	13			10	(10)	946	43.8
33	37	1953	G.Zernial	556	57	4	617	158	21	3	42	.284	.355	.559	914	896	4	0	6	(10)		893	41.8
34	45	1981	D.Murphy	390	73	2	465	98	10	3	15	.251	.372	.408	780	818	10	4	4	10	50	882	41.8
35	35	1971	R.Jackson	567	63	6	636	157	29	3	32	.277	.355	.508	863	891	16	10	(6)	10		895	41.7
36	36	1984	D.Murphy	559	74	3	636	143	18	2	33	.256	.346	.472	818	822	4	5	(9)	10	70	893	41.0
37	39	1903	S.Seybold	522	38	6	566	156	45	8	8	.299	.353	.462	815	888	5					888	40.7
38	31	1901	S.Seybold	449	40	7	496	150	24	14	8	.334	.397	.503	901	903	15					903	39.8
39	29	1988	D.Henderson	507	47	4	558	154	38	1	24	.304	.367	.525	892	907	2	4	(10)		10	907	39.7
40	41	1982	R.Henderson	536	116	2	654	143	24	4	10	.267	.399	.382	782	778	130	42	66	10	30	885	39.7
41	38	1910	D.Murphy	560	31	1	592	168	28	18	4	.300	.338	.436	774	879	18				10	889	39.1
42	43	1916	A.Strunk	544	66	3	613	172	30	9	3	.316	.393	.421	814	891	21	23	(39)	10	20	882	38.4
43	52	1964	R.Colavito	588	83	5	676	161	31	2	34	.274	.368	.507	875	885	3	1	1	(10)		876	38.3
44	42	1974	J.Rudi	593	34	5	632	174	39	4	22	.293	.337	.484	821	860	2	3	(6)		30	884	38.1
45	33	1991	R.Henderson	470	98	7	575	126	17	1	18	.268	.402	.423	825	830	58	18	36	10	20	896	37.9
46	55	1941	B.Johnson	552	95	3	650	152	30	8	22	.275	.385	.478	863	834	6	4	(3)	10	30	871	37.2
47	65	1937	W.Moses	649	54	2	705	208	48	13	25	.320	.374	.550	925	848	9	7	(7)	10	10	861	36.6
48	53	1933	B.Johnson	535	85	0	620	155	44	4	21	.290	.387	.505	892	860	8	3	3	10		873	35.9
49	49	1909	D.Murphy	541	35	6	582	152	28	14	5	.281	.332	.412	744	859	19				20	879	35.6
50	44	1972	R.Jackson	499	59	8	566	132	25	2	25	.265	.352	.473	825	894	9	8	(12)	10	(10)	882	35.5
51	57	1975	R.Jackson	593	67	3	663	150	39	3	36	.253	.332	.511	843	868	17	8	1	10	(10)	869	35.3
52	56	1907	T.Hartsel	507	106	0	613	142	23	6	3	.280	.405	.367	771	891	20				(20)	871	35.0
53	59	1942	B.Johnson	550	82	1	633	160	35	7	13	.291	.384	.451	835	859	3	2	(1)	10		868	34.9
54	47	1911	D.Murphy	508	50	8	566	167	27	11	6	.329	.398	.461	858	870	22				10	880	34.9
55	66	1905	T.Hartsel	538	121	1	660	148	22	8	0	.275	.409	.346	755	869	37			10	(20)	859	33.7
56	68	1981	T.Armas	440	19	2	461	115	24	3	22	.261	.295	.480	775	812	5	1	6		40	859	33.6
57	60	1917	P.Bodie	557	53	3	613	162	28	11	7	.291	.356	.418	774	856	13			10		866	33.5
58	50	1915	A.Strunk	485	56	1	542	144	28	16	1	.297	.371	.427	798	865	17	19	(37)	10	40	878	32.8
59	48	1968	R.Monday	482	72	4	558	132	24	7	8	.274	.373	.402	775	856	14	6	3	10	10	880	32.5
60	51	1905	S.Seybold	492	42	8	542	135	37	4	6	.274	.341	.402	744	856	5				20	876	32.3
61	64	1940	B.Johnson	512	83	4	599	137	25	4	31	.268	.374	.514	888	835	8	2	6	10	10	862	31.3
62	61	1922	B.Miller	535	24	7	566	179	29	12	21	.335	.371	.551	922	873	10	10	(17)		10	866	30.8
63	62	1904	S.Seybold	510	42	4	556	149	26	9	3	.292	.351	.396	747	856	12				10	866	30.2
64	63	1918	T.Walker	414	41	1	456	122	20	0	11	.295	.360	.423	782	855	8				10	865	29.8
65	72	1982	D.Murphy	543	94	3	640	129	15	1	27	.238	.353	.418	771	768	26	8	15	10	60	853	29.1
66	78	1980	D.Murphy	573	102	2	677	157	18	2	13	.274	.386	.380	766	763	26	15	(6)	10	80	847	29.0
67	67	1927	T.Cobb	490	67	5	562	175	32	7	5	.357	.440	.482	921	866	22	16	(17)	10		859	28.6
68	76	1980	T.Armas	628	29	2	659	175	18	8	35	.279	.313	.500	813	809	5	3	(1)		40	848	28.4
69	85	1935	B.Johnson	582	78	2	662	174	29	5	28	.299	.384	.510	894	838	2	4	(9)	10		840	27.2
70	74	1968	R.Jackson	553	50	5	608	138	13	6	29	.250	.317	.452	770	850	14	4	9	10	(20)	849	26.6
71	69	1951	E.Valo	444	75	8	527	134	27	8	7	.302	.412	.446	858	837	11	6	(2)	10	10	856	25.9
72	54	1906	S.Seybold	411	30	3	444	130	21	3	5	.316	.367	.418	786	893	9			(20)		873	25.7
73	40	1997	M.Stairs	352	50	3	405	105	19	0	27	.298	.390	.582	973	918	3	2	(2)	(10)	(20)	886	24.7
74	79	1985	M.Davis	547	50	2	599	157	34	1	24	.287	.349	.484	833	828	24	10	6	10		844	24.7
75	87	1922	T.Walker	565	61	4	630	160	31	4	37	.283	.357	.549	906	857	4	3	(3)		(20)	834	24.2

Philadelphia/Kansas City/Oakland Athletics
Starting Pitchers

V	R	Year	Name	G	GS	IP	W	L	SV	SO	BB	ERA	RA/9	R Wtd RA/9	V Runs /162
1	2	1910	J.Coombs	45	38	353	31	9	1	224	115	1.30	1.89	2.35	90.9
2	1	1931	L.Grove	41	30	289	31	4	5	175	62	2.06	2.62	2.30	76.1
3	3	1971	V.Blue	39	39	312	24	8	0	301	88	1.82	2.11	2.47	72.3
4	6	1902	R.Waddell	33	27	276	24	7	0	210	64	2.05	2.93	2.67	66.9
5	4	1930	L.Grove	50	32	291	28	5	9	209	60	2.54	3.12	2.59	66.9
6	13	1905	R.Waddell	46	34	329	27	10	0	287	90	1.48	2.35	2.87	64.8
7	7	1932	L.Grove	44	30	292	25	10	7	188	79	2.84	3.11	2.69	63.6
8	29	1904	R.Waddell	46	46	383	25	19	0	349	91	1.62	2.56	3.24	58.9
9	39	1918	S.Perry	44	36	332	20	19	2	81	111	1.98	2.63	3.31	58.6
10	9	1981	S.McCatty	22	22	186	14	7	0	91	61	2.33	2.42	2.70	58.2
11	15	1972	C.Hunter	38	37	295	21	7	0	191	70	2.04	2.26	2.96	55.1
12	11	1980	M.Norris	33	33	284	22	9	0	180	83	2.53	2.79	2.81	55.0
13	20	1974	C.Hunter	41	41	318	25	12	0	143	46	2.49	2.75	3.05	53.3
14	17	1909	C.Morgan	40	36	293	18	17	1	111	102	1.81	2.30	3.01	52.9
15	37	1903	R.Waddell	39	38	324	21	16	0	302	85	2.44	3.03	3.30	52.2
16	12	1910	C.Bender	30	28	250	23	5	0	155	47	1.58	2.27	2.83	50.6
17	21	1952	B.Shantz	33	33	280	24	7	0	152	63	2.48	2.80	3.05	49.2
18	14	1911	E.Plank	40	30	257	23	8	4	149	77	2.10	2.98	2.92	49.2
19	22	1929	L.Grove	42	37	275	20	6	4	170	81	2.81	3.40	3.06	48.1
20	23	1976	V.Blue	37	37	298	18	13	0	166	63	2.35	2.72	3.11	48.0
21	16	1990	D.Stewart	36	36	267	22	11	0	166	83	2.56	2.83	2.96	47.2
22	8	1911	C.Bender	31	24	216	17	5	3	114	58	2.16	2.75	2.70	47.0
23	18	1928	L.Grove	39	31	262	24	8	4	183	64	2.58	3.19	3.02	47.0
24	10	1909	H.Krause	32	21	213	18	8	0	139	49	1.39	2.07	2.71	46.0
25	25	1912	E.Plank	37	30	260	26	6	2	110	83	2.22	3.12	3.15	42.7
26	54	1904	E.Plank	44	43	357	26	17	0	201	86	2.17	2.80	3.54	42.3
27	26	1926	L.Grove	45	33	258	13	13	6	194	101	2.51	3.38	3.20	40.9
28	57	1905	E.Plank	41	41	347	24	12	0	210	75	2.26	2.93	3.58	39.6
29	28	1909	C.Bender	34	29	250	18	8	1	161	45	1.66	2.45	3.21	39.4
30	35	1909	E.Plank	34	33	265	19	10	0	132	62	1.76	2.51	3.29	39.3
31	43	1933	L.Grove	45	28	275	24	8	6	114	83	3.20	3.70	3.36	38.5
32	27	1989	M.Moore	35	35	242	19	11	0	172	83	2.61	3.05	3.20	36.4
33	76	1903	E.Plank	43	40	336	23	16	0	176	65	2.38	3.43	3.74	35.3
34	51	1973	K.Holtzman	40	40	297	21	13	0	157	66	2.97	3.30	3.50	35.0
35	5	1994	S.Ontiveros	27	13	115	6	4	0	56	26	2.65	3.04	2.63	34.9
36	32	1998	K.Rogers	34	34	239	16	8	0	138	67	3.17	3.62	3.26	34.4
37	55	1910	C.Morgan	36	34	291	18	12	0	134	117	1.55	2.85	3.55	34.3
38	72	1907	E.Plank	43	40	344	24	16	0	183	85	2.20	3.01	3.71	34.2
39	48	1929	R.Walberg	40	33	268	18	11	4	94	99	3.60	3.86	3.48	33.9
40	40	1947	D.Fowler	36	31	227	12	11	0	75	85	2.81	3.05	3.32	32.9
41	52	1975	V.Blue	39	38	278	22	11	1	189	99	3.01	3.33	3.51	32.3
42	45	1936	H.Kelley	35	27	235	15	12	3	82	75	3.86	4.29	3.39	32.1
43	64	1931	R.Walberg	44	35	291	20	12	3	106	109	3.74	4.11	3.62	32.0
44	46	1980	M.Keough	34	32	250	16	13	0	121	94	2.92	3.38	3.41	31.9
45	38	1968	J.Nash	34	33	229	13	13	0	169	55	2.28	2.48	3.30	31.9
46	19	1914	C.Bender	28	23	179	17	3	2	107	55	2.26	2.46	3.04	31.8
47	50	1929	G.Earnshaw	44	33	255	24	8	1	149	125	3.29	3.88	3.49	31.7
48	62	1906	R.Waddell	43	34	273	15	17	0	196	92	2.21	2.94	3.59	30.8
49	33	1927	J.Quinn	34	26	201	15	10	1	43	37	3.26	3.56	3.26	30.4
50	31	1991	M.Moore	33	33	210	17	8	0	153	105	2.96	3.21	3.26	30.3

Philadelphia/Kansas City/Oakland Athletics
Starting Pitchers

V	R	Year	Name	G	GS	IP	W	L	SV	SO	BB	ERA	RA/9	R Wtd RA/9	V Runs /162
51	44	1907	C.Bender	33	24	219	16	8	3	112	34	2.05	2.75	3.39	29.9
52	49	1913	C.Bender	48	21	237	21	10	13	135	59	2.21	3.03	3.48	29.9
53	67	1931	G.Earnshaw	43	30	282	21	7	6	152	75	3.67	4.15	3.65	29.9
54	61	1976	M.Torrez	39	39	266	16	12	0	115	87	2.50	3.14	3.59	28.7
55	85	1902	E.Plank	36	32	300	20	15	0	107	61	3.30	4.20	3.83	28.1
56	24	1911	H.Krause	27	19	169	11	8	2	85	47	3.04	3.20	3.14	28.1
57	66	1927	L.Grove	51	28	262	20	13	9	174	79	3.19	3.98	3.65	27.8
58	30	1924	S.Baumgartner	36	16	181	13	6	4	45	73	2.88	3.58	3.24	27.8
59	58	1913	E.Plank	41	30	243	18	10	4	151	57	2.60	3.12	3.58	27.7
60	78	1922	E.Rommel	51	33	294	27	13	2	54	63	3.28	3.92	3.75	27.6
61	75	1980	R.Langford	35	33	290	19	12	0	102	64	3.26	3.69	3.72	27.0
62	70	1972	K.Holtzman	39	37	265	19	11	0	134	52	2.51	2.82	3.69	26.8
63	68	1925	S.Harriss	46	33	253	19	12	1	95	95	3.49	4.21	3.65	26.7
64	56	1990	B.Welch	35	35	238	27	6	0	127	77	2.95	3.40	3.56	26.3
65	81	1901	E.Plank	33	32	261	17	13	0	90	68	3.31	4.59	3.78	26.0
66	53	1926	E.Rommel	37	26	219	11	11	0	52	54	3.08	3.74	3.54	25.9
67	77	1988	D.Stewart	37	37	276	21	12	0	192	110	3.23	3.62	3.75	24.8
68	41	1920	E.Rommel	33	12	174	7	7	1	43	43	2.85	3.52	3.35	24.6
69	74	1908	E.Plank	34	28	245	14	16	1	135	46	2.17	2.83	3.72	24.1
70	42	1912	C.Bender	27	19	171	13	8	2	90	33	2.74	3.32	3.35	24.0
71	84	1944	B.Newsom	37	33	265	13	15	1	142	82	2.82	3.40	3.81	23.2
72	59	1925	S.Gray	32	28	204	16	8	3	80	63	3.27	4.13	3.58	23.2
73	34	1970	D.Segui	47	19	162	10	10	2	95	68	2.56	3.00	3.27	23.2
74	83	1925	E.Rommel	52	28	261	21	10	3	67	95	3.69	4.38	3.80	23.0
75	63	1909	J.Coombs	30	24	206	12	11	1	97	73	2.32	2.75	3.60	23.0
76	36	1946	J.Flores	29	15	155	9	7	1	48	38	2.32	2.96	3.29	23.0
77	47	1928	E.Rommel	43	11	174	13	5	4	37	26	3.06	3.62	3.43	22.9
78	65	1906	E.Plank	26	25	212	19	6	0	108	51	2.25	2.98	3.64	22.7
79	95	1947	P.Marchildon	35	35	277	19	9	0	128	141	3.22	3.58	3.89	21.5
80	69	1984	R.Burris	34	28	212	13	10	0	93	90	3.15	3.57	3.66	21.2
81	87	1987	D.Stewart	37	37	261	20	13	0	205	105	3.68	4.17	3.84	20.8
82	73	1928	J.Quinn	31	28	211	18	7	1	43	34	2.90	3.92	3.71	20.8
83	89	1911	C.Morgan	38	30	250	15	7	1	136	113	2.70	3.93	3.85	20.6
84	90	1989	D.Stewart	36	36	258	21	9	0	155	69	3.32	3.67	3.85	20.2
85	71	1989	B.Welch	33	33	210	17	8	0	137	78	3.00	3.52	3.70	20.1
86	80	1969	B.Odom	32	32	231	15	6	0	150	112	2.92	3.39	3.78	20.0
87	97	1960	R.Herbert	37	33	253	14	15	1	122	72	3.28	3.77	3.90	19.3
88	92	1967	C.Hunter	35	35	260	13	17	0	196	84	2.81	3.15	3.89	19.3
89	99	1973	V.Blue	37	37	264	20	9	0	158	105	3.28	3.69	3.91	19.0
90	60	1963	M.Drabowsky	26	22	174	7	13	0	109	64	3.05	3.21	3.59	18.8
91	86	1968	B.Odom	32	31	231	16	10	0	143	98	2.45	2.88	3.84	18.5
92	98	1973	C.Hunter	36	36	256	21	5	0	124	69	3.34	3.69	3.91	18.4
93	103	1971	C.Hunter	37	37	274	21	11	0	181	80	2.96	3.38	3.96	18.2
94	115	1923	E.Rommel	56	31	298	18	19	5	76	108	3.27	4.26	4.04	18.1
95	79	1972	B.Odom	31	30	194	15	6	0	86	87	2.50	2.88	3.77	17.8
96	104	1975	K.Holtzman	39	38	266	18	14	0	122	108	3.14	3.76	3.97	17.5
97	82	2000	T.Hudson	32	32	202	20	6	0	169	82	4.14	4.45	3.80	17.1
98	94	1959	B.Daley	39	29	216	16	13	1	125	62	3.16	3.75	3.89	16.8
99	108	1910	E.Plank	38	32	250	16	10	2	123	55	2.01	3.20	3.98	16.7
100	101	1940	J.Babich	31	30	229	14	13	0	94	80	3.73	4.36	3.93	16.7

Philadelphia/Kansas City/Oakland Athletics
Relief Pitchers

V	R	Year	Name	G	GS	IP	W	L	SV	SO	BB	ERA	RA/9	R Wtd RA/9	V Runs /162
1	3	1970	M.Grant	80	0	135	8	3	24	58	32	1.87	1.93	2.10	36.8
2	1	1990	D.Eckersley	63	0	73	4	2	48	73	4	0.61	1.10	1.15	27.6
3	5	1966	J.Aker	66	0	113	8	4	32	68	28	1.99	2.15	2.51	25.7
4	8	1964	W.Stock	64	0	114	8	3	5	115	42	2.30	2.37	2.65	24.1
5	2	1992	D.Eckersley	69	0	80	7	1	51	93	11	1.91	1.91	2.01	22.7
6	19	1976	R.Fingers	70	0	135	13	11	20	113	40	2.47	2.67	3.05	22.6
7	14	1926	J.Pate	47	2	113	9	0	6	24	51	2.71	3.03	2.87	22.3
8	15	1944	J.Berry	53	0	111	10	8	12	44	23	1.94	2.59	2.90	21.5
9	17	1987	D.Eckersley	54	2	116	6	8	16	113	17	3.03	3.19	2.94	20.9
10	20	1973	R.Fingers	62	2	127	7	8	22	110	39	1.92	2.91	3.08	20.8
11	25	1945	J.Berry	52	0	130	8	7	5	51	38	2.35	2.77	3.21	20.4
12	7	1989	T.Burns	50	2	96	6	5	8	49	28	2.24	2.52	2.65	20.4
13	21	1975	J.Todd	58	0	122	8	3	12	50	33	2.29	2.95	3.11	19.6
14	27	1975	R.Fingers	75	0	127	10	6	24	115	33	2.98	3.06	3.23	18.8
15	4	1972	D.Knowles	54	0	66	5	1	11	36	37	1.37	1.64	2.15	18.6
16	13	1984	B.Caudill	68	0	96	9	7	36	89	31	2.71	2.80	2.87	18.0
17	18	1974	P.Lindblad	45	2	101	4	4	6	46	30	2.06	2.67	2.96	17.9
18	16	1985	J.Howell	63	0	98	9	8	29	68	31	2.85	2.94	2.91	17.9
19	9	2000	J.Tam	72	0	86	3	3	3	46	23	2.63	3.15	2.69	17.8
20	10	1969	J.Roland	39	3	86	5	1	1	48	46	2.19	2.51	2.80	16.8
21	6	1988	D.Eckersley	60	0	73	4	2	45	70	11	2.35	2.48	2.57	16.1
22	34	1977	B.Lacey	64	0	122	6	8	7	69	43	3.03	3.40	3.40	15.7
23	26	1999	D.Jones	70	0	104	5	5	10	63	24	3.55	3.72	3.22	15.4
24	22	1983	T.Burgmeier	49	0	96	6	7	4	39	32	2.81	3.09	3.12	15.4
25	29	1978	E.Sosa	68	0	109	8	2	14	61	44	2.64	3.06	3.29	15.4
26	36	1975	P.Lindblad	68	0	122	9	1	7	58	43	2.72	3.25	3.43	15.3
27	37	1974	R.Fingers	76	0	119	9	5	18	95	29	2.65	3.10	3.44	14.8
28	38	1977	P.Torrealba	41	10	117	4	6	2	51	38	2.62	3.46	3.46	14.3
29	42	1977	J.Coleman	43	12	128	4	4	2	55	49	2.96	3.59	3.59	13.8
30	31	1992	J.Parrett	66	0	98	9	1	0	78	42	3.02	3.20	3.36	13.0
31	39	1988	G.Nelson	54	1	112	9	6	3	67	38	3.06	3.39	3.51	13.0
32	23	1991	D.Eckersley	67	0	76	5	4	43	87	9	2.96	3.08	3.13	12.1
33	30	1973	H.Pina	47	0	88	6	3	8	41	34	2.76	3.17	3.36	11.7
34	24	1989	R.Honeycutt	64	0	77	2	2	12	52	26	2.35	3.05	3.20	11.6
35	48	1971	R.Fingers	48	8	129	4	6	17	98	30	2.99	3.20	3.75	11.6
36	47	1972	R.Fingers	65	0	111	11	9	21	113	32	2.51	2.83	3.71	11.0
37	50	1957	V.Trucks	48	7	116	9	7	7	55	62	3.03	3.49	3.77	10.7
38	54	1982	T.Underwood	56	10	153	10	6	7	79	68	3.29	3.88	3.93	10.7
39	11	1995	R.Honeycutt	52	0	46	5	1	2	21	10	2.96	3.15	2.80	10.1
40	33	1996	J.Corsi	56	0	74	6	0	3	43	34	4.03	4.03	3.39	9.6
41	32	1988	G.Cadaret	58	0	72	5	2	3	64	36	2.89	3.27	3.39	9.4
42	53	1987	G.Nelson	54	6	124	6	5	3	94	35	3.93	4.22	3.88	9.3
43	45	1947	R.Christopher	44	0	81	10	7	12	33	33	2.90	3.33	3.62	8.9
44	43	1968	D.Segui	52	0	83	6	5	6	72	32	2.39	2.71	3.61	8.7
45	12	1992	V.Horsman	58	0	43	2	1	1	18	21	2.49	2.70	2.84	8.2
46	40	2000	D.Jones	54	0	73	4	2	2	54	18	3.93	4.17	3.56	8.1
47	46	1996	B.Groom	72	1	77	5	0	2	57	34	3.84	4.31	3.62	8.0
48	35	1990	R.Honeycutt	63	0	63	2	2	7	38	22	2.70	3.27	3.43	7.9
49	44	1997	B.Taylor	72	0	73	3	4	23	66	36	3.82	3.95	3.61	7.6
50	28	1995	D.Leiper	50	0	45	1	3	2	22	19	3.22	3.63	3.23	7.5

PHILADELPHIA PHILLIES (1900–2000)

The Phillies have the worst winning tradition of the original eight National League teams, with only 33 winning seasons in the past 101 years. They also have only nine postseason appearances, three less than the second worst team, the Cubs. They do, however, have many more winning and postseason teams than the Cubs since 1950.

The Phillies generated three successful periods in their history, beginning with the Dead Ball Era. They began the twentieth century with tremendous potential, as their 1900 roster included Nap Lajoie (.337 average, 974 Total Factor in 1900), Elmer Flick (.367 average and 1,007 Total Factor in his best year in 1900), and Ed Delahanty (.354 average, 1,008 Wtd. Production in 1901). By 1902, these three stars were gone, but the Phillies still settled in as the consistent fourth best team in the league. Philadelphia featured one of the league's early stars in outfielder Sherry Magee, who hit .331 with 49 steals in his best season in 1910. Adjusted for a 6 percent hitter's deflation, Magee batted .351 with 7 home runs, for a 1,009 Wtd. Production. George McQuillan was the team's staff ace, going 23–17 with a 1.53 ERA and a 2.98 Wtd. RA/9 in 1908.

Despite 11 winning seasons in the first 18 years of the century, the Phillies had a difficult time finishing above fourth, with powerhouse dynasties in Chicago, New York, and Pittsburgh usually far above them in the standings. The decline of the Pirates and Cubs after 1913 gave the Phillies one brief period of glory. They finished second in 1913, 1916, and 1917, and they won their first pennant in 1915, before losing the World Series in five games to the Red Sox. Ace pitcher Pete Alexander led the Phillies, winning at least 30 games three straight years from 1915 to 1917. Alexander's best year was in 1915, when he pitched the Phillies into the World Series with a 31–10 record, 1.22 ERA, 2.57 Wtd. RA/9, and 87.2 Runs/162, the league's third best volume of success season ever. Another star was Gavvy Cravath, the best Dead Ball home run hitter with 119 home runs in 11 seasons, including a career high 24 round trippers in 1915. Cravath generated his best season in 1913, hitting .341 with 19 home runs, for a 1,013 Wtd. Production.

Beginning in 1918, Phillies fans endured perhaps the longest stretch of miserable performance in baseball history. Philadelphia put together only one winning season in 31 years from 1918 to 1948. During that period, the team finished in fourth place once—earning a 78–76 record in 1932, in fifth twice, in sixth four times, in seventh eight times, and in dead last 16 times. The Phillies lost 100 or more games in 12 of those seasons, including one season (1930) when they hit .315 as a team in tiny Baker Bowl, while their pitchers gave up nearly seven earned runs a game. Although their pitching was atrocious the entire period, the Phillies had several offensive stars, including 1929's slugging outfielders Chuck Klein (.356, 43 home runs, 94 extra base hits) and Lefty O'Doul (.398, 32 home runs). Other hitters included Spud Davis (.349 average in 1933), Don Hurst (.339, 24 home runs in 1932), and Dolph Camilli (.339, 27 home runs, 1,022 Wtd. Production in 1937). Chuck Klein had the most productive season during this period in 1933, when he hit .368 with 28 home runs. Adjusted for a 4 percent hitter's deflation, Klein hit a career high .383 with 242 hits and 30 home runs, for a 1,065 Wtd. Production, a 1,075 Total Factor, and a 105.6 Hits Contribution.

The Phillies finally turned things around with a third place finish in 1949, and the "Whiz Kids" surprised the nation in 1950 by winning the pennant. The Phillies, with six seasons at or above .500 from 1949 to 1957, were led offensively by Richie Ashburn (.344, 29 steals in 1951), Del Ennis, Willie Jones, and Andy Seminick. The best pitchers were Robin Roberts (28–7, 2.59 ERA, 3.07 Wtd. RA/9 in 1952), Curt Simmons, and Jim Konstanty (16–7, 22 saves, 2.66 ERA, MVP Award in 1950).

After a brief four-year slide, the Phillies produced six consecutive winning seasons from 1962 to 1967. The 1964 team even had a 6½ game lead with two weeks remaining in the schedule, before losing ten straight games to finish one game behind the Cardinals. These Phillies teams featured Richie Allen (.317, 40 home runs, 1,040 Wtd. Production in 1966), Johnny Callison, Jim Bunning (19–14, 2.41 ERA, 2.90 Wtd. RA/9 in 1966), and Chris Short (17–9, 2.20 ERA, 2.90 Wtd. RA/9 in 1964).

The Phillies suffered through seven consecutive losing seasons from 1968 to 1974. Steve Carlton picked the worst of these teams, the 1972 squad, to produce the best rate of success season ever by a Phillies starting pitcher with a 27–10 record, 1.97 ERA, 2.55 Wtd. RA/9, and 81.0 Runs/162. To see just how good Carlton's season was, we need only observe that the rest of the team posted an ugly 32–87 record.

Following this seven-year dip in the road, the Phillies arrived at the best of their three successful periods. From 1975 to 1986, the team finished at or above .500 in 11 of 12 seasons. They won their division five times, plus a playoff appearance as co–division winner in 1981. They even won their first and only World Series championship in 1980. The golden era of Phillies baseball featured the best player in team history and the greatest third baseman of all time, three-time MVP Mike Schmidt. Schmidt unfortunately lost a third of his great 1981 MVP season (.316, 31 home runs) due to a players' strike. Adjusting for a 3 percent hitter's deflation and the impact of the strike, Schmidt hit .326 with 48 home runs, for a 1,114 Wtd. Production and a 1,223 Total Factor, the best rate of success season for any National League player ever. Schmidt's 157.5 Hits Contribution is the National League's second best volume of success result — trailing only Honus Wagner's 158.5 Hits Contribution in 1908. Other impact players of this period include lumbering Greg Luzinski (.309, 39 home runs in 1977), swift Garry Maddox (.330, 29 steals in 1976), veteran Steve Carlton (24–9, 2.34 ERA, 2.92 Wtd. RA/9 in 1980), and Tug McGraw (5–4, 20 saves, 1.46 ERA, 1.76 Wtd. RA/9 in 1980).

Recent Phillies teams are coming up short again, with only one winning season in the past 14 years. The one winning exception was the exciting and rowdy 1993 team that made it to the World Series, led by John Kruk (.316, 14 home runs), Darren Daulton (.257, 24 home runs), and Len Dykstra (.305, 19 home runs, 37 steals). Mike Lieberthal, Scott Rolen, Bobby Abreu and pitcher Curt Schilling also contributed solid seasons in this period.

Philadelphia Phillies — Hitters Volume of Success

Pos	Year	Name	AB	BB	HBP	TAB	H	2B	3B	HR	BA	OB	SA	PRO	Wtd PRO	SB	CS	SBF	SPF	FF	R TF	V HC
C	1992	D.Daulton	485	88	6	579	131	32	5	27	.270	.389	.524	912	939	11	2	11	0	0	950	75.3
1B	1936	D.Camilli	530	116	3	649	167	29	13	28	.315	.441	.577	1,018	995	5			0	0	995	73.3
2B	1900	N.Lajoie	451	10	8	469	152	33	12	7	.337	.362	.510	872	874	22			10	90	974	74.5
SS	1932	D.Bartell	614	64	6	684	189	48	7	1	.308	.379	.414	792	773	8			0	30	803	48.2
3B	1981	M.Schmidt	354	73	4	431	112	19	2	31	.316	.439	.644	1,083	1,114	12	4	9	10	90	1,223	157.5
OF	1933	C.Klein	606	56	1	663	223	44	7	28	.368	.422	.602	1,025	1,065	15			0	10	1,075	105.6
OF	1901	E.Delahanty	542	65	4	611	192	38	16	8	.354	.427	.528	955	1,008	29			10	0	1,018	87.6
OF	1900	E.Flick	545	56	16	617	200	32	16	11	.367	.441	.545	986	987	35			10	10	1,007	84.9
Starters		Averages	516	66	6	588	171	34	10	18	.331	.413	.538	951	965	17	1	3	5	29	1,001	88.4
C	1933	S.Davis	495	32	5	532	173	28	3	9	.349	.395	.473	867	902	2		(10)	(10)		882	54.5
1B	1932	D.Hurst	579	65	7	651	196	41	4	24	.339	.412	.547	959	935	10			0	0	935	53.9
2B	1974	D.Cash	687	46	9	742	206	26	11	2	.300	.352	.378	730	742	20	8	5	10	50	807	42.9
SS	1918	D.Bancroft	499	54	1	554	132	19	4	0	.265	.338	.319	656	726	11			10	40	776	38.4
3B	1966	D.Allen	524	68	3	595	166	25	10	40	.317	.398	.632	1,030	1,040	10	6	(3)	10	(30)	1,017	85.3
OF	1910	S.Magee	519	94	12	625	172	39	17	6	.331	.445	.507	952	1,009	49			10	0	1,019	81.8
OF	1929	L.O'Doul	638	76	4	718	254	35	6	32	.398	.465	.622	1,087	980	2			0	0	980	80.2
OF	1958	R.Ashburn	615	97	4	716	215	24	13	2	.350	.441	.441	882	847	30	12	8	10	90	955	70.9
Reserves		Averages	570	67	6	642	189	30	9	14	.332	.407	.490	897	896	17	3	1	5	18	920	63.5
Totals		Weighted Ave.	534	66	6	606	177	33	9	17	.331	.411	.522	933	942	17	2	2	5	25	974	80.1

Pitchers Volume of Success

Pos	Year	Name	G	GS	IP	W	L	SV	SO	BB	ERA	RA/9	Wtd RA/9	R V Runs /162
SP	1915	P.Alexander	49	42	376	31	10	3	241	64	1.22	2.06	2.57	87.2
SP	1972	S.Carlton	41	41	346	27	10	0	310	87	1.97	2.18	2.55	81.0
SP	1953	R.Roberts	44	41	347	23	16	2	198	61	2.75	3.09	2.90	67.1
SP	1908	G.McQuillan	48	42	360	23	17	2	114	91	1.53	2.17	2.98	66.4
SP	1966	J.Bunning	43	41	314	19	14	1	252	55	2.41	2.61	2.90	57.8
Starters		Averages	45	41	349	25	13	2	223	72	1.95	2.41	2.78	71.9
RP	1950	J.Konstanty	74	0	152	16	7	22	56	50	2.66	3.02	2.92	29.0
RP	1980	T.McGraw	57	0	92	5	4	20	75	23	1.46	1.56	1.76	28.6
RP	1970	D.Selma	73	0	134	8	9	22	153	59	2.75	2.82	2.84	25.6
RP	1995	R.Bottalico	62	0	88	5	3	1	87	42	2.46	2.57	2.52	22.4
Relievers		Averages	67	0	117	9	6	16	93	44	2.41	2.59	2.59	26.4
Totals		Averages	112	41	465	33	19	18	316	115	2.07	2.46	2.73	98.3

Philadelphia Phillies

Hitters Rate of Success

Pos	Year	Name	AB	BB	HBP	TAB	H	2B	3B	HR	BA	OB	SA	PRO	Wtd PRO	SB	CS	SBF	SPF	FF	R TF	V HC
C	1992	D.Daulton	485	88	6	579	131	32	5	27	.270	.389	.524	912	939	11	2	11	0	0	950	75.3
1B	1937	D.Camilli	475	90	2	567	161	23	7	27	.339	.446	.587	1,034	1,022	6		0	0	0	1,022	71.6
2B	1900	N.Lajoie	451	10	8	469	152	33	12	7	.337	.362	.510	872	874	22			10	90	974	74.5
SS	1989	D.Thon	435	33	0	468	118	18	4	15	.271	.323	.434	757	786	6	3	0	10	20	816	34.3
3B	1981	M.Schmidt	354	73	4	431	112	19	2	31	.316	.439	.644	1,083	1,114	12	4	9	10	90	1,223	157.5
OF	1933	C.Klein	606	56	1	663	223	44	7	28	.368	.422	.602	1,025	1,065	15		0	10	0	1,075	105.6
OF	1910	S.Magee	519	94	12	625	172	39	17	6	.331	.445	.507	952	1,009	49			10	0	1,019	81.8
OF	1901	E.Delahanty	542	65	4	611	192	38	16	8	.354	.427	.528	955	1,008	29			10	0	1,018	87.6
Starters		Averages	483	64	5	552	158	31	9	19	.326	.409	.542	951	982	19	1	3	6	26	1,017	86.0
C	1955	S.Lopata	303	58	2	363	82	9	3	22	.271	.391	.538	929	890	4	1	5	(10)	20	905	41.4
1B	1932	D.Hurst	579	65	7	651	196	41	4	24	.339	.412	.547	959	935	10			0	0	935	53.9
2B	1981	M.Trillo	349	26	3	378	100	14	3	6	.287	.341	.395	737	758	10	4	5	0	50	813	34.8
SS	1932	D.Bartell	614	64	6	684	189	48	7	1	.308	.379	.414	792	773	8			0	30	803	48.2
3B	1966	D.Allen	524	68	3	595	166	25	10	40	.317	.398	.632	1,030	1,040	10	6	(3)	10	(30)	1,017	85.3
OF	1900	E.Flick	545	56	16	617	200	32	16	11	.367	.441	.545	986	987	35			10	10	1,007	84.9
OF	1913	G.Cravath	525	55	3	583	179	34	14	19	.341	.407	.568	974	1,013	10			0	(20)	993	68.8
OF	1929	L.O'Doul	638	76	4	718	254	35	6	32	.398	.465	.622	1,087	980	2			0	0	980	80.2
Reserves		Averages	510	59	6	574	171	30	8	19	.335	.409	.538	948	930	11	1	1	1	8	940	62.2
Totals		Weighted Ave.	492	62	5	559	162	30	8	19	.329	.409	.540	950	965	16	1	2	5	20	991	78.1

Pitchers Rate of Success

Pos	Year	Name	G	GS	IP	W	L	SV	SO	BB	ERA	RA/9	Wtd RA/9	R V Runs/162
SP	1972	S.Carlton	41	41	346	27	10	0	310	87	1.97	2.18	2.55	81.0
SP	1915	P.Alexander	49	42	376	31	10	3	241	64	1.22	2.06	2.57	87.2
SP	1964	C.Short	42	31	221	17	9	2	181	51	2.20	2.57	2.90	40.7
SP	1966	J.Bunning	43	41	314	19	14	1	252	55	2.41	2.61	2.90	57.8
SP	1953	R.Roberts	44	41	347	23	16	2	198	61	2.75	3.09	2.90	67.1
Starters		Averages	44	39	321	23	12	2	236	64	2.08	2.49	2.75	66.8
RP	1980	T.McGraw	57	0	92	5	4	20	75	23	1.46	1.56	1.76	28.6
RP	1994	D.Jones	47	0	54	2	4	27	38	6	2.17	2.33	2.28	19.3
RP	1995	R.Bottalico	62	0	88	5	3	1	87	42	2.46	2.57	2.52	22.4
RP	1955	B.Miller	40	0	90	8	4	1	28	28	2.41	2.60	2.59	20.7
Relievers		Averages	52	0	81	5	4	12	57	25	2.11	2.25	2.28	22.8
Totals		Averages	95	39	402	28	16	14	293	88	2.09	2.44	2.65	89.5

Philadelphia Phillies
Catchers

V	R	Year	Name	AB	BB	HBP	TAB	H	2B	3B	HR	BA	OB	SA	PRO	Wtd PRO	SB	CS	SBF	SPF	FF	R TF	V HC
1	1	1992	D.Daulton	485	88	6	579	131	32	5	27	.270	.389	.524	912	939	11	2	11			950	75.3
2	8	1993	D.Daulton	510	117	2	629	131	35	4	24	.257	.397	.482	880	852	5	0	8		10	869	57.5
3	4	1933	S.Davis	495	32	5	532	173	28	3	9	.349	.395	.473	867	902	2			(10)	(10)	882	54.5
4	11	1956	S.Lopata	535	75	1	611	143	33	7	32	.267	.358	.535	893	869	5	2	2	(10)	(10)	851	53.2
5	7	1999	M.Lieberthal	510	44	11	565	153	33	1	31	.300	.368	.551	919	841	0	0	0	(10)	40	871	52.1
6	6	1950	A.Seminick	393	68	6	467	113	15	3	24	.288	.400	.524	925	886	0			(10)		876	46.4
7	5	1932	S.Davis	402	40	2	444	135	23	5	14	.336	.399	.522	921	898	1			(10)	(10)	878	44.6
8	3	1994	D.Daulton	257	33	1	291	77	17	1	15	.300	.381	.549	930	875	4	1	6		20	902	44.0
9	2	1955	S.Lopata	303	58	2	363	82	9	3	22	.271	.391	.538	929	890	4	1	5	(10)	20	905	41.4
10	10	1949	A.Seminick	334	69	5	408	81	11	2	24	.243	.380	.503	883	862	0			(10)		852	35.7
11	9	1954	S.Burgess	345	42	0	387	127	27	5	4	.368	.437	.510	947	897	1	5	(22)	(10)	(10)	855	34.5
12	12	1978	B.Boone	435	46	1	482	123	18	4	12	.283	.353	.425	778	791	2	5	(16)	(10)	50	816	31.7
13	15	1996	B.Santiago	481	49	1	531	127	21	2	30	.264	.333	.503	836	797	2	0	4			800	31.1
14	14	1922	B.Henline	430	36	8	474	136	20	4	14	.316	.380	.479	859	805	2	2	(4)			801	29.4
15	20	1990	D.Daulton	459	72	2	533	123	30	1	12	.268	.370	.416	786	785	7	1	9		(10)	783	26.9
16	13	1952	S.Burgess	371	49	1	421	110	27	2	6	.296	.380	.429	809	819	3	1	2		(20)	801	26.1
17	17	1931	S.Davis	393	36	0	429	128	32	1	4	.326	.382	.443	825	808	0			(10)		798	25.9
18	22	1982	B.Diaz	525	36	3	564	151	29	1	18	.288	.337	.450	786	799	3	6	(15)	(10)		774	25.9
19	16	1979	B.Boone	398	49	2	449	114	21	3	9	.286	.367	.422	790	783	1	4	(15)	(10)	40	798	25.8
20	21	1977	B.Boone	440	42	2	484	125	26	4	11	.284	.349	.436	786	763	5	5	(10)	(10)	40	783	24.3
21	19	2000	M.Lieberthal	389	40	6	435	108	30	0	15	.278	.354	.470	824	752	2	0	4	(10)	40	787	22.6
22	18	1923	B.Henline	330	37	9	376	107	14	3	7	.324	.407	.448	855	819	7	5	(8)		(20)	792	21.6
23	24	1984	O.Virgil	456	45	5	506	119	21	2	18	.261	.334	.434	768	785	1	1	(2)	(10)	(10)	763	20.6
24	23	1962	C.Dalrymple	370	70	4	444	102	13	3	11	.276	.396	.416	813	794	1	3	(11)	(10)	(10)	764	18.3
25	27	1985	O.Virgil	426	49	5	480	105	16	3	19	.246	.331	.432	763	775	0	0	0	(10)	(10)	755	17.8

Philadelphia Phillies
First basemen

V	R	Year	Name	AB	BB	HBP	TAB	H	2B	3B	HR	BA	OB	SA	PRO	Wtd PRO	SB	CS	SBF	SPF	FF	R TF	V HC
1	2	1936	D.Camilli	530	116	3	649	167	29	13	28	.315	.441	.577	1,018	995	5					995	73.3
2	1	1937	D.Camilli	475	90	2	567	161	23	7	27	.339	.446	.587	1,034	1,022	6					1,022	71.6
3	4	1932	D.Hurst	579	65	7	651	196	41	4	24	.339	.412	.547	959	935	10					935	53.9
4	3	1969	D.Allen	438	64	0	502	126	23	3	32	.288	.378	.573	952	973	9	3	6	10	(30)	959	45.2
5	6	1985	M.Schmidt	549	87	3	639	152	31	5	33	.277	.379	.532	911	925	1	3	(7)			917	44.9
6	5	1915	F.Luderus	499	42	7	548	157	36	7	7	.315	.376	.457	833	919	9	7	(9)		10	920	41.2
7	7	1992	J.Kruk	507	92	1	600	164	30	4	10	.323	.428	.458	886	912	3	5	(11)			901	37.3
8	9	1993	J.Kruk	535	111	0	646	169	33	5	14	.316	.433	.475	908	879	6	2	3			882	34.6
9	10	1986	V.Hayes	610	74	1	685	186	46	2	19	.305	.381	.480	861	864	24	12	0	10		874	33.8
10	8	1991	J.Kruk	538	67	1	606	158	27	6	21	.294	.373	.483	856	873	7	0	11			884	33.0
11	12	1941	N.Etten	540	82	3	625	168	27	4	14	.311	.405	.454	859	881	9		10	(20)		871	31.6
12	13	1966	B.White	577	68	3	648	159	23	6	22	.276	.355	.451	806	813	16	6	6	10	40	869	30.7
13	14	1987	V.Hayes	556	121	0	677	154	36	5	21	.277	.406	.473	879	846	16	7	3	10		858	28.5
14	11	1908	K.Bransfield	527	23	2	552	160	25	7	3	.304	.335	.395	730	852	30		10		10	872	28.1
15	16	1979	P.Rose	628	95	2	725	208	40	5	4	.331	.421	.430	851	843	20	11	(3)	10		851	27.9
16	17	1971	D.Johnson	582	72	2	656	154	29	0	34	.265	.348	.490	837	863	0	1	(3)	(10)		850	25.0
17	18	1919	F.Luderus	509	54	4	567	149	30	6	5	.293	.365	.405	770	839	6				10	849	24.6
18	20	1911	F.Luderus	551	40	4	595	166	24	11	16	.301	.353	.472	825	843	6					843	21.6
19	15	1928	D.Hurst	396	68	1	465	113	23	4	19	.285	.391	.508	899	856	3					856	20.1
20	21	1931	D.Hurst	489	64	1	554	149	37	5	11	.305	.386	.468	855	837	8					837	18.5
21	22	1929	D.Hurst	589	80	3	672	179	29	4	31	.304	.390	.525	914	824	10					824	18.3
22	23	1900	E.Delahanty	539	41	7	587	174	32	10	2	.323	.378	.430	809	810	16			10		820	16.1
23	19	1938	P.Weintraub	351	64	4	419	109	23	2	4	.311	.422	.422	844	845	1					845	15.8
24	25	1957	E.Bouchee	574	84	14	672	168	35	8	17	.293	.396	.470	866	845	1	0	1	(10)	(20)	816	15.5
25	28	1981	P.Rose	431	46	3	480	140	18	5	0	.325	.394	.390	784	806	4	4	(8)	10		808	13.3

Philadelphia Phillies
Second basemen

V	R	Year	Name	AB	BB	HBP	TAB	H	2B	3B	HR	BA	OB	SA	PRO	Wtd PRO	SB	CS	SBF	SPF	FF	R TF	V HC
1	1	1900	N.Lajoie	451	10	8	469	152	33	12	7	.337	.362	.510	872	874	22			10	90	974	74.5
2	6	1974	D.Cash	687	46	9	742	206	26	11	2	.300	.352	.378	730	742	20	8	5	10	50	807	42.9
3	8	1987	J.Samuel	655	60	5	720	178	37	15	28	.272	.338	.502	840	808	35	15	7	10	(30)	794	37.4
4	10	1975	D.Cash	699	56	4	759	213	40	3	4	.305	.360	.388	747	756	13	6	1	10	20	787	36.8
5	9	1984	J.Samuel	701	28	7	736	191	36	19	15	.272	.307	.442	749	765	72	15	54	10	(40)	789	36.5
6	2	1981	M.Trillo	349	26	3	378	100	14	3	6	.287	.341	.395	737	758	10	4	5		50	813	34.8
7	4	1980	M.Trillo	531	32	3	566	155	25	9	7	.292	.336	.412	748	758	8	3	3		50	811	33.9
8	3	1970	T.Taylor	439	50	3	492	132	26	9	9	.301	.376	.462	838	817	9	11	(25)	10	10	813	29.8
9	5	1983	J.Morgan	404	89	4	497	93	20	1	16	.230	.374	.403	778	784	18	2	27			811	29.7
10	11	1985	J.Samuel	663	33	6	702	175	31	13	19	.264	.305	.436	741	752	53	19	20	10	(10)	773	29.2
11	13	1929	F.Thompson	623	75	1	699	202	41	3	4	.324	.398	.419	817	736	16			10	20	766	28.4
12	7	1907	O.Knabe	444	52	5	501	113	16	9	1	.255	.339	.338	677	776	18			10	10	796	27.8
13	12	1923	C.Tierney	600	26	3	629	187	36	3	13	.312	.343	.447	790	757	5	5	(8)	10	10	769	26.5
14	18	1963	T.Taylor	640	42	7	689	180	20	10	5	.281	.332	.367	700	736	23	9	7	10		753	22.2
15	17	1986	J.Samuel	591	26	8	625	157	36	12	16	.266	.306	.448	754	756	42	14	21	10	(30)	757	21.4
16	16	1989	T.Herr	561	54	3	618	161	25	6	2	.287	.353	.364	716	744	10	7	(6)	10	10	758	21.3
17	22	1954	G.Hamner	596	53	0	649	178	39	11	13	.299	.356	.466	822	779	1	2	(4)		(30)	745	19.4
18	21	1995	M.Morandini	494	42	9	545	140	34	7	6	.283	.350	.417	767	731	9	6	(5)	10	10	746	17.7
19	23	1922	F.Parkinson	545	55	2	602	150	18	6	15	.275	.344	.413	757	709	3	4	(8)	10	30	742	17.0
20	15	1994	M.Morandini	274	34	4	312	80	16	5	2	.292	.378	.409	787	741	10	5	0	10	10	761	15.9
21	20	1925	L.Fonseca	467	21	3	491	149	30	5	7	.319	.352	.450	802	743	6	2	4	10	(10)	747	15.1
22	24	1965	C.Rojas	521	42	3	566	158	25	3	3	.303	.359	.380	739	759	5	5	(8)		(10)	741	14.9
23	27	1927	F.Thompson	597	34	2	633	181	32	14	1	.303	.343	.409	752	732	19			10	(10)	732	14.7
24	14	1930	B.Friberg	331	47	1	379	113	21	1	4	.341	.425	.447	872	762	1					762	14.5
25	25	1943	D.Murtaugh	451	57	2	510	123	17	4	1	.273	.357	.335	692	727	4			10		737	13.1

Philadelphia Phillies
Shortstops

V	R	Year	Name	AB	BB	HBP	TAB	H	2B	3B	HR	BA	OB	SA	PRO	Wtd PRO	SB	CS	SBF	SPF	FF	R TF	V HC
1	2	1932	D.Bartell	614	64	6	684	189	48	7	1	.308	.379	.414	792	773	8				30	803	48.2
2	5	1934	D.Bartell	604	64	9	677	187	30	4	0	.310	.384	.373	757	735	13			10	40	785	41.6
3	6	1918	D.Bancroft	499	54	1	554	132	19	4	0	.265	.338	.319	656	726	11			10	40	776	38.4
4	7	1978	L.Bowa	654	24	1	679	192	31	5	3	.294	.320	.370	690	701	27	5	24	10	40	775	36.6
5	4	1917	D.Bancroft	478	44	0	522	116	22	5	4	.243	.307	.335	641	715	14			10	70	795	34.8
6	1	1989	D.Thon	435	33	0	468	118	18	4	15	.271	.323	.434	757	786	6	3	0	10	20	816	34.3
7	8	1910	M.Doolan	536	35	6	577	141	31	6	2	.263	.315	.354	670	710	16				60	770	31.2
8	9	1975	L.Bowa	583	24	2	609	178	18	9	2	.305	.335	.377	712	720	24	6	19	10	10	759	28.1
9	3	1919	D.Bancroft	335	31	0	366	91	13	7	0	.272	.333	.352	686	747	8			10	40	797	27.2
10	10	1920	A.Fletcher	550	16	9	575	156	32	9	4	.284	.315	.396	711	739	7	8	(15)	10	20	755	26.7
11	11	1933	D.Bartell	587	56	5	648	159	25	5	1	.271	.340	.336	675	702	6			10	30	742	25.9
12	12	1931	D.Bartell	554	27	3	584	160	43	7	0	.289	.325	.392	717	702	6			10	20	732	20.5
13	13	1952	G.Hamner	596	27	0	623	164	30	5	17	.275	.307	.428	734	744	7	3	2		(20)	725	19.8
14	14	1981	L.Bowa	360	26	0	386	102	14	3	0	.283	.332	.339	670	690	16	7	5	10	20	725	17.5
15	18	1977	L.Bowa	624	32	0	656	175	19	3	4	.280	.316	.340	655	636	32	3	37	10	30	714	16.2
16	15	1927	H.Sand	535	58	1	594	160	22	8	1	.299	.369	.376	744	725	5			10	(20)	715	15.7
17	19	1915	D.Bancroft	563	77	2	642	143	18	2	7	.254	.346	.330	676	746	15	27	(57)	10	10	708	14.9
18	22	1974	L.Bowa	669	23	1	693	184	19	10	1	.275	.300	.338	638	648	39	11	23	10	20	701	12.9
19	21	1902	R.Hulswitt	497	30	2	529	135	11	7	0	.272	.316	.322	638	713	12				(10)	703	12.0
20	20	1929	B.Friberg	455	49	1	505	137	21	10	7	.301	.370	.437	808	728	1			10	(30)	708	11.7
21	16	1961	R.Amaro	381	53	2	436	98	14	9	1	.257	.351	.349	700	672	1	0	2		40	714	11.5
22	27	1926	H.Sand	567	66	2	635	154	30	5	4	.272	.350	.363	713	695	2			10	(10)	695	10.5
23	23	1909	M.Doolan	493	37	2	532	108	12	10	1	.219	.276	.290	566	641	10				60	701	10.3
24	24	1905	M.Doolan	492	24	2	518	125	27	11	1	.254	.292	.360	651	711	17				(10)	701	10.0
25	17	1999	A.Arias	347	36	4	387	105	20	1	4	.303	.375	.401	775	709	2	2	(5)		10	714	9.6

Philadelphia Phillies
Third basemen

V	R	Year	Name	AB	BB	HBP	TAB	H	2B	3B	HR	BA	OB	SA	PRO	Wtd PRO	SB	CS	SBF	SPF	FF	R TF	V HC
1	1	1981	M.Schmidt	354	73	4	431	112	19	2	31	.316	.439	.644	1,083	1,114	12	4	9	10	90	1,223	157.5
2	2	1980	M.Schmidt	548	89	2	639	157	25	8	48	.286	.388	.624	1,012	1,025	12	5	3	10	60	1,098	116.3
3	4	1974	M.Schmidt	568	106	4	678	160	28	7	36	.282	.398	.546	944	959	23	12	(1)	10	70	1,037	103.8
4	7	1976	M.Schmidt	584	100	11	695	153	31	4	38	.262	.380	.524	904	933	14	9	(5)	10	80	1,017	99.7
5	5	1977	M.Schmidt	544	104	9	657	149	27	11	38	.274	.399	.574	972	944	15	8	(1)	10	80	1,033	99.1
6	6	1979	M.Schmidt	541	120	3	664	137	25	4	45	.253	.392	.564	955	947	9	5	(1)	10	70	1,026	97.9
7	3	1982	M.Schmidt	514	107	3	624	144	26	3	35	.280	.407	.547	954	969	14	7	0		70	1,039	95.9
8	9	1983	M.Schmidt	534	128	3	665	136	16	4	40	.255	.402	.524	926	934	7	8	(13)		70	991	87.0
9	10	1975	M.Schmidt	562	101	4	667	140	34	3	38	.249	.367	.523	890	901	29	12	7	10	70	988	86.2
10	8	1966	D.Allen	524	68	3	595	166	25	10	40	.317	.398	.632	1,030	1,040	10	6	(3)	10	(30)	1,017	85.3
11	12	1986	M.Schmidt	552	89	7	648	160	29	1	37	.290	.395	.547	942	945	1	2	(4)		40	980	81.5
12	14	1998	S.Rolen	601	93	11	705	174	45	4	31	.290	.394	.532	927	882	14	7	0	10	50	942	75.8
13	15	1964	D.Allen	632	67	0	699	201	38	13	29	.318	.383	.557	940	966	3	4	(7)	10	(30)	939	74.4
14	13	1984	M.Schmidt	528	92	4	624	146	23	3	36	.277	.388	.536	924	944	5	7	(14)	(10)	40	960	72.5
15	11	1967	D.Allen	463	75	1	539	142	31	10	23	.307	.404	.566	970	1,015	20	5	18	10	(60)	982	68.3
16	16	1987	M.Schmidt	522	83	2	607	153	28	0	35	.293	.392	.548	940	904	2	1	0		30	934	63.0
17	20	1965	D.Allen	619	74	2	695	187	31	14	20	.302	.378	.494	873	897	15	2	15	10	(30)	892	58.1
18	19	1978	M.Schmidt	513	91	4	608	129	27	2	21	.251	.368	.435	803	817	19	6	11	10	60	898	52.6
19	17	2000	S.Rolen	483	51	5	539	144	32	6	26	.298	.371	.551	922	841	8	1	11	10	50	912	50.2
20	21	1997	S.Rolen	561	76	13	650	159	35	3	21	.283	.382	.469	850	807	16	6	6	10	40	863	45.4
21	18	1999	S.Rolen	421	67	3	491	113	28	1	26	.268	.373	.525	898	821	12	2	15	10	60	907	44.5
22	23	1929	P.Whitney	612	61	2	675	200	43	14	8	.327	.390	.482	872	786	7				50	836	40.5
23	24	1992	D.Hollins	586	76	19	681	158	28	4	27	.270	.372	.469	841	865	9	6	(4)		(30)	831	37.3
24	22	1937	P.Whitney	487	43	1	531	166	19	4	8	.341	.395	.446	841	832	6				20	852	36.0
25	25	1951	W.Jones	564	60	4	628	161	28	5	22	.285	.358	.470	828	811	6	2	3		10	824	33.9

Philadelphia Phillies
Outfielders

V	R	Year	Name	AB	BB	HBP	TAB	H	2B	3B	HR	BA	OB	SA	PRO	Wtd PRO	SB	CS	SBF	SPF	FF	R TF	V HC
1	1	1933	C.Klein	606	56	1	663	223	44	7	28	.368	.422	.602	1,025	1,065	15				10	1,075	105.6
2	2	1932	C.Klein	650	60	1	711	226	50	15	38	.348	.404	.646	1,050	1,024	20					1,024	94.8
3	4	1901	E.Delahanty	542	65	4	611	192	38	16	8	.354	.427	.528	955	1,008	29			10		1,018	87.6
4	5	1900	E.Flick	545	56	16	617	200	32	16	11	.367	.441	.545	986	987	35			10	10	1,007	84.9
5	9	1930	C.Klein	648	54	4	706	250	59	8	40	.386	.436	.687	1,123	981	4				10	991	82.7
6	3	1910	S.Magee	519	94	12	625	172	39	17	6	.331	.445	.507	952	1,009	49			10		1,019	81.8
7	11	1929	L.O'Doul	638	76	4	718	254	35	6	32	.398	.465	.622	1,087	980	2					980	80.2
8	7	1901	E.Flick	540	52	7	599	180	32	17	8	.333	.399	.500	899	949	30			10	40	999	79.6
9	18	1958	R.Ashburn	615	97	4	716	215	24	13	2	.350	.441	.441	882	847	30	12	8	10	90	955	70.9
10	6	1907	S.Magee	503	53	4	560	165	28	12	4	.328	.396	.455	852	976	46			10	20	1,006	69.8
11	8	1913	G.Cravath	525	55	3	583	179	34	14	19	.341	.407	.568	974	1,013	10			(20)		993	68.8
12	10	1914	S.Magee	544	55	3	602	171	39	11	15	.314	.380	.509	890	965	25			10	10	985	68.5
13	16	1929	C.Klein	616	54	0	670	219	45	6	43	.356	.407	.657	1,065	960	5					960	68.1
14	13	1963	J.Callison	626	50	2	678	178	36	11	26	.284	.339	.502	841	885	8	3	3	10	70	967	67.8
15	14	1931	C.Klein	594	59	1	654	200	34	10	31	.337	.398	.584	982	961	7					961	66.8
16	12	1915	G.Cravath	522	86	6	614	149	31	7	24	.285	.393	.510	902	995	11	9	(11)		(10)	974	66.7
17	15	1990	L.Dykstra	590	89	7	686	192	35	3	9	.325	.420	.441	861	859	33	5	32	10	60	961	66.5
18	23	1993	L.Dykstra	637	129	2	768	194	44	6	19	.305	.423	.482	905	876	37	12	16	10	30	932	64.0
19	22	2000	B.Abreu	576	100	1	677	182	42	10	25	.316	.418	.554	972	887	28	8	17	10	30	943	60.0
20	21	1999	B.Abreu	546	109	3	658	183	35	11	20	.335	.448	.549	998	913	27	9	13	10	10	946	59.0
21	17	1914	G.Cravath	499	83	3	585	149	27	8	19	.299	.402	.499	901	977	14			(20)		957	58.4
22	30	1951	R.Ashburn	643	50	2	695	221	31	5	4	.344	.393	.426	819	802	29	6	23	10	90	925	58.3
23	27	1905	J.Titus	548	69	12	629	169	36	14	2	.308	.397	.436	834	909	11			10	10	929	54.2
24	19	1976	G.Maddox	531	42	4	577	175	37	6	6	.330	.383	.456	839	866	29	12	8	10	70	954	54.0
25	24	1977	G.Luzinski	554	80	3	637	171	35	3	39	.309	.399	.594	993	964	3	2	(1)	(10)	(20)	932	53.1

Philadelphia Phillies
Outfielders

V	R	Year	Name	AB	BB	HBP	TAB	H	2B	3B	HR	BA	OB	SA	PRO	Wtd PRO	SB	CS	SBF	SPF	FF	R TF	V HC
26	33	1965	J.Callison	619	57	6	682	162	25	16	32	.262	.330	.509	839	862	6	5	(6)	10	50	916	51.6
27	35	1964	J.Callison	654	36	6	696	179	30	10	31	.274	.318	.492	810	832	6	3	0	10	70	912	51.3
28	34	1920	C.Williams	590	32	4	626	192	36	10	15	.325	.364	.497	861	895	18	12	(9)	10	20	916	49.7
29	26	1917	G.Cravath	503	70	1	574	141	29	16	12	.280	.369	.473	842	940	6				(10)	930	49.5
30	37	1975	G.Luzinski	596	89	8	693	179	35	3	34	.300	.398	.540	939	949	3	6	(12)	(10)	(20)	907	49.4
31	25	1968	D.Allen	521	74	1	596	137	17	9	33	.263	.356	.520	876	962	7	7	(11)	10	(30)	930	49.1
32	40	1905	R.Thomas	562	93	4	659	178	11	6	0	.317	.417	.358	775	845	23			10	50	905	48.9
33	31	1947	H.Walker	513	63	4	580	186	29	16	1	.363	.436	.487	924	894	13			10	20	924	48.5
34	36	1955	R.Ashburn	533	105	3	641	180	32	9	3	.338	.449	.448	898	860	12	10	(12)	10	50	908	48.4
35	29	1908	S.Magee	508	49	11	568	144	30	16	2	.283	.359	.417	776	906	40			10	10	926	48.0
36	28	1967	T.Gonzalez	508	47	5	560	172	23	9	9	.339	.400	.472	872	912	10	9	(14)	10	20	929	45.7
37	47	1962	J.Callison	603	54	6	663	181	26	10	23	.300	.363	.491	854	835	10	3	6	10	50	901	45.4
38	45	1989	V.Hayes	540	101	4	645	140	27	2	26	.259	.380	.461	841	873	28	7	21	10		903	44.9
39	41	1904	R.Thomas	496	102	5	603	144	6	6	3	.290	.416	.345	761	855	28			10	40	905	44.7
40	43	1981	G.Matthews	359	59	3	421	108	21	3	9	.301	.404	.451	855	880	15	2	25	10	(10)	905	44.7
41	48	1906	S.Magee	563	52	5	620	159	36	8	6	.282	.348	.407	755	860	55			10	30	900	44.2
42	46	1923	C.Williams	535	59	7	601	157	22	3	41	.293	.371	.576	947	907	11	10	(14)	10		903	43.7
43	44	1930	L.O'Doul	528	63	5	596	202	37	7	22	.383	.453	.604	1,057	924	3				(20)	904	43.7
44	52	1903	R.Thomas	477	107	3	587	156	11	2	1	.327	.453	.365	818	850	17			10	30	890	43.0
45	51	1978	G.Luzinski	540	100	11	651	143	32	2	35	.265	.390	.526	916	932	8	7	(9)	(10)	(20)	893	42.1
46	56	1905	S.Magee	603	44	8	655	180	24	17	5	.299	.354	.420	774	844	48			10	30	884	41.6
47	53	1924	C.Williams	558	67	3	628	183	31	11	24	.328	.403	.552	955	925	7	12	(26)		(10)	889	41.4
48	42	1916	G.Cravath	448	64	5	517	127	21	8	11	.283	.379	.440	819	915	9				(10)	905	38.1
49	50	1914	B.Becker	514	37	0	551	167	25	5	9	.325	.370	.446	816	885	16			10		895	37.9
50	20	1926	C.Williams	336	38	4	378	116	13	4	18	.345	.418	.568	986	962	2				(10)	952	36.8
51	73	1953	R.Ashburn	622	61	5	688	205	25	9	2	.330	.394	.408	802	758	14	6	3	10	90	861	35.7
52	49	1911	S.Magee	445	49	6	500	128	32	5	15	.288	.366	.483	849	867	22			10	20	897	35.1
53	68	1950	D.Ennis	595	56	2	653	185	34	8	31	.311	.372	.551	923	884	2		(10)	(10)		864	35.0
54	65	1941	D.Litwhiler	590	39	2	631	180	29	6	18	.305	.350	.466	816	838	1			10	20	868	34.8
55	54	1925	G.Harper	495	28	6	529	173	35	7	18	.349	.391	.558	949	879	10	8	(11)	10	10	888	34.7
56	32	1977	B.McBride	402	32	3	437	127	25	6	15	.316	.371	.520	891	865	36	7	48	10		922	34.3
57	69	1944	R.Northey	570	67	4	641	164	35	9	22	.288	.367	.496	863	884	1		(10)	(10)		864	34.3
58	38	1913	B.Becker	414	28	0	442	131	24	13	9	.316	.360	.502	862	896	11			10		906	33.0
59	61	1910	J.Bates	498	61	4	563	152	26	11	3	.305	.385	.420	805	853	31			10	10	873	32.7
60	87	1956	R.Ashburn	628	79	5	712	190	26	8	3	.303	.385	.384	769	748	10	1	11	10	80	849	32.7
61	76	1912	D.Paskert	540	91	7	638	170	37	5	2	.315	.420	.413	833	828	36			10	20	858	32.2
62	58	1913	S.Magee	470	38	9	517	144	36	6	11	.306	.369	.479	848	882	23			10	(10)	882	32.2
63	83	1902	R.Thomas	500	107	2	609	143	4	7	0	.286	.414	.322	736	823	17			10	20	853	32.1
64	59	1948	R.Ashburn	463	60	1	524	154	17	4	2	.333	.410	.400	810	800	32			10	70	880	32.1
65	62	1998	B.Abreu	497	84	0	581	155	29	6	17	.312	.411	.497	908	864	19	10	(2)	10		873	31.9
66	80	1922	C.Walker	581	56	4	641	196	36	11	12	.337	.399	.499	899	842	11	4	4	10		857	31.9
67	66	1946	D.Ennis	540	39	4	583	169	30	6	17	.313	.364	.485	849	876	5				(10)	866	31.7
68	63	1934	J.Moore	500	43	1	544	165	35	7	11	.330	.384	.494	878	853	7			10	10	873	31.4
69	84	1949	D.Ennis	610	59	4	673	184	39	11	25	.302	.367	.525	892	871	2		(10)	(10)		851	31.4
70	91	1954	R.Ashburn	559	125	4	688	175	16	8	1	.313	.442	.376	818	775	11	8	(7)	10	70	848	31.2
71	85	1944	B.Adams	584	74	7	665	165	35	3	17	.283	.370	.440	810	830	2			10	10	850	30.8
72	55	1931	B.Arlett	418	45	5	468	131	26	7	18	.313	.387	.538	925	906	3		(10)	(10)		886	30.1
73	81	1908	J.Titus	539	53	14	606	154	24	5	2	.286	.365	.360	725	845	27			10		855	29.8
74	77	1984	V.Hayes	561	59	0	620	164	27	6	16	.292	.360	.447	807	824	48	13	34	10	(10)	858	29.7
75	75	1963	T.Gonzalez	555	53	8	616	170	36	12	4	.306	.375	.436	811	853	13	8	(5)	10		859	29.7

Philadelphia Phillies
Starting Pitchers

V	R	Year	Name	G	GS	IP	W	L	SV	SO	BB	ERA	RA/9	R Wtd RA/9	V Runs /162
1	2	1915	P.Alexander	49	42	376	31	10	3	241	64	1.22	2.06	2.57	87.2
2	3	1916	P.Alexander	48	45	389	33	12	3	167	50	1.55	2.08	2.76	81.9
3	1	1972	S.Carlton	41	41	346	27	10	0	310	87	1.97	2.18	2.55	81.0
4	6	1953	R.Roberts	44	41	347	23	16	2	198	61	2.75	3.09	2.90	67.1
5	9	1908	G.McQuillan	48	42	360	23	17	2	114	91	1.53	2.17	2.98	66.4
6	17	1917	P.Alexander	45	44	388	30	13	0	200	56	1.83	2.48	3.20	61.5
7	11	1954	R.Roberts	45	38	337	23	15	4	185	56	2.97	3.10	3.08	58.3
8	5	1966	J.Bunning	43	41	314	19	14	1	252	55	2.41	2.61	2.90	57.8
9	10	1952	R.Roberts	39	37	330	28	7	2	148	45	2.59	2.84	3.07	57.2
10	7	1980	S.Carlton	38	38	304	24	9	0	286	90	2.34	2.58	2.92	55.4
11	28	1911	P.Alexander	48	37	367	28	13	3	227	129	2.57	3.26	3.33	52.6
12	14	1901	A.Orth	35	33	282	20	12	1	92	32	2.27	3.23	3.15	51.2
13	25	1901	R.Donahue	34	33	295	20	13	1	88	59	2.59	3.37	3.28	48.4
14	18	1950	R.Roberts	40	39	304	20	11	1	146	77	3.02	3.32	3.21	47.8
15	30	1951	R.Roberts	44	39	315	21	15	2	127	64	3.03	3.29	3.35	44.6
16	19	1965	J.Bunning	39	39	291	19	9	0	268	62	2.60	2.85	3.22	43.1
17	26	1967	J.Bunning	40	40	302	17	15	0	253	73	2.29	2.80	3.32	41.4
18	23	1981	S.Carlton	24	24	190	13	4	0	179	62	2.42	2.79	3.27	41.2
19	33	1913	P.Alexander	47	36	306	22	8	2	159	75	2.79	3.12	3.41	41.0
20	4	1964	C.Short	42	31	221	17	9	2	181	51	2.20	2.57	2.90	40.7
21	21	1977	S.Carlton	36	36	283	23	10	0	198	89	2.64	3.15	3.26	40.7
22	22	1905	T.Sparks	34	26	260	14	11	1	98	73	2.18	2.98	3.26	39.3
23	38	1909	E.Moore	38	34	300	18	12	0	173	108	2.10	2.79	3.47	38.0
24	16	1983	J.Denny	36	36	243	19	6	0	139	53	2.37	2.86	3.16	37.6
25	48	1913	T.Seaton	52	35	322	27	12	1	168	136	2.60	3.27	3.57	37.0
26	27	1998	C.Schilling	35	35	269	15	14	0	300	61	3.25	3.38	3.33	36.8
27	20	1947	D.Leonard	32	29	235	17	12	0	103	57	2.68	3.29	3.22	36.6
28	13	1992	C.Schilling	42	26	226	14	11	2	147	59	2.35	2.66	3.12	36.0
29	49	1906	T.Sparks	42	37	317	19	16	3	114	62	2.16	2.87	3.59	35.7
30	8	1967	C.Short	29	26	199	9	11	1	142	74	2.39	2.49	2.95	35.4
31	42	1965	C.Short	47	40	297	18	11	2	237	89	2.82	3.09	3.49	35.1
32	43	1910	E.Moore	46	35	283	22	15	0	185	121	2.58	3.12	3.50	34.9
33	15	1973	W.Twitchell	34	28	223	13	9	0	169	99	2.50	2.87	3.15	34.8
34	29	1997	C.Schilling	35	35	254	17	11	0	319	58	2.97	3.40	3.35	34.2
35	36	1907	T.Sparks	33	31	265	22	8	1	90	51	2.00	2.65	3.46	34.0
36	35	1949	K.Heintzelman	33	32	250	17	10	0	65	93	3.02	3.46	3.44	32.6
37	31	1952	K.Drews	33	30	229	14	15	0	96	52	2.72	3.10	3.36	32.2
38	45	1964	J.Bunning	41	39	284	19	8	2	219	46	2.63	3.14	3.54	32.0
39	54	1911	E.Moore	42	36	308	15	19	1	174	164	2.63	3.59	3.67	32.0
40	50	1934	C.Davis	51	31	274	19	17	5	99	60	2.95	3.74	3.60	30.8
41	56	1901	B.Duggleby	35	29	285	20	12	0	95	41	2.88	3.82	3.72	30.7
42	41	1994	D.Jackson	25	25	179	14	6	0	129	46	3.26	3.56	3.49	30.1
43	34	1948	D.Leonard	34	31	226	12	17	0	92	54	2.51	3.38	3.42	30.0
44	53	1906	B.Duggleby	42	30	280	13	19	2	83	66	2.25	2.92	3.66	29.5
45	46	1954	C.Simmons	34	33	253	14	15	1	125	98	2.81	3.59	3.56	29.4
46	64	1912	P.Alexander	46	34	310	19	17	3	195	105	2.81	3.86	3.78	28.1
47	55	1903	T.Sparks	28	28	248	11	15	0	88	56	2.72	3.96	3.68	27.9
48	12	1912	E.Rixey	23	20	162	10	10	0	59	54	2.50	3.17	3.11	27.5
49	63	1916	E.Rixey	38	33	287	22	10	0	134	74	1.85	2.85	3.78	26.2
50	24	1996	C.Schilling	26	26	183	9	10	0	182	50	3.19	3.39	3.28	26.0

Philadelphia Phillies
Starting Pitchers

V	R	Year	Name	G	GS	IP	W	L	SV	SO	BB	ERA	RA/9	R Wtd RA/9	V Runs /162
51	52	1953	C.Simmons	32	30	238	16	13	0	138	82	3.21	3.86	3.63	25.9
52	37	2000	C.Schilling	29	29	210	11	12	0	168	45	3.81	3.85	3.46	25.6
53	44	1949	R.Meyer	37	28	213	17	8	1	78	70	3.08	3.55	3.53	25.5
54	40	1952	C.Simmons	28	28	201	14	8	0	141	70	2.82	3.22	3.49	25.2
55	57	1944	K.Raffensberger	37	31	259	13	20	0	136	45	3.06	3.51	3.74	24.8
56	86	1914	P.Alexander	46	39	355	27	15	1	214	76	2.38	3.37	3.99	23.6
57	51	1913	A.Brennan	40	25	207	14	12	1	94	46	2.39	3.30	3.61	23.0
58	71	1915	E.Mayer	43	33	275	21	15	2	114	59	2.36	3.08	3.85	22.9
59	58	1957	J.Sanford	33	33	237	19	8	0	188	94	3.08	3.57	3.74	22.6
60	39	1959	G.Conley	25	22	180	12	7	1	102	42	3.00	3.40	3.48	22.6
61	72	1958	R.Roberts	35	34	270	17	14	0	130	51	3.24	3.73	3.85	22.5
62	74	1982	S.Carlton	38	38	296	23	11	0	286	86	3.10	3.47	3.88	22.4
63	32	2000	R.Person	28	28	173	9	7	0	164	95	3.63	3.79	3.41	22.2
64	59	1978	S.Carlton	34	34	247	16	13	0	161	63	2.84	3.31	3.75	22.1
65	73	1926	H.Carlson	35	34	267	17	12	0	55	47	3.23	3.91	3.87	21.3
66	67	1976	S.Carlton	35	35	253	20	7	0	195	72	3.13	3.35	3.83	20.5
67	82	1905	B.Duggleby	38	36	289	18	17	0	75	83	2.46	3.61	3.95	20.4
68	61	1950	C.Simmons	31	27	215	17	8	1	146	88	3.40	3.89	3.76	19.9
69	47	1999	C.Schilling	24	24	180	15	6	0	152	44	3.54	3.69	3.57	19.7
70	68	1935	C.Davis	44	27	231	16	14	2	74	47	3.66	4.01	3.83	19.6
71	81	1974	J.Lonborg	39	39	283	17	13	0	121	70	3.21	3.59	3.94	19.3
72	92	1955	R.Roberts	41	38	305	23	14	3	160	53	3.28	4.04	4.03	18.8
73	77	1931	R.Benge	38	31	247	14	18	2	117	61	3.17	3.90	3.91	18.8
74	79	1909	G.McQuillan	41	28	248	13	16	2	96	54	2.14	3.16	3.93	18.0
75	62	1927	D.Ulrich	32	18	193	8	11	1	42	40	3.17	3.82	3.77	17.8
76	89	1974	S.Carlton	39	39	291	16	13	0	240	136	3.22	3.65	4.01	17.8
77	98	1923	J.Ring	39	36	304	18	16	0	112	115	3.87	4.34	4.06	17.6
78	70	1943	S.Rowe	27	25	199	14	8	1	52	29	2.94	3.30	3.84	16.8
79	66	1993	T.Greene	31	30	200	16	4	0	167	62	3.42	3.78	3.81	16.6
80	85	1900	C.Fraser	29	26	223	15	9	0	58	93	3.14	4.71	3.98	16.5
81	65	1993	T.Mulholland	29	28	191	12	9	0	116	40	3.25	3.77	3.80	16.0
82	60	1951	R.Meyer	28	24	168	8	9	0	65	55	3.48	3.70	3.76	15.6
83	84	1949	R.Roberts	43	31	227	15	15	4	95	75	3.69	4.00	3.98	15.3
84	80	1976	J.Lonborg	33	32	222	18	10	1	118	50	3.08	3.45	3.94	15.2
85	83	1943	D.Barrett	38	24	214	10	13	1	85	79	2.90	3.41	3.96	14.8
86	113	1902	D.White	36	35	306	16	20	1	185	72	2.53	3.71	4.18	14.6
87	69	1915	G.Chalmers	26	20	170	8	9	1	82	45	2.48	3.07	3.83	14.4
88	103	1983	S.Carlton	37	37	284	15	16	0	275	84	3.11	3.71	4.10	14.3
89	88	1932	F.Rhem	32	26	219	15	9	1	53	59	3.58	4.03	4.00	14.2
90	75	1935	S.Johnson	37	18	175	10	8	6	89	31	3.56	4.06	3.88	13.9
91	106	1916	A.Demaree	39	35	285	19	14	1	130	48	2.62	3.13	4.15	13.7
92	91	1978	L.Christenson	33	33	228	13	14	0	131	47	3.24	3.55	4.02	13.5
93	105	1918	B.Hogg	29	25	228	13	13	1	81	61	2.53	3.28	4.14	13.5
94	76	1950	B.Miller	35	22	174	11	6	1	44	57	3.57	4.03	3.90	13.4
95	107	1940	K.Higbe	41	36	283	14	19	1	137	121	3.72	4.01	4.15	13.4
96	94	1959	J.Owens	31	30	221	12	12	1	135	73	3.21	3.95	4.04	13.2
97	99	1955	M.Dickson	36	28	216	12	11	0	92	82	3.50	4.08	4.07	12.3
98	95	1944	B.Lee	31	28	208	10	11	1	50	57	3.15	3.81	4.06	12.2
99	90	1963	R.Culp	34	30	203	14	11	0	176	102	2.97	3.37	4.02	12.1
100	78	1908	L.Richie	25	15	158	7	10	1	58	49	1.83	2.85	3.91	11.9

Philadelphia Phillies
Relief Pitchers

V	R	Year	Name	G	GS	IP	W	L	SV	SO	BB	ERA	RA/9	R Wtd RA/9	V Runs /162
1	12	1950	J.Konstanty	74	0	152	16	7	22	56	50	2.66	3.02	2.92	29.0
2	1	1980	T.McGraw	57	0	92	5	4	20	75	23	1.46	1.56	1.76	28.6
3	9	1970	D.Selma	73	0	134	8	9	22	153	59	2.75	2.82	2.84	25.6
4	5	1963	J.Klippstein	49	1	112	5	6	8	86	46	1.93	2.25	2.68	23.3
5	3	1995	R.Bottalico	62	0	88	5	3	1	87	42	2.46	2.57	2.52	22.4
6	6	1977	G.Garber	64	0	103	8	6	19	78	23	2.35	2.61	2.70	21.2
7	4	1955	B.Miller	40	0	90	8	4	1	28	28	2.41	2.60	2.59	20.7
8	15	1977	R.Reed	60	3	124	7	5	15	84	37	2.75	2.97	3.08	20.4
9	19	1976	R.Reed	59	4	128	8	7	14	96	32	2.46	2.74	3.13	20.3
10	2	1994	D.Jones	47	0	54	2	4	27	38	6	2.17	2.33	2.28	19.3
11	14	1978	R.Reed	66	0	109	3	4	17	85	23	2.24	2.65	3.00	18.8
12	7	1991	M.Williams	69	0	88	12	5	30	84	62	2.34	2.45	2.71	18.1
13	8	1983	A.Holland	68	0	92	8	4	25	100	30	2.26	2.55	2.82	17.8
14	18	1986	K.Tekulve	73	0	110	11	5	4	57	25	2.54	2.86	3.13	17.5
15	11	1978	W.Brusstar	58	0	89	6	3	0	60	30	2.33	2.54	2.88	16.6
16	16	1982	R.Reed	57	2	98	5	5	14	57	24	2.66	2.76	3.08	16.1
17	26	1962	J.Baldschun	67	0	113	12	7	13	95	58	2.96	3.27	3.30	15.8
18	13	1985	D.Carman	71	0	86	9	4	7	87	38	2.08	2.61	2.92	15.6
19	23	1987	K.Tekulve	90	0	105	6	4	3	60	29	3.09	3.26	3.27	15.0
20	10	1964	E.Roebuck	62	0	78	5	3	12	42	27	2.31	2.54	2.87	14.7
21	28	1960	T.Farrell	59	0	103	10	6	11	70	29	2.70	3.15	3.38	14.2
22	27	1988	G.Harris	66	1	107	4	6	1	71	52	2.36	2.86	3.37	14.1
23	20	1996	K.Ryan	62	0	89	3	5	8	70	45	2.43	3.24	3.13	14.1
24	21	1987	S.Bedrosian	65	0	89	5	3	40	74	28	2.83	3.13	3.14	14.0
25	24	1975	T.Hilgendorf	53	0	97	7	3	0	52	38	2.14	2.97	3.28	13.8
26	32	1963	J.Baldschun	65	0	114	11	7	16	89	42	2.30	2.92	3.48	13.6
27	29	1967	T.Farrell	57	1	104	10	6	12	78	22	2.34	2.86	3.39	13.4
28	38	1986	D.Carman	50	14	134	10	5	1	98	52	3.22	3.35	3.66	13.3
29	25	1957	T.Farrell	52	0	83	10	2	10	54	36	2.38	3.14	3.29	12.3
30	34	1949	J.Konstanty	53	0	97	9	5	7	43	29	3.25	3.53	3.51	11.8
31	30	1944	A.Karl	38	0	89	3	2	2	26	21	2.33	3.24	3.45	11.5
32	17	1996	R.Bottalico	61	0	68	4	5	34	74	23	3.19	3.19	3.09	11.1
33	54	1945	A.Karl	67	2	181	8	8	15	51	50	2.99	3.98	4.04	11.0
34	36	1976	T.McGraw	58	0	97	7	6	11	76	42	2.50	3.14	3.59	10.5
35	31	1967	D.Hall	48	1	86	10	8	8	49	12	2.20	2.93	3.48	10.3
36	35	1984	L.Andersen	64	0	91	3	7	4	54	25	2.38	3.18	3.55	10.2
37	40	1975	T.McGraw	56	0	103	9	6	14	55	36	2.98	3.33	3.67	10.1
38	37	1998	M.Leiter	69	0	89	7	5	23	84	47	3.55	3.65	3.59	9.5
39	39	1976	G.Garber	59	0	93	9	3	11	92	30	2.82	3.21	3.67	9.2
40	43	1995	M.Williams	33	8	88	3	3	0	57	29	3.29	3.80	3.72	9.2
41	22	1993	L.Andersen	64	0	62	3	2	0	67	21	2.92	3.21	3.24	9.1
42	44	1966	D.Knowles	69	0	100	6	5	13	88	46	3.05	3.41	3.79	8.5
43	33	1995	H.Slocumb	61	0	65	5	6	32	63	35	2.89	3.58	3.51	8.5
44	47	1972	B.Lersch	36	8	101	4	6	0	48	33	3.04	3.30	3.87	8.2
45	41	1998	J.Spradlin	69	0	82	4	4	1	76	20	3.53	3.75	3.69	7.9
46	50	1994	H.Slocumb	52	0	72	5	1	0	58	28	2.86	3.98	3.90	7.4
47	46	1986	T.Hume	48	1	94	4	1	4	51	34	2.77	3.53	3.86	7.3
48	48	1984	A.Holland	68	0	98	5	10	29	61	30	3.39	3.48	3.89	7.3
49	53	1991	R.McDowell	71	0	101	9	9	10	50	48	2.93	3.55	3.93	7.1
50	42	1997	R.Bottalico	69	0	74	2	5	34	89	42	3.65	3.77	3.71	7.0

PITTSBURGH PIRATES (1900–2000)

Following the 1899 season, the National League decided to reduce the number of franchises from twelve to eight. This decision resulted in an unexpected shift in the league's balance of power over the next decade. Louisville owner Barney Dreyfuss, whose team was to be disbanded, transferred most of his players to the Pittsburgh franchise in which he had part ownership. While the two franchises were .500 clubs in 1899, the combined ball club emerged as a league powerhouse.

Pittsburgh owned the rights to Ginger Beaumont, Sam Leever, Jesse Tannehill, and Jack Chesbro. Coming from Louisville were player-manager Fred Clarke, Tom Leach, Claude Ritchey, Deacon Phillippe, and a young infielder-outfielder named Honus Wagner. Wagner, dubbed "the Flying Dutchman," proceeded to dominate the National League's offensive statistics for the next dozen years, while anchoring the Pirates infield from his shortstop position.

Pittsburgh "only" finished in second place in 1900, but the Pirates then proceeded to win three consecutive pennants in 1901–1903. The best of these squads was a 1902 team that earned a 103–36 record, winning 74 percent of its games while producing the second highest ratio of runs scored to runs given up in modern baseball history. Only the 1906 Cubs, with a 1.85 ratio, beats the 1.76 ratio Pittsburgh achieved that year. This deep Pirates team was led by outfielders Wagner (.330, league-leading 42 steals, 1,008 Total Factor), Beaumont (league-leading .357 average) and Clarke (.316 average). The pitching staff featured a fearsome foursome of Chesbro (28–6, 2.17 ERA, team record 61.8 Runs/162), Tannehill (20–6, 1.95 ERA), Phillippe (20–9, 2.05 ERA), and Leever (15–7, 2.39 ERA).

Only the fact that National League talent was concentrated in three cities kept Pittsburgh from winning eight or ten pennants in a row. While Pittsburgh stayed very competitive from 1904 to 1908, strong teams from Chicago and New York won all the pennants. Pittsburgh finished one game out in Wagner's best season of 1908, with Honus batting .354, hitting 10 home runs, and stealing 53 bases. Adjusted for a National League all-time high 17 percent hitter's deflation that year, Wagner hit .413 with 12 home runs, for a 1,117 Wtd. Production. With his speed and fielding, Wagner achieved a 1,167 Total Factor, the best ever at shortstop. His 158.5 Hits Contribution is the best ever at shortstop and the best volume of success achieved by any National League player.

In 1909, Pittsburgh again reached the top with a 110–42 record, while finishing ahead of an exceptional Cubs team that won 104 games. The 1909 team featured Wagner's league-leading .339 average and 1,088 Total Factor, and a deep rotation of Howie Camnitz (25–6, 1.62 ERA, 2.98 Wtd. RA/9), Vic Willis (22–11, 2.24 ERA), Lefty Leifield, and Babe Adams. Pittsburgh continued to post solid winning seasons through 1912, but age began to take its toll. Wagner continued to be a star through 1916, when he was 42, but the rest of the original Pittsburgh talent pool had either retired or moved on, and the team sank into the second division by 1915.

The Pirates soon re-emerged with a new cast of stars. Veterans Babe Adams (17–10, 1.98 ERA, 2.83 Wtd. RA/9 in 1919) and Max Carey (.329, 51 steals in 53 attempts in 1922) were joined by Pie Traynor (.338, 12 home runs in 1923), Kiki Cuyler, and Wilbur Cooper, as the team finished above .500 from 1918 to 1924.

In 1925, George Grantham joined the team, and the Pirates won the pennant and the World Series. Cuyler had his finest season as a pro with a .357 average, 43 doubles, 26 triples, 18 home runs, and 41 steals, for a 986 Total Factor. Pittsburgh won another pennant in 1927, as young outfielders Paul and Lloyd Waner hit .380 and .355,

147

respectively, to make up for Cuyler's midseason benching by his manager. Paul Waner's efforts earned him the league's MVP Award. Ray Kremer headed up the pitching staff with a 19-8 record, 2.47 ERA, and 2.87 Wtd. RA/9. Although the 1927 squad hit .305 as a team, they hit only 54 home runs, and they were no match for the Yankees Murderer's Row in the World Series, being swept in four games.

Led by Paul Waner, Traynor, and another talented Pirates shortstop in Arky Vaughan, the Pirates remained competitive during the next two decades, but could get no closer than second place finishes in 1932, 1933, 1938, and 1944. Vaughan's 1935 season, when he hit .385 with 19 home runs, stands out as the only shortstop season in modern baseball history to rank with Honus Wagner's eight best seasons at short; Arky cranked out a 1,074 Total Factor and 124.4 Hits Contribution that year.

By the end of World War II, the Pirates laid claim to 38 winning seasons in 46 years. Like the Chicago Cubs, who claimed a similar level of consistent performance, the Pirates expected to field winning clubs every year. In 1946, the Pirates featured a star in third baseman Bob Elliott, and a rookie sensation in left fielder Ralph Kiner. But instead of continued success, the Pirates joined the Cubs at the bottom of the standings. For 12 of the next 13 years, the Pirates finished under .500, including seven years in last place. Poor-fielding Ralph Kiner was not enough, even though he hit 294 home runs from 1946 to 1952 to win seven consecutive home run titles.

The Pirates climbed from last place in 1957 to second place in 1958. Pittsburgh went on to win their first World Series in 35 years in 1960, beating a powerful Yankees team in an exciting seven game series. Bill Mazeroski, the best defensive second baseman ever, became a household name for his winning home run in game seven, while shortstop Dick Groat was the National League's MVP with a league-leading .325 average.

The Pirates of the 1960s were led by 1966 MVP Roberto Clemente, who had his best season the following year, when he batted .357 with 23 home runs. Adjusted for 5 percent hitter's deflation, Clemente batted .374 with 24 home runs, for a 1,070 Total Factor. Other 1960s stars include Mazeroski, Bob Friend, and Roy Face (8-7, 28 saves, 1.88 ERA, 2.29 Wtd. RA/9 in 1962).

The Pirates went from being competitive in the sixties to being dominant in the 1970s. Pittsburgh put together 13 winning seasons in 15 years from 1969 to 1983, while winning their division six times. The best players in this period were Clemente, Willie Stargell (.295, 48 home runs, 1,061 Wtd. Production in 1971), Dave Parker (.334, 30 home runs, 997 Wtd. Production, 1,046 Total Factor, MVP in 1978), and John Candelaria (20-5, 2.34 ERA, Pirates all-time best 2.59 Wtd. RA/9 in 1977). Appearing in just the 1977 season for the Pirates, Goose Gossage went 11-9 with 26 saves, a 1.62 ERA, 1.90 Wtd. RA/9, and Goose saved 39.3 runs from scoring, a league volume of success record for relievers.

The Pirates used a four-year dry spell in the mid-1980s to assemble the nucleus for one of their best lineups ever. The Pirates won their division three consecutive years in 1990-1992, led by 1990 and 1992 MVP Barry Bonds, Andy Van Slyke, Bobby Bonilla, Doug Drabek and yet another talented Pirates shortstop in Jay Bell. Bonds hit .311 with 34 home runs in 1992; he drew 127 walks; he stole 39 bases in 47 attempts; and he played superb defense. Adjusted for 3 percent hitter's deflation, Bonds hit .320 with 35 home runs, for a career-best 1,116 Wtd. Production. Bonds' 1,222 Total Factor that year is second best rate of success in National League history behind Mike Schmidt's 1,223 performance in 1981, and his 134.0 Hits Contribution gives him the best volume of success for any National League outfielder.

For financial reasons, the team was torn apart after the 1992 season, and Barry Bonds' departure for San Francisco was the team's death knell. The struggling organization has finished below .500 ever since Bonds departed, despite the emergence of talented catcher Jason Kendall (.327, 12 home runs, 26 steals in 1998), and outfielder Brian Giles (.315 average, 39 home runs in 1999, followed by another .315 average and 35 home runs in 2000).

Pittsburgh Pirates (1900–2000)

Pittsburgh Pirates — **Hitters Volume of Success**

Pos	Year	Name	AB	BB	HBP	TAB	H	2B	3B	HR	BA	OB	SA	PRO	Wtd PRO	SB	CS	SBF	SPF	FF	R TF	V HC
C	1998	J.Kendall	535	51	31	617	175	36	3	12	.327	.417	.473	889	846	26	5	25	10	20	901	65.7
1B	1941	E.Fletcher	521	118	2	641	150	29	13	11	.288	.421	.457	878	901	5			10	20	931	51.7
2B	1962	B.Mazeroski	572	37	2	611	155	24	9	14	.271	.318	.418	735	719	0	3	(9)	10	110	830	42.0
SS	1908	H.Wagner	568	54	5	627	201	39	19	10	.354	.415	.542	957	1,117	53			10	40	1,167	158.5
3B	1923	P.Traynor	616	34	5	655	208	19	19	12	.338	.377	.489	866	829	28	13	3	10	70	912	64.3
OF	1992	B.Bonds	473	127	5	605	147	36	5	34	.311	.461	.624	1,085	1,116	39	8	36	10	60	1,222	134.0
OF	1949	R.Kiner	549	117	1	667	170	19	5	54	.310	.432	.658	1,089	1,064	6			0	(20)	1,044	95.7
OF	1967	R.Clemente	585	41	3	629	209	26	10	23	.357	.402	.554	956	1,000	9	1	11	10	50	1,070	93.8
Starters		Averages	552	72	7	632	177	29	10	21	.320	.405	.525	930	949	21	4	8	9	44	1,010	88.2
C	1975	M.Sanguillen	481	48	3	532	158	24	4	9	.328	.393	.451	844	854	5	4	(5)	10	0	858	45.8
1B	1982	J.Thompson	550	101	2	653	156	32	0	31	.284	.397	.511	908	922	1	0	1	(10)	0	913	44.6
2B	1906	C.Ritchey	484	68	9	561	130	21	5	1	.269	.369	.339	708	806	6			0	20	826	39.5
SS	1935	A.Vaughan	499	97	7	603	192	34	10	19	.385	.491	.607	1,098	1,074	4			10	(10)	1,074	124.4
3B	1981	B.Madlock	279	34	3	316	95	23	1	6	.341	.418	.495	912	939	18	6	18	10	(10)	957	54.8
OF	1978	D.Parker	581	57	2	640	194	32	12	30	.334	.395	.585	981	997	20	7	9	10	30	1,046	88.1
OF	1927	P.Waner	623	60	3	686	237	42	18	9	.380	.437	.549	986	960	5			10	30	1,000	83.5
OF	1971	W.Stargell	511	83	7	601	151	26	0	48	.295	.401	.628	1,029	1,061	0	0	0	(10)	(10)	1,041	81.1
Subs		Averages	501	69	5	574	164	29	6	19	.328	.413	.525	939	955	7	2	3	4	6	968	70.2
Totals		Weighted Ave.	535	71	6	612	173	29	9	21	.323	.408	.525	933	951	16	3	6	7	31	996	82.2

Pitchers Volume of Success

Pos	Year	Name	G	GS	IP	W	L	SV	SO	BB	ERA	RA/9	Wtd RA/9	V Runs /162
SP	1902	J.Chesbro	35	33	286	28	6	1	136	62	2.17	2.55	2.88	61.8
SP	1906	V.Willis	41	36	322	23	13	1	124	76	1.73	2.35	2.94	60.8
SP	1903	S.Leever	36	34	284	25	7	1	90	60	2.06	3.13	2.91	60.1
SP	1913	B.Adams	43	37	314	21	10	0	144	49	2.15	2.69	2.94	59.4
SP	1909	H.Camnitz	41	30	283	25	6	3	133	68	1.62	2.39	2.98	52.3
Starters		Averages	39	34	298	24	8	1	125	63	1.95	2.62	2.93	58.9
RP	1977	R.Gossage	72	0	133	11	9	26	151	49	1.62	1.83	1.90	39.3
RP	1982	R.Scurry	76	0	104	4	5	14	94	64	1.74	2.26	2.52	23.5
RP	1962	R.Face	63	0	91	8	7	28	45	18	1.88	2.27	2.29	22.9
RP	1968	R.Kline	56	0	113	12	5	7	48	31	1.68	2.07	2.76	22.6
Relievers		Averages	67	0	110	9	7	19	85	41	1.72	2.08	2.35	27.1
Totals		Averages	106	34	408	33	15	20	210	104	1.88	2.47	2.77	86.0

Baseball Players' Best Seasons

Pittsburgh Pirates — **Hitters Rate of Success**

Pos	Year	Name	AB	BB	HBP	TAB	H	2B	3B	HR	BA	OB	SA	PRO	Wtd PRO	SB	CS	SBF	SPF	FF	R TF	V HC
C	1998	J.Kendall	535	51	31	617	175	36	3	12	.327	.417	.473	889	846	26	5	25	10	20	901	65.7
1B	1941	E.Fletcher	521	118	2	641	150	29	13	11	.288	.421	.457	878	901	5			10	20	931	51.7
2B	1929	G.Grantham	349	93	1	443	107	23	10	12	.307	.454	.533	987	890	10		0	(30)		860	38.7
SS	1908	H.Wagner	568	54	5	627	201	39	19	10	.354	.415	.542	957	1117	53			10	40	1,167	158.5
3B	1981	B.Madlock	279	34	3	316	95	23	1	6	.341	.418	.495	912	939	18	6	18	10	(10)	957	54.8
OF	1992	B.Bonds	473	127	5	605	147	36	5	34	.311	.461	.624	1085	1116	39	8	36	10	60	1,222	134.0
OF	1967	R.Clemente	585	41	3	629	209	26	10	23	.357	.402	.554	956	1000	9	1	11	10	50	1,070	93.8
OF	1978	D.Parker	581	57	2	640	194	32	12	30	.334	.395	.585	981	997	20	7	9	10	30	1,046	88.1
Starters		Averages	486	72	7	565	160	31	9	17	.328	.422	.535	957	981	23	3	12	9	23	1,025	85.7
C	1975	M.Sanguillen	481	48	3	532	158	24	4	9	.328	.393	.451	844	854	5	4	(5)	10	0	858	45.8
1B	1950	J.Hopp	345	51	1	397	117	26	6	9	.339	.426	.528	953	913	7	1	0	10	0	923	30.4
2B	1962	B.Mazeroski	572	37	2	611	155	24	9	14	.271	.318	.418	735	719	0	3	(9)	10	110	830	42.0
SS	1935	A.Vaughan	499	97	7	603	192	34	10	19	.385	.491	.607	1098	1074	4			10	(10)	1,074	124.4
3B	1923	P.Traynor	616	34	5	655	208	19	19	12	.338	.377	.489	866	829	28	13	3	10	70	912	64.3
OF	1949	R.Kiner	549	117	1	667	170	19	5	54	.310	.432	.658	1089	1064	6			0	(20)	1,044	95.7
OF	1971	W.Stargell	511	83	7	601	151	26	0	48	.295	.401	.628	1029	1061	0	0	0	(10)	(10)	1,041	81.1
OF	1927	P.Waner	623	60	3	686	237	42	18	9	.380	.437	.549	986	960	5			10	30	1,000	83.5
Subs		Averages	525	66	4	594	174	27	9	22	.331	.409	.540	949	937	7	3	(1)	6	21	963	70.9
Totals		Weighted Ave.	499	70	6	575	164	29	9	19	.329	.417	.537	954	966	17	3	8	8	22	1,004	80.7

Pitchers Rate of Success

Pos	Year	Name	G	GS	IP	W	L	SV	SO	BB	ERA	RA/9	Wtd RA/9	R V Runs /162
SP	1977	J.Candelaria	33	33	231	20	5	0	133	50	2.34	2.50	2.59	50.5
SP	1912	H.Robinson	33	16	175	12	7	2	79	30	2.26	2.78	2.72	37.5
SP	1919	B.Adams	34	29	263	17	10	1	92	23	1.98	2.26	2.83	58.4
SP	1927	R.Kremer	35	28	226	19	8	2	63	53	2.47	2.91	2.87	44.6
SP	1902	J.Chesbro	35	33	286	28	6	1	136	62	2.17	2.55	2.88	61.8
Starters		Averages	34	28	236	19	7	1	101	44	2.23	2.58	2.79	50.6
RP	1977	R.Gossage	72	0	133	11	9	26	151	49	1.62	1.83	1.90	39.3
RP	1972	R.Hernandez	53	0	70	5	0	14	47	22	1.67	1.80	2.11	20.0
RP	1999	S.Sauerbeck	65	0	68	4	1	2	55	38	2.00	2.53	2.28	17.1
RP	1962	R.Face	63	0	91	8	7	28	45	18	1.88	2.27	2.29	22.9
Relievers		Averages	63	0	91	7	4	18	75	32	1.77	2.07	2.11	24.8
Totals		Averages	97	28	327	26	11	19	175	75	2.10	2.44	2.60	75.4

Pittsburgh Pirates (1900–2000)

Pittsburgh Pirates
Catchers

V	R	Year	Name	AB	BB	HBP	TAB	H	2B	3B	HR	BA	OB	SA	PRO	Wtd PRO	SB	CS	SBF	SPF	FF	R TF	V HC
1	1	1998	J.Kendall	535	51	31	617	175	36	3	12	.327	.417	.473	889	846	26	5	25	10	20	901	65.7
2	5	2000	J.Kendall	579	79	15	673	185	33	6	14	.320	.415	.470	884	807	22	12	(3)	10	20	834	50.2
3	2	1975	M.Sanguillen	481	48	3	532	158	24	4	9	.328	.393	.451	844	854	5	4	(5)	10		858	45.8
4	3	1984	T.Pena	546	36	4	586	156	27	2	15	.286	.334	.425	759	776	12	8	(6)		70	839	45.2
5	6	1997	J.Kendall	486	49	31	566	143	36	4	8	.294	.394	.434	828	786	18	6	10	10	20	826	40.1
6	8	1909	G.Gibson	510	44	2	556	135	25	9	2	.265	.326	.361	686	776	9				40	816	38.7
7	7	1971	M.Sanguillen	533	19	3	555	170	26	5	7	.319	.346	.426	772	795	6	4	(3)	10	20	822	38.2
8	10	1983	T.Pena	542	31	0	573	163	22	3	15	.301	.339	.435	774	781	6	7	(13)		30	797	32.7
9	4	1962	S.Burgess	360	31	0	391	118	19	2	13	.328	.381	.500	881	861	0	1	(5)	(10)	(10)	837	29.7
10	11	1986	T.Pena	510	53	1	564	147	26	2	10	.288	.356	.406	762	764	9	10	(18)		40	786	29.2
11	12	1970	M.Sanguillen	486	17	0	503	158	19	9	7	.325	.348	.444	792	773	2	3	(8)	10	10	785	25.8
12	15	1972	M.Sanguillen	520	21	0	541	155	18	8	7	.298	.325	.404	729	755	1	2	(5)	10	10	769	25.0
13	20	1910	G.Gibson	482	47	6	535	125	22	6	3	.259	.333	.349	681	722	7				40	762	22.7
14	13	1959	S.Burgess	377	31	2	410	112	28	5	11	.297	.354	.485	839	815	0	0	0	(10)	(20)	785	22.1
15	17	1982	T.Pena	497	17	4	518	147	28	4	11	.296	.324	.435	759	771	2	5	(15)		10	766	21.9
16	9	1925	E.Smith	329	31	1	361	103	22	3	8	.313	.374	.471	845	783	4	1	5	(10)	20	798	21.8
17	16	1969	M.Sanguillen	459	12	3	474	139	21	6	5	.303	.325	.407	732	749	8	4	0	10	10	769	20.7
18	14	1965	J.Pagliaroni	403	41	3	447	108	15	0	17	.268	.340	.432	772	793	0	0	0	(10)	(10)	773	20.4
19	18	1952	J.Garagiola	344	50	2	396	94	15	4	8	.273	.369	.410	779	789	0	1	(5)	(10)	(10)	764	17.1
20	24	1937	A.Todd	514	16	1	531	158	18	10	8	.307	.330	.428	758	749	2		(10)			739	16.4
21	19	1960	S.Burgess	337	35	0	372	99	15	2	7	.294	.360	.412	773	768	0	1	(5)	(10)	10	763	16.0
22	28	1973	M.Sanguillen	589	17	3	609	166	26	7	12	.282	.305	.411	716	722	2	5	(12)	10	10	730	15.2
23	22	1996	J.Kendall	414	35	15	464	124	23	5	3	.300	.375	.401	776	739	5	2	2	10	(10)	741	14.1
24	21	1993	D.Slaught	377	29	6	412	113	19	2	10	.300	.359	.440	800	774	2	1	0	(10)	(20)	744	13.1
25	25	1922	J.Gooch	353	39	5	397	116	15	3	1	.329	.403	.397	800	750	1	1	(2)		(10)	737	11.9

Pittsburgh Pirates
First basemen

V	R	Year	Name	AB	BB	HBP	TAB	H	2B	3B	HR	BA	OB	SA	PRO	Wtd PRO	SB	CS	SBF	SPF	FF	R TF	V HC
1	2	1941	E.Fletcher	521	118	2	641	150	29	13	11	.288	.421	.457	878	901	5			10	20	931	51.7
2	7	1982	J.Thompson	550	101	2	653	156	32	0	31	.284	.397	.511	908	922	1	0	1	(10)		913	44.6
3	3	1972	W.Stargell	495	65	2	562	145	28	2	33	.293	.377	.558	935	968	1	1	(2)	(10)	(30)	926	43.9
4	8	1942	E.Fletcher	506	105	6	617	146	22	5	7	.289	.417	.393	810	865	0			10	20	895	38.6
5	1	1978	W.Stargell	390	50	7	447	115	18	2	28	.295	.385	.567	951	968	3	2	(2)	(10)	(10)	946	37.4
6	9	1940	E.Fletcher	510	119	9	638	139	22	7	16	.273	.418	.437	856	861	5			10	10	881	35.3
7	6	1970	B.Robertson	390	51	2	443	112	19	4	27	.287	.372	.564	937	913	4	1	4			917	31.1
8	4	1950	J.Hopp	345	51	1	397	117	26	6	9	.339	.426	.528	953	913	7	1		10		923	30.4
9	5	1981	J.Thompson	223	59	0	282	54	13	0	15	.242	.401	.502	903	929	0	0	0	(10)		919	30.3
10	17	1936	G.Suhr	583	95	2	680	182	33	12	11	.312	.410	.467	877	857	8					857	29.7
11	12	1966	D.Clendenon	571	52	2	625	171	22	10	28	.299	.360	.520	880	889	8	7	(9)	10	(20)	870	29.7
12	11	1971	B.Robertson	469	60	4	533	127	18	2	26	.271	.358	.484	842	868	1	2	(5)	(10)	20	873	26.1
13	19	1943	E.Fletcher	544	95	6	645	154	24	5	9	.283	.395	.395	791	830	1				20	850	26.0
14	10	1979	W.Stargell	424	47	3	474	119	19	0	32	.281	.357	.552	908	901	0	1	(4)	(10)	(10)	877	24.1
15	14	1975	W.Stargell	461	58	3	522	136	32	2	22	.295	.377	.516	894	904	0	0	0	(10)	(30)	864	23.3
16	18	1961	D.Stuart	532	34	4	570	160	28	8	35	.301	.347	.581	928	891	0	3	(10)	(10)	(20)	851	23.3
17	15	1926	G.Grantham	449	60	1	510	143	27	13	8	.318	.400	.490	890	868	6				(10)	858	22.4
18	16	1947	H.Greenberg	402	104	4	510	100	13	2	25	.249	.408	.478	885	857	0					857	22.3
19	21	1923	C.Grimm	563	41	0	604	194	29	13	7	.345	.389	.480	869	832	6	9	(19)		30	843	22.2
20	13	1959	D.Stuart	397	42	2	441	118	15	2	27	.297	.367	.549	916	890	1	1	(2)		(20)	868	21.6
21	20	1977	B.Robinson	507	25	3	535	154	32	1	26	.304	.340	.525	865	840	12	6	0	10		850	20.3
22	24	1986	S.Bream	522	60	1	583	140	37	5	16	.268	.345	.450	795	797	13	7	(2)		40	835	18.2
23	23	1928	G.Grantham	440	59	4	503	142	24	9	10	.323	.408	.486	894	852	9				(10)	842	18.0
24	27	1996	J.King	591	70	2	663	160	36	4	30	.271	.350	.497	847	807	15	1	19			826	17.6
25	28	1938	G.Suhr	530	87	0	617	156	35	14	3	.294	.394	.430	824	825	4					825	17.0

Pittsburgh Pirates
Second basemen

V	R	Year	Name	AB	BB	HBP	TAB	H	2B	3B	HR	BA	OB	SA	PRO	Wtd PRO	SB	CS	SBF	SPF	FF	R TF	V HC
1	2	1962	B.Mazeroski	572	37	2	611	155	24	9	14	.271	.318	.418	735	719	0	3	(9)	10	110	830	42.0
2	3	1906	C.Ritchey	484	68	9	561	130	21	5	1	.269	.369	.339	708	806	6				20	826	39.5
3	7	1903	C.Ritchey	506	55	3	564	145	28	10	0	.287	.360	.381	741	771	15				40	811	39.0
4	4	1960	B.Mazeroski	538	40	1	579	147	21	5	11	.273	.325	.392	717	713	4	0	7	10	90	819	38.9
5	1	1929	G.Grantham	349	93	1	443	107	23	10	12	.307	.454	.533	987	890	10				(30)	860	38.7
6	5	1979	P.Garner	549	55	3	607	161	32	8	11	.293	.361	.441	802	795	17	8	2	10	10	816	37.9
7	8	1918	G.Cutshaw	463	27	1	491	132	16	10	5	.285	.326	.395	721	798	25			10		808	36.6
8	11	1966	B.Mazeroski	621	31	1	653	163	22	7	16	.262	.299	.398	696	703	4	3	(3)		100	800	35.8
9	14	1930	G.Grantham	552	81	2	635	179	34	14	18	.324	.413	.534	947	827	5				(30)	797	35.7
10	10	1909	D.Miller	560	39	3	602	156	31	13	3	.279	.329	.396	725	821	14				(20)	801	34.8
11	13	1984	J.Ray	555	37	3	595	173	38	6	6	.312	.358	.434	792	809	11	6	(2)		(10)	798	31.9
12	15	1963	B.Mazeroski	534	32	0	566	131	22	3	8	.245	.288	.343	631	663	2	0	3	10	120	797	30.1
13	9	1902	C.Ritchey	405	53	7	465	112	13	1	2	.277	.370	.328	698	781	10				20	801	29.7
14	16	1964	B.Mazeroski	601	29	0	630	161	22	8	10	.268	.302	.381	683	701	1	1	(2)		80	780	28.4
15	17	1927	G.Grantham	531	74	6	611	162	33	11	8	.305	.396	.454	850	828	9				(50)	778	28.2
16	18	1958	B.Mazeroski	567	25	3	595	156	24	6	19	.275	.309	.439	748	719	1	1	(2)	10	50	777	27.4
17	12	1922	C.Tierney	441	22	2	465	152	26	14	7	.345	.378	.515	893	837	7	8	(18)	10	(30)	799	26.5
18	19	1904	C.Ritchey	544	59	3	606	143	22	12	0	.263	.338	.347	686	771	12					771	26.0
19	6	1933	T.Piet	362	19	6	387	117	21	5	1	.323	.367	.417	784	815	12			10	(10)	815	25.2
20	23	1986	J.Ray	579	58	3	640	174	33	0	7	.301	.367	.394	761	763	6	9	(18)		20	765	24.4
21	21	1913	J.Viox	492	64	3	559	156	32	8	2	.317	.399	.427	826	858	14				(90)	768	23.3
22	25	1983	J.Ray	576	35	0	611	163	38	7	5	.283	.324	.399	723	729	18	9	0		30	759	21.6
23	30	1901	C.Ritchey	540	47	4	591	160	20	4	1	.296	.357	.354	711	750	15					750	21.1
24	26	1907	E.Abbaticchio	496	65	8	569	130	14	7	2	.262	.357	.331	687	788	35			10	(40)	758	20.7
25	28	1961	B.Mazeroski	558	26	3	587	148	21	2	13	.265	.302	.380	681	654	2	1	0	10	90	754	20.4

Pittsburgh Pirates
Shortstops

V	R	Year	Name	AB	BB	HBP	TAB	H	2B	3B	HR	BA	OB	SA	PRO	Wtd PRO	SB	CS	SBF	SPF	FF	R TF	V HC
1	1	1908	H.Wagner	568	54	5	627	201	39	19	10	.354	.415	.542	957	1,117	53			10	40	1,167	158.5
2	4	1905	H.Wagner	548	54	7	609	199	32	14	6	.363	.427	.505	932	1,017	57			10	70	1,097	132.9
3	2	1907	H.Wagner	515	46	5	566	180	38	14	6	.350	.408	.513	921	1,055	61			10	40	1,105	125.7
4	7	1935	A.Vaughan	499	97	7	603	192	34	10	19	.385	.491	.607	1,098	1,074	4			10	(10)	1,074	124.4
5	6	1906	H.Wagner	516	58	10	584	175	38	9	2	.339	.416	.459	875	997	53			10	80	1,087	124.3
6	8	1903	H.Wagner	512	44	7	563	182	30	19	5	.355	.414	.518	931	968	46			10	80	1,058	123.0
7	3	1904	H.Wagner	490	59	4	553	171	44	14	4	.349	.423	.520	944	1,061	53			10	30	1,101	121.6
8	5	1909	H.Wagner	495	66	3	564	168	39	10	5	.339	.420	.489	909	1,028	35			10	50	1,088	120.5
9	9	1901	H.Wagner	549	53	7	609	194	37	11	6	.353	.417	.494	911	961	49			10	50	1,021	120.5
10	11	1912	H.Wagner	558	59	6	623	181	35	20	7	.324	.395	.496	891	886	26			10	80	976	98.1
11	10	1911	H.Wagner	473	67	6	546	158	23	16	9	.334	.423	.507	930	951	20			10	30	991	89.9
12	12	1934	A.Vaughan	558	94	2	654	186	41	11	12	.333	.431	.511	942	915	10			10		925	86.1
13	15	1936	A.Vaughan	568	118	5	691	190	30	11	9	.335	.453	.474	927	906	6			10	(20)	896	81.0
14	14	1938	A.Vaughan	541	104	2	647	174	35	5	7	.322	.433	.444	876	878	14			10	20	908	79.6
15	13	1910	H.Wagner	556	59	5	620	178	34	8	4	.320	.390	.432	822	871	24			10	30	911	77.4
16	16	1933	A.Vaughan	573	64	5	642	180	29	19	9	.314	.388	.478	866	900	3			10	(20)	890	73.5
17	18	1940	A.Vaughan	594	88	3	685	178	40	15	7	.300	.393	.453	846	850	12			10	10	870	71.5
18	19	1993	J.Bell	604	77	6	687	187	32	9	9	.310	.393	.437	830	804	16	10	(6)		70	868	67.5
19	21	1915	H.Wagner	566	39	4	609	155	32	17	6	.274	.325	.422	747	824	22	15	(12)	10	30	852	58.0
20	23	1939	A.Vaughan	595	70	6	671	182	30	11	6	.306	.385	.424	808	791	12			10	20	821	53.5
21	20	1937	A.Vaughan	469	54	2	525	151	17	17	5	.322	.394	.463	857	847	7			10		857	51.4
22	17	1941	A.Vaughan	374	50	2	426	118	20	7	6	.316	.399	.455	854	876	8			10	(10)	876	45.6
23	27	1994	J.Bell	424	49	3	476	117	35	4	9	.276	.355	.441	796	749	2	0	4		40	793	42.1
24	25	1967	G.Alley	550	36	7	593	158	25	7	6	.287	.339	.391	730	763	10	5	0	10	30	803	39.9
25	26	1966	G.Alley	579	27	5	611	173	28	10	7	.299	.336	.418	753	761	8	8	(12)	10	40	799	39.7

Pittsburgh Pirates
Third basemen

V	R	Year	Name	AB	BB	HBP	TAB	H	2B	3B	HR	BA	OB	SA	PRO	Wtd PRO	SB	CS	SBF	SPF	FF	R TF	V HC
1	2	1923	P.Traynor	616	34	5	655	208	19	19	12	.338	.377	.489	866	829	28	13	3	10	70	912	64.3
2	1	1981	B.Madlock	279	34	3	316	95	23	1	6	.341	.418	.495	912	939	18	6	18	10	(10)	957	54.8
3	4	1902	T.Leach	514	45	4	563	143	14	22	6	.278	.341	.426	767	858	25			10	20	888	53.4
4	5	1982	B.Madlock	568	48	4	620	181	33	3	19	.319	.376	.488	863	877	18	6	9	10	(10)	886	50.2
5	6	1927	P.Traynor	573	22	3	598	196	32	9	5	.342	.370	.455	825	803	11			10	70	883	50.1
6	9	1925	P.Traynor	591	52	2	645	189	39	14	6	.320	.377	.464	840	778	15	9	(4)	10	80	864	47.8
7	3	1972	R.Hebner	427	52	6	485	128	24	4	19	.300	.384	.508	892	923	0	0	0	(20)		903	45.4
8	12	1989	B.Bonilla	616	76	1	693	173	37	10	24	.281	.361	.490	851	883	8	8	(11)	(20)		853	45.0
9	11	1988	B.Bonilla	584	85	4	673	160	32	7	24	.274	.370	.476	846	885	3	5	(10)	(20)		855	44.5
10	10	1944	B.Elliott	538	75	0	613	160	28	16	10	.297	.383	.465	848	869	9			(10)		859	43.8
11	17	1910	B.Byrne	602	66	1	669	178	43	12	2	.296	.366	.417	783	830	36			10		840	41.5
12	8	1930	P.Traynor	497	48	1	546	182	22	11	9	.366	.423	.509	932	814	7			10	40	864	40.5
13	15	1943	B.Elliott	581	56	1	638	183	30	12	7	.315	.376	.444	820	862	4			(20)		842	40.1
14	13	1928	P.Traynor	569	28	1	598	192	38	12	3	.337	.370	.462	832	792	12			10	40	842	37.8
15	16	1903	T.Leach	507	40	2	549	151	16	17	7	.298	.352	.438	789	821	22			10	10	841	37.7
16	18	1908	T.Leach	583	54	2	639	151	24	16	5	.259	.324	.381	705	822	24			10		832	37.2
17	19	1926	P.Traynor	574	38	1	613	182	25	17	3	.317	.361	.436	796	776	8			10	40	826	33.8
18	24	1960	D.Hoak	553	74	1	628	156	24	9	16	.282	.368	.445	813	808	3	2	(2)	10		816	31.6
19	7	1940	D.Garms	358	23	1	382	127	23	7	5	.355	.395	.500	895	900	3			(20)		880	31.4
20	27	1904	T.Leach	579	45	5	629	149	15	12	2	.257	.316	.335	651	732	23			10	70	812	30.3
21	20	1932	P.Traynor	513	32	4	549	169	27	10	2	.329	.373	.433	806	786	6			10	30	826	30.2
22	21	1929	P.Traynor	540	30	3	573	192	27	12	4	.356	.393	.472	865	780	13			10	30	820	29.7
23	23	1961	D.Hoak	503	73	3	579	150	27	7	12	.298	.390	.451	842	808	4	2	0	10		818	29.6
24	28	1942	B.Elliott	560	52	2	614	166	26	7	9	.296	.358	.416	774	827	2			(20)		807	27.9
25	14	1901	T.Leach	374	20	4	398	114	12	13	2	.305	.347	.422	769	812	16			10	20	842	27.5

Pittsburgh Pirates
Outfielders

V	R	Year	Name	AB	BB	HBP	TAB	H	2B	3B	HR	BA	OB	SA	PRO	Wtd PRO	SB	CS	SBF	SPF	FF	R TF	V HC
1	1	1992	B.Bonds	473	127	5	605	147	36	5	34	.311	.461	.624	1,085	1,116	39	8	36	10	60	1,222	134.0
2	6	1949	R.Kiner	549	117	1	667	170	19	5	54	.310	.432	.658	1,089	1,064	6			(20)		1,044	95.7
3	2	1990	B.Bonds	519	93	3	615	156	32	3	33	.301	.410	.565	974	973	52	13	40	10	60	1,083	95.3
4	3	1967	R.Clemente	585	41	3	629	209	26	10	23	.357	.402	.554	956	1,000	9	1	11	10	50	1,070	93.8
5	11	1951	R.Kiner	531	137	2	670	164	31	6	42	.309	.452	.627	1,079	1,057	2	1	0	(30)		1,027	90.4
6	9	1900	H.Wagner	527	41	8	576	201	45	22	4	.381	.434	.573	1,007	1,008	38			10	20	1,038	89.2
7	4	1991	B.Bonds	510	107	4	621	149	28	5	25	.292	.419	.514	932	951	43	13	26	10	70	1,057	88.6
8	5	1978	D.Parker	581	57	2	640	194	32	12	30	.334	.395	.585	981	997	20	7	9	10	30	1,046	88.1
9	12	1947	R.Kiner	565	98	2	665	177	23	4	51	.313	.417	.639	1,055	1,022	1			(10)		1,012	84.9
10	14	1927	P.Waner	623	60	3	686	237	42	18	9	.380	.437	.549	986	960	5			10	30	1,000	83.5
11	13	1902	H.Wagner	534	43	14	591	176	30	16	3	.330	.394	.463	857	958	42			10	40	1,008	81.8
12	8	1971	W.Stargell	511	83	7	601	151	26	0	48	.295	.401	.628	1,029	1,061	0	0	0	(10)	(10)	1,041	81.1
13	21	1925	K.Cuyler	617	58	13	688	220	43	26	18	.357	.423	.598	1,021	946	41	13	21	10	10	986	79.0
14	10	1973	W.Stargell	522	80	3	605	156	43	3	44	.299	.395	.646	1,041	1,049	0	0	0	(10)	(10)	1,029	78.4
15	7	1969	R.Clemente	507	56	3	566	175	20	12	19	.345	.413	.544	958	980	4	1	3	10	50	1,043	77.1
16	16	1992	A.Van Slyke	614	58	4	676	199	45	12	14	.324	.386	.505	891	917	12	3	8	10	60	995	76.6
17	22	1928	P.Waner	602	77	5	684	223	50	19	6	.370	.446	.547	992	945	6			10	20	975	74.7
18	15	1961	R.Clemente	572	35	3	610	201	30	10	23	.351	.392	.559	951	914	4	1	3	10	70	997	73.2
19	18	1988	A.Van Slyke	587	57	1	645	169	23	15	25	.288	.352	.506	858	897	30	9	18	10	70	995	72.9
20	23	1966	R.Clemente	638	46	0	684	202	31	11	29	.317	.363	.536	899	907	7	5	(4)	10	60	973	70.4
21	35	1922	M.Carey	629	80	4	713	207	28	12	10	.329	.408	.459	868	813	51	2	62	10	60	946	67.3
22	28	1979	D.Parker	622	67	9	698	193	45	7	25	.310	.385	.526	911	903	20	4	16	10	30	960	67.2
23	31	1977	D.Parker	637	58	7	702	215	44	8	21	.338	.399	.531	929	902	17	19	(28)	10	70	954	65.8
24	26	1964	R.Clemente	622	51	2	675	211	40	7	12	.339	.391	.484	875	899	5	2	1	10	50	961	65.3
25	30	2000	B.Giles	559	114	7	680	176	37	7	35	.315	.437	.594	1,031	940	6	0	8	10		959	65.2

Pittsburgh Pirates
Outfielders

V	R	Year	Name	AB	BB	HBP	TAB	H	2B	3B	HR	BA	OB	SA	PRO	Wtd PRO	SB	CS	SBF	SPF	FF	R TF	V HC
26	32	1936	P.Waner	585	74	3	662	218	53	9	5	.373	.446	.520	965	944	7				10	954	65.1
27	29	1902	G.Beaumont	541	39	4	584	193	21	6	0	.357	.404	.418	822	919	33			10	30	959	65.0
28	17	1968	R.Clemente	502	51	1	554	146	18	12	18	.291	.357	.482	839	922	2	3	(7)	10	70	995	62.6
29	19	1903	F.Clarke	427	41	5	473	150	32	15	5	.351	.414	.532	946	983	21			10		993	61.6
30	38	1934	P.Waner	599	68	2	669	217	32	16	14	.362	.429	.539	968	940	8					940	61.3
31	25	1999	B.Giles	521	95	3	619	164	33	3	39	.315	.423	.614	1,037	949	6	2	3	10		962	60.4
32	27	1902	F.Clarke	459	51	14	524	145	27	14	2	.316	.401	.449	850	950	29			10		960	58.6
33	34	1926	P.Waner	536	66	4	606	180	35	22	8	.336	.413	.528	941	917	11			10	20	947	57.6
34	45	1916	M.Carey	599	59	7	665	158	23	11	7	.264	.337	.374	711	794	63	19	36	10	90	929	57.3
35	44	1901	F.Clarke	527	51	10	588	171	24	15	6	.324	.395	.461	856	903	23			10	20	933	56.9
36	46	1950	R.Kiner	547	122	3	672	149	21	6	47	.272	.408	.590	998	956	2				(30)	926	56.8
37	41	1965	R.Clemente	589	43	5	637	194	21	14	10	.329	.380	.463	843	867	8	0	12	10	50	938	55.0
38	24	1971	R.Clemente	522	26	0	548	178	29	8	13	.341	.372	.502	874	901	1	2	(5)	10	60	966	54.4
39	49	1917	M.Carey	588	58	10	656	174	21	12	1	.296	.369	.378	746	832	46			10	80	922	54.3
40	54	1923	M.Carey	610	73	7	690	188	32	19	6	.308	.388	.452	841	805	51	8	48	10	50	913	53.9
41	53	1932	P.Waner	630	56	2	688	215	62	10	8	.341	.397	.510	906	884	13			10	20	914	53.9
42	37	1988	B.Bonds	538	72	2	612	152	30	5	24	.283	.369	.491	860	899	17	11	(8)	10	40	942	53.7
43	36	1975	D.Parker	558	38	5	601	172	35	10	25	.308	.358	.541	899	909	8	6	(6)	10	30	943	53.1
44	56	1944	J.Russell	580	79	5	664	181	34	14	8	.312	.399	.460	859	881	6			10	20	911	51.0
45	51	1989	B.Bonds	580	93	1	674	144	34	6	19	.248	.353	.426	779	809	32	10	17	10	80	915	50.8
46	48	1963	R.Clemente	600	31	4	635	192	23	8	17	.320	.357	.470	827	871	12	2	12	10	30	922	49.9
47	43	1969	W.Stargell	522	61	6	589	160	31	6	29	.307	.385	.556	941	963	1	0	2	(10)	(20)	934	49.6
48	20	1970	R.Clemente	412	38	2	452	145	22	10	14	.352	.409	.556	965	941	3	0	6	10	30	987	49.5
49	60	1948	R.Kiner	555	112	3	670	147	19	5	40	.265	.391	.533	924	913	1				(10)	903	48.8
50	47	1974	W.Stargell	508	87	6	601	153	37	4	25	.301	.409	.537	947	962	0	2	(6)	(10)	(20)	925	48.1
51	69	1903	G.Beaumont	613	44	5	662	209	30	6	7	.341	.390	.444	833	866	23			10	10	886	47.1
52	66	1929	P.Waner	596	89	3	688	200	43	15	15	.336	.424	.534	958	864	15			10	20	894	47.0
53	57	1925	M.Carey	542	66	4	612	186	39	13	5	.343	.418	.491	909	842	46	11	37	10	20	909	46.6
54	42	1966	W.Stargell	485	48	6	539	153	30	0	33	.315	.384	.581	965	975	2	3	(7)		(30)	938	46.4
55	40	1924	K.Cuyler	466	30	7	503	165	27	16	9	.354	.402	.539	940	910	32	11	19	10		939	45.8
56	52	1907	F.Clarke	501	68	8	577	145	18	13	2	.289	.383	.389	772	885	37			10	20	915	45.6
57	59	1907	T.Leach	547	40	1	588	166	19	12	4	.303	.352	.404	756	866	43			10	30	906	43.9
58	64	1916	B.Hinchman	555	54	2	611	175	18	16	4	.315	.378	.427	805	899	10					899	43.4
59	61	1987	A.Van Slyke	564	56	4	624	165	36	11	21	.293	.361	.507	868	834	34	8	27	10	30	902	42.9
60	73	1933	P.Waner	618	60	2	680	191	38	16	7	.309	.372	.456	828	861	3				20	881	42.2
61	68	1991	B.Bonilla	577	90	2	669	174	44	6	18	.302	.398	.492	890	908	2	4	(8)		(10)	889	42.0
62	63	1987	B.Bonds	551	54	3	608	144	34	9	25	.261	.331	.492	822	791	32	10	19	10	80	900	41.2
63	33	1980	M.Easler	393	43	0	436	133	27	3	21	.338	.404	.583	986	999	5	9	(28)		(20)	951	40.2
64	74	1909	F.Clarke	550	80	6	636	158	16	11	3	.287	.384	.373	756	856	31				20	876	37.7
65	39	1972	R.Clemente	378	29	0	407	118	19	7	10	.312	.361	.479	840	869	0	0	0	10	60	939	37.1
66	67	1976	D.Parker	537	30	2	569	168	28	10	13	.313	.351	.475	826	853	19	7	8	10	20	891	36.2
67	50	1911	F.Clarke	392	53	2	447	127	25	13	5	.324	.407	.492	900	919	10					919	36.2
68	86	1901	G.Beaumont	558	44	2	604	185	14	5	8	.332	.382	.418	800	844	36			10	10	864	35.5
69	55	1906	F.Clarke	417	40	1	458	129	14	13	1	.309	.371	.412	784	892	18			10	10	912	35.5
70	83	1931	P.Waner	559	73	4	636	180	35	10	6	.322	.404	.453	857	839	6				30	869	35.5
71	77	1938	J.Rizzo	555	54	5	614	167	31	9	23	.301	.368	.514	882	883	1			10	(20)	873	35.5
72	81	1974	A.Oliver	617	33	5	655	198	38	12	11	.321	.360	.475	835	848	10	1	12	10		870	35.1
73	80	1912	O.Wilson	583	35	2	620	175	19	36	11	.300	.342	.513	855	850	16			10	10	870	34.9
74	76	1911	O.Wilson	544	41	4	589	163	34	12	12	.300	.353	.472	826	843	10			10	20	873	34.2
75	96	1926	K.Cuyler	614	50	9	673	197	31	15	8	.321	.380	.459	840	819	35			10	30	859	34.2

**Pittsburgh Pirates
Starting Pitchers**

V	R	Year	Name	G	GS	IP	W	L	SV	SO	BB	ERA	RA/9	R Wtd RA/9	V Runs /162
1	5	1902	J.Chesbro	35	33	286	28	6	1	136	62	2.17	2.55	2.88	61.8
2	8	1906	V.Willis	41	36	322	23	13	1	124	76	1.73	2.35	2.94	60.8
3	6	1903	S.Leever	36	34	284	25	7	1	90	60	2.06	3.13	2.91	60.1
4	7	1913	B.Adams	43	37	314	21	10	0	144	49	2.15	2.69	2.94	59.4
5	3	1919	B.Adams	34	29	263	17	10	1	92	23	1.98	2.26	2.83	58.4
6	9	1909	H.Camnitz	41	30	283	25	6	3	133	68	1.62	2.39	2.98	52.3
7	12	1911	B.Adams	40	37	293	22	12	0	133	42	2.33	2.98	3.04	51.8
8	21	1901	J.Chesbro	36	28	288	21	10	1	129	52	2.38	3.25	3.16	51.6
9	1	1977	J.Candelaria	33	33	231	20	5	0	133	50	2.34	2.50	2.59	50.5
10	31	1911	L.Leifield	42	37	318	16	16	1	111	82	2.63	3.23	3.30	46.7
11	35	1903	D.Phillippe	36	33	289	25	9	2	123	29	2.43	3.58	3.33	45.6
12	4	1927	R.Kremer	35	28	226	19	8	2	63	53	2.47	2.91	2.87	44.6
13	26	1909	V.Willis	39	35	290	22	11	1	95	83	2.24	2.61	3.25	44.3
14	45	1901	D.Phillippe	37	32	296	22	12	2	103	38	2.22	3.50	3.41	43.7
15	20	1959	V.Law	34	33	266	18	9	1	110	53	2.98	3.08	3.15	43.6
16	10	1945	P.Roe	33	31	235	14	13	1	148	46	2.87	2.95	2.99	42.9
17	17	1915	A.Mamaux	38	31	252	21	8	0	152	96	2.04	2.50	3.12	42.3
18	27	1901	J.Tannehill	32	30	252	18	10	1	118	36	2.18	3.35	3.26	42.0
19	40	1902	D.Phillippe	31	30	272	20	9	0	122	26	2.05	2.98	3.36	41.8
20	19	1935	C.Blanton	35	31	254	18	13	1	142	55	2.58	3.30	3.15	41.7
21	13	1926	R.Kremer	37	26	231	20	6	5	74	51	2.61	3.08	3.05	40.7
22	41	1912	C.Hendrix	39	32	289	24	9	1	176	105	2.59	3.43	3.36	40.4
23	34	1912	H.Camnitz	41	32	277	22	12	2	121	82	2.83	3.38	3.31	40.3
24	14	1975	J.Reuss	32	32	237	18	11	0	131	78	2.54	2.77	3.06	39.5
25	39	1905	D.Phillippe	38	33	279	20	13	0	133	48	2.19	3.06	3.35	39.3
26	53	1900	D.Phillippe	38	33	279	20	13	0	75	42	2.84	4.10	3.47	39.1
27	23	1986	R.Rhoden	34	34	254	15	12	0	159	76	2.84	2.91	3.18	38.9
28	32	1920	B.Adams	35	33	263	17	13	2	84	18	2.16	2.84	3.30	38.6
29	43	1960	B.Friend	38	37	276	18	12	1	183	45	3.00	3.16	3.39	37.7
30	70	1918	W.Cooper	38	29	273	19	14	3	117	65	2.11	2.84	3.59	37.6
31	2	1912	H.Robinson	33	16	175	12	7	2	79	30	2.26	2.78	2.72	37.5
32	33	1900	S.Leever	30	29	233	15	13	0	84	48	2.71	3.91	3.31	37.5
33	72	1920	W.Cooper	44	37	327	24	15	2	114	52	2.39	3.11	3.62	36.0
34	15	1965	V.Law	29	28	217	17	9	0	101	35	2.15	2.74	3.10	35.2
35	29	1968	B.Veale	36	33	245	13	14	0	171	94	2.05	2.46	3.28	34.8
36	37	1902	S.Leever	28	26	222	15	7	2	86	31	2.39	2.96	3.34	34.8
37	42	1972	S.Blass	33	32	250	19	8	0	117	84	2.49	2.88	3.37	34.6
38	69	1922	W.Cooper	41	36	295	23	14	0	129	61	3.18	3.97	3.58	33.6
39	49	1902	J.Tannehill	26	24	231	20	6	0	100	25	1.95	3.04	3.43	33.5
40	36	1921	W.Glazner	36	25	234	14	5	1	88	58	2.77	3.38	3.33	33.5
41	11	1985	R.Reuschel	31	26	194	14	8	1	138	52	2.27	2.69	3.01	33.3
42	50	1904	S.Leever	34	32	253	18	11	0	63	54	2.17	3.03	3.43	33.2
43	28	1990	D.Drabek	33	33	231	22	6	0	131	56	2.76	3.03	3.26	33.2
44	64	1912	M.O'Toole	37	36	275	15	17	0	150	159	2.71	3.60	3.53	33.1
45	48	1962	B.Friend	39	36	262	18	14	1	144	53	3.06	3.40	3.43	32.9
46	54	1963	B.Friend	39	38	269	17	16	0	144	44	2.34	2.91	3.47	32.4
47	24	1935	B.Swift	39	21	204	15	8	1	74	37	2.70	3.35	3.20	32.3
48	62	1900	J.Tannehill	29	27	234	20	6	0	50	43	2.88	4.15	3.51	31.5
49	73	1904	P.Flaherty	34	33	285	20	11	0	68	69	2.05	3.19	3.62	31.3
50	52	1992	D.Drabek	34	34	257	15	11	0	177	54	2.77	2.95	3.46	31.2

Pittsburgh Pirates
Starting Pitchers

V	R	Year	Name	G	GS	IP	W	L	SV	SO	BB	ERA	RA/9	R Wtd RA/9	V Runs /162
51	65	1924	R.Kremer	41	30	259	18	10	1	64	51	3.19	3.54	3.54	30.9
52	56	1916	W.Cooper	42	23	246	12	11	2	111	74	1.87	2.63	3.48	30.9
53	60	1974	J.Rooker	33	33	263	15	11	0	139	83	2.78	3.19	3.50	30.8
54	80	1914	B.Adams	40	35	283	13	16	1	91	39	2.51	3.08	3.65	30.1
55	46	1984	R.Rhoden	33	33	238	14	9	0	136	62	2.72	3.06	3.42	30.1
56	25	1924	E.Yde	33	22	194	16	3	0	53	62	2.83	3.25	3.25	29.7
57	75	1964	B.Veale	40	38	280	18	12	0	250	124	2.74	3.21	3.62	29.1
58	58	1929	B.Grimes	33	29	233	17	7	2	62	70	3.13	4.17	3.49	29.0
59	93	1922	J.Morrison	45	33	286	17	11	1	104	87	3.43	4.09	3.69	29.0
60	59	1900	R.Waddell	29	22	209	8	13	0	130	55	2.37	4.14	3.50	28.4
61	104	1917	W.Cooper	40	34	298	17	11	1	99	54	2.36	2.90	3.74	28.3
62	100	1933	L.French	47	35	291	18	13	1	88	55	2.72	3.28	3.73	28.2
63	79	1906	S.Leever	36	31	260	22	7	0	76	48	2.32	2.91	3.64	27.8
64	117	1919	W.Cooper	35	32	287	19	13	1	106	74	2.67	3.04	3.81	27.7
65	91	1960	V.Law	35	35	272	20	9	0	120	40	3.08	3.44	3.69	27.6
66	66	1989	D.Drabek	35	34	244	14	12	0	123	69	2.80	3.06	3.54	27.6
67	125	1928	B.Grimes	48	37	331	25	14	3	97	77	2.99	3.97	3.85	27.4
68	18	1932	S.Swetonic	24	19	163	11	6	0	39	55	2.82	3.15	3.13	27.2
69	115	1923	J.Morrison	42	37	302	25	13	2	114	110	3.49	4.05	3.79	27.1
70	105	1944	R.Sewell	38	33	286	21	12	2	87	99	3.18	3.52	3.75	27.0
71	67	1971	S.Blass	33	33	240	15	8	0	136	68	2.85	3.04	3.54	27.0
72	38	1937	R.Bauers	34	19	188	13	6	1	118	80	2.88	3.35	3.34	26.7
73	95	1943	R.Sewell	35	31	265	21	9	3	65	75	2.54	3.19	3.71	26.3
74	16	1970	L.Walker	42	19	163	15	6	3	124	89	3.04	3.09	3.11	26.2
75	57	1968	S.Blass	33	31	220	18	6	0	132	57	2.12	2.62	3.49	26.1
76	22	1921	B.Adams	25	20	160	14	5	0	55	18	2.64	3.21	3.17	26.0
77	44	1934	W.Hoyt	48	15	191	15	6	5	105	43	2.93	3.53	3.39	26.0
78	92	1966	B.Veale	38	37	268	16	12	0	229	102	3.02	3.32	3.69	25.8
79	86	1914	B.Harmon	37	30	245	13	17	3	61	55	2.53	3.09	3.66	25.8
80	124	1908	V.Willis	41	38	305	23	11	0	97	69	2.07	2.80	3.84	25.4
81	77	1959	H.Haddix	31	29	224	12	12	0	149	49	3.13	3.54	3.63	24.4
82	126	1907	V.Willis	39	37	293	21	11	1	107	69	2.34	2.95	3.85	24.1
83	119	1931	H.Meine	36	35	284	19	13	0	58	87	2.98	3.83	3.84	23.9
84	55	1940	R.Sewell	33	23	190	16	5	1	60	67	2.80	3.36	3.48	23.9
85	99	1944	F.Ostermueller	38	28	246	13	8	2	97	77	2.81	3.50	3.73	23.9
86	149	1921	W.Cooper	38	38	327	22	14	0	134	80	3.25	3.99	3.94	23.8
87	106	1965	B.Veale	39	37	266	17	12	0	276	119	2.84	3.32	3.75	23.7
88	63	1943	M.Butcher	33	21	194	10	8	1	45	57	2.60	3.02	3.51	23.7
89	76	1987	R.Reuschel	34	33	227	13	9	0	107	42	3.09	3.61	3.62	23.5
90	137	1927	L.Meadows	40	38	299	19	10	0	84	66	3.40	3.94	3.89	23.4
91	135	1923	W.Cooper	39	38	295	17	19	0	77	71	3.57	4.15	3.88	23.2
92	30	1919	H.Carlson	22	14	141	8	10	0	49	39	2.23	2.62	3.28	23.1
93	51	1936	R.Lucas	27	22	176	15	4	0	53	26	3.18	3.58	3.44	22.9
94	71	1955	B.Friend	44	20	200	14	9	2	98	52	2.83	3.60	3.59	22.6
95	121	1911	H.Camnitz	40	33	268	20	15	1	139	84	3.13	3.76	3.84	22.4
96	90	1905	C.Case	31	24	217	11	11	1	57	66	2.57	3.36	3.68	22.2
97	82	1998	F.Cordova	33	33	220	13	14	0	157	69	3.31	3.71	3.65	22.1
98	85	1996	D.Neagle	33	33	221	16	9	0	149	48	3.50	3.78	3.66	22.1
99	107	1958	R.Kline	32	32	237	13	16	0	109	92	3.53	3.65	3.76	22.0
100	88	1902	E.Doheny	22	21	188	16	4	0	88	61	2.53	3.25	3.67	21.5

Pittsburgh Pirates
Relief Pitchers

V	R	Year	Name	G	GS	IP	W	L	SV	SO	BB	ERA	RA/9	R Wtd RA/9	V Runs /162
1	1	1977	R.Gossage	72	0	133	11	9	26	151	49	1.62	1.83	1.90	39.3
2	6	1982	R.Scurry	76	0	104	4	5	14	94	64	1.74	2.26	2.52	23.5
3	4	1962	R.Face	63	0	91	8	7	28	45	18	1.88	2.27	2.29	22.9
4	10	1968	R.Kline	56	0	113	12	5	7	48	31	1.68	2.07	2.76	22.6
5	12	1965	A.McBean	62	1	114	6	6	18	54	42	2.29	2.61	2.95	20.3
6	9	1983	K.Tekulve	76	0	99	7	5	18	52	36	1.64	2.45	2.71	20.3
7	5	1989	B.Landrum	56	0	81	2	3	26	51	28	1.67	2.00	2.31	20.2
8	2	1972	R.Hernandez	53	0	70	5	0	14	47	22	1.67	1.80	2.11	20.0
9	8	1964	A.McBean	58	0	90	8	3	22	41	17	1.91	2.30	2.59	19.6
10	27	1978	K.Tekulve	91	0	135	8	7	31	77	55	2.33	2.93	3.32	18.5
11	26	1979	K.Tekulve	94	0	134	10	8	31	75	49	2.75	3.08	3.32	18.4
12	11	1959	R.Face	57	0	93	18	1	10	69	25	2.70	2.81	2.88	18.3
13	15	1976	K.Tekulve	64	0	103	5	3	9	68	25	2.45	2.63	3.00	17.8
14	7	1972	D.Giusti	54	0	75	7	4	22	54	20	1.93	2.16	2.53	17.8
15	30	1967	A.McBean	51	8	131	7	4	4	54	43	2.54	2.82	3.35	17.6
16	24	1960	R.Face	68	0	115	10	8	24	72	29	2.90	3.05	3.27	17.3
17	20	1985	C.Guante	63	0	109	4	6	5	92	40	2.72	2.81	3.15	17.1
18	3	1999	S.Sauerbeck	65	0	68	4	1	2	55	38	2.00	2.53	2.28	17.1
19	18	1981	K.Tekulve	45	0	65	5	5	3	34	17	2.49	2.63	3.08	16.1
20	19	1973	D.Giusti	67	0	99	9	2	20	64	37	2.37	2.82	3.10	16.1
21	13	1973	R.Hernandez	59	0	90	4	5	11	64	25	2.41	2.70	2.96	15.9
22	31	1966	B.O'Dell	61	2	113	5	5	10	67	41	2.64	3.04	3.38	14.8
23	37	1975	L.Demery	45	8	115	7	5	4	59	43	2.90	3.13	3.45	14.1
24	29	1970	D.Giusti	66	1	103	9	3	26	85	39	3.06	3.32	3.34	13.9
25	41	1966	P.Mikkelsen	71	0	126	9	8	14	76	51	3.07	3.21	3.57	13.8
26	36	1951	T.Wilks	65	1	101	3	5	13	48	29	2.86	3.39	3.45	13.1
27	14	1990	B.Landrum	54	0	72	7	3	13	39	21	2.13	2.76	2.97	12.7
28	23	1985	A.Holland	56	0	87	1	5	5	62	31	2.90	2.90	3.25	12.7
29	47	1982	K.Tekulve	85	0	129	12	8	20	66	46	2.87	3.29	3.67	12.6
30	39	1987	D.Robinson	67	0	108	11	7	19	79	40	3.42	3.50	3.51	12.5
31	32	1990	B.Patterson	55	5	95	8	5	5	70	21	2.95	3.14	3.38	12.4
32	22	1962	D.Olivo	62	1	84	5	1	7	66	25	2.77	3.21	3.24	12.3
33	25	1958	R.Face	57	0	84	5	2	20	47	22	2.89	3.21	3.31	12.2
34	17	1974	R.Hernandez	58	0	69	5	2	2	33	18	2.75	2.75	3.02	11.8
35	48	1963	A.McBean	55	7	122	13	3	11	74	39	2.57	3.10	3.70	11.6
36	52	1979	E.Romo	84	0	129	10	5	5	106	43	2.99	3.48	3.75	11.6
37	50	1984	D.Robinson	51	1	122	5	6	10	110	49	3.02	3.32	3.71	11.5
38	51	1988	J.Robinson	75	0	125	11	5	9	87	39	3.03	3.18	3.74	11.3
39	16	1998	J.Christiansen	60	0	65	3	3	6	71	27	2.51	3.06	3.01	11.2
40	40	1958	B.Porterfield	39	6	92	4	6	5	40	19	3.33	3.42	3.53	11.1
41	33	1984	K.Tekulve	72	0	88	3	9	13	36	33	2.66	3.07	3.43	11.0
42	28	1967	R.Face	61	0	74	7	5	17	41	22	2.42	2.80	3.32	10.1
43	49	1977	K.Tekulve	72	0	103	10	1	7	59	33	3.06	3.58	3.71	9.7
44	21	1986	P.Clements	65	0	61	0	4	2	31	32	2.80	2.95	3.22	9.0
45	35	1980	G.Jackson	61	0	71	8	4	9	31	20	2.92	3.04	3.44	8.8
46	34	1966	R.Face	54	0	70	6	6	18	67	24	2.70	3.09	3.43	8.7
47	44	1988	B.Jones	59	0	82	3	3	3	48	38	2.84	3.06	3.60	8.7
48	46	1989	B.Kipper	52	0	83	3	4	4	58	33	2.93	3.14	3.63	8.5
49	69	1956	R.Face	68	3	135	12	13	6	96	42	3.52	3.80	4.04	8.2
50	45	1990	S.Ruskin	67	0	75	3	2	2	57	38	2.75	3.35	3.61	7.9

St. Louis Browns/ Baltimore Orioles (1901–2000)

This is the tale of two cities. The St. Louis Browns produced just 12 winning seasons and a single pennant in 53 years. The Browns were unable to compete with the more successful Cardinals for the fan base of a small city, and the team finally moved to Baltimore before the 1954 season. The Baltimore Orioles also failed to win the first six seasons in their new home. Then the Orioles went on a tear, with 24 winning seasons in 26 years, including eight postseason appearances. Although Baltimore's success dropped off since 1985, they still achieved winning records in nearly half their seasons, and they won their division in 1997.

The Browns began their existence in Milwaukee in 1901, featuring veteran fielding star Bobby Wallace at short. They moved to St. Louis in 1902 — at that time the nation's fourth largest city — and added pitcher Jack Powell and aging outfielder Jesse Burkett. George Stone arrived in 1905, and played brilliantly for a few short seasons. In 1906, Stone won the batting title with a .358 average. Since a 14 percent hitter's deflation raged that year, Stone hit for an adjusted .407 average, 1,044 Wtd. Production, and 91.8 Hits Contribution.

The Browns' most successful period was from 1916 to 1929, as the team managed six winning seasons in 14 years. George Sisler was an early star in this period and, over time, the team added Ken Williams, Baby Doll Jacobson, Marty McManus, and Urban Shocker. Sisler had his finest season in 1920, batting .407 with a major-league record 257 hits, 49 doubles, 18 triples, 19 home runs, and 42 stolen bases. Sisler actually finished a distant second to Babe Ruth in home runs that year. Adjusted for a 4 percent hitter's inflation, Sisler batted .392 with 19 home runs, for a 1,101 Total Factor and 112.7 Hits Contribution.

The Browns finished just one game behind the Yankees in 1922, led by league MVP Sisler's .420 average and 51 stolen bases. Williams hit .332 with 39 home runs and 37 stolen bases for a 990 Total Factor, while Shocker went 24–17 with a 2.97 ERA. The Browns floundered in 1923, as Sisler sat out the season with a double vision problem. Williams had his best season that year, batting .357 with 29 home runs and 18 steals, for a career-best 1,015 Wtd. Production and a 1,001 Total Factor.

The Browns failed to produce a winning season from 1930 to 1941. They did take advantage of a talent shortage during World War II to post three winning seasons and their first pennant. Their best players in the 1930s were Harlond Clift (.306, 29 home runs, 967 Total Factor in 1937) and Rick Ferrell. The wartime Browns teams were led by Vern Stephens (.289, league-leading 24 home runs in 1945), George McQuinn, and Nels Potter. After the war, the Browns/Orioles teams produced just one winning season from 1946 to 1959.

The team's resurgence in the 1960s was led by 1964 MVP Brooks Robinson (.317, 28 home runs, 956 Total Factor), Boog Powell, and Milt Pappas. Jim Gentile had one monster year at the plate in 1961, hitting .302 with 46 home runs for a 1,045 Wtd. Production. Frank Robinson was acquired from the Reds in 1966, and he proceeded to post a Triple Crown MVP season, hitting .316 with 49 home runs and 122 RBI, while leading the team to its first pennant in Baltimore. Adjusted for a 4 percent hitter's deflation, Robinson hit .330 with 51 home runs, for a career-best 1,098 Wtd. Production, a 1,105 Total Factor, and 111.6 Hits Contribution. Luis Aparicio, Davy Johnson, Dave McNally, and 20-year-old Jim Palmer also contributed to the 1966 team's success.

Beginning in 1968, the Orioles produced winning seasons for 18 consecutive seasons. The 1969 team won 109 games, but lost to the Miracle Mets in the World Series. The 1970 team won 108 games and the World Series against the Big Red Machine, while Boog Powell (.297, 35 home runs, 971 Wtd. Production) was selected the league's MVP. The 1971 team won "only" 101 games, but featured a pitching rotation of four 20 game winners in Palmer, McNally, Mike Cuellar, and Pat Dobson. The 1973 and 1974 teams won their division, but lost to the A's in the postseason. Jim Palmer produced his best season in 1975, going 23–11 with a 2.09 ERA and 2.55 Wtd. RA/9, while saving a team record 71.9 runs from scoring.

The 1979 team won 102 games and the pennant, but lost the World Series to the Pirates. This team featured steady Eddie Murray (.295, 25 home runs), Ken Singleton (.295, 35 home runs), Doug DeCinces, Mike Flanagan (23–9, 3.08 ERA), Dennis Martinez, and veteran Jim Palmer. Murray led the offense from 1981 to 1984 with four consecutive solid, interchangeable seasons, achieving annual Total Factors of around 970, and Hits Contributions ranging between 63.4 and 64.8.

The Orioles won their last World Series in 1983, led by Murray and MVP shortstop Cal Ripken, who batted .318 with 27 home runs. Ripken won his second MVP Award in 1991 with his best year, as he hit .323 with 34 home runs. Ripken's 1,015 Total Factor is the league's second best rate of success ever for a shortstop, while his 119.1 Hits Contribution is the league's highest volume of success ever at short. Ripken played in every game from early in 1982 to near the end of the 1998 season, setting a new "Iron Man" mark.

Other hitters with solid years in this current period included Chris Hoiles (.310, 29 home runs, 967 Total Factor in 1993), Brady Anderson (.297, 50 home runs, 985 Total Factor in 1996), and Rafael Palmeiro (.310, 39 home runs, 933 Total Factor in 1995). The best starting pitcher was Mike Mussina, who went 16–5 with a 3.06 ERA in 1994. Adjusted for hitter's inflation and a 162 game schedule, Mussina was 23–7 with a 2.78 Wtd. RA/9. The bullpen produced four pitchers with outstanding rates of success: Gregg Olson (1.89 Wtd. RA/9 in 1989), Mark Eichhorn (2.08 Wtd. RA/9 in 1994), Jesse Orosco (2.12 Wtd. RA/9 in 1997), and Randy Myers (1.66 Wtd. RA/9 in 1997).

St. Louis Browns/Baltimore Orioles   **Hitters Volume of Success**

Pos	Year	Name	AB	BB	HBP	TAB	H	2B	3B	HR	BA	OB	SA	PRO	Wtd PRO	SB	CS	SBF	SPF	FF	R TF	V HC
C	1993	C.Hoiles	419	69	9	497	130	28	0	29	.310	.419	.585	1,003	979	1	1	(2)	0	(10)	967	68.6
1B	1920	G.Sisler	631	46	2	679	257	49	18	19	.407	.449	.632	1,082	1,040	42	17	11	10	40	1,101	112.7
2B	1996	R.Alomar	588	90	1	679	193	43	4	22	.328	.418	.527	945	865	17	6	7	10	60	942	83.0
SS	1991	C.Ripken	650	53	5	708	210	46	5	34	.323	.379	.566	945	950	6	1	5	0	60	1,015	119.1
3B	1937	H.Clift	571	98	6	675	175	36	7	29	.306	.413	.546	960	880	8	5	(3)	0	90	967	84.9
OF	1966	F.Robinson	576	87	10	673	182	34	2	49	.316	.415	.637	1,052	1,098	8	5	(3)	10	0	1,105	111.6
OF	1906	G.Stone	581	52	7	640	208	25	20	6	.358	.417	.501	918	1,044	35			10	(10)	1,044	91.8
OF	1922	K.Williams	585	74	7	666	194	34	11	39	.332	.413	.627	1,040	984	37	20	(4)	10	0	990	77.7
Starters		Averages	575	71	6	652	194	37	8	28	.337	.415	.578	993	979	19	7	1	6	29	1,016	93.7
C	2000	C.Johnson	421	52	1	474	128	24	0	31	.304	.382	.582	964	882	2	0	4	(10)	20	896	49.4
1B	1961	J.Gentile	486	96	11	593	147	25	2	46	.302	.428	.646	1,074	1,045	1	1	(2)	(10)	(20)	1,013	68.7
2B	1974	B.Grich	582	90	20	692	153	29	6	19	.263	.380	.431	811	850	17	11	(7)	10	30	883	65.1
SS	1945	V.Stephens	571	55	1	627	165	27	3	24	.289	.352	.473	825	868	2	1	0	0	(10)	858	61.7
3B	1964	B.Robinson	612	51	4	667	194	35	3	28	.317	.373	.521	895	905	1	0	1	0	50	956	76.2
OF	1996	B.Anderson	579	76	22	677	172	37	5	50	.297	.399	.637	1,036	948	21	8	7	10	20	985	73.3
OF	1928	H.Manush	638	39	0	677	241	47	20	13	.378	.414	.575	989	942	17	5	10	10	0	962	69.3
OF	1931	G.Goslin	591	80	4	675	194	42	10	24	.328	.412	.555	967	922	9	6	(4)	10	10	938	61.1
Reserves		Averages	560	67	8	635	174	33	6	29	.311	.393	.550	943	920	9	4	1	3	13	936	65.6
Totals		Weighted Ave.	570	70	7	647	187	36	8	29	.328	.408	.569	976	960	16	6	1	5	23	989	84.3

Pitchers Volume of Success

Pos	Year	Name	G	GS	IP	W	L	SV	SO	BB	ERA	RA/9	Wtd RA/9	R V Runs/162
SP	1975	J.Palmer	39	38	323	23	11	1	193	80	2.09	2.42	2.55	71.9
SP	1959	H.Wilhelm	32	27	226	15	11	0	139	77	2.19	2.55	2.65	50.5
SP	1994	M.Mussina	24	24	176	16	5	0	99	42	3.06	3.22	2.78	49.0
SP	1968	D.McNally	35	35	273	22	10	0	202	55	1.95	2.21	2.94	48.9
SP	1903	W.Sudhoff	38	35	294	21	15	0	104	56	2.27	3.06	3.34	46.2
Starters		Averages	34	32	258	19	10	0	147	62	2.25	2.65	2.86	53.3
RP	1965	S.Miller	67	0	119	14	7	24	104	32	1.89	1.97	2.27	30.3
RP	1994	M.Eichhorn	43	0	71	6	5	1	35	19	2.15	2.41	2.08	27.6
RP	1989	G.Olson	64	0	85	5	2	27	90	46	1.69	1.80	1.89	25.2
RP	1973	B.Reynolds	42	1	111	7	5	9	77	31	1.95	2.19	2.32	27.6
Relievers		Averages	54	0	97	8	5	15	77	32	1.91	2.08	2.17	27.7
Totals		Averages	88	32	355	27	15	15	224	94	2.16	2.50	2.67	81.0

St. Louis Browns/Baltimore Orioles (1901–2000)

St. Louis Browns/Baltimore Orioles — **Hitters Rate of Success**

Pos	Year	Name	AB	BB	HBP	TAB	H	2B	3B	HR	BA	OB	SA	PRO	Wtd PRO	SB	CS	SBF	SPF	FF	R TF	V HC
C	1993	C.Hoiles	419	69	9	497	130	28	0	29	.310	.419	.585	1,003	979	1	1	(2)	0	(10)	967	68.6
1B	1920	G.Sisler	631	46	2	679	257	49	18	19	.407	.449	.632	1,082	1,040	42	17	11	10	40	1,101	112.7
2B	1996	R.Alomar	588	90	1	679	193	43	4	22	.328	.418	.527	945	865	17	6	7	10	60	942	83.0
SS	1991	C.Ripken	650	53	5	708	210	46	5	34	.323	.379	.566	945	950	6	1	5	0	60	1,015	119.1
3B	1937	H.Clift	571	98	6	675	175	36	7	29	.306	.413	.546	960	880	8	5	(3)	0	90	967	84.9
OF	1966	F.Robinson	576	87	10	673	182	34	2	49	.316	.415	.637	1,052	1,098	8	5	(3)	10	0	1,105	111.6
OF	1906	G.Stone	581	52	7	640	208	25	20	6	.358	.417	.501	918	1,044	35			10	(10)	1,044	91.8
OF	1982	J.Lowenstein	322	54	1	377	103	15	2	24	.320	.419	.602	1,022	1,017	7	6	(13)	0	0	1,005	44.4
Starters		Averages	542	69	5	616	182	35	7	27	.336	.416	.573	989	982	16	5	0	5	29	1,016	89.5
C	2000	C.Johnson	421	52	1	474	128	24	0	31	.304	.382	.582	964	882	2	0	4	(10)	20	896	49.4
1B	1961	J.Gentile	486	96	11	593	147	25	2	46	.302	.428	.646	1,074	1,045	1	1	(2)	(10)	(20)	1,013	68.7
2B	1976	B.Grich	518	86	3	607	138	31	4	13	.266	.374	.417	791	844	14	6	3	10	30	887	58.4
SS	1945	V.Stephens	571	55	1	627	165	27	3	24	.289	.352	.473	825	868	2	1	0	0	(10)	858	61.7
3B	1964	B.Robinson	612	51	4	667	194	35	3	28	.317	.373	.521	895	905	1	0	1	0	50	956	76.2
OF	1923	K.Williams	555	79	2	636	198	37	12	29	.357	.439	.623	1,062	1,015	18	17	(24)	10	0	1,001	77.6
OF	1996	B.Anderson	579	76	22	677	172	37	5	50	.297	.399	.637	1,036	948	21	8	7	10	20	985	73.3
OF	1964	B.Powell	424	76	2	502	123	17	0	39	.290	.400	.606	1,007	1,018	0	0	0	(10)	(30)	978	52.7
Reserves		Averages	521	71	6	598	158	29	4	33	.304	.393	.561	954	940	7	4	(1)	0	8	946	64.8
Totals		Weighted Ave.	535	70	5	610	174	33	6	29	.326	.408	.569	977	968	13	5	(0)	3	22	993	81.3

Pitchers Rate of Success

Pos	Year	Name	G	GS	IP	W	L	SV	SO	BB	ERA	RA/9	Wtd RA/9	V Runs /162
SP	1975	J.Palmer	39	38	323	23	11	1	193	80	2.09	2.42	2.55	71.9
SP	1959	H.Wilhelm	32	27	226	15	11	0	139	77	2.19	2.55	2.65	50.5
SP	1992	M.Mussina	32	32	241	18	5	0	130	48	2.54	2.61	2.74	48.6
SP	1981	S.Stewart	29	3	112	4	8	4	57	57	2.32	2.64	2.94	30.4
SP	1968	D.McNally	35	35	273	22	10	0	202	55	1.95	2.21	2.94	48.9
Starters		Averages	33	27	235	16	9	1	144	63	2.19	2.46	2.74	50.1
RP	1997	R.Myers	61	0	60	2	3	45	56	22	1.51	1.81	1.66	19.3
RP	1989	G.Olson	64	0	85	5	2	27	90	46	1.69	1.80	1.89	25.2
RP	1994	M.Eichhorn	43	0	71	6	5	1	35	19	2.15	2.41	2.08	27.6
RP	1997	J.Orosco	71	0	50	6	3	0	46	30	2.32	2.32	2.12	13.5
Relievers		Averages	60	0	67	5	3	18	57	29	1.89	2.06	1.93	21.4
Totals		Averages	93	27	302	21	12	19	201	93	2.12	2.37	2.56	71.5

St. Louis Browns/Baltimore Orioles
Catchers

V	R	Year	Name	AB	BB	HBP	TAB	H	2B	3B	HR	BA	OB	SA	PRO	Wtd PRO	SB	CS	SBF	SPF	FF	R TF	V HC
1	1	1993	C.Hoiles	419	69	9	497	130	28	0	29	.310	.419	.585	1,003	979	1	1	(2)		(10)	967	68.6
2	2	2000	C.Johnson	421	52	1	474	128	24	0	31	.304	.382	.582	964	882	2	0	4	(10)	20	896	49.4
3	3	1989	M.Tettleton	411	73	1	485	106	21	2	26	.258	.371	.509	880	902	3	2	(2)		(30)	870	44.5
4	7	1958	G.Triandos	474	60	1	535	116	10	0	30	.245	.331	.456	787	785	1	0	2	(10)	10	787	29.4
5	6	1956	G.Triandos	452	48	2	502	126	18	1	21	.279	.351	.462	813	779	0	0	0	(10)	20	789	28.0
6	5	1995	C.Hoiles	352	67	4	423	88	15	1	19	.250	.376	.460	836	789	1	0	2			791	25.7
7	9	1932	R.Ferrell	438	66	1	505	138	30	5	2	.315	.406	.420	826	777	5	5	(9)		10	778	25.5
8	4	1963	J.Orsino	379	38	9	426	103	18	1	19	.272	.352	.475	827	841	2	3	(9)	(10)	(30)	792	23.3
9	14	1994	C.Hoiles	332	63	5	400	82	10	0	19	.247	.375	.449	824	769	2	0	5		(10)	764	23.3
10	10	1950	S.Lollar	396	64	8	468	111	22	3	13	.280	.391	.449	841	782	2	0	4	(10)		776	23.1
11	11	1934	R.Hemsley	431	29	2	462	133	31	7	2	.309	.355	.427	782	736	6	2	4	10	20	770	21.4
12	12	1923	H.Severeid	432	31	1	464	133	27	6	3	.308	.356	.419	775	740	3	0	6	(10)	30	766	20.6
13	8	1980	R.Dempsey	362	36	3	401	95	26	3	9	.262	.334	.425	760	756	3	1	2		20	779	19.4
14	13	1931	R.Ferrell	386	56	0	442	118	30	4	3	.306	.394	.427	821	783	2	3	(9)		(10)	765	19.3
15	15	1957	G.Triandos	418	38	3	459	106	21	1	19	.254	.320	.445	765	761	0	0	0	(10)	10	761	19.2
16	23	1922	H.Severeid	517	28	0	545	166	32	7	3	.321	.356	.427	783	741	1	4	(12)	(10)	20	739	16.9
17	19	1959	G.Triandos	393	65	3	461	85	7	1	25	.216	.332	.430	762	759	0	0	0	(10)		749	16.4
18	20	1952	C.Courtney	413	39	1	453	118	24	3	5	.286	.349	.395	743	755	0	2	(8)	(10)	10	747	15.8
19	18	1960	G.Triandos	364	41	1	406	98	18	0	12	.269	.345	.418	762	750	0	0	0	(10)	10	750	14.7
20	22	1996	C.Hoiles	407	57	9	473	105	13	0	25	.258	.362	.474	836	764	0	1	(4)		(20)	741	14.2
21	16	1997	C.Hoiles	320	51	10	381	83	15	0	12	.259	.378	.419	797	752	1	0	2			754	14.0
22	17	1951	S.Lollar	310	43	4	357	78	21	0	8	.252	.350	.397	747	729	1	0	3	(10)	30	752	13.3
23	24	1921	H.Severeid	472	42	0	514	153	23	7	2	.324	.379	.415	795	733	7	2	6	(10)		729	13.2
24	21	1985	R.Dempsey	362	50	1	413	92	19	0	12	.254	.346	.406	752	747	0	1	(5)			743	12.8
25	27	1990	M.Tettleton	444	106	5	555	99	21	2	15	.223	.378	.381	759	772	2	4	(10)		(40)	721	11.7

St. Louis Browns/Baltimore Orioles
First basemen

V	R	Year	Name	AB	BB	HBP	TAB	H	2B	3B	HR	BA	OB	SA	PRO	Wtd PRO	SB	CS	SBF	SPF	FF	R TF	V HC
1	1	1920	G.Sisler	631	46	2	679	257	49	18	19	.407	.449	.632	1,082	1,040	42	17	11	10	40	1,101	112.7
2	2	1922	G.Sisler	586	49	3	638	246	42	18	8	.420	.467	.594	1,061	1,004	51	19	19	10	40	1,073	96.9
3	3	1961	J.Gentile	486	96	11	593	147	25	2	46	.302	.428	.646	1,074	1,045	1	1	(2)	(10)	(20)	1,013	68.7
4	4	1919	G.Sisler	511	27	5	543	180	31	15	10	.352	.390	.530	921	939	28			10	40	989	65.6
5	9	1984	E.Murray	588	107	2	697	180	26	3	29	.306	.415	.509	923	927	10	2	8		30	965	64.8
6	6	1981	E.Murray	378	40	1	419	111	21	2	22	.294	.363	.534	897	941	2	3	(9)		50	982	64.1
7	7	1983	E.Murray	582	86	3	671	178	30	3	33	.306	.398	.538	936	934	5	1	4		30	969	63.5
8	5	1982	E.Murray	550	70	1	621	174	30	1	32	.316	.395	.549	944	940	7	2	5		40	984	63.4
9	8	1921	G.Sisler	582	34	5	621	216	38	18	12	.371	.411	.560	971	896	35	11	20	10	40	966	60.9
10	10	1970	B.Powell	526	104	5	635	156	28	0	35	.297	.417	.549	967	971	1	1	(1)	(10)		959	57.3
11	11	1918	G.Sisler	452	40	5	497	154	21	9	2	.341	.400	.440	841	919	45			10	30	959	57.0
12	14	1995	R.Palmeiro	554	62	3	619	172	30	2	39	.310	.383	.583	966	911	3	1	2		20	933	53.9
13	12	1969	B.Powell	533	72	1	606	162	25	0	37	.304	.388	.559	947	965	1	1	(2)	(10)		953	52.8
14	15	1998	R.Palmeiro	619	79	7	705	183	36	1	43	.296	.382	.565	947	890	11	7	(4)		40	926	52.5
15	13	1917	G.Sisler	539	30	3	572	190	30	9	2	.353	.390	.453	843	932	37			10	10	952	52.2
16	16	1985	E.Murray	583	84	2	669	173	37	1	31	.297	.387	.523	910	904	5	2	1		20	926	49.6
17	20	1994	R.Palmeiro	436	54	2	492	139	32	0	23	.319	.396	.550	947	884	7	3	2			886	38.4
18	19	1980	E.Murray	621	54	2	677	186	36	2	32	.300	.357	.519	876	872	7	2	4		10	887	37.6
19	24	1996	R.Palmeiro	626	95	3	724	181	40	2	39	.289	.385	.546	932	852	8	0	10		10	873	35.4
20	18	1966	B.Powell	491	67	1	559	141	18	0	34	.287	.374	.532	905	945	0	4	(14)	(10)	(20)	902	35.1
21	25	1939	G.McQuinn	617	65	2	684	195	37	13	20	.316	.383	.515	898	836	6	5	(6)		40	870	34.3
22	23	1978	E.Murray	610	70	1	681	174	32	3	27	.285	.360	.480	840	859	6	5	(6)		20	873	33.5
23	17	1990	R.Milligan	362	88	2	452	96	20	1	20	.265	.412	.492	903	918	6	3	0			918	31.9
24	27	1988	E.Murray	603	75	0	678	171	27	2	28	.284	.363	.474	837	851	5	2	1	(10)	20	862	29.9
25	22	1941	G.McQuinn	495	74	0	569	147	28	4	18	.297	.388	.479	867	839	5	4	(5)		40	874	29.5

St. Louis Browns/Baltimore Orioles
Second basemen

V	R	Year	Name	AB	BB	HBP	TAB	H	2B	3B	HR	BA	OB	SA	PRO	Wtd PRO	SB	CS	SBF	SPF	FF	R TF	V HC
1	1	1996	R.Alomar	588	90	1	679	193	43	4	22	.328	.418	.527	945	865	17	6	7	10	60	942	83.0
2	4	1974	B.Grich	582	90	20	692	153	29	6	19	.263	.380	.431	811	850	17	11	(7)	10	30	883	65.1
3	6	1973	B.Grich	581	107	7	695	146	29	7	12	.251	.374	.387	761	781	17	9	(1)	10	80	869	60.9
4	3	1976	B.Grich	518	86	3	607	138	31	4	13	.266	.374	.417	791	844	14	6	3	10	30	887	58.4
5	5	1975	B.Grich	524	107	8	639	136	26	4	13	.260	.393	.399	792	815	14	10	(9)	10	60	876	58.1
6	10	1916	D.Pratt	596	54	3	653	159	35	12	5	.267	.331	.391	722	790	26	17	(12)	10	50	838	50.1
7	9	1948	J.Priddy	560	86	1	647	166	40	9	8	.296	.391	.443	834	805	6	5	(6)		40	839	50.0
8	8	1912	D.Pratt	570	36	4	610	172	26	15	5	.302	.348	.426	774	802	24			10	30	842	48.0
9	2	1997	R.Alomar	412	40	3	455	137	23	2	14	.333	.396	.500	896	845	9	3	6	10	40	902	46.9
10	7	1971	D.Johnson	510	51	5	566	144	26	1	18	.282	.353	.443	796	822	3	1	2		30	854	45.4
11	11	1913	D.Pratt	592	40	1	633	175	31	13	2	.296	.341	.402	743	794	37			10	20	824	43.9
12	12	1923	M.McManus	582	49	4	635	180	35	10	15	.309	.367	.481	848	810	14	10	(9)	10	10	821	43.2
13	14	1914	D.Pratt	584	50	2	636	165	34	13	5	.283	.341	.411	752	827	37	28	(28)	10		809	39.4
14	16	1915	D.Pratt	602	26	3	631	175	31	11	3	.291	.323	.394	717	777	32	23	(21)	10	30	796	35.2
15	19	1922	M.McManus	606	38	6	650	189	34	11	11	.312	.358	.459	817	773	9	6	(4)	10	10	789	33.8
16	18	1998	R.Alomar	588	59	2	649	166	36	1	14	.282	.350	.418	768	722	18	5	12	10	50	794	33.6
17	13	1924	M.McManus	442	55	2	499	147	23	5	5	.333	.409	.441	850	795	13	9	(9)	10	20	815	32.5
18	17	1970	D.Johnson	530	66	0	596	149	27	1	10	.281	.361	.392	753	756	2	1	0		40	796	31.5
19	15	1911	F.LaPorte	507	34	4	545	159	37	12	2	.314	.361	.446	807	819	4				(20)	799	31.0
20	23	1931	O.Melillo	617	37	0	654	189	34	11	2	.306	.346	.407	752	718	7	11	(22)	10	70	776	29.7
21	22	1949	J.Priddy	544	80	1	625	158	26	4	11	.290	.382	.414	796	768	5	3	(2)		10	776	28.4
22	24	1925	M.McManus	587	73	5	665	169	44	8	13	.288	.371	.457	828	761	5	11	(24)	10	20	767	27.2
23	20	1969	D.Johnson	511	57	3	571	143	34	1	7	.280	.356	.391	747	761	3	4	(8)		30	783	26.5
24	30	1908	J.Williams	539	55	3	597	127	20	7	4	.236	.310	.321	631	745	7				10	755	20.8
25	25	1907	H.Niles	492	28	3	523	142	9	5	2	.289	.331	.339	670	774	19			10	(20)	764	20.7

St. Louis Browns/Baltimore Orioles
Shortstops

V	R	Year	Name	AB	BB	HBP	TAB	H	2B	3B	HR	BA	OB	SA	PRO	Wtd PRO	SB	CS	SBF	SPF	FF	R TF	V HC
1	1	1991	C.Ripken	650	53	5	708	210	46	5	34	.323	.379	.566	945	950	6	1	5		60	1,015	119.1
2	2	1984	C.Ripken	641	71	2	714	195	37	7	27	.304	.375	.510	885	889	2	1	0		70	959	101.1
3	3	1983	C.Ripken	663	58	0	721	211	47	2	27	.318	.373	.517	890	889	0	4	(10)		40	919	88.2
4	4	1945	V.Stephens	571	55	1	627	165	27	3	24	.289	.352	.473	825	868	2	1	0		(10)	858	61.7
5	8	1986	C.Ripken	627	70	4	701	177	35	1	25	.282	.358	.461	819	808	4	2	0		30	838	58.7
6	5	1944	V.Stephens	559	62	1	622	164	32	1	20	.293	.365	.462	826	861	2	2	(3)		(10)	847	57.8
7	10	1988	C.Ripken	575	102	2	679	152	25	1	23	.264	.377	.431	808	822	2	2	(3)		10	829	54.0
8	13	1985	C.Ripken	642	67	1	710	181	32	5	26	.282	.351	.469	820	814	2	3	(5)		10	819	53.0
9	11	1905	B.Wallace	587	45	1	633	159	25	9	1	.271	.324	.349	673	775	13				50	825	51.7
10	6	1943	V.Stephens	512	54	0	566	148	27	3	22	.289	.357	.482	839	894	3	2	(2)		(50)	842	51.0
11	7	1908	B.Wallace	487	52	2	541	123	24	4	1	.253	.327	.324	652	769	5				70	839	48.0
12	12	1904	B.Wallace	541	42	2	585	149	29	4	2	.275	.330	.355	685	785	20				40	825	47.7
13	16	1966	L.Aparicio	659	33	1	693	182	25	8	6	.276	.312	.366	677	707	25	11	4	10	80	801	46.0
14	14	1964	L.Aparicio	578	49	3	630	154	20	3	10	.266	.327	.363	690	698	57	17	35	10	70	813	45.2
15	19	1947	V.Stephens	562	70	0	632	157	18	4	15	.279	.359	.406	765	774	8	4	0		20	794	41.7
16	9	1946	V.Stephens	450	35	0	485	138	19	4	14	.307	.357	.460	817	833	0	1	(4)			829	40.6
17	20	1902	B.Wallace	494	45	4	543	141	32	9	1	.285	.350	.393	743	749	18				40	789	38.0
18	15	1906	B.Wallace	476	58	4	538	123	21	7	2	.258	.344	.345	688	783	24				20	803	37.9
19	17	1910	B.Wallace	508	49	1	558	131	19	7	0	.258	.324	.323	647	736	12				60	796	37.4
20	23	1999	M.Bordick	631	54	5	690	175	35	7	10	.277	.339	.403	742	684	14	4	8		80	772	36.3
21	26	1989	C.Ripken	646	57	3	706	166	30	0	21	.257	.320	.401	721	739	3	2	(1)		30	768	35.6
22	21	1982	C.Ripken	598	46	3	647	158	32	5	28	.264	.320	.475	795	792	3	3	(4)		(10)	777	35.5
23	18	1972	B.Grich	460	53	7	520	128	21	3	12	.278	.362	.415	777	842	13	6	2	10	(60)	794	34.4
24	22	1960	R.Hansen	530	69	2	601	135	22	5	22	.255	.343	.440	782	769	3	3	(5)		10	774	33.9
25	24	1942	V.Stephens	575	41	0	616	169	26	6	14	.294	.341	.433	774	796	1	3	(8)		(20)	769	33.0

St. Louis Browns/Baltimore Orioles
Third basemen

V	R	Year	Name	AB	BB	HBP	TAB	H	2B	3B	HR	BA	OB	SA	PRO	Wtd PRO	SB	CS	SBF	SPF	FF	R TF	V HC
1	1	1937	H.Clift	571	98	6	675	175	36	7	29	.306	.413	.546	960	880	8	5	(3)		90	967	84.9
2	3	1938	H.Clift	534	118	5	657	155	25	7	34	.290	.423	.554	977	893	10	5	0		60	953	77.8
3	2	1964	B.Robinson	612	51	4	667	194	35	3	28	.317	.373	.521	895	905	1	0	1		50	956	76.2
4	5	1967	B.Robinson	610	54	4	668	164	25	5	22	.269	.332	.434	767	825	1	3	(7)	(10)	100	908	61.0
5	6	1962	B.Robinson	634	42	1	677	192	29	9	23	.303	.347	.486	833	814	3	1	1		70	886	54.7
6	8	1936	H.Clift	576	115	7	698	174	40	11	20	.302	.424	.514	938	845	12	4	5		20	870	53.8
7	4	1978	D.DeCinces	511	46	2	559	146	37	1	28	.286	.347	.526	873	893	7	7	(12)		30	911	51.9
8	7	1965	B.Robinson	559	47	2	608	166	25	2	18	.297	.354	.445	799	827	3	0	5		40	872	45.0
9	9	1968	B.Robinson	608	44	4	656	154	36	6	17	.253	.308	.416	724	800	1	1	(1)	(10)	70	858	44.4
10	10	1966	B.Robinson	620	56	5	681	167	35	2	23	.269	.335	.444	778	813	2	3	(6)	(10)	50	847	42.5
11	11	1940	H.Clift	523	104	2	629	143	29	5	20	.273	.396	.463	859	808	9	8	(11)		40	838	38.3
12	13	1960	B.Robinson	595	35	0	630	175	27	9	14	.294	.333	.440	774	761	2	2	(3)		70	828	35.2
13	14	1942	H.Clift	541	106	2	649	148	39	4	7	.274	.394	.399	794	817	6	4	(3)		10	824	35.0
14	15	1971	B.Robinson	589	63	3	655	160	21	1	20	.272	.345	.413	758	782	0	0	0	(10)	50	822	33.0
15	12	1974	B.Robinson	553	56	3	612	159	27	0	7	.288	.356	.374	731	765	2	0	3	(10)	70	828	32.7
16	21	1941	H.Clift	584	113	0	697	149	33	9	17	.255	.376	.430	806	779	6	4	(3)		20	796	28.0
17	19	1939	H.Clift	526	111	5	642	142	25	2	15	.270	.402	.411	813	756	4	3	(3)		50	803	27.8
18	18	1908	H.Ferris	555	14	2	571	150	26	7	2	.270	.291	.353	644	760	6				50	810	26.9
19	16	1981	D.DeCinces	346	41	1	388	91	23	2	13	.263	.343	.454	797	835	0	3	(15)		(10)	811	26.5
20	20	1970	B.Robinson	608	53	4	665	168	31	4	18	.276	.338	.429	768	771	1	1	(1)	(10)	40	799	26.3
21	17	1952	J.Dyck	402	50	3	455	108	22	3	15	.269	.354	.450	804	817	0	4	(17)		10	810	21.4
22	22	1969	B.Robinson	598	56	3	657	140	21	3	23	.234	.303	.395	698	711	2	1	0	(10)	80	781	20.1
23	26	1948	B.Dillinger	644	65	1	710	207	34	10	2	.321	.385	.415	799	772	28	11	8	10	(20)	770	19.0
24	23	1935	H.Clift	475	83	6	564	140	26	4	11	.295	.406	.436	842	789	0	3	(10)			779	17.8
25	24	1977	D.DeCinces	522	64	2	588	135	28	3	19	.259	.342	.433	775	766	8	8	(13)		20	774	16.1

Outfielders

V	R	Year	Name	AB	BB	HBP	TAB	H	2B	3B	HR	BA	OB	SA	PRO	Wtd PRO	SB	CS	SBF	SPF	FF	R TF	V HC
1	1	1966	F.Robinson	576	87	10	673	182	34	2	49	.316	.415	.637	1,052	1,098	8	5	(3)	10		1,105	111.6
2	3	1906	G.Stone	581	52	7	640	208	25	20	6	.358	.417	.501	918	1,044	35			10	(10)	1,044	91.8
3	2	1967	F.Robinson	479	71	7	557	149	23	7	30	.311	.408	.576	984	1,059	2	3	(7)	10	10	1,072	83.4
4	6	1922	K.Williams	585	74	7	666	194	34	11	39	.332	.413	.627	1,040	984	37	20	(4)	10		990	77.7
5	5	1923	K.Williams	555	79	2	636	198	37	12	29	.357	.439	.623	1,062	1,015	18	17	(24)	10		1,001	77.6
6	8	1996	B.Anderson	579	76	22	677	172	37	5	50	.297	.399	.637	1,036	948	21	8	7	10	20	985	73.3
7	7	1969	F.Robinson	539	88	13	640	166	19	5	32	.308	.417	.540	957	975	9	3	4	10		989	70.7
8	10	1928	H.Manush	638	39	0	677	241	47	20	13	.378	.414	.575	989	942	17	5	10	10		962	69.3
9	15	1931	G.Goslin	591	80	4	675	194	42	10	24	.328	.412	.555	967	922	9	6	(4)	10	10	938	61.1
10	20	1930	G.Goslin	584	67	3	654	180	36	12	37	.308	.382	.601	983	899	17	11	(7)	10	20	922	53.9
11	11	1942	W.Judnich	457	74	4	535	143	22	6	17	.313	.413	.499	912	938	3	2	(2)		20	957	53.4
12	25	1992	B.Anderson	623	98	9	730	169	28	10	21	.271	.378	.449	828	844	53	16	27	10	30	911	53.4
13	9	1964	B.Powell	424	76	2	502	123	17	0	39	.290	.400	.606	1,007	1,018	0	0	0	(10)	(30)	978	52.7
14	16	1967	P.Blair	552	50	5	607	162	27	12	11	.293	.357	.446	803	864	8	6	(6)	10	70	938	52.2
15	12	1970	F.Robinson	471	69	7	547	144	24	1	25	.306	.402	.520	922	926	2	1	0	10	20	956	51.8
16	26	1907	G.Stone	596	59	6	661	191	13	11	4	.320	.387	.399	787	909	23			10	(10)	909	50.2
17	22	1969	P.Blair	625	40	2	667	178	32	5	26	.285	.330	.477	807	822	20	6	11	10	70	913	49.4
18	21	1977	K.Singleton	536	107	2	645	176	24	0	24	.328	.442	.507	949	939	0	1	(3)	(10)	(10)	916	48.8
19	30	1920	B.Jacobson	609	46	2	657	216	34	14	9	.355	.402	.501	903	868	11	7	(4)	10	30	904	48.2
20	17	1976	R.Jackson	498	54	4	556	138	27	2	27	.277	.353	.502	855	912	28	7	24	10	(10)	936	47.2
21	34	1980	A.Bumbry	645	78	3	726	205	29	9	9	.318	.394	.433	826	823	44	11	29	10	30	892	46.5
22	13	1968	F.Robinson	421	73	12	506	113	27	1	15	.268	.391	.444	835	923	11	2	13	10		946	45.5
23	18	1971	F.Robinson	455	72	9	536	128	16	2	28	.281	.390	.510	900	929	3	0	5	10	(10)	934	45.1
24	29	1942	C.Laabs	520	88	0	608	143	21	7	27	.275	.380	.498	878	903	0	3	(9)	10		904	44.7
25	4	1982	J.Lowenstein	322	54	1	377	103	15	2	24	.320	.419	.602	1,022	1,017	7	6	(13)			1,005	44.4

St. Louis Browns/Baltimore Orioles
Outfielders

V	R	Year	Name	AB	BB	HBP	TAB	H	2B	3B	HR	BA	OB	SA	PRO	Wtd PRO	SB	CS	SBF	SPF	FF	R TF	V HC
26	33	1979	K.Singleton	570	109	1	680	168	29	1	35	.295	.409	.533	942	922	3	1	1	(10)	(20)	893	44.0
27	28	1971	M.Rettenmund	491	87	4	582	156	23	4	11	.318	.424	.448	872	900	15	6	5	10	(10)	905	41.0
28	32	1914	T.Walker	517	51	4	572	154	24	16	6	.298	.365	.441	806	887	29	17	(8)		20	898	40.4
29	24	1971	D.Buford	449	89	7	545	130	19	4	19	.290	.415	.477	891	920	15	7	2	10	(20)	912	40.0
30	37	1941	R.Cullenbine	501	121	2	624	159	29	9	9	.317	.452	.465	917	887	6	4	(3)			884	39.5
31	38	1921	K.Williams	547	74	4	625	190	31	7	24	.347	.429	.561	990	914	20	17	(21)	10	(20)	882	39.2
32	40	1999	B.Anderson	564	96	24	684	159	28	5	24	.282	.408	.477	885	816	36	7	30	10	20	877	38.8
33	42	1905	G.Stone	632	44	5	681	187	25	13	7	.296	.347	.410	756	871	26			10	(10)	871	38.8
34	41	1924	B.Jacobson	579	35	4	618	184	41	12	19	.318	.361	.528	889	832	6	8	(15)	10	50	876	36.8
35	43	1999	A.Belle	610	101	7	718	181	36	1	37	.297	.403	.541	943	870	17	3	14		(20)	865	36.7
36	19	1925	H.Rice	354	54	5	413	127	25	8	11	.359	.450	.568	1,018	936	8	7	(14)		10	932	36.2
37	27	1998	E.Davis	452	44	5	501	148	29	1	28	.327	.393	.582	975	917	7	6	(9)			907	35.8
38	23	1925	K.Williams	411	37	3	451	136	31	5	25	.331	.390	.613	1,003	922	10	5	0	10	(20)	912	35.0
39	47	1975	K.Singleton	586	118	1	705	176	37	4	15	.300	.418	.454	872	898	3	5	(9)	(10)	(20)	859	34.1
40	14	1970	M.Rettenmund	338	38	3	379	109	17	2	18	.322	.396	.544	940	944	13	7	(2)	10	(10)	942	33.2
41	39	1970	P.Blair	480	56	3	539	128	24	2	18	.267	.347	.438	784	788	24	11	4	10	80	881	31.8
42	35	1924	K.Williams	398	69	1	468	129	21	4	18	.324	.425	.533	958	896	20	11	(4)	10	(10)	892	31.5
43	36	1968	D.Buford	426	57	4	487	120	13	4	15	.282	.372	.437	808	893	27	12	6	10	(20)	889	30.5
44	46	1947	J.Heath	491	88	1	580	123	20	7	27	.251	.366	.485	850	860	2	1	0	10	(10)	860	29.8
45	44	1975	D.Baylor	524	53	13	590	148	21	6	25	.282	.363	.489	851	876	32	17	(3)	10	(20)	863	29.8
46	60	1913	B.Shotton	549	99	1	649	163	23	8	1	.297	.405	.373	779	832	43			10		842	27.4
47	45	1965	C.Blefary	462	88	3	553	120	23	4	22	.260	.382	.470	851	881	4	2	0	(10)	(10)	861	27.3
48	52	1978	K.Singleton	502	98	2	602	147	21	2	20	.293	.410	.462	872	892	0	0	0	(10)	(30)	852	27.1
49	31	1973	A.Bumbry	356	34	3	393	120	15	11	7	.337	.399	.500	899	922	23	10	7	10	(40)	899	26.6
50	62	1929	H.Manush	574	43	1	618	204	45	10	6	.355	.401	.500	901	842	9	8	(11)	10		841	25.8
51	68	1980	K.Singleton	583	92	1	676	177	28	3	24	.304	.399	.485	885	881	0	2	(6)	(10)	(30)	836	25.2
52	50	1956	B.Nieman	428	90	0	518	137	21	6	14	.320	.438	.495	934	894	1	6	(20)	(10)	(10)	854	25.1
53	70	1921	B.Jacobson	599	42	3	644	211	38	14	5	.352	.398	.487	885	817	8	8	(12)	10	20	835	25.0
54	59	1940	W.Judnich	519	54	0	573	157	27	7	24	.303	.368	.520	888	836	8	5	(3)		10	843	24.6
55	73	1908	G.Stone	588	55	3	646	165	21	8	5	.281	.345	.369	714	843	20			10	(20)	833	24.5
56	76	1935	M.Solters	631	36	1	668	201	45	7	18	.319	.356	.498	854	800	11	2	10		20	830	24.4
57	84	1932	G.Goslin	572	92	2	666	171	28	9	17	.299	.398	.469	866	815	12	9	(9)	10	10	827	23.2
58	86	1992	M.Devereaux	653	44	4	701	180	29	11	24	.276	.325	.464	789	805	10	8	(8)	10	20	827	23.1
59	88	1902	J.Burkett	553	71	5	629	169	29	9	5	.306	.390	.418	807	814	23			10		824	23.1
60	69	1989	P.Bradley	545	70	7	622	151	23	10	11	.277	.367	.417	783	803	20	6	12	10	10	835	23.0
61	51	1927	K.Williams	423	57	1	481	136	23	6	17	.322	.403	.525	928	872	9	7	(10)	10	(20)	853	22.9
62	85	1997	B.Anderson	590	84	19	693	170	39	7	18	.288	.394	.469	863	815	18	12	(8)	10	10	827	22.9
63	91	1937	B.Bell	642	53	1	696	218	51	8	14	.340	.371	.509	900	825	2	2	(3)			823	22.7
64	79	1906	C.Hemphill	585	43	0	628	169	19	12	4	.289	.338	.383	720	819	33			10		829	22.5
65	61	1919	B.Jacobson	455	24	4	483	147	31	8	4	.323	.362	.453	815	831	9			10		841	22.4
66	67	1934	S.West	482	62	0	544	157	22	10	9	.326	.403	.469	871	820	3	5	(12)	10	20	838	22.0
67	55	1985	M.Young	450	48	4	502	123	22	1	28	.273	.349	.513	862	856	1	5	(17)	10		849	21.9
68	75	1933	S.West	517	59	1	577	155	25	12	11	.300	.373	.458	831	801	10	8	(10)	10	30	832	21.4
69	81	1922	B.Jacobson	555	46	9	610	176	22	16	9	.317	.379	.463	842	797	19	6	11	10	10	827	21.4
70	83	1981	K.Singleton	363	61	0	424	101	16	1	13	.278	.382	.435	817	857	0	0	0	(10)	(20)	827	21.4
71	95	1994	B.Anderson	453	57	10	520	119	25	5	12	.263	.358	.419	777	725	31	1	53	10	30	818	21.3
72	74	1974	P.Blair	552	43	2	597	144	27	4	17	.261	.317	.417	733	768	27	9	14	10	40	832	21.3
73	72	1946	J.Heath	482	73	1	556	134	32	7	16	.278	.374	.473	847	864	0	6	(20)	10	(20)	834	21.3
74	77	1925	B.Jacobson	540	45	1	586	184	30	9	15	.341	.392	.513	905	832	8	11	(23)	10	10	830	21.2
75	54	1982	G.Roenicke	393	70	9	472	106	25	1	21	.270	.392	.499	891	887	6	7	(16)		(20)	851	21.0

St. Louis Browns/ Baltimore Orioles
Starting Pitchers

V	R	Year	Name	G	GS	IP	W	L	SV	SO	BB	ERA	RA/9	R Wtd RA/9	V Runs /162
1	1	1975	J.Palmer	39	38	323	23	11	1	193	80	2.09	2.42	2.55	71.9
2	5	1973	J.Palmer	38	37	296	22	9	1	158	113	2.40	2.61	2.77	58.9
3	9	1977	J.Palmer	39	39	319	20	11	0	193	99	2.91	2.99	2.99	55.6
4	2	1959	H.Wilhelm	32	27	226	15	11	0	139	77	2.19	2.55	2.65	50.5
5	6	1994	M.Mussina	24	24	176	16	5	0	99	42	3.06	3.22	2.78	49.0
6	8	1968	D.McNally	35	35	273	22	10	0	202	55	1.95	2.21	2.94	48.9
7	12	1978	J.Palmer	38	38	296	21	12	0	138	97	2.46	2.86	3.07	48.8
8	4	1992	M.Mussina	32	32	241	18	5	0	130	48	2.54	2.61	2.74	48.6
9	15	1970	J.Palmer	39	39	305	20	10	0	199	100	2.71	2.89	3.15	47.7
10	23	1903	W.Sudhoff	38	35	294	21	15	0	104	56	2.27	3.06	3.34	46.2
11	14	1972	J.Palmer	36	36	274	21	10	0	184	70	2.07	2.39	3.13	45.7
12	11	1945	N.Potter	32	32	255	15	11	0	129	68	2.47	2.65	3.07	44.2
13	38	1902	R.Donahue	35	34	316	22	11	0	63	65	2.76	3.81	3.47	44.1
14	21	1976	J.Palmer	40	40	315	22	13	0	159	84	2.51	2.89	3.30	44.0
15	44	1922	U.Shocker	48	38	348	24	17	3	149	57	2.97	3.65	3.49	43.2
16	17	1969	M.Cuellar	39	39	291	23	11	0	182	79	2.38	2.91	3.24	42.5
17	19	1930	L.Stewart	35	33	271	20	12	0	79	70	3.45	3.95	3.28	40.5
18	62	1902	J.Powell	42	39	328	22	17	2	137	93	3.21	3.95	3.60	40.4
19	13	1995	M.Mussina	32	32	222	19	9	0	158	50	3.29	3.49	3.11	40.3
20	18	1906	B.Pelty	34	30	261	16	11	2	92	59	1.59	2.66	3.25	39.9
21	3	1969	J.Palmer	26	23	181	16	4	0	123	64	2.34	2.39	2.66	38.1
22	28	1908	J.Powell	33	32	256	16	13	1	85	47	2.11	2.57	3.38	35.4
23	25	1984	M.Boddicker	34	34	261	20	11	0	128	81	2.79	3.27	3.35	35.0
24	56	1914	C.Weilman	44	36	299	17	12	1	119	84	2.08	2.89	3.57	34.5
25	16	1997	M.Mussina	33	33	225	15	8	0	218	54	3.20	3.49	3.19	34.1
26	29	1920	U.Shocker	38	28	246	20	10	5	107	70	2.71	3.55	3.38	33.9
27	78	1921	U.Shocker	47	38	327	27	12	4	132	86	3.55	4.16	3.70	32.9
28	46	1971	J.Palmer	37	37	282	20	9	0	184	106	2.68	3.00	3.51	32.7
29	10	1962	R.Roberts	27	25	191	10	9	0	102	41	2.78	2.97	3.04	32.2
30	39	1918	A.Sothoron	29	24	209	12	12	0	71	67	1.94	2.76	3.47	32.1
31	86	1905	H.Howell	38	37	323	15	22	0	198	101	1.98	3.04	3.71	31.8
32	45	1979	M.Flanagan	39	38	266	23	9	0	190	70	3.08	3.62	3.49	31.4
33	37	1906	J.Powell	28	26	244	13	14	1	132	55	1.77	2.84	3.47	31.0
34	32	2000	M.Mussina	34	34	238	11	15	0	210	46	3.79	3.98	3.39	30.7
35	36	1944	N.Potter	32	29	232	19	7	0	91	70	2.83	3.06	3.43	30.7
36	7	1981	S.Stewart	29	3	112	4	8	4	57	57	2.32	2.64	2.94	30.4
37	99	1908	H.Howell	41	32	324	18	18	1	117	70	1.89	2.86	3.76	30.3
38	50	1983	S.McGregor	36	36	260	18	7	0	86	45	3.18	3.50	3.53	29.7
39	67	1916	C.Weilman	46	31	276	17	18	2	91	76	2.15	2.93	3.64	29.6
40	88	1919	A.Sothoron	40	30	270	20	12	3	106	87	2.20	3.37	3.72	29.1
41	34	1982	J.Palmer	36	32	227	15	5	1	103	63	3.13	3.37	3.41	28.9
42	59	1973	D.McNally	38	38	266	17	17	0	87	81	3.21	3.38	3.58	28.8
43	64	1975	M.Torrez	36	36	271	20	9	0	119	133	3.06	3.42	3.61	28.6
44	100	1904	H.Howell	34	33	300	13	21	0	122	60	2.19	2.97	3.76	28.0
45	101	1929	S.Gray	43	37	305	18	15	1	109	96	3.72	4.19	3.77	27.9
46	54	1964	M.Pappas	37	36	252	16	7	0	157	48	2.97	3.18	3.56	27.9
47	51	1919	U.Shocker	30	25	211	13	11	0	86	55	2.69	3.20	3.53	27.8
48	24	1998	M.Mussina	29	29	206	13	10	0	175	41	3.49	3.71	3.34	27.8
49	31	1964	W.Bunker	29	29	214	19	5	0	96	62	2.69	3.03	3.39	27.7
50	27	1999	M.Mussina	31	31	203	18	7	0	172	52	3.50	3.90	3.37	26.7

St. Louis Browns/Baltimore Orioles Starting Pitchers

V	R	Year	Name	G	GS	IP	W	L	SV	SO	BB	ERA	RA/9	R Wtd RA/9	V Runs /162
51	96	1974	R.Grimsley	40	39	296	18	13	1	158	76	3.07	3.38	3.75	26.6
52	76	1950	N.Garver	37	31	260	13	18	0	85	108	3.39	4.15	3.69	26.5
53	89	1920	D.Davis	38	31	269	18	12	0	85	149	3.17	3.91	3.72	26.3
54	75	1944	J.Kramer	33	31	257	17	13	0	124	75	2.49	3.29	3.68	26.2
55	33	1964	R.Roberts	31	31	204	13	7	0	109	52	2.91	3.04	3.40	26.1
56	98	1923	U.Shocker	43	35	277	20	12	5	109	49	3.41	3.96	3.75	26.1
57	47	1984	S.Davis	35	31	225	14	9	1	105	71	3.12	3.44	3.52	25.9
58	68	1980	S.McGregor	36	36	252	20	8	0	119	58	3.32	3.61	3.64	25.7
59	48	1971	D.McNally	30	30	224	21	5	0	91	58	2.89	3.01	3.53	25.7
60	102	1970	D.McNally	40	40	296	24	9	0	185	78	3.22	3.47	3.78	25.5
61	109	1915	C.Weilman	47	31	296	18	19	4	125	83	2.34	3.35	3.83	25.3
62	42	1997	J.Key	34	34	212	16	10	0	141	82	3.43	3.81	3.49	25.2
63	97	1906	F.Glade	35	32	267	15	14	1	96	59	2.36	3.07	3.75	25.2
64	40	1959	B.O'Dell	38	24	199	10	12	1	88	67	2.93	3.35	3.48	25.1
65	30	1995	K.Brown	26	26	172	10	9	0	117	48	3.60	3.81	3.39	25.1
66	20	1983	M.Boddicker	27	26	179	16	8	0	120	52	2.77	3.27	3.30	25.1
67	60	1976	W.Garland	38	25	232	20	7	1	113	64	2.67	3.14	3.59	25.0
68	49	1942	J.Niggeling	28	27	206	15	11	0	107	93	2.66	3.32	3.53	24.8
69	55	1935	I.Andrews	50	20	213	13	7	1	43	53	3.54	4.01	3.56	24.8
70	83	1972	M.Cuellar	35	35	248	18	12	0	132	71	2.57	2.83	3.71	24.7
71	77	1902	W.Sudhoff	30	25	220	12	12	0	42	67	2.86	4.05	3.69	24.5
72	72	1958	J.Harshman	34	29	236	12	15	4	161	75	2.89	3.39	3.67	24.5
73	74	1961	S.Barber	37	34	248	18	12	1	150	130	3.33	3.70	3.68	24.1
74	117	1908	R.Waddell	43	36	286	19	14	3	232	90	1.89	2.93	3.85	23.7
75	52	1943	J.Niggeling	26	26	201	10	10	0	97	74	2.59	3.00	3.55	23.6
76	79	1916	E.Plank	37	26	236	16	15	3	88	67	2.33	2.98	3.70	23.6
77	129	1933	B.Hadley	45	36	317	15	20	3	149	141	3.92	4.32	3.92	23.5
78	112	1979	D.Martinez	40	39	292	15	16	0	132	78	3.66	3.97	3.83	23.5
79	26	1961	M.Pappas	26	23	178	13	9	1	89	78	3.04	3.39	3.37	23.4
80	63	1993	B.McDonald	34	34	220	13	14	0	171	86	3.39	3.76	3.61	23.2
81	92	1957	C.Johnson	35	30	242	14	11	0	177	66	3.20	3.46	3.74	23.2
82	69	1958	B.O'Dell	41	25	221	14	11	8	137	51	2.97	3.38	3.66	23.2
83	130	1907	H.Howell	42	35	316	16	15	3	118	88	1.93	3.19	3.93	23.2
84	90	1980	S.Stone	37	37	251	25	7	0	149	101	3.23	3.70	3.73	23.1
85	22	1961	H.Brown	27	23	167	10	6	1	61	33	3.19	3.34	3.32	22.9
86	43	1959	J.Walker	30	22	182	11	10	4	100	52	2.92	3.36	3.49	22.7
87	70	1959	M.Pappas	33	27	209	15	9	3	120	75	3.27	3.53	3.66	21.8
88	124	1906	H.Howell	35	33	277	15	14	1	140	61	2.11	3.18	3.89	21.8
89	35	1919	C.Weilman	20	20	148	10	6	0	44	45	2.07	3.10	3.42	21.6
90	120	1928	S.Gray	35	31	263	20	12	3	102	86	3.19	4.07	3.86	21.6
91	126	1923	E.Vangilder	41	35	282	16	17	1	74	120	3.06	4.12	3.90	21.5
92	71	1960	M.Pappas	30	27	206	15	11	0	126	83	3.37	3.54	3.67	21.4
93	61	1965	D.McNally	35	29	199	11	6	0	116	73	2.85	3.12	3.59	21.4
94	116	1969	D.McNally	41	40	269	20	7	0	166	84	3.22	3.45	3.84	21.3
95	125	1971	P.Dobson	38	37	282	20	8	1	187	63	2.90	3.32	3.89	20.9
96	85	1994	B.McDonald	24	24	157	14	7	0	94	54	4.06	4.29	3.71	20.9
97	82	1965	S.Barber	37	32	221	15	10	0	130	81	2.69	3.22	3.71	20.9
98	41	1979	S.McGregor	27	23	175	13	6	0	81	23	3.35	3.61	3.49	20.8
99	111	1922	E.Vangilder	43	30	245	19	13	4	63	48	3.42	4.00	3.83	20.8
100	87	1997	S.Erickson	34	33	222	16	7	0	131	61	3.69	4.06	3.72	20.8

St. Louis Browns/ Baltimore Orioles
Relief Pitchers

V	R	Year	Name	G	GS	IP	W	L	SV	SO	BB	ERA	RA/9	R Wtd RA/9	V Runs /162
1	7	1965	S.Miller	67	0	119	14	7	24	104	32	1.89	1.97	2.27	30.3
2	10	1962	D.Hall	43	6	118	6	6	6	71	19	2.28	2.36	2.42	28.1
3	3	1994	M.Eichhorn	43	0	71	6	5	1	35	19	2.15	2.41	2.08	27.6
4	9	1973	B.Reynolds	42	1	111	7	5	9	77	31	1.95	2.19	2.32	27.6
5	2	1989	G.Olson	64	0	85	5	2	27	90	46	1.69	1.80	1.89	25.2
6	8	1991	T.Frohwirth	51	0	96	7	3	3	77	29	1.87	2.24	2.27	24.4
7	6	1964	D.Hall	45	0	88	9	1	7	52	16	1.85	1.94	2.17	23.3
8	13	1991	M.Flanagan	64	1	98	2	7	3	55	25	2.38	2.47	2.51	22.3
9	11	1967	M.Drabowsky	43	0	95	7	5	12	96	25	1.60	1.99	2.46	22.2
10	16	1983	T.Martinez	65	0	103	9	3	21	81	37	2.35	2.61	2.63	22.0
11	22	1961	H.Wilhelm	51	1	110	9	7	18	87	41	2.30	2.86	2.85	20.9
12	21	1967	E.Watt	49	0	104	3	5	8	93	37	2.26	2.26	2.79	20.4
13	1	1997	R.Myers	61	0	60	2	3	45	56	22	1.51	1.81	1.66	19.3
14	25	1992	T.Frohwirth	65	0	106	4	3	4	58	41	2.46	2.80	2.94	19.0
15	18	1997	A.Rhodes	53	0	95	10	3	1	102	26	3.02	3.02	2.76	18.9
16	17	1966	S.Miller	51	0	92	9	4	18	67	22	2.25	2.35	2.75	18.5
17	20	1962	H.Wilhelm	52	0	93	7	10	15	90	34	1.94	2.71	2.78	18.4
18	35	1957	G.Zuverink	56	0	113	10	6	9	36	39	2.48	2.95	3.19	18.1
19	29	1992	A.Mills	35	3	103	10	4	2	60	54	2.61	2.87	3.01	17.7
20	31	1989	M.Williamson	65	0	107	10	5	9	55	30	2.93	2.93	3.08	17.6
21	28	1972	R.Harrison	39	2	94	3	4	4	62	34	2.30	2.30	3.01	17.0
22	12	1997	A.Benitez	71	0	73	4	5	9	106	43	2.45	2.70	2.47	16.9
23	19	1990	M.Williamson	49	0	85	8	2	1	60	28	2.21	2.64	2.77	16.9
24	14	1990	G.Olson	64	0	74	6	5	37	74	31	2.42	2.42	2.54	16.6
25	37	1963	S.Miller	71	0	112	5	8	27	114	53	2.24	2.89	3.23	16.5
26	24	1964	H.Haddix	49	0	90	5	5	10	90	23	2.31	2.60	2.91	16.5
27	26	1969	D.Leonhard	37	3	94	7	4	1	37	38	2.49	2.68	2.99	16.4
28	5	1992	G.Olson	60	0	61	1	5	36	58	24	2.05	2.05	2.15	16.3
29	15	1969	E.Watt	56	0	71	5	2	16	46	26	1.65	2.28	2.54	15.9
30	51	1952	S.Paige	46	6	138	12	10	10	91	57	3.07	3.33	3.63	14.9
31	4	1997	J.Orosco	71	0	50	6	3	0	46	30	2.32	2.32	2.12	13.5
32	40	1993	A.Mills	45	0	100	5	4	4	68	51	3.23	3.50	3.36	13.3
33	46	1963	D.Hall	47	3	112	5	5	12	74	16	2.98	3.13	3.50	13.2
34	36	1955	H.Dorish	48	1	83	5	3	7	28	37	2.83	3.16	3.21	13.0
35	34	1986	D.Aase	66	0	82	6	7	34	67	28	2.98	3.20	3.14	12.9
36	58	1983	S.Stewart	58	1	144	9	4	7	95	67	3.62	3.74	3.77	12.6
37	43	1966	M.Drabowsky	44	3	96	6	0	7	98	29	2.81	2.91	3.40	12.3
38	53	1966	E.Fisher	67	0	107	6	6	19	57	36	2.52	3.11	3.63	11.0
39	23	1998	J.Orosco	69	0	57	4	1	7	50	28	3.18	3.18	2.86	10.7
40	42	1980	T.Martinez	53	0	81	4	4	10	68	34	3.01	3.35	3.38	10.6
41	41	1998	A.Mills	72	0	77	3	4	2	57	50	3.74	3.74	3.37	10.2
42	47	1981	T.Martinez	37	0	59	3	3	11	50	32	2.90	3.20	3.57	9.8
43	27	1996	J.Orosco	66	0	56	3	1	0	52	28	3.40	3.56	2.99	9.7
44	33	1996	R.Myers	62	0	59	4	4	31	74	29	3.53	3.68	3.09	9.6
45	49	1976	D.Miller	49	0	89	2	4	7	37	36	2.94	3.15	3.60	9.5
46	39	1974	B.Reynolds	54	0	69	7	5	7	43	14	2.73	3.00	3.33	9.4
47	30	1995	J.Orosco	65	0	50	2	4	3	58	27	3.26	3.44	3.06	9.3
48	48	1942	G.Caster	39	0	80	8	2	5	34	39	2.81	3.38	3.59	9.0
49	62	1987	M.Williamson	61	2	125	8	9	3	73	41	4.03	4.25	3.91	9.0
50	45	1991	G.Olson	72	0	74	4	6	31	72	29	3.18	3.42	3.47	8.9

St. Louis Cardinals (1900–2000)

The National League began the twentieth century with a stark division between "haves" and "have nots" teams. The Cardinals were, in some ways, the worst of the "have nots," as they put together the least number of winning teams (four) and pennants (none) during the Dead Ball Era. Their best Dead Ball team — and their only winning team in the first decade — was the 1901 squad, which finished in fourth place with a 76–64 record. St. Louis benefited that year from a big season by veteran Jesse Burkett, who hit .376 with 10 home runs, for a 1,012 Total Factor. Shortstop Bobby Wallace hit .324 and anchored the infield defense. By 1908, the Cardinals dropped to last place with a 49–105 record. Following another last place finish in 1913, the team's record improved to 81–72 in 1914, aided by the pitching of Bill Doak (19–6, league leading 1.72 ERA).

Rogers Hornsby helped the Cardinals create a winning tradition in the 1920s that continues to this day, with the Cardinals amassing 57 winning seasons in the past 80 years. In 1922, Hornsby hit .401 with 42 home runs, 102 extra base hits, and 17 steals in his best season, joining Babe Ruth as the only two players up to that time to hit 40 home runs in a season. Adjusted for 7 percent hitter's inflation, Hornsby hit .376 with 42 home runs, for a 1,107 Wtd. Production, a 1,107 Total Factor, and 145.8 Hits Contribution — the league's best volume of success ever at second base. In 1924, he hit .424 with 25 home runs, for a career best 1,165 Wtd. Production. The 1925 team was only 77–76 despite MVP Hornsby's .403 average, 39 home runs, and 1,153 Wtd. Production.

The Cardinals won their first pennant and World Series in 1926 and, amazingly, they did so with Hornsby's worst on-field performance of his career (.317, 11 home runs). A balanced attack led by MVP catcher Bob O'Farrell (.293, 7 home runs) topped the league in most offensive categories. Player-manager Hornsby and owner Sam Breadon clashed during the season, resulting in Hornsby's trade to the Giants for Frankie Frisch after the season ended.

In 1928, the bats of MVP Jim Bottomley (.325, 31 home runs, 93 extra base hits, 981 Wtd. Production) and Chick Hafey (.337, 27 home runs, 943 Wtd. Production) carried the Cardinals to their second pennant. The Cardinals won another pennant in the hitter's year of 1930. St. Louis hit .314 as a team, led by Frisch (.346), Hafey (.336, 26 home runs), and George Watkins (.373, 17 home runs). In 1931, the Cardinals won 100 games and another pennant, led by Bottomley (.348, 9 home runs), Hafey (.349, 16 home runs), and MVP Frisch (.311, league-leading 28 steals).

In 1934, the Cardinals fielded their fifth — and most famous — pennant winning team in nine seasons. The "Gashouse Gang" featured MVP Dizzy Dean, who went 30–7 with a 2.66 ERA and a 3.05 Wtd. RA/9, and his brother Paul, who was 19–11 with a 3.43 ERA. The Dean brothers teamed up in the fall to win four World Series games for the Cardinals. Slugger Ripper Collins hit .333 with 35 home runs for a 989 Total Factor, while 22-year-old Joe Medwick hit .319 with 18 triples and 18 home runs.

In 1937, Medwick produced a career year and won the MVP Award for the Cardinals, hitting .374 with 31 home runs, 97 extra base hits, and a 1,044 Wtd. Production. Fellow slugger Johnny Mize hit .364 with 25 home runs for a 1,010 Wtd. Production, but a lack of pitching resulted in a fourth place finish for the Cardinals, as Dizzy Dean's win totals dropped from 30, 28, and 24 the previous three years to only 13 in 1937. Mize generated his three best seasons in 1938–1940, peaking in 1939 with a .349 average, 28 home runs, and a career-best 1,047 Wtd. Production.

Medwick was traded to Brooklyn during the 1940 season, and Mize departed to the Giants before the 1942 season. The 1942 team proceeded to win 106 games and the pennant, led by pitchers Mort Cooper (22-7, 1.78 ERA, 2.74 Wtd. RA/9, MVP Award) and John Beazley (21-6, 2.13 ERA). Enos Slaughter hit .318 in his best season for a 987 Total Factor, while rookie Stan Musial batted .315.

Musial, Cooper, and the Cardinals dominated the majors during World War II. The team followed up its success in 1942 to win 105 games in both 1943 and 1944, before losing Musial to military service and dropping to 95 wins and second place in 1945. Other stars of these wartime teams included 1944 MVP Marty Marion, Walker Cooper, Whitey Kurowski, Max Lanier, and Harry Breechen. The Cardinals came back in 1946 to win another pennant, as MVP Musial hit .365 with 20 triples and 16 home runs for a 1,054 Wtd. Production, and Howie Pollet won 21 games with a league-leading 2.10 ERA.

In 1948, the 27-year-old Musial added another MVP Award in his peak season, batting .376 with 39 home runs. Adjusted for 1 percent hitter's inflation, Stan the Man hit .372 with 41 home runs, for a 1,138 Wtd. Production, a 1,138 Total Factor, and 132.1 Hits Contribution. Staff ace Harry Breechen was 20-7 with a league leading 2.24 ERA, and an outstanding 2.42 Wtd. RA/9. The Cardinals then struggled to just five winning seasons and one second-place finish in the 1950s, despite impressive seasons from Musial through 1958. In 1962, 41-year-old Musial produced one last outstanding season, hitting .330 with 19 home runs. Musial retired after the 1963 season, and the second place Cardinals completed a streak of 17 Musial-led seasons with no pennants.

The Cardinals won the 1964 pennant behind Ken Boyer (.295, 24 home runs), Bill White (.303, 21 home runs), Gold Glove center fielder Curt Flood (.311 average), and Lou Brock, who hit .348 with 12 home runs and 33 steals after being stolen away from the Cubs. Ray Sadecki won 20 games, while Bob Gibson went 19-12 with a 3.01 ERA.

St. Louis put together consecutive pennant winning teams in 1967 and 1968. In 1967, MVP Orlando Cepeda hit for a .325 average and 25 home runs for a 970 Wtd. Production, Tim McCarver batted .295 with 14 home runs, and Flood batted .335. In 1968, MVP Gibson dominated the league with a 22-9 record and a skimpy 1.12 ERA, while earning the league's third lowest rate of success with a 1.93 Wtd. RA/9, and the league's second best volume of success with 89.0 Runs/162. The remarkable thing about Gibson's record was that while he threw 13 shutouts, he was only 9–9 in decisions where he failed to hold his opponents scoreless. Joe Hoerner was 8-2 with 17 saves and a 1.48 ERA to anchor the bullpen.

The Cardinals failed to win their division in the 1970s, despite standout performances by several individuals. In 1970, Gibson won 23 games. In 1971, MVP third baseman Joe Torre hit .363 with 24 home runs for a 1,009 Wtd. Production. In 1974, Brock hit .306 and stole 118 bases—a record later broken by Rickey Henderson. Ted Simmons was the team's most consistent player, peaking with a .287 average and 22 home runs for the 1978 team. Keith Hernandez was the league's co–MVP in 1979, hitting .344 with 11 home runs, while Garry Templeton hit .314 with 19 triples and 26 steals that year.

Under manager Whitey Herzog, the Cardinals teams of the 1980s emphasized speed, defense, and pitching. Templeton was traded for fielding whiz Ozzie Smith in 1982, and the Cardinals immediately won their division. The Cardinals won the pennant in 1985, as MVP Willie McGee hit .353 with 18 triples, 10 home runs, and 56 stolen bases, for a 989 Total Factor, while rookie Vince Coleman produced the first of three straight seasons with over 100 steals. John Tudor was 21–8 with a 1.93 ERA and a 2.50 Wtd. RA/9, and Joaquin Andujar also won 21 games. The 1987 Cardinals won the pennant with only one power hitter, Jack Clark, who hit .286 with 35 home runs and 136 walks for a 1,017 Wtd. Production. Ozzie Smith hit .303 with 43 steals and his usual incredible fielding in his best season.

Outfielder Ray Lankford led the Cardinals to a division title in 1996. Lankford peaked in 1997, hitting .295 with 31 home runs and 21 steals, for a 967 Total Factor. In 1998, Mark McGwire shattered Roger Maris' home run record with 70 round trippers, while hitting .299, drawing 162 walks, and generating a 1,225 Production for a Cardinals team that won 83 games. Adjusting for 5 percent hitter's inflation, McGwire hit .284 with 68 home runs, earning a 1,166 Wtd. Production. His 1,147 Total Factor and 121.7 Hits Contribution rank as the league's second-best-ever rate and volume of success at first base. McGwire followed this immortalized season with another strong year in 1999, hitting 65 home runs for a losing ball club.

In 2000, the Cardinals won their division behind a deep starting rotation and a stellar season from newly arrived Jim Edmonds (.295, 42 home runs, Gold Glove Award). Knee problems limited McGwire to 32 home runs in just 236 at bats.

St. Louis Cardinals — Hitters Volume of Success

Pos	Year	Name	AB	BB	HBP	TAB	H	2B	3B	HR	BA	OB	SA	PRO	Wtd PRO	SB	CS	SBF	SPF	FF	R TF	V HC
C	1975	T.Simmons	581	63	1	645	193	32	3	18	.332	.398	.491	889	899	1	3	(7)	(10)	0	882	62.8
1B	1998	M.McGwire	509	162	6	677	152	21	0	70	.299	.473	.752	1,225	1,166	1	0	1	(10)	(10)	1,147	121.7
2B	1922	R.Hornsby	623	65	1	689	250	46	14	42	.401	.459	.722	1,181	1,107	17	12	(10)	0	10	1,107	145.8
SS	1901	B.Wallace	550	20	3	573	178	34	15	2	.324	.351	.451	802	846	15		0	80		926	83.4
3B	1971	J.Torre	634	63	4	701	230	34	8	24	.363	.424	.555	979	1,009	4	1	3	(10)	(30)	971	85.2
OF	1948	S.Musial	611	79	3	693	230	46	18	39	.376	.450	.702	1,152	1,138	7		0	0		1,138	132.1
OF	1937	J.Medwick	633	41	2	676	237	56	10	31	.374	.414	.641	1,056	1,044	4		10	30		1,084	110.5
OF	1901	J.Burkett	601	59	10	670	226	20	15	10	.376	.440	.509	949	1,002	27		10	0		1,012	94.0
Starters		Averages	593	69	4	666	212	36	10	30	.358	.428	.603	1,031	1,031	10	2	(2)	(1)	10	1,038	104.4
C	1967	T.McCarver	471	54	5	530	139	26	3	14	.295	.374	.452	826	864	8	8	(14)	10	40	899	56.0
1B	1940	J.Mize	579	82	5	666	182	31	13	43	.314	.404	.636	1,039	1,045	7		0	0		1,045	91.9
2B	1927	F.Frisch	617	43	7	667	208	31	11	10	.337	.387	.472	858	836	48		10	110		956	90.4
SS	1987	O.Smith	600	89	1	690	182	40	4	0	.303	.394	.383	778	748	43	9	34	10	90	882	72.3
3B	1960	K.Boyer	552	56	4	612	168	26	10	32	.304	.373	.562	934	929	8	7	(9)	10	60	989	83.8
OF	1942	E.Slaughter	591	88	6	685	188	31	17	13	.318	.412	.494	906	967	9		10	10		987	78.9
OF	1985	W.McGee	612	34	0	646	216	26	18	10	.353	.387	.503	890	904	56	16	35	10	40	989	71.4
OF	2000	J.Edmonds	525	103	6	634	155	25	0	42	.295	.416	.583	999	912	10	3	6	10	40	968	63.5
Reserves		Averages	568	69	4	641	180	30	10	21	.316	.394	.510	904	901	24	5	6	9	49	965	76.0
Totals		Weighted Ave.	585	69	4	657	201	34	10	27	.344	.417	.573	990	988	14	3	1	2	23	1,014	95.0

Pitchers Volume of Success

Pos	Year	Name	G	GS	IP	W	L	SV	SO	BB	ERA	RA/9	Wtd RA/9	V Runs /162
SP	1968	B.Gibson	34	34	305	22	9	0	268	62	1.12	1.45	1.93	89.0
SP	1985	J.Tudor	36	36	275	21	8	0	169	49	1.93	2.23	2.50	62.9
SP	1942	M.Cooper	37	35	279	22	7	0	152	68	1.78	2.35	2.74	59.3
SP	1948	H.Brecheen	33	30	233	20	7	1	149	49	2.24	2.39	2.42	58.2
SP	1934	D.Dean	50	33	312	30	7	7	195	75	2.66	3.17	3.05	55.0
Starters		Averages	38	34	281	23	8	2	187	61	1.96	2.32	2.53	64.9
RP	1984	B.Sutter	71	0	123	5	7	45	77	23	1.54	1.91	2.13	33.1
RP	1960	L.McDaniel	65	2	116	12	4	26	105	24	2.09	2.17	2.33	30.2
RP	1948	T.Wilks	57	2	131	6	6	13	71	39	2.62	2.75	2.78	27.1
RP	1986	T.Worrell	74	0	104	9	10	36	73	41	2.08	2.52	2.75	20.8
Relievers		Averages	67	1	119	8	7	30	82	32	2.09	2.34	2.49	27.8
Totals		Averages	105	35	399	31	14	32	268	92	2.00	2.33	2.52	92.7

St. Louis Cardinals

Hitters Rate of Success

Pos	Year	Name	AB	BB	HBP	TAB	H	2B	3B	HR	BA	OB	SA	PRO	Wtd PRO	SB	CS	SBF	SPF	FF	R TF	V HC
C	1904	M.Grady	323	31	2	356	101	15	11	5	.313	.376	.474	850	956	6			10	(60)	906	40.7
1B	1998	M.McGwire	509	162	6	677	152	21	0	70	.299	.473	.752	1,225	1,166	1	0	1	(10)	(10)	1,147	121.7
2B	1925	R.Hornsby	504	83	2	589	203	41	10	39	.403	.489	.756	1,245	1,153	5	3	(2)	0	(10)	1,142	134.7
SS	1901	B.Wallace	550	20	3	573	178	34	15	2	.324	.351	.451	802	846	15			0	80	926	83.4
3B	1960	K.Boyer	552	56	4	612	168	26	10	32	.304	.373	.562	934	929	8	7	(9)	10	60	989	83.8
OF	1948	S.Musial	611	79	3	693	230	46	18	39	.376	.450	.702	1,152	1,138	7			0	0	1,138	132.1
OF	1937	J.Medwick	633	41	2	676	237	56	10	31	.374	.414	.641	1,056	1,044	4			10	30	1,084	110.5
OF	1901	J.Burkett	601	59	10	670	226	20	15	10	.376	.440	.509	949	1,002	27			10	0	1,012	94.0
Starters		Averages	535	66	4	606	187	32	11	29	.349	.425	.611	1,035	1,037	9	1	(1)	4	11	1,051	100.1
C	1967	T.McCarver	471	54	5	530	139	26	3	14	.295	.374	.452	826	864	8	8	(14)	10	40	899	56.0
1B	1939	J.Mize	564	92	4	660	197	44	14	28	.349	.444	.626	1,070	1,047	0			0	0	1,047	91.8
2B	1927	F.Frisch	617	43	7	667	208	31	11	10	.337	.387	.472	858	836	48			10	110	956	90.4
SS	1987	O.Smith	600	89	1	690	182	40	4	0	.303	.394	.383	778	748	43	9	34	10	90	882	72.3
3B	1971	J.Torre	634	63	4	701	230	34	8	24	.363	.424	.555	979	1,009	4	1	3	(10)	(30)	971	85.2
OF	1927	C.Hafey	346	36	5	387	114	26	5	18	.329	.401	.590	990	964	12			10	20	994	45.9
OF	1985	W.McGee	612	34	0	646	216	26	18	10	.353	.387	.503	890	904	56	16	35	10	40	989	71.4
OF	1942	E.Slaughter	591	88	6	685	188	31	17	13	.318	.412	.494	906	967	9			10	10	987	78.9
Reserves		Averages	554	62	4	621	184	32	10	15	.332	.404	.506	909	916	23	4	7	6	35	965	74.0
Totals		Weighted Ave.	542	65	4	611	186	32	11	24	.343	.418	.575	993	997	14	2	2	5	19	1,022	91.4

Pitchers Rate of Success

Pos	Year	Name	G	GS	IP	W	L	SV	SO	BB	ERA	Wtd RA/9	R RA/9	V Runs /162
SP	1968	B.Gibson	34	34	305	22	9	0	268	62	1.12	1.45	1.93	89.0
SP	1948	H.Brecheen	33	30	233	20	7	1	149	49	2.24	2.39	2.42	58.2
SP	1985	J.Tudor	36	36	275	21	8	0	169	49	1.93	2.23	2.50	62.9
SP	1942	M.Cooper	37	35	279	22	7	0	152	68	1.78	2.35	2.74	59.3
SP	1969	S.Carlton	31	31	236	17	11	0	210	93	2.17	2.51	2.80	46.0
Starters		Averages	34	33	266	20	8	0	190	64	1.83	2.15	2.46	63.1
RP	1995	T.Fossas	58	0	37	3	0	0	40	10	1.47	1.47	1.44	14.4
RP	1995	T.Henke	52	0	54	1	1	36	48	18	1.82	1.82	1.78	18.7
RP	1966	J.Hoerner	57	0	76	5	1	13	63	21	1.54	1.89	2.10	20.7
RP	1984	B.Sutter	71	0	123	5	7	45	77	23	1.54	1.91	2.13	33.1
Relievers		Averages	60	0	73	4	2	24	57	18	1.58	1.83	1.97	21.7
Totals		Averages	94	33	338	24	11	24	247	82	1.78	2.08	2.35	84.8

St. Louis Cardinals (1900–2000)

St. Louis Cardinals
Catchers

V	R	Year	Name	AB	BB	HBP	TAB	H	2B	3B	HR	BA	OB	SA	PRO	Wtd PRO	SB	CS	SBF	SPF	FF	R TF	V HC
1	5	1975	T.Simmons	581	63	1	645	193	32	3	18	.332	.398	.491	889	899	1	3	(7)	(10)		882	62.8
2	3	1978	T.Simmons	516	77	3	596	148	40	5	22	.287	.383	.512	894	910	1	1	(2)	(10)		898	62.6
3	7	1970	J.Torre	624	70	7	701	203	27	9	21	.325	.399	.498	898	875	2	2	(3)	(10)		863	61.9
4	2	1967	T.McCarver	471	54	5	530	139	26	3	14	.295	.374	.452	826	864	8	8	(14)	10	40	899	56.0
5	4	1980	T.Simmons	495	59	2	556	150	33	2	21	.303	.379	.505	885	896	1	0	2	(10)		888	55.7
6	11	1972	T.Simmons	594	29	2	625	180	36	6	16	.303	.338	.465	802	830	1	3	(8)		20	843	51.8
7	12	1973	T.Simmons	619	61	2	682	192	36	2	13	.310	.374	.438	812	819	2	2	(3)		20	836	51.5
8	9	1977	T.Simmons	516	79	2	597	164	25	3	21	.318	.410	.500	910	884	2	6	(16)	(10)	(10)	848	48.6
9	8	1979	T.Simmons	448	61	4	513	127	22	0	26	.283	.374	.507	881	873	0	1	(4)	(10)		860	44.6
10	1	1904	M.Grady	323	31	2	356	101	15	11	5	.313	.376	.474	850	956	6			10	(60)	906	40.7
11	6	1944	W.Cooper	397	20	1	418	126	25	5	13	.317	.352	.504	855	876	4		(10)			866	39.6
12	10	1943	W.Cooper	449	19	2	470	143	30	4	9	.318	.349	.463	812	853	1		(10)			843	39.0
13	13	1915	F.Snyder	473	39	1	513	141	22	7	2	.298	.353	.387	740	816	3	6	(17)		20	819	36.5
14	16	1974	T.Simmons	599	47	6	652	163	33	6	20	.272	.331	.447	779	791	0	0	0	(10)	10	791	35.3
15	21	1926	B.O'Farrell	492	61	0	553	144	30	9	7	.293	.371	.433	804	784	1		(10)		10	784	29.4
16	14	1942	W.Cooper	438	29	1	468	123	32	7	7	.281	.327	.434	761	812	4		(10)			802	29.3
17	24	1976	T.Simmons	546	73	0	619	159	35	3	5	.291	.375	.394	769	793	0	7	(21)	(10)	10	772	27.8
18	17	1964	T.McCarver	465	40	1	506	134	19	3	9	.288	.346	.400	746	766	2	0	4	10	10	790	27.2
19	20	1983	D.Porter	443	68	4	515	116	24	3	15	.262	.365	.431	796	803	1	3	(9)	(10)		784	26.1
20	22	1988	T.Pena	505	33	1	539	133	23	1	10	.263	.310	.372	682	713	6	2	4		60	777	25.5
21	26	1966	T.McCarver	543	36	2	581	149	19	13	12	.274	.322	.424	745	753	9	6	(5)	10	10	768	25.1
22	23	1971	T.Simmons	510	36	3	549	155	32	4	7	.304	.353	.424	777	801	1	3	(9)	(10)	(10)	772	24.7
23	15	1965	T.McCarver	409	31	1	441	113	17	2	11	.276	.329	.408	737	757	5	1	6	10	20	794	24.5
24	19	1929	J.Wilson	394	43	2	439	128	27	8	4	.325	.394	.464	859	774	4			10		784	23.5
25	18	1934	S.Davis	347	34	2	383	104	22	4	9	.300	.366	.464	830	805	0		(10)	(10)		785	20.7

St. Louis Cardinals
First basemen

V	R	Year	Name	AB	BB	HBP	TAB	H	2B	3B	HR	BA	OB	SA	PRO	Wtd PRO	SB	CS	SBF	SPF	FF	R TF	V HC
1	1	1998	M.McGwire	509	162	6	677	152	21	0	70	.299	.473	.752	1,225	1,166	1	0	1	(10)	(10)	1,147	121.7
2	2	1946	S.Musial	624	73	3	700	228	50	20	16	.365	.434	.587	1,021	1,054	7				10	1,064	103.0
3	4	1940	J.Mize	579	82	5	666	182	31	13	43	.314	.404	.636	1,039	1,045	7					1,045	91.9
4	3	1939	J.Mize	564	92	4	660	197	44	14	28	.349	.444	.626	1,070	1,047	0					1,047	91.8
5	5	1938	J.Mize	531	74	4	609	179	34	16	27	.337	.422	.614	1,036	1,037	0					1,037	81.6
6	7	1999	M.McGwire	521	133	2	656	145	21	1	65	.278	.427	.697	1,124	1,028	0	0	0	(10)	(10)	1,008	74.3
7	11	1934	R.Collins	600	57	2	659	200	40	12	35	.333	.393	.615	1,008	979	2				10	989	72.3
8	6	1957	S.Musial	502	66	2	570	176	38	3	29	.351	.428	.612	1,040	1,014	1	1	(2)			1,012	69.1
9	10	1937	J.Mize	560	56	5	621	204	40	7	25	.364	.427	.595	1,021	1,010	2			(20)		990	68.4
10	12	1979	K.Hernandez	610	80	1	691	210	48	11	11	.344	.421	.513	934	926	11	6	(1)		50	975	67.4
11	9	1967	O.Cepeda	563	62	12	637	183	37	0	25	.325	.403	.524	927	970	11	2	10		10	990	66.8
12	14	1928	J.Bottomley	576	71	3	650	187	42	20	31	.325	.402	.628	1,030	981	10			(20)		961	62.3
13	16	1980	K.Hernandez	595	86	4	685	191	39	8	16	.321	.410	.494	904	916	14	8	(3)		40	953	59.8
14	8	1987	J.Clark	419	136	0	555	120	23	1	35	.286	.461	.597	1,058	1,017	1	2	(5)		(20)	992	58.8
15	13	1941	J.Mize	473	70	1	544	150	39	8	16	.317	.406	.535	941	966	4					966	53.3
16	17	1981	K.Hernandez	376	61	2	439	115	27	4	8	.306	.405	.463	868	893	12	5	4		40	938	53.1
17	18	1955	S.Musial	562	80	8	650	179	30	5	33	.319	.411	.566	977	935	5	4	(4)			931	52.5
18	21	1963	B.White	658	59	0	717	200	26	8	27	.304	.361	.491	852	896	10	9	(11)	10	20	916	49.8
19	24	1925	J.Bottomley	619	47	2	668	227	44	12	21	.367	.413	.578	992	919	3	4	(7)			911	47.4
20	15	1936	J.Mize	414	50	1	465	136	30	8	19	.329	.402	.577	979	958	1					958	43.7
21	25	1935	R.Collins	578	65	3	646	181	36	10	23	.313	.385	.529	915	894	0				10	904	43.5
22	20	1965	B.White	543	63	4	610	157	26	3	24	.289	.367	.481	848	871	3	3	(5)	10	40	917	42.6
23	26	1964	B.White	631	52	1	684	191	37	4	21	.303	.357	.474	831	853	7	6	(7)	10	40	897	41.2
24	23	1993	G.Jeffries	544	62	2	608	186	24	3	16	.342	.411	.485	896	868	46	9	44	10	(10)	912	41.0
25	28	1956	S.Musial	594	75	3	672	184	33	6	27	.310	.390	.522	912	888	2	0	3			891	40.6

St. Louis Cardinals
Second basemen

V	R	Year	Name	AB	BB	HBP	TAB	H	2B	3B	HR	BA	OB	SA	PRO	Wtd PRO	SB	CS	SBF	SPF	FF	R TF	V HC
1	3	1922	R.Hornsby	623	65	1	689	250	46	14	42	.401	.459	.722	1,181	1,107	17	12	(10)		10	1,107	145.8
2	2	1924	R.Hornsby	536	89	2	627	227	43	14	25	.424	.507	.696	1,203	1,165	5	12	(29)			1,136	141.7
3	1	1925	R.Hornsby	504	83	2	589	203	41	10	39	.403	.489	.756	1,245	1,153	5	3	(2)		(10)	1,142	134.7
4	4	1921	R.Hornsby	592	60	7	659	235	44	18	21	.397	.458	.639	1,097	1,052	13	13	(19)		10	1,043	118.2
5	5	1920	R.Hornsby	589	60	3	652	218	44	20	9	.370	.431	.559	990	1,029	12	15	(26)		20	1,023	110.2
6	7	1927	F.Frisch	617	43	7	667	208	31	11	10	.337	.387	.472	858	836	48			10	110	956	90.4
7	6	1923	R.Hornsby	424	55	3	482	163	32	10	17	.384	.459	.627	1,086	1,040	3	7	(22)		(10)	1,008	78.1
8	8	1953	R.Schoendienst	564	60	0	624	193	35	5	15	.342	.405	.502	907	857	3	3	(5)	10	70	933	77.4
9	9	1930	F.Frisch	540	55	0	595	187	46	9	10	.346	.407	.520	927	810	15			10	70	890	61.0
10	11	1952	R.Schoendienst	620	42	0	662	188	40	7	7	.303	.347	.424	772	781	9	6	(4)	10	70	857	57.0
11	10	1985	T.Herr	596	80	2	678	180	38	3	8	.302	.386	.416	803	815	31	3	35	10		860	56.4
12	12	1954	R.Schoendienst	610	54	1	665	192	38	8	5	.315	.371	.428	799	757	4	2	0	10	80	847	54.0
13	13	1989	J.Oquendo	556	79	0	635	162	28	7	1	.291	.380	.372	752	780	3	5	(10)	10	60	840	46.8
14	15	1928	F.Frisch	547	64	1	612	164	29	9	10	.300	.374	.441	815	776	29			10	30	816	40.1
15	18	1933	F.Frisch	585	48	3	636	177	32	6	4	.303	.358	.398	757	787	18			10	10	807	38.7
16	16	1929	F.Frisch	527	53	2	582	176	40	12	5	.334	.397	.484	881	794	24			10	10	814	37.6
17	19	1919	M.Stock	492	49	1	542	151	16	4	0	.307	.371	.356	727	791	17			10		801	34.7
18	20	1926	R.Hornsby	527	61	0	588	167	34	5	11	.317	.388	.463	851	829	3				(30)	799	33.6
19	22	1997	D.DeShields	572	55	3	630	169	26	14	11	.295	.360	.448	808	767	55	14	41	10	(20)	797	33.6
20	26	1910	M.Huggins	547	116	6	669	145	15	6	1	.265	.399	.320	719	762	34			10	10	782	32.5
21	21	1931	F.Frisch	518	45	2	565	161	24	4	4	.311	.368	.396	764	748	28			10	40	798	31.9
22	25	1914	M.Huggins	509	105	7	621	134	17	4	1	.263	.396	.318	714	775	32			10		785	30.9
23	14	1980	K.Oberkfell	422	51	1	474	128	27	6	3	.303	.380	.417	797	807	4	4	(8)	10	10	819	30.2
24	17	1913	M.Huggins	382	92	7	481	109	12	0	0	.285	.432	.317	749	779	23			10	20	809	29.8
25	28	1903	J.Farrell	519	48	2	569	141	25	8	1	.272	.336	.356	692	720	17				60	780	29.6

St. Louis Cardinals
Shortstops

V	R	Year	Name	AB	BB	HBP	TAB	H	2B	3B	HR	BA	OB	SA	PRO	Wtd PRO	SB	CS	SBF	SPF	FF	R TF	V HC
1	1	1917	R.Hornsby	523	45	4	572	171	24	17	8	.327	.385	.484	868	968	17				10	978	90.7
2	2	1901	B.Wallace	550	20	3	573	178	34	15	2	.324	.351	.451	802	846	15				80	926	83.4
3	3	1987	O.Smith	600	89	1	690	182	40	4	0	.303	.394	.383	778	748	43	9	34	10	90	882	72.3
4	6	1963	D.Groat	631	56	6	693	201	43	11	6	.319	.380	.450	830	873	3	1	1	(10)	(10)	854	63.4
5	4	1988	O.Smith	575	74	1	650	155	27	1	3	.270	.354	.336	689	721	57	9	57	10	70	858	60.6
6	5	1918	R.Hornsby	416	40	3	459	117	19	11	5	.281	.349	.416	764	846	8				10	856	54.1
7	10	1979	G.Templeton	672	18	1	691	211	32	19	9	.314	.333	.458	791	784	26	10	8	10	20	823	52.9
8	14	1952	S.Hemus	570	96	20	686	153	28	8	15	.268	.392	.425	817	827	1	5	(12)			815	52.5
9	8	1985	O.Smith	537	65	2	604	148	22	3	6	.276	.356	.361	717	728	31	8	23	10	80	842	51.8
10	9	1991	O.Smith	550	83	1	634	157	30	3	3	.285	.380	.367	747	762	35	9	25	10	30	828	50.1
11	13	1989	O.Smith	593	55	2	650	162	30	8	2	.273	.337	.361	698	724	29	7	22	10	60	816	47.7
12	12	1992	O.Smith	518	59	0	577	153	20	2	0	.295	.367	.342	709	730	43	9	41	10	40	821	43.6
13	7	1984	O.Smith	412	56	2	470	106	20	5	1	.257	.349	.337	686	701	35	7	42	10	100	853	42.8
14	15	1986	O.Smith	514	79	2	595	144	19	4	0	.280	.378	.333	711	713	31	7	27	10	60	810	41.9
15	19	1953	S.Hemus	585	86	12	683	163	32	11	14	.279	.382	.443	825	779	2	1	0			779	40.2
16	11	1980	G.Templeton	504	18	0	522	161	19	9	4	.319	.343	.417	760	769	31	15	2	10	40	821	39.6
17	16	1982	O.Smith	488	68	2	558	121	24	1	2	.248	.342	.314	656	666	25	5	25	10	100	802	37.1
18	17	1904	D.Brain	488	17	0	505	130	24	12	7	.266	.291	.408	699	786	18				10	796	33.8
19	18	1942	M.Marion	485	48	1	534	134	38	5	0	.276	.343	.375	718	767	8				20	787	33.4
20	20	1983	O.Smith	552	64	1	617	134	30	6	3	.243	.323	.335	658	663	34	7	31	10	70	774	32.9
21	24	1977	G.Templeton	621	15	1	637	200	19	18	8	.322	.339	.449	788	765	28	24	(30)	10		746	25.4
22	25	1978	G.Templeton	647	22	1	670	181	31	13	2	.280	.304	.377	682	693	34	11	17	10	20	740	25.0
23	22	1951	S.Hemus	420	75	4	499	118	18	9	2	.281	.395	.381	776	759	7	7	(13)		10	756	23.6
24	21	1943	M.Marion	418	32	2	452	117	15	3	1	.280	.334	.337	671	705	1				60	765	23.4
25	26	1900	B.Wallace	485	40	3	528	130	25	9	4	.268	.328	.381	709	710	7				30	740	22.7

St. Louis Cardinals
Third basemen

V	R	Year	Name	AB	BB	HBP	TAB	H	2B	3B	HR	BA	OB	SA	PRO	Wtd PRO	SB	CS	SBF	SPF	FF	R TF	V HC
1	2	1971	J.Torre	634	63	4	701	230	34	8	24	.363	.424	.555	979	1,009	4	1	3	(10)	(30)	971	85.2
2	1	1960	K.Boyer	552	56	4	612	168	26	10	32	.304	.373	.562	934	929	8	7	(9)	10	60	989	83.8
3	3	1961	K.Boyer	589	68	1	658	194	26	11	24	.329	.400	.533	933	896	6	3	0	10	40	946	75.7
4	6	1959	K.Boyer	563	67	2	632	174	18	5	28	.309	.384	.508	892	867	12	6	0	10	50	927	66.6
5	11	1963	K.Boyer	617	70	2	689	176	28	2	24	.285	.360	.454	814	856	1	0	1	10	30	897	59.5
6	5	1945	W.Kurowski	511	45	5	561	165	27	3	21	.323	.383	.511	894	907	1				20	927	59.2
7	8	1958	K.Boyer	570	49	3	622	175	21	9	23	.307	.365	.496	861	827	11	6	(2)	10	70	906	59.1
8	14	1964	K.Boyer	628	70	2	700	185	30	10	24	.295	.367	.489	856	880	3	5	(9)	10	10	890	58.0
9	9	1947	W.Kurowski	513	87	10	610	159	27	6	27	.310	.420	.544	964	933	4		(10)	(20)		903	57.1
10	12	1919	R.Hornsby	512	48	7	567	163	15	9	8	.318	.384	.430	814	887	17				10	897	56.5
11	10	1999	F.Tatis	537	82	16	635	160	31	2	34	.298	.406	.553	959	878	21	9	4	10	10	902	56.2
12	15	1933	P.Martin	599	67	3	669	189	36	12	8	.316	.387	.456	843	876	26			10	(10)	876	53.7
13	4	1900	J.McGraw	334	85	23	442	115	10	4	2	.344	.505	.416	921	922	29			10		932	52.6
14	13	1946	W.Kurowski	519	72	5	596	156	32	5	14	.301	.391	.462	853	881	2		(10)		20	891	52.1
15	7	1916	R.Hornsby	495	40	4	539	155	17	15	6	.313	.369	.444	814	909	17					909	52.0
16	16	1956	K.Boyer	595	38	1	634	182	30	2	26	.306	.349	.494	843	820	8	3	3	10	30	863	46.8
17	17	1962	K.Boyer	611	75	1	687	178	27	5	24	.291	.370	.470	839	821	12	7	(3)	10	30	858	46.4
18	18	1926	L.Bell	581	54	0	635	189	33	14	17	.325	.383	.518	901	878	9			10	(40)	848	42.0
19	19	1944	W.Kurowski	555	58	2	615	150	25	7	20	.270	.341	.449	790	809	2				20	829	34.9
20	22	1989	T.Pendleton	613	44	0	657	162	28	5	13	.264	.314	.390	703	730	9	5	(1)	10	80	819	32.1
21	23	1943	W.Kurowski	522	31	2	555	150	24	8	13	.287	.330	.439	768	807	3				10	817	28.1
22	21	1950	T.Glaviano	410	90	6	506	117	29	2	11	.285	.421	.446	867	831	6			10	(20)	821	26.5
23	25	1987	T.Pendleton	583	70	2	655	167	29	4	12	.286	.365	.412	777	747	19	12	(7)	10	50	800	26.0
24	24	1910	M.Mowrey	489	67	6	562	138	24	6	2	.282	.375	.368	744	788	21				20	808	25.9
25	20	1998	G.Gaetti	434	43	10	487	122	34	1	19	.281	.359	.495	855	813	1	1	(2)	(10)	20	821	24.4

St. Louis Cardinals
Outfielders

V	R	Year	Name	AB	BB	HBP	TAB	H	2B	3B	HR	BA	OB	SA	PRO	Wtd PRO	SB	CS	SBF	SPF	FF	R TF	V HC
1	1	1948	S.Musial	611	79	3	693	230	46	18	39	.376	.450	.702	1,152	1,138	7					1,138	132.1
2	2	1937	J.Medwick	633	41	2	676	237	56	10	31	.374	.414	.641	1,056	1,044	4			10	30	1,084	110.5
3	3	1943	S.Musial	617	72	2	691	220	48	20	13	.357	.425	.562	988	1,038	9				20	1,058	104.0
4	5	1949	S.Musial	612	107	2	721	207	41	13	36	.338	.438	.624	1,062	1,037	3			(10)		1,027	97.5
5	7	1901	J.Burkett	601	59	10	670	226	20	15	10	.376	.440	.509	949	1,002	27			10		1,012	94.0
6	4	1951	S.Musial	578	98	1	677	205	30	12	32	.355	.449	.614	1,063	1,041	4	5	(8)			1,033	93.4
7	6	1944	S.Musial	568	90	5	663	197	51	14	12	.347	.440	.549	990	1,014	7				10	1,024	88.6
8	8	1936	J.Medwick	636	34	4	674	223	64	13	18	.351	.387	.577	964	943	3			10	50	1,003	82.9
9	11	1942	E.Slaughter	591	88	6	685	188	31	17	13	.318	.412	.494	906	967	9			10	10	987	78.9
10	13	1954	S.Musial	591	103	4	698	195	41	9	35	.330	.433	.607	1,040	986	1	7	(18)		10	978	77.1
11	15	1953	S.Musial	593	105	0	698	200	53	9	30	.337	.437	.609	1,046	988	3	4	(7)		(10)	971	74.9
12	14	1952	S.Musial	578	96	2	676	194	42	6	21	.336	.432	.538	970	982	7	7	(10)			973	72.9
13	12	1950	S.Musial	555	87	3	645	192	41	7	28	.346	.437	.596	1,034	990	5			(10)		980	72.0
14	10	1985	W.McGee	612	34	0	646	216	26	18	10	.353	.387	.503	890	904	56	16	35	10	40	989	71.4
15	20	1935	J.Medwick	634	30	4	668	224	46	13	23	.353	.386	.576	962	940	4			10	10	960	68.0
16	16	2000	J.Edmonds	525	103	6	634	155	25	0	42	.295	.416	.583	999	912	10	3	6	10	40	968	63.5
17	25	1949	E.Slaughter	568	79	1	648	191	34	13	13	.336	.418	.511	929	907	3			10	20	937	58.3
18	21	1998	R.Lankford	533	86	3	622	156	37	1	31	.293	.394	.540	934	889	26	5	24	10	30	953	58.1
19	18	1928	C.Hafey	520	40	2	562	175	46	6	27	.337	.386	.604	990	943	8			10	10	963	57.9
20	17	1997	R.Lankford	465	95	0	560	137	36	3	31	.295	.414	.585	999	948	21	11	(2)	10	10	967	55.8
21	28	1992	R.Lankford	598	72	5	675	175	40	6	20	.293	.373	.480	853	878	42	24	(8)	10	50	930	55.4
22	22	1974	R.Smith	517	71	1	589	160	26	9	23	.309	.394	.528	922	936	4	3	(3)		20	953	54.9
23	31	1900	J.Burkett	559	62	3	624	203	11	15	7	.363	.429	.474	904	905	32			10		915	54.1
24	29	1938	J.Medwick	590	42	2	634	190	47	8	21	.322	.369	.536	905	906	0			10	10	926	53.5
25	24	1929	C.Hafey	517	45	2	564	175	47	9	29	.338	.394	.632	1,026	925	7			10	10	945	53.0

St. Louis Cardinals
Outfielders

															Wtd							R	V
V	R	Year	Name	AB	BB	HBP	TAB	H	2B	3B	HR	BA	OB	SA	PRO	PRO	SB	CS	SBF	SPF	FF	TF	HC
26	27	1944	J.Hopp	527	58	2	587	177	35	9	11	.336	.404	.499	903	925	15		10			935	52.2
27	23	1942	S.Musial	467	62	2	531	147	32	10	10	.315	.397	.490	888	948	6					948	50.7
28	19	1931	C.Hafey	450	39	3	492	157	35	8	16	.349	.404	.569	973	953	11		10			963	50.7
29	41	1946	E.Slaughter	609	69	2	680	183	30	8	18	.300	.374	.465	838	865	9		10	20		895	46.9
30	30	1940	T.Moore	537	42	2	581	163	33	4	17	.304	.356	.475	831	836	18		10	70		916	46.1
31	36	1939	J.Medwick	606	45	2	653	201	48	8	14	.332	.380	.507	886	868	6		10	20		898	46.0
32	9	1927	C.Hafey	346	36	5	387	114	26	5	18	.329	.401	.590	990	964	12		10	20		994	45.9
33	26	1930	C.Hafey	446	46	7	499	150	39	12	26	.336	.407	.652	1,059	925	12		10			935	44.5
34	37	1948	E.Slaughter	549	81	1	631	176	27	11	11	.321	.409	.470	879	868	4		10	20		898	44.3
35	38	1933	J.Medwick	595	26	2	623	182	40	10	18	.306	.337	.497	835	868	5		10	20		898	43.8
36	48	1971	L.Brock	640	76	1	717	200	37	7	7	.313	.386	.425	811	836	64	19	34	10		880	42.0
37	39	1996	R.Lankford	545	79	3	627	150	36	8	21	.275	.370	.486	856	816	35	7	32	10	40	897	41.8
38	44	1939	E.Slaughter	604	44	5	653	193	52	5	12	.320	.371	.482	852	835	2		10		40	885	41.6
39	47	1968	L.Brock	660	46	3	709	184	46	14	6	.279	.329	.418	747	820	62	12	51	10		881	41.6
40	35	1940	E.Slaughter	516	50	2	568	158	25	13	17	.306	.370	.504	874	878	8		10	10		898	40.2
41	42	1901	S.Heidrick	502	21	1	524	170	24	12	6	.339	.366	.470	837	883	32		10			893	39.1
42	51	1965	C.Flood	617	51	6	674	191	30	3	11	.310	.368	.421	789	811	9	3	4	10	50	875	37.8
43	56	1967	L.Brock	689	24	6	719	206	32	12	21	.299	.328	.472	800	837	52	18	21	10		868	37.7
44	33	1925	R.Blades	462	59	6	527	158	37	8	12	.342	.423	.535	958	887	6	8	(18)	10	20	899	37.5
45	46	1998	B.Jordan	564	40	9	613	178	34	7	25	.316	.370	.534	904	860	17	5	11	10		881	36.1
46	49	1995	R.Lankford	483	63	2	548	134	35	2	25	.277	.363	.513	877	835	24	8	14	10	20	879	35.7
47	32	1939	T.Moore	417	43	1	461	123	25	2	17	.295	.362	.487	849	831	6		10		70	911	35.6
48	58	1964	L.Brock	634	40	4	678	200	30	11	14	.315	.360	.464	824	846	43	18	10	10		866	35.1
49	57	1934	J.Medwick	620	21	1	642	198	40	18	18	.319	.343	.529	872	846	3		10		10	866	35.1
50	43	1967	C.Flood	514	37	2	553	172	24	1	5	.335	.382	.414	796	832	2	2	(3)	10	50	889	34.7
51	34	1941	E.Slaughter	425	53	2	480	132	22	9	13	.311	.390	.496	886	909	4		10	(20)		899	34.1
52	63	1963	C.Flood	662	42	2	706	200	34	9	5	.302	.346	.403	749	788	17	12	(9)	10	70	859	34.0
53	52	1905	H.Smoot	534	33	7	574	166	21	16	4	.311	.359	.433	791	864	21			10		874	33.4
54	55	1952	E.Slaughter	510	70	1	581	153	17	12	11	.300	.386	.445	831	841	6	1	7	10	10	868	32.1
55	64	1981	G.Hendrick	394	41	4	439	112	19	3	18	.284	.358	.485	842	867	4	2	0	(10)		857	31.5
56	53	1959	J.Cunningham	458	88	5	551	158	28	6	7	.345	.456	.478	934	907	2	6	(17)	(20)		869	30.9
57	67	1908	R.Murray	593	37	8	638	167	19	15	7	.282	.332	.400	732	854	48		10	(10)		854	30.9
58	65	1956	W.Moon	540	80	1	621	161	22	11	6	.298	.390	.469	858	836	12	9	(9)	10	20	856	30.8
59	50	1975	R.Smith	477	63	3	543	144	26	3	19	.302	.387	.488	875	885	9	7	(9)			876	30.8
60	68	1982	L.Smith	592	64	9	665	182	35	8	8	.307	.383	.434	818	830	68	26	23	(10)		853	30.3
61	45	1962	S.Musial	433	64	3	500	143	18	1	19	.330	.420	.508	928	907	3	0	6	(10)	(20)	883	29.9
62	61	1980	G.Hendrick	572	32	4	608	173	33	2	25	.302	.344	.498	842	853	6	1	6			859	29.4
63	74	1969	L.Brock	655	50	2	707	195	33	10	12	.298	.349	.434	783	801	53	14	33	10		844	29.3
64	40	1930	G.Watkins	391	24	4	419	146	32	7	17	.373	.415	.621	1,037	906	5		10	(20)		896	29.1
65	77	1929	T.Douthit	613	79	5	697	206	42	7	9	.336	.416	.471	888	800	8		10	30		840	28.9
66	66	1957	W.Moon	516	62	1	579	152	28	5	24	.295	.371	.508	879	857	5	6	(11)	10		856	28.5
67	75	1974	L.Brock	635	61	2	698	194	25	7	3	.306	.368	.381	749	761	118	33	70	10		841	27.9
68	72	1968	C.Flood	618	33	5	656	186	17	4	5	.301	.341	.366	707	776	11	6	(1)	10	60	845	27.3
69	60	1996	B.Jordan	513	29	7	549	159	36	1	17	.310	.355	.483	839	799	22	5	21	10	30	860	26.7
70	79	1990	W.McGee	614	48	1	663	199	35	7	3	.324	.374	.419	793	791	31	9	19	10	20	840	26.1
71	82	1965	L.Brock	631	45	10	686	182	35	8	16	.288	.345	.445	791	813	63	27	12	10		835	25.3
72	62	1926	R.Blades	416	62	11	489	127	17	12	8	.305	.409	.462	871	849	6		10			859	24.8
73	88	1972	L.Brock	621	47	1	669	193	26	8	3	.311	.360	.393	753	780	63	18	38	10		828	23.6
74	59	1985	A.Van Slyke	424	47	2	473	110	25	6	13	.259	.336	.439	775	787	34	6	44	10	20	861	23.3
75	71	1983	L.Smith	492	41	9	542	158	31	5	8	.321	.384	.453	837	844	43	18	12	10	(20)	846	22.9

St. Louis Cardinals
Starting Pitchers

V	R	Year	Name	G	GS	IP	W	L	SV	SO	BB	ERA	RA/9	R Wtd RA/9	V Runs /162
1	1	1968	B.Gibson	34	34	305	22	9	0	268	62	1.12	1.45	1.93	89.0
2	4	1969	B.Gibson	35	35	314	20	13	0	269	95	2.18	2.41	2.69	65.1
3	3	1985	J.Tudor	36	36	275	21	8	0	169	49	1.93	2.23	2.50	62.9
4	5	1942	M.Cooper	37	35	279	22	7	0	152	68	1.78	2.35	2.74	59.3
5	2	1948	H.Brecheen	33	30	233	20	7	1	149	49	2.24	2.39	2.42	58.2
6	13	1934	D.Dean	50	33	312	30	7	7	195	75	2.66	3.17	3.05	55.0
7	18	1904	K.Nichols	36	35	317	21	13	1	134	50	2.02	2.75	3.12	53.3
8	8	1944	M.Cooper	34	33	252	22	7	1	97	60	2.46	2.64	2.81	51.4
9	44	1900	C.Young	41	35	321	19	19	0	115	36	3.00	4.03	3.41	47.5
10	15	1943	M.Cooper	37	32	274	21	8	3	141	79	2.30	2.66	3.09	46.9
11	36	1935	D.Dean	50	36	325	28	12	5	190	77	3.04	3.49	3.33	46.5
12	7	1969	S.Carlton	31	31	236	17	11	0	210	93	2.17	2.51	2.80	46.0
13	19	1972	B.Gibson	34	34	278	19	11	0	208	88	2.46	2.69	3.15	45.7
14	17	1927	P.Alexander	37	30	268	21	10	3	48	38	2.52	3.16	3.12	45.1
15	10	1992	B.Tewksbury	33	32	233	16	5	0	91	20	2.16	2.43	2.85	44.1
16	9	1944	T.Wilks	36	21	208	17	4	0	70	49	2.64	2.64	2.81	42.5
17	38	1927	J.Haines	38	36	301	24	10	1	89	77	2.72	3.41	3.36	42.0
18	22	1966	B.Gibson	35	35	280	21	12	0	225	78	2.44	2.89	3.21	41.8
19	27	1946	H.Pollet	40	32	266	21	10	5	107	86	2.10	2.84	3.24	40.8
20	47	1906	J.Taylor	34	33	302	20	12	0	61	86	1.99	2.74	3.43	39.8
21	24	1982	J.Andujar	38	37	266	15	10	0	137	50	2.47	2.88	3.22	39.6
22	16	1949	H.Pollet	39	28	231	20	9	1	108	59	2.77	3.12	3.10	39.2
23	25	1953	H.Haddix	36	33	253	20	9	1	163	69	3.06	3.45	3.24	38.9
24	42	1945	R.Barrett	45	34	285	23	12	2	76	54	3.00	3.35	3.40	38.5
25	57	1936	D.Dean	51	34	315	24	13	11	195	53	3.17	3.66	3.52	38.2
26	33	1914	B.Doak	36	33	256	19	6	1	118	87	1.72	2.78	3.29	37.9
27	12	1943	M.Lanier	32	25	213	15	7	3	123	75	1.90	2.62	3.05	37.6
28	46	1970	B.Gibson	34	34	294	23	7	0	274	88	3.12	3.40	3.42	37.1
29	49	1913	S.Sallee	50	29	276	19	15	5	106	60	2.71	3.16	3.45	35.6
30	53	1914	S.Sallee	46	29	282	18	17	6	105	72	2.10	2.94	3.48	35.5
31	26	1946	H.Brecheen	36	30	231	15	15	3	117	67	2.49	2.84	3.24	35.5
32	39	1928	B.Sherdel	38	27	249	21	10	5	72	56	2.86	3.47	3.36	34.7
33	14	1925	B.Sherdel	32	21	200	15	6	1	53	42	3.11	3.47	3.08	34.6
34	28	1960	E.Broglio	52	24	226	21	9	0	188	100	2.74	3.03	3.25	34.6
35	20	1945	K.Burkhart	42	22	217	18	8	2	67	66	2.90	3.15	3.20	34.5
36	52	1935	P.Dean	46	33	270	19	12	5	143	55	3.37	3.63	3.47	34.4
37	29	1962	B.Gibson	32	30	234	15	13	1	208	95	2.85	3.23	3.26	33.8
38	30	1942	J.Beazley	43	23	215	21	6	3	91	73	2.13	2.80	3.26	32.5
39	6	1945	H.Brecheen	24	18	157	15	4	2	63	44	2.52	2.75	2.79	32.4
40	35	1974	L.McGlothen	31	31	237	16	12	0	142	89	2.69	3.03	3.33	32.4
41	11	1939	B.Bowman	51	15	169	13	5	9	78	60	2.60	2.88	2.92	32.3
42	31	1962	E.Broglio	34	30	222	12	9	0	132	93	3.00	3.24	3.27	31.8
43	80	1912	S.Sallee	48	32	294	16	17	6	108	72	2.60	3.73	3.66	31.0
44	34	1941	E.White	32	25	210	17	7	2	117	70	2.40	3.09	3.30	30.9
45	59	1958	S.Jones	35	35	250	14	13	0	225	107	2.88	3.42	3.53	30.1
46	23	1988	J.Tudor	30	30	198	10	8	0	87	41	2.32	2.73	3.21	29.5
47	74	1920	B.Doak	39	37	270	20	12	1	90	80	2.53	3.13	3.64	29.0
48	108	1904	J.Taylor	41	39	352	20	19	1	103	82	2.22	3.40	3.85	28.9
49	97	1907	E.Karger	39	32	314	15	19	1	137	65	2.04	2.90	3.79	28.3
50	63	1928	J.Haines	33	28	240	20	8	0	77	72	3.18	3.67	3.56	28.0

St. Louis Cardinals
Starting Pitchers

V	R	Year	Name	G	GS	IP	W	L	SV	SO	BB	ERA	RA/9	R Wtd RA/9	V Runs /162
51	55	1944	M.Lanier	33	30	224	17	12	0	141	71	2.65	3.29	3.50	27.6
52	56	1953	V.Mizell	33	33	224	13	11	0	173	114	3.49	3.74	3.51	27.3
53	90	1965	B.Gibson	38	36	299	20	12	1	270	103	3.07	3.31	3.74	27.0
54	64	1934	P.Dean	39	26	233	19	11	2	150	52	3.43	3.71	3.57	27.0
55	51	1967	D.Hughes	37	27	222	16	6	3	161	48	2.67	2.92	3.47	26.9
56	58	1966	A.Jackson	36	30	233	13	15	0	90	45	2.51	3.17	3.52	26.8
57	21	1997	A.Benes	26	26	177	10	7	0	175	61	3.10	3.25	3.20	26.7
58	37	1978	P.Vuckovich	45	23	198	12	12	1	149	59	2.54	2.95	3.34	26.7
59	62	1978	J.Denny	33	33	234	14	11	0	103	74	2.96	3.12	3.54	26.5
60	92	1964	B.Gibson	40	36	287	19	12	1	245	86	3.01	3.32	3.74	25.9
61	41	1944	H.Brecheen	30	22	189	16	5	0	88	46	2.85	3.19	3.40	25.6
62	88	1959	L.Jackson	40	37	256	14	13	0	145	64	3.30	3.62	3.71	25.4
63	50	1937	D.Dean	27	25	197	13	10	1	120	33	2.69	3.47	3.46	25.3
64	40	1950	M.Lanier	27	27	181	11	9	0	89	68	3.13	3.48	3.37	25.2
65	83	1931	B.Hallahan	37	30	249	19	9	4	159	112	3.29	3.69	3.70	25.1
66	68	1989	J.Magrane	34	33	235	18	9	0	127	72	2.91	3.11	3.60	25.1
67	103	1932	D.Dean	46	33	286	18	15	2	191	102	3.30	3.84	3.81	24.9
68	72	1947	H.Brecheen	29	28	223	16	11	1	89	66	3.30	3.71	3.64	24.0
69	60	1976	J.Denny	30	30	207	11	9	0	74	74	2.52	3.09	3.53	23.6
70	67	1997	M.Morris	33	33	217	12	9	0	149	69	3.19	3.65	3.59	23.3
71	70	1921	B.Doak	32	29	209	15	6	1	83	37	2.59	3.66	3.61	23.1
72	43	1949	G.Staley	45	17	171	10	10	6	55	41	2.73	3.42	3.40	23.1
73	32	1997	A.Benes	23	23	162	9	9	0	160	68	2.89	3.34	3.29	22.9
74	45	1947	A.Brazle	44	19	168	14	8	4	85	48	2.84	3.48	3.41	22.5
75	107	1972	R.Wise	35	35	269	16	16	0	142	71	3.11	3.28	3.84	22.5
76	76	1986	J.Tudor	30	30	219	13	7	0	107	53	2.92	3.33	3.64	22.3
77	85	1947	R.Munger	40	31	224	16	5	3	123	76	3.37	3.78	3.70	22.3
78	61	1931	S.Johnson	32	24	186	11	9	2	82	29	3.00	3.53	3.54	22.2
79	98	1928	P.Alexander	34	31	244	16	9	2	59	37	3.36	3.91	3.79	21.8
80	125	1933	D.Dean	48	34	293	20	18	4	199	64	3.04	3.47	3.94	21.0
81	48	1951	M.Lanier	31	23	160	11	9	1	59	50	3.26	3.38	3.44	20.9
82	82	1949	A.Brazle	39	25	206	14	8	0	75	61	3.18	3.71	3.69	20.8
83	104	1911	S.Sallee	36	30	245	15	9	3	74	64	2.76	3.75	3.83	20.8
84	69	1973	B.Gibson	25	25	195	12	10	0	142	57	2.77	3.28	3.60	20.7
85	126	1914	P.Perritt	41	32	286	16	13	2	115	93	2.36	3.34	3.95	20.2
86	101	1985	D.Cox	35	35	241	18	9	0	131	64	2.88	3.40	3.81	20.1
87	93	1931	P.Derringer	35	23	212	18	8	2	134	65	3.36	3.74	3.75	20.1
88	95	1963	C.Simmons	32	32	233	15	9	0	127	48	2.48	3.17	3.78	20.1
89	86	1926	P.Alexander	30	23	200	12	10	2	47	31	3.05	3.74	3.71	19.9
90	89	1968	R.Washburn	31	30	215	14	8	0	124	47	2.26	2.80	3.73	19.7
91	99	2000	D.Kile	34	34	232	20	9	0	192	58	3.91	4.22	3.80	19.7
92	119	1922	J.Pfeffer	44	32	261	19	12	2	83	58	3.58	4.34	3.92	19.5
93	54	1991	J.DeLeon	28	28	163	5	9	0	118	61	2.71	3.15	3.48	19.4
94	77	1929	S.Johnson	42	19	182	13	7	3	80	56	3.60	4.35	3.64	19.4
95	106	1947	M.Dickson	47	25	232	13	16	3	111	88	3.07	3.92	3.84	19.4
96	121	1954	H.Haddix	43	35	260	18	13	4	184	77	3.57	3.95	3.92	19.3
97	94	1957	L.Jackson	41	22	210	15	9	1	96	57	3.47	3.60	3.77	19.3
98	118	1941	L.Warneke	37	30	246	17	9	0	83	82	3.15	3.66	3.91	18.7
99	151	1911	B.Harmon	51	41	348	23	16	4	144	181	3.13	4.01	4.10	18.7
100	110	1950	H.Pollet	37	30	232	14	13	2	117	68	3.29	4.00	3.87	18.6

St. Louis Cardinals
Relief Pitchers

V	R	Year	Name	G	GS	IP	W	L	SV	SO	BB	ERA	RA/9	R Wtd RA/9	V Runs /162
1	4	1984	B.Sutter	71	0	123	5	7	45	77	23	1.54	1.91	2.13	33.1
2	5	1960	L.McDaniel	65	2	116	12	4	26	105	24	2.09	2.17	2.33	30.2
3	19	1948	T.Wilks	57	2	131	6	6	13	71	39	2.62	2.75	2.78	27.1
4	7	1986	R.Horton	42	9	100	4	3	3	49	26	2.24	2.24	2.45	23.4
5	13	1986	T.Worrell	74	0	104	9	10	36	73	41	2.08	2.52	2.75	20.8
6	3	1966	J.Hoerner	57	0	76	5	1	13	63	21	1.54	1.89	2.10	20.7
7	26	1981	B.Sutter	48	0	82	3	5	25	57	24	2.62	2.62	3.07	20.5
8	12	1998	J.Acevedo	50	9	98	8	3	15	56	29	2.56	2.75	2.71	20.1
9	11	1992	M.Perez	77	0	93	9	3	0	46	32	1.84	2.23	2.62	20.0
10	15	1975	A.Hrabosky	65	0	97	13	3	22	82	33	1.66	2.50	2.76	19.4
11	17	1987	T.Worrell	75	0	95	8	6	33	92	34	2.66	2.76	2.77	18.9
12	2	1995	T.Henke	52	0	54	1	1	36	48	18	1.82	1.82	1.78	18.7
13	9	1979	M.Littell	63	0	82	9	4	13	67	39	2.19	2.40	2.59	18.0
14	6	1966	H.Woodeshick	59	0	70	2	1	4	30	23	1.92	2.19	2.43	16.5
15	22	1982	D.Bair	63	0	92	5	3	8	68	36	2.55	2.65	2.96	16.3
16	20	1990	L.Smith	64	0	83	5	5	31	87	29	2.06	2.60	2.80	16.2
17	21	1977	B.Schultz	40	3	85	6	1	1	66	24	2.32	2.75	2.85	16.1
18	23	1965	H.Woodeshick	78	0	92	6	6	18	59	45	2.25	2.64	2.99	16.1
19	10	1991	L.Smith	67	0	73	6	3	47	67	13	2.34	2.34	2.59	16.0
20	27	1953	H.White	59	0	95	6	5	7	34	42	2.94	3.32	3.12	16.0
21	16	1997	J.Frascatore	59	0	80	5	2	0	58	33	2.47	2.81	2.77	15.9
22	37	1970	C.Taylor	56	7	124	6	7	8	64	31	3.11	3.41	3.43	15.5
23	43	1963	R.Taylor	54	9	133	9	7	11	91	30	2.84	2.97	3.54	15.0
24	18	2000	D.Veres	71	0	76	3	5	29	67	25	2.85	3.09	2.78	14.9
25	30	1977	C.Carroll	59	1	101	5	5	5	38	28	2.76	3.12	3.23	14.9
26	8	1992	T.Worrell	67	0	64	5	3	3	64	25	2.11	2.11	2.48	14.8
27	34	1952	A.Brazle	46	6	109	12	5	16	55	42	2.72	3.14	3.40	14.8
28	25	1989	F.DiPino	67	0	88	9	0	0	44	20	2.45	2.65	3.06	14.6
29	1	1995	T.Fossas	58	0	37	3	0	0	40	10	1.47	1.47	1.44	14.4
30	36	1973	O.Pena	53	2	107	5	5	7	61	22	2.91	3.11	3.42	13.6
31	28	1974	M.Garman	64	0	82	7	2	6	45	27	2.64	2.85	3.13	13.0
32	38	1952	E.Yuhas	54	2	99	12	2	6	39	35	2.72	3.18	3.44	12.9
33	24	1993	M.Perez	65	0	73	7	2	7	58	20	2.48	2.97	2.99	12.7
34	39	1973	D.Segui	65	0	100	7	6	17	93	53	2.78	3.15	3.46	12.2
35	33	1985	R.Horton	49	3	90	3	2	1	59	34	2.91	3.01	3.37	11.9
36	35	1974	R.Folkers	55	0	90	6	2	2	57	38	3.00	3.10	3.40	11.5
37	32	1996	T.Mathews	67	0	84	2	6	6	80	32	3.01	3.44	3.33	11.5
38	41	1955	P.LaPalme	56	0	92	4	3	3	39	34	2.75	3.52	3.51	11.3
39	31	1989	D.Quisenberry	63	0	78	3	1	6	37	14	2.64	2.87	3.32	10.7
40	47	1978	M.Littell	72	2	106	4	8	11	130	59	2.79	3.22	3.65	10.7
41	40	1992	C.Carpenter	73	0	88	5	4	1	46	27	2.97	2.97	3.49	10.5
42	29	1994	J.Habyan	52	0	47	1	0	1	46	20	3.23	3.23	3.17	10.3
43	14	1996	R.Honeycutt	61	0	47	2	1	4	30	7	2.85	2.85	2.76	9.4
44	49	1982	B.Sutter	70	0	102	9	8	36	61	34	2.90	3.34	3.73	9.4
45	46	1996	M.Petkovsek	48	6	89	11	2	0	45	35	3.55	3.76	3.64	9.1
46	44	1967	R.Willis	65	0	81	6	5	10	42	43	2.67	3.00	3.56	9.0
47	60	1988	S.Terry	51	11	129	9	6	3	65	34	2.92	3.34	3.93	8.9
48	63	1949	T.Wilks	59	0	118	10	3	9	71	38	3.73	3.97	3.95	8.4
49	45	1989	K.Dayley	71	0	75	4	3	12	40	30	2.87	3.11	3.60	8.0
50	50	1988	T.Worrell	68	0	90	5	9	32	78	34	3.00	3.20	3.77	7.9

Washington Senators/ Minnesota Twins (1901–2000)

Someone has to finish at the bottom of the standings. Washington assumed this position for the first 11 years of its existence. The Senators averaged a 55–92 record during these bleak years, and failed to finish higher than sixth place in the standings. They were only 61–75 in 1902 when Ed Delahanty hit .376 with 10 home runs, for a 1,061 Total Factor and 90.3 Hits Contribution. In 1909, Washington was so bad that 21-year-old Walter Johnson's 2.22 ERA netted him a 13–25 record, while the team's other pitchers had an even more dreadful 29–85 record. That 1909 team earned its 42–110 record by hitting for a .223 average and 9 home runs, and generating just 2.5 runs per game while giving up 4.3 runs per game.

In 1912, the Senators finally earned a winning season, finishing second behind Boston with a 91–61 record. Johnson went 33–12 with a 1.39 ERA and 2.19 Wtd. RA/9, while saving 102.0 runs from scoring over 369 innings. In 1913, the Senators again finished in second place with a 90–64 record, thanks entirely to Walter Johnson. In 346 innings, Johnson was a phenomenal 36–7 with 243 strikeouts, 38 walks, and a sparkling 1.14 ERA. Johnson's 1.68 Wtd. RA/9 is the third best rate of success in major league history. Johnson also saved 116.5 runs from scoring, giving him the highest volume of success since the 1888 season. He even batted .261 that year for a 726 Production, versus his team's .252 average and 643 Production. For his efforts, Johnson won the Chalmers (MVP) Award. Outfielder Clyde Milan chipped in with a .301 average and a league leading 75 stolen bases. The Senators generated four more winning seasons over the next 11 years—a poor showing, given Johnson's continued superb pitching.

In 1924, the Senators ended the Yankees' three-year reign at the top, led by the pitching of Tom Zachary, George Mogridge, Firpo Marberry, and 36-year-old MVP Walter Johnson, who led the league in wins (23) and ERA (2.72), while boasting a 2.84 Wtd. RA/9. The Senators won another pennant in 1925, as Johnson produced his last 20-win season. Veteran Stan Coveleski was 20–5 with a league leading 2.84 ERA and a 2.79 Wtd. RA/9 in his first season for the Senators. Another veteran, shortstop Roger Peckinpaugh (.294, 4 home runs) won the MVP Award in his last full season in the majors. Also contributing were Sam Rice (.350 average), Goose Goslin (.334, 20 triples, 18 home runs, 931 Total Factor), and Joe Judge (.314, 8 home runs). After counting on Walter Johnson's help since 1908, the Senators were unable to stay on top when his performance finally faded in 1926.

Washington staged a comeback with four solid seasons in 1930–1933, as General Crowder won 86 games in those four years. Shortstop Joe Cronin became a star in 1930, hitting .346 with 13 home runs, for a 940 Total Factor and 92.6 Hits Contribution. The Senators won their third pennant in 1933, led by a balanced attack of Goslin, Cronin, Buddy Myer, Heinie Manush (.336 average, 17 triples), Joe Kuhel (.322 average), and part-time help from 43-year-old Sam Rice. The 1933 season capped a 22-year period in which the Senators put together 14 winning seasons.

The Senators then returned to their original losing ways, plunging to seventh place in 1934. Over the 28-year period from 1934 to 1961, the team generated only four winning seasons, and two of the winning records were wartime efforts against weakened competition. The best hitters during these difficult years were Buddy Myer (.349

average in 1935), Cecil Travis (.359 average and 19 triples in 1941), Mickey Vernon (.353 average in 1946), and Roy Sievers (.301 average, 42 home runs, 962 Wtd. Production in 1957). The top pitcher seasons came from Roger Wolff (20–10, 2.12 ERA, 2.84 Wtd. RA/9 in 1945), Camilo Pascual (17–10, 2.64 ERA in 1959), and reliever Dick Hyde (10–3, 18 saves, 1.75 ERA, 2.46 Wtd. RA/9 in 1958).

The franchise moved to Minnesota in 1961, and quickly built a winning tradition. From 1962 to 1979, Minnesota produced 13 seasons of .500 or better ball. In 1965, they won their first World Series in 41 years, with shortstop Zoilo Versalles (.273, 19 home runs, 27 steals) winning the MVP Award. The Twins also captured two division crowns in 1969 and 1970. These winning teams of the sixties and early seventies were built around Harmon Killebrew (.276 average, 49 home runs, 145 walks, 1,032 Wtd. Production, MVP in 1969), Bob Allison, Jimmie Hall, Earl Battey, Jim Perry, and the multitalented Tony Oliva (.323 average, 32 home runs, 958 Total Factor in 1964).

Rod Carew was Rookie of the Year in 1967, and he became the Twins' biggest star in the 1970s after Killebrew faded. Carew's best seasons were in 1975, when he played second and hit .359 with 14 home runs for a 997 Total Factor, and in 1977, when he covered first and hit .388 with 14 home runs for a 1,014 Total Factor, while winning the MVP Award. Pitching ace Bert Blyleven (20–17, 2.52 ERA in 1973) was traded to Texas during the 1976 season, and Carew went to California in 1979, contributing to the Twins' slide to below .500 from 1980 to 1986.

The Twins climbed from sixth place in 1986 to win their third World Series in 1987 with just 85 regular season wins. The 1988 Twins were a better ball club with 91 wins, but they finished in second place in their division. This 1988 squad was paced by Kirby Puckett (.356, 24 home runs, 1,016 Total Factor in his best season), Gary Gaetti (.301, 28 home runs, 959 Total Factor in his best season), Kent Hrbek (.312, 25 home runs), and Frank Viola (24–7, 2.64 ERA, 2.92 Wtd. RA/9). The Twins went from last place in 1990 to win their fourth World Series in 1991, as relief ace Rick Aguilera went 4–5 with 42 saves, a 2.35 ERA, and 2.65 Wtd. RA/9.

The new economics of baseball put a squeeze on the Twins, a small market team, and they were unable to stay competitive in the 1990s. Minnesota lost star Chuck Knoblauch (.341, 13 home runs, 45 steals in 1996) to the Yankees in 1998, and they also lost Kirby Puckett when he retired after the 1995 season with eye problems. The Twins finished the century as they began, fielding teams from 1993 to 1999 that had no chance of winning. The 2000 season saw no change in the Twins fortunes, as they won only 69 games.

Washington Senators/Minnesota Twins — Hitters Volume of Success

Pos	Year	Name	AB	BB	HBP	TAB	H	2B	3B	HR	BA	OB	SA	PRO	Wtd PRO	SB	CS	SBF	SPF	FF	R TF	V HC
C	1963	E.Battey	508	61	8	577	145	17	1	26	.285	.371	.476	847	862	0	0	0	(10)	30	882	56.2
1B	1977	R.Carew	616	69	3	688	239	38	16	14	.388	.452	.570	1,022	1,008	23	13	(4)	10	0	1,014	79.8
2B	1996	C.Knoblauch	578	98	19	695	197	35	14	13	.341	.452	.517	969	884	45	14	23	10	0	917	76.7
SS	1930	J.Cronin	587	72	5	664	203	41	9	13	.346	.422	.513	934	854	17	10	(4)	10	80	940	92.6
3B	1969	H.Killebrew	555	145	5	705	153	20	2	49	.276	.430	.584	1,014	1,032	8	2	5	(10)	(60)	968	84.5
OF	1902	E.Delahanty	473	62	4	539	178	43	14	10	.376	.453	.590	1,043	1,051	16			10	0	1,061	90.3
OF	1988	K.Puckett	657	23	2	682	234	42	5	24	.356	.380	.545	925	937	6	7	(11)	10	80	1,016	84.1
OF	1928	G.Goslin	456	48	3	507	173	36	10	17	.379	.442	.614	1,056	1,006	16	3	19	10	10	1,044	72.9
Starters		Averages	554	72	6	632	190	34	9	21	.344	.425	.549	974	952	16	6	3	5	18	978	79.6
C	1923	M.Ruel	449	55	3	507	142	24	3	0	.316	.394	.383	778	743	4	6	(15)	0	50	778	25.5
1B	1964	B.Allison	492	92	7	591	141	27	4	32	.287	.406	.553	959	970	10	1	13	10	(20)	973	57.0
2B	1935	B.Myer	616	96	4	716	215	36	11	5	.349	.440	.468	907	851	7	6	(7)	10	20	874	67.8
SS	1941	C.Travis	608	52	1	661	218	39	19	7	.359	.410	.520	930	899	2	2	(3)	0	10	906	80.9
3B	1988	G.Gaetti	468	36	5	509	141	29	2	28	.301	.358	.551	909	921	7	4	(2)	0	40	959	59.0
OF	1964	T.Oliva	672	34	6	712	217	43	9	32	.323	.361	.557	918	928	12	6	0	10	20	958	68.0
OF	1944	S.Spence	592	69	4	665	187	31	8	18	.316	.391	.486	877	914	3	7	(16)	0	60	958	66.8
OF	1957	R.Sievers	572	76	7	655	172	23	5	42	.301	.389	.579	968	962	1	1	(1)	(10)	(10)	941	60.3
Reserves		Averages	559	64	5	627	179	32	8	21	.321	.395	.514	909	901	6	4	(4)	3	21	921	60.7
Totals		Weighted Ave.	555	69	6	630	187	33	8	21	.336	.415	.538	953	935	13	5	1	4	19	959	73.3

Pitchers Volume of Success

Pos	Year	Name	G	GS	IP	W	L	SV	SO	BB	ERA	RA/9	Wtd RA/9	R V Runs/162
SP	1913	W.Johnson	48	36	346	36	7	2	243	38	1.14	1.46	1.68	116.5
SP	1932	G.Crowder	50	39	327	26	13	1	103	77	3.33	3.74	3.24	50.3
SP	1945	R.Wolff	33	29	250	20	10	2	108	53	2.12	2.45	2.84	50.1
SP	1925	S.Coveleski	32	32	241	20	5	0	58	73	2.84	3.21	2.79	49.9
SP	1973	B.Blyleven	40	40	325	20	17	0	258	67	2.52	3.02	3.20	49.0
Starters		Averages	41	35	298	24	10	1	154	62	2.36	2.75	2.73	63.2
RP	1980	D.Corbett	73	0	136	8	6	23	89	42	1.98	2.05	2.07	37.6
RP	1979	M.Marshall	90	1	143	10	15	32	81	48	2.65	2.96	2.86	27.0
RP	1963	B.Dailey	66	0	109	6	3	21	72	19	1.99	2.15	2.40	26.1
RP	1958	D.Hyde	53	0	103	10	3	18	49	35	1.75	2.27	2.46	25.3
Relievers		Averages	71	0	123	9	7	24	73	36	2.13	2.38	2.46	29.0
Totals		Averages	111	35	421	33	17	25	227	98	2.29	2.64	2.65	92.2

Washington Senators/Minnesota Twins (1901–2000)

Washington Senators/Minnesota Twins — **Hitters Rate of Success**

Pos	Year	Name	AB	BB	HBP	TAB	H	2B	3B	HR	BA	OB	SA	PRO	Wtd PRO	SB	CS	SBF	SPF	FF	R TF	V HC
C	1963	E.Battey	508	61	8	577	145	17	1	26	.285	.371	.476	847	862	0	0	0	(10)	30	882	56.2
1B	1964	B.Allison	492	92	7	591	141	27	4	32	.287	.406	.553	959	970	10	1	13	10	(20)	973	57.0
2B	1975	R.Carew	535	64	1	600	192	24	4	14	.359	.428	.497	926	950	35	9	27	10	10	997	89.0
SS	1930	J.Cronin	587	72	5	664	203	41	9	13	.346	.422	.513	934	854	17	10	(4)	10	80	940	92.6
3B	1969	H.Killebrew	555	145	5	705	153	20	2	49	.276	.430	.584	1,014	1,032	8	2	5	(10)	(60)	968	84.5
OF	1902	E.Delahanty	473	62	4	539	178	43	14	10	.376	.453	.590	1,043	1,051	16		10		0	1,061	90.3
OF	1928	G.Goslin	456	48	3	507	173	36	10	17	.379	.442	.614	1,056	1,006	16	3	19	10	10	1,044	72.9
OF	1988	K.Puckett	657	23	2	682	234	42	5	24	.356	.380	.545	925	937	6	7	(11)	10	80	1,016	84.1
Starters		Averages	533	71	4	608	177	31	6	23	.333	.415	.545	960	956	14	4	6	5	16	983	78.3
C	1923	M.Ruel	449	55	3	507	142	24	3	0	.316	.394	.383	778	743	4	6	(15)	0	50	778	25.5
1B	1946	M.Vernon	587	49	0	636	207	51	8	8	.353	.403	.508	910	928	14	10	(9)	10	0	930	50.9
2B	1996	C.Knoblauch	578	98	19	695	197	35	14	13	.341	.452	.517	969	884	45	14	23	10	0	917	76.7
SS	1941	C.Travis	608	52	1	661	218	39	19	7	.359	.410	.520	930	899	2	2	(3)	0	10	906	80.9
3B	1988	G.Gaetti	468	36	5	509	141	29	2	28	.301	.358	.551	909	921	7	4	(2)	0	40	959	59.0
OF	1971	T.Oliva	487	25	2	514	164	30	3	22	.337	.372	.546	918	947	4	1	4	10	10	971	52.3
OF	1944	S.Spence	592	69	4	665	187	31	8	18	.316	.391	.486	877	914	3	7	(16)	0	60	958	66.8
OF	1957	R.Sievers	572	76	7	655	172	23	5	42	.301	.389	.579	968	962	1	1	(1)	(10)	(10)	941	60.3
Reserves		Averages	543	58	5	605	179	33	8	17	.329	.398	.513	912	902	10	6	(2)	3	20	922	59.0
Totals		Weighted Ave.	536	66	5	607	178	32	7	21	.332	.410	.534	944	938	12	5	3	4	18	963	71.9

Pitchers Rate of Success

Pos	Year	Name	G	GS	IP	W	L	SV	SO	BB	ERA	RA/9	Wtd RA/9	V Runs/162
SP	1913	W.Johnson	48	36	346	36	7	2	243	38	1.14	1.46	1.68	116.5
SP	1925	S.Coveleski	32	32	241	20	5	0	58	73	2.84	3.21	2.79	49.9
SP	1945	R.Wolff	33	29	250	20	10	2	108	53	2.12	2.45	2.84	50.1
SP	1988	F.Viola	35	35	255	24	7	0	193	54	2.64	2.82	2.92	46.4
SP	1924	T.Zachary	33	27	203	15	9	2	45	53	2.75	3.28	2.97	37.6
Starters		Averages	36	32	259	23	8	1	129	54	2.19	2.53	2.56	60.1
RP	1980	D.Corbett	73	0	136	8	6	23	89	42	1.98	2.05	2.07	37.6
RP	1963	B.Dailey	66	0	109	6	3	21	72	19	1.99	2.15	2.40	26.1
RP	1958	D.Hyde	53	0	103	10	3	18	49	35	1.75	2.27	2.46	25.3
RP	1991	R.Aguilera	63	0	69	4	5	42	61	30	2.35	2.61	2.65	14.6
Relievers		Averages	64	0	104	7	4	26	68	32	1.99	2.22	2.35	25.9
Totals		Averages	100	32	363	30	12	27	197	86	2.13	2.44	2.50	86.0

Washington Senators/Minnesota Twins
Catchers

V	R	Year	Name	AB	BB	HBP	TAB	H	2B	3B	HR	BA	OB	SA	PRO	Wtd PRO	SB	CS	SBF	SPF	FF	R TF	V HC
1	1	1963	E.Battey	508	61	8	577	145	17	1	26	.285	.371	.476	847	862	0	0	0	(10)	30	882	56.2
2	2	1961	E.Battey	460	53	3	516	139	24	1	17	.302	.378	.470	847	824	3	3	(5)	(10)	40	849	42.1
3	3	1965	E.Battey	394	50	2	446	117	22	2	6	.297	.379	.409	788	815	0	0	0	(10)	10	815	29.3
4	5	1923	M.Ruel	449	55	3	507	142	24	3	0	.316	.394	.383	778	743	4	6	(15)		50	778	25.5
5	6	1960	E.Battey	466	48	8	522	126	24	2	15	.270	.349	.427	776	763	4	5	(11)	(10)	30	772	24.7
6	4	1964	E.Battey	405	51	1	457	110	17	1	12	.272	.354	.407	762	771	1	1	(2)	(10)	20	778	22.0
7	13	1962	E.Battey	522	57	0	579	146	20	3	11	.280	.351	.393	743	727	0	0	0	(10)	40	757	21.9
8	15	1976	B.Wynegar	534	79	2	615	139	21	2	10	.260	.358	.363	721	767	0	0	0	(20)		747	20.4
9	12	1990	B.Harper	479	19	7	505	141	42	3	6	.294	.331	.432	763	773	3	2	(2)	(10)		761	20.2
10	8	1926	M.Ruel	368	61	2	431	110	22	4	1	.299	.401	.389	790	751	7	6	(11)	(10)	40	770	19.9
11	10	1991	B.Harper	441	14	6	461	137	28	1	10	.311	.341	.447	787	789	1	2	(6)	(10)	(10)	763	18.8
12	11	1921	P.Gharrity	387	45	3	435	120	19	8	7	.310	.386	.455	841	776	4	3	(4)		(10)	762	18.4
13	9	1989	B.Harper	385	13	6	404	125	24	0	8	.325	.356	.449	806	824	2	4	(14)	(10)	(30)	770	17.7
14	7	1985	M.Salas	360	18	1	379	108	20	5	9	.300	.335	.458	793	786	0	1	(5)		(10)	771	16.8
15	17	1992	B.Harper	502	26	7	535	154	25	0	9	.307	.350	.410	760	772	0	1	(4)	(10)	(20)	739	15.7
16	18	1927	M.Ruel	428	63	5	496	132	16	5	1	.308	.403	.376	779	733	9	6	(6)	(10)	20	737	14.8
17	14	1983	D.Engle	374	28	1	403	114	22	4	8	.305	.355	.449	804	800	2	1	0		(50)	750	14.0
18	20	1943	J.Early	423	53	4	480	109	23	3	5	.258	.346	.362	708	753	5	3	(2)		(20)	731	13.0
19	16	1941	J.Early	355	24	3	382	102	20	7	10	.287	.338	.468	805	779	0	1	(5)		(30)	744	12.7
20	21	1973	G.Mitterwald	432	39	5	476	112	15	0	16	.259	.328	.405	733	749	3	1	2	(10)	(10)	731	12.2
21	19	1916	J.Henry	305	49	6	360	76	12	3	0	.249	.364	.308	672	736	12					736	10.5
22	23	1925	M.Ruel	393	63	4	460	122	9	2	0	.310	.411	.344	754	693	4	5	(12)		40	721	10.1
23	24	1938	R.Ferrell	411	75	0	486	120	24	5	1	.292	.401	.382	783	715	1	0	2	(10)	10	717	9.7
24	22	1988	T.Laudner	375	36	1	412	94	18	1	13	.251	.318	.408	726	736	0	0	0	(10)		726	9.5
25	27	1979	B.Wynegar	504	74	2	580	136	20	0	7	.270	.366	.351	717	699	2	2	(3)	(10)	20	706	7.9

Washington Senators/Minnesota Twins
First basemen

V	R	Year	Name	AB	BB	HBP	TAB	H	2B	3B	HR	BA	OB	SA	PRO	Wtd PRO	SB	CS	SBF	SPF	FF	R TF	V HC
1	2	1977	R.Carew	616	69	3	688	239	38	16	14	.388	.452	.570	1,022	1,008	23	13	(4)	10		1,014	79.8
2	1	1967	H.Killebrew	547	131	3	681	147	24	1	44	.269	.413	.558	970	1,044	1	0	1	(10)	(20)	1,015	79.6
3	3	1964	B.Allison	492	92	7	591	141	27	4	32	.287	.406	.553	959	970	10	1	13	10	(20)	973	57.0
4	4	1961	H.Killebrew	541	107	3	651	156	20	7	46	.288	.409	.606	1,015	987	1	2	(4)	(10)	(30)	942	53.5
5	5	1946	M.Vernon	587	49	0	636	207	51	8	8	.353	.403	.508	910	928	14	10	(9)	10		930	50.9
6	6	1976	R.Carew	605	67	1	673	200	29	12	9	.331	.398	.463	861	916	49	22	7	10	(10)	923	49.1
7	9	1953	M.Vernon	608	63	4	675	205	43	11	15	.337	.403	.518	921	903	4	6	(11)	10	10	912	48.0
8	10	1984	K.Hrbek	559	65	4	628	174	31	3	27	.311	.387	.522	909	910	1	1	(2)			909	41.5
9	11	1978	R.Carew	564	78	1	643	188	26	10	5	.333	.415	.441	857	873	27	7	19	10		902	40.5
10	8	1988	K.Hrbek	510	67	0	577	159	31	0	25	.312	.392	.520	911	924	0	3	(10)	(10)	10	914	39.5
11	13	1987	K.Hrbek	477	84	0	561	136	20	1	34	.285	.392	.545	937	896	5	2	2			898	34.2
12	14	1990	K.Hrbek	492	69	7	568	141	26	0	22	.287	.382	.474	856	867	5	2	2	(10)	30	889	32.2
13	7	1989	K.Hrbek	375	53	1	429	102	17	0	25	.272	.364	.517	881	900	3	0	7	(10)	20	917	30.1
14	15	1917	J.Judge	393	50	2	445	112	15	15	2	.285	.369	.415	783	867	17			10	10	887	26.0
15	18	1930	J.Judge	442	60	3	505	144	29	11	10	.326	.410	.509	919	840	13	6	2		30	872	25.9
16	16	1965	H.Killebrew	401	72	4	477	108	16	1	25	.269	.386	.501	887	918	0	0	0	(10)	(30)	878	24.6
17	12	1925	J.Harris	319	56	5	380	100	21	10	13	.313	.424	.564	988	908	6	3	0		(10)	898	24.4
18	26	1933	J.Kuhel	602	59	2	663	194	34	10	11	.322	.385	.467	851	821	17	8	1	10	10	842	24.1
19	27	1954	M.Vernon	597	61	5	663	173	33	14	20	.290	.360	.492	853	852	1	4	(10)			842	23.8
20	22	1983	K.Hrbek	515	57	3	575	153	41	5	16	.297	.370	.489	860	856	4	6	(13)		10	853	22.7
21	19	1960	H.Killebrew	442	71	1	514	122	19	1	31	.276	.377	.534	911	896	1	0	2	(10)	(30)	858	22.6
22	20	1972	H.Killebrew	433	94	1	528	100	13	2	26	.231	.369	.450	820	889	0	1	(4)	(10)	(20)	855	22.5
23	17	1969	R.Reese	419	23	5	447	135	24	4	16	.322	.365	.513	878	894	1	5	(19)			875	22.4
24	29	1936	J.Kuhel	588	64	4	656	189	42	8	16	.321	.392	.502	893	804	15	7	1	10	20	836	21.7
25	25	1913	C.Gandil	550	36	3	589	175	25	8	1	.318	.363	.398	762	813	22				30	843	21.6

Washington Senators/Minnesota Twins
Second basemen

V	R	Year	Name	AB	BB	HBP	TAB	H	2B	3B	HR	BA	OB	SA	PRO	Wtd PRO	SB	CS	SBF	SPF	FF	R TF	V HC
1	1	1975	R.Carew	535	64	1	600	192	24	4	14	.359	.428	.497	926	950	35	9	27	10	10	997	89.0
2	3	1974	R.Carew	599	74	1	674	218	30	5	3	.364	.435	.446	880	919	38	16	8	10	10	948	84.3
3	2	1973	R.Carew	580	62	2	644	203	30	11	6	.350	.415	.471	885	905	41	16	13	10	20	948	80.6
4	4	1996	C.Knoblauch	578	98	19	695	197	35	14	13	.341	.452	.517	969	884	45	14	23	10		917	76.7
5	5	1995	C.Knoblauch	538	78	10	626	179	34	8	11	.333	.427	.487	914	859	46	18	15	10	10	894	70.0
6	6	1935	B.Myer	616	96	4	716	215	36	11	5	.349	.440	.468	907	851	7	6	(7)	10	20	874	67.8
7	9	1997	C.Knoblauch	611	84	17	712	178	26	10	9	.291	.392	.411	803	758	62	10	56	10	30	853	57.0
8	7	1938	B.Myer	437	93	1	531	147	22	8	6	.336	.454	.465	918	839	9	5	(2)		20	857	45.7
9	12	1994	C.Knoblauch	445	41	10	496	139	45	3	5	.312	.383	.461	844	785	35	6	44	10	(20)	819	44.7
10	11	1972	R.Carew	535	43	2	580	170	21	6	0	.318	.371	.379	750	813	12	6	0	10		823	40.1
11	10	1969	R.Carew	458	37	3	498	152	30	4	8	.332	.386	.467	853	869	19	8	6	10	(40)	844	37.7
12	8	1979	R.Wilfong	419	29	2	450	131	22	6	9	.313	.360	.458	818	798	11	4	6	10	40	854	36.3
13	15	1905	C.Hickman	573	21	7	601	159	37	12	4	.277	.311	.405	716	825	6				(30)	795	32.9
14	14	1933	B.Myer	530	60	1	591	160	29	15	4	.302	.374	.436	810	781	6	8	(16)	10	20	795	32.5
15	18	1934	B.Myer	524	102	1	627	160	33	8	3	.305	.419	.416	835	786	6	6	(9)	10	(10)	777	28.9
16	19	1992	C.Knoblauch	600	88	5	693	178	19	6	2	.297	.391	.358	749	762	34	13	11	10	(10)	773	28.8
17	13	1906	L.Schlafly	426	50	14	490	105	13	8	2	.246	.345	.329	674	766	29			10	20	796	27.1
18	17	1907	J.Delahanty	499	41	14	554	139	21	7	2	.279	.350	.361	711	821	24				(40)	781	26.7
19	20	1983	J.Castino	563	62	1	626	156	30	4	11	.277	.350	.403	753	750	4	2	0		20	770	25.2
20	16	1911	K.Elberfeld	404	65	25	494	110	19	4	0	.272	.405	.339	744	755	24			10	20	785	24.6
21	23	1943	J.Priddy	560	67	1	628	152	31	3	4	.271	.350	.359	709	755	5	5	(8)		10	758	22.8
22	26	1901	J.Farrell	555	52	1	608	151	32	11	3	.272	.336	.386	721	723	25			10	20	753	22.7
23	21	1967	R.Carew	514	37	2	553	150	22	7	8	.292	.342	.409	750	807	5	9	(22)	10	(30)	765	21.0
24	28	1923	B.Harris	532	50	13	595	150	21	13	2	.282	.358	.382	740	706	23	16	(14)	10	50	752	19.9
25	24	1945	G.Myatt	490	63	2	555	145	17	7	1	.296	.378	.365	744	782	30	11	14	10	(50)	756	19.7

Washington Senators/Minnesota Twins
Shortstops

V	R	Year	Name	AB	BB	HBP	TAB	H	2B	3B	HR	BA	OB	SA	PRO	Wtd PRO	SB	CS	SBF	SPF	FF	R TF	V HC
1	1	1930	J.Cronin	587	72	5	664	203	41	9	13	.346	.422	.513	934	854	17	10	(4)	10	80	940	92.6
2	2	1941	C.Travis	608	52	1	661	218	39	19	7	.359	.410	.520	930	899	2	2	(3)		10	906	80.9
3	3	1965	Z.Versalles	666	41	7	714	182	45	12	19	.273	.322	.462	785	812	27	5	23	10	40	885	75.7
4	5	1931	J.Cronin	611	81	4	696	187	44	13	12	.306	.391	.480	870	830	10	9	(11)	10	40	869	72.3
5	6	1933	J.Cronin	602	87	2	691	186	45	11	5	.309	.398	.445	843	813	5	4	(4)	10	50	869	71.7
6	4	1932	J.Cronin	557	66	3	626	177	43	18	6	.318	.393	.492	885	833	7	5	(5)	10	40	878	67.9
7	8	1979	R.Smalley	621	80	4	705	168	28	3	24	.271	.357	.441	799	779	2	3	(5)		60	834	57.7
8	7	1978	R.Smalley	586	85	1	672	160	31	3	19	.273	.366	.433	800	815	2	8	(20)		40	835	55.5
9	10	1969	L.Cardenas	578	66	4	648	162	24	4	10	.280	.358	.388	746	759	5	6	(10)		70	819	48.5
10	11	1934	J.Cronin	504	53	1	558	143	30	9	7	.284	.353	.421	774	728	8	0	14	10	60	812	41.9
11	9	1980	R.Smalley	486	65	2	553	135	24	1	12	.278	.365	.405	771	765	3	3	(5)		60	820	41.6
12	14	1964	Z.Versalles	659	42	8	709	171	33	10	20	.259	.312	.431	743	751	14	4	8	10		769	36.2
13	12	1971	L.Cardenas	554	51	1	606	146	25	4	18	.264	.327	.421	747	771	3	3	(5)		20	787	36.0
14	16	1963	Z.Versalles	621	33	5	659	162	31	13	10	.261	.303	.401	704	717	7	4	(1)	10	40	765	32.4
15	13	1910	G.McBride	514	61	8	583	118	19	4	1	.230	.321	.288	609	692	11				80	772	32.1
16	17	1929	J.Cronin	494	85	1	580	139	29	8	8	.281	.388	.421	809	755	5	9	(21)	10	20	764	29.7
17	19	1938	C.Travis	567	58	4	629	190	30	5	5	.335	.401	.432	833	760	6	5	(6)			754	29.1
18	18	1908	G.McBride	518	41	3	562	120	10	6	0	.232	.292	.274	566	668	12				90	758	27.1
19	20	1937	C.Travis	526	39	5	570	181	27	7	3	.344	.395	.439	834	764	3	2	(2)		(10)	753	25.9
20	15	1989	G.Gagne	460	17	2	479	125	29	7	9	.272	.301	.424	725	741	11	4	6	10	10	766	23.8
21	22	1907	D.Altizer	540	34	6	580	145	15	5	2	.269	.319	.326	645	745	38			10	(20)	735	21.2
22	25	1962	Z.Versalles	568	37	2	607	137	18	3	17	.241	.290	.373	663	648	5	5	(8)	10	70	721	17.0
23	21	1987	G.Gagne	437	25	4	466	116	28	7	10	.265	.311	.430	741	709	6	6	(12)	10	30	737	16.6
24	27	1904	J.Cassidy	581	15	4	600	140	12	19	1	.241	.265	.332	597	684	17			10	20	714	15.7
25	26	1976	R.Smalley	513	76	2	591	133	18	3	3	.259	.357	.324	681	724	2	4	(10)			715	14.8

Washington Senators/Minnesota Twins
Third basemen

V	R	Year	Name	AB	BB	HBP	TAB	H	2B	3B	HR	BA	OB	SA	PRO	Wtd PRO	SB	CS	SBF	SPF	FF	R TF	V HC
1	1	1969	H.Killebrew	555	145	5	705	153	20	2	49	.276	.430	.584	1,014	1,032	8	2	5	(10)	(60)	968	84.5
2	3	1966	H.Killebrew	569	103	2	674	160	27	1	39	.281	.393	.538	931	972	0	2	(6)	(10)	(40)	917	64.3
3	2	1988	G.Gaetti	468	36	5	509	141	29	2	28	.301	.358	.551	909	921	7	4	(2)		40	959	59.0
4	4	1986	G.Gaetti	596	52	6	654	171	34	1	34	.287	.350	.518	869	854	14	15	(23)		50	881	51.4
5	5	1970	H.Killebrew	527	128	2	657	143	20	1	41	.271	.416	.546	962	966	0	3	(9)	(10)	(70)	877	50.4
6	9	1959	H.Killebrew	546	90	7	643	132	20	2	42	.242	.356	.516	873	869	3	2	(1)	(10)	(30)	827	35.8
7	10	1939	B.Lewis	536	72	2	610	171	23	16	10	.319	.402	.478	879	818	10	9	(12)	10	10	825	33.4
8	12	1951	E.Yost	568	126	11	705	161	36	4	12	.283	.423	.424	847	827	6	4	(3)	10	(30)	804	31.1
9	11	1954	E.Yost	539	131	5	675	138	26	4	11	.256	.406	.380	786	785	7	3	1	10	10	806	30.5
10	8	1980	J.Castino	546	29	0	575	165	17	7	13	.302	.337	.430	768	762	7	5	(5)	10	60	827	30.4
11	7	1975	E.Soderholm	419	53	0	472	120	17	2	11	.286	.367	.415	782	802	3	5	(14)	10	40	838	27.5
12	17	1953	E.Yost	577	123	4	704	157	30	7	9	.272	.403	.395	799	783	7	4	(1)	10		792	26.6
13	19	1950	E.Yost	573	141	8	722	169	26	2	11	.295	.440	.405	845	786	6	6	(8)	10		788	26.1
14	6	1973	S.Braun	361	74	3	438	102	28	5	6	.283	.409	.438	846	865	4	3	(4)	10	(30)	841	26.0
15	13	1940	C.Travis	528	48	2	578	170	37	11	2	.322	.381	.445	826	777	0	1	(3)		30	804	25.4
16	14	1963	R.Rollins	531	36	8	575	163	23	1	16	.307	.360	.444	804	818	2	0	3		(20)	802	23.4
17	16	1902	B.Coughlin	469	26	8	503	141	27	4	6	.301	.348	.414	762	768	29			10	20	798	22.7
18	18	1987	G.Gaetti	584	37	3	624	150	36	2	31	.257	.304	.485	789	755	10	7	(6)		40	789	21.5
19	15	1942	B.Estralella	429	85	3	517	119	24	5	8	.277	.400	.413	813	837	5	2	2		(40)	798	21.3
20	22	1983	G.Gaetti	584	54	4	642	143	30	3	21	.245	.313	.414	727	724	7	1	7		50	782	20.0
21	27	1962	R.Rollins	624	75	6	705	186	23	5	16	.298	.379	.428	807	789	3	1	1		(20)	770	18.1
22	23	1928	O.Bluege	518	46	8	572	154	33	7	2	.297	.364	.400	763	727	18	6	10	10	30	777	17.4
23	20	1974	E.Soderholm	464	48	5	517	128	18	3	10	.276	.350	.392	742	775	7	3	2	10		787	17.4
24	34	1912	E.Foster	618	53	4	675	176	34	9	2	.285	.345	.379	724	750	27			10		760	14.9
25	28	1935	C.Travis	534	41	9	584	170	27	8	0	.318	.377	.399	776	727	4	2	0		40	767	14.9

Washington Senators/Minnesota Twins
Outfielders

V	R	Year	Name	AB	BB	HBP	TAB	H	2B	3B	HR	BA	OB	SA	PRO	Wtd PRO	SB	CS	SBF	SPF	FF	R TF	V HC
1	1	1902	E.Delahanty	473	62	4	539	178	43	14	10	.376	.453	.590	1,043	1,051	16			10		1,061	90.3
2	3	1988	K.Puckett	657	23	2	682	234	42	5	24	.356	.380	.545	925	937	6	7	(11)	10	80	1,016	84.1
3	2	1928	G.Goslin	456	48	3	507	173	36	10	17	.379	.442	.614	1,056	1,006	16	3	19	10	10	1,044	72.9
4	6	1964	T.Oliva	672	34	6	712	217	43	9	32	.323	.361	.557	918	928	12	6	0	10	20	958	68.0
5	5	1944	S.Spence	592	69	4	665	187	31	8	18	.316	.391	.486	877	914	3	7	(16)		60	958	66.8
6	7	1926	G.Goslin	568	63	7	638	201	26	15	17	.354	.425	.542	967	919	8	8	(12)	10	40	957	63.8
7	12	1986	K.Puckett	680	34	7	721	223	37	6	31	.328	.366	.537	903	888	20	12	(5)	10	50	943	63.7
8	9	1989	K.Puckett	635	41	3	679	215	45	4	9	.339	.381	.465	846	865	11	4	4	10	70	949	61.9
9	14	1957	R.Sievers	572	76	7	655	172	23	5	42	.301	.389	.579	968	962	1	1	(1)	(10)	(10)	941	60.3
10	11	1966	T.Oliva	622	42	5	669	191	32	7	25	.307	.356	.502	857	895	13	7	(1)	10	40	944	59.4
11	16	1992	K.Puckett	639	44	6	689	210	38	4	19	.329	.377	.490	867	881	17	7	4	10	40	936	58.5
12	17	1925	G.Goslin	601	53	6	660	201	34	20	18	.334	.394	.547	941	865	27	8	16	10	40	931	57.4
13	10	1963	B.Allison	527	90	3	620	143	25	4	35	.271	.381	.533	914	930	6	1	6	10		946	55.6
14	18	1970	T.Oliva	628	38	3	669	204	36	7	23	.325	.366	.514	881	884	5	4	(4)	10	40	930	55.0
15	13	1967	T.Oliva	557	44	8	609	161	34	6	17	.289	.350	.463	813	875	11	3	8	10	50	943	53.7
16	4	1971	T.Oliva	487	25	2	514	164	30	3	22	.337	.372	.546	918	947	4	1	4	10	10	971	52.3
17	19	1965	T.Oliva	576	55	4	635	185	40	5	16	.321	.384	.491	876	906	19	9	1	10	10	928	51.5
18	21	1987	K.Puckett	624	32	6	662	207	32	5	28	.332	.370	.534	904	864	12	7	(3)	10	40	911	48.6
19	8	1968	T.Oliva	470	45	7	522	136	24	5	18	.289	.360	.477	837	924	10	9	(14)	10	30	950	47.9
20	20	1977	L.Bostock	593	51	6	650	199	36	12	14	.336	.394	.508	901	889	16	7	3	10	10	912	47.8
21	23	1992	S.Mack	600	64	15	679	189	31	6	16	.315	.395	.467	861	875	26	14	(3)	10	20	903	47.0
22	25	1969	T.Oliva	637	45	3	685	197	39	4	24	.309	.358	.496	854	870	10	13	(22)	10	40	898	45.7
23	26	1964	H.Killebrew	577	93	8	678	156	11	1	49	.270	.379	.548	927	937	0	0	0	(10)	(30)	897	45.2
24	22	1977	L.Hisle	546	56	6	608	165	36	3	28	.302	.373	.533	906	894	21	10	2	10		905	42.8
25	15	1994	S.Mack	303	32	6	341	101	21	2	15	.333	.408	.564	972	905	4	1	6	10	20	940	42.0

Washington Senators/Minnesota Twins (1901–2000)

Washington Senators/Minnesota Twins
Outfielders

V	R	Year	Name	AB	BB	HBP	TAB	H	2B	3B	HR	BA	OB	SA	PRO	Wtd PRO	SB	CS	SBF	SPF	FF	R TF	V HC
26	28	1982	G.Ward	570	37	1	608	165	33	7	28	.289	.334	.519	853	847	13	1	17	10	20	894	39.6
27	34	1924	G.Goslin	579	68	9	656	199	30	17	12	.344	.421	.516	937	876	15	14	(19)	10	10	877	39.5
28	31	1946	S.Spence	578	62	4	644	169	50	10	16	.292	.365	.497	861	879	1	7	(19)		20	880	39.5
29	30	1958	R.Sievers	550	53	4	607	162	18	1	39	.295	.361	.544	904	903	3	1	2	(10)	(10)	885	38.7
30	39	1920	S.Rice	624	39	4	667	211	29	9	3	.338	.381	.428	809	778	63	30	4	10	80	872	38.3
31	29	1963	H.Killebrew	515	72	3	590	133	18	0	45	.258	.353	.555	908	923	0	0	0	(10)	(20)	893	38.2
32	35	1927	G.Goslin	581	50	5	636	194	37	15	13	.334	.392	.516	908	853	21	6	13	10		877	38.0
33	38	1994	K.Puckett	439	28	7	474	139	32	3	20	.317	.367	.540	907	844	6	3	0		30	874	37.3
34	37	1998	M.Lawton	557	86	15	658	155	36	6	21	.278	.389	.478	867	815	16	8	0	10	50	875	36.8
35	47	1942	S.Spence	629	62	1	692	203	27	15	4	.323	.384	.432	817	841	5	2	1		20	862	36.2
36	32	1990	K.Puckett	551	57	3	611	164	40	3	12	.298	.367	.446	813	824	5	4	(5)	10	50	879	35.5
37	43	1991	K.Puckett	611	31	4	646	195	29	6	15	.319	.356	.460	816	818	11	5	1	10	40	869	34.5
38	27	1936	J.Stone	437	60	0	497	149	22	11	15	.341	.421	.545	965	869	8	0	15	10		894	34.1
39	48	1995	K.Puckett	538	56	3	597	169	39	0	23	.314	.382	.515	897	843	3	2	(2)		20	862	33.3
40	41	1962	B.Allison	519	84	4	607	138	24	8	29	.266	.372	.511	883	863	8	5	(3)	10		870	32.6
41	24	1991	S.Mack	442	34	6	482	137	27	8	18	.310	.367	.529	897	899	13	9	(10)	10		899	32.5
42	55	1911	C.Milan	616	74	7	697	194	24	8	3	.315	.395	.394	789	800	58			10	40	850	32.4
43	36	1967	B.Allison	496	74	2	572	128	21	6	24	.258	.357	.470	826	889	6	4	(3)		(10)	876	32.3
44	50	1932	H.Manush	625	36	5	666	214	41	14	14	.342	.383	.520	903	850	7	2	4			854	32.3
45	40	1942	G.Case	513	44	3	560	164	26	2	5	.320	.377	.407	784	807	44	6	54	10		871	31.9
46	46	1934	H.Manush	556	36	3	595	194	42	11	11	.349	.392	.523	915	861	7	3	2			863	31.4
47	33	1982	T.Brunansky	463	71	8	542	126	30	1	20	.272	.378	.471	849	843	1	2	(5)		40	878	31.1
48	54	1923	S.Rice	595	57	6	658	188	35	18	3	.316	.381	.450	832	795	20	8	6	10	40	850	30.7
49	45	1931	S.West	526	30	0	556	175	43	13	3	.333	.369	.481	850	811	6	8	(17)	10	60	864	29.6
50	57	1962	H.Killebrew	552	106	4	662	134	21	1	48	.243	.369	.545	914	893	1	2	(4)	(10)	(30)	849	29.0
51	63	1919	S.Rice	557	42	7	606	179	23	9	3	.321	.376	.411	787	803	26			10	30	843	28.7
52	56	1910	C.Milan	531	71	15	617	148	17	6	0	.279	.379	.333	713	810	44			10	30	850	28.6
53	60	1917	S.Rice	586	50	3	639	177	25	7	0	.302	.360	.369	729	806	35			10	30	846	28.4
54	44	1963	J.Hall	497	63	0	560	129	21	5	33	.260	.343	.521	864	879	3	3	(5)	10	(20)	864	28.4
55	58	2000	M.Lawton	561	91	7	659	171	44	2	13	.305	.408	.460	868	795	23	7	13	10	30	848	28.3
56	42	1976	L.Bostock	474	33	1	508	153	21	9	4	.323	.368	.430	798	850	12	6	0	10	10	870	27.1
57	49	1974	L.Hisle	510	48	8	566	146	20	7	19	.286	.357	.465	822	858	12	6	0	10	(10)	858	27.1
58	59	1921	S.Rice	561	38	9	608	185	39	13	4	.330	.382	.467	849	783	26	12	3	10	50	846	27.0
59	69	1943	G.Case	613	41	3	657	180	36	5	1	.294	.341	.374	715	761	61	14	47	10	20	838	26.6
60	68	1993	K.Puckett	622	47	7	676	184	39	3	22	.296	.352	.474	826	804	8	6	(6)	10	30	838	26.1
61	52	1965	J.Hall	522	51	1	574	149	25	4	20	.285	.350	.464	814	842	14	7	0	10		852	25.9
62	64	1995	M.Cordova	512	52	10	574	142	27	4	24	.277	.355	.486	842	791	20	7	10	10	30	841	25.8
63	66	1953	J.Busby	586	38	4	628	183	28	7	6	.312	.358	.415	773	758	13	6	2	10	70	839	25.8
64	61	1930	H.Manush	554	31	0	585	194	49	12	9	.350	.385	.531	915	837	7	4	(2)	10		845	25.8
65	62	1947	S.Spence	506	81	0	587	141	22	6	16	.279	.378	.441	819	828	2	2	(3)		20	845	25.8
66	53	1964	J.Hall	510	44	1	555	144	20	3	25	.282	.341	.480	821	830	5	2	2	10	10	852	25.0
67	51	1943	B.Johnson	438	64	3	505	116	22	8	7	.265	.362	.400	762	811	11	5	2	10	30	853	24.2
68	67	1902	J.Ryan	484	43	7	534	155	32	6	6	.320	.384	.448	832	839	10					839	24.1
69	75	1943	S.Spence	570	84	5	659	152	23	10	12	.267	.366	.405	771	821	8	1	9			829	23.8
70	71	1959	J.Lemon	531	46	1	578	148	18	3	33	.279	.337	.510	848	844	5	2	2		(10)	836	22.7
71	79	1950	I.Noren	542	67	2	611	160	27	10	14	.295	.375	.459	834	776	5	2	2	10	40	827	21.4
72	74	1996	R.Becker	525	68	2	595	153	31	4	12	.291	.375	.434	809	738	19	5	14	10	70	832	21.2
73	80	1960	J.Lemon	528	67	7	602	142	10	1	38	.269	.359	.508	866	852	2	0	3	(10)	(20)	825	20.4
74	70	1942	R.Cullenbine	427	92	0	519	118	33	1	6	.276	.405	.400	805	828	1	4	(13)		20	836	20.4
75	73	1976	D.Ford	514	36	10	560	137	24	7	20	.267	.327	.457	784	834	17	6	8	10	(20)	833	20.0

Washington Senators/ Minnesota Twins
Starting Pitchers

V	R	Year	Name	G	GS	IP	W	L	SV	SO	BB	ERA	RA/9	R Wtd RA/9	V Runs /162
1	1	1913	W.Johnson	48	36	346	36	7	2	243	38	1.14	1.46	1.68	116.5
2	2	1912	W.Johnson	50	37	369	33	12	2	303	76	1.39	2.17	2.19	102.0
3	3	1918	W.Johnson	39	29	326	23	13	3	162	70	1.27	1.96	2.47	96.6
4	6	1914	W.Johnson	51	40	372	28	18	1	225	74	1.72	2.13	2.63	83.8
5	5	1915	W.Johnson	47	39	337	27	13	4	203	56	1.55	2.22	2.54	79.6
6	4	1919	W.Johnson	39	29	290	20	14	2	147	51	1.49	2.26	2.49	76.9
7	8	1910	W.Johnson	45	42	370	25	17	1	313	76	1.36	2.24	2.79	76.5
8	21	1916	W.Johnson	48	38	370	25	20	1	228	82	1.90	2.56	3.18	59.6
9	10	1924	W.Johnson	38	38	278	23	7	0	158	77	2.72	3.14	2.84	55.6
10	28	1932	G.Crowder	50	39	327	26	13	1	103	77	3.33	3.74	3.24	50.3
11	9	1945	R.Wolff	33	29	250	20	10	2	108	53	2.12	2.45	2.84	50.1
12	7	1925	S.Coveleski	32	32	241	20	5	0	58	73	2.84	3.21	2.79	49.9
13	30	1911	W.Johnson	40	37	322	25	13	1	207	70	1.90	3.32	3.25	49.1
14	23	1973	B.Blyleven	40	40	325	20	17	0	258	67	2.52	3.02	3.20	49.0
15	11	1988	F.Viola	35	35	255	24	7	0	193	54	2.64	2.82	2.92	46.4
16	14	1987	F.Viola	36	36	252	17	10	0	197	66	2.90	3.25	2.99	43.8
17	32	1921	G.Mogridge	38	36	288	18	14	0	101	66	3.00	3.72	3.30	42.2
18	16	1963	C.Pascual	31	31	248	21	9	0	202	81	2.46	2.76	3.08	40.6
19	17	1959	C.Pascual	32	30	239	17	10	0	185	69	2.64	3.01	3.12	40.0
20	29	1929	F.Marberry	49	26	250	19	12	11	121	69	3.06	3.60	3.24	38.4
21	15	1928	G.Braxton	38	24	218	13	11	6	94	44	2.51	3.22	3.05	38.4
22	19	1991	K.Tapani	34	34	244	16	9	0	135	40	2.99	3.10	3.15	38.2
23	12	1924	T.Zachary	33	27	203	15	9	2	45	53	2.75	3.28	2.97	37.6
24	37	1933	E.Whitehill	39	37	270	22	8	1	96	100	3.33	3.73	3.39	37.0
25	13	1927	B.Hadley	30	27	199	14	6	0	60	86	2.85	3.26	2.99	36.5
26	35	1969	J.Perry	46	36	262	20	6	0	153	66	2.82	2.99	3.33	35.7
27	27	1925	W.Johnson	30	29	229	20	7	0	108	78	3.07	3.73	3.24	35.3
28	71	1917	W.Johnson	47	34	326	23	16	3	188	68	2.21	2.90	3.64	34.9
29	20	1978	D.Goltz	29	29	220	15	10	0	116	67	2.49	2.94	3.16	34.2
30	58	1918	H.Harper	35	32	244	11	10	1	78	104	2.18	2.84	3.58	34.0
31	24	1915	D.Ayers	40	16	211	14	9	3	96	38	2.21	2.81	3.21	33.2
32	50	1922	W.Johnson	41	31	280	15	16	4	105	99	2.99	3.70	3.54	33.2
33	22	1944	J.Niggeling	24	24	206	10	8	0	121	88	2.32	2.84	3.18	33.2
34	83	1919	J.Shaw	45	37	307	17	17	5	128	101	2.73	3.37	3.72	33.1
35	40	1908	W.Johnson	36	30	256	14	14	1	160	53	1.65	2.63	3.45	33.0
36	52	1930	G.Crowder	40	35	280	18	16	2	107	96	3.89	4.29	3.56	32.6
37	47	1974	B.Blyleven	37	37	281	17	17	0	249	77	2.66	3.17	3.51	32.5
38	34	1931	F.Marberry	45	25	219	16	4	7	88	63	3.45	3.78	3.33	31.5
39	38	1952	B.Porterfield	31	29	231	13	14	0	80	85	2.72	3.12	3.40	31.2
40	36	1928	S.Jones	30	27	225	17	7	0	63	78	2.84	3.56	3.37	31.1
41	56	1939	D.Leonard	34	34	269	20	8	0	88	59	3.54	4.15	3.57	31.1
42	49	1930	B.Hadley	42	34	260	15	11	2	162	105	3.73	4.26	3.54	31.0
43	55	1915	B.Gallia	43	29	260	17	11	1	130	64	2.29	3.12	3.56	30.2
44	51	1953	B.Porterfield	34	32	255	22	10	0	77	73	3.35	3.49	3.55	30.0
45	25	1988	A.Anderson	30	30	202	16	9	0	83	37	2.45	3.11	3.22	30.0
46	60	1975	B.Blyleven	35	35	276	15	10	0	233	84	3.00	3.40	3.59	29.8
47	61	1971	B.Blyleven	38	38	278	16	15	0	224	59	2.81	3.07	3.60	29.7
48	33	1936	P.Appleton	38	20	202	14	9	3	77	77	3.53	4.19	3.31	29.5
49	53	1979	J.Koosman	37	36	264	20	13	0	157	83	3.38	3.69	3.56	29.2
50	57	1962	C.Pascual	34	33	258	20	11	0	206	59	3.32	3.49	3.57	28.2

Washington Senators/Minnesota Twins Starting Pitchers

V	R	Year	Name	G	GS	IP	W	L	SV	SO	BB	ERA	RA/9	R Wtd RA/9	V Runs /162
51	18	1934	B.Burke	37	15	168	8	8	0	52	72	3.21	3.59	3.15	27.7
52	31	1948	R.Scarborough	31	26	185	15	8	1	76	72	2.82	3.45	3.28	27.6
53	67	1962	J.Kaat	39	35	269	18	14	1	173	75	3.14	3.55	3.64	27.5
54	74	1923	W.Johnson	42	34	261	17	12	4	130	73	3.48	3.86	3.66	27.5
55	43	1945	D.Leonard	31	29	216	17	7	1	96	35	2.13	3.00	3.48	27.2
56	64	1984	F.Viola	35	35	258	18	12	0	149	73	3.21	3.53	3.61	27.0
57	97	1912	B.Groom	43	40	316	24	13	1	179	94	2.62	3.79	3.83	26.9
58	41	1999	B.Radke	33	33	219	12	14	0	121	44	3.75	3.99	3.46	26.7
59	45	1967	J.Merritt	37	28	228	13	7	0	161	30	2.53	2.84	3.51	26.6
60	80	1921	W.Johnson	35	32	264	17	14	1	143	92	3.51	4.16	3.70	26.6
61	79	1931	L.Brown	42	32	259	15	14	0	79	79	3.20	4.20	3.69	26.1
62	76	1916	H.Harper	36	34	250	14	10	0	149	101	2.45	2.96	3.68	25.8
63	82	1940	K.Chase	35	34	262	15	17	0	129	143	3.23	4.12	3.72	25.7
64	94	1933	G.Crowder	52	35	299	24	15	4	110	81	3.97	4.21	3.82	25.7
65	92	1972	B.Blyleven	39	38	287	17	17	0	228	69	2.73	2.91	3.81	25.0
66	95	1940	D.Leonard	35	35	289	14	19	0	124	78	3.49	4.24	3.83	24.7
67	96	1977	D.Goltz	39	39	303	20	11	0	186	91	3.36	3.83	3.83	24.6
68	73	1992	J.Smiley	34	34	241	16	9	0	163	65	3.21	3.47	3.64	24.5
69	26	1963	L.Stange	32	20	165	12	5	0	100	43	2.62	2.89	3.23	24.4
70	75	1913	J.Boehling	38	25	235	17	7	4	110	82	2.14	3.20	3.67	24.3
71	66	1938	D.Leonard	33	31	223	12	15	0	68	53	3.43	4.40	3.63	24.1
72	39	1922	T.Zachary	32	25	185	15	10	1	37	43	3.12	3.60	3.45	24.0
73	42	1954	J.Schmitz	29	23	185	11	8	1	56	64	2.91	3.21	3.47	23.6
74	99	1908	T.Hughes	43	31	276	18	15	4	165	77	2.21	2.93	3.85	22.9
75	78	1925	D.Ruether	30	29	223	18	7	0	68	105	3.87	4.24	3.68	22.9
76	69	1923	G.Mogridge	33	30	211	13	13	1	62	56	3.11	3.84	3.64	22.7
77	89	1947	W.Masterson	35	31	253	12	16	1	135	97	3.13	3.49	3.80	22.5
78	70	1917	D.Ayers	40	15	208	11	10	1	78	59	2.17	2.90	3.64	22.3
79	59	1991	S.Erickson	32	32	204	20	8	0	108	71	3.18	3.53	3.58	22.1
80	44	1966	J.Perry	33	25	184	11	7	0	122	53	2.54	2.98	3.48	22.0
81	85	1961	J.Kralick	33	33	242	13	11	0	137	64	3.61	3.76	3.74	21.9
82	87	1963	D.Stigman	33	33	241	15	15	0	193	81	3.25	3.36	3.75	21.5
83	88	1946	M.Haefner	33	27	228	14	11	1	85	80	2.85	3.39	3.77	21.0
84	113	1966	J.Kaat	41	41	305	25	13	0	205	55	2.75	3.37	3.94	21.0
85	81	1924	G.Mogridge	30	30	213	16	11	0	48	61	3.76	4.10	3.71	21.0
86	90	1946	B.Newsom	34	31	237	14	13	1	114	90	2.93	3.42	3.80	20.9
87	54	1931	B.Hadley	55	11	180	11	10	8	124	92	3.06	4.05	3.56	20.9
88	77	1924	F.Marberry	50	14	195	11	12	15	68	70	3.09	4.06	3.68	20.0
89	48	1943	M.Candini	28	21	166	11	7	1	67	65	2.49	2.98	3.53	20.0
90	65	1952	C.Marrero	22	22	184	11	8	0	77	53	2.88	3.33	3.63	19.9
91	114	1968	D.Chance	43	39	292	16	16	1	234	63	2.53	2.96	3.94	19.9
92	46	1965	J.Perry	36	19	168	12	7	0	88	47	2.63	3.05	3.51	19.5
93	109	1926	W.Johnson	33	33	261	15	16	0	125	73	3.63	4.14	3.92	19.4
94	107	1941	D.Leonard	34	33	256	18	13	0	91	54	3.45	4.11	3.91	19.4
95	112	1970	J.Perry	40	40	279	24	12	0	168	57	3.04	3.61	3.94	19.3
96	103	1978	G.Zahn	35	35	252	14	14	0	106	81	3.03	3.60	3.87	19.3
97	68	1958	C.Pascual	31	27	177	8	12	0	146	60	3.15	3.36	3.64	19.0
98	101	1928	B.Hadley	33	31	232	12	13	0	80	100	3.54	4.07	3.86	19.0
99	118	1936	B.Newsom	43	38	286	17	15	2	156	146	4.32	5.05	3.99	19.0
100	62	1952	S.Shea	22	21	169	11	7	0	65	92	2.93	3.30	3.60	19.0

Washington Senators/ Minnesota Twins
Relief Pitchers

V	R	Year	Name	G	GS	IP	W	L	SV	SO	BB	ERA	RA/9	R Wtd RA/9	V Runs /162
1	1	1980	D.Corbett	73	0	136	8	6	23	89	42	1.98	2.05	2.07	37.6
2	8	1970	T.Hall	52	11	155	11	6	4	184	66	2.55	2.67	2.91	28.4
3	7	1979	M.Marshall	90	1	143	10	15	32	81	48	2.65	2.96	2.86	27.0
4	2	1963	B.Dailey	66	0	109	6	3	21	72	19	1.99	2.15	2.40	26.1
5	3	1958	D.Hyde	53	0	103	10	3	18	49	35	1.75	2.27	2.46	25.3
6	5	1969	R.Perranoski	75	0	120	9	10	31	62	52	2.11	2.40	2.67	25.1
7	22	1927	G.Braxton	58	2	155	10	9	13	96	33	2.95	3.58	3.28	23.1
8	10	1933	J.Russell	50	3	124	12	6	13	28	32	2.69	3.27	2.97	23.0
9	9	1970	S.Williams	68	0	113	10	1	15	76	32	1.99	2.71	2.95	20.1
10	17	1974	B.Campbell	63	0	120	8	7	19	89	55	2.62	2.77	3.07	19.8
11	26	1926	F.Marberry	64	5	138	12	7	22	43	66	3.00	3.59	3.40	18.6
12	23	1981	D.Corbett	54	0	88	2	6	17	60	34	2.57	2.98	3.32	18.3
13	31	1977	T.Johnson	71	0	147	16	7	15	87	47	3.13	3.49	3.49	17.5
14	19	1976	T.Burgmeier	57	0	115	8	1	1	45	29	2.50	2.81	3.21	17.2
15	16	1978	M.Marshall	54	0	99	10	12	21	56	37	2.45	2.82	3.03	16.8
16	21	1997	G.Swindell	65	1	116	7	4	1	75	25	3.58	3.58	3.28	16.5
17	14	1966	A.Worthington	65	0	91	6	3	16	93	27	2.46	2.57	3.00	15.7
18	11	2000	L.Hawkins	66	0	88	2	5	14	59	32	3.39	3.49	2.98	15.4
19	6	1988	J.Reardon	63	0	73	2	4	42	56	15	2.47	2.59	2.68	15.2
20	24	1970	R.Perranoski	67	0	111	7	8	34	55	42	2.43	3.08	3.36	14.8
21	4	1991	R.Aguilera	63	0	69	4	5	42	61	30	2.35	2.61	2.65	14.6
22	12	1992	C.Willis	59	0	79	7	3	1	45	11	2.72	2.84	2.98	13.8
23	18	1991	C.Willis	40	0	89	8	3	2	53	19	2.63	3.13	3.18	13.6
24	40	1973	R.Corbin	51	7	148	8	5	14	83	60	3.03	3.53	3.74	13.4
25	34	1969	B.Miller	48	11	119	5	5	3	57	32	3.02	3.18	3.54	13.4
26	15	1965	J.Klippstein	56	0	76	9	3	5	59	31	2.24	2.61	3.00	13.1
27	44	1976	B.Campbell	78	0	168	17	5	20	115	62	3.01	3.38	3.86	13.0
28	13	1993	R.Aguilera	65	0	72	4	3	34	59	14	3.11	3.11	2.98	12.6
29	28	1998	M.Trombley	77	1	97	6	5	1	89	41	3.63	3.82	3.44	12.0
30	20	1965	A.Worthington	62	0	80	10	7	21	59	41	2.13	2.81	3.23	11.8
31	37	1979	P.Redfern	40	6	108	7	3	1	85	35	3.49	3.74	3.61	11.4
32	29	1983	R.Davis	66	0	89	5	8	30	84	33	3.34	3.44	3.47	10.8
33	30	2000	B.Wells	76	0	86	0	7	10	76	15	3.65	4.07	3.47	10.4
34	42	1987	J.Berenguer	47	6	112	8	1	4	110	47	3.94	4.10	3.77	9.7
35	36	1998	G.Swindell	81	0	90	5	6	2	63	31	3.59	3.99	3.59	9.6
36	27	1992	M.Guthrie	54	0	75	2	3	5	76	23	2.88	3.24	3.40	9.6
37	35	1990	T.Leach	55	0	82	2	5	2	46	21	3.20	3.42	3.58	8.9
38	38	1999	B.Wells	76	0	87	8	3	1	44	28	3.81	4.23	3.66	8.7
39	25	2000	E.Guardado	70	0	62	7	4	9	52	25	3.94	3.94	3.36	8.2
40	51	1934	A.McColl	42	2	112	3	4	1	29	36	3.86	4.50	3.94	8.0
41	32	1997	R.Aguilera	61	0	68	5	4	26	68	22	3.82	3.82	3.50	8.0
42	41	1999	M.Trombley	75	0	87	2	8	24	82	28	4.33	4.33	3.75	7.8
43	46	1941	A.Carrasquel	35	5	97	6	2	2	30	49	3.44	4.08	3.88	7.7
44	47	1957	B.Byerly	47	0	95	6	6	6	39	22	3.13	3.60	3.89	7.4
45	50	1989	J.Berenguer	56	0	106	9	3	3	93	47	3.48	3.74	3.93	7.4
46	49	1985	P.Filson	40	6	96	4	5	2	42	30	3.67	3.95	3.91	6.9
47	33	1993	L.Casian	54	0	57	5	3	1	31	14	3.02	3.65	3.50	6.7
48	39	1989	G.Wayne	60	0	71	3	4	1	41	36	3.30	3.55	3.73	6.5
49	54	1927	B.Burke	36	6	100	3	2	0	20	32	3.96	4.36	4.00	6.5
50	43	1998	R.Aguilera	68	0	74	4	9	38	57	15	4.24	4.24	3.82	6.1

AMERICAN LEAGUE EXPANSION TEAMS (1961–2000)

Perhaps the most significant event for major league baseball during the second half of the twentieth century was the expansion to 14 new cities. More teams meant more fans, more players, more hitting due to the thinning of pitching staffs, and the eventual realignment of leagues into the current three division format. In 1961, the Los Angeles Angels and Washington Senators expansion clubs of the American League kicked off this process. In 1969, the Kansas City Royals and Seattle Pilots–turned–Milwaukee Brewers joined the league. In 1977, the Toronto Blue Jays and Seattle Mariners were added. Finally, in 1998, Milwaukee moved to the National League, allowing for the addition of the Tampa Bay Devil Rays to the American League. Tampa Bay's three seasons will not be covered here; the other teams are discussed below.

Los Angeles/California/ Anaheim Angels (1961–2000)

Initially, the Angels played well for an expansion team, with four winning seasons in their first ten years, and no last place finishes. The Angels were two games over .500 in 1964, thanks to the outstanding pitching of Dean Chance (20–9 record, 1.65 ERA, 2.03 Wtd. RA/9) and Bob Lee (6–5, 19 saves, 1.51 ERA, 2.28 Wtd. RA/9). The 1970 team finished in third place, led by shortstop Jim Fregosi, who hit .278 with 22 home runs, and pitcher Clyde Wright, who was 22–12 with a 2.83 ERA.

The Angels finally suffered through expansion blues with seven straight losing seasons from 1971 to 1977, including two last place finishes. The team's only strength was found in their starting rotation, where two flame-throwers held center stage. Nolan Ryan was 21–16 with a 2.87 ERA in 1973, while setting a major league record with 383 strikeouts in 326 innings. Frank Tanana went 16–9 with a 2.62 ERA in 1975, 19–10 with a 2.43 ERA in 1976, and 15–9 with a league-leading 2.54 ERA and a 2.69 Wtd. RA/9 in 1977, before hurting his arm.

The Angels went through their golden era from 1978 to 1986, with six winning seasons and three division titles. The 1979 division winner featured Bobby Grich (.294, 30 home runs) and MVP Don Baylor (.296, 36 home runs, 22 steals), while Ryan posted a 16–14 record. The Angels won another division title in 1982, as Doug DeCinces hit .301 with 30 home runs for a 953 Total Factor, Fred Lynn hit .299 with 21 home runs, and Reggie Jackson hit a league-leading 39 home runs. The 1986 division winners were led by rookie Wally Joyner (.290, 22 home runs) and Mike Witt (18–10, 2.84 ERA).

The Angels struggled recently, with four winning seasons in the past 13 years. The 1989 team finished in third place, as veteran Bert Blyleven went 17–5 with a 2.73 ERA and 2.98 Wtd. RA/9, while Chuck Finley posted a 16–9 record, 2.57 ERA, and 3.02 Wtd. RA/9. The 1995 team finished one game out, led by outfielders Tim Salmon (.330, 34 home runs, 1,000 Total Factor), Jim Edmonds (.290, 33 home runs), and rookie Garret Anderson (.321, 16 home runs), while Troy Percival was 3–2 with 3 saves, a 1.95 ERA, and 2.06 Wtd. RA/9. Darin Erstad starred for the 2000 team, with a .355 batting average, 240 hits, 25 home runs, and a 948 Total Factor, while teammate Troy Glaus hit .284 with a league-leading 47 home runs.

191

Washington Senators/Texas Rangers (1961–2000)

The old Washington Senators departed for Minnesota in 1961, and a new team was added to fill the void in the nation's capitol. During its first eight years, this new Senators team fared even worse than the old Senators team, as the Senators finished in last place four times. Then, in 1969, Ted Williams managed the team to a surprising 86–76 record, as slugger Frank Howard batted .296 with 48 home runs for a 996 Wtd. Production, Mike Epstein hit 30 home runs, and Dick Bosman was 14–5 with a league-leading 2.19 ERA and a 3.06 Wtd. RA/9. The Senators fell under .500 in 1970 and 1971 despite Howard's big bat, giving the team just one winning season in 11 years.

The franchise departed for Texas in 1972. Howard was traded away in midyear, and the new Rangers finished dead last with 100 losses in 1972 and 105 losses in 1973. The 1974 team improved by 27 wins and finished in second place, as Ferguson Jenkins went 25–12 with a 2.82 ERA, and MVP Jeff Burroughs hit .301 with 25 home runs. The Rangers slid under .500 in 1975 and 1976, completing a 16-year stretch with just two winning seasons.

The Rangers produced four winning seasons from 1977 to 1981, but failed to make the postseason. Al Oliver hit over .300 four times, while Buddy Bell hit .329 with 17 home runs in 1980. In 1979, Jim Kern was 13–5 with 29 saves, a 1.57 ERA, and a 2.12 Wtd. RA/9. The Rangers then posted only one winning season from 1982 to 1988, giving them only seven winning seasons in their first 28 years.

The Rangers are currently in their most productive period, with eight winning seasons from 1989 to 2000. In 1989, Ruben Sierra hit .306 with 29 home runs, while a new Ranger, 42-year-old Nolan Ryan, went 16–10 with 301 strikeouts in only 239 innings. The team finished in third place in both 1990 and 1991, as the remarkable Ryan continued to pitch well. The Rangers struggled to just one winning season from 1992 to 1994, even though Ivan Rodriguez emerged as the league's best catcher, and Juan Gonzalez twice led the league in home runs. Gonzalez's best season was in 1993, when he batted .310 with 46 home runs, for a 977 Wtd. Production and 970 Total Factor.

The Rangers won the division title for the first time ever in 1996, as Gonzalez hit .314 with 47 home runs to win the league's MVP Award, and Rusty Greer hit .332 with 18 home runs. The Rangers won another division title in 1998, with Gonzalez achieving another MVP Award by hitting .318 with 45 home runs for a 943 Wtd. Production, while John Wetteland went 3–1 with 42 saves, a 2.03 ERA, and a 2.22 Wtd. RA/9. Rodriguez and Rafael Palmeiro produced their best volume of success seasons for the 1999 division winners. MVP Rodriguez won his eighth straight Gold Glove Award, and hit .332 with 35 home runs for a 937 Total Factor. Palmeiro batted .324 with 47 home runs for a 995 Total Factor. Rodriguez lost the last third of the 2000 season to an injury, but he first managed to hit .347 with 27 home runs in 383 total at bats for a 1,047 Total Factor, the highest rate of success ever for a catcher.

Kansas City Royals (1969–2000)

The Royals started their existence with two very successful decades, before their poor-man economic status turned the team into an also-ran status in the 1990s. Kansas City finished as high as second place three times by 1975, while putting together the pieces for a winning tradition. In 1971, 24-year-old Amos Otis emerged as the team's first star, hitting .301 with 15 home runs and 52 steals.

The Royals won their division in 1976, 1977, and 1978. In 1976, George Brett led the league with a .333 average, while Hal McRae finished a close second at .332. In 1977, Dennis Leonard was 20–12 with a 3.04 ERA, while Brett and Al Cowens each hit .312 with over 20 home runs. In 1978, Leonard was 21–17, Paul Splittorff was 19–13, and Larry Gura went 16–4 with a 2.72 ERA. Otis provided power and speed that season with a .298 average, 22 home runs, and 32 steals, for a 1,019 Total Factor in his best season.

The Royals won the pennant in 1980, led by MVP Brett's stratospheric .390 average and 24 home runs. Brett generated a 1,120 Wtd. Production, the league's best ever rate of success at third with a 1,155 Total Factor, and the league's second best volume of success at third with a 106.3 Hits Contribution — despite playing in only 117 games. The 1980 team also received a great leadoff performance from Willie Wilson, who hit .326 with 79 steals. Leonard won 20 games, while Dan Quisenberry emerged as the bullpen stopper, going 12–7 with 33 saves and a 3.09 ERA.

The Royals won their first World Series in 1985. Brett was the team's only consistent hitter, batting .335 with 30 home runs for the league's best ever 110.8 Hits Contribution at third base, and he carried the team in the World Series as well. Twenty-one-year-old Bret Saberhagen went 20–6 with a 2.87 ERA and 2.99 Wtd. RA/9, while Quisenberry went 8–9 with 37 saves, a 2.37 ERA, and 2.83 Wtd. RA/9.

The Royals and star George Brett both faded slowly, although the Royals still managed six winning seasons in the next nine years. In 1989, Saberhagen led the league in wins (23) and ERA (2.16), while earning a 2.67 Wtd. RA/9 in his best season. Also in 1989, reliever Jeff Montgomery was 7–3 with 18 saves, a 1.37 ERA, and a 1.63 Wtd. RA/9 for his best season. In 1990, 37-year-old George Brett won his third batting title with a .329 average. The Royals failed to win their division from 1986 to 2000 despite these fine individual performances, and the ball club became a perennial loser in 1995.

Milwaukee Brewers (1969–2000)

The franchise posted losing seasons in its first nine seasons from 1969 to 1977, a typical performance for an expansion team. The Seattle Pilots experiment lasted just one season, before the organization moved on to Milwaukee in 1970. Tommy Harper led the 1970 squad with his career year, hitting .296 with 31 home runs and 38 steals, for a 923 Total Factor. Bullpen closer Ken Sanders saved a total of 44 games in 1970 and 1971, with an ERA below 2.00 each year. George Scott came from Boston, and anchored the infield with solid seasons in 1973–1976, including a league leading 36 home runs in 1975.

The Brewers put together 11 seasons of .500 or better records from 1978 to 1992. They also played in a very tough Eastern Division, as demonstrated by the 87 wins, fifth place finish of the 1983 Brewers. In 1978, Larry Hisle hit .290 with 34 home runs, while pitcher Mike Caldwell went 22–9 with a 2.36 ERA and a 2.97 Wtd. RA/9. In 1979, Sixto Lezcano batted .321 with 28 home runs for a 1,008 Total Factor. The 1980 team featured Cecil Cooper, who hit .352 with 25 home runs for a 974 Total Factor, and Robin Yount, who hit .293 with 23 home runs. The 1981 squad had the league's best record in a strike-shortened season, as MVP Award winner Rollie Fingers blew away all comers with a 6–3 record, 28 saves, 1.04 ERA, the third-best-ever 1.16 Wtd. RA/9, and the second-best-ever 44.6 Runs/162 for relief pitchers.

The Brewers went to the World Series in 1982. MVP shortstop Robin Yount hit .331 with 210 hits, 46 doubles, 12 triples, and 29 home runs, for a 1,009 Total Factor and 114.1 Hits Contribution — second only to Cal Ripken's 1991 season in volume of success. Cooper hit .313 with 32 home runs; Paul Molitor batted .302 with 19 home runs and 41 steals; Pete Vukovich was 18–6 with a 3.34 ERA; and Fingers saved 29 games with a 2.60 ERA.

The Brewers then slid below .500 for three seasons (1984–1986), while Yount moved from shortstop to the outfield. The Brewers produced winning seasons from 1987 to 1992, led by Molitor's best season in 1987 (.353, 16 home runs, 45 steals, 997 Total Factor), Teddy Higuera's pitching in 1988 (16–9 record, 2.45 ERA, 2.70 Wtd. RA/9), and another MVP season from Yount in 1989 (.318, 21 home runs).

Molitor left for Toronto after the 1992 season, and Yount retired at the end of the 1993 season. The Brewers suffered through losing seasons from 1993 to 1997, before switching to the National League and struggling through three more losing seasons. The team's best players in this period were Jeff Cirillo and Jeromy Burnitz.

Toronto Blue Jays (1977–2000)

The Blue Jays finished last in their first six seasons (1977–1982). Toronto then put together 11 consecutive winning seasons from 1983 to 1993, winning their division four times. The 1985 division champions won 99 games, as Doyle Alexander went 17–10, Stieb was 14–13 with a league-leading 2.48 ERA and 2.99 Wtd. RA/9, Jimmy Key was 14–6, and Dennis Lamp finished 11–0. Jesse Barfield led the offense with a .289 average, 27 home runs and 22 steals for a 980 Total Factor. In 1986, Barfield hit .289 with a league-leading 40 home runs for a 986 Total Factor, while reliever Mark Eichhorn worked 157 innings, posting a 14–6 record with 10 saves, a 1.72 ERA, 1.79 Wtd. RA/9, and a major league best 48.2 Runs/162 for a relief pitcher. The 1987 team finished two games out, as George Bell hit .308 with 47 home runs and won the MVP Award, even though his 922 Wtd. Production and porous fielding were lackluster MVP performances. The 1989 squad won the division with just 89 wins, as McGriff led the league with 36 home runs, while reliever Tom Henke (8–3, 20 saves, 1.92 ERA, 2.09 Wtd. RA/9) anchored the bullpen.

The Blue Jays won the division in 1991, and the World Series in 1992 and 1993. In 1991, Joe Carter hit .273 with 33 home runs. In 1992, veteran Jack Morris was the staff ace with a 21–6 record. In 1993, the Blue Jays lineup boasted John Olerud (.363, 24 home runs, 1,051 Wtd. Production), Roberto Alomar (.326, 17 home runs, 55 steals, 957 Total Factor), and Paul Molitor (.332, 22 home runs). Pat Hentgen earned a 19–9 record in 1993, and reliever Duane Ward was 2–3 with 45 saves, 2.13 ERA, and 2.04 Wtd. RA/9.

The Blue Jays slumped to three winning seasons from 1994 to 2000. In 1997, Roger Clemens enjoyed the best season of his outstanding career, going 21–7 with a sparking 2.05 ERA. Clemens' 2.03 Wtd. RA/9 ranks fifth in league rate of success, while his 74.1 runs saved from scoring ranks just 22nd in league volume of success, but it also ranks an impressive second best over the past half century. The 1998 team won 88 games, as Jose Canseco,

Carlos Delgado, and Shawn Green hit a combined 119 home runs, and Clemens was 20–6 with a 2.65 ERA and 2.69 Wtd. RA/9. The 1999 team won 84 games, as Green hit .309 with 42 home runs for a 957 Total Factor. The 2000 team hit 244 home runs, but missed the playoffs. Carlos Delgado batted .344 with 41 home runs and 99 extra base hits, for a 1,041 Wtd. Production.

Seattle Mariners (1977–2000)

The Mariners entered the league the same year as the Blue Jays. Unlike Toronto, the Mariners needed 15 years to put together a winning season. Part of Seattle's problem was the team's inability to develop star players. In 1989, 19-year-old Ken Griffey, Jr., became the Mariners' first true star in his rookie season, and he led the Mariners to their first winning season two years later. Griffey achieved the best of his many fine seasons in the strike-shortened 1994 season, hitting .323 with 40 home runs, for a 1,078 Production. Adjusted for 7 percent hitter's inflation and a 162 game schedule, Junior batted .302 with 54 home runs, for a career-best 1,006 Wtd. Production, 1,066 Total Factor, and 102.0 Hits Contribution.

The Mariners won their division in 1995, as Edgar Martinez hit .356 with 52 doubles, 29 home runs, and 116 walks, for a 1,110 Production. Adjusted for 6 percent hitter's inflation, Martinez batted .336 with 31 home runs, for a 1,047 Wtd. Production, 1,014 Total Factor, and 101.3 Hits Contribution. Randy Johnson overpowered opponents, winning 90 percent of his decisions with an 18–2 record, a league-leading 2.48 ERA, 2.43 Wtd. RA/9, and 294 strikeouts in just 214 innings.

In 1996, 20-year-old rookie shortstop Alex Rodriguez impressed the baseball world with a .358 batting average, 36 home runs, and 91 extra base hits, for a 980 Total Factor and 100.5 Hits Contribution. Griffey and Jay Buhner each hit over 40 home runs that year, but the team finished in second place due to Randy Johnson's injuries that limited him to 61 innings and a 5–0 record. The Mariners won the division in 1997, led by MVP Griffey (.304, 56 home runs, 1,057 Total Factor) and Johnson (20–4, 2.28 ERA, 2.32 Wtd. RA/9).

Rodriguez hit .310 with 42 home runs and 46 steals in 1998, while Griffey led the league in home runs in 1998 and in 1999, and he won his tenth consecutive Gold Glove Award, before being traded to Cincinnati after the 1999 season at his request. In 2000, the Mariners earned a playoff spot without Johnson and Griffey, as Rodriguez (.316, 41 home runs, league record 1,016 Total Factor at short) and Martinez (.324, 37 home runs) excelled.

American League Expansion Teams (1961–2000)

AL Expansion — **Hitters Volume of Success**

Pos	Year	Name	T	L	AB	BB	HBP	TAB	H	2B	3B	HR	BA	OB	SA	PRO	Wtd PRO	SB	CS	SBF	SPF	FF	R TF	V HC
C	1999	I.Rodriguez	Tex	AL	600	24	1	625	199	29	1	35	.332	.358	.558	917	846	25	12	2	0	90	937	77.3
1B	2000	C.Delgado	Tor	AL	569	123	15	707	196	57	1	41	.344	.472	.664	1,137	1,041	0	1	(3)	0	(10)	1,028	86.9
2B	1993	R.Alomar	Tor	AL	589	80	5	674	192	35	6	17	.326	.411	.492	903	882	55	15	35	10	30	957	87.1
SS	1982	R.Yount	Mil	AL	635	54	1	690	210	46	12	29	.331	.384	.578	962	958	14	3	11	10	30	1,009	114.1
3B	1985	G.Brett	KC	AL	550	103	3	656	184	38	5	30	.335	.442	.585	1,028	1,021	9	1	10	0	40	1,071	110.8
OF	1994	K.Griffey Jr.	Sea	AL	433	56	2	491	140	24	4	40	.323	.403	.674	1,078	1,006	11	3	10	10	40	1,066	102.0
OF	1995	T.Salmon	Cal	AL	537	91	6	634	177	34	3	34	.330	.432	.594	1,026	968	5	5	(7)	0	40	1,000	82.6
OF	1986	J.Barfield	Tor	AL	589	69	8	666	170	35	2	40	.289	.371	.559	929	917	8	8	(11)	10	70	986	72.4
Starters		Averages			563	75	5	643	184	37	4	33	.326	.410	.585	995	954	16	6	6	5	41	1,006	91.6
C	1979	D.Porter	KC	AL	533	121	8	662	155	23	10	20	.291	.429	.484	913	893	3	4	(7)	0	10	896	69.0
1B	1993	J.Olerud	Tor	AL	551	114	7	672	200	54	2	24	.363	.478	.599	1,077	1,051	0	2	(6)	(10)	0	1,035	84.9
2B	1981	B.Grich	Cal	AL	352	40	4	396	107	14	2	22	.304	.381	.543	924	969	2	4	(14)	0	30	985	85.5
SS	2000	A.Rodriguez	Sea	AL	554	100	7	661	175	34	2	41	.316	.427	.606	1,033	946	15	4	10	10	50	1,016	111.4
3B/DH	1995	E.Martinez	Sea	AL	511	116	8	635	182	52	0	29	.356	.482	.628	1,110	1,047	4	3	(3)	0	(30)	1,014	101.3
OF	1978	A.Otis	KC	AL	486	66	4	556	145	30	7	22	.298	.387	.525	911	932	32	8	27	10	50	1,019	69.3
OF	2000	D.Erstad	Ana	AL	676	64	1	741	240	39	6	25	.355	.412	.541	953	872	28	8	15	10	50	948	67.2
OF	1979	S.Lezcano	Mil	AL	473	77	3	553	152	29	3	28	.321	.420	.573	992	971	4	3	(3)	10	30	1,008	66.0
Reserves		Averages			517	87	5	610	170	34	4	26	.326	.427	.562	989	958	11	5	2	4	24	988	81.8
Totals		Weighted Ave.			548	79	5	632	179	36	4	31	.326	.416	.577	993	956	14	6	5	5	35	1,000	88.4

Pitchers Volume of Success

Pos	Year	Name	T	L	G	GS	IP	W	L	SV	SO	BB	ERA	RA/9	Wtd RA/9	V Runs/162
SP	1964	D.Chance	LA	AL	46	35	278	20	9	4	207	86	1.65	1.81	2.03	78.2
SP	1997	R.Clemens	Tor	AL	34	34	264	21	7	0	292	68	2.05	2.22	2.03	74.1
SP	1995	R.Johnson	Sea	AL	30	30	214	18	2	0	294	65	2.48	2.73	2.43	56.9
SP	1989	B.Saberhagen	KC	AL	36	35	262	23	6	0	193	43	2.16	2.54	2.67	55.0
SP	1978	M.Caldwell	Mil	AL	37	34	293	22	9	1	131	54	2.36	2.76	2.97	51.8
Starters		Averages			37	34	262	21	7	1	223	63	2.13	2.40	2.43	63.2
RP	1986	M.Eichhorn	Tor	AL	69	0	157	14	6	10	166	45	1.72	1.83	1.79	48.2
RP	1981	R.Fingers	Mil	AL	47	0	78	6	3	28	61	13	1.04	1.04	1.16	44.6
RP	1979	J.Kern	Tex	AL	71	0	143	13	5	29	136	62	1.57	2.20	2.12	38.7
RP	1983	D.Quisenberry	KC	AL	69	0	139	5	3	45	48	11	1.94	2.27	2.29	35.0
Relievers		Averages			64	0	129	10	4	28	103	33	1.64	1.93	1.92	41.6
Totals		Averages			101	34	391	30	11	29	326	96	1.96	2.25	2.26	104.8

AL Expansion

Hitters Rate of Success

Pos	Year	Name	T	L	AB	BB	HBP	TAB	H	2B	3B	HR	BA	OB	SA	PRO	Wtd PRO	SB	CS	SBF	SPF	FF	R TF	V HC
C	2000	I.Rodriguez	Tex	AL	363	19	1	383	126	27	4	27	.347	.381	.667	1,048	959	5	5	(12)	0	100	1,047	67.4
1B	1993	J.Olerud	Tor	AL	551	114	7	672	200	54	2	24	.363	.478	.599	1,077	1,051	0	2	(6)	(10)	0	1,035	84.9
2B	1981	B.Grich	Cal	AL	352	40	4	396	107	14	2	22	.304	.381	.543	924	969	2	4	(14)	0	30	985	85.5
SS	2000	A.Rodriguez	Sea	AL	554	100	7	661	175	34	2	41	.316	.427	.606	1,033	946	15	4	10	10	50	1,016	111.4
3B	1980	G.Brett	KC	AL	449	58	1	508	175	33	9	24	.390	.461	.664	1,124	1,120	15	6	6	10	20	1,155	106.3
OF	1994	K.Griffey Jr.	Sea	AL	433	56	2	491	140	24	4	40	.323	.403	.674	1,078	1,006	11	3	10	10	40	1,066	102.0
OF	1978	A.Otis	KC	AL	486	66	4	556	145	30	7	22	.298	.387	.525	911	932	32	8	27	10	50	1,019	69.3
OF	1979	S.Lezcano	Mil	AL	473	77	3	553	152	29	3	28	.321	.420	.573	992	971	4	3	(3)	10	30	1,008	66.0
Starters		Averages			458	66	4	528	153	31	4	29	.333	.422	.605	1,027	995	11	4	2	5	40	1,042	86.6
C	1979	D.Porter	KC	AL	533	121	8	662	155	23	10	20	.291	.429	.484	913	893	3	4	(7)	0	10	896	69.0
1B	2000	C.Delgado	Tor	AL	569	123	15	707	196	57	1	41	.344	.472	.664	1,137	1,041	0	1	(3)	0	(10)	1,028	86.9
2B	1993	R.Alomar	Tor	AL	589	80	5	674	192	35	6	17	.326	.411	.492	903	882	55	15	35	10	30	957	87.1
SS	1982	R.Yount	Mil	AL	635	54	1	690	210	46	12	29	.331	.384	.578	962	958	14	3	11	10	30	1,009	114.1
3B/DH	1995	E.Martinez	Sea	AL	511	116	8	635	182	52	0	29	.356	.482	.628	1,110	1,047	4	3	(3)	0	(30)	1,014	101.3
OF	1995	T.Salmon	Cal	AL	537	91	6	634	177	34	3	34	.330	.432	.594	1,026	968	5	5	(7)	0	40	1,000	82.6
OF	1986	J.Barfield	Tor	AL	589	69	8	666	170	35	2	40	.289	.371	.559	929	917	8	8	(11)	10	70	986	72.4
OF	1993	J.Gonzalez	Tex	AL	536	37	13	586	166	33	1	46	.310	.369	.632	1,001	977	4	1	3	0	(10)	970	59.4
Reserves		Averages			562	86	8	657	181	39	4	32	.322	.419	.579	998	960	12	5	2	4	16	982	84.1
Totals		Weighted Ave.			493	73	5	571	162	34	4	30	.329	.421	.596	1,017	984	11	5	2	5	32	1,022	85.8

Pitchers Rate of Success

Pos	Year	Name	T	L	G	GS	IP	W	L	SV	SO	BB	ERA	RA/9	Wtd RA/9	R V Runs /162
SP	1964	D.Chance	LA	AL	46	35	278	20	9	4	207	86	1.65	1.81	2.03	78.2
SP	1997	R.Clemens	Tor	AL	34	34	264	21	7	0	292	68	2.05	2.22	2.03	74.1
SP	1997	R.Johnson	Sea	AL	30	29	213	20	4	0	291	77	2.28	2.54	2.32	52.8
SP	1989	B.Saberhagen	KC	AL	36	35	262	23	6	0	193	43	2.16	2.54	2.67	55.0
SP	1993	K.Appier	KC	AL	34	34	239	18	8	0	186	81	2.56	2.79	2.68	49.9
Starters		Averages			36	33	251	20	7	1	234	71	2.12	2.36	2.34	62.0
RP	1981	R.Fingers	Mil	AL	47	0	78	6	3	28	61	13	1.04	1.04	1.16	44.6
RP	1969	K.Tatum	Cal	AL	45	0	86	7	2	22	65	39	1.36	1.36	1.52	29.1
RP	1989	J.Montgomery	KC	AL	63	0	92	7	3	18	94	25	1.37	1.57	1.63	30.0
RP	1986	M.Eichhorn	Tor	AL	69	0	157	14	6	10	166	45	1.72	1.83	1.79	48.2
Relievers		Averages			56	0	103	9	4	20	97	31	1.44	1.53	1.58	38.0
Totals		Averages			92	33	354	29	10	20	330	102	1.92	2.12	2.12	100.0

American League Expansion Teams (1961–2000)

LA/California/Anaheim Angels (AL Expansion)   **Hitters Volume of Success**

Pos	Year	Name	T	L	AB	BB	HBP	TAB	H	2B	3B	HR	BA	OB	SA	PRO	Wtd PRO	SB	CS	SBF	SPF	FF	R TF	V HC
C	1990	L.Parrish	Cal	AL	470	46	5	521	126	14	0	24	.268	.340	.451	791	804	2	2	(4)	(10)	30	820	35.5
1B	1967	D.Mincher	Cal	AL	487	69	4	560	133	23	3	25	.273	.368	.487	855	920	0	3	(10)	(10)	0	899	34.5
2B	1981	B.Grich	Cal	AL	352	40	4	396	107	14	2	22	.304	.381	.543	924	969	2	4	(14)	0	30	985	85.5
SS	1970	J.Fregosi	Cal	AL	601	69	3	673	167	33	5	22	.278	.355	.459	814	818	0	2	(6)	10	20	842	57.7
3B	1982	D.DeCinces	Cal	AL	575	66	1	642	173	42	5	30	.301	.374	.548	922	918	7	5	(4)	0	40	953	72.6
OF	1995	T.Salmon	Cal	AL	537	91	6	634	177	34	3	34	.330	.432	.594	1,026	968	5	5	(7)	0	40	1,000	82.6
OF	2000	D.Erstad	Ana	AL	676	64	1	741	240	39	6	25	.355	.412	.541	953	872	28	8	15	10	50	948	67.2
OF	1995	J.Edmonds	Cal	AL	558	51	5	614	162	30	4	33	.290	.355	.536	891	840	1	4	(11)	10	60	899	46.8
Starters		Averages			532	62	4	598	161	29	4	27	.302	.379	.520	899	885	6	4	(5)	1	34	915	60.3
C	1979	B.Downing	Cal	AL	509	77	5	591	166	27	3	12	.326	.420	.462	881	862	3	3	(5)	0	(60)	798	33.8
1B	1987	W.Joyner	Cal	AL	564	72	5	641	161	33	1	34	.285	.371	.528	900	863	8	2	6	0	10	879	33.3
2B	1999	R.Velarde	Ana	AL	631	70	6	707	200	25	7	16	.317	.390	.455	845	780	24	8	11	0	0	790	35.4
SS	1981	R.Burleson	Cal	AL	430	42	3	475	126	17	1	5	.293	.360	.372	732	768	4	6	(16)	0	50	802	47.9
3B	2000	T.Glaus	Ana	AL	563	112	2	677	160	37	1	47	.284	.405	.604	1,009	923	14	11	(11)	0	10	922	66.4
OF	1977	B.Bonds	Cal	AL	592	74	2	668	156	23	9	37	.264	.347	.520	868	858	41	18	7	10	20	895	43.9
OF	1979	D.Baylor	Cal	AL	628	71	11	710	186	33	3	36	.296	.377	.530	908	888	22	12	(3)	10	(10)	886	43.4
OF/DH	1994	C.Davis	Cal	AL	392	69	1	462	122	18	1	26	.311	.416	.561	977	912	3	2	(2)	0	(40)	870	35.0
Reserves		Averages			539	73	4	616	160	27	3	27	.297	.386	.504	890	858	15	8	(2)	3	(3)	856	42.4
Totals		Weighted Ave.			534	66	4	604	160	28	3	27	.300	.381	.515	896	876	9	5	(4)	2	22	896	54.3

Pitchers Volume of Success

Pos	Year	Name	T	L	G	GS	IP	W	L	SV	SO	BB	ERA	RA/9	Wtd RA/9	R V Runs/162
SP	1964	D.Chance	LA	AL	46	35	278	20	9	4	207	86	1.65	1.81	2.03	78.2
SP	1977	F.Tanana	Cal	AL	31	31	241	15	9	0	205	61	2.54	2.69	2.69	50.0
SP	1973	N.Ryan	Cal	AL	41	39	326	21	16	1	383	162	2.87	3.12	3.31	45.3
SP	1986	M.Witt	Cal	AL	34	34	269	18	10	0	208	73	2.84	3.18	3.12	43.1
SP	1989	B.Blyleven	Cal	AL	33	33	241	17	5	0	131	44	2.73	2.84	2.98	42.2
Starters		Averages			37	34	271	18	10	1	227	85	2.53	2.74	2.84	51.8
RP	1969	K.Tatum	Cal	AL	45	0	86	7	2	22	65	39	1.36	1.36	1.52	29.1
RP	1964	B.Lee	LA	AL	64	5	137	6	5	19	111	58	1.51	2.04	2.28	34.6
RP	1985	S.Cliburn	Cal	AL	44	0	99	9	3	6	48	26	2.09	2.27	2.25	25.4
RP	1985	D.Moore	Cal	AL	65	0	103	8	8	31	72	21	1.92	2.45	2.43	24.4
Relievers		Averages			55	1	106	8	5	20	74	36	1.71	2.06	2.16	28.4
Totals		Averages			92	36	377	26	14	21	301	121	2.30	2.54	2.65	80.1

LA/California/Anaheim Angels (AL Expansion)

Hitters Rate of Success

Pos	Year	Name	T	L	AB	BB	HBP	TAB	H	2B	3B	HR	BA	OB	SA	PRO	Wtd PRO	SB	CS	SBF	SPF	FF	R TF	V HC
C	1990	L.Parrish	Cal	AL	470	46	5	521	126	14	0	24	.268	.340	.451	791	804	2	2	(4)	(10)	30	820	35.5
1B	1967	D.Mincher	Cal	AL	487	69	4	560	133	23	3	25	.273	.368	.487	855	920	0	3	(10)	(10)	0	899	34.5
2B	1981	B.Grich	Cal	AL	352	40	4	396	107	14	2	22	.304	.381	.543	924	969	2	4	(14)	0	30	985	85.5
SS	1964	J.Fregosi	LA	AL	505	72	4	581	140	22	9	18	.277	.372	.463	835	845	8	3	3	10	0	858	54.2
3B	1982	D.DeCinces	Cal	AL	575	66	1	642	173	42	5	30	.301	.374	.548	922	918	7	5	(4)	0	40	953	72.6
OF	1995	T.Salmon	Cal	AL	537	91	6	634	177	34	3	34	.330	.432	.594	1,026	968	5	5	(7)	0	40	1,000	82.6
OF	2000	D.Erstad	Ana	AL	676	64	1	741	240	39	6	25	.355	.412	.541	953	872	28	8	15	10	50	948	67.2
OF	1996	J.Edmonds	Cal	AL	431	46	4	481	131	28	3	27	.304	.376	.571	947	866	4	0	8	10	40	924	38.2
Starters		Averages			504	62	4	570	153	27	4	26	.304	.384	.526	910	894	7	4	(2)	1	29	923	58.8
C	1961	E.Averill	LA	AL	323	62	2	387	86	9	0	21	.266	.388	.489	877	852	1	0	2	(10)	(40)	805	23.5
1B	1987	W.Joyner	Cal	AL	564	72	5	641	161	33	1	34	.285	.371	.528	900	863	8	2	6	0	10	879	33.3
2B	1999	R.Velarde	Ana	AL	631	70	6	707	200	25	7	16	.317	.390	.455	845	780	24	8	11	0	0	790	35.4
SS	1981	R.Burleson	Cal	AL	430	42	3	475	126	17	1	5	.293	.360	.372	732	768	4	6	(16)	0	50	802	47.9
3B	2000	T.Glaus	Ana	AL	563	112	2	677	160	37	1	47	.284	.405	.604	1,009	923	14	11	(11)	0	10	922	66.4
OF	1977	B.Bonds	Cal	AL	592	74	2	668	156	23	9	37	.264	.347	.520	868	858	41	18	7	10	20	895	43.9
OF	1982	F.Lynn	Cal	AL	472	58	3	533	141	38	1	21	.299	.379	.517	896	892	7	8	(16)	0	10	886	32.7
OF	1979	D.Baylor	Cal	AL	628	71	11	710	186	33	3	36	.296	.377	.530	908	888	22	12	(3)	10	(10)	886	43.4
Reserves		Averages			525	70	4	600	152	27	3	27	.288	.377	.502	879	855	15	8	(2)	1	6	860	40.8
Totals		Weighted Ave.			511	65	4	580	153	27	4	26	.299	.382	.518	900	881	10	5	(2)	1	21	902	52.8

Pitchers Rate of Success

Pos	Year	Name	T	L	G	GS	IP	W	L	SV	SO	BB	ERA	RA/9	Wtd RA/9	R V Runs /162
SP	1964	D.Chance	LA	AL	46	35	278	20	9	4	207	86	1.65	1.81	2.03	78.2
SP	1977	F.Tanana	Cal	AL	31	31	241	15	9	0	205	61	2.54	2.69	2.69	50.0
SP	1989	B.Blyleven	Cal	AL	33	33	241	17	5	0	131	44	2.73	2.84	2.98	42.2
SP	1989	C.Finley	Cal	AL	29	29	200	16	9	0	156	82	2.57	2.88	3.02	34.1
SP	1986	M.Witt	Cal	AL	34	34	269	18	10	0	208	73	2.84	3.18	3.12	43.1
Starters		Averages			35	32	246	17	8	1	181	69	2.45	2.66	2.75	49.5
RP	1969	K.Tatum	Cal	AL	45	0	86	7	2	22	65	39	1.36	1.36	1.52	29.1
RP	1996	T.Percival	Cal	AL	62	0	74	0	2	36	100	31	2.31	2.43	2.04	20.7
RP	1985	S.Cliburn	Cal	AL	44	0	99	9	3	6	48	26	2.09	2.27	2.25	25.4
RP	1989	G.Minton	Cal	AL	62	0	90	4	3	8	42	37	2.20	2.20	2.28	22.8
Relievers		Averages			53	0	87	5	3	18	64	33	1.99	2.06	2.03	24.5
Totals		Averages			88	32	333	22	11	19	245	102	2.33	2.50	2.56	74.0

American League Expansion Teams (1961–2000)

Washington Senators/Texas Rangers (AL Expansion)

Hitters Volume of Success

Pos	Year	Name	T	L	AB	BB	HBP	TAB	H	2B	3B	HR	BA	OB	SA	PRO	Wtd PRO	SB	CS	SBF	SPF	FF	R TF	V HC
C	1999	I.Rodriguez	Tex	AL	600	24	1	625	199	29	1	35	.332	.358	.558	917	846	25	12	2	0	90	937	77.3
1B/DH	1999	R.Palmeiro	Tex	AL	565	97	3	665	183	30	1	47	.324	.426	.630	1,056	974	2	4	(9)	(10)	40	995	71.3
2B	1991	J.Franco	Tex	AL	589	65	3	657	201	27	3	15	.341	.409	.474	883	888	36	9	26	10	(40)	884	62.2
SS	1975	T.Harrah	Tex	AL	522	98	1	621	153	24	1	20	.293	.406	.458	864	889	23	9	8	10	20	927	78.4
3B	1981	B.Bell	Tex	AL	360	42	3	405	106	16	1	10	.294	.373	.428	801	840	3	3	(7)	0	80	913	57.4
OF	1969	F.Howard	Was	AL	592	102	5	699	175	17	2	48	.296	.403	.574	978	996	1	0	1	(10)	(40)	947	63.2
OF	1993	J.Gonzalez	Tex	AL	536	37	13	586	166	33	1	46	.310	.369	.632	1,001	977	4	1	3	0	(10)	970	59.4
OF	1989	R.Sierra	Tex	AL	634	43	2	679	194	35	14	29	.306	.352	.543	895	917	8	2	6	10	(10)	923	53.5
Starters		Averages			550	64	4	617	172	26	3	31	.313	.388	.543	931	920	13	5	4	1	16	941	65.3
C	1978	J.Sundberg	Tex	AL	518	64	3	585	144	23	6	6	.278	.361	.380	741	758	2	5	(13)	(10)	90	825	41.0
1B	1969	M.Epstein	Was	AL	403	85	10	498	112	18	1	30	.278	.416	.551	967	985	2	5	(15)	(10)	(10)	949	42.5
2B	1977	B.Wills	Tex	AL	541	65	0	606	155	28	6	9	.287	.363	.410	773	765	28	12	6	10	0	781	27.7
SS	1986	S.Fletcher	Tex	AL	530	47	4	581	159	34	5	3	.300	.361	.400	761	751	12	11	(16)	10	0	745	22.9
3B	1969	K.McMullen	Was	AL	562	70	1	633	153	25	2	19	.272	.354	.425	779	794	4	5	(9)	(10)	40	815	29.7
OF	1974	J.Burroughs	Tex	AL	554	91	5	650	167	33	2	25	.301	.405	.504	908	951	2	3	(6)	0	(20)	925	52.0
OF	1978	B.Bonds	Tex	AL	565	79	2	646	151	19	4	31	.267	.359	.480	839	858	43	22	(1)	10	10	876	36.5
OF	1996	R.Greer	Tex	AL	542	62	3	607	180	41	6	18	.332	.404	.530	933	854	9	0	14	0	10	878	34.8
Reserves		Averages			527	70	4	601	153	28	4	18	.289	.378	.460	838	838	13	8	(5)	0	15	848	35.9
Totals		Weighted Ave.			542	66	4	612	166	27	3	27	.305	.385	.515	900	893	13	6	1	1	16	910	55.5

Pitchers Volume of Success

Pos	Year	Name	T	L	G	GS	IP	W	L	SV	SO	BB	ERA	RA/9	Wtd RA/9	R Runs/162
SP	1977	B.Blyleven	Tex	AL	30	30	235	14	12	0	182	69	2.72	3.11	3.11	37.8
SP	1978	J.Matlack	Tex	AL	35	33	270	15	13	1	157	51	2.27	3.10	3.33	36.8
SP	1974	F.Jenkins	Tex	AL	41	41	328	25	12	0	225	45	2.82	3.21	3.56	36.4
SP	1996	K.Hill	Tex	AL	35	35	251	16	10	0	170	95	3.63	3.95	3.32	34.5
SP	1969	D.Bosman	Was	AL	31	26	193	14	5	1	99	39	2.19	2.75	3.06	32.0
Starters		Averages			34	33	255	17	10	0	167	60	2.75	3.24	3.31	35.5
RP	1979	J.Kern	Tex	AL	71	0	143	13	5	29	136	62	1.57	2.20	2.12	38.7
RP	1999	J.Zimmerman	Tex	AL	65	0	88	9	3	3	67	23	2.36	2.46	2.13	23.6
RP	1985	G.Harris	Tex	AL	58	0	113	5	4	11	111	43	2.47	2.79	2.76	22.5
RP	1970	D.Knowles	Was	AL	71	0	119	2	14	27	71	58	2.04	2.72	2.97	21.0
Relievers		Averages			66	0	116	7	7	18	96	47	2.06	2.53	2.50	26.5
Totals		Averages			101	33	371	24	17	18	263	106	2.53	3.02	3.05	62.0

Washington Senators/Texas Rangers (AL Expansion)   **Hitters Rate of Success**

Pos	Year	Name	T	L	AB	BB	HBP	TAB	H	2B	3B	HR	BA	OB	SA	PRO	Wtd PRO	SB	CS	SBF	SPF	FF	R TF	V HC
C	2000	I.Rodriguez	Tex	AL	363	19	1	383	126	27	4	27	.347	.381	.667	1,048	959	5	5	(12)	0	100	1,047	67.4
1B/DH	1999	R.Palmeiro	Tex	AL	565	97	3	665	183	30	1	47	.324	.426	.630	1,056	974	2	4	(9)	(10)	40	995	71.3
2B	1989	J.Franco	Tex	AL	548	66	1	615	173	31	5	13	.316	.390	.462	852	873	2	3	23	10	(10)	896	61.9
SS	1975	T.Harrah	Tex	AL	522	98	1	621	153	24	1	20	.293	.406	.458	864	889	23	9	8	10	20	927	78.4
3B	1980	B.Bell	Tex	AL	490	40	0	530	161	24	4	17	.329	.379	.498	877	874	3	1	2	0	60	935	55.3
OF	1993	J.Gonzalez	Tex	AL	536	37	13	586	166	33	1	46	.310	.369	.632	1,001	977	4	1	3	0	(10)	970	59.4
OF	1969	F.Howard	Was	AL	592	102	5	699	175	17	2	48	.296	.403	.574	978	996	1	0	1	(10)	(40)	947	63.2
OF	1974	J.Burroughs	Tex	AL	554	91	5	650	167	33	2	25	.301	.405	.504	908	951	2	3	(6)	0	(20)	925	52.0
Starters		Averages			521	69	4	594	163	27	3	30	.313	.397	.550	946	938	8	3	1	0	18	957	63.6
C	1978	J.Sundberg	Tex	AL	518	64	3	585	144	23	6	6	.278	.361	.380	741	758	2	5	(13)	(10)	90	825	41.0
1B	1969	M.Epstein	Was	AL	403	85	10	498	112	18	1	30	.278	.416	.551	967	985	2	5	(15)	(10)	(10)	949	42.5
2B	1977	B.Wills	Tex	AL	541	65	0	606	155	28	6	9	.287	.363	.410	773	765	28	12	6	10	0	781	27.7
SS	1986	S.Fletcher	Tex	AL	530	47	4	581	159	34	5	3	.300	.361	.400	761	751	12	11	(16)	10	0	745	22.9
3B	1991	S.Buechele	Tex	AL	530	49	7	586	139	22	3	22	.262	.333	.440	772	777	0	5	(16)	0	60	821	29.1
OF	1989	R.Sierra	Tex	AL	634	43	2	679	194	35	14	29	.306	.352	.543	895	917	8	2	6	10	(10)	923	53.5
OF	1996	R.Greer	Tex	AL	542	62	3	607	180	41	6	18	.332	.404	.530	933	854	9	0	14	0	10	878	34.8
OF	1978	B.Bonds	Tex	AL	565	79	2	646	151	19	4	31	.267	.359	.480	839	858	43	22	(1)	10	10	876	36.5
Reserves		Averages			533	62	4	599	154	28	6	19	.289	.369	.467	835	832	13	8	(5)	3	19	849	36.0
Totals		Weighted Ave.			525	66	4	595	160	27	4	26	.305	.387	.522	909	903	9	5	(1)	1	18	921	54.4

Pitchers Rate of Success

Pos	Year		T	L	G	GS	IP	W	L	SV	SO	BB	ERA	RA/9	Wtd RA/9	V Runs /162
SP	1969	D.Bosman	Was	AL	31	26	193	14	5	1	99	39	2.19	2.75	3.06	32.0
SP	1991	N.Ryan	Tex	AL	27	27	173	12	6	0	203	72	2.91	3.02	3.07	28.7
SP	1977	B.Blyleven	Tex	AL	30	30	235	14	12	0	182	69	2.72	3.11	3.11	37.8
SP	1961	D.Donovan	Was	AL	23	22	169	10	10	0	62	35	2.40	3.20	3.18	25.8
SP	1996	K.Hill	Tex	AL	35	35	251	16	10	0	170	95	3.63	3.95	3.32	34.5
Starters					29	28	204	13	9	0	143	62	2.82	3.25	3.16	31.8
RP	1992	J.Russell	Tex	AL	59	0	66	4	3	30	48	25	1.63	1.90	2.00	18.8
RP	1979	J.Kern	Tex	AL	71	0	143	13	5	29	136	62	1.57	2.20	2.12	38.7
RP	1999	J.Zimmerman	Tex	AL	65	0	88	9	3	3	67	23	2.36	2.46	2.13	23.6
RP	1998	J.Wetteland	Tex	AL	63	0	62	3	1	42	72	14	2.03	2.47	2.22	16.1
Relievers					65	0	90	7	3	26	81	31	1.85	2.26	2.12	24.3
Totals					94	28	294	20	12	26	224	93	2.53	2.94	2.84	56.1

Kansas City Royals (AL Expansion)

Hitters Volume of Success

Pos	Year	Name	T	L	AB	BB	HBP	TAB	H	2B	3B	HR	BA	OB	SA	PRO	Wtd PRO	SB	CS	SBF	SPF	FF	R TF	V HC
C	1979	D.Porter	KC	AL	533	121	8	662	155	23	10	20	.291	.429	.484	913	893	3	4	(7)	0	10	896	69.0
1B	1975	J.Mayberry	KC	AL	554	119	4	677	161	38	1	34	.291	.419	.547	966	995	5	3	(1)	(10)	0	984	68.9
2B	1998	J.Offerman	KC	AL	607	89	5	701	191	28	13	7	.315	.407	.438	845	794	45	12	28	10	(20)	813	42.5
SS	1997	J.Bell	KC	AL	573	71	4	648	167	28	3	21	.291	.373	.461	834	787	10	6	(3)	0	30	814	47.1
3B	1985	G.Brett	KC	AL	550	103	3	656	184	38	5	30	.335	.442	.585	1,028	1,021	9	1	10	0	40	1,071	110.8
OF	1978	A.Otis	KC	AL	486	66	4	556	145	30	7	22	.298	.387	.525	911	932	32	8	27	10	50	1,019	69.3
OF	1980	W.Wilson	KC	AL	705	28	6	739	230	28	15	3	.326	.357	.421	779	775	79	10	75	10	60	921	57.5
OF	1991	D.Tartabull	KC	AL	484	65	3	552	153	35	3	31	.316	.400	.593	993	999	6	3	0	(10)	(30)	959	53.0
Starters		Averages			562	83	5	649	173	31	7	21	.309	.402	.501	903	895	24	6	16	1	18	930	64.8
C	1993	M.MacFarlane	KC	AL	388	40	16	444	106	27	0	20	.273	.365	.497	862	842	2	5	(17)	(10)	10	824	31.1
1B/DH	1994	B.Hamelin	KC	AL	312	56	1	369	88	25	1	24	.282	.393	.599	992	926	4	3	(5)	(10)	(10)	901	32.6
2B	1986	F.White	KC	AL	566	43	2	611	154	37	3	22	.272	.326	.465	790	780	4	4	(6)	0	40	813	37.3
SS	1971	F.Patek	KC	AL	591	44	5	640	158	21	11	6	.267	.323	.371	694	716	49	14	31	10	20	777	35.1
3B	1987	K.Seitzer	KC	AL	641	80	2	723	207	33	8	15	.323	.400	.470	869	834	12	7	(3)	0	0	831	39.6
OF	2000	J.Damon	KC	AL	655	65	1	721	214	42	10	16	.327	.388	.495	883	808	46	9	37	10	40	895	47.3
OF	1977	A.Cowens	KC	AL	606	41	8	655	189	32	14	23	.312	.363	.525	888	878	16	12	(12)	10	30	907	46.7
OF	2000	J.Dye	KC	AL	601	69	3	673	193	41	2	33	.321	.394	.561	954	874	0	1	(3)	0	30	901	46.0
Reserves		Averages			545	55	5	605	164	32	6	20	.297	.369	.498	867	827	17	7	3	1	20	851	39.5
Totals		Weighted Ave.			556	73	5	634	170	31	7	21	.305	.391	.500	891	872	21	6	12	1	18	903	56.3

Pitchers Volume of Success

Pos	Year	Name	T	L	G	GS	IP	W	L	SV	SO	BB	ERA	RA/9	Wtd RA/9	R V Runs /162
SP	1989	B.Saberhagen	KC	AL	36	35	262	23	6	0	193	43	2.16	2.54	2.67	55.0
SP	1993	K.Appier	KC	AL	34	34	239	18	8	0	186	81	2.56	2.79	2.68	49.9
SP	1994	D.Cone	KC	AL	23	23	172	16	5	0	132	54	2.94	3.15	2.72	49.6
SP	1988	M.Gubicza	KC	AL	35	35	270	20	8	0	183	83	2.70	3.14	3.25	39.1
SP	1972	R.Nelson	KC	AL	34	19	173	11	6	3	120	31	2.08	2.13	2.79	35.7
Starters		Averages			32	29	223	18	7	1	163	58	2.48	2.77	2.84	45.9
RP	1983	D.Quisenberry	KC	AL	69	0	139	5	3	45	48	11	1.94	2.27	2.29	35.0
RP	1989	J.Montgomery	KC	AL	63	0	92	7	3	18	94	25	1.37	1.57	1.63	30.0
RP	1990	S.Farr	KC	AL	57	6	127	13	7	1	94	48	1.98	2.27	2.38	30.7
RP	1976	M.Littell	KC	AL	60	1	104	8	4	16	92	60	2.08	2.25	2.57	23.0
Relievers		Averages			62	2	116	8	4	20	82	36	1.87	2.13	2.25	29.7
Totals		Averages			95	31	339	26	11	21	245	94	2.27	2.55	2.64	75.5

Kansas City Royals (AL Expansion) — Hitters Rate of Success

Pos	Year	Name	T	L	AB	BB	HBP	TAB	H	2B	3B	HR	BA	OB	SA	PRO	Wtd PRO	SB	CS	SBF	SPF	FF	R TF	V HC
C	1979	D.Porter	KC	AL	533	121	8	662	155	23	10	20	.291	.429	.484	913	893	3	4	(7)	0	10	896	69.0
1B	1975	J.Mayberry	KC	AL	554	119	4	677	161	38	1	34	.291	.419	.547	966	995	5	3	(1)	(10)	0	984	68.9
2B	1984	F.White	KC	AL	479	27	2	508	130	22	5	17	.271	.313	.445	758	761	5	5	(9)	10	60	821	33.0
SS	1997	J.Bell	KC	AL	573	71	4	648	167	28	3	21	.291	.373	.461	834	787	10	6	(3)	0	30	814	47.1
3B	1980	G.Brett	KC	AL	449	58	1	508	175	33	9	24	.390	.461	.664	1,124	1,120	15	6	6	10	20	1,155	106.3
OF	1978	A.Otis	KC	AL	486	66	4	556	145	30	7	22	.298	.387	.525	911	932	32	8	27	10	50	1,019	69.3
OF	1991	D.Tartabull	KC	AL	484	65	3	552	153	35	3	31	.316	.400	.593	993	999	6	3	0	(10)	(30)	959	53.0
OF	1980	W.Wilson	KC	AL	705	28	6	739	230	28	15	3	.326	.357	.421	779	775	79	10	75	10	60	921	57.5
Starters		Averages			533	69	4	606	165	30	7	22	.309	.392	.510	903	902	19	6	11	3	25	940	63.0
C	1993	M.MacFarlane	KC	AL	388	40	16	444	106	27	0	20	.273	.365	.497	862	842	2	5	(17)	(10)	10	824	31.1
1B/DH	1994	B.Hamelin	KC	AL	312	56	1	369	88	25	1	24	.282	.393	.599	992	926	4	3	(5)	(10)	(10)	901	32.6
2B	1998	J.Offerman	KC	AL	607	89	5	701	191	28	13	7	.315	.407	.438	845	794	45	12	28	10	(20)	813	42.5
SS	1971	F.Patek	KC	AL	591	44	5	640	158	21	11	6	.267	.323	.371	694	716	49	14	31	10	20	777	35.1
3B	1987	K.Seitzer	KC	AL	641	80	2	723	207	33	8	15	.323	.400	.470	869	834	12	7	(3)	0	0	831	39.6
OF	1990	B.Jackson	KC	AL	405	44	2	451	110	16	1	28	.272	.346	.523	869	884	15	9	(6)	10	20	908	32.3
OF	1977	A.Cowens	KC	AL	606	41	8	655	189	32	14	23	.312	.363	.525	888	878	16	12	(12)	10	30	907	46.7
OF	2000	J.Dye	KC	AL	601	69	3	673	193	41	2	33	.321	.394	.561	954	874	0	1	(3)	0	30	901	46.0
Reserves		Averages			519	58	5	582	155	28	6	20	.296	.374	.498	872	837	18	8	2	3	10	851	38.2
Totals		Weighted Ave.			528	66	4	598	161	29	7	21	.304	.386	.506	892	880	19	6	8	3	20	910	54.8

Pitchers Rate of Success

Pos	Year	Name	T	L	G	GS	IP	W	L	SV	SO	BB	ERA	RA/9	Wtd RA/9	R Runs /162
SP	1989	B.Saberhagen	KC	AL	36	35	262	23	6	0	193	43	2.16	2.54	2.67	55.0
SP	1993	K.Appier	KC	AL	34	34	239	18	8	0	186	81	2.56	2.79	2.68	49.9
SP	1994	D.Cone	KC	AL	23	23	172	16	5	0	132	54	2.94	3.15	2.72	49.6
SP	1972	R.Nelson	KC	AL	34	19	173	11	6	3	120	31	2.08	2.13	2.79	35.7
SP	1978	L.Gura	KC	AL	35	26	222	16	4	0	81	60	2.72	2.96	3.18	33.9
Starters		Averages			32	27	214	17	6	1	142	54	2.48	2.72	2.81	44.8
RP	1989	J.Montgomery	KC	AL	63	0	92	7	3	18	94	25	1.37	1.57	1.63	30.0
RP	1994	B.Brewer	KC	AL	50	0	39	4	1	3	25	16	2.56	2.56	2.21	14.4
RP	1983	D.Quisenberry	KC	AL	69	0	139	5	3	45	48	11	1.94	2.27	2.29	35.0
RP	1990	S.Farr	KC	AL	57	6	127	13	7	1	94	48	1.98	2.27	2.38	30.7
Relievers		Averages			60	2	99	7	4	17	65	25	1.88	2.14	2.16	27.5
Totals		Averages			92	29	313	24	9	17	208	79	2.29	2.53	2.60	72.3

American League Expansion Teams (1961–2000)

Seattle Pilots/Milwaukee Brewers (AL Expansion)   **Hitters Volume of Success**

Pos	Year	Name	T	L	AB	BB	HBP	TAB	H	2B	3B	HR	BA	OB	SA	PRO	Wtd PRO	SB	CS	SBF	SPF	FF	R TF	V HC
C	1975	D.Porter	Mil	AL	409	89	5	503	95	12	5	18	.232	.376	.418	794	817	2	5	(15)	0	(10)	792	27.5
1B	1980	C.Cooper	Mil	AL	622	39	2	663	219	33	4	25	.352	.392	.539	931	927	17	6	7	0	40	974	64.5
2B	1977	D.Money	Mil	AL	570	57	7	634	159	28	3	25	.279	.352	.470	822	813	8	5	(3)	10	(10)	810	37.7
SS	1982	R.Yount	Mil	AL	635	54	1	690	210	46	12	29	.331	.384	.578	962	958	14	3	11	10	30	1,009	114.1
3B/DH	1987	P.Molitor	Mil	AL	465	69	2	536	164	41	5	16	.353	.438	.566	1,004	963	45	10	44	10	(20)	997	71.8
OF	1979	S.Lezcano	Mil	AL	473	77	3	553	152	29	3	28	.321	.420	.573	992	971	4	3	(3)	10	30	1,008	66.0
OF	1980	B.Oglivie	Mil	AL	592	54	5	651	180	26	2	41	.304	.367	.563	930	926	11	9	(10)	10	20	946	58.4
OF	1978	L.Hisle	Mil	AL	520	67	5	592	151	24	0	34	.290	.377	.533	909	930	10	6	(3)	0	(10)	917	44.9
Starters	Averages				536	63	4	603	166	30	4	27	.310	.387	.533	920	914	14	6	3	6	9	933	60.6
C	1983	T.Simmons	Mil	AL	600	41	2	643	185	39	3	13	.308	.355	.448	803	802	4	2	0	(10)	(40)	752	22.8
1B	1973	G.Scott	Mil	AL	604	61	2	667	185	30	4	24	.306	.372	.488	860	882	9	5	(1)	10	30	921	47.8
2B	1991	W.Randolph	Mil	AL	431	75	0	506	141	14	3	0	.327	.427	.374	800	805	4	2	0	0	10	815	31.2
SS	1996	J.Valentin	Mil	AL	552	66	0	618	143	33	7	24	.259	.338	.475	813	744	17	4	14	10	0	767	31.0
3B	1970	T.Harper	Mil	AL	604	77	4	685	179	35	4	31	.296	.380	.522	901	905	38	16	8	10	0	923	67.5
OF	1979	G.Thomas	Mil	AL	557	98	2	657	136	29	0	45	.244	.359	.539	898	879	1	5	(13)	10	20	896	43.3
OF	1997	J.Burnitz	Mil	AL	494	75	5	574	139	37	8	27	.281	.382	.553	934	882	20	13	(10)	0	(20)	852	25.8
OF	1973	D.May	Mil	AL	624	44	5	673	189	23	4	25	.303	.354	.473	826	847	6	7	(11)	10	(10)	836	25.2
Reserves	Averages				558	67	3	628	162	30	4	24	.291	.371	.484	854	845	12	7	(2)	5	(1)	847	36.8
Totals	Weighted Ave.				543	65	3	611	165	30	4	26	.304	.382	.517	898	891	13	6	2	6	5	904	52.7

Pitchers Volume of Success

Pos	Year	Name	T	L	G	GS	IP	W	L	SV	SO	BB	ERA	RA/9	Wtd RA/9	R Runs /162	V
SP	1978	M.Caldwell	Mil	AL	37	34	293	22	9	1	131	54	2.36	2.76	2.97	51.8	
SP	1988	T.Higuera	Mil	AL	31	31	227	16	9	0	192	59	2.45	2.61	2.70	46.8	
SP	1980	M.Haas	Mil	AL	33	33	252	16	15	0	146	56	3.10	3.42	3.45	31.1	
SP	1994	R.Bones	Mil	AL	24	24	171	10	9	0	57	45	3.43	4.01	3.47	29.3	
SP	1996	B.McDonald	Mil	AL	35	35	221	12	10	0	146	67	3.90	4.23	3.56	24.6	
Starters	Averages				32	31	233	15	10	0	134	56	2.99	3.34	3.21	36.7	
RP	1981	R.Fingers	Mil	AL	47	0	78	6	3	28	61	13	1.04	1.04	1.16	44.6	
RP	1974	T.Murphy	Mil	AL	70	0	123	10	10	20	47	51	1.90	1.98	2.20	32.3	
RP	1971	K.Sanders	Mil	AL	83	0	136	7	12	31	80	34	1.91	2.32	2.72	27.8	
RP	1997	D.Jones	Mil	AL	75	0	80	6	6	36	82	9	2.02	2.24	2.05	22.3	
Relievers	Averages				69	0	104	7	8	29	68	27	1.77	1.96	2.15	31.8	
Totals	Averages				101	31	337	22	18	29	202	83	2.61	2.91	2.88	68.5	

Seattle Pilots/Milwaukee Brewers (AL Expansion)

Hitters Rate of Success

Pos	Year	Name	T	L	AB	BB	HBP	TAB	H	2B	3B	HR	BA	OB	SA	PRO	Wtd PRO	SB	CS	SBF	SPF	FF	R TF	V HC
C	1973	D.Porter	Mil	AL	350	57	4	411	89	19	2	16	.254	.365	.457	822	843	5	2	2	0	(30)	815	27.0
1B	1980	C.Cooper	Mil	AL	622	39	2	663	219	33	4	25	.352	.392	.539	931	927	17	6	7	0	40	974	64.5
2B	1991	W.Randolph	Mil	AL	431	75	0	506	141	14	3	0	.327	.427	.374	800	805	4	2	0	0	10	815	31.2
SS	1982	R.Yount	Mil	AL	635	54	1	690	210	46	12	29	.331	.384	.578	962	958	14	3	11	10	30	1,009	114.1
3B/DH	1987	P.Molitor	Mil	AL	465	69	2	536	164	41	5	16	.353	.438	.566	1,004	963	45	10	44	10	(20)	997	71.8
OF	1979	S.Lezcano	Mil	AL	473	77	3	553	152	29	3	28	.321	.420	.573	992	971	4	3	(3)	10	30	1,008	66.0
OF	1980	B.Oglivie	Mil	AL	592	54	5	651	180	26	2	41	.304	.367	.563	930	926	11	9	(10)	10	20	946	58.4
OF	1978	L.Hisle	Mil	AL	520	67	5	592	151	24	0	34	.290	.377	.533	909	930	10	6	(3)	0	(10)	917	44.9
Starters		Averages			511	62	3	575	163	29	4	24	.319	.395	.530	926	920	14	5	6	5	9	940	59.7
C	1984	J.Sundberg	Mil	AL	348	38	0	386	91	19	4	7	.261	.334	.399	734	737	1	1	(2)	(10)	50	774	17.8
1B	1973	G.Scott	Mil	AL	604	61	2	667	185	30	4	24	.306	.372	.488	860	882	9	5	(1)	10	30	921	47.8
2B	1977	D.Money	Mil	AL	570	57	7	634	159	28	3	25	.279	.352	.470	822	813	8	5	(3)	10	(10)	810	37.7
SS	1994	J.Valentin	Mil	AL	285	38	2	325	68	19	0	11	.239	.332	.421	753	703	12	3	17	10	50	781	26.0
3B	1970	T.Harper	Mil	AL	604	77	4	685	179	35	4	31	.296	.380	.522	901	905	38	16	8	10	0	923	67.5
OF	1979	G.Thomas	Mil	AL	557	98	2	657	136	29	0	45	.244	.359	.539	898	879	1	5	(13)	10	20	896	43.3
OF	1972	J.Briggs	Mil	AL	418	54	1	473	111	14	1	21	.266	.351	.455	805	873	1	2	(6)	0	(10)	857	23.7
OF	1997	J.Burnitz	Mil	AL	494	75	5	574	139	37	8	27	.281	.382	.553	934	882	20	13	(10)	0	(20)	852	25.8
Reserves		Averages			485	62	3	550	134	26	3	24	.272	.358	.481	838	848	11	6	(1)	5	14	866	36.2
Totals		Weighted Ave.			502	62	3	567	153	28	4	24	.304	.383	.514	897	896	13	6	4	5	10	915	51.9

Pitchers Rate of Success

Pos	Year	Name	T	L	G	GS	IP	W	L	SV	SO	BB	ERA	RA/9	Wtd RA/9	R V Runs /162
SP	1988	T.Higuera	Mil	AL	31	31	227	16	9	0	192	59	2.45	2.61	2.70	46.8
SP	1978	M.Caldwell	Mil	AL	37	34	293	22	9	1	131	54	2.36	2.76	2.97	51.8
SP	1983	M.Haas	Mil	AL	25	25	179	13	3	0	75	42	3.27	3.32	3.35	24.1
SP	1994	R.Bones	Mil	AL	24	24	171	10	9	0	57	45	3.43	4.01	3.47	29.3
SP	1996	B.McDonald	Mil	AL	35	35	221	12	10	0	146	67	3.90	4.23	3.56	24.6
Starters		Averages			30	30	218	15	8	0	120	53	3.01	3.31	3.17	35.3
RP	1981	R.Fingers	Mil	AL	47	0	78	6	3	28	61	13	1.04	1.04	1.16	44.6
RP	1970	K.Sanders	Mil	AL	50	0	92	5	2	13	64	25	1.75	1.86	2.03	25.9
RP	1997	D.Jones	Mil	AL	75	0	80	6	6	36	82	9	2.02	2.24	2.05	22.3
RP	1974	T.Murphy	Mil	AL	70	0	123	10	10	20	47	51	1.90	1.98	2.20	32.3
Relievers		Averages			61	0	93	7	5	24	64	25	1.71	1.81	1.91	31.3
Totals		Averages			91	30	311	21	13	24	184	78	2.62	2.86	2.80	66.6

Toronto Blue Jays (AL Expansion)

Hitters Volume of Success

Pos	Year	Name	T	L	AB	BB	HBP	TAB	H	2B	3B	HR	BA	OB	SA	PRO	Wtd PRO	SB	CS	SBF	SPF	FF	R TF	V HC
C	1983	E.Whitt	Tor	AL	344	50	0	394	88	15	2	17	.256	.350	.459	810	808	1	1	(2)	(10)	20	816	26.0
1B	2000	C.Delgado	Tor	AL	569	123	15	707	196	57	1	41	.344	.472	.664	1,137	1,041	0	1	(3)	0	(10)	1,028	86.9
2B	1993	R.Alomar	Tor	AL	589	80	5	674	192	35	6	17	.326	.411	.492	903	882	55	15	35	10	30	957	87.1
SS	1987	T.Fernandez	Tor	AL	578	51	5	634	186	29	8	5	.322	.382	.426	807	774	32	12	12	10	30	826	49.6
3B	1990	K.Gruber	Tor	AL	592	48	8	648	162	36	6	31	.274	.336	.512	848	862	14	2	15	10	30	917	62.0
OF	1986	J.Barfield	Tor	AL	589	69	8	666	170	35	2	40	.289	.371	.559	929	917	8	8	(11)	10	70	986	72.4
OF	1999	S.Green	Tor	AL	614	66	11	691	190	45	0	42	.309	.386	.588	974	899	20	7	8	10	40	957	65.7
OF	1984	L.Moseby	Tor	AL	592	78	8	678	166	28	15	18	.280	.372	.470	841	845	39	9	29	10	40	924	53.8
Starters	Averages				558	71	8	637	169	35	5	26	.302	.388	.525	912	884	21	7	10	6	31	932	62.9
C	2000	D.Fletcher	Tor	AL	416	20	5	441	133	19	1	20	.320	.358	.514	873	799	1	0	2	(10)	0	791	23.9
1B	1993	J.Olerud	Tor	AL	551	114	7	672	200	54	2	24	.363	.478	.599	1,077	1,051	0	2	(6)	(10)	0	1,035	84.9
2B	1982	D.Garcia	Tor	AL	597	21	5	623	185	32	3	5	.310	.339	.399	737	734	54	20	21	10	20	786	29.8
SS	1999	T.Batista	Tor	AL	519	38	6	563	144	30	1	31	.277	.334	.518	852	786	4	0	7	10	30	833	45.8
3B/DH	1988	R.Mulliniks	Tor	AL	337	56	0	393	101	21	1	12	.300	.399	.475	874	889	1	0	2	(10)	(40)	841	23.4
OF	1987	G.Bell	Tor	AL	610	39	7	656	188	32	4	47	.308	.357	.605	962	922	5	1	4	10	(20)	917	49.8
OF	1991	D.White	Tor	AL	642	55	7	704	181	40	10	17	.282	.345	.455	800	804	33	10	17	10	70	902	48.4
OF	1991	J.Carter	Tor	AL	638	49	10	697	174	42	3	33	.273	.334	.503	837	842	20	9	3	10	0	855	32.3
Reserves	Averages				539	49	6	594	163	34	3	24	.304	.368	.508	877	856	15	5	6	3	8	873	42.3
Totals	Weighted Ave.				552	63	7	622	167	35	4	25	.303	.381	.519	900	875	19	6	9	5	23	912	56.1

Pitchers Volume of Success

Pos	Year	Name	T	L	G	GS	IP	W	L	SV	SO	BB	ERA	RA/9	R Wtd RA/9	V Runs /162
SP	1997	R.Clemens	Tor	AL	34	34	264	21	7	0	292	68	2.05	2.22	2.03	74.1
SP	1987	J.Key	Tor	AL	36	36	261	17	8	0	161	66	2.76	3.21	2.96	46.5
SP	1996	P.Hentgen	Tor	AL	35	35	266	20	10	0	177	94	3.22	3.56	2.99	46.2
SP	1984	D.Stieb	Tor	AL	35	35	267	16	8	0	198	88	2.83	2.93	3.00	46.2
SP	1996	J.Guzman	Tor	AL	27	27	188	11	8	0	165	53	2.93	3.26	2.74	37.9
Starters	Averages				33	33	249	17	8	0	199	74	2.75	3.02	2.74	50.2
RP	1986	M.Eichhorn	Tor	AL	69	0	157	14	6	10	166	45	1.72	1.83	1.79	48.2
RP	1989	T.Henke	Tor	AL	64	0	89	8	3	20	116	25	1.92	2.02	2.09	24.4
RP	1992	D.Ward	Tor	AL	79	0	101	7	4	12	103	39	1.95	2.40	2.52	22.9
RP	1994	T.Castillo	Tor	AL	41	0	68	5	2	1	43	28	2.51	2.91	2.52	21.8
Relievers	Averages				63	0	104	9	4	11	107	34	1.95	2.19	2.15	29.3
Totals	Averages				97	33	353	26	12	11	306	108	2.51	2.78	2.57	79.5

Toronto Blue Jays (AL Expansion) — Hitters Rate of Success

Pos	Year	Name	T	L	AB	BB	HBP	TAB	H	2B	3B	HR	BA	OB	SA	PRO	Wtd PRO	SB	CS	SBF	SPF	FF	R TF	V HC
C	1983	E.Whitt	Tor	AL	344	50	0	394	88	15	2	17	.256	.350	.459	810	808	1	1	(2)	(10)	20	816	26.0
1B	1993	J.Olerud	Tor	AL	551	114	7	672	200	54	2	24	.363	.478	.599	1,077	1,051	0	2	(6)	(10)	0	1,035	84.9
2B	1993	R.Alomar	Tor	AL	589	80	5	674	192	35	6	17	.326	.411	.492	903	882	55	15	35	10	30	957	87.1
SS	1999	T.Batista	Tor	AL	519	38	6	563	144	30	1	31	.277	.334	.518	852	786	4	0	7	10	30	833	45.8
3B	1990	K.Gruber	Tor	AL	592	48	8	648	162	36	6	31	.274	.336	.512	848	862	14	2	15	10	30	917	62.0
OF	1986	J.Barfield	Tor	AL	589	69	8	666	170	35	2	40	.289	.371	.559	929	917	8	8	(11)	10	70	986	72.4
OF	1999	S.Green	Tor	AL	614	66	11	691	190	45	0	42	.309	.386	.588	974	899	20	7	8	10	40	957	65.7
OF	1983	L.Moseby	Tor	AL	539	51	5	595	170	31	7	18	.315	.380	.499	879	878	27	8	17	10	20	925	47.6
Starters		Averages			542	65	6	613	165	35	3	28	.303	.384	.532	916	892	16	5	8	5	30	935	61.4
C	2000	D.Fletcher	Tor	AL	416	20	5	441	133	19	1	20	.320	.358	.514	873	799	1	0	2	(10)	0	791	23.9
1B	2000	C.Delgado	Tor	AL	569	123	15	707	196	57	1	41	.344	.472	.664	1,137	1,041	0	1	(3)	0	(10)	1,028	86.9
2B	1982	D.Garcia	Tor	AL	597	21	5	623	185	32	3	5	.310	.339	.399	737	734	54	20	21	10	20	786	29.8
SS	1987	T.Fernandez	Tor	AL	578	51	5	634	186	29	8	5	.322	.382	.426	807	774	32	12	12	10	30	826	49.6
3B/DH	1988	R.Mulliniks	Tor	AL	337	56	0	393	101	21	1	12	.300	.399	.475	874	889	1	0	2	(10)	(40)	841	23.4
OF	1987	G.Bell	Tor	AL	610	39	7	656	188	32	4	47	.308	.357	.605	962	922	5	1	4	10	(20)	917	49.8
OF	1991	D.White	Tor	AL	642	55	7	704	181	40	10	17	.282	.345	.455	800	804	33	10	17	10	70	902	48.4
OF	1984	D.Collins	Tor	AL	441	33	9	483	136	24	15	2	.308	.369	.444	813	816	60	14	63	10	0	889	30.3
Reserves		Averages			524	50	7	580	163	32	5	19	.312	.378	.498	875	851	23	7	15	4	6	876	42.8
Totals		Weighted Ave.			536	60	6	602	164	34	4	25	.306	.382	.521	903	879	19	6	10	5	22	915	55.2

Pitchers Rate of Success

Pos	Year	Name	T	L	G	GS	IP	W	L	SV	SO	BB	ERA	RA/9	Wtd RA/9	R V Runs/162
SP	1997	R.Clemens	Tor	AL	34	34	264	21	7	0	292	68	2.05	2.22	2.03	74.1
SP	1996	J.Guzman	Tor	AL	27	27	188	11	8	0	165	53	2.93	3.26	2.74	37.9
SP	1987	J.Key	Tor	AL	36	36	261	17	8	0	161	66	2.76	3.21	2.96	46.5
SP	1985	D.Stieb	Tor	AL	36	36	265	14	13	0	167	96	2.48	3.02	2.99	46.1
SP	1996	P.Hentgen	Tor	AL	35	35	266	20	10	0	177	94	3.22	3.56	2.99	46.2
Starters		Averages			34	34	249	17	9	0	192	75	2.67	3.04	2.74	50.2
RP	1986	M.Eichhorn	Tor	AL	69	0	157	14	6	10	166	45	1.72	1.83	1.79	48.2
RP	1993	D.Ward	Tor	AL	71	0	72	2	3	45	97	25	2.13	2.13	2.04	20.1
RP	1989	T.Henke	Tor	AL	64	0	89	8	3	20	116	25	1.92	2.02	2.09	24.4
RP	1997	P.Quantrill	Tor	AL	77	0	88	6	7	5	56	17	1.94	2.56	2.34	21.7
Relievers		Averages			70	0	102	8	5	20	109	28	1.88	2.08	2.02	28.6
Totals		Averages			104	34	350	24	14	20	301	103	2.44	2.76	2.53	78.8

American League Expansion Teams (1961–2000)

Seattle Mariners (AL Expansion) **Hitters Volume of Success**

Pos	Year	Name	T	L	AB	BB	HBP	TAB	H	2B	3B	HR	BA	OB	SA	PRO	Wtd PRO	SB	CS	SBF	SPF	FF	R TF	V HC
C	1993	D.Valle	Sea	AL	423	48	17	488	109	19	0	13	.258	.357	.395	751	733	1	0	2	(10)	30	755	18.1
1B	1989	A.Davis	Sea	AL	498	101	6	605	152	30	1	21	.305	.428	.496	924	947	0	1	(3)	(10)	(10)	924	44.5
2B	1989	H.Reynolds	Sea	AL	613	55	3	671	184	24	9	0	.300	.361	.369	729	748	25	18	(15)	10	60	802	37.4
SS	2000	A.Rodriguez	Sea	AL	554	100	7	661	175	34	2	41	.316	.427	.606	1,033	946	15	4	10	10	50	1,016	111.4
3B/DH	1995	E.Martinez	Sea	AL	511	116	8	635	182	52	0	29	.356	.482	.628	1,110	1,047	4	3	(3)	0	(30)	1,014	101.3
OF	1994	K.Griffey Jr.	Sea	AL	433	56	2	491	140	24	4	40	.323	.403	.674	1,078	1,006	11	3	10	10	40	1,066	102.0
OF	1981	T.Paciorek	Sea	AL	405	35	4	444	132	28	2	14	.326	.385	.509	894	937	13	10	(15)	0	(10)	913	49.7
OF	1985	P.Bradley	Sea	AL	641	55	12	708	192	33	8	26	.300	.366	.498	863	858	22	9	5	10	20	893	45.7
Starters		Averages			510	71	7	588	158	31	3	23	.310	.402	.518	920	902	11	6	(1)	3	19	922	63.8
C	1995	D.Wilson	Sea	AL	399	33	2	434	111	22	3	9	.278	.336	.416	752	710	2	1	0	(10)	40	740	14.5
1B	1995	T.Martinez	Sea	AL	519	62	4	585	152	35	3	31	.293	.373	.551	924	871	0	0	0	(10)	0	861	28.6
2B	1981	J.Cruz	Sea	AL	352	39	3	394	90	12	3	2	.256	.335	.324	659	691	43	8	65	10	30	796	31.4
SS	1978	C.Reynolds	Sea	AL	548	36	3	587	160	16	7	5	.292	.339	.374	713	729	9	6	(5)	10	0	734	20.2
3B	1985	J.Presley	Sea	AL	570	44	1	615	157	33	1	28	.275	.328	.484	813	807	2	2	(3)	0	10	814	28.7
OF	1994	J.Buhner	Sea	AL	358	66	5	429	100	23	4	21	.279	.399	.542	941	878	0	1	(4)	0	30	904	42.3
OF	1978	L.Roberts	Sea	AL	472	41	8	521	142	21	7	22	.301	.367	.515	881	901	6	3	0	(10)	0	891	33.2
OF	1979	R.Jones	Sea	AL	622	85	3	710	166	29	9	21	.267	.358	.444	801	784	33	12	12	10	20	826	23.3
Reserves		Averages			480	51	4	534	135	24	5	17	.280	.354	.456	811	799	12	4	8	0	16	824	27.8
Totals		Weighted Ave.			500	64	6	570	150	28	4	21	.300	.386	.498	884	867	12	5	2	2	18	889	51.8

Pitchers Volume of Success

Pos	Year	Name	T	L	G	GS	IP	W	L	SV	SO	BB	ERA	RA/9	Wtd RA/9	V Runs/162
SP	1995	R.Johnson	Sea	AL	30	30	214	18	2	0	294	65	2.48	2.73	2.43	56.9
SP	1998	J.Moyer	Sea	AL	34	34	234	15	9	0	158	42	3.53	3.80	3.42	29.5
SP	1990	E.Hansen	Sea	AL	33	33	236	18	9	0	211	68	3.24	3.36	3.52	27.2
SP	1985	M.Moore	Sea	AL	35	34	247	17	10	0	155	70	3.46	3.64	3.61	26.1
SP	1982	F.Bannister	Sea	AL	35	35	247	12	13	0	209	77	3.43	3.64	3.69	23.9
Starters		Averages			33	33	236	16	9	0	205	64	3.25	3.45	3.36	32.7
RP	1995	J.Nelson	Sea	AL	62	0	79	7	3	2	96	27	2.17	2.40	2.14	23.9
RP	1991	B.Swift	Sea	AL	71	0	90	1	2	17	48	26	1.99	2.19	2.22	23.3
RP	1982	B.Caudill	Sea	AL	70	0	96	12	9	26	111	35	2.35	2.35	2.38	23.2
RP	1982	E.Vande Berg	Sea	AL	78	0	76	9	4	5	60	32	2.37	2.49	2.52	17.2
Relievers		Averages			70	0	85	7	5	13	79	30	2.22	2.35	2.31	21.9
Totals		Averages			104	33	321	23	13	13	284	94	2.97	3.16	3.08	54.6

Baseball Players' Best Seasons

Seattle Mariners (AL Expansion) — **Hitters Rate of Success**

Pos	Year	Name	T	L	AB	BB	HBP	TAB	H	2B	3B	HR	BA	OB	SA	PRO	Wtd PRO	SB	CS	SBF	SPF	FF	R TF	V HC
C	1993	D.Valle	Sea	AL	423	48	17	488	109	19	0	13	.258	.357	.395	751	733	1	0	2	(10)	30	755	18.1
1B	1989	A.Davis	Sea	AL	498	101	6	605	152	30	1	21	.305	.428	.496	924	947	0	1	(3)	(10)	(10)	924	44.5
2B	1989	H.Reynolds	Sea	AL	613	55	3	671	184	24	9	0	.300	.361	.369	729	748	25	18	(15)	10	60	802	37.4
SS	2000	A.Rodriguez	Sea	AL	554	100	7	661	175	34	2	41	.316	.427	.606	1,033	946	15	4	10	10	50	1,016	111.4
3B/DH	1995	E.Martinez	Sea	AL	511	116	8	635	182	52	0	29	.356	.482	.628	1,110	1,047	4	3	(3)	0	(30)	1,014	101.3
OF	1994	K.Griffey Jr.	Sea	AL	433	56	2	491	140	24	4	40	.323	.403	.674	1,078	1,006	11	3	10	10	40	1,066	102.0
OF	1981	T.Paciorek	Sea	AL	405	35	4	444	132	28	2	14	.326	.385	.509	894	937	13	10	(15)	0	(10)	913	49.7
OF	1994	J.Buhner	Sea	AL	358	66	5	429	100	23	4	21	.279	.399	.542	941	878	0	1	(4)	0	30	904	42.3
Starters		Averages			474	72	7	553	147	29	3	22	.309	.408	.524	932	906	9	5	(2)	1	20	925	63.3
C	1995	D.Wilson	Sea	AL	399	33	2	434	111	22	3	9	.278	.336	.416	752	710	2	1	0	(10)	40	740	14.5
1B	1986	K.Phelps	Sea	AL	344	88	6	438	85	16	4	24	.247	.409	.526	935	922	2	3	(9)	(10)	(30)	874	21.6
2B	1981	J.Cruz	Sea	AL	352	39	3	394	90	12	3	2	.256	.335	.324	659	691	43	8	65	10	30	796	31.4
SS	1985	S.Owen	Sea	AL	352	34	0	386	91	10	6	6	.259	.324	.372	696	691	11	5	2	10	60	764	18.7
3B	1993	M.Blowers	Sea	AL	379	44	2	425	106	23	3	15	.280	.358	.475	833	813	1	5	(20)	10	30	833	23.6
OF	1985	P.Bradley	Sea	AL	641	55	12	708	192	33	8	26	.300	.366	.498	863	858	22	9	5	10	20	893	45.7
OF	1978	L.Roberts	Sea	AL	472	41	8	521	142	21	7	22	.301	.367	.515	881	901	6	3	0	(10)	0	891	33.2
OF/DH	1981	R.Zisk	Sea	AL	357	28	3	388	111	12	1	16	.311	.366	.485	851	892	0	2	(10)	(10)	(40)	832	21.0
Reserves		Averages			412	45	5	462	116	19	4	15	.279	.357	.451	809	817	11	5	4	0	14	835	26.2
Totals		Weighted Ave.			454	63	6	523	137	26	3	20	.299	.391	.500	891	877	9	5	(0)	1	18	895	51.0

Pitchers Rate of Success

Pos	Year	Name	T	L	G	GS	IP	W	L	SV	SO	BB	ERA	RA/9	Wtd RA/9	V Runs /162
SP	1997	R.Johnson	Sea	AL	30	29	213	20	4	0	291	77	2.28	2.54	2.32	52.8
SP	1998	J.Moyer	Sea	AL	34	34	234	15	9	0	158	42	3.53	3.80	3.42	29.5
SP	1990	E.Hansen	Sea	AL	33	33	236	18	9	0	211	68	3.24	3.36	3.52	27.2
SP	1985	M.Moore	Sea	AL	35	34	247	17	10	0	155	70	3.46	3.64	3.61	26.1
SP	1982	F.Bannister	Sea	AL	35	35	247	12	13	0	209	77	3.43	3.64	3.69	23.9
Starters		Averages			33	33	235	16	9	0	205	67	3.21	3.42	3.34	31.9
RP	1995	J.Nelson	Sea	AL	62	0	79	7	3	2	96	27	2.17	2.40	2.14	23.9
RP	1991	B.Swift	Sea	AL	71	0	90	1	2	17	48	26	1.99	2.19	2.22	23.3
RP	1982	B.Caudill	Sea	AL	70	0	96	12	9	26	111	35	2.35	2.35	2.38	23.2
RP	1982	E.Vande Berg	Sea	AL	78	0	76	9	4	5	60	32	2.37	2.49	2.52	17.2
Relievers		Averages			70	0	85	7	5	13	79	30	2.22	2.35	2.31	21.9
Totals		Averages			104	33	321	24	14	13	284	97	2.95	3.13	3.07	53.8

American League Expansion Teams (1961–2000)

AL Expansion Catchers

V	R	Year	Name	T	L	AB	BB	HBP	TAB	H	2B	3B	HR	BA	OB	SA	PRO	Wtd PRO	SB	CS	SBF	SPF	FF	R TF	V HC
1	2	1999	I.Rodriguez	Tex	AL	600	24	1	625	199	29	1	35	.332	.358	.558	917	846	25	12	2		90	937	77.3
2	3	1998	I.Rodriguez	Tex	AL	579	32	3	614	186	40	4	21	.321	.360	.513	873	821	9	0	14		90	925	72.3
3	4	1979	D.Porter	KC	AL	533	121	8	662	155	23	10	20	.291	.429	.484	913	893	3	4	(7)		10	896	69.0
4	1	2000	I.Rodriguez	Tex	AL	363	19	1	383	126	27	4	27	.347	.381	.667	1,048	959	5	5	(12)		100	1,047	67.4
5	5	1997	I.Rodriguez	Tex	AL	597	38	8	643	187	34	4	20	.313	.362	.484	846	799	7	3	1		90	890	65.3
6	7	1996	I.Rodriguez	Tex	AL	639	38	4	681	192	47	3	19	.300	.344	.473	816	747	5	0	7		100	854	57.2
7	6	1994	I.Rodriguez	Tex	AL	363	31	7	401	108	19	1	16	.298	.364	.488	852	795	6	3	0	10	80	885	56.1
8	8	1978	J.Sundberg	Tex	AL	518	64	3	585	144	23	6	6	.278	.361	.380	741	758	2	5	(13)	(10)	90	825	41.0
9	11	1978	D.Porter	KC	AL	520	75	2	597	138	27	6	18	.265	.360	.444	804	822	0	5	(16)		10	817	39.6
10	16	1995	I.Rodriguez	Tex	AL	492	16	4	512	149	32	2	12	.303	.330	.449	779	735	0	2	(7)		80	808	35.7
11	10	1990	L.Parrish	Cal	AL	470	46	5	521	126	14	0	24	.268	.340	.451	791	804	2	2	(4)	(10)	30	820	35.5
12	19	1979	B.Downing	Cal	AL	509	77	5	591	166	27	3	12	.326	.420	.462	881	862	3	3	(5)		(60)	798	33.8
13	15	1977	J.Sundberg	Tex	AL	453	53	2	508	132	20	3	6	.291	.368	.389	757	748	2	2	(7)	(10)	80	811	32.3
14	9	1993	M.MacFarlane	KC	AL	388	40	16	444	106	27	0	20	.273	.365	.497	862	842	2	5	(17)	(10)	10	824	31.1
15	14	1977	D.Porter	KC	AL	425	53	1	479	117	21	3	16	.275	.357	.452	809	800	1	0	2		10	812	30.7
16	18	1993	I.Rodriguez	Tex	AL	473	29	4	506	129	28	4	10	.273	.320	.412	732	715	8	7	(11)	10	90	804	30.4
17	25	1981	J.Sundberg	Tex	AL	339	50	1	390	94	17	2	3	.277	.372	.366	738	774	2	5	(19)	(10)	40	784	30.0
18	26	1980	J.Sundberg	Tex	AL	505	64	1	570	138	24	1	10	.273	.356	.384	740	737	2	2	(3)	(10)	60	784	28.9
19	22	1994	M.MacFarlane	KC	AL	314	35	18	367	80	17	3	14	.255	.362	.462	824	769	1	0	3	(10)	30	792	28.3
20	21	1975	D.Porter	Mil	AL	409	89	5	503	95	12	5	18	.232	.376	.418	794	817	2	5	(15)		(10)	792	27.5
21	13	1973	D.Porter	Mil	AL	350	57	4	411	89	19	2	16	.254	.365	.457	822	843	5	2	2		(30)	815	27.0
22	12	1983	E.Whitt	Tor	AL	344	50	0	394	88	15	2	17	.256	.350	.459	810	808	1	1	(2)	(10)	20	816	26.0
23	27	1980	J.Watham	KC	AL	453	50	3	506	138	14	7	6	.305	.377	.406	784	780	17	3	21	10	(30)	781	25.0
24	20	1972	E.Kirkpatrick	KC	AL	364	51	3	418	100	15	1	9	.275	.368	.396	764	828	3	5	(16)		(20)	793	24.1
25	23	2000	D.Fletcher	Tor	AL	416	20	5	441	133	19	1	20	.320	.358	.514	873	799	1	0	2	(10)		791	23.9

AL Expansion First basemen

V	R	Year	Name	T	L	AB	BB	HBP	TAB	H	2B	3B	HR	BA	OB	SA	PRO	Wtd PRO	SB	CS	SBF	SPF	FF	R TF	V HC
1	2	2000	C.Delgado	Tor	AL	569	123	15	707	196	57	1	41	.344	.472	.664	1,137	1,041	0	1	(3)		(10)	1,028	86.9
2	1	1993	J.Olerud	Tor	AL	551	114	7	672	200	54	2	24	.363	.478	.599	1,077	1,051	0	2	(6)	(10)		1,035	84.9
3	3	1975	J.Mayberry	KC	AL	554	119	4	677	161	38	1	34	.291	.419	.547	966	995	5	3	(1)	(10)		984	68.9
4	5	1980	C.Cooper	Mil	AL	622	39	2	663	219	33	4	25	.352	.392	.539	931	927	17	6	7		40	974	64.5
5	4	1972	J.Mayberry	KC	AL	503	78	3	584	150	24	3	25	.298	.396	.507	903	979	0	2	(6)		10	982	62.1
6	6	1993	R.Palmiero	Tex	AL	597	73	5	675	176	40	2	37	.295	.376	.554	931	908	22	3	22		30	961	61.3
7	9	1989	F.McGriff	Tor	AL	551	119	4	674	148	27	3	36	.269	.402	.525	927	950	7	4	(1)			949	57.3
8	10	1990	F.McGriff	Tor	AL	557	94	2	653	167	21	1	35	.300	.403	.530	932	948	5	3	(1)			947	54.9
9	7	1988	F.McGriff	Tor	AL	536	79	4	619	151	35	4	34	.282	.378	.552	930	946	6	1	6			952	53.6
10	12	1991	R.Palmiero	Tex	AL	631	68	6	705	203	49	3	26	.322	.393	.532	925	930	4	3	(3)			928	53.0
11	14	1973	G.Scott	Mil	AL	604	61	2	667	185	30	4	24	.306	.372	.488	860	882	9	5	(1)	10	30	921	47.8
12	15	1988	G.Brett	KC	AL	589	82	3	674	180	42	3	24	.306	.393	.509	903	918	14	3	11		(10)	919	47.8
13	16	1975	G.Scott	Mil	AL	617	51	3	671	176	26	4	36	.285	.343	.515	858	884	6	5	(6)	10	30	918	47.3
14	11	1990	G.Brett	KC	AL	544	56	0	600	179	45	7	14	.329	.392	.515	906	922	9	2	8			929	45.6
15	13	1989	A.Davis	Sea	AL	498	101	6	605	152	30	1	21	.305	.428	.496	924	947	0	1	(3)	(10)	(10)	924	44.5
16	19	1981	C.Cooper	Mil	AL	416	28	3	447	133	35	1	12	.320	.367	.495	862	904	5	4	(6)		10	908	44.4
17	17	1973	J.Mayberry	KC	AL	510	122	2	634	142	20	2	26	.278	.420	.478	898	921	3	0	4	(10)		915	43.8
18	8	1969	M.Epstein	Was	AL	403	85	10	498	112	18	1	30	.278	.416	.551	967	985	2	5	(15)	(10)	(10)	949	42.5
19	21	1979	C.Cooper	Mil	AL	590	56	0	646	182	44	1	24	.308	.368	.508	877	858	15	3	13		30	901	40.4
20	20	1998	C.Delgado	Tor	AL	530	73	11	614	155	43	1	38	.292	.389	.592	982	923	3	0	5		(20)	908	40.3
21	23	1983	W.Upshaw	Tor	AL	579	61	5	645	177	26	7	27	.306	.377	.515	891	890	10	7	(6)	10		894	38.2
22	24	2000	R.Palmiero	Tex	AL	565	103	3	671	163	29	3	39	.288	.401	.558	958	877	2	1	0	(10)	20	887	37.5
23	25	1982	C.Cooper	Mil	AL	654	32	0	686	205	38	3	32	.313	.345	.528	873	869	2	3	(6)		20	884	37.2
24	27	1984	A.Davis	Sea	AL	567	97	7	671	161	34	3	27	.284	.395	.497	892	896	5	4	(4)		(10)	882	35.7
25	28	1994	W.Clark	Tex	AL	389	71	3	463	128	24	2	13	.329	.436	.501	938	875	5	1	6			881	34.7

AL Expansion
Second basemen

V	R	Year	Name	T	L	AB	BB	HBP	TAB	H	2B	3B	HR	BA	OB	SA	PRO	Wtd PRO	SB	CS	SBF	SPF	FF	R TF	V HC
1	2	1993	R.Alomar	Tor	AL	589	80	5	674	192	35	6	17	.326	.411	.492	903	882	55	15	35	10	30	957	87.1
2	1	1981	B.Grich	Cal	AL	352	40	4	396	107	14	2	22	.304	.381	.543	924	969	2	4	(14)		30	985	85.5
3	3	1992	R.Alomar	Tor	AL	571	87	5	663	177	27	8	8	.310	.406	.427	833	849	49	9	44	10	40	944	81.6
4	8	1991	R.Alomar	Tor	AL	637	57	4	698	188	41	11	9	.295	.357	.436	793	798	53	11	42	10	30	879	64.6
5	6	1991	J.Franco	Tex	AL	589	65	3	657	201	27	3	15	.341	.409	.474	883	888	36	9	26	10	(40)	884	62.2
6	4	1989	J.Franco	Tex	AL	548	66	1	615	173	31	5	13	.316	.390	.462	852	873	21	3	23	10	(10)	896	61.9
7	5	1979	B.Grich	Cal	AL	534	59	2	595	157	30	5	30	.294	.366	.537	904	884	1	0	2		10	896	59.7
8	9	1995	R.Alomar	Tor	AL	517	47	0	564	155	24	7	13	.300	.358	.449	807	761	30	3	40	10	50	861	53.2
9	11	1979	P.Molitor	Mil	AL	584	48	2	634	188	27	16	9	.322	.375	.469	845	826	33	13	10	10		847	48.8
10	14	1994	R.Alomar	Tor	AL	392	51	2	445	120	25	4	8	.306	.389	.452	840	784	19	8	6		50	841	46.6
11	13	1982	B.Grich	Cal	AL	506	82	8	596	132	28	5	19	.261	.372	.449	821	818	3	3	(5)		30	843	44.8
12	7	1983	B.Grich	Cal	AL	387	76	7	470	113	17	0	16	.292	.417	.460	877	876	2	4	(12)		20	884	44.4
13	20	1998	J.Offerman	KC	AL	607	89	5	701	191	28	13	7	.315	.407	.438	845	794	45	12	28	10	(20)	813	42.5
14	17	1990	J.Franco	Tex	AL	582	82	2	666	172	27	1	11	.296	.384	.402	786	800	31	10	16	10	(10)	815	41.2
15	10	1980	P.Molitor	Mil	AL	450	48	3	501	137	29	2	9	.304	.375	.438	813	810	34	7	38	10		857	41.1
16	21	1977	D.Money	Mil	AL	570	57	7	634	159	28	3	25	.279	.352	.470	822	813	8	5	(3)	10	(10)	810	37.7
17	23	1989	H.Reynolds	Sea	AL	613	55	3	671	184	24	9	0	.300	.361	.369	729	748	25	18	(15)	10	60	802	37.4
18	19	1986	F.White	KC	AL	566	43	2	611	154	37	3	22	.272	.326	.465	790	780	4	4	(6)		40	813	37.3
19	26	1999	R.Velarde	Ana	AL	631	70	6	707	200	25	7	16	.317	.390	.455	845	780	24	8	11			790	35.4
20	12	1990	P.Molitor	Mil	AL	418	37	1	456	119	27	6	12	.285	.344	.464	808	822	18	3	25	10	(10)	847	35.1
21	16	1982	F.White	KC	AL	524	16	2	542	156	45	6	11	.298	.321	.469	790	787	10	7	(7)	10	30	820	34.9
22	15	1984	F.White	KC	AL	479	27	2	508	130	22	5	17	.271	.313	.445	758	761	5	5	(9)	10	60	821	33.0
23	25	1981	J.Cruz	Sea	AL	352	39	3	394	90	12	3	2	.256	.335	.324	659	691	43	8	65	10	30	796	31.4
24	18	1991	W.Randolph	Mil	AL	431	75	0	506	141	14	3	0	.327	.427	.374	800	805	4	2	0		10	815	31.2
25	28	1982	D.Garcia	Tor	AL	597	21	5	623	185	32	3	5	.310	.339	.399	737	734	54	20	21	10	20	786	29.8

AL Expansion
Shortstops

V	R	Year	Name	T	L	AB	BB	HBP	TAB	H	2B	3B	HR	BA	OB	SA	PRO	Wtd PRO	SB	CS	SBF	SPF	FF	R TF	V HC
1	2	1982	R.Yount	Mil	AL	635	54	1	690	210	46	12	29	.331	.384	.578	962	958	14	3	11	10	30	1,009	114.1
2	1	2000	A.Rodriguez	Sea	AL	554	100	7	661	175	34	2	41	.316	.427	.606	1,033	946	15	4	10	10	50	1,016	111.4
3	3	1996	A.Rodriguez	Sea	AL	601	59	4	664	215	54	1	36	.358	.419	.631	1,049	960	15	4	10	10		980	100.5
4	6	1998	A.Rodriguez	Sea	AL	686	45	10	741	213	35	5	42	.310	.362	.560	921	866	46	13	26	10	20	922	91.7
5	5	1975	T.Harrah	Tex	AL	522	98	1	621	153	24	1	20	.293	.406	.458	864	889	23	9	8	10	20	927	78.4
6	7	1983	R.Yount	Mil	AL	578	72	3	653	178	42	10	17	.308	.387	.503	891	890	12	5	3	10	10	913	78.0
7	4	1999	A.Rodriguez	Sea	AL	502	56	5	563	143	25	0	42	.285	.362	.586	948	874	21	7	12	10	40	936	73.5
8	10	1984	R.Yount	Mil	AL	624	67	1	692	186	27	7	16	.298	.367	.441	808	811	14	4	8	10	30	859	65.0
9	8	1980	R.Yount	Mil	AL	611	26	1	638	179	49	10	23	.293	.323	.519	842	838	20	5	15	10	10	873	64.2
10	9	1981	R.Yount	Mil	AL	377	22	2	401	103	15	5	10	.273	.317	.419	736	772	4	1	5	10	80	866	59.1
11	13	1970	J.Fregosi	Cal	AL	601	69	3	673	167	33	5	22	.278	.355	.459	814	818	0	2	(6)	10	20	842	57.7
12	12	1997	A.Rodriguez	Sea	AL	587	41	5	633	176	40	3	23	.300	.351	.496	846	799	29	6	25	10	10	844	55.0
13	11	1964	J.Fregosi	LA	AL	505	72	4	581	140	22	9	18	.277	.372	.463	835	845	8	3	3	10		858	54.2
14	14	1967	J.Fregosi	Cal	AL	590	49	5	644	171	23	6	9	.290	.349	.395	744	801	9	6	(4)	10	30	837	53.5
15	17	1987	T.Fernandez	Tor	AL	578	51	5	634	186	29	8	5	.322	.382	.426	807	774	32	12	12	10	30	826	49.6
16	19	1981	R.Burleson	Cal	AL	430	42	3	475	126	17	1	5	.293	.360	.372	732	768	4	6	(16)		50	802	47.9
17	18	1997	J.Bell	KC	AL	573	71	4	648	167	28	3	21	.291	.373	.461	834	787	10	6	(3)		30	814	47.1
18	20	1986	T.Fernandez	Tor	AL	687	27	4	718	213	33	9	10	.310	.340	.428	768	757	25	12	1	10	30	799	46.8
19	22	1990	T.Fernandez	Tor	AL	635	71	7	713	175	27	17	4	.276	.355	.391	745	758	26	13	0	10	30	798	46.1
20	15	1999	T.Batista	Tor	AL	519	38	6	563	144	30	1	31	.277	.334	.518	852	786	4	0	7	10	30	833	45.8
21	23	1988	T.Fernandez	Tor	AL	648	45	4	697	186	41	4	5	.287	.337	.386	723	735	15	5	7	10	40	792	43.1
22	21	1965	J.Fregosi	Cal	AL	602	54	4	660	167	19	7	15	.277	.341	.407	748	774	13	5	4	10	10	798	42.9
23	16	1978	R.Yount	Mil	AL	502	24	1	527	147	23	9	9	.293	.326	.428	755	772	16	5	11	10	40	832	42.8
24	25	1976	T.Harrah	Tex	AL	584	91	3	678	152	21	1	15	.260	.363	.377	740	789	8	5	(3)			786	40.2
25	26	1966	J.Fregosi	Cal	AL	611	67	2	680	154	32	7	13	.252	.328	.391	719	751	17	8	1	10	20	782	39.0

American League Expansion Teams (1961-2000)

AL Expansion Third basemen

V	R	Year	Name	T	L	AB	BB	HBP	TAB	H	2B	3B	HR	BA	OB	SA	PRO	Wtd PRO	SB	CS	SBF	SPF	FF	R TF	V HC
1	2	1985	G.Brett	KC	AL	550	103	3	656	184	38	5	30	.335	.442	.585	1,028	1,021	9	1	10		40	1,071	110.8
2	1	1980	G.Brett	KC	AL	449	58	1	508	175	33	9	24	.390	.461	.664	1,124	1,120	15	6	6	10	20	1,155	106.3
3	5	1979	G.Brett	KC	AL	645	51	0	696	212	42	20	23	.329	.378	.563	941	920	17	10	(4)	10	20	946	76.3
4	3	1992	E.Martinez	Sea	AL	528	54	4	586	181	46	3	18	.343	.408	.544	951	970	14	4	10			980	73.6
5	4	1982	D.DeCinces	Cal	AL	575	66	1	642	173	42	5	30	.301	.374	.548	922	918	7	5	(4)		40	953	72.6
6	7	1970	T.Harper	Mil	AL	604	77	4	685	179	35	4	31	.296	.380	.522	901	905	38	16	8	10		923	67.5
7	10	1976	G.Brett	KC	AL	645	49	1	695	215	34	14	7	.333	.381	.462	843	900	21	11	(1)	10	10	919	67.0
8	8	2000	T.Glaus	Ana	AL	563	112	2	677	160	37	1	47	.284	.405	.604	1,009	923	14	11	(11)		10	922	66.4
9	11	1990	K.Gruber	Tor	AL	592	48	8	648	162	36	6	31	.274	.336	.512	848	862	14	2	15	10	30	917	62.0
10	9	1977	G.Brett	KC	AL	564	55	2	621	176	32	13	22	.312	.375	.532	907	897	14	12	(15)	10	30	922	60.9
11	12	1981	B.Bell	Tex	AL	360	42	3	405	106	16	1	10	.294	.373	.428	801	840	3	3	(7)		80	913	57.4
12	6	1980	B.Bell	Tex	AL	490	40	0	530	161	24	4	17	.329	.379	.498	877	874	3	1	2		60	935	55.3
13	15	1982	G.Brett	KC	AL	552	71	1	624	166	32	9	21	.301	.381	.505	887	883	6	1	6			889	51.4
14	16	1984	B.Bell	Tex	AL	553	63	3	619	174	36	5	11	.315	.388	.458	845	849	2	1	0		40	889	50.9
15	18	1988	P.Molitor	Mil	AL	609	71	2	682	190	34	6	13	.312	.386	.452	837	851	41	10	29	10	(20)	870	50.1
16	14	1981	G.Brett	KC	AL	347	27	1	375	109	27	7	6	.314	.365	.484	849	891	14	6	5	10	(10)	896	48.6
17	25	1982	P.Molitor	Mil	AL	666	69	1	736	201	26	8	19	.302	.368	.450	819	815	41	9	30	10		855	48.6
18	22	1989	P.Molitor	Mil	AL	615	64	4	683	194	35	4	11	.315	.384	.439	823	843	27	11	7	10		860	46.9
19	17	1982	B.Bell	Tex	AL	537	70	2	609	159	27	2	13	.296	.379	.426	806	802	5	4	(5)		80	878	46.9
20	13	1983	G.Brett	KC	AL	464	57	1	522	144	38	2	25	.310	.387	.563	949	948	0	1	(4)		(40)	905	46.8
21	21	1988	K.Gruber	Tor	AL	569	38	7	614	158	33	5	16	.278	.331	.438	768	781	23	5	20	10	50	861	42.4
22	24	1991	E.Martinez	Sea	AL	544	84	8	636	167	35	1	14	.307	.407	.452	859	864	0	3	(9)			855	42.1
23	31	1987	K.Seitzer	KC	AL	641	80	2	723	207	33	8	15	.323	.400	.470	869	834	12	7	(3)			831	39.6
24	20	1978	G.Brett	KC	AL	510	39	1	550	150	45	8	9	.294	.345	.467	812	830	23	7	15		20	866	39.2
25	29	1975	G.Brett	KC	AL	634	46	2	682	195	35	13	11	.308	.356	.456	812	836	13	10	(10)	10		836	39.1

AL Expansion Outfielders

V	R	Year	Name	T	L	AB	BB	HBP	TAB	H	2B	3B	HR	BA	OB	SA	PRO	Wtd PRO	SB	CS	SBF	SPF	FF	R TF	V HC
1	1	1994	K.Griffey Jr.	Sea	AL	433	56	2	491	140	24	4	40	.323	.403	.674	1,078	1,006	11	3	10	10	40	1,066	102.0
2	3	1997	K.Griffey Jr.	Sea	AL	608	76	8	692	185	34	3	56	.304	.389	.646	1,035	977	15	4	10	10	60	1,057	98.6
3	4	1993	K.Griffey Jr.	Sea	AL	582	96	6	684	180	38	3	45	.309	.412	.617	1,029	1,004	17	9	(1)	10	40	1,053	96.3
4	2	1996	K.Griffey Jr.	Sea	AL	545	78	7	630	165	26	2	49	.303	.397	.628	1,024	937	16	1	21	10	90	1,058	90.2
5	7	1998	K.Griffey Jr.	Sea	AL	633	76	7	716	180	33	3	56	.284	.367	.611	979	920	20	5	13	10	70	1,053	87.3
6	9	1995	T.Salmon	Cal	AL	537	91	6	634	177	34	3	34	.330	.432	.594	1,026	968	5	5	(7)		40	1,000	82.6
7	6	1991	K.Griffey Jr.	Sea	AL	548	71	1	620	179	42	1	22	.327	.405	.527	932	937	18	6	9	10	60	1,016	76.5
8	10	1986	J.Barfield	Tor	AL	589	69	8	666	170	35	2	40	.289	.371	.559	929	917	8	8	(11)	10	70	986	72.4
9	14	1999	K.Griffey Jr.	Sea	AL	606	91	7	704	173	26	3	48	.285	.385	.576	961	886	24	7	13	10	60	970	71.2
10	5	1978	A.Otis	KC	AL	486	66	4	556	145	30	7	22	.298	.387	.525	911	932	32	8	27	10	50	1,019	69.3
11	19	2000	D.Erstad	Ana	AL	676	64	1	741	240	39	6	25	.355	.412	.541	953	872	28	8	15	10	50	948	67.2
12	11	1992	K.Griffey Jr.	Sea	AL	565	44	5	614	174	39	4	27	.308	.363	.535	898	915	10	5	0	10	60	985	66.6
13	8	1979	S.Lezcano	Mil	AL	473	77	3	553	152	29	3	28	.321	.420	.573	992	971	4	3	(3)	10	30	1,008	66.0
14	17	1999	S.Green	Tor	AL	614	66	11	691	190	45	0	42	.309	.386	.588	974	899	20	7	8	10	40	957	65.7
15	16	1989	R.Yount	Mil	AL	614	63	6	683	195	38	9	21	.318	.387	.511	898	921	19	3	18	10	10	959	65.5
16	12	1985	J.Barfield	Tor	AL	539	66	4	609	156	34	9	27	.289	.371	.536	907	901	22	8	9		60	980	64.7
17	20	1969	F.Howard	Was	AL	592	102	5	699	175	17	2	48	.296	.403	.574	978	996	1	0	1	(10)	(40)	947	63.2
18	13	1993	J.Gonzalez	Tex	AL	536	37	13	586	166	33	1	46	.310	.369	.632	1,001	977	4	1	3		(10)	970	59.4
19	21	1968	F.Howard	Was	AL	598	54	6	658	164	28	3	44	.274	.340	.552	892	986	0	0	0	(10)	(30)	946	59.0
20	22	1980	B.Oglivie	Mil	AL	592	54	5	651	180	26	2	41	.304	.367	.563	930	926	11	9	(10)	10	20	946	58.4
21	31	1980	W.Wilson	KC	AL	705	28	6	739	230	28	15	3	.326	.357	.421	779	775	79	10	75	10	60	921	57.5
22	18	1971	A.Otis	KC	AL	555	40	2	597	167	26	4	15	.301	.350	.443	793	819	52	8	57	10	70	956	56.4
23	24	1970	F.Howard	Was	AL	566	132	2	700	160	15	1	44	.283	.420	.546	966	970	1	2	(4)	(10)	(30)	926	56.2
24	23	1998	J.Gonzalez	Tex	AL	606	46	6	658	193	50	2	45	.318	.372	.630	1,003	943	2	1	0		(10)	933	55.0
25	28	1984	L.Moseby	Tor	AL	592	78	8	678	166	28	15	18	.280	.372	.470	841	845	39	9	29	10	40	924	53.8

AL Expansion
Outfielders

V	R	Year	Name	T	L	AB	BB	HBP	TAB	H	2B	3B	HR	BA	OB	SA	PRO	Wtd PRO	SB	CS	SBF	SPF	FF	R TF	V HC
26	30	1988	R.Yount	Mil	AL	621	63	3	687	190	38	11	13	.306	.373	.465	838	852	22	4	19	10	40	921	53.6
27	29	1989	R.Sierra	Tex	AL	634	43	2	679	194	35	14	29	.306	.352	.543	895	917	8	2	6	10	(10)	923	53.5
28	15	1991	D.Tartabull	KC	AL	484	65	3	552	153	35	3	31	.316	.400	.593	993	999	6	3	0	(10)	(30)	959	53.0
29	25	1974	J.Burroughs	Tex	AL	554	91	5	650	167	33	2	25	.301	.405	.504	908	951	2	3	(6)		(20)	925	52.0
30	33	1987	G.Bell	Tor	AL	610	39	7	656	188	32	4	47	.308	.357	.605	962	922	5	1	4	10	(20)	917	49.8
31	35	1981	T.Paciorek	Sea	AL	405	35	4	444	132	28	2	14	.326	.385	.509	894	937	13	10	(15)		(10)	913	49.7
32	41	1991	D.White	Tor	AL	642	55	7	704	181	40	10	17	.282	.345	.455	800	804	33	10	17	10	70	902	48.4
33	26	1983	L.Moseby	Tor	AL	539	51	5	595	170	31	7	18	.315	.380	.499	879	878	27	8	17	10	20	925	47.6
34	49	2000	J.Damon	KC	AL	655	65	1	721	214	42	10	16	.327	.388	.495	883	808	46	9	37	10	40	895	47.3
35	45	1995	J.Edmonds	Cal	AL	558	51	5	614	162	30	4	33	.290	.355	.536	891	840	1	4	(11)	10	60	899	46.8
36	39	1977	A.Cowens	KC	AL	606	41	8	655	189	32	14	23	.312	.363	.525	888	878	16	12	(12)	10	30	907	46.7
37	32	1993	T.Salmon	Cal	AL	515	82	5	602	146	35	1	31	.283	.387	.536	923	901	5	6	(11)		30	920	46.6
38	38	1973	A.Otis	KC	AL	583	63	1	647	175	21	4	26	.300	.369	.484	853	875	13	9	(7)	10	30	907	46.2
39	43	2000	T.Salmon	Ana	AL	568	104	6	678	165	36	2	34	.290	.406	.540	946	866	0	2	(6)		40	900	46.2
40	42	2000	J.Dye	KC	AL	601	69	3	673	193	41	2	33	.321	.394	.561	954	874	0	1	(3)		30	901	46.0
41	53	1985	P.Bradley	Sea	AL	641	55	12	708	192	33	8	26	.300	.366	.498	863	858	22	9	5	10	20	893	45.7
42	34	1978	L.Hisle	Mil	AL	520	67	5	592	151	24	0	34	.290	.377	.533	909	930	10	6	(3)		(10)	917	44.9
43	61	1991	R.Sierra	Tex	AL	661	56	0	717	203	44	5	25	.307	.361	.502	863	868	16	4	11	10		889	44.9
44	55	1970	A.Otis	KC	AL	620	68	1	689	176	36	9	11	.284	.356	.424	780	783	33	2	40	10	60	893	44.4
45	48	1977	B.Bonds	Cal	AL	592	74	2	668	156	23	9	37	.264	.347	.520	868	858	41	18	7	10	20	895	43.9
46	50	1990	K.Griffey Jr.	Sea	AL	597	63	2	662	179	28	7	22	.300	.369	.481	849	863	16	11	(9)	10	30	895	43.4
47	64	1979	D.Baylor	Cal	AL	628	71	11	710	186	33	3	36	.296	.377	.530	908	888	22	12	(3)	10	(10)	886	43.4
48	47	1979	G.Thomas	Mil	AL	557	98	2	657	136	29	0	45	.244	.359	.539	898	879	1	5	(13)	10	20	896	43.3
49	36	1996	J.Gonzalez	Tex	AL	541	45	3	589	170	33	2	47	.314	.370	.643	1,013	927	2	0	3		(20)	910	42.9
50	44	1972	A.Otis	KC	AL	540	50	3	593	158	28	2	11	.293	.356	.413	769	834	28	12	6	10	50	900	42.4
51	40	1994	J.Buhner	Sea	AL	358	66	5	429	100	23	4	21	.279	.399	.542	941	878	0	1	(4)		30	904	42.3
52	58	1997	J.Buhner	Sea	AL	540	119	5	664	131	18	2	40	.243	.384	.506	890	840	0	0	0		50	890	41.8
53	46	1979	W.Wilson	KC	AL	588	28	7	623	185	18	13	6	.315	.353	.420	773	757	83	12	89	10	40	896	41.2
54	57	1976	A.Otis	KC	AL	592	55	5	652	165	40	2	18	.279	.345	.444	789	842	26	7	17	10	20	890	41.1
55	54	1974	A.Otis	KC	AL	552	58	2	612	157	31	9	12	.284	.355	.438	793	831	18	5	12	10	40	893	39.5
56	73	1997	T.Salmon	Ana	AL	582	95	7	684	172	28	1	33	.296	.401	.517	918	866	9	12	(21)		30	876	38.5
57	27	1996	J.Edmonds	Cal	AL	431	46	4	481	131	28	3	27	.304	.376	.571	947	866	4	0	8	10	40	924	38.2
58	68	1996	J.Buhner	Sea	AL	564	84	9	657	153	29	0	44	.271	.374	.557	931	852	0	1	(3)		30	879	38.0
59	70	1987	D.Tartabull	KC	AL	582	79	1	662	180	27	3	34	.309	.393	.541	934	896	9	4	1		(20)	877	37.8
60	63	1999	J.Gonzalez	Tex	AL	562	51	4	617	183	36	1	39	.326	.386	.601	987	911	3	3	(5)		(20)	886	37.8
61	72	1978	B.Bonds	Tex	AL	565	79	2	646	151	19	4	31	.267	.359	.480	839	858	43	22	(1)	10	10	876	36.5
62	66	1986	R.Yount	Mil	AL	522	62	4	588	163	31	7	9	.312	.389	.450	840	828	14	5	6	10	40	885	35.7
63	87	1987	R.Yount	Mil	AL	635	76	1	712	198	25	9	21	.312	.386	.479	865	830	19	9	1	10	20	861	35.2
64	71	1982	W.Wilson	KC	AL	585	26	6	617	194	19	15	3	.332	.366	.431	797	794	37	11	23	10	50	877	35.1
65	69	1996	R.Greer	Tex	AL	542	62	3	607	180	41	6	18	.332	.404	.530	933	854	9	0	14		10	878	34.8
66	86	1997	R.Greer	Tex	AL	601	83	3	687	193	42	3	26	.321	.406	.531	937	884	9	5	(1)		(20)	863	34.5
67	78	1998	J.Edmonds	Ana	AL	599	57	1	657	184	42	1	25	.307	.368	.506	874	822	7	5	(4)	10	40	868	34.5
68	74	1981	G.Thomas	Mil	AL	363	50	2	415	94	22	0	21	.259	.352	.493	845	886	4	5	(14)	(10)	10	873	34.5
69	67	1988	D.Tartabull	KC	AL	507	76	4	587	139	38	3	26	.274	.373	.515	888	903	8	5	(3)		(20)	879	34.1
70	79	1979	A.Otis	KC	AL	577	68	3	648	170	28	2	18	.295	.372	.444	816	798	30	5	29	10	30	867	33.9
71	52	1978	B.Oglivie	Mil	AL	469	52	0	521	142	29	4	18	.303	.372	.497	869	889	11	7	(5)	10		893	33.7
72	88	1986	G.Bell	Tor	AL	641	41	2	684	198	38	6	31	.309	.352	.532	884	872	7	8	(12)	10	(10)	860	33.4
73	56	1978	L.Roberts	Sea	AL	472	41	8	521	142	21	7	22	.301	.367	.515	881	901	6	3	0	(10)		891	33.2
74	60	1978	G.Thomas	Mil	AL	452	73	2	527	111	24	1	32	.246	.353	.515	868	888	3	4	(9)	10		889	33.0
75	62	1982	F.Lynn	Cal	AL	472	58	3	533	141	38	1	21	.299	.379	.517	896	892	7	8	(16)		10	886	32.7

American League Expansion Teams (1961–2000)

AL Expansion
Starting Pitchers

V	R	Year	Name	T	L	G	GS	IP	W	L	SV	SO	BB	ERA	RA/9	R Wtd RA/9	V Runs /162
1	1	1964	D.Chance	LA	AL	46	35	278	20	9	4	207	86	1.65	1.81	2.03	78.2
2	2	1997	R.Clemens	Tor	AL	34	34	264	21	7	0	292	68	2.05	2.22	2.03	74.1
3	4	1995	R.Johnson	Sea	AL	30	30	214	18	2	0	294	65	2.48	2.73	2.43	56.9
4	5	1989	B.Saberhagen	KC	AL	36	35	262	23	6	0	193	43	2.16	2.54	2.67	55.0
5	3	1997	R.Johnson	Sea	AL	30	29	213	20	4	0	291	77	2.28	2.54	2.32	52.8
6	18	1978	M.Caldwell	Mil	AL	37	34	293	22	9	1	131	54	2.36	2.76	2.97	51.8
7	8	1977	F.Tanana	Cal	AL	31	31	241	15	9	0	205	61	2.54	2.69	2.69	50.0
8	6	1993	K.Appier	KC	AL	34	34	239	18	8	0	186	81	2.56	2.79	2.68	49.9
9	11	1994	D.Cone	KC	AL	23	23	172	16	5	0	132	54	2.94	3.15	2.72	49.6
10	9	1998	R.Clemens	Tor	AL	33	33	235	20	6	0	271	88	2.65	2.99	2.69	48.7
11	10	1988	T.Higuera	Mil	AL	31	31	227	16	9	0	192	59	2.45	2.61	2.70	46.8
12	17	1987	J.Key	Tor	AL	36	36	261	17	8	0	161	66	2.76	3.21	2.96	46.5
13	23	1996	P.Hentgen	Tor	AL	35	35	266	20	10	0	177	94	3.22	3.56	2.99	46.2
14	24	1984	D.Stieb	Tor	AL	35	35	267	16	8	0	198	88	2.83	2.93	3.00	46.2
15	22	1985	D.Stieb	Tor	AL	36	36	265	14	13	0	167	96	2.48	3.02	2.99	46.1
16	16	1975	F.Tanana	Cal	AL	34	33	257	16	9	0	269	73	2.62	2.80	2.95	45.8
17	32	1976	F.Tanana	Cal	AL	34	34	288	19	10	0	261	73	2.43	2.75	3.14	45.3
18	48	1973	N.Ryan	Cal	AL	41	39	326	21	16	1	383	162	2.87	3.12	3.31	45.3
19	15	1994	R.Johnson	Sea	AL	23	23	172	13	6	0	204	72	3.19	3.40	2.94	43.7
20	19	1986	T.Higuera	Mil	AL	34	34	248	20	11	0	207	74	2.79	3.04	2.98	43.5
21	7	1992	K.Appier	KC	AL	30	30	208	15	8	0	150	68	2.46	2.55	2.68	43.4
22	30	1986	M.Witt	Cal	AL	34	34	269	18	10	0	208	73	2.84	3.18	3.12	43.1
23	20	1989	B.Blyleven	Cal	AL	33	33	241	17	5	0	131	44	2.73	2.84	2.98	42.2
24	49	1977	N.Ryan	Cal	AL	37	37	299	19	16	0	341	204	2.77	3.31	3.31	41.5
25	21	1985	B.Saberhagen	KC	AL	32	32	235	20	6	0	158	38	2.87	3.02	2.99	40.9
26	52	1972	N.Ryan	Cal	AL	39	39	284	19	16	0	329	157	2.28	2.54	3.33	40.9
27	40	1988	M.Gubicza	KC	AL	35	35	270	20	8	0	183	83	2.70	3.14	3.25	39.1
28	36	1987	B.Saberhagen	KC	AL	33	33	257	18	10	0	163	53	3.36	3.47	3.19	38.9
29	28	1990	C.Finley	Cal	AL	32	32	236	18	9	0	177	81	2.40	2.94	3.08	38.7
30	12	1996	J.Guzman	Tor	AL	27	27	188	11	8	0	165	53	2.93	3.26	2.74	37.9
31	29	1977	B.Blyleven	Tex	AL	30	30	235	14	12	0	182	69	2.72	3.11	3.11	37.8
32	33	1991	T.Candiotti	Tor	AL	34	34	238	13	13	0	167	73	2.65	3.10	3.15	37.3
33	53	1978	J.Matlack	Tex	AL	35	33	270	15	13	1	157	51	2.27	3.10	3.33	36.8
34	37	1991	J.Abbott	Cal	AL	34	34	243	18	11	0	158	73	2.89	3.15	3.20	36.7
35	88	1974	F.Jenkins	Tex	AL	41	41	328	25	12	0	225	45	2.82	3.21	3.56	36.4
36	41	1969	A.Messersmith	Cal	AL	40	33	250	16	11	2	211	100	2.52	2.92	3.25	36.2
37	44	1993	R.Johnson	Sea	AL	35	34	255	19	8	1	308	99	3.24	3.42	3.28	36.1
38	13	1972	R.Nelson	KC	AL	34	19	173	11	6	3	120	31	2.08	2.13	2.79	35.7
39	66	1980	L.Gura	KC	AL	36	36	283	18	10	0	113	76	2.95	3.40	3.43	35.5
40	50	1995	D.Cone	Tor	AL	30	30	229	18	8	0	191	88	3.57	3.73	3.32	35.4
41	38	1985	C.Leibrandt	KC	AL	33	33	238	17	9	0	108	68	2.69	3.26	3.23	35.1
42	67	1983	D.Stieb	Tor	AL	36	36	278	17	12	0	187	93	3.04	3.40	3.43	34.9
43	45	1994	P.Hentgen	Tor	AL	24	24	175	13	8	0	147	59	3.40	3.81	3.29	34.7
44	51	1996	K.Hill	Tex	AL	35	35	251	16	10	0	170	95	3.63	3.95	3.32	34.5
45	46	1991	M.Langston	Cal	AL	34	34	246	19	8	0	183	96	3.00	3.25	3.30	34.4
46	25	1989	C.Finley	Cal	AL	29	29	200	16	9	0	156	82	2.57	2.88	3.02	34.1
47	34	1978	L.Gura	KC	AL	35	26	222	16	4	0	81	60	2.72	2.96	3.18	33.9
48	58	1993	M.Langston	Cal	AL	35	35	256	16	11	0	196	85	3.20	3.51	3.37	33.8
49	31	1996	K.Appier	KC	AL	32	32	211	14	11	0	207	75	3.62	3.71	3.12	33.7
50	14	1992	J.Guzman	Tor	AL	28	28	181	16	5	0	165	72	2.64	2.79	2.93	32.7

213

AL Expansion
Starting Pitchers

V	R	Year	Name	T	L	G	GS	IP	W	L	SV	SO	BB	ERA	RA/9	R Wtd RA/9	V Runs /162
51	26	1969	D.Bosman	Was	AL	31	26	193	14	5	1	99	39	2.19	2.75	3.06	32.0
52	60	1998	R.Johnson	Sea	AL	34	34	244	19	11	0	329	86	3.28	3.76	3.39	31.7
53	54	1995	K.Rogers	Tex	AL	31	31	208	17	7	0	140	76	3.38	3.76	3.35	31.5
54	56	1997	K.Appier	KC	AL	34	34	236	9	13	0	196	74	3.40	3.67	3.36	31.4
55	39	1985	J.Key	Tor	AL	35	32	213	14	6	0	85	50	3.00	3.26	3.23	31.4
56	98	1977	D.Leonard	KC	AL	38	37	293	20	12	1	244	79	3.04	3.60	3.60	31.2
57	69	1980	M.Haas	Mil	AL	33	33	252	16	15	0	146	56	3.10	3.42	3.45	31.1
58	75	1984	D.Alexander	Tor	AL	36	35	262	17	6	0	139	59	3.13	3.41	3.49	31.0
59	71	1993	D.Cone	KC	AL	34	34	254	11	14	0	191	114	3.33	3.61	3.46	30.9
60	70	1983	C.Hough	Tex	AL	34	33	252	15	13	0	152	95	3.18	3.43	3.46	30.8
61	42	1989	K.McCaskill	Cal	AL	32	32	212	15	10	0	107	59	2.93	3.10	3.26	30.7
62	77	1975	S.Busby	KC	AL	34	34	260	18	12	0	160	81	3.08	3.32	3.50	30.5
63	43	1992	J.Abbott	Cal	AL	29	29	211	7	15	0	130	68	2.77	3.11	3.27	30.3
64	112	1976	B.Blyleven	Tex	AL	36	36	298	13	16	0	219	81	2.87	3.20	3.65	29.9
65	65	1998	J.Moyer	Sea	AL	34	34	234	15	9	0	158	42	3.53	3.80	3.42	29.5
66	72	1994	R.Bones	Mil	AL	24	24	171	10	9	0	57	45	3.43	4.01	3.47	29.3
67	47	1990	D.Stieb	Tor	AL	33	33	209	18	6	0	125	64	2.93	3.15	3.30	29.2
68	86	1981	L.Gura	KC	AL	23	23	172	11	8	0	61	35	2.72	3.19	3.55	29.0
69	27	1991	N.Ryan	Tex	AL	27	27	173	12	6	0	203	72	2.91	3.02	3.07	28.7
70	78	1986	K.McCaskill	Cal	AL	34	33	246	17	10	0	202	92	3.36	3.58	3.51	28.7
71	85	1984	B.Black	KC	AL	35	35	257	17	12	0	140	64	3.12	3.47	3.55	28.7
72	128	1973	B.Singer	Cal	AL	40	40	316	20	14	0	241	130	3.22	3.53	3.74	28.7
73	68	1970	D.Bosman	Was	AL	36	34	231	16	12	0	134	71	3.00	3.16	3.45	28.5
74	115	1982	D.Stieb	Tor	AL	38	38	288	17	14	0	141	75	3.25	3.62	3.67	28.5
75	97	1985	D.Alexander	Tor	AL	36	36	261	17	10	0	142	67	3.45	3.63	3.60	27.9
76	62	1994	K.Appier	KC	AL	23	23	155	7	6	0	145	63	3.83	3.95	3.42	27.8
77	105	1997	P.Hentgen	Tor	AL	35	35	264	15	10	0	160	71	3.68	3.95	3.61	27.6
78	144	1974	N.Ryan	Cal	AL	42	41	333	22	16	0	367	202	2.89	3.44	3.81	27.5
79	82	1987	J.Clancy	Tor	AL	37	37	241	15	11	0	180	80	3.54	3.84	3.54	27.4
80	79	1990	E.Hansen	Sea	AL	33	33	236	18	9	0	211	68	3.24	3.36	3.52	27.2
81	93	1978	F.Jenkins	Tex	AL	34	30	249	18	8	0	157	41	3.04	3.33	3.58	27.1
82	59	1998	R.Arrojo	TB	AL	32	32	202	14	12	0	152	65	3.56	3.74	3.37	26.7
83	111	1970	C.Wright	Cal	AL	39	39	261	22	12	0	110	88	2.83	3.35	3.65	26.2
84	84	1979	M.Caldwell	Mil	AL	30	30	235	16	6	0	89	39	3.29	3.68	3.55	26.2
85	63	1988	D.Stieb	Tor	AL	32	31	207	16	8	0	147	79	3.04	3.30	3.42	26.2
86	57	1965	G.Brunet	Cal	AL	41	26	197	9	11	2	141	69	2.56	2.92	3.36	26.2
87	102	1985	M.Moore	Sea	AL	35	34	247	17	10	0	155	70	3.46	3.64	3.61	26.1
88	83	1981	K.Forsch	Cal	AL	20	20	153	11	7	0	55	27	2.88	3.18	3.54	26.1
89	94	1987	C.Leibrandt	KC	AL	35	35	240	16	11	0	151	74	3.41	3.89	3.58	26.0
90	35	1961	D.Donovan	Was	AL	23	22	169	10	10	0	62	35	2.40	3.20	3.18	25.8
91	80	1998	C.Finley	Ana	AL	34	34	223	11	9	0	212	109	3.39	3.91	3.52	25.7
92	108	1985	C.Hough	Tex	AL	34	34	250	14	16	0	141	83	3.31	3.67	3.64	25.6
93	73	1971	M.Hedlund	KC	AL	32	30	206	15	8	0	76	72	2.71	2.97	3.48	24.7
94	92	1995	K.Appier	KC	AL	31	31	201	15	10	0	185	80	3.89	4.02	3.58	24.6
95	87	1996	B.McDonald	Mil	AL	35	35	221	12	10	0	146	67	3.90	4.23	3.56	24.6
96	64	1965	P.Richert	Was	AL	34	29	194	15	12	0	161	84	2.60	2.97	3.42	24.6
97	109	1995	M.Gubicza	KC	AL	33	33	213	12	14	0	81	62	3.75	4.09	3.64	24.4
98	106	1989	C.Bosio	Mil	AL	33	33	235	15	10	0	173	48	2.95	3.45	3.62	24.4
99	76	1995	A.Leiter	Tor	AL	28	28	183	11	11	0	153	108	3.64	3.93	3.50	24.2
100	120	1989	M.Gubicza	KC	AL	36	36	255	15	11	0	173	63	3.04	3.53	3.71	24.1

American League Expansion Teams (1961–2000)

AL Expansion Relief Pitchers

V	R	Year	Name	T	L	G	GS	IP	W	L	SV	SO	BB	ERA	RA/9	R Wtd RA/9	V Runs /162
1	4	1986	M.Eichhorn	Tor	AL	69	0	157	14	6	10	166	45	1.72	1.83	1.79	48.2
2	1	1981	R.Fingers	Mil	AL	47	0	78	6	3	28	61	13	1.04	1.04	1.16	44.6
3	12	1979	J.Kern	Tex	AL	71	0	143	13	5	29	136	62	1.57	2.20	2.12	38.7
4	25	1983	D.Quisenberry	KC	AL	69	0	139	5	3	45	48	11	1.94	2.27	2.29	35.0
5	24	1964	B.Lee	LA	AL	64	5	137	6	5	19	111	58	1.51	2.04	2.28	34.6
6	16	1974	T.Murphy	Mil	AL	70	0	123	10	10	20	47	51	1.90	1.98	2.20	32.3
7	29	1990	S.Farr	KC	AL	57	6	127	13	7	1	94	48	1.98	2.27	2.38	30.7
8	3	1989	J.Montgomery	KC	AL	63	0	92	7	3	18	94	25	1.37	1.57	1.63	30.0
9	2	1969	K.Tatum	Cal	AL	45	0	86	7	2	22	65	39	1.36	1.36	1.52	29.1
10	49	1971	K.Sanders	Mil	AL	83	0	136	7	12	31	80	34	1.91	2.32	2.72	27.8
11	54	1965	B.Lee	Cal	AL	69	0	131	9	7	23	89	42	1.92	2.40	2.76	26.1
12	6	1970	K.Sanders	Mil	AL	50	0	92	5	2	13	64	25	1.75	1.86	2.03	25.9
13	63	1982	D.Quisenberry	KC	AL	72	0	137	9	7	35	46	12	2.57	2.83	2.87	25.7
14	56	1984	D.Quisenberry	KC	AL	72	0	129	6	3	44	41	12	2.64	2.71	2.78	25.5
15	20	1985	S.Cliburn	Cal	AL	44	0	99	9	3	6	48	26	2.09	2.27	2.25	25.4
16	61	1985	D.Quisenberry	KC	AL	84	0	129	8	9	37	54	16	2.37	2.86	2.83	24.7
17	33	1985	D.Moore	Cal	AL	65	0	103	8	8	31	72	21	1.92	2.45	2.43	24.4
18	11	1989	T.Henke	Tor	AL	64	0	89	8	3	20	116	25	1.92	2.02	2.09	24.4
19	14	1995	J.Nelson	Sea	AL	62	0	79	7	3	2	96	27	2.17	2.40	2.14	23.9
20	13	1999	J.Zimmerman	Tex	AL	65	0	88	9	3	3	67	23	2.36	2.46	2.13	23.6
21	18	1991	B.Swift	Sea	AL	71	0	90	1	2	17	48	26	1.99	2.19	2.22	23.3
22	30	1982	B.Caudill	Sea	AL	70	0	96	12	9	26	111	35	2.35	2.35	2.38	23.2
23	10	1995	T.Percival	Cal	AL	62	0	74	3	2	3	94	26	1.95	2.31	2.06	23.1
24	15	1993	J.Montgomery	KC	AL	69	0	87	7	5	45	66	23	2.27	2.27	2.18	23.0
25	39	1976	M.Littell	KC	AL	60	1	104	8	4	16	92	60	2.08	2.25	2.57	23.0
26	35	1992	D.Ward	Tor	AL	79	0	101	7	4	12	103	39	1.95	2.40	2.52	22.9
27	23	1989	G.Minton	Cal	AL	62	0	90	4	3	8	42	37	2.20	2.20	2.28	22.8
28	31	1987	T.Henke	Tor	AL	72	0	94	0	6	34	128	25	2.49	2.59	2.38	22.7
29	55	1985	G.Harris	Tex	AL	58	0	113	5	4	11	111	43	2.47	2.79	2.76	22.5
30	9	1997	D.Jones	Mil	AL	75	0	80	6	6	36	82	9	2.02	2.24	2.05	22.3
31	34	1994	T.Castillo	Tor	AL	41	0	68	5	2	1	43	28	2.51	2.91	2.52	21.8
32	27	1997	P.Quantrill	Tor	AL	77	0	88	6	7	5	56	17	1.94	2.56	2.34	21.7
33	76	1987	M.Eichhorn	Tor	AL	89	0	128	10	6	4	96	52	3.17	3.31	3.05	21.5
34	41	1981	D.Aase	Cal	AL	39	0	65	4	4	11	38	24	2.34	2.34	2.61	21.3
35	70	1970	D.Knowles	Was	AL	71	0	119	2	14	27	71	58	2.04	2.72	2.97	21.0
36	40	1981	D.Quisenberry	KC	AL	40	0	62	1	4	18	20	15	1.73	2.31	2.57	20.7
37	7	1996	T.Percival	Cal	AL	62	0	74	0	2	36	100	31	2.31	2.43	2.04	20.7
38	32	1984	D.Corbett	Cal	AL	45	1	85	5	1	4	48	30	2.12	2.33	2.39	20.5
39	28	1991	M.Eichhorn	Cal	AL	70	0	82	3	3	1	49	13	1.98	2.31	2.34	20.2
40	8	1993	D.Ward	Tor	AL	71	0	72	2	3	45	97	25	2.13	2.13	2.04	20.1
41	26	1991	B.Harvey	Cal	AL	67	0	79	2	4	46	101	17	1.60	2.29	2.32	19.6
42	53	1997	B.Wickman	Mil	AL	74	0	96	7	6	1	78	41	2.73	3.01	2.75	19.2
43	21	1990	T.Henke	Tor	AL	61	0	75	2	4	32	75	19	2.17	2.17	2.27	19.0
44	62	1987	D.Mohorcic	Tex	AL	74	0	99	7	6	16	48	19	2.99	3.08	2.84	18.9
45	5	1992	J.Russell	Tex	AL	59	0	66	4	3	30	48	25	1.63	1.90	2.00	18.8
46	36	1980	J.Garvin	Tor	AL	61	0	83	4	7	8	52	27	2.29	2.50	2.52	18.8
47	38	1996	M.James	Cal	AL	69	0	81	5	5	1	65	42	2.67	3.00	2.52	18.3
48	79	1980	D.Darwin	Tex	AL	53	2	110	13	4	8	104	50	2.63	3.04	3.06	18.2
49	95	1977	E.Romo	Sea	AL	58	3	114	8	10	16	105	39	2.83	3.15	3.15	17.8
50	42	1992	J.Montgomery	KC	AL	65	0	83	1	6	39	69	27	2.18	2.50	2.63	17.8

National League Expansion Teams (1962–2000)

The first National League expansion teams, the Houston Astros and the New York Mets, began playing ball in 1962 — one year after the first American League expansion teams were added. The Montreal Expos and San Diego Padres were added in 1969; this expansion to 12 teams resulted in the creation of the two-division format. While the American League expanded again in 1977, the National League waited until 1993 to add the Colorado Rockies and Florida Marlins. The next season a three division format was created. Two more teams were added in 1998, with the Tampa Bay Devil Rays going to the American League and the Arizona Diamondbacks to the National League. The Milwaukee Brewers volunteered to switch leagues to maintain an even number of teams in each league.

Houston Astros (1962–2000)

The Houston Astros (originally the Colt 45s) began their existence with seven losing seasons from 1962 to 1968. In 1969, Jimmy Wynn led the Astros to their first .500 season with a .269 average, 33 home runs, and 148 walks, for a 1,022 Total Factor. The Astros continued to play around .500 ball, winning 79, 80, 81, or 82 games in seven seasons from 1969 to 1978. The 1972 team was 84–69, achieving the best record of this period. Twenty-one-year-old Cesar Cedeno led the offense with a .320 average, 22 home runs, 55 steals, and he won a Gold Glove for his defense, while generating a 1,026 Total Factor. The pitching staff featured two 15 game winners in Larry Dierker and Don Wilson.

The Astros posted seven winning seasons from 1979 to 1992. Houston won its first division title in 1980 with 93 victories. Cedeno came back from a knee injury to hit .309 with 48 steals, and Jose Cruz batted .302 with 36 steals, while a deep bullpen was led by Joe Sambito (8–4, 17 saves, 2.19 ERA) and Dave Smith (7–5, 10 saves, 1.93 ERA, 2.37 Wtd. RA/9). The 1981 team made the playoffs in a strike-shortened season, as Nolan Ryan overpowered opponents with an 11–5 record, league-leading 1.69 ERA, and 2.40 Wtd. RA/9 in the best year of his long career. The Astros also won the division with 96 wins in 1986. Mike Scott starred with an 18–10 record, a league leading 2.22 ERA and a 2.61 Wtd. RA/9, and he struck out a league high 306 batters in 275 innings.

The Astros are in their most successful period, with seven straight winning seasons from 1993 to 1999, including division titles in 1997, 1998, and 1999 — but still no pennants to show for their efforts. The current team is built around two players. Jeff Bagwell had the best season ever by a National League first baseman in 1994, when he hit .368 with 39 home runs before breaking a bone in his hand just as the players' strike wiped out the last third of the season. Bagwell also won his only Gold Glove and the league's MVP Award that season. Adjusted for 6 percent hitter's inflation and a 162 game schedule, Bagwell batted .346 with 53 home runs, for a 1,139 Wtd. Production, a 1,203 Total Factor, and 137.0 Hits Contribution. The other star, Craig Biggio, is a catcher-turned–second baseman with several Gold Glove awards. Biggio's best season was in 1997, when he hit .309 with 22 home runs and 47 steals, while earning a 968 Total Factor and 99.2 Hits Contribution. Other players with solid seasons for recent winning teams include:

216

Mark Portugal (SP)	(18–4, 2.77 ERA in 1993)
Darryl Kile (SP)	(19–7, 2.57 ERA in 1997)
Moises Alou (OF)	(.312, 38 home runs, 944 Total Factor in 1998)
Carl Everett (OF)	(.325, 25 home runs, 925 Total Factor in 1999)
Mike Hampton (SP)	(22–4, 2.90 ERA, 2.93 Wtd. RA/9 in 1999)
Billy Wagner (RP)	(4–1, 39 saves, 1.57 ERA, 1.53 Wtd. RA/9 in 1999)

New York Mets (1962–2000)

The New York Mets began as a hopelessly inept team, losing 120, 111, 109, 112, 95, 101, and 89 games in their first seven seasons. Then a "miracle" occurred in 1969, as the amazing Mets won 100 games, the pennant and the World Series. The Mets achieved their miracle with the pitching of Tom Seaver (25–7, 2.21 ERA, 2.76 Wtd. RA/9) and Jerry Koosman (17–9, 2.28 ERA, 2.75 Wtd. RA/9).

In 1971, Seaver won 20 games, and his 1.76 ERA was the best by any qualifying National League pitcher in the 1970s. Seaver's 2.24 Wtd. RA/9 that year ranks seventh all time in league rate of success, and he saved 73.7 runs from scoring. Tug McGraw was just as effective out of the bullpen, with an 11–4 record, 8 saves, a 1.70 ERA, and 2.07 Wtd. RA/9, while saving 30.6 runs from scoring.

The Mets won just 82 games in 1973, but managed to win their division in a tight race with four other teams. Seaver (19–10, 2.08 ERA, 2.53 Wtd. RA/9) and Koosman (14–15, 2.84 ERA) pitched these hitless wonders into the World Series.

The Mets fell apart when Seaver was traded during the 1977 season, while Koosman went 8–20 in 1977 and 3–15 in 1978. New York finished last in last or next-to-last place from 1977 to 1983. The one standout performance in this period was by reliever Jesse Orosco, who went 13–7 with 17 saves, a 1.47 ERA and a 2.44 Wtd. RA/9 in 1983.

From 1984 to 1990, the Mets experienced their golden period, with two first place and five second place finishes. In 1984, 19-year-old Dwight Gooden sparkled with a 17–9 record and 2.60 ERA. In 1985, Gooden overpowered opponents with a 24–4 record and 1.53 ERA. Gooden's 1.86 Wtd. RA/9 was the league's second best ever rate of success, while he saved 83.0 runs from scoring. The 1986 Mets went 108–54, and won a memorable World Series battle with the Red Sox. This team was deep in pitching, featuring starters Bob Ojeda (18–5, 2.47 ERA), Gooden (17–6, 2.84 ERA), Ron Darling (15–6, 2.81 ERA), and reliever Orosco (8–6, 21 saves, 2.33 ERA). In 1988, the Mets won 100 games and their division. David Cone was 20–3 with a 2.22 ERA and a 3.07 Wtd. RA/9, while reliever Randy Myers went 7–3 with 26 saves, a 1.72 ERA and 2.34 Wtd. RA/9. Darryl Strawberry hit .269 with a league leading 39 home runs and 29 steals, for a 959 Total Factor.

New York struggled through six losing seasons from 1991 to 1996, as Strawberry was traded and Gooden faded. The Mets then finished the decade with three winning seasons. In 1998, Al Leiter went 17–6 with a 2.47 ERA and a solid 2.52 Wtd. RA/9. The Mets captured a wild card spot in 1999, as Robin Ventura experienced his best season with a .301 average and 32 home runs, while Mike Piazza batted .303 with 40 home runs.

The Mets began the new century with a World Series appearance against their crosstown rivals, the Yankees. Piazza batted .324 with 38 home runs, for a 925 Wtd. Production, and Edgar Alfonso hit .324 with 25 home runs. Leiter (16–8, 3.20 ERA) and Mike Hampton (15–10, 3.14 ERA) headed up the starting rotation.

Montreal Expos (1969–2000)

The Montreal Expos were baseball's first foray into Canada. The Expos started the way most expansion teams began, with ten losing records from 1969 to 1978. The 1969 team was only 52–110, but fans found a hero in Rusty Staub, who hit .302 with 29 home runs, for a 975 Wtd. Production. In 1972, Mike Marshall was 14–8 with 18 saves, a 1.78 ERA, a 2.37 Wtd. RA/9, and he saved 29.7 runs from scoring. In 1977, 23-year-old catcher Gary Carter had a breakout season, hitting .284 with 31 home runs.

The Expos put together a run of 14 winning seasons in 18 years from 1979 to 1996. In 1979, the Expos won 95 games and finished just 2 games out, as Larry Parrish hit .307 with 30 home runs. The Expos finished just one game out in 1980, as Andre Dawson hit .308 with 17 home runs and 34 steals, and Steve Rogers was 16–11 with a 2.98 ERA. Montreal made the playoffs in 1981 with a 60–48 record. Dawson starred in his best season with a .302 average, 24 home runs, and 26 steals, for a 1,078 Total Factor and 100.9 Hits Contribution, while 21-year-old rookie Tim Raines hit .304 with 71 steals for a 995 Total Factor.

The Expos finished no higher than third place from 1982 to 1991. In 1982, Carter led the Expos in his best season, batting .293 with 29 home runs, for a 967 Total Factor and 88.6 Hits Contribution. From 1982 through 1986, Raines stole 78, 90, 75, 70, and 70 bases. In 1987, the Expos won 91 games as Raines hit .330 with 18 home runs and 50 more steals, for a 1,031 Total Factor. Teammate Tim Burke was 7–0 with 18 saves, a 1.19 ERA, and 1.79 Wtd. RA/9.

The Expos finished in second in 1992, as Larry Walker hit .301 with 23 home runs, while Dennis Martinez went 16–11 with a 2.47 ERA, and Mel Rojas was 7–1 with 10 saves, a 1.43 ERA, and 1.79 Wtd. RA/9, and he saved 31.1 runs from scoring. The Expos finished in second in 1993, as Jeff Fassero was 12–5 with a 2.29 ERA, and John Wetteland went 9–3 with 43 saves, a 1.37 ERA and a 1.80 Wtd. RA/9. Montreal's best season ever was wiped out by the players' strike of 1994. This 74–40 team had the league's best record, with Walker batting .322 with 19 home runs, and Moises Alou hitting .339 with 22 home runs.

The Expos were forced to reduce their player payroll to survive in a small city market, resulting in just one winning season after 1994. Montreal even lost ace pitcher Pedro Martinez to Boston following a 1997 season where he went 17–8 with a 1.90 ERA and 2.38 Wtd. RA/9. In 1998, Ugueth Urbina was 6–3 with 34 saves, a 1.30 ERA, and the league's best ever rate of success with a 1.41 Wtd. RA/9. Vladimir Guerrero hit 38 home runs in 1998, 42 home runs in 1999, and 44 home runs in 2000, which, along with a .345 batting average, earned him a 982 Wtd. Production.

San Diego Padres (1969–2000)

The Padres began with nine losing seasons from 1969 to 1977. Cito Gaston produced by far his best season in 1970, hitting .318 with 29 home runs. In 1975, Randy Jones led the league with a 2.24 ERA, while going 20–12. Jones then led the league in wins in 1976 with a 22–14 record, and he achieved a 2.74 ERA.

The 1978 team won 84 games, as Dave Winfield hit .308 with 24 home runs and 21 steals, while 39-year-old Gaylord Perry was 21–6 with a 2.73 ERA. In 1979, Winfield hit .308 with 34 home runs for a 1,002 Total Factor. Winfield left for the Yankees before the 1981 season.

In 1984, the Padres won their first division title and the pennant. Twenty-four-year-old Tony Gwynn led the league with a .351 average and stole 33 bases for a 929 Total Factor, while bullpen stars Goose Gossage (10–6 record, 25 saves, 2.90 ERA) and Craig Lefferts (3–4 record, 10 saves, 2.13 ERA, 2.76 Wtd. RA/9) anchored the pitching.

The Padres produced uneven results from 1985 to 1995, with five winning and six losing seasons. Gwynn was the team's star during this period, winning batting titles with averages of .370 (1987), .313 (1988), .336 (1989), .394 (1994), and .368 (1995). Gwynn's .394 average in 1994 was the highest batting average since Ted Williams hit .406 in 1941. Gwynn was a better all-around player in 1987, as he won a Gold Glove and hit .370 with 56 steals and a career high 82 walks, for a 1,019 Total Factor. The best pitching performance in this period was by Mark Davis in 1989. Davis was 4–3 with 44 saves, a 1.85 ERA, and a 2.36 Wtd. RA/9. Two sluggers starred in 1992, as Fred McGriff led the league with 35 home runs, and Gary Sheffield batted .330 with 33 home runs for a 1,017 Total Factor.

Gwynn won his seventh batting title with a .353 average in 1996, as the Padres won their second division title. Ken Caminiti earned a Gold Glove and a MVP Award, batting .326 with 40 home runs for a 1,037 Total Factor. Trevor Hoffman was 9–5 with 42 saves, a 2.25 ERA and a 2.27 Wtd. RA/9.

In 1998, the Padres won 98 games, their third division title, and their second pennant, paced by three exceptional performances. Greg Vaughn hit .272 with 50 home runs. Kevin Brown arrived from the Marlins to go 18–7 with a 2.38 ERA and a 2.66 Wtd. RA/9. Ace reliever Hoffman went 4–2 with 53 saves, a 1.48 ERA and a sharp 1.46 Wtd. RA/9, the league's third lowest rate of success among relief pitchers.

Colorado Rockies (1993–2000)

The Rockies are a fun team to watch, as baseballs travel a long way in Denver's thin air. This is especially true in a period of high hitter's inflation tied to a major increase in the number of home runs being hit out of every ballpark. Rockies pitching suffers as a result, but the team generated enough hitting to achieve four winning seasons in their first eight years, including a wild card winner in 1995.

Colorado's first big hitter was Andres Galarraga, who won the batting title in 1993 with a .370 average, while hitting 22 home runs, for a 987 Total Factor. Galarraga went on to hit .304 with a league leading 47 home runs in 1996, and .318 with 41 home runs in 1997.

Dante Bichette went from being a below-average hitter with Milwaukee to a power-hitting threat with Colorado. His best season was in 1995, when he hit .340 with 40 home runs for a 942 Wtd. Production.

Ellis Burks achieved some success with other teams before he came to Colorado, and he starred for the Giants after leaving the Rockies. Burks produced a huge season with the Rockies in 1996, when he hit .344 with 40 home runs, 93 extra base hits, and 32 steals, for a 1,026 Total Factor.

Todd Helton hit .315 with 25 home runs to finish second in the Rookie of the Year voting in 1998. Helton produced a mega-season in 2000, batting .372 with 42 home runs and 103 extra base hits, for a 1,085 Total Factor and 103.0 Hits Contribution.

Larry Walker achieved one of the greatest seasons ever in the National League in 1997, hitting .366 with 49 home runs, 99 extra base hits, and 33 steals in 41 attempts, while winning MVP and Gold Glove awards. Adjusted for 5 percent hitter's inflation, Walker batted .348 with 47 home runs, for a 1,115 Wtd. Production, a 1,179 Total Factor, and 132.6 Hits Contribution. In 1998, Walker won another Gold Glove while hitting for a league-leading .363 average with 23 home runs, for a 1,075 Total Factor. In 1999, Walker had another impressive season, leading the league with a .379 average, hitting 37 home runs in just 438 at bats, and winning another Gold Glove, for a 1,119 Total Factor.

Florida Marlins (1993–2000)

The Marlins have just one winning season in their eight-year history. The 1996 team finished two games under .500, but had more star performances than during their championship season. Kevin Brown was 17–11 with a league-leading 1.89 ERA and a stellar 2.24 Wtd. RA/9, Al Leiter was 16–12 with a 2.93 ERA and a 2.99 Wtd. RA/9, and reliever Robb Nen was 5–1 with 35 saves, a 1.95 ERA, and a 2.21 Wtd. RA/9. Gary Sheffield hit .314 with 42 home runs, while drawing 142 walks, for a 1,042 Wtd. Production and a 1,029 Total Factor.

The Marlins spent millions to assemble a powerful team in 1997, and they went on to win 92 games and the wild card spot. They then surprised in the playoffs, going on to win the World Series. Brown led the pitching staff with a 16–8 record, 2.69 ERA, and 2.87 Wtd. RA/9.

The team's owner suffered a huge financial loss in 1997. Having won the World Series, he sold and traded the best players on the Marlins, and the team nosedived to a 54–108 record in 1998. By 2000, new ownership and a group of talented young players brought the Marlins back to nearly .500.

NL Expansion   **Hitters Volume of Success**

Pos	Year	Name	T	L	AB	BB	HBP	TAB	H	2B	3B	HR	BA	OB	SA	PRO	Wtd PRO	SB	CS	SBF	SPF	FF	R TF	V HC
C	1982	G.Carter	Mon	NL	557	78	6	641	163	32	1	29	.293	.385	.510	895	909	2	5	(12)	0	70	967	88.6
1B	1994	J.Bagwell	Hou	NL	400	65	4	469	147	32	2	39	.368	.461	.750	1,211	1,139	15	4	14	10	40	1,203	137.0
2B	1997	C.Biggio	Hou	NL	619	84	34	737	191	37	8	22	.309	.419	.501	920	873	47	10	35	10	40	968	99.2
SS	1983	D.Thon	Hou	NL	619	54	2	675	177	28	9	20	.286	.345	.457	802	809	34	16	3	10	30	852	61.1
3B	1996	K.Caminiti	SD	NL	546	78	4	628	178	37	2	40	.326	.414	.621	1,035	986	11	5	2	0	50	1,037	96.1
OF	1997	L.Walker	Col	NL	568	78	14	660	208	46	4	49	.366	.455	.720	1,175	1,115	33	8	24	10	30	1,179	132.6
OF	1981	A.Dawson	Mon	NL	394	35	7	436	119	21	3	24	.302	.369	.553	923	949	26	4	39	10	80	1,078	100.9
OF	1996	E.Burks	Col	NL	613	61	6	680	211	45	8	40	.344	.409	.639	1,048	999	32	6	28	0	0	1,026	87.2
Starters		Averages			540	67	10	616	174	35	5	33	.323	.407	.587	994	965	25	7	17	6	44	1,032	100.3
C	1998	M.Piazza	NY	NL	561	58	2	621	184	38	1	32	.328	.393	.570	963	917	1	0	2	(10)	(10)	898	65.3
1B	2000	T.Helton	Col	NL	580	103	4	687	216	59	2	42	.372	.470	.698	1,168	1,066	5	3	(1)	0	20	1,085	103.0
2B	2000	E.Alfonso	NY	NL	544	95	5	644	176	40	2	25	.324	.429	.542	971	886	3	2	(1)	0	30	914	70.3
SS	1994	W.Cordero	Mon	NL	415	41	6	462	122	30	3	15	.294	.366	.489	855	805	16	3	20	10	(40)	795	41.5
3B	1992	G.Sheffield	SD	NL	557	48	6	611	184	34	3	33	.330	.390	.580	969	998	5	6	(11)	10	20	1,017	87.5
OF	1987	T.Gwynn	SD	NL	589	82	3	674	218	36	13	7	.370	.450	.511	961	924	56	12	45	10	40	1,019	83.9
OF	1972	C.Cedeno	Hou	NL	559	56	5	620	179	39	8	22	.320	.387	.537	924	956	55	21	20	10	40	1,026	83.4
OF	1985	T.Raines	Mon	NL	575	81	3	659	184	30	13	11	.320	.407	.475	881	895	70	9	75	10	40	1,020	82.4
Reserves		Averages			548	71	4	622	183	38	6	23	.334	.414	.553	967	936	26	7	18	5	18	977	77.2
Totals		Weighted Ave.			542	68	8	618	177	36	5	30	.327	.409	.576	985	955	25	7	17	6	35	1,013	92.6

Pitchers Volume of Success

Pos	Year	Name	T	L	G	GS	IP	W	L	SV	SO	BB	ERA	RA/9	Wtd RA/9	R V Runs /162
SP	1985	D.Gooden	NY	NL	35	35	277	24	4	0	268	69	1.53	1.66	1.86	83.0
SP	1971	T.Seaver	NY	NL	36	35	286	20	10	0	289	61	1.76	1.92	2.24	73.7
SP	1996	K.Brown	Fla	NL	32	32	233	17	11	0	159	33	1.89	2.32	2.24	59.9
SP	1999	R.Johnson	Ari	NL	35	35	272	17	9	0	364	70	2.48	2.85	2.58	59.8
SP	1986	M.Scott	Hou	NL	37	37	275	18	10	0	306	72	2.22	2.39	2.61	59.4
Starters		Averages			35	35	269	19	9	0	277	61	1.98	2.22	2.31	67.2
RP	1992	M.Rojas	Mon	NL	68	0	101	7	1	10	70	34	1.43	1.52	1.79	31.1
RP	1972	M.Marshall	Mon	NL	65	0	116	14	8	18	95	47	1.78	2.02	2.37	29.7
RP	1971	T.McGraw	NY	NL	51	1	111	11	4	8	109	41	1.70	1.78	2.07	30.6
RP	1987	T.Burke	Mon	NL	55	0	91	7	0	18	58	17	1.19	1.78	1.79	28.0
Relievers		Averages			60	0	105	10	3	14	83	35	1.55	1.78	2.02	29.9
Totals		Averages			95	35	373	29	12	14	360	96	1.85	2.10	2.23	97.0

National League Expansion Teams (1962–2000)

NL Expansion — **Hitters Rate of Success**

Pos	Year	Name	T	L	AB	BB	HBP	TAB	H	2B	3B	HR	BA	OB	SA	PRO	Wtd PRO	SB	CS	SBF	SPF	FF	R TF	V HC
C	1982	G.Carter	Mon	NL	557	78	6	641	163	32	1	29	.293	.385	.510	895	909	2	5	(12)	0	70	967	88.6
1B	1994	J.Bagwell	Hou	NL	400	65	4	469	147	32	2	39	.368	.461	.750	1,211	1,139	15	4	14	10	40	1,203	137.0
2B	1997	C.Biggio	Hou	NL	619	84	34	737	191	37	8	22	.309	.419	.501	920	873	47	10	35	10	50	968	99.2
SS	1983	D.Thon	Hou	NL	619	54	2	675	177	28	9	20	.286	.345	.457	802	809	34	16	3	10	30	852	61.1
3B	1996	K.Caminiti	SD	NL	546	78	4	628	178	37	2	40	.326	.414	.621	1,035	986	11	5	2	0	50	1,037	96.1
OF	1997	L.Walker	Col	NL	568	78	14	660	208	46	4	49	.366	.455	.720	1,175	1,115	33	8	24	10	30	1,179	132.6
OF	1981	A.Dawson	Mon	NL	394	35	7	436	119	21	3	24	.302	.369	.553	923	949	26	4	39	10	80	1,078	100.9
OF	1987	T.Raines	Mon	NL	530	90	4	624	175	34	8	18	.330	.431	.526	958	921	50	5	61	10	40	1,031	81.5
Starters		Averages			529	70	9	609	170	33	5	30	.321	.410	.572	982	955	27	7	21	8	49	1,032	99.6
C	2000	M.Piazza	NY	NL	482	58	3	543	156	26	0	38	.324	.400	.614	1,014	925	4	2	0	(10)	(10)	905	58.9
1B	2000	T.Helton	Col	NL	580	103	4	687	216	59	2	42	.372	.470	.698	1,168	1,066	5	3	(1)	0	20	1,085	103.0
2B	2000	E.Alfonso	NY	NL	544	95	5	644	176	40	2	25	.324	.429	.542	971	886	3	2	(1)	0	30	914	70.3
SS	1994	W.Cordero	Mon	NL	415	41	6	462	122	30	3	15	.294	.366	.489	855	805	16	3	20	10	(40)	795	41.5
3B	1992	G.Sheffield	SD	NL	557	48	6	611	184	34	3	33	.330	.390	.580	969	998	5	6	(11)	10	20	1,017	87.5
OF	1996	E.Burks	Col	NL	613	61	6	680	211	45	8	40	.344	.409	.639	1,048	999	32	6	28	0	0	1,026	87.2
OF	1972	C.Cedeno	Hou	NL	559	56	5	620	179	39	8	22	.320	.387	.537	924	956	55	21	20	10	40	1,026	83.4
OF	1969	J.Wynn	Hou	NL	495	148	3	646	133	17	1	33	.269	.440	.507	947	969	23	7	13	10	30	1,022	81.3
Reserves		Averages			531	76	5	612	172	36	3	31	.324	.414	.581	995	957	18	6	8	4	11	981	76.6
Totals		Weighted Ave.			530	72	8	610	171	34	4	30	.322	.411	.575	986	956	24	7	17	6	36	1,015	92.0

Pitchers Rate of Success

Pos	Year	Name	T	L	G	GS	IP	W	L	SV	SO	BB	ERA	RA/9	Wtd RA/9	R Runs/162
SP	1985	D.Gooden	NY	NL	35	35	277	24	4	0	268	69	1.53	1.66	1.86	83.0
SP	1971	T.Seaver	NY	NL	36	35	286	20	10	0	289	61	1.76	1.92	2.24	73.7
SP	1996	K.Brown	Fla	NL	32	32	233	17	11	0	159	33	1.89	2.32	2.24	59.9
SP	1997	P.Martinez	Mon	NL	31	31	241	17	8	0	305	67	1.90	2.42	2.38	58.2
SP	1981	N.Ryan	Hou	NL	21	21	149	11	5	0	140	68	1.69	2.05	2.40	54.0
Starters		Averages			31	31	237	18	8	0	232	60	1.75	2.06	2.20	65.8
RP	1998	U.Urbina	Mon	NL	64	0	69	6	3	34	94	33	1.30	1.43	1.41	24.1
RP	1998	T.Hoffman	SD	NL	66	0	73	4	2	53	86	21	1.48	1.48	1.46	25.1
RP	1999	B.Wagner	Hou	NL	66	0	75	4	1	39	124	23	1.57	1.69	1.53	25.1
RP	1999	A.Benitez	NY	NL	77	0	78	4	3	22	128	41	1.85	1.96	1.77	24.1
Relievers		Averages			68	0	74	5	2	37	108	30	1.56	1.65	1.55	24.6
Totals		Averages			99	31	311	22	10	37	340	89	1.71	1.96	2.05	90.4

Houston Astros (NL Expansion)

Hitters Volume of Success

Pos	Year	Name	T	L	AB	BB	HBP	TAB	H	2B	3B	HR	BA	OB	SA	PRO	Wtd PRO	SB	CS	SBF	SPF	FF	R TF	V HC
C	1977	J.Ferguson	Hou	NL	421	85	0	506	108	21	3	16	.257	.381	.435	816	792	6	2	4	(10)	(10)	776	23.8
1B	1994	J.Bagwell	Hou	NL	400	65	4	469	147	32	2	39	.368	.461	.750	1,211	1,139	15	4	14	10	40	1,203	137.0
2B	1997	C.Biggio	Hou	NL	619	84	34	737	191	37	8	22	.309	.419	.501	920	873	47	10	35	10	50	968	99.2
SS	1983	D.Thon	Hou	NL	619	54	2	675	177	28	9	20	.286	.345	.457	802	809	34	16	3	10	30	852	61.1
3B	1994	K.Caminiti	Hou	NL	406	43	2	451	115	28	2	18	.283	.355	.495	850	800	4	3	(4)	0	30	826	33.3
OF	1972	C.Cedeno	Hou	NL	559	56	5	620	179	39	8	22	.320	.387	.537	924	956	55	21	20	10	40	1,026	83.4
OF	1969	J.Wynn	Hou	NL	495	148	3	646	133	17	1	33	.269	.440	.507	947	969	23	7	13	10	30	1,022	81.3
OF	2000	R.Hidalgo	Hou	NL	558	56	21	635	175	42	3	44	.314	.397	.636	1,033	943	13	6	1	10	30	984	68.6
Starters		Averages			510	74	9	592	153	31	5	27	.300	.398	.535	934	908	25	9	11	6	30	955	73.5
C	2000	M.Meluskey	Hou	NL	337	55	4	396	101	21	0	14	.300	.404	.487	891	813	1	0	2	0	(20)	795	22.2
1B	1989	G.Davis	Hou	NL	581	69	7	657	156	26	1	34	.269	.353	.492	845	878	4	2	0	(10)	0	868	30.5
2B	1971	J.Morgan	Hou	NL	583	88	1	672	149	27	11	13	.256	.354	.407	761	784	40	8	34	10	20	848	52.0
SS	1970	D.Menke	Hou	NL	562	82	5	649	171	26	6	13	.304	.398	.441	839	818	6	5	(6)	10	(30)	792	40.2
3B	1972	D.Rader	Hou	NL	553	57	5	615	131	24	7	22	.237	.314	.425	739	765	5	5	(8)	10	50	817	31.1
OF	1998	M.Alou	Hou	NL	584	84	5	673	182	34	5	38	.312	.403	.582	985	937	11	3	7	10	(10)	944	59.9
OF	1984	J.Cruz	Hou	NL	600	73	0	673	187	28	13	12	.312	.386	.462	848	866	22	8	8	10	20	905	47.2
OF	1999	C.Everett	Hou	NL	464	50	11	525	151	33	3	25	.325	.404	.571	975	892	27	7	23	10	0	925	42.0
Reserves		Averages			533	70	5	608	154	27	6	21	.288	.375	.481	857	845	15	5	8	6	4	863	40.6
Totals		Weighted Ave.			517	73	8	597	153	29	5	25	.296	.390	.517	907	887	21	7	10	6	21	924	62.5

Pitchers Volume of Success

Pos	Year	Name	T	L	G	GS	IP	W	L	SV	SO	BB	ERA	RA/9	Wtd RA/9	R V Runs /162
SP	1986	M.Scott	Hou	NL	37	37	275	18	10	0	306	72	2.22	2.39	2.61	59.4
SP	1981	N.Ryan	Hou	NL	21	21	149	11	5	0	140	68	1.69	2.05	2.40	54.0
SP	1982	J.Niekro	Hou	NL	35	35	270	17	12	0	130	64	2.47	2.63	2.94	48.6
SP	1981	B.Knepper	Hou	NL	22	22	157	9	5	0	75	38	2.18	2.36	2.76	47.3
SP	1969	L.Dierker	Hou	NL	39	37	305	20	13	0	232	72	2.33	2.86	3.19	46.2
Starters		Averages			31	30	231	15	9	0	177	63	2.23	2.52	2.83	51.1
RP	1995	D.Veres	Hou	NL	72	0	103	5	1	1	94	30	2.26	2.53	2.48	26.7
RP	1999	B.Wagner	Hou	NL	66	0	75	4	1	39	124	23	1.57	1.69	1.53	25.1
RP	1980	D.Smith	Hou	NL	57	0	103	7	5	10	85	32	1.93	2.10	2.37	25.0
RP	1990	L.Andersen	Hou	NL	65	0	96	5	2	7	93	27	1.79	2.07	2.23	24.8
Relievers		Averages			65	0	94	5	2	14	99	28	1.91	2.13	2.20	25.4
Totals		Averages			96	30	325	20	11	14	276	91	2.14	2.41	2.65	76.5

National League Expansion Teams (1962–2000)

Houston Astros (NL Expansion) **Hitters Rate of Success**

Pos	Year	Name	T	L	AB	BB	HBP	TAB	H	2B	3B	HR	BA	OB	SA	PRO	Wtd PRO	SB	CS	SBF	SPF	FF	R TF	V HC
C	2000	M.Meluskey	Hou	NL	337	55	4	396	101	21	0	14	.300	.404	.487	891	813	1	0	2	0	(20)	795	22.2
1B	1994	J.Bagwell	Hou	NL	400	65	4	469	147	32	2	39	.368	.461	.750	1,211	1,139	15	4	14	10	40	1,203	137.0
2B	1997	C.Biggio	Hou	NL	619	84	34	737	191	37	8	22	.309	.419	.501	920	873	47	10	35	10	50	968	99.2
SS	1983	D.Thon	Hou	NL	619	54	2	675	177	28	9	20	.286	.345	.457	802	809	34	16	3	10	30	852	61.1
3B	1986	D.Walling	Hou	NL	382	36	0	418	119	23	1	13	.312	.371	.479	850	852	1	1	(2)	0	0	850	26.6
OF	1972	C.Cedeno	Hou	NL	559	56	5	620	179	39	8	22	.320	.387	.537	924	956	55	21	20	10	40	1,026	83.4
OF	1969	J.Wynn	Hou	NL	495	148	3	646	133	17	1	33	.269	.440	.507	947	969	23	7	13	10	30	1,022	81.3
OF	2000	R.Hidalgo	Hou	NL	558	56	21	635	175	42	3	44	.314	.397	.636	1,033	943	13	6	1	10	30	984	68.6
Starters		Averages			496	69	9	575	153	30	4	26	.308	.402	.541	943	918	24	8	11	8	25	961	72.4
C	1977	J.Ferguson	Hou	NL	421	85	0	506	108	21	3	16	.257	.381	.435	816	792	6	2	4	(10)	(10)	776	23.8
1B	1990	G.Davis	Hou	NL	327	46	8	381	82	15	4	22	.251	.357	.523	880	879	8	3	5	(10)	0	873	18.8
2B	1967	J.Morgan	Hou	NL	494	81	2	577	136	27	11	6	.275	.380	.411	790	827	29	5	31	10	(10)	858	47.4
SS	1970	D.Menke	Hou	NL	562	82	5	649	171	26	6	13	.304	.398	.441	839	818	6	5	(6)	10	(30)	792	40.2
3B	1992	K.Caminiti	Hou	NL	506	44	1	551	149	31	2	13	.294	.352	.441	793	816	10	4	3	0	10	829	29.7
OF	2000	M.Alou	Hou	NL	454	52	2	508	161	28	2	30	.355	.423	.623	1,047	955	3	3	(6)	10	0	959	48.9
OF	1999	C.Everett	Hou	NL	464	50	11	525	151	33	3	25	.325	.404	.571	975	892	27	7	23	10	0	925	42.0
OF	1984	J.Cruz	Hou	NL	600	73	0	673	187	28	13	12	.312	.386	.462	848	866	22	8	8	10	20	905	47.2
Reserves		Averages			479	64	4	546	143	26	6	17	.299	.386	.484	870	853	14	5	8	4	(3)	863	37.2
Totals		Weighted Ave.			490	68	7	565	150	29	5	23	.305	.397	.522	919	896	20	7	10	6	16	928	60.7

Pitchers Rate of Success

Pos	Year	Name	T	L	G	GS	IP	W	L	SV	SO	BB	ERA	RA/9	Wtd RA/9	R Runs /162
SP	1981	N.Ryan	Hou	NL	21	21	149	11	5	0	140	68	1.69	2.05	2.40	54.0
SP	1990	D.Darwin	Hou	NL	48	17	163	11	4	2	109	31	2.21	2.32	2.50	37.3
SP	1986	M.Scott	Hou	NL	37	37	275	18	10	0	306	72	2.22	2.39	2.61	59.4
SP	1981	B.Knepper	Hou	NL	22	22	157	9	5	0	75	38	2.18	2.36	2.76	47.3
SP	1999	M.Hampton	Hou	NL	34	34	239	22	4	0	177	101	2.90	3.24	2.93	43.3
Starters		Averages			32	26	197	14	6	0	161	62	2.30	2.53	2.66	48.3
RP	1999	B.Wagner	Hou	NL	66	0	75	4	1	39	124	23	1.57	1.69	1.53	25.1
RP	1997	T.Martin	Hou	NL	55	0	56	5	3	2	36	23	2.09	2.09	2.06	15.6
RP	1979	J.Sambito	Hou	NL	63	0	91	8	7	22	83	23	1.77	1.97	2.12	24.6
RP	1990	L.Andersen	Hou	NL	65	0	96	5	2	7	93	27	1.79	2.07	2.23	24.8
Relievers		Averages			62	0	80	6	3	18	84	24	1.79	1.96	2.00	22.5
Totals		Averages			95	26	276	20	9	18	245	86	2.15	2.36	2.47	70.8

New York Mets (NL Expansion) — **Hitters Volume of Success**

Pos	Year	Name	T	L	AB	BB	HBP	TAB	H	2B	3B	HR	BA	OB	SA	PRO	Wtd PRO	SB	CS	SBF	SPF	FF	R TF	V HC
C	1998	M.Piazza	NY	NL	561	58	2	621	184	38	1	32	.328	.393	.570	963	917	1	0	2	(10)	(10)	898	65.3
1B	1998	J.Olerud	NY	NL	557	96	4	657	197	36	4	22	.354	.452	.551	1,003	955	2	2	(3)	(10)	20	962	60.0
2B	2000	E.Alfonso	NY	NL	544	95	5	644	176	40	2	25	.324	.429	.542	971	886	3	2	(1)	0	30	914	70.3
SS	1971	B.Harrelson	NY	NL	547	53	2	602	138	16	6	0	.252	.321	.303	624	643	28	7	22	10	40	715	15.2
3B	1989	H.Johnson	NY	NL	571	77	1	649	164	41	3	36	.287	.373	.559	932	967	41	8	36	10	(60)	953	73.4
OF	1987	D.Strawberry	NY	NL	532	97	7	636	151	32	5	39	.284	.401	.583	984	946	36	12	18	10	(10)	964	62.5
OF	1996	B.Gilkey	NY	NL	571	73	4	648	181	44	3	30	.317	.398	.562	960	915	17	9	(1)	10	30	953	60.5
OF	1969	C.Jones	NY	NL	483	64	7	554	164	25	4	12	.340	.424	.482	907	927	16	8	0	10	20	957	52.8
Starters		Averages			546	77	4	626	169	34	4	25	.310	.399	.520	919	896	18	6	9	4	8	916	57.5
C	1985	G.Carter	NY	NL	555	69	6	630	156	17	1	32	.281	.367	.488	855	868	1	1	(2)	(10)	30	887	62.9
1B	1984	K.Hernandez	NY	NL	550	97	1	648	171	31	0	15	.311	.415	.449	864	883	2	3	(6)	0	50	927	48.5
2B	1994	J.Kent	NY	NL	415	23	10	448	121	24	5	14	.292	.344	.475	818	770	1	4	(15)	10	10	776	27.3
SS	1995	J.Vizcaino	NY	NL	509	35	1	545	146	21	5	3	.287	.334	.365	699	666	8	3	3	0	30	700	11.0
3B	1999	R.Ventura	NY	NL	588	74	3	665	177	38	0	32	.301	.382	.529	911	833	1	1	(1)	(10)	90	912	62.0
OF	1988	K.McReynolds	NY	NL	552	38	4	594	159	30	2	27	.288	.338	.496	835	873	21	0	33	10	20	936	50.7
OF	1996	L.Johnson	NY	NL	682	33	1	716	227	31	21	9	.333	.365	.479	844	804	50	12	34	10	30	878	41.3
OF	1979	L.Mazzilli	NY	NL	597	93	0	690	181	34	4	15	.303	.397	.449	846	839	34	12	14	10	10	872	37.8
Reserves		Averages			556	58	3	617	167	28	5	18	.301	.370	.468	838	821	15	5	8	3	34	865	42.7
Totals		Weighted Ave.			549	70	4	623	169	32	4	22	.307	.389	.503	892	871	17	6	9	3	16	899	52.6

Pitchers Volume of Success

Pos	Year	Name	T	L	G	GS	IP	W	L	SV	SO	BB	ERA	RA/9	Wtd RA/9	R V Runs /162
SP	1985	D.Gooden	NY	NL	35	35	277	24	4	0	268	69	1.53	1.66	1.86	83.0
SP	1971	T.Seaver	NY	NL	36	35	286	20	10	0	289	61	1.76	1.92	2.24	73.7
SP	1969	J.Koosman	NY	NL	32	32	241	17	9	0	180	68	2.28	2.46	2.75	48.5
SP	1994	B.Saberhagen	NY	NL	24	24	177	14	4	0	143	13	2.74	2.94	2.88	46.6
SP	1974	J.Matlack	NY	NL	34	34	265	13	15	0	195	76	2.41	2.78	3.05	44.3
Starters		Averages			32	32	249	18	8	0	215	57	2.09	2.29	2.52	59.2
RP	1971	T.McGraw	NY	NL	51	1	111	11	4	8	109	41	1.70	1.78	2.07	30.6
RP	1983	J.Orosco	NY	NL	62	0	110	13	7	17	84	38	1.47	2.21	2.44	25.8
RP	1999	A.Benitez	NY	NL	77	0	78	4	3	22	128	41	1.85	1.96	1.77	24.1
RP	1975	B.Apodaca	NY	NL	46	0	85	3	4	13	45	28	1.49	1.91	2.11	23.1
Relievers		Averages			59	0	96	8	5	15	92	37	1.62	1.97	2.12	25.9
Totals		Averages			91	32	345	25	13	15	307	94	1.96	2.20	2.41	85.1

National League Expansion Teams (1962–2000)

New York Mets (NL Expansion) — **Hitters Rate of Success**

Pos	Year	Name	T	L	AB	BB	HBP	TAB	H	2B	3B	HR	BA	OB	SA	PRO	Wtd PRO	SB	CS	SBF	SPF	FF	R TF	V HC
C	2000	M.Piazza	NY	NL	482	58	3	543	156	26	0	38	.324	.400	.614	1,014	925	4	2	0	(10)	(10)	905	58.9
1B	1998	J.Olerud	NY	NL	557	96	4	657	197	36	4	22	.354	.452	.551	1,003	955	2	2	(3)	(10)	20	962	60.0
2B	2000	E.Alfonso	NY	NL	544	95	5	644	176	40	2	25	.324	.429	.542	971	886	3	2	(1)	0	30	914	70.3
SS	1971	B.Harrelson	NY	NL	547	53	2	602	138	16	6	0	.252	.321	.303	624	643	28	7	22	10	40	715	15.2
3B	1989	H.Johnson	NY	NL	571	77	1	649	164	41	3	36	.287	.373	.559	932	967	41	8	36	10	(60)	953	73.4
OF	1985	D.Strawberry	NY	NL	393	73	1	467	109	15	4	29	.277	.392	.557	949	964	26	11	8	10	0	982	50.0
OF	1969	C.Jones	NY	NL	483	64	7	554	164	25	4	12	.340	.424	.482	907	927	16	8	0	10	20	957	52.8
OF	1996	B.Gilkey	NY	NL	571	73	4	648	181	44	3	30	.317	.398	.562	960	915	17	9	(1)	10	30	953	60.5
Starters		Averages			519	74	3	596	161	30	3	24	.310	.399	.520	919	897	17	6	8	4	9	917	55.1
C	1985	G.Carter	NY	NL	555	69	6	630	156	17	1	32	.281	.367	.488	855	868	1	1	(2)	(10)	30	887	62.9
1B	1984	K.Hernandez	NY	NL	550	97	1	648	171	31	0	15	.311	.415	.449	864	883	2	3	(6)	0	50	927	48.5
2B	1964	R.Hunt	NY	NL	475	29	11	515	144	19	6	6	.303	.357	.406	764	785	6	2	4	0	(10)	778	22.8
SS	1995	J.Vizcaino	NY	NL	509	35	1	545	146	21	5	3	.287	.334	.365	699	666	8	3	3	0	30	700	11.0
3B	1999	R.Ventura	NY	NL	588	74	3	665	177	38	0	32	.301	.382	.529	911	833	1	1	(1)	(10)	90	912	62.0
OF	1988	K.McReynolds	NY	NL	552	38	4	594	159	30	2	27	.288	.338	.496	835	873	21	0	33	10	20	936	50.7
OF	1986	L.Dykstra	NY	NL	431	58	0	489	127	27	7	8	.295	.378	.445	824	826	31	7	33	10	10	879	28.3
OF	1996	L.Johnson	NY	NL	682	33	1	716	227	31	21	9	.333	.365	.479	844	804	50	12	34	10	30	878	41.3
Reserves		Averages			543	54	3	600	163	27	5	17	.301	.368	.461	829	820	15	4	12	1	31	865	40.9
Totals		Weighted Ave.			527	67	3	597	162	29	4	22	.307	.389	.500	888	871	16	5	9	3	16	899	50.4

Pitchers Rate of Success

Pos	Year	Name	T	L	G	GS	IP	W	L	SV	SO	BB	ERA	RA/9	Wtd RA/9	V Runs /162
SP	1985	D.Gooden	NY	NL	35	35	277	24	4	0	268	69	1.53	1.66	1.86	83.0
SP	1971	T.Seaver	NY	NL	36	35	286	20	10	0	289	61	1.76	1.92	2.24	73.7
SP	1998	A.Leiter	NY	NL	28	28	193	17	6	0	174	71	2.47	2.56	2.52	43.7
SP	1969	J.Koosman	NY	NL	32	32	241	17	9	0	180	68	2.28	2.46	2.75	48.5
SP	1994	B.Saberhagen	NY	NL	24	24	177	14	4	0	143	13	2.74	2.94	2.88	46.6
Starters		Averages			31	31	235	18	7	0	211	56	2.08	2.23	2.40	59.1
RP	1999	A.Benitez	NY	NL	77	0	78	4	3	22	128	41	1.85	1.96	1.77	24.1
RP	1971	T.McGraw	NY	NL	51	1	111	11	4	8	109	41	1.70	1.78	2.07	30.6
RP	1975	B.Apodaca	NY	NL	46	0	85	3	4	13	45	28	1.49	1.91	2.11	23.1
RP	1988	R.Myers	NY	NL	55	0	68	7	3	26	69	17	1.72	1.99	2.34	16.7
Relievers		Averages			57	0	86	6	4	17	88	32	1.69	1.90	2.07	23.6
Totals		Averages			88	31	320	25	10	17	299	88	1.97	2.14	2.31	82.7

226 Baseball Players' Best Seasons

Montreal Expos (NL Expansion) **Hitters Volume of Success**

Pos	Year	Name	T	L	AB	BB	HBP	TAB	H	2B	3B	HR	BA	OB	SA	PRO	Wtd PRO	SB	CS	SBF	SPF	FF	R TF	V HC
C	1982	G.Carter	Mon	NL	557	78	6	641	163	32	1	29	.293	.385	.510	895	909	2	5	(12)	0	70	967	88.6
1B	1988	A.Galarraga	Mon	NL	609	39	10	658	184	42	8	29	.302	.354	.540	894	935	13	4	7	0	20	962	60.3
2B	2000	J.Vidro	Mon	NL	606	49	2	657	200	51	2	24	.330	.382	.540	922	841	5	4	(4)	0	(10)	827	44.2
SS	1994	W.Cordero	Mon	NL	415	41	6	462	122	30	3	15	.294	.366	.489	855	805	16	3	20	10	(40)	795	41.5
3B	1979	L.Parrish	Mon	NL	544	41	2	587	167	39	2	30	.307	.358	.551	909	901	5	1	5	0	(10)	896	50.4
OF	1981	A.Dawson	Mon	NL	394	35	7	436	119	21	3	24	.302	.369	.553	923	949	26	4	39	10	80	1,078	100.9
OF	1985	T.Raines	Mon	NL	575	81	3	659	184	30	13	11	.320	.407	.475	881	895	70	9	75	10	40	1,020	82.4
OF	1969	R.Staub	Mon	NL	549	110	9	668	166	26	5	29	.302	.427	.526	953	975	3	4	(7)	(10)	(10)	948	60.6
Starters		Averages			531	59	6	596	163	34	5	24	.307	.383	.523	906	903	18	4	15	3	18	939	66.1
C	1990	M.Fitzgerald	Mon	NL	313	60	2	375	76	18	1	9	.243	.368	.393	761	760	8	1	15	0	0	775	17.4
1B	1982	A.Oliver	Mon	NL	617	61	4	682	204	43	2	22	.331	.394	.514	908	922	5	2	1	0	(20)	904	43.5
2B	1992	D.Deshields	Mon	NL	530	54	3	587	155	19	8	7	.292	.361	.398	759	781	46	15	26	10	(20)	797	31.3
SS	1989	S.Owen	Mon	NL	437	76	3	516	102	17	4	6	.233	.351	.332	683	709	3	2	(2)	0	30	737	18.4
3B	1970	B.Bailey	Mon	NL	352	72	1	425	101	19	3	28	.287	.409	.597	1,006	981	5	3	(2)	0	(30)	949	47.1
OF	1994	L.Walker	Mon	NL	395	47	4	446	127	44	2	19	.322	.399	.587	986	928	15	5	11	10	10	959	60.6
OF	2000	V.Guerrero	Mon	NL	571	58	8	637	197	28	11	44	.345	.413	.664	1,077	982	9	10	(16)	10	(20)	956	60.3
OF	1994	M.Alou	Mon	NL	422	42	2	466	143	31	5	22	.339	.401	.592	994	935	7	6	(10)	10	0	935	55.8
Reserves		Averages			455	59	3	517	138	27	5	20	.304	.388	.513	901	878	12	6	3	5	(6)	880	41.8
Totals		Weighted Ave.			506	59	5	570	155	32	5	22	.306	.384	.520	904	895	16	5	11	3	10	919	58.0

Pitchers Volume of Success

Pos	Year	Name	T	L	G	GS	IP	W	L	SV	SO	BB	ERA	RA/9	Wtd RA/9	R Runs /162	V
SP	1997	P.Martinez	Mon	NL	31	31	241	17	8	0	305	67	1.90	2.42	2.38	58.2	
SP	1982	S.Rogers	Mon	NL	35	35	277	19	8	0	179	65	2.40	2.73	3.05	46.4	
SP	1991	D.Martinez	Mon	NL	31	31	222	14	11	0	123	62	2.39	2.84	3.14	34.9	
SP	1990	O.Boyd	Mon	NL	31	31	191	10	6	0	113	52	2.93	3.02	3.25	27.7	
SP	1994	K.Hill	Mon	NL	23	23	155	16	5	0	85	44	3.32	3.55	3.48	26.3	
Starters		Averages			30	30	217	15	8	0	161	58	2.51	2.85	3.02	38.7	
RP	1992	M.Rojas	Mon	NL	68	0	101	7	1	10	70	34	1.43	1.52	1.79	31.1	
RP	1972	M.Marshall	Mon	NL	65	0	116	14	8	18	95	47	1.78	2.02	2.37	29.7	
RP	1987	T.Burke	Mon	NL	55	0	91	7	0	18	58	17	1.19	1.78	1.79	28.0	
RP	1993	J.Wetteland	Mon	NL	70	0	85	9	3	43	113	28	1.37	1.79	1.80	26.0	
Relievers		Averages			65	0	98	9	3	22	84	32	1.46	1.79	1.96	28.7	
Totals		Averages			95	30	315	24	11	22	245	90	2.19	2.52	2.69	67.4	

National League Expansion Teams (1962–2000)

Montreal Expos (NL Expansion) — Hitters Rate of Success

Pos	Year	Name	T	L	AB	BB	HBP	TAB	H	2B	3B	HR	BA	OB	SA	PRO	Wtd PRO	SB	CS	SBF	SPF	FF	R TF	V HC
C	1982	G.Carter	Mon	NL	557	78	6	641	163	32	1	29	.293	.385	.510	895	909	2	5	(12)	0	70	967	88.6
1B	1988	A.Galarraga	Mon	NL	609	39	10	658	184	42	8	29	.302	.354	.540	894	935	13	4	7	0	20	962	60.3
2B	2000	J.Vidro	Mon	NL	606	49	2	657	200	51	2	24	.330	.382	.540	922	841	5	4	(4)	0	(10)	827	44.2
SS	1994	W.Cordero	Mon	NL	415	41	6	462	122	30	3	15	.294	.366	.489	855	805	16	3	20	10	(40)	795	41.5
3B	1970	B.Bailey	Mon	NL	352	72	1	425	101	19	3	28	.287	.409	.597	1,006	981	5	3	(2)	0	(30)	949	47.1
OF	1981	A.Dawson	Mon	NL	394	35	7	436	119	21	3	24	.302	.369	.553	923	949	26	4	39	10	80	1,078	100.9
OF	1987	T.Raines	Mon	NL	530	90	4	624	175	34	8	18	.330	.431	.526	958	921	50	5	61	10	40	1,031	81.5
OF	1994	L.Walker	Mon	NL	395	47	4	446	127	44	2	19	.322	.399	.587	986	928	15	5	11	10	10	959	60.6
Starters		Averages			482	56	5	544	149	34	4	23	.309	.387	.540	926	906	17	4	15	5	18	944	65.6
C	1990	M.Fitzgerald	Mon	NL	313	60	2	375	76	18	1	9	.243	.368	.393	761	760	8	1	15	0	0	775	17.4
1B	1982	A.Oliver	Mon	NL	617	61	4	682	204	43	2	22	.331	.394	.514	908	922	5	2	1	0	(20)	904	43.5
2B	1992	D.Deshields	Mon	NL	530	54	3	587	155	19	8	7	.292	.361	.398	759	781	46	15	26	10	(20)	797	31.3
SS	1992	S.Owen	Mon	NL	386	50	0	436	104	16	3	7	.269	.353	.381	734	755	9	4	2	0	(10)	748	17.8
3B	1979	L.Parrish	Mon	NL	544	41	2	587	167	39	2	30	.307	.358	.551	909	901	5	1	5	0	(10)	896	50.4
OF	2000	V.Guerrero	Mon	NL	571	58	8	637	197	28	11	44	.345	.413	.664	1,077	982	9	10	(16)	10	(20)	956	60.3
OF	1969	R.Staub	Mon	NL	549	110	9	668	166	26	5	29	.302	.427	.526	953	975	3	4	(7)	(10)	(10)	948	60.6
OF	1994	M.Alou	Mon	NL	422	42	2	466	143	31	5	22	.339	.401	.592	994	935	7	6	(10)	10	0	935	55.8
Reserves		Averages			492	60	4	555	152	28	5	21	.308	.387	.513	900	889	12	5	2	3	(11)	882	42.1
Totals		Weighted Ave.			485	57	5	547	150	32	4	23	.309	.387	.531	917	900	15	5	11	4	8	923	57.8

Pitchers Rate of Success

Pos	Year	Name	T	L	G	GS	IP	W	L	SV	SO	BB	ERA	RA/9	Wtd RA/9	V Runs /162
SP	1997	P.Martinez	Mon	NL	31	31	241	17	8	0	305	67	1.90	2.42	2.38	58.2
SP	1978	S.Rogers	Mon	NL	30	29	219	13	10	1	126	64	2.47	2.63	2.98	38.3
SP	1991	D.Martinez	Mon	NL	31	31	222	14	11	0	123	62	2.39	2.84	3.14	34.9
SP	1990	O.Boyd	Mon	NL	31	31	191	10	6	0	113	52	2.93	3.02	3.25	27.7
SP	1988	P.Perez	Mon	NL	27	27	188	12	8	0	131	44	2.44	2.82	3.32	25.8
Starters		Averages			30	30	212	13	9	0	160	58	2.40	2.73	2.99	37.0
RP	1998	U.Urbina	Mon	NL	64	0	69	6	3	34	94	33	1.30	1.43	1.41	24.1
RP	1992	M.Rojas	Mon	NL	68	0	101	7	1	10	70	34	1.43	1.52	1.79	31.1
RP	1987	T.Burke	Mon	NL	55	0	91	7	0	18	58	17	1.19	1.78	1.79	28.0
RP	1993	J.Wetteland	Mon	NL	70	0	85	9	3	43	113	28	1.37	1.79	1.80	26.0
Relievers		Averages			64	0	87	7	2	26	84	28	1.33	1.64	1.72	27.3
Totals		Averages			94	30	299	20	10	26	243	86	2.09	2.41	2.62	64.3

San Diego Padres (NL Expansion)   **Hitters Volume of Success**

Pos	Year	Name	T	L	AB	BB	HBP	TAB	H	2B	3B	HR	BA	OB	SA	PRO	Wtd PRO	SB	CS	SBF	SPF	FF	R TF	V HC
C	1982	T.Kennedy	SD	NL	562	26	5	593	166	42	1	21	.295	.332	.486	818	831	1	0	2	(10)	(10)	812	38.1
1B	1992	F.McGriff	SD	NL	531	96	1	628	152	30	4	35	.286	.396	.556	952	980	8	6	(6)	0	0	974	60.9
2B	1988	R.Alomar	SD	NL	545	47	3	595	145	24	6	9	.266	.328	.382	709	742	24	6	19	10	50	821	38.4
SS	1980	O.Smith	SD	NL	609	71	5	685	140	18	5	0	.230	.315	.276	591	599	57	15	37	10	100	746	27.4
3B	1996	K.Caminiti	SD	NL	546	78	4	628	178	37	2	40	.326	.414	.621	1,035	986	11	5	2	0	50	1,037	96.1
OF	1987	T.Gwynn	SD	NL	589	82	3	674	218	36	13	7	.370	.450	.511	961	924	56	12	45	10	40	1,019	83.9
OF	1979	D.Winfield	SD	NL	597	85	2	684	184	27	10	34	.308	.396	.558	954	946	15	9	(4)	10	50	1,002	79.6
OF	1996	S.Finley	SD	NL	655	56	4	715	195	45	9	30	.298	.357	.531	888	846	22	8	8	10	40	904	49.9
Starters		Averages			579	68	3	650	172	32	6	22	.297	.374	.489	863	856	24	8	13	5	40	914	59.3
C	1979	G.Tenace	SD	NL	463	105	7	575	122	16	4	20	.263	.407	.445	852	845	2	6	(16)	(10)	(10)	808	35.8
1B	1990	J.Clark	SD	NL	334	104	2	440	89	12	1	25	.266	.443	.533	976	975	4	3	(4)	(10)	(10)	950	37.8
2B	1998	Q.Veras	SD	NL	517	84	6	607	138	24	2	6	.267	.376	.356	732	696	24	9	9	10	20	735	14.5
SS	1991	T.Fernandez	SD	NL	558	55	0	613	152	27	5	4	.272	.338	.360	698	712	23	9	8	10	10	740	22.7
3B	1992	G.Sheffield	SD	NL	557	48	6	611	184	34	3	33	.330	.390	.580	969	998	5	6	(11)	10	20	1,017	87.5
OF	1998	G.Vaughn	SD	NL	573	79	5	657	156	28	4	50	.272	.365	.597	962	916	11	4	4	0	(10)	910	47.7
OF	1982	S.Lezcano	SD	NL	470	78	2	550	136	26	6	16	.289	.393	.472	865	879	2	1	0	0	50	929	44.9
OF	1970	C.Gaston	SD	NL	584	41	2	627	186	26	9	29	.318	.365	.543	908	885	4	1	3	10	0	898	42.1
Reserves		Averages			507	74	4	585	145	24	4	23	.287	.382	.486	868	860	9	5	(1)	3	9	870	41.6
Totals		Weighted Ave.			555	70	4	629	163	30	6	22	.294	.376	.488	865	857	19	7	8	4	30	899	53.4

Pitchers Volume of Success

Pos	Year	Name	T	L	G	GS	IP	W	L	SV	SO	BB	ERA	RA/9	Wtd RA/9	R V Runs /162
SP	1998	K.Brown	SD	NL	36	35	257	18	7	0	257	49	2.38	2.70	2.66	54.2
SP	1971	D.Roberts	SD	NL	37	34	270	14	17	0	135	61	2.10	2.64	3.08	44.4
SP	1975	R.Jones	SD	NL	37	36	285	20	12	0	103	56	2.24	2.97	3.28	40.5
SP	1990	E.Whitson	SD	NL	32	32	229	14	9	0	127	47	2.60	2.87	3.09	37.3
SP	1991	A.Benes	SD	NL	33	33	223	15	11	0	167	59	3.03	3.07	3.40	28.8
Starters		Averages			35	34	253	16	11	0	158	54	2.44	2.84	3.10	41.0
RP	1998	T.Hoffman	SD	NL	66	0	73	4	2	53	86	21	1.48	1.48	1.46	25.1
RP	1982	L.DeLeon	SD	NL	61	0	102	9	5	15	60	16	2.03	2.21	2.47	23.7
RP	1981	G.Lucas	SD	NL	57	0	90	7	7	13	53	36	2.00	2.60	3.05	22.9
RP	1989	M.Davis	SD	NL	70	0	93	4	3	44	92	31	1.85	2.04	2.36	22.7
Relievers		Averages			64	0	90	6	4	31	73	26	1.86	2.12	2.38	23.6
Totals		Averages			99	34	342	22	15	31	231	80	2.29	2.65	2.91	64.6

National League Expansion Teams (1962–2000)

San Diego Padres (NL Expansion) **Hitters Rate of Success**

Pos	Year	Name	T	L	AB	BB	HBP	TAB	H	2B	3B	HR	BA	OB	SA	PRO	Wtd PRO	SB	CS	SBF	SPF	FF	R TF	V HC
C	1982	T.Kennedy	SD	NL	562	26	5	593	166	42	1	21	.295	.332	.486	818	831	1	0	2	(10)	(10)	812	38.1
1B	1992	F.McGriff	SD	NL	531	96	1	628	152	30	4	35	.286	.396	.556	952	980	8	6	(6)	0	0	974	60.9
2B	1988	R.Alomar	SD	NL	545	47	3	595	145	24	6	9	.266	.328	.382	709	742	24	6	19	10	50	821	38.4
SS	1980	O.Smith	SD	NL	609	71	5	685	140	18	5	0	.230	.315	.276	591	599	57	15	37	10	100	746	27.4
3B	1996	K.Caminiti	SD	NL	546	78	4	628	178	37	2	40	.326	.414	.621	1,035	986	11	5	2	0	50	1,037	96.1
OF	1987	T.Gwynn	SD	NL	589	82	3	674	218	36	13	7	.370	.450	.511	961	924	56	12	45	10	40	1,019	83.9
OF	1979	D.Winfield	SD	NL	597	85	2	684	184	27	10	34	.308	.396	.558	954	946	15	9	(4)	10	50	1,002	79.6
OF	1982	S.Lezcano	SD	NL	470	78	2	550	136	26	6	16	.289	.393	.472	865	879	2	1	0	0	50	929	44.9
Starters		Averages			556	70	3	630	165	30	6	20	.296	.379	.481	859	860	22	7	12	4	41	917	58.7
C	1979	G.Tenace	SD	NL	463	105	7	575	122	16	4	20	.263	.407	.445	852	845	2	6	(16)	(10)	(10)	808	35.8
1B	1990	J.Clark	SD	NL	334	104	2	440	89	12	1	25	.266	.443	.533	976	975	4	3	(4)	(10)	(10)	950	37.8
2B	1998	Q.Veras	SD	NL	517	84	6	607	138	24	2	6	.267	.376	.356	732	696	24	9	9	10	20	735	14.5
SS	1991	T.Fernandez	SD	NL	558	55	0	613	152	27	5	4	.272	.338	.360	698	712	23	9	8	10	10	740	22.7
3B	1992	G.Sheffield	SD	NL	557	48	6	611	184	34	3	33	.330	.390	.580	969	998	5	6	(11)	10	20	1,017	87.5
OF	1998	G.Vaughn	SD	NL	573	79	5	657	156	28	4	50	.272	.365	.597	962	916	11	4	4	0	(10)	910	47.7
OF	1996	S.Finley	SD	NL	655	56	4	715	195	45	9	30	.298	.357	.531	888	846	22	8	8	10	40	904	49.9
OF	1970	C.Gaston	SD	NL	584	41	2	627	186	26	9	29	.318	.365	.543	908	885	4	1	3	10	0	898	42.1
Reserves		Averages			530	72	4	606	153	27	5	25	.288	.377	.495	872	855	12	6	0	4	8	867	42.2
Totals		Weighted Ave.			547	71	3	622	161	29	5	22	.294	.378	.485	863	858	18	6	8	4	30	900	53.2

Pitchers Rate of Success

Pos	Year	Name	T	L	G	GS	IP	W	L	SV	SO	BB	ERA	RA/9	Wtd RA/9	R Runs /162
SP	1998	K.Brown	SD	NL	36	35	257	18	7	0	257	49	2.38	2.70	2.66	54.2
SP	1971	D.Roberts	SD	NL	37	34	270	14	17	0	135	61	2.10	2.64	3.08	44.4
SP	1990	E.Whitson	SD	NL	32	32	229	14	9	0	127	47	2.60	2.87	3.09	37.3
SP	1975	R.Jones	SD	NL	37	36	285	20	12	0	103	56	2.24	2.97	3.28	40.5
SP	1991	A.Benes	SD	NL	33	33	223	15	11	0	167	59	3.03	3.07	3.40	28.8
Starters		Averages			35	34	253	16	11	0	158	54	2.44	2.84	3.10	41.0
RP	1998	T.Hoffman	SD	NL	66	0	73	4	2	53	86	21	1.48	1.48	1.46	25.1
RP	1989	M.Davis	SD	NL	70	0	93	4	3	44	92	31	1.85	2.04	2.36	22.7
RP	1982	L.DeLeon	SD	NL	61	0	102	9	5	15	60	16	2.03	2.21	2.47	23.7
RP	1971	B.Miller	SD	NL	56	0	99	8	5	10	51	40	1.64	2.19	2.55	22.1
Relievers		Averages			63	0	92	6	4	31	72	27	1.77	2.02	2.26	23.4
Totals		Averages			98	34	345	22	15	31	230	81	2.26	2.62	2.88	64.4

Colorado Rockies (NL Expansion)   **Hitters Volume of Success**

Pos	Year	Name	T	L	AB	BB	HBP	TAB	H	2B	3B	HR	BA	OB	SA	PRO	Wtd PRO	SB	CS	SBF	SPF	FF	R TF	V HC
C	1996	J.Reed	Col	NL	341	43	2	386	97	20	1	8	.284	.368	.419	787	750	2	2	(5)	(10)	(40)	695	3.2
1B	2000	T.Helton	Col	NL	580	103	4	687	216	59	2	42	.372	.470	.698	1,168	1,066	5	3	(1)	0	20	1,085	103.0
2B	1996	E.Young	Col	NL	568	47	21	636	184	23	4	8	.324	.396	.421	817	778	53	19	22	10	60	871	56.1
SS	1997	W.Weiss	Col	NL	393	66	2	461	106	23	5	4	.270	.377	.384	762	723	5	2	2	0	60	785	27.0
3B	1998	V.Castilla	Col	NL	645	40	6	691	206	28	4	46	.319	.365	.589	954	908	5	9	(18)	0	30	920	67.1
OF	1997	L.Walker	Col	NL	568	78	14	660	208	46	4	49	.366	.455	.720	1,175	1,115	33	8	24	10	30	1,179	132.6
OF	1996	E.Burks	Col	NL	613	61	6	680	211	45	8	40	.344	.409	.639	1,048	999	32	6	28	0	0	1,026	87.2
OF	1995	D.Bichette	Col	NL	579	22	4	605	197	38	2	40	.340	.369	.620	989	942	13	9	(8)	10	(10)	934	57.3
Starters	Averages				536	58	7	601	178	35	4	30	.332	.404	.578	983	928	19	7	6	3	19	955	66.7
C	2000	B.Mayne	Col	NL	335	47	1	383	101	21	0	6	.301	.389	.418	807	736	1	3	(12)	(10)	(20)	694	3.0
1B	1997	A.Galarraga	Col	NL	600	54	17	671	191	31	3	41	.318	.390	.585	975	926	15	8	(1)	0	10	934	52.6
2B	1998	M.Lansing	Col	NL	584	39	5	628	161	39	2	12	.276	.326	.411	737	702	10	3	6	10	20	738	15.7
SS	2000	N.Perez	Col	NL	651	30	0	681	187	39	11	10	.287	.319	.427	746	680	3	6	(12)	10	60	738	24.6
3B	1993	C.Hayes	Col	NL	573	43	5	621	175	45	2	25	.305	.359	.522	881	853	11	6	(2)	0	20	871	45.9
OF	1994	M.Kingery	Col	NL	301	30	2	333	105	27	8	4	.349	.411	.532	943	888	5	7	(26)	10	(20)	852	21.2
OF	2000	J.Hammonds	Col	NL	454	44	5	503	152	24	2	20	.335	.400	.529	928	847	14	7	0	0	(20)	827	16.7
OF	1999	D.Hamilton	Col	NL	505	57	2	564	159	19	4	9	.315	.387	.422	808	739	6	8	(17)	10	30	763	1.4
Reserves	Averages				500	43	5	548	154	31	4	16	.308	.368	.480	848	793	8	6	(8)	4	10	799	22.6
Totals	Weighted Ave.				524	53	6	583	170	34	4	25	.324	.393	.547	940	883	15	7	1	3	16	903	52.0

Pitchers Volume of Success

Pos	Year	Name	T	L	G	GS	IP	W	L	SV	SO	BB	ERA	RA/9	Wtd RA/9	R Runs /162
SP	2000	B.Bohanon	Col	NL	34	26	177	12	10	0	98	79	4.68	5.14	4.62	(1.2)
SP	1995	K.Ritz	Col	NL	31	28	173	11	11	2	120	65	4.21	4.72	4.63	(1.5)
SP	1997	R.Bailey	Col	NL	29	29	191	9	10	0	84	70	4.29	4.85	4.77	(4.6)
SP	1993	A.Reynoso	Col	NL	30	30	189	12	11	0	117	63	4.00	4.81	4.85	(6.1)
SP	2000	P.Astacio	Col	NL	32	32	196	12	9	0	193	77	5.27	5.46	4.90	(7.5)
Starters	Averages				31	29	185	11	10	0	122	71	4.50	5.00	4.76	(4.2)
RP	2000	G.White	Col	NL	68	0	84	11	2	5	84	15	2.36	2.46	2.21	21.9
RP	1995	S.Reed	Col	NL	71	0	84	5	2	3	79	21	2.14	2.57	2.51	21.4
RP	2000	M.Myers	Col	NL	78	0	45	0	1	1	41	24	1.99	1.99	1.78	14.0
RP	1995	C.Leskanic	Col	NL	76	0	98	6	3	10	107	33	3.40	3.49	3.41	13.9
Relievers	Averages				73	0	78	6	2	5	78	23	2.57	2.75	2.61	17.8
Totals	Averages				104	29	263	17	12	5	200	94	3.93	4.34	4.12	13.6

National League Expansion Teams (1962–2000)

Colorado Rockies (NL Expansion) — Hitters Rate of Success

Pos	Year	Name	T	L	AB	BB	HBP	TAB	H	2B	3B	HR	BA	OB	SA	PRO	Wtd PRO	SB	CS	SBF	SPF	FF	R TF	V HC
C	1996	J.Reed	Col	NL	341	43	2	386	97	20	1	8	.284	.368	.419	787	750	2	2	(5)	(10)	(40)	695	3.2
1B	2000	T.Helton	Col	NL	580	103	4	687	216	59	2	42	.372	.470	.698	1,168	1,066	5	3	(1)	0	20	1,085	103.0
2B	1996	E.Young	Col	NL	568	47	21	636	184	23	4	8	.324	.396	.421	817	778	53	19	22	10	60	871	56.1
SS	1997	W.Weiss	Col	NL	393	66	2	461	106	23	5	4	.270	.377	.384	762	723	5	2	2	0	60	785	27.0
3B	1998	V.Castilla	Col	NL	645	40	6	691	206	28	4	46	.319	.365	.589	954	908	5	9	(18)	0	30	920	67.1
OF	1997	L.Walker	Col	NL	568	78	14	660	208	46	4	49	.366	.455	.720	1,175	1,115	33	8	24	10	30	1,179	132.6
OF	1996	E.Burks	Col	NL	613	61	6	680	211	45	8	40	.344	.409	.639	1,048	999	32	6	28	0	0	1,026	87.2
OF	1995	D.Bichette	Col	NL	579	22	4	605	197	38	2	40	.340	.369	.620	989	942	13	9	(8)	10	(10)	934	57.3
Starters		Averages			536	58	7	601	178	35	4	30	.332	.404	.578	983	928	19	7	6	3	19	955	66.7
C	2000	B.Mayne	Col	NL	335	47	1	383	101	21	0	6	.301	.389	.418	807	736	1	3	(12)	(10)	(20)	694	3.0
1B	1993	A.Galarraga	Col	NL	470	24	6	500	174	35	4	22	.370	.408	.602	1,010	978	2	4	(11)	0	20	987	51.6
2B	1995	J.Bates	Col	NL	322	42	2	366	86	17	4	8	.267	.355	.419	774	738	3	6	(23)	0	30	745	11.6
SS	2000	N.Perez	Col	NL	651	30	0	681	187	39	11	10	.287	.319	.427	746	680	3	6	(12)	10	60	738	24.6
3B	1993	C.Hayes	Col	NL	573	43	5	621	175	45	2	25	.305	.359	.522	881	853	11	6	(2)	0	20	871	45.9
OF	1994	M.Kingery	Col	NL	301	30	2	333	105	27	8	4	.349	.411	.532	943	888	5	7	(26)	10	(20)	852	21.2
OF	2000	J.Hammonds	Col	NL	454	44	5	503	152	24	2	20	.335	.400	.529	928	847	14	7	0	0	(20)	827	16.7
OF	1999	D.Hamilton	Col	NL	505	57	2	564	159	19	4	9	.315	.387	.422	808	739	6	8	(17)	10	30	763	1.4
Reserves		Averages			451	40	3	494	142	28	4	13	.315	.374	.484	858	803	6	6	(13)	3	13	805	22.0
Totals		Weighted Ave.			508	52	6	565	166	33	4	24	.327	.396	.550	946	887	14	7	(1)	3	17	905	51.8

Pitchers Rate of Success

Pos	Year	Name	T	L	G	GS	IP	W	L	SV	SO	BB	ERA	RA/9	Wtd RA/9	R Runs /162	V
SP	2000	B.Bohanon	Col	NL	34	26	177	12	10	0	98	79	4.68	5.14	4.62	(1.2)	
SP	1995	K.Ritz	Col	NL	31	28	173	11	11	2	120	65	4.21	4.72	4.63	(1.5)	
SP	1997	R.Bailey	Col	NL	29	29	191	9	10	0	84	70	4.29	4.85	4.77	(4.6)	
SP	1993	A.Reynoso	Col	NL	30	30	189	12	11	0	117	63	4.00	4.81	4.85	(6.1)	
SP	2000	P.Astacio	Col	NL	32	32	196	12	9	0	193	77	5.27	5.46	4.90	(7.5)	
Starters		Averages			31	29	185	11	10	0	122	71	4.50	5.00	4.76	(4.2)	
RP	2000	M.Myers	Col	NL	78	0	45	0	1	1	41	24	1.99	1.99	1.78	14.0	
RP	2000	G.White	Col	NL	68	0	84	11	2	5	84	15	2.36	2.46	2.21	21.9	
RP	1995	S.Reed	Col	NL	71	0	84	5	2	3	79	21	2.14	2.57	2.51	21.4	
RP	1998	C.McElroy	Col	NL	78	0	68	6	4	2	61	24	2.90	3.03	2.98	11.9	
Relievers		Averages			74	0	70	6	2	3	66	21	2.37	2.56	2.42	17.3	
Totals		Averages			105	29	255	17	12	3	189	92	3.91	4.33	4.11	13.1	

Florida Marlins (NL Expansion)

Hitters Volume of Success

Pos	Year	Name	T	L	AB	BB	HBP	TAB	H	2B	3B	HR	BA	OB	SA	PRO	Wtd PRO	SB	CS	SBF	SPF	FF	R TF	V HC
C	1997	C.Johnson	Fla	NL	416	60	3	479	104	26	1	19	.250	.349	.454	803	762	0	2	(8)	(10)	60	804	28.9
1B	1999	D.Lee	Fla	NL	477	63	4	544	134	18	3	28	.281	.369	.507	877	800	0	3	(10)	0	0	790	5.1
2B	1995	Q.Veras	Fla	NL	440	80	9	529	115	20	7	5	.261	.386	.373	758	722	56	21	25	10	10	767	23.3
SS	1996	E.Renteria	Fla	NL	431	33	2	466	133	18	3	5	.309	.361	.399	760	724	16	2	24	10	30	788	28.0
3B	2000	M.Lowell	Fla	NL	508	54	9	571	137	38	0	22	.270	.350	.474	825	752	4	0	7	0	20	779	17.1
OF	1996	G.Sheffield	Fla	NL	519	142	10	671	163	33	1	42	.314	.469	.624	1,094	1,042	16	9	(3)	10	(20)	1,029	86.9
OF	1995	J.Conine	Fla	NL	483	66	1	550	146	26	2	25	.302	.387	.520	907	864	2	0	3	0	(10)	857	29.5
OF	1997	M.Alou	Fla	NL	538	70	4	612	157	29	5	23	.292	.377	.493	870	826	9	5	(2)	10	(10)	824	19.5
Starters		Averages			477	71	5	553	136	26	3	21	.286	.384	.485	869	821	13	5	5	4	10	839	29.8
C	1994	B.Santiago	Fla	NL	337	25	1	363	92	14	2	11	.273	.325	.424	749	705	1	2	(8)	0	30	728	12.3
1B	1999	K.Millar	Fla	NL	351	40	7	398	100	17	4	9	.285	.369	.433	802	734	1	0	2	0	10	746	(4.5)
2B	2000	L.Castillo	Fla	NL	539	78	0	617	180	17	3	2	.334	.418	.388	806	735	62	22	28	10	(10)	763	22.8
SS	1995	K.Abbott	Fla	NL	420	36	5	461	107	18	7	17	.255	.321	.452	773	737	4	3	(4)	10	(30)	713	12.5
3B	1997	B.Bonilla	Fla	NL	562	73	5	640	167	39	3	17	.297	.383	.468	851	807	6	6	(9)	0	(50)	749	9.9
OF	2000	C.Floyd	Fla	NL	420	50	8	478	126	30	0	22	.300	.385	.529	914	833	24	3	36	10	(40)	839	18.6
OF	2000	P.Wilson	Fla	NL	605	55	8	668	160	35	3	31	.264	.334	.486	820	748	36	14	11	10	10	779	7.0
OF	1996	D.White	Fla	NL	552	38	8	598	151	37	6	17	.274	.329	.455	784	747	22	6	16	10	0	773	4.4
Reserves		Averages			473	49	5	528	135	26	4	16	.286	.360	.455	815	758	20	7	9	6	(10)	764	10.4
Totals		Weighted Ave.			475	64	5	544	136	26	3	19	.286	.376	.475	851	800	15	6	6	5	3	814	23.3

Pitchers Volume of Success

Pos	Year	Name	T	L	G	GS	IP	W	L	SV	SO	BB	ERA	Wtd RA/9	RA/9	R V Runs /162
SP	1996	K.Brown	Fla	NL	32	32	233	17	11	0	159	33	1.89	2.32	2.24	59.9
SP	1996	A.Leiter	Fla	NL	33	33	215	16	12	0	200	119	2.93	3.09	2.99	37.4
SP	2000	R.Dempster	Fla	NL	33	33	226	14	10	0	209	97	3.66	4.06	3.65	22.9
SP	1997	A.Fernandez	Fla	NL	32	32	221	17	12	0	183	69	3.59	3.79	3.72	20.3
SP	1995	P.Rapp	Fla	NL	28	28	167	14	7	0	102	76	3.44	3.87	3.79	15.9
Starters		Averages			32	32	212	16	10	0	155	79	3.07	3.40	3.24	31.2
RP	1996	R.Nen	Fla	NL	75	0	83	5	1	35	92	21	1.95	2.28	2.21	21.7
RP	1993	B.Harvey	Fla	NL	59	0	69	1	5	45	73	13	1.70	1.83	1.84	20.8
RP	1999	A.Alfonseca	Fla	NL	73	0	78	4	5	21	46	29	3.24	3.24	2.93	14.0
RP	1995	T.Mathews	Fla	NL	57	0	83	4	4	3	72	27	3.38	3.48	3.41	11.9
Relievers		Averages			66	0	78	4	4	26	71	23	2.60	2.74	2.63	17.1
Totals		Averages			98	32	291	19	14	26	225	101	2.95	3.22	3.08	48.3

National League Expansion Teams (1962–2000)

Florida Marlins (NL Expansion)   **Hitters Rate of Success**

Pos	Year	Name	T	L	AB	BB	HBP	TAB	H	2B	3B	HR	BA	OB	SA	PRO	Wtd PRO	SB	CS	SBF	SPF	FF	R TF	V HC
C	1997	C.Johnson	Fla	NL	416	60	3	479	104	26	1	19	.250	.349	.454	803	762	0	2	(8)	(10)	60	804	28.9
1B	1999	D.Lee	Fla	NL	477	63	4	544	134	18	3	28	.281	.369	.507	877	800	0	3	(10)	0	0	790	5.1
2B	1995	Q.Veras	Fla	NL	440	80	9	529	115	20	7	5	.261	.386	.373	758	722	56	21	25	10	10	767	23.3
SS	1996	E.Renteria	Fla	NL	431	33	2	466	133	18	3	5	.309	.361	.399	760	724	16	2	24	10	30	788	28.0
3B	2000	M.Lowell	Fla	NL	508	54	9	571	137	38	0	22	.270	.350	.474	825	752	4	0	7	0	20	779	17.1
OF	1996	G.Sheffield	Fla	NL	519	142	10	671	163	33	1	42	.314	.469	.624	1,094	1,042	16	9	(3)	10	(20)	1,029	86.9
OF	1995	J.Conine	Fla	NL	483	66	1	550	146	26	2	25	.302	.387	.520	907	864	2	0	3	0	(10)	857	29.5
OF	2000	C.Floyd	Fla	NL	420	50	8	478	126	30	0	22	.300	.385	.529	914	833	24	3	36	10	(40)	839	18.6
Starters	Averages				462	69	6	536	132	26	2	21	.286	.385	.489	874	821	15	5	9	4	6	841	29.7
C	1994	B.Santiago	Fla	NL	337	25	1	363	92	14	2	11	.273	.325	.424	749	705	1	2	(8)	0	30	728	12.3
1B	1999	K.Millar	Fla	NL	351	40	7	398	100	17	4	9	.285	.369	.433	802	734	1	0	2	0	10	746	(4.5)
2B	2000	L.Castillo	Fla	NL	539	78	0	617	180	17	3	2	.334	.418	.388	806	735	62	22	28	10	(10)	763	22.8
SS	1995	K.Abbott	Fla	NL	420	36	5	461	107	18	7	17	.255	.321	.452	773	737	4	3	(4)	10	(30)	713	12.5
3B	1997	B.Bonilla	Fla	NL	562	73	5	640	167	39	3	17	.297	.383	.468	851	807	6	6	(9)	0	(50)	749	9.9
OF	1997	M.Alou	Fla	NL	538	70	4	612	157	29	5	23	.292	.377	.493	870	826	9	5	(2)	10	(10)	824	19.5
OF	2000	P.Wilson	Fla	NL	605	55	8	668	160	35	3	31	.264	.334	.486	820	748	36	14	11	10	10	779	7.0
OF	1996	D.White	Fla	NL	552	38	8	598	151	37	6	17	.274	.329	.455	784	747	22	6	16	10	0	773	4.4
Reserves	Averages				488	52	5	545	139	26	4	16	.285	.360	.453	812	760	18	7	4	6	(6)	764	10.5
Totals	Weighted Ave.				471	63	5	539	135	26	3	19	.286	.377	.476	853	801	16	6	8	5	2	815	23.3

Pitchers Rate of Success

Pos	Year	Name	T	L	G	GS	IP	W	L	SV	SO	BB	ERA	RA/9	Wtd RA/9	R V Runs/162
SP	1996	K.Brown	Fla	NL	32	32	233	17	11	0	159	33	1.89	2.32	2.24	59.9
SP	1996	A.Leiter	Fla	NL	33	33	215	16	12	0	200	119	2.93	3.09	2.99	37.4
SP	2000	R.Dempster	Fla	NL	33	33	226	14	10	0	209	97	3.66	4.06	3.65	22.9
SP	1997	A.Fernandez	Fla	NL	32	32	221	17	12	0	183	69	3.59	3.79	3.72	20.3
SP	1995	P.Rapp	Fla	NL	28	28	167	14	7	0	102	76	3.44	3.87	3.79	15.9
Starters	Averages				32	32	212	16	10	0	155	79	3.07	3.40	3.24	31.2
RP	1993	B.Harvey	Fla	NL	59	0	69	1	5	45	73	13	1.70	1.83	1.84	20.8
RP	1996	R.Nen	Fla	NL	75	0	83	5	1	35	92	21	1.95	2.28	2.21	21.7
RP	1999	A.Alfonseca	Fla	NL	73	0	78	4	5	21	46	29	3.24	3.24	2.93	14.0
RP	1993	M.Turner	Fla	NL	55	0	68	4	5	0	59	26	2.91	3.04	3.06	11.3
Relievers	Averages				66	0	75	4	4	25	68	22	2.45	2.60	2.51	17.0
Totals	Averages				97	32	287	19	14	25	222	101	2.91	3.19	3.05	48.2

NL Expansion
Catchers

V	R	Year	Name	T	L	AB	BB	HBP	TAB	H	2B	3B	HR	BA	OB	SA	PRO	Wtd PRO	SB	CS	SBF	SPF	FF	R TF	V HC
1	1	1982	G.Carter	Mon	NL	557	78	6	641	163	32	1	29	.293	.385	.510	895	909	2	5	(12)		70	967	88.6
2	2	1980	G.Carter	Mon	NL	549	58	1	608	145	25	5	29	.264	.336	.486	822	832	3	2	(2)		80	911	67.6
3	5	1984	G.Carter	Mon	NL	596	64	6	666	175	32	1	27	.294	.368	.487	854	873	2	2	(3)	(10)	30	890	67.5
4	4	1998	M.Piazza	NY	NL	561	58	2	621	184	38	1	32	.328	.393	.570	963	917	1	0	2	(10)	(10)	898	65.3
5	6	1985	G.Carter	NY	NL	555	69	6	630	156	17	1	32	.281	.367	.488	855	868	1	1	(2)	(10)	30	887	62.9
6	3	2000	M.Piazza	NY	NL	482	58	3	543	156	26	0	38	.324	.400	.614	1,014	925	4	2	0	(10)	(10)	905	58.9
7	7	1977	G.Carter	Mon	NL	522	58	5	585	148	29	2	31	.284	.361	.525	886	860	5	5	(8)		20	872	54.2
8	10	1996	T.Hundley	NY	NL	540	79	3	622	140	32	1	41	.259	.357	.550	907	864	1	3	(8)			856	53.0
9	9	1979	G.Carter	Mon	NL	505	40	5	550	143	26	5	22	.283	.342	.485	827	820	3	2	(2)		40	858	47.4
10	11	1983	G.Carter	Mon	NL	541	51	7	599	146	37	3	17	.270	.341	.444	784	791	1	1	(2)	(10)	60	839	46.2
11	8	1997	T.Hundley	NY	NL	417	83	3	503	114	21	2	30	.273	.398	.549	947	899	2	3	(8)		(30)	861	44.0
12	12	1999	M.Piazza	NY	NL	534	51	1	586	162	25	0	40	.303	.365	.575	940	860	2	2	(3)	(10)	(20)	827	41.7
13	14	1982	T.Kennedy	SD	NL	562	26	5	593	166	42	1	21	.295	.332	.486	818	831	1	0	2	(10)	(10)	812	38.1
14	18	1981	G.Carter	Mon	NL	374	35	1	410	94	20	2	16	.251	.317	.444	761	783	1	5	(21)	(10)	50	802	36.9
15	16	1979	G.Tenace	SD	NL	463	105	7	575	122	16	4	20	.263	.407	.445	852	845	2	6	(16)	(10)	(10)	808	35.8
16	19	1978	G.Carter	Mon	NL	533	62	5	600	136	27	1	20	.255	.338	.422	760	774	10	6	(3)		30	800	35.1
17	15	1986	G.Carter	NY	NL	490	62	6	558	125	14	2	24	.255	.346	.439	785	787	1	0	2	(10)	30	808	34.8
18	22	1978	J.Stearns	NY	NL	477	70	8	555	126	24	1	15	.264	.368	.413	781	794	25	13	(2)	10	(10)	792	30.4
19	17	1997	C.Johnson	Fla	NL	416	60	3	479	104	26	1	19	.250	.349	.454	803	762	0	2	(8)	(10)	60	804	28.9
20	20	1989	C.Biggio	Hou	NL	443	49	6	498	114	21	2	13	.257	.339	.402	741	769	21	3	28	10	(10)	798	28.6
21	26	1987	B.Santiago	SD	NL	546	16	5	567	164	33	2	18	.300	.326	.467	793	763	21	12	(5)	10	10	778	27.2
22	13	1999	D.Nilsson	Mil	NL	343	53	2	398	106	19	1	21	.309	.405	.554	958	877	1	2	(7)	(10)	(40)	820	27.0
23	32	1983	T.Kennedy	SD	NL	549	51	2	602	156	27	2	17	.284	.347	.434	781	787	1	3	(8)	(10)		769	26.4
24	27	1977	J.Ferguson	Hou	NL	421	85	0	506	108	21	3	16	.257	.381	.435	816	792	6	2	4	(10)	(10)	776	23.8
25	24	1968	J.Grote	NY	NL	404	44	3	451	114	18	0	3	.282	.357	.349	706	775	1	5	(19)		30	786	23.4

First basemen

V	R	Year	Name	T	L	AB	BB	HBP	TAB	H	2B	3B	HR	BA	OB	SA	PRO	Wtd PRO	SB	CS	SBF	SPF	FF	R TF	V HC
1	1	1994	J.Bagwell	Hou	NL	400	65	4	469	147	32	2	39	.368	.461	.750	1,211	1,139	15	4	14	10	40	1,203	137.0
2	2	2000	T.Helton	Col	NL	580	103	4	687	216	59	2	42	.372	.470	.698	1,168	1,066	5	3	(1)		20	1,085	103.0
3	3	1996	J.Bagwell	Hou	NL	568	135	10	713	179	48	2	31	.315	.454	.570	1,025	976	21	7	9	10	20	1,016	83.4
4	4	1997	J.Bagwell	Hou	NL	566	127	16	709	162	40	2	43	.286	.430	.592	1,022	970	31	10	15	10	20	1,015	82.7
5	5	1999	J.Bagwell	Hou	NL	562	149	11	722	171	35	0	42	.304	.458	.591	1,049	960	30	11	10	10	30	1,010	82.6
6	8	2000	J.Bagwell	Hou	NL	590	107	15	712	183	37	1	47	.310	.428	.615	1,044	952	9	6	(4)	10	20	978	70.6
7	7	1998	J.Bagwell	Hou	NL	540	109	7	656	164	33	1	34	.304	.427	.557	984	937	19	7	7	10	30	984	66.8
8	9	1992	F.McGriff	SD	NL	531	96	1	628	152	30	4	35	.286	.396	.556	952	980	8	6	(6)			974	60.9
9	10	1988	A.Galarraga	Mon	NL	609	39	10	658	184	42	8	29	.302	.354	.540	894	935	13	4	7	0	20	962	60.3
10	11	1998	J.Olerud	NY	NL	557	96	4	657	197	36	4	22	.354	.452	.551	1,003	955	2	2	(3)	(10)	20	962	60.0
11	13	1997	A.Galarraga	Col	NL	600	54	17	671	191	31	3	41	.318	.390	.585	975	926	15	8	(1)		10	934	52.6
12	14	1996	A.Galarraga	Col	NL	626	40	17	683	190	39	3	47	.304	.362	.601	962	917	18	8	3		10	929	51.9
13	6	1993	A.Galarraga	Col	NL	470	24	6	500	174	35	4	22	.370	.408	.602	1,010	978	2	4	(11)		20	987	51.6
14	15	1984	K.Hernandez	NY	NL	550	97	1	648	171	31	0	15	.311	.415	.449	864	883	2	3	(6)		50	927	48.5
15	16	1986	K.Hernandez	NY	NL	551	94	4	649	171	34	1	13	.310	.414	.446	861	863	2	1	0		50	913	44.3
16	21	1982	A.Oliver	Mon	NL	617	61	4	682	204	43	2	22	.331	.394	.514	908	922	5	2	1		(20)	904	43.5
17	17	1994	A.Galarraga	Col	NL	417	19	8	444	133	21	0	31	.319	.360	.592	953	897	8	3	4		10	911	42.2
18	22	1999	T.Helton	Col	NL	578	68	6	652	185	39	5	35	.320	.397	.587	984	900	7	6	(7)		10	903	41.2
19	20	1991	F.McGriff	SD	NL	528	105	2	635	147	19	1	31	.278	.400	.494	894	912	4	1	3		(10)	905	40.9
20	18	1995	J.Bagwell	Hou	NL	448	79	6	533	130	29	0	21	.290	.403	.496	899	856	12	5	4	10	40	910	40.0
21	19	1993	J.Bagwell	Hou	NL	535	62	3	600	171	37	4	20	.320	.393	.516	909	880	13	4	8	10	10	908	39.5
22	12	1990	J.Clark	SD	NL	334	104	2	440	89	12	1	25	.266	.443	.533	976	975	4	3	(4)	(10)	(10)	950	37.8
23	25	1972	N.Colbert	SD	NL	563	70	2	635	141	27	2	38	.250	.335	.508	843	873	15	6	4	10		887	37.4
24	26	1993	F.McGriff	SD	NL	557	76	2	635	162	29	2	37	.291	.378	.549	927	898	5	3	(1)		(10)	886	35.2
25	29	1985	K.Hernandez	NY	NL	593	77	2	672	183	34	4	10	.309	.390	.430	820	833	3	3	(4)		50	879	34.7

National League Expansion Teams (1962–2000)

NL Expansion
Second basemen

V	R	Year	Name	T	L	AB	BB	HBP	TAB	H	2B	3B	HR	BA	OB	SA	PRO	Wtd PRO	SB	CS	SBF	SPF	FF	R TF	V HC
1	1	1997	C.Biggio	Hou	NL	619	84	34	737	191	37	8	22	.309	.419	.501	920	873	47	10	35	10	50	968	99.2
2	2	1994	C.Biggio	Hou	NL	437	62	8	507	139	44	5	6	.318	.412	.483	895	842	39	4	58	10	30	940	87.1
3	3	1998	C.Biggio	Hou	NL	646	64	23	733	210	51	2	20	.325	.405	.503	908	864	50	8	44	10	10	928	84.8
4	4	1995	C.Biggio	Hou	NL	553	80	22	655	167	30	2	22	.302	.411	.483	894	851	33	8	25	10	30	916	80.9
5	5	2000	E.Alfonso	NY	NL	544	95	5	644	176	40	2	25	.324	.429	.542	971	886	3	2	(1)		30	914	70.3
6	6	1999	E.Alfonso	NY	NL	628	85	3	716	191	41	1	27	.304	.390	.502	891	815	9	2	7		50	872	63.6
7	7	1996	E.Young	Col	NL	568	47	21	636	184	23	4	8	.324	.396	.421	817	778	53	19	22	10	60	871	56.1
8	11	1971	J.Morgan	Hou	NL	583	88	1	672	149	27	11	13	.256	.354	.407	761	784	40	8	34	10	20	848	52.0
9	9	1967	J.Morgan	Hou	NL	494	81	2	577	136	27	11	6	.275	.380	.411	790	827	29	5	31	10	(10)	858	47.4
10	13	1993	C.Biggio	Hou	NL	610	77	10	697	175	41	5	21	.287	.376	.474	850	823	15	17	(26)	10	20	827	47.0
11	16	1996	C.Biggio	Hou	NL	605	75	27	707	174	24	4	15	.288	.390	.415	805	767	25	7	15	10	.30	822	46.0
12	12	1985	B.Doran	Hou	NL	578	71	0	649	166	31	6	14	.287	.365	.434	799	812	23	15	(10)	10	20	832	45.3
13	19	1999	C.Biggio	Hou	NL	639	88	11	738	188	56	0	16	.294	.389	.457	846	774	28	14	0	10	30	814	45.2
14	15	1999	J.Bell	Ari	NL	589	82	4	675	170	32	6	38	.289	.379	.557	936	856	7	4	(1)		(30)	825	44.9
15	14	2000	J.Vidro	Mon	NL	606	49	2	657	200	51	2	24	.330	.382	.540	922	841	5	4	(4)		(10)	827	44.2
16	18	1965	J.Morgan	Hou	NL	601	97	3	701	163	22	12	14	.271	.375	.418	793	815	20	9	3	10	(10)	817	44.1
17	21	1998	F.Vina	Mil	NL	637	54	25	716	198	39	7	7	.311	.387	.427	814	775	22	16	(13)	10	40	811	43.0
18	20	1970	J.Morgan	Hou	NL	548	102	1	651	147	28	9	8	.268	.384	.396	780	761	42	13	23	10	20	814	39.8
19	8	1995	E.Young	Col	NL	366	49	5	420	116	21	9	6	.317	.405	.473	877	836	35	12	25	10	(10)	861	39.5
20	17	1988	R.Alomar	SD	NL	545	47	3	595	145	24	6	9	.266	.328	.382	709	742	24	6	19	10	50	821	38.4
21	10	1990	B.Doran	Hou	NL	403	79	0	482	121	29	2	7	.300	.415	.434	849	848	23	9	10	10	(20)	848	37.3
22	24	1989	R.Alomar	SD	NL	623	53	1	677	184	27	1	7	.295	.352	.376	727	755	42	17	11	10	20	796	35.7
23	23	1969	J.Morgan	Hou	NL	535	110	1	646	126	18	5	15	.236	.367	.372	739	756	49	14	31	10		797	34.2
24	28	1997	E.Young	Col	NL	622	71	9	702	174	33	8	8	.280	.362	.397	759	720	45	14	23	10	30	783	32.7
25	22	1992	D.Deshields	Mon	NL	530	54	3	587	155	19	8	7	.292	.361	.398	759	781	46	15	26	10	(20)	797	31.3

NL Expansion
Shortstops

V	R	Year	Name	T	L	AB	BB	HBP	TAB	H	2B	3B	HR	BA	OB	SA	PRO	Wtd PRO	SB	CS	SBF	SPF	FF	R TF	V HC
1	1	1983	D.Thon	Hou	NL	619	54	2	675	177	28	9	20	.286	.345	.457	802	809	34	16	3	10	30	852	61.1
2	2	1994	W.Cordero	Mon	NL	415	41	6	462	122	30	3	15	.294	.366	.489	855	805	16	3	20	10	(40)	795	41.5
3	4	1970	D.Menke	Hou	NL	562	82	5	649	171	26	6	13	.304	.398	.441	839	818	6	5	(6)	10	(30)	792	40.2
4	3	1982	D.Thon	Hou	NL	496	37	1	534	137	31	10	3	.276	.328	.397	725	736	37	8	37	10	10	793	33.4
5	5	1996	E.Renteria	Fla	NL	431	33	2	466	133	18	3	5	.309	.361	.399	760	724	16	2	24	10	30	788	28.0
6	9	1980	O.Smith	SD	NL	609	71	5	685	140	18	5	0	.230	.315	.276	591	599	57	15	37	10	100	746	27.4
7	6	1997	W.Weiss	Col	NL	393	66	2	461	106	23	5	4	.270	.377	.384	762	723	5	2	2		60	785	27.0
8	7	1969	D.Menke	Hou	NL	553	87	4	644	149	25	5	10	.269	.373	.387	760	777	2	7	(18)	10	(20)	750	26.9
9	13	2000	N.Perez	Col	NL	651	30	0	681	187	39	11	10	.287	.319	.427	746	680	3	6	(12)	10	60	738	24.6
10	11	1978	O.Smith	SD	NL	590	47	0	637	152	17	6	1	.258	.312	.312	624	635	40	12	24	10	70	739	23.3
11	10	1991	T.Fernandez	SD	NL	558	55	0	613	152	27	5	4	.272	.338	.360	698	712	23	9	8	10	10	740	22.7
12	12	1985	G.Templeton	SD	NL	546	41	1	588	154	30	2	6	.282	.333	.377	711	722	16	6	6		10	738	21.3
13	15	1995	W.Weiss	Col	NL	427	98	5	530	111	17	3	1	.260	.404	.321	725	690	15	3	16		30	736	21.1
14	14	1989	S.Owen	Mon	NL	437	76	3	516	102	17	4	6	.233	.351	.332	683	709	3	2	(2)		30	737	18.4
15	8	1992	S.Owen	Mon	NL	386	50	0	436	104	16	3	7	.269	.353	.381	734	755	9	4	2		(10)	748	17.8
16	16	1996	W.Weiss	Col	NL	517	80	6	603	146	20	2	8	.282	.385	.375	760	724	10	2	9		(10)	723	17.6
17	18	1998	J.Bell	Ari	NL	549	81	7	637	138	29	5	20	.251	.355	.432	786	748	3	5	(10)		(20)	718	17.0
18	22	1998	N.Perez	Col	NL	647	38	1	686	177	25	9	9	.274	.315	.382	697	663	5	6	(10)	10	50	713	16.8
19	25	1996	M.Grudzielanek	Mon	NL	657	26	9	692	201	34	4	6	.306	.341	.397	738	703	33	7	26	10	(30)	709	15.6
20	20	1971	B.Harrelson	NY	NL	547	53	2	602	138	16	6	0	.252	.321	.303	624	643	28	7	22	10	40	715	15.2
21	28	1999	N.Perez	Col	NL	690	28	1	719	193	27	11	12	.280	.309	.403	712	651	13	5	4	10	40	705	14.7
22	19	2000	D.Jackson	SD	NL	470	62	3	535	120	27	6	6	.255	.346	.377	722	659	28	6	28	10	20	717	14.1
23	23	1995	K.Abbott	Fla	NL	420	36	5	461	107	18	7	17	.255	.321	.452	773	737	4	3	(4)	10	(30)	713	12.5
24	26	1984	C.Reynolds	Hou	NL	527	22	0	549	137	15	11	6	.260	.290	.364	654	668	7	1	9		30	707	11.7
25	31	1995	J.Vizcaino	NY	NL	509	35	1	545	146	21	5	3	.287	.334	.365	699	666	8	3	3		30	700	11.0

NL Expansion
Third basemen

V	R	Year	Name	T	L	AB	BB	HBP	TAB	H	2B	3B	HR	BA	OB	SA	PRO	Wtd PRO	SB	CS	SBF	SPF	FF	R TF	V HC
1	1	1996	K.Caminiti	SD	NL	546	78	4	628	178	37	2	40	.326	.414	.621	1,035	986	11	5	2		50	1,037	96.1
2	2	1992	G.Sheffield	SD	NL	557	48	6	611	184	34	3	33	.330	.390	.580	969	998	5	6	(11)	10	20	1,017	87.5
3	3	1989	H.Johnson	NY	NL	571	77	1	649	164	41	3	36	.287	.373	.559	932	967	41	8	36	10	(60)	953	73.4
4	5	1998	V.Castilla	Col	NL	645	40	6	691	206	28	4	46	.319	.365	.589	954	908	5	9	(18)		30	920	67.1
5	6	1999	R.Ventura	NY	NL	588	74	3	665	177	38	0	32	.301	.382	.529	911	833	1	1	(1)	(10)	90	912	62.0
6	8	1996	V.Castilla	Col	NL	629	35	5	669	191	34	0	40	.304	.345	.548	894	851	7	2	4		50	906	60.4
7	11	1995	K.Caminiti	SD	NL	526	69	1	596	159	33	0	26	.302	.384	.513	898	855	12	5	3		30	888	54.9
8	12	1997	V.Castilla	Col	NL	612	44	8	664	186	25	2	40	.304	.358	.547	906	860	2	4	(9)		30	881	52.2
9	7	1997	K.Caminiti	SD	NL	486	80	3	569	141	28	0	26	.290	.394	.508	902	856	11	2	12		40	908	51.9
10	9	1979	L.Parrish	Mon	NL	544	41	2	587	167	39	2	30	.307	.358	.551	909	901	5	1	5		(10)	896	50.4
11	14	1999	M.Williams	Ari	NL	627	41	2	670	190	37	2	35	.303	.348	.536	884	808	2	0	3		60	871	49.5
12	16	1995	B.Bonilla	NY	NL	554	54	2	610	182	37	8	28	.329	.390	.576	966	920	0	5	(15)		(40)	865	48.6
13	15	1991	H.Johnson	NY	NL	564	78	1	643	146	34	4	38	.259	.350	.535	885	903	30	16	(3)		(30)	870	47.2
14	17	1998	J.Cirillo	Mil	NL	604	79	4	687	194	31	1	14	.321	.403	.445	849	808	10	4	3		50	860	47.2
15	4	1970	B.Bailey	Mon	NL	352	72	1	425	101	19	3	28	.287	.409	.597	1,006	981	5	3	(2)		(30)	949	47.1
16	13	1993	C.Hayes	Col	NL	573	43	5	621	175	45	2	25	.305	.359	.522	881	853	11	6	(2)		20	871	45.9
17	21	1995	V.Castilla	Col	NL	527	30	4	561	163	34	2	32	.309	.351	.564	915	871	2	8	(24)			848	39.6
18	20	1973	B.Bailey	Mon	NL	513	88	1	602	140	25	4	26	.273	.380	.489	870	877	5	8	(17)		(10)	850	38.3
19	23	1999	J.Cirillo	Mil	NL	607	75	5	687	198	35	1	15	.326	.405	.461	866	792	7	4	(1)		40	831	37.5
20	10	1987	R.Ready	SD	NL	350	67	3	420	108	26	6	12	.309	.424	.520	944	908	7	3	2		(20)	890	34.8
21	30	2000	J.Cirillo	Col	NL	598	67	6	671	195	53	2	11	.326	.399	.477	876	799	3	4	(7)		30	822	33.9
22	26	1987	T.Wallach	Mon	NL	593	37	7	637	177	42	4	26	.298	.347	.514	861	828	9	5	(1)	(10)	10	827	33.6
23	27	1994	K.Caminiti	Hou	NL	406	43	2	451	115	28	2	18	.283	.355	.495	850	800	4	3	(4)		30	826	33.3
24	24	1985	T.Wallach	Mon	NL	569	38	5	612	148	36	3	22	.260	.312	.450	762	774	9	9	(14)	(10)	80	830	33.2
25	28	1987	H.Johnson	NY	NL	554	83	5	642	147	22	1	36	.265	.366	.504	870	836	32	10	18	10	(40)	824	33.0

Outfielders

V	R	Year	Name	T	L	AB	BB	HBP	TAB	H	2B	3B	HR	BA	OB	SA	PRO	Wtd PRO	SB	CS	SBF	SPF	FF	R TF	V HC
1	1	1997	L.Walker	Col	NL	568	78	14	660	208	46	4	49	.366	.455	.720	1,175	1,115	33	8	24	10	30	1,179	132.6
2	3	1981	A.Dawson	Mon	NL	394	35	7	436	119	21	3	24	.302	.369	.553	923	949	26	4	39	10	80	1,078	100.9
3	2	1999	L.Walker	Col	NL	438	57	12	507	166	26	4	37	.379	.464	.710	1,174	1,074	11	4	6	10	30	1,119	87.4
4	7	1996	E.Burks	Col	NL	613	61	6	680	211	45	8	40	.344	.409	.639	1,048	999	32	6	28			1,026	87.2
5	6	1996	G.Sheffield	Fla	NL	519	142	10	671	163	33	1	42	.314	.469	.624	1,094	1,042	16	9	(3)	10	(20)	1,029	86.9
6	11	1987	T.Gwynn	SD	NL	589	82	3	674	218	36	13	7	.370	.450	.511	961	924	56	12	45	10	40	1,019	83.9
7	8	1972	C.Cedeno	Hou	NL	559	56	5	620	179	39	8	22	.320	.387	.537	924	956	55	21	20	10	40	1,026	83.4
8	10	1985	T.Raines	Mon	NL	575	81	3	659	184	30	13	11	.320	.407	.475	881	895	70	9	75	10	40	1,020	82.4
9	5	1987	T.Raines	Mon	NL	530	90	4	624	175	34	8	18	.330	.431	.526	958	921	50	5	61	10	40	1,031	81.5
10	9	1969	J.Wynn	Hou	NL	495	148	3	646	133	17	1	33	.269	.440	.507	947	969	23	7	13	10	30	1,022	81.3
11	13	1979	D.Winfield	SD	NL	597	85	2	684	184	27	10	34	.308	.396	.558	954	946	15	9	(4)	10	50	1,002	79.6
12	4	1998	L.Walker	Col	NL	454	64	4	522	165	46	3	23	.363	.446	.630	1,076	1,024	14	4	11	10	30	1,075	79.0
13	14	1986	T.Raines	Mon	NL	580	78	2	660	194	35	10	9	.334	.415	.476	891	893	70	9	74	10	20	998	75.6
14	15	1994	T.Gwynn	SD	NL	419	48	2	469	165	35	1	12	.394	.458	.568	1,026	966	5	0	10	10	10	996	75.5
15	12	1973	C.Cedeno	Hou	NL	525	41	7	573	168	35	2	25	.320	.377	.537	914	922	56	15	43	10	40	1,015	70.2
16	22	1983	T.Raines	Mon	NL	615	97	2	714	183	32	8	11	.298	.395	.429	824	831	90	14	82	10	40	963	70.0
17	21	1984	T.Raines	Mon	NL	622	87	2	711	192	38	9	8	.309	.395	.437	833	850	75	10	73	10	30	964	69.8
18	17	2000	R.Hidalgo	Hou	NL	558	56	21	635	175	42	3	44	.314	.397	.636	1,033	943	13	6	1	10	30	984	68.6
19	19	1995	L.Walker	Col	NL	494	49	14	557	151	31	5	36	.306	.384	.607	991	945	16	3	17	10	10	981	66.9
20	28	1983	A.Dawson	Mon	NL	633	38	9	680	189	36	10	32	.299	.347	.539	886	893	25	11	4	10	50	957	64.8
21	35	1986	T.Gwynn	SD	NL	642	52	3	697	211	33	7	14	.329	.382	.467	849	851	37	9	26	10	60	947	63.0
22	20	1987	D.Strawberry	NY	NL	532	97	7	636	151	32	5	39	.284	.401	.583	984	946	36	12	18	10	(10)	964	62.5
23	29	1965	J.Wynn	Hou	NL	564	84	5	653	155	30	7	22	.275	.374	.470	844	867	43	4	51	10	30	957	62.2
24	16	1981	T.Raines	Mon	NL	313	45	2	360	95	13	7	5	.304	.394	.438	832	856	71	11	129	10		995	61.7
25	31	1982	A.Dawson	Mon	NL	608	34	8	650	183	37	7	23	.301	.346	.498	845	858	39	10	28	10	60	955	61.3

National League Expansion Teams (1962–2000)

NL Expansion Outfielders

V	R	Year	Name	T	L	AB	BB	HBP	TAB	H	2B	3B	HR	BA	OB	SA	PRO	Wtd PRO	SB	CS	SBF	SPF	FF	R TF	V HC
26	23	1980	A.Dawson	Mon	NL	577	44	6	627	178	41	7	17	.308	.364	.492	856	867	34	9	24	10	60	961	60.8
27	24	1988	D.Strawberry	NY	NL	543	85	3	631	146	27	3	39	.269	.371	.545	916	958	29	14	1	10	(10)	959	60.7
28	34	1969	R.Staub	Mon	NL	549	110	9	668	166	26	5	29	.302	.427	.526	953	975	3	4	(7)	(10)	(10)	948	60.6
29	26	1994	L.Walker	Mon	NL	395	47	4	446	127	44	2	19	.322	.399	.587	986	928	15	5	11	10	10	959	60.6
30	32	1996	B.Gilkey	NY	NL	571	73	4	648	181	44	3	30	.317	.398	.562	960	915	17	9	(1)	10	30	953	60.5
31	30	2000	V.Guerrero	Mon	NL	571	58	8	637	197	28	11	44	.345	.413	.664	1,077	982	9	10	(16)	10	(20)	956	60.3
32	36	1998	M.Alou	Hou	NL	584	84	5	673	182	34	5	38	.312	.403	.582	985	937	11	3	7	10	(10)	944	59.9
33	40	1995	D.Bichette	Col	NL	579	22	4	605	197	38	2	40	.340	.369	.620	989	942	13	9	(8)	10	(10)	934	57.3
34	37	1968	J.Wynn	Hou	NL	542	90	5	637	146	23	5	26	.269	.378	.474	853	936	11	17	(34)	10	30	942	56.0
35	39	1994	M.Alou	Mon	NL	422	42	2	466	143	31	5	22	.339	.401	.592	994	935	7	6	(10)	10		935	55.8
36	45	1974	C.Cedeno	Hou	NL	610	64	4	678	164	29	5	26	.269	.342	.461	803	815	57	17	32	10	70	927	54.9
37	42	1984	T.Gwynn	SD	NL	606	59	2	667	213	21	10	5	.351	.411	.444	855	873	33	18	(4)	10	50	929	54.5
38	44	1970	J.Wynn	Hou	NL	554	106	1	661	156	32	2	27	.282	.398	.493	891	868	24	5	20	10	30	928	53.9
39	27	1969	C.Jones	NY	NL	483	64	7	554	164	25	4	12	.340	.424	.482	907	927	16	8	0	10	20	957	52.8
40	33	1992	L.Walker	Mon	NL	528	41	6	575	159	31	4	23	.301	.358	.506	864	889	18	6	10	10	40	949	52.5
41	41	1976	C.Cedeno	Hou	NL	575	55	1	631	171	26	5	18	.297	.360	.454	814	840	58	15	42	10	40	932	52.4
42	49	1972	J.Wynn	Hou	NL	542	103	2	647	148	29	3	24	.273	.391	.470	862	892	17	7	4	10	10	916	51.5
43	38	1988	K.McReynolds	NY	NL	552	38	4	594	159	30	2	27	.288	.338	.496	835	873	21	0	33	10	20	936	50.7
44	18	1985	D.Strawberry	NY	NL	393	73	1	467	109	15	4	29	.277	.392	.557	949	964	26	11	8	10		982	50.0
45	55	1996	S.Finley	SD	NL	655	56	4	715	195	45	9	30	.298	.357	.531	888	846	22	8	8	10	40	904	49.9
46	25	2000	M.Alou	Hou	NL	454	52	2	508	161	28	2	30	.355	.423	.623	1,047	955	3	3	(6)	10		959	48.9
47	52	1989	T.Gwynn	SD	NL	604	56	1	661	203	27	7	4	.336	.393	.424	817	848	40	16	11	10	40	910	48.0
48	51	1998	G.Vaughn	SD	NL	573	79	5	657	156	28	4	50	.272	.365	.597	962	916	11	4	4		(10)	910	47.7
49	54	1984	J.Cruz	Hou	NL	600	73	0	673	187	28	13	12	.312	.386	.462	848	866	22	8	8	10	20	905	47.2
50	63	1973	K.Singleton	Mon	NL	560	123	2	685	169	26	2	23	.302	.429	.479	908	915	2	8	(19)			896	45.3
51	58	1967	J.Wynn	Hou	NL	594	74	2	670	148	29	3	37	.249	.334	.495	829	867	16	4	11	10	10	899	45.0
52	43	1982	S.Lezcano	SD	NL	470	78	2	550	136	26	6	16	.289	.393	.472	865	879	2	1	0		50	929	44.9
53	61	1978	D.Winfield	SD	NL	587	55	2	644	181	30	5	24	.308	.370	.499	869	884	21	9	4	10		898	43.1
54	48	1980	C.Cedeno	Hou	NL	499	66	1	566	154	32	8	10	.309	.390	.465	855	866	48	15	30	10	10	916	42.9
55	60	1997	T.Gwynn	SD	NL	592	43	3	638	220	49	2	17	.372	.417	.547	964	915	12	5	3		(20)	898	42.8
56	56	1989	T.Raines	Mon	NL	517	93	3	613	148	29	6	9	.286	.398	.418	816	847	41	9	35	10	10	902	42.3
57	59	1970	C.Gaston	SD	NL	584	41	2	627	186	26	9	29	.318	.365	.543	908	885	4	1	3	10		898	42.1
58	46	1999	C.Everett	Hou	NL	464	50	11	525	151	33	3	25	.325	.404	.571	975	892	27	7	23	10		925	42.0
59	53	1977	C.Cedeno	Hou	NL	530	47	11	588	148	36	8	14	.279	.350	.457	807	784	61	14	53	10	60	907	41.8
60	47	1993	T.Gwynn	SD	NL	489	36	1	526	175	41	3	7	.358	.403	.497	900	871	14	1	22	10	20	923	41.5
61	82	1996	L.Johnson	NY	NL	682	33	1	716	227	31	21	9	.333	.365	.479	844	804	50	12	34	10	30	878	41.3
62	71	1998	V.Guerrero	Mon	NL	623	42	7	672	202	37	7	38	.324	.374	.589	963	916	11	9	(10)	10	(30)	886	41.2
63	74	1971	R.Staub	Mon	NL	599	74	9	682	186	34	6	19	.311	.394	.482	877	904	9	5	(1)		(20)	882	40.6
64	73	1983	J.Cruz	Hou	NL	594	65	1	660	189	28	8	14	.318	.386	.463	849	856	30	16	(3)	10	20	884	39.7
65	65	1978	J.Cruz	Hou	NL	565	57	0	622	178	34	9	10	.315	.378	.460	838	852	37	9	29	10		891	39.7
66	50	1994	G.Sheffield	Fla	NL	322	51	6	379	89	16	1	27	.276	.385	.584	969	912	12	6	0	10	(10)	912	39.5
67	64	1967	R.Staub	Hou	NL	546	60	3	609	182	44	1	10	.333	.402	.473	875	915	0	4	(12)		(10)	892	39.2
68	67	1990	D.Strawberry	NY	NL	542	70	4	616	150	18	1	37	.277	.364	.518	882	881	15	8	(2)	10		889	38.7
69	76	1995	T.Gwynn	SD	NL	535	35	1	571	197	33	1	9	.368	.408	.484	892	850	17	5	12	10	10	881	38.0
70	84	1999	V.Guerrero	Mon	NL	610	55	7	672	193	37	5	42	.316	.379	.600	979	896	14	7	0	10	(30)	876	38.0
71	85	1979	L.Mazzilli	NY	NL	597	93	0	690	181	34	4	15	.303	.397	.449	846	839	34	12	14	10	10	872	37.8
72	77	1980	D.Winfield	SD	NL	558	79	2	639	154	25	6	20	.276	.368	.450	818	828	23	7	13	10	30	881	37.7
73	62	1976	D.Winfield	SD	NL	492	65	3	560	139	26	4	13	.283	.370	.431	801	826	26	7	20	10	40	896	37.1
74	66	1975	C.Cedeno	Hou	NL	500	62	7	569	144	31	3	13	.288	.374	.440	814	824	50	17	27	10	30	890	36.0
75	91	1992	M.Grissom	Mon	NL	653	42	5	700	180	39	6	14	.276	.324	.418	742	764	78	13	70	10	20	864	35.6

NL Expansion
Starting Pitchers

V	R	Year	Name	T	L	G	GS	IP	W	L	SV	SO	BB	ERA	RA/9	R Wtd RA/9	V Runs /162
1	1	1985	D.Gooden	NY	NL	35	35	277	24	4	0	268	69	1.53	1.66	1.86	83.0
2	2	1971	T.Seaver	NY	NL	36	35	286	20	10	0	289	61	1.76	1.92	2.24	73.7
3	8	1973	T.Seaver	NY	NL	36	36	290	19	10	0	251	64	2.08	2.30	2.53	65.5
4	3	1996	K.Brown	Fla	NL	32	32	233	17	11	0	159	33	1.89	2.32	2.24	59.9
5	9	1999	R.Johnson	Ari	NL	35	35	272	17	9	0	364	70	2.48	2.85	2.58	59.8
6	10	1986	M.Scott	Hou	NL	37	37	275	18	10	0	306	72	2.22	2.39	2.61	59.4
7	4	1997	P.Martinez	Mon	NL	31	31	241	17	8	0	305	67	1.90	2.42	2.38	58.2
8	14	1969	T.Seaver	NY	NL	36	35	273	25	7	0	208	82	2.21	2.47	2.76	54.5
9	11	1998	K.Brown	SD	NL	36	35	257	18	7	0	257	49	2.38	2.70	2.66	54.2
10	5	1981	N.Ryan	Hou	NL	21	21	149	11	5	0	140	68	1.69	2.05	2.40	54.0
11	16	1975	T.Seaver	NY	NL	36	36	280	22	9	0	243	88	2.38	2.60	2.87	52.5
12	21	1982	J.Niekro	Hou	NL	35	35	270	17	12	0	130	64	2.47	2.63	2.94	48.6
13	13	1969	J.Koosman	NY	NL	32	32	241	17	9	0	180	68	2.28	2.46	2.75	48.5
14	15	1981	B.Knepper	Hou	NL	22	22	157	9	5	0	75	38	2.18	2.36	2.76	47.3
15	18	1994	B.Saberhagen	NY	NL	24	24	177	14	4	0	143	13	2.74	2.94	2.88	46.6
16	25	1982	S.Rogers	Mon	NL	35	35	277	19	8	0	179	65	2.40	2.73	3.05	46.4
17	36	1969	L.Dierker	Hou	NL	39	37	305	20	13	0	232	72	2.33	2.86	3.19	46.2
18	19	2000	R.Johnson	Ari	NL	35	35	249	19	7	0	347	76	2.64	3.22	2.90	45.9
19	29	1971	D.Roberts	SD	NL	37	34	270	14	17	0	135	61	2.10	2.64	3.08	44.4
20	17	1997	K.Brown	Fla	NL	33	33	237	16	8	0	205	66	2.69	2.92	2.87	44.3
21	27	1974	J.Matlack	NY	NL	34	34	265	13	15	0	195	76	2.41	2.78	3.05	44.3
22	24	1997	D.Kile	Hou	NL	34	34	256	19	7	0	205	94	2.57	3.06	3.01	44.0
23	7	1998	A.Leiter	NY	NL	28	28	193	17	6	0	174	71	2.47	2.56	2.52	43.7
24	38	1970	T.Seaver	NY	NL	37	36	291	18	12	0	283	83	2.82	3.19	3.21	43.6
25	20	1999	M.Hampton	Hou	NL	34	34	239	22	4	0	177	101	2.90	3.24	2.93	43.3
26	35	1968	T.Seaver	NY	NL	36	35	278	16	12	1	205	48	2.20	2.37	3.16	43.2
27	32	1971	D.Wilson	Hou	NL	35	34	268	16	10	0	180	79	2.45	2.69	3.14	42.3
28	34	1976	T.Seaver	NY	NL	35	34	271	14	11	0	235	77	2.59	2.76	3.15	42.3
29	41	1979	J.Richard	Hou	NL	38	38	292	18	13	0	313	98	2.71	3.02	3.25	42.3
30	49	1975	R.Jones	SD	NL	37	36	285	20	12	0	103	56	2.24	2.97	3.28	40.5
31	22	1978	S.Rogers	Mon	NL	30	29	219	13	10	1	126	64	2.47	2.63	2.98	38.3
32	28	1988	D.Cone	NY	NL	35	28	231	20	3	0	213	80	2.22	2.61	3.07	38.1
33	51	1977	J.Richard	Hou	NL	36	36	267	18	12	0	214	104	2.97	3.17	3.28	37.8
34	31	1994	D.Drabek	Hou	NL	23	23	165	12	6	0	121	45	2.84	3.17	3.11	37.6
35	50	1968	J.Koosman	NY	NL	35	34	264	19	12	0	178	69	2.08	2.46	3.28	37.5
36	23	1996	A.Leiter	Fla	NL	33	33	215	16	12	0	200	119	2.93	3.09	2.99	37.4
37	30	1990	E.Whitson	SD	NL	32	32	229	14	9	0	127	47	2.60	2.87	3.09	37.3
38	6	1990	D.Darwin	Hou	NL	48	17	163	11	4	2	109	31	2.21	2.32	2.50	37.3
39	39	1990	F.Viola	NY	NL	35	35	250	20	12	0	182	60	2.67	2.99	3.22	37.1
40	86	1976	R.Jones	SD	NL	40	40	315	22	14	0	93	50	2.74	3.11	3.55	35.2
41	33	1991	D.Martinez	Mon	NL	31	31	222	14	11	0	123	62	2.39	2.84	3.14	34.9
42	26	1978	C.Swan	NY	NL	29	28	207	9	6	0	125	58	2.43	2.69	3.05	34.7
43	12	2000	J.D'Amico	Mil	NL	23	23	162	12	7	0	101	46	2.66	3.05	2.74	32.8
44	64	1972	J.Matlack	NY	NL	34	32	244	15	10	0	169	71	2.32	2.91	3.41	32.7
45	59	1976	J.Koosman	NY	NL	34	32	247	21	10	0	200	66	2.69	2.95	3.37	32.6
46	37	1987	N.Ryan	Hou	NL	34	34	212	8	16	0	270	87	2.76	3.19	3.20	31.9
47	43	1986	B.Ojeda	NY	NL	32	30	217	18	5	0	148	52	2.57	2.98	3.26	31.4
48	60	1981	D.Sutton	Hou	NL	23	23	159	11	9	0	104	29	2.61	2.89	3.39	31.3
49	44	1991	P.Harnisch	Hou	NL	33	33	217	12	9	0	172	83	2.70	2.95	3.26	31.2
50	76	1973	J.Koosman	NY	NL	35	35	263	14	15	0	156	76	2.84	3.18	3.49	31.1

National League Expansion Teams (1962–2000)

NL Expansion Starting Pitchers

V	R	Year	Name	T	L	G	GS	IP	W	L	SV	SO	BB	ERA	RA/9	R Wtd RA/9	V Runs /162
51	68	1987	M.Scott	Hou	NL	36	36	248	16	13	0	233	79	3.23	3.42	3.43	31.0
52	63	1962	T.Farrell	Hou	NL	43	29	242	10	20	4	203	55	3.02	3.38	3.41	30.9
53	40	1997	R.Reed	NY	NL	33	31	208	13	9	0	113	31	2.89	3.28	3.23	30.7
54	53	2000	M.Hampton	NY	NL	33	33	218	15	10	0	151	99	3.14	3.68	3.31	30.2
55	58	1974	L.Dierker	Hou	NL	33	33	224	11	10	0	150	82	2.90	3.05	3.35	30.1
56	55	1984	D.Gooden	NY	NL	31	31	218	17	9	0	276	73	2.60	2.97	3.32	30.0
57	52	1992	S.Fernandez	NY	NL	32	32	215	14	11	0	193	67	2.73	2.81	3.30	30.0
58	45	2000	A.Leiter	NY	NL	31	31	208	16	8	0	200	76	3.20	3.63	3.27	29.8
59	48	1993	M.Portugal	Hou	NL	33	33	208	18	4	0	131	77	2.77	3.25	3.28	29.6
60	61	1991	A.Benes	SD	NL	33	33	223	15	11	0	167	59	3.03	3.07	3.40	28.8
61	102	1980	S.Rogers	Mon	NL	37	37	281	16	11	0	147	85	2.98	3.23	3.65	28.2
62	74	1986	R.Darling	NY	NL	34	34	237	15	6	0	184	81	2.81	3.19	3.49	28.2
63	69	1990	D.Martinez	Mon	NL	32	32	226	10	11	0	156	49	2.95	3.19	3.44	28.1
64	42	1990	O.Boyd	Mon	NL	31	31	191	10	6	0	113	52	2.93	3.02	3.25	27.7
65	114	1976	J.Richard	Hou	NL	39	39	291	20	15	0	214	151	2.75	3.25	3.71	27.3
66	72	1966	M.Cuellar	Hou	NL	38	28	227	12	10	2	175	52	2.22	3.13	3.48	27.2
67	88	1999	J.Lima	Hou	NL	35	35	246	21	10	0	187	44	3.58	3.95	3.57	27.1
68	90	1989	B.Hurst	SD	NL	33	33	245	15	11	0	179	66	2.69	3.09	3.57	26.8
69	78	1992	D.Martinez	Mon	NL	32	32	226	16	11	0	147	60	2.47	2.98	3.50	26.5
70	71	1989	S.Fernandez	NY	NL	35	32	219	14	5	0	198	75	2.83	3.00	3.47	26.5
71	126	1977	S.Rogers	Mon	NL	40	40	302	17	16	0	206	81	3.10	3.64	3.77	26.4
72	80	1998	A.Ashby	SD	NL	33	33	227	17	9	0	151	58	3.34	3.57	3.51	26.3
73	85	1982	T.Lollar	SD	NL	34	34	233	16	9	0	150	87	3.13	3.17	3.54	26.3
74	73	1994	K.Hill	Mon	NL	23	23	155	16	5	0	85	44	3.32	3.55	3.48	26.3
75	112	1972	T.Seaver	NY	NL	35	35	262	21	12	0	249	77	2.92	3.16	3.70	26.2
76	96	1967	T.Seaver	NY	NL	35	34	251	16	13	0	170	78	2.76	3.05	3.62	26.1
77	95	1986	D.Gooden	NY	NL	33	33	250	17	6	0	200	80	2.84	3.31	3.62	26.1
78	98	1989	M.Langston	Mon	NL	34	34	250	16	14	0	235	112	2.74	3.13	3.62	26.0
79	70	1990	Z.Smith	Mon	NL	33	31	215	12	9	0	130	50	2.55	3.22	3.47	26.0
80	82	1989	E.Whitson	SD	NL	33	33	227	16	11	0	117	48	2.66	3.05	3.53	26.0
81	56	1988	P.Perez	Mon	NL	27	27	188	12	8	0	131	44	2.44	2.82	3.32	25.8
82	77	1993	P.Harnisch	Hou	NL	33	33	218	16	9	0	185	79	2.98	3.47	3.50	25.6
83	75	1999	O.Daal	Ari	NL	32	32	215	16	9	0	148	79	3.65	3.86	3.49	25.5
84	89	1996	J.Fassero	Mon	NL	34	34	232	15	11	0	222	55	3.30	3.69	3.57	25.4
85	57	1971	K.Forsch	Hou	NL	33	23	188	8	8	0	131	53	2.53	2.87	3.34	25.3
86	110	1976	J.Matlack	NY	NL	35	35	262	17	10	0	153	57	2.95	3.23	3.69	25.3
87	100	1973	D.Roberts	Hou	NL	39	36	249	17	11	0	119	62	2.85	3.32	3.65	25.2
88	47	1994	S.Reynolds	Hou	NL	33	14	124	8	5	0	110	21	3.05	3.34	3.27	25.0
89	79	1998	R.Reed	NY	NL	31	31	212	16	11	0	153	29	3.48	3.56	3.50	24.8
90	97	1981	B.Gullickson	Mon	NL	22	22	157	7	9	0	115	34	2.80	3.09	3.62	24.8
91	67	1994	J.Fassero	Mon	NL	21	21	139	8	6	0	119	40	2.99	3.50	3.43	24.6
92	103	1972	D.Wilson	Hou	NL	33	33	228	15	10	0	172	66	2.68	3.12	3.65	24.0
93	91	1995	P.Martinez	Mon	NL	30	30	195	14	10	0	174	66	3.51	3.65	3.58	23.9
94	119	1979	J.Niekro	Hou	NL	38	38	264	21	11	0	119	107	3.00	3.48	3.75	23.7
95	92	1988	M.Scott	Hou	NL	32	32	219	14	8	0	190	53	2.92	3.05	3.59	23.5
96	54	1985	S.Fernandez	NY	NL	26	26	170	9	9	0	180	80	2.80	2.96	3.31	23.5
97	46	1998	O.Daal	Ari	NL	33	23	163	8	12	0	132	51	2.88	3.32	3.27	23.4
98	122	1978	G.Perry	SD	NL	37	37	261	21	6	0	154	66	2.73	3.31	3.75	23.3
99	81	1964	B.Bruce	Hou	NL	35	29	202	15	9	0	135	33	2.76	3.12	3.52	23.3
100	83	1994	P.Martinez	Mon	NL	24	23	145	11	5	1	142	45	3.42	3.61	3.54	23.2

NL Expansion
Relief Pitchers

V	R	Year	Name	T	L	G	GS	IP	W	L	SV	SO	BB	ERA	RA/9	R Wtd RA/9	V Runs /162
1	6	1992	M.Rojas	Mon	NL	68	0	101	7	1	10	70	34	1.43	1.52	1.79	31.1
2	11	1971	T.McGraw	NY	NL	51	1	111	11	4	8	109	41	1.70	1.78	2.07	30.6
3	21	1972	M.Marshall	Mon	NL	65	0	116	14	8	18	95	47	1.78	2.02	2.37	29.7
4	7	1987	T.Burke	Mon	NL	55	0	91	7	0	18	58	17	1.19	1.78	1.79	28.0
5	30	1995	D.Veres	Hou	NL	72	0	103	5	1	1	94	30	2.26	2.53	2.48	26.7
6	8	1993	J.Wetteland	Mon	NL	70	0	85	9	3	43	113	28	1.37	1.79	1.80	26.0
7	26	1983	J.Orosco	NY	NL	62	0	110	13	7	17	84	38	1.47	2.21	2.44	25.8
8	76	1993	J.Fassero	Mon	NL	56	15	150	12	5	1	140	54	2.29	3.01	3.03	25.4
9	3	1999	B.Wagner	Hou	NL	66	0	75	4	1	39	124	23	1.57	1.69	1.53	25.1
10	2	1998	T.Hoffman	SD	NL	66	0	73	4	2	53	86	21	1.48	1.48	1.46	25.1
11	44	1985	T.Burke	Mon	NL	78	0	120	9	4	8	87	44	2.39	2.39	2.68	25.1
12	29	1974	C.Taylor	Mon	NL	61	0	108	6	2	11	43	25	2.17	2.25	2.47	25.0
13	22	1980	D.Smith	Hou	NL	57	0	103	7	5	10	85	32	1.93	2.10	2.37	25.0
14	16	1990	L.Andersen	Hou	NL	65	0	96	5	2	7	93	27	1.79	2.07	2.23	24.8
15	13	1979	J.Sambito	Hou	NL	63	0	91	8	7	22	83	23	1.77	1.97	2.12	24.6
16	38	1972	T.McGraw	NY	NL	54	0	106	8	6	27	92	40	1.70	2.21	2.59	24.4
17	1	1998	U.Urbina	Mon	NL	64	0	69	6	3	34	94	33	1.30	1.43	1.41	24.1
18	4	1999	A.Benitez	NY	NL	77	0	78	4	3	22	128	41	1.85	1.96	1.77	24.1
19	37	1982	J.Reardon	Mon	NL	75	0	109	7	4	26	86	36	2.06	2.31	2.58	23.9
20	28	1982	L.DeLeon	SD	NL	61	0	102	9	5	15	60	16	2.03	2.21	2.47	23.7
21	34	1981	J.Reardon	Mon	NL	43	0	70	3	0	8	49	21	2.18	2.18	2.55	23.6
22	24	1979	E.Sosa	Mon	NL	62	0	97	8	7	18	59	37	1.96	2.23	2.40	23.2
23	12	1975	B.Apodaca	NY	NL	46	0	85	3	4	13	45	28	1.49	1.91	2.11	23.1
24	46	1963	H.Woodeshick	Hou	NL	55	0	114	11	9	10	94	42	1.97	2.29	2.73	23.1
25	79	1981	G.Lucas	SD	NL	57	0	90	7	7	13	53	36	2.00	2.60	3.05	22.9
26	27	1984	B.Dawley	Hou	NL	60	0	98	11	4	5	47	35	1.93	2.20	2.46	22.9
27	59	1987	A.McGaffigan	Mon	NL	69	0	120	5	2	12	100	42	2.39	2.84	2.85	22.8
28	20	1989	M.Davis	SD	NL	70	0	93	4	3	44	92	31	1.85	2.04	2.36	22.7
29	48	1992	D.Jones	Hou	NL	80	0	112	11	8	36	93	17	1.85	2.34	2.75	22.5
30	17	1989	L.Andersen	Hou	NL	60	0	88	4	4	3	85	24	1.54	1.95	2.26	22.5
31	131	1973	M.Marshall	Mon	NL	92	0	179	14	11	31	124	75	2.66	3.12	3.43	22.5
32	64	1989	D.Darwin	Hou	NL	68	0	122	11	4	7	104	33	2.36	2.51	2.90	22.4
33	18	1996	T.Hoffman	SD	NL	70	0	88	9	5	42	111	31	2.25	2.35	2.27	22.3
34	33	1971	B.Miller	SD	NL	56	0	99	8	5	10	51	40	1.64	2.19	2.55	22.1
35	15	2000	G.White	Col	NL	68	0	84	11	2	5	84	15	2.36	2.46	2.21	21.9
36	61	1990	G.Harris	SD	NL	73	0	117	8	8	9	97	49	2.30	2.68	2.89	21.7
37	14	1996	R.Nen	Fla	NL	75	0	83	5	1	35	92	21	1.95	2.28	2.21	21.7
38	39	1988	M.Davis	SD	NL	62	0	98	5	10	28	102	42	2.01	2.20	2.59	21.4
39	31	1995	S.Reed	Col	NL	71	0	84	5	2	3	79	21	2.14	2.57	2.52	21.4
40	49	1984	C.Lefferts	SD	NL	62	0	106	3	4	10	56	24	2.13	2.47	2.76	21.2
41	9	1993	B.Harvey	Fla	NL	59	0	69	1	5	45	73	13	1.70	1.83	1.84	20.8
42	36	1976	K.Forsch	Hou	NL	52	0	92	4	3	19	49	26	2.15	2.25	2.57	20.3
43	52	1994	T.Jones	Hou	NL	48	0	73	5	2	5	63	26	2.72	2.85	2.79	20.2
44	41	1978	J.D'Acquisto	SD	NL	45	3	93	4	3	10	104	56	2.13	2.32	2.63	19.9
45	69	1992	X.Hernandez	Hou	NL	77	0	111	9	1	7	96	42	2.11	2.51	2.95	19.8
46	55	1981	J.Sambito	Hou	NL	49	0	64	5	5	10	41	22	1.84	2.40	2.81	18.8
47	122	1986	A.McGaffigan	Mon	NL	48	14	143	10	5	2	104	55	2.65	3.09	3.38	18.8
48	109	1986	L.McCullers	SD	NL	70	7	136	10	10	5	92	58	2.78	3.04	3.32	18.7
49	108	1989	G.Harris	SD	NL	56	8	135	8	9	6	106	52	2.60	2.87	3.32	18.6
50	81	1983	L.DeLeon	SD	NL	63	0	111	6	6	13	90	27	2.68	2.76	3.05	18.6

Nineteenth Century Players

The early days of baseball were filled with major instability. Teams frequently switched cities, sometimes in mid-season. New leagues formed, and just as quickly folded. The rules of the game constantly changed. And players either learned to cope with change, or were swept aside. Early superstar Ross Barnes was one of the players who could not adjust. Barnes learned how to get on base by bunting a ball into fair territory that would then roll foul. Barnes used this legal trick to hit .397 over six National Association and National League seasons from 1871 to 1876, including a .429 batting average in the first National League season of 1876. After the rule change in 1877, his average plunged below .300 the remainder of his career.

By the 1890s the game's rules were pretty much the same as today, but the facilities, equipment, player violence, and other factors were still dramatically different. Perhaps the biggest difference was the high rate of errors, affecting pitcher earned run averages positively and runs allowed averages negatively.

The Chicago club dominated the early days of the National League, finishing first in 1876, 1880, 1881, 1882, 1885, and 1886. Cap Anson, a big man for his day at six feet and 227 pounds, was Chicago's best player for most of the 22 years he played, and its manager for the last 19 of those seasons. Other Chicago stars included Barnes, Ned Williamson, manager/ace pitcher Al Spalding (47 wins in 1876), King Kelly, Abner Dalrymple, George Gore, and Jack Clarkson. The 1884 Chicago team finished in fourth place, but the offense hit 142 home runs, with most of these home runs traveling over a very shallow right field fence. Williamson hit 27 home runs (a record for home runs that stood until 1919), Fred Pfeffer hit 25, Dalrymple hit 22, and Anson hit 21. Dan Brouthers, Anson's chief rival for best nineteenth century hitter, led players on all other teams with 14 home runs.

St. Louis fielded the best American Association teams, with titles in 1885, 1886, 1887, and 1888. This fiesty club featured several talented players. Arlie Latham "stole" 129 bases in 1887. (In the 1880s, advancing an extra base on a hit was considered a steal.) That same year, Tip O'Neill hit .435 with 14 home runs for a 1,183 Wtd. Production. Pitchers Bob Caruthers and Dave Foutz were excellent hitters, with Caruthers achieving one of the league's top five batting averages in both 1886 and 1887. Other St. Louis stars included player-manager Charles Comiskey, Yank Robinson, Bill Gleason, and catcher Jocko Milligan, who hit .366 in 1889.

Boston beat out Baltimore for the title of best team of the 1890s, with first place finishes in 1891, 1892, 1893, 1897, and 1898. Kid Nichols, Boston's best player, was a seven-time 30 game winner who won 297 games in the 1890s. In hit-crazy 1894, center fielder Hugh Duffy batted .440 with 51 doubles and 18 home runs, for a 1,196 Production. After adjusting for 15 percent hitter's inflation and a 162 game schedule, Duffy hit only .381 with 20 home runs, for a 1,037 Wtd. Production. Veterans Harry Stovey, King Kelly, and Dan Brouthers—along with Jimmy Collins, Herman Long, Fred Tenney, Bobby Lowe, Billy Hamilton, and Chick Stahl—also contributed to these great Boston teams.

The Baltimore club won in 1894, 1895, and 1896. This team featured a lineup of talented hitters at the peak of the hitter's era of the 1890s. Willie Keeler, Joe Kelley, Hughie Jennings, John McGraw, and Wilbert Robinson all hit for high averages, while Bill Hoffer was 56–13 over the two seasons of 1895 and 1896.

In 1894, Philadelphia assembled one of the most impressive outfields ever, with four .400 hitters! Speedy Billy Hamilton batted .404 with 126 walks, a .523 on-base percentage, and a league-leading 98 stolen bases. Hamilton's 931 Total Factor does not reflect the potential value of his stolen bases. Slugging Sam Thompson batted .407 with 29 doubles, 27 triples and 13 home runs in 437 at bats, for a 1,023 Total Factor. The team's best player of the 1890s, Ed Delahanty, hit .407 with 61 extra-base hits, for a 972 Total Factor. And Tuck Turner hit a team high .416 with 30 extra-base hits in 339 at bats—but he couldn't break into a starting lineup that featured three Hall of Fame outfielders.

1876 - 1887   **Hitters Volume of Success**

Pos	Year	Name	T	L	AB	BB	HBP	TAB	H	2B	3B	HR	BA	OB	SA	PRO	Wtd PRO	SB	CS	SBF	SPF	FF	R TF	V HC
C	1876	D.White	Chi	NL	303	7	0	310	104	18	1	1	.343	.358	.419	777	917				0	40	957	103.1
1B	1886	D.Brouthers	Det	NL	489	66	0	555	181	40	15	11	.370	.445	.581	1,026	1,130	21			0	(10)	1,120	120.8
2B	1876	R.Barnes	Chi	NL	322	20	0	342	138	21	14	1	.429	.462	.590	1,052	1,242				10	50	1,302	250.4
SS	1878	B.Ferguson	Chi	NL	259	10	0	269	91	10	2	0	.351	.375	.405	781	922				0	80	1,002	115.6
3B	1876	C.Anson	Chi	NL	309	12	0	321	110	9	7	2	.356	.380	.450	830	980				0	50	1,030	119.5
OF	1887	T.O'Neill	StL	AA	517	50	5	572	225	52	19	14	.435	.490	.691	1,180	1,183	30			10	(10)	1,183	136.7
OF	1886	K.Kelly	Chi	NL	451	83	0	534	175	32	11	4	.388	.483	.534	1,018	1,121	53			10	10	1,141	127.3
OF	1879	C.Jones	Bos	NL	355	29	0	384	112	22	10	9	.315	.367	.510	877	1,034				0	50	1,084	120.8
Starters	Averages				376	35	1	411	142	26	10	5	.378	.431	.540	972	1,086	13	0	0	4	33	1,123	136.8
C	1881	C.Bennett	Det	NL	299	18	0	317	90	18	7	7	.301	.341	.478	819	922				0	100	1,022	100.4
1B	1885	R.Connor	NY	NL	455	51	0	506	169	23	15	1	.371	.435	.495	929	1,082				0	10	1,092	113.5
2B	1884	F.Dunlap	StL	U	449	29	0	478	185	39	8	13	.412	.448	.621	1,069	1,283				0	100	1,383	240.7
SS	1882	J.Glasscock	Cle	NL	358	13	0	371	104	27	9	4	.291	.315	.450	765	868				10	100	978	107.2
3B	1884	N.Williamson	Chi	NL	417	42	0	459	116	18	8	27	.278	.344	.554	898	1,013				10	70	1,093	117.0
OF	1884	O.Shaffer	StL	U	467	30	0	497	168	40	10	2	.360	.398	.501	899	1,080				0	0	1,080	115.6
OF	1885	P.Browning	Lou	AA	481	25	0	506	174	34	10	9	.362	.393	.530	923	1,051				10	20	1,081	114.0
OF	1879	P.Hines	Pro	NL	409	8	0	417	146	25	10	2	.357	.369	.482	851	1,003				0	30	1,033	110.8
Reserves	Averages				417	27	0	444	144	28	10	8	.345	.385	.517	902	1,050	0	0	0	4	54	1,107	127.4
Totals	Weighted Ave.				389	32	0	422	143	26	10	6	.367	.416	.533	949	1,074	9	0	0	4	40	1,117	133.7

Pitchers Volume of Success

Pos	Year	Name	T	L	G	GS	IP	W	L	SV	SO	BB	ERA	RA/9	Wtd RA/9	R V Runs /162
SP	1876	G.Bradley	StL	NL	64	64	573	45	19	0	103	38	1.23	3.60	2.82	275.0
SP	1884	O.Radbourn	Pro	NL	75	73	679	59	12	1	441	98	1.38	2.86	2.32	239.9
SP	1876	A.Spalding	Chi	NL	61	60	529	47	12	0	39	26	1.75	3.85	3.02	225.2
SP	1882	W.White	Cin	AA	54	54	480	40	12	0	122	71	1.54	3.08	2.58	219.5
SP	1884	G.Hecker	Lou	AA	75	73	671	52	20	0	385	56	1.80	3.09	2.61	213.5
SP	1879	T.Bond	Bos	NL	64	64	555	43	19	0	155	24	1.96	3.34	2.88	209.8
SP	1883	T.Keefe	NY	AA	68	68	619	41	27	0	359	108	2.41	3.55	2.78	202.6
SP	1876	J.Devlin	Lou	NL	68	68	622	30	35	0	122	37	1.56	4.47	3.51	181.0
SP	1884	P.Galvin	Buf	NL	72	72	636	46	22	0	369	63	1.99	3.59	2.91	165.3
Totals	Averages - 9 Starters				67	66	596	45	20	0	233	58	1.74	3.49	2.82	214.6

1876 - 1887 — Hitters Rate of Success

Pos	Year	Name	T	L	AB	BB	HBP	TAB	H	2B	3B	HR	BA	OB	SA	PRO	Wtd PRO	SB	CS	SBF	SPF	FF	R TF	V HC
C	1881	C.Bennett	Det	NL	299	18	0	317	90	18	7	7	.301	.341	.478	819	922				0	100	1,022	100.4
1B	1886	D.Brouthers	Det	NL	489	66	0	555	181	40	15	11	.370	.445	.581	1,026	1,130	21			0	(10)	1,120	120.8
2B	1884	F.Dunlap	StL	U	449	29	0	478	185	39	8	13	.412	.448	.621	1,069	1,283				0	100	1,383	240.7
SS	1884	F.Fennelly	Was	AA	379	31	2	412	118	22	15	4	.311	.367	.480	847	990				10	20	1,020	103.4
3B	1884	N.Williamson	Chi	NL	417	42	0	459	116	18	8	27	.278	.344	.554	898	1,013				10	70	1,093	117.0
OF	1887	T.O'Neill	StL	AA	517	50	5	572	225	52	19	14	.435	.490	.691	1,180	1,183	30			10	(10)	1,183	136.7
OF	1886	K.Kelly	Chi	NL	451	83	0	534	175	32	11	4	.388	.483	.534	1,018	1,121	53			10	10	1,141	127.3
OF	1879	C.Jones	Bos	NL	355	29	0	384	112	22	10	9	.315	.367	.510	877	1,034				0	50	1,084	120.8
Starters		Averages			420	44	1	464	150	30	12	11	.358	.420	.566	985	1,099	13	0	0	5	41	1,145	133.4
C	1885	B.Ewing	NY	NL	342	13	0	355	104	15	12	6	.304	.330	.471	800	932				0	60	992	77.7
1B	1885	R.Connor	NY	NL	455	51	0	506	169	23	15	1	.371	.435	.495	929	1,082				0	10	1,092	113.5
2B	1876	R.Barnes	Chi	NL	322	20	0	342	138	21	14	1	.429	.462	.590	1,052	1,242				10	50	1,302	250.4
SS	1878	B.Ferguson	Chi	NL	259	10	0	269	91	10	2	0	.351	.375	.405	781	922				0	80	1,002	115.6
3B	1876	C.Anson	Chi	NL	309	12	0	321	110	9	7	2	.356	.380	.450	830	980				0	50	1,030	119.5
OF	1885	P.Browning	Lou	AA	481	25	0	506	174	34	10	9	.362	.393	.530	923	1,051				10	20	1,081	114.0
OF	1884	O.Shaffer	StL	U	467	30	0	497	168	40	10	2	.360	.398	.501	899	1,080				0	0	1,080	115.6
OF	1876	G.Hall	Phi	NL	268	8	0	276	98	7	13	5	.366	.384	.545	929	1,096				0	(20)	1,076	104.6
Reserves		Averages			363	21	0	384	132	20	10	3	.362	.397	.501	899	1,054	0	0	0	3	31	1,087	126.3
Totals		Weighted Ave.			401	36	1	437	144	27	11	9	.360	.412	.544	956	1,084	9	0	0	4	38	1,126	131.0

Pitchers Rate of Success

Pos	Year	Name	T	L	G	GS	IP	W	L	SV	SO	BB	ERA	RA/9	Wtd RA/9	R Runs /162
SP	1880	T.Keefe	Tro	NL	12	12	105	6	6	0	39	16	0.86	2.31	2.21	52.2
SP	1884	O.Radbourn	Pro	NL	75	73	679	59	12	1	441	98	1.38	2.86	2.32	239.9
SP	1882	W.White	Cin	AA	54	54	480	40	12	0	122	71	1.54	3.08	2.58	219.5
SP	1884	C.Sweeney	StL	U	60	56	492	41	15	1	337	42	1.70	3.33	2.59	163.2
SP	1884	G.Hecker	Lou	AA	75	73	671	52	20	0	385	56	1.80	3.09	2.61	213.5
SP	1886	C.Ferguson	Phi	NL	48	45	396	30	9	2	212	69	1.98	3.30	2.74	104.2
SP	1885	M.Welch	NY	NL	56	55	492	44	11	1	258	131	1.66	3.11	2.79	141.0
SP	1882	D.Driscoll	Pit	AA	23	23	201	13	9	0	59	12	1.21	3.27	2.79	81.9
SP	1884	C.Buffinton	Bos	NL	67	67	587	48	16	0	417	76	2.15	3.45	2.80	163.1
Totals		Averages - 9 Starters			52	51	456	37	12	1	252	63	1.69	3.14	2.62	153.2

Nineteenth Century Players

1876-1887
Catchers

V	R	Year	Name	T	L	AB	BB	HBP	TAB	H	2B	3B	HR	BA	OB	SA	PRO	Wtd PRO	SB	CS	SBF	SPF	FF	R TF	V HC
1	5	1876	D.White	Chi	NL	303	7		310	104	18	1	1	.343	.358	.419	777	917					40	957	103.1
2	1	1881	C.Bennett	Det	NL	299	18		317	90	18	7	7	.301	.341	.478	819	922					100	1,022	100.4
3	8	1882	C.Bennett	Det	NL	342	20		362	103	16	10	5	.301	.340	.450	790	897					40	937	85.7
4	7	1878	L.Brown	Pro	NL	243	7		250	74	21	6	1	.305	.324	.453	777	917				(10)	30	937	82.1
5	10	1879	D.White	Cin	NL	333	6		339	110	16	6	1	.330	.342	.423	766	902					20	922	80.1
6	9	1883	B.Ewing	NY	NL	376	20		396	114	11	13	10	.303	.338	.481	820	890					40	930	78.1
7	2	1885	B.Ewing	NY	NL	342	13		355	104	15	12	6	.304	.330	.471	800	932					60	992	77.7
8	17	1877	C.McVey	Chi	NL	266	8		274	98	9	7	0	.368	.387	.455	842	948				10	(60)	898	77.6
9	3	1882	J.O'Brien	Phi	AA	241	13		254	73	13	3	3	.303	.339	.419	758	919					60	979	75.8
10	6	1885	C.Bennett	Det	NL	349	47		396	94	24	13	5	.269	.356	.456	812	945						945	73.8
11	14	1886	J.Kerins	Lou	AA	487	66	3	556	131	19	9	4	.269	.360	.370	729	820	26				90	910	71.7
12	16	1883	C.Bennett	Det	NL	371	26		397	113	34	7	5	.305	.350	.474	825	895					10	905	70.6
13	13	1886	F.Carroll	Pit	AA	486	52	4	542	140	28	11	5	.288	.362	.422	783	881	20				30	911	70.2
14	11	1884	B.Ewing	NY	NL	382	28		410	106	15	20	3	.277	.327	.445	772	870					50	920	67.4
15	18	1880	J.Clapp	Cin	NL	323	21		344	91	16	4	1	.282	.326	.365	691	831					60	891	66.7
16	20	1882	P.Snyder	Cin	AA	309	9		318	90	12	2	1	.291	.311	.353	664	805					80	885	65.5
17	21	1884	J.Rowe	Buf	NL	400	23		423	126	14	14	4	.315	.352	.450	802	905					(20)	885	59.3
18	22	1882	B.Taylor	Pit	AA	299	7		306	84	16	13	3	.281	.297	.452	749	908					(40)	868	57.8
19	4	1884	F.Carroll	Col	AA	252	13	5	270	70	13	5	6	.278	.326	.440	766	896					70	966	54.6
20	27	1879	S.Flint	Chi	NL	324	6		330	92	22	6	1	.284	.297	.398	695	819					20	839	51.5
21	30	1876	J.Clapp	StL	NL	298	8		306	91	4	2	0	.305	.324	.332	656	774					40	814	49.7
22	19	1881	J.Rowe	Buf	NL	246	1		247	82	11	11	1	.333	.336	.480	816	918					(30)	888	47.9
23	29	1883	J.O'Brien	Phi	AA	390	25		415	113	14	10	0	.290	.333	.377	709	817						817	45.9
24	15	1884	J.Milligan	Phi	AA	268	8	0	276	77	20	3	3	.287	.308	.418	726	848				(10)	70	908	44.7
25	12	1886	B.Ewing	NY	NL	275	16		291	85	11	7	4	.309	.347	.444	791	871	18				40	911	42.3

1876-1887
First basemen

V	R	Year	Name	T	L	AB	BB	HBP	TAB	H	2B	3B	HR	BA	OB	SA	PRO	Wtd PRO	SB	CS	SBF	SPF	FF	R TF	V HC
1	1	1886	D.Brouthers	Det	NL	489	66		555	181	40	15	11	.370	.445	.581	1,026	1,130	21				(10)	1,120	120.8
2	2	1881	C.Anson	Chi	NL	343	26		369	137	21	7	1	.399	.442	.510	952	1,072					40	1,112	115.9
3	6	1885	R.Connor	NY	NL	455	51		506	169	23	15	1	.371	.435	.495	929	1,082					10	1,092	113.5
4	5	1886	C.Anson	Chi	NL	504	55		559	187	35	11	10	.371	.433	.544	977	1,075	29				20	1,095	113.2
5	4	1882	D.Brouthers	Buf	NL	351	21		372	129	23	11	6	.368	.403	.547	950	1,078					20	1,098	111.6
6	9	1877	D.White	Bos	NL	266	8		274	103	14	11	2	.387	.405	.545	950	1,070						1,070	105.7
7	3	1885	D.Brouthers	Buf	NL	407	34		441	146	32	11	7	.359	.408	.543	951	1,108						1,108	103.6
8	8	1884	H.Stovey	Phi	AA	448	26	4	478	146	22	23	10	.326	.368	.545	913	1,067					10	1,077	102.9
9	7	1884	L.Reilly	Cin	AA	448	5	14	467	152	24	19	11	.339	.366	.551	918	1,072					10	1,082	102.3
10	10	1883	D.Brouthers	Buf	NL	425	16		441	159	41	17	3	.374	.397	.572	969	1,052					10	1,062	100.4
11	12	1886	R.Connor	NY	NL	485	41		526	172	29	20	7	.355	.405	.540	945	1,041	17				20	1,061	95.2
12	13	1884	C.Anson	Chi	NL	475	29		504	159	30	3	21	.335	.373	.543	916	1,033					10	1,043	93.2
13	11	1884	D.Brouthers	Buf	NL	398	33		431	130	22	15	14	.327	.378	.563	941	1,061						1,061	84.9
14	19	1885	H.Stovey	Phi	AA	486	39	4	529	153	27	9	13	.315	.371	.488	858	977				10	10	997	83.5
15	17	1883	E.Swartwood	Pit	AA	412	25		437	147	24	8	3	.357	.394	.476	869	1,001					10	1,011	83.4
16	15	1882	C.Anson	Chi	NL	348	20		368	126	29	8	1	.362	.397	.500	897	1,018						1,018	83.3
17	14	1884	D.Orr	NY	AA	458	5	1	464	162	32	13	9	.354	.362	.539	901	1,053			(10)	(20)	1,023	82.5
18	18	1883	H.Stovey	Phi	AA	421	27		448	128	31	6	14	.304	.346	.506	852	981				10	10	1,001	81.9
19	16	1882	R.Connor	Tro	NL	349	13		362	115	22	18	4	.330	.354	.530	884	1,003					10	1,013	80.3
20	22	1883	R.Connor	NY	NL	409	25		434	146	28	15	1	.357	.394	.506	900	978					10	988	73.6
21	23	1887	D.Brouthers	Det	NL	500	71	6	577	169	36	20	12	.338	.426	.562	988	987	34				(10)	977	72.5
22	21	1886	D.Orr	NY	AA	571	17	5	593	193	25	31	7	.338	.363	.527	890	1,000	16		(10)			990	72.5
23	20	1885	D.Orr	NY	AA	444	8	3	455	152	29	21	6	.342	.358	.543	901	1,026			(10)	(20)		996	71.5
24	24	1887	C.Anson	Chi	NL	472	60	1	533	164	33	13	7	.347	.422	.517	939	938	27				30	968	64.0
25	26	1885	C.Anson	Chi	NL	464	34		498	144	35	7	7	.310	.357	.461	819	954						954	63.6

1876-1887
Second basemen

V	R	Year	Name	T	L	AB	BB	HBP	TAB	H	2B	3B	HR	BA	OB	SA	PRO	Wtd PRO	SB	CS	SBF	SPF	FF	R TF	V HC
1	2	1876	R.Barnes	Chi	NL	322	20		342	138	21	14	1	.429	.462	.590	1,052	1,242				10	50	1,302	250.4
2	1	1884	F.Dunlap	StL	U	449	29		478	185	39	8	13	.412	.448	.621	1,069	1,283					100	1,383	240.7
3	3	1882	P.Browning	Lou	AA	288	26		314	109	17	3	5	.378	.430	.510	940	1,141				10	50	1,201	160.1
4	4	1884	F.Pfeffer	Chi	NL	467	25		492	135	10	10	25	.289	.325	.514	839	946				10	120	1,076	130.2
5	6	1884	S.Barkley	Tol	AA	435	22	2	459	133	39	9	1	.306	.342	.444	786	918					70	988	97.6
6	5	1885	H.Richardson	Buf	NL	426	20		446	136	19	11	6	.319	.350	.458	808	941				10	40	991	94.7
7	7	1886	B.McPhee	Cin	AA	560	59	5	624	150	23	12	8	.268	.343	.395	738	829	40			10	90	929	84.5
8	8	1881	F.Dunlap	Cle	NL	351	18		369	114	25	4	3	.325	.358	.444	802	903					20	923	80.6
9	9	1883	H.Richardson	Buf	NL	399	22		421	124	34	7	1	.311	.347	.439	785	853				10	60	923	78.0
10	11	1883	J.Farrell	Pro	NL	420	15		435	128	24	11	3	.305	.329	.436	764	830					80	910	76.3
11	10	1883	F.Dunlap	Cle	NL	396	22		418	129	34	2	4	.326	.361	.452	813	883					30	913	74.3
12	14	1880	F.Dunlap	Cle	NL	373	7		380	103	27	9	4	.276	.289	.429	718	864					30	894	72.0
13	15	1887	H.Richardson	Det	NL	543	31	2	576	178	25	18	8	.328	.366	.484	851	849	29				40	889	71.4
14	12	1884	H.Richardson	Buf	NL	439	22		461	132	27	9	6	.301	.334	.444	778	878				10	20	908	69.4
15	18	1884	R.Connor	NY	NL	477	38		515	151	28	4	4	.317	.367	.417	784	884						884	69.4
16	13	1883	J.Burdock	Bos	NL	400	14		414	132	27	8	5	.330	.353	.475	828	899						899	68.9
17	16	1883	P.Smith	Col	AA	405	22		427	106	14	17	4	.262	.300	.410	710	817				10	60	887	68.2
18	17	1877	J.Gerhardt	Lou	NL	250	5		255	76	6	5	1	.304	.318	.380	698	785					100	885	65.6
19	21	1884	B.McPhee	Cin	AA	450	27	6	483	125	8	7	5	.278	.327	.360	687	803				10	50	863	60.2
20	19	1885	F.Dunlap	StL	NL	423	41		464	114	11	5	2	.270	.334	.333	667	777					90	867	58.8
21	23	1884	P.Smith	Col	AA	445	20	12	477	106	18	10	6	.238	.289	.364	653	764				10	80	854	56.3
22	25	1882	H.Richardson	Buf	NL	354	11		365	96	20	8	2	.271	.293	.390	683	775				10	60	845	53.3
23	22	1886	Y.Robinson	StL	AA	481	64	15	560	132	26	9	3	.274	.377	.385	761	856	51			10	(10)	856	53.0
24	24	1887	F.Pfeffer	Chi	NL	479	34	1	514	133	21	6	16	.278	.327	.447	774	772	57			10	70	852	52.2
25	26	1886	F.Dunlap	Det	NL	481	44		525	132	23	5	7	.274	.335	.387	722	795	20				50	845	52.2

1876-1887
Shortstops

V	R	Year	Name	T	L	AB	BB	HBP	TAB	H	2B	3B	HR	BA	OB	SA	PRO	Wtd PRO	SB	CS	SBF	SPF	FF	R TF	V HC
1	2	1878	B.Ferguson	Chi	NL	259	10		269	91	10	2	0	.351	.375	.405	781	922					80	1,002	115.6
2	3	1882	J.Glasscock	Cle	NL	358	13		371	104	27	9	4	.291	.315	.450	765	868				10	100	978	107.2
3	6	1876	J.Peters	Chi	NL	316	3		319	111	14	2	1	.351	.357	.418	775	915				10	20	945	107.2
4	1	1884	F.Fennelly	Was	AA	379	31	2	412	118	22	15	4	.311	.367	.480	847	990				10	20	1,020	103.4
5	8	1876	G.Wright	Bos	NL	335	8		343	100	18	6	1	.299	.315	.397	712	840				10	60	910	101.1
6	4	1884	J.Glasscock	Cle	NL	453	33		486	142	13	9	3	.313	.360	.402	762	859				10	80	949	94.5
7	5	1886	J.Glasscock	StL	NL	486	38		524	158	29	7	3	.325	.374	.432	806	888	38			10	50	948	93.2
8	7	1884	S.Houck	Phi	AA	472	7	8	487	140	19	14	0	.297	.318	.396	714	835				10	70	915	86.4
9	13	1879	G.Wright	Pro	NL	388	13		401	107	15	10	1	.276	.299	.374	673	793				10	80	883	85.5
10	9	1887	O.Burns	Bal	AA	551	63	5	619	188	33	19	9	.341	.414	.519	933	935	58			10	(40)	905	84.5
11	11	1883	M.Moynahan	Phi	AA	400	31		431	124	18	10	1	.310	.360	.413	772	889				10		899	80.9
12	10	1887	S.Wise	Bos	NL	467	36	7	510	156	27	17	9	.334	.390	.522	913	911	43				(10)	901	74.2
13	14	1877	J.Peters	Chi	NL	265	1		266	84	10	3	0	.317	.320	.377	697	785				10	80	875	72.7
14	16	1882	K.Kelly	Chi	NL	377	10		387	115	37	4	1	.305	.323	.432	755	857				10		867	72.5
15	12	1885	S.Wise	Bos	NL	424	25		449	120	20	10	4	.283	.323	.406	729	849					40	889	70.8
16	17	1885	F.Fennelly	Cin	AA	454	38	3	495	124	14	17	10	.273	.333	.445	778	886				10	(30)	866	70.2
17	21	1887	M.Ward	NY	NL	545	29	4	578	184	16	5	1	.338	.375	.391	766	765	111			10	80	855	67.8
18	15	1886	F.Fennelly	Cin	AA	497	60	18	575	124	13	17	6	.249	.351	.380	732	822	32			10	40	872	67.2
19	18	1883	J.Richmond	Col	AA	385	25		410	109	7	8	0	.283	.327	.343	670	771					90	861	64.6
20	23	1882	B.Gleason	StL	AA	347	6		353	100	11	6	1	.288	.300	.363	663	805				10	30	845	63.8
21	22	1885	J.Glasscock	StL	NL	446	29		475	125	18	3	1	.280	.324	.341	665	775				10	70	855	63.6
22	24	1880	A.Irwin	Wor	NL	352	11		363	91	19	4	1	.259	.281	.344	625	751					90	841	59.1
23	20	1885	G.Smith	Bkn	AA	419	10	0	429	108	17	11	4	.258	.275	.379	655	745					110	855	57.6
24	29	1883	C.Nelson	NY	AA	417	31		448	127	19	6	0	.305	.353	.379	732	842					(20)	822	56.9
25	25	1885	T.Burns	Chi	NL	445	16		461	121	23	9	7	.272	.297	.411	708	825				10		835	55.5

Nineteenth Century Players

1876-1887
Third basemen

V	R	Year	Name	T	L	AB	BB	HBP	TAB	H	2B	3B	HR	BA	OB	SA	PRO	Wtd PRO	SB	CS	SBF	SPF	FF	R TF	V HC
1	2	1879	K.Kelly	Cin	NL	345	8		353	120	20	12	2	.348	.363	.493	855	1,008				10	50	1,068	119.8
2	3	1876	C.Anson	Chi	NL	309	12		321	110	9	7	2	.356	.380	.450	830	980					50	1,030	119.5
3	1	1884	N.Williamson	Chi	NL	417	42		459	116	18	8	27	.278	.344	.554	898	1,013				10	70	1,093	117.0
4	4	1879	N.Williamson	Chi	NL	320	24		344	94	20	13	1	.294	.343	.447	790	931				10	70	1,011	97.8
5	5	1882	H.Carpenter	Cin	AA	351	10		361	120	15	5	1	.342	.360	.422	782	948				10	20	978	93.6
6	6	1884	E.Sutton	Bos	NL	468	29		497	162	28	7	3	.346	.384	.455	839	947					10	957	80.9
7	9	1887	D.Lyons	Phi	AA	570	47	6	623	209	43	14	6	.367	.421	.523	943	946	73			10	(10)	946	80.3
8	8	1884	P.Browning	Lou	AA	447	13	2	462	150	33	8	4	.336	.357	.472	829	969				10	(30)	949	75.5
9	7	1880	R.Connor	Tro	NL	340	13		353	113	18	8	3	.332	.357	.459	816	981					(30)	951	75.3
10	12	1884	D.Esterbrook	NY	AA	477	12	10	499	150	29	11	1	.314	.345	.428	772	903					20	923	72.3
11	11	1877	C.Anson	Chi	NL	255	9		264	86	19	1	0	.337	.360	.420	779	878					50	928	71.8
12	13	1882	N.Williamson	Chi	NL	348	27		375	98	27	4	3	.282	.333	.408	741	841				10	70	921	70.3
13	10	1884	J.Gleason	StL	U	395	23		418	128	30	2	4	.324	.361	.441	802	963					(20)	943	68.2
14	17	1884	A.Latham	StL	AA	474	18	6	498	130	17	12	1	.274	.309	.367	676	790				10	100	900	64.4
15	15	1883	E.Sutton	Bos	NL	414	17		431	134	28	15	3	.324	.350	.486	836	908						908	64.4
16	14	1876	L.Meyerle	Phi	NL	256	3		259	87	12	8	0	.340	.347	.449	797	940					(20)	920	62.8
17	16	1887	J.Denny	Ind	NL	510	13	3	526	165	34	12	11	.324	.344	.502	846	845	29				60	905	60.3
18	18	1884	Y.Robinson	Bal	U	415	37		452	111	24	4	3	.267	.327	.366	694	833				10	50	893	57.6
19	20	1885	E.Sutton	Bos	NL	457	17		474	143	23	8	4	.313	.338	.425	762	888						888	56.5
20	21	1883	N.Williamson	Chi	NL	402	22		424	111	49	5	2	.276	.314	.438	751	816				10	60	886	56.2
21	19	1884	F.Corey	Phi	AA	439	17	2	458	121	17	16	5	.276	.306	.421	727	850					40	890	55.8
22	22	1884	D.White	Buf	NL	452	32		484	147	16	11	5	.325	.370	.442	812	916			(10)	(20)		886	55.6
23	23	1876	J.Battin	StL	NL	283	6		289	85	11	4	0	.300	.315	.367	682	805					70	875	54.7
24	28	1886	A.Latham	StL	AA	578	55	6	639	174	23	8	1	.301	.368	.374	741	833	60			10		843	45.1
25	27	1885	N.Williamson	Chi	NL	407	75		482	97	16	5	3	.238	.357	.324	681	793				10	40	843	42.7

1876-1887
Outfielders

V	R	Year	Name	T	L	AB	BB	HBP	TAB	H	2B	3B	HR	BA	OB	SA	PRO	Wtd PRO	SB	CS	SBF	SPF	FF	R TF	V HC
1	1	1887	T.O'Neill	StL	AA	517	50	5	572	225	52	19	14	.435	.490	.691	1,180	1,183	30			10	(10)	1,183	136.7
2	2	1886	K.Kelly	Chi	NL	451	83		534	175	32	11	4	.388	.483	.534	1,018	1,121	53			10	10	1,141	127.3
3	3	1879	C.Jones	Bos	NL	355	29		384	112	22	10	9	.315	.367	.510	877	1,034					50	1,084	120.8
4	5	1884	O.Shaffer	StL	U	467	30		497	168	40	10	2	.360	.398	.501	899	1,080						1,080	115.6
5	4	1885	P.Browning	Lou	AA	481	25	0	506	174	34	10	9	.362	.393	.530	923	1,051				10	20	1,081	114.0
6	14	1879	P.Hines	Pro	NL	409	8		417	146	25	10	2	.357	.369	.482	851	1,003				30		1,033	110.8
7	6	1876	G.Hall	Phi	NL	268	8		276	98	7	13	5	.366	.384	.545	929	1,096					(20)	1,076	104.6
8	8	1884	K.Kelly	Chi	NL	452	46		498	160	28	5	13	.354	.414	.524	938	1,058				10	(10)	1,058	101.3
9	10	1885	H.Larkin	Phi	AA	453	26	5	484	149	37	14	8	.329	.372	.525	897	1,022				30		1,052	99.0
10	19	1886	H.Richardson	Det	NL	538	46		584	189	27	11	11	.351	.402	.504	906	998	42			20		1,018	94.7
11	16	1878	O.Shaffer	Ind	NL	266	13		279	90	19	6	0	.338	.369	.455	824	973				10	40	1,023	93.7
12	9	1880	G.Gore	Chi	NL	322	21		343	116	23	2	2	.360	.399	.463	862	1,037					20	1,057	93.2
13	15	1887	P.Browning	Lou	AA	547	55	8	610	220	35	16	4	.402	.464	.547	1,011	1,013	103			10		1,023	91.0
14	18	1882	E.Swartwood	Pit	AA	325	21		346	107	18	11	4	.329	.370	.489	859	1,042				10	(30)	1,022	90.6
15	20	1887	S.Thompson	Det	NL	545	32	9	586	203	29	23	10	.372	.416	.565	982	980	22			10	20	1,010	90.0
16	22	1884	C.Jones	Cin	AA	472	37	10	519	148	19	17	7	.314	.376	.470	846	989					10	999	87.9
17	17	1878	P.Hines	Pro	NL	257	2		259	92	13	4	4	.358	.363	.486	849	1,003					20	1,023	86.9
18	12	1879	J.O'Rourke	Bos	NL	317	8		325	108	17	11	6	.341	.357	.521	877	1,034			(10)		10	1,034	86.7
19	24	1885	G.Gore	Chi	NL	441	68		509	138	21	13	5	.313	.405	.454	858	1,000				(10)		990	82.2
20	26	1878	A.Dalrymple	Mil	NL	271	6		277	96	10	4	0	.354	.368	.421	789	931				10	40	981	78.4
21	28	1877	J.O'Rourke	Bos	NL	265	20		285	96	14	4	0	.362	.407	.445	852	960				10		970	77.8
22	27	1880	A.Dalrymple	Chi	NL	382	3		385	126	25	12	0	.330	.335	.458	793	954					20	974	75.7
23	29	1885	C.Jones	Cin	AA	487	21	9	517	157	19	17	5	.322	.362	.462	824	938					30	968	75.6
24	25	1877	C.Jones	Cin	NL	240	15		255	75	12	10	2	.313	.353	.471	824	927					60	987	75.5
25	30	1876	P.Hines	Chi	NL	305	1		306	101	21	3	2	.331	.333	.439	773	912				10	40	962	74.4

1876-1887
Outfielders

V	R	Year	Name	T	L	AB	BB	HBP	TAB	H	2B	3B	HR	BA	OB	SA	PRO	Wtd PRO	SB	CS	SBF	SPF	FF	R TF	V HC
26	33	1879	J.O'Rourke	Pro	NL	362	13		375	126	19	9	1	.348	.371	.459	829	977					10	(30)	957	72.3
27	32	1886	T.O'Neill	StL	AA	579	47	7	633	190	28	14	3	.328	.385	.440	826	928	9				10	20	958	70.6
28	11	1887	B.Caruthers	StL	AA	364	66	6	436	130	23	11	8	.357	.463	.547	1,010	1,013	49					30	1,043	69.8
29	35	1878	T.York	Pro	NL	269	8		277	83	19	10	1	.309	.329	.465	793	936						20	956	69.7
30	40	1884	A.Dalrymple	Chi	NL	521	14		535	161	18	9	22	.309	.327	.505	832	938						10	948	69.1
31	36	1886	H.Larkin	Phi	AA	565	59	7	631	180	36	16	2	.319	.390	.450	839	944	32					10	954	68.7
32	34	1886	G.Gore	Chi	NL	444	102		546	135	20	12	6	.304	.434	.444	878	967	23					(10)	957	67.7
33	7	1886	B.Caruthers	StL	AA	317	64	1	382	106	21	14	4	.334	.448	.527	974	1,095	26					(20)	1,075	67.4
34	37	1884	J.O'Rourke	Buf	NL	467	35		502	162	33	7	5	.347	.392	.480	872	983						(30)	953	66.6
35	39	1876	L.Pike	StL	NL	282	8		290	91	19	10	1	.323	.341	.472	813	960					10	(20)	950	66.2
36	38	1883	G.Gore	Chi	NL	392	27		419	131	30	9	2	.334	.377	.472	849	922						30	952	63.6
37	23	1881	D.Brouthers	Buf	NL	270	18		288	86	18	9	8	.319	.361	.541	902	1,015						(20)	995	63.0
38	53	1876	J.O'Rourke	Bos	NL	312	15		327	102	17	3	2	.327	.358	.420	778	918					10	(10)	918	62.4
39	44	1884	E.Seery	Bal	U	467	21		488	146	26	7	2	.313	.342	.411	753	904					10	20	934	62.3
40	41	1885	K.Kelly	Chi	NL	438	46		484	126	24	7	9	.288	.355	.436	791	922					10	10	942	62.1
41	52	1885	A.Dalrymple	Chi	NL	492	46		538	135	27	12	11	.274	.336	.445	782	910						10	920	61.0
42	31	1883	P.Browning	Lou	AA	358	23		381	121	15	9	4	.338	.378	.464	842	969					10	(20)	959	60.9
43	21	1884	B.Hoover	Phi	U	317	16		333	108	21	8	1	.341	.372	.467	839	1,008							1,008	60.1
44	42	1877	J.Cassidy	Har	NL	251	3		254	95	10	5	0	.378	.386	.458	844	950					10	(20)	940	59.7
45	54	1882	G.Gore	Chi	NL	367	29		396	117	15	7	3	.319	.369	.422	791	898						20	918	58.0
46	48	1878	C.Jones	Cin	NL	261	4		265	81	11	7	3	.310	.321	.441	761	899						30	929	57.4
47	45	1884	G.Gore	Chi	NL	422	61		483	134	18	4	5	.318	.404	.415	818	923						10	933	57.4
48	47	1883	C.Jones	Cin	AA	391	20		411	115	15	12	10	.294	.328	.471	799	920						10	930	56.2
49	43	1886	H.Stovey	Phi	AA	489	64	1	554	144	28	11	7	.294	.377	.440	817	918	68				10	10	938	55.6
50	50	1886	S.Thompson	Det	NL	503	35		538	156	18	13	8	.310	.355	.445	800	881	13				10	30	921	54.9
51	57	1880	P.Hines	Pro	NL	374	13		387	115	20	2	3	.307	.331	.396	726	874						40	914	54.9
52	59	1882	P.Hines	Pro	NL	379	10		389	117	28	10	4	.309	.326	.467	793	901						10	911	54.4
53	62	1884	P.Hines	Pro	NL	490	44		534	148	36	10	3	.302	.360	.435	794	896						10	906	53.6
54	13	1885	S.Thompson	Det	NL	254	16		270	77	11	9	7	.303	.344	.500	844	984					10	40	1,034	51.9
55	63	1882	M.Mansell	Pit	AA	347	7		354	96	18	16	2	.277	.291	.438	729	884					10	10	904	51.4
56	66	1886	P.Hines	Was	NL	487	35		522	152	30	8	9	.312	.358	.462	820	903	21					10	913	50.7
57	65	1884	H.Moore	Was	U	461	19		480	155	23	5	1	.336	.363	.414	777	933						(30)	903	50.3
58	60	1881	H.Richardson	Buf	NL	344	12		356	100	18	9	2	.291	.315	.413	727	819					10	80	909	49.6
59	67	1880	J.O'Rourke	Bos	NL	363	21		384	100	20	11	6	.275	.315	.441	756	909						(10)	899	49.4
60	72	1878	D.Higham	Pro	NL	281	5		286	90	22	1	1	.320	.332	.416	749	884						10	894	49.3
61	46	1884	F.Mann	Col	AA	366	25	11	402	101	12	18	7	.276	.341	.464	805	941					10	(20)	931	49.0
62	61	1885	N.Hanlon	Det	NL	424	47		471	128	18	8	1	.302	.372	.389	761	886					10	10	906	48.7
63	74	1883	G.Wood	Det	NL	441	25		466	133	26	11	5	.302	.339	.444	784	851					10	30	891	48.5
64	66	1885	T.Brown	Pit	AA	437	34	7	478	134	16	12	4	.307	.366	.426	792	901					10	(10)	901	47.9
65	71	1879	T.York	Pro	NL	342	19		361	106	25	5	1	.310	.346	.421	767	904						(10)	894	47.7
66	76	1885	J.O'Rourke	NY	NL	477	40		517	143	21	16	5	.300	.354	.442	796	928						(40)	888	46.8
67	70	1881	K.Kelly	Chi	NL	353	16		369	114	27	3	2	.323	.352	.433	786	885					10		895	46.5
68	49	1886	P.Browning	Lou	AA	467	30	7	504	159	29	6	2	.340	.389	.441	830	933	26				10	(20)	923	46.3
69	78	1884	D.Rowe	StL	U	485	10		495	142	32	11	4	.293	.307	.429	736	883							883	45.0
70	81	1877	G.Hall	Lou	NL	269	12		281	87	15	8	0	.323	.352	.439	791	891						(10)	881	44.5
71	90	1876	D.Higham	Har	NL	312	2		314	102	21	2	0	.327	.331	.407	738	871							871	42.5
72	75	1884	C.Crane	Bos	U	428	14		442	122	23	6	12	.285	.308	.451	759	911						(20)	891	42.5
73	68	1880	J.O'Rourke	Bos	NL	313	18		331	86	22	8	3	.275	.314	.425	739	889					(10)	20	899	42.5
74	84	1887	J.Fogarty	Phi	NL	495	82	10	587	129	26	12	8	.261	.376	.410	787	785	102				10	80	875	42.1
75	79	1880	H.Stovey	Wor	NL	355	12		367	94	21	14	6	.265	.289	.454	742	893					10	(20)	883	41.8

Nineteenth Century Players

1876-1887
Starting Pitchers

V	R	Year	Name	T	L	G	GS	IP	W	L	SV	SO	BB	ERA	RA/9	R Wtd RA/9	V Runs /162
1	12	1876	G.Bradley	StL	NL	64	64	573	45	19	0	103	38	1.23	3.60	2.82	275.0
2	2	1884	O.Radbourn	Pro	NL	75	73	679	59	12	1	441	98	1.38	2.86	2.32	239.9
3	25	1876	A.Spalding	Chi	NL	61	60	529	47	12	0	39	26	1.75	3.85	3.02	225.2
4	3	1882	W.White	Cin	AA	54	54	480	40	12	0	122	71	1.54	3.08	2.58	219.5
5	5	1884	G.Hecker	Lou	AA	75	73	671	52	20	0	385	56	1.80	3.09	2.61	213.5
6	15	1879	T.Bond	Bos	NL	64	64	555	43	19	0	155	24	1.96	3.34	2.88	209.8
7	7	1883	T.Keefe	NY	AA	68	68	619	41	27	0	359	108	2.41	3.55	2.78	202.6
8	42	1878	T.Bond	Bos	NL	59	59	533	40	19	0	182	33	2.06	3.75	3.31	195.8
9	13	1876	T.Bond	Har	NL	45	45	408	31	13	0	88	13	1.68	3.62	2.84	194.1
10	58	1876	J.Devlin	Lou	NL	68	68	622	30	35	0	122	37	1.56	4.47	3.51	181.0
11	23	1883	O.Radbourn	Pro	NL	76	68	632	48	25	1	315	56	2.05	3.91	3.01	177.2
12	51	1877	T.Bond	Bos	NL	58	58	521	40	17	0	170	36	2.11	4.28	3.45	173.7
13	17	1884	P.Galvin	Buf	NL	72	72	636	46	22	0	369	63	1.99	3.59	2.91	165.3
14	4	1884	C.Sweeney	StL	U	60	56	492	41	15	1	337	42	1.70	3.33	2.59	163.2
15	10	1884	C.Buffinton	Bos	NL	67	67	587	48	16	0	417	76	2.15	3.45	2.80	163.1
16	44	1880	M.Ward	Pro	NL	70	67	595	39	24	1	230	45	1.74	3.48	3.33	154.4
17	32	1883	W.White	Cin	AA	65	64	577	43	22	0	141	104	2.09	3.98	3.12	152.9
18	14	1884	B.Taylor	StL	U	63	59	523	43	16	4	284	84	2.10	3.70	2.87	148.2
19	8	1885	M.Welch	NY	NL	56	55	492	44	11	1	258	131	1.66	3.11	2.79	141.0
20	52	1882	J.McCormick	Cle	NL	68	67	596	36	30	0	200	103	2.37	4.14	3.46	139.1
21	85	1877	J.Devlin	Lou	NL	61	61	559	35	25	0	141	41	2.25	4.64	3.74	137.7
22	31	1885	E.Morris	Pit	AA	63	63	581	39	24	0	298	101	2.35	3.80	3.12	135.4
23	68	1880	J.McCormick	Cle	NL	74	74	658	45	28	0	260	75	1.85	3.75	3.59	134.7
24	66	1879	M.Ward	Pro	NL	70	60	587	47	19	1	239	36	2.15	4.14	3.57	130.8
25	41	1885	J.Clarkson	Chi	NL	70	70	623	53	16	0	308	97	1.85	3.68	3.30	126.9
26	11	1884	E.Morris	Col	AA	52	52	430	34	13	0	302	51	2.18	3.33	2.82	122.5
27	22	1885	B.Caruthers	StL	AA	53	53	482	40	13	0	190	57	2.07	3.66	3.01	121.3
28	57	1880	L.Corcoran	Chi	NL	63	60	536	43	14	2	268	99	1.95	3.66	3.50	119.5
29	29	1884	T.Keefe	NY	AA	58	58	483	37	17	0	334	71	2.25	3.64	3.08	116.9
30	49	1882	O.Radbourn	Pro	NL	55	52	474	33	20	0	201	51	2.09	4.08	3.41	115.7
31	20	1886	L.Baldwin	Det	NL	56	56	487	42	13	0	323	100	2.24	3.59	2.99	111.1
32	59	1882	T.Mullane	Lou	AA	55	55	460	30	24	0	170	78	1.88	4.14	3.53	108.7
33	46	1884	J.McCormick	Cle	NL	66	65	569	40	25	0	343	89	2.37	4.16	3.37	106.4
34	30	1886	E.Morris	Pit	AA	64	63	555	41	20	1	326	118	2.45	3.95	3.09	105.6
35	6	1886	C.Ferguson	Phi	NL	48	45	396	30	9	2	212	69	1.98	3.30	2.74	104.2
36	71	1884	D.Shaw	Bos	U	67	66	643	30	33	0	451	109	2.30	4.65	3.61	102.4
37	24	1886	D.Foutz	StL	AA	59	57	504	41	16	1	283	144	2.11	3.86	3.02	100.5
38	38	1882	L.Corcoran	Chi	NL	39	39	356	27	12	0	170	63	1.95	3.87	3.24	100.2
39	55	1883	J.Whitney	Bos	NL	62	56	514	37	21	2	345	35	2.24	4.52	3.49	100.2
40	48	1883	T.Mullane	StL	AA	53	49	461	35	15	1	191	74	2.19	4.34	3.40	98.1
41	37	1883	J.McGinnis	StL	AA	45	45	383	28	16	0	128	69	2.33	4.09	3.21	95.4
42	69	1878	M.Ward	Pro	NL	37	37	334	22	13	0	116	34	1.51	4.07	3.59	94.9
43	33	1885	T.Keefe	NY	NL	46	46	400	32	13	0	227	102	1.58	3.48	3.12	93.1
44	28	1883	J.McCormick	Cle	NL	43	41	342	28	12	1	145	65	1.84	3.97	3.06	93.0
45	21	1887	E.Smith	Cin	AA	52	52	447	34	17	0	176	126	2.94	4.51	3.00	91.3
46	53	1884	J.Lynch	NY	AA	55	53	496	37	15	0	292	42	2.67	4.10	3.47	88.5
47	108	1879	P.Galvin	Buf	NL	66	66	593	37	27	0	136	31	2.28	4.54	3.91	86.2
48	67	1882	F.Goldsmith	Chi	NL	45	45	405	28	17	0	109	38	2.42	4.27	3.57	85.1
49	54	1886	T.Keefe	NY	NL	64	64	535	42	20	0	297	102	2.56	4.17	3.47	84.6
50	70	1884	M.Welch	NY	NL	65	65	557	39	21	0	345	146	2.50	4.44	3.60	84.1

1876-1887
Starting Pitchers

V	R	Year	Name	T	L	G	GS	IP	W	L	SV	SO	BB	ERA	RA/9	R Wtd RA/9	V Runs /162
51	34	1876	C.Cummings	Har	NL	24	24	216	16	8	0	26	14	1.67	4.04	3.17	83.0
52	9	1882	D.Driscoll	Pit	AA	23	23	201	13	9	0	59	12	1.21	3.27	2.79	81.9
53	102	1883	P.Galvin	Buf	NL	76	75	656	46	29	0	279	50	2.72	5.03	3.88	80.9
54	27	1884	J.Whitney	Bos	NL	38	37	336	23	14	0	270	27	2.09	3.75	3.04	80.4
55	81	1884	T.Mullane	Tol	AA	67	65	567	36	26	0	325	89	2.52	4.38	3.70	79.2
56	19	1886	B.Caruthers	StL	AA	44	43	387	30	14	0	166	86	2.32	3.81	2.98	79.1
57	26	1882	H.McCormick	Cin	AA	25	25	220	14	11	0	33	42	1.52	3.56	3.04	77.1
58	63	1886	T.Ramsey	Lou	AA	67	67	589	38	27	0	499	207	2.45	4.54	3.55	76.9
59	61	1887	J.Clarkson	Chi	NL	60	59	523	38	21	0	237	92	3.08	4.87	3.54	75.4
60	75	1887	M.Kilroy	Bal	AA	69	69	589	46	19	0	217	157	3.07	4.98	3.62	72.3
61	87	1882	S.Wiedman	Det	NL	46	45	411	25	20	0	161	39	2.63	4.47	3.74	71.7
62	16	1880	G.Bradley	Pro	NL	28	20	196	13	8	1	54	6	1.38	3.03	2.90	68.7
63	65	1887	T.Keefe	NY	NL	56	56	477	35	19	0	189	108	3.12	4.89	3.55	67.8
64	89	1882	S.Weaver	Phi	AA	42	41	371	26	15	0	104	35	2.74	4.42	3.77	67.2
65	97	1884	B.Sweeney	Bal	U	62	60	538	40	21	0	374	74	2.59	4.92	3.82	66.7
66	50	1884	F.Mountain	Col	AA	42	41	361	23	17	1	156	78	2.45	4.07	3.44	65.9
67	134	1877	T.Larkin	Har	NL	56	56	501	29	25	0	96	53	2.14	5.12	4.12	65.3
68	45	1887	T.Mullane	Cin	AA	48	48	416	31	17	0	97	121	3.24	5.06	3.36	65.1
69	60	1883	H.Daily	Cle	NL	45	43	379	23	19	1	171	99	2.42	4.59	3.54	64.9
70	88	1884	H.Daily	C-P	U	58	58	501	28	28	0	483	72	2.43	4.82	3.74	64.5
71	124	1880	L.Richmond	Wor	NL	74	66	591	32	32	3	243	74	2.15	4.24	4.06	62.3
72	76	1885	D.Foutz	StL	AA	47	46	408	33	14	0	147	92	2.63	4.42	3.63	61.4
73	86	1884	W.White	Cin	AA	52	52	456	34	18	0	118	74	3.32	4.42	3.74	61.2
74	39	1887	B.Caruthers	StL	AA	39	39	341	29	9	0	74	61	3.30	4.88	3.24	58.7
75	122	1881	J.McCormick	Cle	NL	59	58	526	26	30	0	178	84	2.45	4.57	4.04	57.8
76	40	1880	F.Goldsmith	Chi	NL	26	24	210	21	3	1	90	18	1.75	3.42	3.27	57.0
77	92	1885	O.Radbourn	Pro	NL	49	49	446	28	21	0	154	83	2.20	4.22	3.79	55.8
78	120	1877	T.Nichols	StL	NL	42	39	350	18	23	0	80	53	2.60	5.01	4.03	54.9
79	96	1887	T.Ramsey	Lou	AA	65	64	561	37	27	0	355	167	3.43	5.74	3.81	54.6
80	128	1881	J.Whitney	Bos	NL	66	63	552	31	33	0	162	90	2.48	4.63	4.10	54.4
81	123	1881	G.Derby	Det	NL	56	55	495	29	26	0	212	86	2.20	4.58	4.05	53.5
82	101	1885	G.Hecker	Lou	AA	53	53	480	30	23	0	209	54	2.18	4.72	3.88	53.0
83	1	1880	T.Keefe	Tro	NL	12	12	105	6	6	0	39	16	0.86	2.31	2.21	52.2
84	62	1887	S.King	StL	AA	46	44	390	32	12	1	128	109	3.78	5.33	3.54	51.9
85	84	1887	E.Seward	Phi	AA	55	52	471	25	25	0	155	140	4.13	5.60	3.72	51.6
86	64	1886	J.McCormick	Chi	NL	42	42	348	31	11	0	172	100	2.82	4.27	3.55	50.8
87	47	1887	C.Ferguson	Phi	NL	37	33	297	22	10	1	125	47	3.00	4.66	3.39	49.3
88	82	1886	P.Galvin	Pit	AA	50	50	435	29	21	0	72	75	2.67	4.74	3.71	48.0
89	105	1885	E.Daily	Phi	NL	50	50	440	26	23	0	140	90	2.21	4.34	3.89	47.4
90	36	1878	J.McCormick	Ind	NL	14	14	117	5	8	0	36	15	1.69	3.62	3.20	47.0
91	72	1887	M.Welch	NY	NL	40	40	346	22	15	0	115	91	3.36	4.97	3.61	46.3
92	56	1879	B.Mathews	Pro	NL	27	25	189	12	6	1	90	26	2.29	4.05	3.49	45.4
93	154	1878	W.White	Cin	NL	52	52	468	30	21	0	169	45	1.79	4.79	4.23	45.1
94	99	1887	P.Galvin	Pit	NL	49	48	441	28	21	0	76	67	3.29	5.29	3.84	44.5
95	95	1882	M.Ward	Pro	NL	33	32	278	19	12	1	72	36	2.59	4.56	3.81	44.1
96	116	1885	H.Porter	Bkn	AA	54	54	482	33	21	0	197	107	2.78	4.88	4.01	43.0
97	77	1885	L.McKeon	Cin	AA	33	33	290	20	13	0	117	50	2.86	4.44	3.65	42.9
98	145	1879	T.Larkin	Chi	NL	58	58	513	31	23	0	142	30	2.44	4.86	4.19	42.8
99	121	1884	L.Corcoran	Chi	NL	60	59	517	35	23	0	272	116	2.40	4.98	4.04	42.4
100	94	1884	D.Burns	Cin	U	40	40	330	23	15	0	167	47	2.46	4.89	3.80	42.2

1888 - 1899

Hitters Volume of Success

Pos	Year	Name	T	L	AB	BB	HBP	TAB	H	2B	3B	HR	BA	OB	SA	PRO	Wtd PRO	SB	CS	SBF	SPF	FF	R TF	V HC
C	1888	K.Kelly	Bos	NL	440	31	4	475	140	22	11	9	.318	.368	.480	848	983	56			10	0	993	85.0
1B	1888	C.Anson	Chi	NL	515	47	1	563	177	20	12	12	.344	.400	.499	899	1,042	28			0	40	1,082	99.6
2B	1890	C.Childs	Syr	AA	493	72	6	571	170	33	14	2	.345	.434	.481	915	976	56			10	20	1,006	104.6
SS	1896	H.Jennings	Bal	NL	521	19	51	591	209	27	9	0	.401	.472	.488	960	914	70			10	90	1,014	121.7
3B	1890	D.Lyons	Phi	AA	339	57	10	406	120	29	5	7	.354	.461	.531	992	1,057	21			10	40	1,107	90.8
OF	1896	E.Delahanty	Phi	NL	499	62	9	570	198	44	17	13	.397	.472	.631	1,103	1,051	37			10	40	1,101	114.5
OF	1894	H.Duffy	Bos	NL	539	66	1	606	237	51	16	18	.440	.502	.694	1,196	1,037	48			10	10	1,057	106.1
OF	1888	J.Ryan	Chi	NL	549	35	5	589	182	33	10	16	.332	.377	.515	892	1,034	60			10	30	1,074	106.0
Starters		Averages			487	49	11	546	179	32	12	10	.368	.437	.542	979	1,010	47	0	0	9	34	1,053	103.5
C	1888	B.Ewing	NY	NL	415	24	3	442	127	18	15	6	.306	.348	.465	813	943	53			0	50	993	79.1
1B	1892	D.Brouthers	Bkn	NL	588	84	16	688	197	30	20	5	.335	.432	.480	911	999	31			0	20	1,019	86.1
2B	1890	B.McPhee	Cin	NL	528	82	6	616	135	16	22	3	.256	.362	.386	748	787	55			10	90	887	71.1
SS	1896	B.Dahlen	Chi	NL	474	64	8	546	167	30	19	9	.352	.438	.553	990	944	51			10	70	1,024	115.4
3B	1899	J.Williams	Pit	NL	617	60	6	683	219	28	27	9	.355	.417	.532	949	943	26			0	10	953	81.5
OF	1895	S.Thompson	Phi	NL	538	31	5	574	211	45	21	18	.392	.430	.654	1,085	1,006	27			10	30	1,046	96.1
OF	1896	J.Kelley	Bal	NL	519	91	12	622	189	31	19	8	.364	.469	.543	1,013	965	87			10	10	985	82.7
OF	1889	H.Stovey	Phi	AA	556	77	1	634	171	38	13	19	.308	.393	.525	918	943	63			10	40	993	82.4
Reserves		Averages			529	64	7	601	177	30	20	10	.334	.413	.518	932	942	49	0	0	6	40	988	86.8
Totals		Weighted Ave.			501	54	10	564	178	31	14	10	.357	.429	.534	963	987	48	0	0	8	36	1,031	98.0

Pitchers Volume of Success

Pos	Year	Name	T	L	G	GS	IP	W	L	SV	SO	BB	ERA	RA/9	Wtd RA/9	R Runs /162
SP	1888	S.King	StL	AA	66	65	586	45	21	0	258	76	1.64	3.15	2.72	141.5
SP	1894	A.Rusie	NY	NL	54	50	444	36	13	1	195	200	2.78	4.62	2.75	109.5
SP	1889	J.Clarkson	Bos	NL	73	72	620	49	19	1	284	203	2.73	4.06	3.08	107.1
SP	1888	E.Seward	Phi	AA	57	57	519	35	19	0	272	127	2.01	3.52	3.04	103.6
SP	1888	T.Keefe	NY	NL	51	51	434	35	12	0	335	90	1.74	2.90	2.85	98.2
SP	1892	C.Young	Cle	NL	53	49	453	36	12	0	168	118	1.93	3.14	2.73	97.3
SP	1890	K.Nichols	Bos	NL	48	47	424	27	19	0	222	112	2.23	3.71	2.97	89.9
SP	1890	B.Rhines	Cin	NL	46	45	401	28	17	0	182	113	1.95	3.66	2.93	87.2
SP	1890	S.Stratton	Lou	AA	50	49	431	34	14	0	207	61	2.36	3.88	3.04	87.0
Totals		Averages - 9 Starters			55	54	479	36	16	0	236	122	2.16	3.63	2.90	102.4

1888 - 1899

Hitters Rate of Success

Pos	Year	Name	T	L	AB	BB	HBP	TAB	H	2B	3B	HR	BA	OB	SA	PRO	Wtd PRO	SB	CS	SBF	SPF	FF	R TF	V HC
C	1890	B.Ewing	NY	P	352	39	1	392	119	19	15	8	.338	.406	.545	951	921	36			0	100	1,021	78.7
1B	1888	C.Anson	Chi	NL	515	47	1	563	177	20	12	12	.344	.400	.499	899	1,042	28			0	40	1,082	99.6
2B	1890	C.Childs	Syr	AA	493	72	6	571	170	33	14	2	.345	.434	.481	915	976	56			10	20	1,006	104.6
SS	1896	B.Dahlen	Chi	NL	474	64	8	546	167	30	19	9	.352	.438	.553	990	944	51			10	70	1,024	115.4
3B	1890	D.Lyons	Phi	AA	339	57	10	406	120	29	5	7	.354	.461	.531	992	1,057	21			10	40	1,107	90.8
OF	1896	E.Delahanty	Phi	NL	499	62	9	570	198	44	17	13	.397	.472	.631	1,103	1,051	37			10	40	1,101	114.5
OF	1888	J.Ryan	Chi	NL	549	35	5	589	182	33	10	16	.332	.377	.515	892	1,034	60			10	30	1,074	106.0
OF	1894	H.Duffy	Bos	NL	539	66	1	606	237	51	16	18	.440	.502	.694	1,196	1,037	48			10	10	1,057	106.1
Starters		Averages			470	55	5	530	171	32	14	11	.364	.437	.559	995	1,010	42	0	0	8	44	1,061	102.0
C	1888	K.Kelly	Bos	NL	440	31	4	475	140	22	11	9	.318	.368	.480	848	983	56			10	0	993	85.0
1B	1892	D.Brouthers	Bkn	NL	588	84	16	688	197	30	20	5	.335	.432	.480	911	999	31			0	20	1,019	86.1
2B	1892	B.McPhee	Cin	NL	573	84	7	664	157	19	12	4	.274	.373	.370	743	815	44			10	70	895	70.0
SS	1896	H.Jennings	Bal	NL	521	19	51	591	209	27	9	0	.401	.472	.488	960	914	70			10	90	1,014	121.7
3B	1899	J.McGraw	Bal	NL	399	124	14	537	156	13	3	1	.391	.547	.446	994	988	73			10	10	1,008	78.8
OF	1895	S.Thompson	Phi	NL	538	31	5	574	211	45	21	18	.392	.430	.654	1,085	1,006	27			10	30	1,046	96.1
OF	1893	B.Hamilton	Phi	NL	355	63	13	431	135	22	7	5	.380	.490	.524	1,014	972	43			10	20	1,002	62.1
OF	1895	B.Lange	Chi	NL	478	55	4	537	186	27	16	10	.389	.456	.575	1,032	957	67			10	30	997	74.6
Reserves		Averages			487	61	14	562	174	26	12	7	.357	.444	.501	945	951	51	0	0	9	34	993	84.3
Totals		Weighted Ave.			476	57	8	541	172	30	13	9	.362	.439	.539	978	990	45	0	0	8	40	1,039	96.1

Pitchers Rate of Success

Pos	Year	Name	T	L	G	GS	IP	W	L	SV	SO	BB	ERA	RA/9	Wtd RA/9	R Runs /162
SP	1896	B.Rhines	Cin	NL	19	17	143	8	6	0	32	48	2.45	3.27	2.38	42.4
SP	1898	A.Maul	Bal	NL	28	28	240	20	7	0	31	49	2.10	2.78	2.46	59.0
SP	1898	C.Griffith	Chi	NL	38	38	326	24	10	0	97	64	1.88	2.90	2.57	76.1
SP	1888	S.King	StL	AA	66	65	586	45	21	0	258	76	1.64	3.15	2.72	141.5
SP	1892	C.Young	Cle	NL	53	49	453	36	12	0	168	118	1.93	3.14	2.73	97.3
SP	1894	A.Rusie	NY	NL	54	50	444	36	13	1	195	200	2.78	4.62	2.75	109.5
SP	1899	V.Willis	Bos	NL	41	38	343	27	8	2	120	117	2.50	3.31	2.75	72.6
SP	1897	K.Nichols	Bos	NL	46	40	368	31	11	3	127	68	2.64	3.72	2.77	87.9
SP	1895	B.Hoffer	Bal	NL	41	38	314	31	6	0	80	124	3.21	4.18	2.78	75.7
Totals		Averages - 9 Starters			43	40	357	29	10	1	123	96	2.29	3.49	2.69	84.7

1888-1899
Catchers

V	R	Year	Name	T	L	AB	BB	HBP	TAB	H	2B	3B	HR	BA	OB	SA	PRO	Wtd PRO	SB	CS	SBF	SPF	FF	R TF	V HC
1	3	1888	K.Kelly	Bos	NL	440	31	4	475	140	22	11	9	.318	.368	.480	848	983	56				10	993	85.0
2	2	1888	B.Ewing	NY	NL	415	24	3	442	127	18	15	6	.306	.348	.465	813	943	53				50	993	79.1
3	1	1890	B.Ewing	NY	P	352	39	1	392	119	19	15	8	.338	.406	.545	951	921	36				100	1,021	78.7
4	4	1889	B.Ewing	NY	NL	407	37	0	444	133	23	13	4	.327	.383	.477	860	876	34				90	966	74.2
5	7	1891	J.Milligan	Phi	AA	455	56	15	526	138	35	12	11	.303	.397	.505	903	934	2			(10)		924	71.6
6	5	1889	F.Carroll	Pit	NL	318	85	11	414	105	21	11	2	.330	.486	.484	970	988	19			(30)		958	67.4
7	10	1890	J.O'Connor	Col	AA	457	38	1	496	148	14	10	2	.324	.377	.411	788	841	29				40	881	57.6
8	9	1890	J.Clements	Phi	NL	381	45	3	429	120	23	8	7	.315	.392	.472	864	909	10		(10)			899	54.3
9	6	1895	J.Clements	Phi	NL	322	22	8	352	127	27	2	13	.394	.446	.612	1,058	981	3		(10)	(30)		941	53.9
10	21	1895	D.McGuire	Was	NL	533	40	5	578	179	30	8	10	.336	.388	.478	866	803	16		(10)		30	823	48.9
11	12	1891	L.Cross	Phi	AA	402	38	3	443	121	20	14	5	.301	.366	.458	823	852	14			10		862	45.1
12	8	1899	E.McFarland	Phi	NL	324	36	2	362	108	22	9	2	.333	.403	.475	879	874	9				50	924	44.8
13	16	1891	J.Clements	Phi	NL	423	43	5	471	131	29	4	4	.310	.380	.426	806	853	3		(10)			843	43.5
14	11	1891	K.Kelly	Cin	AA	350	57	3	410	100	16	7	2	.286	.390	.389	779	806	29				60	866	42.7
15	15	1890	K.Kelly	Bos	P	340	52	2	394	111	18	6	4	.326	.419	.450	869	841	51			10		851	40.1
16	22	1890	D.Farrell	Chi	P	451	42	1	494	131	21	12	2	.290	.352	.404	756	732	8				80	812	38.8
17	14	1895	C.Zimmer	Cle	NL	315	33	9	357	107	21	2	5	.340	.417	.467	884	820	14				40	860	37.8
18	19	1892	C.Zimmer	Cle	NL	413	32	7	452	108	29	13	1	.262	.325	.402	727	797	18				40	837	36.3
19	13	1889	J.Keenan	Cin	AA	300	48	6	354	86	10	11	6	.287	.395	.453	849	872	18		(10)			862	36.1
20	18	1892	J.Clements	Phi	NL	402	43	3	448	106	25	6	8	.264	.339	.415	755	827	7		(10)		20	837	36.0
21	23	1891	D.McGuire	Was	AA	413	43	10	466	125	22	10	3	.303	.382	.426	808	836	10		(10)	(20)		806	33.2
22	17	1897	D.McGuire	Was	NL	327	21	2	350	112	17	7	4	.343	.386	.474	860	819	9		(10)		30	839	32.3
23	20	1890	D.McGuire	Roc	AA	331	21	8	360	99	16	4	4	.299	.356	.408	763	814	8		(10)		30	834	32.2
24	30	1891	J.Boyle	StL	AA	439	47	12	498	123	18	8	5	.280	.365	.392	757	801	19			(30)		771	26.2
25	41	1897	K.Douglas	StL	NL	516	52	12	580	170	15	3	6	.329	.403	.405	808	770	12			(20)		750	24.1

1888-1899
First basemen

V	R	Year	Name	T	L	AB	BB	HBP	TAB	H	2B	3B	HR	BA	OB	SA	PRO	Wtd PRO	SB	CS	SBF	SPF	FF	R TF	V HC
1	1	1888	C.Anson	Chi	NL	515	47	1	563	177	20	12	12	.344	.400	.499	899	1,042	28				40	1,082	99.6
2	2	1892	D.Brouthers	Bkn	NL	588	84	16	688	197	30	20	5	.335	.432	.480	911	999	31				20	1,019	86.1
3	6	1888	D.Brouthers	Det	NL	522	68	12	602	160	33	11	9	.307	.399	.464	862	999	34					999	78.4
4	3	1891	D.Brouthers	Bos	AA	486	87	24	597	170	26	19	5	.350	.471	.512	983	1,017	31			(10)		1,007	78.2
5	7	1890	R.Connor	NY	P	484	88	1	573	169	24	15	14	.349	.450	.548	998	966	22				30	996	75.8
6	4	1888	R.Connor	NY	NL	481	73	4	558	140	15	17	14	.291	.389	.480	869	1,007	27					1,007	75.2
7	5	1888	L.Reilly	Cin	AA	527	17	18	562	169	28	14	13	.321	.363	.501	864	996	82			10		1,006	74.9
8	8	1889	D.Brouthers	Bos	NL	485	66	14	565	181	26	9	7	.373	.462	.507	969	987	22					987	71.2
9	10	1892	R.Connor	Phi	NL	564	116	6	686	166	37	11	12	.294	.420	.463	883	967	22					967	68.1
10	9	1889	T.Tucker	Bal	AA	527	42	33	602	196	22	11	5	.372	.450	.484	934	960	63			10		970	66.3
11	11	1889	R.Connor	NY	NL	496	93	2	591	157	32	17	13	.317	.426	.528	955	972	21			(10)		962	66.0
12	13	1890	P.Werden	Tol	AA	498	78	13	589	147	22	20	6	.295	.404	.456	860	917	59			10	10	937	56.2
13	16	1889	C.Anson	Chi	NL	518	86	5	609	161	32	7	7	.311	.414	.440	854	870	27				40	910	49.4
14	15	1897	N.Lajoie	Phi	NL	545	15	12	572	197	40	23	9	.361	.392	.569	960	915	20			10	(10)	915	47.4
15	17	1890	C.Anson	Chi	NL	504	113	6	623	157	14	5	7	.312	.443	.401	844	888	29				10	898	45.5
16	19	1890	D.Brouthers	Bos	P	460	99	18	577	152	36	9	1	.330	.466	.454	921	891	28					891	41.0
17	18	1891	R.Connor	NY	NL	479	83	4	566	139	29	13	7	.290	.399	.449	848	898	27					898	40.4
18	12	1892	B.Ewing	NY	NL	393	38	0	431	122	10	15	8	.310	.371	.473	845	926	42				30	956	40.2
19	21	1890	J.Beckley	Pit	P	516	42	6	564	167	38	22	9	.324	.381	.535	916	887	18			10	(10)	887	38.6
20	22	1899	F.Tenney	Bos	NL	603	63	3	669	209	19	17	1	.347	.411	.439	851	846	28			10	20	876	35.5
21	20	1890	D.Orr	Bkn	P	464	30	4	498	172	32	13	6	.371	.414	.534	948	918	10		(10)	(20)		888	34.4
22	14	1893	D.Brouthers	Bkn	NL	282	52	6	340	95	21	11	2	.337	.450	.511	961	921	9				10	931	32.3
23	23	1895	E.Cartwright	Was	NL	472	54	1	527	156	34	17	3	.331	.400	.494	894	829	50			10	30	869	30.4
24	28	1889	H.Larkin	Phi	AA	516	83	16	615	164	23	12	3	.318	.428	.426	854	877	11		(10)	(10)		857	29.7
25	29	1894	D.Brouthers	Bal	NL	525	67	5	597	182	39	23	9	.347	.425	.560	985	855	38					855	29.5

1888-1899
Second basemen

V	R	Year	Name	T	L	AB	BB	HBP	TAB	H	2B	3B	HR	BA	OB	SA	PRO	Wtd PRO	SB	CS	SBF	SPF	FF	R TF	V HC
1	1	1890	C.Childs	Syr	AA	493	72	6	571	170	33	14	2	.345	.434	.481	915	976	56			10	20	1,006	104.6
2	2	1896	C.Childs	Cle	NL	498	100	4	602	177	24	9	1	.355	.467	.446	913	869	25			10	100	979	103.5
3	3	1892	C.Childs	Cle	NL	558	117	9	684	177	14	11	3	.317	.443	.398	841	922	26			10	(10)	922	81.3
4	5	1890	B.McPhee	Cin	NL	528	82	6	616	135	16	22	3	.256	.362	.386	748	787	55			10	90	887	71.1
5	8	1893	C.Childs	Cle	NL	485	120	4	609	158	19	10	3	.326	.463	.425	888	851	23			10	20	881	70.4
6	4	1892	B.McPhee	Cin	NL	573	84	7	664	157	19	12	4	.274	.373	.370	743	815	44			10	70	895	70.0
7	10	1893	B.McPhee	Cin	NL	491	94	4	589	138	17	11	3	.281	.401	.379	779	748	25			10	110	868	63.3
8	7	1888	F.Pfeffer	Chi	NL	517	32	3	552	129	22	10	8	.250	.297	.377	674	782	64			10	90	882	61.5
9	11	1889	B.McPhee	Cin	AA	540	60	4	604	145	25	7	5	.269	.346	.369	715	734	63			10	120	864	59.6
10	6	1899	T.Daly	Bkn	NL	498	69	12	579	156	24	9	5	.313	.409	.428	837	832	43			10	40	882	57.3
11	12	1898	N.Lajoie	Phi	NL	608	21	7	636	197	43	11	6	.324	.354	.461	814	844	25			10	10	864	57.2
12	13	1889	L.Bierbauer	Phi	AA	549	29	4	582	167	27	7	7	.304	.344	.417	761	782	17				80	862	56.6
13	9	1897	C.Childs	Cle	NL	444	74	2	520	150	15	9	1	.338	.435	.419	854	813	25			10	50	873	55.8
14	15	1889	H.Richardson	Bos	NL	536	48	5	589	163	33	10	6	.304	.367	.437	803	818	47				30	848	55.7
15	18	1891	B.McPhee	Cin	NL	562	74	2	638	144	14	16	6	.256	.345	.370	715	757	33			10	70	837	54.0
16	19	1894	B.McPhee	Cin	NL	474	90	5	569	144	21	9	5	.304	.420	.418	838	727	33			10	100	837	50.3
17	21	1890	H.Collins	Bkn	NL	510	85	3	598	142	32	7	3	.278	.385	.386	771	811	85			10	10	831	49.8
18	14	1888	B.McPhee	Cin	AA	458	43	5	506	110	12	10	4	.240	.312	.336	648	748	54			10	100	858	49.2
19	24	1894	C.Childs	Cle	NL	479	107	5	591	169	21	12	2	.353	.475	.459	935	811	17			10		821	46.8
20	20	1890	A.Myers	Phi	NL	487	57	10	554	135	29	7	2	.277	.365	.378	742	781	44			10	40	831	46.4
21	17	1894	H.Reitz	Bal	NL	446	42	7	495	135	22	31	2	.303	.372	.504	876	760	18				80	840	44.7
22	26	1893	S.Wise	Was	NL	521	49	4	574	162	27	17	5	.311	.375	.457	831	797	20	(10)			30	817	44.7
23	28	1890	L.Bierbauer	Bkn	P	589	40	0	629	180	31	11	7	.306	.350	.431	781	756	16				50	806	44.5
24	33	1894	B.Lowe	Bos	NL	613	50	6	669	212	34	11	17	.346	.401	.520	921	799	23			10	(10)	799	44.4
25	30	1891	C.Childs	Cle	NL	551	97	7	655	155	21	12	2	.281	.395	.374	769	814	39			10	(20)	804	43.5

1888-1899
Shortstops

V	R	Year	Name	T	L	AB	BB	HBP	TAB	H	2B	3B	HR	BA	OB	SA	PRO	Wtd PRO	SB	CS	SBF	SPF	FF	R TF	V HC
1	2	1896	H.Jennings	Bal	NL	521	19	51	591	209	27	9	0	.401	.472	.488	960	914	70			10	90	1,014	121.7
2	1	1896	B.Dahlen	Chi	NL	474	64	8	546	167	30	19	9	.352	.438	.553	990	944	51			10	70	1,024	115.4
3	3	1895	H.Jennings	Bal	NL	529	24	32	585	204	41	7	4	.386	.444	.512	957	887	53			10	100	997	113.9
4	5	1889	J.Glasscock	Ind	NL	582	31	5	618	205	40	3	7	.352	.390	.467	857	873	57			10	90	973	111.6
5	6	1894	B.Dahlen	Chi	NL	502	76	3	581	179	32	14	15	.357	.444	.566	1,010	876	42			10	80	966	103.2
6	4	1897	H.Jennings	Bal	NL	439	42	46	527	156	26	9	2	.355	.463	.469	932	888	60			10	90	988	98.2
7	9	1890	J.Glasscock	NY	NL	512	41	9	562	172	32	9	1	.336	.395	.439	834	878	54			10	60	948	91.8
8	10	1897	G.Davis	NY	NL	519	41	7	567	183	31	10	10	.353	.407	.509	916	873	65			10	60	943	91.0
9	11	1898	H.Jennings	Bal	NL	534	78	46	658	175	25	11	1	.328	.454	.421	876	908	28			10	10	928	87.9
10	15	1891	H.Long	Bos	NL	577	80	8	665	163	21	12	9	.282	.377	.407	785	830	60			10	40	880	81.3
11	12	1892	B.Dahlen	Chi	NL	581	45	5	631	169	23	19	5	.291	.347	.422	769	843	60			10	60	913	79.5
12	14	1888	E.McKean	Cle	AA	548	28	6	582	164	21	15	6	.299	.340	.425	765	883	52			10		893	75.7
13	13	1899	B.Wallace	StL	NL	577	54	2	633	170	28	14	12	.295	.357	.454	811	806	17				90	896	74.6
14	20	1890	B.Shindle	Phi	P	584	40	4	628	189	21	21	10	.324	.371	.483	854	827	51			10	20	857	71.5
15	18	1894	H.Jennings	Bal	NL	501	37	27	565	168	28	16	4	.335	.411	.479	890	772	37			10	90	872	69.2
16	21	1890	M.Ward	Bkn	P	561	51	2	614	188	15	12	4	.335	.393	.426	819	793	63			10	50	853	68.4
17	8	1899	G.Davis	NY	NL	416	37	2	455	140	21	5	1	.337	.393	.418	812	807	34			10	140	957	67.5
18	17	1898	B.Dahlen	Chi	NL	521	58	23	602	151	35	8	1	.290	.385	.393	779	807	27			10	60	877	65.2
19	26	1890	E.McKean	Cle	NL	530	87	6	623	157	15	14	7	.296	.401	.417	818	861	23			10	(40)	831	60.1
20	24	1896	G.DeMontreville	Was	NL	533	29	3	565	183	24	5	8	.343	.381	.452	833	793	28			10	40	843	59.9
21	29	1889	H.Long	KC	AA	574	64	10	648	158	32	6	3	.275	.358	.368	726	746	89			10	70	826	58.4
22	23	1896	H.Long	Bos	NL	502	26	5	533	173	26	8	6	.345	.383	.464	847	807	38			10	30	847	57.6
23	7	1897	B.Dahlen	Chi	NL	276	43	7	326	80	18	8	6	.290	.399	.478	877	835	15			10	120	965	56.6
24	16	1899	B.Dahlen	Bkn	NL	428	67	15	510	121	22	7	4	.283	.398	.395	793	788	29			10	80	878	55.5
25	31	1892	H.Long	Bos	NL	646	44	8	698	181	33	6	6	.280	.334	.378	712	780	57			10	30	820	55.4

1888-1899
Third basemen

V	R	Year	Name	T	L	AB	BB	HBP	TAB	H	2B	3B	HR	BA	OB	SA	PRO	Wtd PRO	SB	CS	SBF	SPF	FF	R TF	V HC
1	1	1890	D.Lyons	Phi	AA	339	57	10	406	120	29	5	7	.354	.461	.531	992	1,057	21			10	40	1,107	90.8
2	4	1899	J.Williams	Pit	NL	617	60	6	683	219	28	27	9	.355	.417	.532	949	943	26				10	953	81.5
3	6	1893	G.Davis	NY	NL	549	42	9	600	195	22	27	11	.355	.410	.554	964	924	37			10	10	944	80.6
4	2	1899	J.McGraw	Bal	NL	399	124	14	537	156	13	3	1	.391	.547	.446	994	988	73			10	10	1,008	78.8
5	7	1896	B.Joyce	Was	NL	475	101	22	598	158	25	12	13	.333	.470	.518	988	941	45			10	(10)	941	78.6
6	3	1894	B.Joyce	Was	NL	355	87	12	454	126	25	14	17	.355	.496	.648	1,143	992	21			10		1,002	75.8
7	5	1898	J.Collins	Bos	NL	597	40	7	644	196	35	5	15	.328	.377	.479	856	888	12			10	50	948	75.0
8	8	1889	D.Lyons	Phi	AA	510	79	7	596	168	36	4	9	.329	.426	.469	895	919	10				20	939	73.3
9	10	1888	B.Nash	Bos	NL	526	50	4	580	149	18	15	4	.283	.350	.397	747	866	20				70	936	72.4
10	11	1897	J.Collins	Bos	NL	529	41	7	577	183	28	13	6	.346	.400	.482	882	841	14			10	70	921	67.4
11	9	1891	D.Farrell	Bos	AA	473	59	4	536	143	19	13	12	.302	.384	.474	858	888	21				50	938	65.5
12	14	1899	H.Wagner	Lou	NL	571	40	11	622	192	43	13	7	.336	.391	.494	885	879	37			10	20	909	60.4
13	12	1891	D.Lyons	StL	AA	451	88	18	557	142	24	3	11	.315	.445	.455	900	931	9			(20)		911	59.9
14	15	1895	B.Joyce	Was	NL	474	96	14	584	148	25	13	17	.312	.442	.527	969	899	29			10	(20)	889	58.6
15	19	1889	L.Marr	Col	AA	546	87	6	639	167	26	15	1	.306	.407	.414	821	843	29				30	873	55.4
16	13	1895	G.Davis	NY	NL	430	55	2	487	146	36	9	5	.340	.417	.500	917	850	48			10	50	910	54.9
17	16	1898	J.McGraw	Bal	NL	515	112	19	646	176	8	10	0	.342	.475	.396	871	903	43			10	(30)	883	54.2
18	18	1894	L.Cross	Phi	NL	529	29	3	561	204	34	9	7	.386	.421	.524	944	819	21			10	50	879	53.4
19	21	1891	A.Latham	Cin	NL	533	74	11	618	145	20	10	7	.272	.372	.386	759	803	87			10	50	863	50.7
20	20	1897	B.Wallace	Cle	NL	516	48	2	566	173	33	21	4	.335	.394	.504	898	855	14			10		865	48.3
21	22	1894	G.Davis	NY	NL	477	66	4	547	168	26	19	8	.352	.435	.537	972	843	40			10	10	863	46.9
22	24	1890	G.Pinkney	Bkn	NL	485	80	4	569	150	20	9	7	.309	.411	.431	842	886	47			10	(40)	856	45.5
23	17	1895	J.McGraw	Bal	NL	388	60	5	453	143	13	6	2	.369	.459	.448	908	842	61			10	30	882	43.6
24	25	1888	J.Denny	Ind	NL	524	9	2	535	137	27	7	12	.261	.277	.408	685	794	32				60	854	41.8
25	27	1896	G.Davis	NY	NL	494	50	4	548	158	25	12	5	.320	.387	.449	836	797	48			10	40	847	41.8

1888-1899
Outfielders

V	R	Year	Name	T	L	AB	BB	HBP	TAB	H	2B	3B	HR	BA	OB	SA	PRO	Wtd PRO	SB	CS	SBF	SPF	FF	R TF	V HC
1	1	1896	E.Delahanty	Phi	NL	499	62	9	570	198	44	17	13	.397	.472	.631	1,103	1,051	37			10	40	1,101	114.5
2	7	1893	E.Delahanty	Phi	NL	595	47	10	652	219	35	18	19	.368	.423	.583	1,007	965	37			10	60	1,035	106.8
3	3	1894	H.Duffy	Bos	NL	539	66	1	606	237	51	16	18	.440	.502	.694	1,196	1,037	48			10	10	1,057	106.1
4	2	1888	J.Ryan	Chi	NL	549	35	5	589	182	33	10	16	.332	.377	.515	892	1,034	60			10	30	1,074	106.0
5	5	1895	S.Thompson	Phi	NL	538	31	5	574	211	45	21	18	.392	.430	.654	1,085	1,006	27			10	30	1,046	96.1
6	6	1895	E.Delahanty	Phi	NL	480	86	6	572	194	49	10	11	.404	.500	.617	1,117	1,036	46			10		1,046	95.7
7	4	1899	E.Delahanty	Phi	NL	581	55	4	640	238	55	9	9	.410	.464	.582	1,046	1,040	30			10		1,050	94.1
8	12	1896	J.Kelley	Bal	NL	519	91	12	622	189	31	19	8	.364	.469	.543	1,013	965	87			10	10	985	82.7
9	11	1889	H.Stovey	Phi	AA	556	77	1	634	171	38	13	19	.308	.393	.525	918	943	63			10	40	993	82.4
10	27	1896	J.Burkett	Cle	NL	586	49	7	642	240	27	16	6	.410	.461	.541	1,002	955	34			10		965	77.8
11	19	1890	T.McCarthy	StL	AA	548	66	11	625	192	28	9	6	.350	.430	.467	898	944	83			10	20	974	77.5
12	24	1894	J.Kelley	Bal	NL	507	107	5	619	199	48	20	6	.393	.502	.602	1,104	957	46			10		967	76.0
13	16	1897	W.Keeler	Bal	NL	564	35	7	606	239	27	19	0	.424	.464	.539	1,003	955	64			10	10	975	75.5
14	10	1895	B.Lange	Chi	NL	478	55	4	537	186	27	16	10	.389	.456	.575	1,032	957	67			10	30	997	74.6
15	23	1895	J.Kelley	Bal	NL	518	77	10	605	189	26	19	10	.365	.456	.546	1,003	930	54			10	30	970	74.6
16	22	1889	M.Tiernan	NY	NL	499	96	5	600	167	23	14	10	.335	.447	.497	944	961	33			10		971	74.4
17	8	1894	S.Thompson	Phi	NL	437	40	1	478	178	29	27	13	.407	.458	.686	1,145	993	24			10	20	1,023	74.1
18	29	1889	J.Ryan	Chi	NL	576	70	6	652	177	31	14	17	.307	.388	.498	886	903	45			10	40	953	73.9
19	13	1897	F.Clarke	Lou	NL	518	45	24	587	202	30	13	6	.390	.462	.533	994	947	57			10	20	977	73.8
20	17	1897	E.Delahanty	Phi	NL	530	60	3	593	200	40	15	5	.377	.444	.538	981	935	26			10	30	975	73.7
21	21	1888	H.Stovey	Phi	AA	530	62	3	595	152	25	20	9	.287	.365	.460	825	952	87			10	10	972	71.8
22	18	1888	T.O'Neill	StL	AA	529	44	4	577	177	24	10	5	.335	.390	.446	836	964	26			10		974	70.5
23	15	1890	E.Swartwood	Tol	AA	462	80	17	559	151	23	11	3	.327	.444	.444	887	946	53			10	20	976	69.9
24	20	1894	E.Delahanty	Phi	NL	489	60	7	556	199	39	18	4	.407	.478	.585	1,063	922	21			10	40	972	69.8
25	26	1890	P.Browning	Cle	P	493	75	3	571	184	40	8	5	.373	.459	.517	976	945	35			10	10	965	69.4

1888-1899
Outfielders

V	R	Year	Name	T	L	AB	BB	HBP	TAB	H	2B	3B	HR	BA	OB	SA	PRO	Wtd PRO	SB	CS	SBF	SPF	FF	R TF	V HC
26	35	1895	J.Burkett	Cle	NL	550	74	8	632	225	22	13	5	.409	.486	.524	1,009	936	41			10		946	69.3
27	45	1894	B.Hamilton	Phi	NL	544	126	9	679	220	25	15	4	.404	.523	.528	1,050	911	98			10	10	931	68.9
28	31	1891	H.Stovey	Bos	NL	544	79	2	625	152	31	20	16	.279	.373	.498	871	922	57			10	20	952	67.9
29	37	1891	B.Hamilton	Phi	NL	527	102	7	636	179	23	7	2	.340	.453	.421	874	925	111			10	10	945	66.8
30	25	1899	J.Burkett	StL	NL	558	67	2	627	221	21	8	7	.396	.463	.500	963	957	25			10		967	66.1
31	34	1890	C.Wolf	Lou	AA	543	43	12	598	197	29	11	4	.363	.421	.479	900	947	46					947	64.8
32	28	1892	B.Hamilton	Phi	NL	554	81	8	643	183	21	7	3	.330	.423	.410	833	913	57			10	30	953	63.2
33	33	1888	H.Collins	Lou	AA	527	50	5	582	162	31	12	2	.307	.373	.423	796	918	71			10	20	948	62.5
34	9	1893	B.Hamilton	Phi	NL	355	63	13	431	135	22	7	5	.380	.490	.524	1,014	972	43			10	20	1,002	62.1
35	46	1893	E.Smith	Pit	NL	518	77	5	600	179	26	23	7	.346	.435	.525	960	921	26				10	931	61.3
36	43	1896	M.Tiernan	NY	NL	521	77	2	600	192	24	16	7	.369	.452	.516	968	922	35			10		932	61.3
37	52	1893	S.Thompson	Phi	NL	600	50	6	656	222	37	13	11	.370	.424	.530	954	915	18			10	(10)	915	60.8
38	39	1896	E.Smith	Pit	NL	484	74	8	566	175	21	14	6	.362	.454	.500	954	909	33				30	939	60.1
39	49	1895	B.Hamilton	Phi	NL	517	96	7	620	201	22	6	7	.389	.490	.495	985	914	97			10		924	60.0
40	44	1888	D.Johnston	Bos	NL	585	15	1	601	173	31	18	12	.296	.314	.472	786	911	35				20	931	59.3
41	41	1899	C.Stahl	Bos	NL	576	72	4	652	202	23	19	7	.351	.426	.493	919	914	33			10	10	934	57.9
42	50	1891	M.Tiernan	NY	NL	542	69	3	614	166	30	12	16	.306	.388	.494	882	934	53			10	(20)	924	57.0
43	14	1892	E.Delahanty	Phi	NL	477	31	9	517	146	30	21	6	.306	.360	.495	855	937	29			10	30	977	57.0
44	42	1898	E.Delahanty	Phi	NL	548	77	11	636	183	36	9	4	.334	.426	.454	880	913	58			10	10	933	56.0
45	55	1893	J.Burkett	Cle	NL	511	98	7	616	178	25	15	6	.348	.459	.491	951	912	39			10	(10)	912	56.0
46	51	1889	T.O'Neill	StL	AA	534	72	5	611	179	33	8	9	.335	.419	.478	897	921	28					921	55.2
47	53	1896	W.Keeler	Bal	NL	544	37	7	588	210	22	13	4	.386	.432	.496	928	884	67			10	20	914	54.0
48	60	1890	M.Tiernan	NY	NL	553	68	5	626	168	25	21	13	.304	.385	.495	880	926	56			10	(30)	906	53.3
49	54	1895	J.Stenzel	Pit	NL	514	57	11	582	192	38	13	7	.374	.447	.539	986	914	53			10	(10)	914	53.0
50	36	1888	M.Tiernan	NY	NL	443	42	7	492	130	16	8	9	.293	.364	.427	790	916	52			10	20	946	52.7
51	58	1897	J.Burkett	Cle	NL	517	76	7	600	198	28	7	2	.383	.468	.476	944	899	28			10		909	52.2
52	59	1892	S.Thompson	Phi	NL	609	59	11	679	186	28	11	9	.305	.377	.432	809	887	28			10	10	907	50.9
53	38	1898	E.Flick	Phi	NL	453	86	15	554	137	16	13	8	.302	.430	.448	878	910	23			10	20	940	50.8
54	70	1895	M.Griffin	Bkn	NL	519	93	10	622	173	38	7	4	.333	.444	.457	900	835	27			10	50	895	49.7
55	47	1892	J.Ryan	Chi	NL	505	61	5	571	148	21	11	10	.293	.375	.438	812	890	27			10	30	930	49.7
56	75	1896	B.Hamilton	Bos	NL	524	110	2	636	192	24	10	3	.366	.478	.468	946	901	83			10	(20)	891	49.6
57	68	1894	J.Stenzel	Pit	NL	522	75	6	603	185	39	20	13	.354	.441	.580	1,022	886	61			10		896	48.8
58	63	1897	J.Kelley	Bal	NL	505	70	7	582	183	31	9	5	.362	.447	.489	936	892	44			10		902	48.0
59	67	1890	S.Johnson	Col	AA	538	48	10	596	186	23	18	1	.346	.409	.461	870	928	43			10	(40)	898	47.9
60	64	1891	H.Duffy	Bos	AA	536	61	4	601	180	20	8	9	.336	.408	.453	861	891	85			10		901	47.6
61	48	1889	W.Wilmot	Was	NL	432	51	2	485	125	19	19	9	.289	.367	.484	851	867	40			10	50	927	47.6
62	57	1892	O.Burns	Bkn	NL	542	65	6	613	171	27	18	4	.315	.395	.454	849	930	33			10	(30)	910	47.1
63	82	1891	T.Brown	Bos	AA	589	70	4	663	189	30	21	5	.321	.397	.469	865	896	106			10	(20)	886	46.9
64	32	1888	P.Browning	Lou	AA	383	37	4	424	120	22	8	3	.313	.380	.436	816	941	36			10		951	46.2
65	40	1898	B.Hamilton	Bos	NL	417	87	2	506	154	16	5	3	.369	.480	.453	933	968	54			10	(40)	938	45.8
66	71	1890	B.Hamilton	Phi	NL	496	83	9	588	161	13	9	2	.325	.430	.399	829	873	102			10	10	893	45.5
67	61	1890	J.O'Rourke	NY	P	478	33	8	519	172	37	5	9	.360	.410	.515	925	896	23				10	906	45.0
68	69	1895	M.Tiernan	NY	NL	476	66	1	543	165	23	21	7	.347	.427	.527	955	885	36			10		895	43.5
69	90	1889	E.Seery	Ind	NL	526	67	10	603	165	26	12	8	.314	.401	.454	856	872	19			10		882	43.5
70	56	1896	T.McCreery	Lou	NL	441	42	1	484	155	23	21	7	.351	.409	.546	956	910	26					910	43.3
71	99	1895	W.Keeler	Bal	NL	565	37	14	616	213	24	15	4	.377	.429	.494	922	856	47			10	10	876	42.2
72	89	1889	B.Holliday	Cin	AA	563	43	2	608	181	28	7	19	.321	.372	.497	869	893	46			10	(20)	883	42.1
73	77	1899	B.Freeman	Was	NL	588	23	18	629	187	19	25	25	.318	.362	.563	925	920	21				(30)	890	42.0
74	112	1890	H.Duffy	Chi	P	596	59	2	657	191	36	16	7	.320	.384	.470	853	826	78			10	30	866	41.8
75	104	1896	G.Van Haltren	NY	NL	562	55	2	619	197	18	21	5	.351	.410	.484	894	852	39			10	10	872	41.5

Nineteenth Century Players

1888-1899
Starting Pitchers

V	R	Year	Name	T	L	G	GS	IP	W	L	SV	SO	BB	ERA	RA/9	R Wtd RA/9	V Runs /162
1	4	1888	S.King	StL	AA	66	65	586	45	21	0	258	76	1.64	3.15	2.72	141.5
2	6	1894	A.Rusie	NY	NL	54	50	444	36	13	1	195	200	2.78	4.62	2.75	109.5
3	25	1889	J.Clarkson	Bos	NL	73	72	620	49	19	1	284	203	2.73	4.06	3.08	107.1
4	20	1888	E.Seward	Phi	AA	57	57	519	35	19	0	272	127	2.01	3.52	3.04	103.6
5	16	1890	S.King	Chi	P	56	56	461	30	22	0	185	163	2.69	4.55	2.93	102.1
6	11	1888	T.Keefe	NY	NL	51	51	434	35	12	0	335	90	1.74	2.90	2.85	98.2
7	5	1892	C.Young	Cle	NL	53	49	453	36	12	0	168	118	1.93	3.14	2.73	97.3
8	18	1890	K.Nichols	Bos	NL	48	47	424	27	19	0	222	112	2.23	3.71	2.97	89.9
9	8	1897	K.Nichols	Bos	NL	46	40	368	31	11	3	127	68	2.64	3.72	2.77	87.9
10	15	1890	B.Rhines	Cin	NL	46	45	401	28	17	0	182	113	1.95	3.66	2.93	87.2
11	21	1890	S.Stratton	Lou	AA	50	49	431	34	14	0	207	61	2.36	3.88	3.04	87.0
12	13	1895	C.Young	Cle	NL	47	40	370	35	10	0	121	75	3.26	4.31	2.86	84.8
13	44	1893	A.Rusie	NY	NL	56	52	482	33	21	1	208	218	3.23	4.85	3.30	83.3
14	22	1894	J.Meekin	NY	NL	52	48	409	33	9	2	133	171	3.70	5.15	3.06	83.3
15	10	1898	K.Nichols	Bos	NL	50	42	388	31	12	4	138	85	2.13	3.15	2.79	80.5
16	32	1889	B.Caruthers	Bkn	AA	56	50	445	40	11	1	118	104	3.13	4.35	3.16	80.1
17	12	1891	C.Buffinton	Bos	AA	48	43	364	29	9	1	158	120	2.55	3.79	2.85	79.9
18	36	1893	K.Nichols	Bos	NL	52	44	425	34	14	1	94	118	3.52	4.70	3.20	79.4
19	23	1888	C.Buffinton	Phi	NL	46	46	400	28	17	0	199	59	1.91	3.12	3.06	79.0
20	41	1895	P.Hawley	Pit	NL	56	50	444	31	22	1	142	122	3.18	4.90	3.26	78.2
21	3	1898	C.Griffith	Chi	NL	38	38	326	24	10	0	97	64	1.88	2.90	2.57	76.1
22	9	1895	B.Hoffer	Bal	NL	41	38	314	31	6	0	80	124	3.21	4.18	2.78	75.7
23	29	1893	T.Breitenstein	StL	NL	48	42	383	19	24	1	102	156	3.18	4.63	3.15	74.1
24	39	1888	M.Welch	NY	NL	47	47	425	26	19	0	167	108	1.93	3.30	3.24	74.0
25	24	1891	G.Haddock	Bos	AA	51	47	380	34	11	1	169	137	2.49	4.08	3.07	72.7
26	7	1899	V.Willis	Bos	NL	41	38	343	27	8	2	120	117	2.50	3.31	2.75	72.6
27	48	1891	P.Knell	Col	AA	58	52	462	28	27	0	228	226	2.92	4.44	3.34	72.4
28	47	1893	C.Young	Cle	NL	53	46	423	34	16	1	102	103	3.36	4.90	3.33	71.2
29	26	1890	O.Radbourn	Bos	P	41	38	343	27	12	0	80	100	3.31	4.80	3.09	68.4
30	19	1897	A.Rusie	NY	NL	38	37	322	28	10	0	135	87	2.54	3.99	2.97	68.3
31	33	1896	N.Cuppy	Cle	NL	46	40	358	25	14	1	86	75	3.12	4.35	3.17	67.6
32	83	1891	A.Rusie	NY	NL	61	57	500	33	20	1	337	262	2.55	4.39	3.55	65.9
33	55	1896	C.Young	Cle	NL	51	46	414	28	15	3	140	62	3.24	4.65	3.39	65.9
34	108	1891	B.Hutchison	Chi	NL	66	58	561	44	19	1	261	178	2.81	4.54	3.67	65.0
35	96	1890	K.Gleason	Phi	NL	60	55	506	38	17	2	222	167	2.63	4.50	3.60	64.7
36	127	1890	B.Hutchison	Chi	NL	71	66	603	42	25	2	289	199	2.70	4.70	3.76	64.3
37	65	1891	G.Weyhing	Phi	AA	52	51	450	31	20	0	219	161	3.18	4.62	3.47	62.7
38	56	1889	E.Chamberlain	StL	AA	53	51	422	32	15	1	202	165	2.97	4.70	3.41	62.2
39	62	1893	F.Killen	Pit	NL	55	48	415	36	14	0	99	140	3.64	5.10	3.47	62.1
40	30	1898	D.McJames	Bkn	NL	45	42	374	27	15	0	178	113	2.36	3.56	3.15	61.7
41	66	1894	C.Young	Cle	NL	52	47	409	26	21	1	108	106	3.94	5.84	3.47	60.4
42	54	1889	J.Duryea	Cin	AA	53	48	401	32	19	1	183	127	2.56	4.67	3.39	60.2
43	2	1898	A.Maul	Bal	NL	28	28	240	20	7	0	31	49	2.10	2.78	2.46	59.0
44	57	1896	P.Hawley	Pit	NL	49	43	378	22	21	0	137	157	3.57	4.69	3.42	58.6
45	60	1895	K.Nichols	Bos	NL	47	42	380	26	16	3	140	86	3.41	5.19	3.45	57.1
46	37	1896	B.Hoffer	Bal	NL	35	35	309	25	7	0	93	95	3.38	4.40	3.21	56.8
47	82	1892	G.Weyhing	Phi	NL	59	49	470	32	21	3	202	168	2.66	4.08	3.54	56.0
48	119	1890	M.Baldwin	Chi	P	58	56	492	33	24	0	206	249	3.35	5.78	3.73	55.8
49	70	1888	B.Caruthers	Bkn	AA	44	43	392	29	15	0	140	53	2.39	4.04	3.49	55.1
50	72	1890	J.Clarkson	Bos	NL	44	44	383	26	18	0	138	140	3.27	4.37	3.49	54.3

1888-1899
Starting Pitchers

V	R	Year	Name	T	L	G	GS	IP	W	L	SV	SO	BB	ERA	RA/9	R Wtd RA/9	V Runs /162
51	122	1891	S.McMahon	Bal	AA	61	58	503	35	24	1	219	149	2.81	4.63	3.74	52.8
52	27	1899	N.Hahn	Cin	NL	38	34	309	23	8	0	145	68	2.68	3.73	3.10	52.7
53	106	1889	S.King	StL	AA	56	53	458	35	16	1	188	125	3.14	5.05	3.66	52.6
54	92	1890	H.Gastright	Col	AA	48	45	401	30	14	0	199	135	2.94	4.57	3.58	52.0
55	49	1899	J.McGinnity	Bal	NL	48	41	366	28	16	2	74	93	2.68	4.03	3.35	51.8
56	103	1891	J.Stivetts	StL	AA	64	56	440	33	22	1	259	232	2.86	4.85	3.65	51.5
57	71	1888	M.Hughes	Bkn	AA	40	40	363	25	13	0	159	98	2.13	4.04	3.49	51.0
58	34	1899	J.Tannehill	Pit	NL	40	35	313	24	14	1	61	51	2.73	3.82	3.18	50.7
59	43	1896	F.Dwyer	Cin	NL	36	34	289	24	11	1	57	60	3.15	4.49	3.27	50.6
60	113	1896	F.Killen	Pit	NL	52	50	432	30	18	0	134	119	3.41	5.08	3.70	50.3
61	28	1899	J.Hughes	Bkn	NL	35	35	292	28	6	0	99	119	2.68	3.73	3.10	49.8
62	42	1899	F.Kitson	Bal	NL	40	37	328	22	16	0	75	65	2.77	3.93	3.27	49.6
63	59	1892	E.Stein	Bkn	NL	48	42	377	27	16	1	190	150	2.84	3.96	3.44	49.5
64	38	1888	B.Sanders	Phi	NL	31	29	275	19	10	0	121	33	1.90	3.27	3.21	49.0
65	102	1892	K.Nichols	Bos	NL	53	51	453	35	16	0	192	121	2.84	4.19	3.64	48.9
66	143	1890	B.Barr	Roc	AA	57	54	493	28	24	0	209	219	3.25	4.87	3.82	48.5
67	35	1891	J.Ewing	NY	NL	33	30	269	21	8	0	138	105	2.27	3.94	3.18	48.2
68	84	1895	N.Cuppy	Cle	NL	47	40	353	26	14	2	91	95	3.54	5.35	3.55	47.9
69	52	1899	K.Nichols	Bos	NL	42	37	343	21	19	1	108	82	2.99	4.06	3.38	47.5
70	104	1890	E.Healy	Tol	AA	46	46	389	22	21	0	225	127	2.89	4.65	3.65	47.2
71	89	1890	R.Ehret	Lou	AA	43	38	359	25	14	2	174	79	2.53	4.56	3.58	46.9
72	110	1890	H.Staley	Pit	P	46	46	388	21	25	0	145	74	3.23	5.71	3.68	46.4
73	77	1889	C.Buffinton	Phi	NL	47	43	380	28	16	0	153	121	3.24	4.64	3.52	46.0
74	76	1898	C.Young	Cle	NL	46	41	378	25	13	0	101	41	2.53	3.98	3.52	45.9
75	174	1890	A.Rusie	NY	NL	67	62	549	29	34	1	341	289	2.56	4.92	3.93	45.6
76	75	1899	C.Young	StL	NL	44	42	369	26	16	1	111	44	2.58	4.22	3.51	45.3
77	121	1891	K.Nichols	Bos	NL	52	48	425	30	17	3	240	103	2.39	4.63	3.74	45.2
78	45	1898	T.Lewis	Bos	NL	41	33	313	26	8	2	72	109	2.90	3.76	3.33	45.1
79	116	1890	G.Weyhing	Bkn	P	49	46	390	30	16	0	177	179	3.60	5.77	3.72	44.6
80	50	1890	F.Knauss	Col	AA	37	34	276	17	12	2	148	106	2.81	4.28	3.36	44.2
81	148	1894	T.Breitenstein	StL	NL	56	50	447	27	23	0	140	191	4.79	6.46	3.84	43.5
82	88	1889	M.Welch	NY	NL	45	41	375	27	12	2	125	149	3.02	4.70	3.57	43.4
83	190	1892	B.Hutchison	Chi	NL	75	70	622	36	36	1	312	190	2.76	4.57	3.97	43.1
84	58	1894	S.McMahon	Bal	NL	35	33	276	25	8	0	60	111	4.21	5.75	3.42	42.8
85	115	1896	K.Nichols	Bos	NL	49	43	372	30	14	1	102	101	2.83	5.10	3.72	42.5
86	1	1896	B.Rhines	Cin	NL	19	17	143	8	6	0	32	48	2.45	3.27	2.38	42.4
87	153	1891	J.Clarkson	Bos	NL	55	51	461	33	19	3	141	154	2.79	4.77	3.85	42.3
88	130	1895	A.Rusie	NY	NL	49	47	393	23	23	0	201	159	3.73	5.67	3.77	42.0
89	147	1888	P.Galvin	Pit	NL	50	50	437	23	25	0	107	53	2.63	3.91	3.84	41.5
90	94	1897	T.Breitenstein	Cin	NL	40	39	320	23	12	0	98	91	3.62	4.83	3.59	41.2
91	99	1888	N.Hudson	StL	AA	39	37	333	25	10	0	130	59	2.54	4.19	3.62	41.2
92	14	1889	J.Stivetts	StL	AA	26	20	192	12	7	1	143	68	2.25	3.99	2.90	41.0
93	93	1891	H.Staley	Bos	NL	40	37	324	24	13	0	139	80	2.58	4.44	3.59	41.0
94	101	1892	N.Cuppy	Cle	NL	47	42	376	28	13	1	103	121	2.51	4.19	3.64	40.6
95	69	1896	R.Ehret	Cin	NL	34	33	277	18	14	0	60	74	3.42	4.78	3.49	40.5
96	138	1888	G.Weyhing	Phi	AA	47	47	404	28	18	0	204	111	2.25	4.41	3.81	39.9
97	114	1894	G.Hemming	Lou	NL	41	38	340	17	19	1	70	159	4.27	6.23	3.71	39.4
98	194	1890	S.McMahon	Phi	AA	60	57	509	36	21	1	291	166	3.27	5.07	3.98	39.4
99	139	1893	B.Kennedy	Bkn	NL	46	44	383	25	20	1	107	168	3.72	5.60	3.81	39.4
100	91	1898	J.Powell	Cle	NL	42	41	342	23	15	0	93	112	3.00	4.05	3.58	39.0

ALL TIME GREAT PLAYER SEASONS

The preceding chapters present the all time single season lineups for each team. This chapter summarizes these results into the all time volume and rate of success lineups for the American and National leagues. Just imagine these all time American and National League teams squaring off in a historic All-Star game!

For the *volume of success* contest, the American League team lineup includes the best seasons from Ruth, Mantle, Williams, Gehrig, Brett, Lajoie, Ripken, Freehan, and Walter Johnson. Reserves include seasons from Cobb, Foxx, Collins, Speaker, and Yount, as well as pitchers Young, Walsh, Eichhorn, and Fingers. Their National League opponents include the best seasons from Wagner, Hornsby, Schmidt, Barry Bonds, Musial, Walker, Bench, Bagwell, and Joe McGinnity. Reserves include seasons from Mays, Aaron, McGwire, Joe Morgan, and Campanella, as well as pitchers Gibson, Alexander, Mathewson, Maddux, and Gossage. The American League's strength lies in its outfield and pitching, while the National League features the best infield, especially at short and third.

These volume of success stars come from every decade of the twentieth century, with the only real imbalance being that starting pitchers come almost exclusively from the innings-heavy hurlers of the 1900s and 1910s, while relief pitchers come exclusively from the 1970s, 1980s, and 1990s. The most remarkable appearance on this volume of success team is made by Greg Maddux, who started only every fifth game and, yet, still earns a spot among the top five National League volume of success starters.

For the *rate of success* contest, the American League draws upon the best seasons from Ruth, Williams, Mantle, Gehrig, Lajoie, Brett, Ivan Rodriguez, Alex Rodriguez, and Pedro Martinez. Although six of these players also start on the volume of success team, only two of the six—Gehrig and Lajoie—feature the same season on each team. Reserves include the best seasons from Cobb, Foxx, Yastrzemski, Ripken, and Fisk, as well as pitchers Johnson, Clemens, Mesa and Eckersley. The National League starts the same seasons from Bench, Bagwell, Wagner, Schmidt, Bonds, and Walker, while also starting Mays, Joe Morgan, and Maddux. Reserves include the best seasons from Musial, Hornsby, McGwire, and Caminiti, as well as pitchers Gooden, Gibson, Koufax, Seaver, and Urbina.

These rate of success stars represent every decade of the twentieth century and the year 2000, with a relatively even distribution except for relief pitchers, who come almost exclusively from among the 1990s closer specialists.

The next logical step is to summarize the best single season results of every league into a "dream team" lineup that features the best single season performances of all time. The all time *volume of success* lineup of the eight greatest infielder and outfielder seasons is historically balanced, with only one nineteenth century player, and with at most one player season from each decade of the twentieth century. And what a lineup it is, with seasons from Ruth, Mantle, Williams, Wagner, Schmidt, Bench, Bagwell, and Ross Barnes!

In contrast, the five volume of success starting pitcher seasons all come from the 1870s and early 1880s, as these pitchers benefited from starting nearly every game. Not even the best season from Walter Johnson or Cy Young can make the all time volume of success team. And the four volume of success relief pitcher seasons all come from the 1970s and 1980s, the peak volume period for relief innings worked by talented relievers.

The all time *rate of success* team features only three players from the 1800s, and none of these is a pitcher! The starting lineup of eight infielders and outfielders represents eight different decades, while the reserves also feature players from eight different decades. Except for relief pitchers, there is a fairly equal distribution of players through time. Seasons from every decade except the 1890s and the 1960s are represented on the all time rate of success team:

1870s	1	Barnes
1880s	2	Dunlap, O'Neill
1890s	0	
1900s	1	Wagner
1910s	3	Cobb, Johnson, Leonard
1920s	2	Ruth, Gehrig
1930s	1	Vaughan
1940s	1	Williams
1950s	1	Mantle
1960s	0	
1970s	1	Bench
1980s	4	Schmidt, Brett, Gooden, Fingers
1990s	6	Bagwell, Bonds, Maddux, Mesa, Eckersley, Jackson
2000	2	Rodriguez, Martinez

This chapter also ranks the 25 best seasons for each infield position, the 75 best outfielder seasons, the 100 best starting pitcher seasons, and the 50 best relief pitcher seasons. This information is provided for the American League, the National League, and the all time greatest seasons ever. These rankings are a salute to the finest player seasons in major league history.

All Time Great Player Seasons

American League Greatest   **Hitters Volume of Success**

Pos	Year	Name	T	L	AB	BB	HBP	TAB	H	2B	3B	HR	BA	OB	SA	PRO	Wtd PRO	SB	CS	SBF	SPF	FF	R TF	V HC
C	1968	B.Freehan	Det	AL	540	65	24	629	142	24	2	25	.263	.367	.454	821	907	0	1	(3)	10	80	994	94.8
1B	1927	L.Gehrig	NY	AL	584	109	3	696	218	52	18	47	.373	.474	.765	1,240	1,165	10	8	(8)	0	0	1,157	135.0
2B	1901	N.Lajoie	Phi	AL	544	24	13	581	232	48	14	14	.426	.463	.643	1,106	1,109	27			10	80	1,199	164.7
SS	1991	C.Ripken	Bal	AL	650	53	5	708	210	46	5	34	.323	.379	.566	945	950	6	1	5	0	60	1,015	119.1
3B	1985	G.Brett	KC	AL	550	103	3	656	184	38	5	30	.335	.442	.585	1,028	1,021	9	1	10	0	40	1,071	110.8
OF	1923	B.Ruth	NY	AL	522	170	4	696	205	45	13	41	.393	.545	.764	1,309	1,250	17	21	(34)	10	40	1,266	177.5
OF	1956	M.Mantle	NY	AL	533	112	2	647	188	22	5	52	.353	.467	.705	1,172	1,123	10	1	12	10	70	1,214	148.2
OF	1946	T.Williams	Bos	AL	514	156	2	672	176	37	8	38	.342	.497	.667	1,164	1,188	0	0	0	0	0	1,188	144.9
Starters		Averages			555	99	7	661	194	39	9	35	.350	.455	.642	1,097	1,090	10	4	(2)	5	46	1,139	136.9
C	1972	C.Fisk	Bos	AL	457	52	4	513	134	28	9	22	.293	.370	.538	909	985	5	2	2	0	40	1,027	89.9
1B	1932	J.Foxx	Phi	AL	585	116	0	701	213	33	9	58	.364	.469	.749	1,218	1,146	3	7	(15)	0	20	1,152	134.1
2B	1909	E.Collins	Phi	AL	571	62	6	639	198	30	10	3	.347	.416	.450	866	1,001	67			10	70	1,081	126.7
SS	1982	R.Yount	Mil	AL	635	54	1	690	210	46	12	29	.331	.384	.578	962	958	14	3	11	10	30	1,009	114.1
3B/DH	1995	E.Martinez	Sea	AL	511	116	8	635	182	52	0	29	.356	.482	.628	1,110	1,047	4	3	(3)	0	(30)	1,014	101.3
OF	1917	T.Cobb	Det	AL	588	61	4	653	225	44	24	6	.383	.444	.570	1,014	1,122	55			10	40	1,172	135.6
OF	1967	C.Yastrzemski	Bos	AL	579	91	4	674	189	31	4	44	.326	.421	.622	1,043	1,122	10	8	(8)	0	60	1,174	133.8
OF	1912	T.Speaker	Bos	AL	580	82	6	668	222	53	12	10	.383	.464	.567	1,031	1,069	52			10	70	1,149	131.1
Reserves		Averages			563	79	4	647	197	40	10	25	.349	.433	.589	1,022	1,059	26	3	(2)	5	38	1,100	120.8
Totals		Weighted Ave.			558	92	6	656	195	39	9	32	.350	.447	.624	1,072	1,080	15	4	(2)	5	43	1,126	131.5

Pitchers Volume of Success

Pos	Year	Name	T	L	G	GS	IP	W	L	SV	SO	BB	ERA	RA/9	Wtd RA/9	R V Runs /162
SP	1913	W.Johnson	Was	AL	48	36	346	36	7	2	243	38	1.14	1.46	1.68	116.5
SP	1901	C.Young	Bos	AL	43	41	371	33	10	0	158	37	1.62	2.71	2.23	110.8
SP	1908	E.Walsh	Chi	AL	66	49	464	40	15	6	269	56	1.42	2.17	2.85	92.6
SP	1910	J.Coombs	Phi	AL	45	38	353	31	9	1	224	115	1.30	1.89	2.35	90.9
SP	1917	E.Cicotte	Chi	AL	49	35	347	28	12	4	150	70	1.53	1.98	2.49	84.0
Starters		Averages			50	40	376	34	11	3	209	63	1.39	2.03	2.30	99.0
RP	1986	M.Eichhorn	Tor	AL	69	0	157	14	6	10	166	45	1.72	1.83	1.79	48.2
RP	1981	R.Fingers	Mil	AL	47	0	78	6	3	28	61	13	1.04	1.04	1.16	44.6
RP	1973	J.Hiller	Det	AL	65	0	125	10	5	38	124	39	1.44	1.51	1.60	41.1
RP	1984	W.Hernandez	Det	AL	80	0	140	9	3	32	112	36	1.92	1.92	1.97	40.3
Relievers		Averages			65	0	125	10	4	27	116	33	1.66	1.71	1.76	43.6
Totals		Averages			115	40	501	43	15	30	325	97	3.87	4.78	5.21	142.5

Baseball Players' Best Seasons

American League Greatest — **Hitters Rate of Success**

Pos	Year	Name	T	L	AB	BB	HBP	TAB	H	2B	3B	HR	BA	OB	SA	PRO	Wtd PRO	SB	CS	SBF	SPF	FF	R TF	V HC
C	2000	I.Rodriguez	Tex	AL	363	19	1	383	126	27	4	27	.347	.381	.667	1,048	959	5	5	(12)	0	100	1,047	67.4
1B	1927	L.Gehrig	NY	AL	584	109	3	696	218	52	18	47	.373	.474	.765	1,240	1,165	10	8	(8)	0	0	1,157	135.0
2B	1901	N.Lajoie	Phi	AL	544	24	13	581	232	48	14	14	.426	.463	.643	1,106	1,109	27			10		1,199	164.7
SS	2000	A.Rodriguez	Sea	AL	554	100	7	661	175	34	2	41	.316	.427	.606	1,033	946	15	4	10	10	50	1,016	111.4
3B	1980	G.Brett	KC	AL	449	58	1	508	175	33	9	24	.390	.461	.664	1,124	1,120	15	6	6	10	20	1,155	106.3
OF	1920	B.Ruth	NY	AL	458	148	3	609	172	36	9	54	.376	.530	.847	1,378	1,325	14	14	(22)	10	10	1,323	172.7
OF	1941	T.Williams	Bos	AL	456	145	3	604	185	33	3	37	.406	.551	.735	1,286	1,244	2	4	(9)	0	0	1,234	144.3
OF	1957	M.Mantle	NY	AL	474	146	0	620	173	28	6	34	.365	.515	.665	1,179	1,172	16	3	15	10	30	1,228	146.1
Starters		Averages			485	94	4	583	182	36	8	35	.375	.480	.698	1,178	1,137	13	6	(3)	6	36	1,177	131.0
C	1972	C.Fisk	Bos	AL	457	52	4	513	134	28	9	22	.293	.370	.538	909	985	5	2	2	0	40	1,027	89.9
1B	1932	J.Foxx	Phi	AL	585	116	0	701	213	33	9	58	.364	.469	.749	1,218	1,146	3	7	(15)	0	20	1,152	134.1
2B	1909	E.Collins	Phi	AL	571	62	6	639	198	30	10	3	.347	.416	.450	866	1,001	67			10	70	1,081	126.7
SS	1991	C.Ripken	Bal	AL	650	53	5	708	210	46	5	34	.323	.379	.566	945	950	6	1	5	0	60	1,015	119.1
3B	1912	F.Baker	Phi	AL	577	50	6	633	200	40	21	10	.347	.404	.541	945	980	40			10	40	1,030	99.5
OF	1910	T.Cobb	Det	AL	506	64	4	574	194	35	13	8	.383	.456	.551	1,008	1,146	65			10	30	1,186	123.2
OF	1967	C.Yastrzemski	Bos	AL	579	91	4	674	189	31	4	44	.326	.421	.622	1,043	1,122	10	8	(8)	0	60	1,174	133.8
OF	1990	R.Henderson	Oak	AL	489	97	4	590	159	33	3	28	.325	.441	.577	1,017	1,034	65	10	72	10	40	1,156	112.2
Reserves		Averages			552	73	4	629	187	35	9	26	.339	.420	.576	996	1,046	33	4	7	5	45	1,103	117.3
Totals		Weighted Ave.			507	87	4	598	184	36	9	32	.363	.460	.658	1,117	1,107	20	5	1	6	39	1,153	126.4

Pitchers Rate of Success

Pos	Year	Name	T	L	G	GS	IP	W	L	SV	SO	BB	ERA	RA/9	Wtd RA/9	R V Runs /162
SP	2000	P.Martinez	Bos	AL	29	29	217	18	6	0	284	32	1.74	1.82	1.55	72.3
SP	1913	W.Johnson	Was	AL	48	36	346	36	7	2	243	38	1.14	1.46	1.68	116.5
SP	1914	D.Leonard	Bos	AL	36	25	225	19	5	3	176	60	.96	1.36	1.68	75.7
SP	1964	D.Chance	LA	AL	46	35	278	20	9	4	207	86	1.65	1.81	2.03	78.2
SP	1997	R.Clemens	Tor	AL	34	34	264	21	7	0	292	68	2.05	2.22	2.03	74.1
Starters		Averages			39	32	266	23	7	2	240	57	1.30	1.50	1.56	83.4
RP	1995	J.Mesa	Cle	AL	62	0	64	3	0	46	58	17	1.13	1.27	1.13	27.4
RP	1990	D.Eckersley	Oak	AL	63	0	73	4	2	48	73	4	.61	1.10	1.15	27.6
RP	1981	R.Fingers	Oak	AL	47	0	78	6	3	28	61	13	1.04	1.04	1.16	44.6
RP	1998	M.Jackson	Cle	AL	69	0	64	1	1	40	55	13	1.55	1.55	1.40	22.5
Relievers		Averages			60	0	70	4	2	41	62	12	1.06	1.19	1.15	30.5
Totals		Averages			99	32	336	26	8	42	302	69	2.48	2.83	2.86	113.9

All Time Great Player Seasons

American League Greatest Catchers

V	R	Year	Name	T	L	AB	BB	HBP	TAB	H	2B	3B	HR	BA	OB	SA	PRO	Wtd PRO	SB	CS	SBF	SPF	FF	R TF	V HC
1	5	1968	B.Freehan	Det	AL	540	65	24	629	142	24	2	25	.263	.367	.454	821	907	0	1	(3)	10	80	994	94.8
2	2	1972	C.Fisk	Bos	AL	457	52	4	513	134	28	9	22	.293	.370	.538	909	985	5	2	2		40	1,027	89.9
3	8	1932	M.Cochrane	Phi	AL	518	100	4	622	152	35	4	23	.293	.412	.510	921	867	0	1	(3)	10	90	964	89.3
4	4	1933	M.Cochrane	Phi	AL	429	106	3	538	138	30	4	15	.322	.459	.515	974	940	8	6	(7)	10	60	1,002	87.7
5	3	1931	M.Cochrane	Phi	AL	459	56	3	518	160	31	6	17	.349	.423	.553	976	931	2	3	(7)	10	80	1,014	87.4
6	9	1937	B.Dickey	NY	AL	530	73	4	607	176	35	2	29	.332	.417	.570	987	904	3	2	(2)	(10)	70	963	86.9
7	11	1967	B.Freehan	Det	AL	517	73	20	610	146	23	1	20	.282	.392	.447	839	902	1	2	(5)	10	50	958	81.5
8	6	1930	M.Cochrane	Phi	AL	487	55	1	543	174	42	5	10	.357	.424	.526	949	868	5	0	9	10	90	977	81.4
9	12	1977	C.Fisk	Bos	AL	536	75	9	620	169	26	3	26	.315	.408	.521	929	919	7	6	(8)		30	941	77.8
10	13	1999	I.Rodriguez	Tex	AL	600	24	1	625	199	29	1	35	.332	.358	.558	917	846	25	12	2		90	937	77.3
11	22	1954	Y.Berra	NY	AL	584	56	4	644	179	28	6	22	.307	.371	.488	859	858	0	1	(3)		50	905	73.4
12	17	1956	Y.Berra	NY	AL	521	65	5	591	155	29	2	30	.298	.381	.534	914	876	3	2	(2)		50	924	73.1
13	16	1998	I.Rodriguez	Tex	AL	579	32	3	614	186	40	4	21	.321	.360	.513	873	821	9	0	14		90	925	72.3
14	30	1950	Y.Berra	NY	AL	597	55	4	656	192	30	6	28	.322	.383	.533	915	851	4	2	0		40	891	70.3
15	27	1979	D.Porter	KC	AL	533	121	8	662	155	23	10	20	.291	.429	.484	913	893	3	4	(7)		10	896	69.0
16	7	1993	C.Hoiles	Bal	AL	419	69	9	497	130	23	0	29	.310	.419	.585	1,003	979	1	1	(2)		(10)	967	68.6
17	18	1939	B.Dickey	NY	AL	480	77	4	561	145	23	3	24	.302	.403	.513	915	851	5	0	8	(10)	70	920	68.1
18	26	1978	C.Fisk	Bos	AL	571	71	7	649	162	39	5	20	.284	.370	.475	844	863	7	2	4		30	898	68.1
19	10	1936	B.Dickey	NY	AL	423	46	3	472	153	26	8	22	.362	.428	.617	1,045	941	0	2	(8)	(10)	40	963	67.5
20	15	1938	B.Dickey	NY	AL	454	75	2	531	142	27	4	27	.313	.412	.568	981	896	3	0	5	(10)	40	931	67.5
21	1	2000	I.Rodriguez	Tex	AL	363	19	1	383	126	27	4	27	.347	.381	.667	1,048	959	5	5	(12)		100	1,047	67.4
22	31	1997	I.Rodriguez	Tex	AL	597	38	8	643	187	34	4	20	.313	.362	.484	846	799	7	3	1		90	890	65.3
23	25	1929	M.Cochrane	Phi	AL	514	69	2	585	170	37	8	7	.331	.412	.475	887	828	7	6	(8)	10	70	900	65.2
24	29	1952	Y.Berra	NY	AL	534	66	4	604	146	17	1	30	.273	.358	.478	835	848	2	3	(6)		50	892	65.0
25	21	1953	Y.Berra	NY	AL	503	50	3	556	149	23	5	27	.296	.363	.523	886	869	0	3	(10)		50	909	64.4

American League Greatest First Basemen

V	R	Year	Name	T	L	AB	BB	HBP	TAB	H	2B	3B	HR	BA	OB	SA	PRO	Wtd PRO	SB	CS	SBF	SPF	FF	R TF	V HC
1	1	1927	L.Gehrig	NY	AL	584	109	3	696	218	52	18	47	.373	.474	.765	1,240	1,165	10	8	(8)			1,157	135.0
2	2	1932	J.Foxx	Phi	AL	585	116	0	701	213	33	9	58	.364	.469	.749	1,218	1,146	3	7	(15)		20	1,152	134.1
3	4	1933	J.Foxx	Phi	AL	573	96	1	670	204	37	9	48	.356	.449	.703	1,153	1,111	2	2	(3)		20	1,129	120.4
4	3	1961	N.Cash	Det	AL	535	124	9	668	193	22	8	41	.361	.488	.662	1,150	1,118	11	5	1		20	1,139	117.5
5	6	1994	F.Thomas	Chi	AL	399	109	2	510	141	34	1	38	.353	.494	.729	1,223	1,142	2	3	(7)		(30)	1,105	115.0
6	8	1934	L.Gehrig	NY	AL	579	109	2	690	210	40	6	49	.363	.465	.706	1,172	1,103	9	5	(1)			1,101	114.6
7	9	1920	G.Sisler	StL	AL	631	46	2	679	257	49	18	19	.407	.449	.632	1,082	1,040	42	17	11	10	40	1,101	112.7
8	11	1938	J.Foxx	Bos	AL	565	119	0	684	197	33	9	50	.349	.462	.704	1,166	1,065	5	4	(4)		20	1,081	106.6
9	5	1972	D.Allen	Chi	AL	506	99	1	606	156	28	5	37	.308	.422	.603	1,025	1,112	19	8	5	10	(10)	1,116	105.2
10	13	1930	L.Gehrig	NY	AL	581	101	3	685	220	42	17	41	.379	.473	.721	1,194	1,092	12	14	(22)			1,070	102.9
11	19	1931	L.Gehrig	NY	AL	619	117	0	736	211	31	15	46	.341	.446	.662	1,108	1,057	17	12	(9)			1,048	102.5
12	18	1936	L.Gehrig	NY	AL	579	130	7	716	205	37	7	49	.354	.478	.696	1,174	1,057	3	4	(7)			1,050	100.5
13	15	1970	C.Yastrzemski	Bos	AL	566	128	1	695	186	29	0	40	.329	.453	.592	1,045	1,049	23	13	(4)	10	10	1,065	97.8
14	12	1922	G.Sisler	StL	AL	586	49	3	638	246	42	18	8	.420	.467	.594	1,061	1,004	51	19	19	10	40	1,073	96.9
15	14	1934	J.Foxx	Phi	AL	539	111	1	651	180	28	6	44	.334	.449	.653	1,102	1,037	11	2	10		20	1,067	96.9
16	7	1939	J.Foxx	Bos	AL	467	89	2	558	168	31	10	35	.360	.464	.694	1,158	1,077	4	3	(3)		30	1,104	93.3
17	17	1935	J.Foxx	Phi	AL	535	114	0	649	185	33	7	36	.346	.461	.636	1,096	1,028	6	4	(3)		30	1,055	92.6
18	25	1937	H.Greenberg	Det	AL	594	102	3	699	200	49	14	40	.337	.436	.668	1,105	1,013	8	3	3		10	1,025	89.5
19	22	1938	H.Greenberg	Det	AL	556	119	3	678	175	23	4	58	.315	.438	.683	1,122	1,024	7	5	(4)		10	1,030	88.3
20	20	1928	L.Gehrig	NY	AL	562	95	4	661	210	47	13	27	.374	.467	.648	1,115	1,062	4	11	(26)			1,037	88.3
21	24	2000	C.Delgado	Tor	AL	569	123	15	707	196	57	1	41	.344	.472	.664	1,137	1,041	0	1	(3)		(10)	1,028	86.9
22	21	1993	J.Olerud	Tor	AL	551	114	7	672	200	54	2	24	.363	.478	.599	1,077	1,051	0	2	(6)	(10)		1,035	84.9
23	29	1937	L.Gehrig	NY	AL	569	127	4	700	200	37	9	37	.351	.473	.643	1,116	1,023	4	3	(3)		(10)	1,010	84.4
24	10	1996	M.McGwire	Oak	AL	423	116	8	547	132	21	0	52	.312	.468	.730	1,199	1,096	0	0	0	(10)		1,086	82.4
25	23	1929	J.Foxx	Phi	AL	517	103	2	622	183	23	9	33	.354	.463	.625	1,088	1,016	9	7	(8)	10	10	1,028	80.5

American League Greatest
Second basemen

V	R	Year	Name	T	L	AB	BB	HBP	TAB	H	2B	3B	HR	BA	OB	SA	PRO	Wtd PRO	SB	CS	SBF	SPF	FF	R TF	V HC
1	1	1901	N.Lajoie	Phi	AL	544	24	13	581	232	48	14	14	.426	.463	.643	1,106	1,109	27			10	80	1,199	164.7
2	2	1910	N.Lajoie	Cle	AL	591	60	5	656	227	51	7	4	.384	.445	.514	960	1,091	26				80	1,171	159.6
3	3	1904	N.Lajoie	Cle	AL	553	27	8	588	208	49	15	5	.376	.413	.546	959	1,099	29			10	50	1,159	139.7
4	6	1909	E.Collins	Phi	AL	571	62	6	639	198	30	10	3	.347	.416	.450	866	1,001	67			10	70	1,081	126.7
5	7	1906	N.Lajoie	Cle	AL	602	30	6	638	214	48	9	0	.355	.392	.465	857	974	20			10	90	1,074	124.3
6	8	1914	E.Collins	Phi	AL	526	97	6	629	181	23	14	2	.344	.452	.452	904	994	58	30	(3)	10	50	1,051	115.3
7	5	1903	N.Lajoie	Cle	AL	485	24	3	512	167	41	11	7	.344	.379	.518	896	977	21			10	100	1,087	113.2
8	9	1913	E.Collins	Phi	AL	534	85	7	626	184	23	13	3	.345	.441	.453	894	955	55			10	80	1,045	112.8
9	10	1915	E.Collins	Chi	AL	521	119	5	645	173	22	10	4	.332	.460	.436	896	972	46	30	(21)	10	70	1,031	111.8
10	11	1910	E.Collins	Phi	AL	581	49	6	636	188	16	15	3	.324	.382	.418	800	910	81			10	110	1,030	109.8
11	21	1944	S.Stirnweiss	NY	AL	643	73	1	717	205	35	16	8	.319	.389	.460	849	884	55	11	43	10	40	978	105.1
12	14	1912	E.Collins	Phi	AL	543	101	0	644	189	25	11	0	.348	.450	.435	885	917	63			10	70	997	100.7
13	23	1936	C.Gehringer	Det	AL	641	83	4	728	227	60	12	15	.354	.431	.555	987	888	4	1	3		70	961	100.6
14	16	1999	R.Alomar	Cle	AL	563	99	7	669	182	40	3	24	.323	.430	.533	963	889	37	6	35	10	60	994	98.3
15	17	1908	N.Lajoie	Cle	AL	581	47	9	637	168	32	6	2	.289	.352	.375	727	858	15			10	120	988	96.6
16	22	1920	E.Collins	Chi	AL	602	69	2	673	224	38	13	3	.372	.438	.493	932	896	20	8	6	10	60	972	96.6
17	26	1945	S.Stirnweiss	NY	AL	632	78	1	711	195	32	22	10	.309	.385	.476	862	906	33	17	(1)	10	40	955	96.1
18	13	1911	E.Collins	Phi	AL	493	62	15	570	180	22	13	3	.365	.451	.481	932	945	38			10	50	1,005	91.3
19	31	1934	C.Gehringer	Det	AL	601	99	3	703	214	50	7	11	.356	.450	.517	967	910	11	8	(7)		40	943	90.9
20	15	1975	R.Carew	Min	AL	535	64	1	600	192	24	4	14	.359	.428	.497	926	950	35	9	27	10	10	997	89.0
21	4	1902	N.Lajoie	Cle	AL	352	19	6	377	133	35	5	7	.378	.419	.565	984	993	20			10	110	1,113	88.8
22	24	1993	R.Alomar	Tor	AL	589	80	5	674	192	35	6	17	.326	.411	.492	903	882	55	15	35	10	30	957	87.1
23	27	1937	C.Gehringer	Det	AL	564	90	1	655	209	40	1	14	.371	.458	.520	978	896	11	4	4		50	950	87.0
24	19	1981	B.Grich	Cal	AL	352	40	4	396	107	14	2	22	.304	.381	.543	924	969	2	4	(14)		30	985	85.5
25	36	1929	C.Gehringer	Det	AL	634	64	6	704	215	45	19	13	.339	.405	.532	936	874	27	9	12	10	30	926	85.1

American League Greatest
Shortstop

V	R	Year	Name	T	L	AB	BB	HBP	TAB	H	2B	3B	HR	BA	OB	SA	PRO	Wtd PRO	SB	CS	SBF	SPF	FF	R TF	V HC
1	2	1991	C.Ripken	Bal	AL	650	53	5	708	210	46	5	34	.323	.379	.566	945	950	6	1	5		60	1,015	119.1
2	4	1982	R.Yount	Mil	AL	635	54	1	690	210	46	12	29	.331	.384	.578	962	958	14	3	11	10	30	1,009	114.1
3	1	2000	A.Rodriguez	Sea	AL	554	100	7	661	175	34	2	41	.316	.427	.606	1,033	946	15	4	10	10	50	1,016	111.4
4	3	1969	R.Petrocelli	Bos	AL	535	98	1	634	159	32	2	40	.297	.407	.589	996	1,014	3	5	(10)	(10)	20	1,014	106.3
5	7	1948	L.Boudreau	Cle	AL	560	98	2	660	199	34	6	18	.355	.453	.534	987	953	3	2	(1)	(10)	40	982	105.7
6	9	1944	L.Boudreau	Cle	AL	584	73	5	662	191	45	5	3	.327	.406	.437	843	878	11	3	7		90	975	103.8
7	11	1984	C.Ripken	Bal	AL	641	71	2	714	195	37	7	27	.304	.375	.510	885	889	2	1	0		70	959	101.1
8	8	1996	A.Rodriguez	Sea	AL	601	59	4	664	215	54	1	36	.358	.419	.631	1,049	960	15	4	10	10		980	100.5
9	10	1987	A.Trammell	Det	AL	597	60	3	660	205	34	3	28	.343	.406	.551	957	918	21	2	24	10	10	962	94.5
10	14	1999	D.Jeter	NY	AL	627	91	12	730	219	37	9	24	.349	.441	.552	993	916	19	8	4	10		930	93.1
11	12	1930	J.Cronin	Was	AL	587	72	5	664	203	41	9	13	.346	.422	.513	934	854	17	10	(4)	10	80	940	92.6
12	5	1999	N.Garciaparra	Bos	AL	532	51	8	591	190	42	4	27	.357	.421	.603	1,025	945	14	3	13	10	20	988	91.8
13	16	1998	A.Rodriguez	Sea	AL	686	45	10	741	213	35	5	42	.310	.362	.560	921	866	46	13	26	10	20	922	91.7
14	6	2000	N.Garciaparra	Bos	AL	529	61	2	592	197	51	3	21	.372	.439	.599	1,038	951	5	2	2	10	20	982	90.3
15	18	1983	C.Ripken	Bal	AL	663	58	0	721	211	47	2	27	.318	.373	.517	890	889	0	4	(10)		40	919	88.2
16	24	1949	V.Stephens	Bos	AL	610	101	0	711	177	31	2	39	.290	.391	.539	930	897	2	2	(3)		10	905	86.4
17	25	1943	L.Appling	Chi	AL	585	90	1	676	192	33	2	3	.328	.419	.407	825	879	27	8	15		10	904	82.1
18	17	1917	R.Chapman	Cle	AL	563	61	0	624	170	28	13	2	.302	.370	.409	779	862	52			10	50	922	81.2
19	22	1941	C.Travis	Was	AL	608	52	1	661	218	39	19	7	.359	.410	.520	930	899	2	2	(3)		10	906	80.9
20	21	1995	J.Valentin	Bos	AL	520	81	10	611	155	37	2	27	.298	.403	.533	935	882	20	5	15		10	908	80.4
21	15	1975	T.Harrah	Tex	AL	522	98	1	621	153	24	1	20	.293	.406	.458	864	889	23	9	8	10	20	927	78.4
22	28	1923	J.Sewell	Cle	AL	553	98	7	658	195	41	10	3	.353	.456	.479	935	893	9	6	(4)		10	899	78.1
23	20	1983	R.Yount	Mil	AL	578	72	3	653	178	42	10	17	.308	.387	.503	891	890	12	5	3	10	10	913	78.0
24	23	1938	J.Cronin	Bos	AL	530	91	5	626	172	51	5	17	.325	.428	.536	964	880	7	5	(5)	10	20	906	76.5
25	33	1965	Z.Versalles	Min	AL	666	41	7	714	182	45	12	19	.273	.322	.462	785	812	27	5	23	10	40	885	75.7

All Time Great Player Seasons

American League Greatest Third basemen

V	R	Year	Name	T	L	AB	BB	HBP	TAB	H	2B	3B	HR	BA	OB	SA	PRO	Wtd PRO	SB	CS	SBF	SPF	FF	R TF	V HC
1	2	1985	G.Brett	KC	AL	550	103	3	656	184	38	5	30	.335	.442	.585	1,028	1,021	9	1	10		40	1,071	110.8
2	1	1980	G.Brett	KC	AL	449	58	1	508	175	33	9	24	.390	.461	.664	1,124	1,120	15	6	6	10	20	1,155	106.3
3	3	1912	F.Baker	Phi	AL	577	50	6	633	200	40	21	10	.347	.404	.541	945	980	40			10	40	1,030	99.5
4	4	1987	W.Boggs	Bos	AL	551	105	2	658	200	40	6	24	.363	.467	.588	1,055	1,012	1	3	(7)		20	1,024	96.6
5	7	1988	W.Boggs	Bos	AL	584	125	3	712	214	45	6	5	.366	.480	.490	970	986	2	3	(5)		10	991	93.2
6	6	1913	F.Baker	Phi	AL	564	63	10	637	190	34	9	12	.337	.413	.493	906	967	34			10	20	997	89.7
7	5	1953	A.Rosen	Cle	AL	599	85	4	688	201	27	5	43	.336	.422	.613	1,034	1,014	8	7	(8)			1,006	85.6
8	10	1937	H.Clift	StL	AL	571	98	6	675	175	36	7	29	.306	.413	.546	960	880	8	5	(3)		90	967	84.9
9	9	1969	H.Killebrew	Min	AL	555	145	5	705	153	20	2	49	.276	.430	.584	1,014	1,032	8	2	5	(10)	(60)	968	84.5
10	19	1985	W.Boggs	Bos	AL	653	96	4	753	240	42	3	8	.368	.452	.478	929	923	2	1	0		20	943	81.4
11	15	1938	H.Clift	StL	AL	534	118	5	657	155	25	7	34	.290	.423	.554	977	893	10	5	0		60	953	77.8
12	18	1979	G.Brett	KC	AL	645	51	0	696	212	42	20	23	.329	.378	.563	941	920	17	10	(4)	10	20	946	76.3
13	13	1964	B.Robinson	Bal	AL	612	51	4	667	194	35	3	28	.317	.373	.521	895	905	1	0	1		50	956	76.2
14	16	1983	W.Boggs	Bos	AL	582	91	2	675	210	44	7	5	.361	.449	.486	935	934	3	3	(4)		20	950	75.1
15	8	1992	E.Martinez	Sea	AL	528	54	4	586	181	46	3	18	.343	.408	.544	951	970	14	4	10			980	73.6
16	14	1982	D.DeCinces	Cal	AL	575	66	1	642	173	42	5	30	.301	.374	.548	922	918	7	5	(4)		40	953	72.6
17	23	1986	W.Boggs	Bos	AL	580	105	0	685	207	47	2	8	.357	.455	.486	942	929	0	4	(11)		10	928	69.1
18	28	1901	J.Collins	Bos	AL	564	34	5	603	187	42	16	6	.332	.375	.495	869	872	19			10	40	922	68.4
19	22	1911	F.Baker	Phi	AL	592	40	2	634	198	42	14	11	.334	.379	.508	887	900	38			10	20	930	67.8
20	24	1970	T.Harper	Mil	AL	604	77	4	685	179	35	4	31	.296	.380	.522	901	905	38	16	8	10		923	67.5
21	29	1976	G.Brett	KC	AL	645	49	1	695	215	34	14	7	.333	.381	.462	843	900	21	11	(1)	10	10	919	67.0
22	26	2000	T.Glaus	Ana	AL	563	112	2	677	160	37	1	47	.284	.405	.604	1,009	923	14	11	(11)		10	922	66.4
23	46	1989	W.Boggs	Bos	AL	621	107	7	735	205	51	7	3	.330	.434	.449	883	906	2	6	(13)		10	903	65.3
24	25	1914	F.Baker	Phi	AL	570	53	3	626	182	23	10	9	.319	.380	.442	822	904	19	20	(32)	10	40	922	64.7
25	32	1966	H.Killebrew	Min	AL	569	103	2	674	160	27	1	39	.281	.393	.538	931	972	0	2	(6)	(10)	(40)	917	64.3

American League Greatest Outfielders

V	R	Year	Name	T	L	AB	BB	HBP	TAB	H	2B	3B	HR	BA	OB	SA	PRO	Wtd PRO	SB	CS	SBF	SPF	FF	R TF	V HC
1	3	1923	B.Ruth	NY	AL	522	170	4	696	205	45	13	41	.393	.545	.764	1,309	1,250	17	21	(34)	10	40	1,266	177.5
2	2	1921	B.Ruth	NY	AL	540	144	4	688	204	44	16	59	.378	.512	.846	1,358	1,253	17	13	(12)	10	20	1,271	177.0
3	1	1920	B.Ruth	NY	AL	458	148	3	609	172	36	9	54	.376	.530	.847	1,378	1,325	14	14	(22)	10	10	1,323	172.7
4	9	1927	B.Ruth	NY	AL	540	138	0	678	192	29	8	60	.356	.487	.772	1,259	1,183	7	6	(7)		20	1,196	149.2
5	7	1956	M.Mantle	NY	AL	533	112	2	647	188	22	5	52	.353	.467	.705	1,172	1,123	10	1	12	10	70	1,214	148.2
6	6	1957	M.Mantle	NY	AL	474	146	0	620	173	28	6	34	.365	.515	.665	1,179	1,172	16	3	15	10	30	1,228	146.1
7	11	1946	T.Williams	Bos	AL	514	156	2	672	176	37	8	38	.342	.497	.667	1,164	1,188	0	0	0			1,188	144.9
8	4	1941	T.Williams	Bos	AL	456	145	3	604	185	33	3	37	.406	.551	.735	1,286	1,244	2	4	(9)			1,234	144.3
9	8	1926	B.Ruth	NY	AL	495	144	3	642	184	30	5	47	.372	.516	.737	1,253	1,190	11	9	(10)		20	1,200	142.4
10	14	1942	T.Williams	Bos	AL	522	145	4	671	186	34	5	36	.356	.499	.648	1,147	1,180	3	2	(1)			1,179	141.6
11	17	1924	B.Ruth	NY	AL	529	142	4	675	200	39	7	46	.378	.513	.739	1,252	1,170	9	13	(24)		20	1,167	138.4
12	16	1917	T.Cobb	Det	AL	588	61	4	653	225	44	24	6	.383	.444	.570	1,014	1,122	55			10	40	1,172	135.6
13	15	1967	C.Yastrzemski	Bos	AL	579	91	4	674	189	31	4	44	.326	.421	.622	1,043	1,122	10	8	(8)		60	1,174	133.8
14	21	1947	T.Williams	Bos	AL	528	162	2	692	181	40	9	32	.343	.499	.634	1,133	1,146	0	1	(3)			1,143	133.8
15	20	1912	T.Speaker	Bos	AL	580	82	6	668	222	53	12	10	.383	.464	.567	1,031	1,069	52			10	70	1,149	131.1
16	10	1919	B.Ruth	Bos	AL	432	101	6	539	139	34	12	29	.322	.456	.657	1,114	1,136	7			10	50	1,196	130.4
17	5	1957	T.Williams	Bos	AL	420	119	5	544	163	28	1	38	.388	.528	.731	1,259	1,251	0	1	(3)	(10)	(10)	1,228	128.2
18	37	1949	T.Williams	Bos	AL	566	162	2	730	194	39	3	43	.343	.490	.650	1,141	1,100	1	1	(1)			1,099	124.8
19	22	1911	T.Cobb	Det	AL	591	44	8	643	248	47	24	8	.420	.467	.621	1,088	1,103	83			10	30	1,143	124.3
20	18	1961	M.Mantle	NY	AL	514	126	0	640	163	16	6	54	.317	.452	.687	1,138	1,107	12	1	15	10	30	1,162	123.2
21	12	1910	T.Cobb	Det	AL	506	64	4	574	194	35	13	8	.383	.456	.551	1,008	1,146	65			10	30	1,186	123.2
22	36	1915	T.Cobb	Det	AL	563	118	10	691	208	31	13	3	.369	.486	.487	973	1,055	96	38	27	10	10	1,102	119.5
23	29	1931	B.Ruth	NY	AL	534	128	1	663	199	31	3	46	.373	.495	.700	1,195	1,140	5	4	(4)		(20)	1,116	119.1
24	31	1928	B.Ruth	NY	AL	536	135	3	674	173	29	8	54	.323	.461	.709	1,170	1,115	4	5	(8)			1,107	117.9
25	27	1909	T.Cobb	Det	AL	573	48	6	627	216	33	10	9	.377	.431	.517	947	1,094	76			10	20	1,124	115.3

American League Greatest Outfielders

V	R	Year	Name	T	L	AB	BB	HBP	TAB	H	2B	3B	HR	BA	OB	SA	PRO	Wtd PRO	SB	CS	SBF	SPF	FF	R TF	V HC
26	25	1941	J.DiMaggio	NY	AL	541	76	4	621	193	43	11	30	.357	.440	.643	1,083	1,047	4	2	0	10	70	1,127	115.1
27	58	1981	D.Evans	Bos	AL	412	85	1	498	122	19	4	22	.296	.418	.522	940	985	3	2	(2)	10	80	1,073	113.5
28	30	1955	M.Mantle	NY	AL	517	113	3	633	158	25	11	37	.306	.433	.611	1,044	1,024	8	1	9	10	70	1,113	112.7
29	19	1990	R.Henderson	Oak	AL	489	97	4	590	159	33	3	28	.325	.441	.577	1,017	1,034	65	10	72	10	40	1,156	112.2
30	32	1966	F.Robinson	Bal	AL	576	87	10	673	182	34	2	49	.316	.415	.637	1,052	1,098	8	5	(3)	10		1,105	111.6
31	40	1930	B.Ruth	NY	AL	518	136	1	655	186	28	9	49	.359	.493	.732	1,225	1,120	10	10	(14)		(10)	1,095	111.0
32	33	1912	J.Jackson	Cle	AL	572	54	12	638	226	44	26	3	.395	.458	.579	1,036	1,074	35			10	20	1,104	110.9
33	42	1914	T.Speaker	Bos	AL	571	77	7	655	193	46	18	4	.338	.423	.503	926	1,018	42	29	(23)	10	90	1,095	110.7
34	34	1911	J.Jackson	Cle	AL	571	56	8	635	233	45	19	7	.408	.468	.590	1,058	1,073	41			10	20	1,103	110.0
35	43	1958	M.Mantle	NY	AL	519	129	2	650	158	21	1	42	.304	.445	.592	1,036	1,035	18	3	17	10	30	1,092	109.0
36	35	1968	C.Yastrzemski	Bos	AL	539	119	2	660	162	32	2	23	.301	.429	.495	924	1,021	13	6	1		80	1,102	108.5
37	62	1937	J.DiMaggio	NY	AL	621	64	5	690	215	35	15	46	.346	.412	.673	1,085	994	3	0	4	10	60	1,069	107.6
38	28	1913	T.Speaker	Bos	AL	520	65	7	592	189	35	22	3	.363	.441	.533	974	1,040	46			10	70	1,120	107.5
39	55	1923	T.Speaker	Cle	AL	574	93	4	671	218	59	11	17	.380	.469	.610	1,079	1,031	8	9	(14)	10	50	1,077	107.4
40	41	1916	T.Speaker	Cle	AL	546	82	4	632	211	41	8	2	.386	.470	.502	972	1,064	35	27	(28)	10	50	1,095	107.0
41	51	1948	T.Williams	Bos	AL	509	126	3	638	188	44	3	25	.369	.497	.615	1,112	1,074	4	0	6			1,080	103.0
42	38	1912	T.Cobb	Det	AL	553	43	5	601	226	30	23	7	.409	.456	.584	1,040	1,078	61			10	10	1,098	102.6
43	46	1913	J.Jackson	Cle	AL	528	80	5	613	197	39	17	7	.373	.460	.551	1,011	1,080	26			10		1,090	102.1
44	63	1994	K.Griffey Jr.	Sea	AL	433	56	2	491	140	24	4	40	.323	.403	.674	1,078	1,006	11	3	10	10	40	1,066	102.0
45	49	1916	T.Cobb	Det	AL	542	78	2	622	201	31	10	5	.371	.452	.493	944	1,034	68	24	30	10	10	1,084	101.8
46	23	1954	T.Williams	Bos	AL	386	136	1	523	133	23	1	29	.345	.516	.635	1,151	1,149	0	0	0		(10)	1,139	100.1
47	44	1930	A.Simmons	Phi	AL	554	39	1	594	211	41	16	36	.381	.423	.708	1,130	1,033	9	2	8		50	1,091	99.4
48	52	1985	R.Henderson	NY	AL	547	99	3	649	172	28	5	24	.314	.422	.516	938	931	80	10	87	10	50	1,079	99.3
49	68	1997	K.Griffey Jr.	Sea	AL	608	76	8	692	185	34	3	56	.304	.389	.646	1,035	977	15	4	10	10	60	1,057	98.6
50	24	1939	J.DiMaggio	NY	AL	462	52	4	518	176	32	6	30	.381	.448	.671	1,119	1,041	3	0	5	10	80	1,136	98.3
51	47	1917	T.Speaker	Cle	AL	523	67	7	597	184	42	11	2	.352	.432	.486	918	1,016	30			10	60	1,086	98.2
52	69	1993	K.Griffey Jr.	Sea	AL	582	96	6	684	180	38	3	45	.309	.412	.617	1,029	1,004	17	9	(1)	10	40	1,053	96.3
53	70	1994	A.Belle	Cle	AL	412	58	5	475	147	35	2	36	.357	.442	.714	1,156	1,079	9	6	(6)		(20)	1,053	94.6
54	54	1979	F.Lynn	Bos	AL	531	82	4	617	177	42	1	39	.333	.426	.637	1,063	1,040	2	2	(3)		40	1,077	93.9
55	77	1920	T.Speaker	Cle	AL	552	97	5	654	214	50	11	8	.388	.483	.562	1,045	1,005	10	13	(23)	10	50	1,042	93.2
56	76	1906	G.Stone	StL	AL	581	52	7	640	208	25	20	6	.358	.417	.501	918	1,044	35			10	(10)	1,044	91.8
57	50	1931	A.Simmons	Phi	AL	513	47	3	563	200	37	13	22	.390	.444	.641	1,085	1,035	3	3	(5)		50	1,080	91.1
58	64	1910	T.Speaker	Bos	AL	538	52	6	596	183	20	14	7	.340	.404	.468	873	992	35			10	60	1,062	91.0
59	86	1940	H.Greenberg	Det	AL	573	93	1	667	195	50	8	41	.340	.433	.670	1,103	1,039	6	3	0		(10)	1,029	90.6
60	65	1902	E.Delahanty	Was	AL	473	62	4	539	178	43	14	10	.376	.453	.590	1,043	1,051	16			10		1,061	90.3
61	67	1996	K.Griffey Jr.	Sea	AL	545	78	7	630	165	26	2	49	.303	.397	.628	1,024	937	16	1	21	10	90	1,058	90.2
62	57	1918	T.Cobb	Det	AL	421	41	2	464	161	19	14	3	.382	.440	.515	955	1,044	34			10	20	1,074	89.2
63	66	1932	B.Ruth	NY	AL	457	130	2	589	156	13	5	41	.341	.489	.661	1,150	1,082	2	2	(3)		(20)	1,059	89.0
64	88	1995	A.Belle	Cle	AL	546	73	6	625	173	52	1	50	.317	.403	.690	1,094	1,031	5	2	2		(10)	1,023	89.0
65	13	1955	T.Williams	Bos	AL	320	91	2	413	114	21	3	28	.356	.501	.703	1,204	1,181	2	0	5			1,185	88.6
66	84	1969	R.Jackson	Oak	AL	549	114	12	675	151	36	3	47	.275	.410	.608	1,019	1,038	13	5	4	10	(20)	1,032	88.3
67	60	1975	F.Lynn	Bos	AL	528	62	3	593	175	47	7	21	.331	.405	.566	971	1,000	10	5	0	10	60	1,070	88.2
68	26	1962	M.Mantle	NY	AL	377	122	1	500	121	15	1	30	.321	.488	.605	1,093	1,068	9	0	17	10	30	1,125	87.7
69	99	1998	K.Griffey Jr.	Sea	AL	633	76	7	716	180	33	3	56	.284	.367	.611	979	920	20	5	13	10	70	1,013	87.3
70	79	1929	A.Simmons	Phi	AL	581	31	1	613	212	41	9	34	.365	.398	.642	1,040	971	4	2	0		70	1,041	87.2
71	105	1994	K.Lofton	Cle	AL	459	52	2	513	160	32	9	12	.349	.417	.536	953	890	60	12	66	10	40	1,006	86.0
72	39	1922	T.Speaker	Cle	AL	426	77	1	504	161	48	8	11	.378	.474	.606	1,080	1,022	8	3	4	10	60	1,096	85.4
73	98	1972	B.Murcer	NY	AL	585	63	2	650	171	30	7	33	.292	.363	.537	900	976	11	9	(10)	10	40	1,016	84.1
74	96	1988	K.Puckett	Min	AL	657	23	2	682	234	42	5	24	.356	.380	.545	925	937	6	7	(11)	10	80	1,016	84.1
75	81	1923	H.Heilmann	Det	AL	524	74	5	603	211	44	11	18	.403	.481	.632	1,113	1,063	9	7	(8)	(10)	(10)	1,035	83.9

American League Greatest DH's

V	R	Year	Name	T	L	AB	BB	HBP	TAB	H	2B	3B	HR	BA	OB	SA	PRO	Wtd PRO	SB	CS	SBF	SPF	FF	R TF	V HC
1	1	1995	E.Martinez	Sea	AL	511	116	8	635	182	52	0	29	.356	.482	.628	1,110	1,047	4	3	(3)		(30)	1,014	101.3
2	4	1991	F.Thomas	Chi	AL	559	138	1	698	178	31	2	32	.318	.454	.553	1,007	1,012	1	2	(4)	10	(30)	988	72.6
3	2	1987	P.Molitor	Mil	AL	465	69	2	536	164	41	5	16	.353	.438	.566	1,004	963	45	10	44	10	(20)	997	71.8
4	3	1999	R.Palmeiro	Tex	AL	565	97	3	665	183	30	1	47	.324	.426	.630	1,056	974	2	4	(9)	(10)	40	995	71.3
5	7	1977	J.Rice	Bos	AL	644	53	8	705	206	29	15	39	.320	.379	.593	972	961	5	4	(4)		(20)	937	60.4
6	5	2000	F.Thomas	Chi	AL	582	112	5	699	191	44	0	43	.328	.441	.625	1,066	976	1	3	(7)	(10)	(20)	939	56.3
7	8	1996	E.Martinez	Sea	AL	499	123	8	630	163	52	2	26	.327	.467	.595	1,062	971	3	3	(5)		(30)	937	50.1
8	9	1997	E.Martinez	Sea	AL	542	119	11	672	179	35	1	28	.330	.460	.554	1,013	956	2	4	(8)		(30)	918	47.4
9	10	1993	P.Molitor	Tor	AL	636	77	3	716	211	37	5	22	.332	.406	.509	916	894	22	4	18	10	(20)	902	45.1
10	14	1994	P.Molitor	Tor	AL	454	55	1	510	155	30	4	14	.341	.414	.518	931	869	20	0	37	10	(20)	896	43.5
11	17	1991	P.Molitor	Mil	AL	665	77	6	748	216	32	13	17	.325	.400	.489	888	893	19	8	4	10	(20)	887	41.7
12	12	1976	H.McRae	KC	AL	527	64	8	599	175	34	5	8	.332	.412	.461	873	932	22	12	(3)		(30)	899	40.4
13	6	1977	O.Gamble	Chi	AL	408	54	6	468	121	22	2	31	.297	.387	.588	975	964	1	2	(6)	10	(30)	938	40.3
14	13	1998	E.Martinez	Sea	AL	556	106	3	665	179	46	1	29	.322	.433	.565	998	938	1	1	(1)	(10)	(30)	897	40.2
15	16	1992	P.Molitor	Mil	AL	609	73	3	685	195	36	7	12	.320	.396	.461	857	874	31	6	26	10	(20)	890	39.2
16	18	2000	E.Martinez	Sea	AL	556	96	5	657	180	31	0	37	.324	.428	.579	1,007	922	3	0	4	(10)	(30)	886	36.3
17	26	1994	C.Davis	Cal	AL	392	69	1	462	122	18	1	26	.311	.416	.561	977	912	3	2	(2)		(40)	870	35.0
18	15	1999	E.Martinez	Sea	AL	502	97	6	605	169	35	1	24	.337	.450	.554	1,003	925	7	2	5	(10)	(30)	890	34.6
19	29	1982	H.McRae	KC	AL	613	55	5	673	189	46	8	27	.308	.370	.542	912	908	4	4	(6)		(40)	862	33.6
20	31	1994	J.Canseco	Tex	AL	429	69	5	503	121	19	2	31	.282	.388	.552	940	878	15	8	(2)		(20)	856	33.3
21	11	1994	B.Hamelin	KC	AL	312	56	1	369	88	25	1	24	.282	.393	.599	992	926	4	3	(5)	(10)	(10)	901	32.6
22	28	1984	M.Easler	Bos	AL	601	58	4	663	188	31	5	27	.313	.377	.516	893	897	1	1	(1)		(30)	865	30.0
23	24	1998	T.Salmon	Ana	AL	463	90	3	556	139	28	1	26	.300	.417	.533	951	894	0	1	(3)	(10)	(10)	871	30.0
24	19	1999	J.Jaha	Oak	AL	457	101	9	567	126	23	0	35	.276	.416	.556	972	897	2	0	3	(10)	(10)	880	29.7
25	36	1992	D.Winfield	Tor	AL	583	82	1	666	169	33	3	26	.290	.378	.491	869	886	2	3	(6)	(10)	(20)	850	29.5

AL All Time Greats
Starting Pitchers

V	R	Year	Name	T	L	G	GS	IP	W	L	SV	SO	BB	ERA	RA/9	R Wtd RA/9	V Runs /162
1	2	1913	W.Johnson	Was	AL	48	36	346	36	7	2	243	38	1.14	1.46	1.68	116.5
2	11	1901	C.Young	Bos	AL	43	41	371	33	10	0	158	37	1.62	2.71	2.23	110.8
3	9	1912	W.Johnson	Was	AL	50	37	369	33	12	2	303	76	1.39	2.17	2.19	102.0
4	24	1918	W.Johnson	Was	AL	39	29	326	23	13	3	162	70	1.27	1.96	2.47	96.6
5	99	1908	E.Walsh	Chi	AL	66	49	464	40	15	6	269	56	1.42	2.17	2.85	92.6
6	14	1910	J.Coombs	Phi	AL	45	38	353	31	9	1	224	115	1.30	1.89	2.35	90.9
7	26	1917	E.Cicotte	Chi	AL	49	35	347	28	12	4	150	70	1.53	1.98	2.49	84.0
8	42	1914	W.Johnson	Was	AL	51	40	372	28	18	1	225	74	1.72	2.13	2.63	83.8
9	111	1902	C.Young	Bos	AL	45	43	385	32	11	0	160	53	2.15	3.18	2.90	82.1
10	28	1919	E.Cicotte	Chi	AL	40	35	307	29	7	1	110	49	1.82	2.26	2.49	81.4
11	31	1915	W.Johnson	Was	AL	47	39	337	27	13	4	203	56	1.55	2.22	2.54	79.6
12	66	1946	B.Feller	Cle	AL	48	42	371	26	15	4	348	153	2.18	2.45	2.72	79.5
13	68	1910	E.Walsh	Chi	AL	45	36	370	18	20	5	258	61	1.27	2.19	2.73	79.2
14	4	1964	D.Chance	LA	AL	46	35	278	20	9	4	207	86	1.65	1.81	2.03	78.2
15	20	1945	H.Newhouser	Det	AL	40	36	313	25	9	2	212	110	1.81	2.10	2.44	77.6
16	27	1919	W.Johnson	Was	AL	39	29	290	20	14	2	147	51	1.49	2.26	2.49	76.9
17	108	1912	E.Walsh	Chi	AL	62	41	393	27	17	10	254	94	2.15	2.86	2.89	76.6
18	83	1910	W.Johnson	Was	AL	45	42	370	25	17	1	313	76	1.36	2.24	2.79	76.5
19	37	1921	R.Faber	Chi	AL	43	39	331	25	15	1	124	87	2.48	2.91	2.58	76.3
20	12	1931	L.Grove	Phi	AL	41	30	289	31	4	5	175	62	2.06	2.62	2.30	76.1
21	3	1914	D.Leonard	Bos	AL	36	25	225	19	5	3	176	60	0.96	1.36	1.68	75.7
22	5	1997	R.Clemens	Tor	AL	34	34	264	21	7	0	292	68	2.05	2.22	2.03	74.1
23	64	1972	G.Perry	Cle	AL	41	40	343	24	16	1	234	82	1.92	2.07	2.71	74.0
24	39	1940	B.Feller	Cle	AL	43	37	320	27	11	4	261	118	2.61	2.87	2.59	73.6
25	8	1978	R.Guidry	NY	AL	35	35	274	25	3	0	248	72	1.74	2.01	2.16	73.0
26	72	1912	J.Wood	Bos	AL	43	38	344	34	5	1	258	82	1.91	2.72	2.75	72.7
27	1	2000	P.Martinez	Bos	AL	29	29	217	18	6	0	284	32	1.74	1.82	1.55	72.3
28	25	1971	V.Blue	Oak	AL	39	39	312	24	8	0	301	88	1.82	2.11	2.47	72.3
29	273	1904	J.Chesbro	NY	AL	55	51	455	41	12	0	239	88	1.82	2.53	3.20	72.0
30	32	1975	J.Palmer	Bal	AL	39	38	323	23	11	1	193	80	2.09	2.42	2.55	71.9
31	16	1934	L.Gomez	NY	AL	38	33	282	26	5	1	158	96	2.33	2.74	2.40	71.1
32	36	1910	R.Ford	NY	AL	36	33	300	26	6	1	209	70	1.65	2.07	2.58	69.4
33	236	1907	E.Walsh	Chi	AL	56	46	422	24	18	4	206	87	1.60	2.56	3.15	69.3
34	19	1937	L.Gomez	NY	AL	34	34	278	21	11	0	194	93	2.33	2.85	2.43	69.0
35	150	1911	E.Walsh	Chi	AL	56	37	369	27	18	4	255	72	2.22	3.05	2.99	67.6
36	51	1902	R.Waddell	Phi	AL	33	27	276	24	7	0	210	64	2.05	2.93	2.67	66.9
37	38	1930	L.Grove	Phi	AL	50	32	291	28	5	9	209	60	2.54	3.12	2.59	66.9
38	86	1908	A.Joss	Cle	AL	42	35	325	24	11	2	130	30	1.16	2.13	2.80	66.8
39	44	1946	H.Newhouser	Det	AL	37	34	293	26	9	1	275	98	1.94	2.37	2.63	65.9
40	57	1908	C.Young	Bos	AL	36	33	299	21	11	2	150	37	1.26	2.05	2.69	65.2
41	141	1944	D.Trout	Det	AL	49	40	352	27	14	0	144	83	2.12	2.66	2.98	65.0
42	107	1905	R.Waddell	Phi	AL	46	34	329	27	10	0	287	90	1.48	2.35	2.87	64.8
43	209	1904	C.Young	Bos	AL	43	41	380	26	16	1	200	29	1.97	2.46	3.11	64.1
44	103	1916	B.Ruth	Bos	AL	44	41	324	23	12	1	170	118	1.75	2.31	2.87	64.0
45	59	1932	L.Grove	Phi	AL	44	30	292	25	10	7	188	79	2.84	3.11	2.69	63.6
46	69	1939	B.Feller	Cle	AL	39	35	297	24	9	1	246	142	2.85	3.18	2.73	63.3
47	85	1941	T.Lee	Chi	AL	35	34	300	22	11	1	130	92	2.37	2.94	2.80	61.7
48	112	1913	R.Russell	Chi	AL	52	36	317	22	16	4	122	79	1.90	2.53	2.90	61.2
49	17	1911	V.Gregg	Cle	AL	34	26	245	23	7	0	125	86	1.80	2.47	2.42	61.2
50	30	1936	L.Grove	Bos	AL	35	30	253	17	12	2	130	65	2.81	3.20	2.53	60.0

All Time Great Player Seasons

AL All Time Greats
Starting Pitchers

V	R	Year	Name	T	L	G	GS	IP	W	L	SV	SO	BB	ERA	RA/9	R Wtd RA/9	V Runs /162
51	23	1968	L.Tiant	Cle	AL	34	32	258	21	9	0	264	73	1.60	1.85	2.47	60.0
52	253	1916	W.Johnson	Was	AL	48	38	370	25	20	1	228	82	1.90	2.56	3.18	59.6
53	6	1999	P.Martinez	Bos	AL	31	29	213	23	4	0	313	37	2.07	2.36	2.05	59.5
54	216	1922	R.Faber	Chi	AL	43	38	352	21	17	2	148	83	2.81	3.26	3.12	59.1
55	194	1920	J.Bagby	Cle	AL	48	38	340	31	12	0	73	79	2.89	3.23	3.07	59.0
56	297	1904	R.Waddell	Phi	AL	46	46	383	25	19	0	349	91	1.62	2.56	3.24	58.9
57	77	1973	J.Palmer	Bal	AL	38	37	296	22	9	1	158	113	2.40	2.61	2.77	58.9
58	365	1918	S.Perry	Phi	AL	44	36	332	20	19	2	81	111	1.98	2.63	3.31	58.6
59	61	1981	S.McCatty	Oak	AL	22	22	186	14	7	0	91	61	2.33	2.42	2.70	58.2
60	123	1927	T.Thomas	Chi	AL	40	36	308	19	16	1	107	94	2.98	3.21	2.94	58.1
61	159	1971	W.Wood	Chi	AL	44	42	334	22	13	1	210	62	1.91	2.56	3.00	57.8
62	148	1920	S.Coveleski	Cle	AL	41	38	315	24	14	2	133	65	2.49	3.14	2.99	57.8
63	40	1943	S.Chandler	NY	AL	30	30	253	20	4	0	134	54	1.64	2.21	2.62	57.4
64	18	1995	R.Johnson	Sea	AL	30	30	214	18	2	0	294	65	2.48	2.73	2.43	56.9
65	327	1918	S.Coveleski	Cle	AL	38	33	311	22	13	1	87	76	1.82	2.60	3.27	56.6
66	10	1955	B.Pierce	Chi	AL	33	26	206	15	10	1	157	64	1.97	2.18	2.22	56.3
67	15	1906	D.White	Chi	AL	28	24	219	18	6	0	95	38	1.52	1.93	2.36	56.3
68	128	1917	S.Coveleski	Cle	AL	45	36	298	19	14	4	133	94	1.81	2.35	2.95	56.0
69	188	1968	D.McLain	Det	AL	41	41	336	31	6	0	280	63	1.96	2.30	3.06	55.7
70	183	1926	G.Uhle	Cle	AL	39	36	318	27	11	1	159	118	2.83	3.23	3.06	55.6
71	97	1924	W.Johnson	Was	AL	38	38	278	23	7	0	158	77	2.72	3.14	2.84	55.6
72	149	1977	J.Palmer	Bal	AL	39	39	319	20	11	0	193	99	2.91	2.99	2.99	55.6
73	170	1944	H.Newhouser	Det	AL	47	34	312	29	9	2	187	102	2.22	2.71	3.03	55.5
74	356	1903	C.Young	Bos	AL	40	35	342	28	9	2	176	37	2.08	3.03	3.30	55.1
75	131	1972	C.Hunter	Oak	AL	38	37	295	21	7	0	191	70	2.04	2.26	2.96	55.1
76	88	1980	M.Norris	Oak	AL	33	33	284	22	9	0	180	83	2.53	2.79	2.81	55.0
77	50	1989	B.Saberhagen	KC	AL	36	35	262	23	6	0	193	43	2.16	2.54	2.67	55.0
78	173	1974	G.Perry	Cle	AL	37	37	322	21	13	0	216	99	2.51	2.74	3.04	54.3
79	145	1949	M.Parnell	Bos	AL	39	33	295	25	7	2	122	134	2.77	3.11	2.98	54.3
80	89	1920	B.Shawkey	NY	AL	38	31	268	20	13	2	126	85	2.45	2.97	2.83	54.2
81	202	1905	N.Altrock	Chi	AL	38	34	316	23	12	0	97	63	1.88	2.53	3.09	54.1
82	467	1902	B.Dinneen	Bos	AL	42	42	371	21	21	0	136	99	2.93	3.76	3.43	53.9
83	279	1941	B.Feller	Cle	AL	44	40	343	25	13	2	260	194	3.15	3.38	3.22	53.8
84	79	1946	S.Chandler	NY	AL	34	32	257	20	8	2	138	90	2.10	2.49	2.77	53.8
85	22	1990	R.Clemens	Bos	AL	31	31	228	21	6	0	209	54	1.93	2.33	2.44	53.6
86	234	1917	B.Ruth	Bos	AL	41	38	326	24	13	2	128	108	2.01	2.51	3.15	53.6
87	134	1924	H.Pennock	NY	AL	40	34	286	21	9	3	101	64	2.83	3.27	2.96	53.3
88	179	1974	C.Hunter	Oak	AL	41	41	318	25	12	0	143	46	2.49	2.75	3.05	53.3
89	114	1956	E.Wynn	Cle	AL	38	35	278	20	9	2	158	91	2.72	3.01	2.92	53.2
90	52	1986	R.Clemens	Bos	AL	33	33	254	24	4	0	238	67	2.48	2.73	2.68	53.1
91	204	1975	C.Hunter	NY	AL	39	39	328	23	14	0	177	83	2.58	2.94	3.10	53.1
92	162	1909	C.Morgan	Phi	AL	40	36	293	18	17	1	111	102	1.81	2.30	3.01	52.9
93	13	1997	R.Johnson	Sea	AL	30	29	213	20	4	0	291	77	2.28	2.54	2.32	52.8
94	167	1948	B.Lemon	Cle	AL	43	37	294	20	14	2	147	129	2.82	3.18	3.03	52.6
95	94	1905	D.White	Chi	AL	36	33	260	17	13	0	120	58	1.76	2.32	2.83	52.3
96	243	1917	J.Bagby	Cle	AL	49	37	321	23	13	7	83	73	1.96	2.52	3.16	52.3
97	355	1903	R.Waddell	Phi	AL	39	38	324	21	16	0	302	85	2.44	3.03	3.30	52.2
98	320	1907	C.Young	Bos	AL	43	37	343	21	15	1	147	51	1.99	2.65	3.26	51.8
99	136	1978	M.Caldwell	Mil	AL	37	34	293	22	9	1	131	54	2.36	2.76	2.97	51.8
100	280	1903	B.Dinneen	Bos	AL	37	34	299	21	13	2	148	66	2.26	2.95	3.22	51.5

AL All Time Greats
Relief Pitchers

V	R	Year	Name	T	L	G	GS	IP	W	L	SV	SO	BB	ERA	RA/9	R Wtd RA/9	V Runs /162
1	13	1986	M.Eichhorn	Tor	AL	69	0	157	14	6	10	166	45	1.72	1.83	1.79	48.2
2	3	1981	R.Fingers	Mil	AL	47	0	78	6	3	28	61	13	1.04	1.04	1.16	44.6
3	7	1973	J.Hiller	Det	AL	65	0	125	10	5	38	124	39	1.44	1.51	1.60	41.1
4	19	1984	W.Hernandez	Det	AL	80	0	140	9	3	32	112	36	1.92	1.92	1.97	40.3
5	35	1979	J.Kern	Tex	AL	71	0	143	13	5	29	136	62	1.57	2.20	2.12	38.7
6	39	1975	R.Gossage	Chi	AL	62	0	142	9	8	26	130	70	1.84	2.03	2.14	38.1
7	29	1980	D.Corbett	Min	AL	73	0	136	8	6	23	89	42	1.98	2.05	2.07	37.6
8	33	1970	M.Grant	Oak	AL	80	0	135	8	3	24	58	32	1.87	1.93	2.10	36.8
9	63	1983	D.Quisenberry	KC	AL	69	0	139	5	3	45	48	11	1.94	2.27	2.29	35.0
10	62	1964	B.Lee	LA	AL	64	5	137	6	5	19	111	58	1.51	2.04	2.28	34.6
11	87	1965	H.Wilhelm	Chi	AL	66	0	144	7	7	20	106	32	1.81	2.13	2.45	33.7
12	12	1996	M.Rivera	NY	AL	61	0	108	8	3	5	130	34	2.09	2.09	1.76	33.6
13	46	1974	T.Murphy	Mil	AL	70	0	123	10	10	20	47	51	1.90	1.98	2.20	32.3
14	75	1963	D.Radatz	Bos	AL	66	0	132	15	6	25	162	51	1.97	2.11	2.36	32.3
15	78	1990	S.Farr	KC	AL	57	6	127	13	7	1	94	48	1.98	2.27	2.38	30.7
16	88	1979	S.Monge	Cle	AL	76	0	131	12	10	19	108	64	2.40	2.54	2.45	30.6
17	74	1962	D.Radatz	Bos	AL	62	0	125	9	6	24	144	40	2.24	2.30	2.36	30.6
18	54	1965	S.Miller	Bal	AL	67	0	119	14	7	24	104	32	1.89	1.97	2.27	30.3
19	182	1964	D.Radatz	Bos	AL	79	0	157	16	9	29	181	58	2.29	2.52	2.82	30.3
20	8	1989	J.Montgomery	KC	AL	63	0	92	7	3	18	94	25	1.37	1.57	1.63	30.0
21	30	1999	K.Foulke	Chi	AL	67	0	105	3	3	9	123	21	2.22	2.39	2.07	29.1
22	5	1969	K.Tatum	Cal	AL	45	0	86	7	2	22	65	39	1.36	1.36	1.52	29.1
23	105	1979	A.Lopez	Det	AL	61	0	127	10	5	21	106	51	2.41	2.62	2.53	28.6
24	224	1968	W.Wood	Chi	AL	88	2	159	13	12	16	74	33	1.87	2.21	2.94	28.5
25	138	1977	S.Lyle	NY	AL	72	0	137	13	5	26	68	33	2.17	2.69	2.69	28.4
26	213	1970	T.Hall	Min	AL	52	11	155	11	6	4	184	66	2.55	2.67	2.91	28.4
27	192	1947	J.Page	NY	AL	56	2	141	14	8	17	116	72	2.48	2.62	2.85	28.1
28	83	1962	D.Hall	Bal	AL	43	6	118	6	6	6	71	19	2.28	2.36	2.42	28.1
29	147	1971	K.Sanders	Mil	AL	83	0	136	7	12	31	80	34	1.91	2.32	2.72	27.8
30	2	1990	D.Eckersley	Oak	AL	63	0	73	4	2	48	73	4	0.61	1.10	1.15	27.6
31	31	1994	M.Eichhorn	Bal	AL	43	0	71	6	5	1	35	19	2.15	2.41	2.08	27.6
32	68	1973	B.Reynolds	Bal	AL	42	1	111	7	5	9	77	31	1.95	2.19	2.32	27.6
33	1	1995	J.Mesa	Cle	AL	62	0	64	3	0	46	58	17	1.13	1.27	1.13	27.4
34	178	1949	J.Page	NY	AL	60	0	135	13	8	27	99	75	2.59	2.93	2.81	27.4
35	137	1964	H.Wilhelm	Chi	AL	73	0	131	12	9	27	95	30	1.99	2.40	2.69	27.2
36	195	1979	M.Marshall	Min	AL	90	1	143	10	15	32	81	48	2.65	2.96	2.86	27.0
37	15	1996	R.Hernandez	Chi	AL	72	0	85	6	5	38	85	38	1.91	2.23	1.87	26.6
38	111	1961	L.Arroyo	NY	AL	65	0	119	15	5	29	87	49	2.19	2.57	2.56	26.4
39	160	1965	B.Lee	Cal	AL	69	0	131	9	7	23	89	42	1.92	2.40	2.76	26.1
40	82	1963	B.Dailey	Min	AL	66	0	109	6	3	21	72	19	1.99	2.15	2.40	26.1
41	23	1970	K.Sanders	Mil	AL	50	0	92	5	2	13	64	25	1.75	1.86	2.03	25.9
42	197	1982	D.Quisenberry	KC	AL	72	0	137	9	7	35	46	12	2.57	2.83	2.87	25.7
43	98	1966	J.Aker	KC	AL	66	0	113	8	4	32	68	28	1.99	2.15	2.51	25.7
44	164	1984	D.Quisenberry	KC	AL	72	0	129	6	3	44	41	12	2.64	2.71	2.78	25.5
45	52	1985	S.Cliburn	Cal	AL	44	0	99	9	3	6	48	26	2.09	2.27	2.25	25.4
46	95	1957	G.Staley	Chi	AL	47	0	105	5	1	7	44	27	2.06	2.31	2.49	25.3
47	36	1990	B.Thigpen	Chi	AL	77	0	89	4	6	57	70	32	1.83	2.03	2.13	25.3
48	90	1958	D.Hyde	Was	AL	53	0	103	10	3	18	49	35	1.75	2.27	2.46	25.3
49	16	1989	G.Olson	Bal	AL	64	0	85	5	2	27	90	46	1.69	1.80	1.89	25.2
50	133	1969	R.Perranoski	Min	AL	75	0	120	9	10	31	62	52	2.11	2.40	2.67	25.1

All Time Great Player Seasons

National League Greatest — **Hitters Volume of Success**

Pos	Year	Name	T	L	AB	BB	HBP	TAB	H	2B	3B	HR	BA	OB	SA	PRO	Wtd PRO	SB	CS	SBF	SPF	FF	R TF	V HC
C	1972	J.Bench	Cin	NL	538	100	2	640	145	22	2	40	.270	.386	.541	927	959	6	6	(9)	0	90	1,040	116.4
1B	1994	J.Bagwell	Hou	NL	400	65	4	469	147	32	2	39	.368	.461	.750	1,211	1,139	15	4	14	10	40	1,203	137.0
2B	1922	R.Hornsby	StL	NL	623	65	1	689	250	46	14	42	.401	.459	.722	1,181	1,107	17	12	(10)	0	10	1,107	145.8
SS	1908	H.Wagner	Pit	NL	568	54	5	627	201	39	19	10	.354	.415	.542	957	1,117	53			10	40	1,167	158.5
3B	1981	M.Schmidt	Phi	NL	354	73	4	431	112	19	2	31	.316	.439	.644	1,083	1,114	12	4	9	10	90	1,223	157.5
OF	1992	B.Bonds	Pit	NL	473	127	5	605	147	36	5	34	.311	.461	.624	1,085	1,116	39	8	36	10	60	1,222	134.0
OF	1997	L.Walker	Col	NL	568	78	14	660	208	46	4	49	.366	.455	.720	1,175	1,115	33	8	24	10	30	1,179	132.6
OF	1948	S.Musial	StL	NL	611	79	3	693	230	46	18	39	.376	.450	.702	1,152	1,138	7		0	0		1,138	132.1
Starters		Averages			517	80	5	602	180	36	8	36	.348	.440	.655	1,096	1,099	23	5	8	6	45	1,158	139.2
C	1953	R.Campanella	Bkn	NL	519	67	4	590	162	26	3	41	.312	.395	.611	1,006	950	4	2	0	0	50	1,000	95.5
1B	1998	M.McGwire	StL	NL	509	162	6	677	152	21	0	70	.299	.473	.752	1,225	1,166	1	0	1	(10)	(10)	1,147	121.7
2B	1976	J.Morgan	Cin	NL	472	114	1	587	151	30	5	27	.320	.453	.576	1,029	1,062	60	9	68	10	20	1,160	132.8
SS	1935	A.Vaughan	Pit	NL	499	97	7	603	192	34	10	19	.385	.491	.607	1,098	1,074	4			10	(10)	1,074	124.4
3B	1964	R.Santo	Chi	NL	592	86	2	680	185	33	13	30	.313	.401	.564	966	992	3	4	(7)	(10)	60	1,035	103.4
OF	1955	W.Mays	NY	NL	580	79	4	663	185	18	13	51	.319	.404	.659	1,063	1,018	24	4	23	10	80	1,131	124.1
OF	1905	C.Seymour	Cin	NL	581	51	2	634	219	40	21	8	.377	.429	.559	988	1,078	21			10	40	1,128	117.9
OF	1963	H.Aaron	Mil	NL	631	78	0	709	201	29	4	44	.319	.394	.586	980	1,031	31	5	28	10	20	1,089	112.0
Reserves		Averages			548	92	3	643	181	29	9	36	.330	.429	.613	1,042	1,047	19	3	14	4	31	1,096	116.4
Totals		Weighted Ave.			527	84	4	615	180	33	8	36	.342	.436	.641	1,078	1,082	21	5	10	5	40	1,138	131.6

Pitchers Volume of Success

Pos	Year	Name	T	L	G	GS	IP	W	L	SV	SO	BB	ERA	RA/9	Wtd RA/9	R V Runs/162
SP	1904	J.McGinnity	NY	NL	51	44	408	35	8	5	144	86	1.61	2.27	2.57	94.6
SP	1968	B.Gibson	StL	NL	34	34	305	22	9	0	268	62	1.12	1.45	1.93	89.0
SP	1915	P.Alexander	Phi	NL	49	42	376	31	10	3	241	64	1.22	2.06	2.57	87.2
SP	1908	C.Mathewson	NY	NL	56	44	391	37	11	5	259	42	1.43	1.96	2.69	85.3
SP	1994	G.Maddux	Atl	NL	25	25	202	16	6	0	156	31	1.56	1.96	1.92	83.7
Starters		Averages			43	38	336	28	9	3	214	57	1.43	2.00	2.39	88.0
RP	1977	R.Gossage	Pit	NL	72	0	133	11	9	26	151	49	1.62	1.83	1.90	39.3
RP	1984	B.Sutter	StL	NL	71	0	123	5	7	45	77	23	1.54	1.91	2.13	33.1
RP	1974	M.Marshall	LA	NL	106	0	208	15	12	21	143	56	2.42	2.85	3.13	33.0
RP	1966	P.Regan	LA	NL	65	0	117	14	1	21	88	24	1.62	1.85	2.06	32.5
Relievers		Averages			79	0	145	11	7	28	115	38	2.05	2.41	2.63	34.5
Totals		Averages			122	38	482	39	16	31	328	95	3.14	3.99	4.56	122.4

Baseball Players' Best Seasons

National League Greatest   **Hitters Rate of Success**

Pos	Year	Name	T	L	AB	BB	HBP	TAB	H	2B	3B	HR	BA	OB	SA	PRO	Wtd PRO	SB	CS	SBF	SPF	FF	R Wtd TF	V HC
C	1972	J.Bench	Cin	NL	538	100	2	640	145	22	2	40	.270	.386	.541	927	959	6	6	(9)	0	90	1,040	116.4
1B	1994	J.Bagwell	Hou	NL	400	65	4	469	147	32	2	39	.368	.461	.750	1,211	1,139	15	4	14	10	40	1,203	137.0
2B	1976	J.Morgan	Cin	NL	472	114	1	587	151	30	5	27	.320	.453	.576	1,029	1,062	60	9	68	10	20	1,160	132.8
SS	1908	H.Wagner	Pit	NL	568	54	5	627	201	39	19	10	.354	.415	.542	957	1,117	53			10	40	1,167	158.5
3B	1981	M.Schmidt	Phi	NL	354	73	4	431	112	19	2	31	.316	.439	.644	1,083	1,114	12	4	9	10	90	1,223	157.5
OF	1992	B.Bonds	Pit	NL	473	127	5	605	147	36	5	34	.311	.461	.624	1,085	1,116	39	8	36	10	60	1,222	134.0
OF	1997	L.Walker	Col	NL	568	78	14	660	208	46	4	49	.366	.455	.720	1,175	1,115	33	8	24	10	30	1,179	132.6
OF	1965	W.Mays	SF	NL	558	76	0	634	177	21	3	52	.317	.399	.645	1,044	1,073	9	4	1	10	80	1,164	122.9
Starters		Averages			491	86	4	582	161	31	5	35	.328	.432	.627	1,059	1,084	28	5	18	9	56	1,167	136.5
C	1951	R.Campanella	Bkn	NL	505	53	4	562	164	33	1	33	.325	.393	.590	983	963	1	2	(5)	0	50	1,008	93.0
1B	1998	M.McGwire	StL	NL	509	162	6	677	152	21	0	70	.299	.473	.752	1,225	1,166	1	0	1	(10)	(10)	1,147	121.7
2B	1925	R.Hornsby	StL	NL	504	83	2	589	203	41	10	39	.403	.489	.756	1,245	1,153	5	3	(2)	0	(10)	1,142	134.7
SS	1935	A.Vaughan	Pit	NL	499	97	7	603	192	34	10	19	.385	.491	.607	1,098	1,074	4			10	(10)	1,074	124.4
3B	1996	K.Caminiti	SD	NL	546	78	4	628	178	37	2	40	.326	.414	.621	1,035	986	11	5	2	0	50	1,037	96.1
OF	1948	S.Musial	StL	NL	611	79	3	693	230	46	18	39	.376	.450	.702	1,152	1,138	7			0	0	1,138	132.1
OF	1905	C.Seymour	Cin	NL	581	51	2	634	219	40	21	8	.377	.429	.559	988	1,078	21			10	40	1,128	117.9
OF	1987	E.Davis	Cin	NL	474	84	1	559	139	23	4	37	.293	.401	.593	994	956	50	6	64	10	60	1,090	88.5
Reserves		Averages			529	86	4	618	185	34	8	36	.349	.443	.648	1,091	1,068	13	2	8	3	21	1,100	113.5
Totals		Weighted Ave.			504	86	4	594	169	32	6	35	.335	.436	.634	1,069	1,079	23	4	14	7	45	1,144	128.8

Pitchers Rate of Success

Pos	Year	Name	T	L	G	GS	IP	W	L	SV	SO	BB	ERA	R Wtd RA/9	V RA/9	Runs /162
SP	1995	G.Maddux	Atl	NL	28	28	210	19	2	0	181	23	1.63	1.67	1.64	76.7
SP	1985	D.Gooden	NY	NL	35	35	277	24	4	0	268	69	1.53	1.66	1.86	83.0
SP	1968	B.Gibson	StL	NL	34	34	305	22	9	0	268	62	1.12	1.45	1.93	89.0
SP	1964	S.Koufax	LA	NL	29	28	223	19	5	1	223	53	1.74	1.98	2.23	57.6
SP	1971	T.Seaver	NY	NL	36	35	286	20	10	0	289	61	1.76	1.92	2.24	73.7
Starters		Averages			32	32	260	21	6	0	246	54	1.52	1.70	1.95	76.0
RP	1998	U.Urbina	Mon	NL	64	0	69	6	3	34	94	33	1.30	1.43	1.41	24.1
RP	1995	T.Fossas	StL	NL	58	0	37	3	0	0	40	10	1.47	1.47	1.44	14.4
RP	1998	T.Hoffman	SD	NL	66	0	73	4	2	53	86	21	1.48	1.48	1.46	25.1
RP	1999	B.Wagner	Hou	NL	66	0	75	4	1	39	124	23	1.57	1.69	1.53	25.1
Relievers		Averages			64	0	64	4	2	32	86	22	1.33	1.39	1.34	22.2
Totals		Averages			96	32	324	25	8	32	332	75	2.92	3.17	3.35	98.2

All Time Great Player Seasons

National League Greatest Catchers

V	R	Year	Name	T	L	AB	BB	HBP	TAB	H	2B	3B	HR	BA	OB	SA	PRO	Wtd PRO	SB	CS	SBF	SPF	FF	R TF	V HC
1	1	1972	J.Bench	Cin	NL	538	100	2	640	145	22	2	40	.270	.386	.541	927	959	6	6	(9)		90	1,040	116.4
2	2	1970	J.Bench	Cin	NL	605	54	0	659	177	35	4	45	.293	.351	.587	937	914	5	2	1		100	1,015	106.1
3	9	1974	J.Bench	Cin	NL	621	80	3	704	174	38	2	33	.280	.365	.507	872	886	5	4	(4)		90	972	98.8
4	5	1953	R.Campanella	Bkn	NL	519	67	4	590	162	26	3	41	.312	.395	.611	1,006	950	4	2	0		50	1,000	95.5
5	3	1975	J.Bench	Cin	NL	530	65	2	597	150	39	1	28	.283	.363	.519	882	892	11	0	17		100	1,010	94.5
6	6	1997	M.Piazza	LA	NL	556	69	3	628	201	32	1	40	.362	.435	.638	1,073	1,019	5	1	5	(10)	(20)	993	94.4
7	4	1951	R.Campanella	Bkn	NL	505	53	4	562	164	33	1	33	.325	.393	.590	983	963	1	2	(5)		50	1,008	93.0
8	10	1982	G.Carter	Mon	NL	557	78	6	641	163	32	1	29	.293	.385	.510	895	909	2	5	(12)		70	967	88.6
9	11	1966	J.Torre	Atl	NL	546	60	2	608	172	20	3	36	.315	.385	.560	945	955	0	4	(12)	(10)	20	952	79.6
10	8	1955	R.Campanella	Bkn	NL	446	56	6	508	142	20	1	32	.318	.402	.583	985	943	2	3	(7)	(10)	50	976	75.9
11	12	1992	D.Daulton	Phi	NL	485	88	6	579	131	32	5	27	.270	.389	.524	912	939	11	2	11			950	75.3
12	14	1969	J.Bench	Cin	NL	532	49	4	585	156	23	1	26	.293	.357	.487	844	864	6	6	(10)		90	944	74.3
13	17	1930	G.Hartnett	Chi	NL	508	55	1	564	172	31	3	37	.339	.404	.630	1,034	903	0		(10)		40	933	72.4
14	25	1980	G.Carter	Mon	NL	549	58	1	608	145	25	5	29	.264	.336	.486	822	832	3	2	(2)		80	911	67.6
15	41	1984	G.Carter	Mon	NL	596	64	6	666	175	32	1	27	.294	.368	.487	854	873	2	2	(3)	(10)	30	890	67.5
16	33	1996	M.Piazza	LA	NL	547	81	1	629	184	16	0	36	.336	.423	.563	986	939	0	3	(9)	(10)	(20)	900	66.8
17	20	1977	J.Bench	Cin	NL	494	58	1	553	136	34	2	31	.275	.353	.540	893	867	2	4	(10)		70	927	65.7
18	32	1998	J.Kendall	Pit	NL	535	51	31	617	175	36	3	12	.327	.417	.473	889	846	26	5	25	10	20	901	65.7
19	35	1998	M.Piazza	NY	NL	561	58	2	621	184	38	1	32	.328	.393	.570	963	917	1	0	2	(10)	(10)	898	65.3
20	42	1964	J.Torre	Mil	NL	601	36	7	644	193	36	5	20	.321	.366	.498	864	888	2	4	(9)	(10)	20	889	64.9
21	18	1995	M.Piazza	LA	NL	434	39	1	474	150	17	0	32	.346	.401	.606	1,007	959	1	0	2	(10)	(20)	931	64.5
22	43	1973	J.Bench	Cin	NL	557	83	0	640	141	17	3	25	.253	.350	.429	779	786	4	1	3		100	889	64.4
23	30	1965	J.Torre	Mil	NL	523	61	8	592	152	21	1	27	.291	.373	.489	863	887	0	1	(3)	(10)	30	903	63.7
24	47	1985	G.Carter	NY	NL	555	69	6	630	156	17	1	32	.281	.367	.488	855	868	1	1	(2)	(10)	30	887	62.9
25	52	1975	T.Simmons	StL	NL	581	63	1	645	193	32	3	18	.332	.398	.491	889	899	1	3	(7)	(10)		882	62.8

National League Greatest First Basemen

V	R	Year	Name	T	L	AB	BB	HBP	TAB	H	2B	3B	HR	BA	OB	SA	PRO	Wtd PRO	SB	CS	SBF	SPF	FF	R TF	V HC
1	1	1994	J.Bagwell	Hou	NL	400	65	4	469	147	32	2	39	.368	.461	.750	1,211	1,139	15	4	14	10	40	1,203	137.0
2	2	1998	M.McGwire	StL	NL	509	162	6	677	152	21	0	70	.299	.473	.752	1,225	1,166	1	0	1	(10)	(10)	1,147	121.7
3	3	1969	W.McCovey	SF	NL	491	121	4	616	157	26	2	45	.320	.458	.656	1,114	1,139	0	0	0	(10)		1,129	105.4
4	5	2000	T.Helton	Col	NL	580	103	4	687	216	59	2	42	.372	.470	.698	1,168	1,066	5	3	(1)		20	1,085	103.0
5	6	1946	S.Musial	StL	NL	624	73	3	700	228	50	20	16	.365	.434	.587	1,021	1,054	7				10	1,064	103.0
6	4	1971	H.Aaron	Atl	NL	495	71	2	568	162	22	3	47	.327	.414	.669	1,082	1,115	1	1	(2)	10		1,124	95.7
7	8	1940	J.Mize	StL	NL	579	82	5	666	182	31	13	43	.314	.404	.636	1,039	1,045	7					1,045	91.9
8	7	1939	J.Mize	StL	NL	564	92	4	660	197	44	14	28	.349	.444	.626	1,070	1,047	0					1,047	91.8
9	14	1996	J.Bagwell	Hou	NL	568	135	10	713	179	48	2	31	.315	.454	.570	1,025	976	21	7	9	10	20	1,016	83.4
10	15	1997	J.Bagwell	Hou	NL	566	127	16	709	162	40	2	43	.286	.430	.592	1,022	970	31	10	15	10	20	1,015	82.7
11	18	1999	J.Bagwell	Hou	NL	562	149	11	722	171	35	0	42	.304	.458	.591	1,049	960	30	11	10	10	30	1,010	82.6
12	11	1989	W.Clark	SF	NL	588	74	5	667	196	38	9	23	.333	.412	.546	958	995	8	3	3	10	20	1,028	81.8
13	9	1938	J.Mize	StL	NL	531	74	4	609	179	34	16	27	.337	.422	.614	1,036	1,037	0					1,037	81.6
14	13	1970	W.McCovey	SF	NL	495	137	3	635	143	39	2	39	.289	.446	.612	1,058	1,031	0	0	0	(10)		1,021	76.0
15	20	1999	M.McGwire	StL	NL	521	133	2	656	145	21	1	65	.278	.427	.697	1,124	1,028	0	0	0	(10)	(10)	1,008	74.3
16	24	1936	D.Camilli	Phi	NL	530	116	3	649	167	29	13	28	.315	.441	.577	1,018	995	5					995	73.3
17	23	1941	D.Camilli	Bkn	NL	529	104	4	637	151	29	6	34	.285	.407	.556	962	987	3				10	997	72.6
18	28	1934	R.Collins	StL	NL	600	57	2	659	200	40	12	35	.333	.393	.615	1,008	979	2				10	989	72.3
19	12	1937	D.Camilli	Phi	NL	475	90	2	567	161	23	7	27	.339	.446	.587	1,034	1,022	6					1,022	71.6
20	32	2000	J.Bagwell	Hou	NL	590	107	15	712	183	37	1	47	.310	.428	.615	1,044	952	9	6	(4)	10	20	978	70.6
21	17	1957	S.Musial	StL	NL	502	66	2	570	176	38	3	29	.351	.428	.612	1,040	1,014	1	1	(2)			1,012	69.1
22	27	1937	J.Mize	StL	NL	560	56	5	621	204	40	7	25	.364	.427	.595	1,021	1,010	2				(20)	990	68.4
23	19	1968	W.McCovey	SF	NL	523	72	5	600	153	16	4	36	.293	.383	.545	928	1,019	4	2	0	(10)		1,009	68.3
24	16	1960	F.Robinson	Cin	NL	464	82	9	555	138	33	6	31	.297	.413	.595	1,007	1,002	13	6	2	10		1,013	67.7
25	33	1979	K.Hernandez	StL	NL	610	80	1	691	210	48	11	11	.344	.421	.513	934	926	11	6	(1)		50	975	67.4

National League Greatest
Second basemen

V	R	Year	Name	T	L	AB	BB	HBP	TAB	H	2B	3B	HR	BA	OB	SA	PRO	Wtd PRO	SB	CS	SBF	SPF	FF	R TF	V HC
1	5	1922	R.Hornsby	StL	NL	623	65	1	689	250	46	14	42	.401	.459	.722	1,181	1,107	17	12	(10)		10	1,107	145.8
2	3	1924	R.Hornsby	StL	NL	536	89	2	627	227	43	14	25	.424	.507	.696	1,203	1,165	5	12	(29)			1,136	141.7
3	2	1925	R.Hornsby	StL	NL	504	83	2	589	203	41	10	39	.403	.489	.756	1,245	1,153	5	3	(2)		(10)	1,142	134.7
4	1	1976	J.Morgan	Cin	NL	472	114	1	587	151	30	5	27	.320	.453	.576	1,029	1,062	60	9	68	10	20	1,160	132.8
5	4	1975	J.Morgan	Cin	NL	498	132	3	633	163	27	6	17	.327	.471	.508	979	990	67	10	70	10	40	1,110	128.1
6	7	1921	R.Hornsby	StL	NL	592	60	7	659	235	44	18	21	.397	.458	.639	1,097	1,052	13	13	(19)		10	1,043	118.2
7	9	1929	R.Hornsby	Chi	NL	602	87	1	690	229	47	8	39	.380	.459	.679	1,139	1,027	2					1,027	118.1
8	8	1927	R.Hornsby	NY	NL	568	86	4	658	205	32	9	26	.361	.448	.586	1,035	1,007	9				20	1,027	112.8
9	6	1928	R.Hornsby	Bos	NL	486	107	1	594	188	42	7	21	.387	.498	.632	1,130	1,076	5				(20)	1,056	110.5
10	10	1920	R.Hornsby	StL	NL	589	60	3	652	218	44	20	9	.370	.431	.559	990	1,029	12	15	(26)		20	1,023	110.2
11	12	1984	R.Sandberg	Chi	NL	636	52	3	691	200	36	19	19	.314	.369	.520	889	909	32	7	25	10	70	1,013	108.0
12	14	1973	J.Morgan	Cin	NL	576	111	4	691	167	35	2	26	.290	.408	.493	901	909	67	15	51	10	40	1,009	106.7
13	13	1951	J.Robinson	Bkn	NL	548	79	9	636	185	33	7	19	.338	.429	.527	957	937	25	8	13	10	50	1,010	103.5
14	11	1974	J.Morgan	Cin	NL	512	120	3	635	150	31	3	22	.293	.430	.494	924	939	58	12	51	10	20	1,019	101.0
15	16	1985	R.Sandberg	Chi	NL	609	57	1	667	186	31	6	26	.305	.366	.504	870	884	54	11	45	10	60	999	99.7
16	21	1997	C.Biggio	Hou	NL	619	84	34	737	191	37	8	22	.309	.419	.501	920	873	47	10	35	10	50	968	99.2
17	17	1990	R.Sandberg	Chi	NL	615	50	1	666	188	30	3	40	.306	.359	.559	918	917	25	7	16	10	50	992	97.4
18	22	1949	J.Robinson	Bkn	NL	593	86	8	687	203	38	12	16	.342	.432	.528	960	937	37			10	20	967	97.1
19	19	1991	R.Sandberg	Chi	NL	585	87	2	674	170	32	2	26	.291	.384	.485	870	887	22	8	8	10	70	976	93.2
20	24	1972	J.Morgan	Cin	NL	552	115	6	673	161	23	4	16	.292	.419	.435	854	884	58	17	34	10	30	957	91.8
21	26	1927	F.Frisch	StL	NL	617	43	7	667	208	31	11	10	.337	.387	.472	858	836	48			10	110	956	90.4
22	25	1992	R.Sandberg	Chi	NL	612	68	1	681	186	32	8	26	.304	.374	.510	884	910	17	6	7	10	30	957	88.1
23	31	1994	C.Biggio	Hou	NL	437	62	8	507	139	44	5	6	.318	.412	.483	895	842	39	4	58	10	30	940	87.1
24	23	1952	J.Robinson	Bkn	NL	510	107	13	630	157	17	3	19	.308	.440	.465	904	916	24	7	15	10	20	961	87.0
25	34	1998	C.Biggio	Hou	NL	646	64	23	733	210	51	2	20	.325	.405	.503	908	864	50	8	44	10	10	928	84.8

National League Greatest
Shortstop

V	R	Year	Name	T	L	AB	BB	HBP	TAB	H	2B	3B	HR	BA	OB	SA	PRO	Wtd PRO	SB	CS	SBF	SPF	FF	R TF	V HC
1	1	1908	H.Wagner	Pit	NL	568	54	5	627	201	39	19	10	.354	.415	.542	957	1,117	53			10	40	1,167	158.5
2	4	1905	H.Wagner	Pit	NL	548	54	7	609	199	32	14	6	.363	.427	.505	932	1,017	57			10	70	1,097	132.9
3	2	1907	H.Wagner	Pit	NL	515	46	5	566	180	38	14	6	.350	.408	.513	921	1,055	61			10	40	1,105	125.7
4	7	1935	A.Vaughan	Pit	NL	499	97	7	603	192	34	10	19	.385	.491	.607	1,098	1,074	4			10	(10)	1,074	124.4
5	6	1906	H.Wagner	Pit	NL	516	58	10	584	175	38	9	2	.339	.416	.459	875	997	53			10	80	1,087	124.3
6	8	1903	H.Wagner	Pit	NL	512	44	7	563	182	30	19	5	.355	.414	.518	931	968	46			10	80	1,058	123.0
7	3	1904	H.Wagner	Pit	NL	490	59	4	553	171	44	14	4	.349	.423	.520	944	1,061	53			10	30	1,101	121.6
8	5	1909	H.Wagner	Pit	NL	495	66	3	564	168	39	10	5	.339	.420	.489	909	1,028	35			10	50	1,088	120.5
9	9	1901	H.Wagner	Pit	NL	549	53	7	609	194	37	11	6	.353	.417	.494	911	961	49			10	50	1,021	120.5
10	14	1959	E.Banks	Chi	NL	589	64	7	660	179	25	6	45	.304	.379	.596	975	946	2	4	(9)	10	30	978	104.5
11	10	1996	B.Larkin	Cin	NL	517	96	7	620	154	32	4	33	.298	.415	.567	981	935	36	10	24	10	40	1,009	102.5
12	16	1958	E.Banks	Chi	NL	617	52	4	673	193	23	11	47	.313	.370	.614	984	945	4	4	(6)	10	10	960	100.4
13	15	1912	H.Wagner	Pit	NL	558	59	6	623	181	35	20	7	.324	.395	.496	891	886	26			10	80	976	98.1
14	18	1960	E.Banks	Chi	NL	597	71	4	672	162	32	7	41	.271	.353	.554	907	902	1	3	(7)		40	935	91.9
15	13	1917	R.Hornsby	StL	NL	523	45	4	572	171	24	17	8	.327	.385	.484	868	968	17				10	978	90.7
16	12	1911	H.Wagner	Pit	NL	473	67	6	546	158	23	16	9	.334	.423	.507	930	951	20			10	30	991	89.9
17	19	1957	E.Banks	Chi	NL	594	70	3	667	169	34	6	43	.285	.363	.579	942	918	8	4	0	10		928	89.0
18	17	1995	B.Larkin	Cin	NL	496	61	3	560	158	29	6	15	.319	.396	.492	888	846	51	5	69	10	30	955	88.1
19	23	1934	A.Vaughan	Pit	NL	558	94	2	654	186	41	11	12	.333	.431	.511	942	915	10			10		925	86.1
20	20	1955	E.Banks	Chi	NL	596	45	2	643	176	29	9	44	.295	.347	.596	942	903	9	3	4	10	10	927	85.4
21	11	1991	B.Larkin	Cin	NL	464	55	3	522	140	27	4	20	.302	.379	.506	886	904	24	6	22	10	70	1,005	85.4
22	22	1901	B.Wallace	StL	NL	550	20	3	573	178	34	15	2	.324	.351	.451	802	846	15				80	926	83.4
23	27	1936	A.Vaughan	Pit	NL	568	118	5	691	190	30	11	9	.335	.453	.474	927	906	6			10	(20)	896	81.0
24	26	1938	A.Vaughan	Pit	NL	541	104	2	647	174	35	5	7	.322	.433	.444	876	878	14			10	20	908	79.6
25	25	1910	H.Wagner	Pit	NL	556	59	5	620	178	34	8	4	.320	.390	.432	822	871	24			10	30	911	77.4

All Time Great Player Seasons

National League Greatest Third basemen

V	R	Year	Name	T	L	AB	BB	HBP	TAB	H	2B	3B	HR	BA	OB	SA	PRO	Wtd PRO	SB	CS	SBF	SPF	FF	R TF	V HC
1	1	1981	M.Schmidt	Phi	NL	354	73	4	431	112	19	2	31	.316	.439	.644	1,083	1,114	12	4	9	10	90	1,223	157.5
2	2	1980	M.Schmidt	Phi	NL	548	89	2	639	157	25	8	48	.286	.388	.624	1,012	1,025	12	5	3	10	60	1,098	116.3
3	4	1974	M.Schmidt	Phi	NL	568	106	4	678	160	28	7	36	.282	.398	.546	944	959	23	12	(1)	10	70	1,037	103.8
4	6	1964	R.Santo	Chi	NL	592	86	2	680	185	33	13	30	.313	.401	.564	966	992	3	4	(7)	(10)	60	1,035	103.4
5	10	1999	C.Jones	Atl	NL	567	126	2	695	181	41	1	45	.319	.445	.633	1,078	986	25	3	26	10		1,022	101.2
6	9	1938	M.Ott	NY	NL	527	118	5	650	164	23	6	36	.311	.442	.583	1,024	1,025	2					1,025	100.7
7	11	1976	M.Schmidt	Phi	NL	584	100	11	695	153	31	4	38	.262	.380	.524	904	933	14	9	(5)	10	80	1,017	99.7
8	7	1977	M.Schmidt	Phi	NL	544	104	9	657	149	27	11	38	.274	.399	.574	972	944	15	8	(1)	10	80	1,033	99.1
9	8	1979	M.Schmidt	Phi	NL	541	120	3	664	137	25	4	45	.253	.392	.564	955	947	9	5	(1)	10	70	1,026	97.9
10	15	1967	R.Santo	Chi	NL	586	96	3	685	176	23	4	31	.300	.401	.512	913	955	1	5	(12)	(10)	80	1,013	96.8
11	5	1996	K.Caminiti	SD	NL	546	78	4	628	178	37	2	40	.326	.414	.621	1,035	986	11	5	2		50	1,037	96.1
12	3	1982	M.Schmidt	Phi	NL	514	107	3	624	144	26	3	35	.280	.407	.547	954	969	14	7	0		70	1,039	95.9
13	14	1966	R.Santo	Chi	NL	561	95	6	662	175	21	8	30	.312	.417	.538	955	965	4	5	(9)	(10)	70	1,016	94.6
14	20	1959	E.Mathews	Mil	NL	594	80	3	677	182	16	8	46	.306	.391	.593	984	955	2	1	0	10	20	985	91.4
15	22	1973	D.Evans	Atl	NL	595	124	3	722	167	25	8	41	.281	.407	.556	964	972	6	3	0		10	982	91.3
16	13	1992	G.Sheffield	SD	NL	557	48	6	611	184	34	3	33	.330	.390	.580	969	998	5	6	(11)	10	20	1,017	87.5
17	17	1983	M.Schmidt	Phi	NL	534	128	3	665	136	16	4	40	.255	.402	.524	926	934	7	8	(13)		70	991	87.0
18	19	1975	M.Schmidt	Phi	NL	562	101	4	667	140	34	3	38	.249	.367	.523	890	901	29	12	7	10	70	988	86.2
19	12	1966	D.Allen	Phi	NL	524	68	3	595	166	25	10	40	.317	.398	.632	1,030	1,040	10	6	(3)	10	(30)	1,017	85.3
20	26	1971	J.Torre	StL	NL	634	63	4	701	230	34	8	24	.363	.424	.555	979	1,009	4	1	3	(10)	(30)	971	85.2
21	18	1960	K.Boyer	StL	NL	552	56	4	612	168	26	10	32	.304	.373	.562	934	929	8	7	(9)	10	60	989	83.8
22	27	1965	R.Santo	Chi	NL	608	88	5	701	173	30	4	33	.285	.379	.510	889	914	3	1	1	(10)	60	965	83.1
23	32	1953	E.Mathews	Mil	NL	579	99	2	680	175	31	8	47	.302	.406	.627	1,033	976	1	3	(7)	10	(20)	959	82.8
24	16	1954	E.Mathews	Mil	NL	476	113	2	591	138	21	4	40	.290	.428	.603	1,031	977	10	3	6	10		993	82.1
25	34	1917	H.Groh	Cin	NL	599	71	8	678	182	39	11	1	.304	.385	.411	796	887	15			10	60	957	81.9

National League Greatest Outfielders

V	R	Year	Name	T	L	AB	BB	HBP	TAB	H	2B	3B	HR	BA	OB	SA	PRO	Wtd PRO	SB	CS	SBF	SPF	FF	R TF	V HC
1	1	1992	B.Bonds	Pit	NL	473	127	5	605	147	36	5	34	.311	.461	.624	1,085	1,116	39	8	36	10	60	1,222	134.0
2	2	1997	L.Walker	Col	NL	568	78	14	660	208	46	4	49	.366	.455	.720	1,175	1,115	33	8	24	10	30	1,179	132.6
3	5	1948	S.Musial	StL	NL	611	79	3	693	230	46	18	39	.376	.450	.702	1,152	1,138	7					1,138	132.1
4	3	1993	B.Bonds	SF	NL	539	126	2	667	181	38	4	46	.336	.463	.677	1,140	1,104	29	12	7	10	50	1,171	131.6
5	6	1955	W.Mays	NY	NL	580	79	4	663	185	18	13	51	.319	.404	.659	1,063	1,018	24	4	23	10	80	1,131	124.1
6	4	1965	W.Mays	SF	NL	558	76	0	634	177	21	3	52	.317	.399	.645	1,044	1,073	9	4	1	10	80	1,164	122.9
7	7	1905	C.Seymour	Cin	NL	581	51	2	634	219	40	21	8	.377	.429	.559	988	1,078	21			10	40	1,128	117.9
8	8	1996	B.Bonds	SF	NL	517	151	1	669	159	27	3	42	.308	.465	.615	1,080	1,029	40	7	37	10	50	1,126	117.3
9	10	1954	W.Mays	NY	NL	565	66	2	633	195	33	13	41	.345	.415	.667	1,083	1,026	8	5	(3)	10	80	1,113	112.8
10	16	1963	H.Aaron	Mil	NL	631	78	0	709	201	29	4	44	.319	.394	.586	980	1,031	31	5	28	10	20	1,089	112.0
11	11	1964	W.Mays	SF	NL	578	82	1	661	171	21	9	47	.296	.384	.607	992	1,019	19	5	13	10	70	1,112	111.6
12	18	1937	J.Medwick	StL	NL	633	41	2	676	237	56	10	31	.374	.414	.641	1,056	1,044	4			10	30	1,084	110.5
13	17	1962	W.Mays	SF	NL	621	78	4	703	189	36	5	49	.304	.385	.615	1,001	978	18	2	19	10	80	1,087	110.4
14	13	1963	W.Mays	SF	NL	596	66	2	664	187	32	7	38	.314	.384	.582	966	1,017	8	3	3	10	70	1,099	108.2
15	24	1958	W.Mays	SF	NL	600	78	1	679	208	33	11	29	.347	.423	.583	1,006	966	31	6	26	10	70	1,073	107.3
16	20	1957	W.Mays	NY	NL	585	76	1	662	195	26	20	35	.333	.411	.626	1,037	1,011	38	19	0	10	60	1,081	107.2
17	14	1994	B.Bonds	SF	NL	391	74	6	471	122	18	1	37	.312	.429	.647	1,076	1,013	29	9	22	10	50	1,095	107.1
18	22	1933	C.Klein	Phi	NL	606	56	1	663	223	44	7	28	.368	.422	.602	1,025	1,065	15			10		1,075	105.6
19	27	1959	H.Aaron	Mil	NL	629	51	4	684	223	46	7	39	.355	.406	.636	1,042	1,012	8	0	11	10	30	1,063	104.8
20	31	1943	S.Musial	StL	NL	617	72	2	691	220	48	20	13	.357	.425	.562	988	1,038	9				20	1,058	104.0
21	29	1995	B.Bonds	SF	NL	506	120	5	631	149	30	7	33	.294	.434	.577	1,011	963	31	10	16	10	70	1,060	102.3
22	26	1962	F.Robinson	Cin	NL	609	76	11	696	208	51	2	39	.342	.424	.624	1,048	1,024	18	9	0	10	30	1,064	101.8
23	21	1981	A.Dawson	Mon	NL	394	35	7	436	119	21	3	24	.302	.369	.553	923	949	26	4	39	10	80	1,078	100.9
24	28	1997	B.Bonds	SF	NL	532	145	8	685	155	26	5	40	.291	.450	.585	1,034	982	37	8	29	10	40	1,061	98.9
25	12	2000	B.Bonds	SF	NL	480	117	3	600	147	28	4	49	.306	.445	.688	1,133	1,033	11	3	8	10	50	1,101	98.3

National League Greatest Outfielders

V	R	Year	Name	T	L	AB	BB	HBP	TAB	H	2B	3B	HR	BA	OB	SA	PRO	Wtd PRO	SB	CS	SBF	SPF	FF	R TF	V HC
26	34	1998	B.Bonds	SF	NL	552	130	8	690	167	44	7	37	.303	.442	.609	1,051	1,000	28	12	5	10	40	1,055	98.0
27	58	1949	S.Musial	StL	NL	612	107	2	721	207	41	13	36	.338	.438	.624	1,062	1,037	3				(10)	1,027	97.5
28	50	1945	T.Holmes	Bos	NL	636	70	4	710	224	47	6	28	.352	.420	.577	997	1,011	15				20	1,031	97.3
29	37	1901	J.Sheckard	Bkn	NL	554	47	5	606	196	29	19	11	.354	.409	.534	944	996	35			10	40	1,046	96.3
30	33	1972	B.Williams	Chi	NL	574	62	6	642	191	34	6	37	.333	.403	.606	1,010	1,045	3	1	1	10		1,057	96.3
31	39	1949	R.Kiner	Pit	NL	549	117	1	667	170	19	5	54	.310	.432	.658	1,089	1,064	6				(20)	1,044	95.7
32	19	1990	B.Bonds	Pit	NL	519	93	3	615	156	32	3	33	.301	.410	.565	974	973	52	13	40	10	60	1,083	95.3
33	64	1932	C.Klein	Phi	NL	650	60	1	711	226	50	15	38	.348	.404	.646	1,050	1,024	20					1,024	94.8
34	84	1901	J.Burkett	StL	NL	601	59	10	670	226	20	15	10	.376	.440	.509	949	1,002	27			10		1,012	94.0
35	25	1967	R.Clemente	Pit	NL	585	41	3	629	209	26	10	23	.357	.402	.554	956	1,000	9	1	11	10	50	1,070	93.8
36	48	1951	S.Musial	StL	NL	578	98	1	677	205	30	12	32	.355	.449	.614	1,063	1,041	4	5	(8)			1,033	93.4
37	30	1989	K.Mitchell	SF	NL	543	87	3	633	158	34	6	47	.291	.392	.635	1,027	1,066	3	4	(7)	10	(10)	1,059	90.9
38	74	1930	H.Wilson	Chi	NL	585	105	1	691	208	35	6	56	.356	.454	.723	1,177	1,029	3				(10)	1,019	90.5
39	59	1951	R.Kiner	Pit	NL	531	137	2	670	164	31	6	42	.309	.452	.627	1,079	1,057	2	1	0		(30)	1,027	90.4
40	38	1961	F.Robinson	Cin	NL	545	71	10	626	176	32	7	37	.323	.411	.611	1,022	981	22	3	24	10	30	1,045	90.3
41	46	1959	W.Mays	SF	NL	575	65	2	642	180	43	5	34	.313	.385	.583	967	939	27	4	28	10	60	1,037	90.0
42	45	1900	H.Wagner	Pit	NL	527	41	8	576	201	45	22	4	.381	.434	.573	1,007	1,008	38			10	20	1,038	89.2
43	32	1991	B.Bonds	Pit	NL	510	107	4	621	149	28	5	25	.292	.419	.514	932	951	43	13	26	10	70	1,057	88.6
44	63	1944	S.Musial	StL	NL	568	90	5	663	197	51	14	12	.347	.440	.549	990	1,014	7			10		1,024	88.6
45	15	1987	E.Davis	Cin	NL	474	84	1	559	139	23	4	37	.293	.401	.593	994	956	50	6	64	10	60	1,090	88.5
46	72	1954	D.Snider	Bkn	NL	584	84	4	672	199	39	10	40	.341	.427	.647	1,074	1,018	6	6	(8)		10	1,020	88.3
47	47	1967	H.Aaron	Atl	NL	600	63	0	663	184	37	3	39	.307	.373	.573	946	989	17	6	7	10	30	1,036	88.1
48	36	1978	D.Parker	Pit	NL	581	57	2	640	194	32	12	30	.334	.395	.585	981	997	20	7	9	10	30	1,046	88.1
49	73	1932	M.Ott	NY	NL	566	100	4	670	180	30	8	38	.318	.424	.601	1,025	999	6				20	1,019	87.8
50	66	1960	W.Mays	SF	NL	595	61	4	660	190	29	12	29	.319	.386	.555	941	936	25	10	7	10	70	1,023	87.8
51	78	1901	E.Delahanty	Phi	NL	542	65	4	611	192	38	16	8	.354	.427	.528	955	1,008	29			10		1,018	87.6
52	9	1999	L.Walker	Col	NL	438	57	12	507	166	26	4	37	.379	.464	.710	1,174	1,074	11	4	6	10	30	1,119	87.4
53	56	1955	D.Snider	Bkn	NL	538	104	1	643	166	34	6	42	.309	.421	.628	1,050	1,005	9	7	(7)		30	1,028	87.2
54	60	1996	E.Burks	Col	NL	613	61	6	680	211	45	8	40	.344	.409	.639	1,048	999	32	6	28			1,026	87.2
55	53	1996	G.Sheffield	Fla	NL	519	142	10	671	163	33	1	42	.314	.469	.624	1,094	1,042	16	9	(3)	10	(20)	1,029	86.9
56	62	1983	D.Murphy	Atl	NL	589	90	2	681	178	24	4	36	.302	.396	.540	936	944	30	4	31	10	40	1,025	86.8
57	67	1936	M.Ott	NY	NL	534	111	5	650	175	28	6	33	.328	.448	.588	1,036	1,013	6				10	1,023	86.4
58	42	1969	H.Aaron	Atl	NL	547	87	2	636	164	30	3	44	.300	.398	.607	1,005	1,028	9	10	(16)	10	20	1,042	86.1
59	85	1953	D.Snider	Bkn	NL	590	82	3	675	198	38	4	42	.336	.419	.627	1,046	989	16	7	3		20	1,012	86.0
60	51	1962	H.Aaron	Mil	NL	592	66	3	661	191	28	6	45	.323	.393	.618	1,012	989	15	7	1	10	30	1,030	86.0
61	41	1965	H.Aaron	Mil	NL	570	60	1	631	181	40	1	32	.318	.384	.560	943	969	24	4	24	10	40	1,043	85.9
62	65	1968	H.Aaron	Atl	NL	606	64	1	671	174	33	4	29	.287	.356	.498	855	938	28	5	25	10	50	1,023	85.1
63	79	1987	D.Murphy	Atl	NL	566	115	7	688	167	27	1	44	.295	.420	.580	1,000	961	16	6	5	10	40	1,017	85.0
64	88	1900	E.Flick	Phi	NL	545	56	16	617	200	32	16	11	.367	.441	.545	986	987	35			10	10	1,007	84.9
65	83	1947	R.Kiner	Pit	NL	565	98	2	665	177	23	4	51	.313	.417	.639	1,055	1,022	1		(10)			1,012	84.9
66	75	1987	T.Gwynn	SD	NL	589	82	3	674	218	36	13	7	.370	.450	.511	961	924	56	12	45	10	40	1,019	83.9
67	44	1941	P.Reiser	Bkn	NL	536	46	11	593	184	39	17	14	.343	.406	.558	964	989	4			10	40	1,039	83.8
68	80	1977	G.Foster	Cin	NL	615	61	5	681	197	31	2	52	.320	.386	.631	1,017	988	6	4	(3)	10	20	1,015	83.5
69	97	1927	P.Waner	Pit	NL	623	60	3	686	237	42	18	9	.380	.437	.549	986	960	5			10	30	1,000	83.5
70	61	1972	C.Cedeno	Hou	NL	559	56	5	620	179	39	8	22	.320	.387	.537	924	956	55	21	20	10	40	1,026	83.4
71	86	1961	W.Mays	SF	NL	572	81	2	655	176	32	3	40	.308	.395	.584	979	941	18	9	0	10	60	1,011	83.1
72	92	1936	J.Medwick	StL	NL	636	34	4	674	223	64	13	18	.351	.387	.577	964	943	3			10	50	1,003	82.9
73	118	1930	C.Klein	Phi	NL	648	54	4	706	250	59	8	40	.386	.436	.687	1,123	981	4				10	991	82.7
74	95	1970	B.Williams	Chi	NL	636	72	2	710	205	34	4	42	.322	.393	.586	979	955	7	1	7	10	30	1,002	82.6
75	68	1964	F.Robinson	Cin	NL	568	79	9	656	174	38	6	29	.306	.399	.548	947	973	23	5	19	10	20	1,022	82.6

NL All Time Greats
Starting Pitchers

V	R	Year	Name	T	L	G	GS	IP	W	L	SV	SO	BB	ERA	RA/9	R Wtd RA/9	V Runs /162
1	36	1904	J.McGinnity	NY	NL	51	44	408	35	8	5	144	86	1.61	2.27	2.57	94.6
2	4	1968	B.Gibson	StL	NL	34	34	305	22	9	0	268	62	1.12	1.45	1.93	89.0
3	34	1915	P.Alexander	Phi	NL	49	42	376	31	10	3	241	64	1.22	2.06	2.57	87.2
4	54	1908	C.Mathewson	NY	NL	56	44	391	37	11	5	259	42	1.43	1.96	2.69	85.3
5	3	1994	G.Maddux	Atl	NL	25	25	202	16	6	0	156	31	1.56	1.96	1.92	83.7
6	2	1985	D.Gooden	NY	NL	35	35	277	24	4	0	268	69	1.53	1.66	1.86	83.0
7	16	1923	D.Luque	Cin	NL	41	37	322	27	8	2	151	88	1.93	2.52	2.36	82.8
8	25	1905	C.Mathewson	NY	NL	43	37	339	31	9	3	206	64	1.28	2.26	2.48	82.5
9	10	1933	C.Hubbell	NY	NL	45	33	309	23	12	5	156	47	1.66	2.01	2.28	82.1
10	66	1916	P.Alexander	Phi	NL	48	45	389	33	12	3	167	50	1.55	2.08	2.76	81.9
11	11	1966	S.Koufax	LA	NL	41	41	323	27	9	0	317	77	1.73	2.06	2.29	81.4
12	33	1972	S.Carlton	Phi	NL	41	41	346	27	10	0	310	87	1.97	2.18	2.55	81.0
13	32	1909	T.Brown	Chi	NL	50	34	343	27	9	7	172	53	1.31	2.05	2.55	80.4
14	12	1936	C.Hubbell	NY	NL	42	34	304	26	6	3	123	57	2.31	2.40	2.31	79.9
15	208	1903	J.McGinnity	NY	NL	55	48	434	31	20	2	171	109	2.43	3.36	3.12	79.9
16	53	1902	J.Taylor	Chi	NL	36	33	325	23	11	1	83	43	1.33	2.38	2.68	78.2
17	1	1995	G.Maddux	Atl	NL	28	28	210	19	2	0	181	23	1.63	1.67	1.64	76.7
18	15	1963	S.Koufax	LA	NL	40	40	311	25	5	0	306	58	1.88	1.97	2.35	76.3
19	69	1920	P.Alexander	Chi	NL	46	40	363	27	14	5	173	69	1.91	2.38	2.77	76.0
20	30	1908	T.Brown	Chi	NL	44	31	312	29	9	5	123	49	1.47	1.84	2.53	74.1
21	9	1906	T.Brown	Chi	NL	36	32	277	26	6	3	144	61	1.04	1.82	2.28	73.8
22	7	1971	T.Seaver	NY	NL	36	35	286	20	10	0	289	61	1.76	1.92	2.24	73.7
23	20	1905	E.Reulbach	Chi	NL	34	29	292	18	14	1	152	73	1.42	2.19	2.40	73.7
24	14	1909	C.Mathewson	NY	NL	37	33	275	25	6	2	149	36	1.14	1.88	2.34	71.2
25	41	1924	D.Vance	Bkn	NL	35	34	308	28	6	0	262	77	2.16	2.60	2.60	70.5
26	24	1928	D.Vance	Bkn	NL	38	32	280	22	10	2	200	72	2.09	2.54	2.46	68.5
27	62	1965	S.Koufax	LA	NL	43	41	336	26	8	2	382	71	2.04	2.41	2.73	68.4
28	195	1903	C.Mathewson	NY	NL	45	42	366	30	13	2	267	100	2.26	3.34	3.11	68.3
29	18	1953	W.Spahn	Mil	NL	35	32	266	23	7	3	148	70	2.10	2.54	2.39	67.5
30	104	1953	R.Roberts	Phi	NL	44	41	347	23	16	2	198	61	2.75	3.09	2.90	67.1
31	131	1908	G.McQuillan	Phi	NL	48	42	360	23	17	2	114	91	1.53	2.17	2.98	66.4
32	118	1918	H.Vaughn	Chi	NL	35	33	290	22	10	0	148	76	1.74	2.33	2.94	66.4
33	40	1909	O.Overall	Chi	NL	38	32	285	20	11	3	205	80	1.42	2.08	2.59	65.5
34	75	1939	B.Walters	Cin	NL	39	36	319	27	11	0	137	109	2.29	2.76	2.80	65.5
35	29	1973	T.Seaver	NY	NL	36	36	290	19	10	0	251	64	2.08	2.30	2.53	65.5
36	71	1934	C.Hubbell	NY	NL	49	34	313	21	12	8	118	37	2.30	2.88	2.77	65.4
37	57	1969	B.Gibson	StL	NL	35	35	314	20	13	0	269	95	2.18	2.41	2.69	65.1
38	45	1947	W.Spahn	Bos	NL	40	35	290	21	10	3	123	84	2.33	2.70	2.65	64.8
39	23	1919	P.Alexander	Chi	NL	30	27	235	16	11	1	121	38	1.72	1.95	2.44	63.9
40	109	1914	B.James	Bos	NL	46	37	332	26	7	3	156	118	1.90	2.47	2.92	63.4
41	26	1985	J.Tudor	StL	NL	36	36	275	21	8	0	169	49	1.93	2.23	2.50	62.9
42	93	1902	J.Chesbro	Pit	NL	35	33	286	28	6	1	136	62	2.17	2.55	2.88	61.8
43	83	1975	A.Messersmith	LA	NL	42	40	322	19	14	1	213	96	2.29	2.57	2.84	61.6
44	251	1917	P.Alexander	Phi	NL	45	44	388	30	13	0	200	56	1.83	2.48	3.20	61.5
45	178	1902	N.Hahn	Cin	NL	36	36	321	23	12	0	142	58	1.77	2.72	3.07	61.4
46	56	1965	J.Marichal	SF	NL	39	37	295	22	13	1	240	46	2.13	2.38	2.69	61.2
47	5	1997	G.Maddux	Atl	NL	33	33	233	19	4	0	177	20	2.20	2.24	2.20	60.9
48	119	1906	V.Willis	Pit	NL	41	36	322	23	13	1	124	76	1.73	2.35	2.94	60.8
49	106	1903	S.Leever	Pit	NL	36	34	284	25	7	1	90	60	2.06	3.13	2.91	60.1
50	92	1964	D.Drysdale	LA	NL	40	40	321	18	16	0	237	68	2.18	2.55	2.88	59.9

NL All Time Greats
Starting Pitchers

V	R	Year	Name	T	L	G	GS	IP	W	L	SV	SO	BB	ERA	RA/9	R Wtd RA/9	V Runs /162
51	8	1996	K.Brown	Fla	NL	32	32	233	17	11	0	159	33	1.89	2.32	2.24	59.9
52	37	1999	R.Johnson	Ari	NL	35	35	272	17	9	0	364	70	2.48	2.85	2.58	59.8
53	158	1919	H.Vaughn	Chi	NL	38	37	307	21	14	1	141	62	1.79	2.43	3.04	59.8
54	59	1932	L.Warneke	Chi	NL	35	32	277	22	6	0	106	64	2.37	2.73	2.71	59.8
55	42	1986	M.Scott	Hou	NL	37	37	275	18	10	0	306	72	2.22	2.39	2.61	59.4
56	116	1913	B.Adams	Pit	NL	43	37	314	21	10	0	144	49	2.15	2.69	2.94	59.4
57	63	1942	M.Cooper	StL	NL	37	35	279	22	7	0	152	68	1.78	2.35	2.74	59.3
58	101	1940	B.Walters	Cin	NL	36	36	305	22	10	0	115	92	2.48	2.80	2.90	59.1
59	128	1911	N.Rucker	Bkn	NL	48	33	316	22	18	4	190	110	2.71	2.91	2.97	58.5
60	82	1919	B.Adams	Pit	NL	34	29	263	17	10	1	92	23	1.98	2.26	2.83	58.4
61	187	1954	R.Roberts	Phi	NL	45	38	337	23	15	4	185	56	2.97	3.10	3.08	58.3
62	13	1915	F.Toney	Cin	NL	36	23	223	17	6	2	108	73	1.58	1.86	2.32	58.2
63	17	1997	P.Martinez	Mon	NL	31	31	241	17	8	0	305	67	1.90	2.42	2.38	58.2
64	22	1948	H.Brecheen	StL	NL	33	30	233	20	7	1	149	49	2.24	2.39	2.42	58.2
65	70	1963	D.Ellsworth	Chi	NL	37	37	291	22	10	0	185	75	2.11	2.32	2.77	57.9
66	103	1966	J.Bunning	Phi	NL	43	41	314	19	14	1	252	55	2.41	2.61	2.90	57.8
67	159	1918	L.Tyler	Chi	NL	33	30	269	19	8	1	102	67	2.00	2.41	3.04	57.8
68	60	1907	O.Overall	Chi	NL	36	30	268	23	7	3	141	69	1.68	2.08	2.72	57.7
69	87	1966	J.Marichal	SF	NL	37	36	307	25	6	0	222	36	2.23	2.58	2.87	57.6
70	6	1964	S.Koufax	LA	NL	29	28	223	19	5	1	223	53	1.74	1.98	2.23	57.6
71	48	1930	D.Vance	Bkn	NL	35	31	259	17	15	0	173	55	2.61	3.38	2.66	57.3
72	183	1952	R.Roberts	Phi	NL	39	37	330	28	7	2	148	45	2.59	2.84	3.07	57.2
73	134	1928	L.Benton	NY	NL	42	35	310	25	9	4	90	71	2.73	3.08	2.99	56.9
74	55	1954	J.Antonelli	NY	NL	39	37	259	21	7	2	152	94	2.30	2.71	2.69	56.5
75	50	1992	G.Maddux	Chi	NL	35	35	268	20	11	0	199	70	2.18	2.28	2.68	56.0
76	156	1948	J.Sain	Bos	NL	42	39	315	24	15	1	137	83	2.60	3.00	3.04	55.9
77	107	1980	S.Carlton	Phi	NL	38	38	304	24	9	0	286	90	2.34	2.58	2.92	55.4
78	149	1913	C.Mathewson	NY	NL	40	35	306	25	11	2	93	21	2.06	2.76	3.02	55.1
79	163	1934	D.Dean	StL	NL	50	33	312	30	7	7	195	75	2.66	3.17	3.05	55.0
80	578	1902	V.Willis	Bos	NL	51	46	410	27	20	3	225	101	2.20	3.12	3.52	54.7
81	164	1912	C.Mathewson	NY	NL	43	34	310	23	12	4	134	34	2.12	3.11	3.05	54.7
82	136	1912	N.Rucker	Bkn	NL	45	34	298	18	21	4	151	72	2.21	3.05	2.99	54.6
83	67	1969	T.Seaver	NY	NL	36	35	273	25	7	0	208	82	2.21	2.47	2.76	54.5
84	47	1998	K.Brown	SD	NL	36	35	257	18	7	0	257	49	2.38	2.70	2.66	54.2
85	35	1907	T.Brown	Chi	NL	34	27	233	20	6	3	107	40	1.39	1.97	2.57	54.1
86	21	1981	N.Ryan	Hou	NL	21	21	149	11	5	0	140	68	1.69	2.05	2.40	54.0
87	172	1911	C.Mathewson	NY	NL	45	37	307	26	13	3	141	38	1.99	2.99	3.06	53.9
88	235	1901	V.Willis	Bos	NL	38	35	305	20	17	0	133	78	2.36	3.27	3.18	53.8
89	124	1933	L.Warneke	Chi	NL	36	34	287	18	13	1	133	75	2.00	2.60	2.95	53.8
90	52	1993	J.Rijo	Cin	NL	36	36	257	14	9	0	227	62	2.48	2.66	2.68	53.5
91	127	1941	W.Wyatt	Bkn	NL	38	35	288	22	10	1	176	82	2.34	2.78	2.97	53.5
92	135	1925	D.Luque	Cin	NL	36	36	291	16	18	0	140	78	2.63	3.37	2.99	53.4
93	204	1904	K.Nichols	StL	NL	36	35	317	21	13	1	134	50	2.02	2.75	3.12	53.3
94	46	1998	G.Maddux	Atl	NL	34	34	251	18	9	0	204	45	2.22	2.69	2.65	53.3
95	130	1974	P.Niekro	Atl	NL	41	39	302	20	13	1	195	88	2.38	2.71	2.98	53.1
96	74	1937	J.Turner	Bos	NL	33	30	257	20	11	1	69	52	2.38	2.80	2.79	53.0
97	77	1933	H.Schumacher	NY	NL	35	33	259	19	12	1	96	84	2.16	2.47	2.81	53.0
98	166	1969	B.Singer	LA	NL	41	40	316	20	12	1	247	74	2.34	2.73	3.05	52.9
99	365	1904	C.Mathewson	NY	NL	48	46	368	33	12	1	212	78	2.03	2.94	3.33	52.7
100	363	1911	P.Alexander	Phi	NL	48	37	367	28	13	3	227	129	2.57	3.26	3.33	52.6

All Time Great Player Seasons

NL All Time Greats
Relief Pitchers

V	R	Year	Name	T	L	G	GS	IP	W	L	SV	SO	BB	ERA	RA/9	R Wtd RA/9	V Runs /162
1	16	1977	R.Gossage	Pit	NL	72	0	133	11	9	26	151	49	1.62	1.83	1.90	39.3
2	29	1984	B.Sutter	StL	NL	71	0	123	5	7	45	77	23	1.54	1.91	2.13	33.1
3	276	1974	M.Marshall	LA	NL	106	0	208	15	12	21	143	56	2.42	2.85	3.13	33.0
4	20	1966	P.Regan	LA	NL	65	0	117	14	1	21	88	24	1.62	1.85	2.06	32.5
5	13	1977	B.Sutter	Chi	NL	62	0	107	7	3	31	129	23	1.34	1.76	1.82	32.5
6	17	1967	T.Abernathy	Cin	NL	70	0	106	6	3	28	88	41	1.27	1.61	1.91	31.2
7	10	1992	M.Rojas	Mon	NL	68	0	101	7	1	10	70	34	1.43	1.52	1.79	31.1
8	22	1971	T.McGraw	NY	NL	51	1	111	11	4	8	109	41	1.70	1.78	2.07	30.6
9	52	1960	L.McDaniel	StL	NL	65	2	116	12	4	26	105	24	2.09	2.17	2.33	30.2
10	136	1952	J.Black	Bkn	NL	56	2	142	15	4	15	85	41	2.15	2.54	2.75	30.0
11	61	1982	G.Minton	SF	NL	78	0	123	10	4	30	58	42	1.83	2.12	2.37	29.9
12	60	1972	M.Marshall	Mon	NL	65	0	116	14	8	18	95	47	1.78	2.02	2.37	29.7
13	82	1963	R.Perranoksi	LA	NL	69	0	129	16	3	21	75	43	1.67	2.09	2.49	29.6
14	189	1950	J.Konstanty	Phi	NL	74	0	152	16	7	22	56	50	2.66	3.02	2.92	29.0
15	5	1980	T.McGraw	Phi	NL	57	0	92	5	4	20	75	23	1.46	1.56	1.76	28.6
16	57	1981	R.Camp	Atl	NL	48	0	76	9	3	17	47	12	1.78	2.01	2.35	28.2
17	11	1987	T.Burke	Mon	NL	55	0	91	7	0	18	58	17	1.19	1.78	1.79	28.0
18	152	1948	T.Wilks	StL	NL	57	2	131	6	6	13	71	39	2.62	2.75	2.78	27.1
19	36	1983	L.Smith	Chi	NL	66	0	103	4	10	29	91	41	1.65	2.00	2.21	26.8
20	79	1995	D.Veres	Hou	NL	72	0	103	5	1	1	94	30	2.26	2.53	2.48	26.7
21	7	1956	M.Grissom	NY	NL	43	2	81	1	1	7	49	16	1.56	1.67	1.77	26.3
22	126	1954	M.Grissom	NY	NL	56	3	122	10	7	19	64	50	2.35	2.73	2.71	26.3
23	166	1982	S.Bedrosian	Atl	NL	64	3	138	8	6	11	123	57	2.42	2.55	2.85	26.2
24	180	1959	B.Henry	Chi	NL	65	0	134	9	8	12	115	26	2.68	2.82	2.89	26.1
25	12	1993	J.Wetteland	Mon	NL	70	0	85	9	3	43	113	28	1.37	1.79	1.80	26.0
26	31	1990	R.Dibble	Cin	NL	68	0	98	8	3	11	136	34	1.74	2.02	2.18	25.9
27	73	1983	J.Orosco	NY	NL	62	0	110	13	7	17	84	38	1.47	2.21	2.44	25.8
28	95	1954	H.Wilhelm	NY	NL	57	0	111	12	4	7	64	52	2.10	2.59	2.57	25.8
29	165	1970	D.Selma	Phi	NL	73	0	134	8	9	22	153	59	2.75	2.82	2.84	25.6
30	72	1980	R.Camp	Atl	NL	77	0	108	6	4	22	33	29	1.91	2.16	2.44	25.4
31	233	1993	J.Fassero	Mon	NL	56	15	150	12	5	1	140	54	2.29	3.01	3.03	25.4
32	4	1999	B.Wagner	Hou	NL	66	0	75	4	1	39	124	23	1.57	1.69	1.53	25.1
33	3	1998	T.Hoffman	SD	NL	66	0	73	4	2	53	86	21	1.48	1.48	1.46	25.1
34	117	1973	P.Borbon	Cin	NL	80	0	121	11	4	14	60	35	2.16	2.45	2.69	25.1
35	114	1985	T.Burke	Mon	NL	78	0	120	9	4	8	87	44	2.39	2.39	2.68	25.1
36	77	1974	C.Taylor	Mon	NL	61	0	108	6	2	11	43	25	2.17	2.25	2.47	25.0
37	62	1980	D.Smith	Hou	NL	57	0	103	7	5	10	85	32	1.93	2.10	2.37	25.0
38	39	1990	L.Andersen	Hou	NL	65	0	96	5	2	7	93	27	1.79	2.07	2.23	24.8
39	54	1978	D.Bair	Cin	NL	70	0	100	7	6	28	91	38	1.97	2.06	2.34	24.7
40	27	1979	J.Sambito	Hou	NL	63	0	91	8	7	22	83	23	1.77	1.97	2.12	24.6
41	19	1990	J.Brantley	SF	NL	55	0	87	5	3	19	61	33	1.56	1.87	2.01	24.6
42	301	1979	T.Hume	Cin	NL	57	12	163	10	9	17	80	33	2.76	2.98	3.21	24.4
43	100	1972	T.McGraw	NY	NL	54	0	106	8	6	27	92	40	1.70	2.21	2.59	24.4
44	23	1998	R.Nen	SF	NL	78	0	89	7	7	40	110	25	1.52	2.13	2.10	24.3
45	32	1993	G.McMichael	Atl	NL	74	0	92	2	3	19	89	29	2.06	2.16	2.18	24.3
46	1	1998	U.Urbina	Mon	NL	64	0	69	6	3	34	94	33	1.30	1.43	1.41	24.1
47	6	1999	A.Benitez	NY	NL	77	0	78	4	3	22	128	41	1.85	1.96	1.77	24.1
48	97	1982	J.Reardon	Mon	NL	75	0	109	7	4	26	86	36	2.06	2.31	2.58	23.9
49	50	1983	T.Niedenfuer	LA	NL	66	0	95	8	3	11	66	29	1.90	2.09	2.31	23.7
50	55	1967	F.Linzy	SF	NL	57	0	96	7	7	17	38	34	1.51	1.97	2.34	23.7

Baseball Players' Best Seasons

All Time Greatest

Hitters Volume of Success

Pos	Year	Name	T	L	AB	BB	HBP	TAB	H	2B	3B	HR	BA	OB	SA	PRO	Wtd PRO	SB	CS	SBF	SPF	FF	R TF	V HC
C	1972	J.Bench	Cin	NL	538	100	2	640	145	22	2	40	.270	.386	.541	927	959	6	6	(9)	0	90	1,040	116.4
1B	1994	J.Bagwell	Hou	NL	400	65	4	469	147	32	2	39	.368	.461	.750	1,211	1,139	15	4	14	10	40	1,203	137.0
2B	1876	R.Barnes	Chi	NL	322	20	0	342	138	21	14	1	.429	.462	.590	1,052	1,242	0			10	50	1,302	250.4
SS	1908	H.Wagner	Pit	NL	568	54	5	627	201	39	19	10	.354	.415	.542	957	1,117	53			10	40	1,167	158.5
3B	1981	M.Schmidt	Phi	NL	354	73	4	431	112	19	2	31	.316	.439	.644	1,083	1,114	12	4	9	10	90	1,223	157.5
OF	1923	B.Ruth	NY	AL	522	170	4	696	205	45	13	41	.393	.545	.764	1,309	1,250	17	21	(34)	10	40	1,266	177.5
OF	1956	M.Mantle	NY	AL	533	112	2	647	188	22	5	52	.353	.467	.705	1,172	1,123	10	1	12	10	70	1,214	148.2
OF	1946	T.Williams	Bos	AL	514	156	2	672	176	37	8	38	.342	.497	.667	1,164	1,188	0	0	0	0	0	1,188	144.9
Starters		Averages			469	94	3	566	164	30	8	32	.350	.461	.649	1,110	1,138	14	5	(1)	8	53	1,197	161.3
C	1876	D.White	Chi	NL	303	7	0	310	104	18	1	1	.343	.358	.419	777	917	0			0	40	957	103.1
1B	1927	L.Gehrig	NY	AL	584	109	3	696	218	52	18	47	.373	.474	.765	1,240	1,165	10	8	(8)	0	0	1,157	135.0
2B	1884	F.Dunlap	StL	U	449	29	0	478	185	39	8	13	.412	.448	.621	1,069	1,283	0			0	100	1,383	240.7
SS	1935	A.Vaughan	Pit	NL	499	97	7	603	192	34	10	19	.385	.491	.607	1,098	1,074	4			10	(10)	1,074	124.4
3B	1879	K.Kelly	Cin	NL	345	8	0	353	120	20	12	2	.348	.363	.493	855	1,008	0			10	50	1,068	119.8
OF	1887	T.O'Neill	StL	AA	517	50	5	572	225	52	19	14	.435	.490	.691	1,180	1,183	30			10	50	1,183	136.7
OF	1917	T.Cobb	Det	AL	588	61	4	653	225	44	24	6	.383	.444	.570	1,014	1,122	55			10	(10)	1,172	135.6
OF	1992	B.Bonds	Pit	NL	473	127	5	605	147	36	5	34	.311	.461	.624	1,085	1,116	39	8	36	10	60	1,222	134.0
Reserves		Averages			470	61	3	534	177	37	12	17	.377	.452	.615	1,067	1,123	17	2	3	6	34	1,167	141.2
Totals		Weighted Ave.			469	83	3	555	168	32	9	27	.359	.458	.638	1,096	1,133	15	4	0	7	46	1,187	154.6

Pitchers Volume of Success

Pos	Year	Name	T	L	G	GS	IP	W	L	SV	SO	BB	ERA	RA/9	Wtd RA/9	R V Runs /162
SP	1876	G.Bradley	StL	NL	64	64	573	45	19	0	103	38	1.23	3.60	2.82	275.0
SP	1884	O.Radbourn	Pro	NL	75	73	679	59	12	1	441	98	1.38	2.86	2.32	239.9
SP	1876	A.Spalding	Chi	NL	61	60	529	47	12	0	39	26	1.75	3.85	3.02	225.2
SP	1882	W.White	Cin	AA	54	54	480	40	12	0	122	71	1.54	3.08	2.58	219.5
SP	1884	G.Hecker	Lou	AA	75	73	671	52	20	0	385	56	1.80	3.09	2.61	213.5
Starters		Averages			66	65	586	49	15	0	218	58	1.42	3.04	2.46	234.6
RP	1986	M.Eichhorn	Tor	AL	69	0	157	14	6	10	166	45	1.72	1.83	1.79	48.2
RP	1981	R.Fingers	Mil	AL	47	0	78	6	3	28	61	13	1.04	1.04	1.16	44.6
RP	1973	J.Hiller	Det	AL	65	0	125	10	5	38	124	39	1.44	1.51	1.60	41.1
RP	1984	W.Hernandez	Det	AL	80	0	140	9	3	32	112	36	1.92	1.92	1.97	40.3
Relievers		Averages			65	0	125	10	4	27	116	33	1.39	1.43	1.48	43.6
Totals		Averages			131	65	711	58	19	27	334	91	3.10	4.98	4.38	278.2

All Time Greatest — Hitters Rate of Success

Pos	Year	Name	T	L	AB	BB	HBP	TAB	H	2B	3B	HR	BA	OB	SA	PRO	Wtd PRO	SB	CS	SBF	SPF	FF	R TF	V HC
C	2000	I.Rodriguez	Tex	AL	363	19	1	383	126	27	4	27	.347	.381	.667	1,048	959	5	5	(12)	0	100	1,047	67.4
1B	1994	J.Bagwell	Hou	NL	400	65	4	469	147	32	2	39	.368	.461	.750	1,211	1,139	15	4	14	10	40	1,203	137.0
2B	1884	F.Dunlap	StL	U	449	29	0	478	185	39	8	13	.412	.448	.621	1,069	1,283	0			0	100	1,383	240.7
SS	1908	H.Wagner	Pit	NL	568	54	5	627	201	39	19	10	.354	.415	.542	957	1,117	53			10	40	1,167	158.5
3B	1981	M.Schmidt	Phi	NL	354	73	4	431	112	19	2	31	.316	.439	.644	1,083	1,114	12	4	9	10	90	1,223	157.5
OF	1920	B.Ruth	NY	AL	458	148	3	609	172	36	9	54	.376	.530	.847	1,378	1,325	14	14	(22)	10	10	1,323	172.7
OF	1941	T.Williams	Bos	AL	456	145	3	604	185	33	3	37	.406	.551	.735	1,286	1,244	2	4	(9)	0	0	1,234	144.3
OF	1957	M.Mantle	NY	AL	474	146	0	620	173	28	6	34	.365	.515	.665	1,179	1,172	16	3	15	10	30	1,228	146.1
Starters		Averages			440	85	3	528	163	32	7	31	.369	.474	.680	1,154	1,180	15	4	(1)	6	51	1,237	153.0
C	1972	J.Bench	Cin	NL	538	100	2	640	145	22	2	40	.270	.386	.541	927	959	6	6	(9)	0	90	1,040	116.4
1B	1927	L.Gehrig	NY	AL	584	109	3	696	218	52	18	47	.373	.474	.765	1,240	1,165	10	8	(8)	0	0	1,157	135.0
2B	1876	R.Barnes	Chi	NL	322	20	0	342	138	21	14	1	.429	.462	.590	1,052	1,242	0			10	50	1,302	250.4
SS	1935	A.Vaughan	Pit	NL	499	97	7	603	192	34	10	19	.385	.491	.607	1,098	1,074	4			10	(10)	1,074	124.4
3B	1980	G.Brett	KC	AL	449	58	1	508	175	33	9	24	.390	.461	.664	1,124	1,120	15	6	6	10	20	1,155	106.3
OF	1992	B.Bonds	Pit	NL	473	127	5	605	147	36	5	34	.311	.461	.624	1,085	1,116	39	8	36	10	60	1,222	134.0
OF	1910	T.Cobb	Det	AL	506	64	4	574	194	35	13	8	.383	.456	.551	1,008	1,146	65			10	30	1,186	123.2
OF	1887	T.O'Neill	StL	AA	517	50	5	572	225	52	19	14	.435	.490	.691	1,180	1,183	30			10	(10)	1,183	136.7
Reserves		Averages			486	78	3	568	179	36	11	23	.369	.459	.633	1,092	1,118	21	4	3	8	29	1,157	140.8
Totals		Weighted Ave.			456	83	3	541	168	33	8	28	.369	.469	.664	1,133	1,159	17	4	1	7	44	1,210	148.9

Pitchers Rate of Success

Pos	Year	Name	T	L	G	GS	IP	W	L	SV	SO	BB	ERA	RA/9	Wtd RA/9	R V Runs/162
SP	2000	P.Martinez	Bos	AL	29	29	217	18	6	0	284	32	1.74	1.82	1.55	72.3
SP	1995	G.Maddux	Atl	NL	28	28	210	19	2	0	181	23	1.63	1.67	1.64	76.7
SP	1913	W.Johnson	Was	AL	48	36	346	36	7	2	243	38	1.14	1.46	1.68	116.5
SP	1914	D.Leonard	Bos	AL	36	25	225	19	5	3	176	60	0.96	1.36	1.68	75.7
SP	1985	D.Gooden	NY	NL	35	35	277	24	4	0	268	69	1.53	1.66	1.86	83.0
Starters		Averages			35	31	255	23	5	1	230	45	1.57	1.78	1.86	84.8
RP	1995	J.Mesa	Cle	AL	62	0	64	3	0	46	58	17	1.13	1.27	1.13	27.4
RP	1990	D.Eckersley	Oak	AL	63	0	73	4	2	48	73	4	0.61	1.10	1.15	27.6
RP	1981	R.Fingers	Mil	AL	47	0	78	6	3	28	61	13	1.04	1.04	1.16	44.6
RP	1998	M.Jackson	Cle	AL	69	0	64	1	1	40	55	13	1.55	1.55	1.40	22.5
Relievers		Averages			60	0	70	4	2	41	62	12	.92	1.04	1.01	30.5
Totals		Averages			95	31	325	27	6	42	292	56	2.08	2.35	2.38	115.4

All Time Greatest Catchers

V	R	Year	Name	T	L	AB	BB	HBP	TAB	H	2B	3B	HR	BA	OB	SA	PRO	Wtd PRO	SB	CS	SBF	SPF	FF	R TF	V HC
1	2	1972	J.Bench	Cin	NL	538	100	2	640	145	22	2	40	.270	.386	.541	927	959	6	6	(9)		90	1,040	116.4
2	6	1970	J.Bench	Cin	NL	605	54	0	659	177	35	4	45	.293	.351	.587	937	914	5	2	1		100	1,015	106.1
3	31	1876	D.White	Chi	NL	303	7		310	104	18	1	1	.343	.358	.419	777	917					40	957	103.1
4	4	1881	C.Bennett	Det	NL	299	18		317	90	18	7	7	.301	.341	.478	819	922					100	1,022	100.4
5	21	1974	J.Bench	Cin	NL	621	80	3	704	174	38	2	33	.280	.365	.507	872	886	5	4	(4)		90	972	98.8
6	11	1953	R.Campanella	Bkn	NL	519	67	4	590	162	26	3	41	.312	.395	.611	1,006	950	4	2	0		50	1,000	95.5
7	12	1968	B.Freehan	Det	AL	540	65	24	629	142	24	2	25	.263	.367	.454	821	907	0	1	(3)	10	80	994	94.8
8	8	1975	J.Bench	Cin	NL	530	65	2	597	150	39	1	28	.283	.363	.519	882	892	11	0	17		100	1,010	94.5
9	13	1997	M.Piazza	LA	NL	556	69	3	628	201	32	1	40	.362	.435	.638	1,073	1,019	5	1	5	(10)	(20)	993	94.4
10	9	1951	R.Campanella	Bkn	NL	505	53	4	562	164	33	1	33	.325	.393	.590	983	963	1	2	(5)		50	1,008	93.0
11	3	1972	C.Fisk	Bos	AL	457	52	4	513	134	28	9	22	.293	.370	.538	909	985	5	2	2		40	1,027	89.9
12	26	1932	M.Cochrane	Phi	AL	518	100	4	622	152	35	4	23	.293	.412	.510	921	867	0	1	(3)	10	90	964	89.3
13	22	1982	G.Carter	Mon	NL	557	78	6	641	163	32	1	29	.293	.385	.510	895	909	2	5	(12)		70	967	88.6
14	10	1933	M.Cochrane	Phi	AL	429	106	3	538	138	30	4	15	.322	.459	.515	974	940	8	6	(7)	10	60	1,002	87.7
15	7	1931	M.Cochrane	Phi	AL	459	56	3	518	160	31	6	17	.349	.423	.553	976	931	2	3	(7)	10	80	1,014	87.4
16	27	1937	B.Dickey	NY	AL	530	73	4	607	176	35	2	29	.332	.417	.570	987	904	3	2	(2)	(10)	70	963	86.9
17	41	1882	C.Bennett	Det	NL	342	20		362	103	16	10	5	.301	.340	.450	790	897					40	937	85.7
18	15	1888	K.Kelly	Bos	NL	440	31	4	475	140	22	11	9	.318	.368	.480	848	983	56			10		993	85.0
19	40	1878	L.Brown	Pro	NL	243	7		250	74	21	6	1	.305	.324	.453	777	917			(10)		30	937	82.1
20	30	1967	B.Freehan	Det	AL	517	73	20	610	146	23	1	20	.282	.392	.447	839	902	1	2	(5)	10	50	958	81.5
21	19	1930	M.Cochrane	Phi	AL	487	55	1	543	174	42	5	10	.357	.424	.526	949	868	5	0	9	10	90	977	81.4
22	55	1879	D.White	Cin	NL	333	6		339	110	16	6	1	.330	.342	.423	766	902					20	922	80.1
23	32	1966	J.Torre	Atl	NL	546	60	2	608	172	20	3	36	.315	.385	.560	945	955	0	4	(12)	(10)	20	952	79.6
24	14	1888	B.Ewing	NY	NL	415	24	3	442	127	18	15	6	.306	.348	.465	813	943	53				50	993	79.1
25	5	1890	B.Ewing	NY	P	352	39	1	392	119	19	15	8	.338	.406	.545	951	921	36				100	1,021	78.7

All Time Greatest First Basemen

V	R	Year	Name	T	L	AB	BB	HBP	TAB	H	2B	3B	HR	BA	OB	SA	PRO	Wtd PRO	SB	CS	SBF	SPF	FF	R TF	V HC
1	1	1994	J.Bagwell	Hou	NL	400	65	4	469	147	32	2	39	.368	.461	.750	1,211	1,139	15	4	14	10	40	1,203	137.0
2	2	1927	L.Gehrig	NY	AL	584	109	3	696	218	52	18	47	.373	.474	.765	1,240	1,165	10	8	(8)			1,157	135.0
3	3	1932	J.Foxx	Phi	AL	585	116	0	701	213	33	9	58	.364	.469	.749	1,218	1,146	3	7	(15)		20	1,152	134.1
4	4	1998	M.McGwire	StL	NL	509	162	6	677	152	21	0	70	.299	.473	.752	1,225	1,166	1	0	1	(10)	(10)	1,147	121.7
5	9	1886	D.Brouthers	Det	NL	489	66		555	181	40	15	11	.370	.445	.581	1,026	1,130	21			(10)		1,120	120.8
6	7	1933	J.Foxx	Phi	AL	573	96	1	670	204	37	9	48	.356	.449	.703	1,153	1,111	2	2	(3)		20	1,129	120.4
7	5	1961	N.Cash	Det	AL	535	124	9	668	193	22	8	41	.361	.488	.662	1,150	1,118	11	5	1		20	1,139	117.5
8	11	1881	C.Anson	Chi	NL	343	26		369	137	21	7	1	.399	.442	.510	952	1,072					40	1,112	115.9
9	13	1994	F.Thomas	Chi	AL	399	109	2	510	141	34	1	38	.353	.494	.729	1,223	1,142	2	3	(7)		(30)	1,105	115.0
10	15	1934	L.Gehrig	NY	AL	579	109	2	690	210	40	6	49	.363	.465	.706	1,172	1,103	9	5	(1)			1,101	114.6
11	19	1885	R.Connor	NY	NL	455	51		506	169	23	15	1	.371	.435	.495	929	1,082					10	1,092	113.5
12	18	1886	C.Anson	Chi	NL	504	55		559	187	35	11	10	.371	.433	.544	977	1,075	29				20	1,095	113.2
13	16	1920	G.Sisler	StL	AL	631	46	2	679	257	49	18	19	.407	.449	.632	1,082	1,040	42	17	11	10	40	1,101	112.7
14	17	1882	D.Brouthers	Buf	NL	351	21		372	129	23	11	6	.368	.403	.547	950	1,078					20	1,098	111.6
15	24	1938	J.Foxx	Bos	AL	565	119	0	684	197	33	9	50	.349	.462	.704	1,166	1,065	5	4	(4)		20	1,081	106.6
16	28	1877	D.White	Bos	NL	266	8		274	103	14	11	2	.387	.405	.545	950	1,070						1,070	105.7
17	6	1969	W.McCovey	SF	NL	491	121	4	616	157	26	2	45	.320	.458	.656	1,114	1,139	0	0	0	(10)		1,129	105.4
18	10	1972	D.Allen	Chi	AL	506	99	1	606	156	28	5	37	.308	.422	.603	1,025	1,112	19	8	5	10	(10)	1,116	105.2
19	12	1885	D.Brouthers	Buf	NL	407	34		441	146	32	11	7	.359	.408	.543	951	1,108						1,108	103.6
20	21	2000	T.Helton	Col	NL	580	103	4	687	216	59	2	42	.372	.470	.698	1,168	1,066	5	3	(1)		20	1,085	103.0
21	31	1946	S.Musial	StL	NL	624	73	3	700	228	50	20	16	.365	.434	.587	1,021	1,054	7				10	1,064	103.0
22	27	1930	L.Gehrig	NY	AL	581	101	3	685	220	42	17	41	.379	.473	.721	1,194	1,092	12	14	(22)			1,070	102.9
23	25	1884	H.Stovey	Phi	AA	448	26	4	478	146	22	23	10	.326	.368	.545	913	1,067					10	1,077	102.9
24	38	1931	L.Gehrig	NY	AL	619	117	0	736	211	31	15	46	.341	.446	.662	1,108	1,057	17	12	(9)			1,048	102.5
25	22	1884	L.Reilly	Cin	AA	448	5	14	467	152	24	19	11	.339	.366	.551	918	1,072					10	1,082	102.3

All Time Greatest Second basemen

V	R	Year	Name	T	L	AB	BB	HBP	TAB	H	2B	3B	HR	BA	OB	SA	PRO	Wtd PRO	SB	CS	SBF	SPF	FF	R TF	V HC
1	2	1876	R.Barnes	Chi	NL	322	20		342	138	21	14	1	.429	.462	.590	1,052	1,242				10	50	1,302	250.4
2	1	1884	F.Dunlap	StL	U	449	29		478	185	39	8	13	.412	.448	.621	1,069	1,283					100	1,383	240.7
3	4	1901	N.Lajoie	Phi	AL	544	24	13	581	232	48	14	14	.426	.463	.643	1,106	1,109	27			10	80	1,199	164.7
4	3	1882	P.Browning	Lou	AA	288	26		314	109	17	3	5	.378	.430	.510	940	1,141				10	50	1,201	160.1
5	5	1910	N.Lajoie	Cle	AL	591	60	5	656	227	51	7	4	.384	.445	.514	960	1,091	26				80	1,171	159.6
6	12	1922	R.Hornsby	StL	NL	623	65	1	689	250	46	14	42	.401	.459	.722	1,181	1,107	17	12	(10)		10	1,107	145.8
7	1	1924	R.Hornsby	StL	NL	536	89	2	627	227	43	14	25	.424	.507	.696	1,203	1,165	5	12	(29)			1,136	141.7
8	7	1904	N.Lajoie	Cle	AL	553	27	8	588	208	49	15	5	.376	.413	.546	959	1,099	29			10	50	1,159	139.7
9	8	1925	R.Hornsby	StL	NL	504	83	2	589	203	41	10	39	.403	.489	.756	1,245	1,153	5	3	(2)		(10)	1,142	134.7
10	6	1976	J.Morgan	Cin	NL	472	114	1	587	151	30	5	27	.320	.453	.576	1,029	1,062	60	9	68	10	20	1,160	132.8
11	15	1884	F.Pfeffer	Chi	NL	467	25		492	135	10	10	25	.289	.325	.514	839	946				10	120	1,076	130.2
12	11	1975	J.Morgan	Cin	NL	498	132	3	633	163	27	6	17	.327	.471	.508	979	990	67	10	70	10	40	1,110	128.1
13	14	1909	E.Collins	Phi	AL	571	62	6	639	198	30	10	3	.347	.416	.450	866	1,001	67			10	70	1,081	126.7
14	16	1906	N.Lajoie	Cle	AL	602	30	6	638	214	48	9	0	.355	.392	.465	857	974	20			10	90	1,074	124.3
15	20	1921	R.Hornsby	StL	NL	592	60	7	659	235	44	18	21	.397	.458	.639	1,097	1,052	13	13	(19)		10	1,043	118.2
16	24	1929	R.Hornsby	Chi	NL	602	87	1	690	229	47	8	39	.380	.459	.679	1,139	1,027	2					1,027	118.1
17	18	1914	E.Collins	Phi	AL	526	97	6	629	181	23	14	2	.344	.452	.452	904	994	58	30	(3)	10	50	1,051	115.3
18	13	1903	N.Lajoie	Cle	AL	485	24	3	512	167	41	11	7	.344	.379	.518	896	977	21			10	100	1,087	113.2
19	23	1927	R.Hornsby	NY	NL	568	86	4	658	205	32	9	26	.361	.448	.586	1,035	1,007	9				20	1,027	112.8
20	19	1913	E.Collins	Phi	AL	534	85	7	626	184	23	13	3	.345	.441	.453	894	955	55			10	80	1,045	112.8
21	21	1915	E.Collins	Chi	AL	521	119	5	645	173	22	10	4	.332	.460	.436	896	972	46	30	(21)	10	70	1,031	111.8
22	17	1928	R.Hornsby	Bos	NL	486	107	1	594	188	42	7	21	.387	.498	.632	1,130	1,076	5				(20)	1,056	110.5
23	25	1920	R.Hornsby	StL	NL	589	60	3	652	218	44	20	9	.370	.431	.559	990	1,029	12	15	(26)		20	1,023	110.2
24	22	1910	E.Collins	Phi	AL	581	49	6	636	188	16	15	3	.324	.382	.418	800	910	81			10	110	1,030	109.8
25	28	1984	R.Sandberg	Chi	NL	636	52	3	691	200	36	19	19	.314	.369	.520	889	909	32	7	25	10	70	1,013	108.0

All Time Greatest Shortstop

V	R	Year	Name	T	L	AB	BB	HBP	TAB	H	2B	3B	HR	BA	OB	SA	PRO	Wtd PRO	SB	CS	SBF	SPF	FF	R TF	V HC
1	1	1908	H.Wagner	Pit	NL	568	54	5	627	201	39	19	10	.354	.415	.542	957	1,117	53			10	40	1,167	158.5
2	4	1905	H.Wagner	Pit	NL	548	54	7	609	199	32	14	6	.363	.427	.505	932	1,017	57			10	70	1,097	132.9
3	2	1907	H.Wagner	Pit	NL	515	46	5	566	180	38	14	6	.350	.408	.513	921	1,055	61			10	40	1,105	125.7
4	7	1935	A.Vaughan	Pit	NL	499	97	7	603	192	34	10	19	.385	.491	.607	1,098	1,074	4			10	(10)	1,074	124.4
5	6	1906	H.Wagner	Pit	NL	516	58	10	584	175	38	9	2	.339	.416	.459	875	997	53			10	80	1,087	124.3
6	8	1903	H.Wagner	Pit	NL	512	44	7	563	182	30	19	5	.355	.414	.518	931	968	46			10	80	1,058	123.0
7	14	1896	H.Jennings	Bal	NL	521	19	51	591	209	27	9	0	.401	.472	.488	960	914	70			10	90	1,014	121.7
8	3	1904	H.Wagner	Pit	NL	490	59	4	553	171	44	14	4	.349	.423	.520	944	1,061	53			10	30	1,101	121.6
9	5	1909	H.Wagner	Pit	NL	495	66	3	564	168	39	10	5	.339	.420	.489	909	1,028	35			10	50	1,088	120.5
10	10	1901	H.Wagner	Pit	NL	549	53	7	609	194	37	11	6	.353	.417	.494	911	961	49			10	50	1,021	120.5
11	13	1991	C.Ripken	Bal	AL	650	53	5	708	210	46	5	34	.323	.379	.566	945	950	6	1	5		60	1,015	119.1
12	19	1878	B.Ferguson	Chi	NL	259	10		269	91	10	2	0	.351	.375	.405	781	922					80	1,002	115.6
13	9	1896	B.Dahlen	Chi	NL	474	64	8	546	167	30	19	9	.352	.438	.553	990	944	51			10	70	1,024	115.4
14	17	1982	R.Yount	Mil	AL	635	54	1	690	210	46	12	29	.331	.384	.578	962	958	14	3	11	10	30	1,009	114.1
15	20	1895	H.Jennings	Bal	NL	529	24	32	585	204	41	7	4	.386	.444	.512	957	887	53			10	100	997	113.9
16	32	1889	J.Glasscock	Ind	NL	582	31	5	618	205	40	3	7	.352	.390	.467	857	873	57			10	90	973	111.6
17	12	2000	A.Rodriguez	Sea	AL	554	100	7	661	175	34	2	41	.316	.427	.606	1,033	946	15	4	10	10	50	1,016	111.4
18	28	1882	J.Glasscock	Cle	NL	358	13		371	104	27	9	4	.291	.315	.450	765	868				10	100	978	107.2
19	43	1876	J.Peters	Chi	NL	316	3		319	111	14	2	1	.351	.357	.418	775	915				10	20	945	107.2
20	15	1969	R.Petrocelli	Bos	AL	535	98	1	634	159	32	2	40	.297	.407	.589	996	1,014	3	5	(10)	(10)	20	1,014	106.3
21	25	1948	L.Boudreau	Cle	AL	560	98	2	660	199	34	6	18	.355	.453	.534	987	953	3	2	(1)	(10)	40	982	105.7
22	29	1959	E.Banks	Chi	NL	589	64	7	660	179	25	6	45	.304	.379	.596	975	946	2	4	(9)	10	30	978	104.5
23	31	1944	L.Boudreau	Cle	AL	584	73	5	662	191	45	5	3	.327	.406	.437	843	878	11	3	7		90	975	103.8
24	11	1884	F.Fennelly	Was	AA	379	31	2	412	118	22	15	4	.311	.367	.480	847	990				10	20	1,020	103.4
25	33	1894	B.Dahlen	Chi	NL	502	76	3	581	179	32	14	15	.357	.444	.566	1,010	876	42			10	80	966	103.2

All Time Greatest Third basemen

V	R	Year	Name	T	L	AB	BB	HBP	TAB	H	2B	3B	HR	BA	OB	SA	PRO	Wtd PRO	SB	CS	SBF	SPF	FF	R TF	V HC
1	1	1981	M.Schmidt	Phi	NL	354	73	4	431	112	19	2	31	.316	.439	.644	1,083	1,114	12	4	9	10	90	1,223	157.5
2	7	1879	K.Kelly	Cin	NL	345	8		353	120	20	12	2	.348	.363	.493	855	1,008				10	50	1,068	119.8
3	14	1876	C.Anson	Chi	NL	309	12		321	110	9	7	2	.356	.380	.450	830	980					50	1,030	119.5
4	5	1884	N.Williamson	Chi	NL	417	42		459	116	18	8	27	.278	.344	.554	898	1,013				10	70	1,093	117.0
5	4	1980	M.Schmidt	Phi	NL	548	89	2	639	157	25	8	48	.286	.388	.624	1,012	1,025	12	5	3	10	60	1,098	116.3
6	6	1985	G.Brett	KC	AL	550	103	3	656	184	38	5	30	.335	.442	.585	1,028	1,021	9	1	10		40	1,071	110.8
7	2	1980	G.Brett	KC	AL	449	58	1	508	175	33	9	24	.390	.461	.664	1,124	1,120	15	6	6	10	20	1,155	106.3
8	9	1974	M.Schmidt	Phi	NL	568	106	4	678	160	28	7	36	.282	.398	.546	944	959	23	12	(1)	10	70	1,037	103.8
9	11	1964	R.Santo	Chi	NL	592	86	2	680	185	33	13	30	.313	.401	.564	966	992	3	4	(7)	(10)	60	1,035	103.4
10	18	1999	C.Jones	Atl	NL	567	126	2	695	181	41	1	45	.319	.445	.633	1,078	986	25	3	26	10		1,022	101.2
11	16	1938	M.Ott	NY	NL	527	118	5	650	164	23	6	36	.311	.442	.583	1,024	1,025	2					1,025	100.7
12	19	1976	M.Schmidt	Phi	NL	584	100	11	695	153	31	4	38	.262	.380	.524	904	933	14	9	(5)	10	80	1,017	99.7
13	13	1912	F.Baker	Phi	AL	577	50	6	633	200	40	21	10	.347	.404	.541	945	980	40			10	40	1,030	99.5
14	12	1977	M.Schmidt	Phi	NL	544	104	9	657	149	27	11	38	.274	.399	.574	972	944	15	8	(1)	10	80	1,033	99.1
15	15	1979	M.Schmidt	Phi	NL	541	120	3	664	137	25	4	45	.253	.392	.564	955	947	9	5	(1)	10	70	1,026	97.9
16	24	1879	N.Williamson	Chi	NL	320	24		344	94	20	13	1	.294	.343	.447	790	931				10		1,011	97.8
17	23	1967	R.Santo	Chi	NL	586	96	3	685	176	23	4	31	.300	.401	.512	913	955	1	5	(12)	(10)	80	1,013	96.8
18	17	1987	W.Boggs	Bos	AL	551	105	2	658	200	40	6	24	.363	.467	.588	1,055	1,012	1	3	(7)		20	1,024	96.6
19	10	1996	K.Caminiti	SD	NL	546	78	4	628	178	37	2	40	.326	.414	.621	1,035	986	11	5	2		50	1,037	96.1
20	8	1982	M.Schmidt	Phi	NL	514	107	3	624	144	26	3	35	.280	.407	.547	954	969	14	7	0		70	1,039	95.9
21	22	1966	R.Santo	Chi	NL	561	95	6	662	175	21	8	30	.312	.417	.538	955	965	4	5	(9)	(10)	70	1,016	94.6
22	40	1882	H.Carpenter	Cin	AA	351	10		361	120	15	5	1	.342	.360	.422	782	948				10	20	978	93.6
23	30	1988	W.Boggs	Bos	AL	584	125	3	712	214	45	6	5	.366	.480	.490	970	986	2	3	(5)		10	991	93.2
24	34	1959	E.Mathews	Mil	NL	594	80	3	677	182	16	8	46	.306	.391	.593	984	955	2	1	0	10	20	985	91.4
25	36	1973	D.Evans	Atl	NL	595	124	3	722	167	25	8	41	.281	.407	.556	964	972	6	3	0		10	982	91.3

All Time Greatest Outfielders

V	R	Year	Name	T	L	AB	BB	HBP	TAB	H	2B	3B	HR	BA	OB	SA	PRO	Wtd PRO	SB	CS	SBF	SPF	FF	R TF	V HC
1	3	1923	B.Ruth	NY	AL	522	170	4	696	205	45	13	41	.393	.545	.764	1,309	1,250	17	21	(34)	10	40	1,266	177.5
2	2	1921	B.Ruth	NY	AL	540	144	4	688	204	44	16	59	.378	.512	.846	1,358	1,253	17	13	(12)	10	20	1,271	177.0
3	1	1920	B.Ruth	NY	AL	458	148	3	609	172	36	9	54	.376	.530	.847	1,378	1,325	14	14	(22)	10	10	1,323	172.7
4	10	1927	B.Ruth	NY	AL	540	138	0	678	192	29	8	60	.356	.487	.772	1,259	1,183	7	6	(7)		20	1,196	149.2
5	8	1956	M.Mantle	NY	AL	533	112	2	647	188	22	5	52	.353	.467	.705	1,172	1,123	10	1	12	10	70	1,214	148.2
6	6	1957	M.Mantle	NY	AL	474	146	0	620	173	28	6	34	.365	.515	.665	1,179	1,172	16	3	15	10	30	1,228	146.1
7	12	1946	T.Williams	Bos	AL	514	156	2	672	176	37	8	38	.342	.497	.667	1,164	1,188	0	0	0			1,188	144.9
8	4	1941	T.Williams	Bos	AL	456	145	3	604	185	33	3	37	.406	.551	.735	1,286	1,244	2	4	(9)			1,234	144.3
9	9	1926	B.Ruth	NY	AL	495	144	3	642	184	30	5	47	.372	.516	.737	1,253	1,190	11	9	(10)		20	1,200	142.4
10	17	1942	T.Williams	Bos	AL	522	145	4	671	186	34	5	36	.356	.499	.648	1,147	1,180	3	2	(1)			1,179	141.6
11	21	1924	B.Ruth	NY	AL	529	142	4	675	200	39	7	46	.378	.513	.739	1,252	1,170	9	13	(24)		20	1,167	138.4
12	15	1887	T.O'Neill	StL	AA	517	50	5	572	225	52	19	14	.435	.490	.691	1,180	1,183	30			10	(10)	1,183	136.7
13	19	1917	T.Cobb	Det	AL	588	61	4	653	225	44	24	6	.383	.444	.570	1,014	1,122	55			10	40	1,172	135.6
14	7	1992	B.Bonds	Pit	NL	473	127	5	605	147	36	5	34	.311	.461	.624	1,085	1,116	39	8	36	10	60	1,222	134.0
15	18	1967	C.Yastrzemski	Bos	AL	579	91	4	674	189	31	4	44	.326	.421	.622	1,043	1,122	10		(8)		60	1,174	133.8
16	26	1947	T.Williams	Bos	AL	528	162	2	692	181	40	9	32	.343	.499	.634	1,133	1,146	0	1	(3)			1,143	133.3
17	16	1997	L.Walker	Col	NL	568	78	14	660	208	46	4	49	.366	.455	.720	1,175	1,115	33	8	24	10	30	1,179	132.6
18	30	1948	S.Musial	StL	NL	611	79	3	693	230	46	18	39	.376	.450	.702	1,152	1,138	7					1,138	132.1
19	20	1993	B.Bonds	SF	NL	539	126	2	667	181	38	4	46	.336	.463	.677	1,140	1,104	29	12	7	10	50	1,171	131.6
20	25	1912	T.Speaker	Bos	AL	580	82	6	668	222	53	12	10	.383	.464	.567	1,031	1,069	52				70	1,149	131.1
21	11	1919	B.Ruth	Bos	AL	432	101	6	539	139	34	12	29	.322	.456	.657	1,114	1,136	7			10	50	1,196	130.4
22	5	1957	T.Williams	Bos	AL	420	119	5	544	163	28	1	38	.388	.528	.731	1,259	1,251	0	1	(3)	(10)	(10)	1,228	128.2
23	28	1886	K.Kelly	Chi	NL	451	83		534	175	32	11	4	.388	.483	.534	1,018	1,121	53			10	10	1,141	127.3
24	53	1949	T.Williams	Bos	AL	566	162	2	730	194	39	3	43	.343	.490	.650	1,141	1,100	1	1	(1)			1,099	124.8
25	27	1911	T.Cobb	Det	AL	591	44	8	643	248	47	24	8	.420	.467	.621	1,088	1,103	83			10	30	1,143	124.3

All Time Greatest Outfielders

V	R	Year	Name	T	L	AB	BB	HBP	TAB	H	2B	3B	HR	BA	OB	SA	PRO	Wtd PRO	SB	CS	SBF	SPF	FF	R TF	V HC
26	32	1955	W.Mays	NY	NL	580	79	4	663	185	18	13	51	.319	.404	.659	1,063	1,018	24	4	23	10	80	1,131	124.1
27	23	1961	M.Mantle	NY	AL	514	126	0	640	163	16	6	54	.317	.452	.687	1,138	1,107	12	1	15	10	30	1,162	123.2
28	13	1910	T.Cobb	Det	AL	506	64	4	574	194	35	13	8	.383	.456	.551	1,008	1,146	65			10	30	1,186	123.2
29	22	1965	W.Mays	SF	NL	558	76	0	634	177	21	3	52	.317	.399	.645	1,044	1,073	9	4	1	10	80	1,164	122.9
30	71	1879	C.Jones	Bos	NL	355	29		384	112	22	10	9	.315	.367	.510	877	1,034					50	1,084	120.8
31	49	1915	T.Cobb	Det	AL	563	118	10	691	208	31	13	3	.369	.486	.487	973	1,055	96	38	27	10	10	1,102	119.5
32	40	1931	B.Ruth	NY	AL	534	128	1	663	199	31	3	46	.373	.495	.700	1,195	1,140	5	4	(4)		(20)	1,116	119.1
33	44	1928	B.Ruth	NY	AL	536	135	3	674	173	29	8	54	.323	.461	.709	1,170	1,115	4	5	(8)			1,107	117.9
34	33	1905	C.Seymour	Cin	NL	581	51	2	634	219	40	21	8	.377	.429	.559	988	1,078	21			10	40	1,128	117.9
35	35	1996	B.Bonds	SF	NL	517	151	1	669	159	27	3	42	.308	.465	.615	1,080	1,029	40	7	37	10	50	1,126	117.3
36	76	1884	O.Shaffer	StL	U	467	30		497	168	40	10	2	.360	.398	.501	899	1,080						1,080	115.6
37	37	1909	T.Cobb	Det	AL	573	48	6	627	216	33	10	9	.377	.431	.517	947	1,094	76			10	20	1,124	115.3
38	34	1941	J.DiMaggio	NY	AL	541	76	4	621	193	43	11	30	.357	.440	.643	1,083	1,047	4	2	0	10	70	1,127	115.1
39	51	1896	E.Delahanty	Phi	NL	499	62	9	570	198	44	17	13	.397	.472	.631	1,103	1,051	37			10	40	1,101	114.5
40	73	1885	P.Browning	Lou	AA	481	25	0	506	174	34	10	9	.362	.393	.530	923	1,051				10	20	1,081	114.0
41	90	1981	D.Evans	Bos	AL	412	85	1	498	122	19	4	22	.296	.418	.522	940	985	3	2	(2)	10	80	1,073	113.5
42	41	1954	W.Mays	NY	NL	565	66	2	633	195	33	13	41	.345	.415	.667	1,083	1,026	8	5	(3)	10	80	1,113	112.8
43	42	1955	M.Mantle	NY	AL	517	113	3	633	158	25	11	37	.306	.433	.611	1,044	1,024	8	1	9	10	70	1,113	112.7
44	24	1990	R.Henderson	Oak	AL	489	97	4	590	159	33	3	28	.325	.441	.577	1,017	1,034	65	10	72	10	40	1,156	112.2
45	65	1963	H.Aaron	Mil	NL	631	78	0	709	201	29	4	44	.319	.394	.586	980	1,031	31	5	28	10	20	1,089	112.0
46	45	1966	F.Robinson	Bal	AL	576	87	10	673	182	34	2	49	.316	.415	.637	1,052	1,098	8	5	(3)	10		1,105	111.6
47	43	1964	W.Mays	SF	NL	578	82	1	661	171	21	9	47	.296	.384	.607	992	1,019	19	5	13	10	70	1,112	111.6
48	56	1930	B.Ruth	NY	AL	518	136	1	655	186	28	9	49	.359	.493	.732	1,225	1,120	10	10	(14)		(10)	1,095	111.0
49	46	1912	J.Jackson	Cle	AL	572	54	12	638	226	44	26	3	.395	.458	.579	1,036	1,074	35			10	20	1,104	110.9
50	151	1879	P.Hines	Pro	NL	409	8		417	146	25	10	2	.357	.369	.482	851	1,003					30	1,033	110.8
51	59	1914	T.Speaker	Bos	AL	571	77	7	655	193	46	18	4	.338	.423	.503	926	1,018	42	29	(23)	10	90	1,095	110.7
52	70	1937	J.Medwick	StL	NL	633	41	2	676	237	56	10	31	.374	.414	.641	1,056	1,044	4			10	30	1,084	110.5
53	66	1962	W.Mays	SF	NL	621	78	4	703	189	36	5	49	.304	.385	.615	1,001	978	18	2	19	10	80	1,087	110.4
54	47	1911	J.Jackson	Cle	AL	571	56	8	635	233	45	19	7	.408	.468	.590	1,058	1,073	41			10	20	1,103	110.0
55	60	1958	M.Mantle	NY	AL	519	129	2	650	158	21	1	42	.304	.445	.592	1,036	1,035	18	3	17	10	30	1,092	109.0
56	48	1968	C.Yastrzemski	Bos	AL	539	119	2	660	162	32	2	23	.301	.429	.495	924	1,021	13	6	1		80	1,102	108.5
57	52	1963	W.Mays	SF	NL	596	66	2	664	187	32	7	38	.314	.384	.582	966	1,017	8	3	3	10	70	1,099	108.2
58	96	1937	J.DiMaggio	NY	AL	621	64	5	690	215	35	15	46	.346	.412	.673	1,085	994	3	0	4	10	60	1,069	107.6
59	38	1913	T.Speaker	Bos	AL	520	65	7	592	189	35	22	3	.363	.441	.533	974	1,040	46			10	70	1,120	107.5
60	82	1923	T.Speaker	Cle	AL	574	93	4	671	218	59	11	17	.380	.469	.610	1,079	1,031	8	9	(14)	10	50	1,077	107.4
61	91	1958	W.Mays	SF	NL	600	78	1	679	208	33	11	29	.347	.423	.584	1,006	966	31	6	26	10	70	1,073	107.3
62	74	1957	W.Mays	NY	NL	585	76	1	662	195	26	20	35	.333	.411	.626	1,037	1,011	38	19	0	10	60	1,081	107.2
63	58	1994	B.Bonds	SF	NL	391	74	6	471	122	18	1	37	.312	.429	.647	1,076	1,013	29	9	22	10	50	1,095	107.1
64	57	1916	T.Speaker	Cle	AL	546	82	4	632	211	41	8	2	.386	.470	.502	972	1,064	35	27	(28)	10	50	1,095	107.0
65	145	1893	E.Delahanty	Phi	NL	595	47	10	652	219	35	18	19	.368	.423	.583	1,007	965	37			10	60	1,035	106.8
66	111	1894	H.Duffy	Bos	NL	539	66	1	606	237	51	16	18	.440	.502	.694	1,196	1,037	48			10	10	1,057	106.1
67	88	1888	J.Ryan	Chi	NL	549	35	5	589	182	33	10	16	.332	.377	.515	892	1,034	60			10	30	1,074	106.0
68	86	1933	C.Klein	Phi	NL	606	56	1	663	223	44	7	28	.368	.422	.602	1,025	1,065	15			10		1,075	105.6
69	99	1959	H.Aaron	Mil	NL	629	51	4	684	223	46	7	39	.355	.406	.636	1,042	1,012	8	0	11	10	30	1,063	104.8
70	83	1876	G.Hall	Phi	NL	268	8		276	98	7	13	5	.366	.384	.545	929	1,096					(20)	1,076	104.6
71	108	1943	S.Musial	StL	NL	617	72	2	691	220	48	20	13	.357	.425	.562	988	1,038	9				20	1,058	104.0
72	77	1948	T.Williams	Bos	AL	509	126	3	638	188	44	3	25	.369	.497	.615	1,112	1,074	4	0	6			1,080	103.0
73	54	1912	T.Cobb	Det	AL	553	43	5	601	226	30	23	7	.409	.456	.584	1,040	1,078	61			10	10	1,098	102.6
74	103	1995	B.Bonds	SF	NL	506	120	5	631	149	30	7	33	.294	.434	.577	1,011	963	31	10	16	10	70	1,060	102.3
75	63	1913	J.Jackson	Cle	AL	528	80	5	613	197	39	17	7	.373	.460	.551	1,011	1,080	26			10		1,090	102.1

All Time Greatest Starting Pitchers

V	R	Year	Name	T	L	G	GS	IP	W	L	SV	SO	BB	ERA	RA/9	R Wtd RA/9	V Runs /162
1	190	1876	G.Bradley	StL	NL	64	64	573	45	19	0	103	38	1.23	3.60	2.82	275.0
2	26	1884	O.Radbourn	Pro	NL	75	73	679	59	12	1	441	98	1.38	2.86	2.32	239.9
3	359	1876	A.Spalding	Chi	NL	61	60	529	47	12	0	39	26	1.75	3.85	3.02	225.2
4	77	1882	W.White	Cin	AA	54	54	480	40	12	0	122	71	1.54	3.08	2.58	219.5
5	89	1884	G.Hecker	Lou	AA	75	73	671	52	20	0	385	56	1.80	3.09	2.61	213.5
6	228	1879	T.Bond	Bos	NL	64	64	555	43	19	0	155	24	1.96	3.34	2.88	209.8
7	168	1883	T.Keefe	NY	AA	68	68	619	41	27	0	359	108	2.41	3.55	2.78	202.6
8	799	1878	T.Bond	Bos	NL	59	59	533	40	19	0	182	33	2.06	3.75	3.31	195.8
9	200	1876	T.Bond	Har	NL	45	45	408	31	13	0	88	13	1.68	3.62	2.84	194.1
10	1,255	1876	J.Devlin	Lou	NL	68	68	622	30	35	0	122	37	1.56	4.47	3.51	181.0
11	351	1883	O.Radbourn	Pro	NL	76	68	632	48	25	1	315	56	2.05	3.91	3.01	177.2
12	1,094	1877	T.Bond	Bos	NL	58	58	521	40	17	0	170	36	2.11	4.28	3.45	173.7
13	249	1884	P.Galvin	Buf	NL	72	72	636	46	22	0	369	63	1.99	3.59	2.91	165.3
14	81	1884	C.Sweeney	StL	U	60	56	492	41	15	1	337	42	1.70	3.33	2.59	163.2
15	180	1884	C.Buffinton	Bos	NL	67	67	587	48	16	0	417	76	2.15	3.45	2.80	163.1
16	834	1880	M.Ward	Pro	NL	70	67	595	39	24	1	230	45	1.74	3.48	3.33	154.4
17	481	1883	W.White	Cin	AA	65	64	577	43	22	0	141	104	2.09	3.98	3.12	152.9
18	224	1884	B.Taylor	StL	U	63	59	523	43	16	4	284	84	2.10	3.70	2.87	148.2
19	134	1888	S.King	StL	AA	66	65	586	45	21	0	258	76	1.64	3.15	2.72	141.5
20	174	1885	M.Welch	NY	NL	56	55	492	44	11	1	258	131	1.66	3.11	2.79	141.0
21	1,122	1882	J.McCormick	Cle	NL	68	67	596	36	30	0	200	103	2.37	4.14	3.46	139.1
22	1,990	1877	J.Devlin	Lou	NL	61	61	559	35	25	0	141	41	2.25	4.64	3.74	137.7
23	478	1885	E.Morris	Pit	AA	63	63	581	39	24	0	298	101	2.35	3.80	3.12	135.4
24	1,508	1880	J.McCormick	Cle	NL	74	74	658	45	28	0	260	75	1.85	3.75	3.59	134.7
25	1,430	1879	M.Ward	Pro	NL	70	60	587	47	19	1	239	36	2.15	4.14	3.57	130.8
26	776	1885	J.Clarkson	Chi	NL	70	70	623	53	16	0	308	97	1.85	3.68	3.30	126.9
27	188	1884	E.Morris	Col	AA	52	52	430	34	13	0	302	51	2.18	3.33	2.82	122.5
28	341	1885	B.Caruthers	StL	AA	53	53	482	40	13	0	190	57	2.07	3.66	3.01	121.3
29	1,253	1880	L.Corcoran	Chi	NL	63	60	536	43	14	2	268	99	1.95	3.66	3.50	119.5
30	436	1884	T.Keefe	NY	AA	58	58	483	37	17	0	334	71	2.25	3.64	3.08	116.9
31	3	1913	W.Johnson	Was	AL	48	36	346	36	7	2	243	38	1.14	1.46	1.68	116.5
32	1,009	1882	O.Radbourn	Pro	NL	55	52	474	33	20	0	201	51	2.09	4.08	3.41	115.7
33	319	1886	L.Baldwin	Det	NL	56	56	487	42	13	0	323	100	2.24	3.59	2.99	111.1
34	17	1901	C.Young	Bos	AL	43	41	371	33	10	0	158	37	1.62	2.71	2.23	110.8
35	149	1894	A.Rusie	NY	NL	54	50	444	36	13	1	195	200	2.78	4.62	2.75	109.5
36	1,331	1882	T.Mullane	Lou	AA	55	55	460	30	24	0	170	78	1.88	4.14	3.53	108.7
37	443	1889	J.Clarkson	Bos	NL	73	72	620	49	19	1	284	203	2.73	4.06	3.08	107.1
38	925	1884	J.McCormick	Cle	NL	66	65	569	40	25	0	343	89	2.37	4.16	3.37	106.4
39	445	1886	E.Morris	Pit	AA	64	63	555	41	20	1	326	118	2.45	3.95	3.09	105.6
40	146	1886	C.Ferguson	Phi	NL	48	45	396	30	9	2	212	69	1.98	3.30	2.74	104.2
41	375	1888	E.Seward	Phi	AA	57	57	519	35	19	0	272	127	2.01	3.52	3.04	103.6
42	1,574	1884	D.Shaw	Bos	U	67	66	643	30	33	0	451	109	2.30	4.65	3.61	102.4
43	265	1890	S.King	Chi	P	56	56	461	30	22	0	185	163	2.69	4.55	2.93	102.1
44	13	1912	W.Johnson	Was	AL	50	37	369	33	12	2	303	76	1.39	2.17	2.19	102.0
45	355	1886	D.Foutz	StL	AA	59	57	504	41	16	1	283	144	2.11	3.86	3.02	100.5
46	639	1882	L.Corcoran	Chi	NL	39	39	356	27	12	0	170	63	1.95	3.87	3.24	100.2
47	1,190	1883	J.Whitney	Bos	NL	62	56	514	37	21	2	345	35	2.24	4.52	3.49	100.2
48	205	1888	T.Keefe	NY	NL	51	51	434	35	12	0	335	90	1.74	2.90	2.85	98.2
49	986	1883	T.Mullane	StL	AA	53	49	461	35	15	1	191	74	2.19	4.34	3.40	98.1
50	139	1892	C.Young	Cle	NL	53	49	453	36	12	0	168	118	1.93	3.14	2.73	97.3

All Time Greatest Starting Pitchers

V	R	Year	Name	T	L	G	GS	IP	W	L	SV	SO	BB	ERA	RA/9	R Wtd RA/9	V Runs /162
51	52	1918	W.Johnson	Was	AL	39	29	326	23	13	3	162	70	1.27	1.96	2.47	96.6
52	602	1883	J.McGinnis	StL	AA	45	45	383	28	16	0	128	69	2.33	4.09	3.21	95.4
53	1,528	1878	M.Ward	Pro	NL	37	37	334	22	13	0	116	34	1.51	4.07	3.59	94.9
54	75	1904	J.McGinnity	NY	NL	51	44	408	35	8	5	144	86	1.61	2.27	2.57	94.6
55	482	1885	T.Keefe	NY	NL	46	46	400	32	13	0	227	102	1.58	3.48	3.12	93.1
56	409	1883	J.McCormick	Cle	NL	43	41	342	28	12	1	145	65	1.84	3.97	3.06	93.0
57	206	1908	E.Walsh	Chi	AL	66	49	464	40	15	6	269	56	1.42	2.17	2.85	92.6
58	334	1887	E.Smith	Cin	AA	52	52	447	34	17	0	176	126	2.94	4.51	3.00	91.3
59	31	1910	J.Coombs	Phi	AL	45	38	353	31	9	1	224	115	1.30	1.89	2.35	90.9
60	297	1890	K.Nichols	Bos	NL	48	47	424	27	19	0	222	112	2.23	3.71	2.97	89.9
61	7	1968	B.Gibson	StL	NL	34	34	305	22	9	0	268	62	1.12	1.45	1.93	89.0
62	1,133	1884	J.Lynch	NY	AA	55	53	496	37	15	0	292	42	2.67	4.10	3.47	88.5
63	158	1897	K.Nichols	Bos	NL	46	40	368	31	11	3	127	68	2.64	3.72	2.77	87.9
64	73	1915	P.Alexander	Phi	NL	49	42	376	31	10	3	241	64	1.22	2.06	2.57	87.2
65	260	1890	B.Rhines	Cin	NL	46	45	401	28	17	0	182	113	1.95	3.66	2.93	87.2
66	383	1890	S.Stratton	Lou	AA	50	49	431	34	14	0	207	61	2.36	3.88	3.04	87.0
67	2,653	1879	P.Galvin	Buf	NL	66	66	593	37	27	0	136	31	2.28	4.54	3.91	86.2
68	118	1908	C.Mathewson	NY	NL	56	44	391	37	11	5	259	42	1.43	1.96	2.69	85.3
69	1,444	1882	F.Goldsmith	Chi	NL	45	45	405	28	17	0	109	38	2.42	4.27	3.57	85.1
70	212	1895	C.Young	Cle	NL	47	40	370	35	10	0	121	75	3.26	4.31	2.86	84.8
71	1,137	1886	T.Keefe	NY	NL	64	64	535	42	20	0	297	102	2.56	4.17	3.47	84.6
72	1,548	1884	M.Welch	NY	NL	65	65	557	39	21	0	345	146	2.50	4.44	3.60	84.1
73	55	1917	E.Cicotte	Chi	AL	49	35	347	28	12	4	150	70	1.53	1.98	2.49	84.0
74	92	1914	W.Johnson	Was	AL	51	40	372	28	18	1	225	74	1.72	2.13	2.63	83.8
75	6	1994	G.Maddux	Atl	NL	25	25	202	16	6	0	156	31	1.56	1.96	1.92	83.7
76	770	1893	A.Rusie	NY	NL	56	52	482	33	21	1	208	218	3.23	4.85	3.30	83.3
77	412	1894	J.Meekin	NY	NL	52	48	409	33	9	2	133	171	3.70	5.15	3.06	83.3
78	5	1985	D.Gooden	NY	NL	35	35	277	24	4	0	268	69	1.53	1.66	1.86	83.0
79	542	1876	C.Cummings	Har	NL	24	24	216	16	8	0	26	14	1.67	4.04	3.17	83.0
80	33	1923	D.Luque	Cin	NL	41	37	322	27	8	2	151	88	1.93	2.52	2.36	82.8
81	54	1905	C.Mathewson	NY	NL	43	37	339	31	9	3	206	64	1.28	2.26	2.48	82.5
82	238	1902	C.Young	Bos	AL	45	43	385	32	11	0	160	53	2.15	3.18	2.90	82.1
83	22	1933	C.Hubbell	NY	NL	45	33	309	23	12	5	156	47	1.66	2.01	2.28	82.1
84	175	1882	D.Driscoll	Pit	AA	23	23	201	13	9	0	59	12	1.21	3.27	2.79	81.9
85	153	1916	P.Alexander	Phi	NL	48	45	389	33	12	3	167	50	1.55	2.08	2.76	81.9
86	57	1919	E.Cicotte	Chi	AL	40	35	307	29	7	1	110	49	1.82	2.26	2.49	81.4
87	23	1966	S.Koufax	LA	NL	41	41	323	27	9	0	317	77	1.73	2.06	2.29	81.4
88	70	1972	S.Carlton	Phi	NL	41	41	346	27	10	0	310	87	1.97	2.18	2.55	81.0
89	2,519	1883	P.Galvin	Buf	NL	76	75	656	46	29	0	279	50	2.72	5.03	3.88	80.9
90	171	1898	K.Nichols	Bos	NL	50	42	388	31	12	4	138	85	2.13	3.15	2.79	80.5
91	378	1884	J.Whitney	Bos	NL	38	37	336	23	14	0	270	27	2.09	3.75	3.04	80.4
92	67	1909	T.Brown	Chi	NL	50	34	343	27	9	7	172	53	1.31	2.05	2.55	80.4
93	526	1889	B.Caruthers	Bkn	AA	56	50	445	40	11	1	118	104	3.13	4.35	3.16	80.1
94	25	1936	C.Hubbell	NY	NL	42	34	304	26	6	3	123	57	2.31	2.40	2.31	79.9
95	487	1903	J.McGinnity	NY	NL	55	48	434	31	20	2	171	109	2.43	3.36	3.12	79.9
96	207	1891	C.Buffinton	Bos	AA	48	43	364	29	9	1	158	120	2.55	3.79	2.85	79.9
97	65	1915	W.Johnson	Was	AL	47	39	337	27	13	4	203	56	1.55	2.22	2.54	79.6
98	135	1946	B.Feller	Cle	AL	48	42	371	26	15	4	348	153	2.18	2.45	2.72	79.5
99	582	1893	K.Nichols	Bos	NL	52	44	425	34	14	1	94	118	3.52	4.70	3.20	79.4
100	1,872	1884	T.Mullane	Tol	AA	67	65	567	36	26	0	325	89	2.52	4.38	3.70	79.2

All Time Greatest Relief Pitchers

V	R	Year	Name	T	L	G	GS	IP	W	L	SV	SO	BB	ERA	RA/9	R Wtd RA/9	V Runs /162
1	24	1986	M.Eichhorn	Tor	AL	69	0	157	14	6	10	166	45	1.72	1.83	1.79	48.2
2	3	1981	R.Fingers	Mil	AL	47	0	78	6	3	28	61	13	1.04	1.04	1.16	44.6
3	11	1973	J.Hiller	Det	AL	65	0	125	10	5	38	124	39	1.44	1.51	1.60	41.1
4	37	1984	W.Hernandez	Det	AL	80	0	140	9	3	32	112	36	1.92	1.92	1.97	40.3
5	32	1977	R.Gossage	Pit	NL	72	0	133	11	9	26	151	49	1.62	1.83	1.90	39.3
6	62	1979	J.Kern	Tex	AL	71	0	143	13	5	29	136	62	1.57	2.20	2.12	38.7
7	68	1975	R.Gossage	Chi	AL	62	0	142	9	8	26	130	70	1.84	2.03	2.14	38.1
8	50	1980	D.Corbett	Min	AL	73	0	136	8	6	23	89	42	1.98	2.05	2.07	37.6
9	57	1970	M.Grant	Oak	AL	80	0	135	8	3	24	58	32	1.87	1.93	2.10	36.8
10	106	1983	D.Quisenberry	KC	AL	69	0	139	5	3	45	48	11	1.94	2.27	2.29	35.0
11	104	1964	B.Lee	LA	AL	64	5	137	6	5	19	111	58	1.51	2.04	2.28	34.6
12	161	1965	H.Wilhelm	Chi	AL	66	0	144	7	7	20	106	32	1.81	2.13	2.45	33.7
13	16	1996	M.Rivera	NY	AL	61	0	108	8	3	5	130	34	2.09	2.09	1.76	33.6
14	65	1984	B.Sutter	StL	NL	71	0	123	5	7	45	77	23	1.54	1.91	2.13	33.1
15	574	1974	M.Marshall	LA	NL	106	0	208	15	12	21	143	56	2.42	2.85	3.13	33.0
16	48	1966	P.Regan	LA	NL	65	0	117	14	1	21	88	24	1.62	1.85	2.06	32.5
17	26	1977	B.Sutter	Chi	NL	62	0	107	7	3	31	129	23	1.34	1.76	1.82	32.5
18	80	1974	T.Murphy	Mil	AL	70	0	123	10	10	20	47	51	1.90	1.98	2.20	32.3
19	132	1963	D.Radatz	Bos	AL	66	0	132	15	6	25	162	51	1.97	2.11	2.36	32.3
20	33	1967	T.Abernathy	Cin	NL	70	0	106	6	3	28	88	41	1.27	1.61	1.91	31.2
21	22	1992	M.Rojas	Mon	NL	68	0	101	7	1	10	70	34	1.43	1.52	1.79	31.1
22	140	1990	S.Farr	KC	AL	57	6	127	13	7	1	94	48	1.98	2.27	2.38	30.7
23	162	1979	S.Monge	Cle	AL	76	0	131	12	10	19	108	64	2.40	2.54	2.45	30.6
24	52	1971	T.McGraw	NY	NL	51	1	111	11	4	8	109	41	1.70	1.78	2.07	30.6
25	131	1962	D.Radatz	Bos	AL	62	0	125	9	6	24	144	40	2.24	2.30	2.36	30.6
26	94	1965	S.Miller	Bal	AL	67	0	119	14	7	24	104	32	1.89	1.97	2.27	30.3
27	343	1964	D.Radatz	Bos	AL	79	0	157	16	9	29	181	58	2.29	2.52	2.82	30.3
28	121	1960	L.McDaniel	StL	NL	65	2	116	12	4	26	105	24	2.09	2.17	2.33	30.2
29	291	1952	J.Black	Bkn	NL	56	2	142	15	4	15	85	41	2.15	2.54	2.75	30.0
30	12	1989	J.Montgomery	KC	AL	63	0	92	7	3	18	94	25	1.37	1.57	1.63	30.0
31	137	1982	G.Minton	SF	NL	78	0	123	10	4	30	58	42	1.83	2.12	2.37	29.9
32	136	1972	M.Marshall	Mon	NL	65	0	116	14	8	18	95	47	1.78	2.02	2.37	29.7
33	176	1963	R.Perranoksi	LA	NL	69	0	129	16	3	21	75	43	1.67	2.09	2.49	29.6
34	51	1999	K.Foulke	Chi	AL	67	0	105	3	3	9	123	21	2.22	2.39	2.07	29.1
35	8	1969	K.Tatum	Cal	AL	45	0	86	7	2	22	65	39	1.36	1.36	1.52	29.1
36	407	1950	J.Konstanty	Phi	NL	74	0	152	16	7	22	56	50	2.66	3.02	2.92	29.0
37	194	1979	A.Lopez	Det	AL	61	0	127	10	5	21	106	51	2.41	2.62	2.53	28.6
38	17	1980	T.McGraw	Phi	NL	57	0	92	5	4	20	75	23	1.46	1.56	1.76	28.6
39	419	1968	W.Wood	Chi	AL	88	2	159	13	12	16	74	33	1.87	2.21	2.94	28.5
40	254	1977	S.Lyle	NY	AL	72	0	137	13	5	26	68	33	2.17	2.69	2.69	28.4
41	400	1970	T.Hall	Min	AL	52	11	155	11	6	4	184	66	2.55	2.67	2.91	28.4
42	130	1981	R.Camp	Atl	NL	48	0	76	9	3	17	47	12	1.78	2.01	2.35	28.2
43	359	1947	J.Page	NY	AL	56	2	141	14	8	17	116	72	2.48	2.62	2.85	28.1
44	150	1962	D.Hall	Bal	AL	43	6	118	6	6	6	71	19	2.28	2.36	2.42	28.1
45	23	1987	T.Burke	Mon	NL	55	0	91	7	0	18	58	17	1.19	1.78	1.79	28.0
46	274	1971	K.Sanders	Mil	AL	83	0	136	7	12	31	80	34	1.91	2.32	2.72	27.8
47	2	1990	D.Eckersley	Oak	AL	63	0	73	4	2	48	73	4	0.61	1.10	1.15	27.6
48	53	1994	M.Eichhorn	Bal	AL	43	0	71	6	5	1	35	19	2.15	2.41	2.08	27.6
49	119	1973	B.Reynolds	Bal	AL	42	1	111	7	5	9	77	31	1.95	2.19	2.32	27.6
50	1	1995	J.Mesa	Cle	AL	62	0	64	3	0	46	58	17	1.13	1.27	1.13	27.4

Index

Aaron, Hank 12, 259
Abreu, Bobby 137
Adams, Babe 147
Aguilera, Rick 181
Alexander, Doyle 193
Alexander, Pete 47, 136, 259
Alfonso, Edgar 217
Allen, Dick 58, 137
Allen, Johnny 79
Allison, Bob 181
Alomar, Roberto 80, 193
Alou, Felipe 12
Alou, Moises 217–218
Altrock, Nick 57
Anderson, Brady 159
Anderson, Garret 191
Andrews, Mike 23
Andujar, Joaquin 170
Anson, Cap 8, 241
Antonelli, Johnny 102
Aparicio, Luis 57, 158
Appling, Luke 57
Arroyo, Luis 114
Ashburn, Richie 137
Averill, Earl 79
Avila, Bobby 80

Bagby, Jim 79
Bagwell, Jeff 216, 259–260
Bailey, Ed 69
Baines, Harold 58
Baker, Dusty 35
Baker, Frank 113, 125
Bancroft, Dave 101
Bando, Sal 126
Banks, Ernie 1–2, 47
Bannister, Floyd 58
Barfield, Jesse 193
Barnes, Ross 8, 241, 259–260
Bartell, Dick 102
Bassler, Johnny 90
Battey, Earl 181
Baylor, Don 191
Bearden, Gene 80
Beaumont, Ginger 147
Beazley, John 170
Beck, Rod 103
Beckert, Glenn 1
Bell, Buddy 80, 192

Bell, George 193
Bell, Gus 69
Bell, Jay 148
Belle, Albert 5, 80
Bench, Johnny 5, 69, 259–260
Bender, Chief 125
Berger, Wally 11
Berra, Yogi 113–114
Bichette, Dante 218
Biggio, Craig 216
Black, Joe 35
Blue, Vida 126
Blyleven, Bert 181, 191
Boggs, Wade 9, 24
Bonds, Barry 102–103, 148, 259–260
Bonds, Bobby 102
Bonilla, Bobby 148
Bosman, Dick 192
Bottomley, Jim 68, 169
Boudreau, Lou 80
Bowa, Larry 5
Boyer, Ken 170
Bradley, Bill 79
Breadon, Sam 169
Breechen, Harry 170
Bresnahan, Roger 101
Brett, George 192–193, 259–260
Brewer, Jim 35
Bridges, Tommy 90–91
Brock, Lou 170
Brouthers, Dan 241
Brown, Kevin 218–219
Brown, Three Finger 2, 46
Buhner, Jay 194
Bunning, Jim 91, 137
Burke, Tim 217
Burkett, Jesse 158, 169
Burkett, John 103
Burks, Ellis 24, 218
Burleson, Rick 23
Burnitz, Jeromy 193
Burns, George (Cle) 79
Burns, George (NY) 101
Burroughs, Jeff 192

Caldwell, Mike 193
Callison, Johnny 58, 137
Camilli, Dolph 34–35, 136

Caminiti, Ken 218, 259
Camnitz, Howie 147
Campanella, Roy 34–35, 259
Campaneris, Bert 126
Candelaria, John 148
Canseco, Jose 5, 126, 193
Carbo, Bernie 69
Carew, Rod 181
Carey, Max 147
Carlton, Steve 137
Carroll, Clay 69
Carter, Gary 217
Carter, Joe 193
Carty, Rico 12
Caruthers, Bob 241
Cash, Norm 58, 91
Cavaretta, Phil 47
Cedeno, Cesar 216
Cepeda, Orlando 102, 170
Cey, Ron 35
Chance, Dean 191
Chance, Frank 1, 46
Chandler, Spud 114
Chapman, Ray 79
Chase, Hal 5
Cheney, Larry 34
Chesbro, Jack 113, 147
Cicotte, Eddie 22, 57
Cirillo, Jeff 193
Clark, Jack 102, 170
Clark, Will 102
Clarke, Fred 147
Clarkson, John 241
Clemens, Roger 24, 193–194, 259
Clemente, Roberto 148
Clift, Harlond 158
Cobb, Ty 5, 10, 46, 57, 90, 259–260
Cochrane, Mickey 90–91, 126
Colavito, Rocky 91
Coleman, Vince 170
Collins, Eddie 57, 125, 259
Collins, Jimmy 241
Collins, Ray 22
Collins, Ripper 169
Combs, Earle 113
Comiskey, Charles 241
Concepcion, Dave 5, 69
Cone, David 115, 217

Conigliaro, Tony 23
Connolly, Joe 11
Coombs, Jack 125
Cooper, Cecil 23, 193
Cooper, Mort 170
Cooper, Walker 102, 170
Cooper, Wilbur 147
Coveleski, Stan 79, 180
Cowens, Al 192
Cravath, Gavvy 136
Crawford, Sam 68, 90
Cree, Birdie 113
Cronin, Joe 23, 180
Cross, Lave 34
Crowder, General 180
Cruz, Jose 216
Cuellar, Mike 159
Cullenbine, Roy 91
Cuyler, Kiki 47, 147–148

Dahlen, Bill 34
Dalrymple, Abner 241
Daly, Tom 34
Daniels, Kal 69
Darling, Ron 217
Daubert, Jake 34
Daulton, Darren 137
Davis, Eric 69
Davis, Harry 125
Davis, Mark 218
Davis, Spud 136
Davis, Tommy 35
Davis, Willie 35
Dawson, Andre 47, 217
Dean, Dizzy 169–170
Dean, Paul 169
DeCinces, Doug 159, 191
Delahanty, Ed 136, 180, 242
Delgado, Carlos 194
Derringer, Paul 68
Dibble, Rob 69
Dickey, Bill 113–114
Dierker, Larry 216
DiMaggio, Dom 23
DiMaggio, Joe 2, 5, 113–115
Dinneen, Bill 22
Doak, Bill 169
Dobson, Joe 23
Dobson, Pat 159

Index

Doby, Larry 80
Doerr, Bobby 23
Donlin, Mike 101
Donovan, Wild Bill 90
Dotson, Richard 58
Doyle, Larry 101
Drabek, Doug 148
Dreyfuss, Barney 147
Dropo, Walt 23
Drysdale, Don 34–35
Duffy, Hugh 241
Dunlap, Fred 260
Duren, Ryne 114
Dykstra, Len 137

Eckersley, Dennis 23, 126, 259–260
Edmonds, Jim 170, 191
Eichhorn, Mark 159, 193, 259
Eller, Hod 68
Elliott, Bob 12, 148
Ennis, Del 137
Epstein, Mike 192
Erskine, Carl 35
Erstad, Darin 191
Evans, Darrell 12
Evans, Dwight 23–24
Everett, Carl 217
Evers, Johnny 1, 11, 46

Faber, Red 57
Face, Roy 148
Fain, Ferris 126
Fassero, Jeff 218
Feller, Bob 80
Felsch, Happy 57
Ferrell, Rick 158
Ferrell, Wes 79
Fingers, Rollie 126, 193, 259–260
Finley, Charlie 125–126
Finley, Chuck 191
Fisk, Carlton 23, 58, 259
Fitzsimmons, Freddie 102
Flanagan, Mike 159
Flick, Elmer 79, 136
Flood, Curt 170
Ford, Russ 113
Ford, Whitey 113–114
Foster, George 69
Foster, Rube 22
Fournier, Jack 34
Foutz, Dave 241
Fox, Nellie 57
Foxx, Jimmie 23, 126, 259
Franco, John 69
Franco, Julio 80
Frazee, Harry 22
Freehan, Bill 91, 259
Freeman, Buck 22
Fregosi, Jim 191
Friend, Bob 148
Frisch, Frank 101, 169
Furillo, Carl 35

Gaetti, Gary 181
Galarraga, Andres 12, 218
Garcia, Mike 80
Garciaparra, Nomar 24
Garvey, Steve 35
Gaston, Cito 218
Gehrig, Lou 2, 113–114, 259–260
Gehringer, Charlie 90–91
Gentile, Jim 158
Geronimo, Cesar 69

Giambi, Jason 126
Gibson, Bob 2, 7, 170
Gibson, Kirk 36, 91, 259
Giles, Brian 148
Glaus, Troy 191
Glavine, Tom 12
Gleason, Bill 241
Gomez, Lefty 113–114
Gonzalez, Juan 192
Gooden, Dwight 217, 259–260
Goodman, Billy 23
Gordon, Joe 80, 114
Gore, George 241
Goslin, Goose 180
Gossage, Goose 58, 115, 148, 218, 259
Grace, Mark 1, 47
Granger, Wayne 69
Grantham, George 68, 147
Green, Shawn 194
Greenberg, Hank 90–91
Greenwell, Mike 24
Greer, Rusty 192
Gregg, Vean 79
Grich, Bobby 191
Griffey, Ken, Jr. 194
Griffey, Ken, Sr. 69
Griffith, Clark 57
Grimes, Burleigh 34
Grimes, Ray 47
Grissom, Marv 102
Groat, Dick 148
Groh, Heinie 68
Grove, Lefty 7, 23, 126
Guerrero, Pedro 35–36
Guerrero, Vladimir 218
Guidry, Ron 115
Gullett, Don 69
Gura, Larry 192
Gwynn, Tony 218

Hack, Stan 47
Hafey, Chick 68, 169
Hale, Odell 79
Hall, Jimmie 181
Hamilton, Billy 241
Hampton, Mike 217
Harder, Mel 79
Hargrave, Bubbles 68
Harper, Tommy 193
Hartnett, Gabby 2, 47
Hartsel, Topsy 125
Heath, Jeff 12, 80
Heilmann, Harry 68, 90
Helton, Todd 218
Henderson, Rickey 115, 126, 170
Henke, Tom 193
Henrich, Tommy 114
Hentgen, Pat 193
Herman, Babe 34, 68
Herman, Billy 1, 47
Hernandez, Keith 170
Hernandez, Willie 91
Hershiser, Orel 36
Herzog, Whitey 170
Higbe, Kirby 35
Higuera, Teddy 193
Hiller, John 91
Hisle, Larry 193
Hodges, Gil 34–35
Hoerner, Joe 170
Hoffer, Bill 241
Hoffman, Trevor 218
Hogan, Shanty 102

Hoiles, Chris 159
Hollocher, Charlie 47
Holmes, Tommy 11–12
Hooper, Harry 22
Hooton, Burt 35
Horlen, Joe 58
Hornsby, Rogers 1–2, 11, 47, 101, 169, 259
Horton, Willie 91
Howard, Elston 114
Howard, Frank 5, 192
Hoyt, La Marr 58
Hrbek, Kent 181
Hubbell, Carl 102
Hudson, Tim 126
Hunter, Catfish 114, 126
Hurst, Don 136
Hyde, Dick 181

Jackson, Mike 80, 260
Jackson, Reggie 114–115, 126, 191
Jackson, Shoeless Joe 57, 79
Jackson, Travis 101–102
Jacobson, Baby Doll 158
James, Bill 11
Jansen, Larry 102
Jenkins, Ferguson 2, 10, 47, 192
Jennings, Hughie 34, 241
Jensen, Jackie 23
Jeter, Derek 115
John, Tommy 35
Johnson, Bob 126
Johnson, Davy 12, 158
Johnson, Randy 194
Johnson, Walter 7, 180, 259–260
Jones, Chipper 12
Jones, Doug 80
Jones, Fielder 34, 57
Jones, Randy 218
Jones, Willie 137
Joost, Eddie 126
Joss, Addie 79
Joyner, Wally 191
Judge, Joe 180

Kaline, Al 91
Kauff, Benny 101
Keeler, Willie 34, 241
Kell, George 91
Keller, Charlie 114
Kelley, Joe 34, 241
Kelly, George 101
Kelly, King 241
Keltner, Ken 80
Kendall, Jason 148
Kent, Jeff 103
Kern, Jim 192
Key, Jimmy 193
Kile, Darryl 217
Killebrew, Harmon 5, 181
Killian, Ed 90
Kinder, Ellis 23
Kiner, Ralph 148
Klein, Chuck 136
Kling, Johnny 46
Kluszewski, Ted 68–69
Knoblauch, Chuck 181
Konstanty, Jim 137
Koosman, Jerry 217
Koufax, Sandy 34–35, 259
Kremer, Ray 148
Kruk, John 137
Kuhel, Joe 180

Kuhn, Bowie 126
Kurowski, Whitey 170

Lajoie, Nap 79, 125, 136, 259
Lamp, Dennis 193
Lanier, Max 170
Lankford, Ray 170
Larkin, Barry 69
Larry, Frank 91
Latham, Arlie 241
Lazzeri, Tony 113
Leach, Freddy 102
Leach, Tom 147
Lee, Bob 191
Leever, Sam 147
Lefferts, Craig 218
Leifield, Lefty 147
Leiter, Al 217, 219
Lemon, Bob 80
Lemon, Chet 91
Leonard, Dennis 192
Leonard, Dutch 22, 260
Lewis, Duffy 22
Lezcano, Sixto 193
Liebenthal, Mike 137
Lindstrom, Fred 102
Linzy, Frank 102
Lofton, Kenny 80
Lolich, Mickey 91
Lollar, Sherm 57
Lombardi, Ernie 68
Lonborg, Jim 23
Long, Herman 241
Lopes, Davy 35
Lowe, Bobby 241
Lundgren, Carl 7, 46
Luque, Dolf 68
Luzinski, Greg 137
Lyle, Sparky 114
Lynn, Fred 10, 23, 191
Lyons, Ted 57

McCarver, Tim 170
McCormick, Frank 68
McCovey, Willie 102
McDougald, Gil 114
McDowell, Jack 58
McDowell, Sam 80
McGee, Willie 170
McGinnity, Joe 34, 101, 259
McGraw, John 101, 241
McGraw, Tug 137, 217
McGriff, Fred 12, 193, 218
McGwire, Mark 1–2, 4, 126, 170, 259
Mack, Connie 125–126
McLain, Denny 91
McManus, Marty 158
McNally, Dave 158–159
McQuillan, George 136
McQuinn, George 158
McRae, Hal 192
Maddox, Garry 137
Maddux, Greg 7–8, 12, 47, 259–260
Magee, Sherry 136
Maglie, Sal 102
Maloney, Jim 69
Malzone, Frank 23
Mantle, Mickey 2, 5, 113–115, 259–260
Manush, Heinie 90, 180
Maranville, Rabbit 11
Marberry, Firpo 180

Index

Marichal, Juan 102
Marion, Marty 170
Maris, Roger 1, 5, 113–114, 170
Marquard, Rube 34, 101
Marshall, Mike 35, 217
Martin, Billy 126
Martinez, Dennis 159, 217
Martinez, Edgar 194, 260
Martinez, Pedro 2, 7–8, 12, 24, 218, 259–260
Martinez, Ramon 36
Mathews, Eddie 12
Mathewson, Christy 7, 101–102, 259
Mattingly, Don 115
May, Lee 69
Mays, Carl 22
Mays, Willie 1, 102, 259
Mazeroski, Bill 5, 148
Medwick, Joe 34–35, 169–170
Melton, Bill 5
Melton, Cliff 102
Merkle, Fred 101
Mesa, Jose 80, 259–260
Messersmith, Andy 35
Meusel, Bob 68, 113
Meusel, Irish 101
Meyers, Chief 101
Milan, Clyde 180
Milligan, Jocko 241
Millwood, Kevin 12
Minoso, Minnie 57
Minton, Greg 102
Mitchell, Kevin 102
Mize, Johnny 102, 169–170
Mogridge, George 180
Molitor, Paul 193
Mondesi, Raul 36
Montgomery, Jeff 193
Moon, Wally 35
Morgan, Joe 69, 259
Morris, Hal 69
Morris, Jack 91, 193
Mullin, George 90
Munson, Thurman 114
Murcer, Bobby 114
Murphy, Dale 12
Murphy, Danny 125
Murphy, Johnny 114
Murray, Eddie 159
Musial, Stan 2, 170, 259
Mussina, Mike 159
Myer, Buddy 180
Myers, Randy 69, 159, 217

Nen, Robb 103, 219
Nettles, Graig 80, 114
Newcombe, Don 35
Newhouser, Hal 91
Newsome, Bobo 91
Nichols, Kid 241
Niekro, Phil 12
Nolan, Gary 69
Nomo, Hideo 36
Northrup, Jim 91

O'Doul, Lefty 136
O'Farrell, Bob 169
Ojeda, Bob 217
Olerud, John 193
Oliva, Tony 181
Oliver, Al 192
Olson, Gregg 159
O'Neill, Paul 115

O'Neill, Tip 241, 260
Orosco, Jesse 159, 217
Otis, Amos 192
Ott, Mel 101–102
Overall, Orvie 46
Owen, Frank 57

Page, Joe 114
Palmeiro, Rafael 159, 192
Palmer, Jim 158–159
Pappas, Milt 158
Parker, Dave 69, 148
Parnell, Mel 23
Parrish, Lance 91
Parrish, Larry 217
Pascual, Camilo 181
Peckinpaugh, Roger 113, 180
Pendleton, Terry 12
Pennock, Herb 113
Percival, Troy 191
Perez, Tony 69
Perranoski, Ron 35
Perry, Gaylord 80, 102, 218
Perry, Jim 181
Pesky, Johnny 23
Peters, Gary 58
Petrocelli, Rico 23
Pettitte, Andy 115
Pfeffer, Fred 241
Pfeffer, Jeff 34
Pfiester, Jack 7, 46
Phillippe, Deacon 147
Piazza, Mike 36, 217
Pierce, Billy 57, 102
Pinson, Vada 69
Plank, Eddie 125
Pollet, Howie 170
Portugal, Mark 216
Post, Wally 69
Potter, Nels 158
Powell, Boog 158–159
Powell, Jack 158
Puckett, Kirby 181

Quisenberry, Dan 192

Radatz, Dick 23
Radbourn, Old Hoss 7–8
Raines, Tim 217
Ramirez, Manny 80
Regan, Phil 35
Reiser, Pete 35
Reulbach, Ed 46
Reuschel, Rick 102
Reynolds, Allie 114
Rhodes, Dusty 102
Rice, Jim 5, 22–24
Rice, Sam 180
Richards, Paul 57
Ripken, Cal 1, 159, 193, 259
Ritchey, Claude 147
Rivera, Mariano 115
Rixey, Eppa 68
Rizzuto, Phil 113–114
Roberts, Robin 137
Robinson, Brooks 158
Robinson, Frank 69, 158
Robinson, Jackie 34–35
Robinson, Wilbert 241
Robinson, Yank 241
Rodriguez, Alex 194, 259
Rodriguez, Ivan 192, 259–260
Roe, Preacher 35
Rogers, Steve 217

Rojas, Mel 217
Rolen, Scott 137
Rolfe, Red 114
Romano, Johnny 80
Rose, Pete 69
Rosen, Al 80
Roush, Edd 68
Rowe, Schoolboy 90–91
Rucker, Nap 34
Rudi, Joe 126
Rudolph, Dick 11
Ruether, Dutch 68
Ruffing, Red 113–114
Ruppert, Colonel 113
Ruth, Babe 1–2, 8, 22, 90, 113–115, 125, 158, 169, 259–260
Ryan, Nolan 191–192, 216

Saberhagen, Bret 192–193
Sabo, Chris 69
Sadecki, Ray 170
Sain, Johnny 11–12
Sallee, Slim 68
Salmon, Tim 191
Sambito, Joe 216
Sandberg, Ryne 1, 47
Sanders, Ken 193
Sanders, Reggie 69
Sanford, Jack 102
Santo, Ron 47
Sauer, Hank 47
Schalk, Ray 57
Schilling, Curt 137
Schmidt, Mike 4–6, 137, 148, 259–260
Schulte, Wildfire 46
Schumacher, Hal 102
Schupp, Ferdie 101
Scott, George 23, 193
Scott, Mike 216
Seaver, Tom 69, 217, 259
Selbach, Kip 22
Seminick, Andy 137
Sewell, Joe 79
Seybold, Socks 125
Seymour, Cy 68
Shantz, Bobby 126
Shaw, Bob 58
Shawkey, Bob 113
Sheckard, Jimmy 34, 46
Sheffield, Gary 218–219
Shocker, Urban 158
Shore, Ernie 22
Short, Chris 137
Sierra, Ruben 192
Sievers, Roy 181
Simmons, Al 126
Simmons, Curt 137
Simmons, Ted 170
Singleton, Ken 159
Sisler, George 158
Slaughter, Enos 170
Smith, Dave 216
Smith, Ozzie 1, 170
Smith, Reggie 23, 35
Smoltz, John 12
Snider, Duke 34–35
Sosa, Sammy 1–2, 46–47
Spahn, Warren 11–12
Spalding, Al 8, 241
Speaker, Tris 22, 79, 259
Splittorff, Paul 192
Stahl, Chick 22, 241
Stargell, Willie 148

Staub, Rusty 217
Steinbrenner, George 114
Steinfeldt, Harry 46
Stephens, Vern 23, 158
Stewart, Dave 126
Stieb, Dave 193
Stirnweiss, Snuffy 114
Stone, George 158
Stovey, Harry 241
Strawberry, Darryl 217
Stuart, Dick 23
Summers, Ed 90
Sutter, Bruce 2, 47
Sutton, Don 35
Sweeney, Bill 11
Swift, Bob 103

Tanana, Frank 191
Tannehill, Jesse 22, 147
Taylor, Dummy 101
Taylor, Jack 46
Tejeda, Miguel 126
Templeton, Garry 170
Tenace, Gene 126
Tenney, Fred 241
Terry, Bill 102
Tesreau, Jeff 101
Thomas, Frank 58
Thome, Jim 80
Thompson, Rob 103
Thompson, Sam 242
Thomson, Bobby 102
Tiant, Luis 23, 80
Tinker, Joe 1, 46
Tolan, Bobby 69
Toney, Fred 68
Torre, Joe 12, 170
Trammell, Alan 91
Travis, Cecil 181
Traynor, Pie 147–148
Trosky, Hal 79–80
Trout, Dizzy 91
Trucks, Virgil 91
Tudor, John 170
Turner, Jim 11
Turner, Tuck 242
Tyler, Lefty 47

Uhle, George 79
Urbina, Ugueth 218, 259

Valdes, Ismael 36
Valenzuela, Fernando 35
Valo, Elmer 126
Van Slyke, Andy 148
Vance, Dazzy 34
Vaughan, Arky 24, 148, 260
Vaughn, Greg 218
Vaughn, Hippo 47
Vaughn, Mo 24
Veach, Bobby 90
Ventura, Robin 58, 217
Vernon, Mickey 181
Versalles, Zoilo 181
Viola, Frank 181
Vizquel, Omar 80
Vosmik, Joe 79
Vukovich, Pete 193

Waddell, Rube 125
Wagner, Billy 217
Wagner, Honus 1, 137, 147–148, 259–260
Walker, Larry 9, 217–219, 259

Index

Wallace, Bobby 158, 169
Walsh, Ed 57, 259
Walters, Bucky 68
Waner, Lloyd 147
Waner, Paul 147–148
Ward, Duane 193
Warneke, Lon 47
Watkins, George 169
Weaver, Buck 57
Webb, Earl 22
Wertz, Vic 91
Wetteland, John 192, 218
Wheat, Zach 34
Whitaker, Lou 91
White, Bill 170
White, Doc 57
White, Roy 114
Wilhelm, Hoyt 58, 102
Williams, Bernie 115
Williams, Billy 2, 47
Williams, Jimmy 113
Williams, Ken 158
Williams, Lefty 57
Williams, Matt 103
Williams, Ted 1, 11, 22–23, 192, 218, 259–260
Williamson, Ned 241
Williamson, Scott 69
Willis, Vic 11, 147
Wills, Maury 35
Wilson, Don 216
Wilson, Hack 1, 9, 47
Wilson, Willie 192
Wiltse, Hooks 101
Winfield, Dave 115, 218
Witt, Mike 191
Wolff, Roger 181
Wood, Smokey Joe 22
Wood, Wilbur 58
Wright, Clyde 191
Wyatt, Whit 35
Wynn, Early 80
Wynn, Jimmy 216

Yastrzemski, Carl 22–23, 259
Yawkey, Tom 22–23
York, Rudy 91
Young, Cy 7, 22, 259
Youngs, Ross 101
Yount, Robin 193, 259

Zachary, Tom 180